S0-BOS-247

ENGLISH-CAYUGA / CAYUGA-ENGLISH DICTIONARY

Shagohędéhta' Reginald Henry (1923-1993)

FRANCES FROMAN, ALFRED KEYE, LOTTIE KEYE (language consultants)
and CARRIE DYCK (compiler)

English-Cayuga / Cayuga-English Dictionary

Gayogo̱ho:nǫˀ / Hnyǫˀǫhneha:ˀ Wadęwęnaga:da:s Ohyadǫ̱hsrǫ:dǫˀ

UNIVERSITY OF TORONTO PRESS
Toronto Buffalo London

Published by the University of Toronto Press Incorporated 2002
Toronto Buffalo London
Printed in Canada

ISBN 0-8020-3618-X

Printed on acid-free paper

National Library of Canada Cataloguing in Publication

English-Cayuga/Cayuga-English dictionary / Frances Froman, Alfred Keye, Lottie Keye, Carrie Dyck.

ISBN 0-8020-3618-X

1. Cayuga language – Dictionaries – English. 2. English language – Dictionaries – Cayuga. I. Title.

PM757.Z5E64 2002 497′.55 C2002-904450-2

University of Toronto Press acknowledges the financial assistance to its publishing program of the Canada Council for the Arts and the Ontario Arts Council.

University of Toronto Press acknowledges the financial support for its publishing activities of the Government of Canada through the Book Publishing Industry Development Program (BPIDP).

Financial support for this publication has been provided by the Ontario Ministry of Education, Ministry of Training, Colleges and Universities; and also by Memorial University of Newfoundland; Six Nations of the Grand River Band Council; Social Sciences and Humanities Research Council of Canada (Postdoctoral research fellowship #756-94-0716); Student Career Programme, Government of Canada; Sweetgrass First Nations Language Council, Inc.; University of Calgary; Woodland Cultural Centre, Brantford, Ontario.

Contents

Preface

This Cayuga dictionary is dedicated to the memory of Sagohędéhta' Mr. Reg Henry (1923-1993). A Faithkeeper, Cayuga linguist, and scholar, Reg Henry was the designer of the Cayuga writing system, which is now in general use at the Six Nations of the Grand River Indian Reserve in southern Ontario.

Though familiar with linguistic writing conventions, Reg Henry chose to design a writing system that would resemble the English writing system more closely (this, for the many speakers of Cayuga who were already familiar with English) and yet still represent the Cayuga language in a linguistically sound manner.

Reg Henry's work on the writing system began some 30 years ago while he was working with scholars at the Rochester Museum in New York State. The writing system underwent many changes during its development, and it has been subtly changing since, as people become more familiar with it.

Reg Henry's legacy included major retranscriptions of Ǫgwehǫ́:weh (Iroquoian) works, which were previously scattered in various archaic texts, writing systems, and styles of orature. He also transcribed and translated between other Ǫgwehǫ́:weh languages and English.

It is fitting, then, that the Creator bestowed upon him the great name Sagohędéhta', *He Leads the People*, for he certainly did just that!

ACKNOWLEDGEMENTS

This dictionary was a long-term project covering the period of 1994-2001. It was completed with the financial support, generosity, and dedication of many people, many of whom are listed below. Any omissions are unintentional. Nyá:węh.

The sponsors of the dictionary, signing the agreement which started the dictionary-making process, included the Sweetgrass First Nations Language Council Inc., the Ontario Ministry of Education, (Ministry of Training, Colleges and Universities), and Six Nations of the Grand River Band Council.

Special thanks must go out to Amos Key Jr., Language Program Director of the Woodland Cultural Centre, who steered the project from the initial writing of the proposal to its completion, and who chaired the steering committee for the Cayuga dictionary.

Thanks to John Stanley of the Ontario Ministry of Education, (Ministry of Training, Colleges and Universities) for his role in obtaining financial support for the dictionary. Financial support was provided mainly by the the Ontario Ministry of Education, (Ministry of Training, Colleges and Universities). Grants to students were provided by the Government of Canada, the University of Calgary, and Memorial University of Newfoundland. The summer students who worked on the project were Jill Perry, Edward Smith, and Rhonda West.

Other administrative support, including meeting space and materials, was provided by the Woodland Cultural Centre in Brantford, Ontario (near Six Nations).

Special mention goes to Angie Monture (secretary for the language program at the Woodland Cultural Centre), who has often gone beyond the call of duty to provide support, and to coordinate the dictionary meetings. Niá:wen.

The steering committee members for the dictionary at various times included Betsy Buck, Carrie Dyck (project coordinator, dictionary compiler), Frances Froman, Louise Hill, Ken Jacobs, Cindy John (former project coordinator), Eileen Johnson, Amos Key Jr. (Chair), Alfred Keye, Lottie Keye, and Cheryl Porter.

The linguistic consultants for the dictionary included Carrie Dyck, Hazel Dean John (a Seneca-speaking linguist), and Michael Foster (who provided invaluable linguistic notes and workshops on Cayuga grammar).

Language consultants for the dictionary included Alta Doxtator, Frances Froman, Arnie General, Cleveland General, Halsie Isaacs, Cassie Jacobs, Oliver Jacobs, Elva Jamieson, Alfred Keye, Lottie Keye, Irene Longboat, Huron Miller, Elizabeth Sandy, Pat Sandy, Elizabeth Silversmith, and Jimmy Styres. We are indebted to these people for their valuable knowledge of the Cayuga language.

Editors and administrative assistants at various times included Betsy Buck, Hubert Buck, Carrie Dyck, Frances Froman, Elva Jamieson, Cindy John (former project coordinator), Lottie Keye, Alfred Keye, and Angie Monture. Frances Froman, Lottie Keye, and Alfred Keye painstakingly corrected the spelling of the Cayuga words in the dictionary.

Nya:wę́h swagwé:gǫh!

Some of the Elders who were consultants for the dictionary.
Back row (left to right): Oliver Jacobs, Halsie Isaacs, Arnie General, Pat Sandy.
Front row (left to right): Cassie Jacobs, Elizabeth Silversmith, Alta Doxtator.

Introduction

The Hodinǫhsǫ́:nih (People of the Longhouse) traditionally lived along the Mohawk River valley and around the Finger Lakes district in present-day New York State. The Ganyę'gęhó:nǫ' (Mohawk people or Keepers of the Eastern Door) lived between the Allegheny and Catskill Mountains. The Onǫdowá'ga:' (Seneca people or Keepers of the Western Door) were settled along the Genessee River. In between, the Onǫdagehó:nǫ' (Onondaga people) lived near present-day Syracuse, New York, and the Ohnyahęhó:nǫ' (Oneida people) lived near Lake Oneida, New York. The Gayogǫhó:nǫ' (People of the Pipe or Cayuga people) lived in an area between Lake Cayuga and Lake Owasco in present-day Cayuga County, New York. Together, these peoples formed the original Hwíhs Niyǫhwęjá:ge: (Five Nations Iroquois Confederacy or League of the Iroquois). The Dahsgáo:wę' (Tuscarora people) joined the League (afterwards known as Hyeí Niyǫhwęjá:ge: or Six Nations) after losing their homelands in present-day North Carolina.

The original Cayuga villages were destroyed by the Sullivan Campaign of 1779, in retaliation for the Cayuga having sided with the British during the American Revolution. Many Cayuga people subsequently moved to Fort Niagara, and later, to Six Nations of the Grand River, lands granted by the Crown to the Iroquois in 1784.

Before the American Revolution, some Cayugas had settled with a western branch of the Senecas on the Lower Sandusky River in Ohio. The Cayugas and Senecas in Ohio were collectively known as the 'Sandusky Senecas'. In 1831, the Sandusky Senecas moved to present-day Miami, Oklahoma (Michelson 1988:5; Mithun 1979:149). The variety of Cayuga spoken in Oklahoma was called Seneca and few, if any, speakers of this dialect remain. However, Cayuga is still spoken by approximately 100 people at Six Nations, where Mohawk and Onondaga are also spoken. (This figure is from the Speakers of Aboriginal Languages Survey, conducted by Sweetgrass First Nations Language Council Inc. in 1995 and updated in 1999).

Cayuga (Gayogǫho:nǫhnéha:', or Gayogǫhó:nǫ' for short, or Ǫgwehǫwéhnęha:') is most closely related to Seneca, and is also related to the other Northern Iroquoian languages of Mohawk, Oneida, Onondaga, and Tuscarora. Older Cayuga speakers frequently speak more than one Iroquoian language (as well as English) and they often understand one or two more Iroquoian languages besides. For example, the late Reginald Henry (to whom this dictionary is dedicated) was a fluent speaker of Cayuga, Onondaga, and English, and he understood Mohawk and Oneida as well.

Two varieties of Cayuga are spoken at Six Nations. Lower Cayuga (Ganedagehó:nǫʼ) is spoken at the Lower End of Six Nations (Ganédageh *in the valley*). Upper Cayuga (Dagęhyatgehó:nǫʼ) is spoken at the Upper End (Dagę́hya:t *top of the mountain*). All of the speakers consulted for this dictionary were Lower Cayuga speakers over 40 years of age.

Pronunciation differences separate Lower and Upper Cayuga: Lower Cayuga speakers say <gy> where Upper Cayugas use <dy>. For example, the number *nine* is pronounced as gyǫhdǫ: in Lower Cayuga, and as dyohdǫ: in Upper Cayuga. Lower Cayuga also has devoiced (whispered) vowels, such as the <ǫ> in gyǫhdǫ:. Devoiced vowels occur in odd-numbered syllables containing <h>. Similarly, in odd-numbered syllables containing a glottal stop, Lower Cayuga speakers either omit the glottal stop or pronounce it simultaneously with other segments in the syllable: for example, in the word dʼęʼóyanreʼ *it is not good*, the first syllable <dʼęʼ> has an ejective [t'] followed by an [e] with creaky voice phonation or with a single glottal catch. (Se §5 of the User Guide for further information on pronunciation).

Other pronunciation differences are characteristic of individuals or families, rather than of the two dialects of Cayuga. For example, some people pronounce the <sr> in words like ganǫ́hkwahsraʼ *love* as <fr>, while others prefer the pronunciation <shr>, as in *shrink*. Also, the prefix meaning *you (singular)* can be pronounced either as English <sh> before <r> (spelled <sr> in Cayuga), as in dasrá:tęh *you climb over here!*, or as <d> before <r>, as in dadrá:tęh *you climb over here!* Furthermore, some people pronounce certain words with an <o> where others prefer a <u> sound. Examples include dago:s / dagu:s *cat*, swayóʼtsʼageh / swayúʼtsʼa-geh *on your chins*, and ohyoʼtí:yeht / oh-yuʼtí:yeht *it is sharp*.

Other sources of variation arise from vocabulary and prefix choice. Differences in vocabulary choice include using either ganǫhsadaiháʼtaʼ or hǫhji for *stove*. Differences in prefix choice include the word for *brooch, safety pin*, which is either gajíhoha:ʼ with the prefix ga- or ojíhoha:ʼ with the prefix o-.

Two spelling systems were developed for Cayuga, the linguistic orthography and the Henry orthography (used in this dictionary). The linguistic one was developed for Native Language Teacher Certification programs in the 1970s, and is also used in the Watęwayę́stanih grammar (Mithun and Henry 1984). The Henry orthography was developed in the early 1980s by the late Reginald Henry. It has been widely adopted and is currently used in the Cayuga immersion school at Six Nations and for other Cayuga language courses. The main differences between the two systems are in the representation of consonants: where the linguistic orthography uses <th, t, kh, k, tsh, and ts>, the Henry orthography uses <t, d, k, g, ts, and j>. Cayuga speakers also tend to write <s> for <sh>. For example, Reg Henry's name can be spelled as Shagohędéhtaʼ or Sagohędéhtaʼ.

The dictionary begins with a user guide describing the dictionary entries and the

Cayuga sound and spelling system. Following the user guide are the English-Cayuga sections of the dictionary, the Cayuga-English sections, and several appendices. The appendices are organized by themes, including time periods (appendix A), numbers and money (B), terms for kin and nationalities (C), chiefs' names (D), place names (E), traditional and ceremonial language (F), government and business terms (G), vocabulary from the Ganǫ́hǫnyǫhk or Thanksgiving Address (H), particles (I), and a grammatical sketch (J).

REFERENCES

Foster, M. 1974. *From the earth to beyond the sky: An ethnographic approach to four Longhouse Iroquois speech events.* (The Mercury Series, Ethnology Division, Paper 20). Ottawa: National Museum of Man.

Michelson, K. 1988. *A comparative study of Lake-Iroquoian accent.* (Studies in Natural Language and Linguistic Theory). Dordrecht: Kluwer Academic Publishers.

Mithun, M. 1979. Iroquoian. In L. Campbell and M. Mithun (eds)., *The languages of Native America*, 133-212. Austin: University of Texas Press.

Mithun, M., and R. Henry. 1984. Watęwayę́stanih. *A Cayuga teaching grammar.* Brantford, Ontario: Woodland Indian Cultural Educational Centre.

User Guide

1 DICTIONARY ENTRIES

The dictionary contains four types of entries: English-Cayuga entries and cross-references, and Cayuga-English entries and cross-references. Each is described below.

1.1 ENGLISH-CAYUGA ENTRIES

English-Cayuga dictionary entries have the components illustrated below. (Diacritics are described in later sections; the raised dot in §5.8, the colon in §5.5, and the acute accent in §5.6-5.7).

able
 ę·ha:gwé:niʼ he can do it
 [(N+) stem: -gweni, gweny$_V$- be able to do s.t., succeed]
 ę·ga·eg·wé:niʼ they (f/m) can do it; they are able to do it
 ę·ga:gwé:niʼ it can be; that is enough
 ęh·se:gwé:niʼ you will succeed
 de·yo·yʼa·dó·węh·dǫʼ it is able
 [de+yo+ stem: -yaʼdowehd$_V$- think about, consider]

English-Cayuga entries begin with an English keyword (such as, *able*). Following each keyword are Cayuga words with meanings similar to the English keyword (such as, deyoyʼadówęhdǫʼ *it is able*). Grammatical information in square brackets (such as, [de+yo+ stem: -yaʼdowehd$_V$- *think about, consider*]) appears after the first instance of any Cayuga stem. For example, it appears after the words ęha:gwé:niʼ and deyoyʼadówęhdǫʼ in the preceding example but not after the words ęgaegwé:niʼ and ęhse:gwé:niʼ, which have the same stem (and basic meaning) as ęha:gwé:niʼ.

A key to interpreting the grammatical information is provided in §2.3 of this user guide. See also the list of abbreviations provided at the end of this user guide.

1.2 ENGLISH-CAYUGA CROSS-REFERENCES

Another type of entry is the English-Cayuga cross-reference:

able see: accomplish
 sa·ih·wag·wé:nyǫ: you are able to perform (that is, run, dance, orate, etc).

Cross-references point to other Cayuga words with related meanings; for example, more words with a meaning like *able* can be found under the entry *accomplish*.

Cross-references do not include grammatical information in square brackets; the grammatical information is, instead, found in the original entry (in the above case, under *accomplish*).

1.3 CAYUGA-ENGLISH DICTIONARY ENTRIES

Cayuga-English dictionary entries are headed by a stem, which is not a word, followed by a colloquial translation. In the following example, the stem is -ganye(:)-, and variants of this stem occur in each of the words listed below the stem.

-ganye(:) shuffle
 ǫhsganyehahk she used to shuffle H
 ęyǫhsganye:ʼ she will shuffle P
 gohsga:nye:ʼ she has shuffled S
 desahsganye: shuffle I

For the Cayuga-English verb entries, the *habitual* (H), *punctual* (P), *stative* (S), and *imperative* (I) forms of the verb are often listed. (The imperative is typically the second person or 'you' singular form). For more information about these aspect forms, see §8.7-8.11 of Appendix J (Cayuga Grammar).

In Cayuga-English entries, the grammatical information appears below the stem, in square brackets. For example, in the following entry, the verb stem -ga'- obligatorily takes [P+] (patient) pronominal prefixes. (A key to interpreting the grammatical information is provided in §2.3 of this user guide).

·ga' like the taste of s.t
[P+]
age:ga's I like the taste of it H
ǫge'ga' I liked the taste of it P
oga'ǫh it tastes good S

The verb stem requires any obligatory prefixes listed in order to convey the meaning that appears beside the stem. To illustrate, in the following examples the same verb stem -ga'de' has different (but related) meanings depending on which prefixes are used with the verb stem.

·ga'de' often, many, lots
[o+at+]
otga'de' often; many; lots S
·ga'de' have much, many, lots
[P+(ad+)N+]
aknǫhsaga'de' I have many houses S

In the above examples, -ga'de' means *often, etc.* only when it takes the prefixes [o+] and [at+]; in contrast, the same stem means *to have a lot, etc.* when it takes a [P+] (patient) pronominal prefix, an incorporated noun [N+], and, optionally, the prefix [ad+] or [at+]. (A key to interpreting the grammatical information is provided in §2.3 of this user guide).

1.4 CAYUGA-ENGLISH CROSS-REFERENCES

Cross-references in the Cayuga-English section of the dictionary point to related forms of a stem:

·ę' a group of things lying on the ground
see: (y)ę' [A/P+(N+)] a group of things lying on the ground; to be lying on the ground covering a large area
ganawaę:' a swamp; a pond S

In the previous example, the verb stem -ę'- is related to a form of the verb which begins with a <y>, namely -(y)ę'-. Looking up the stem -(y)ę'- yields additional, related forms such as the following:

·(y)ę' lie on the ground
[ga+]
ga:yę' it is lying on the ground S

Cayuga entries are organized by stems, with information about bases (obligatory prefixes, etc.) also being listed.

2 GENERAL INFORMATION ABOUT DICTIONARY ENTRIES

Conventions for translations and for grammatical information are discussed below.

2.1 TRANSLATIONS

The Cayuga words were translated by a committee working over a five-year period. The translations are colloquial and are often taken out of context. So, for example, many nouns such as o’nhǫ́hsa’ can be translated as singular (*egg*) or plural (*eggs*), depending on the context in which the word was used. In the dictionary, therefore, nouns are sometimes translated as singular, and sometimes as plural; the original context has since been omitted. The dictionary user will want to compare several related Cayuga words in order to gain a better idea of the meaning of any given Cayuga stem.

2.2 TWO TYPES OF SPELLING IN DICTIONARY ENTRIES; ALPHABETIZATION

The spelling of the Cayuga words was determined by a committee working over a five-year period. In current practice, the spellings tend to be more variable or more phonetic (that is, more closely mirroring the pronunciation).

In contrast, the spellings in the grammatical portions of the dictionary entries are phonemic or linguistic. To illustrate, in the following grammatical information there is a glottal stop before the <d> of the verb stem -ya’dowehd$_V$-.

[de+yo+ stem: -ya’dowehd$_V$- *think about, consider*]

If this glottal stop is in an even-numbered syllable (counting from beginning of the word), then speakers typically spell the word as shown in the grammatical entry. For example, in the word ga·ya’do·wéh·dǫ:’ *the idea of thinking*, the second syllable has the glottal stop after the vowel <a> and before the <d>. However, if the glottal stop is in an odd-numbered syllable, then speakers will either *not* spell the glottal stop at all (as in the third syllable in de·yo·ya·dó·wę̱h·dǫ’ *it is able*) or they will switch the glottal stop with the odd-numbered vowel (as in the third syllable in de·yo·y’a·dó·wę̱h·dǫ’ *it is able*). These spelling practices reflect the operation of a phonetic rule called laryngeal metathesis, which is discussed in §5.9 under the consonants <h> and <’>.

Also as a result of laryngeal metathesis, in the spelling of Cayuga words, odd-numbered vowels followed by <h> are underlined to show devoicing, whereas even-numbered vowels followed by <h> are not devoiced or underlined. In contrast, in the spelling of grammatical information, vowels are not underlined because devoicing is predictable. (See §5.4 for details).

By another phonetic rule, accented vowels are frequently lengthened. Length is typically included in Cayuga spellings. In contrast, in the grammatical information, predictable vowel length is not included; however unpredictable vowel length is included, following linguistic or phonemic principles. (See §5.5 and §5.7 for a description of predictable vowel length).

Noun and verb stems listed in the grammatical information sections in dictionary entries end with a ‘d’ or a ‘g’. Such stems are pronounced as, and written with, ‘t’ or ‘k’ when they are word-final. For example, the stem -ya’dowehd$_V$- occurs at the end of the following word, where it is spelled with a final ‘t’.

dę̱hsya’do:weht *you will be a seer, thinker*

Alphabetization in the Cayuga-English section of the dictionary takes into account speakers’ tendencies to omit length (:), glottal stop, and <h> in the spelling:

alphabetization ignores length (:), and any h's or glottal stops (ʼ) that are not between vowels. However, main entries are listed twice, once as if <h, ʼ, and :> were ignored, and once as if they were included. For example, stems with the segments <ʼs> are alphabetized under <ʼ> and also under <s>.

Otherwise, vowels are alphabetized in the order <a, e, ę, o, ǫ, u> and consonants occur in the order <ˀ, d, g, h, j, k, n, r, s, t, w, y>.

segments	**dictionary alphabetization**
a, a:, ah, aʼ	a
ad, ahd, aʼd	ad
ae	ae
aę	aę
ag, ahg, aʼg	ag
aha	aha
aj, ahj, aʼj	aj
ak, ahk, aʼk	ak
an, ahn, aʼn	an
ao	ao
aǫ	aǫ
ar, ahr, aʼr	ar
as, ahs, aʼs	as
at, aht, aʼt	at
aw, ahw, aʼw	aw
ay, ahy, aʼy	ay

2.3 GRAMMATICAL INFORMATION

Minimal grammatical information (essentially, noun stems, verb stems, and prefixes obligatory to bases) is provided in dictionary entries. Grammatical information is always contained in square brackets [ ]. Elements within square brackets are generally not whole Cayuga words; instead, they include prefixes and other parts which are obligatory for the meaning of the word or base.

Look in §3 to find out more about the prefixes listed in dictionary entries. Look in §4 to find out about endings, which are often not listed in dictionary entries, but whose presence can be inferred by comparing noun or verb stems with actual words.

Grammatical information is presented in the following order (but not all parts will occur in a given entry): particles, prepronominal prefixes, pronominal prefixes, semireflexive or reflexive prefixes, stems, incorporated nouns, verbs.

The various grammatical parts are described in the following sections, but a few general conventions remain to be discussed first. See Appendix J (Cayuga Grammar) for more details about the grammatical parts.

A slash / indicates an obligatory choice. For example, [X/Y] means that either part X or part Y must be included in the word. See §2.3.5 for an example.

A plus sign + indicates that the word in question requires an affix. See §2.3.5 for an example.

Parentheses ( ) are used either for: (1) an optional grammatical element (for example, see §1.3); or (2) a vowel or consonant which can be absent in related forms of a word. In the latter case, material in brackets typically consists of a joiner vowel or a noun increment. To illustrate, the noun stem for *house* is listed as -nǫhs(a)-. The bracketed 'a' is not technically part of the noun; it is a euphonic element (the joiner vowel) that appears between the noun and some verb stems, and elsewhere. Examples in which the joiner vowel appears or doesn't appear are as follows (the joiner vowel is doubly underlined, the noun stem is bolded): dęgat**nǫhs**áhsnyeʼs *I'm a housekeeper*; ga**nǫ́hs**gǫ: *in the house*; godí**nǫhs**o:t *their (f/m) house*.

The bracketing convention can also indicate a noun increment and joiner vowel combination, such as (-ʼd-a-), which appears after some incorporated nouns and before the verb, for example, in the noun stem -ǫgwe(ʼda)-$_{N}$; compare ǫ́:gweh *person, human*, which lacks the noun increment and joiner vowel, and ǫgweʼdagwé:gǫh *all the people*, which has both.

2.3.1 Particles

Particles include small words such as tó: *that*, or tsę́h, shę́h *that, of, because, etc.* When these are obligatory for the meaning of the base, they are included with the grammatical information. Appendix I also contains a list of particles with example sentences to illustrate particle meaning.

2.3.2 Prepronominal prefixes

Obligatory prepronominal prefixes are shown in their most commonly occurring form for the verb in question; the prepronominals are listed in §3 of this guide. They are also described in §8.2 of Appendix J (Cayuga Grammar).

2.3.3 Pronominal prefixes

Pronominal prefixes are listed in two ways:

(1) if a specific prefix is needed in order to convey the meaning of the word, then that prefix is listed; for example, if the third person feminine indefinite ǫ+ *she, someone* is required for the meaning of a particular word, then ǫ+ appears in the grammatical information.

(2) If the word requires a *class* of prefixes, on the other hand, then the class, either [A+] (*agent*), [P+] (*patient*), or [TR+] (*transitive* or *interactive*) is given. The three classes of pronominal prefix are listed and described in §8.3 of Appendix J (Cayuga Grammar).

Verbs whose prefix class is *not* specified take the [A+] series in the *habitual* and *punctual* aspects, and the [P+] series in the *stative* aspect (see for example the entry -ganye(:) in §1.3). In contrast, verbs whose prefix class *is* specified must take only the prefix type listed (for example, [P+] in all aspects; see -gaʼ in §1.3).

Nouns whose prefix class is not specified are *inalienable* (that is, designating *body parts)*; when unpossessed, these take the third neuter [P+] pronominal prefix (generally [o+]); when possessed—the usual case—they take an [A+] pronominal prefix and the external locative suffix [–aʼgeh], listed in §3 of the User Guide and described in §7.5 of Appendix J (Cayuga Grammar).

Finally, the designation [A/P+(N+)] or [A/P+N+] indicates that the class of the pronominal prefix required by the verb changes (to either [A] or [P]), depending on the type of noun that is incorporated. See §3.1, §3.4, §4 and §8.5 of Appendix J (Cayuga Grammar).

2.3.4 *Semireflexive and reflexive prefixes*

Obligatory semireflexive and reflexive prefixes are shown in their most commonly occurring form for the verb in question. See §8.4, Appendix J (Cayuga Grammar) for both types of prefixes.

The forms of the semireflexive prefix are: [-(a)d+, -(a)de+, -(a)t+, -(a)g+, -(a)k+]. (The use of parentheses is discussed in §2.3 of this user guide).

The forms of the reflexive prefix are: [-(a)dad+, -(a)dade+, -(a)dat+, -(a)dag+, and -(a)dak+].

2.3.5 *Incorporated nouns*

Some verbs require incorporated nouns, in which case they are designated as [N+]; other verbs *optionally* take incorporated nouns, in which case they are designated as [(N+)].

In some cases, a verb incorporates a meaningless noun if no other noun has been incorporated. For example, the verb ga̲hǫʼji: *it is dark* requires the meaningless noun -hǫʼ- when no other noun is incorporated. For such verbs, the obligatory choice is indicated by means of a slash; thus, the grammatical information for ga̲hǫʼji: *it is dark* includes the elements [N/hǫʼ+], which can be translated as *either a noun or* –hǫʼ- *must be incorporated*. An example of the same verb with the incorporated noun -geʼa(:)- *hair* is:

hogéʼaji: *he has dark hair*

See §4 and §8.5 of Appendix J (Cayuga Grammar) for further discussion of noun incorporation.

3 PREFIXES

This section lists prefixes, prefix combinations, and the section of Appendix J (Cayuga Grammar) in which they are discussed or listed.

a, a:	8.2, 8.3
ad(i)	8.2
ae	8.2
ag(e)	8.3
ago	8.3
agw(a)	8.3
agy	8.3
ak	8.3
aki(y)	8.2, 8.3
akn(i)	8.2, 8.3
aǫ	8.3, 8.2
aǫda	8.2
aǫsa	8.2
at	8.2
da, da:	8.2
daǫda	8.2
daǫsa	8.2
de(ʼ), dʼe	8.2
dedi	8.2
deg	8.2
dʼej(i)	8.2
des, dʼes	8.2
det, dʼet	8.2
dę	8.2
dędi	8.2
dęg	8.2
dęj(i)	8.2
dęs	8.2
dęt	8.2
di	8.2
dǫ	8.2
dǫda	8.2
dǫ:da	8.2
dǫsa	8.2
dǫ:sa	8.2
dw(a)	8.2, 8.3
e	8.2, 8.3
edi	8.2
ehy(a)	8.3
esa	8.3
esgw(a)	8.3
eskni(y)	8.3
esę	8.3
eti(y)	8.3

etsi(y)	8.2, 8.3	hǫsa	8.2
ę	8.2	hǫwa	8.3
ędi	8.2	hǫwadi	8.3
ęg	8.2	hǫwę	8.3
ęj(i)	8.2	hǫwęn	8.3
ęs	8.2	hy(a)	8.3
ęt	8.2	hyę	8.3
g	8.3	j(a)	8.2, 8.3
ga	8.3	ji	8.2
gadi	8.3	k	8.3
gae	8.3	kake	8.3
gaesa	8.3	kashe(y)	8.3
gaesę	8.3	ke(y)	8.2, 8.3
ga:g	8.3	kni(y)	8.2, 8.3
gake(y)	8.2, 8.3	na, na:	8.2
gaǫ	8.3	naʼ, nʼa	8.2
gaǫdad(e)	8.3	naʼdaǫda	8.2
gaǫdat	8.3	naʼde, nʼade	8.2
gaǫg(e)	8.2, 8.3	naʼdeg	8.2
gaǫk	8.3	naʼdet	8.2
gashe(y)	8.2, 8.3	naʼdǫda	8.2
gaw	8.3	naʼdǫ:da	8.2
gǫ(y)	8.2, 8.3	naʼdęt	8.2
go	8.3	naǫsa	8.2
godi	8.3	nę	8.2
gon	8.3	nhe	8.2
gęn	8.3	ni	8.2
gwa(y)	8.2, 8.3	nidi	8.2
gwę	8.3	nig	8.2
gy	8.3	nij	8.2
h	8.3	nis	8.2
ha, ha:	8.2, 8.3	nit	8.2
haʼ	8.2	nǫ	8.2
haʼde	8.2	nǫda	8.2
haʼdę	8.2	nǫdi	8.2
hadi	8.3	nǫsa	8.2
hag(e)	8.2, 8.3	o	8.3
haʼt	8.2	odi	8.3
hak	8.3	on	8.3
haǫsa	8.2	ǫ	8.2, 8.3
he(y), heʼ	8.2, 8.3	ǫ:da	8.2
hehs(e)	8.2, 8.3	ǫdad(e)	8.3
hes	8.2	ǫdat	8.3
hej(i)	8.2	ǫg	8.3
hę	8.2	ǫge	8.3
hęj(i)	8.2	ǫgw(a)	8.3
hęn	8.3	ǫgwę	8.3
hęs	8.2	ǫgy	8.3
hęt	8.2	ǫk	8.3
ho	8.3	ǫki(y)	8.2, 8.3
hodi	8.3	ǫkn(i)	8.2, 8.3
hon	8.3	ǫ:sa	8.2

s(a)	8.3, 8.2
sę	8.3
sg	8.3
sge	8.3
sgwa	8.3
sgwę	8.3
shago	8.3
shagodi	8.3
shagon	8.3
shagwa	8.3
shagwę	8.3
shakni(y)	8.2, 8.3
she(y)	8.3
shedwa(y)	8.3
shedwę	8.3
shegy	8.3
shej	8.3
shesni	8.3
shesw(a)	8.3
sheswę	8.3
shetni(y)	8.3
shetw(a)	8.3
shetwę	8.3
shǫgw(a)	8.3
shǫgwę	8.3
shǫgy	8.3
shǫkn(i)	8.3
sk	8.3
skni(y)	8.3
sky	8.3
sn(i)	8.2, 8.3
sw(a)	8.2, 8.3
swę	8.3
t	8.2
ta(ʼ)	8.2
ta:	8.2
tae	8.2
taʼde	8.2
taʼdę	8.2
te(ʼ), te:	8.2
tę	8.2
ti	8.2
tn(i)	8.3
tǫde	8.2
tǫdi	8.2
tsaʼ	8.2
tsaʼde	8.2
tsaʼdeg	8.2
tsaʼdę	8.2
tsi	8.2
w(a)	8.3

4 ENDINGS

This section lists verbs and endings which commonly occur word-finally, and the section in Appendix J (Cayuga Grammar) or in the Cayuga-English Dictionary (CED) in which these are listed or discussed. Alphabetization in this table ignores glottal stop and [h], as described in §2.2 of this user guide.

-(a)deʼ see CED
a verb meaning *exist* or *stick out;* also used in expressions meaning *different* or *unusual*

-(a)denyǫʼ see -(a)deʼ in CED
the verb *exist* or *stick out* with distributive; denotes *the existence of several objects*

-(a)dęs see CED
a verb denoting an object that is *thick*

-(a)dih see CED
a verb denoting a *side* of an object

(a)dihǫh see CED
a verb denoting objects that are *leaning*

-(a)ęʼ see CED
the verb *lie*; denotes an object *lying on the ground*

-(a)ędahkwaʼ see CED, 7.5 in Appendix J
the verb *lie* with instrumental; denotes *a place where certain objects are put*

-(a)ędǫʼ see CED
the verb *lie* with distributive; denotes several objects *lying on the ground*

-(a)ędǫnyǫʼ see CED
the verb *lie* with distributive; denotes many objects *lying on the ground*

-(a)gahdeh see CED
a verb denoting an object that is *raw*

-(a)ge: see CED
the verb *be more than one*; appears after many incorporated nouns; used in expressions for counting objects; also used

in expressions meaning *many, all kinds of, a variety of*

-(a)ʼgeh see, 7.5 in Appendix J
external locative; denotes *on, etc.*

-(a)gehagyeʼ see -(a)ge: in CED; 8.6 in Appendix J
the verb *be more than one* in the progressive; denotes *several objects at a time*

-(a)ʼgeho:nǫʼ see, 7.5 in Appendix J
external locative plus populative; denotes people who live on or near a place

-(a)goʼ see, 8.6, 8.7 in Appendix J
reversive and punctual suffixes; denote that the action is the *opposite* of some other action

-(a)gǫ: see, 7.5 in Appendix J
internal locative suffix; means *in*, *on*, or *under*

-(a)gwahs see, 8.6, 8.7 in Appendix J
reversive and habitual suffixes; denote that the action is the *opposite* of some other action

-(a)gwęhdę see CED
a verb denoting an object that is *flat, dented*

-(a)gwęh see, 8.6, 8.7 in Appendix J
reversive and stative suffixes; denote that the action is the *opposite* of some other action

-(ʼ)ah see, 7.5 in Appendix J
diminutive suffix; can denote smallness; present in many kinship terms

-(a)haʼ see, 8.6, 8.7 in Appendix J
dislocative and habitual suffixes; denote *to go and do something*

-(a)haʼ see, 8.6, 8.7 in Appendix J
dislocative and punctual suffixes; denote *to go and do something*

-(a)he:ʼ see -(h)e:ʼ in CED
a verb denoting an object that is *sitting on top of something*

-(a)he:ʼ see, 8.6, 8.11 in Appendix J
purposive past

-(a)heʼ see, 8.6, 8.11 in Appendix J
purposive

-(a)hęh see -(h)ęh in CED
a verb denoting the *middle* of an object

-(a)hǫh see -(adi)hǫh in CED
a verb denoting objects that are *leaning*

-(a)kaʼ see, 8.6, 8.7 in Appendix J
dislocative, punctual

-(a):ʼkʼah see, 7.5 in Appendix J
locative suffix; means *beside* or *alongside*

-(a):kʼah see CED
a verb denoting an object that is *short*

-(a)kdagyeʼ see, 7.5 in Appendix J
locative; means *beside* or *alongside*

-(a)ke:ʼ see, 8.6, 8.11 in Appendix J
purposive past

-(a)keʼ see, 8.6, 8.11 in Appendix J
purposive, punctual

-(a)hnaʼ see, 8.6, 8.7 in Appendix J
dislocative and punctual suffixes

-(a)hne:ʼ see, 8.6, 8.11 in Appendix J
purposive past

-(a)hneʼ see, 8.6, 8.11 in Appendix J
factual purposive

-(a)hneʼs see, 8.6, 8.7 in Appendix J
habitual purposive

-(a)hneʼse:k see, 8.6, 8.11 in Appendix J
future habitual purposive or optative habitual purposive

-(a)hneʼsgęhę:ʼ see, 8.6, 8.11 in Appendix J
habitual past, purposive

-(a)hnǫʼ see, 8.6, 8.7 in Appendix J
dislocative plus plural

-(a)hnǫh see, 8.6, 8.7 in Appendix J
stative, dislocative stem

-(a)hnǫhk see, 8.6, 8.7 in Appendix J
stative past, dislocative stem

-(a)hnǫ:k see, 8.6, 8.7 in Appendix J
future stative, dislocative stem
optative stative, dislocative stem

-(a)hsa' see, 8.6, 8.7 in Appendix J
dislocative, punctual

-(a)hsde' see CED
a verb denoting an object that is *heavy*

-(a)hse:' see, 8.6, 8.11 in Appendix J
purposive past

-(a)hse' see, 8.6, 8.11 in Appendix J
purposive, punctual

-(a)se: see CED
a verb denoting an object that is *new*

-(a)hse:k see, 8.6, 8.7
future habitual; optative habitual

-(a)hsę: see, 8.6, 8.7
a verb denoting an object that is *fat*

-(a)hshę: see CED
a verb denoting an object that is *slow-moving*

-(a)hsi see, 8.6 in Appendix J
reversive; denotes that the action is the opposite of some other action

-(a):t see -d in CED
the verb *stand*; appears after many incorporated nouns; used in expressions for counting objects

-(a)ta' see, 8.6, 8.7 in Appendix J
dislocative, punctual

-(a)te' see CED
a verb denoting an object that is *bright, clear*

-(a)te:' see, 8.6, 8.11 in Appendix J
purposive past

-(a)te' see, 8.6, 8.11 in Appendix J
purposive, punctual

-(a)tshǫ' see -tsǫ' in CED
the verb *stand* with pluralizer; used in expressions meaning *each* or *individually* or *one after another*

-(')d see, 8.6 in Appendix J
inchoative suffix; means *come into being*

-(h)d see, 8.6 in Appendix J
causative suffix; means *cause someone to do something*

-da' see CED
the verb *stand* with inchoative; meaning *stand up*

-dagǫh see CED
a verb denoting an object that is *dark*

-dagye' see CED
the verb *stand* with progressive; meaning *to continue on*

-(')daihę: see CED
a verb denoting an object that is *hot*

-deht, -dehd see -dehd in CED
a verb denoting an object that is *bold, bright, strong*

-dę' see CED
the verb *stand* with benefactive and inchoative; meaning *to come to be standing*

-dęhda:' see CED
a verb denoting *to lie spread out on the ground*

-dǫ' see CED
the verb *stand* with distributive; denotes *a group of similar standing objects*

-(')dǫh see, 8.6, 8.7 in Appendix J
causative and stative suffixes; means *cause someone to do something*

-(h)dǫh see, 8.6, 8.7 in Appendix J
causative and stative suffixes; *cause someone to do something*

-(h)dǫh see, 8.6, 8.7 in Appendix J
causative and stative suffixes; means *cause someone to do something*

-(')dr(a) see, 8.6, 8.7 in Appendix J
dislocative suffix

-(')dra' see, 8.6, 8.7 in Appendix J
dislocative and punctual suffixes

-(')drah see, 8.6, 8.7 in Appendix J
dislocative and imperative suffixes

-(')dre:' see, 8.6, 8.11 in Appendix J
purposive past

-(ʼ)dreʼ see, 8.6, 8.11 in Appendix J
purposive and punctual

-(ʼ)drǫh see, 8.6, 8.7 in Appendix J
dislocative and stative

-e:s see CED
a verb denoting an object that is *long*

-e:sʼah see CED
a verb denoting an object that is *short in length*

-e:sǫʼs see CED
a verb denoting several objects that are *long*

-e:t see CED
the verb *stand*

-ęʼ see, 8.6, 8.7 in Appendix J
benefactive and punctual suffixes; meaning an *action is done for someone's benefit*

-ęʼ see -(y)ę in CED
the verb *to be lying on the ground*

-ęʼ see, 8.6 in Appendix J
inchoative suffix; meaning to *come into being*

-ʼę:ʼ see CED
a verb denoting an object that is *coloured*

-ędaʼ see -(y)ędaʼ in CED
the verb *lie* with inchoative; meaning: *come to have* or *finish*

-ędahkwaʼ see CED
the verb *to be lying on the ground* with instrumental, denoting *a place where something is put*

-ędǫʼ see CED
the verb *to be lying on the ground* with pluralizer, denoting several objects lying on the ground

-ędǫnyǫʼ see CED
the verb *to be lying on the ground* with pluralizers, denoting many objects lying on the ground

-ęgyeʼs see, 8.6, 8.9 in Appendix J
habitual, progressive stem

-ęh see, 8.7 in Appendix J
stative

-ęh see, 8.6, 8.7 in Appendix J
benefactive and imperative suffixes; meaning an *action is done for someone's benefit*

-ęhęgye:ʼ see, 8.6, 8.9 in Appendix J
purposive past, progressive

-ęhęgyeʼ see, 8.6, 8.9 in Appendix J
punctual, progressive stem

-ęhęgyeʼ see, 8.6, 8.9 in Appendix J
stative, progressive stem

-ęhęgye:k see, 8.6, 8.9 in Appendix J
optative stative, progressive stem

-ęhęgyeʼse:k see, 8.6, 8.9 in Appendix J
optative habitual, progressive stem

-ęhęgyeʼsgęhę:ʼ see, 8.6, 8.9 in Appendix J
habitual past, progressive stem

-ęhk see, 8.7 in Appendix J
stative past

-ę:k see, 8.7 in Appendix J
future stative, optative stative

-ęhne:ʼ see, 8.7 in Appendix J
stative past

-gaʼdeʼ see CED
a verb denoting *many* or *few* objects

-gaęh(eʼ) see CED
a verb denoting an object that is *crossed, bent*

-gayǫh see CED
a verb denoting an object that is *old*

-ge: see, 8.6 in Appendix J
augmentative suffix; denotes *largeness* or *greatness*

-(ʼ)geh see, 7.5 in Appendix J
external locative suffix; denotes a *place*

-geha:ʼ see, 7.5 in Appendix J
customary suffix; denotes a typical *way* or *kind* of thing

-gehǫʼ see CED
a verb denoting objects that are *lying around*

-gę: see CED
a verb denoting an object that is *light-coloured, white*

-(ʼ)gęd, -(ʼ)gęt see CED
a verb denoting an object that is *light-coloured, white*

-gęhę:ʼ see, 7.5 in Appendix J
decessive; denotes something that *used to exist* or that *existed formerly*

-go:wah see, 7.5 in Appendix J
augmentative suffix; denotes *largeness*

-gowanęh see CED
a verb denoting an object that is *big*

-griʼ see CED
a verb denoting an object that is *juiced, liquid*

-gwegǫh see CED
a verb denoting *all* or *everything*

-h see, 8.7 in Appendix J
habitual suffix

-(h)aʼ see, 8.7 in Appendix J
habitual suffix

-(h)ah see, 7.5 in Appendix J
diminutive suffix; means *fairly, etc.*

-(h)eʼ see, 8.6 in Appendix J
inchoative suffix; means to *come into being*

-(h)e:ʼ see CED
a verb denoting an object that is *sitting on top of something*

-he:tgę see -(hr)etgę in CED
a verb denoting an object that is *evil, bad, ugly*

-(h)onǫʼ see, 7.5 in Appendix J
populative suffix; denotes *people who live on or near a place*

-(h)ǫʼ see, 8.6, 8.7 in Appendix J
dislocative plus plural suffixes; denotes *going and doing several actions*

-i:ʼ see CED
a verb denoting an object that is *stuck onto something*

-i:yo: see CED
a verb denoting an object that is *nice, good*

-jih see, 8.6 in Appendix J
intensifier suffix; meaning: *really* or *even more so*

-ka:ʼ see, 7.5 in Appendix J
customary suffix; denotes a *typical way or kind* of thing

-(h)kwaʼ see, 7.5 in Appendix J
instrumental suffix; the object denoted is an *instrument*

-(ʼ)n(a) see, 8.6 in Appendix J
dislocative

-(h)n(a) see, 8.6 in Appendix J
dislocative

-(ʼ)naʼ see, 8.6, 8.7 in Appendix J
dislocative and punctual

-nahnǫh see CED
a verb denoting an object that is *full*

-nawę: see CED
a verb denoting an object that is *wet*

-(ʼ)ne:ʼ see, 8.6, 8.11 in Appendix J
purposive past

-(ʼ)neʼ see, 8.6, 8.11 in Appendix J
purposive punctual

-(h)neh see, 7.5 in Appendix J
external locative suffix; denotes a place

-neha:ʼ see,
customary; denotes a typical *way or kind* of thing

-nha:ʼ see CED
a verb denoting that an object is *sticking out*

-ni: see, 8.6, 8.7 in Appendix J
benefactive and stative suffixes; denote an *action is done for someone's benefit*

-nih see, 8.6, 8.7 in Appendix J
benefactive and habitual suffixes; denote an *action is done for someone's benefit*

-(h)niyǫh see CED
a verb denoting an object that is *hard, tough*

-niyǫ:t see -niyǫd in CED
a verb denoting an object that is *hanging*

-no:ʼ see CED
a verb denoting an object that is *cold, cool*

-(h)nǫʼ see, 7.5 in Appendix J
distributive suffix

-nǫ:ʼ see CED
a verb denoting an object that is *costly, dear, expensive*

-(ʼ)nǫht see -(ʼ)nǫhd in CED
a verb denoting an object that is *in something*

-nǫht see -nǫhd in CED
a verb denoting an object that is *spooky*

-nyǫ see, 8.6 in Appendix J
distributive suffix; denotes *several objects or actions*

-odaʼ see CED
the verb *stand* with inchoative; meaning an object that *comes to be put in or on*

-ogaʼd see CED
a verb denoting an object that is *rough*

-odagyeʼ(s) see CED; 8.6 in Appendix J
the verb *stand* in the progressive; denotes *going along and doing something*

-odahkwaʼ see CED, 7.5 in Appendix J
the verb *stand* with instrumental; denotes *an instrument*

-odęʼ see CED; 8.6 in Appendix J
the verb *stand* with benefactive and inchoative; meaning an object that *comes to be put in or on for someone*

-oʼdę: see CED
a verb denoting a *type of* object

-odǫʼ see CED; 8.6 in Appendix J
the verb *stand* with distributive; denotes *a group of objects or actions*

-odǫnyǫʼ see CED; 8.6
the verb *stand* with distributive; denotes many *objects* or *actions*

-ogę: see -ogę: in CED
a verb denoting objects that are *together, between*

-o:t see -od in CED
a verb denoting objects that are *standing*

-owanęh see CED
a verb denoting an object that is *big*

-ǫ: see, 8.7 in Appendix J
stative suffix

-ǫʼ see, 8.6 in Appendix J
distributive suffix; denotes *several objects or actions*

-ǫ: see CED
a verb denoting an object that *resembles something*

-ǫdahkwaʼ see CED; 7.5 in Appendix J
the verb *attached* with instrumental; denotes an *instrument* or *tool*

-ǫdǫʼ see -ǫd in CED
the verb *attached* with distributive; denotes *several attached objects*

-ǫdǫnyǫʼ see -ǫd in CED; 8.6 in Appendix J
the verb *attached* with distributives; denotes *several (attached) objects*

-ǫgyeʼs see, 8.6, 8.9 in Appendix J
habitual with progressive stem

-ǫh see, 8.7 in Appendix J
stative suffix

-ǫhǫgye:ʼ see, 8.9 in Appendix J
purposive past, progressive stem

-ǫhǫgyeʼ see, 8.9 in Appendix J
punctual, progressive stem

-ǫhǫgyeʼ see, 8.9 in Appendix J
stative, progressive stem

-ǫhǫgye:k see, 8.9 in Appendix J
optative stative, progressive stem

-ǫhǫgyeʼse:k see, 8.9 in Appendix J
optative habitual, progressive stem

-o̧ho̧gye'sgę̧hę̧:' see, 8.9 in Appendix J
habitual past, progressive stem

-o̧hk see, 8.7 in Appendix J
stative past

-o̧hne:' see, 8.7 in Appendix J
stative past

-o̧nyahno̧' see CED
the verb *make* plus dislocative plus plural; denotes *growing objects* or *several objects*

-o̧nyo̧' see, 8.6 in Appendix J
distributive suffixes; denotes *several objects or actions*

-o̧:t see -o̧d in CED
a verb denoting objects that are *attached* or *rooted*

-o̧:weh see, 7.5 in Appendix J
typicalizer suffix; denotes something that is typically *Indian, ceremonial, or traditional*

-(h)s see, 8.7 in Appendix J
habitual suffix

-(h)s see, 8.6, 8.7 in Appendix J
causative-instrumental and punctual suffixes; means *make something be or become a certain way*

-(')s see, 8.7 in Appendix J
habitual suffix

-(')s see, 8.6 in Appendix J
pluralizer suffix; denotes *several objects*

-(h)sd see, 8.6, 8.7 in Appendix J
causative-instrumental and stative suffixes; means *make something be or become a certain way*

-(h)sdo̧h see, 8.6, 8.7 in Appendix J
causative-instrumental and stative suffixes; means *make something be or become a certain way*

-(h)se:h see, 8.6, 8.7 in Appendix J
benefactive and stative suffixes; means *action is done for someone's benefit*

-(h)sgę̧hę̧:' see, 8.6, 8.7 in Appendix J
habitual and past suffixes; means *used to*

-(h)sgo̧: see, 8.6 in Appendix J
facilitative suffix; means *prone to, easily,* or *tend to*

-sho̧', -so̧' see, 7.5 in Appendix J
pluralizer suffix; denotes *a number of objects or actions*

-sho̧:'o̧h, -so̧:'o̧h, -sho̧:'ah, -so̧:'ah see, 7.5 in Appendix J
pluralizer suffix; denotes *a number of objects*

-(h)siha:' see CED
a verb denoting objects that are *congregated or standing in a group*

-(h)snowe' see CED
a verb denoting an object that is *fast*

-so̧', -sho̧' see, 7.5 in Appendix J
pluralizer suffix; denotes *a number of objects or actions*

-so̧:'o̧h, -sho̧:'o̧h, -sho̧:'ah, -so̧:'ah see, 7.5 in Appendix J
pluralizer suffix; denotes *a number of objects*

-(h)sra' see, 7.5 in Appendix J
nominalizer; occurs at the end of some nouns

-(h)sta' see, 8.6, 8.7 in Appendix J
causative-instrumental and habitual suffixes; means *make something be or become a certain way*

-(')t see, 8.6, 8.7 in Appendix J
causative and punctual suffixes; means *cause someone to do something*

-(')t see, 8.6 in Appendix J
inchoative suffix; means *come into being*

-(h)t see, 8.6 in Appendix J
causative suffix, meaning *to cause someone to do something*

-(h)ta' see, 8.6, 8.7 in Appendix J
causative and habitual suffixes; means *cause someone to do something*

-(ˊ)taʼ see, 8.6, 8.7 in Appendix J
causative and habitual suffixes; means *cause someone to do something*

-tʼah see CED
the verb *stand* with diminutive; used in expressions meaning *odd* or *unusual*

-tę: see CED
a verb denoting an object that is *dry*

-tgiʼ see CED
a verb denoting an object that is *dirty, ugly*

-traʼ see, 7.5 in Appendix J
nominalizer; occurs at the end of some nouns

-u:kʼuh see -u:ʼuh in CED
the verb *small*, with modalizer; used with factual, future, or optative prefixes

-u:sʼuh see CED
the verb *small*, with pluralizer; denotes *several small objects*

-u:ʼuh see CED
a verb denoting an object that is *small*

-(hwęʼga)ʼoh see CED
a verb denoting an object that is *notched*

-yanoweʼ see CED
a verb denoting an object that is *fast*

5 THE CAYUGA SOUND AND SPELLING SYSTEM

This description has been revised and expanded from the one in Mithun and Henry (1982).

5.1 ORTHOGRAPHY

The Henry orthography, used in this dictionary, is named after Reg Henry (Shagohędéhtaʼ; also spelled Sagohędéhtaʼ). The symbols used in the Henry orthography are listed next.

Vowel symbols:

i		u
e, ę		o, ǫ
	a	

Vowels are discussed in §5.2.

Vowel diacritics include:

ˊ an acute accent, stress marker, or stress point (discussed in §5.6-5.7)

: a colon or lengthener, indicating vowel length (discussed in §5.5)

_ underlining, indicating devoiced or whispered vowels (discussed in §5.4)

Consonant symbols:

	t,d		k,g	ʼ
	s			h
		ts, j		
	n			
	r			
w	y			

Consonants are discussed in §5.9.

5.2 VOWELS

a sounds like the <a> in father

sga:t *one*
aha:k *he ate it*
dasha: *pass it here*

e sounds like the <e> in hey, or like the <ay> in way, say

é:ʼ *again*
ehswe:ʼ *you all thought*

i sounds like the <i> in police, or like the <ea> in eat

i:ʼ *I, myself*
í:wi: *I want*

o sounds like the <o> in so, or like the <oa> in boat

ó: *oh*
ó:nęh *now*

u sounds like the <u> in blue, or like the <oo> in boot

The [u] sound is rare; it occurs most commonly in three words:

niwú:ʼuh *it is small*
niwuʼdrugyé:ʼah *it is narrow*
dá:gu:s *cat*

In some words, either <u> or <o> is used, depending on the speaker's choice; both pronunciations are correct, but it is best to consistently use either [o] or [u]:

swanóʼjʼageh, swanúʼjʼageh *on your (p) teeth*
swayóʼtsaʼgeh, swayúʼtsaʼgeh *on your (p) chins*
dago:s, dagu:s *cat*

5.3 NASALIZED VOWELS

The nasal vowels of Cayuga have no exact counterparts in English. <ę> varies between [ɛ̃] and a more centralized [ʌ̃]; <ǫ> varies between [õ] and [ũ] in pronunciation.

ę sounds somewhat like the <e> before <n> in encounter, men, or like the nasal vowel sound in French frein *brake*.

ęhę:ʼ *yes*
gę́:s *generally*

ǫ sounds somewhat like the <o> before <n> in known or noon, or like the nasal vowel sound in French don *gift*.

ǫ́:dǫh *she is saying*
sǫ́:deʼ *last night*

ę:, ǫ: After long <ę:> and <ǫ:>, an [n] sound can be heard, especially when these vowels are before <t,d,k,g,ts,j>. For example, the word <nę:dah> *here, take it!* can sound like [nę:^{n}dah].

When <ę> and <ǫ> are short, they are pronounced without a following consonantal [n] sound.

[ɑ̃] A nasalized <a> (pronounced as in French an *year*) can be heard in a very few words, such as in the particle hwaʼ (which occurs in the phrase neʼ hwaʼ *this one this time, this one next*). Nasalization of <a> is not spelled, as it occurs very infrequently.

5.4 DEVOICED (WHISPERED) VOWELS

Counting from the beginning of the word, vowels are pronounced as devoiced (or whispered) when they are odd-numbered and followed by <h>. Whispered vowels result from a rule known as laryngeal metathesis, discussed in §5.9 under the consonants <h> and <ʼ>. Whispered vowels are underlined in the Henry orthography. Examples of devoiced and voiced vowels are contrasted in the following pairs of related words:

a̲ sa̲hwíhsdaęʼ *you have money*
a akwíhsdaęʼ *I have money*

i̲ si̲hsa:k *look for it*
i ęhsíhsa:k *you will look for it*

e̲ ęknége̲haʼ *I will drink it*
e ęyehnegéhaʼ *she will drink*

o̱ go̱hgáhę: *she is jealous*
o hohgáhę: *he is jealous*

ę̱ ahshéhdehnyę̱ht *you knocked someone over*
ę shehdéhnyęhtaʼ *you are knocking someone over right now*

ǫ̱ agę́nǫ̱hdǫʼ *I know*
ǫ honǫ́hdǫʼ *he knows*

In the combinations <e̱haʼ>, <ę̱haʼ>, <o̱haʼ> and <ǫ̱haʼ>, the vowels <e> and <ę> sound like whispered y's, and the vowels <o> and <ǫ> sound like whispered w's; furthermore, the <a> in the combinations <ę̱haʼ> and <ǫ̱haʼ> is nasalized. For example, the word ęknége̱haʼ *I will drink it* sounds like [ęknéky̥aʼ], that is, with the initial [ky] sound heard before the <u> in 'cure'. Similarly, the word ehyádo̱haʼ *she is a secretary* sounds like [ehyátw̥ãʼ], that is, with the initial [tw] sound heard in 'twice,' followed by a nasalized [ã] as in the French word 'an' *year.*

5.5 LONG VOWELS

Vowels followed by a colon or *lengthener* take about twice as long to pronounce as a short vowel. Sometimes length alone makes a difference in the meaning of a word. Some examples include:

e haʼseʼ *you are going*
e: haʼse:ʼ *you went*
a oyę́ʼgwaʼ *tobacco*
a: oyę́ʼgwa:ʼ *smoke*

Cayuga speakers also write a lengthener after two consecutive vowels, such as after <ae> in the following example.

satgǫhso̱háe: *wash your face!*

See §5.3 for further notes on pronouncing long nasalized vowels.

5.6 ACCENT (GENERAL DESCRIPTION)

Most words have an accented vowel, which is pronounced with higher pitch. (Some words are accentless; these are described below). Accented vowels have the acute accent mark ´, also called a *stress point* by Cayuga speakers.

The placement of accent depends on where the word is in a phrase. In words that are pronounced in isolation, and in words that are at the end of a phrase, accent falls on the second-last vowel, the third-last vowel, or, occasionally, on the fourth vowel from the end. Accented vowels are often long, particularly if they are even-numbered (counting from the beginning of the word).

hahá:wiʼ *he is carrying it*
hodá:węʼ *he has swum*
hahé:haʼ *he sets it*

hnéganohs *water*
dewáhǫhde:s *deer*

ganagáeda̱hkwaʼ *a whistle*
sayaʼdodrǫhgwáǫnihsgǫ: *you are always shivering*

Particles typically have only one vowel, which is accented when the particles are pronounced in isolation.

tę́ʼ *not*
ní:ʼ *I, me*

For nouns or verbs that are *not* at the end of a phrase, the accent falls on the final vowel. For example, the accent is on the final vowel of aga:tǫ:déʼ when this word is at the beginning of the following phrase:

> Aga:tǫ:dé' tsǫ:, tę' ni:' degé:gę:'.
> *I just heard it, I didn't see it.*

However, the accent falls on the second last vowel of the same word when it is phrase-final:

> Negitsǫ́: aga:tǫ́:de' *I just heard it*

In contrast to the above words, some nouns and verbs are accentless when they are pronounced alone or at the end of a phrase; consequently, both the vowels in such words have the same lower pitch:

> ganyo:' *wild animal*
> ahsęh *three*

However, such words have an accent on the final syllable when they are *not* phrase-final. For example, the word ahsęh *three* has a final accent when it is phrase-medial:

> ahsę́h niwáhshę: *thirty*

Finally, groups of particles in a phrase tend to share one accent; consequently, Cayuga speakers spell particle groups as if they were one word. For example, the following groups, which have been taken out of their sentence contexts, each contain three particles.

> Negitsǫ́:... *it's just that ... (non-phrase-final particle group; consists of* ne' gi' tsǫ:)
> gyę'nétsǫ:, ... *just that, ... (phrase-final particle group; consists of* gyę' ne' tsǫ:)

Note in particular that the particle tsǫ: *just* is accented when it is at the end of the phrase-medial particle group negitsǫ́:, while the same particle is unaccented when it is at the the end of the phrase-final particle group gyę'nétsǫ:.

In summary, in nouns, verbs, and particle groups which are not phrase-final, the accent is on the final vowel. Otherwise, in accentable words, the accent falls anywhere within the last four vowels from the end of the word. Rules of accent placement for phrase-final words follow below.

5.7 ACCENTING INDIVIDUAL WORDS

As mentioned in the previous section, words in isolation or words at the end of a phrase are accented on the second, third, or fourth vowel from the end of the word. The rules for word accent are complex but regular.

1. Counting from the beginning of the word to determine whether a vowel is even- or odd-numbered, accent the second-to-last vowel if it is also even-numbered. Also lengthen this vowel if it is followed immediately by any consonant except for <h> or <'>.

   satgǫhsǫháe: *wash your face! (<a> is the fourth vowel from the beginning of the word, second from the end, and immediately followed by another vowel; it is accented but not lengthened).*

   d'ehǫgw'edí:yo' *he is not a nice man (<i> is the fourth vowel from the beginning of the word, second from the end, and followed by the consonant <y>; it is accented and lengthened).*

   ętsǫ́'ne:k *you will subtract (<ǫ> is the second vowel from the beginning of the word and the second vowel from the end; this vowel is accented but* not *lengthened because it is followed by a glottal stop).*

ga̱hsǫ́hdaʼ *wire, nail, needle (<ǫ> is the second vowel from the beginning of the word and the second vowel from the end; this vowel is accented but* not *lengthened because it is followed by <h>).*

2. Counting from the beginning of the word, accent the second-to-last vowel if it is odd-numbered and a) *not* followed by a consonant cluster, b) *not* followed by <t> <k>, or <j>, c) *not* followed by <h> or <ʼ>, and d) it is *not* the vowel <a>. Also lengthen this vowel if it is immediately followed by <d, g, s, n, r, w, y>. If the accented vowel has been lengthened, then also lengthen the previous vowel, if it is not followed by <h> or <ʼ>.

dó:gaʼ *I don't know (<o> is the first vowel from the beginning of the word, second-to-last, and is followed by <g>; hence, it is accented and lengthened).*

ęhsnaʼjó:dęʼ *you will boil (<o> is the third vowel from the beginning of the word, second-to-last, and is followed by by <d>; hence, it is accented and lengthened; the preceding vowel is not lengthened because it is followed by a glottal stop).*

aga:tǫ́:deʼ *I heard it (<ǫ> is the third vowel from the beginning of the word, second-to-last, and is followed by by <d>; <ǫ> is consequently accented and lengthened; in addition, the third-to-last vowel is* not *followed by <h> or <ʼ> and so it is lengthened as well).*

3. If the odd-numbered, second-to-last vowel is followed by a consonant cluster, by <t>, <k>, <j>, <h> or <ʼ>, or if it is the vowel <a>, then accent the third-to-last vowel instead. Do not lengthen this vowel, even though it is accented.

asatgǫhsóhae:ʼ *you have washed your face (the second-to-last vowel is an odd-numbered <a> and cannot be accented, so the third-to-last vowel is accented instead).*

hoyáne taʼ *the chief's clan mother (the second-to-last vowel is odd-numbered and followed by <t>, and so cannot be accented; the third-to-last vowel is accented instead).*

degrǫʼ *eight (the first vowel is also second-to-last, but is followed by a consonant cluster, <gr>; there is no third-to-last vowel, so the word remains unaccented).*

agiʼ *I said (the first vowel is second-to-last, but it is also the vowel <a> and so it cannot be accented; there is no third-to-last vowel, so the word remains unaccented).*

4. If the vowel that is normally accented according to the above rules is immediately preceded by another vowel, then the accent shifts to the preceding vowel.

ganagáeda̱hkwaʼ *a whistle (the fourth vowel <e> would normally be accented, but since it is immediately preceded by a vowel, <a>, the <a> is accented instead).*

5. Exceptions exist:

a. Vowels before the suffixes -kʼah and -sʼah are always accented and lengthened (even when odd-numbered).

ganǫhsá:kʼah *beside the house*
onǫhsatgí:sʼah *an ugly house*

b. The vowel of the suffix -shǫ́:ʼǫh / -sǫ́:ʼǫh or -shǫ́:ʼah / -sǫ́:ʼah is always lengthened and accented. (Length is underlying).

(o)gwẹni̱hshǫ́:ʼǫh *change (money)*

c. The vowels in some words or stems are always lengthened, and are accented if they are second-to-last, even though they are before <h> or <ʼ>. (Length is underlying).

knó:haʼ *my mother*
hahé:haʼ *he sets it*

d. The vowel <a> can sometimes be accented and lengthened even if it is odd-numbered, as long as it is followed by only one consonant; this is particularly true if <a> is the first vowel of the word.

gá:yẹʼ *it is lying there*
sá:weh *it is yours*

6. Laryngeal metathesis (described in §5.4, §5.9) affects odd-numbered vowels followed by <h> or <ʼ>, counting from the beginning of the word.

5.8 SYLLABLE BOUNDARIES

Cayuga speakers requested that syllable boundaries be included in Cayuga words, and so this has been done in the English-Cayuga side of the dictionary. Syllable boundaries are indicated either by raised dots, the colon (vowel length), or the glottal stop. For example, in the word ẹt·sǫ́ʼne:k *you will subtract*, the raised dot indicates a syllable boundary between the <t> and the <s>. *Raised dots are not used in the Cayuga spelling system and should be removed when spelling Cayuga words.*

Other syllable boundaries are not specifically indicated by a dot, but can be inferred from the placement of the glottal stop or the lengthener. For example, there is a syllable break:

- After any glottal stop that appears between vowels; for example, after the <ʼ> in the word a·hod·ri̱h·wáʼe:s *he was accused.*
- Between any glottal stop and a following consonant, for example, between <ʼ> and <n> in the word ẹt·sǫ́ʼne:k *you will subtract*, or between <ʼ> and <d> in the word ẹh·sǫg·weʼdá·nẹ̱hs·goʼ *you will kidnap someone.*
- Immediately after a colon (vowel length marker) if a single consonant follows the colon. For example, there is a syllable boundary after the colon in the word grǫh·yá:gẹhs *I am always in pain.*
- Between the first and second consonant following a colon. For example, there is a syllable boundary between the <t> and the <g> in the word ohs·wá:tgẹhs *black sucker (fish).*
- Note, however, that if the colon is nearly word-final, as in the word ẹt·sǫ́ʼne:k *you will subtract*, then the syllable boundary is at the end of the word rather than immediately after the colon. The same point holds for near-word-final glottal stop <ʼ>.

5.9 CONSONANTS

d sounds like <d> in dad before regular (voiced) vowels:

drę́:na: *skunk*
dó:gaˀ *I don't know*

d sounds like <t> before whispered (devoiced) vowels:

dehadí:hwahkwaˀ *choir*
ganǫhsagę́drahgǫh *foundation*

There are no d's word-finally. Any stem-final d's listed in the grammatical sections of dictionary entries are pronounced and written as <t> when the stems in question occur word-finally. An example is discussed at the end of §2.2 of this user guide.

t sounds like <t> in take

satǫ: *lie down!*
sahsnęht *get down!*

g sounds like hard <g> before regular (voiced) vowels:

degrǫˀ *eight*
agiˀ *I said*

g sounds like <k> before whispered (devoiced) vowels:

gahsǫ́hdaˀ *wire; nail; needle*
grahe:t *tree*

There are no g's word-finally. Any stem-final g's listed in the grammatical sections of dictionary entries are pronounced and written as <k> when the stems in question occur word-finally. An analogous example is discussed at the end of §2.2.

k sounds like the <k> in king.

knó:haˀ *my mother*
odé:kaˀ *it is burning*

s sounds like the <sh> in shirt when it is before y or r:

sahsyǫˀ *you returned*
ęhsręˀ *you will set it on something*

s otherwise sounds like the <s> in sing:

só:wa:s *dog*
sgę́:nǫˀ *hello*

h sounds like <h> in hello. Unlike English, Cayuga allows 'h' before consonants and word-finally.

knó:haˀ *my mother*
hahdo:s *he dives*

When <h> appears after <s> in Cayuga, it is pronounced separately from the <s>, *not* like English <sh>. The <sh> combination sounds like the <sh> in the phrase *less heat*:

shę́h *how (this word is also written as* tsęh *and pronounced* tshęh*)*
shehó:wi: *tell her*

Because of laryngeal metathesis, a vowel devoices if the vowel and a following <h> are in an odd-numbered syllable (counting from the beginning of the word). Devoiced vowels are underlined in the spelling system.

ehyádǫhkwaˀ *a pencil*

In contrast, a vowel followed by <h> is voiced when it is in an even-numbered syllable.

ęgakyadǫ́hnaˀ *I'm going to go and have a reading*

A vowel followed by <h> is also voiced when it is in absolute word-initial position or in word-final position, or preceded by another <h>.

ehyá:dǫh *she writes*

shehó:wih *tell her*

j can sound like the <j> in judge, or the soft <g> in Gerald, especially before the vowels <i> and <e>; it can also sound like the <dz> sound in adze or the <ds> sound in leads, especially before the vowels <a> and <o>. However, speakers will also use the two <j> sounds interchangeably.

onájagę:t *rice*
hęjéhehs *birthdays*
ęhsnaʼjó:dęʼ *you will boil s.t.*

j can sound like the <ch> in church, or like the <ts> in cats before whispered vowels:

jo̱hsíʼda:t *one*
jo̱hsra:t *one year*

ts has no comparable sound in English; it is made by pronouncing the three consonants <t s h> quickly, as in the phrase *let's hit*.

gadi:tsé:nęʼ *farm animals*
tsisédẹhjih *earlier this morning*

n sounds like the <n> in nod.

neʼ *that*
í:nǫh *it is far*

n sounds like the <n> in snore before <h> or whispered vowels:

gǫnheʼ *I am alive*
deganǫhsá:ge: *two houses*

r sounds like the <r> in unrest, drain, or grow:

onráhdaʼ *leaf*
gwadre:ʼ *my grandchild*
oʼgraʼ *snow; snowflake*

r sounds like the <r> in train when it is spelled as <tr> or when it is spelled as <dr> before a whispered vowel:

atriht *you broke*
hęnódra̱hstaʼ *they (m) sprinkle on*

r sounds like the <r> in creek when it is spelled as <kr> or when it is spelled as <gr> before a whispered vowel:

ękręʼ *I will set it*
gra̱he:t *tree*

w sounds like the <w> in wash:

waʼne:ʼ *today*
ǫ́:wi: *I think so*

w before devoiced vowels sounds like the <w> in swish, or like the sound you make when you blow out a candle:

wa̱hshę: *ten*
niyohwi̱hsdáʼe: *o'clock*

hw sounds like <h> followed by <w> (the same sounds you hear at the beginning of words such as what and which in some varieties of British English):

hwihs *five*
ganéhwaʼ *hide; animal skin*

y sounds like the <y> in yes:

í:yę: *she wants, wishes*
ó:yaʼ *other*

y Before whispered vowels, <y> sounds like the <y> in the expression 'Can I help you?' or like the <y> sound occurring before the 'oo' sound in English pure or cure:

gyo̱hdǫ: *nine*
dęʼ ni̱hságye̱haʼ? *what are you doing?*

hy sounds like [h] followed by [y]. You can also hear these sounds before the ‘oo’ sound in English h̲uman or h̲umour in some varieties of English:

hyéi:ˀ *six*
ohyaˀ *fruit, berries*

ˀ is the *glottal stop* or *slow marker* (as Cayuga speakers call it). This sound is heard in English before the vowels in the words uh-uh (meaning *no*) and oh-oh (meaning *oops*). When you pronounce this sound, you can feel the vocal folds deliberately closing in the Adam’s apple.

haˀnih *my father*
onǫ́ˀa:ˀ *a head*

In Cayuga, the glottal stop is as important as any other consonant; for example, it can make the difference between a statement and a command:

satgǫhsǫ̱háe: *wash your face! (command; no glottal stop at the end)*

asatgǫhsóhae:ˀ *you have washed your face (statement; ends with a glottal stop)*

ˀ Reflecting the operation of laryngeal metathesis, the slow marker (glottal stop) will be spelled either before or after the same vowel of related words, and it can even be deleted in the spelling and in pronunciation. It typically occurs after the vowel if the vowel is even-numbered (counting from the beginning of the word). For example, the slow marker is after <e>, the second vowel, in the following word:

hǫgweˀdí:yoˀ *he is a nice man*

However, the slow marker is spelled in front of the same vowel or is deleted, reflecting pronunciation changes described below, if the vowel is odd-numbered (counting from the beginning of the word). For example, the slow marker is before the second <e> in the following word.

dˀehǫgwˀedí:yoˀ *he is not a nice man*

However, the glottal stop does not move if the vowel before it is preceded by another glottal stop or by <h>. It also does not move in a small number of suffixes. Examples include the following, which end with the suffixes -kˀah and -sˀah.

ganǫhsá:kˀah *beside the house*
onǫhsatgí:sˀah *an ugly house*

ˀ In pronunciation, when the slow marker occurs with an odd-numbered vowel, the vowel can sound as if it were ‘swallowed’. (It is pronounced either with creaky voice phonation or with a single glottal catch, which can alsobe inaudible or omitted in faster speech). Occasionally, speakers highlight this pronunciation by underlining the affected vowel, as in the following example, or even by deleting the vowel or the glottal stop in the spelling.

dę̱ˀóyanreˀ *it is not nice*

This word sounds almost like dˀóyanreˀ or tˀóyanreˀ when the vowel is ‘swallowed’.

5.10 COMMON VOWEL COMBINATIONS

Common vowel combinations include: <ei, oi, ęi, ǫi, ie, ia, ea, io, eo, ię, oę, iǫ, ęǫ>.

5.11 COMMON SYLLABLES

	i	e	a	o	u	ę	ǫ
d	di	de	da	do	du	dę	dǫ
g	gi	ge	ga	go	gu	gę	gǫ
h	hi	he	ha	ho	hu	hę	hǫ
j	ji	je	ja	jo	ju	ję	jǫ
k	ki	ke	ka	ko	ku	kę	kǫ
n	ni	ne	na	no	nu	nę	nǫ
r	ri	re	ra	ro	ru	rę	rǫ
s	si	se	sa	so	su	sę	sǫ
t	ti	te	ta	to	tu	tę	tǫ
w	wi	we	wa	wo	wu	wę	wǫ
y	yi	ye	ya	yo	yu	yę	yǫ
ʼ	ʼi	ʼe	ʼa	ʼo	ʼu	ʼę	ʼǫ
dr	dri	dre	dra	dro	dru	drę	drǫ
gr	gri	gre	gra	gro	gru	grę	grǫ
kr	kri	kre	kra	kro	kru	krę	krǫ
nr	nri	nre	nra	nro	nru	nrę	nrǫ
sr	sri	sre	sra	sro	sru	srę	srǫ
tr	tri	tre	tra	tro	tru	trę	trǫ
dw	dwi	dwc	dwa	dwo	dwu	dwę	dwǫ
gw	gwi	gwe	gwa	gwo	gwu	gwę	gwǫ
kw	kwi	kwe	kwa	kwo	kwu	kwę	kwǫ
nw	nwi	nwe	nwa	nwo	nwu	nwę	nwǫ
sw	swi	swe	swa	swo	swu	swę	swǫ
tw	twi	twe	twa	two	twu	twę	twǫ
dy	dyi	dye	dya	dyo	dyu	dyę	dyǫ
gy	gyi	gye	gya	gyo	gyu	gyę	gyǫ
ky	kyi	kye	kya	kyo	kyu	kyę	kyǫ
ny	nyi	nye	nya	nyo	nyu	nyę	nyǫ
sy	syi	sye	sya	syo	syu	syę	syǫ
sd	sdi	sde	sda	sdo	sdu	sdę	sdǫ
sg	sgi	sge	sga	sgo	sgu	sgę	sgǫ
sh	shi	she	sha	sho	shu	shę	shǫ
sn	sni	sne	sna	sno	snu	snę	snǫ
sgr	sgri	sgre	sgra	sgro	sgru	sgrę	sgrǫ
sgw	sgwi	sgwe	sgwa	sgwo	sgwu	sgwę	sgwǫ
sgy	sgyi	sgye	sgya	sgyo	sgyu	sgyę	sgyǫ
ts	tsi	tse	tsa	tso	tsu	tsę	tsǫ

LIST OF ABBREVIATIONS

A+	the verb requires an agent pronominal prefix; see Appendix J, §8.3.1
A, B, C, D, E, F, G, H, I, J	Appendices A, B, C, D, E, F, G, H, I, and J
A/P+N+	the verb requires an incorporated noun, and in addition, the type of pronominal prefix—agent or patient—depends on which noun is incorporated; see Appendix J, §8.5
-(a)di, ogy- (illustrative example)	the hyphen signifies a stem or part-word
at+ (illustrative example)	the verb requires the prefix specified (here, the semireflexive prefix whose form is at+ in most forms of this word)
de+yo+ (illustrative example)	the word requires the particular prefixes shown, as described in §2.3 of the User Guide; see §3 of the User Guide for a listing of all prefixes
(f/m)	referring to a group that is either all female, or mixed male and female; see Appendix J, §8.3
gwahs g+yo+ (illustrative example)	the verb requires a particle (here, *gwahs*) plus the several prefixes listed
H	habitual aspect verb form; see Appendix J, §8.7
I	imperative verb form; see Appendix J , §8.7
-k(wa)$_{N}$- (illustrative example)	the stem is either -kwa- or -k-; the material in brackets does not occur in some words
(m)	referring to an all-male group; see Appendix J, §8.3
N (subscript)	noun stem
(N+) (illustrative example)	the verb optionally takes an incorporated noun; in general, a grammatical term listed in brackets is optional (that is, not required to express the meaning of the verb)
-nehagwa(h,ʼ), nehago$_{V}$-	the stem in question has several related forms, -nehagwah-, -nehagwaʼ- and -nehago-; look up such entries in the Cayuga-English dictionary section for details on variants
P	punctual aspect verb form; see Appendix J, §8.7
P+	the verb requires a patient pronominal prefix; see Appendix J, §8.3.2
S	stative aspect verb form; see Appendix J, §8.7
s.o.	someone
s.t.	something
TR/ę+ (illustrative example)	either a TR (transitive or interactive) pronominal prefix or the semireflexive prefix ę+ is required by the verb; in general, a slash indicates that the verb requires either one prefix or the other
TR+	the verb requires transitive or interactive pronominal prefixes; see Appendix J, §8.3.3
V (subscript)	verb stem
we all (excl).	several of them and I; or one of them and we; see Appendix J, §8.3
we all (incl).	several of you and I; or one of you and we; see Appendix J, §8.3
we two (excl).	you and she, he, or it; see Appendix J, §8.3
we two (incl).	you and I; see Appendix J, §8.3
(z)	zoic; referring to animals or things; see Appendix J, §8.3

English-Cayuga Dictionary

A

abandon

ęhs·he:yá:diʼ you will abandon s.o., let them go
[TR+ stem: -(a)di, ogy, -ǫdi, -ǫgy$_V$- throw, abandon]

ęh·sá:diʼ you will get rid of s.t., abandon it, throw it out

a·hot·wa.ji:yǫ́:diʼ he abandoned his family
[at+ stem: -(h)wajiy(a)$_N$- family -(a)di, ogy, -ǫdi, -ǫgy$_V$- throw]

ęh·sad·wi·yǫ́:diʼ you will abandon your baby, child
[ad+ stem: -wiy(a)$_N$- baby -(a)di, ogy, -ǫdi, -ǫgy$_V$- throw]

a·hǫ·wag·yé:saht he abandoned her; he left her
[TR+ stem: -yesahd- abandon s.o.; consists of: -yes$_V$- easy]

abandon a child see: miscarriage

a·go·wi:yǫ́:diʼ she abandoned her child, had an abortion

abasement see: feel bad

o·dé·haʼt a shame; an embarrassment

abashed see: feel bad

ga·dé·hęhs I am embarrassed, ashamed

abcess

a·gég·wa·ǫ:t I have an abscess, a boil
[P+ stem: -gwaǫd- abcess, bulge; consists of: -g(wa)$_N$- lump, boil -ǫd$_V$- attached]

abdomen see: belly, gut, stomach

ek·wá:hk·waʼ a stomach

abduct see: kidnap

ęh·sǫg·weʼdá·nęhs·goʼ you will kidnap s.o. (lit.: steal a person)

aberrant see: unusual

ti·yó:t·ah it is queer, unusual, odd

abhor see: hate

gǫhs·wá·hęhs I hate you

abhorrence see: hatred

ohs·wá·hęh·de:ʼ hatred

abide see: live

ha·dí·nag·reʼ they (m) live here

able

ę·ha:gwé:niʼ he can do it
[(N+) stem: -gweni, gweny$_V$- able to do s.t., succeed]

ę·ga·eg·wé:niʼ they (f/m) can do it; they are able to do it

ę·ga:gwé:niʼ it can be; that is enough

ęh·se:gwé:niʼ you will succeed

de·yo·yʼa·dó·węh·dǫʼ it is able
[de+yo+ stem: -yaʼdowehd$_V$- think about, consider]

able see: accomplish

sa·ih·wag·wé:nyǫ: you are able to perform (that is, run, dance, orate, etc.)

Cayuga pronunciation guide: /a/ father /e/ weigh /ę/ men (nasalized) /i/ police /o/ hole /ǫ/ home (nasalized) /u/ blue. Underlined vowels are voiceless or whispered. /´/ high pitch. /t/ too /d/ do /k/ king /g/ good (never soft g) /j/ judge or adze /s/ soon /sh/ less heat (never the sh in shirt) /sr/ shrine /sy/ sure /hw/ which (the sound made when you blow out a candle) /h/ hi /ts/ cats hide /ʼ/ (the sound before the first vowel in 'uh-uh') /n/ noon /r/ round /w/ way /y/ yes.

abnormal see: unusual
ti·yó:tʼah it is queer, unusual, odd
Aboriginal see: C (Ǫg·we·hǫ:weh)
[-ǫ:weh typicalizer suffix; denotes something that is typically 'Aboriginal, Indian, ceremonial, or traditional']
Aboriginal Affairs see: G (Ǫg·we·hǫ·weh O·ih·wa·geh·sǫʼ)
Aboriginal Education Council see: G
Aboriginal Trappers' Federation see: G
abort
ǫ·dad·wi·yáh·dǫ·taʼ an abortion
[adad+ stem: -wiyahdǫʼd- abort; consists of: -wiy(a)$_N$- child, offspring -(a)hdǫ(:)$_V$- lose, disappear]
a·ga·dad·wí·yah·dǫʼt I had an abortion
a·ga·dad·wi·yah·dǫ́ʼdǫh I did have an abortion
abort see: miscarriage
a·go·wi·yǫ́:diʼ she abandoned her child, had an abortion
about see: be someplace
gę́·neʼs they (z) are around; they are here; they are together
above see: I (he:tgęh)
above average see: exceptional
á·ǫ·gǫh·dǫh exceptional; above average; too much
above the water
oh·ne·ga·gę́h·ya:t just above the water
[o+ stem: -(h)negagęhyad- above the water; consists of: -(h)neg(a)$_N$- water, liquid -gęhyad$_V$- beside]
abruptly
tsaʼdwáht·ge: abruptly
[tsaʼ+d+wa+ stem: -(a)hd$_V$- like, resemble, abruptly]
tsaʼdwaht it is abrupt
abruptly see: suddenly
da·wę́:nǫhk sudden; all of a sudden
absolution see: repentance
a·dat·re·wáh·dǫ:ʼ repentance, etc.

abstain see: remove
de·se·nęt·sǫ́ʼne:k remove your arms (that is, retract them); remove your support
absurd
onówęht it is absurd, unbelievable
[o+ stem: -nowęhd- lie; be absurd, unbelievable; consists of: -nowę(:)$_V$- liar]
abundant see: I (much; i:soʼ)
abuse
dehs·ha·god·rǫ́ʼwehs·taʼ he abuses s.o.
[de+TR+ad+ stem: -(r)ǫʼwęsd$_V$- abuse]
gagęhętrǫ́:niʼ it has been abused
[stem: -gęhęʼtrǫni- be cruel, mean; consists of: -gęhęʼtr(a)$_N$- abuse -ǫni, ǫny$_V$- make]
se·gę́·hę·nih you abuse it; you are mean to it; you are an abuser
[TR+ stem: -gęhęnih$_V$- abuse s.o., be mean to s.o., annoy s.o.]
she·gę́·hę·nih you are mean to her
ha·di·gę·hę́:nih they (m) are mean to s.t.
abusive see: mean
ęh·se·gę·hęʼtrǫ́:nih you will be mean, abusive
abutting see: beside
ak·dá:gyeʼ beside; the edge
accede see: affirm
ęhs·rih·wah·ní:ya:t you will affirm it, agree
accept see: catch
ga·yé:nahs it catches, receives, accepts, holds it
accept advice
ag·rih·wa·yé:na:ʼ I accept your word
[stem: -(r)ihwayena(w)- accept advice; consists of: -(r)ih(wa)$_N$- word -yena(w), yenaǫ, yena(:)$_V$- catch, receive, accept]
ęhs·ri:hwa·yé:na:ʼ you will accept advice, a suggestion, etc.

accessory
ga·ǫg·yáːˀdahk·waˀ their (f/m) accessories
[gaǫ+ag+ stem: -yaˀdahkwaˀ- accessory; consists of: -yaˀd(a)$_{N}$- body]
accessory see: work together
a·ta·di·yéːnaˀ they (m) did it together (that is, they were accomplices)
accident
wad·rih·wag·yá·ǫːs continuous accidents
[ad+ stem: -(r)ihwagyaǫ- accident; consists of: -(r)ih(wa)$_{N}$- word -(a)gyaǫˀ$_{V}$- tricked, fooled]
a·wad·rih·wág·ya·ǫˀ there was an accident
god·rih·wag·yá·ǫˀǫh s.o. had an accident
accidental see: do unintentionally, err
taˀde·wa·géh·dǫːˀ I did not mean or intend it
aˀón·hiˀk it was a mistake, accidental
acclaim see: praise s.o.
ęhs·he·ho·wáːnaht you will praise her, uplift her spirits, flatter her
accommodate see: adjust
ęt·saːdóːgęhs you will adjust s.t.
accompany see: escort
hęhs·he·ha·wíh·dahk you will escort her, take her with you
accomplice see: work together
a·ta·di·yéːnaˀ they (m) did it together (that is, they were accomplices)
accomplish
ęhs·rih·wag·wę́ːniˀ you will accomplish
[stem: -(r)ihwagweny- accomplish, achieve, lead; consists of: -(r)ih(wa)$_{N}$- word -gweni, gweny$_{V}$- able to do s.t., succeed]
sa·ih·wag·wéːnyǫː you are able to perform (that is, run, dance, orate, etc.)
o·ih·wag·wéːnyǫː to perform (lit.: it is able to perform)

accomplish (continued)
ę·sa·dad·rih·wag·wéːnyęˀs you will achieve
[adad+ stem: -(r)ihwagwenyę- accomplish, achieve, lead; consists of: -(r)ih(wa)$_{N}$- word -gweni, gweny$_{V}$- able to do s.t., succeed]
ah·sa·dad·rih·wag·wéːnyaˀs you are a success
accomplish see: able
ęh·seːgwéːniˀ you will succeed
accountability see: responsibility
ga·ih·wa·géh·deˀ responsibility
accoutrements see: clothes
at·rǫ́·nˀidaˀ clothes
accumulate
ęh·sa·dad·ro·héːgęˀ you will accumulate (things, ideas, etc.) for yourself
[adad+ stem: -(r)ohegę- accumulate for oneself; consists of: -(r)oheg$_{V}$- gather]
accumulate see: gather, store
ęhs·ró·heːk you will gather
sęh·sęːnǫ́ːnih store it; put it away
accurate see: right
tgaːyé·iː it is right, correct
accuse
a·hod·rih·wáˀeːs he was accused
[P+ad+ stem: -(r)ihwaˀe- accuse s.o.; consists of: -(r)ih(wa)$_{N}$- word -(ˀ)ehsd$_{V}$- be hit by s.t.]
accuse see: blame
ęhs·héh·waˀehs you will blame s.o.
ache
ga·nǫ·hǫk·déhs·raˀ an ache
[ga+ stem: -nǫhǫkdehsr(a)$_{N}$- ache -nǫhǫkd(ę,anih)$_{V}$- sick]
ag·yaˀda·nǫ́h·waːs I am sore; I ache
[P+ stem: -yaˀdanǫhwag- ache; consists of: -yaˀd(a)$_{N}$- body -nǫhwag$_{V}$- sore, ache]
ǫg·yaˀda·nǫ́h·waːk I ached

Cayuga pronunciation guide: /a/ father /e/ weigh /ę/ men (nasalized) /i/ police /o/ hole /ǫ/ home (nasalized) /u/ blue. Underlined vowels are voiceless or whispered. /ˊ/ high pitch. /t/ too /d/ do /k/ king /g/ good (never soft g) /j/ judge or adze /s/ soon /sh/ less heat (never the sh in shirt) /sr/ shrine /sy/ sure /hw/ which (the sound made when you blow out a candle) /h/ hi /ts/ cats hide /ˀ/ (the sound before the first vowel in 'uh-uh') /n/ noon /r/ round /w/ way /y/ yes.

ache see: agony, headache, stomach ache, painful
grǫh·yá:gęhs I am always in pain
ak·nǫʼá:nǫh·wa:s I have a headache
a·gek·se·dá·nǫh·wa:s I have a stomach ache
o·nó·hǫk·deʼ it is painful
achieve see: accomplish
ęhs·rih·wag·wę́·niʼ you will accomplish
acknowledge see: recognize, thank
ęg·yę́:de:ʼ I will recognize it
dęd·wa·nǫ·hǫ́:nyǫ:ʼ we all (incl.) will thank (s.t.)
acquire
ę·sa:yę́:daʼ you will acquire, obtain
[P+ (N) stem: -(y)ędaʼ- become, acquire, finish; consists of: -(y)ę$_{V}$- lie on the ground]
acquire see: gather, buy
haʼhá:goʼ he went and got it
ęh·sní:nǫʼ you will buy, purchase
acre
sgá:t é:gęh one acre
[consists of: sga:t one; e:gęh s.o. has seen it]
acrid see: bitter
de·yós·gan·yeʼs it is bitter
across (go across)
at·sa:dǫ́:goht you went across; you have completed s.t.
[de+...ad+ stem: -ǫgohd$_{V}$- surpass, go across, complete s.t.]
across (go across) see: cross
a·ta·hę·dí:yaʼk he went across the field
act see: do, slow
nig·ya:gó:yę: the way she does s.t.
a·gáhs·hę: I am slow to act
activate see: begin
ęht·sáh·sa·węʼ you will begin, start
active
ha·yaʼt·gá·ǫ:ʼ he is quick to move; he is active, always moving around

active (continued)
[A+ stem: -yaʼd(a)$_{N}$- body -gaǫ$_{V}$- active, quick]
ag·yáʼda·deht I am nimble, active, energetic
[P+ stem: -yaʼdadehd- active, nimble, energetic; consists of: -yaʼd(a)$_{N}$- body -dehd$_{V}$- bold, bright, strong]
go·yáʼda·deht she is agile
ho·yáʼda·deht he is agile, fleet of foot, nimble, quick-moving
active see: agile
ha·yaʼt·gá·i·yeʼ he is agile
actor, actress
hag·yę́·nʼa·taʼ he is an actor, clown, etc.
[A+ag+ stem: -yęnaʼtaʼ, yanaʼtaʼ- actor, actress; consists of: -yęnaʼd, yanaʼd$_{V}$- mark s.t.]
ǫg·yá·nʼa·taʼ actress
ga·ǫg·ya·náʼtaʼ they (f/m) are performers (for example, figure skaters, actors, etc.)
actual see: right
dó:gęhs sure; truly; right; it is a fact
acute see: extreme
he·yod·rah·héhs·dǫh it is extreme
add
ęt·yehs you will add
[(heʼ+)... stem: -yehsd$_{V}$- add]
hęt·yehs you will add
haʼdę́:syehs you will put them all together
[haʼde+... stem: -yehsd$_{V}$- add]
add see: resume, count
hęt·sáh·sǫd·ręʼ you will resume, add on
ęd·wáhs·he:t we all (incl.) will count
addicted
hog·yá·naʼǫh he is possessed, addicted (with gambling, women, etc.)
[P+ag+ stem: -yanaʼ, yanǫʼ$_{V}$- be addicted]

addicted (continued)
tsaʼho:ya:t he can't help himself; it's become a habit with him
[tsaʼ+P+…-ad$_V$- be unable to help oneself]
additional see: another
he·jó:yaʼ another thing
adequate see: enough
sag·yé·nih·dǫh you have enough
adhere see: stick
o·waʼnę́:da:s it sticks to it; it adheres to it
adhesive see: glue
et·séhs·da·taʼ glue
adjacent see: near
i·wá:kʼah near
adjoining see: along
o·ha·hak·dá:gyeʼ along the edge of the road
adjunct see: assistant
gǫn·háʼtraʼ s.o.'s assistant
adjust
ęt·sa:dó:gęhs you will adjust s.t.
[d+…ad+ stem: -dogęhsd- arrange things, right s.t.; consists of: -dogę(:)$_V$- right, true]
administer see: G (ha·di:h·wa·hę:deʼ)
administration building see: G (ga·nǫh·sag·wę:ni:yoʼ)
admiration see: respect
ga·gǫ́n·yǫhs·de:ʼ respect
admire see: revere
dęd·wa·dad·rih·wa·nǫ́hk·wa:k we all (incl.) will show respect for one another
admonish see: scold
ęhs·he·dahs·wá·hęd·rǫ:ʼ you will scold her or s.o.
adolescent see: teenager
ek·saʼda·sé:ʼah teenage girl
adopt
ęh·sa·dǫg·weʼdá·ǫ·goʼ you will adopt a person

adopt (continued)
[ad+(N) stem: -ǫgwe(ʼda)$_N$- person -(r)ǫgw$_V$- keep]
sad·wi·yá·ǫg·wahs you adopt babies
[stem: -wiy(a)$_N$- child, offspring -(r)ǫgw$_V$- keep]
ęh·sad·wi·yá·ǫ·goʼ you will adopt a baby
a·gad·wi·yá·ǫg·węh I have adopted a baby
adore see: revere
de·ke·nǫ·hǫ́k·waʼ she who I revere as…
advantage see: benefit
ę·ya:gó:dǫʼs it will be for her benefit
adverse see: bad
tęʼ det·ga:yé·iʼ it is bad, false, wrong
advise see: counsel, suggest
ho·ha·hah·sę́·hęg·yeʼ he is counselling
ęht·se·yęʼni·gǫ·hó:tahs you will suggest to her, advise her
advisor see: counsel
ha·háhs·hę·hęʼ he is a counsellor
Advisory Council see: G (Tę·nęʼni·gǫ·ho:taʼ)
advocate
ha·dihs·waʼné:taʼ they (m) are advocates, backers, supporters
[A+ stem: -(h)swaʼned- support s.o., s.t., agree with s.o., back s.o.; consists of: -(h)swaʼn(a), (h)sweʼn(a)$_N$- upper back -d- stand]
advocate see: argue for s.o.
des·ha·go·dih·wa·gé·n·hahs they argue for us
adze see: axe
a·dó:gęʼ axe, tomahawk
affair see: G (hę·nahs·he:dahs o·ih·wa·geh·sǫʼ), word, etc.
go·íh·wa·geh s.o.'s affairs
[stem: -(r)ih(wa)$_N$- word]
o·íh·waʼ message; it matters; it is its fault; word; affair; business

Cayuga pronunciation guide: /a/ father /e/ weigh /ę/ men (nasalized) /i/ police /o/ hole /ǫ/ home (nasalized) /u/ blue. Underlined vowels are voiceless or whispered. /ʼ/ high pitch. /t/ too /d/ do /k/ king /g/ good (never soft g) /j/ judge or adze /s/ soon /sh/ less heat (never the sh in shirt) /sr/ shrine /sy/ sure /hw/ which (the sound made when you blow out a candle) /h/ hi /ts/ cats hide /ʼ/ (the sound before the first vowel in 'uh-uh') /n/ noon /r/ round /w/ way /y/ yes.

affirm

ęhs·rih·wa̲h·ní:ya:t you will affirm it, agree

[stem: -(r)ihwahniyaʼd- affirm, agree; consists of: -(r)ih(wa)$_N$- word -(h)niyaʼd$_V$- harden, toughen]

ęg·rih·wa̲h·ní:ya:t I will affirm it, agree, defend it

affix see: attach

ęh·só·ha·ęʼ you will attach s.t.

affluent see: wealthy

a·gat·ga·nǫ́:nih I am wealthy

afford

ę·ge·ga:gwé:niʼ I will afford it

[stem: -gagweni- afford s.t.; consists of: -ga:$_N$- price -gweni, gweny$_V$- able to do s.t., succeed]

afghan see: bedspread

e·nak·do·wé:k·taʼ bedspread

African-American see: C (ha·hǫʼjiʼ)

afraid see: frightened, scared

a·sét·sa̲h·niʼk you are afraid

ęh·sáhd·rǫʼk you will be afraid of s.t.; it will frighten you

after all see: I (seʼ)

afternoon

o·dǫ·go̲h·dǫ́h ga·ǫ́hya̲·hęh, ga·ǫhya̲·hę́h o·dǫ́·go̲h·dǫh afternoon

[consists of: odǫgohdǫh it has passed by; gaǫ:hya̲hęh noon, mid sky]

afterwards see: I (waʼji:hah)

again see: I (e:ʼ)

age

hat·gę́·ji̲h·taʼ he is getting old

[at+ stem: -gęhjih(s)d- age; consists of: -gęhjih$_V$- old (person)]

ot·gęh·jihs·dǫ́·hǫg·yeʼ it is getting old, aging

ni·sohs·ri·yáʼgǫh you are a certain number of years old

[ni+P+ stem: -ohsriyaʼgǫh- be a certain age; consists of: -(o)hsr(a)$_N$- year, winter -(i)yaʼg$_V$- cut, break, cross]

age see: ripen, mature, old (in years)

ę·wáh·ya·iʼ it will ripen

ę·yǫg·ya·díh·sa:ʼ she has matured, completed her life cycle

dó: ni·ya·go·nohs·ri·yáʼgǫh how old are they (f/m)?

agency see: association, G

gęg·yohg·wa·gé·hǫʼ associations; councils; agencies; groups (lit.: crowds lying about)

agent

ho·nad·ri̲·hǫ́:dǫʼ they (m) are agents

[A+ ad+ stem: -(r)ihǫd- appoint, faithkeeper, agent; consists of: -(r)ih(wa)$_N$- word -ǫd$_V$- attached]

aggravating see: maddening

o·náʼkwa:t it is irritating, maddening

agile

ha·yaʼt·gá·i·yeʼ he is agile

[A+ stem: -yaʼtgaiyeʼ- agile; consists of: -yaʼd(a)$_N$- body -gaiyeʼ$_V$-]

agitate see: stir

deh·sá·węn·ye:ʼ beat; mix; stir

agonize see: suffer

de·sęʼni·gǫ́h·ga·eʼ you suffer

agonizing see: painful

o·nǫ́·hǫk·deʼ it is painful

agony: see: pain

ęg·rǫ́h·ya·gęʼ I will be in pain; I will labour; I will be in agony

agree see: affirm, charge (be in charge), decide, reconcile, support

ęhs·rih·wa̲h·ní:ya:t you will affirm it, agree

ę·jad·ri̲h·wahs·rǫ́:niʼ you two will come to an agreement

dęhs·ni:h·wá·ę·daʼ you two will decide, come to an agreement

ę·ji·jad·ri̲h·wahs·rǫ́:niʼ you two will reconcile

a·héh·wa·waʼs I agree with him, support him

agreeable see: nice
hǫg·weʼdí:yo: he is a charming, polite, nice person
agreement
ga·íh·wi̲h·saʼ an agreement
[ga+ stem: -(r)ihwahsʼ- plan; make an agreement; consists of: -(r)ih(wa)$_N$- word -(h)sʼ$_V$- plan, promise]
agressive see: bad
de·ta·ih·wa:yé·i: he is corrupt; he has no scruples; he is aggressive
aha! see: I (hoho:)
ahead
o·hę́:dǫ: ahead, in front, the front
[o+ stem: -(h)ęd$_V$- lead]
he·yo·dʼag·wá·is·hǫ: straight ahead
[heʼ+yo+ stem: -d(a)$_N$- way -gwaihs(i)$_V$- straight; straight ahead]
Ahkwesahsne see: E (Gwe·sa̲hs·neh, Og·we·sa̲hs·neh)
aid see: help
ga·yę·na·wáhs·raʼ help
aide see: assistant
gǫn·háʼtraʼ s.o.'s assistant
AIDS
ga·yaʼda·dǫ́:gwahs AIDS
[ga+ stem: -yaʼdadǫhgwahs- AIDS, HIV consists of: -yaʼd(a)$_N$- body -dǫhgwa(ʼ,h)$_V$- fever]
AIDS see: disease
ga·noh·soh·dá·nǫ:ʼ AIDS; disease
ail see: sick
tęʼ de·sa·da·gá·i·deʼ you feel sick
ak·nǫ·hǫk·dá:nih I am sick
air
ó:wa:ʼ air, wind
[o+ stem: -w(a:)$_N$- air, wind]
air conditioner
ga·nǫh·sa·nóhs·da̲hk·waʼ air conditioner
[ga+ stem: -nǫhsanohsdahkwaʼ- air conditioner; consists of: -nǫhs(a)$_N$- house -nohsdahkwaʼ$_V$- s.t. that cools]
airplane
de·gá:dęhs airplane
[de+ga+ stem: -dęhs- plane, airplane; consists of: -dę$_V$- fly, take off]
airplane see: jet
ot·sa:dó:t de·gá:dęh jet; plane
alarm clock
go·yéh·taʼ alarm clock
[go+ stem: -yehtaʼ- alarm clock; consists of: ye(h,:)$_V$- wake up, awaken]
alarm clock
go·yeh·táʼ ga̲h·wíhs·daʼehs alarm clock
[consists of: goyehtaʼ alarm clock; ga̲hwihsdʼa̲ehs clock]
Albany, N.Y. see: E (Sga·nę·da:dih)
alcohol see: liquor
de·gaʼni·gǫ·ha·dé:nyǫhs alcoholic beverages (lit.: mind-altering substance)
alert see: quick-witted
haʼde·ho·íh·wa·ge: he is quick-witted; he has lots of business, different ideas, many ideas; he is into everything
Algonquians see: C (Tsaʼgan·haʼ)
alight see: land
dę·gęʼdrǫ́:daʼ it will land
alike see: like, same, similar
ní:yoht what it is like (must be preceded by a particle such as deʼ, neʼ)
tsaʼdé:yoht they are (lit.: it is) the same
tó:hah tsaʼdé:yoht it is similar
alive
a·gá·dǫn·hi: I am alive; I am born; I am full of life
[ad+ stem: -ǫnhi:(ʼ)- alive; consists of: -ǫnheʼ$_V$- alive]
a·gǫ́:nheʼ she is alive
[P+ stem: -ǫnheʼ$_V$- alive]
ǫn·heʼ it is alive
alive see: born
sa·gá·dǫn·he:t I am alive again
alkaline see: salty
o·ji·keʼdá:weht it is salty

Cayuga pronunciation guide: /a/ father /e/ weigh /ę/ men (nasalized) /i/ police /o/ hole /ǫ/ home (nasalized) /u/ blue. Underlined vowels are voiceless or whispered. /ʹ/ high pitch. /t/ too /d/ do /k/ king /g/ good (never soft g) /j/ judge or adze /s/ soon /sh/ less heat (never the sh in shirt) /sr/ shrine /sy/ sure /hw/ which (the sound made when you blow out a candle) /h/ hi /ts/ cats hide /ʼ/ (the sound before the first vowel in 'uh-uh') /n/ noon /r/ round /w/ way /y/ yes.

all
og·wé:gǫh, gwé:gǫh, ag·wé:gǫh everything, all
[(o+) stem: -gwegǫh$_V$- all]
ti·yog·wé:gǫh all of it
[ti+yo+ stem: -gwegǫh$_V$- all]
allege see: say
aʼá:gęʼ she did say
allegory see: tale
oʼga:ʼ a parable; a tale; a story; a legend
all gone
haʼwá:tsʼaht it is all gone
[heʼ+...(N) stem: -atsʼahd- all gone; consists of: -(a)tsʼ$_V$- use up]
he·yót·sʼah·dǫh it is all gone
all gone see: use up
a·wá:tsʼa:ʼ it is worn out, all gone, burnt up; it went down to nothing
allocate see: include
há·ǫn·ya̱h·nǫʼ he has included or designated
all over
ti·ga:gwé:gǫh all over the place; here and there
[ti+ga+ stem: -gwegǫh$_V$- all, all over, here and there]
tsi·yoh·wę·ja:gwé:gǫh all over the earth
[tsi+yo+ stem: -ǫhwęj(a)$_N$- earth, land -gwegǫh$_V$- all, all over]
allow see: agree
ęhs·rih·wa̱h·ní:ya:t you will affirm it, agree
alloy see: metal
ga·í:sdaʼ tin, metal
Allegheny, N.Y. see: E (O·hi:yoʼ)
allergic reaction
ęh·sa·wę·nóhg·ra:ʼ it will give you an allergic reaction
[TR+ stem: -węnohgr(a)$_N$- weed -węnohgra:$_V$- cause an allergic reaction]

alliance
de·ga·ih·wá·ka·hǫʼ alliance
[de+ga+ stem: -(r)ihwakahǫʼ- alliance consists of: -(r)ih(wa)$_N$- word -kahǫ$_V$- adjoin, assemble, put together]
alligator
de·gaʼnǫ́:dǫ:t alligator
[de+ga+ stem: -(ʼ)nǫdǫd- alligator consists of: -(ʼ)nǫd(a)$_N$- -ǫd$_V$- attached]
alluring see: enticing
ohs·gá:naʼt it is enticing, alluring, attractive, tempting
almost see: I (o:nę to:hah)
alone
neʼ a·ǫ·hę́:ʼęh all alone; the most
[neʼ a+ stem: -ǫhę:ʼęh- alone; consists of: -(r)ǫhę$_V$- alone, most]
along
o·ha·hak·dá:gyeʼ along the edge of the road
[o+ stem: -(h)ah(a)$_N$- road -(a)kdagyeʼ$_V$- edge]
wa·dę·hę́:kʼah alongside of the fence
[wa+ stem: -(a)dęʼh(ę)$_N$- fence -kʼah alongside]
along
[-a:ʼkʼah locative suffix; means 'beside' or 'alongside']
[-akdagyeʼ locative; means 'beside' or 'alongside']
also see: I (gwatoh)
altar
ha·ji·hęhs·da:jíʼ had·rę·ná·ę:da̱hk·waʼ altar; pulpit
[consists of: hajihęhsda:jiʼ minister; hadręnaę:da̱hkwaʼ he uses it to pray]
alter see: change
dęk·dé:niʼ I am going to change s.t.
altercation see: argue
de·ga·ih·wá·gen·hęh there is an argument

altitude see: height
ni·tgá:deʼ how high it is (inanimate object); the height of s.t.
always
gyot·gǫ:t always
[g+yo+at+ stem: -gǫd$_V$- persevere, linger, always]
haʼdę·wat·gǫ́:dęʼ always; forever
[haʼde+wa+at+ stem: -gǫdęʼ- always, forever; consists of: -gǫd$_V$- persevere, linger]
amateur see: learn
ǫ·de·wa·yę́:staʼ she is a novice, learner, beginner
amazed see: surprised
ak·né·hag·wahs I'm always amazed
amazing
o·né·hag·waht it is amazing, awesome
[o+ stem: -nehagwahd- amazing; consists of: -nehagwa(h,ʼ), nehago$_V$- surprised, amazed]
ambassador see: G (gon·haʼtraʼ sha·gog·yaʼda·nǫhg·wa:nih), represent
ęhs·ha·gog·yaʼdǫ́:dahk he will be an ambassador, represent s.o.
ambulance driver
god·rih·wag·ya·ǫʼǫ́h
go·yaʼda·nęhg·wíh ha·dó:wih ambulance driver
[consists of: godrihwagyaǫʼǫh s.o. had an accident; goyaʼdanęhgwih transportation, bus, elevator; hado:wih he drives]
ambush see: catch
ę·hǫ·wa·di:yé:na:ʼ they will arrest or catch him, them (m)
amend see: repair
sa·sehs·rǫ́:niʼ you repaired it
American see: C (Gwahs·dǫ·hon·ǫh·ge·ho:nǫʼ)
amid see: middle
de·yó:gę: between, in the middle

ammunition
ǫʼgę́·hohk·waʼ ammunition
[ǫ+ stem: -(ʼ)gęhohkwaʼ- ammunition; consists of: -(a)ʼgęh(ęda)$_N$- ash, dust, bullet -(h)gw$_V$- lift, pick up]
amount
shę·ní:yǫ: the amount of
[shęh ni+y+ stem: -ǫ$_V$- number (of things)]
ni·gá:gǫ: three or more people; how many of them (f/m)
[ni+A+ stem: -ǫ$_V$- number (of things)]
ni·ga·hǫhs·rá:ge: amount of boxes
[ni+ga+ stem: -(h)ǫhsr(a)$_N$- box -(a)ge:$_V$- two or more, three or more, an amount]
amount see: cost, volume
ni·gá:nǫ:ʼ how much it costs
tsę́h ni·gá:dę:s volume; density; how thick it is; mass
amount
[-dǫʼ the verb 'stand' with distributive; denotes 'a group of similar standing objects']
[+odǫʼ the verb 'stand' with distributive; denotes 'a group of objects or actions']
[+odǫnyǫʼ the verb 'stand' with distributive; denotes many objects or actions]
[-ǫʼ distributive suffix; denotes 'several objects or actions']
[+ǫdǫʼ the verb 'attached' with distributive; denotes 'several attached objects']
[+ǫdǫnyǫʼ the verb 'attached' with distributives; denotes 'several attached objects']
[+ǫnyahnǫʼ the verb 'make' plus dislocative plus plural; denotes 'growing' or 'several objects']
[-ǫnyǫʼ distributive suffixes; denote 'several objects or actions']

amount (continued)
[-(h)s(h)ǫʼ pluralizer; denotes several objects]
[-(h)s(h)ǫːʼah, (h)s(h)ǫːʼǫh pluralizer; denotes several objects]
[-ʼs pluralizer suffix; denotes 'several objects']
[-adenyǫʼ the verb 'exist' with distributive; denotes 'the existence of several objects']
[-agehagyeʼ the verb 'be more than one' in the progressive; denotes 'several objects at a time']
amphibian see: frog
sgwaʼáh·daʼ frog
ample see: enough
a·sag·yéːniht you got enough
amplify see: big
a·ga·go·wáːn·heʼ, **a·gó·wan·heʼ** it became big
amusement see: game, recreation
at·gáhn·yeht·raʼ sports; games
de·yǫʼni·gǫ·ha·wę́n·yʼe·taʼ recreation; hobbies
amusing
o·yǫ́ːgyat it is amusing, laughable
[o+ stem: -yǫgyaʼd- amusing, laughable; consists of: -yǫdi, yǫgy$_V$- smile]
amusing see: comical
o·yǫːgyę́·niː it is comical
analogous see: same
tsaʼdéːyoht they are (lit.: it is) the same
analyse see: investigate
ęhs·ríh·wi̱h·saːk you will investigate, inquire
Ancaster, Ont. see: E (Tga·naʼjo·haːʼ)
ancestor
ha·di·gęh·jih·sǫʼgę́·hęːʼ they (m) are our grandfathers, our ancestors
[A+ stem: -gęhjihsǫʼgęhęːʼ- ancestor, grandfather; consists of: -gęhjih$_V$- old (person); -sǫʼ plural -gęhęːʼ former, deceased]
ancestor (continued)
ǫg·weʼda·gáːyǫh our ancestor
[stem: -ǫgweʼdagayǫh- ancestor; consists of: -ǫgwe(ʼda)$_N$- person -gayǫh$_V$- old]
ancestral
[-gęhęːʼ decessive; denotes something that 'used to exist' or that 'existed formerly']
ancient see: old (thing)
o·gáːyǫh it is old
and see: I, hniʼ
anecdote see: tale
oʼgaːʼ a parable; tale; story; legend
anaesthetized see: numb
ot·sís·da̱ʼǫh it is numb
angel
de·yǫ·ki·yę́ʼnya·dǫʼ they protect us with their hands; angels
[de+TR/...ę+ stem: -ʼnyadǫʼ- angel; consists of: -(ʼ)ny(a)$_N$- finger, hand -(ʼ)nyadǫ(ː)$_V$- protect, embrace]
de·ga·eːwáːyǫːt they (f/m) are angels
[de+gae+ stem: -wayǫd- angel; consists of: -way(a)$_N$- fin, wing -ǫd$_V$- attached]
anger
ohs·rǫ́·hęʼdaʼ angry person; temper
[o+ stem: -(a)hsrǫhę(ʼda)$_N$- anger, temper -(h)srǫhęː$_V$- cross, angry]
ak·náʼk·węhs s.t. makes me angry
[P+ stem: -naʼkwę(h,ʼ), naʼgǫ$_V$- angry]
a·hó·nak·węh he became very angry
ak·náʼkwęʼǫh I am angry
anger see: testy
sa·tíʼyahs·gǫː you hold grudges; you get angry easily
angle see: corner
he·yóʼwiː a corner
angry
gahs·rę́·hęʼdoːt a standing, angry person
[ga+ stem: -(a)hsrǫhę(ʼda)$_N$- anger, temper -od$_V$- stand]

anguish see: pain
ęg·rǫ́h·ya·gę' I will be in pain; I will labour, be in agony
animal (tame)
ga·náhsg·wa' tame animal; pet; domestic animal
[ga+ stem: -nahsg(wa)$_N$- domestic animal]
gat·sé:nę' animal; pet
[ga+ stem: -tsenę$_N$- tame animal]
ga·di:tsé:nę' farm animals (lit.: they (z) are domesticated, tame)
animal (wild)
gan·yo:' wild animal(s)
[ga+ stem: -nyo:'- animal; consists of: -nyo:'$_N$- wild animal -(r)iyo, nyo$_V$- kill someting]
ga·dí:nyo:' wild animals
animal
gę·na·dag·wę:ní:yo' they (z) are wild
[A+adag+ stem: -nyo:'$_N$- wild animal -węniyo'$_V$- be wild]
animosity see: hatred
ohs·wá·hęh·de:' hatred
ankle
o·já·ho'gwa' ankle
[o+ stem: -jaoho'(s)g(wa)$_N$- ankle]
se·ja·o·hó'gw'a·geh on your ankle
sa·ja·o·hó'sg·wa' your ankle
ge·ja·ǫ·hó'sg·w'a·geh on my ankle
announce see: proclaim
ęt·ri·ho·wá:naht you will proclaim, announce s.t.
annoy see: bother
dęhs·ni·gǫ·há:ha' you are annoying me, bothering me
annoyed
sge·gę·hę'dá:nih you are sick of me, annoyed wih me, bored with me
[TR+ stem: -gęhę'd(ę, anih)- be annoyed, disgusted, sick of s.t.; consists of: -gęhę$_V$- abuse s.o., be mean to s.o., annoy s.o.]

annoyed (continued)
gǫ·gę·hę'dá:nih I am sick of you
ęh·sa·gę·hę́'dę' you will be disgusted
as·ge·gę·hę́'dę' you got sick of me; you are bored with me
annoyed
ǫ·ge·gę·hę́'dę' I am annoyed
ǫ'k·nǫ's I am sick of it, bored, fed up; I got sick of it
[P+ stem: -nǫ's$_V$- tire of s.t., get sick of s.t.]
anoint see: oil s.o.
a·hat·na:sǫ' he did oil himself
anomalous see: unusual
ti·yó:t'ah it is queer, unusual, odd
another
he·jó:ya' another thing
[he'+s+yo+ stem: -y(a)$_N$- other, different]
he·jo:yá' tsǫ: another thing again; elsewhere; on a tangent
[consists of: hejoya' another thing; tsǫ: just]
another see: other
ó:ya' other; another
answer
dęhs·rih·wad·rá:go' you will answer, reply
[(de+)... stem: -(r)ihwadragw- answer, reply; consists of: -(r)ih(wa)$_N$- word -(r)agw$_V$- choose, take out]
ga·ih·wad·rá:gwę:' an answer
ant
jin·hǫ́hg·wa·hęh ants
[stem: -jinhǫhgwahęh- ant; consists of: -jinhǫhgw(a)$_N$- -(h)ęh$_V$- mid]
antagonize see: offend
ęhs·he'ni·gǫ́·ha'e:k you will offend s.o.
anterior see: ahead
o·hę́:dǫ: ahead; in front; the front
anticipate see: expect
kni·gǫ́:ha:' I am expecting, watching

Cayuga pronunciation guide: /a/ father /e/ weigh /ę/ men (nasalized) /i/ police /o/ hole /ǫ/ home (nasalized) /u/ blue. Underlined vowels are voiceless or whispered. /'/ high pitch. /t/ too /d/ do /k/ king /g/ good (never soft g) /j/ judge or adze /s/ soon /sh/ less heat (never the sh in shirt) /sr/ shrine /sy/ sure /hw/ which (the sound made when you blow out a candle) /h/ hi /ts/ cats hide /'/ (the sound before the first vowel in 'uh-uh') /n/ noon /r/ round /w/ way /y/ yes.

antifreeze
wat·ne·gǫh·dá:s de·ga·nǫn·yá·ę·hę' antifreeze
[consists of: watnegǫhda:s it cleans up with liquid; deganǫnyaę:hę' it does not freeze]
antique
ho'dreh·da·gá:yǫh his old (antique) car
[stem: -(')drehd(a)$_N$- car, vehicle -gayǫh$_V$- old (thing); antique]
antique see: old (thing)
o·gá:yǫh it is old
antler see: horn
o·ná·ga' horns, antlers
anus
o·hét·ga·hę:t anus
[o+ stem: -(h)etgahęd- anus; consists of: -(h)etg(a)$_N$- anus -gahęd$_V$- drill, hole]
o·hét·ga'a:' rear end, posterior
[o+ stem: -(h)etga'a:'- posterior; consists of: -(h)etg(a)$_N$- anus]
sę·het·ga'á'geh on your anus
anxiety see: worry
ęh·sę·ni·gǫ́·hod·rǫ:' you will worry, despair; you will be desperate
any see: amount
shę·ní:yǫ: the amount of
anything see: I (sgahǫ'dę')
apart see: distance; unjoin
na'de·gę·ná:dre' how far apart they (z) are
de·wa·dah·sǫd·rá:gwahs they come apart (lit.: it comes apart)
apologize
tsa·dat·re·wáh·ta' you are repenting right now; you repent all the time
[s+...adat+ stem: -(hr)ewahd$_V$- punish, apologize, repent]
ęs·ga·dat·ré:waht I will apologize, repent
sa·hę·na·da:tré:waht they (m) repented
ęs·gǫ·ya·dat·re·wáh·dę' I will repent to you
[s+...adat+ stem: -(hr)ewahdę$_V$- punish, apologize, repent to s.o.]
appalling see: terrible
de·yo·dę·nǫh·ya·níh·dǫh it is overwhelming, terrible
apparatus see: tool
ehs·ta'shǫ́:'ǫh tools, utensils
apparel see: clothes
at·rǫ́·n'i·da' clothes
apparent see: recognizable
o·yę́:deht it is recognizable, plain to be seen, conspicuous
apparition see: ghost, vision
jihs·gę: a ghost
ad·wag·yá·ǫn·yo:' a haunted apparition
appeal see: plead, tempt
ęh·sa·dę·ní:dęht you will plead
ęhs·he·yahs·gá·nek·dę',
ęhs·hehs·ga·né:kdę' you will tempt s.o.
ohs·gá:na't it is enticing, alluring, attractive, tempting
appear unintentionally
ta'sa·do·dáh·si' you appeared unintentionally
[ti+...ad+ stem: -odahsi- appear unintentionally; consists of: -od$_V$- stand]
tęhsa·do·dáh·si' you will appear unintentionally
appear unintentionally see: originate
tę·wa·da·dǫ́:ni' it will emerge or appear unintentionally; it will do it by itself
appease see: reconcile
ę·ji·jad·rih·wahs·rǫ́:ni' you two will reconcile
appendage see: arm, leg, fin, hand
snęt·sá'geh on your arm
sęh·sín'a·geh on your leg
o·wá:ya' fin of a fish, wings
sęh·sóh·d'a·geh on your hand
appetizing see: smell, taste good
gad·rę·na·gá'ǫh it smells good, sweet, appetizing
o·gá'ǫh it tastes good

applaud see: praise s.o.
ęhs·he·ho·wá:naht you will praise her, uplift her spirits, flatter her

apple
gahn·yǫ'ǫ́h oh·ya' apples
[consists of: gahnyǫ'ǫh it is white; ohya' fruit]
swah·yó:wa:' apples; crabapples
[s+wa+ stem: -(a)hyowa:'- apple; consists of: -(a)hy(a)$_{N}$- fruit, berry -owa:'$_{V}$- bitter]
swah·yo·wá:' oh·yá' grahe:t apple tree
[consists of: swahyo:wa:' ohya' apples or crabapples; grahe:t living tree]

appliance
e·kǫn·ya·ta'géh oh·sǫ·wah·da·da·i·hę́: ehs·ta'shǫ́:'ǫh electric kitchen appliances
[consists of: ekǫnyata'geh kitchen; ohsǫwahdadai:hę: electricity; ehs·ta'shǫ:'ǫh appliance]

appoint
a·hǫ·wá·i·hǫ·dę' they delegated him a duty
[TR+ stem: -(r)ihǫd- appoint; consists of: -ǫdę$_{V}$- put in]
ni·hǫ·wá·i·hǫ:t he has appointed him
shǫg·wá·i·hǫ:t he has appointed us

appoint see: include
há·ǫn·ya·hnǫ' he has included, designated s.o.

apportion see: share
dęh·sé·kah·si' you will share, divide

appreciate see: thank
dęhs·he·nǫ·hǫ́:nyǫ:' you will welcome, greet, thank s.o.

apprehend see: catch
ah·sa·go·di:yé:na:' they arrested, caught her

apprehensive see: frightened, scared
a·sét·sah·ni'k you are afraid
ęh·sáhd·rǫ'k you will be afraid of s.t.; it will frighten you

approach
ęh·sad·r'a·nę́:da:k you will get close to s.t., approach it
[ad+ stem: -(ra')nęd(a:'g), (ya')nęd(a:'g)$_{V}$- stick, cling]

approve see: affirm, decide
ęhs·rih·wah·ní:ya:t you will affirm it, agree
dęhs·ni:hwá·ę·da' you will decide, come to an agreement

April see: A (Ga·nęsg·wa·ǫ:ta'go:wah)

apron
ǫ·nih·no·dáhk·wa' apron
[ǫ+ stem: -nihnodahkwa'- apron; consists of: -(i)hn(a)$_{N}$- material, skin -odahkwa'$_{V}$- something standing]
ha·nǫh·sǫ:níh hę·nih·nę·dǫ́hk·wa' carpenter's apron
[consists of: hanǫhsǫ:nih he is a carpenter; ǫnihnodahkwa' apron]

apt see: able
a:hag·wé:ni' he was able to do it

arbitrate see: G (dę·ha·di:h·wa·ge:n·ha')

arboretum see: greenhouse
hę·nah·do·gáh·ta'geh greenhouse

archaic see: old (thing)
o·gá:yǫh it is old

archery
dę·hę·na·de'dra·gę́:nyǫhs archery (lit. they (m) are competing)
[de+…ade+ stem: -(')dragęny- practice archery; consists of: -(')dr(a)$_{N}$- case, quiver -gęni, gęny$_{V}$- compete]

archetype see: pattern
gyǫ·den·yę·dę́hs·dahk·wa' pattern

archive see: G (o·ih·wa·ga:yǫh)

Arctic see: north
o·to·we'géh·neh North place

ardour see: love
ga·nǫ́hk·wahs·ra' love

arduous see: difficult
wę́:do:' it is difficult

Cayuga pronunciation guide: /a/ father /e/ weigh /ę/ men (nasalized) /i/ police /o/ hole /ǫ/ home (nasalized) /u/ blue. Underlined vowels are voiceless or whispered. /´/ high pitch. /t/ too /d/ do /k/ king /g/ good (never soft g) /j/ judge or adze /s/ soon /sh/ less heat (never the sh in shirt) /sr/ shrine /sy/ sure /hw/ which (the sound made when you blow out a candle) /h/ hi /ts/ cats hide /'/ (the sound before the first vowel in 'uh-uh') /n/ noon /r/ round /w/ way /y/ yes.

area
og·ye·na·wáh·dǫh area (lit.: s.t. is clinging to s.t.)
[o+ag+ stem: -yenawahdǫh- area; consists of: -yenawahd$_{V}$- cause to catch, receive, accept]

arena
de·ta·di·jihg·wʼa̲·éhs·taʼ arena
[de+t+hadi+ stem: -jihgwaʼehsta- arena; consists of: -jihg(wa)$_{N}$- porridge, mush -(ʼ)ehsd$_{V}$- be hit with s.t.]

argue
des·ha·go·dih·wa·gé:nhahs they argue for us
[de+...(r)ihwa/N+ stem: -(r)ih(wa)$_{N}$- word -genh$_{V}$- argue for, advocate]
dęhs·rih·wa·gé:nhaʼ you will argue, debate, protest
de·ya·go·dih·wa·gé:nhęh they (f/m) are arguing
de·ga·ih·wá·gen·hęh there is an argument
dęh·sá·dat·sʼa:ʼ you will quarrel
[de+...ad+ stem: -(a)tsʼ$_{V}$- use up, argue, quarrel]
de·wá·dat·sʼǫh a quarrel; an argument

arid see: dry
o·háʼdǫh it is dry (that is, fields, weather); a drought

aridity see: drought
o·haʼdǫ́:ge: a drought

arise see: get up; wake up
sat·gęh get up
í:jeh wake up

aristocracy see: G, royalty
gwa:gó:wah royalty, king; the King; the Crown

arm
o·nę́:tsaʼ arm (said, for example, when holding up a doll's arm for show)
[o+ stem: -nęts(a)$_{N}$- arm]
go·nę́:tsaʼ her arm (that is, a doll's)
snęt·sáʼgeh on your arm
sa·nę́:tso:t, snę́:tso:t you have an arm; your attached arm
[stem: -nęts(a)$_{N}$- arm -od$_{V}$- stand, attached object]

arm (of an organization) see: G (he·ga·nęt·sa:deʼ de·yǫ·ki·yǫh·wę·jaʼnya:ʼ)

arm (take s.o. by the arm)
ęt·gǫ·nę:tsí:neʼ I will take you by the arm
[d+TR+ stem: -nętsineʼ- take s.o. by the arm, lead by the arm; consists of: -nęts(a)$_{N}$- arm; -ine$_{V}$- go]
ęt·knę:tsí:neʼ I will pull it by the arm, lead it by the arm

armband
ǫ·nęt·san·háhs·taʼ bracelet; armband
[ǫ+ stem: -nętsanhahstaʼ- armband; consists of: -nęts(a)$_{N}$- arm -nhahsd$_{V}$- encircle]

armpit
on·hǫ́h·daʼ armpit
[o+ stem: -(ʼ)nhǫhd(a)$_{N}$- armpit]
sen·hǫ́h·da:gǫ: your underarm, armpit

arms see: weapon
ǫd·ri·yǫh·dáhk·waʼ weapon

aroma see: perfume, smell
gad·rę:ní:yoʼs perfume
o·de:d·rę́:na:ʼ, o·ded·rę·ná·i:ʼ a smell; an odour

aromatic see: strong-smelling
gad·rę·nahs·há:s·deʼ it is a strong smell; it is strong-smelling

around see: be someplace
gę́:neʼs they (z) are around; they are here; they are together

arouse
ę·déhs·raʼ sexual arousal
[stem: -ędehsr(a)$_{N}$- sexual arousal]
hoʼdeh he is horny
[P+ stem: -(ni)ʼd(a)$_{N}$- privates -(ʼ)deh$_{V}$- aroused]
goʼdeh she is horny

arouse see: wake up, incite
a·hé:yeht I woke him up
ęt·ri·hǫ́:niʼ you will incite, be the cause of s.t.

arrange
ęhs·dó:gęhs you will arrange (things, flowers, etc.)
[(ad+rihwa+) stem: -dogęhsd- arrange things, right s.t.; consists of: -dogę(:)$_V$- right, true]
ęh·sad·rih·wa:dó:gęhs you will right a wrong

arrange see: charge (be in charge), plan
ęhs·rih·wahs·rǫ́:niʼ you will come to an arrangement
ęhs·ríh·wahsʼa:ʼ you will plan an idea; you will promise, make an agreement

array see: spread out
ag·rá·hǫh I did spread it already

arrears see: debt
sat·gá·o:t you have a debt

arrest see: catch
ah·sa·go·di:yé·na:ʼ they arrested, caught her

arrive
é:yǫhs she arrives (at the same time)
[stem: -yǫ$_V$- arrive]
aʼé:yǫʼ she arrived
gó:yǫ: she has arrived
ę·ga·e·yǫ́·hǫ:ʼ they (f/m) will arrive

arrive early see: fast
ohs·no:wé:ʼah it is fairly fast; to arrive a little bit early

arrogant see: conceited
ha·dá:ta:ʼ he is conceited

arrow
gʼa·nǫh arrow
[ga+ stem: -(ʼ)nǫh$_N$- arrow]

artifice see: trick
og·yá·ǫhs·raʼ, ag·yá·ǫhs·raʼ a trick

artificial
ti·gahs·rǫ́:niʼ man-made; artificial
[ti+ga+ stem: -(h)srǫni- artificial; consists of: -hsr$_N$- -ǫni, ǫny$_V$- make]

artist, arts see: G, arts
hę·nag·ye·náh·taʼ the arts (lit.:they (m) perform)

arts council see: G (Hę·nag·ye·nah·taʼ Gęg·yohg·wa·ęʼ)

arts foundation see: G (O·ih·wag·we:gǫh Ha·di·yʼa·dahs·dah·nǫh Ho·nahs·di:hs·dǫh)

ascend see: climb, rise
ag·rá:tę: I did climb
wa·tá:da:s it rises up

ascertain see: learn
ęh·sa·de·wá:yę:s you will learn

ash
oʼgę́·hęʼ ashes; bullet; dust
[o+ stem: -(a)ʼgęh(ęda)$_N$- ash, dust, bullet]

ashamed see: feel bad
ga·dé·hęhs I am embarrassed, ashamed

ashtray
ǫʼgę·hę:kwaʼ ashtray
[ǫ+ stem: -(ʼ)gęhęhkwaʼ- ashtray; consists of: -(a)ʼgęh(ęda)$_N$- ash, dust -(h)kwaʼ$_V$- instrument]

asinine see: stupid
de·saʼni·gǫ́·ha:t you are stupid, foolish

ask
ga·ǫ·da·hǫ́·dǫ·haʼ they (f/m) are asking
[TR/ad+ stem: -(a)hǫdǫ(:)$_V$- ask]
wa·da·hǫ·dó·haʼ it is asking; the questioner
ę·sa·da·hǫ́:dǫʼ you will ask
sa·da:hǫ́:dǫ: ask; inquire
a·hǫ·wa·há·ǫ·dǫ:ʼ they or s/he asked him, them (m)
a·gak·wa·hǫ́:dǫ:ʼ it asked for food
[stem: -k(wa)$_N$- food -(a)hǫdǫ(:)$_V$- ask for s.t.]
o·da·hǫ·dǫ́hs·raʼ the act of asking
[o+ ad+ stem: -(a)hǫdǫhsr(a)$_N$- asking -(a)hǫdǫ(:)$_V$- ask]

Cayuga pronunciation guide: /a/ father /e/ weigh /ę/ men (nasalized) /i/ police /o/ hole /ǫ/ home (nasalized) /u/ blue. Underlined vowels are voiceless or whispered. /ʼ/ high pitch. /t/ too /d/ do /k/ king /g/ good (never soft g) /j/ judge or adze /s/ soon /sh/ less heat (never the sh in shirt) /sr/ shrine /sy/ sure /hw/ which (the sound made when you blow out a candle) /h/ hi /ts/ cats hide /ʼ/ (the sound before the first vowel in ‘uh-uh’) /n/ noon /r/ round /w/ way /y/ yes.

asleep see: sleep
a·gí·d'a·ǫh I was asleep; I am sleeping
aspire see: want
de·sa·dǫh·wę·jo·níhs·gǫ: you always want s.t.
ass see: anus, buttock
o·hét·ga·hę:t anus
o·hét·ga'a:' rear end; posterior
oh·ná'tsa' buttock; ass; behind; posterior
assassinate see: kill s.t., s.o.
ho·dę́:nyo: he has killed s.o.
assault see: rape, beat up
ahs·ha·got·go·ho·wá·nah·dę' he raped her (lit.: he forced her in a big way)
a·hǫ·wę·dá:nyo' s.o. beat him up, broke his spirit
assemble
dęh·sé·ka·hǫ' you will assemble, put together
[de+...(N) stem: -kahǫ$_V$- adjoin, abut, assemble, put together]
assemble see: congregate
ęd·wád·rohe:k we all (incl.) will gather together
assembly see: crowd, G (Ho·nǫh·wę·jag·wę:ni:yo')
gęg·yóh·go:t a crowd
Assembly of First Nations see: G (Ho·nǫh·wę·jag·wę:ni:yo' Ho·nę·nig·yohg·wahs·rǫ:ni:)
assert see: demand, say
ęt·ríh·wa·he:k you will demand s.t., insist on s.t., force s.t.
a'á:gę' she did say
assign see: appoint
há·ǫ·nyah·nǫ' he has included, designated
assist see: help, support
ga·ǫ·dag·ye·na·wá'seh they help her
heh·wá·w'a·seh I did agree with him, support him

assistant, associate
gǫn·há'tra' s.o.'s assistant
[stem: -nha'tr(a)$_N$- employee, civil servant, minister -nha'$_V$- command, hire]
association
gęg·yohg·wa·gé·hǫ' associations; councils; agencies; groups (lit.: crowds lying about)
[ga+ stem: -(i)gyohgwagehǫ'- association, etc.; consists of: -(i)gyohg(wa)$_N$- crowd -gehǫ'$_V$- lie about]
assume see: believe
ta·wéh·dah·gǫh he believes
assure see: encourage
ęh·sas·gyá·ǫn·yǫ' you will encourage
asthma
de·ya·go'áh·sa·w'ehs she has asthma
[de+P+ stem: -('a)hsawehs- have asthma; consists of: -('a)hsa(w)$_N$- chest -(')e$_V$- hit]
to'á'sah·w'ehs he has asthma
astonish see: surprised
ǫk·ne·há:go' I was amazed, surprised
asylum see: hospital
ǫ·te·y'ǫ·da·ę·dáhk·w'a·geh hospital
at
[-'geh, -hneh external locative suffixes; denote a place]
atmosphere see: air
ó:wa:' air; wind
attach
ęh·só·ha·ę' you will attach s.t.
[(N) stem: -oha(:,ę)$_V$- attach]
o·ha:' it is attached to s.t.
á·ǫ:t it is attached; it is sticking out
[a+ stem: -ǫd$_V$- attached]
ga·gę'dó:'a·ę:' it is attached to s.t.
[ga+ stem: -gę'do:'aę:'- attached; consists of: -gę'do:'$_V$- stuck]
attach see: join
dęh·sáh·sǫd·rę' you will join two things together

attack see: rape, beat up
ahs·ha·got·go·ho·wá·nah·dę' he raped her (lit.: he forced her in a big way)
a·hǫ·wę·dá:nyo' s.o. beat him up, broke his spirit
attain see: accomplish
ęhs·rih·wag·wę́:ni' you will accomplish
attempt see: try
a:ga·d'en·yę́·dę' I might try, attempt s.t.
attend to see: care for
ęhs·he·ya·de·wa·yę:nǫ́:ni' you will take care of them, care for them (for a while)
attendant see: nurse
de·yǫ·te·yǫ'dahs·nyé·ha' nurse
attention (pay attention)
sat·gá·hǫ·ha' you are paying attention, watching right now
[P+(N) stem: -(a)tgahǫ(:), (a)tgaha(:)$_V$- pay attention, watch]
ęh·sát·ga·hǫ:' you will pay attention, keep a close eye on s.t.
sat·gá·hǫ: pay attention
attic see: upstairs
o·nák·da·he: loft, etc.
attire see: clothes
ahg·wę́:nya' clothing; clothes
attitude
tsęh ni·sa'ni·gǫ́·ho'dę: your attitude, mood
[tsęh ni+P+ stem: -(')nigǫho'dę'- think a certain way; have an attitude, mood; consists of: -(')nigǫh(a)$_N$- mind -o'dę:$_V$- type of]
attorney see: lawyer
dę·ha·ih·wá·gen·hahs he is a lawyer
attorney general see: G (Dę·ha·ih·wa·gen·has·go:wah)
attractive see: enticing; pretty
ohs·gá:na't it is enticing, alluring, attractive, tempting
ek·sa'gó:wah she is pretty
auction
de·hę·nat·wihs·da·gę:nyǫ́hs wat·gé·hǫ' an auction
[consists of: dehęnatwihsdagę:nyǫhs they are competing for money; watgehǫ' sales]
ho·na·dek·wát·gę·hǫ' they (m) are auctioning off the food
[ade+ stem: -kwatgehǫ- auction; consists of: -k(wa)$_N$- food -(a)tgehǫ$_V$- sell]
auctioneer
hat·gé·hǫ·ha' he is an auctioneer
[A+ stem: -(a)tgehǫha'- auctioneer, seller; consists of: -(a)tgehǫ$_V$- sell]
ha·wę·nahs·nó:we' he is an auctioneer
[A+ stem: -węnahsnowe'- auctioneer; consists of: -węn(a)$_N$- voice, word -(h)snowe'$_V$- fast]
audience see: crowd, demand (an audience from s.o.)
ni·gęg·yoh·gó'dę: assembled crowd; a kind of crowd
ę·hǫ·wa·dih·wa'éhs·dę' they will unravel his message, demand an audience from him
auditor see: G (hę·nat·wihs·da·nǫh ha·dik·dǫ·ha')
auditor general see: G (Hat·wihs·da·nǫh·go:wah o·hę:dǫ:)
auger
ga·na'ja·dáhg·wahs grain auger
[ga+ stem: -na'jadahgwahs- auger; consists of: -na(')ja(da)$_N$- wheat, grain -(h)gw$_V$- remove s.t.]
gana'jawę́hę:s grain auger
[ga+ stem: -na'jawęhęs- auger; consists of: -na(')ja(da)$_N$- wheat, grain -węhę(h)d$_V$- climb s.t.]
augment see: amplify
a·ga·go·wá:n·he', **a·gó·wan·he'** it became big
August see: A (Jihs·gęh·neh)

Cayuga pronunciation guide: /a/ father /e/ weigh /ę/ men (nasalized) /i/ police /o/ hole /ǫ/ home (nasalized) /u/ blue. Underlined vowels are voiceless or whispered. /´/ high pitch. /t/ too /d/ do /k/ king /g/ good (never soft g) /j/ judge or adze /s/ soon /sh/ less heat (never the sh in shirt) /sr/ shrine /sy/ sure /hw/ which (the sound made when you blow out a candle) /h/ hi /ts/ cats hide /'/ (the sound before the first vowel in 'uh-uh') /n/ noon /r/ round /w/ way /y/ yes.

aunt see: C
knoh·á:ʼah my aunt (maternal)
authentic see: right
tga:yé·i: it is right, correct
authority
dwę·nǫ́h·twaʼ (**dwę·nǫ́h·dǫ·haʼ**) it is the boss, the authority
[d+A+ stem: -ęnǫhdǫhaʼ- be demanding, strict; consists of: -ęnǫhdǫ(:)$_{V}$- know]
authorize see: delegate, sanction
há·ǫn·ya̲h·nǫʼ he has included or designated s.o.
ęhs·rih·wag·wę:ní:yohs you will sanction, charter, give authority to s.o.
automobile see: vehicle
gʼad·réh·daʼ car; vehicle
auto shop see: garage
sha·diʼdre̲h·dǫ́·nihs·geh garage; auto shop
autumn see: A
gę·nę·na·géh·neh autumn; fall
[stem: -(gę)nęn(a)- fall, autumn -(h)neh at -(ʼ)geh on]
avalanche
a·waʼgra·nę́ht·ge: there was an avalanche (of snow)
[a+wa+ stem: -(a)ʼgranęhtge:- avalanche; consists of: -(a)ʼgr(a)$_{N}$- snow; -(y)ęhd$_{V}$- hit, knock, strike -ge: big]
a·gahs·den·yę́ʼgeh there were falling rocks
[a+ga+ stem: -(h)sdenyęʼgeh- avalanche; consists of: -(h)sd(ęha)$_{N}$- stone -yagęʼ$_{V}$- go out -(ʼ)geh on]
avenge see: cure
a·hé:jęʼt I fixed (lit. cured) him; I got even with him
avenue see: road
o·há·haʼ road
aversion see: hatred
ohs·wá·hęh·de:ʼ hatred
avian see: bird
ji·dę́:ʼęh bird
Avocet Blue Stocking
ga·yóhg·waʼ Avocet Blue Stocking (a type of bird)
[ga+ stem: -(ʼ)yohg(wa)$_{N}$- tail, skirt]
avoid
sa·deʼgwę·hę́:gyeʼs you are avoiding
[ade+ stem: -(ʼ)gwęhęgyeʼs- avoid; consists of: -(ʼ)gw$_{V}$- run away, flee]
avoid see: run away
ęh·sá·dʼe·goʼ you will flee, run away
await see: expect
ga·ęʼni·gǫ́·haʼ they (f/m) are waiting for s.t.
awake
a·ga·did·rę·ta·od·rǫ: (**a·ga·did·ręh·da̲·hóʼdrǫ:**) I had to stay awake
[ad+ stem: -(i)dręhdahoʼdrǫ- stay awake; consists of: -(i)dręhd(a)$_{N}$- dream -(w)idręhd(a:)$_{V}$- sleepy]
awake see: up
a·gát·gę·hǫh I am up now
awaken see: get up, wake up
sat·gęh get up
í:jeh wake up
awesome see: amazing
o·né·hag·waht it is amazing, awesome
awful see: terrible
de·yo·dę·nǫh·ya·níh·dǫh it is overwhelming, terrible
axe
a·dó:gęʼ axe; tomahawk
[stem: -(a)dogęʼ$_{N}$- axe]
axe see: chop
ęh·sáʼo:k it will chop you

B

baby
o·wi·ya:ʼáh ek·sá:ʼah baby girl
[consists of: owi:ya:ʼah baby; eksa:ʼah she is a child under 12]
o·wi·ya:ʼáh hak·sá:ah baby boy
[consists of: owi:ya:ʼah baby; haksa:ʼah he is a child]
baby see: child
o·wi·yá:ʼah baby
baby food
o·wi·ya:ʼáh gok·waʼ baby's food
[consists of: owi:ya:ʼah baby; gokwaʼ her food]
babysit
sad·wi·yá:nǫh you babysit all the time; you are babysitting right now
[ad+ stem: -wiyanǫ(:)- babysit; consists of: -wiy(a)$_N$- child, offspring -nǫ(:)$_V$- guard]
ę·gad·wi·yá:nǫ:ʼ I will babysit
ga·dę́·gahn·yeh I am babysitting
[adę+ stem: -gahnye$_V$- play, comfort a child, babysit, rock a child]
ęh·sa·dę·gáhn·yeʼ you will comfort, rock a child; you are babysitting
back. see: advocate, reinforce an idea, support s.o.
ha·dihs·waʼné:taʼ they (m) are advocates, backers, supporters
ęt·ríh·wa·waʼs you will back up the idea (that is, reinforce it)
a·héh·wa·waʼs I agree with him, support him
back (lower)
sęhs·hǫ́h·neh on your lower back
[stem: -(ę)hshǫ$_N$- lower back -(h)neh- at]
gęhs·hǫ́h·neh my lower back
back (rounded)
ę·sa·no·wag·wá·ǫ·dęʼ you will get a rounded back
[stem: -nowagwaǫdę- get a rounded back; consists of: -nowa(gwa)$_N$- rounded back -ǫd$_V$- attached]
back (upper)
ohs·wéʼnaʼ upper bcck
[o+ stem: -(h)swaʼn(a), (h)sweʼn(a)$_N$- upper back]
sęhs·wéʼnʼa·geh on your upper back
backbone
ses·hǫh·néh sehs·węʼnʼa·géh ohsg·yę́ʼda·geh backbone, spine
[consists of: sęhshǫhneh on your lower back; sęhsweʼnʼageh on your upper back; ohsgyęʼdageh on your bones]
backhoe
(wa·da·ded·réʼs) ga·yaʼdǫ́:nihs backhoe
[consists of: wadadedreʼs it drives itself; gaya:ʼdǫ:nihs it makes a hole, a track]
backing see: reinforcement
gahs·wáʼne:t reinforcement; backing
back then
swe·gé·haʼ back then; long ago
[stem: -swegehaʼ- back then, long ago]
back then see: past
oh·náʼgę·jih way back in the past; back then
backwoods see: forest
ga·há:gǫ: in the bush
bacon
gah·yęʼgwaʼikdǫ́h oʼwá·hǫh bacon
[consists of: gayęʼgwaikdǫh bacon; oʼwahǫh meat]
gwisgwís oʼwá·hǫh bacon
[consists of: gwihsgwihs pig; oʼwahǫh meat]

bad
tę́ʼ det·ga:yé·iʼ it is bad, false, wrong
[tęʼ deʼ+ not t/d+A+((r)ih(wa)+) stem: -yei, (y)i$_V$- true; bad, false, wrong]
de·ta·ih·wa:yé·i: he is corrupt, he has no scruples, he is aggressive
de·ta·dih·wa:yé·i: they (m) are corrupt, impish, bad
de·yoh·ne·gí:yo: it is not good water
[deʼ+ not yo+ stem: -(h)neg(a)$_N$- water, liquid -iyo:$_V$- be nice, good; bad]
hah·si·na̱·hé:t·gęh he has a bad leg
[A+ stem: -(h)sin(a)$_N$- leg -(hr)etgęh$_V$- evil, bad, ugly]
a·wá·het·geʼ it got no good
[(N+) stem: -(hr)etgęʼ- go bad, get wrecked; consists of: -(hr)etgę$_V$- evil, bad, ugly]
ę·wá·het·gęʼ it (an idea) will spoil, go bad
o·hét·gęʼǫh it is wrecked, ruined
ǫ·geʼdre̱h·dá·het·gęʼ my car broke down
[(N+) stem: -(ʼ)drehdahetgęʼ- have a car break-down consists of: -(ʼ)drehd(a)$_N$- car, etc. -(hr)etgę$_V$- evil, bad, ugly]
a·goʼdre̱h·dá·het·gęʼs her car broke down
od·reh·da̱·hét·gʼę·ǫh a car is broken down
da·wá·teht·gęht it went bad
[de+...at+ stem: -(hr)etgęhd- ruin, wreck, damage; consists of: -(hr)etgę$_V$- evil, bad, ugly, turn bad]
bad cf. evil, feel bad, ugly
wa̱·hét·gęh it is evil (in mind), bad
ga·dé·hęhs I am embarrassed, ashamed
ę·wá·det·giht it will be bad weather
bad medicine see: evil power
ot·gǫhs·hǫ́:ʼǫh things with evil power

baffled see: confused
de·wag·yad·ri·ho·dáh·se:ʼ I am confused; I cannot make up my mind
bag
gá:ya:ʼ bag, mattress, pouch, tick (that is, a mattress bag into which straw is stuffed)
[ga+ stem: -ya:$_N$- bag]
ga·yá:gǫ: in the bag
baggage see: wallet
gatg·wę́·daʼ wallet, purse, pocketbook, suitcase
bail elevator
ga̱·heh·na·wę́·hę:s bail elevator
[ga+ stem: -(h)ehnawęhę:s- bail elevator; consists of: -(hr)ehn(a)$_N$- cargo, bundle -węhę(h)d$_V$- climb s.t.]
bailer
de·gahs·tǫd·róha:s a bailer (for hay, straw)
[-(h)stǫdr(a)$_N$- hay, straw -ohag$_V$- squeeze]
ball
[ni+w+ -ęʼnhotr(a)$_N$- wheel -u:sʼuh$_V$- several small objects]
niwęʼnhotru:sʼuh a number of small balls
ball deer
de·węʼnhé:ga:ʼ ball deer (so called because they roll up in a ball)
[de+w+ stem: -ęʼnhe:ga:ʼ- ball deer; consists of: -ęʼnh(otra)$_N$- ball -iga:ʼ$_V$-]
ball diamond
de·yǫʼnhok·táʼgeh ball diamond
[de+yo+ stem: -ǫʼnhoktaʼgeh- ball diamond; consists of: -ęnh(otra)- ball -oʼkd$_V$- end -(ʼ)geh- on, at]
ball of foot
á:gwa̱h·daʼ, og·wáh·daʼ the sole; the ball of the foot
[(o+) stem: -(r)agwahd(a)$_N$- ball of foot, sole]
gra:gwa̱h·dáʼgeh on the ball of my foot

ball of foot (continued)
gra:gwah·dá:gǫ: on the sole of my foot
balloon
wa·de·wa·ǫ·dá:s de·wa·di·yǫ́:taʼ, de·wa·di·yǫ:táʼ wa·de·wá·ǫ·da:s balloon [consists of: wadewaǫda:s air is put in it; dewadiyǫ:taʼ it stretches]
balloon see: rubber band
de·wa·di·yǫ́:taʼ it stretches (shortened form of 'rubber band'); balloon; elastic
balls see: testicles
hahsg·wáʼgeh his testicles
banana
o·naʼgáʼ oh·yaʼ banana [consists of: onaʼga:ʼ horns, antlers; ohyaʼ fruit]
de·yo·dah·yá:k·dǫ: banana [de+yo+ad+ stem: -(a)hyakdǫ:- banana; consists of: -(a)hy(a)$_{N}$- fruit, berry -(a)ʼkdǫ$_{V}$- bent, crooked]
o·naʼgá:ʼ oh·yáʼ grahe:t banana tree [consists of: onaʼgaʼ ohyaʼ banana; grahe:t living tree]
band
hę·nad·rę·nó:taʼ male singers; a band; a musical group [A+ad+ stem: -(r)ęnod- play music, sing; consists of: -(r)ęn(a)$_{N}$- song, music -od$_{V}$- stand]
bandage
o·yę́h·sa:ʼ bandage [o+ stem: -yęhs(a:)$_{N}$- bandage]
sag·yę́h·sa·ǫ bandage yourself [(ag+) stem: -yęhsaǫ- bandage (oneself); consists of: -yęhs(a)$_{N}$- bandage -(r)ǫ$_{V}$- bead s.t.]
bandit see: rob
sha·góh·sęh·taʼ he is a robber
bang
a·gan·ho·há:yęht noise made by banging a door
bang (continued)
[stem: -nhohayęhd- bang a door; consists of: -nho(ha)$_{N}$- door -(y)ęhd$_{V}$- hit, knock down, strike]
bang see: knock, noise
sen·hó·haʼe:k knock on the door
bank see: G (eh·wihs·da·ę·dahk·waʼ)
Bank of Canada see: G (Eh·wihs·da·ę·dahk·waʼgo·wah·neh)
banned see: forbidden
o·nǫ́ʼne:ʼ it is forbidden, sacred, holy
banner see: flag
ga·yę́hs·ro:t flag
bannock
ti·wat·naʼdá·ǫt bannock (coal-baked) [ti+wa+at+ stem: -naʼdaǫd- bannock; consists of: -naʼd(a:)$_{N}$- bread -ǫd$_{V}$- attached, roasted]
baptize
hǫ·wá·dʼis·gohs baptism (lit.: he baptizes them) [TR+ stem: -(ʼ)sgoh$_{V}$- immerse, drown, baptize]
a·hǫ·wa·díʼsgoʼ they (m) have baptized him, them (m)
baptize
ho·wa·dih·né·god·rahs baptism; to christen (lit.: they sprinkle him, them) [TR/at+ stem: -(h)negodrah- baptize, christen; consists of: -(h)neg(a)$_{N}$- water, liquid -odrah$_{V}$- sprinkle]
hǫ·wat·ni·gód·ra·hǫh they (m) have been baptized
banquet see: feast
ęh·sa·de·kǫ́·ni·ge: you will feast
bar
ǫt·ne·gah·ní:nǫh(geh) hotel; pub; bar; saloon [ǫ+at+ stem: -(h)negahninǫh- bar; consists of: -(h)neg(a)$_{N}$- water, liquid -(h)ninǫ$_{V}$- buy -(ʼ)geh- on, at]
gahn·yǫ́ʼsraʼ a bar; a stick-like object [ga+stem: -(h)nyǫhsr(a)$_{N}$- bar]

Cayuga pronunciation guide: /a/ father /e/ weigh /ę/ men (nasalized) /i/ police /o/ hole /ǫ/ home (nasalized) /u/ blue. Underlined vowels are voiceless or whispered. /´/ high pitch. /t/ too /d/ do /k/ king /g/ good (never soft g) /j/ judge or adze /s/ soon /sh/ less heat (never the sh in shirt) /sr/ shrine /sy/ sure /hw/ which (the sound made when you blow out a candle) /h/ hi /ts/ cats hide /ʼ/ (the sound before the first vowel in 'uh-uh') /n/ noon /r/ round /w/ way /y/ yes.

bar (continued)
de·gahn·yǫhs·rá:dǫh bars on a window
[de+ga+ stem: -(h)nyǫhsr(a)$_N$- bar -dǫʼ- several attached objects]
dęhs·rǫ́h·węʼ you will bar s.t., put up a barrier
[de+... stem: -(r)ǫhwęʼ- bar a pathway; consists of: -(hr)ǫhw$_V$- cause to wait]
dę·wát·rǫh·węʼ it will bar your pathway
ęts·he·ya̱h·si·no·dáh·dęʼ, dę̱hs·he·ya̱h·si·no·dáh·dęʼ you will trip s.o., bar s.o.'s way with your leg
[de+TR+ stem: -(a)hsinodahd(ę,ani)- bar s.o.'s way; consists of: -(a)hsin(a)$_N$- leg (ę)hs(a)$_N$- foot -odahd(ę, ani)$_V$- trip]
barbecue
ǫ·deʼs·gǫ·dáhk·waʼ barbecue equipment
[ǫ+ade+ stem: -(ʼ)sgǫdahkwaʼ- barbeque equipment; consists of: -ʼsg$_N$- roast -ǫd$_V$- attached, cooked]
ahs·deh·ká:ʼ ǫ·deʼsgǫ·dáhk·waʼ outdoor barbecue
[consists of: ahsdehka:ʼ outside type; ǫdeʼsgǫdahkwaʼ barbecue equipment]
bare see: naked
ga·jíʼgwaʼ it is naked
barely see: I, trǫhgeh tsǫ:
barf see: vomit
ǫ·gen·yag·wá·hǫ: I vomited
bargain
wag·yé:sęh it is a bargain; it is cheap
[wa+ag+ stem: -yesęh- bargain, cheap; consists of: -yes$_V$- be easy]
bargain see: barter
dęhs·nǫ́·wa·yęht you will barter, bargain, affirm a deal
bark
ga̱h·nih it is barking
[stem: -(h)ni$_V$- bark]
bark see: peelings
o·wá·ji̱hs·daʼ peelings, bark of a tree

barn
ha·diʼdrǫ·dáhk·waʼ a place where they (m) live; a stable, a barn
[A+ stem: -(ʼ)drǫdahkwaʼ- barn, stable; consists of: -(i)ʼdrǫ$_V$- live, dwell, be at home]
ha·dihs·tǫd·ra·ę·dáhk·waʼ barn
[hadi/e+ stem: -(h)stǫdraędahkwaʼ- barn; consists of: -(h)stǫdr(a)$_N$- straw, hay -ędahkwaʼ- place where s.t. is put]
ehs·tǫd·rá·ę·da̱hk·waʼ barn
barn see: stable
de·ga·di·dáhs·taʼ stable; barn; bus stop
barn raising see: working bee
dę·ha·di·nę́·hę·da:s working bee; barn raising
barn swallow
gwi·yó:gęʼ barn swallow
[stem: -gwiyogęʼ$_V$- barn swallow]
barrel
ga·nah·go·wá:nęh big barrel
[ga+ stem: -nahg(wa)$_N$- drum, barrel -owanęh$_V$- be big]
barren
tę́ʼ de·yǫ·twa·ji:yǫ́:nih she is barren
[(tęʼ) deʼ+ not A+at+ stem: -(h)wajiyǫnih- be barren; consists of: -(h)wajiy(a)$_N$- family -ǫni, ǫny$_V$- make]
de·ha·twa·ji:yǫ́:nih he is barren
barrette see: bobby pin
ǫ·den·yat·so·da̱hk·wáʼ ga·jí·ho·ha:ʼ bobby pin; barrette
barrier
de·wat·rǫh·wák·waʼ a barrier
[de+wa+at+ stem: -(h)rǫhwahkwaʼ- barrier; consists of: -(hr)ǫhw$_V$- cause to wait]
barrier see: partition
wa·dę·nǫh·sa·we·tá·hǫh a partition
barrister see: lawyer
de̱·ha·ih·wá·gen·hahs he is a lawyer

bartender
hat·ne·gah·ní:nǫhs bartender
[A+at+ stem: -(h)negahninǫhs- bartender; consists of: -(h)neg(a)$_N$- water, liquid -(h)ninǫ$_V$- sell]
hah·né:kaʼ bartender
[A+ stem: -(h)nekaʼ- barmaid, bartender; consists of: -(h)neg(a)$_N$- water, liquid]

barter
dehs·nǫ·wa·yę́h·taʼ you are a bargainer
[de+... stem: -nǫwayęhd$_V$- barter]
dęhs·nǫ́·wa·yęht you will barter, bargain, affirm a deal

barter see: trade
dę·hę·nę·dá·da·wihs trades; commerce; barter

base see: bottom, foundation
heh·dáʼ geg·wá·i where it starts; the bottom
ga·nǫh·sa·gę́d·rah·gǫh foundation (of a building)

baseball bat
ęʼn·ho:tráʼ eh·wáʼehs·taʼ baseball bat
[consists of: ęʼnho:traʼ ball; ehwaʼestaʼ drumstick; baseball bat]

baseball game
de·wę́ʼnho: baseball game
[de+w+ stem: -ęʼnho:- baseball game; consists of: -ęʼnh(otra)$_N$- ball]

basement
o·yá:daʼ basement; track
[o+ stem: -yad(a)$_N$- hole, track, ditch]
o·yá:deʼ basement; track; ditch
[o+ stem: -yadeʼ- basement; consists of: -yad(a)$_N$- hole, track, ditch -deʼ$_V$- exist]
o·yá·da·gǫ: in the track; in the basement, ditch, hole

bashful see: shy
go·díʼgrǫʼ she is shy

basin see: bowl, sink
de·yoh·sé:s ga·jęʼ bowl
ǫh·jo·há·iʼtaʼgeh sink; wash basin

basket
gaʼáhd·raʼ basket
[ga+ stem: -(ʼ)ahdr(a)$_N$- basket]
e·ga·heh·do·ha·iʼtáʼ gaʼáhd·raʼ lyed corn basket (for washing)
[consists of: egahehdohaiʼtaʼ s.o. washes or lyes corn; gaʼahdraʼ basket]
o·nę·hę́ʼ e·yahk·wáʼ gaʼáhd·raʼ corn basket
[consists of: onęhę:ʼ corn; eyahkwaʼ containers; gaʼahdraʼ basket]
o·hǫ·nʼa·dáʼ e·yahk·wáʼ gaʼáhd·raʼ potato basket
[consists of: (o)hǫnʼadaʼ potato; eyahkwaʼ containers; gaʼahdraʼ basket]
e·ga·heh·dę́h·dahk·waʼ lyed corn basket (for lying corn)
[stem: -gahehd(a)$_N$- eyelash, stem (of a berry), eye (of a corn kernel) -ęhdahkwaʼ$_V$- s.t. used for hitting]

basket
gaʼahd·ro·wá:nęh bushel basket
[ga+ stem: -(ʼ)ahdrowanęh- bushel basket; consists of: -(ʼ)ahdr(a)$_N$- basket +owanęh$_V$- be big]
e·nę·ho·ha·tóʼ gaʼáhd·rah lying corn basket
[consists of: enęhotatoʼ s.t. used for washing corn; gaʼahdrah basket]

basketball
gaʼahd·raʼni:yǫ́t ęʼnhóʼtraʼ basketball
[consists of: gaʼahdraʼni:yǫ:t a hanging basket; ęʼnhoʼtraʼ ball]
gaʼahd·ra·ni:yǫ́t hę·nęʼhot·ró·iʼa:s they (m) play basketball
[consists of: gaʼahdraʼni:yǫ:t a hanging basket; hęnęhotroiʼa:s they (m) throw the ball in]

bass
sga̲h·sá·ga̲·hǫ꞉ʼ large mouth bass
[s+ga+ stem: -(h)sagahaǫ꞉ʼ- large mouth bass; consists of: -(h)sag(a)$_N$- mouth
-haǫ$_N$- be beaded, strung up]
oʼnó꞉ksaʼ bass (fish); oysters; shellfish; sea shells
[o+stem: -(ʼ)noks(a)$_N$- bass, etc.]
bassinet see: cradle
o·wi꞉ya꞉ʼáh de·yǫt·ga꞉hǫ́hk·waʼ baby's cradle
basswood
o·hó꞉draʼ basswood
[o+ stem: -(h)odr(a)$_N$- basswood]
bastard see: foundling
ga·wi·yat·sę́꞉nyǫ꞉ child born out of wedlock; foundling; illegitimate child
bat
ad·ráʼwi̲hs·daʼ bat (mammal)
[ad+stem: -(ra)hwisd(a)$_N$- a thin slice of s.t., a bat (mammal)]
bat see: drumstick
eh·wáʼes·taʼ drumstick; baseball bat
bat one's eyes see: flirt
ęh·sat·ga̲·hǫ́꞉nyǫʼ you will flirt, bat your eyes
bath powder
ǫ·de·teʼtro·há꞉taʼ bath powder
[ǫ+ade+ stem: -teʼtrohataʼ- bath powder; consists of: -teʼtr(a)$_N$- flour, powder -ohaeʼd$_V$- cause to clean, wash]
bathroom
ǫg·yaʼdǫ̲·ha·iʼtáʼgeh bathroom
[ǫ+ag+ stem: -yaʼdohaiʼtaʼgeh- bathroom; consists of: -yaʼd(a)$_N$- body
-ohaeʼd$_V$- cause to clean, wash
-(ʼ)geh- on, at]
bath tub
ǫg·yaʼdǫ̲·há·iʼtaʼ, ǫg·yaʼdǫ̲·háʼtaʼ bath tub
[ǫ+ag+ -yaʼd(a)$_N$- body -ohaʼd$_V$- cause to clean, wash]

bathe
ǫg·yaʼdǫ̲·há·i꞉ she is bathing
[ag+ stem: -yaʼdohae- bathe; consists of: -yaʼd(a)$_N$- body -ohae$_V$- clean, wash]
gag·yaʼdǫ̲·háe꞉ I am taking a bath
a·wag·yaʼdó·ha·i꞉ʼ it washed its body
sag·yaʼdǫ̲·há·i꞉ you take a bath
syaʼdó·ha·i꞉ give it a bath
bathe see: swim
hę·ná·da·węhs they (m) are swimming
bathing suit
ǫ·da·wʼę·dáhk·waʼ bathing suit; s.t. used for swimming
[ǫ+ad+ stem: -(a)węʼdahkwaʼ- bathing suit; consists of: -(a)węʼd$_V$- cause to swim]
batter see: beat up
a·hǫ·wę·dá꞉nyoʼ s.o. beat him up, broke his spirit
battle see: fight
wad·rí꞉yo꞉ war; fight
bawl see: cry
gahs·dá꞉haʼ I am crying
bay
a·wad·wę·nó꞉dęʼ it did bay, howl
[ad+ stem: -węnod- bay, howl; consists of: -węn(a)$_N$- voice, word -od$_V$- stand]
od·wę́꞉no꞉d it is baying
bayou see: swamp
ga·ná·wa·ę꞉ʼ swamp; pond
be see: I (is), exist, see
ę·yǫh·wę·já꞉de꞉k the earth will exist
á꞉gę·hę꞉k it should be
be a certain length or depth
ni·yo꞉yá꞉de꞉s how deep the hole, trench, ditch is
[ni+yo+ stem: -yad(a)$_N$- hole, track, ditch -es$_V$- long, be a certain length, depth]

be someplace
gę́:neʼs they (z) are around; they are here; they are together
[A+ stem: -eʼ(s)- be someplace; consists of: -e$_{V}$- go]
í:geʼs I am here
beach see: lake
gan·ya·dak·dá:gyeʼ along the lake or shoreline
bead
ó:yę:ʼ beads
[o+ stem: -yę:$_{N}$- bead]
de·ye·há·ǫ·haʼ she is beading
[de+… stem: -haǫ, yaǫ- bead s.t.; consists of: -ha$_{N}$- -(r)ǫ$_{V}$- bead s.t.]
des·yá·ǫ·haʼ you are beading
de·gá·ya·ǫ:ʼ it is beaded
beak
gahn·yę́·dah·saʼ, ohn·yę́·dah·saʼ beak
[ga/o+ stem: -(h)nyędahs(a)$_{N}$- beak]
gahn·yę·dah·sáʼgeh on its beak
beam
gá·ǫ·da·deʼ beam
[ga+ stem: -(r)ǫdadeʼ- beam; consists of: -(r)ǫd(a)$_{N}$- log -deʼ$_{V}$- exist]
(de)·gahn·yǫhs·rá:deʼ iron beams
[(de+) ga+ stem: -(h)nyǫhsradeʼ- iron beams; consists of: -(h)nyǫhsr(a)$_{N}$- bar -deʼ$_{V}$- exist]
de·ga·ǫ·dá·hǫh beam
[de+ga+ stem: -(r)ǫdahǫh- beam; consists of: -(r)ǫd(a)$_{N}$- log -(adi)hǫh$_{V}$- lean against]
bean
oh·sá·heʼdaʼ beans
[o+ stem: -(h)saheʼd(a)$_{N}$- bean]
oh·sa·heʼdá:gę:t white bean
[o+ stem: -(h)saheʼd(a)$_{N}$- bean -(ʼ)gęd$_{V}$- light-coloured, white]
o·sa·heʼdá:ji: black bean
[o+ stem: -(h)saheʼd(a)$_{N}$- bean -ji(:,h)$_{V}$- be dark]

bean (continued)
oh·sa·heʼdá:se: string beans (yellow, green)
[o+ stem: -(h)saheʼdase- string bean, yellow bean, green bean; consists of: -(h)saheʼd(a)$_{N}$- bean -(a)se$_{V}$- new]
de·ga·jihg·wá·hih·dǫh mashed beans
[de+ga+ stem: -jihg(wa)$_{N}$- mash -(hr)ihd$_{V}$- slice, mash, grind]
bear
hnyag·wá·iʼ bear
[stem: -(h)nyagwai(ʼda)$_{N}$- bear]
bear see: polar bear
gahn·yag·wá·iʼda·gę:t polar bear
Bear Clan see: C (hahn·yag·wa·i)
beard
de·ha·gǫhs·twę́ʼo:t he has a beard
[de+A+ stem: -gǫhstwęʼod- have a beard; consists of: -gǫhstǫʼ(a), gǫhstwęʼ(ę)$_{N}$- whiskers -od$_{V}$- stand]
beard see: whiskers
o·gǫhs·twę́:ʼę:ʼ a beard; whiskers
beast see: animal (wild)
gan·yo: wild animals
beat
ohn·yah·snó:weʼ a fast beat
[o+ stem: -(h)ny(a)$_{N}$- stick -(h)snoweʼ$_{V}$- fast]
ohn·yáhs·hę: a slow beat
[o+ stem: -(h)ny(a)$_{N}$- stick -(a)hshę:$_{V}$- slow-moving]
ho·nahg·wáʼe·hag·yeʼ he is beating the drum as he moves along
[stem: -(ʼ)nahgwaʼe- beat a drum; consists of: -nahg(wa)$_{N}$- drum, barrel -(ʼ)e$_{V}$- hit]
a·haʼnǫhg·wáʼe:k he beat the drum, the barrel
ęhs·he·yaʼt·gę́:niʼ you will beat s.o. (in a race)
[TR+ stem: -yaʼtgęni- beat s.o. in a physical contest; consists of: -yaʼd(a)$_{N}$- body -gęni, gęny$_{V}$- compete]

Cayuga pronunciation guide: /a/ father /e/ weigh /ę/ men (nasalized) /i/ police /o/ hole /ǫ/ home (nasalized) /u/ blue. Underlined vowels are voiceless or whispered. /ˊ/ high pitch. /t/ too /d/ do /k/ king /g/ good (never soft g) /j/ judge or adze /s/ soon /sh/ less heat (never the sh in shirt) /sr/ shrine /sy/ sure /hw/ which (the sound made when you blow out a candle) /h/ hi /ts/ cats hide /ʼ/ (the sound before the first vowel in ‘uh-uh’) /n/ noon /r/ round /w/ way /y/ yes.

beat see: pound, rhythm, stir, stamp one's foot
  ę·gé:teʼt I will pound
  de·yóhk·waʼ a steady rhythm, beat; a throbbing sound
  deh·sá·węn·ye:ʼ beat; mix; stir
  ho·wę́:sęh·dǫh he is keeping a beat with his feet

beat up
  a·hǫ·wę·dá:nyoʼ s.o. beat him up, broke his spirit
  [TR+ stem: -(i)ʼdanyo- beat up; consists of: -(ni)ʼd(a)$_{N}$- feces -(r)iyo, nyo$_{V}$- kill s.t.]
  hǫ·węʼdan·yóhs·rǫh he is beating him up

beautician see: hairdresser
  e·ge·aʼs·rǫ́:ni:ʼ she is a hairdresser

beautiful see: good, handsome, pretty
  o·yá:n·reʼ it is nice, good, beautiful
  o·jínʼa·dǫ: it is handsome; s.t. / s.o. handsome or attractive
  ek·saʼgó:wah she is pretty

beaver
  na·gán·yʼa·gǫʼ beaver
  [na+ga+ stem: -nyaʼgǫʼ- beaver; consists of: -(ʼ)ny(a)$_{N}$- finger, hand]

because see: I (giʼ gyę:ʼ, shęh)

beckon
  gá:jih come here; it beckons
  [ga+ stem: -jih$_{V}$- beckon]

become (become well)
  sa·gá:dǫʼ I became (well) again
  [stem: -(a)dǫʼ$_{V}$- become well]
  ęt·sá:dǫʼ you will become healthy again
  a·wá:dǫʼ it has become; it became
  o·dǫ́ʼǫh·ne:ʼ it became
  tsaʼga:yę́:daʼ when it became
  [stem: -(y)ędaʼ- become, acquire, finish; consists of: -(y)ę$_{V}$- lie on the ground]

become see: present
  ęh·sá:dǫʼ you will present, offer s.t.; you will become s.t.

bed
  ga·ná:k·daʼ bed
  [ga+ stem: -nakd(a)$_{N}$- bed, seat]
  ga·nák·da·geh on the bed

bed see: lake bed, sleep
  haʼde·yo·nǫh·wa·ęʼda̲ʼóh oh·né·ga·gǫ: lake bed
  sę·dáʼdrah go to bed; go to sleep

bed bug
  jiʼnǫh·dó:yaʼ bed bug
  [stem: -jiʼnǫhdoy(a)$_{N}$- bed bug; consists of: -(ʼ)nǫhd$_{N}$- be in s.t.]

bed (go to bed)
  eh·sę́·dʼa̲d·reʼ you are going to bed
  [aʼ+P+ stem: -idaʼdreʼ- go to bed; consists of: -(i)daʼ$_{V}$- sleep]

bed-and-breakfast see: motel
  ǫ·nǫh·wehs·táʼgeh motel; inn; bed-and-breakfast; hotel

bedding
  gęts·gaʼshǫ́:ʼǫh bedding
  [ga+stem: -(n)itsg(wa)$_{N}$- bedding]

bed linen see: sheet
  ǫ·nits·gá:kwaʼ sheets

bedroom
  o·nǫ́h·wes·taʼ(geh) bedroom
  [o+ stem: -nǫhwehstaʼ(geh)- bedroom; consists of: -nǫhwehsd$_{V}$- cause to sleep over]
  tsę·nǫ́h·wehs·taʼ your (p) bedroom

bedspread
  e·nak·do·wé:ktaʼ bedspread
  [e+ stem: -nakdowektaʼ- bedspread; consists of: -nakd(a)$_{N}$- bed, seat +owekd$_{V}$- cause to cover]

bee
  gʼa·náh·gǫ·taʼ bee
  [ga+ stem: -(ʼ)nahgǫtaʼ- bee; consists of: -(ʼ)nahg(a)$_{N}$- sting -ǫd$_{V}$- attached]

bee sting
ę·saʼnah·gǫ́:dęʼ you will get a bee sting [P+ stem: -(ʼ)nahgǫd- bee sting; consists of: -(ʼ)nahg(a)$_{N}$- sting -ǫd$_{V}$- attached]

beech
o·no·hots·gę́ʼęʼ beech [o+ stem: -nohotsgęʼęʼ$_{N}$- beech]
ohsg·yǫ́ʼwaʼ blue beech [o+ stem: -(h)sgyǫʼ(wa)$_{N}$- blue beech]

beef
gyǫn·hohs·gwa·ǫ́t oʼwá·hǫh beef [consists of: gyonhohsgwaǫ:t cow; oʼwahǫh meat]

beer
gah·wę́ʼs·do·taʼ beer [ga+ stem: -(h)węʼsdotaʼ- beer; consists of: -(h)węʼsd(a)$_{N}$- foam -od$_{V}$- stand]

beet
ot·gwęh·jʼi·áʼ ok·de·ho·wá·nęʼs beets [consists of: otgwęhjʼia:ʼ red; okdehowa:nęʼs big edible roots]

beetle see: insect
o·jiʼnǫ́:waʼ bug, insect, worm

before see: I (gao:ʼ), previously
ga·óʼ na·wá:dih previously

beg
de·sat·sá·i·deʼs you are a freeloader [de+…at+ stem: -saide(:)$_{V}$- beg, freeload]
dę·gat·sá·i·de:ʼ I will freeload
de·wa·gat·sá·i·de:ʼ I did freeload
de·sat·sá·i·de: beg

beg see: plead
ęh·sa·dę·ní:dęht you will plead

begin
ęt·sáh·sa·węʼ you will begin, start [d/g+...stem: -(a)hsawę, (a)hsa:$_{V}$- begin, start; consists of: -(h)s(a)$_{N}$- mouth]
to·hsa:ʼ he has begun
gyoh·sa:ʼ the beginning of s.t.
deh·sáh·sa·węh begin; start

begin (continued)
da·wá:gyę:t the first one; the beginner [t/d/g+wa+ag+ stem: -yęhd- begin, be first; consists of: -(y)ę$_{V}$- lie on the ground]
gyog·yę́h·dǫh the first one, the beginning

beginner see: learn
ǫ·de·wa·yę́·s·taʼ she is a novice, learner, beginner

beguile see: bewitch, deceive
ę·gǫ·yat·gǫ́ʼtra:s I will bewitch you
dęhs·hé·gah·gwe:k you will pull the wool over her eyes, outsmart her, deceive her

behave see: conduct
na·ǫ·sa·ǫg·wa·yę́·hę:k what we all should be doing; how we all should conduct ourselves

behind
(oh)naʼgę́:ʼ shę́h ga·nǫ́h·so:t behind the house [(oh)naʼgę:ʼ shęh ga+ stem: -nǫhs(a)$_{N}$- house -od$_{V}$- stand]
gah·náʼtso:t its attached ass; a bare ass (said of children with no clothes on, etc.) [ga+ stem: -(h)naʼts(a)$_{N}$- buttock -od$_{V}$- attached object]
a·hǫ·we·no·wah·sǫ́:dręʼ he's right behind him [TR+ stem: -nowa(gwa)$_{N}$- rounded back -(a)hsǫdrę, (a)hsǫdre$_{V}$- join together, be behind s.o.]

behind see: late, anus, next
ę·wák·nihs·goʼ I will be late
o·hét·gaʼa:ʼ rear end; posterior
sho·nǫ́ʼne:t he is behind him; he is next in line

being see: person
ǫ́:gweh a person; a human

belch see: burp
at·gę·nin·yáʼgyaʼk I burped, belched

Cayuga pronunciation guide: /a/ father /e/ weigh /ę/ men (nasalized) /i/ police /o/ hole /ǫ/ home (nasalized) /u/ blue. Underlined vowels are voiceless or whispered. /ʹ/ high pitch. /t/ too /d/ do /k/ king /g/ good (never soft g) /j/ judge or adze /s/ soon /sh/ less heat (never the sh in shirt) /sr/ shrine /sy/ sure /hw/ which (the sound made when you blow out a candle) /h/ hi /ts/ cats hide /ʼ/ (the sound before the first vowel in 'uh-uh') /n/ noon /r/ round /w/ way /y/ yes.

belief
tsę́h hǫ:wéh gyǫg·wéh·da̱h·gǫh our belief; religion
[consists of: tsęh hǫ:weh the reason for; gyǫgwehda̱hgǫh our belief]

believable see: righteous
od·rih·wag·wá·ih·sǫ: it is believable, credible, righteous, fair, honest

believe
ta·wéh·da̱h·gǫh he believes
dih·séh·da̱h·gǫh you are credulous, gullible; you believe in s.t.
[d+A+ stem: -ehdahgw- believe; consists of: -ehdahgw$_{V}$- escort]
dih·seh·da̱h·gǫ́hs·gǫh you are really gullible

believe see: will
sé:ǫ:ʼ you wanted; you believed

belittle see: jeer
ęh·sad·wę·ná:yęht you will jeer, jest, throw words at s.o.

bell
o·jíh·wę·daʼ bell
[o+ stem: -jihwęd(a)$_{N}$- bell]

belly
ok·séʼdaʼ a belly
[o+ stem: -kseʼd(a)$_{N}$- belly]
sek·séʼdaʼgeh on your belly

belly see: stomach
ek·wá:hk·waʼ a stomach

belly button see: navel
ek·séʼdo:t her belly button

belongings
sa·wę́h·sǫʼ your belongings, property
[P+ stem: -(a)węhsǫʼ- belongings, property; consists of: -(a)węh$_{V}$- have -sǫʼ plural]

beloved see: love
shed·wá·nǫ̱hk·waʼ we love him

below see: underneath
oh·na·gǫ́h tgá:yęh it lies underneath, below

belt
at·naʼga·wíhd·raʼ belt
[at+ stem: -naʼgawihdr(a)$_{N}$- belt; consists of: -naʼg(a)$_{N}$- horn -(a)wihd$_{N}$- be inserted]

bench
wak·yę·da̱hk·wé:sǫʼs benches; pews
[wa+ stem: -(a)kyędahkwesǫʼs- bench, pew; consists of: -(a)kyędahkw(a)$_{N}$- chair -es$_{V}$- long; -ǫʼs- several objects]

bend
de·wáʼt·saʼkdǫhs it bends all the time; it is flexible
[de+...at+ stem: -shaʼged, shaʼkdǫ$_{V}$- bend, bend (forwards)]
de·yót·saʼkdǫh it is bent; a curve, a bend
de·sát·saʼge:t bend forwards
oh·naʼgę́:ʼ haʼde·sat·sáʼge:t bend backward
[ohnaʼgę:ʼ haʼde+...at+ stem: -shaʼged, shaʼkdǫ$_{V}$- bend]
de·sat·si·náʼk·dǫh your legs are bent, crooked
[de+P+(at+) N+ stem: -(h)sin(a)$_{N}$- leg -(a)ʼkdǫ$_{V}$- bent, crooked]
haʼhiʼya·gá·ę·heʼ his body trunk is crooked; he is bent over
[A+ stem: -(h)iʼyagaęheʼ- bent over; consists of: -(h)iʼy(a)$_{N}$- trunk, form -gaęh(eʼ)$_{V}$- cross]

bend see: fold
de·séh·sa·ge:t you will fold it once, bend it

beneath see: under
oh·ná:gǫ: under

benediction see: prayer
ga·ih·wa·né:gę:ʼ prayer; to pray

benefit
go·dǫ́ʼstaʼ it always benefits her
[P+ad+ stem: -ǫʼsd- benefit s.o.; consists of: -ǫʼs$_{V}$- be beneficial]
ę·ya:gó:dǫʼs it will be for her benefit

benefit (continued)
go·dǫ́ˀse:ˀ it did benefit her
berate see: scold
ęhs·he·da̲hs·wá·hęd·rǫ:ˀ you will scold her, s.o.
bereaved
sat·ga·ǫ·níˀǫh you are bereaved
[P+at+ stem: -gaǫniˀǫh$_V$- be bereaved, be in mourning]
berry see: fruit
oh·yaˀ fruit;, berry
beseech see: beg
de·sat·sá·i·de: beg
beside
ak·dá:gyeˀ the edge; beside
[stem: -(a)kdagyeˀ$_V$- edge, beside]
beside see: along, near
o·ha·hak·dá:gyeˀ along the edge of the road
i·wá:kˀah near
beside
[-a:ˀkˀah locative suffix; means 'beside' or 'alongside']
[-akdagyeˀ locative; means 'beside' or 'alongside']
best
gwahs gyo·yá:nreˀ the best
[gwahs g+yo+ stem: -yanreˀ$_V$- be good, nice, beautiful]
naˀga:tgwé:niˀ the best I could do
[naˀ+A+at+ stem: -gweni, gweny$_V$- be able to do s.t., succeed, do s.t. to the best of one's ability
best see: greatest
neˀ gya·ǫ·hę́:ˀęh the greatest
bestow see: give
shǫg·wá:wi: he has given us
bet see: gamble
de·to·dí:yęˀ they (m) are gambling, betting

betray
ęh·sní·gǫ̲·haˀt you will betray
[stem: -(ˀ)nigǫhaˀd- betray; consists of: -(ˀ)nigǫh(a)$_N$- mind]
betray see: cheat
ęhs·heˀni·gǫ́·haˀdęˀ you will cheat her, betray her
betroth see: marry
hon·yá:kd·reˀ he is getting married
Better Business Bureau see: G (Ho-nah-dęg-yaˀdǫh Ta-di-dag-wa-ihs-hǫhs)
between
det·ni·yˀa·da:dó:gę: between you and me; between our bodies
[de+...adad+ stem: -yaˀd(a)$_N$- body -ogę$_V$- together, between]
between see: duel, middle
de·yo·do·gę́ˀǫh it is in between; a duel between two people
de·yó:gę: between; in the middle
bewitch
ę·gǫ·yat·gǫ́ˀtra:s I will bewitch you
[TR+ at+ stem: -gǫˀtra:- bewitch; consists of: -gǫˀtr(a)$_N$- ominous medicine -a:ˀ$_V$- hold, contain, include]
ę·gǫ·yat·gǫ́ˀtra:ˀ I will bewitch you
bewitch see: persuade
aˀe·sˀa·ni·gǫ·hó·dagoˀ she bested your mind, bewitched you
betwixt see: between
det·ni·yˀa·da:dó:gę: between you and me; between our bodies
bewildered see: confused
de·wa·gad·ri·ho·dá·hǫh I am confused or mixed up; s.t. is blocking my thinking
bib
o·wi·ya:ˀáh ǫt·géh·dahs·taˀ baby's bib
[consists of: owi:ya:ˀah baby; ǫtgehdahstaˀ scarf, bib]

Bible
ga̱h·ya·dǫhs·ra·do·gę́h·di',
oh·ya·dǫhs·ra·do·gę́h·di' Bible
[ga+/o+ stem: -(h)yadǫhsradogęhdi'- Bible; consists of: -(h)yadǫhsr(a)$_N$- paper -dogęhd$_V$- make right, true]
bicker see: argue
dęh·sá·dat·s'a:' you will quarrel
bicycle
dek·ní: de·wę'ni̱hs·gá·ǫ:t bicycle
[consists of: dekni: two dewę'ni̱hsgaǫ:t it has two wheels]
big
go·wá:nęh, ga·gó·wa·nęh it is big
[(ga+) stem: -gowanęh$_V$- be big]
ga·di·go·wá:nę's they (z) are big
ga·di·go·wá:nęh they (z) are big
go·wa:nę́:hah it is fairly big
[A+ stem: -gowanęhah- fairly big; consists of: -gowanęh$_V$- be big]
ga̱h·wa·ji·yó·wa·nęh a large family
[A+ stem: -(h)wajiy(a)$_N$- family -owanęh$_V$- be big]
ge̱h·wa·ji·o·wa·nę́:hah my family is fairly big
e·go·wa·nęh·gó:wah she is really big
[A+ stem: -gowanęhgowah- be really big; consists of: -gowanęh$_V$- be big -gowah- big]
a·ga·go·wá:n·he', a·gó·wan·he' it became big
[(ga+) stem: -gowanhe'- become big; consists of: -gowanęh$_V$- be big]
big see: size
shę́h ní:wa's sizes; how big they are (lit.: how big it is)
big
[-ge: augmentative suffix; denotes 'largeness' or 'greatness']
[-go:wah augmentative suffix; denotes 'largeness']
bigger
he·yo·hé: wak·yę·da̱h·gó·wa·nęh it is a bigger chair
[heyohe: wa+ stem: -(a)kyędahk(wa)$_N$- chair -owanęh$_V$- be big, bigger]
biggest
gwáhs tgo·wá:nęh the biggest
[(ne:') gwahs t+ stem: -gowanęh$_V$- be big; biggest]
né:' gwáhs dwak·yę·da̱h·gó·wa·nęh it is the biggest chair
[ne:' gwahs d/t/g+A/P+N+ stem: (a)kyędahk(wa)$_N$- chair -owanęh$_V$- be big, biggest]
bike see: bicycle
dek·ní: de·wę'ni̱hs·gá·ǫ:t bicycle
bilingualism see: G (de·ga·wę·na:ge:)
bill see: beak, B (money)
gahn·yę́·da̱h·sa', ohn·yę́·da̱h·sa' beak
oh·wihs·da' money
Bill of Rights see: G (Tǫ·wa:na:wi: Ga·ya'da·gęn·hahs·ra' Ga·ya·nęhs·ra')
billboard see: sign
ga·néhs·da·ot headboards; grave markers; billboards; signs (lit.: standing board)
billfold see: wallet
gat·gwę́·da' wallet; purse; pocketbook; suitcase
binder
o·wi:ya:'áh de·yǫg·y'a·dán·hahs·ta' baby's binder (to keep in the belly button)
[consists of: owi:ya:'ah baby; deyǫgy'adanhahsta' s.t. that binds the body]
bingo
hę·nahs·he·dá·da̱hg·wahs bingo
[A+ stem: -(a)hshedadahgwahs- bingo; consists of: -(a)hshedad(a)$_N$- number -(h)gw$_V$- lift, pick up]

bingo see: call, cards
tgyah·sǫ́·haʼ I call them; I am a bingo caller
de·yeh·ya·dǫhs·rá·ę·dahk·waʼ playing cards; bingo
birch
de·yoʼwa·jihs·daʼǫh a birch tree
[de+yo+ contains: -wajihsd(a)$_N$- peelings, rind -(hwęʼga)ʼoh$_V$- notch]
bird
ji·dę́:ʼęh bird
[stem: -jidęʼęh$_N$- bird]
birth
a·dǫ́n·hehs·raʼ birth
[stem: -(a)dǫnhehsr(a)$_N$- birth; consists of: -ǫnheʼ$_V$- alive]
ǫ·ná:gra:s the birthing
[-nagreʼ, nagrad$_V$- live]
aʼǫ́·naʼgra:t birth (lit.: s.o. was born)
birth see: child-bearing, due
ǫ·déʼdǫ·haʼ she is child-bearing; she is giving birth right now
ǫ·déʼdǫh·neʼ she is about to give birth
birth cord see: tendon
o·jíhn·yaʼdaʼ tendon; ligament; birth cord
birthday
he·jé·hehs her birth date
[heʼ+s/j+… stem: -hę(:)$_V$- be day]
het·sehs it is your birthday
hehs·gé·hehs it is my birthday
hę·jé·he:ʼ it will be her birthday (lit.: she will come to her birth time)
hę·jé·hehs it will be her birthday
[heʼ+s/j+… stem: -hehsd$_V$- cause to be day]
bisect see: cross
de·ha·di·hę:di:yaʼs they (m) cut across fields
bite
ǫt·só·hihs she bites it
[at+ stem: -(sho)hih$_V$- bite]

bite (continued)
ę·wát·so·hih it will bite (as a way of clinging on)
got·so·hi·hǫh I have bit it
saht·só·hih bite it
hat·só·hihs·rǫh he is biting
ę·sa:gá·i:ʼ you will bite s.o., s.t.
[TR+ stem: -gai(:)- bite s.o.; consists of: -(sho)hih$_V$- bite]
dahs·ge:gá·i: bite me; take a bite
bite see: snack
ę·jid·wa·naʼdá·ik·sǫ:ʼ we all (incl.) will snack
bitter
de·yos·ga:n·yeʼs it is bitter
[deʼ+ not yo+ stem: -(a)hsganyeʼs$_V$- bitter; consists of: (ahs)gan(eg)$_V$- want, desire, long for]
bitter see: sour
o·jí·wa·gę: it is sour, salty, bitter
bizarre see: strange
og·yá:nǫhk it is strange, bizarre
blabbermouth see: chatterbox
go·ih·wa·gáʼdeʼ she is a chatterbox
black
swę́ʼdʼa·ę:ʼ black
[stem: -(h)swęʼdaę:ʼ- black; consists of: -(h)swęʼd(a)$_N$- coal, ember -ʼę:ʼ$_V$- be coloured]
ga·hǫ́ʼjih·gę·ha:ʼ the black kind
[ga+ stem: -(h)ǫʼjihgeha:ʼ- black; consists of: -(hǫʼ)ji(:,h)$_V$- dark]
Black see: C (ha·hǫʼjiʼ)
blackberry see: blueberry
oh·yá:jih dark fruit; blueberries, blackberries
blackbird
jog·rihs blackbird
[j+o+ stem: -grihs$_V$- dark]
blackcap
tǫ·dá:k·dǫ: blackcaps
[t+hǫ+ stem: -(a)dakdǫ:- blackcap; consists of: -(a)ʼkdǫ$_V$- bent, crooked]

Cayuga pronunciation guide: /a/ father /e/ weigh /ę/ men (nasalized) /i/ police /o/ hole /ǫ/ home (nasalized) /u/ blue. Underlined vowels are voiceless or whispered. /ʼ/ high pitch. /t/ too /d/ do /k/ king /g/ good (never soft g) /j/ judge or adze /s/ soon /sh/ less heat (never the sh in shirt) /sr/ shrine /sy/ sure /hw/ which (the sound made when you blow out a candle) /h/ hi /ts/ cats hide /ʼ/ (the sound before the first vowel in 'uh-uh') /n/ noon /r/ round /w/ way /y/ yes.

black eye
de·se·ga̱·hǫ́ʼji: you have a black eye
[de+A+ stem: -gahǫʼji:- black eye; consists of: -gah(a)$_N$- eye -(hǫʼ)ji(:,h)$_V$- dark]
de·ye·ga̱·há·hǫʼji: she has a black eye

blade
o·hę́·nʼat·raʼ a blade
[o+ stem: -(hr)enaʼtr(a)$_N$- knife]
o·hę́·nʼat·rǫ:t blade
[o+ stem: -(hr)enaʼtrǫd- blade; consists of: -(hr)enaʼtr(a)$_N$- knife -ǫd$_V$- attached]

blame
ahs·ríh·waʼehs you are blaming s.t.
[TR+ stem: -(r)ihwaʼehsd- demand a report, an account; blame s.o.; consists of: -(r)ih(wa)$_N$- word -(ʼ)ehsd$_V$- cause to hit]
ęhs·héh·waʼehs you will blame s.o.

blamed see: guilty
a·god·ri̱h·wáʼehs she got blamed

blameless see: sinless
de·ho·i:hwa·neʼá·gǫh he is sinless

blanch see: pale, boil
de·sahs·gyę·náʼgya·gǫh you are pale, ashen
sęn·yá·haʼt boil s.t.

blanket
o·yę́hs·raʼ blankets
[o+ stem: -yęhsr(a)$_N$- blanket]

blaring see: noisy
oʼtgáiʼni: it is noisy, loud

blaze see: fire
o·dé:kaʼ fire; it is burning

bleach
gahs·dag·wá:da̱hg·wahs bleach; javex
[ga+ stem: -(h)sdagwadahgwahs- bleach; consists of: -(h)sdag(wa)$_N$- dirt, dirty clothes -(h)gw$_V$- remove]

bleached see: pale
de·sahs·gyę·náʼgya·gǫh you are pale, ashen

blemish see: blight, bruise, infected
o·dág·wa·sę̱h it is bruised
goʼnó:drahs she has open, weeping sores

blend see: mix
dę̱s·yehs you will mix them all together

blessed see: forbidden
o·nǫ́ʼne:ʼ it is forbidden, sacred, holy

blight
oh·ya:gwá·ǫt fruit with bumps or blight
[o+ stem: -ahy(a)- fruit -g(wa)$_N$- bump -ǫd$_V$- attached]

blind
de·ha·ga̱h·gwé:gǫh he is blind
[de+A+ stem: -gahgwegǫh- blind; consists of: -gah(a)$_N$- eye -gwegǫh$_V$- all]
de·ga·ga̱h·gwé:gǫh it is blind
de·ye·ga̱h·gwé:gǫh she is blind
(o·nǫh·sa·ga·hę́t) eh·si·há·ǫ:kwaʼ window blind
[consists of: onǫhsagahęt window; ehsihaǫ:kwaʼ a blind]

blink see: wink
de·sat·gwi·áʼe:k wink

blister
ǫg·rá:do:k I blistered my heel
[(N+) stem: -o:g- blister s.t.; consists of: -(r)a(k)d(a)$_N$- heel -o(:)$_V$- submerge, boil, cook]

block see: square, bar (a door)
ge·í: naʼde·yo·da·gá·ǫ·deʼ a square
dęhs·rǫ́h·węʼ you will bar s.t., put up a barrier

blond see: fair haired
go·nǫ́h·gę:t she is fair haired, she has light hair

blood see: bloodroot, Métis, pure-bred
[stem: -tgwęhs(a)$_N$- blood]
de̱·ho·na·det·gwę̱h·sá·ye̱hs·dǫh Métis (lit.: they have mixed blood)
[de+hon+ade+ stem: -tgwęhsayehsdǫh- Métis; consists of: -tgwęhs(a)$_N$- blood -yehsd$_V$- mix]

blood (continued)
gat·gwęh·sa·náh·nǫh pure-bred (lit.: full of the same blood)
[ga+ stem: -tgwęhsanahnǫh- pure-bred; consists of: -tgwęhs(a)$_N$- blood -nahnǫh$_V$- full]

bloodroot
gat·gwęh·sa·há·iʼs bloodroot
[ga+ stem: -tgwęhsahaiʼs- bloodroot; consists of: -tgwęhs(a)$_N$- blood -es$_V$- long]

blood sucker
jag·wa·dihs blood suckers
[stem: -jagwahdihs- blood sucker]

bloom
ga·wę́·hǫ·taʼ flowering plant
[ga+ stem: -węhǫd- bloom; consists of: -(a)węh(ę)$_N$- flower -ǫd$_V$- attached]
ga·wę·hó:daʼs blooming plant, flower
a·ga·wę·hǫ́:dęʼ a flower bloomed
ag·ya·wę·hę́h·gwa·it opening bloom
[de+...+ya+ stem: -(a)węhęhgwaid- bloom; consists of: -(a)węh(ę)$_N$- flower -g(wa)$_N$- bumb (hr)ihd$_V$- break up]

blossom see: flower
a·wę́·hęʼ flower

blouse
a·déhs·waʼ blouse, middy
[stem: -(a)dehsw(a)$_N$- blouse]

blow
gá·ǫ·da:s I blow
[stem: -ǫʼdad$_V$- blow]
hęh·sá·ǫ·da:t you will blow
a·ga·ǫ·dá:dǫh I am blowing now; I have blown

blow one's nose
sa·jiʼ nǫ·gé:wahs you are blowing your nose
[P+ stem: -jiʼnǫgew- blow one's nose; consists of: -jinǫhgr(a)$_N$- mucus -(r)age(:,w)$_V$- wipe]

blue
á·ǫh·ya·ę:ʼ, ǫh·yáʼę:ʼ blue
[(a+) stem: -(r)ǫhyaʼę:ʼ- blue; consists of: -(r)ǫhy(a)$_N$- sky -ʼę:ʼ$_V$- coloured]
á·ǫh·yʼa·gę:t light blue
[a+ stem: -(r)ǫhy(a)$_N$- sky -(ʼ)gęd$_V$- light-coloured, white]

blueberry
oh·yá:jih dark fruit; blueberries, blackberries
[o+ stem: -(a)hyajih- blueberry, blackberry; consists of: -(a)hy(a)$_N$- fruit, berry -ji(:,h)$_V$- dark]

bluebird
jǫ́·n·yǫ:ʼ bluebird
[stem: -jǫnyǫ:ʼ$_N$- bluebird]

blue jay
diʼdi:ʼ blue jay
[stem: -diʼdi:ʼ$_N$- blue jay]

blues
oʼni·gǫh·sa·dǫhk·gę·há:ʼ ni·ga·ę·nóʼdęʼs blues music
[consists of: oʼnigǫhsadǫhka:ʼ the sad kind; nigaęnoʼdęʼs a kind of music]

blunder see: err
ęh·sá:nhiʼk you will err, make a mistake

blurred vision
at·gat·ga·há·węn·ye:ʼ I had blurred vision
[de+...at+ stem: -gahawęnye:ʼ- blurred vision; consists of: -gah(a)$_N$- eye -(a)węnye(:)$_V$- stir, mix]

blurry see: fuzzy
taʼde·yo·ga·há·ę·daht it is fuzzy, out of focus, opaque, unclear

blush see: make-up
ǫt·goʼjon·yáh·taʼ make-up, blush, rouge

blustery see: windy
o·wá:deʼ windy; wind; a breeze

board
ga·néhs·da:ʼ a board
[ga+ stem: -nehsd(a:)$_N$- floor, board]

Cayuga pronunciation guide: /a/ father /e/ weigh /ę/ men (nasalized) /i/ police /o/ hole /ǫ/ home (nasalized) /u/ blue. Underlined vowels are voiceless or whispered. /ʹ/ high pitch. /t/ too /d/ do /k/ king /g/ good (never soft g) /j/ judge or adze /s/ soon /sh/ less heat (never the sh in shirt) /sr/ shrine /sy/ sure /hw/ which (the sound made when you blow out a candle) /h/ hi /ts/ cats hide /ʼ/ (the sound before the first vowel in 'uh-uh') /n/ noon /r/ round /w/ way /y/ yes.

board see: G, stay, tree
ho·nad·rih·wahs·dí:hs·dǫh board, bureau, office, department, foundation, institute, etc.
hot·wá'ehs·dǫh he is a boarder; he is homeless
o·héh·sa' decayed tree; log; wood; board
boast see: proud
i·gé:hah I am gloating, boastful
boastfulness see: pride
ga·ná·i: pride; boastfulness
boat
ga̱·hǫ́:wa' boat
[ga+ stem: -(h)ǫw(a)$_N$- boat]
ga̱·hǫ́·wa·gǫ: in a boat
bobby pin
ǫ·den·yat·so·da̱hk·wá' ga·jí·ho·ha:' bobby pin; barrette
[consists of: ǫdenyatsoda̱hkwa' bobby pin, barrette; gajihoha:' pin, etc.]
bobcat
o·gǫh·sa̱h·sę́: da·gu:sgó:wah bobcat
[consists of: ogǫhsa̱hsę: it has a fat face; dagu:sgo:wah big cat]
body
o·yá'da' a body
[o+ stem: -ya'd(a)$_N$- body]
gy'a·dá'geh on my body
sya'dá'geh on your body
heh·dá' geg·wa·í sya'dá'geh your lower body
[consists of: hehda' gegwai the bottom; sya'da'geh on your body]
body see: cadaver, corpse, trunk
o·gán·y'ę·da' cadaver; dead body
o·yǫ́'da' a dead body; cadaver
o·hí'ya' the body's trunk, form
body pad
hę·nat·gǫd·ráhk·wa' body pads (protectors)
body pad (continued)
[A+at+ stem: -gǫdrahkwa'- body pad; consists of: -gǫ'dr(a)$_N$- pillow, cushion, cotton batting]
bog see: swamp
ga·ná·wa·ę:' swamp; pond
boil
on·yá·hęhs it is boiling
[o+(N+) stem: -nyahę(h,')$_V$- boil]
ęg·yǫ́n·ya̱·hęh it will boil
on·yá·hę'ǫh it has boiled
ohsg·wán·ya̱·hęhs rocks are boiling
[o+(N+) stem: -(h)sg(wa:)$_N$- stone, bullet, rock -nyahę(h,')$_V$- boil]
shǫna'do: boil the potatoes I
[-(h)ǫna'd(a)$_N$ - potato -o(:)$_V$- submerge, cook, boil]
sęn·yá·ha't boil s.t.
[ę+ stem: -nyaha'd- boil s.t.; consists of: -nyahę(h,')$_V$- boil]
ęhs·na'jó:dę' you will boil
[stem: -na'jod- boil; consists of: -na'j(a)$_N$- pail, drum -od$_V$- stand]
ga·ná'jo:t it is boiled (lit.: it is a standing pot)
wa̱·hyo' cooked fruit, stewed fruit
[wa+ stem: -(a)hy(a)$_N$- fruit, berry -o'$_V$- boiled, stewed]
boil see: abcess, water
a·gég·wa·ǫ:t I have an abscess, a boil
í:yo' it is in the water, submerged in liquid
boil dry see: evaporate
a·wá:sdehs it evaporated, dried up, boiled dry
boisterous see: loud
ag·ri's·do·wá·nęh I am loud and noisy
bold see: self-centred
ha·dág·y'a·da:s he has a high opinion of himself; he is self-centred; he is bold; he is conceited, boastful, bragging
bologna see: sausage
o·he:tsá·i: cooked wieners; bologna

bolster see: double
dęhs·ná'net'a:' you will double it, reinforce it, line it
bolt see: lock
e'no·wa·ni·yǫ·dáhk·wa lock
bonds see: G (sa·yę:dǫ')
bone
ohsg·yę́'da:' bone; bare bones
[o+ stem: -(h)sgyę'd(a:)$_N$- bone]
ohsg·yę́'da·gǫ: in the bones
ohsg·yę́'da·de' bones
[o+ stem: -(h)sgyę'd(a:)$_N$- bone -de'$_V$- exist]
ohsg·yę́'dǫ:t bone
[o+ stem: -(h)sgyę'd(a:)$_N$- bone -ǫd$_V$- attached]
bone marrow
ohsg·yę'da·gǫ́: gah·né:ga:t bone marrow
[onsists of: ohsgyę'dagǫ: in the bones; gahne:ga:t it is watery]
bonnet
o·wi:ya:'áh go·na·há·o·tra' baby's bonnet, hat
[consists of: owi:ya:'ah baby; gonahaotra' her hat]
book
oh·ya·dǫhs·rǫ́:dǫ' book
[o+ stem: -(h)yadǫhsrǫdǫ'- book; consists of: -(h)yadǫhsr(a)$_N$- paper -ǫdǫ'$_V$- several attached objects]
book see: reserve
wag·ye·na·wáh·dǫh a reserved or booked venue
ęh·sag·ye·ná:waht you will retain or book a venue; you will hold onto s.t., you will cling to s.t.
boost see: pick up, uphold
at·ga·ke·yá'dahk I picked them up
dę·yehg·wa·dáh·nǫ:' she will raise or lift things up
boot
de·yoh·dahg·wá:se:s boots

boot (continued)
[de+yo+ stem: -(a)hdahgwase:s- boot; consists of: -(a)hdahg(wa)$_N$- shoe -es$_V$- long]
gǫhs·reh·ká:' ah·dáhg·wa' winter boots
[consists of: gǫhsrehka:' winter kind; ahdahgwa' shoes]
bootie
o·wi:ya:'áh go·dáh·d'it·ra' baby's booties, socks
[consists of: owi:ya:'ah baby; godahd'itra' her socks]
border see: edge, hem, boundary
tsę́h hǫ́ he·yo·d'ok·dá'ǫh the edge
de·gág·wat·węh a hem
de·ga·ihs·dí'dra·hǫh boundary
bore see: drill, bother
se·ga·hę́:dę' drill
dęhs·ni·gǫ·há:ha' you are annoying me, bothering me
boring
o·gę́·hę't it is boring, disgusting
[o+ stem: -gęhę'd- be boring, annoying, disgusting; consists of: -gęhę$_V$- abuse s.o., be mean to s.o., annoy s.o., disgust s.o.]
o·nó's·hes·de:' it is boring, tiring
[o+ stem: -no'shehsde:'- be boring, tiring; consists of: -nǫ's$_V$- tire of s.t., be sick of s.t.]
born
sa·gá·dǫn·he:t I am alive again
[ad+ stem: -ǫnhed- be born; consists of: -ǫnhe'$_V$- alive]
tsa'sá·dǫn·he:t when you became alive
sa·dǫ:nhé:dǫh you were born
a·gę·nag·rá:dǫh I was born
[ę+ stem: -nagrad- born; consists of: -nagre', nagrad$_V$- live]
born see: alive
a·gá·dǫn·hi: I am alive; I am born; I am full of life

Cayuga pronunciation guide: /a/ father /e/ weigh /ę/ men (nasalized) /i/ police /o/ hole /ǫ/ home (nasalized) /u/ blue. Underlined vowels are voiceless or whispered. /'/ high pitch. /t/ too /d/ do /k/ king /g/ good (never soft g) /j/ judge or adze /s/ soon /sh/ less heat (never the sh in shirt) /sr/ shrine /sy/ sure /hw/ which (the sound made when you blow out a candle) /h/ hi /ts/ cats hide /'/ (the sound before the first vowel in 'uh-uh') /n/ noon /r/ round /w/ way /y/ yes.

borrow
sę̱.ní.hahs.gǫ: you are a habitual borrower
[ę/N+ stem: -niha$_V$- borrow, rent]
ęh.sę́.ni̱.ha' you will borrow, rent
sheh.wihs.da.ní.hahs you borrow money from her
[ę/N+ stem: -(h)wihsd(a), (hr)ihsd(a)$_N$- metal, money -niha$_V$- borrow (money)]
ęk.wihs.da.ní.ha' I will borrow money
bosom see: breast, chest
e.nǫ́'gwa'geh on her breast
g'ah.sá'geh on my chest
boss see: authority, truth
dwę.nǫ́h.dǫ̱.ha' it is the boss, the authority
grih.wag.wę.ní:yo' (where) I reside, dwell; (where) I'm the boss
both
de.ga.e.já.ǫ: both of them (f/m)
[de+A+ stem: -jaǫ:$_V$- both]
both see: I (dejaǫ:)
bother
dęhs.ni.gǫ̱.há:ha' you are annoying me, bothering me
[de+TR+ stem: -(')nigǫha(ę,nih)- bother s.o., annoy s.o.; consists of: -(')nigǫh(a)$_N$- mind]
dęh.sni.gǫ̱.há.ę:' you will be annoying
bother with s.o. see: pay attention
ę.sáhs.di:s you will pay attention
bottle
gat.sé'da', gęt.sé'da' bottle; jar
[ga+ stem: -(i)tse(')da)$_N$- bottle]
gat.sé'do:t standing bottle; belly button
[ga+ stem: -(i)tse(')da)$_N$- bottle -od$_V$- attached]
e.nǫ'gę̱.ha'da̱hk.wá' gat.sé'da' nursing bottle
[consists of: enǫ'gę̱ha'da̱hkwa' nursing bottle; gatse'da' bottle; jar]
bottle see: preserve
sa.dah.ya̱h.sę:nǫ́:nih preserve fruit
bottom
heh.dá' geg.wá.i where it starts; the bottom
[consists of: (o)hehda' dirt; earth; gegwai a direction; a side]
bottom see: buttock
oh.ná'tsa' buttock; ass; behind; posterior; rear
bough see: branch
og.wí:ya' a limb, twig, branch
boulder
gahs.gwa.o.wá:nęh boulder
[ga+ stem: -(h)sgwaowanęh- boulder; consists of: -(h)sg(wa:)$_N$- stone, rock +owanęh$_V$- be big]
boulder see: stone
gahs.gwa:' stone; rock; boulder; bullet
boulevard see: road
o.há.ha' road
boundary
de.ga.ihs.dí'dra̱.hǫh boundary (lit.: it has been surveyed)
[de+ga+ stem: -(r)ihsdi'drahǫh- be surveyed; be a boundary; consists of: -(hr)ihsd(a)$_N$- metal, -(i)'drah$_V$- go and drag s.t.]
bovine see: cow
gyon.hóhsg.wa.ǫ:t cow
bow
a.dó:da:' bow (as in bow and arrow)
[stem: -(a)dod(a:)$_N$- bow]
bow see: bend, hang one's head
de.sát.sa'ge:t bend forwards
de.yo.nǫ̱.há:kdǫ: it is hanging its head (for example, in sadness or shame)
bowl
de.yoh.sé:s ga.ję' bowl
[consists of: deyohse:s it has a wide mouth; gaję' dish, plate, bowl]
bowl see: dish
ga.ję' dish; plate; bowl

box
de̱·hę·na·dát·gǫ̱·heːs boxers; they (m) are boxing
[de+...+adat+ stem: -gǫhe- punch, box; consists of: -gǫh(a)$_{N}$- fist -(ʼ)e$_{V}$- hit]
ga̱·hǫ́hs·raʼ a box
[ga+ stem: -(h)ǫhsr(a)$_{N}$- box]
ga̱·hǫ́hs·ra·gǫː in the box

boy see: man, twin, male
hǫ́ːgweh a man; a boy
de̱·há·di·kęh twin boys
de̱·ha·di·yáhs·heː two males; they (m) are two

boyfriend see: C
ǫg·yáːtsih my friend, my boyfriend, my girl friend

bra
de·yǫt·nǫ·gó·hak·taʼ bra
[de+yǫ+at+ stem: -nǫʼgohaktaʼ- bra; consists of: -nǫʼg(wa)$_{N}$- breast, -ohakd$_{V}$- cause to squeeze]

bracelet see: armband
ǫ·nęt·san·háhs·taʼ bracelet; armband

brag see: proud
ha·ná·iː he is proud, boastful, bragging or conceited

braid
gan·yaːtsǫ́ːniː it is braided
[stem: -nyatsǫni- braid s.t.; consists of: -nyats(a)$_{N}$- braid -ǫni, ǫny$_{V}$- make]

brain
o·jiʼdrǫ·wáh·daʼ the brain
[o+ stem: -jiʼdrǫwahd(a)$_{N}$- brain]

brain see: mind
gaʼní·gǫ·haʼ the mind

brain-wracking see: consequences
de·yo·yʼa·dó·we̱h·deːʼ to weigh the consequences; it is brain-wracking

branch
og·wíːyaʼ a limb; twig; branch
[o+ stem: -gwiy(a)$_{N}$- branch, limb, twig]

branch (continued)
ohs·gó·haʼ branch
[o+ stem: -(h)sgoh(a)$_{N}$- branch]

branch (of an organization) see: G (he·ga·nęt·saːdeʼ de·yǫ·ki·yǫh·wę·jaʼnyaːʼ)

Brantford, Ont. see: E (Tga·na·da̱·ha·eːʼ)

brassier see: bra
de·yǫt·nǫ·gó·hak·taʼ bra

brave see: masculine
ha·jíːnah he is masculine, brave; his genitals

brawl see: fight
wad·ríːyoː war; fight

bread
o·náʼdaːʼ bread
[o+ stem: -naʼd(aː)$_{N}$- bread]
ga·naʼdaːgiːdá·ǫ fried bread
[ga+ stem: -naʼd(aː)$_{N}$- bread -gidaǫ$_{V}$- fry]
ga·jíh·yoːt type of bread baked in a shallow pan; pan bread, which has bumps like porridge; oven bread
[ga+ stem: -jih(nyowa)$_{N}$- spot, bump -od$_{V}$- stand]

bread pan
e·naʼdáːkwaʼ bread container
[e+ stem: -naʼdaːkwaʼ- bread container; consists of: -naʼd(aː)$_{N}$- bread -(h)kwaʼ$_{N}$- instrument]
ǫt·naʼdá·ǫːda̱hk·waʼ bread pan
[ǫ+at+ stem: -naʼdaǫdahkwaʼ- bread pan; consists of: -naʼd(aː)$_{N}$- bread -ǫdahkwaʼ$_{V}$- attached instrument]

bread steamer
e·naʼdaːna·wę́h·da̱hk·waʼ bread steamer
[e+ stem: -naʼdaːnawęhdahkwaʼ- bread steamer; consists of: -naʼd(aː)$_{N}$- bread -nawęhdahkwaʼ$_{V}$- wetting instrument]

Cayuga pronunciation guide: /a/ father /e/ weigh /ę/ men (nasalized) /i/ police /o/ hole /ǫ/ home (nasalized) /u/ blue. Underlined vowels are voiceless or whispered. /ʹ/ high pitch. /t/ too /d/ do /k/ king /g/ good (never soft g) /j/ judge or adze /s/ soon /sh/ less heat (never the sh in shirt) /sr/ shrine /sy/ sure /hw/ which (the sound made when you blow out a candle) /h/ hi /ts/ cats hide /ʼ/ (the sound before the first vowel in ʻuh-uhʼ) /n/ noon /r/ round /w/ way /y/ yes.

break

de·gá·hiʼs it breaks; it is breakable [de+...(N+) stem: -(hr)iʼ$_V$- break up]

dę·gá·hiʼ it will break

de·yó·hiʼǫh it is broken

de·gá·yʼak·sǫʼ it is broken [de+... stem: -(i)yaʼksǫʼ- several broken pieces; consists of: -(i)yaʼg$_V$- cut, break -sǫʼ plural]

haʼde·ga·yáʼksǫʼ it is broken up in different ways [haʼde+... stem: -(i)yaʼksǫʼ- several broken pieces; consists of: -(i)yaʼg$_V$- cut, break]

de·gá·yęg·yaʼs it cuts wood [de+...(N+) stem: -yęd(a)$_N$- wood -(i)yaʼg$_V$- cut, break, break apart, cut across]

dę·gat·nęt·sí:yaʼk I will break my arm [de+...ad+N+ stem: -nęts(a)$_N$- arm -(i)yaʼg$_V$- cut, break, break one's limb in two]

a·teh·si·ní:yaʼk you broke his leg [de+TR+N+ stem: -(h)sin(a)$_N$- leg -(i)yaʼg$_V$- cut, break, break s.o.'s body part]

break down see: bad

ǫ·geʼdrȩh·dá·he:t·gęʼ my car broke down

break s.o.'s spirit

a·to·wa·yę·ní:yaʼk it broke his spirit [de+TR+N+ stem: -wayę(n)$_N$- heart, spirit -(i)yaʼg$_V$- cut, break, break s.o.'s body part]

break s.o.'s spirit see: beat up

a·hǫ·wę·dá:nyoʼ s.o. beat him up, broke his spirit

breakfast

se·deh·ji·háh ni·yǫ·de·kǫ́:niʼ breakfast [consists of: sedehji:hah early morning; niyǫdekǫ:niʼ what s.o. eats]

breast

e·nǫ́ʼgwʼa·geh on her breast [e+ stem: -nǫʼg(wa)$_N$- breast]

e·nǫ́ʼgo:t her breast (attached) [e+ stem: -nǫʼg(wa)$_N$- breast, milk -od$_V$- stand]

breast see: chest

sʼah·sáʼgeh on your chest

breast-feed

ęhs·he·nǫ·gé·haʼt you will breast-feed [TR+ stem: -nǫgehaʼd- breast-feed; consists of: -nǫʼg(wa)$_N$- breast, milk -(h)negeha$_V$- drink]

breathe

sa·dǫ́:nyeʼs you are breathing [ad+ stem: -ǫwi, ǫny$_V$- breathe]

wa·dǫ́:n·yeʼs it is breathing; the pumping action of the gill

ǫ·dǫ́:nyeʼs she is breathing

sa·dǫ́:wih breathe

ę·yǫ·do·wíhs·ręht she will breathe [ad+ stem: -ǫwihsręhd- breathe; consists of: -ǫhwihsr(a)$_N$- breath -(y)ęhd$_V$- hit, knock down, strike]

aʼǫ·do·wíhs·ręht, aʼǫ·do·íhs·ręht she did breathe (that is, when she was born)

go·do·ihs·rę́h·dǫh she is breathing

breathe see: gill

wa·dǫ́n·ye·taʼ how it breathes; its a breather; the gill

breathless

de·ha·ǫh·wihs·hé:yohs he is out of breath; his breath is ebbing away [de+A+ stem: -ǫhwihsheyohs- breathless; consists of: -ǫhwihsr(a)$_N$- breath -(ga)hey, (gę)hey, (i)hey, (ga)he:, (gę)he:, (i)he:$_V$- die, be weak, be exhausted]

ha·dǫh·wihs·róʼktaʼ he is out of breath [ad+ stem: -ǫhwihsroʼkd- be breathless; consists of: -ǫhwihsr(a)$_N$- breath -oʼkd$_V$- end]

breathless (continued)
ha·dǫ·wi̱hs·rí:yaʼs he is out of breath; he is dying
[ad+ stem: -ǫwihsriyaʼ(g)s- breathless; consists of: -ǫhwihsr(a)$_N$- breath -(i)yaʼg$_V$- cut, break]
breathless see: short of breath
ha·dǫ́hs·weh·taʼ he is short of breath
breathtaking see: amazing
o·né·hag·waht it is amazing; awesome
breech cloth
ǫ·deʼká·ǫ·da̱hk·waʼ a breech cloth
[ǫ+ade+ stem: -(ʼ)kaǫdahkwaʼ- breech cloth; consists of: -(ʼ)k(a:)$_N$- skirt, slip -ǫdahkwaʼ$_V$- attached instrument]
breeze see: air, wind
ó:wa:ʼ air; wind
o·wá:deʼ windy; wind; a breeze
brew see: ferment, beer
ęh·saht·ne·gǫ́:niʼ you will ferment s.t.
ga̱h·wę́ʼs·do·taʼ beer
bribe see: persuade
ęs·hǫg·waʼni·gǫ̱·hó·da·goʼ he will influence or bribe us/s.o.
brick
oʼdá·iʼ brick
[o+ stem: -(i)ʼd(a:)$_N$- clay, mud, mortar -i:ʼ$_V$- stuck onto s.t.]
bricklayer
oʼda·íʼ dę̱·haʼsgwá:dǫ̱·haʼ he is a bricklayer
[consists of: oʼda:iʼ brick; dę̱haʼsgwa:dǫ̱haʼ he is a bricklayer]
bride
gon·yá:kdreʼ a bride to be (lit.: she is getting married)
[P+ stem: -nyakdre- get married; consists of: -nyag$_V$- marry]
bridegroom see: husband
he·gę́h·jih my husband

bridge
wahs·gó·hǫh a bridge
[w+ stem: -(a)hsg(wa)$_N$- roof, bridge -(adi)hǫh$_V$- lean against]
bridge of the nose
o·gǫ́ʼdaʼ bridge of one's nose
[o+ stem: -gǫʼd(a)$_N$- bridge of nose]
ge·gǫ́ʼdʼa·geh on the bridge of my nose
swa·gǫ́ʼdʼa·geh on the bridge of your (p) noses
bridle see: harness
wa·deʼn·heh·só·dahk·waʼ a harness (for an animal)
bright
oh·sóhg·wa·deht vibrant colours; florescent, neon colours
[o+ stem: -(a)hsoh(gwa)$_N$- colour, paint, crayon -dehd$_V$- bold, bright, strong]
oh·sohg·wa·dehts·hǫ́:ʼǫh bold, bright colours
de·yó·ha·teʼ it is bright (for example, sunlight)
[de+P+N/h+ stem: -(a)te$_V$- bright, clear]
dę·to·ha·téʼdǫ·hǫk he will brighten from over there
[de+d+P+N/h+ stem: -(a)teʼd- brighten up; consists of: -(a)te$_V$- bright, clear]
brilliant see: bright
brim
de·yoʼnihs·gá:deʼ brim of a hat
[de+yo+ stem: -(ʼ)nihsg(a)$_N$- brim -deʼ$_V$- exist]
bring
ę·ta·há:wiʼ he is going to bring s.t.
[d+... stem: -(h)awi, (h)a:$_V$- hold, include, carry, bring (s.t.)]
dę·ta·há:wiʼ he will bring it back
[de+d+... stem: -(h)awi, (h)a:$_V$- hold, include, carry, bring, bring s.t. back]
sha·há:wiʼ he brought it with him
[s+... stem: -(h)awi, (h)a:$_V$- hold, include, carry, bring, bring s.t. with oneself]

Cayuga pronunciation guide: /a/ father /e/ weigh /ę/ men (nasalized) /i/ police /o/ hole /ǫ/ home (nasalized) /u/ blue. Underlined vowels are voiceless or whispered. /ˊ/ high pitch. /t/ too /d/ do /k/ king /g/ good (never soft g) /j/ judge or adze /s/ soon /sh/ less heat (never the sh in shirt) /sr/ shrine /sy/ sure /hw/ which (the sound made when you blow out a candle) /h/ hi /ts/ cats hide /ʼ/ (the sound before the first vowel in 'uh-uh') /n/ noon /r/ round /w/ way /y/ yes.

bring (continued)
a·há:yǫ:t he scored; he brought it
[stem: -yǫʼd- bring s.t.; consists of: -yǫ$_{V}$- arrive]
ęhs·gá·e·yǫʼt they (f/m) will bring it back
[s+... stem: -yǫʼd- bring s.t. back; consists of: -yǫ$_{V}$- arrive]
bring see: hold, escort
e·há:wiʼ she carried it here; she brought it here
hęhs·he·ha·wíh·dahk you will escort her, take her with you
bring about see: do, produce
tsę́h ni·yǫg·wag·yáh·sǫh what we have done
a·ha·i·hǫ́n·ya̱h·nǫ:ʼ he produced s.t. (lit.: he started the idea)
bring together see: gather
gá·e·yo·he:s they (f/m) are gathering
bring down see: hand down
ęt·sáʼsęht you will bring it down
broad see: long, thick, wide
ǫ́:sʼǫhs lengthy objects
gá:dę:s it is thick, dense
de·yóh·se:s it has a wide mouth
broadcast
de̱·ha·ih·wá·ę·twahs he brings forth the message all the time
[de+(s+)... stem: -(r)ihwaętwahd- spread the news, bring forth a message; consists of: -(r)ih(wa)$_{N}$- word -(y)ętw(ahd)$_{V}$- spread (seeds), seed s.t.]
dęs·ha·ih·wá·ę·twaht he will bring forth a message
dehs·ho·ih·wá·ę·twęh he is bringing forth the message right now
broadcast see: movie, scatter s.t.
ga·yáʼtaʼ movies; television
de·wa·dog·wáh·dǫh it has been spread out, distributed, scattered
broaden see: stretch
de̱·ho:dí:yǫ:t he is stretching it

broad-minded
sni·gǫ·ho·wá:nęh you have a broad mind
[A+ stem: -(ʼ)nigǫhowanęh- broad-minded; consists of: -(ʼ)nigǫh(a)$_{N}$- mind -owanęh$_{V}$- be big]
broadcloth
o·nih·ga·hęhs·rí:yo: broad cloth
[o+ stem: -nihgahęhsriyo:- broadcloth; consists of: -niga:hęh(sra)$_{N}$- fabric -iyo:$_{V}$- be nice, good]
broil see: roast
wa·déʼsgǫ:t it is roasting, frying
broke see: poor
a·gí:dęht I am poor, poverty-stricken, in poverty
broken-hearted see: grieve
de·wak·ni·gǫ́h·nyʼa·gǫh I am broken-hearted, grieving
brooch
de·yǫ·de·ji·ho·háʼda̱hk·waʼ brooch
[de+yǫ+ade+ stem: -jihohaʼdahkwaʼ- brooch; consists of: -jihoh(a:)$_{N}$- pin -dahkwaʼ$_{V}$- standing instrument]
brooch see: pin
ga·jí·ho·ha:ʼ, o·jí·ho·ha:ʼ straight pin; pin; brooch; safety pin
brood see: child
o·wí:yaʼ young; offspring
brook see: river
gi·hę́:deʼ creek; river; stream
broom
ga·nóhs·gwi·ta:ʼ broom
[ga+ stem: -noʼsgwita:ʼ- broom; consists of: -onoʼsgwiʼd$_{V}$- sweep up]
de·ya·ga·nóʼsgwi·ta:ʼ broom
[de+yag+ stem: -noʼsgwita:ʼ- broom; consists of: -anoʼsgwiʼd$_{V}$- sweep up]
brother see: C
de·yag·ya·dęh·nǫ́:de:ʼ my brother, my sister
heh·jíʼah my older brother
heʼgę́:ʼęh my younger brother

brother-in-law see: C
ǫg·yá:gyoh my brother-in-law, sister-in-law
brow (upper) see: hairline
se·gę́ʼs·dʼa·geh on your hairline, upper brow
brown
héh·sʼa·ę:ʼ brown
[stem: -(h)ehsaʼę:ʼ- brown; consists of: -(h)ehs(a)$_{N}$- decayed tree -ʼę:ʼ$_{V}$- coloured]
bruise
o·dág·wa·sęh it is bruised
[o+ad(e)+(N/da)+ stem: -(a)gwasęh$_{V}$- be bruised]
a·wá·dag·wa:s it got bruised
[ad(e)+(N/da)+ stem: -(a)gwasd- get bruised; consists of: -(a)gwas$_{V}$- bruise]
ę·wá·dag·wa:s it will get bruised
o·de·dag·wá:sdǫh it is bruised
brush
ę·dę́·dahk·waʼ brush
[stem: -ędędahkwaʼ- brush]
ot·geʼahs·rǫ́n·yʼa·taʼ hair brush
[o+at+ stem: -geʼahsrǫnyʼataʼ- brush; consists of: -geʼ(a:), geh(a)$_{N}$- hair -ǫnyaʼd$_{V}$- make up]
ǫt·geʼęh·dáhk·waʼ hair brush
[ǫ+at+ stem: -geʼęhdahkwaʼ- brush; consists of: -geʼ(a:), geh(a)$_{N}$- hair -ęhdahkwaʼ$_{V}$- s.t. used for hitting]
brush see: sweep
de·gó·nohs·gwihs I am sweeping
brush one's teeth see: clean
ę·gat·noʼjó·ha·i:ʼ I am going to brush (lit.: wash) my teeth
bucket see: pail
ga·náʼjaʼ pail
bud see: sprout
a·gag·wi·yǫ́:dęʼ it got buds
buddy see: C
ǫg·wa·dá·oʼshǫʼ we all are buddies, friends
buff see: shine s.t.
dę·gehs·dá:teʼt I am going to shine it
buffalo
deg·rí·yaʼgǫʼ buffalo
[de+gr+stem: -(i)yaʼg$_{V}$- cut, break]
Buffalo, N.Y. see: E (Kyod·ro:wę:, Gyod·ro:wę:)
buffet
gak·si:yóʼs ek·sa·ę·dáhk·waʼ buffet, hutch
[consists of: gaksi:yoʼs good dishes; eksaędahkwaʼ place where dishes are put]
bug see: insect
o·jíʼnǫ·waʼ bug; insect; worm
build see: make
as·ha·go·nǫh·sǫ́:niʼ he built a house for her
building
gat·se:nę́ʼ ga·díʼdrǫʼ farm yard buildings
[consists of: gatse:nęʼ one animal or pet; gadiʼdrǫʼ they (z) live (designates a shed, dog house; etc.)]
building see: house, live
ga·nǫ́h·saʼ a house
ga·díʼdrǫʼ they (z) live (designates a shed, dog house; etc.)
bulb see: root
ok·dé·haʼ edible roots
bulemic see: vomit
ga·den·yag·wáh·taʼ I make myself vomit; I am bulemic
bulge see: lump
og·wá·ǫt it has a lump, a bulge
bulk see: mass
tsęh ni·yó:s·deʼ mass (lit.: how much it weighs; how heavy it is)
bulky see: thick
gá:dę:s it is thick, dense

Cayuga pronunciation guide: /a/ father /e/ weigh /ę/ men (nasalized) /i/ police /o/ hole /ǫ/ home (nasalized) /u/ blue. Underlined vowels are voiceless or whispered. /ʹ/ high pitch. /t/ too /d/ do /k/ king /g/ good (never soft g) /j/ judge or adze /s/ soon /sh/ less heat (never the sh in shirt) /sr/ shrine /sy/ sure /hw/ which (the sound made when you blow out a candle) /h/ hi /ts/ cats hide /ʼ/ (the sound before the first vowel in 'uh-uh') /n/ noon /r/ round /w/ way /y/ yes.

bulldozer
ga̱·heh·dǫ́:ne:s bulldozer
[ga+ stem: -(h)ehdǫne:s- bulldozer; consists of: -(h)ehd(a)$_N$- land, dirt, earth, ground -ǫ'n(eg)$_V$- remove, take away]

bullet see: ash, stone
o'gę́·hę' ashes; bullet; dust
gahs·gwa:' stone; rock; boulder; bullet

bump
a·hé·hihs I bumped him (for example, with a car)
[TR+ stem: -(hr)ihsd$_V$- bump s.o.; consists of: -(hr)i'$_V$- break up]

bumpy see: lump, rough
og·wá·ǫt it has a lump; a bulge
á·o·ga't it is rough

bundle
swa·tóhg·wa:t one bundle
[s+wa+ stem: -(a)tohg(wa)$_N$- bundle -d$_V$- stand; one]
wa·toh·gǫn·yáh·nǫ' bundles
[wa+ stem: -(a)tohg(wa)$_N$- bundle -ǫni, ǫnyahnǫ'$_V$- several made objects]

bundle see: cargo, package
o·héh·na', ga̱·héh·na' cargo; bundle; load
ga·hó:tra' a package

bunk see: bed
ga·ná:k·da' bed

bur
o'nǫ́h·da' bur
[o+ stem: -(')nǫhd(a)$_N$- bur]

burden
o·íh·wa̱hs·de' mental burden; preoccupation
[o+ stem: -(r)ihwahsde'- burden, preoccupation; consists of: -(r)ih(wa)$_N$- word -(a)hsde'$_V$- heavy]

burden see: cargo
o·héh·na', ga̱·héh·na' cargo; bundle; load

burden strap
dę·sat·no'á:nha' you will have a burden strap
[de+…at+ stem: -no'a:nha'- burden strap, strap; consists of: -nǫ'(a:), nǫh(a)$_N$- head -nha:'$_V$- stick out]

bureau see: G (ho·nad·rih·wahs·di:hs·dǫh), desk
ǫk·ya·dǫhs·rá·hahk·wa' desk

burdock
o'nǫh·da·gó:wah burdock
[o+stem: -(')nǫhd(a)$_N$- bur -gowah big]

burglar see: rob
sha·góh·se̱h·ta' he is a robber

Burlington, Ont. see: E (Deg·yo'ne̱h·sa·hǫh)

burn
krę'da:s I always burn s.t.
[stem: -(hr)ę'da:$_V$- burn s.t.]
ęhs·rę́'da:' you will burn s.t.
ak·rę́'da: I did burn it
ǫ·dé·g'a·ta' s.o. burns up s.t.
[A+ stem: -(a)dega'd- burn s.t. up, start a fire; consists of: -(a)deg$_V$- burn up]
ę·ga:dé:ga't I will start a fire

burn see: fire
o·dé:ka' fire; it is burning

burn up
ha'wá·dats'ǫh it is empty, burnt up, used up
[ha'+ … stem: -(a)ts'$_V$- use up]
a'ó:de:k it did burn
[P+(N+) stem: -(a)deg$_V$- burn up]
o·dé·gęh it is burnt
a'o·ga̱·hó·ja·de:k the grass burned; a grass fire
[P+(N+) stem: -gaho'j(a)$_N$- grass -(a)deg$_V$- burn up]
ǫ·ge·ge̱'á:de:k my hair got burnt, singed
[P+(N+) stem: -ge'(a:), geh(a)$_N$- hair -(a)deg$_V$- burn up]

burn up (continued)
wa·dǫ́:twahs what it burns (in the way of fuel)
[ad+ stem: -ǫtw$_{V}$- burn up]
burn up see: use up
a·wá:tsʼa:ʼ it is worn out, all gone, burnt up; it went down to nothing
burp
at·gę·nin·yáʼgyaʼk I burped, belched
[de+...ęn+ stem: -(i)nyaʼgyaʼg$_{V}$- burp, belch; consists of: -(i)yaʼg$_{V}$- cut]
burro see: jackass
de·wa·hǫh·dá·hǫʼ a jackass; a donkey
burial see: hide
ę·yǫ́h·seht there will be a burial (lit.: it will be hidden)
bury an object
ę·hę·nat·sá:dǫʼ they (m) will bury it
[at+ stem: -(h)sadǫ(:)$_{V}$- bury an object]
ę·gát·sa·dǫ:ʼ I will bury s.t. over there
a·gát·sa·dǫʼ I buried it (an object)
bury s.o., an animal
ę·géh·sa·dǫ:ʼ I will bury it (an animal)
[stem: -(h)sadǫ(:)$_{V}$- bury s.o., an animal]
a·géh·sa·dǫʼ I buried it (an animal)
ę·hǫ·wa·díh·sa·dǫ:ʼ they will bury him, them (m)
bus
ga·na·da·gǫh·ká:ʼ
go·yaʼda·nę́h·gwʼi·taʼ city bus
[consists of: ganadagǫhgę̲ha:ʼ urban; goyaʼdanęhgwʼitaʼ elevator, bus]
go·yaʼda·nę́h·gwʼi·taʼ bus; elevator (lit.: people mover)
[go+ stem: -yaʼdanęhgwiʼtaʼ- transportation, bus, elevator; consists of: -yaʼd(a)$_{N}$- body -nęhgwiʼd$_{V}$- cause to be carried]
bus see: transportation
go·yaʼda·nę́hg·wih transportation; bus; elevator (lit.: people mover)
bus driver
go·yaʼda·nęhg·wíh ha·dó:nyeʼs bus driver
[consists of: goyaʼdanęhgwih transportation, bus, elevator; hado:nyeʼs he drives continually]
bus stop see: stable
de·ga·di·dáhs·taʼ stable; barn; bus stop
bush
o·hǫ́:daʼ a bush; a whip
[o+ stem: -(h)ǫd(a)$_{N}$- bush]
o·hǫ́·da·gǫ: in the bushes
o·hǫ:dá:kʼah near or by the bushes
o·hǫ́·da·ę:ʼ a bush; a shrub
[o+ stem: consists of: -(h)ǫd(a)$_{N}$- bush -ę$_{V}$- lie on the ground]
bush see: forest
ga̲·há:gǫ: in the bush
business see: G, occupation, word
ni·sa·i·hoʼdęhs·róʼdę: your occupation, your type of work
ha·diʼnhah·gyáʼs ho·nah·dęg·yáʼdǫh business, industry
o·íh·waʼ message; it matters; it is its fault; word; affair; business
business association see: G
(ho·nah·dęg·yʼa·dǫh gęg·yohg·wa·ęʼ)
butcher
ga·dit·se:nę́ʼ han·yohs butcher
[consists of: gadi:tse:nęʼ farm animals; hanyohs he kills s.t.]
had·wa·ha·hní:nǫh he is a butcher, a seller of meat
[A+ad+ stem: -(ʼ)wahahninǫh- butcher; consists of: -(ʼ)wah(a)$_{N}$- meat -(h)ninǫ$_{V}$- sell]
had·wá·haʼ he is a butcher
[A+ad+ stem: -(ʼ)wahaʼ- butcher; consists of: -(ʼ)wah(a)$_{N}$- meat]
butcher see: kill s.t., s.o.
a·há:nyoʼ he killed (an animal)

butter
o·wíd·ra·ta' butter
[o+ stem: -widrata'- butter; consists of: -widr(a)$_N$- ice -ta'- dried up]
butterfly
ji'da·ná:wę: butterfly (lit.: s.t. is wet; referring to the transformation)
[stem: -ji'dana:wę:- butterfly; consists of: -ji'd(a)- cry -nawę:$_V$- wet]
buttock
oh·ná'tsa' buttock; ass; behind; posterior
[o+ stem: -(h)na'ts(a)$_N$- buttock]
sn'at·sá'geh on your buttocks
geh·ná't·sa'geh on my buttocks
sn'at·so:t your buttocks
[A+ stem: -(h)na'ts(a)$_N$- buttock -od$_V$- attached]
button
ęh·nyáhs·ga:' button
[stem: -ęhnyahsg(a:)$_N$- button]
buy
hah·ní:nǫh he is a buyer
[stem: -(h)ninǫ$_V$- buy]
a'eh·ní:nǫ' she purchased
ęhs·ní:nǫ' you will buy, purchase
tę' de·wa:kní:nǫh, tę' de'a:kní:nǫh I did not buy it
buzzard
ga·ję́·hęh·da:s buzzards; vultures
[ga+ stem: -jęhęhdas- buzzard, vulture; consists of: -jęhęhd(a)$_N$- flesh -g$_V$- eat]
by
[-a:'k'ah locative suffix; means 'beside' or 'alongside']
[-akdagye' locative; means 'beside' or 'alongside']
by see: near
i·wá:k'ah near

C

cab see: taxi
wa·dǫg·we·dá·nęhg·wih taxi
cabbage
o·nǫ'á·o·sa' cabbage
[o+ stem: -nǫ'aosa'- cabbage; consists of: -nǫ'(a:), nǫh(a)$_N$- head -osa'-]
Cabinet see: G (Gwa·go:wah Ga·ǫg·we'da' Gęg·yohg·wa·ge·hǫ')
cabinet see: buffet, cupboard, medicine cabinet
gak·si:yó's ek·sa·ę·dáhk·wa' buffet, hutch
ek·wa·ę·dáhk·wa' cupboard, pantry
e·nǫh·gwat·ra·ę·dáhk·wa' medicine cabinet
cable see: thread
oh·sí:ya' thread; string; cord
cadaver
o·gán·y'ę·da' cadaver; dead body
[o+ stem: -ganyę'd(a)$_N$- cadaver]
cadaver see: corpse
o·yǫ́'da' a dead body; a cadaver
cafeteria see: restaurant
ǫ·de·kǫn·yá'ta'geh restaurant; cafeteria; dining room; dining hall
cage
de·gahn·yohs·ra:dǫ́' ga·din·hó:dǫh caged animals
[consists of: degahnyohsra:dǫ' a cage; gadinho:dǫh they (z) are locked up]
cake
de·ga'nhǫh·sá·yehs·dǫh cake
[de+ga+ stem: -(')nhǫhs(a)$_N$- egg -yehsd$_V$- add]
cake pan
de·ga'nhǫh·sa·yehs·dǫ́h ǫt·na'dá·ǫ·dahk·wa' cake pan
[consists of: dega'nhǫhsayehsdǫh cake; ǫtna'daǫ:dahkwa' bread pan]

calamity
ad·wá·dęn·hiht a calamity (lit.: it happened all of a sudden, all at once)
[de+...wa+adę+ stem: -nhihd- have a calamity; consists of: -nhi'$_V$- err, mistake]
calamity see: disaster
ad·rih·wag·yá·ǫhs·ra' disaster
calculate see: count
ęd·wáhs·he:t we all (incl.) will count
calculator
oh·sno:wé' wa̱hs·hé:dahs calculator
[consists of: ohsno:we' it is fast; wa̱she:dahs it counts]
Caledonia, Ont. see: E (Tga·na·daę:')
calendar
at·só:gę' calendar
[stem: -(a)tsogę'$_N$- calendar]
calf
ohs·twa:s'áh gyǫn·hóhsg·wa·ǫt calf
[consists of: ohstwa:s'ah an animal's young; gyǫnhohsgwaǫt a cow]
calf (body part)
se̱hs·ná'd'a·geh on your calf
[stem: -(h)sna('da)$_N$- muscle, hamstring, calf]
geh·sná'd'a·geh on my calf (of leg)
swah·sná'd'a·geh on your (p) calves
calico
og·ya·na·dáh·nǫ' patterned material; calico
[o+ag+ stem: -yana'dahnǫ'- calico; consists of: -yęna'd, yana'd$_V$- mark s.t.]
call
ta·gíh·nǫ:s he is calling me
[he'/d/t+TR+ stem: -(i)hnǫg$_V$- call]
ha's·héh·nǫ:k call s.o. / her
he·wa·gi̱h·nǫ́:gǫh I have called it; it has called me
ha'síh·nǫ:k call it
ha'héhs·nǫ:k call him
call (continued)
tgyah·sǫ́·ha' I call them; I am a bingo caller
[he'/d/t+A+ stem: -yahsǫ(:)$_V$- named]
hęhs·hé·yah·sǫ:' you will be calling s.o.'s name
tse·yáh·sǫn·yǫh you are going along calling s.o.'s name; you call s.o.'s name all the time
call see: name
e:dwa̱h·sę́:nǫ' we all (incl.) should give it a name
call girl see: prostitute
wa·dat·ge·hǫ́·ha' she (lit.: it) is a prostitute
call upon see: visit, appoint
a·gag·y'ǫ·sé·he' I am going to go visit
ni̱·hǫ·wá·i·hǫ:t he has appointed him
calm see: quiet
ta'dé·yo:gyę: quietness; quiet; stillness
camp
ęh·sę·na·dá·ę:' you will camp
[ę+ stem: -nadaę'- camp; consists of: -nad(a)$_N$- town, community -ę$_V$- lie on the ground]
can see: able, garbage can, may, preserve
ę·ga·e·gwé:ni' they (f/m) can do it; they are able to do it
gog·yé's e·yáhk·wa' garbage can
ę·wá:dǫ' yes, you may
sa·dah·ya̱h·sę·nǫ́:nih preserve fruit
candid see: righteous
od·rih·wag·wá·ih·sǫ: it is believable, credible, righteous, fair, honest
canine see: dog
só:wa:s dog
can opener
e·ji·ho·dág·wa̱h·ta' can, bottle opener
[e+ stem: -jihodagwahta'- can opener; consists of: -jih(wa), jihy$_N$- hammer -odagwahd$_V$- cause to remove, detach]
canopy see: roof
ahsg·wa' roof

Canada see: E (Canadagwa:di, Kanadagwa:di)
Canada Act see: G (Ga·ya·nẹhs·ra' Ọg·wahs·ha·i·ne')
Canada Council see: G (Oh·wihs·da' Tẹ·naht·ga's)
Canada Post Corporation see: G (Gah·ya·dọhs·ra·nẹhg·wih Gẹg·yohg·wa·ẹ')
cancer
ga'wá·ha:s, go'wá·ha:s cancer
[ga+ / go+ stem: -(')waha:s- cancer; consists of: -(')wah(a)$_N$- meat -g$_V$- eat]
candelabra
ga·na'na·wẹ́'s ọ·de·jihs·do·dahk·wá' ga·yé:nahs candelabra
[consists of: gana'nawẹ's it melts; ọdejihsdodahkwa' s.t. that holds lights; ga·ye:nahs it holds it]
candidate see: G (dẹ·hẹh·da:t)
candles
ga·na'na·wẹ́hs ọ·de·jihs·dó·dahk·wa' candles
[consists of: gana'nawẹ's it melts; ọdejihsdodahkwa' s.t. that holds lights]
cane
a·dá'dit·ra' cane
[a+ stem: -(a)'ditr(a)$_N$- cane]
canister
ga·na'johg·wa'shọ:'ọ́h e·yáhk·wa' canisters
[consists of: gana'johsgwa'shọ:'ọh cup; eyahkwa' containers]
cannon
ga·ho'da·gó:wah cannon; missile
[ga+ stem: -(h)o'dagowah- cannon, missile; consists of: -(h)o'd(a)$_N$- gun]
canoe see: spoon
gan·yó:da' spoon; canoe; birch bark canoe
cantaloupe
wah·yá·is a musk melon; a cantaloupe (lit.: fruit is beginning to ripen)
cantaloupe (continued)
[wa+ stem: -(a)hyais- cantaloupe, musk melon; consists of: -(a)hy(a)$_N$- fruit, berry -(r)i, (w)i$_V$- ripe]
cantankerous
e·nọ́·wẹhd·ra' she is cantankerous
[A+ stem: -nọwẹhdra'$_V$- cantankerous]
cantankerous see: grumpy
de·di·sa'ni·gọ·hí:yo: you are grumpy, grouchy, not happy
canyon
he·yo·heh·dẹ́'ọ·ge: canyon
[he+yo+ stem: -(h)ehdẹ'ọge:- canyon; consists of: -(h)ehd(a)$_N$- land, dirt, earth, ground -(a's)ẹ'$_V$- fall, drop, reduce;
-ge:- big]
cap
gat·gwẹ́h·do:t cap (a type of hat)
[ga+ stem: -tgwẹhdod- cap; consists of: -tgwẹhd(a)$_N$- scalp -od$_V$- stand]
cap see: hat
a·na·há·ot·ra' hat
capability see: power
gahs·háhs·dẹhs·ra', ohs·háhs·dẹhs·ra' power; strength
cape see: point
he·yo·doh·wẹ'ok·dá'ọh a point of land; a cape; a peninsula
capital see: G, equity
ga·na·dag·wẹ·ní:yo' capital city
tsẹ́h ni·yó:ga:' equity; capital; value, worth
captive see: slave
ha·dit·sé:nẹ' they (m) are slaves (lit.: they (m) are animals)
capture see: catch
ah·sa·go·di:yé:na:' they arrested, caught her
car
g'ad·réh·da' car; vehicle
[ga+ stem: -(')drehd(a)$_N$- vehicle, car]
de·ga'dreh·dá:ge: two cars

car (continued)
[de+ga+ stem: -(ʼ)drehd(a)$_N$- car, vehicle -(a)ge:$_V$- two]
od·reh·da·ga·yǫh·géh·a:ʼ an antique car
[o+ stem: -(ʼ)drehdagayǫhgeha:ʼ- antique car, car; consists of: -(ʼ)drehd(a)$_N$- vehicle, car -gayǫh$_V$- old (thing)]
wa·déʼdreʼs a drag; a car (old word) (lit.: it is dragging itself)
[w+ade+ stem: -(i)ʼdre(:)$_V$- drag, drive]

car race
gad·reh·dáʼ de·gę·ná·ǫ·haʼ car races
[consists of: gʼadrehdaʼ vehicle, car; degęnaǫ:haʼ they (z) are racers]

car seat
o·wi:ya:ʼáh gad·reh·da·gǫ́: ǫg·yę́·dahk·waʼ baby's car seat
[consists of: owi:ya:ʼah a baby; gadrehdagǫ: in the car; ǫkyędahkwaʼ her chair]

carafe see: bottle
gat·séʼdaʼ, gęt·séʼdaʼ bottle; jar

carcass see: cadaver, corpse
o·gán·yʼę·daʼ cadaver; dead body
o·yǫ́ʼdaʼ a dead body; cadaver

cardinal
gah·di·só:da: cardinal (bird)
[ga+ stem: -(h)disoda:- cardinal; consists of: -oda(:,h)$_V$- drape]

cardinal see: beginning
gyog·yę́h·dǫh the first one; the beginning

cards
de·yeh·ya·dǫhs·rá·ę·dahk·waʼ playing cards; bingo
[de+ye+ stem: -(h)yadǫhsraędahkwaʼ- cards, bingo; consists of: -(h)yadǫhsr(a)$_N$- paper -ędahkwaʼ$_V$- things that are laid down]

care for
ta·dihs·nyé:gyeʼs they (m) look after all
[de+TR+ stem: -(h)snye$_V$- care for, look after]

care for (continued)
dę·hǫ·wa·díhs·nyeʼ they care for them
a:go·ih·wa·nǫ́hk·wa:k I should care for, respect your ideas
[stem: -(r)ihwanǫhkw- care for, respect; consists of: -(r)ih(wa)$_N$- word -nǫhkw$_V$- love]
sa·de·wa·yę:nǫ́:nih you care for it all the time
[ade+ stem: -wayę(n)$_N$- heart, spirit -wayęnǫni$_V$- care for, do carefully]
ęhs·he·ya·de·wa·yę:nǫ́:niʼ you will take care of them, care for them
ęd·wa·de·wa·yę·nǫ́:niʼ we all (incl.) will do it carefully; we all will do right
ho·de·wa·yę:nǫ́:ni: he has done it carefully

caress
hehs·yaʼdahd·rǫ́:gwahs you are caressing him now
[TR+ stem: -yaʼd(a)$_N$- body -(a)hdrǫgw$_V$- caress]
ę·hes·yʼa·dahd·rǫ́:gǫʼ you will caress him
hehs·yaʼdahd·rǫ́:gwęh you did caress him

carefree see: happy-go-lucky
ho·dę·dǫn·yáʼdahs·gǫ: he is a joker, happy-go-lucky; he is obnoxious

caregiver see: nurse
de·yǫ·te·yǫʼdahs·nyé·haʼ nurse

careless see: neglect
dehs·gáhs·dihs·taʼ I no longer pay attention

cargo
o·héh·naʼ, ga·héh·naʼ cargo; bundle; load
[o/ga+ stem: -(hr)ehn(a)$_N$- cargo, bundle]

carp
de·yo·nǫ·gę́ʼdǫ:t carp
[de+yo+ stem: -nǫgęʼdǫ:t- carp; consists of: -nǫgęʼd(a)$_N$- -ǫd$_V$- attached]

Cayuga pronunciation guide: /a/ father /e/ weigh /ę/ men (nasalized) /i/ police /o/ hole /ǫ/ home (nasalized) /u/ blue. Underlined vowels are voiceless or whispered. /ʼ/ high pitch. /t/ too /d/ do /k/ king /g/ good (never soft g) /j/ judge or adze /s/ soon /sh/ less heat (never the sh in shirt) /sr/ shrine /sy/ sure /hw/ which (the sound made when you blow out a candle) /h/ hi /ts/ cats hide /ʼ/ (the sound before the first vowel in 'uh-uh') /n/ noon /r/ round /w/ way /y/ yes.

carpenter

ha·nọh·sǫ́·nih he is a carpenter

[A+ stem: -nọhsọnih- carpenter; consists of: -nọhs(a)$_N$- house -ọni, ọny$_V$- make]

carpet see: rug

ga·nehs·da:géh e·dęh·dá:kwa' rug

carriage

o·wi:ya:'áh ọt·nǫ́·da̱hs·ta' baby carriage; stroller

[consists of: owi:ya:'ah baby; ọtnọdahsta' she / s.o. is put in there]

carrot see: root

ok·dé·ha' edible roots

carry

ę·ha·ha·wíh·sọ:' he will carry s.t. around

[stem: -(h)awihsọ:'- carry around; consists of: -(h)awi, (h)a:$_V$- hold, include, carry, bring]

ęhs·héh·sa·dę' you will carry s.o. on your back

[TR+ stem: -(h)sadę- mount a horse; carry s.o. on one's back; consists of: -(h)se'$_V$- ride horseback]

carry see: hold

ká:wi' I am carrying

carry on see: persevere

ęh·se:já:gọ:' you will persevere

carton see: box

ga̱·hǫ́hs·ra' a box

cartwheel

de·sę'tsih·gáhg·ya'ks you do cartwheels

[de+...ę+ stem: -tsigahgya'g- cartwheel; consists of: -tsigahd(a)- -(i)ya'g$_V$- cut, break]

de·sę'tsi·gáhg·ya'k you will do a cartwheel

de·sę'tsi·gáhg·y'a·kọ:' you are going along doing cartwheels

cash see: B (gwę·nihs·họ:'ọh, oh·wihs·da')

cashier

e·gá:gwahs cashier

[e+ stem: -ga:gw- tax s.o., be a cashier; consists of: -ga:$_N$- price -gw$_V$- gather, pick, get]

casket

ọg·weh·gę̱·hę́:' ọg·yá'da̱hkwa' casket

[consists of: ọgwegę̱hę:' a former human; ọgya'dahkwa' s.t. that takes away the body]

castigate see: punish

ęh·gahs·he·hé:waht you will punish them

cast lots see: vote

dęh·sę·nig·yohg·wa·gę́:ni' you will vote, cast lots

casualty see: accident

da·wad·ri̱h·wág·ya·ọ: there was an accident over there

cat

da·gu:s cat

[stem: -dagu:s$_N$- cat]

Cat O' Nine Tails

họ·wa·di̱·họ·da·yę́h·da̱hk·wa' Cat O' Nine Tails

[họwadi+ stem: -(h)ọdayęhdahkwa'- Cat O' Nine Tails; consists of: -(h)ọd(a)$_N$- bush -ęhdahkwa'$_V$- s.t. used for hitting]

catch

ga·yé:nahs it catches, receives, accepts, holds it

[TR+(N+) stem: -yena(w), yenaọ, yena(:)$_V$- catch, receive, accept]

a·ga·e·yé:na:' they (f/m) caught, received, accepted it

ah·sa·go·di:yé:na:' they arrested, caught her

ę·hǫ·wa·di:yé:na:' they will arrest, catch him, them (m)

ag·ye:ná·ọ: I have caught it, received it

jé:na: grip, hold it

catch see: trap
hę·nad·rihs·dá·ę·hę' they (m) are trappers
cater see: serve
ęhs·hé:hahs you will serve s.o.
catfish
o·nǫ́g'ę·da' catfish
[o+ stem: -nǫgę'd(a)$_N$- catfish]
tgwi·yó:gę' channel catfish
[stem: -tgwiyogę'- catfish; consists of: -gwiy(a)$_N$- branch, limb, twig -ogę$_V$- between]
Catholic
dę·ha·di·yáh·sǫ·ta' Catholics (lit.: they (m) cross themselves)
[de+A+ stem: -yahsǫta'- Catholic; cross oneself; consists of: -yahs(a)$_N$- cross -ǫd$_V$- attached]
dę·ga·e·yáh·sǫ·ta' Catholics; nuns (lit.: they (f/m) cross themselves)
catnip
da·gú:s ga·dín·rah·da:s catnip
[consists of: da:gu:s cat; gadinrahda:s they (z) eat the leaves]
cattail
ot·jíhs·da·gę:t cattail
[o+at+ stem: -jihsdagęd- cattail; consists of: -jihsd(a)$_N$- light -(')gęd$_V$- light-coloured, white]
Cattaraugus, N.Y. see: E (Ga·da:grahs·gę·hę:')
cattle see: herd
gahs·yá·o:t a standing herd
Caucasian see: C
hah·nyǫ́'ǫh he is a white man
Caughnawaga, Que. see: E (Gah·na·wa·geh)
cause see: incite
ęt·ri·hǫ́:ni' you will incite, be the cause of s.t.
cautious see: wary
wa·dat·ni·gǫ́·ha:' it is wary, cautious
cave
oh·wę·ja'gá·hę:t cave
[o+ stem: -ǫhwęjagahęd- cave; consists of: -ǫhwęj(a)$_N$- earth, land -gahęd$_V$- drill, hole]
oh·wę·ja·gá·hęt·ge: cavern; cavity; big cave
[o+ stem: -ǫhwęjagahętge:- cavern, cave; consists of: -ǫhwęj(a)$_N$- earth, land -gahęd$_V$- drill, hole]
cave in see: landslide
ę·yǫ́h·wę·ję' it will cave in
cavern see: cave
cavity (tooth)
o·no'ja·gá·hę:t tooth cavity
[o+ stem: -no'jagahęd- tooth cavity; consists of: -no'j(a)$_N$- tooth -gahęd$_V$- drill, hole]
Cayuga, Ont. see: E (Ni·ga·na'jú:'uh)
Cayuga people see: C (Ga·yo·go·ho:nǫ')
cease see: end, finish, quit
he·yo·d'ok·dá'ǫh it ends over there
hę·só'kdę' you will finish s.t.
a·gę́·ni·hę' I stopped, quit
ceiling
o·dáhs·gwa·de' ceiling
[o+ad+ stem: -(a)hsgwade'- ceiling; consists of: -(a)hsg(wa)$_N$- roof, bridge -de'$_V$- exist]
celebrate
sa·dę́'nyo·ta' you celebrate all the time; you are celebrating
[adę+ stem: -(')nyod- celebrate, party; consists of: -(')ny(a)$_N$- finger, hand -od$_V$- stand]
ęh·sa·dę'nyó:dę' you will celebrate
wa·dę́'nyo:t a celebration; a party
celebration
o·dǫt·ga·déhs·ra' celebration
[o+ad+ stem: -adǫtgadehsr(a)$_N$- celebration -ǫtgad(ǫ:)$_V$- enjoy]

Cayuga pronunciation guide: /a/ father /e/ weigh /ę/ men (nasalized) /i/ police /o/ hole /ǫ/ home (nasalized) /u/ blue. Underlined vowels are voiceless or whispered. /´/ high pitch. /t/ too /d/ do /k/ king /g/ good (never soft g) /j/ judge or adze /s/ soon /sh/ less heat (never the sh in shirt) /sr/ shrine /sy/ sure /hw/ which (the sound made when you blow out a candle) /h/ hi /ts/ cats hide /'/ (the sound before the first vowel in 'uh-uh') /n/ noon /r/ round /w/ way /y/ yes.

celebration (continued)
de·yog·yǫ̲hg·wę́ːdǫhs upheaval of a crowd of people; a celebration; a riot [de+yo+ stem: -(i)gyohgwędǫhs- celebration, riot; consists of: -(i)gyohg(wa)$_N$- crowd -ędǫh$_V$- shake s.t.]
celebration see: feast
ęh·sa·de·kǫ́·ni·geː you will feast
celery
ǫːda·gáh·deh celery
[ǫ+ad+ stem: -(a)gahdeh- celery; consists of: -(a)gahdeh$_V$- raw]
celestial see: heaven
ha·di·ǫh·yaʼge̲hóːnǫʼ they (m) are the heavenly kind
cell see: prison
de·gahn·yǫhs·ráːdeʼ prison
cellar see: basement
o·yáːdeʼ basement; track; ditch
censure see: condemn, denounce
ęhs·yéːsaht you will condemn, slander, insult s.o.
dęhs·ríh·wa·yaʼk you will denounce it, disapprove of it
census see: G (hę·na·dǫg·weʼda̲hs·heːdahs)
cent see: B (sgag·we·niʼdaːt)
central see: middle
de·yóːgęː between; in the middle
cereal see: porridge
o·jíhg·waʼ porridge; mush
ceremonial
[-ǫːweh typicalizer suffix; denotes something that is typically ‘Indian, ceremonial, or traditional’]
ceremonial friend see: C (ǫg·yaːda·oː)
ceremony
ę·wad·ri̲h·wah·dę́ːdiʼ the ceremony will start
[ad+ stem: -(r)ihwahdędi, (r)ihwahdęgy- start a ceremony; consists of: -(r)ih(wa)$_N$- word -(a)hdędi, (a)hdęgy$_V$- leave, go away]

ceremony (continued)
od·rih·wa̲h·dę́ːgyǫː the ceremony
ed·wad·ri̲h·wáh·dęg·yaʼt we all (incl.) did the ceremony
[ad+ stem: -(r)ihwahdęgyaʼd- do a ceremony; consists of: -(r)ih(wa)$_N$- word -(a)hdędi, (a)hdęgy$_V$- leave, go away]
certain
o·ih·wíːyoʼ it is certain, for sure
[o+ stem: -(r)ihwiyoʼ- certain, sure; consists of: -(r)ih(wa)$_N$- word -iyoː$_V$- be nice, good]
certain see: certain type or kind of thing, right, which
ga·dóːgęː a certain way; together; a certain thing
ga·ę́ níːgaːʼ which one; a specific thing
certain type or kind of thing
ni·ga·ę·nóʼdęː a type of song
[ni+ga+ stem: -(r)ęn(a)$_N$- song, music -oʼdęː$_V$- type of]
chaff see: winnow
ęh·sa·ge̲·hę́ːwaːk you will winnow the chaff (of corn, beans)
chagrin see: shame
o·dé·haʼt a shame; an embarrassment
chain
de·ga·ihs·dó·da̲·hǫh chain
[de+ga+ stem: -(r)ihsdodahǫh- chain; consists of: -(h)wihsd(a), (hr)ihsd(a)$_N$- metal, money -oda(ː,h)$_V$- drape]
chain saw
wat·ga·ha·dǫ́hs de·gá·yęg·yaʼs chainsaw
[consists of: watgahadǫhs it rolls; degayęgyaʼs it cuts wood]
chair
ak·yę́·da̲hk·waʼ, ag·yę́·da̲hk·waʼ chair
[a+ stem: -(a)kyędahkw(a)$_N$- chair]
ak·yę·da̲hk·wáʼgeh on the chair
ak·yę·dahk·wáːʼkʼah beside the chair
chairman see: G (hod·rih·wahs·dihs·dǫh)

chalk
ohs·dę́·hę'geh on the chalk
[o+ stem: -(a)hsdęh(a)$_N$- dust]

chalk board
ohs·dę·hę'géh eh·yá·dǫhk·wa' chalk board
[consists of: ohsdęhę'geh on the chalk; ehyadǫhkwa' a pencil]

chalk brush
ohs·dę·hę'géh e·ya:gé·wah·ta' chalk brush
[consists of: ohsdęhę'geh on the chalk; eya:gewahta' an eraser]

chamber see: room
o·nǫ́h·sǫ:t a room; a vault

chance see: luck
ad·rá'swa' luck

change
dęk·dé:ni' I am going to change s.t.
[de+...(N+) stem: -deni, deny$_V$- change]
a·ta·ę·na:dé:ni' he changed the song
[de+... stem: -(r)ęn(a)$_N$- song, music -deni, deny$_V$- change]
dęhs·wíhs·da·hiht you will make change
[de+... stem: -(h)wihsdahihd- make change; consists of: -(h)wihsd(a), (hr)ihsd(a)$_N$- metal, money -(hr)i'$_V$- break up]
ęh·sat·gwęn·ya:dé:ni' you will change your clothes
[at+ stem: -(a)hgwęny(a)$_N$- clothes -deni, deny$_V$- change]
ęhs·na:dé:ni' you will change the oil, fluid
[stem: -(h)n(a)$_N$- oil, gas -deni, deny$_V$- change]

change see: B (gwę·nihs·hǫ:'ǫh)

change purse
og·wę·ni'dah·sǫ:'ǫ́h wad·ráhk·wa' a change purse

change purse (continued)
[consists of: ogwęn'ida'shǫ:'ǫh pennies; wadrahkwa' a container]

chant
ęhs·wa·ę·nága·nye:' you all will yodel, chant
[stem: -(r)ęnaganye(:)- chant, yodel; consists of: -(r)ęn(a)$_N$- song, music -ganye(:)$_V$- chant, trill]

chaos
de·yó·dog·węh disorder; chaos (lit.: it is scattered)
[de+yo+ad+ stem: -ogwęh- chaos, disorder; consists of: -ogw$_V$- scatter]

char see: burn, roast
ęhs·rę́'da:' you will burn s.t.
ęh·sa·d'e·s·gǫ́:dę' you will roast s.t.

character
tsę́h ni·hǫ́n·ho'dę: what type of character they have
[tsęh ni+A+h+ stem: -o'dę:$_V$- type of]

charge
ę·yǫ·ki·gá:go' they will charge us
[TR+ stem: -ga:gw- charge s.o. a price; consists of: -ga:$_N$- price -gw$_V$- gather, pick, get]

charge see: blame, price
ęhs·héh·wa'ehs you will blame s.o.
ga·gá·he:' the price of s.t.

charge (be in charge)
ha·dih·wahs·rǫ́:nih they (m) who are in charge
[A+ stem: -(r)ihwahsrǫni- arrange; be in charge; consists of: -(r)ih(wa)$_N$- word -(h)srǫni$_V$- fix, repair]
ę·jad·rih·wahs·rǫ́:ni' you two will come to an agreement
sa·ih·wahs·rǫ·ni·há:gye' you are making up the rules as you go along
wad·rih·wahs·rǫ́:ni: peace; to make peace with s.o.

charitable see: generous
gog·yés'a·geh she is generous to a fault

Cayuga pronunciation guide: /a/ father /e/ weigh /ę/ men (nasalized) /i/ police /o/ hole /ǫ/ home (nasalized) /u/ blue. Underlined vowels are voiceless or whispered. /´/ high pitch. /t/ too /d/ do /k/ king /g/ good (never soft g) /j/ judge or adze /s/ soon /sh/ less heat (never the sh in shirt) /sr/ shrine /sy/ sure /hw/ which (the sound made when you blow out a candle) /h/ hi /ts/ cats hide /'/ (the sound before the first vowel in 'uh-uh') /n/ noon /r/ round /w/ way /y/ yes.

charming see: nice
hǫg·w'e·dí:yo: he is a charming, polite, nice person
charter see: hire, sanction
ę·sá·dęn·ha' you will order s.t., hire s.t.
ęhs·rih·wag·wę:ní:yohs you will sanction, charter, give authority to
Charter of Rights and Freedoms see: G (Tǫ·wa:na:wi: Ga·ya'da·gęn·hahs·ra' Ga·ya·nęhs·ra')
chase see: follow, hunt
a·gá·kehs·re:' I chased them, followed them
hę·na:dó:wa:s they (m) are hunting
chasm see: canyon
he·yo·heh·dę́'ǫ·ge: canyon
chastise see: punish, scold
ęh·gahs·he·hé:waht you will punish them
ęhs·he·dahs·wá·hęd·rǫ:' you will scold her, s.o.
chatterbox
go·ih·wa·gá'de' she is a chatterbox
[P+ stem: -(r)ihwaga'de'- chatterbox, talkative; consists of: -(r)ih(wa)$_N$- word -ga'de'$_V$- many]
chatterbox see: mockingbird
sa'sa' mockingbird; chatterbox
cheap see: bargain, inexpensive, stingy, terrible
wag·yé·sęh it is a bargain; it is cheap
tę́' de·gá:nǫ:' it is not costly
sa·ní'ǫh you are stingy, greedy, cheap
de·yo·nǫh·yá:niht it is terrible, frugal, cheap
cheat
gas·he'ni·gǫ·ha'dá:nih,
gas·he'ni·gǫ́·ha'ta' you betray them continually
[TR/adę+ stem: -(')nigǫh(a)$_N$- mind -(')nigǫha'd(ę, anih)$_V$- cheat, betray]
ęhs·ni·gǫ·há'dę' you will cheat
ęh·sa·dę·ni·gǫ·há'dę' you will betray

cheat (continued)
ęhs·he'ni·gǫ́·ha'dę' you will cheat her, betray her
ęhs·he'ni·gǫ́·ha't you will cheat s.o.
check see: examine
ę·sat·ga·hí:yohs you will look closely at s.t., peer at s.t.
cheek
o·yó'gwa:' cheeks
[stem: -yo'g(wa)$_N$- cheek]
sy'ogwá'geh on your cheeks
swa·yó'gw'a·geh on your (p) cheeks
gy'og·wá:'geh on my cheek
cheerful see: happy
a·gat·sę·nǫ́:ni: I am glad, happy
cheerless see: sad
de·sa'ni·gǫ́·hęh·dǫh you are sad
cheese
ga·nǫg·was·téhs·dǫ' cheese
[ga+ stem: -nǫgwastehsdǫ'- cheese; consists of: -nǫ'g(wa)$_N$- breast, milk -(a)hsde(hsd)$_V$- evaporate, boil down]
ó:ji:s cheese
[o+ stem: -ji:s$_N$- cheese]
chef see: baker
ha·na'dá·ǫ·nihs he is a baker
cherish see: value
ak·nǫhs·de' I value it
Cherokee people see: C (O·ya·d'a·ge·ho:nǫ')
cherry
e·i'gó:wah cherries
[stem: -ei'$_N$- cherry -gowah- big]
e·i'go:wáh gra̲he:t cherry tree
[consists of: ei'go:wah cherries; gra̲he:t living tree]
chest
o'áhs'a' chest
[stem: -(')a)hsa(w)$_N$- chest, cough]
g'ah·sá'geh on my chest
s'ah·sá'geh on your chest
chest see: breast
e·nǫ́'gw'a·geh on her breast

chew
de·yóts·ga'hǫ' it is chewing, it is a chewer (for example, a cow)
[de+P+ stem: -(a)tsga'hǫ$_V$- chew]
de·wa·gats·gá'hǫ: I am chewing right now
de·sáts·g'a·hǫ: chew it
chickadee
jik·jí:ye:' chickadee
[stem: -jikjiye:'$_N$- chickadee]
chicken
daks·há·e'dohs chicken
[stem: -dakshae'dohs$_N$- chicken]
chicken coop
daks·ha·e'dóhs o·dí·nǫh·so:t chicken coop
[consists of: dakshae:'dohs chicken; odinǫhso:t they (z) dwell]
chief see: authority, G, leader
dwę·nǫ́h·dǫ·ha' it is the boss, the authority
ha·di·go·wá:nę's they (m) are big; chiefs
ha·hę́:dǫ' he is the front, leader
Chief Justice see: G (Sha·go·dęn·yeh·ta'go:wah)
child
a·gék·s'a·da' my child
[stem: -ksa('da)$_N$- child]
hak·sá:'ah he is a child
ha·di:k·sá:'ah they (m) are two boys
ek·sá:'ah she is a child (under twelve)
ek·sa'shǫ́'ǫh she/they are children
ga·ek·sá:'ah they (f/m) are two girls
ga·ek·sa'shǫ́:'ǫh they (f/m) are children
ha·dik·sa'shǫ́:'ǫh they (m) are) children
o·wí:ya' young; offspring (of an animal)
[o+ stem: -wiy(a)$_N$- child, offspring]
o·wi:yá:'ah baby
ag·wí:ya' my baby
o·wi:ya:'áh hak·sá:'ah baby boy

child (continued)
[consists of: owi:ya:'ah baby; haksa:'ah he is a child]
o·wi:ya:'áh ek·sá:'ah baby girl
[consists of: owi:ya:'ah baby; eksa:'ah she is a child]
ga·ke·ha·waks·hǫ́:'ǫh my children
[TR+ stem: -(h)awahg$_V$- offspring]
swag·wi·yá·ę·dad·rę' I am going to have another child
[stem: -wiyaęda'(dre')- ; consists of: -wiy(a)$_N$- child, offspring -ę$_V$- lie on the ground]
child-bearing
ǫ·dé'dǫ·ha' she is child-bearing; she is giving birth right now
[o+ade+ stem: -(')dǫha'- child-bearing; consists of: -(')dǫ(:)$_V$- due]
childish
ǫ·dek·sa'dǫ́:nih she is childish
[A+ade+ stem: -ksa'dǫni- childish, immature; consists of: -ksa('da)$_N$- child -ǫni, ǫny$_V$- make]
sa·dek·s'a·dǫ́:nih you are immature, childish
Children's Aid office see: G (Ha·dik·sa·shǫ'ǫh Dę·hǫ·wa·dihsn·ye')
Child Welfare see: G (Ek·sa'shǫ:'ǫh Hǫ·wa·dihs·wa'ne·ta')
chill see: cold (become cold)
dęt·gá·n'a·nuhs it becomes cold again
chilly see: cold
jo·ná'nǫhs·dǫh it is chilly
chime see: bell
o·jíh·wę·da' bell
chimney
gan·yę́·ho:t a standing chimney
[ga+ stem: -nyęh(a)$_N$- chimney -od$_V$- stand]
chimpanzee see: monkey
ga·jí'nǫh·da:s monkey (lit.: it eats bugs)

Cayuga pronunciation guide: /a/ father /e/ weigh /ę/ men (nasalized) /i/ police /o/ hole /ǫ/ home (nasalized) /u/ blue. Underlined vowels are voiceless or whispered. /´/ high pitch. /t/ too /d/ do /k/ king /g/ good (never soft g) /j/ judge or adze /s/ soon /sh/ less heat (never the sh in shirt) /sr/ shrine /sy/ sure /hw/ which (the sound made when you blow out a candle) /h/ hi /ts/ cats hide /'/ (the sound before the first vowel in 'uh-uh') /n/ noon /r/ round /w/ way /y/ yes.

chin
oʼyóʼtsaʼ a chin
[stem: -yoʼts(a)$_{N}$-, -yuʼts(a)$_{N}$- chin]
syʼot·sáʼgeh on your chin
gyʼot·sáʼgeh on my chin
swa·yúʼt·saʼgeh on your (p) chins

chip see: wood chip
o·wę́ʼga:ʼ wood chips

chipmunk
jíh·nyʼo·gęʼ chipmunk
[stem: -jihnyʼogęʼ- chipmunk; consists of: -jihnew(a)$_{N}$- stripe -ogę$_{V}$- between]

chisel
eh·węʼga:gwah·dáhk·waʼ chisel
[e+ stem: -(h)węʼga:gwahdahkwaʼ- chisel; consists of: -(h)węʼg(a:)$_{N}$- chip -(r)agw$_{V}$- choose, take out]

choice see: choose
ag·rá:gwęh I have picked it out; I have chosen that one

choir
dę·ha·dí:h·wa̱hk·waʼ a choir; they (m) are gospel singers
[de+A+ stem: -(r)ihwahkwaʼ- choir; consists of: -(r)ih(wa)$_{N}$- word -(h)gw$_{V}$- lift, pick up]

choke
de·sáh·si̱·haʼs you are choking
[de+P+ stem: -(a)hsihaʼs$_{V}$- choke]
a·tóh·si̱·ha:ʼs he did choke
dę·héhs·hǫn·yaʼk you will strangle him
[TR+ stem: -(h)ǫnyaʼg$_{V}$- choke s.o.]

chokecherries
on·yá·taht·ne chokecherries
[o+ stem: -nyadahneh- chokecherries; consists of: -nyad(a:)$_{N}$- lake]
nęs·dag·węh·dę: chokecherries
[stem: -nęhsdagwęhdę:- chokecherries; consists of: -nehsd(a:)$_{N}$- floor, board -(a)gwęhdę$_{V}$- flat, dented]

chomp see: bite
ę·sa:gá·i:ʼ you will bite s.o., s.t.

choose
grag·wahs I am taking it out right now; I always take it out
[stem: -(r)agw$_{V}$- choose, take out]
ęhs·rá:goʼ you will choose it; take it out
ag·rá:gwęh I have picked it out; I have chosen that one
ę·yę·sa·yáʼda·goʼ they (f/m) will choose you to do s.t.
[stem: -yaʼd(a)$_{N}$- body -(r)agw$_{V}$- choose, take out]
ęh·sa·dad·rá:gwahs you will choose for yourself
[adad+ stem: -(r)agwahsd$_{V}$- choose for oneself]

choose see: gather
ęhs·ró·he:k you will gather

choosy
ho·dǫg·wʼe·dá·gǫn·yǫhs he is choosy about who he associates with; he discriminates
[P+ad+ stem: -ǫgweʼdagǫnyǫhsd- choosy, discriminate; consists of: -ǫgwe(ʼda)$_{N}$- person -gǫnyǫ$_{V}$- clean, discriminating]

chop
ge̱ʼohs I am a chopper
[stem: -(ʼ)og$_{V}$- axe, chop]
a·ha·da·déʼo:k he axed himself
ęh·sáʼo:k it will chop you
a·geʼó:gǫh I did chop; I have chopped

chop see: slice
deh·sáh·ya̱·hiht dice, cut, mash, etc. the fruit

chore see: work
ga·i·ho·dę́s·rahs·deʼ, o·i·ho·dę́s·rahs·deʼ heavy work; hard work

chosen see: lucky
sę·dá·ǫ: you are chosen, special, fortunate

chow see: food
gak·waʼ food

christen see: baptize
ho·wa·di̲h·né·god·rahs baptism; to christen (lit.: they sprinkle him, them)

Christian
ahs·rih·wí:yohs you became a Christian; you converted to Christianity
[stem: -(r)ihwiyohsd- become a Christian, convert; consists of: -(r)ih(wa)$_N$- word -iyo:$_V$- be nice, good]

Christian see: kneel
dę·yǫ·dǫt·só:dę' she will become a Christian; she will kneel in prayer

Christianity see: religion
ga·ih·wi·yóhs·dęhs·ra' religion; the Christian faith

chuckle see: giggle, laugh
sa·yǫ'gyé·ni:, sa·yǫ'gyę́·ni: you have the giggles
gyǫg·yáh·ta' I am really laughing

church
ǫd·rę·ná·ę·dahk·wa' church
[ǫ+ad+ stem: -(r)ęnaęda̲hkwa'- church; consists of: -(r)ęn(a)$_N$- song, music -ędahkwa'$_V$- place where s.t. is laid down]

cigarettes see: tobacco
o·yę́'gwa' tobacco; cigarettes

cinch see: belt
at·na'ga·wíhd·ra' belt

cinder see: ash, coal
o'gę́·hę' ashes; bullet; dust
de·yohs·wę·da:nę́:yǫ:t coals; embers

cinema see: movie
ga·yá'ta' movies; television

circle
de·wę'nya̲hs·gá·ǫni:
(**de·wę'ni̲hs·gá·ǫni:**) a circle
[de+w+ stem: -ę'nihsgaǫni- circle, hoop; consists of: -ę'nihsg(a)$_N$- wheel -ǫni, ǫny$_V$- make]

circle see: wheel
ę·níhs·ga:', wę·níhs·ga:' wheel; circle; hoop

circular see: round
de·yot·w'ę·nǫ́:nih it is round

circumcise
ę·ha·di·neh·wí:ya'k they (m) will circumcise it
[stem: -nehwiya'g- circumcise; consists of: -neh(wa)$_N$- skin, hide, leather, rawhide -(i)ya'g$_V$- cut, break]

circus
dę·hę·nag·yá:dǫhs circus (lit.: they (m) put up tents)
[de+hęn+ag+ stem: -yadǫ's- circus; consists of: -ya:$_N$- bag -d$_V$- stand]

citizenship see: G (de̲·hǫ·wa·di·den·ye's tsęh ni·ho·nǫh·wę·jo'dę:h)

city
ga·na·do·wá:nęh city
[ga+ stem: -nadowanęh- city; consists of: -nad(a)$_N$- town, community -owanęh$_V$- be big]

city see: town
ga·ná:da' town

city dwellers see: urban
ga·na·da·ge̲·hó:nǫ' urban dwellers; city people; urbanites

claim see: affirm
ęg·rih·wa̲h·ní:ya:t I will affirm it, defend it, agree

clairvoyant see: fortune teller
de̲·ha·y'a·dó·we̲h·ta' he is a fortune teller, seer, thinker

clan see: C (o'sya:de:nyǫ')

clan mother see: C (Ho·na'ga:' e·ha:')

clap
de·sę́'nya̲'we:k, de·sę́'nya̲'ok clap
[de+...ę+ stem: -(')nyaweg- clap; consists of: -(')ny(a)$_N$- finger, hand -(')e$_V$- hit]

clarify see: explain
dęg·ríh·wa·te't I will explain an idea

clasp see: hold, pin
e·ha:' she is holding s.t. right now
ga·jí·ho·ha:', o·jí·ho·ha:' pin, etc.

Cayuga pronunciation guide: /a/ father /e/ weigh /ę/ men (nasalized) /i/ police /o/ hole /ǫ/ home (nasalized) /u/ blue. Underlined vowels are voiceless or whispered. /´/ high pitch. /t/ too /d/ do /k/ king /g/ good (never soft g) /j/ judge or adze /s/ soon /sh/ less heat (never the sh in shirt) /sr/ shrine /sy/ sure /hw/ which (the sound made when you blow out a candle) /h/ hi /ts/ cats hide /'/ (the sound before the first vowel in 'uh-uh') /n/ noon /r/ round /w/ way /y/ yes.

classify see: arrange
ęhs·dó:gęhs you will arrange (i.e., things, flowers, etc.)

claw
de·ga·ji̲ʼéh·de:s claw
[de+ga+ stem: -jiʼehdes- claw; consists of: -jiʼohd(a), jiʼehd(a)$_N$- fingernail, toenail -es$_V$- long]

claw see: scratch
de·wa·gah·jí:yoʼ I am digging in my nails; I am scratching

claw (of a hammer)
gah·sǫ·wa̲h·dó·dag·wahs the claw of a hammer
[ga+ stem: -(h)sǫwahdodagwahs- claw (of a hammer); consists of: -(h)sǫwahd(a)$_N$- wire, nail, needle -odagw$_V$- remove, detach]

clay
oʼda:ʼ clay; mud; mortar
[o+ stem: -(i)ʼd(a:)$_N$- clay, mud, mortar]
oʼdá:gǫ: in the mud
o·ná·wa·daʼ clay; plaster; white-wash
[o+ stem: -nawad(a)$_N$- clay, plaster, white-wash]

clean
sat·gǫ́:nyohs you are very clean
[P+at+ stem: -gǫnyǫ$_V$- clean, discriminating]
got·gǫ́:nyohs she has high standards
o·dę·nǫ̲·há·i:ʼ it is washed, clean
[(ad+) n/N+ stem: -ohae$_V$- clean, wash]
ę·sah·yǫ̲·há·i:ʼ you will wash fruit
[stem: -(a)hy(a)$_N$- fruit, berry -ohae$_V$- clean, wash]
sa·des·ge̲·hó·ha·e: wash your lousy self
[ade+ stem: -(h)sgeh(a)$_N$- louse -ohae$_V$- clean, wash]
gek·so·há·i·hǫh I am washing dishes
[stem: -ks(a)$_N$- dish -ohae$_V$- clean, wash]
ę·gat·noʼjó·ha·i:ʼ I am going to brush (lit.: wash) my teeth

clean (continued)
[at+ stem: -noʼj(a)$_N$- tooth -ohae$_V$- clean, wash]
de·gat·nǫ̲h·sáhs·nyeʼs I am always cleaning my house; I'm a housecleaner
[de+...at+ stem: -nǫhs(a)$_N$- house -(h)snye(h,ʼ)$_V$- clean s.t. up]
de·gat·nǫ̲h·sáhs·nyeh I am cleaning up the house
dę·gat·nǫ̲h·sáhs·nyeʼ I will clean up the house
at·gat·nǫ̲h·sáhs·nyeʼ I did clean up the house
de·gáhs·nyeʼǫ:ʼ it cleans up
de·sa·da·déhs·nyeh tidy up; groom yourself

clean see: tidy up
dę·sá·do̲h·da:ʼ you will tidy it up, clean it

clear
de·yo·ih·wá:teʼ it is a clear idea
[de+yo+ stem: -(r)ih(wa)$_N$- word -(a)te$_V$- bright, clear]
ęhs·waʼni·gǫ́·hohs·gǫhk you all will have clear minds
[stem: -(ʼ)nigǫh(a)$_N$- mind -ohsgaʼ(w)$_V$- clear]
dęh·seh·wę́:daht you will make a clearing
[de+... stem: -(h)wędahd- clear out; consists of: -(h)węd(a)$_N$- hole, opening -(a)hd$_V$- like, resemble]

clear see: sound, understand
o·hǫ́:gaʼt a clear sound
o·ni·gǫ̲·há·ę·dahk, o·ni·gǫ̲·há·ę·daht it is clearly understood

clear-cut
a·ha·di·ha·do·dá:goʼ they (m) cut the forest right out
[stem: -(h)adodagw- clear-cut; consists of: -(h)ad(a)$_N$- forest -odagw$_V$- remove, detach]

clearing
de·yo·ha·dág·wę̲h·deʼ a clearing in the forest
[de+yo+ stem: -(h)adagwędeʼ- clearing; consists of: -(h)ad(a)$_{N}$- forest -(a)gwęhdę$_{V}$- flat, dented]
clearly see: I (gwaʼ ti:gę:)
cleft see: gap
de·ya·ǫh·wę́:deʼ a gap; an opening
clench see: hold
e·ha:ʼ she is holding s.t. right now
clerk see: secretary
eh·yá·dǫ·haʼ she is a secretary, stenographer, court recorder, transcriber
clever
sa·wa·yęn·héʼsgǫ: you are clever, educated
[P+ stem: -wayę(n)$_{N}$- heart, spirit -wayęnheʼsgǫ:$_{V}$- clever, educated]
ho·wa·yęn·héʼsgǫ: he is a fast learner, a quick study
clever see: smart
saʼní·gǫ̲·ha:t you are smart, brilliant
cliff
he·yóʼs·gwa·ǫ:t a rock formation that protrudes; a cliff
[he+yo+ stem: -(h)sgwaǫd- cliff; consists of: -(h)sg(wa:)$_{N}$- stone, bullet, rock -ǫd$_{V}$- attached]
climate see: weather
shę́h ni·węh·ni̲hs·róʼdęʼs seasonal weather conditions
climb
gra·tęhs I climb
[stem: -(r)atę, (r)adeʼ$_{V}$- climb]
ęhs·rá:tęʼ you will climb
ag·rá:tę: I did climb
srá:deʼ you are climbing
das·rá:tęh, dad·rá:tęh climb (over here)
haʼsrá:tęh, haʼdrá:tęh climb over there
srá:tęh climb

climb (continued)
ad·wa·dę·hę́·wę·hę:t it has gone over the fence
[de+... stem: -(a)dęʼh(ę)$_{N}$- fence -węhę(h)d$_{V}$- climb s.t.]
dę·wa·dʼa·wę́·hę:t it will go over the fence
de·yo·dʼawę́·hęh·dǫh it went over the fence; it is going over the fence
climb see: uphill (go uphill)
ęh·se·ne·dá·wę·hę:t you will go uphill
cling
sag·yé·na·waht cling to it; hang on
[ag+ stem: -yenawahd- cling; consists of: -yena(w), yenaǫ, yena(:)$_{V}$- catch, receive, accept, book a venue]
cling see: stick
sag·yaʼda·nę́·da·gǫh cling to it
clinic
ga·né:yǫhs a medical clinic; a healing place
[ga+ stem: -neyǫhs- medical clinic, clinic; consists of: -neyǫ(:)$_{V}$- heal]
clip see: paper clip
de·yeh·ya·dǫhs·ra·ę·da̲h·kwáʼ ga̲h·só·wa̲h·daʼ paper clip
clippers see: nail clippers
ǫ·de·ji̲ʼóhg·yʼak·taʼ nail clippers
clock
ga̲h·wíhs·dʼa̲ehs clock
[ga+ stem: -(h)wihsdʼaehs- clock; consists of: -(h)wihsd(a), (h)rihsd(a)$_{N}$- metal, money -(ʼ)e$_{V}$- hit]
clock radio
go·yeh·táʼ wad·rę́·no·taʼ clock radio
[consists of: goyehtaʼ alarm clock; wadręnotaʼ stereo; radio]
close
se·ji·hó:dęhs you close it all the time
[stem: -jihod$_{V}$- close, turn off]
ge·jí·ho·taʼ I am closing it right now; I am going along closing things
ę·ge·ji̲·hó:dęʼ I will close it

Cayuga pronunciation guide: /a/ father /e/ weigh /ę/ men (nasalized) /i/ police /o/ hole /ǫ/ home (nasalized) /u/ blue. Underlined vowels are voiceless or whispered. /´/ high pitch. /t/ too /d/ do /k/ king /g/ good (never soft g) /j/ judge or a̲d̲z̲e /s/ soon /sh/ le̲s̲s̲ h̲eat (never the sh in shirt) /sr/ s̲h̲r̲ine /sy/ s̲ure /hw/ w̲h̲ich (the sound made when you blow out a candle) /h/ hi /ts/ ca̲t̲s̲ h̲ide /ʼ/ (the sound before the first vowel in ‘uh-uh’) /n/ noon /r/ round /w/ way /y/ yes.

close (continued)

se·jihó:dęh close it

gen·hó·ha:s I close the door

[stem: -nhoha:$_V$- close (the door)]

ę·gén·ho·ha: I will close the door

a·gen·ho·há·hǫh, a·gen·ho·há:hǫh I have closed the door

sen·hó·ha: close the door

dę·sát·ga̱hg·we:k you will close your eyes

[de+...at+ stem: -gahgweg- close one's eyes; consists of: -gah(a)$_N$- eye -gweg$_V$- close]

close see: along, approach, near

o·ha·hak·dá:gyeʼ along the edge of the road

ęh·sad·rʼa·nę́:da:k you will get close to s.t., approach it

i·wá:kʼah near

closet

ahg·węn·yá·ę·da̱hk·waʼ closet

[stem: -(a)hgwęnya- closet; consists of: -(a)hgwęny(a)$_N$- clothes -ędahkwaʼ$_V$- place where things are put]

cloth

ni·gę́h·ne:s a length of cloth, material

[ni+ga+ stem: -(i)hn(a)$_N$- material, skin -es$_V$- long]

ni·gęh·né:sʼah a short length of cloth

cloth see: fabric, material

o·ni·ga:hę́hs·raʼ material; cloth

ni·ga·hę́:hah it is thin (for example, material)

clothe

sag·yaʼda·wíʼtaʼ you are always putting it on; you are putting it on right now

[ag+ stem: -yaʼdawiʼd$_V$- put on (clothes), clothe oneself; consists of: [ag+ -yaʼd(a)$_N$- body -awiʼd$_V$- insert]

ę·sag·yaʼdá:wi:t you will put on (clothes)

sag·yaʼda·wíʼdǫh you have on clothes

clothes

at·rǫ́·nʼi·daʼ clothes

[stem: -(a)trǫniʼd(a)$_N$- clothes]

ahg·wę́:nyaʼ clothing; clothes

[stem: -(a)hgwęny(a)$_N$- clothes]

ahg·wę:ní:yǫt hanging clothes

[stem: -(a)hgwęny(a)$_N$- clothes -niyǫd$_V$- hang]

ahg·węn·ya·gé·hǫʼ clothes lying around

[stem: -(a)hgwęny(a)$_N$- clothes -gehǫʼ$_V$- lie about]

ahg·węn·ya·seʼs·hǫ́:ʼǫh new clothes

[+ stem: -(a)hgwęny(a)$_N$- clothes -(a)se$_V$- new]

ahg·węn·ya·gá:yǫh ohg·węn·ya·gá:yǫh old clothes

[/o+ stem: -(a)hgwęny(a)$_N$- clothes -gayǫh$_V$- old (thing)]

de·yohg·węn·yá·hiʼǫh torn clothes

[de+yo+ stem: -(a)hgwęny(a)$_N$- clothes -(hr)iʼ$_V$- break up]

ohg·wę́n·yat·giʼ ugly clothes; dirty clothes

[o+ stem: -(a)hgwęny(a)$_N$- clothes -tgi$_V$- dirty, ugly]

gahs·dág·wa·grahs dirty, smelly clothes

[ga+ stem: -(h)sdag(wa)$_N$- dirt, dirty clothes -grahs$_V$- stink]

ǫd·ri·hoʼdahs**táʼ ahg·wę́:nyaʼ** work clothes

[consists of: ǫdrihoʼdahstaʼ tools, equipment; ahgwę:nyaʼ clothing, clothes]

otg·ríhs·rǫʼ wrinkled clothes; it is wrinkled up

[o+at+ stem: -grihsrǫʼ- several wrinkled items; consists of: -gri$_V$- wrinkle]

ǫg·yaʼda̱hs·rǫnyʼa·táʼ ahg·wę́:nyaʼ dress clothes; Sunday best

[consists of: ǫgyaʼda̱hsrǫnyʼataʼ (s.o. dresses up); ahgwę:nyaʼ clothing, clothes]

clothes brush
e·gę·hę·dáhk·waʼ clothes brush
[e+ stem: -(ʼ)gęhędahkwaʼ- clothes brush; consists of: -(a)ʼgęh(ęda)$_N$- ash, dust -(h)gw$_V$- lift, pick up]

clothes dryer
ahg·wę:nyáʼ **ga̲·há**ʼ**ta**ʼ clothes dryer
[consists of: ahgwę:nyaʼ clothing; clothes; ga̲haʼtaʼ it dries s.t.]
wa̲hg·węn·ya·táʼ**ta**ʼ clothes dryer
[w+stem: -(a)hgwęnyataʼtaʼ- clothes dryer; consists of: -(a)hgwęny(a)$_N$- clothes -taʼd$_V$- dry s.t.]

clothes hamper
es·dág·wa̲hkwaʼ dirty clothes hamper; laundry basket
[e+ stem: -(h)sdagwahkwaʼ- clothes hamper; consists of: -(h)sdag(wa)$_N$- dirt, dirty clothes -(h)gw$_V$- lift, pick up]

clothes hanger
ga̲h·sǫh·dáʼ
ǫhg·węn·ya·ni·yǫ·dáhk·waʼ wire clothes hangers
[consists of: ga̲hsǫhdaʼ wire; ǫhgwęnyaniyǫdahkwaʼ s.t. used for hanging clothes]

clothesline
e·ha·da̲hk·wáʼ **ga̲h·sí·ya·de**ʼ clothesline
[consists of: ehada̲hkwaʼ s.t. used for drying; ga̲hsiyadeʼ suspended line]
ga̲·háʼ**do̲h·nǫ**ʼ clothesline; it is hanging up to dry
[ga+ stem: -(h)aʼdohnǫʼ- clothesline; consists of: -(h)aʼd$_V$- dry]

clothespin
gʼ**a·wáhs·da**ʼ clothespin
[ga+ stem: -(ʼ)wahsd(a)$_N$- pin]
eʼ**wahs·do·dáhk·wa**ʼ clothespin
[e+ stem: -(ʼ)wahsd(a)$_N$- pin -odahkwaʼ$_V$- s.t. that stands attached]

clothespin bag
ga·wahs·dáʼ **e·yáhk·wa**ʼ clothespin bag
[consists of: gawahsdaʼ clothespin; eyahkwaʼ containers]

clothing see: clothes
at·rǫ́·nʼ**i·da**ʼ clothes

cloud
oh·jíʼ**gra**ʼ cloud
[o+ stem: -(a)hjiʼgr(a)$_N$- cloud]

cloudy
ga·góh·da̲h·sʼ**ǫhs** cloudy intervals
[ga+ stem: -gohdahsʼǫhs- cloudy]
oh·jíʼ**gre**ʼ it is cloudy
[o+ stem: -(a)hjiʼgreʼ- cloudy; consists of: -(a)hjiʼgr(a)$_N$- cloud -e$_V$- go]

club see: drumstick
eh·wáʼ**es·ta**ʼ drumstick; baseball bat

clubhouse see: meeting place
ǫd·ró·hek·taʼ meeting place; gathering place

clumsy see: slow
sad·ri·hó:wi: you are a klutz; you're slow-moving; you are feeble, clumsy

clutch see: hold
e·ha:ʼ she is holding s.t. right now

coal
ohs·wę́·daʼ coal; embers
[o+ stem: -(h)swęʼd(a)$_N$- coal, ember]
de·yohs·wʼ**ę·da:nę́:yǫ:t** coals; embers
[de+yo+ stem: -(h)swęʼd(a)$_N$- coal, ember -niyǫd$_V$- hang]

coalition see: G (sgęg·yohg·wa:t o·dǫʼǫh)

coat
so̲h·ga:s you coat s.t. all the time (that is, for a living)
[stem: -ohga(:,h)$_V$- coat, clean]
ęh·sóh·ga:ʼ you will coat s.t. (with a paste, etc.)
so̲h·gá:hǫh you have coated it
go̲hs·reh·ká:ʼ **ag·yaʼda·wí**ʼ**tra**ʼ winter coat
[consists of: go̲hsrehka:ʼ winter kind; agyaʼdawiʼtraʼ coat, dress]

coat (continued)
oh·né·gag·re' rubber coat
[o+ stem: -(h)negagre'- rubber coat, coat; consists of: -(h)neg(a)$_N$- water, liquid -gri'$_V$- juice, liquid]
coat see: dress
ag·ya'da·wí'tra' coat; dress
cob
o·nǫ́hg·we' corn cob
[o+ stem: -nǫhg(wę)$_N$- cob]
code see: G (ga·ya·nęhs·ra')
coffee
oh·sa·he'dá:gri' bean soup; coffee
[o+ stem: -(h)sahe'dagri'- coffee, bean soup; consists of: -(h)sahe'd(a)$_N$- bean -gri'$_V$- juice, liquid]
coffee maker
oh·sǫ·wah·da·da·i·hę́: o·sa·he'da:grí' gahs·rǫ́:nihs electric coffee-maker
[consists of: ohsǫwahdadai:hę: electricity; osahe'da:gri' coffee; gahsrǫ:nihs it makes it]
coffee table
ni·wa·dek·wa·hahs·rú:s'uh coffee tables
[ni+wa+ade+ stem: -kwahahsru:s'uh- coffee table; consists of: -(a)dekwahahsr(a)$_N$- table -u:s'uh$_V$- small items]
cohere see: stick
o·wa'nę́:da:s it sticks to it; it adheres to it
coil see: curl
de·yó·jits·grǫ:t flat curls; flat curls on a basket
cold
o·tó:we' it is cold
[o+ stem: -(a)tow(e')$_V$- cold (weather)]
jo·tó:we' it is cold again
o·ni'da·tó:we' it is a shitty cold
[o+ stem: -(ni)'d(a)$_N$- feces-(a)tow(e')$_V$- cold (weather)]
a·ga·to·wáhs·ta' I am cold
[stem: -atowahsd- cold; consists of: -(a)tow(e')$_V$- cold (weather)]

cold (continued)
o·ná'no:' it is cold, cool
[o+ N/na'+ stem: -no:'$_V$- cold, cool]
sa'n·yǫ́h·sa·no:' you have a cold nose
[P+ stem: -(')nyǫhs(a)$_N$- nose -no:'$_V$- cold, cool]
o·wá:no: it is a cold wind
[o+ stem: -w(a:)$_N$- air -no:'$_V$- cold, cool]
dęt·gá·na·nuhs it becomes cold again
[N/na'+ stem: -nohsd- become cold, chill; consists of: -no:'$_V$- cold, cool]
jo·ná'nǫhs·dǫh it is chilly
o·wa:nóhs·dǫh it got cold (weather)
[stem: -w(a:)$_N$- air -nohsd$_V$- become cold, chill]
sa·ga·wá:nohs it became cooler
he·yǫg·wag·ya'da·núhs·dǫ·hǫ:k we all will be cooling off over there
[N/na'+ stem: -nohsd- become cold, chill; consists of: -ya'd(a)$_N$- body -no$_V$- cold, cool]
a·ga·to·wíny'ǫ·se: I have a cold
[P+at+ stem: -(h)owinyǫ'se:$_V$- cold]
ǫg·ya·to·wíny'ǫse: we all have a cold
sa·to·win·yǫ́'se: you have a cold
ho·to·win·yǫ́'se: he has a cold
cold packing
gęt·sé'do' cold packing (part of the process of canning)
[ga+ stem: -(i)tse'do'- cold packing; consists of: -(i)tse('da)$_N$- bottle -o(:)$_V$- submerge, boil, cook]
Cold Spring, N.Y. see: E (Gyoh·ne·ga·no:)
collaborate see: work together
ded·wa:yé:na: let's work together, help each other
collar
de·gán·ya·he:' collar
[de+ga+ stem: -nyahe:'- collar; consists of: -(h)nya('sa)$_N$- neck, throat -(h)e:'$_V$- sitting up on top of s.t.]

collect see: accumulate, gather
ęh·sa·dad·ro·hé:gę' you will accumulate (things, ideas, etc.) for yourself
ęhs·ró·he:k you will gather
e·ga:gwáh·ta' s.o. collects money
collection plate
e·ga:gwah·tá' ga·ję' collection plate
[consists of: ega:gwahta' s.o. collects mone); gaję' dish; plate; bowl]
cologne see: perfume
gad·rę:ní:yo's perfume
colonist see: pioneer
a·ta·di·hę́·dohs·ga:' they (m) were pioneers
colour
ǫh·sóh·ta' colour; paints; crayons
[ǫ+ stem: -(a)hsoh(gwa)$_N$- colour, paint, crayon -(a)hsohd$_V$- colour]
oh·sohg·wí:yo: nice colour
[o+ stem: -(a)hsoh(gwa)$_N$- colour, paint, crayon -iyo:$_V$- be nice, good]
de·yoh·sǫhg·wá:teh bright colours
[de+yo+ stem: -(a)hsoh(gwa)$_N$- colour, paint, crayon -(a)te$_V$- bright, clear]
oh·sohg·wa·dá:gǫh dark colour
[o+ stem: -(a)hsoh(gwa)$_N$- colour, paint, crayon -dagǫh$_V$- dark]
oh·sohg·wa·dé:nyǫ' different kinds of colours
[o+ stem: consists of: -(a)hsoh(gwa)$_N$- colour, paint, crayon -denyǫ'$_V$- several existing things]
coloured
wah·só·hǫ:t it is coloured, dyed
[wa+ stem: -(a)hsohǫd- coloured, dyed; consists of: -(a)hsoh(gwa)$_N$- colour, paint, crayon -ǫd$_V$- attached]
coloured see: dyed
wah·sá·hǫh it is dyed, coloured
colourless see: transparent
he·yó:gę't it is transparent

colts foot
ohsg·wá·ę'da', sgwá·ę'da' colts foot (a type of herb)
[o+ stem: -(h)sgwaę('da)$_N$- colts foot]
comb
ga·náh·da' comb
[ga+ stem: -nahd(a)$_N$- comb]
o·wi:ya:'áh go·náh·da' baby's comb
[consists of: owi:ya:'ah baby; gonahda' her comb]
ǫt·nah·do·dáhk·wa' hair combs
[ǫ+at+ stem: -nahdodahkwa'- comb; consists of: -nahd(a)$_N$- comb -od$_V$- stand]
on·ráhs·ro:t rooster comb
[o+ stem: -nrahsrod- rooster comb; consists of: -nrahsr(a)$_N$- mushroom -od$_V$- stand]
de·ga·do·dá·is·hǫhs I am combing my hair
[de+ad+ stem: -odais(i)$_V$- comb; comb one's own hair]
de·yǫ·do·dá·is·hǫhs she is combing her hair
dę·ga·do·dá·isi' I am going to comb my hair
de·wa·ga·do·da·ih·sǫ·hǫ́:gye' I am going along combing my hair
combat see: fight, wrestle
ę·gas·he·ya'dri·yóh·dę' you will make them fight
ęh·sa·dag·yé·na:' you will wrestle
combine
ga·na'ji:yá's ga·ná·j'a·ehs a combine (machine)
[consists of: gana'ji:ya's a combine; ganaj'aehs grain threshing machine]
combine see: mix
dęs·yehs you will mix them all together
come
ę·te' he will come this way
[d+ stem: -e$_V$- go, come this way]
ęt·gá·ę:' they (f/m) will come

Cayuga pronunciation guide: /a/ father /e/ weigh /ę/ men (nasalized) /i/ police /o/ hole /ǫ/ home (nasalized) /u/ blue. Underlined vowels are voiceless or whispered. /'/ high pitch. /t/ too /d/ do /k/ king /g/ good (never soft g) /j/ judge or adze /s/ soon /sh/ less heat (never the sh in shirt) /sr/ shrine /sy/ sure /hw/ which (the sound made when you blow out a candle) /h/ hi /ts/ cats hide /'/ (the sound before the first vowel in 'uh-uh') /n/ noon /r/ round /w/ way /y/ yes.

come (continued)
da·gę́:neʼ they (z) are coming
dá:geʼ I am coming
come see: arrive, come again, come apart, come back, come from, come here, come in, come on, come out
gó:yǫ: she has arrived
come again see: return
shá:yǫʼ he returned
come apart see: unjoin
de·wa·dah·sǫd·rá:gwahs they come apart (lit.: it comes apart)
come back
dǫ·dá·sah·ge:t you should come back
[de+d+... stem: -(a)hge(h)d$_V$- return, go back, come back]
ǫ́:da̲·heʼ, **a·ǫ́·da̲·heʼ** he would come this way
naʼdę́:t·ge:ʼ I will come back over here, return
[ni+de+d+ stem: -e$_V$- go, come back here, return]
naʼdǫ:dá:geʼ I should come this way
dǫ·dá·ę:ʼ she is coming back
[de+d+ stem: -e$_V$- go, come back this way]
dǫ·dá·heʼ he is coming back
det·geʼ I will come this way; I will come back; I am coming back
dǫ́:da:ge:ʼ I would come back
dǫ·dá:geʼ I am coming back
come by horseback
ęd·ya·go̲h·sá:dęʼ she will come by horseback
[de+P+ stem: -(h)sadę- mount a horse; consists of: -(h)seʼ$_V$- ride horseback, come by horseback]
ę·tóhsa·dęʼ he will come by horseback
come by vehicle see: drag
ęd·ya·go·díʼdrę:ʼ they (f/m) will come by vehicle

come for a purpose
sen·yę́ʼdeʼ you came for a purpose
[A+ stem: -(ʼ)nyędeʼ- come for a purpose; consists of: -(ʼ)nyędę$_V$- try]
come from
tę·né·da̲hk·waʼ where they (m) come from
[d+ stem: -edahkw- come from; consists of: -e$_V$- go, come from]
nǫ·dá:kne:ʼ where we two (excl.) came from
[ni+d+ stem: -e$_V$- go, come from somewhere]
nǫ·dá:ge:ʼ I come from; I came from
ga·óʼ nǫ·dáh·se:ʼ come this way
come from see: originate from
dwa·gáh·dęg·yǫ: I come from
come here see: beckon
gá:jih it beckons (used in the sense of 'come here')
come in
it·gyǫhs I come in (from the same place) all the time
[d+... stem: -yǫ$_V$- arrive, come in]
da̲·ha:dí:yǫʼ they (m) came in
da·jǫh come in
come on see: I (haoʼ)
come out
a·ga·ya·gę́h·dahk it came out (suddenly)
[d+... stem: -yagęhd- come out suddenly; consists of: -yagęʼ$_V$- go out, come out]
comet see: star
o·jih·sǫ·doh·go·dá:gyeʼ a shooting star
comfort see: console, forget
ęhs·heʼni·gǫ́·hoʼdrǫ:ʼ you will console s.o. (lit.: you will caress s.o.'s mind)
ęhs·heʼni·gǫ́·hęh·dęʼ you will make s.o. feel better, comfort s.o. (lit.: you will make s.o. forget s.t.)

comfortable
ęh·saʼni·gǫ·hí:yohs your mind will adjust (that is, become comfortable)
[P+ stem: -(ʼ)nigǫhiyoh(sd)- become comfortable, be at ease; consists of: -(ʼ)nigǫh(a)$_{N}$- mind -iyo:$_{V}$- be nice, good]
ę·sat·nahs·gǫ́:niʼ you will get comfortable in bed
[at+ stem: -nahsgǫni- make oneself comfortable; consists of: -naʼsg(wa)$_{N}$- mattress -ǫni, ǫny$_{V}$- make]
a·gat·nak·dí:yohs I made myself comfortable
[(at+) stem: -nakdiyohsd- make oneself comfortable; consists of: -nakd(a)$_{N}$- bed, seat -iyo:$_{V}$- be nice, good]
ęh·sa·nak·dí:yohs you will become physically comfortable (lit.: you'll be comfortable with your bed)
comical
o·yǫ:gyę́·ni: it is comical
[o+ stem: -yǫgyęni:- comical; have the giggles; consists of: -yǫdi, yǫgy$_{V}$- smile]
comical see: amusing
o·yǫ́ʼgyaʼt it is amusing, laughable
command
ken·haʼs I hire her
[TR+ stem: -nhaʼ$_{V}$- command, hire]
ęhs·hé:nhaʼ you will command, hire her
ę·gás·hen·haʼ you will command, hire them
gan·háʼǫh it is hired
ken·háʼǫh I have hired her
command see: demand, hire
ęt·ríh·wa·hek you will demand s.t., insist, force s.t.
ę·sá·dęn·haʼ you will order s.t., hire s.t.
commendation see: special
o·i·ho·wá:nęh it is important; a great, worthy commendation it is special

commemorate see: celebrate
ęh·sa·dʼęn·yó:dęʼ you will celebrate
commence see: begin
deh·sáh·sa·węh begin; start it
comment see: say
ę·hęʼ he will say
commerce see: trade
dę·hę·nę·dá·da·wihs trades; commerce; barter
commiseration see: pity
gę·dę́·ǫʼ to help each other; compassion; helpfulness
commissioner see: G (gon·haʼtraʼ sha·gog·yaʼda·nǫhg·wa:nih)
commit a crime
a·tad·rih·wá·hęʼ he went afoul of the law; he did s.t. wrong
[de+...ad+ stem: -(r)ihwahę- commit a crime, do wrong, consists of: -(r)ih(wa)$_{N}$- word -(hr)e, (hr)ę$_{V}$- put, place]
commitment see: responsibility
sad·rih·wa·géh·deʼ your responsibility
common-law
go·nat·nahg·wá·ǫ·ni: they (f/m) are common-law
[at+ stem: -(ʼ)nahgwaǫni- common-law consists of: -(ʼ)ahgw(a)$_{N}$- wife, marriage -ǫni, ǫny$_{V}$- make]
commons see: town square
tsaʼde·ga·ná·da·hęh village square; village centre; town square
communicable
go·wa:ʼs it is communicable (that is, a disease, vermin)
[go+ stem: -wa:ʼs$_{V}$- communicable]
communicate see: say, talk
a·hęʼ he said
ę·géh·ta·ęʼ I will talk

community hall
de·tę·nat·gwá'ta' community hall [de+t+hęn+at+ stem: -gwa'ta'- community hall; consists of: -gw$_{V}$- gather, pick, get]

compact see: volume
tsę́h ni·gá:dę:s volume; density; how thick it is; mass

companion see: wife, husband
ke·gę́h·jih my wife
ak·nág·wa' my wife
he·gę́h·jih my husband

companionship see: friendship
a·dá·o'tra' friendship; also refers to a ceremonial friend

compare see: copy
dah·sa·den·yę́:dęhs copy; compare

compassion see: kindness, mercy, pity
a·dę·ni·dę́·ǫs·ra' the act of kindness
gę·dá·ǫhs·ra' mercy
gę·dę́·ǫ' compassion; helpfulness

compensate see: pay, repay
a'é·gan·ya'k she paid
ęt·sé·gan·ya'k you will repay, refund

compete
dę·ho·nat·gę́:nyǫ: they (m) compete [de+...at+ stem: -gęni, gęny$_{V}$- compete]

competition
de·wát·gęn·yǫ: a competition

complain
sa·ih·wa·gę́:nya't you will complain; you are a complainer [P+ stem: -(r)ihwagęnya'd- complain, instigate; consists of: -(r)ih(wa)$_{N}$- word -gęni, gęny$_{V}$- compete]

complain see: instigate, whine
ho·ih·wa·gę́:nya't he is an instigator
at·ga·ji·dá·ga·i: there was whining, crying, repetitive complaining

complete
ha·wa·yę·nę́:da's he finishes [stem: -wayęnęda'- complete, finish; consists of: -wayę(n)$_{N}$- heart, spirit -ęda'$_{V}$- finish]
a'e·wa·yę:nę́:da' she finished
ęh·se·wa·yę:nę́:da' you will complete
tsa'ha·wa·yę:nę́:da' when he finished, completed it
ga·wa·ya·nę́·da̲'ǫh it is ready, prepared

complete see: accomplish, across (go), finish
ęhs·rih·wag·wę́:ni' you will accomplish
hę·só'kdę' you will finish s.t.
at·sa:dǫ́:goht you went across; you have completed s.t.

compliant see: willing
ho·gá·ę:s he is willing

complicit see: work together
a·ta·di·yé:na' they (m) did it together (for example, accomplices)

compliment s.o. see: praise s.o.
ęhs·he·ho·wá:naht you will praise her, uplift her spirits, flatter her

complimentary
gǫ·wah·sę·ní·yo̲hs·ta' it is complimentary, flattering [TR+ stem: -(h)sęniyohsd- compliment, flatter; consists of: -(h)sęn(a)$_{N}$- name -iyo:$_{V}$- be nice, good]

comply see: listen
ęh·sa·da̲·hǫh·si·yóhs·ta:k you will listen, obey

compose
gǫ·nad·rę·nǫ́:nih they (f/m) are composers [ad+ stem: -(r)ęnǫni- compose; consists of: -(r)ęn(a)$_{N}$- song, music -ǫni, ǫny$_{V}$- make]
a·had·rę·nǫ́:ni' he made a song
a'ǫd·rę·nǫ́:ni' she made a song
go·nad·rę·nǫ́:ni: they (f/m) composed a song

compose oneself
a·ga·dǫg·we'dí:yohs I made myself nice (that is, I put on my public face, facade)
[ad+ stem: -ǫgwe'diyohsd- compose oneself; consists of: -ǫgwe('da)$_N$- person -iyo:$_V$- be nice, good]

computer
de·ga·i·hó:węhs computer
[de+ga+ stem: -(r)ihowęhs- computer; consists of: -(r)ih(wa)$_N$- word -owę(:)$_V$- split in two]

composure see: patience
ga·dę'ni·gǫ·hah·ní·yahs·ta' I have patience

comprehend see: understand
ak·ni·gǫ·há·ę·da's I understand

compress see: squeeze
dęhs·tó·ha:k you will squeeze it

computation see: count
ęd·wáhs·he:t we all (incl.) will count

comrade see: friend
ǫg·wa·dá·o'shǫ' we all are buddies, friends

conceal see: hide oneself
ę·gá·da̱h·seht I will hide

concealed see: secret
ad·rih·wa̱h·séh·dǫ:' a secret

concede see: affirm, give up
ęhs·rih·wa̱h·ní:ya:t you will affirm it, agree
ę·sa:wę́:na't you will give up

conceit see: pride
ga·ná·i: pride; boastfulness

conceited
ha·dá:ta:' he is conceited
[A+ad+ stem: -(a)ta:'- conceited, snob; consists of: -(a)d$_V$- be contained, in s.t.]
wa·dá:ta:' a snob

conceive see: think about, child-bearing
de·wag·y'a·dó·we̱h·dǫh I have already thought about it; I am thinking about it
ǫ·dé'dǫ̱·ha' she is child-bearing; she is giving birth right now

concentrate see: pay attention
ę·sáhs·di:s you will pay attention

concept see: idea
o·íh·wa·geh the reason, idea for s.t.

conception see: birth
a·dǫ́n·hehs·ra' birth

concern see: care for, worry
ęhs·he·ya·de·wa·yę:nǫ́:ni' you will take care of them, care for them
ęh·sę·ni·gǫ́·hod·rǫ:' you will worry, despair; you will be desperate

concession
sgá:t he·yo·ta·hí:nǫ: one concession (a measurement)
[sga:t one he+yo+at+ stem: -(h)ahinǫ:- concession; consists of: -(h)ah(a)$_N$- road -ine$_V$- go]

conciliate see: reconcile
ę·ji·jad·rih·wa̱hs·rǫ́:ni' you two will reconcile

conclude see: decide, finish
a·to·ih·wá·ę·da's he came to a decision, a conclusion
hę·só'kdę' you will finish s.t.

concoct see: plan
ę·jad·rih·wáhs'a:' you two will plan

concur see: affirm
ęhs·rih·wa̱h·ní:ya:t you will affirm it, agree

condemn
she·yéh·sa̱h·ta' you always condemn, insult, slander s.o.
[stem: -yesahd$_V$- condemn, slander, insult]
ęhs·yé:saht you will condemn, slander, insult s.o.
she·yeh·sa̱h·dáh·nǫh you are slandering, insulting s.o.

condemn see: blame, denounce, sentence
ęhs·héh·wa'ehs you will blame s.o.
dęhs·ríh·wa·ya:'k you will denounce it, disapprove of it

Cayuga pronunciation guide: /a/ father /e/ weigh /ę/ men (nasalized) /i/ police /o/ hole /ǫ/ home (nasalized) /u/ blue. Underlined vowels are voiceless or whispered. /'/ high pitch. /t/ too /d/ do /k/ king /g/ good (never soft g) /j/ judge or adze /s/ soon /sh/ less heat (never the sh in shirt) /sr/ shrine /sy/ sure /hw/ which (the sound made when you blow out a candle) /h/ hi /ts/ cats hide /'/ (the sound before the first vowel in 'uh-uh') /n/ noon /r/ round /w/ way /y/ yes.

condemn (continued)

a·hǫ·wa·dę́:nyeht he was sentenced (lit.: they sent him)

condemned see: guilty

a·ho·nǫ·dá:nhaʼ he was found guilty

condensation see: fog

ot·sá:daʼ fog; steam

condiment see: pepper, salt, herb

de·yóh·sa·it pepper

o·jí·kʼe·daʼ salt

de·ga·yehs·dáh·nǫʼ mixture; it is mixed together to make it good (for example, herbs, spices, etc.)

condom

ǫ·den·ro·wé:k·taʼ condom

[ǫ+ade+ stem: -nrowektaʼ- condom; consists of: -nr(a)$_N$- phallus, penis -(hr)oweg$_V$- cover]

conduct

na·ǫ·sa·ǫg·wa·yę́·hę:k what we all should be doing; how we all should conduct ourselves

[naǫsa+P+ stem: -ye(:)$_V$- do, conduct]

conduct see: do

nig·ya:gó:yę: the way she does s.t.

cone see: pine cone

o·nę́ʼdǫ:t pine cone

confer see: discuss

dęd·wah·tá:goʼ we all (incl.) will discuss

conference see: meet

ęhs·wat·ge·níh·sa:ʼ you all will have a meeting

confidential see: secret

od·rih·wa·séh·dǫh it is secret

confirm see: affirm

ęhs·rih·wa̲h·ní:ya:t you will affirm it, agree

conflict see: fight, war

od·ri·yo̲h·dę́·daʼǫh war

wad·rí:yo: a war; a fight

conform see: adjust, listen

ęt·sa:dó:gęhs you will adjust s.t.

ęh·sa·da̲·hǫh·si·yóhs·ta:k you will listen, obey

confront see: argue

dęhs·rih·wa·gé:nhaʼ you will argue, debate, protest

confused

de·wa·ga·da·wę̱n·yáʼseh I am confused and doubtful (lit: my thinking is going around in circles)

[de+P+ad+ stem: -(a)węnyaʼseh- confused, doubtful; consists of: -(a)węnye(:)$_V$- stir, mix]

de·wag·yad·ri·ho·dáh·se:ʼ I am confused; I cannot make up my mind

[de+P+ad+ stem: -(r)ihodahse:ʼ- confused; consists of: -(r)ih(wa)$_N$- word -oda(h)$_V$- draped]

de·wa·gad·ri·ho·dá·hǫh I am confused, mixed up; s.t. is blocking my thinking

congested see: breathless

ha·dǫh·wi̲hs·róʼktaʼ he is out of breath

congregate

ęd·wád·ro̲·he:k we all (incl.) will gather together

[ad+ stem: -(r)oheg$_V$- gather, congregate]

gę·nád·ro̲·he:s they (z) are flocking

congregate see: gather, stand in a bunch, group

gá·e·yo̲·he:s they (f/m) are gathering

ga·díh·si̲·ha:ʼ they (z) are congregated

conifer see: pine

o·nę́ʼdaʼ evergreen; conifer

conjurer see: evil power

go·ná:t·gǫh they (f/m) are a force to be reckoned with; they (f/m) are ominous; they are bad medicine people

connect see: attach, join

ęh·só·ha·ęʼ you will attach s.t.

dęh·sáh·sǫd·ręʼ you will join two things together

consciousness (lose consciousness)
hęh·sah·dǫ́:ʼ ęh·saʼni·gǫ́·hah·dǫʼ you will lose consciousness
[consists of: hęhsahdǫ:ʼ you will lose it there; ęhsaʼnigǫhahdǫʼ you will faint]
consecrated see: forbidden
o·nǫ́ʼne:ʼ it is forbidden, sacred, holy
consensus see: G (de·ga·ih·wa·ę·daʼs)
consent see: affirm, listen, willing
ęhs·rih·wah·ní·ya·t you will affirm it, agree
ę·ga·tǫ́·da·t I will consent
ę·wa·ge·gá·ęʼ I will consent
conservation see: G
(de·hę·nǫh·wę·jahsn·yeʼ)
consider see: think
de·wag·yʼa·dó·węh·dǫh I have already thought about it; I am thinking about it
consideration see: kindness
a·dę·ni·dé·ǫs·raʼ the act of kindness
consign see: appoint
ni·hǫ·wá·i·hǫ·t he has appointed him
console
ęhs·heʼni·gǫ́·hoʼdrǫ:ʼ you will console s.o. (lit.: you will caress s.o.'s mind)
[ę+ stem: -(ʼ)nigǫhoʼdrǫ- console s.o.; consists of: -(ʼ)nigǫh(a)$_{N}$- mind -(a)hdrǫ(gw)$_{V}$- caress]
conspicuous see: recognizable
o·yę́·deht it is recognizable, plain to be seen, conspicuous
conspire see: work together
at·ga·e·yé·naʼ they (f/m) did it together (for example, accomplices)
constable see: police
sha·go·di·yé·nahs policemen
constantly see: always
gyot·gǫ·t always
constipate
ǫg·yáʼdag·we·s she gets bound up, constipated

constipate (continued)
[ag+ stem: -yaʼdagweg- constipate; consists of: -yaʼd(a)$_{N}$- body -gweg$_{V}$- close]
hag·yáʼdag·we·s he gets bound up,constipated
ę·sag·yʼa·dá·gwe·k you will get constipated
gog·yaʼdag·wé·gǫh she is constipated
Constitution see: G
(Ga·ya·nęhs·raʼgo:wah)
Constitution Act see: G,
(Gah·ya·dǫhs·rag·wę·ni:yoʼ)
construct see: assemble, make
dęh·sé·ga·hǫʼ you will assemble, put together
a·gǫ́·niʼ I did make, earn
consult see: discuss
dęd·wah·tá·goʼ we all (incl.) will discuss
consume see: digest, eat
dę·gák·wa·hiht it will digest
a·ha·k he ate it
consumed see: use up, all gone
a·wá·tsʼa:ʼ it is worn out, all gone, burnt up; it went down to nothing
haʼwá·tsʼaht it is all gone
Consumer's Affairs see: G
(Gah·ni·nǫhn·yǫʼ
O·de·dag·wa·ih·sǫ·hag·yeʼ)
consumption
gah·ní·nǫh·nyǫʼ consumption
[stem: -(h)ninǫ$_{V}$- buy]
contact see: touch
haʼgye:ʼ I touched it
contain
wa·dǫ·dá·taʼ it contains s.t.; a container
[wa+ad+ stem: -ǫdataʼ- contain; consists of: -ǫda:(h)$_{V}$- put in, attached]
í·wa·t it is contained; it (z) is in there; solid matter
[(i+)wa+ stem: -(a)d$_{V}$- be contained, in s.t.]

Cayuga pronunciation guide: /a/ father /e/ weigh /ę/ men (nasalized) /i/ police /o/ hole /ǫ/ home (nasalized) /u/ blue. Underlined vowels are voiceless or whispered. /ˊ/ high pitch. /t/ too /d/ do /k/ king /g/ good (never soft g) /j/ judge or adze /s/ soon /sh/ less heat (never the sh in shirt) /sr/ shrine /sy/ sure /hw/ which (the sound made when you blow out a candle) /h/ hi /ts/ cats hide /ʼ/ (the sound before the first vowel in 'uh-uh') /n/ noon /r/ round /w/ way /y/ yes.

contain (continued)
ní:ga:ʼ how much (liquid) is contained in it
[(ni+)ga+ stem: -a:$_V$- contain (liquid)]
í:ga:ʼ it contains (liquid)
container
wad·ráhk·waʼ a container
[e/wa+ad+ stem: -(r)ahkwaʼ, yahkwaʼ- container; consists of: -(r)a(:,h)$_V$- spread]
e·yáhk·waʼ containers
contaminate see: infect
oʼnó:draʼ it is infected; an infection
aʼa·go·nó:drahs she / s.o. got chicken pox, a skin infection, allergic reactions; she became infected
contemplate see: think
de·wag·yʼa·dó·we̲h·dǫh I have already thought about it; I am thinking about it
contemptible see: evil
wa̲·hé:tgęh it is evil (in mind), bad
contend see: compete
dę·ho·nat·gę́:nyǫ: they (m) compete
contented see: fun, satisfied
o·dǫ́t·gadeʼ it is fun; a good feeling
dwak·ni·go̲·hí:yo: I am satisfied, peaceful
contentment see: satisfaction
oʼni·go̲h·sí·yo̲hs·de:ʼ satisfaction
contest see: competition
de·wát·gęn·yǫ: a competition
continually see: always
gyot·gǫ:t always
continue
hę·gá·dag·yeʼ it will continue on
[heʼ+ga stem: -dagyeʼ(s)- continue on, be ongoing; consists of: -d$_V$- stand]
wa·dę·hę:dá:gyeʼ the fence is continuing
[ad+ stem: consists of: -(a)dęʼh(ę)$_N$- fence -dagyeʼ(s)$_V$- continue on, be ongoing]

continue see: restart
deg·yóh·sa:ʼ it has resumed
continue
[-dagyeʼ the verb 'stand' with progressive; meaning 'to continue on']
consequences
de·yo·yʼa·dó·we̲h·de:ʼ to weigh the consequences; it is brain-wracking
[de+yo+ stem: -yaʼdowehde:ʼ- contemplation, pondering; consists of: -yaʼdowehd$_V$- think about, consider]
contortion see: convulse
go·yé·na̲h·sǫhs a convulsion
contract see: agreement
ga·íh·wi̲h·saʼ an agreement
contradict see: disagree
taʼde·gri̲h·wáhs·nyeʼ I oppose it; I do not agree
contribute see: work together
ded·wa·ye·ná·wʼa·kǫʼ we all (incl.) are working united for one cause
contrite see: feel bad
ga·dé·hęhs I am embarrassed, ashamed
contrive see: plan
ę·jad·ri̲h·wáh·sʼa:ʼ you two will plan, make a plan
control see: oversee
ęh·sad·ri̲h·wát·ga̲·hǫ:ʼ you will oversee, supervise
controversy see: argue
de·ga·ih·wá·gen·hęh there is an argument
convene see: congregate
ęd·wád·ro̲·he:k we all (incl.) will gather together
convention see: crowd
ni·gęg·yo̲h·góʼdę: an assembled crowd; a kind of crowd
converge
de·yo·na·ta·hoʼd·ráʼǫh converging roads
[de+yon+at+ stem: -(h)ah(a)$_N$- road -(aʼ)draʼ$_V$- meet]

converge see: meet
de·gę́·nad·ra'·s they (z) meet all the time
converse see: talk
ę·géh·ta·ę' I will talk
convert see: Christian, trade
ahs·rih·wí:yohs you became a Christian; you converted to Christianity
dę·sá·da·dǫ' you will trade, exchange
convey see: bring, send
ę·ta·há:wi' he is going to bring s.t.
he·wa·ga·dę́n·yeh·dǫh I sent it
conveyance see: transportation
go·ya'da·nę́hg·wih transportation; bus; elevator (lit.: people mover)
convict see: send
a·hǫ·wa·dę́:nyeht he was sentenced (lit.: they sent him)
conviction see: belief
tsę́h hǫ:wéh gyǫg·wéh·dah·gǫh our belief; religion
convulse
go·yé·nah·sǫhs a convulsion
[P+ stem: -yęnahsǫ'$_V$- convulse, convulsion]
ǫg·yé·nah·sǫ:' I had convulsions
a·ho·yé·nah·sǫ:' he had convulsions
ę·sa·yę·náh·sǫ:' you are an epileptic (lit.: you will have convulstions)
go·dę·dǫn·yá'ta' convulsions
[P+ad+ stem: -ędǫnya'd- tease, joke, jest, have convulsions; consists of: -(w)ędǫnya'd$_V$- cause s.t. to shake]
cook
ga·kǫ́:nihs it cooks
[stem: -kǫni- cook; consists of: -k(wa)$_N$- food -ǫni, ǫny$_V$- make]
ge·kǫ·nihs·gę́·hę:' I used to cook
ga·kǫ́:ni: cooking
go·kǫ́:ni: she is cooking
a·ge·kǫ·níh·ne:' I have cooked
se·kǫ́:nih cook
e·kǫ́n·y'a·ta' what one cooks with

cook (continued)
[stem: -kǫnya'd- cause to cook; consists of: -k(wa)$_N$- food -ǫni, ǫny$_V$- make]
cook see: boil, roast, bake, endure
ęg·yǫ́n·ya·hęh it will boil
wa·dé's·gǫ:t it is roasting, frying
wa·tǫ́n'a·dǫ:t baked potatoes
ę·ga·ǫ·dáh·gahs·dǫ: they (f/m) will endure; used in the sense of 'go and cook in the cookhouse'
cooker
gak·wahs·nó:we' fast-food cooker
[ga+ stem: -kwahsnowe'- fast-food cooker; consists of: -k(wa)$_N$- food -(h)snowe'$_V$- fast]
cookie
ni·yo·n'a·da·ó:s'uh cookies
[ni+yo+ stem: -na'daos'uh- cookie; consists of: -na'd(a:)$_N$- bread -u:'uh$_V$- small]
cookout see: barbecue
ahs·deh·ká:' ǫ·de'sgǫ·dáhk·wa' outdoor barbecue
cool see: cold
o·ná'no:' it is cold, cool
coop see: chicken coop
daks·ha·e'dóhs o·dí·nǫh·so:t chicken coop
cooperate see: participate, work together
dę·ya·go'nya:gwę́·hęg·ye' she will have a hand in it
ded·wa:yé·na: let's (incl.) work together, help one another
copulate see: mate
o·ná·da'i:s they (z) are mating
copy
ęt·sa·den·yę́:dęhs you will copy, use as a model, pattern
[de+...ade+ stem: -(')nyędęhsd- measure; copy, compare; consists of: -(')nyędę$_V$- try]
dah·sa·den·yę́:dęhs copy; compare

cord see: thread, rope
oh·sí:ya' thread; string; cord
ga:ts·g'ę·da' a rope
copy see: imitate
ęts·ná'gyę:' you will imitate, mock, mimic s.t.
cord (of wood)
wa·dę·hí:' o·yę́:da' cord of wood
[consists of: wadęhi:' it is stacked; oyę:da' wood, firewood]
corn
o·nę́·hę:' corn
[o+ stem: -nęh(ę)$_N$- corn]
nawę'dawéht o·nę́·hę'se: sweet corn
[consists of: nawę'daweht it is sweet, rich; onęhę'se: new corn]
wa·dęh·sǫ́' o·nę́·hę:' roasted white corn
[consists of: wadęhsǫ' it is roasted; onęhę'se: new corn]
ohn·yǫ́hg·wihs·da' braided corn
[o+ stem: -(h)nyǫhgwihsd(a)$_N$- braided corn]
o·nę́·hę'gę:t white corn
[o+ stem: -nęh(ę)$_N$- corn -(')gęd$_V$- light-coloured, white]
o·nę́·hę·se:' green corn; new corn
[o+ stem: -nęh(ę)$_N$- corn -(a)se:$_V$- new]
ǫ·nę́·hę·jih black, dark corn
[o+ stem: -nęh(ę)$_N$- corn -ji(:,h)$_V$- dark]
wat·nę́·hęs·dǫ:t whole corn roasted on an open fire
[w+at+ stem: -nęh(ę)$_N$- corn -(h)sdǫd$_V$- roasted]
o·nę́·hęt·gi' dirty corn
[o+ stem: -nęh(ę)$_N$- corn -tgi$_V$- dirty, ugly]
e·ne·ho·há·to lyed corn
[e+ stem: -nęhohato- corn (lyed); consists of: -nęh(ę)$_N$- corn -ohae$_V$- clean, wash]
ga·nę́·ho' boiled corn
[ga+ stem: -nęh(ę)$_N$- corn -o'- boiled, stewed]

corn (continued)
o·jitg·wa:'ę:' yellow corn
[o+ stem: -jitgw(a:)$_N$- yellow -'ę:'$_V$- be coloured]
ga·ga·heh·dę́h·dǫh lyed corn
[ga+ stem: -gahehdęhd- lye corn; consists of: -gahehd(a)$_N$- eye (of a corn kernel) -(y)ęhd$_V$- hit, knock down, strike]
corn see: soup
o·gę́:nye:' roasted green corn; dried corn soup (made with roasted green corn)
corn bread
o·nę·hę́' o·ná'da:' corn bread
[consists of: onęhę:' corn; ona'da:' bread]
corn bug
ga·nę·há·i·ta' corn bug; corn napper
[ga+ stem: -nęhaita'- corn bug; consists of: -nęh(ę)$_N$- corn -(hr)i'$_V$- break up]
corn flour
o·nę·hę́:' o·té'tra' corn flour
[consists of: onęhę:' corn; ote'tra' flour, powder]
onęhę'sé:' gate'trǫ́:ni: cornmeal flour (made with yellow corn)
[consists of: onęhę'se: new corn; gate'trǫ:ni: it is made into flour]
corn oil
o·nę·hę́' oh·na' corn oil
[consists of: onęhę:' corn; ohna' oil]
corn soup see: soup
o·gę́:nye:' roasted green corn; dried corn soup (made with roasted green corn)
o·nę́·hohg·wa' lyed corn soup
ohn·yé:ha' flint corn soup
corn stalk
o·hé:ya' a corn stalk
[o+ stem: -(h)ey(a)$_N$- corn stalk]

corn stalk (continued)
ga·he·yá·o·dǫ’ a standing bunch of corn stalks
[ga+ stem: -(h)ey(a)$_N$- corn stalk -od$_V$- stand]

corn tassel
tsa’gę́:da’ corn tassel
[stem: -tsa’gęd(a)$_N$- corn tassel]

corner
he·yó’wi: a corner
[he+yo+ stem: -(’)wi:- corner]

corner see: recourse (without)
a·to·da·níh·s’a·e:k he got cornered, up against the wall with no recourse

Cornplanter Reserve, Pennsylvania see: E (Ga·yę·twah·geh)

corporation see: G (dę·ho·nag.yehs·dǫh)

corpse
o·yǫ́’da’ a dead body; a cadaver
[o+ stem: -(he)yǫ(’da)$_N$- corpse, cadaver]

corpulent see: fat
gǫh·sę: she is fat

corral see: stable
de·ga·di·dę́hs·dahk·wa’ stable

correct see: arrange, punish, right
ęh·sad·rih·wa:dó:gęhs you will right a wrong
ęh·gahs·he·hé:waht you will punish them
tga:yé·i: it is right, correct

Correctional Services see: G (Ǫ·da·dęn·ho·dǫhk·wa’ O·ih·wa·geh)

correlate see: same, resemble
tsa’dé:yoht they are (lit.: it is) the same
sgá:yę: it resembles

correspond see: write
eh·yá:dǫh she writes

corrode see: rust
ohs·gę́’dra·he:’ it is rusting, rusty

corrupt
des·ha·g’o·ni·gǫ·há·gęn·yǫhs he intimidates people all the time
[de+TR+ stem: -(’)nigǫhagęni- corrupt, intimidate; consists of: -(’)nigǫh(a)$_N$- mind -gęni, gęny$_V$- compete]
dęhs·he’ni·gǫ·ha·gę́:ni’ you will corrupt s.o.’s mind
dęs·ha·g’o·ni·gǫ·ha:gę́:ni’ he will overcome their mind, intimidate s.o.
ęhs·ni·gǫ·ha:gę́:ni’ you will beat s.o. (mentally)
ęhs·he·ya·dáh·dǫ’t you will corrupt her/them
[TR+ad+ stem: -(a)hdǫ’d- lose s.t., corrupt s.o.; consists of: -(a)hdǫ(:)$_V$- lose, disappear]

corrupt see: bad
de·ta·dih·wa:yé·i: they (m) are corrupt, impish, bad

corset see: girdle
de·yǫg·y’a·dó·hak·ta’ girdle

cosmetics see: make-up
ǫt·go’jon·yáh·ta’ make-up; blush; rouge

cost
ni·gá:nǫ:’ how much it costs
[(ni+) ga+(N+) stem: -nǫ:’$_V$- costly, dear, expensive]
ga·nǫ:’ it is expensive, dear, precious
ǫ·ge:gá:h·dę’ that’s how much it cost me
[P+ stem: -gahdę- cost s.o.; consists of: -ga(:)$_N$- price -(a)hd$_V$- like, resemble]

cost see: price
ga·gá·he:’ the price of s.t.

costume see: clothes
ahg·wę́:nya’ clothing; clothes

cot see: bed
ga·ná:kda’ bed

cottager see: lake
gan·ya·da:ge·hó:nǫ’ lake people; cottagers

Cayuga pronunciation guide: /a/ father /e/ weigh /ę/ men (nasalized) /i/ police /o/ hole /ǫ/ home (nasalized) /u/ blue. Underlined vowels are voiceless or whispered. /´/ high pitch. /t/ too /d/ do /k/ king /g/ good (never soft g) /j/ judge or adze /s/ soon /sh/ less heat (never the sh in shirt) /sr/ shrine /sy/ sure /hw/ which (the sound made when you blow out a candle) /h/ hi /ts/ cats hide /’/ (the sound before the first vowel in ‘uh-uh’) /n/ noon /r/ round /w/ way /y/ yes.

cotton
ga·ni·ga:hęhs·rí:yo: cotton, silk
[ga+ stem: -niga:hęhsriyo:- cotton, silk; consists of: -niga:hęh(sra)$_{N}$- fabric -iyo:$_{V}$- be nice, good]

cotton batting
o·gǫ́:draʼ cotton batting; q-tips
[o+ stem: -gǫʼdr(a)$_{N}$- pillow, cushion, cotton batting]
o·naʼgwí:yaʼ cotton batting
[o+ stem: -naʼgwiy(a)$_{N}$- cotton batting]

couch
ǫg·yaʼgye·nę́·da̱hk·waʼ couch
[ǫ+ag+ stem: -yaʼgyenęhdahkwaʼ- couch; consists of: -yaʼd(a)$_{N}$- body -(raʼ)nęd(a:ʼg), (yaʼ)nęd(a:ʼg)$_{V}$- stick, cling]

cough
ga̱h·sáʼkaʼ I have a cough; I am coughing
[stem: -(a)hsaʼg- cough; consists of: -(ʼa)hsa(w)$_{N}$- chest -(ʼ)g$_{V}$- cough]
ǫh·sáʼkaʼ she is coughing

council see: association
gęg·yohg·wa·gé·hǫʼ associations; councils; agencies; groups

council chamber see: court
ha·di·hahs·hę́ʼda̱hk·waʼ a court; a council chamber

counsel
ęhs·he·ta·háhs ęhs·heʼni·gǫ·hah·ní:ya:t you counsel her
[consists of: ęhshetahahs you talk to her; ęhsheʼnigǫhahni:ya:t you strengthen her mind]
ha·háhs·hę·hęʼ he is a counsellor
[stem: -(h)ahshę$_{V}$- counsel]
ę·ha·hah·sę́·hę:k he will be a counsellor
ho·ha·hah·sę́·hęg·yeʼ he is counselling

counselor see: G (ha·hahs·hę·hęʼ)

count
hę·nahs·hé:dahs they (m) count things
[stem: -(a)hshed$_{V}$- count]
ęd·wáhs·he:t we all (incl.) will count
ę·yág·wa̱hs·he:t we all (excl.) will count
jid·wáhs·he:t let us all (incl.) count again
ęd·wahs·hé:dǫh will all (incl.) qill give a number; we all will number
[stem: -(a)hshedǫh$_{V}$- number; consists of: -(a)hshed$_{V}$- count]

count on see: rely on
ke·yáʼdaʼs I rely on her

counter see: shelf, table
wę·níhs·rǫʼ shelves; shelving

country
o·dǫh·wę·já:deʼ country
[o+ad+ stem: -ǫhwęjadeʼ- country; consists of: -ǫhwęj(a)$_{N}$- earth -deʼ$_{V}$- exist]
gyoh·wę́·ja·deʼ a country
[g+yo+ stem: -ǫhwęj(a)$_{N}$- earth, land -deʼ$_{V}$- exist]

country see: forest, G (o·dǫh·wę·ja·deʼ)
ga̱·há:gǫ: in the bush

couple see: pair, C (ǫg·ya:tsih)
o·ná:tsih a pair (of shoes, socks)

courageous see: masculine
ha·jí:nah he is masculine, brave; his genitals

courier
ha·nę́hg·wih (he is a) courier
[A+ stem: -nęhgwih- courier; consists of: -nęhgwi$_{V}$- haul]
ha·heh·na·nę́hg·wih he is a courier
[stem: -hehnanęhgwih- courier; consists of: -(hr)ehn(a)$_{N}$- cargo, bundle -nęhgwi$_{V}$- haul]
ha·ih·wa·nę́hg·wih he is a courier
[A+ stem: -(r)ihwanęhgwih- courier; consists of: -(r)ih(wa)$_{N}$- word -nęhgwi$_{V}$- haul]

court
ha·di·hahs·hę́ˀdahk·waˀ a court; a council chamber
[hadi+ stem: -(h)ahshęˀdahkwaˀ- court, council chamber; consists of: -(h)ahshę$_{V}$- counsel]
court recorder see: secretary
eh·yá·dǫ·haˀ she is a secretary, stenographer, court recorder, transcriber
courthouse see: G
(dę·ha·di·hah·sę·dahk·waˀ)
cousin see: C
ǫg·waˀsé:shǫˀ our cousins (lit.: we all are cousins)
covenant see: promise
ga·ih·wih·sá·hǫh a promise
cover
geˀhó:we:s I am covering s.t.
[TR+(N+) stem: -(ˀh)oweg$_{V}$- cover s.t.]
ęhs·heˀhó:we:k you will cover s.o.
ęh·seˀhó:we:k you will cover s.t.
a·geˀho·wé:gǫh I did cover s.t.
ęh·snahs·gó:we:k cover your bed
[TR+ stem: -naˀsg(wa)$_{N}$- mattress +oweg$_{V}$- cover]
ęhs·he·yęhs·ró:we:k you will cover s.o. with a blanket
[TR+ stem: -yęhsr(a)$_{N}$- blanket -oweg$_{V}$- cover]
ęhs·he·yęhs·ráhg·wa:s you will cover s.o. with a blanket
[stem: -yęhsr(a)$_{N}$- blanket -(h)gwahsd$_{V}$- lift, pick up]
cover see: bedspread, blanket
e·nak·do·wé:k·taˀ bedspread
o·yęhs·raˀ blankets
covet see: want
gahs·gá:ne:s I have longings for; I want; I desire

cow
gyon·hóhsg·wa·ǫ:t cow
[g+yo+ stem: -nhohsgwaǫd- cow; consists of: -nhohsg(wa)$_{N}$- s.t. to do with the cud -ǫd$_{V}$- attached]
coward see: timid
totg·ri: he's a wimp; he pulls back
cozy see: comfortable
ęh·sa·nak·dí:yohs you will become physically comfortable (lit.: you'll be comfortable with your bed)
crab
jiˀo: a crab
[stem: -jiˀo:- crab; consists of: -jiˀ(a)$_{N}$- crab -o(:)$_{V}$- submerge]
crabapple
oh·ya·ji·wá:gę: crabapples; tart, sour fruit
[o+ stem: -(a)hyajiwagę:- crabapple; consists of: -(a)hy(a)$_{N}$- fruit, berry -jiwagę:$_{V}$- sour, bitter, salty]
oh·ya·ji·wa:gę́: oh·yáˀ grahe:t crabapple tree
[consists of: ohyaji:wa:gę: crabapples; ohyaˀ fruit, berry; grahe:t living tree]
crabby see: grumpy
de·di·sˀa·ni·gǫ·hí:yo: you are grumpy, grouchy, unhappy
cracker
o·naˀdá:tę: crackers
[o+ stem: -naˀda:ˀtę:- cracker; consists of: -naˀd(a:)$_{N}$- bread -tę(:)$_{V}$- dry]
cradle
o·wi:ya:ˀáh de·yǫt·gá:hǫhk·waˀ baby's cradle
[consists of: owi:ya:ˀah baby; deyǫtga:hǫhkwaˀ rocking chair]
cradle-robber
oh·náh·tęhs·dǫh dried-up skin (a derogatory term referring to s.o. associating with a younger woman or man)

Cayuga pronunciation guide: /a/ father /e/ weigh /ę/ men (nasalized) /i/ police /o/ hole /ǫ/ home (nasalized) /u/ blue. Underlined vowels are voiceless or whispered. /´/ high pitch. /t/ too /d/ do /k/ king /g/ good (never soft g) /j/ judge or adze /s/ soon /sh/ less heat (never the sh in shirt) /sr/ shrine /sy/ sure /hw/ which (the sound made when you blow out a candle) /h/ hi /ts/ cats hide /ˀ/ (the sound before the first vowel in 'uh-uh') /n/ noon /r/ round /w/ way /y/ yes.

cradle-robber (continued)
[o+ stem: -(h)natęhsdǫh- cradle-robber; consists of: -(i)hn(a)$_N$- material, skin -tęhsd$_V$- be dried out]

cradleboard
ga:hǫ́hs·raʼ cradleboard
[ga+stem: -(h)ǫhsr(a)$_N$- box]
oh·węʼgʼa·géh go·yaʼdo·nę́·da·gǫh baby on a cradleboard (high language)
[consists of: ohwęʼgʼageh on a splint; goyaʼdonędagǫh her body is stuck on it]

craft see: boat, occupation
ga̲·hǫ́:waʼ boat
ni·sa·i·hoʼdęhs·róʼdę: your occupation; your type of work

craft shop
ti·gahs·rǫn·yah·nǫʼshǫ́:ʼǫh craft shops
[ti+ga+ stem: -(h)srǫnyahnǫʼ- craft shop; consists of: -hsr$_N$- noun -ǫni, ǫny$_V$- make]

craftsman see: work
hę·nad·ri̲·hóʼda:s they (m) work; they are workers

cramp
ǫ·géhs·nag·ri:k I had muscle cramps; I got a cramp
[P+ stem: -(h)snagri- cramp; consists of: -(h)sna(ʼda)$_N$- muscle, hamstring, calf (body part) -gri$_V$- wrinkle]
ǫ·gehs·nag·rík·sǫ:ʼ I got cramps

crane (bird)
de·gá·hǫh marsh crane (lit.: it leans; referring to its legs); a bar; a barrier
[de+ga+ stem: -hǫh- crane; consists of: -(adi)hǫh$_V$- lean against]
de·ga·ǫh·yá·ga̲h·ne:ʼ a stream crane
[de+ga+ stem: -ǫhyagahne:ʼ- stream crane; consists of: -(r)ǫhy(a)$_N$- sky]

crane (machine)
wa·da·dʼed·réʼs de·gáhg·wa·taʼ crane (hoisting machine)
[consists of: wadadedreʼs (it drives itself); degahgwataʼ it raises things up]

cranky see: cantankerous
e·nǫ́·wę̱hd·raʼ she is cantankerous

crate see: basket, box
gaʼáhd·raʼ basket
ga̲·hǫ́hs·raʼ a box

crater see: hole
ǫh·wę·ja·gá·hę·taʼ, ga̲h·wę·ja·gá·hę·taʼ a hole in the earth

crave
knǫ́:wa:s I crave s.t.
[stem: -nǫwag$_V$- crave]
ęk·nǫ́:wa:k I will crave s.t.
ak·nǫ́:wa:k I did get hungry for it

crave see: want
ga̲hs·gá:ne:s I have longings for; I want; I desire

crawl
at·sák·yo̲hs·gwi:ʼ you did crawl
[de+…ak+ stem: -(h)yohs(a)$_N$- elbow -(h)yohsgwi(:)$_V$- crawl]
ag·yǫ́k·yohs·gwi:ʼ she did crawl (that is, she learned how to crawl)
de·sák·yo̲hs·gwi: crawl

crayon see: colour
ǫh·sóh·taʼ colour; paints; crayons

crazy
te·haʼni·gǫ·ha·yé·i:ʼ he is not right in the mind
[(tęʼ not) teʼ+A+ stem: -(ʼ)nigǫhayei- be crazy, mentally ill; consists of: -(ʼ)nigǫh(a)$_N$- mind -yei, (y)i̲$_V$- right, correct]
tę́ʼ teʼsni·go̲·ha·yé·i:ʼ you are crazy (comical); you lose control of your mind
de·ge·na̲·ha:wé:nyeʼ I am crazy
[de+A+ stem: -nahawenye(:)- crazy, insane; consists of: -nǫh(a), nah(a)$_N$- scalp -(a)węnye(:)$_V$- stir, mix]
de·sę·na̲·ha:wę́:nyeʼ you are crazy (not right in the mind)
dęsęna̲ha:wę́:nye:ʼ you will go insane

cream separator
de·ga·wid·rá·gę̱d·rǫhs cream separator [de+ga+ stem: -widragędrǫhs- cream separator; consists of: -widr(a)$_N$- ice, cream -gędrǫ(:)$_V$- separate]
crease see: wrinkle
ohs·gwí'dra' a prune; wrinkles
create
tsa'hǫh·wę·já:da:t when he made the earth
[stem: -ǫhwęj(a)$_N$- earth, land -dad$_V$- create]
hǫh·wę·ja·dá·dǫh he has created the earth
create see: make
ę·ya:gǫ́:ni' she will make, earn
creature see: animal (tame), animal (wild)
gat·sé:nę' an animal; a pet
credible see: righteous
od·rih·wag·wá·ih·sǫ: it is believable, credible, righteous, fair, honest
credulous see: believe
dih·séh·da̱h·gǫh you are credulous, gullible; you believe in s.t.
creed see: belief
tsę́h hǫ:wéh gyǫg·wéh·da̱h·gǫh our belief; religion
creek see: river
gi·hę́:de' creek, river, stream
creep see: sneak around
sgę:nǫ:'ǫ́h hot·rihs·dǫ·hǫ́:gye' he is sneaking around slowly
cremate
a·hǫ·wa·di·y'a·dę́'da:' they burned the body, cremated him
[TR+ stem: -ya'dę'da:- cremate; consists of: -ya'd(a)$_N$- body -(hr)ę'da:$_V$- burn s.t.]
crevasse see: canyon
he·yo·heh·dę́'ǫ·ge: canyon

crib
o·wi:ya:'áh gǫ·ná:kda' baby's crib [consists of: owi:ya:'ah baby; gǫna:kda' her bed]
crib see: cradle
o·wi:ya:'áh de·yǫt·gá:hǫhk·wa' baby's cradle
cricket
ji·nǫ́h·sa·nǫh cricket
[ji+ stem: -nǫhsa'nǫh- cricket; consists of: -nǫhs(a)$_N$- house -(')nǫh$_V$- put in]
crime see: commit a crime
a·tad·ri̱h·wá·hę' he went afoul of the law; he did s.t. wrong
crimp see: fold
dę·seh·sak·da:nyǫ́:go' you will fold s.t.up
crimson see: red
ot·gwę́h·j'ia:' red
crippled
ho·jí:yo' he is crippled
[P+(N+) stem: -jiyo'$_V$- crippled, lame]
a·ge:jí:yo' I am crippled, lame
goh·si·na·jí:yo' she has a bad leg
[P+ stem: -(h)sin(a)$_N$- leg -jiyo'$_V$- crippled, lame]
crooked see: bend
ha'hi'ya·gá·ę·he' his body trunk is crooked; he is bent over
crop see: harvest
ga·yę́t·wag·węh a harvest
cross
es·ró·hę: she is habitually cross; cantankerous
[A+ stem: -(h)srǫhę:$_V$- cross, angry]
ǫd·rę·na·ę·da̱hk·wa'géh de·gá·ya̱h·sǫ:t church cross
[consists of: ǫdręnaę:da̱hkwa'geh in the church; degaya̱hsǫ:t a cross]
dę·ha·di·hę:dí:ya's they (m) cut across fields
[de+... stem: -(h)ęd(a)$_N$- field -(i)ya'g$_V$- cut, break, cut across]

Cayuga pronunciation guide: /a/ father /e/ weigh /ę/ men (nasalized) /i/ police /o/ hole /ǫ/ home (nasalized) /u/ blue. Underlined vowels are voiceless or whispered. /'/ high pitch. /t/ too /d/ do /k/ king /g/ good (never soft g) /j/ judge or adze /s/ soon /sh/ less heat (never the sh in shirt) /sr/ shrine /sy/ sure /hw/ which (the sound made when you blow out a candle) /h/ hi /ts/ cats hide /'/ (the sound before the first vowel in 'uh-uh') /n/ noon /r/ round /w/ way /y/ yes.

cross see: put together
dęhs·wat·nęt·sá'drǫ:' you all will cross your arms
cross-country meet
dę̱·ha·di·hę:di:yá's dę̱·hę·ná·ǫ·ha' cross-country meet
[consists of: dę̱hadihędiya's they (m) cut across fields; dę̱hęnaǫ:ha' they (m) race; they are racing (right now)]
cross-eyed
ha·gah·gá·ę·heh he is cross eyed
[A+ stem: -gahgaęhe'- cross-eyed; consists of: -gah(a)$_N$- eye -gaęh(e')$_V$- cross]
e·gah·gá·ę·he' she is cross eyed
ga·gah·gá·ę·heh it is cross eyed
crossroad
de·yo·ha·híy'ak·sǫ' crossroads
[de+yo+ stem: -(h)ahiya'g- crossroad; consists of: -(h)ah(a)$_N$- road -(i)ya'g$_V$- cut, break, cross]
de·yo·ha·hí·y'a·gǫh a crossroad
crow
ga'ga:' crow, raven
[stem: -ga'ga:'$_N$- crow, raven]
crowd
gęg·yóh·go:t a crowd
[stem: -(i)gyohg(wa)$_N$- crowd -od$_V$- stand]
gęg·yohg·wí:yǫ: it is a nice big crowd
[ga+ stem: -(i)gyohg(wa)$_N$- crowd -iyo:$_V$- be nice, good]
ni·gęg·yǫ̱h·gó'dę: an assembled crowd; a kind of crowd
[ni+ga+ stem: -(i)gyohg(wa)$_N$- crowd -o'dę:$_V$- type of]
og·yohg·wa·ní·dęht a poor crowd
[o+ stem: -(i)gyohgwanidęhd- poor crowd; consists of: -(i)gyohg(wa)$_N$- crowd -nidęhd$_V$- pitiful]
crown see: G (gwa:go:wah)
Crown corporation see: G (Gwa:go:wah Dę̱·ho·nag·yehs·dǫh)
Crown Council see: G (Gwa:go:wah Des·ha·go·dih·wa·ge:n·hahs)
cruel see: mean
a·gǫg·w'e·dá·het·gę' she is a mean person
crush see: mash, pound
dęh·se·ji̱hs·gǫ́:ni' you will mash it up
ę·gé:te't I will pound
cry
de·gáhs·hę·twahs I am crying
[de+ stem: -(a)hshętw$_V$- cry]
dę·gáhs·hę·to' I will cry
ag·yǫ́h·sęh·to' she cried
o:nę́h ní: de·wa·ga̱hs·hę́:twęh I've already cried
gahs·dá:ha' I am crying
[stem: -(h)sd(a:)$_N$- drop (of water) -(a)hsda:ha', (a)hsdaę'$_V$- cry]
ohs·tá·ha'ge: it is really crying
ę·sáhs·da·ę:' you will cry
ę·gáhs·da·ę:' I will cry
ga·jí'do:t it is crying
[stem: -ji'dod- cry; consists of: -ji'd(a)$_N$- cry -od$_V$- stand]
ga·ji'do·dá:gye' s.o. is going along crying
se·ji'dę́:da' stop crying
[stem: -ji'dęda'- stop crying; consists of: -ji'd(a)$_N$- cry -ęda'$_V$- finish]
go·ji'do·wá:nęh she's a great big crybaby
[P+ stem: -ji'dowanęh- cry a great deal; consists of: -ji'd(a)$_N$- cry -owanęh$_V$- be big]
ga·ji'da·náh·nǫ' you (lit.: it) is about to cry
[stem: -ji'danahnǫ'- be about to cry; consists of: -ji'd(a)$_N$- cry -nahnǫh$_V$- full]
go·jí'da·i:' she's a cry-baby
[P+ stem: -ji'd(a)$_N$- cry -i:'$_V$- stuck onto s.t.]

cry (continued)
sa.jí'da.wi's you are a cry-baby
[P+ stem: -ji'dawi's- cry-baby; consists of: -ji'd(a)$_N$- cry]
cry see: shed tears, whine, sob, yell
ęh.sa.gahd.rá.hi' you will shed tears
at.ga.ji.dá.ga.i: there was whining, crying, repetitive complaining
g'o.ni.gǫ.há.het.gę's she is sobbing
ha.dęh.sa.he:t you will scream, yell over there
cry out see: scream, yell
ha.dęh.sa.he:t you will scream, yell over there
crystalline see: transparent
he.yó:gę't it is transparent
CSIS see: G (de.ha.di.nę.hę.da:s ho.nad.rih.wah.seh.dǫh oh.wę.ja.ę:dǫ:nyǫ')
cube see: slice, square
deh.sáh.ya.hiht dice, cut, mash, etc. the fruit
ge.í: na'de.yo.da.gá.ǫ.de' a square
cucumber
oh.nyǫhs.gwa.e' cucumber
[o+ stem: -(h)nyǫhsgwae'- cucumber; consists of: -(h)nyǫhs(a)$_N$- melon, squash -gw(a)$_N$- lump]
cultivate see: hoe
at.keh.da.węn.ye:' I hoed, tilled the earth
cultivator
de.ga.heh.dá.węn.yeh cultivator
[de+ga+ stem: -(h)ehdawęnyeh- cultivator; cultivate, hoe s.t., till s.t.; consists of: -(h)ehd(a)$_N$- land, dirt, earth, ground -(a)węnye(:)$_V$- stir, mix]
Cultural Affairs see: G (Ti.yǫg.we'da.de.jih Go.ih.wa.geh)
culture see: G (Ti.yǫg.we'da.de.jih Go.ih.wa.geh)
culvert see: gulley
o.yá.dag.ye' gulley
cup
ga.ná'jǫhs.gwa' cup
[ga+stem: -na'j(oh(s)gwa)$_N$- cup]
ga.na'jǫhs.gwá:gǫ:' in the cup
cup see: measuring cup
ǫ.de'nyę.dęhs.dahk.wá'
ga.ná'jǫhs.gwa' measuring cup
cupboard
ek.wa.ę.dáhk.wa' cupboard; pantry
[e+ stem: -kwaędahkwa'- pantry; consists of: -k(wa)$_N$- food -ędahkwa'$_V$- place for laying things away]
ek.sa.ę.dáhk.wa' s.t. into which dishes are put
[e+ stem: -ksaędahkwa'- cupboard; consists of: -ks(a)$_N$- dish -ędahkwa'$_V$- place for laying things away]
curator see: G (ek.dǫ.tahk.wa'geh hohs.dihs.dǫh)
cure
ske.ję́'ta' you cure me (all the time)
[stem: -ję'd$_V$- cure, practice medicine]
ę.jí.sa.ję't it will cure you again
a.gé:jęt it cured me
a.hé:ję't I fixed (lit. cured) him; I got even with him
ahs.ké:ję't you cured me; you got even with me
swa.gé.j'ę.dǫh it did cure me again
cure see: heal
ę.ji.sa.né:yǫ:' it will heal you
curious see: inquisitive, unusual
sa.da.hǫh.dǫ́hs.gǫh you are inquisitive
ti.yó:t'ah it is queer, unusual, odd
curl
de.yó.jits.grǫ:t flat curls; flat curls on a basket
[de+yo+ stem: -jitsgr(a)$_N$- curl -ǫd$_V$- attached]

Cayuga pronunciation guide: /a/ father /e/ weigh /ę/ men (nasalized) /i/ police /o/ hole /ǫ/ home (nasalized) /u/ blue. Underlined vowels are voiceless or whispered. /´/ high pitch. /t/ too /d/ do /k/ king /g/ good (never soft g) /j/ judge or adze /s/ soon /sh/ less heat (never the sh in shirt) /sr/ shrine /sy/ sure /hw/ which (the sound made when you blow out a candle) /h/ hi /ts/ cats hide /'/ (the sound before the first vowel in 'uh-uh') /n/ noon /r/ round /w/ way /y/ yes.

curling iron
de·yǫ·de·ji'sg·rihs·dáhk·wa' curling iron
[de+yǫ+ade+ stem: -ji'sgrihsdahkwa'- curling iron; consists of: -jitsgr(a)$_N$- curl -(r)ihsdahkwa'- implement for ironing]
curly hair
de·yó·jits·gri: it has curly hair
[de+P+ stem: -jitsgri:- have curly hair; consists of: -jitsgr(a)$_N$- curl -i:'$_V$- stuck onto s.t.]
de·ya·go·jíts·gri: she has curly hair
de·hó·jits·gri: he has curly hair
current
oh·ná·wa·deht strong currents
[o+ stem: -(h)nawadehd- strong current; consists of: -(h)naw(a)$_N$- running water -dehd$_V$- bold, bright, strong]
current see: rapids, stream
gah·na·wahs·háhs·de' fast flowing currents; rapids
gi·hę́·den·yǫ' streams; rivers; creeks
currency see: B (gwę·nihs·hǫ́:'ǫh)
curse
ęhs·he·yá·ę·na:' you will curse, hex s.o.
[TR+ stem: -(a)'ęn(a)$_N$- stick, pole, rod -(a)'ęna(:)$_V$- curse, hex]
curse see: swear
ęhs·rih·wa·né'ak·sǫ:' you will swear, use profane language
curtain
o·jí'a:' curtains; lace
[o+ stem: -ji'(a:)$_N$- curtain, lace]
curve
de·yo·ta·há'k·dǫ: a curve in the road
[de+yo+at+ stem: -(h)aha'kdǫ:- curve; consists of: -(h)ah(a)$_N$- road -(a)'kdǫ$_V$- bent, crooked]
curve see: bend
de·yót·sa'k·dǫh it is bent; a curve, a bend
cushion see: pillow
ga·gǫ́'dra' pillow; cushion
cusp see: tooth
o·nó'ja' teeth
custom see: manner
tsę́h ni·yǫg·wá·i·ho'dę: our ways; our beliefs
cut
kré·nahs I cut it all the time
[(N+) stem: -(hr)e(n)$_V$- cut]
ę́·kre:' I will cut it
a·hǫ́·wa·he:' he slashed him with a sharp instrument
ak·ré·nęh I did cut it
as·ha·go·di·hen·yáh·nǫ:' they cut up s.o.
a·hę·na·tǫ́:gya'k they (m) cut the bush down
[at+ stem: -(h)ǫd(a)$_N$- bush -(i)ya'g$_V$- cut, break]
swá·ǫg·y'a·gǫh you all have cut the log
[stem: -(r)ǫd(a)$_N$- log -(i)ya'g$_V$- cut, break]
ęhs·ríhs·gy'ak·sǫ' you will slice s.t. up
[stem: -(r)ihsgya'ksǫ'- cut up s.t.; consists of: -(h)wihsd(a), (hr)ihsd(a)$_N$- metal -(i)ya'g$_V$- cut, break]
cut see: break, chop, halve, trim, split
de·gá·y'ak·sǫ' it is broken
a·ge'ó:gǫh I did chop; I have chopped
de·só:wę: halve it
ęt·só·ha·go' you will cut down, trim s.t.
at·gó:wę:' I split it open
cut across see: cross
dę·ha·di·hę:dí:ya's they (m) cut across fields
cut hair
gat·nǫ́h·ga·ǫ:s I always cut my hair; I am cutting my hair
[at+ stem: -nǫh(a), nah(a)$_N$- scalp -nǫhgaǫ, nǫhga(:)$_V$- cut hair]
a·gat·nǫh·gá·ǫ:' I did get my hair cut
ę·gát·nǫh·ga:' I am going to cut my hair
ę·wát·nǫh·ga:' it is going to cut its hair

cut one's nails
ga·de·ji'óhg·ya's I am cutting my nails [ade+ stem: -ji'ohd(a), ji'ehd(a)$_N$- fingernail, toenail, claw, nail -(i)ya'g$_V$- cut, break, cut for oneself]
ę·ga·de·jí'ohg·ya'k I am going to cut my nails
sa·de·ji'óhg·ya'k you cut your nails
cylinder see: tube
ga̱·hó·w'e·da' a tube; a cylinder

D

daft see: crazy
te·ha'ni·gǫ·ha·yé·i: he is not right in the mind
dagger see: blade
o·hę́·n'at·rǫ:t blade
dam
de·gáh·n'e·ka:' a dam [de+ga+ stem: -hne'ka:'- dam; consists of: -(h)neg(a)$_N$- water, liquid -(h)awi, (h)a:$_V$- hold, include, carry, bring]
damage see: hurt, ruin
ęhs·hé·nǫhn·ya'k you will hurt s.o.
ęhs·hé:tgęht you will damage, ruin, wreck s.t.
damp
ot·sá·dę'ǫh it is damp [o+ at+ stem: -(h)sad(a)$_N$- fog -(a's)ę'$_V$- fall, drop, reduce]
damp see: wet
o·nǫ́hg·wi·ja' it is soaking wet, saturated
dance
ga·nǫ́:nya' a dance [ga+ stem: -nǫny(a)$_N$- dance]
dę·hę́:na:t they (m) will dance [de+…at+ stem: -(h)gw$_V$- lift, pick up]
dę·jíd·wa:t we all (incl.) will dance again
dance (continued)
dęh·sa:t you will dance
dę́:ga:t I will dance
de·wá:tgwęh the act of dancing
de·hę·nat·gwáh·ne' they (m) are going to dance
go·nǫ́n·yat·gi' she does not dance very well [P+ stem: -nǫnyatgi'- be a bad dancer; consists of: -nǫny(a)$_N$- dance -tgi$_V$- dirty, ugly]
a·hah·si·ya·ǫ·nyáh·nǫ:' he is a fluid dancer [stem: -(h)siyaǫnyahnǫ:'- fluid dancer; consists of: -(h)siy(a)$_N$- line, string -ǫni, ǫny$_V$- make]
dandruff
sa·ga·heh·dá·ę: you have dandruff [P+ stem: -gahehdaę:- have dandruff; consists of: -gahehd(a)$_N$- fluff, eyelash, stem (of a berry), eye (of a corn kernel) -ę$_V$- lie on the ground]
danger see: scared
ohd·rǫhk it is frightening, fierce, scary; danger
dangle see: hang
tga·ní:yǫ:t it is hanging over there
daring see: masculine
ha·jí:nah he is masculine, brave; his genitals
dark
ga̱·hǫ́'ji: it is dark-coloured [A/P+N/(hǫ')+ stem: -ji(:,h)$_V$- dark]
a·kǫ́'jih·ne' I got dark, black (that is, really tanned)
ę·kǫ́'jih·ne' I am going to get dark
dark see: black, dim, night
swę́'d'a·ę:' black
ga·jihs·da̱hk·wáh·dǫh,
ga·jihs·da̱hk·wáh·twęh it is dim
ha'dę·wa̱h·sǫ·dá·ę·da' when night has set in

Cayuga pronunciation guide: /a/ father /e/ weigh /ę/ men (nasalized) /i/ police /o/ hole /ǫ/ home (nasalized) /u/ blue. Underlined vowels are voiceless or whispered. /'/ high pitch. /t/ too /d/ do /k/ king /g/ good (never soft g) /j/ judge or adze /s/ soon /sh/ less heat (never the sh in shirt) /sr/ shrine /sy/ sure /hw/ which (the sound made when you blow out a candle) /h/ hi /ts/ cats hide /'/ (the sound before the first vowel in 'uh-uh') /n/ noon /r/ round /w/ way /y/ yes.

dark hair
a·ge·gʼe·á·jiː I have dark hair
[P+ stem: -geʼ(aː), geh(a)$_N$- hair -ji(ː,h)$_V$- dark]
ho·géʼa·jiː he has dark hair
go·géʼaʼjiː she has dark hair

dart see: arrow
gʼa·nǫh arrow

dash see: rush
deh·seʼdrá·i·haʼt you rush s.t., hurry s.t. up

daughter see: C (ke·haːwahk)

daughter-in-law see: C (keh·seːyǫh)

dawn see: A, sunrise
da·węːdóːdęʼ sunrise
da·gaːgwíːtgęʼ sunrise; the sun did rise

day
ę·déh·kaːʼ day kind (things used during the day)
[stem: -ęd(a)$_N$- day]
węh·nihs·rag·wéːgǫh all day
[w+ stem: -ęhnihsr(a)$_N$- day -gwegǫh$_V$- all]
węh·nihs·riːyoː nice day
[w+ stem: -ęhnihsr(a)$_N$- day -iyoː$_V$- be nice, good]

daybreak see: A (sunrise)
da·węːdóːdęʼ sunrise
da·gaːgwíːt·gęʼ sunrise; the sun did rise

daylight see: sunshine
o·dę́·ha·oːt sunshine

dead see: cadaver, corpse, death, die
hǫh·sá·go̱·haːʼ it (death) took her
o·gán·yʼę·daʼ cadaver; dead body
ga̱·héːyǫːʼ death
ha·hę·héːyaʼt he died suddenly
o·yǫ́ʼdaʼ a dead body; cadaver

dead end
o·ha·ho·(k)dáʼǫh dead end (lit.: where the road goes onto another road)
[o+ stem: -(h)aho(k)daʼǫh- dead end; consists of: -(h)ah(a)$_N$- road -oʼkd$_V$- end]

deadened see: numb
ot·sís·da̱ʼǫh it is numb

deaf
de·gáʼsweːs I am getting deaf
[de+A+ stem: -(a)ʼsweg$_V$- deaf]
dę·gáʼsweːk I will be deaf
de·gaʼswéːgǫh I am deaf
de·haʼswéːgǫh he is deaf
de·yǫʼswéːgǫh she is deaf
de·waʼswéːgǫh it is deaf

deal see: agreement, bargain, sale
gá·ih·wi̱h·saʼ an agreement
wag·yé·sęh it is a bargain; it is cheap
wag·yé·sa̱hs·dǫh sales, bargains

dear see: cost
ga·nǫːʼ it is expensive, dear, precious

death
ga̱·héːyǫːʼ death
[ga+ stem: -(h)eyǫː- death; consists of: -(ga)hey, (gę)hey, (i)hey, (ga)heː, (gę)heː, (i)heː$_V$- die, be weak, be exhausted]

debate see: argue
dęhs·rih·wa·géːnhaʼ you will argue, debate, protest

debt
o·gá·ot a debt
[o+ stem: -gaod- have a debt; consists of: -ga$_N$- price -od$_V$- stand]
sat·gá·ot you have a debt
wat·gá·ot a debt, a price

decay
o·nę́·hęt·gęː decayed corn
[o+ stem: -nęh(ę)$_N$- corn -tgę$_V$- spoiled, rotten]

decay see: bad, decomposition, spoiled
ę·wá·het·gęʼ it (an idea) will spoil, go bad
o·ya·ǫʼdáːtgęː a state of decomposition
ot·gęh it is rotten, decayed; spoilage

deceased
[-gęhę:ʼ decessive; denotes something that 'used to exist' or that 'existed formerly']
deceive
ęh·se·ya·dó·goh·dęʼ you will outdo s.o.; you will go right over her, go right past her, deceive her
[TR+ad+ stem: -ǫgohdę- deceive; consists of: -ǫgohd$_V$- surpass]
dęhs·hé·gahg·we:k you will pull the wool over her eyes, outsmart her, deceive her
[de+TR+ stem: -gahgweg- close one's eyes, outsmart, deceive; consists of: -gah(a)$_N$- eye -gweg$_V$- close]
deceive see: betray, cheat, trick
ęh·sní·gǫ·haʼt you will betray
ęhs·heʼni·gǫ́·haʼdęʼ you will cheat her, betray her
eh·sa:gyá·ǫʼ you were tricked, fooled
December see: A (Jo:to:ʼgo:wah)
decide
dę·ho·di:hwá·ę·dʼa·seh they (m) are deciding
[stem: -(r)ihwaędaʼs- decide, agree, conclude; consists of: -(r)ih(wa)$_N$- word -ędaʼ$_V$- finish]
a·to·ih·wá·ę·daʼs he came to a decision, a conclusion
ad·wag·rih·wá·ę·daʼs I came to a decision
dęhs·ni:hwá·ę·daʼ you will come to an agreement
deh·sa·ih·wá·ę·daʼs you decide
decide see: settle
haʼhoʼni·gó·haʼehs his mind settled on s.t.; he decided
decimal point
o·jihs·da·nóhg·waʼ decimal point; point; dot
[o+ stem: -jihsdanohg(wa)$_N$- spot]

deck (of cards) see: cards
de·yeh·ya·dǫhs·rá·ę·dahk·waʼ playing cards; bingo
declare see: proclaim, say, tell
ęt·ri·ho·wá:naht you will proclaim, announce s.t.
a·hęʼ he said
a·ga:tró:wi: I have told
decomposition
o·ya·ǫʼdá:tgę: a state of decomposition
[o+ stem: -yaǫʼdatgę:- decomposed; consists of: -(he)yǫ(ʼda)$_N$- corpse, cadaver
-tgę$_V$- spoiled, rotten]
decorticate see: peel, shell s.t.
ęhs·ra·wihs·dó:tsiʼ you will peel
ęh·sék·dot·sih you will shell (eggs, etc.)
decrease see: use up
a·wá:tsʼa:ʼ it is worn out, all gone, burnt up; it went down to nothing
decrepit see: ragged
ge·géʼa:ʼ I am raggedy
deduce see: decide
a·to·ih·wá·ę·daʼs he came to a decision, a conclusion
deduct see: subtract
ęt·sǫ́ʼne:k you will subtract
deep
oh·nó:de:s deep water
[o+ stem: -(h)nodes- deep; consists of: -(h)nod(a)$_N$- water -es$_V$- long]
o·yá:de:s deep hole
[o+ stem: -yad(a)$_N$- hole, track, ditch -es$_V$- long]
deep see: be a certain length, depth
ni·yó:ya·de:s how deep the hole, trench, ditch is
deer
de·wá·hǫh·de:s deer
[de+wa+ stem: -(a)hǫhde:s- deer; consists of: -(a)hǫhd(a)$_N$- ear -es$_V$- long]

deer (continued)
de·yo·ji·á·n'ę·dǫ:t stag deer
[de+yo+ stem: -jianę'dǫt- stag deer; consists of: -jianę'd(a)- -ǫd$_V$- attached]
defame see: gossip, scandal
dę·sad·ri̱h·wá·ę·dǫhk,
dęh·sad·ri̱h·wá·ę·dǫh you will gossip
o·ih·wat·gí:nyǫ' scandalous news; rumours
defeat see: beat
ęhs·he·y'at·gę́:ni' you will beat s.o. (in a race)
defend see: argue, protect
ho·na·d'ę·ní·gǫ·ha:' they (m) are protecting, watching
des·ha·go·dih·wa·gé:nhahs they argue for us
defer see: move
ęd·wa:gę́·is we all (incl.) will postpone
deficiency see: lack
da·wá·dok·dahs it lacks; it is not enough
defile see: bad, corrupt, rape
da·wá·teht·gęht it went bad
ęhs·he·ya·dáh·dǫ't you will corrupt her/them
ahs·ha·got·go·ho·wá·na̱h·dę' he raped her (lit.: he forced her in a big way)
definite see: which
ga·ę́ ní:ga:' which one; a specific thing
deflate
a·wa·de·wa:dáh·go' it deflated
[(ade+) stem: -wadahgw- deflate; consists of: -w(a:)$_N$- air -dahgw$_V$- remove]
ga·wá:da̱hg·węh it is deflated
deformed see: back (rounded), bend, crippled
ę·sa·no·wag·wá·ǫ·dę' you will get a rounded back
ha'hi'ya·gá·ę·he' his body trunk is crooked; he is bent over
ho·jí:yo' he is crippled
dehydrated see: dry, skin
o·hę: it is dry
ge̱h·ná:tę:, gi̱h·ná:tę: I have dry skin
Delaware see: C (De·wa'gan·ha')
delay see: move
sa·gę́·ihs·dǫh you have postponed it
delayed see: late
ę·wák·ni̱hs·go' I will be late
delectable see: taste good
o·gá'ǫh it tastes good
delegate see: appoint, responsibility
a·hǫ·wá·i·hǫ·dę' they delegated him a duty
ga·ih·wa·ę·da̱hg·wáh·nǫ' their (f/m) collective responsibility; delegations
deliberate see: discuss, do on purpose
dęd·wah·tá:go' we all (incl.) will discuss
tsa'seht you did it on purpose; it was premeditated; it was done in spite
delicious see: taste good
o·gá'ǫh it tastes good
delighted see: happy
a·gat·sę·nǫ́:ni: I am glad, happy
delightful see: good, nice
o·yá:n·re' it is nice, good, beautiful
hǫg·we'dí:yo: he is a charming, polite, nice person
deliver see: bring
ę·ta·há:wi' he is going to bring s.t.
delude see: deceive
ęh·se·ya·dó·go̱h·dę' you will outdo s.o.; you will go right over her, go right past her; deceive her
deluge see: rain
a·gas·dá·o·wa·naht it rained hard
delve see: dig
ę·yó'gwa:t it will dig

demand
ę·t·ríh·wa·hek you will demand s.t., insist on s.t., force s.t.
[de+… stem: -(r)ihwaʼe- demand s.t., insist on s.t.; consists of: -(r)ih(wa)$_N$- word -(ʼ)e$_V$- hit]
dahs·ríh·waʼek you insisted
at·ga·ǫg·ríh·waʼehs they wanted a report
[stem: -(r)ihwaʼehsd- demand a report, an account; consists of: -(r)ih(wa)$_N$- word -(ʼ)ehsd$_V$- cause to hit]
ę·hǫ·wa·dih·waʼéhs·dęʼ they will unravel his message, demand an audience from him
ga·ih·waʼéhs·dǫ꞉ʼ a report
demanding
tgę·nǫ́h·dǫ·haʼ I make the decisions; I am a strict person
[d+A+ stem: -ęnǫhdǫhaʼ- be demanding, strict; consists of: -ęnǫhdǫ(꞉)$_V$- know]
dyo·nǫ́h·dǫ·haʼ she is a bossy woman
demeanour see: attitude, manner
tsę́h ni·saʼni·gǫ́·hoʼdę꞉ your attitude, mood
ni·sa·i·hóʼdę꞉ your manner
demented see: crazy
te·haʼni·gǫ·ha·yé·i꞉ʼ he is not right in the mind
demise see: death
ga·hé꞉yǫ꞉ʼ death
demolish see: wreck
ęhsré꞉tgęh you will wreck it
demonstrate see: explain, show
dęhs·ríh·wa·teʼt you will explain
gǫ·yǫh·wa·dá꞉nih I am showing you s.t.
demure see: shy
go·díʼgrǫʼ she is shy
den see: hole, room
ǫh·wę·ja·gá·hę·taʼ, gah·wę·ja·gá·hę·taʼ a hole in the earth
o·nǫ́h·sǫ꞉t a room; a vault

denigrate see: jeer, shit on s.o.
ęh·sad·wę·ná꞉yęht you will jeer, jest, throw words at s.o.
ta·ha·gę·ní·da·hęh he won't shit on me
[ę+ stem: -niʼdahęh- shit on s.o.; consists of: -(ni)ʼd(a)$_N$- feces, privates -(hr)e, (hr)ę$_V$- put, place]
denounce
dęhs·ríh·wa·yaʼk you will denounce it, disapprove of it
[de+… stem: -(r)ihwayaʼg- denounce, disapprove; consists of: -(r)ih(wa)$_N$- word -(i)yaʼg$_V$- cut, break]
ę·t·ríh·węht you will bring the idea down
[stem: -(r)ihwęhd- bring down an idea; consists of: -(r)ih(wa)$_N$- word -(y)ęhd$_V$- hit, knock down, strike]
denounce see: blame, condemn
ęhs·héh·waʼehs you will blame s.o.
ęhs·yé꞉saht you will condemn, slander, insult s.o.
dense see: thick, volume
gá꞉dę꞉s it is thick, dense
tsę́h ni·gá꞉dę꞉s volume, density; how thick it is; mass
dent see: flat
ad·wa·dag·wę́h·dę꞉ it became dented
dentist
ha·dę·nʼo·jó·dag·wahs he is a dentist
[A+adę+ stem: -nʼojodagwahs- dentist; consists of: -noʼj(a)$_N$- tooth -odagw$_V$- remove, detach]
ha·dę·nʼo·jo·dag·wáhs·geh a dentist's office
deny
a·ga·dę·ná꞉węʼ I denied
[adę+ consists of: -nowę(꞉)$_V$- deny]
ga·dę·no·wę́h·taʼ I am in denial; I am denying
[adę+ stem: -nowęhd- lie, be in denial; consists of: -nowę(꞉)$_V$- deny]
ęh·sa·dę·nó꞉węht you will deny

Cayuga pronunciation guide: /a/ father /e/ weigh /ę/ men (nasalized) /i/ police /o/ hole /ǫ/ home (nasalized) /u/ blue. Underlined vowels are voiceless or whispered. /´/ high pitch. /t/ too /d/ do /k/ king /g/ good (never soft g) /j/ judge or adze /s/ soon /sh/ less heat (never the sh in shirt) /sr/ shrine /sy/ sure /hw/ which (the sound made when you blow out a candle) /h/ hi /ts/ cats hide /ʼ/ (the sound before the first vowel in 'uh-uh') /n/ noon /r/ round /w/ way /y/ yes.

depart see: go out, leave
gyá:gęʼs I am going out
sgah·dę́:gyeʼs I am leaving again
department see: G
(ho·nad·rih·wahs·di:hs·dǫh)
Department of Energy and Mines see: G
(Oh·wę·ja·geh Wah·dęg·yaʼtaʼ
Oh·wę·ja·gǫh·sǫʼ)
dependable see: reliable
ho·yaʼda·dá:ni: he is reliable, dependable
dependent see: child
a·gék·sʼa·daʼ my child
depleted see: all gone
haʼwá:tsʼaht it is all gone
deposit see: place
ę·há·hęʼ he will place it on s.t.
deprecate see: jeer
ęh·sad·wę·ná:yęht you will jeer, jest, throw words at s.o.
depressed
ęt·sní·gǫ·hęʼ you will be depressed
[de+... stem: -(ʼ)nigǫhęʼ- be depressed, sad; consists of: -(ʼ)nigǫh(a)$_{N}$- mind -(h)ę(h,ʼ)$_{V}$- feel bad]
dwak·ni·gǫ·hę́ʼǫh I am in sorrow, in mourning; I am sad
deranged see: crazy
de·sę·na̲·háwęn·yeʼ you are crazy (not right in the mind)
descend
ę·gá:s·nęht I will get off, dismount
[stem: -(ah)snęhd$_{V}$- descend]
ę·sá:s·nęht you will get down
sah·snęh·dǫ·hǫ́:gyeʼ you are getting down from there right now
sas·nęht get down from there
describe see: recount, tell
ęt·sa:tró:wiʼ you will recount, retell
ęd·wa:tró:wiʼ we all (incl.) will tell

description
tsę́h ni·yóh·dǫʼs descriptions
[tsęh ni+yo+ stem: -(a)hd$_{V}$- be like, resemble]
deseed
ęh·sets·gęʼę́·da̲h·goʼ you will remove seeds
[N+ stem: -tsgęʼędahgw- deseed; consists of: -tsgęʼęd(a)$_{N}$- pit -(h)gw$_{V}$- remove]
Deseronto, N.Y. see: E (Ta·yę·da·ne:gęʼ)
desert
o·neh·sa·dá·i·hę: desert
[o+ stem: -(ʼ)nehsadaihę:- desert; consists of: -(ʼ)nehs(a)$_{N}$- sand -(ʼ)daihę:$_{V}$- be hot]
oʼneh·sa·da·i·hę·go·wáh·neh a desert
[o+ stem: -(ʼ)nehsadaiʼhęgowahneh- desert; consists of: -(ʼ)nehs(a)$_{N}$- sand -(ʼ)daihę:$_{V}$- be hot -(h)neh- on, at]
gyo·neh·sa·da·i·hę·go·wáh·neh Sahara Desert
[g+yo+ stem: -(ʼ)nehsadaiʼhęgowahneh- Sahara; consists of: -(ʼ)nehs(a)$_{N}$- sand -(ʼ)daihę:$_{V}$- be hot -(h)neh - on, at]
deserter see: traitor
de̲·ho·ih·wa·dó:gę: he is a traitor
deserve see: earn (money), meet, same
de·sá·dęht·sʼǫh you've earned it; you deserve it; you've paid your dues
de·ya·go·nád·raʼǫh they deserve each other (said in anger); they (f/m) are meeting right now
tsaʼgá·nǫʼa:t they deserve each other (lit.: it is the same kind of head)
designate see: include, point out
há·ǫ:nya̲h·nǫʼ he has included, designated
ęhs·hę́ʼnyʼa·da:t you will point s.o. out
desirable see: enticing
ohs·gá:naʼt it is enticing, alluring, attractive, tempting

desire see: crave, want
ęk·nǫ́:wa:k I will crave s.t.
dęh·sa·dǫh·wę:jǫ́:ni' you will want s.t.
desist see: quit
a·gę́·ni·hę' I stopped, quit
desk
ǫk·ya·dǫhs·rá·hahk·wa' desk
[ǫ+ak+ stem: -(h)yadǫhsrahahkwa'- desk; consists of: -(h)yadǫhsr(a)$_N$- paper -(h)ahkwa'$_V$- s.t. that supports s.t.]
despair see: worry
ęh·sę·ni·gǫ́·hod·rǫ:' you will worry, despair; you will be desperate
desperate
de·yǫ́t·gan·yahs she is desperate, desperately wanting s.t., in dire need; she will settle for just anyone (that is, a mate)
[de+…at+ stem: -gany$_V$- be desperate]
dę·hát·gan·yahs he is desperate, desperately wanting s.t.; in dire need; he will settle for just anyone (that is, a mate)
dę·hat·gan·yáh·se:k he will be desperate
de·hot·gan·yǫ́hs·gǫ: he is desperate
de·hót·gan·yęh he is really desperate
de·yót·gan·yęh it is in dire need
despicable see: evil
wa·hé:tgęh it is evil (in mind); it is bad
despise see: hate
kehs·wá·hęhs I hate her
despondent see: depressed
dwak·ni·gǫ·hę́'ǫh I am in sorrow, in mourning; I am sad
dessert
na·wę'da·wehts·hǫ́:'ǫh dessert (lit. sweet things)
[stem: -nawę'dawehtshǫ:'ǫh- dessert; consists of: -(rę)nawę'd(a)$_N$- sugar, candy -nawęhd$_V$- wet s.t., be saturated]
dessert see: goodies
o·ga'ǫhs·hǫ́:'ǫh goodies, dessert

destitute see: poor
a·gí:dęht I am poor, poverty-stricken, in poverty
destroy see: ruin, wreck
ęhs·hé:tgęht you will damage, ruin, wreck s.t.
ęhsré:tgęh you will wreck it
detach see: remove
ę·sǫ́·da·go' you will remove, detach s.t.
detain see: catch
ah·sa·go·di:yé:na:' they arrested, caught her, s.o.
detect see: find, recognize
a·gét·sęn·yǫ: I have found it
ęg·yę́·de:' I will recognize it
deter see: quit
a·gę́·ni·hę' I stopped, quit
determine see: find, learn
a·gét·sęn·yǫ: I have found it
ęh·sa·de·wá:yę:s you will learn
detest see: hate
kehs·wá·hęhs I hate her
devastate see: ruin, wreck
ęhs·hé:tgęht you will damage, ruin, wreck s.t.
ęhs·ré:tgęh you will wreck it
develop see: mature, ripen
ę·wáh·ya·i' it will ripen
a·wát·sihs'a:' it did mature (said of plants); it completed its life-cycle
development see: G (ho·dis·rǫ·ni·hag·ye')
device see: tool
ehs·ta'shǫ́:'ǫh tools, utensils (what one uses)
devil
ga·jí·ha·ya' the devil
[ga+ consists of: -jihay(a)$_N$- devil]
devise see: make, plan
gǫ́:nih I make, earn
ęd·wad·rih·wáh·s'a:' we all (incl.) will plan s.t.
devotion see: love
ga·nǫ́hk·wahs·ra' love

Cayuga pronunciation guide: /a/ father /e/ weigh /ę/ men (nasalized) /i/ police /o/ hole /ǫ/ home (nasalized) /u/ blue. Underlined vowels are voiceless or whispered. /'/ high pitch. /t/ too /d/ do /k/ king /g/ good (never soft g) /j/ judge or adze /s/ soon /sh/ less heat (never the sh in shirt) /sr/ shrine /sy/ sure /hw/ which (the sound made when you blow out a candle) /h/ hi /ts/ cats hide /'/ (the sound before the first vowel in 'uh-uh') /n/ noon /r/ round /w/ way /y/ yes.

devour see: eat, glutton
a·ha:k he ate it
ęh·sá·det·sęhs you will be a glutton; you will gobble, gorge yourself
dew
o'á·wa·ye' there is dew on s.t.
[o+ stem: -(a)'aw(a)$_N$- dew]
diabetes
ad·wa·de·jitg·wá·o·go:' diabetes
[a+de+w+ade+ stem: -jitgwaogo:'- diabetes; consists of: -jitgw(a:)$_N$- yellow -ogw$_V$- scatter]
dialect see: language
ni·ga·wę·nó:dę' language
dialogue see: talk
ęhs·hé·ta·hahs you talk to her
diamond
de·yo·wid·ra:téh ga·nǫ:' diamonds
[consists of: deyowi'dra:teh it is icy, glassy; ganǫ:' it is expensive, dear]
diaper
g'ad·ró:da:' a diaper
[ga+ stem: -(i)'drǫda:'- diaper; consists of: -(ni)'d(a)$_N$- feces -oda(:)$_V$- put in]
ni·ga·hę:hęh g'ad·ró·da:' cloth diapers
[consists of: nigahę:hęh material; g'adroda:' diaper]
gog·yé's g'ad·ró·da:' disposable diapers
[consists of: gogye's to get rid of s.t; g'adroda:' diaper]
diaper bag
e'dro·dá:kwa' diaper bag
[e+ stem: -(')drodahkwa'- diaper bag; consists of: -(ni)'d(a)$_N$- feces -oda:hkwa'$_V$- s.t. into which things are put]
diction see: language
ni·ga·wę·nó:dę' language
dictionary
wa·dę·wę·na·ga:dá:s oh·ya·dǫhs·rǫ́:dǫ' dictionary
[consists of: wadwęnaga:da:s it raises up words; ohyadǫhsrǫ:dǫ' book]
de·ga·ih·wá·te'ta' dictionary
[de+ga+ stem: -(r)ihwate'ta'- dictionary; consists of: -(r)ih(wa)$_N$- word -(a)te'd$_V$- clarify, explain]
die
e·hé:yǫhs she is dying, on her deathbed
[stem: -(ga)hey, (gę)hey, (i)hey, (ga)he:, (gę)he:, (i)he:$_V$- die, be weak, be exhausted]
hę·hé:yǫhs he is dying
gi·hé:yǫhs I am dying
ę·gí·he:' I will die
a·we:t'á:' a·gi·hé:yǫ: I'm pretending I am dead
a·go·wi·ya·ge·hé:ya's her baby died
[-wiy(a)$_N$- child, offspring -(ga)hey, (gę)hey, (i)hey, (ga)he:, (gę)he:, (i)he:$_V$- die, weak, exhausted]
ha·hę·hé:ya't he died suddenly
[ha'+...stem: -(i)heya'd- die suddenly, play dead, pretend to be dead; consists of: -(ga)hey, (gę)hey, (i)hey, (ga)he:, (gę)he:, (i)he:$_V$- die, weak, exhausted]
hǫ·sá·gǫ·ha:' it (death) took her
[he'+s+P+...stem: -(h)awi, (h)a:$_V$- hold, include, carry, bring]
he·ja·gǫ·há·ǫ: it (death) took her
ta·di·yę·dá·e:si' they (m) broke the tie (that is, they died suddenly)
[d+... stem: -yędaihs(i)- die suddenly; consists of: -(y)ęda'$_V$- finish]
die see: breathless
ha·dǫ·wihs·rí:ya's he is out of breath; he is dying

diet
ǫ·dehs·gyǫ·wá·ta'ta' s.o. loses weight, diets
[ade+ stem: -(h)sgyǫ'wata'd- diet, lose weight; consists of: -(h)sgyǫ'w(a), (h)sgyę'w(a)$_N$- bone -ta'd$_V$- dry]
a·ga·ǫ:dehs·gyǫ·wá:ta't they (f/m) dieted, lost weight
ę·sas·gyę·wá:ta't it will make you skinny, take you to the bare bones
differ see: disagree
ta'deg·rih·wáhs·nye' I oppose it; I do not agree
different
de·sáh·dį·hęh you are different
[de+A+ stem: -(a)hdihęh$_V$- different]
de·wáh·dį·hęh the difference; it is different
deg·yáh·dį·hęh we two are different
ha'dé:yǫ: many different things
[ha'de+y+ stem: -ǫ$_V$- a number of things, many different things]
ti·ga'dręh·dá:de' a different car
[ti+ga+ stem: -(')drehd(a)$_N$- vehicle, car -de'$_V$- exist, be different]
ti·sǫg·w'e·dá:de' you are a different person
[ti+A+ stem: -ǫgwe('da)$_N$- person -de'$_V$- exist, be different]
o·yá' ní:yoht different
[consists of: oya' another; niyoht a certain way]
different see: odd, other
ti·yo·yęhs·rá:de' it is an odd-ball blanket
ó:ya' other; another
difficult
wę́:do:' it is difficult
[w+ stem: -ędo:'$_V$- difficult]
difficult see: demanding
tgę·nǫ́h·dǫ·ha' I make the decisions; I am a strict person
diffuse see: spread, sprinkle
e·yá:ta' s.o. spreads it
ę·hę́·nod·rahs they (m) will sprinkle on
dig
o'gwa:s it digs, uncovers
[P+ stem: -o'gwad$_V$- dig]
a'ó'gwa:t it dug
ę·yó'gwa:t it will dig
dig see: unearth
ęt·sat·sa·dǫ́:go' you will unearth it
digest
de·gak·wa·híh·ta' food processor
[de+... stem: -kwahihd- digest; consists of: -k(wa)$_N$- food -(hr)ihd$_V$- cause to break up]
dę·gák·wa·hiht it will digest
digit see: finger, number, thumb
o'nya' fingers
ohs·hé:da' number
a·wę'yǫh·ga:' thumb
dike see: dam
de·gáh·n'e·ka:' a dam
diligent see: active, work well
ag·yá'da·deht I am nimble, active, energetic
got·sáh·niht she is a good worker, tireless, active, industrious, etc.
dilute
dehs·né·ga·yehs dilute it
[de+... stem: -(h)negayehsd- dilute; consists of: -(h)neg(a)$_N$- water, liquid -yehsd$_V$- add]
dim
ga·jihs·dahk·wáh·dǫh, ga·jihs·dahk·wáh·twęh it is dim
[ga+ stem: -jihsd(a)$_N$- light -(h)gwahd$_V$- cause to lift, pick up]
dim see: extinguish
ęh·si'dǫhg·wáhs·twaht you will dim the lights
dime see: B (wahs·hę:gwę·nihs)
dimension see: size
shę́h ní:wa's sizes; how big they are

Cayuga pronunciation guide: /a/ father /e/ weigh /ę/ men (nasalized) /i/ police /o/ hole /ǫ/ home (nasalized) /u/ blue. Underlined vowels are voiceless or whispered. /´/ high pitch. /t/ too /d/ do /k/ king /g/ good (never soft g) /j/ judge or adze /s/ soon /sh/ less heat (never the sh in shirt) /sr/ shrine /sy/ sure /hw/ which (the sound made when you blow out a candle) /h/ hi /ts/ cats hide /'/ (the sound before the first vowel in 'uh-uh') /n/ noon /r/ round /w/ way /y/ yes.

diminish see: shrink

ohs·twá'ọh it has shrunk

diminutive see: small

ni·ya·gú:'uh she is small; a small girl

dine see: eat

a·ha:k he ate it

dingy see: dirty

ot·gi' it is ugly, dirty, soiled

dining hall

deh·kọn·yá'ta' dining hall

[(a)de+ stem: -kọnya'ta'- dining hall; consists of: -k(wa)$_N$- food -ọni, ọny$_V$- make]

dining hall see: restaurant

ọ·de·kọn·yá'ta'geh restaurant; cafeteria; dining room; dining hall

dining room

o·de·kọn·ya'ta'géh o·nọ́h·sọ:t dining room

[consists of: ọdekọnya'ta'geh restaurant, cafeteria, dining room; onọhsọ:t a room]

dining room see: restaurant

ọ·de·kọn·yá'ta'geh restaurant; cafeteria; dining room; dining hall

dinosaur

de·ga'ni·gọh·dẹ́:dọhs dinosaurs

[de+ga+ stem: -(')nigọhdẹdọhs- dinosaur; consists of: -(')nigọh(a)$_N$- mind -ẹdọh$_V$- shake s.t.]

dip

hé:gohs I am dipping it in all the time

[he'+... stem: -oh$_V$- dip in liquid]

hẹ́:goh I will put (dip) it in

he·wá·gọ·họh I have already dipped, submerged it

direct see: lead, oversee, refer, straight

ẹ·há·hẹ:t he will lead

ẹh·sad·rih·wát·ga·họ:' you will oversee, supervise

hẹ·gọ·ya·dẹ́:nyeht I will refer you (to s.o. else)

o·de·dag·wá·ih·sọ: it is straight

direction

tsẹ́h ni·yó·y'a·dọh a direction

[tsẹh ni+yo+ stem: -ya'dọh$_V$- direction]

tga·ye·í' tga·ẹg·wá·dih from the right (correct) direction

[consists of: tga:yei: it is right, correct; tgaẹgwadih they (f/m) are going in a direction]

directly see: suddenly

tó: hé:yoht suddenly

director see: G (gohs·dihs·dọh)

dirt see: land, loam, soil

o·héh·da' dirt; earth

ni·yo·heh·dó'dẹ: loam

oh·né'dr'a·geh on the ground

dirty

ot·gi' it is ugly, dirty, soiled

[P+(N+) stem: -tgi$_V$- dirty, ugly]

ho·yá'dat·gi' he is dirty, has dirty ways

[P+ stem: -ya'd(a)$_N$- body -tgi$_V$- dirty, ugly]

o·yá'dat·gi' it is hideous, ugly

a'ohs·dag·wá·ẹ: it got dirty, soiled, stained

[P+ stem: -(h)sdagwaẹ:- dirty, soiled; consists of: -(h)sdag(wa)$_N$- dirt, dirty -ẹ$_V$- lie on the ground]

ohs·dág·wa·ẹ: it is soiled, dirty, stained

dẹ·hó'da·i:' he got dirty (lit.: covered with manure)

[P+ stem: -(')dai:'- dirty; consists of: -(i)'d(a:)$_N$- mud, manure -i:'$_V$- stuck onto s.t.(be)]

a·ha·d'e·dá·ọ·ni' he got dirty

[stem: -(')daọni- dirty, muddy; consists of: -(i)'d(a:)$_N$- clay, mud, mortar, manure -ọni, ọny$_V$- make]

a·ga'dá·ọ·ni' it got muddy

ẹ·ga·d'e·dá·ọ:ni' I am going to get muddy

dirty see: ugly

ẹh·sé:tgiht you will dirty it up

dirty clothes
gahs·dá:gwa', ohs·dá:gwa' dirty clothes
[ga/o+ stem: -(h)sdag(wa)$_N$- dirt, dirty clothes]

dirty clothes see: laundry, rags
gahs·dag·wa:ni·yǫ́:dǫ' hanging dirty laundry
de·yot·ge'ó:gwęh clothes; rags scattered all over

disabled see: crippled
go·jí:yo' she is crippled

disagree
de·wag·ri̲·hó'da̲·hǫh I am not in complete agreement
[de+P+ stem: -(ri)ho'dahǫh- disagree; consists of: -(ri)ho'd$_V$- work]
ta'deg·rih·wa̲hs·nye' I oppose it; I do not agree
[ta'de+... stem: -(r)ihwahsnye- disagree, oppose; consists of: -(r)ih(wa)$_N$- word -(h)snye$_V$- care for, look after]

disagreeable see: unpleasant
de·a·ǫ·wé:saht it is unpleasant

disagreement see: argue
de·wá·dat·s'ǫh a quarrel; an argument

disappear
wa̲h·dǫhs it disappears
[stem: -(a)hdǫ$_V$- disappear]
ęh·sáh·dǫ' you will disappear

disapprove
des·rih·wa·nǫ́h·we's you disapprove
[de'+A+ stem: -(r)ihwanǫhwe's- disapprove; consists of: -(r)ih(wa)$_N$- word -nǫhwe'$_V$- like]

disapprove see: denounce, disagree
dęhs·ríh·wa·ya:'k you will denounce it, disapprove of it
ta'deg·ri̲h·wáhs·nye' I oppose it; I do not agree

disassemble see: take apart
de·wa·ge·káhs·hǫ: I have taken one object apart

disaster
ad·rih·wag·yá·ǫhs·ra' disaster
[a+ad+ stem: -rihwagyaǫhsr(a)$_N$- disaster; -rihwagyaǫ$_V$- accident]
sa·wad·ri̲h·wat·wa̲h·dáh·nǫ:' natural disasters
[s+...wa+ad+ stem: -(r)ihwatwahdahnǫ:'- disaster; consists of: -(r)ih(wa)$_N$- word -(a)twahd, (a)dwahd$_V$- miss s.t.]

disburse see: give, spread
shǫg·wá:wi: he has given us
e·yá:ta' s.o. spreads it

discard see: throw
wag·yǫ: s.t. thrown away; discards

discernible see: recognizable, visible
o·yę́:deht it is recognizable, plain to be seen, conspicuous
ó:gę't it is visible

discharge see: release, shoot
sa·ga·e·sáht·ga' they released you (s), fired you, let you go
ęhsí:'a'k you will shoot

discipline see: punish
ę·sa:tré:waht you will be punished

discomfort see: pain
ęg·rǫ́h·ya·gę' I will be in pain; I will labour, in agony

disconnect see: unjoin
dę·gę·na·dah·sǫd·rá:go' they (z) will be unjoined (for example, a train, a chain); they will come apart

disconsolate see: unhappy
de·a·ga·dǫt·gá:de', de·wa·ga·dǫt·gá:dǫ' I am not happy

discontent
deg·yo'ni·gǫ·hi·yóhs·dę:' it is discontent
[de'+d/g+P+ stem: -(')nigǫhiyohsdę:'- discontent; consists of: -(')nigǫh(a)$_N$- mind -iyohsd$_V$- make nice, good]

discount see: bargain, sale
wag·yé:sęh it is a bargain; it is cheap
wag·yé·sa̲hs·dǫh sales; bargains

discourage s.o.
dęhs·heʼni·gǫ́hn·yaʼk you will discourage s.o.
[de+TR+ stem: -(ʼ)nigǫhnyaʼg- discourage s.o.; consists of: -(ʼ)nigǫh(a)$_N$- mind -(i)yaʼg$_V$- cut, break]
discover see: find, learn
a·gét·sęn·yǫ: I have found it
ęh·sa·de·wá:yę:s you will learn
discriminate see: choosy
ho·dǫg·wʼe·dá·gǫn·yǫhs he is choosy about who he associates with; he discriminates
discuss
dęd·wah·tá:goʼ we all (incl.) will discuss
[de+… stem: -(h)ta:gw- discuss; consists of: -(h)ta:$_V$- talk, speak]
discuss see: argue, talk
dęhs·rih·wa·gé:nhaʼ you will argue, debate, protest
ę·géh·ta·ęʼ I will talk
disease
ga·noh·so·dá:nǫ:ʼ AIDS; disease
[ga+ stem: -nǫhsod(a)$_N$- sickness -nǫ:ʼ$_V$- costly, dear, expensive]
disease see: sickness
o·nǫh·so·dá·i:yǫ:ʼ sickness; illness; epidemic; plague
disembark
ę·gat·nǫh·dáh·goʼ I will disembark, get out of a vehicle
[at+ stem: -nǫhdahgw- disembark; consists of: -(ʼ)nǫhd$_V$- be in]
disembowel see: eviscerate
ęhs·yǫ·wa·dáh·goʼ you will gut s.t.
disgrace see: scandal, shame
o·ih·wat·gí:nyǫʼ scandalous news; rumours
o·dé·haʼt a shame; an embarrassment
disguise see: hide oneself, mask, recognize
ę·gá·da̱h·seht I will hide
disguise (continued)
ga·gǫ́h·saʼ the mask
ta:ga·e·sa·yę́:de: they will not recognize you (that is, a disguise)
disgust see: annoyed, boring, dislike, hate
ęh·sa·gę̱·hę́ʼdęʼ you will be disgusted
o·gę́·hęʼt it is boring, disgusting
deh·snǫ́h·weʼs you dislike
ęh·séhs·wa̱·hęh you will hate, dislike
dish
ga·jęʼ dish; plate; bowl
[ga+ stem: -jęʼ$_N$- dish, plate, bowl]
sgak·sa:t one dish
[s+ga+ stem: -ks(a)$_N$- dish -d$_V$- stand]
ga·ksí:yoʼs good dishes
[ga+ stem: -ks(a)$_N$- dish -iyo:$_V$- be nice, good]
de·gak·sa·gę́:drǫhs it scrapes dishes
[de+ga+ stem: -ks(a)$_N$- dish -gędrǫ(:)$_V$- separate]
sek·so·há·i·hǫ: wash the dishes
[stem: -ks(a)$_N$- dish -ohae$_V$- clean, wash]
dishonest see: two-faced
sa·gǫh·sa̱h·ní:yǫh you are two-faced
dishonor see: shame
o·dé·haʼt a shame; an embarrassment
dish pan see: sink
ek·so·ha·i·hǫʼdáhk·waʼ kitchen sink; dish pan
dish washer
gak·só·ha·ehs dish washer
[ga+ stem: -ksohaehs- dish washer; consists of: -ks(a)$_N$- dish -ohae$_V$- clean, wash]
disjointed see: divide, unjoin
dęh·se·kah·sǫ́:goʼ you will divide it into parts
de·yo·da̱h·sǫ́d·rag·węh it is disjointed
disk see: circle
de·węʼnya̱hs·gá·ǫ·ni:
(de·węʼni̱hs·gá·ǫ·ni:) a circle

dislike
tę' dek·nǫ́h·we's I do not like it
[(tę') de'+ not ... stem: -nǫhwe'$_V$- like, dislike]
dehs·nǫ́h·we's you dislike
dislike see: hate
ęh·séhs·wa̱·hęh you will hate, dislike
dislocate
a·sat·nęt·sá·da̱h·go' your arm came out of its socket
[at+ stem: -nętsadahgw- dislocate; consists of: -nęts(a)$_N$- arm -(h)gw$_V$- remove]
ad·wat·nęt·só·da·goh our (incl.) arm came out of its socket
[at+ stem: -nętsodagw- dislocate; consists of: -nęts(a)$_N$- arm -odagw$_V$- remove, detach]
dislodge see: remove
ę·sǫ́·da·go' you will remove, detach s.t.
dismal see: mournful
o'ni·gǫh·sá:dǫhk it is mournful
dismantle see: take apart
de·wa·ge·káhs·hǫ: I have taken one object apart
dismount see: descend
ę·gá:s·nęht I will get off, dismount
disobedient
de·sa:tǫ́:da:s you are disobedient
[de'+A+ stem: -(a)tǫda'd- do not listen to s.t., be disobedient; consists of: -(a)tǫdę(h,'), (a)tǫde'$_V$- hear]
disorder see: chaos
de·yó·dog·węh disorder; chaos
disparage see: jeer
ęh·sad·wę·ná:yęht you will jeer, jest, throw words at s.o.
dispatch see: send
he·wa·ga·dę́n·ye̱h·dǫh I sent it
dispensary see: clinic
ga·né:yǫhs a medical clinic
dispense see: give
dahs·gǫh give it to me
disperse see: scatter, spread
de·wa·dog·wáh·dǫh it has been spread out, distributed, scattered
ęhs·ra:' you will spread
displace see: remove
ę·sǫ́·da·go' you will remove, detach s.t.
display see: show
gǫ·yǫh·wa·dá:nih I am showing you s.t.
disposition see: attitude
tsę́h ni·sa'ni·gǫ́·ho'dę: your attitude, mood
dispute see: argue, disagree
dęhs·rih·wa·gé:nha' you will argue, debate, protest
ta'deg·ri̱h·wáhs·nye' I oppose it; I do not agree
disregard see: neglect
dehs·gahs·dí:s·ta' I no longer pay attention
disrepute see: scandal
o·ih·wat·gí:nyǫ' scandalous news; rumours
disrobe see: undress
ę·sat·rǫn·yáh·si' you will take your clothes off
dissatisfaction see: discontent
deg·yo'ni·gǫ·hi·yóhs·dę:' it is discontent
dissatisfied
dǫ·gá·d'ok·tahs I was not satisfied; I didn't get enough
[d+P+ad+ stem: -o'kd(ę,ani)- finish s.t., be dissatisfied; consists of: -o'kd$_V$- end]
dwa·ga·dok·dá:nih I am dissatisfied
dissemble see: lie
a·gę·nó:węht I lied
disseminate see: spread out, scatter
e·yá:ta' s.o. spreads it
de·wa·dog·wáh·dǫh it has been spread out, distributed, scattered
dissent see: disagree
ta'deg·ri̱h·wáhs·nye' I oppose it; I do not agree

dissimilar see: different, other
de·wáh·di·hęh the difference; it is different
ó:ya' other; another
dissipate see: use up
a·wá:ts'a:' it is worn out, all gone, burnt up; it went down to nothing
dissolve see: wet
ęhs·ná·na·wę't you will melt, liquefy s.t.
dissuade see: persuade
ęhs·he'ni·gǫ·hǫ́:ni' you will influence, persuade s.o.
distance
ni·yó:we' how far (distance)
[ni+y+ stem: -o:', we'$_V$- distance, amount]
shę́ ni·yó:we' up to there; until
to ni·yó:we' that far
na'de·gę·ná:dre' how far apart they (z) are
[na'de+A+ stem: -(a)dre'$_V$- be a certain distance apart]
na'de·gá·ǫd·re' how far apart they (f/m) are
distill see: evaporate, ferment
a·wá:sdehs it evaporated, dried up, boiled dry
ęh·sat·ne·gǫ́:ni' you will ferment s.t.
distinct see: different, special
de·sáh·di·hęh you are different
o·i·ho·wá:nęh it is important; a great, worthy commendation; it is special
distinguish see: recognize
ęg·yę́:de:' I will recognize it
distinguished see: distinct
o·i·ho·wá:nęh it is important; a great, worthy commendation; it is special
distress see: unhappy
de·a·ga·dǫt·gá:de', de·wa·ga·dǫt·gá:dǫ' I am not happy

distribute see: scatter
de·wa·dog·wáh·dǫh it has been spread out, distributed, scattered
disturb see: bother
dęhs·ni·ga̱ǫ·há:ha' you are annoying me, bothering me
disturbance see: riot
ga·nǫ́hs·gan·yęh a riot
ditch see: basement
o·yá:de' basement; track; ditch
dive
hah·do:s he dives; he is a diver
[stem: -(a)hdo(:)$_V$- dive]
a·háh·do: he dove, he dived
ę·háh·do: he will dive
sa̱h·do: you dive
dive see: swim
a:yǫ·dá:wę:' she might swim
divergent see: different
de·wáh·di̱·hęh the difference; it is different
diversity see: variety
ha·de·yo̱h·yá:ge: a variety of fruit
divide
de·gá·kah·sǫ: division; it is separated
[de+...+ stem: -kahsǫ:- division; consists of: -kahs(i)$_V$- share, divide]
dęh·se·kah·sǫ́:go' you will divide it into parts
[stem: -kahsǫgw- divide into parts; consists of: -kahs(i)$_V$- share, divide]
ho·ih·wa·káhs·hǫg·weh he has divided into parts, duties
de·seh·kah·sǫ́·gwa̱·hǫ: divide them (several objects) up into categories
[de+...(N+) stem: -kahsǫgwah- go and divide into parts; consists of: -kahs(i)$_V$- share, divide]
dę·seh·kah·sǫ́g·wa̱·hǫ' you will divide them (several objects) up into categories
divide see: share
dęh·sé·kah·si' you will share, divide

divider see: partition
wa·dę·nǫh·sa·we·tá·hǫh partition
divine
ha·dih·ne·gát·sęn·yǫhs they (m) divine, witch for water
[stem: -(h)negatsęny- divine, witch for water; consists of: -(h)neg(a)$_N$- water, liquid -tsęi, tsęny$_V$- find]
divine see: forbidden
o·nǫ́ˀne:ˀ it is forbidden, sacred, holy
division see: partition
wa·dę·nǫh·sa·we·tá·hǫh partition
division (of an organization) see: G (he·ga·nęt·sa:deˀ de·yǫ·ki·yǫh·wę·jaˀnya:ˀ)
dizzy
a·gah·sǫ·wá·den·yeˀs, a·gat·sǫ·wá·den·yeˀs I am dizzy
[P+ (at)+ stem: -(a)hsǫwadenyeˀs- dizzy; consists of: -(a)hsǫw(a)$_N$- -deni, deny$_V$- change]
do
hę·nág·ye·hęˀ they (m) do it
[(ni+) (d+)P+(ag+) stem: -ye(:)$_V$- do]
ni·to·dí:yę: as they (m) are doing (continually)
nig·ya:gó:yę: the way she does s.t.
ni·yó:yę: what it is doing
tsę́h ni·yǫg·wag·yáh·sǫh what we have done
do see: do carefully, do on purpose, do right, do unintentionally
do carefully see: care for
ęd·wa·de·wa·yę·nǫ́:niˀ we all (incl.) will do it carefully; we all will do right
do on purpose
tsi·géh·taˀ I do it on purpose all the time
[tsi+ stem: -ehd$_V$- do on purpose]
tsaˀgeht I did it on purpose
tsaˀseht you did it on purpose; it was premeditated; it was done in spite
tsi·wá·geh·dǫh I did it on purpose
tsi·wéh·dǫh it was planned on purpose
do right
dęhs·yí:dahs you do things right
[de+... stem: -yidahsd- do s.t. right; consists of: -yei, (y)i$_V$- right, correct]
do right see: care for
ęd·wa·de·wa·yę·nǫ́:niˀ we all (incl.) will do it carefully; we all will do right
do unintentionally
taˀde·wa·géh·dǫ:ˀ I did not mean it, intend it
[(te') ta'+de+P+ stem: -ehd$_V$- do on purpose, do unintentionally]
tęˀ taˀde·ha·wéh·dǫ: he did not mean it
dock
wa·tǫ·wa·ę:dahk·wáˀgeh a dock
[w+at+ stem: -(h)ǫwayędahkwa - dock; consists of: -(h)ǫw(a)$_N$- boat -ędahkwaˀ$_V$- place where things are put]
a·hę·na·tǫ·wa·nę́:da:k they (m) docked a boat
[at+ stem: -(h)ǫwanęda:ˀg- dock a boat; consists of: -(h)ǫw(a)$_N$- boat -(raˀ)nęd(a:ˀg), (yaˀ)nęd(a:ˀg)$_V$- stick, cling]
doctor
ha·dé:jęˀs he is a doctor
[A+ade+ stem: -jęˀs- doctor; consists of: -jęˀd$_V$- cure, practice medicine]
doctor's office
ha·dé·jęhs·geh doctor's office; clinic
[A+ade+ stem: -jęˀsgeh- doctor's office, clinic; consists of: -jęˀd$_V$- cure, practice medicine]
doctrine see: belief, religion
tsę́h hǫ:wéh gyǫg·wéh·dah·gǫh our belief; religion
ga·ih·wi·yóhs·dęhs·raˀ religion; the Christian faith
document see: paper
gah·yá·dǫhs·raˀ paper

dog
só:wa:s dog
[stem: -sowa:s$_{N}$- dog]
so·wa:s·gó:wah great dog
wa·dad·wę:ni:yóʼ só:wa:s wild dog, stray dog
[consists of: wadadwę:ni:yoʼ a stray animal; so:wa:s dog]
dogfish
ga·néhs·hę·hęʼ dogfish
[ga+ stem: -nehshęhę$_{N}$- dogfish]
dogfish see: mud puppy
nǫh·so·dá·i:yǫ: mud puppies; dogfish
doll
ga·yáʼdaʼ doll
[ga+ stem: -yaʼd(a)$_{N}$- body]
dollar see: B (sgah·wihs·da:t)
dolt see: stupid
de·hoʼni·gǫ́·ha:t he is ignorant, unthinkingly foolish
domain see: area
og·ye·na·wáh·dǫh area
domestic
go·nǫ́hs·gǫh·ka:ʼ anything that belongs in a house
[ga+ stem: -nǫhs(a)$_{N}$- house]
domestic see: animal (tame), tame
ga·náhsg·waʼ tame animal; pet; domestic animal
wat·nahs·gǫ́:ni: it has been made into a pet
donate
da·sáht·gaʼ you donated
[d+... stem: -(a)htga(w)$_{V}$- release, let go, donate]
donate see: give
dahs·gǫh give it to me
donkey see: jackass
de·wa·hǫh·dá·hǫʼ a jackass; a donkey
don't see: I (ahgwih)
door
gan·hó·haʼ door
[ga+ stem: -nho(ha)$_{N}$- door]
door see: gate
gan·ho·ha·ní:yǫ:t gate; door
doorstep
ǫhs·hę́·dahk·waʼ doorstep
[ǫ+ stem: -(a)hshędahkwaʼ- doorstep; consists of: -(a)shęd$_{V}$- step]
doorway
gan·hó·ga·hę:t doorway
[ga+ stem: -nhogahęd- doorway; consists of: -nho(ha)$_{N}$- door -gahęd$_{V}$- drill, hole]
dormant see: sleep
o·dáʼǫh it is asleep
dot see: decimal point
o·jihs·da·nóhg·waʼ decimal point; point; dot
double
dęhs·náʼnetʼa:ʼ you will double it, reinforce it, line it
[de+ stem: -naʼnetʼa:ʼ$_{V}$- double, reinforce, line (with material)]
de·gá·yʼa·se:ʼ it is doubled
[de+A+ stem: -(a)ʼse:ʼ$_{V}$- cousin, be double]
double see: fold
de·séh·sa·ge:t you will fold it once, bend it
double back
ǫ:sa·gat·ga·ę·hę́:goʼ I should turn around and go back the way I came
[s+...at+ stem: -gaęhęgw- double back, return; consists of: -gaęh(eʼ)$_{V}$- cross]
doubtful see: confused
de·wa·ga·da·węn·yáʼseh I am confused and doubtful
dough
ohs·héʼaʼ dough
[o+ stem: -(h)sheʼ(a)$_{N}$- dough]
douse see: extinguish, wet
waʼswáh·dǫh it is extinguished
ahs·náʼna·węht you wet it

down see: descend, drink
ę·sá:s·nęht you will get down
ę·yeh·ne·gé·ha' she will drink
downwind see: windward
nig·yo·wá·ę·hę: the direction of the wind
draft see: air
ó:wa:' air; wind
drag
ak·ní'dre' we two (excl.) are dragging s.t.; we are riding along
[(N+) stem: -(i)'dre(:)$_V$- drag, drive]
ha'dre' he is dragging
s'ad·re' you are driving
a·gé'dre' I am riding along
ǫk·ní'dre:' we two are riding along in s.t.
ęd·ya·go·dí'drę:' they (f/m) will come by vehicle
a·gé'dre:' I dragged it
dę·díh·s'ad·re:' you will drive over here
de·sá'dre: drive over here
he'sá'dre: drive over there
hǫ·wę·y'a·dí'drehs·rǫh s.o. is going along dragging him
[TR+ stem: -ya'd(a)$_N$- body -(i)'drehsr- drag along]
ęd·wa·ǫ·dí'dre:' we all (incl.) will drag the log
[stem: -(r)ǫd(a)$_N$- log -(i)'dre(:)$_V$- drag, drive]
dragon
he·gę'dǫh·gó·i'a:s dragon (lit.: flame thrower)
[he+ga+ stem: -(i')dǫhgoi'a:s- dragon; consists of: -i'dǫhg(wa)$_N$- flame -oi'a:s$_V$- throw s.t.]
drain
sne·ga:dé:nih drain s.t. (potatoes, etc.)
[N+ stem: -(h)negadeni- drain; consists of: -(h)neg(a)$_N$- water, liquid -deni, deny$_V$- change]

drape
gó:da:s I drape it all the time
[(N+) stem: -oda(:,h)$_V$- drape]
de·wa:dó:da:s it drapes itself
ę·gó:da: I will drape it
o·dá·hǫh it is draped
drape see: hang, string up
ga·ní:yǫ:t it is hanging
ik·da:s I am stringing it, draping it
drapery see: curtain
o·jí'a:' curtains; lace
draw see: write
eh·yá:dǫh she writes
drawn out see: take time
tó na'ǫ́·nis·he' it took that long
draw water
eh·ne·ga·nęhg·wih·ta' s.t.to draw water with
[e+ stem: -(h)neganęhgwihta'- draw water; consists of: -(h)neg(a)$_N$- water, liquid -nęhgwi$_V$- haul]
dreadful see: terrible
de·yo·dę·nǫh·ya·níh·dǫh it is overwhelming, terrible
dream
og·yá:nǫ's it dreams
[P+ag+ stem: -yanǫ'$_V$- dream]
ę·yóg·ya·nǫ'k it will dream
ǫ·gág·ya·nǫ'k I did have a dream
hog·yán'ǫd·rǫh he is dreaming
[P+ag+ stem: -yanǫ'dr$_V$- go along dreaming]
dream see: nightmare, sleep
ǫ·ga·ded·ręh·dat·gí:dę' I had a bad dream
o·wid·ręh·dá:gǫ: it came through a dream
dreary
de·yot·gręg·ręh·dǫh the sky is dreary, grey
[de+...at+ stem: -gręgręhdǫh- dreary, overcast; consists of: -gręgręhd$_V$- frown, sneer]

Cayuga pronunciation guide: /a/ father /e/ weigh /ę/ men (nasalized) /i/ police /o/ hole /ǫ/ home (nasalized) /u/ blue. Underlined vowels are voiceless or whispered. /'/ high pitch. /t/ too /d/ do /k/ king /g/ good (never soft g) /j/ judge or adze /s/ soon /sh/ less heat (never the sh in shirt) /sr/ shrine /sy/ sure /hw/ which (the sound made when you blow out a candle) /h/ hi /ts/ cats hide /'/ (the sound before the first vowel in 'uh-uh') /n/ noon /r/ round /w/ way /y/ yes.

drench see: wet
a·ha·n'a·ná:węht he wet it
dress
sat·rǫ́:nih get dressed
[stem: -(a)trǫni, (a)trǫny$_V$- dress]
ag·ya'da·wí'tra' coat; dress
[ag+ stem: -(a)gya'dawi'tr(a)$_N$- dress, coat, shirt; consists of: -ya'dawi'd$_V$- put on (clothes), clothe oneself]
o·wi:ya:'áh gog·ya'da·wí'tra' baby's dress, sweater, coat
[consists of: owi:ya:'ah baby; gogya'dawi'tra' her coat, dress]
dress clothes see: clothes
ǫg·ya'da̱hs·rǫn·y'a·tá' ahg·wę́:nya' dress clothes; Sunday best
dress s.t. up
ga·ya'da̱hs·rǫ́:nih it dresses it up
[stem: -ya'dahsrǫnih- dress s.t.up; consists of: -ya'd(a)$_N$- body -(h)srǫni$_V$- fix, repair]
ǫg·ya'da̱hs·rǫ́n·y'a·ta' s.o. dresses up
[ag+ stem: -ya'dahsrǫnya'd- dress up; consists of: -ya'd(a)$_N$- body -(h)srǫnya'd$_V$- fix up, repair]
dresser
(o·hǫhs·rǫ:dǫ́') ǫhg·wę́n·yah·kwa' dresser
[consists of: ohǫhsrǫ:dǫ' lots of boxes; ǫhgwęnyahkwa' place where clothes are put]
dressing see: bandage
o·yę́h·sa:' bandage
drill
e·ga·hę·dáhk·wa' drill
[e+ stem: -gahędahkwa'- drill; consists of: -gahęd$_V$- drill, hole]
se·ga̱·hę́:dę' drill it
[stem: -gahędę- drill a hole; consists of: -gahęd$_V$- drill, hole]
drill bit
ga·gá·hę·ta' a drill bit
[ga+ stem: -gahęta'- drill bit; consists of: -gahęd$_V$- drill, hole]
drink
gah·né·ge̱·ha' it is drinking
[stem: -(h)neg(a)$_N$- water, liquid -(h)negeha$_V$- drink]
ę·yeh·ne·gé·ha' she will drink
sne·gé·hah drink
drink see: quench one's thirst, sip, smell
ę·ka'da·ná:wę' I will quench my thirst, wet my throat
ęts·ne·ga̱hg·yę́·hę·to' you will sip through a straw
had·rę·no·wá:ne' he has a big smell, odour, scent; he has been drinking
drip see: leak
o·kahs it leaks
drip sweat
ęh·sa·ga̱hd·ró:dę' you will drip tears, shed tears
[P+ stem: -gahdrod- drip sweat, tears; consists of: -gahdr(a)$_N$- tear -od$_V$- stand]
o·gáhd·ro:t it is tearing (as in a teardrop)
sa·gáhd·ro:t you are tearing (shedding tear-drops)
drive
ga·dó:wih, ga·dó:wihs
ga·dǫ́·nye's I drive all the time
[ad+ stem: -owi, ǫny$_V$- drive]
ha·dó:nye's he drives it; he is a driver
hę·sa:dó:wih you will drive over there
a·ga:dó:wi: I did the driving
ha'sa:dó:wih drive it over there; herd the animals
drive see: drag
s'ad·re' you are driving
drizzle
a·wa·yǫ́:gyǫ: it is drizzling; misty rain; fine rain
[stem: -(a)'awayǫdi- drizzle; consists of: -(a)'aw(a)$_N$- dew -ǫdi, -ǫgy$_V$- throw]

drop see: fall
da·wáʼsęʼ it dropped, reduced

drool
sęts·gro:t you are drooling
[P+ stem: -(n)itsgrod- drool; consists of: -(n)itsgr(a)$_N$- saliva -od$_V$- stand]

drool see: saliva
ots·graʼ saliva; spit; sputum

droplet see: leak
ohs·dá·o·kahs one drop at a time (is falling)

drought
o·háʼdǫ·ge: a drought
[stem: -(h)aʼd- drought; consists of: -(h)aʼd$_V$- dry; ge:- big]
a·gá·haʼtge: a big drought

drowse see: sleep
ę·sę́:daʼ you will sleep

drum
ga·náʼjǫ: drum; water drum
[ga+ stem: -naʼjǫ:- water drum; consists of: -naʼj(a)$_N$- pail, drum -oʼ$_N$- be submerged]
ga·náhg·waʼ bass drum
[ga+ stem: -nahg(wa)$_N$- drum, barrel]
ga·naʼjo·wíʼtraʼ water drum
[ga+ stem: -naʼjowiʼtr(a)$_N$- water drum]
ga·naʼjo·wá:nęh bass drum, big kettle drum, big pail
[ga+ stem: -naʼj(a)$_N$- pail, drum -owanęh$_V$- big]

drum (beat a drum)
ha·di·na̲hg·wáʼehs they (m) are drummers
[stem: -nahgwaʼe- beat the drum; consists of: -nahg(wa)$_N$- drum, barrel -(ʼ)e$_V$- hit]
ho·nahg·wáʼe·hag·yeʼ he is beating the drum as he moves along

drumstick
eh·wáʼes·taʼ drumstick; baseball bat
[e+ stem: -(r)ihwaʼestaʼ- drumstick; consists of: -(r)ih(wa)$_N$- word -(ʼ)ehsd$_V$- hit with s.t.]

drunk
dih·sa:t·hné:ga:t you are not level; you are tipsy
[deʼ+ not …at+ stem: -(h)negad- watery, drunk, tipsy; consists of: -(h)neg(a)$_N$- water, liquid -d$_V$- stand]

dry
o·hę: it is dry
[o+ stem: -(h)ę:- ; consists of: -tę(:), hę(:)$_V$- dry]
ga̱·háʼtaʼ it dries
[stem: -(h)aʼd, taʼd$_V$- dry out]
ęh·sé:haʼt you will dry s.t.
o·háʼdǫh it is dry (for example, fields, weather); drought
ga̱·háʼdǫh it is drying (right now)
gyo·háʼdǫh it is dry over there (refers to the American Southwest)
ę·sad·wa·há·taʼt you will dry out the meat
[N+ stem: -(ʼ)wah(a)$_N$- meat : -taʼd$_V$- dry s.t.out]
wa·dah·ya·táʼdǫh dried fruit
[wa+ad+ stem: -(a)hy(a)$_N$- fruit, berry +taʼd$_V$- dry s.t.out]
ga·neh·wa·táʼdǫh dried, drying hides
[stem: -nehw(a)$_N$- hide -taʼd$_V$- dry s.t.out]
ęh·snę́·hę·taʼt you will dry corn
[stem: -nęh(ę)$_N$- corn -taʼd$_V$- dry s.t.out]
ga·nę·hę·táʼdǫh dried corn
ga̱·hę́hs·taʼ it is drying out
[stem: consists of: -(h)ęhsd$_V$- dry out, evaporate]
sa·ga·ga̱·hóʼja·tęhs the grass dried up
[N+ stem: consists of: -gahoʼj(a)$_N$- grass -tęhsd$_V$- dry out, evaporate]

Cayuga pronunciation guide: /a/ father /e/ weigh /ę/ men (nasalized) /i/ police /o/ hole /ǫ/ home (nasalized) /u/ blue. Underlined vowels are voiceless or whispered. /ˊ/ high pitch. /t/ too /d/ do /k/ king /g/ good (never soft g) /j/ judge or adze /s/ soon /sh/ less heat (never the sh in shirt) /sr/ shrine /sy/ sure /hw/ which (the sound made when you blow out a candle) /h/ hi /ts/ cats hide /ʼ/ (the sound before the first vowel in 'uh-uh') /n/ noon /r/ round /w/ way /y/ yes.

dry (continued)
o·hę́h·jih·węh it is really dried out
[o+ stem: -(h)ęhjihwęh- really dried out; consists of: -tę(:), hę(:)$_V$- be dry]
dry skin see: skin
sęh·ná·tę:, sih·ná·tę: you have dry skin
dry up see: evaporate
a·wá:sdehs it evaporated, dried up, boiled dry
dryer
a·tá'dahk·wa' dryer
[stem: -ta'dahkwa'- dryer; consists of: ta'd- dry s.t.out]
e·há·dahk·wa' dryer
[e+ stem: -(h)a'dahkwa'- dryer; consists of: -(h)a'd$_V$- dry s.t. out]
dryer see: clothes dryer, hair dryer
ahg·wę:nyá' ga·há'ta' clothes dryer
ǫt·gé' a·tá'tkwa' hair dryer
dryness see: drought
o·há'dǫ·ge: a drought
dubious see: confused
de·wa·ga·da·węn·yá'seh I am confused, doubtful
duck
twę́:twę:t duck
[stem: -twętwęt$_N$- duck]
duck pen
twę:twę́:t de·wa·tę·hę:dǫ́' ha·dí'drǫ·ta' duck pen
[consists of: twę:twę:t duck; dewatęhę:dǫ' gadi'drǫ' they (z) live (designates a shed, dog house; etc.)]
due
ę·yǫ́·d'e·dǫ:' when she will be due
[ade+ stem: -(')dǫ(:)$_V$- due]
ę·wá·d'e·dǫ:' when it (animal) is due
ǫ·dé'dǫh·ne' she is about to give birth
duel
de·yo·do·gę́'ǫh it is in between; a duel between two people
[de+yo+ad+ stem: -ogę'ǫh- duel; consists of: -ogę$_V$- together, between]

dull see: sharp
oh·yu'tí:yeht it is sharp
dumb see: stupid
de·sa'ni·gǫ́·ha:t you are stupid, foolish
dumbfound see: startle
ę·sę'ni·gǫ·ha·né'wa: you will be mentally startled
dunce see: trick
eh·sa:gyá·ǫ' you were tricked, fooled
dungeon see: prison
de·gahn·yǫhs·rá·de' prison
Dunnville, Ont. see: E .
(Det·gah·ne·ga·ha'go:wah)
duplicate see: copy
ęt·sa·den·yę́:dęhs you will copy, use as a model, a pattern
durable see: hard
oh·ní:yǫh it is hard
duration see: take time
tó na'ǫ́·nis·he' it took that long
dusk
shę́h ni·ye·jihs·dó:ta' the time when s.o. turns the lights on
[shęh ni+ye+ stem: -jihsdod- turn on; consists of: -jihsd(a)$_N$- light -od$_V$- stand]
dusk see: night, sun-down
ah·sǫ́·heh·ka:' night kind
he·gáhg·wę's to the setting sun; the direction of the sunset; west
dust
ę·sá'gę·hęt you will take the dust off
[stem: -(a)'gęhęd- dust s.t.; consists of: -(a)'gęh(ęda)$_N$- ash, dust]
dust see: ash, powder
o'gę́·hę' ashes; bullet; dust
ǫ·de·te'tráh·ta' powder
duster
ǫ'gę·hęh·dáhk·wa' duster
[ǫ+ stem: -(a)'gęhęhdahkwa'- duster; consists of: -(a)'gęh(ęda)$_N$- ash, dust -(h)kwa'$_V$- s.t. that picks things up]

dust pan
de·yọ·gẹ·hẹ́h·dahk·wa' dust pan
[de+yọ+ stem: -gẹhẹhdahkwa'- dust pan; consists of: -(a)'gẹh(ẹda)$_N$- ash, dust-(h)kwa'$_V$- s.t. that picks things up]
Dutch see: C (Oh·wẹ'ga:' De·ho·nẹ:so·we:k·sọ')
duty see: necessity
tgá:gọ:t a compelling must
dwarf
ni·hẹ·nọg·we'dú:s'uh dwarves
[ni+A+ stem: -ọgwe du:s'uh dwarf; consists of: -ọgwe('da)$_N$- person -u:'uh$_V$- small]
dwell
tsẹ́h dwak·nọ́h·so:t where I dwell (lit.: where my house is)
[(d)+P+ stem: -nọhsod- dwell; consists of: -nọhs(a)$_N$- house -od$_V$- stand]
o·dí·nọh·so:t they (z) dwell
nẹ·yak·n'i·drọ́:da'k where we two (excl.) will dwell
[stem: -(i)'drọd- be placed; consists of: -(i)'drọ$_V$- live, dwell, be at home]
ẹhs·ni'drọ́:da'k you two will stay home
nẹ·gi'drọ́:da'k where I will dwell, live
a·ọ·da·gi'drọ́:da'k I should have stayed at home
ẹ·gi'drọ́:da'k I will be at home; I will stay at home
hẹ·gi'drọ́:da'k where I will live (over there)
tgi'drọ́:da'k where I lived
ha·di'drọ́:dọ' how they (m) are placed
dwell see: live, inhabit, truth
shẹ́h tgi'drọ' where I live
ẹ·sat·hna·dá·ẹ' you will inhabit
nẹ·yak·n'i·drọ́:da'k where we two (excl.) will dwell
grih·wag·wẹ·ní:yo' where I reside, dwell (lit.: where I'm the boss)
dwelling see: house
ga·nọ́h·sa' a house
dwindle see: shrink
ẹ·wáhs·twa' it will shrink (that is, wool)
dye see: colour
ọh·sóh·ta' colour; paints; crayons
dyed
wah·sá·họh it is dyed, coloured
[wa+ stem: -(a)hsoh(gwa)$_N$- colour, paint, crayon -(a)hsahọh$_V$- dyed, coloured]
dyed see: coloured
wah·só·họ:t it is coloured, dyed
dynasty
gah·wa·ji·ya:dó:gẹ: a certain family, dynasty
[ga+ stem: -(h)wajiyadogẹ:- dynasty, species; consists of: -(h)wajiy(a)$_N$- family -dogẹ(:)$_V$- right, true]

E

eager see: willing, work well
ho·gá·ẹ:s he is willing
got·sáh·niht she is a good worker, tireless, active, industrious, etc.
each
[-tsọ' the verb 'stand' with pluralizer; used in expressions meaning 'each' or 'individually' or 'one after another']
eagle
a·wẹ·he'gó:wah eagle
[stem: -(a)wẹhe'$_N$- eagle]
os·wẹ'gá·i:yo' a hawk; a small eagle
[o+ stem: -swẹ'g(a)$_N$- hawk -iyo:$_V$- be nice, good]
ear
o·họ́h·da' ears
[stem: -(a)họhd(a)$_N$- ear]
sa·họ́h·d'a·geh on your ears

Cayuga pronunciation guide: /a/ father /e/ weigh /ẹ/ men (nasalized) /i/ police /o/ hole /ọ/ home (nasalized) /u/ blue. Underlined vowels are voiceless or whispered. /´/ high pitch. /t/ too /d/ do /k/ king /g/ good (never soft g) /j/ judge or adze /s/ soon /sh/ less heat (never the sh in shirt) /sr/ shrine /sy/ sure /hw/ which (the sound made when you blow out a candle) /h/ hi /ts/ cats hide /'/ (the sound before the first vowel in 'uh-uh') /n/ noon /r/ round /w/ way /y/ yes.

ear (inner)
o·hǫ́h·da·gǫ: inner ear
[o+ stem: -(a)hǫhdagǫ:- inner ear; consists of: -(a)hǫhd(a)$_N$- ear -(a)gǫ:- in]
ear of corn
oh·wę́h·da:ʼ corn ears
[o+ stem: -(h)węhd(a:)$_N$- ear of corn]
earache
a·ga·hǫh·dá·nǫh·wa:s I have an earache
[P+ stem: -(a)hǫhd(a)$_N$- ear -nǫhwag$_V$- be sore, ache]
early
o·hę:dǫ́: ih·seʼ you are the first to arrive; you are early
[consists of: ohę:dǫ: ahead; ihseʼ you are here]
oh·sno:wéʼ ahs·yǫʼ you got here early
[consists of: ohsno:weʼ it is fast; ahsyǫʼ you arrived]
early see: ahead, fast, premature
o·hę́:dǫ: ahead; in front; the front
ohs·no:wé:ʼah it is fairly fast; to arrive a little bit early
to·dǫ́:noʼk he is mentally challenged; he was born premature
earn see: acquire, make
ę·sa:yę́·daʼ you will acquire, obtain
gǫ́:nih I make, earn
earn money
dęh·sá·dęt·sʼa:ʼ you will earn it (money)
[de+...adę+ stem: -(a)tsʼ$_V$- use up; earn (money)]
de·sá·dęht·sʼǫh you've earned it; you deserve it; you've paid your dues
a·tad·rih·wá:tsʼa:ʼ he earned it; he fulfilled it
[de+...(ad+) stem: -(r)ihwatsʼa:ʼ- earn s.t., fulfill s.t.; consists of: -(r)ih(wa)$_N$- word -(a)tsʼ$_V$- use up]
de·ho·dí:h·wat·sa:ʼ they are earning, fulfilling it

earring
gʼa·wáhs·ha:ʼ earrings
[ga+ stem: -(ʼ)wahs(a:)$_N$- earring]
de·yǫt·wah·sá·ǫ:kwaʼ earrings
[de+yǫ+at+ stem: -(ʼ)wahsaǫkwaʼ- earring; consists of: -(ʼ)wahs(a:)$_N$- earring]
earth
oh·wę́·ja·geh on earth
[o+ stem: -ǫhwęj(a)$_N$- earth, land]
oh·wę́·ja·gǫ: under the earth, ground
oh·wę́·ja·deʼ existing earth, land
[o+ stem: -ǫhwęj(a)$_N$- earth, land -deʼ$_V$- exist]
gyǫh·wę́·ja:deʼ existing land
de·yǫg·węh·siʼda·gę́d·rahg·węh earth (lit.: where we put our feet)
[de+yǫgw+ stem: -ęhsiʼdagędrahgwęh- earth; consists of: -(a)hsi(ʼda), (ę)hs(a)$_N$- foot -gędrahgw$_V$- support]
earth see: land, world
o·héh·daʼ dirt; earth
o·ih·wa·gę́h·yat·geʼ to the edge of the world (in the last days)
easily
[-(h)sgǫ: facilitative suffix; means 'prone to,' 'easily' or 'really']
easy
wag·yé:sęh it is easy
[w+ag+ -yesęh - easy]
ease see: comfortable
a·gat·nak·dí:yohs I made myself comfortable
east see: sunrise
tgá:g·wit·gęʼs east (a direction); the sun rises there
tga:gwit·gę́ʼs·geh the east; where the sun rises
earthquake
ag·yǫh·węh·ję́:dǫh earthquake
[a+g+yo+ stem: -ǫhwęhjędǫh- earthquake; consists of: -ǫhwęj(a)$_N$- earth, land -ędǫh$_V$- shake s.t.]

eat
í:ge:s I eat
[stem: -g$_{V}$- eat]
á:se:k you should eat
a·ha:k he ate it
a·gáh·ya·gǫh I am eating fruit
[stem: -(a)hy(a)$_{N}$- fruit, berry -g$_{V}$- eat]
hon·ráh·da·gǫh he is eating lettuce
[stem: -nrahd(a)$_{N}$- leaf -g$_{V}$- eat]
í:se:k eat it
ga·ǫ:de·kǫ́:nih they (f/m) eat
[ade+ stem: -kǫni- eat; consists of: -k(wa)$_{N}$- food -ǫni, ǫny$_{V}$- make]
a·gę·na·de·kǫ́:niʼ they (z) ate
ho·de:kǫ́:ni: he is eating
sa·de:kǫ́:nih you eat
ę·ji·sa·de·kǫ·ní·hag·yeʼ you can (lit.: will) eat while you are going along
ę·ga:kwę́:daʼ it is going to finish eating
[stem: -kwędaʼ- finish eating; consists of: -k(wa)$_{N}$- food -ędaʼ$_{V}$- finish]
a·gek·wę·dáʼǫh I have finished eating
ebony see: black
swę́ʼdʼa·ę:ʼ black
eclipse
a·wad·ri̲hg·wáh·dǫʼ an eclipse took place (lit.: the moon got lost)
[a+wa+ad+ stem: -(r)ihgwahdǫʼ- eclipse; consists of: -(r)ihg(wa)$_{N}$- moon -(a)hdǫ(:)$_{V}$- lose, disappear]
economical see: frugal, inexpensive
de·ya·go·nǫ́h·ya·ni:s she is frugal
tęʼ de·gá:nǫ:ʼ it is not costly
Economic Development (office) see: G (O·hę:dǫ: Haʼwa·ta·hi:neʼ Got·ga·nǫ·ni·hag·yeʼ)
economize
ęh·sat·wihs·dá·nʼi·ǫhs you will economize
[at+ stem: -(h)wihsdaniʼǫhsd- economize; consists of: -(h)wihsd(a), (hr)ihsd(a)$_{N}$- metal, money -niʼǫh$_{V}$- be stingy, greedy, cheap]
sat·wihs·da·níʼǫhs you economize
economize see: reserve
ęh·sa·do̲h·wíhs·da·ęʼ you will economize
edge
o·ha·há:kʼah by the edge of the road
[o+ stem: -(h)aha:kʼah- edge of the road; consists of: -(h)ah(a)$_{N}$- road]
o·dóʼk·dag·yeʼ rim; outer and inner rim splint; along the edge
[o+ad+ stem: -oʼkdagyeʼ- along the edge; consists of: -oʼkd$_{V}$- end]
tsęh hǫ́ he·yo·dʼok·dáʼǫh the edge
[tsęh hǫ: he+yo+ad+ stem: -oʼkdaʼǫh- end of s.t.; consists of: -oʼkd$_{V}$- end]
edge see: beside, blade, hem
ak·dá:gyeʼ the edge; beside
o·hę́·nʼat·rǫ:t blade
de·gág·wat·węh a hem
edit see: arrange
ęhs·dó:gęhs you will arrange (things, flowers, etc.)
edition see: book
oh·ya·dǫhs·rǫ́:dǫʼ book
educated see: clever, smart
sa·wa·yęn·héʼs·gǫ: you are clever, educated
sya·dǫhs·rá·ę·diʼ you are smart (educated)
ga·i:hǫn·yá:ni:ʼ education
[ga+ stem: -(r)ihǫnyani:- education consists of: -(r)ih(wa)$_{N}$- word of -ǫni, ǫnyani$_{V}$- make for oneself]
education (postsecondary) see: G (he:t·gęh tga:deh hę·na·de·wa·yęhs·taʼ)
education office
ga·i:hǫn·ya:ní:ʼ tga·yaʼdag·wę·ni·yóʼgeh education office; education
[consists of: gai:hǫnya:ni:ʼ education; tgayaʼdagwęniyoʼgeh head office]

Cayuga pronunciation guide: /a/ father /e/ weigh /ę/ men (nasalized) /i/ police /o/ hole /ǫ/ home (nasalized) /u/ blue. Underlined vowels are voiceless or whispered. /ˊ/ high pitch. /t/ too /d/ do /k/ king /g/ good (never soft g) /j/ judge or adze /s/ soon /sh/ less heat (never the sh in shirt) /sr/ shrine /sy/ sure /hw/ which (the sound made when you blow out a candle) /h/ hi /ts/ cats hide /ʼ/ (the sound before the first vowel in ‘uh-uh’) /n/ noon /r/ round /w/ way /y/ yes.

eel
gǫ́:deh eel
[stem: -gǫdeh$_{V}$- eel]
eerie see: odd
og·ya·nǫh·sá:nǫht weird, odd, spooky house
effective see: useful
o·í·hǫ:t it is useful
efficient see: work well
got·sáh·niht she is a good worker, tireless, active, industrious, etc.
effortless see: easy
wag·yé:sęh it is easy
egg
oʼnhǫ́h·saʼ eggs
[o+ stem: -(ʼ)nhǫhs(a)$_{N}$- egg]
egocentric, egotistical see: self-centered, conceited
ha·dág·yʼa·da:s he has a high opinion of himself; he is self-centred; he is bold; he is conceited, boastful, bragging
eight see: B (deg·rǫʼ)
eighteen see: B (deg·rǫʼ sga·eʼ)
eighty see: B (deg·rǫʼ ni·wahs·hę:)
elaborate see: explain
dęhs·ríh·wa·teʼt you will explain
elapse see: past
o·dǫ́·gǫh·dǫh it has passed by; the past
elastic see: rubber band
de·wa·di·yǫ́:taʼ it stretches (shortened form of 'rubber band'); balloon; elastic
de·wa·di·yǫ:táʼ oh·ná:griʼ rubber band; elastic
elbow
kyoh·sáʼgeh on my elbow
[stem: -(h)yohs(a)$_{N}$- elbow]
swah·yóh·sʼa·geh on your (p) elbows
elder
ga·e·gę̱h·jih·sǫ́:ʼǫh they (f/m) are elderly
[A+ stem: -gęhjihsǫ:ʼǫh- elder; consists of: -gęhjih$_{V}$- old (person)]
ha·di·gę̱h·jiʼsǫ́:ʼǫh they (m) are old men, male elders
elder see: old (person), old (living thing)
ha·gęh·jí:hah he is an old man; he is getting old, getting on
hohs·dę́:ʼęh he is old; he is an old man
elderberry
ot·goʼdáʼ oh·yaʼ elderberry
[consists of: otgoʼdaʼ sumac; ohyaʼ fruit]
elect
a·hǫ·wa·díʼd·rǫʼ they placed, elected him
[TR+ stem: -(i)ʼdrǫ$_{V}$- live, dwell, elect]
a·hǫ·wa·dits·gó:dęʼ they elected him, them (m)
[TR+ stem: -(i)tsgodęʼ- elect; consists of: -(n)itsg(wa)$_{N}$- body -odę$_{V}$- put in]
elect see: appoint, vote
a·hǫ·wa·i·hǫ́:dęʼ they delegated him a duty
dęh·sę·nig·yohg·wa·gę́:niʼ you will vote, cast lots
electrician
(oh·sǫ·wa̱h·da·da·i:hę́:)
hah·sǫ·wa̱h·dá:da:s electrician
[consists of: ohsǫwa̱hdadai:hę: electricity; hahsǫwa̱hda:da:s electrician (lit.: he puts up the wires)]
electricity
oh·sǫ·wa̱h·da·dá·i:hę: electricity
[o+ stem: -(h)sǫwahdaʼdaihę:- electricity; consists of: -(h)sǫwahd(a)$_{N}$- wire, nail, needle -(ʼ)daihę:$_{V}$- hot]
dewę̱ni̱hoks, dewę̱ni̱hoʼs electricity H
elephant
gʼan·yoʼse:sgó:wah elephant
[ga+ stem: -(ʼ)nyohsesgowah- elephant; consists of: -(ʼ)nyǫhs(a)$_{N}$- nose -es$_{V}$- long -gowah- big]
elevate see: pick up, uphold
at·gehk I picked s.t. up
dę·yehg·wa·dáh·nǫ:ʼ she will raise things, lift things up

elevator
de·ya·go·ya'dahk·wá' ǫ́:gweh elevator [consists of: deyagoya'dahkwa' s.t.that lifts things; ǫ:gweh person]
elevator see: transportation
go·ya'da·nę́hg·wih transportation; bus; elevator (lit.: people mover)
eleven see: B (sga:t sga·e')
elixir see: mix
de·gah·ne·gá·yęhs·dǫh water is mixed in it
elm
ga·hǫ́:ga:' elm [ga+ stem: -(h)ǫg(a:)$_N$- elm]
o·hóhsg·ra' slippery elm [o+ stem: -(h)ohsgr(a)$_N$- slippery elm]
elope
a·ga·e'nya:gę́' a'a·go·dí:nya'k they eloped [consists of: agae'nya:gę' they (f/m) escaped; a'agodi:nya'k they (f/m) cut across]
elongate see: stretch
de·ya·go·dí:yǫ:t she is stretching it
elsewhere
ga·ęg·wa'nhǫ́: ó:ya' elsewhere [consists of: gaęgwa'nhǫ: somewhere; o:ya' other, another]
elsewhere see: another
he.jo:yá' tsǫ: another thing again; elsewhere; on a tangent
elude see: run away
ę·gę·na·dé'go' they (z) will flee, run away
emanate see: originate from, start from
nig·ya·wé:nǫ: where it came from
dwa·da:dǫ́:nih where it starts from
emancipate see: release
sa·ga·e·sáht·ga' they released you again
embankment see: dam
de·gáh·n'e·ka:' a dam
embarassment see: shame
o·dé·ha't a shame; an embarrassment

embark
ęt·ga·ǫ:t·nǫ́h·da:' they (f/m) will get into a vehicle and come towards us [at+ stem: -(')nǫhda(:,h)- get into a vehicle, embark; consists of: -(')nǫh$_V$- put in, get into]
ę·gát·nǫh·da:' I will embark, get in s.t.
embarrassed see: feel bad
ęh·sá·dę·hęh you will become embarrassed, ashamed
embrace see: hold
e·ha:' she is holding s.t. right now
embryo see: egg
o'nhǫ́h·sa' eggs
emerge unintentionally
ę·yǫ·yę·déh·te' it will emerge unintentionally [stem: -yędehte'- emerge unintentionally; consists of: -(y)ęde(:,')$_V$- recognize]
a·ǫ·yę·déh·te' it emerged unintentionally
emerge see: appear unintentionally, originate
ta'sa·do·dáh·si' you appeared unintentionally
tę·wa·da·dǫ́:ni' it will emerge, appear unintentionally; it will do it by itself
employ see: hire, use
ę·sá·dęn·ha' you will order s.t., hire s.t.
ęh·sehs you will use it
employee see: G (sen-ha'tra')
employment see: occupation
ni·sa·i·ho'dęhs·ró'dę: your occupation; your type of work
Employment and Immigration see: G (Hę·na·dęn·ha's Dę·hę·na·dǫg·we'da·den·ye's)
Employment Office see: G (Dę·ha·di·ho'dęhs·rag·wę·ni:yo')

Cayuga pronunciation guide: /a/ father /e/ weigh /ę/ men (nasalized) /i/ police /o/ hole /ǫ/ home (nasalized) /u/ blue. Underlined vowels are voiceless or whispered. /´/ high pitch. /t/ too /d/ do /k/ king /g/ good (never soft g) /j/ judge or adze /s/ soon /sh/ less heat (never the sh in shirt) /sr/ shrine /sy/ sure /hw/ which (the sound made when you blow out a candle) /h/ hi /ts/ cats hide /'/ (the sound before the first vowel in 'uh-uh') /n/ noon /r/ round /w/ way /y/ yes.

empty
a·ha:dé:ni' he emptied s.t. (lit.: he changed it)
[(d+)...(N+)stem: -deni, deny$_{V}$- change, empty s.t.]
a·ta:dé:ni' he changed s.t.
ga·dé:nyǫ: it is empty
empty see: all gone, deflate
ha'wá:ts'aht it is all gone
a·wa·de·wa:dáh·go' it deflated
enchant see: bewitch, evil power
ę·gǫ·yat·gǫ́'tra:s I will bewitch you
ot·gǫhs·hǫ́:'ǫh things with evil power
encircle
dę·wat·wa·dáh·se·dahk it will encircle it
[de+...at+ stem: -(h)wadahsed- encircle; consists of: -(h)wad(a)$_{N}$- year -(a)hsed$_{V}$-hide s.t.]
enclosure see: yard
wa·dę·hę́:gǫ:, a·dę·hę́:gǫ: in the yard
encounter see: meet
a·tę́n'ad·ra' they (m) met
encourage
ęh·sasg·yá·ǫn·yǫ' you will encourage
[stem: -(a)hsgyaǫnyǫ- encourage; consists of: -(ah)sgyaǫ$_{V}$- walk fast]
gahsg·yá·ǫ:nyǫ:' words of encouragement
encourage see: walk fast
ęh·sáhsg·ya·ǫ:' you will walk fast; you will encourage
end
he·wá·d'ok·ta' a word suffix; it ends over there; it ends it
[he+w+ad+ stem: -o'kd$_{V}$- end]
he·yo·dok·dá'ǫh it ends over there
he·yó·ta·ho'k end of the trail, path, row
[he'+yo+at+ stem: -(h)ah(a)$_{N}$- road -o'kd$_{V}$- end]
he·yoh·tę́:do'k end of the field
[he'+yo+at+ stem: -(h)ęd(a)$_{N}$- field -o'kd$_{V}$- end]

end (continued)
ǫ·ga·ta·hó'k·tahs I came to the end of the trail, row
[ad+(N)+ stem: -(h)ah(a)$_{N}$- road -o'kdahsd$_{V}$- come to the end]
o·ih·wa·gę́h·ya:t it is almost to the end
[o+ stem: -(r)ih(wa)$_{N}$- word -gęhyad$_{V}$- beside]
end see: finish, stop
hę·só'k·dę' you will finish s.t.
a·ta:dahs he stopped it, prevented it
endeavor see: try
a:ga·d'en·yę́:dę' I might try, attempt
endless see: always
ha'dę·wat·gǫ́:dę' always; forever
endorse see: uphold
de·yǫg·wa̲hg·wá:dǫh we all are upholding it (a thing, idea)
endow see: give
dahs·gǫh give it to me
endowment see: power, present
ga̲hs·háhs·dęhs·ra', ohs·háhs·dęhs·ra' power; strength
wa·dá·wi̲·hǫ' presents
endure
sa·dáh·ga̲hs·ta' you do endure
[ad+ stem: -(a)hgahsd(ǫ)$_{V}$- endure]
ę·ga·ǫ·dáh·gahs·dǫ: they (f/m) will endure; used in the sense of, 'go and cook in the cookhouse'
ęh·sę'ni·gǫ·hah·ní:ya:t you will endure (lit. toughen, strengthen your mind)
[adę+ stem: -(')nigǫhahniyad- endure; consists of: -(')nigǫh(a)$_{N}$- mind -(h)niyad$_{V}$- harden, toughen]
sa·dę'ni·gǫ·hah·ní:ya:t keep your mind strong
energetic see: work well
got·sáh·niht she is a good worker, tireless, active, industrious, etc.
energy see: electricity, power
oh·sǫ·wa̲h·da·dá·i:hę: electricity

energy (continued)
ga̱hs·háhs·dę̱hs·raʼ, ohs·háhs·dę̱hs·raʼ power; strength
engine
ga̱·hǫ́ʼji̱hs·daʼ a motor; an engine
[ga+ stem: -(h)ǫjihsd(a)$_{N}$- engine, motor -(h)ǫʼjihsd$_{V}$- cause to darken]
England see: E (Gwagowaʼhneh)
engulf see: flood
ę·węh·nó:dǫ:ʼ it will flood
enjoy
ęhs·wa·dǫt·gá:dǫ:ʼ you all will have a good time, enjoy yourselves, have fun
[ad+ stem: -ǫtgad(ǫ:)$_{V}$- enjoy]
a·gǫʼwe̱hsg·wá:nih I enjoy it
[P+ stem: -ǫʼwes(ę,gwani)- enjoy s.t.; consists of: -ǫʼwes$_{V}$- enjoy]
ę·wa·gʼǫ·wé:sęʼ I will enjoy myself
enjoy see: fun
a·gǫ́ʼwe̱h·sahs I am having a good time, enjoying s.t.
enjoyable
a·ǫʼwé:sęh(t), aǫʼwé:sah(t) it is enjoyable; a good feeling
[P+ stem: -ǫʼwesahd, ǫʼwesęh(d)- enjoyable; consists of: -ǫʼwes$_{V}$- enjoy]
enlarge
ga·go·wa·náh·taʼ it makes things big
[stem: -gowanahd, gowanęhd- enlarge s.t.; consists of: -owanęh$_{V}$- be big]
ę·sehs·go̱·ha·o·wá:neht branch it out (that is, add particles, etc. to 'dress up' speech.)
[stem: -(h)sgoh(a)$_{N}$- branch -owanahd$_{V}$- enlarge]
enormous see: big
go·wá:nęh, ga·gó·wa·nęh it is big
enough
sag·yé·ni̱h·dǫh you have enough
[ag+ stem: -yenihd$_{V}$- have enough]
a·sa:gyé:·niht you got enough

enough (continued)
tóh haʼde·ga·yé·i:ʼ you get enough (lit.: it is enough)
[toh haʼde+ga+ stem: -i:ʼ$_{V}$- be stuck onto s.t.; get enough]
wag·yaʼda·wíʼtri:ʼ enough material for a full dress
[wa+ stem: -(a)gyaʼdawiʼtr(a)$_{N}$- dress, coat, shirt -i:ʼ$_{V}$- stuck onto s.t.]
enough see: able, I (to tsǫ:)
ę·ga:gwé:niʼ it can be; that is enough
enraged see: anger
ak·náʼk·węhs s.t. makes me angry
enter see: come in, go in
da̱·ha:dí:yǫʼ they (m) came in
haʼjǫh, haʼsyǫh go in; enter
enterprising see: active, quick-witted, work well
ag·yáʼda·deht I am nimble, active, energetic
haʼde·ho·íh·wa·ge: he is quick-witted; he has lots of business, different ideas, many ideas; he is into everything
sat·sáh·niht you are overzealous, ambitious
entertain
des·heʼni·gǫ·ha·wę́:nye: entertain her/them
[de+...ę+ stem: -(ʼ)nigǫhawęnye- entertain; consists of: -(ʼ)nigǫh(a)$_{N}$- mind -(a)węnye(:)$_{V}$- stir, mix]
de·yoʼni·gǫ·ha·wę́:nyaʼt it is entertaining
[de+...ę+ stem: -(ʼ)nigǫhawęnyaʼd- entertaining; consists of: -(ʼ)nigǫh(a)$_{N}$- mind -(a)węnye(:)$_{V}$- stir, mix]
entertainment see: recreation
de·yǫʼni·gǫ·ha·wę́n·yʼe·taʼ recreation; hobbies
enthusiastic see: work well
got·sáh·niht she is a good worker, tireless, active, industrious, etc.

Cayuga pronunciation guide: /a/ father /e/ weigh /ę/ men (nasalized) /i/ police /o/ hole /ǫ/ home (nasalized) /u/ blue. Underlined vowels are voiceless or whispered. /ˊ/ high pitch. /t/ too /d/ do /k/ king /g/ good (never soft g) /j/ judge or adze /s/ soon /sh/ less heat (never the sh in shirt) /sr/ shrine /sy/ sure /hw/ which (the sound made when you blow out a candle) /h/ hi /ts/ cats hide /ʼ/ (the sound before the first vowel in 'uh-uh') /n/ noon /r/ round /w/ way /y/ yes.

enticing
ohs·gá:na' t it is enticing, alluring, attractive, tempting
[o+ stem: -(a)hsgana'd- enticing, attractive; consists of: -(ahs)gan(eg)$_V$- want, desire, long for]
entire see: all
og·wé:gǫh, gwé:gǫh, ag·wé:gǫh everything, all
entrails see: gut
o·yǫ́:wa' guts; intestines
entrance see: doorway
gan·hó·ga·hę:t doorway
entrap see: catch, trap
ah·sa·go·di·yé·na:' they arrested, caught her
hę·nad·rihs·dá·ę·hę' they (m) are trappers
entrust see: appoint
a·hǫ·wa·i·hǫ́:dę' they delegated him a duty
entry see: doorway
gan·hó·ga·hę:t doorway
enumerate see: count
ęd·wáhs·he:t we all (incl.) will count
envious see: jealous
ak·nó:s·hę: I am envious
environment see: G (tsęh ni·yoh·dǫ·hǫg·ye' sęh hǫh·wę·ja·da·dǫh)
epicure see: glutton
a·gá·det·sę: I am a glutton
epidemic see: sickness
o·nǫh·so·dá·i:yǫ:' sickness; illness; epidemic; plague
epilepsy see: convulse
ę·sa·yę·náh·sǫ:' you are an epileptic (lit.: you will have convulstions)
epoxy see: glue
et·sehs·dá:ta' glue
equal
tsa'dé:yǫ: of equal number, amount
[tsa'de+y+ stem: -ǫ$_V$- number (of things), equal number, amount]

equal (continued)
tsa'de·yo·sháhs·dęhs·ra' of equal strength, power
[tsa'de+yo+ stem: -shasdęhsr(a)$_N$- power, strength]
equal see: same
tsa'de·yo·yę́hs·ra·ge: they are (lit. it is) two of the same kind of blanket
equality
tsa'de·ga·ya'dag·wę·ní:yo' equality
[tsa'de+ga+ stem: -ya'dagwęniyo'- equality; consists of: -ya'd(a)$_N$- body -gwęniyo'$_V$- main]
equilibrium see: harmony
dę·ga·ih·wá·ę·dad·re' harmony
equipment
o·i·ho'dęhs·ras·dé' gę·nad·ri·hó'da:s heavy equipment
[consists of: oiho'dęhsrahsde' heavy work; gęnadriho'da:s they (z) work]
equipment see: tool
ǫd·ri·ho'dá:sta' tools; equipment
equitable see: righteous
od·rih·wag·wá·ih·sǫ: it is believable, credible, righteous, fair, honest
equity
tsę́h ni·yó:ga:' equity; capital; value; worth
[tsęh ni+yo+ stem: -ga:'- equity, value; consists of: -ga:$_N$- price]
equivalent see: same
tsa'dé:yoht they are (lit.: it is) the same
erase see: wipe
ęg·rá:ge:' I will erase, wipe it
eraser
e·ya:gé·wah·ta' an eraser
[e+ stem: -ya:gewahta'- eraser; consists of: -(r)age(:,w)$_V$- wipe]
erect
ę·wa·d'a·yó:dę' it will be erect (poised to strike)
[ad+ -(a)'yod$_V$- erect]

erection
ę·ha·da·gę·hó:dę' he will get an erection
[ad+ stem: -(a)'gehod$_V$- erection]
ho·dá'gę·ho:t he has an erection
sa·dá'gę·ho:t you have an erection
ho·da'gę·hó:da'k he did have erections (but he doesn't any more)
erode
wa·téhg·ya's it is eroding
[at+ stem: -(h)ehgya'g- erode; consists of: -(h)ehd(a)$_N$- land, dirt, earth, ground -(i)ya'g$_V$- cut, break]
ę·wáh·tehg·ya'k it will erode
erosion
o·heh·dę'ǫ́·hǫg·ye' continually falling earth; erosion
[o+ stem: -(h)ehdę'ǫhǫgye'- erosion consists of: -(h)ehd(a)$_N$- land (etc.) -(a's)ę'ǫhǫgye'$_V$- fall, drop continuously]
err
a·gé:nhi's I err, make mistakes
[stem: -nhi'$_V$- err, mistake]
a'ón·hi'k it was a mistake; accidental
a·hó:nhi'k he made a mistake
ęh·sá:nhi'k you will err, make a mistake
a·gén·hi'ǫh I have made a mistake, an error
escape
ge'nyá:gę's I'm an escaper
[stem: -(')nyagę'$_V$- escape, run away]
sha'nyá:gę' he escaped again
go·di'ny'a·gę́'ǫh they (f/m) ran away
ęhs·hé'ny'a·gęht you will help s.o. escape
[TR+ stem: -(')nyagęhd- help s.o. escape; consists of: -(')nyagę'$_V$- escape, run away]
escape see: rescue, run away
a·ha·do·dá·i·si: he got loose, escaped
ęh·sá·de'go' you will flee, run away
escarpment
de·gahs·dę·hę́·dag·ye' escarpment
[de+ga+ stem: -(h)sdęhędagye'- escarpment; consists of: -(h)sd(ęha)$_N$- stone -(h)ędagye'$_V$- lead along]
escort
ęhs·néh·dahk you will escort
[stem: -ehdahgw$_V$- escort]
hęhs·he·ha·wíh·dahk you will escort her, take her with you
[he+...TR+ stem: -(h)awihd- escort, take s.o. with; consists of: -(h)awi, (h)a:$_V$- hold, include, carry, bring]
dęhs·he·ya̱·ha·hi·yá'k·dę' you will escort her across the road
[TR+ stem: -(h)ahahiya'kd(ę, ani)- escort s.o.; consists of: -(h)ah(a)$_N$- road -(i)ya'g$_V$- cut, break]
Eskimo see: C (O·to·we·ge·ho:nǫ')
esophagus see: throat
o·há'da' quill; plume; feather; voice; throat; larynx; esophagus
espouse see: marry
ę·wá·gen·ya:k I will be married
essence see: smell
o·ded·rę·na:', o·ded·rę·ná·i:' a smell
essential see: necessity
tgá:gǫ:t a compelling must
esteem see: respect
ga·gǫ́n·yǫhs·de:' respect
ethical see: righteous
god·rih·wag·wá·eh·sǫh she is fair, righteous
Europe see: E (Sgan·ya·da:di·go:wah, Ǫh·wę·ja·ga·yǫh·neh)
evade see: escape, run away
sha'nyá:gę' he escaped
ę·gę·na·dé'go' they (z) will flee, run away

evaporate
wahs·déhs·ta' it is evaporating; it evaporates
[stem: -(a)hsde(hsd)$_V$- evaporate, boil down]
a·wá:sdehs it evaporated, dried up, boiled dry
ę·wá:stehs it will evaporate
ohs·déhs·dǫh it has evaporated; it is all dried up
os·déhs·da̲h·ne:' it has gone down (that is, the water level)
os·de: it is empty, evaporated
[o+ stem: -(a)hsde:$_V$- evaporated, empty]
he·yó:sde: it has boiled down
even see: equal, flat
tsa'dé:yǫ: of equal number, amount
de·yo·dag·wę́h·dę:, de·wa·dag·wę́h·dę: it is flat
even (get even) see: cure
ahs·ké:ję't you cured me; you got even with me
evening see: A (oga:s'ah)
evening bird
ga·jí·dęht·ra:s evening bird
[ga+ stem: -jidęhtra:s- evening bird; consists of: -jidę'ęh$_N$- bird]
evening star
ga·jihs·dǫ·dá:ha' evening star; morning star; Venus
[ga+ stem: -jihsdǫda:ha'- Venus; consists of: -jihsd(anohgwa)$_N$- spot, spark -ǫda:(h)$_V$- put in, be attached]
o·jihs·da·nóhg·wa:' evening star; a star
[o+ stem: -jihsdanohgwa:'- star, evening star; consists of: -jihsdanohg(wa)$_N$- spot]
ever see: I (hwę:dǫh)
evergreen see: pine tree
o·nę́'da' evergreen; conifer
everyday use
o·hę'dron·yóh·ka:' everyday use
[stem: -(h)ę'dronyohka:'- everyday use; consists of: -(h)ędrǫnyǫ'$_V$- several leading items]
everything
o·i·hwag·wé:gǫh everything; the whole idea
[o+ stem: -(r)ih(wa)$_N$- word -gwegǫh$_V$- all]
everything see: all
og·wé:gǫh, gwé:gǫh, ag·wé:gǫh everything; all
everywhere
ha'de·ho·nǫh·wę·já:ge: they (m) are all over the earth
[ha'de+hon+ stem: -ǫhwęj(a)$_N$- earth, land -(a)ge:$_V$- many different things]
evident see: recognizable, visible
o·yę́:deht it is recognizable, plain to be seen, conspicuous
ó:gę't it is visible
evil
wa̲·hé:t·gęh evil (in mind); bad
[A+(N+) stem: -(hr)etgę$_V$- evil, bad, ugly]
ga̲·hé:t·gę' it is ugly
e·hé:t·gę' she is ugly, unruly
evil power
go·ná:t·gǫh they (f/m) are a force to be reckoned with; they (f/m) are ominous; they are bad medicine people
[P+ stem: -(a)tgǫ'$_V$- have evil power, bad medicine; be a witch, a warlock; be ominous]
ot·gǫhs·hǫ́:'ǫh things with evil power
[o+ stem: -(a)tgǫ'$_V$- have evil power, bad medicine; be a witch, a warlock; be ominous]

evil-minded

e'ni.gǫ.há.het.gę' she is evil-minded [A+ stem: -(')nigǫhahetgę'- evil-minded; consists of: -(')nigǫh(a)$_N$- mind -(hr)etgę$_V$- evil, bad, ugly]

g'a.ni.gǫ.há.het.gę' a bad-thinking mind

eviscerate

ęhs.yǫ.wa.dáh.go' you will gut s.t. [stem: -yǫwadahgw- eviscerate; consists of: -yǫw(a'da)$_N$- gut, intestine -(h)gw$_V$- remove]

exacting see: demanding

tgę.nǫ́h.dǫ.ha' I make the decisions; I am a strict person

exaggerate

hęhsǫ́:goht you will exaggerate go above and beyond [he'+... stem: -ǫgohd$_V$- surpass, exaggerate]

ha'sǫ́:goht you are going above and beyond

exaggerate see: overdo

e.sá'dra.hehs you are exaggerating

exalt see: praise s.o.

ęhs.he.ho.wá:naht you will praise her, uplift her spirits, flatter her

examine

ę.sat.ga.hí:yohs you will look closely at s.t., peer at s.t. [at+ stem: -gahiyohsd- examine closely; consists of: -gah(a)$_N$- eye -iyohsd$_V$- make nice, good]

a.gat.ga.hí.yohs.dǫh I am staring at it, examining it closely

ęh.sék.dǫn.yǫ' you will fully examine it [stem: -kdǫnyǫ- examine fully; consists of: -kdǫ(:)$_V$- taste, examine, look closely at s.t.]

dwak.dǫ́:nyǫ: let's examine it

examine see: try

a:ga.d'en.yę́:dę' I might try, attempt

example see: pattern

ęt.sa.d.en.yę́:dęhs you will copy, use as a model, pattern

excavate see: dig

ę.yǫ́'gwa:t it will dig

excellent see: worthy

od.rih.wa.ga:nǫ́:ni: a worthy idea; s.t. excellent

exceptional

a.ǫ́.gǫh.dǫh exceptional; above average; too much [stem: -ǫgohd$_V$- surpass]

excess see: extreme, surplus

he.yod.rah.héhs.dǫh it is extreme

he.yó.gǫh.so:t a surplus

exchange see: trade

dę.sá.da.dǫ' you will trade, exchange

excrement see: feces

o'da' feces; shit; excrement; manure

excruciating see: painful

o.nó.hǫk.de' it is painful

excuse me see: I (wa'gyęh)

execute see: kill

ęhs.rí:yo' you will kill s.t.

executive see: G (director, gohs.dihs.dǫh)

exercise see: strength (use one's strength)

ęh.sa.d'es.há:s.dǫh you will use your strength

exert see: struggle

ęh.sá.det.sa't you will struggle, squirm to get loose, revolt

exhale see: breathe

ǫ.dǫ́:nye's she is breathing

exhaust see: use up

a.wá:ts'a:' it is worn out, all gone, burnt up; it went down to nothing

exhausted

ęk.ni.gǫ.há.ga.he:' I will be mentally exhausted [stem: -(')nigǫhagahe(y)- be exhausted (mentally); consists of: -(')nigǫh(a)$_N$- mind -(ga)he:, (gę)he:, (i)he:$_V$- die, be weak, be exhausted]

exhausted (continued)
ak·ni·gǫ·ha·ga·hé:yǫh I am mentally exhausted
exhausted see: all gone, tired
haʼwá:tsʼaht it is all gone
a·gá·ǫ:tsęht they (f/m) were tired, sleepy
exhibit see: show
gǫ·yǫh·wa·dá:nih I am showing you s.t.
exhilarated see: happy
a·gat·sę·nǫ́:ni: I am glad, happy
exist
ę·yǫh·wę·já:de:k the earth will exist
[P+ stem: -ǫhwęj(a)$_N$- earth, land -deʼ$_V$- exist]
exist see: I (be)
exit see: come out, go out, leave
a·ga·ya·gę́h·dahk it came out (suddenly)
ęhs·yá:gęʼ you will go out
sgah·dę́:gyeʼs I am leaving again
exorbitant see: cost
ga·nǫ:ʼ it is expensive, dear, precious
expand see: inflate, swell up
ga·wa·ǫ:dá:hǫh it is inflated
a·wáh·dę·goh it swelled up
expect
kni·gǫ́:ha:ʼ I am expecting, watching
[stem: -(ʼ)nigǫha(:)$_V$- expect, watch]
tęʼ dek·ní·gǫ·ha: I am not expecting
sha·go·diʼní·gǫ·ha:ʼ they are protecting, watching over s.o.
ga·ęʼni·gǫ́·ha:ʼ they (f/m) are waiting for s.t.
kni·gǫ́·haʼk I was waiting
ęk·ní·gǫ·haʼk I will expect it, be watching out for s.t.
sni·gǫ́·haʼk watch out for yourself
expect see: wish
a:yá:węh I wish, hope
expeditious see: fast
ohs·nó:weʼ it is fast, quick

expend see: use up
a·wá:tsʼa:ʼ it is worn out, all gone, burnt up; it went down to nothing
expensive see: cost
ga·nǫ:ʼ it is expensive, dear, precious
experience see: feel
ni·wa·de·dróʼdę: an experience
expire see: die
hę·hé:yǫhs he is dying
explain
de·ga·ih·wá·teʼtaʼ dictionary (lit.: it explains)
[de+… stem: -(r)ihwateʼtaʼ- dictionary; consists of: -(r)ih(wa)$_N$- word -(a)teʼd$_V$- clarify, explain]
dęhs·ríh·wa·teʼt you will explain
dęg·ríh·wa·teʼt I will explain an idea
explode
de·wad·ra·né·ga·ǫ:s it is exploding
[de+…ad+ stem: -(wa)negaǫ, (wa)nega(:), (ra)negaǫ, (ra)nega(:)$_V$- explode, split]
exploit see: use
ęh·sehs you will use it
explorer see: pioneer
a·ta·di·hę́·dohs·ga:ʼ they (m) were pioneers
exponents
tsęh ni·gáʼshahs·deʼ exponents
[tsęh ni+ga+ stem: -sha(h)sdeʼ- exponents; consists of: -sha(h)sd$_V$- be strong]
expose see: naked, uncover
ga·jíʼgwaʼ it is naked
ęh·snahs·go·wé:ksih you will uncover the bed
expound see: explain, proclaim
dęhs·ríh·wa·teʼt you will explain
ęt·ri·ho·wá:naht you will proclaim, announce s.t.
expression see: word
ga·wę́·na·gǫ:ʼ in the words, voice; in the speech

expressway
de·wa·ta·há'drǫ' expressway; interchanges
[de+wa+at+ stem: -(h)aha'drǫ'- expressway, interchange; consists of: -(h)ah(a)$_N$- road -(a)dre'$_V$- be a certain distance apart]
extend see: go out, protrude, stretch
gyo·yá·gę'ǫh it comes out here; it is sticking out, protruding
he·yá·ǫ:t it protrudes
de·ho:dí:yǫ:t he is stretching it
extension see: postponement
ga·gę́·ihs·dǫh postponement
extensive see: big, long
go·wá:nęh, ga·gó·wa·nęh it is big
í:yǫ:s it is long
exterior see: outdoor
ahs·déh·gę·ha:' the outside type
external see: outdoor
ahs·deh·gę·ha:' outside type
extinct
o·ih·wah·dǫ́'ǫh it is extinct
[stem: -(r)ihwahdǫ'ǫh- be extinct; consists of: -(r)ih(wa)$_N$- word -(a)hdǫ(:)$_V$- lose, disappear]
dehs·gę́·ne:s it is extinct
[de'+s+A+ stem: -ines- extinct; consists of: -ine$_V$- go]
extinguish
wa'swáh·dǫh it is extinguished
[stem: -(a)hswahd, -(a)hstwahd$_V$- extinguish, dim]
sahs·waht put the light out
ęh·si'dǫhg·wáhs·twaht you will dim the lights
[stem: -idǫhg(wa)$_N$- flame -(a)hswahd, -(a)hstwahd$_V$- extinguish, dim]
gę·dǫ'gwahs·twáh·dǫh the flame is turned down
si·dǫ́hg·wahs·twaht lower the flame (on a kerosene lamp, etc.)

extinguish (continued)
se·jíhs·dahs·twaht dim the light
[stem: -jihsd(a)$_N$- light -(a)hswahd, -(a)hstwahd$_V$- extinguish, dim]
extra see: another, extreme, surplus
he·jó:ya' another thing
he·yod·rah·héhs·dǫh it is extreme
he·yó·gǫh·so:t it is a surplus
extraordinary see: exceptional
á·ǫ·gǫh·dǫh exceptional; above average; too much
extravagant
gog·yéh·sahs·dǫ: she is extravagant, wasteful
[P+ag+ stem: -yesahsdǫ:- extravagant, wasteful; consists of: -yes$_V$- be easy]
extreme
he·yod·rah·héhs·dǫh it is extreme
[he'+yo+ stem: -(')drahehsdǫh- extreme; consists of: -(')drahehsd$_V$- overdo, exaggerate]
extremity see: arm, leg, limb
snęt·sá'geh on your arm
sęh·sín'a·geh on your leg
og·wí:ya' a limb, twig, branch
exultation see: happiness
ot·sę́·nǫn·ya't a happy feeling; gratefulness; thankfulness; joy
eye
o·gá·ha' eye
[stem: -gah(a)$_N$- eye]
se·gá·ha'geh on your eyes
swa·gá·ha'geh on your (p) eyes
ge·gá·ha'geh on my eye
eyebrow
o·gahg·wá·o·sa' eyebrow
[stem: -gahgwaos(a)$_N$- eyebrow]
se·gahg·wá·o:s'a·geh on your eyebrow
eyebrow pencil
e·ga'gwa·o:s'a·géh ǫh·sóh·ta' an eyebrow pencil
[consists of: egahgwaohs'ageh on her eyebrow; ǫhsohta' colour pencil]

Cayuga pronunciation guide: /a/ father /e/ weigh /ę/ men (nasalized) /i/ police /o/ hole /ǫ/ home (nasalized) /u/ blue. Underlined vowels are voiceless or whispered. /'/ high pitch. /t/ too /d/ do /k/ king /g/ good (never soft g) /j/ judge or adze /s/ soon /sh/ less heat (never the sh in shirt) /sr/ shrine /sy/ sure /hw/ which (the sound made when you blow out a candle) /h/ hi /ts/ cats hide /'/ (the sound before the first vowel in 'uh-uh') /n/ noon /r/ round /w/ way /y/ yes.

eye glasses
ga·gá·hihs·da' eye glasses
[ga+ stem: -gahihsd(a)- eyeglasses consists of: -gah(a)$_N$- eye -(h)wihsd(a), (hr)ihsd(a)- metal]
eyelash
o·gá·heh·da' eyelash; the stem of a berry; the eye of the corn kernel
[stem: -gahehd(a)$_N$- eyelash, stem (of a berry), eye (of a corn kernel)]
se·gá·heh·do:t you have eyelashes
[A+ stem: -gahehd(a)$_N$- eyelash -od$_V$- attached object]
ge·ga·heh·dá'geh on my eyelashes
se·ga·heh·dá'geh on your eyelashes
swa·ga·heh·dá'geh on your (p) eyelashes
ad·wa·ge·gá·ho's I got an eyelash in my eye
[de+P+ stem: -gaho'sd- get an eyelash in one's eye; consists of: -gah(a)$_N$- eye -o'sd$_V$- cause to be submerged]
eyeliner
ǫt·ga·hah·sóh·ta' eyeliner
[ǫ+at+ stem: -gahahsohta'- eyeliner; consists of: -gah(a)$_N$- eye -(a)hsohd$_V$- colour]
eye patch
ǫt·ga·ho·wé:kta' eye patch
[ǫ+at+ stem: -gahowekta'- eye patch; consists of: -gah(a)$_N$- eye -(hr)oweg$_V$- cover]

F

fable see: tale
o'ga:' a parable; a tale; a story; a legend
fabric
o·ni·gá:hęhs·ra' material; cloth
[o+ stem: -niga:hęh(sra)$_N$- fabric]
fabricate see: make
gǫ́:nih I make, earn
fabrication see: lie
o·nó·w'ę·da' a lie
fabric softener
ga·ni·ga:hęhs·ra·ho'dęhs·ta' fabric softener
[ga+ stem: -niga:hęhsraho'dęhsta'- fabric softener; consists of: -niga:hęh(sra)$_N$- fabric -(ri)ho'dęhsd$_V$- work s.t., soften s.t.]
façade see: ahead
o·hę́:dǫ: ahead; in front; the front
face
o·gǫ́h·sa' face
[o+ stem: -gǫhs(a)$_N$- face]
ge·gǫ́h·s'a·geh on my face
se·gǫ́h·s'a·geh on your face
swa·gǫ́h·s'a·geh on your (p) faces
o·gǫ́h·sah·sę: it has a fat face
[o+ stem: -gǫhs(a)$_N$- face -(a)hsę:$_V$- fat]
face cloth
ǫt·gǫh·sǫ·há·i'ta' face cloth
[ǫ+at+ stem: -gǫhsohai'ta'- face cloth; consists of: -gǫhs(a)$_N$- face -ohae'd$_V$- cause to clean, wash]
facetious see: two-faced
sa·gǫh·sah·ní:yǫh you are two-faced
facility see: house
ga·nǫ́h·sa' a house
facsimilie see: fax
dehs·ga·yá·ǫ'da' a facsimilie
fact see: I (hne:')
fade
ę·wa·dah·só:go' it will lose its colour (for example, old paint)
[ad+ stem: -(a)hsogw- fade, lose colour; consists of: -(a)hsoh(gwa)$_N$- colour, paint, crayon -ogw$_V$- scatter]
o·dáh·sog·węh it is faded

fail see: unable
ęh·sáːnǫːʼ you will fail
[P+ stem: -nǫːʼ$_{V}$- be unable]
faint
ǫk·ni·gǫ·háh·dǫʼ I fainted
[P+ stem: -(ʼ)nigǫhahdǫ- faint; consists of: -(ʼ)nigǫh(a)$_{N}$- mind -(a)hdǫ(ː)$_{V}$- lose, disappear]
ęh·saʼni·gǫ́·hah·dǫʼ you will faint (lit.: you will lose your mind)
fair
dę·hę·nat·gę́ːnyǫhs a fair (lit. they (m) compete there)
[de+hęn+at+ stem: -gęnyǫhs- fair; consists of: -gęni, gęny$_{V}$- compete]
fair see: light-coloured, righteous
haʼgęː he is light-skinned
god·rih·wag·wá·eh·sǫh she is fair, righteous
fairly
[-hah diminutive suffix; can mean 'fairly']
fair-haired
go·nǫ́h·gęːt she is fair haired, she has light hair
[P+ stem: -nǫhgęd- fair haired; consists of: -nǫh(a), nah(a)$_{N}$- scalp -(ʼ)gęd$_{V}$- light-coloured, white]
ho·nǫ́h·gęːt he is fair haired
fairgrounds
deg·yǫt·gęn·yáʼtaʼgeh fairgrounds
[de+g+yǫ+at+ stem: -gęnyaʼtaʼgeh- fairgrounds; consists of: -gęnyaʼd- cause to compete]
fairy tale see: tale
oʼgaːʼ a parable; a tale; a story; a legend
faith see: belief, religion
tsęh hǫːwéh gyǫg·wéh·dah·gǫh our belief; religion
ga·ih·wi·yóhs·dęhs·raʼ religion; the Christian faith

faithful see: reliable
ho·yaʼda·dáːniː he is reliable, dependable
faithkeeper see: C (god·ri·hǫːt)
fake see: make-believe
aːwetʼahs·hǫ́ːʼǫh make-believe; pretend
fall
e·dáːgraʼs she is forever falling (for example, an old person)
[stem: -(i)dagraʼ$_{V}$- fall]
gye·dáːgraʼs she falls there (that is, always at the same spot)
ę·yé·dag·raʼ she will fall down
a·gi·dag·ráʼǫh I have fallen
da·wáʼsęʼ it dropped, reduced
[d/g+...(a)ʼs/N+ stem: -(aʼs)ęʼ$_{V}$- fall, drop, reduce]
dwa·sęʼs it falls; it's a dropper
gyo·sę́ʼǫh it has fallen off s.t.
he·wáʼsęʼs it falls in (all the time)
[heʼ+...(a)ʼs/N+ stem: -(aʼs)ęʼ$_{V}$- fall, drop, reduce, fall in]
hę·wáʼsęʼ it will fall in
he·yóʼsęʼǫh it has fallen in
he·yoh·ne·gę́ʼǫh falling water
[heʼ/g+yo+ stem: -(h)neg(a)$_{N}$- water, liquid -(aʼs)ęʼ$_{V}$- fall, drop, reduce]
gyǫh·né·gʼęǫh falling water
go·géʼęs her hair is falling out
[P+ stem: -geʼ(aː), geh(a)$_{N}$- hair -(aʼs)ęʼ$_{V}$- fall, drop, reduce]
a·wáh·yęʼ fruit fell down
[stem: -(a)hy(a)$_{N}$- fruit, berry -ę$_{V}$- lie on the ground]
fall see: A (gę·nę·na·geh·neh), trip s.o.
de·sah·sig·yáʼksgǫː you are always stumbling, tripping, stubbing your toe; you are a klutz
fall short see: fail
ęh·sáːnǫːʼ you will fail
false see: bad
tę́ʼ det·gaːyé·iʼ it is bad, false, wrong

falsehood see: lie
o·nó·w'ę·da' a lie
false teeth
ti·gahs·ro:ní' o·nó'ja' false teeth [consists of: tigahsro:ni' s.t.that is artificially made; ono'ja' teeth]
ohsg·yę́'dan·hǫ:t false teeth (lit.: a mouth full of bones)
[o+ stem: -(h)sgyę'danhǫd- false teeth; consists of: -(h)sgyę'd(a:)$_N$- bone -nhǫd(a:,ę)$_V$- put in]
o·no'jat·gí:s'ah false teeth
[o+ stem: -no'jatgi:s'ah- false teeth; consists of: -no'j(a)$_N$- tooth -tgi$_V$- dirty, ugly]
ti·ga·nǫ·jǫ́:ni: false teeth
[ti+ga+ stem: -no'jǫni:- false teeth; consists of: -no'j(a)$_N$- tooth -ǫni, ǫny$_V$- make, artificial]
falter see: stagger, trip
hehs·hohs·hę·dá'ǫh tsǫ: he is staggering
de·sah·sig·yá'ksgǫ: you are always stumbling, tripping, stubbing your toe; you are a klutz
family
swah·wa:jí:ya' your (p) families
[stem: -(h)wajiy(a)$_N$- family]
ga̲h·wa·ji·yá:de' a matrilineal family
[ga+ stem: -(h)wajiy(a)$_N$- family -de'$_V$- exist]
ga̲h·wa·ji·yá·ge̲·hǫ' families
[ga+ stem: -(h)wajiy(a)$_N$- family -gehǫ'$_V$- lie about]
ga̲h·wa·ji·yó·wa·nęh large family
[ga+ stem: -(h)wajiy(a)$_N$- family -owanęh$_V$- be big]
ga̲h·wa·ji·ya:do:gę́: ji·dę·'ęs·hǫ:'ǫ́h ga·'ga:' the crow family, species
[consists of: ga̲hwajiya:do:gę: a certain family, dynasty; jidę'shǫ:'ǫh birds; ga'ga:' crow]
family see: dynasty
ga̲h·wa·ji·ya:dó:gę: a certain family, dynasty
famine
o·dǫ́hs·we'dęht famine; hunger
[o+ad+ stem: -ǫhswe'dęhd- famine; consists of: -ǫhswe'd(ę,ani)$_V$- be hungry, short of breath]
a'a·go·dǫhs·we'dę́'ge: there was a big famine
famous see: important
hah·sę·no·wá:nęh he is an important person; he is famous, prominent (lit.: he has made a name for himself)
fang see: tooth
o·nó'ja' teeth
fantasy see: make-believe
a:wet'ahs·hǫ́:'ǫh make-believe; pretend
far see: distance
ni·yó:we' how far (distance)
farmer
ha·hę·da·ge·hó:nǫ' farmer
[A+ stem: -(h)ędagehonǫ'- farmer; consists of: -(h)ęd(a)$_N$- field]
fart
ǫ·ní'den·yǫhs she farts
[ę+ stem: -ni'deni, ni'deny$_V$- fart]
a'ǫ·n'i·dé:ni' she farted
ę·yǫ·n'i·dé:ni' she will fart
a'wę·n'i·dé:ni' it farted
a·gę·n'i·dé:nyǫ: I have farted
a·ho·n'i·do·dá·eh·sę' he farted
[P+ stem: -(')nidodaehsę- fart; consists of: -(i)'d(a)$_N$- feces, -odaihsę$_V$- remove for oneself]
fast
ohs·nó:we' it is fast, quick
[A/P+(N+) stem: -(h)snowe'$_V$- fast]
ohs·no:wé:'ah it is fairly fast; to arrive a little bit early
gy'a·dahs·nó:we' I am fast, quick
[A+ stem: -ya'd(a)$_N$- body -(h)snowe'$_V$- fast]

fast see: diet
a·ga·ǫ:dehsg·yǫ·wá:ta'ť they (f/m) dieted, lost weight
fasten see: attach
ah·só·ha·ę:' you have attached it
fastener see: pin
ga·jí·ho·ha:', o·jí·ho·ha:' straight pin; pin; brooch; safety pin
fat
oh·sę: it is fat
[P+(N+) stem: -(a)hsę:$_V$- fat]
ho·hsę: he is fat
a·gáh·sę: I am fat
goh·sę: she is fat
o'dǫ́:dra' it is fat; gristle; rind
[o+ stem: -(')dǫdr(a)$_N$- fat, gristle, rind]
o'dróhs·ra' fat; pig rinds
[o+ stem: -(')drohsr(a)$_N$- fat, rind]
father see: C
ha'nih my father
father-in-law see: C
hak·né:nhǫ:s my father-in-law
fatigue see: tired
a·gá·ǫ:t·sęht they (f/m) were tired, sleepy
fatten
ęh·sah·sęt·rǫ́:ni' it will make you fat
[TR+ stem: -(h)sętrǫni- fatten; consists of: -(h)sętr(a)$_N$- fat -ǫni, ǫny$_V$- make]
fatty see: oily
oh·ná·i:' it is oily, greasy
fault
de·yot·wę·ja·kah·sǫ́:ge: a fault (in the earth)
[de+yo+at+ stem: -(h)węjakahsǫge:- fault; consists of: -(ǫh)węj(a)$_N$- earth -kahsǫ$_V$- share, divide several items -ge:- big]
o·íh·wa' a message; it matters; it is its fault
[o+ stem: -(r)ih(wa)$_N$- word]
sa·íh·wa' your fault

fault (continued)
sa·ih·wat·sę́n·yahs·gǫ: you find faults
[P+ stem: -(r)ihwahtsęnyahsgǫ:- find fault; consists of: -(r)ih(wa)$_N$- word -tsęi, tsęny$_V$- find -sgǫ:- easily]
favored see: lucky
go·dá·ǫ: she is lucky, fortunate
fawn
ohs·twa:s'áh de·wá·hǫh·de:s fawn
[consists of: ohstwa:s'ah young animal; dewahǫhde:s deer]
fax
dehs·ga·yá·ǫ'da' a facsimilie
[de+s+ga+ stem: -yaǫda:- be similar; be a fax, an imitation; consists of: -y(a)$_N$- other, different -ǫda:(h)$_V$- put in, attached]
FBI see: G (de·ha·di·nę·hę·da:s ho·nad·rih·wah·sęh·dǫh oh·wę·ja·ę:dǫ:nyǫ')
fear see: frightened, frightening, scared
a·sét·sah·ni'k you are afraid
ǫ·gáhd·rǫ'k it frightened me; I got frightened
fearful see: frightened, frightening
a·sét·sah·ni'k you are afraid
fearless see: masculine
ha·jí:nah he is masculine, brave; his genitals
feasible see: maybe
ę·wa:dǫ́' gis·hęh maybe; a possibility
feast
ęh·sa·de·kǫ́·ni·ge: you will feast
[ade+ stem: -kǫnige:- feast; consists of: -k(wa)$_N$- food -ǫni, ǫny$_V$- make -ge:- big]
feast see: mealtime
ni·jǫ·de·kǫ́:nih the time to eat; mealtime
feather
ohs·dó'dr'a·geh on its feathers
[stem: -(h)sto'dr(a)$_N$- feather]

feather (continued)
gahs·do'dro·wá:nęh a large feather [ga+ stem: -(h)sto'dr(a)$_N$- feather -owanęh$_V$- be big]

feather see: tail, throat
o'yóhg·wa' skirt; tail; feather
o·há'da' quill; plume; feather; voice; throat; larynx; esophagus

February see: A (Gan·rah·dah·gah)

feces
o'da' feces; shit; excrement; manure [o+ stem: -(ni)'d(a)$_N$- feces]

feces see: undergarment
de·yó·da·gę:t dirty undergarments; soil; fecal matter

fed up see: annoyed
ǫ'k·nǫ's I am sick of it, bored, fed up; I got sick of it

federal see: G (ha·di·go·wahs·hǫ')

federation see: G (De·ga·na·da·węn·ye'ta'geh)

feeble see: slow, weak
sad·ri·hó:wi: you are a klutz; you are slow-moving; you are feeble, clumsy
ag·ya'da·gę·hé:yǫ: I am physically weak, slow

feed
ęk·nǫ:t I will give it s.t.to eat [TR+(N+) stem: -nǫd$_V$- feed]
ęhs·nǫ:t you will feed
ahs·ha·gǫh·yá:nǫ:t he gave her fruit [TR+ stem: -(a)hy(a)$_N$- fruit, berry -nǫd$_V$- feed]
ę·gék·wa·nǫ:t I will feed it [TR+ stem: -k(wa)$_N$- food -nǫd$_V$- feed]
sek·wá:nǫ:t feed it
ęg·wa·dę·ná'tra·nǫ:t we will give you food [TR+adę+ stem: -na'tr(a)$_N$- food, lunch -nǫd$_V$- feed]

feed (continued)
shǫg·wa·dę·na'trá·ę:ni: the food he has given us [TR+adę+ stem: -na'traęni- feed; consists of: -na'tr(a)$_N$- food, lunch -ęni$_V$- lay down for s.o.'s benefit]

feel
ni·wa·ded·ró'dę: an experience [ni+wa+(a)de+ stem: -(')dro'dę:- feel, experience; consists of: -(')dr(a)$_N$- case, quiver -o'dę:$_V$- type of]
shęh ni·wa·ga·dé'dr'o·dę: how I feel about s.t., s.o.

feel see: caress, grope, think, touch
ę·hes·y'a·dahd·rǫ́:gǫ' you will caress him
hęhs·yáh·nǫ:' you will grope, touch, pick at s.t.
sgę:nǫ́: se·nǫ́h·dǫn·yǫh (you are) safe; you are feeling well; you are at peace with yourself
ha'ga:ké:ye:' I touched them

feel bad
ga·dé·hęhs I am embarrassed, ashamed [stem: -(h)ę(h,')$_V$- feel bad]
a·há·dę·hęh he felt shame
ęh·sá·dę·hęh you will become embarrassed, ashamed
ho·dé·hę'ǫh he is embarrassed right now

feel good see: enjoyable, fun
a·ǫ'wé:sęh(t), a·ǫ'wé:sah(t) it is enjoyable; a good feeling
ga·ǫ·wéhs·hahs she is pleased; a good feeling

feign see: make-believe, pretend
a:wet'ahs·hǫ́:'ǫh make-believe; pretend
a:we:t'áh tsǫ́: dę·sá't·sǫhs pretend to sneeze

feline see: cat
da·gu:s cat

fell see: cut, hit, knock down
a·hę·na·tǫ́:gyaʼk they (m) cut the bush down
ęhs·yaʼg·yé:nęht you can knock it down
da̲·hǫ·wag·yę·da̲hk·wá·hag·waht s.o. knocked him out of his chair

felt
ohs·dí:st·rat·giʼ felt
[o+ stem: -(h)sdi:stratgiʼ- felt; consists of: -hsdi:str(a)$_N$- trade cloth -tgi$_V$- dirty, ugly]

female
je·yáʼda:t one person (female)
[s/j+e+ stem: -yaʼdad- one person; consists of: -yaʼd(a)$_N$- body -d$_V$- stand]

female see: genitals, woman
oʼn·héhg·yęʼ it is a female animal; the genitals (of a female animal)
a·gǫ́:gweh girl; woman; the female gender

fence
a·dę́·hęʼ fence
[a+ stem: -(a)dęʼh(ę)$_N$- fence]
a·dę́ʼhęʼgeh on the fence
a·dęʼhę́:kʼah by the fence
wa·dę́·hę·deʼ fence
[w+ stem: -(a)dęʼh(ę)$_N$- fence -deʼ$_V$- exist]
de·waʼdę·hǫ́·dag·yeʼ wood fence; rail and stump fence
[de+w+ stem: -(a)dęʼh(ę)$_N$- fence -ǫdagyeʼ$_V$- continue on]
de·ga·nehs·dá:dǫʼ board fence
[de+ga+ stem: -nehsd(a:)$_N$- floor, board -dǫʼ$_V$- several standing objects]

ferment
ęh·sat·ne·gǫ́:niʼ you will ferment s.t.
[at+ stem: -(h)negǫni- ferment, brew; consists of: -(h)neg(a)$_N$- water, liquid -ǫni, ǫny$_V$- make]

fern
wa·dáʼkę·dahs ladies' fern
[wa+ stem: -(a)daʼkędahs- ladies' fern; consists of: -(ʼ)k(a:)$_N$- skirt, slip -ędahsd$_V$- cause s.t. to lie on the ground]

ferret
ga·yaʼda·dáhg·wahs ferret
[ga+ stem: -yaʼdadahgwahs- ferret; consists of: -yaʼd(a)$_N$- body -(h)gw$_V$- remove]

fertile see: child-bearing, mature
ǫ·dé:dǫ̲·haʼ she is child-bearing; she is giving birth right now
ot·sih·sʼǫ̲hǫ́:gyeʼ it is getting mature

festivity see: celebration
o·dǫt·ga·déhs·raʼ celebration

fetish
ot·gǫt·ras·hǫ́:ʼǫh object used for witchcraft
[o+ stem: -(a)tgǫʼtraʼsǫ:ʼǫh- witchcraft; consists of: -gǫʼtr(a)$_N$- weight, fetish]

fever
ǫ·gíʼdǫhg·wa: I got a fever
[P+ stem: -(i)dǫhgwa(ʼ,h)$_V$- fever]
ak·dǫhg·wá:hǫh I have a fever
o·dǫ́hg·wa: fever

few
ni·yǫ́:hah a few; a little bit
[ni+yo+ stem: -ǫ:hah- few, little; consists of: -ǫ$_V$- number (of things) -hah- a little]
de̲·yo·dʼed·re̲h·da·gáʼdeʼ not many cars
[deʼ+yo+ade+ stem: -(ʼ)drehd(a)$_N$- car, vehicle -gaʼdeʼ$_V$- many, few]
deʼo·da̲h·yǫ́:ni: not much fruit on the trees
[deʼ+ not o+ad+ stem: -(a)hy(a)$_N$- fruit, berry -ǫni, ǫny$_V$- make; be little, few]

fidgety
sat·naʼt·sa·gę́·nyeʼ you are fidgety
[P+at+ stem: -(h)naʼtsagęnyeʼ- fidgety; consists of: -(h)naʼts(a)$_N$- buttock -gęni, gęny$_V$- compete]

Cayuga pronunciation guide: /a/ father /e/ weigh /ę/ men (nasalized) /i/ police /o/ hole /ǫ/ home (nasalized) /u/ blue. Underlined vowels are voiceless or whispered. /ˊ/ high pitch. /t/ too /d/ do /k/ king /g/ good (never soft g) /j/ judge or a<u>dz</u>e /s/ soon /sh/ le<u>ss h</u>eat (never the sh in shirt) /sr/ <u>shr</u>ine /sy/ <u>s</u>ure /hw/ <u>wh</u>ich (the sound made when you blow out a candle) /h/ hi /ts/ ca<u>ts h</u>ide /ʼ/ (the sound before the first vowel in 'uh-uh') /n/ noon /r/ round /w/ way /y/ yes.

field
ga̱·hę́·da·gǫ: in the field; meadow
[ga+ stem: -(h)ęd(a)$_N$- field]
ga̱·hę·dá:ʼkʼah by the field
ga̱·hęh·dí:yo: good ground
[ga+ stem: -(h)ęd(a)$_N$- field -iyo:$_V$- be nice, good]
ohn·yǫhsg·wa·éʼ ga·yę́:twęh cucumber field
[consists of: ohnyǫhsgwaeʼ cucumber; gayę:twęh it is planted]
jih·sǫ:dáhk ga·yę́:twęh strawberry field
[consists of: jihsǫ:dahk strawberry; gayę:twęh it is planted]
oh·ya·ka·hǫ́ʼ ga·yę́:twęh tomato field
[consists of: ohyaka̱hǫʼ tomatoes; gayę:twęh it is planted]
ga̱·hǫ·na·dá·yęt·węh potato field
[stem: -(h)ǫnaʼd(a)$_N$- potato -yętw, yęto$_V$- plant]
ga̱hs·tǫd·ra·yę́:twęh hay field
[stem: -(h)stǫdr(a)$_N$- straw, hay -yętw, yęto$_V$- plant]
ga·na·ja·yę́:twęh wheat field, oat field
[stem: -na(ʼ)ja(da)$_N$- wheat, grain -yętw, yęto$_V$- plant]
ga·yęʼgwa·yę́:twęh tobacco field
[stem: -yęʼg(wa)$_N$- tobacco, smoke, cigarettes -yętw, yęto$_V$- plant]
field see: meadow, pasture
ga̱·hę́·da·ęʼ meadow; pasture; field
ga·di:ʼtse:nę́ʼ ha·diʼdrǫ·dáhk·waʼ pasture
fifteen see: B (hwihs sga·eʼ)
fifty see: B (hwihs ni·wahs·hę:)
fight
wad·rí:yo: war; fight
[w+ad+ stem: -(r)iyo, nyo$_V$- kill someting]

fight (continued)
ę·gas·he·yaʼdri·yóh·dęʼ you will make them fight
[TR+ad+ stem: -(r)iyohdę- make s.o. fight; consists of: -(r)iyo, nyo$_V$- kill someting]
sa·ǫh·wę·jáhs·gęn·hęh you are fighting over the land right now
[stem: consists of: -ǫhwęj(a)$_N$- earth, land -(h)sgenh$_V$- argue for, advocate]
fight see: wrestle
ęh·sa·dag·yé:na:ʼ you will wrestle
figure see: number, trunk
ohs·hé:daʼ number
o·híʼyaʼ the body's trunk, form
filament see: line, thread, wire
oh·sí:yǫ:t attached cord; string; umbilical cord
oh·sí:yaʼ thread; string; cord
ga̱h·sǫ́·wa̱h·daʼ nails; wire; needle
file see: grate, paper
ęh·sé:ge:t you will grate, scrape, file
ga̱h·yá·dǫhs·raʼ paper
fill
ga·nǫ́n·heʼs it fills up all the time
[stem: -nǫnhe$_V$- fill]
a·gá·nǫn·heʼ it filled up
ę·gá·nǫn·heʼ it will fill up
ęhs·nǫ́:nheht, ęh·snę́:nheht you will fill in
[stem: -nǫnhehd, nęnhehd- fill s.t.up; consists of: -nǫnhe$_V$- fill]
á:knǫn·heht I would fill it up
filling
oh·daht it is filling
[o+ stem: -(a)hdahd- filling; consists of: -(a)hdaʼ$_V$- get full of food]
film see: movie
ga·yáʼtaʼ movies; television

filter
dę·sǫ́:goht you will penetrate
[de+...(N+) stem: -ǫgohd$_{V}$- surpass, filter, strain, penetrate]
deh·sǫ́:goht filter it; strain it
deyǫ́:goht, deyáǫgoht to penetrate (lit.: it has penetrated)
dęh·sne:gǫ́:goht you will filter, strain liquid
[de+...(at+) stem: -(h)negǫgohd- filter, strain liquid; consists of: -(h)neg(a)$_{N}$- water, liquid -ǫgohd$_{V}$- surpass]
de·yot·ne·gǫ́·go̱h·dǫh strained water
de·gah·ne·gǫ́·go̱h·dǫh water that is being strained
ęh·snǫ·wá·ęh·dahk you will filter the water
[stem: -(h)nawaędahgw- filter water; consists of: -(h)naw(a)$_{N}$- water, running -ędahgw$_{V}$- raise from the ground]
filthy
de·wá·ge·jǫ:t I am filthy
[de+P+ stem: -(i)jǫd$_{V}$- be filthy]
fin
o·wá:yaʼ fin of a fish; wings
[o+ stem: -way(a)$_{N}$- fin, wing]
final see: last
hes·gá:gǫ:t the last
finally see: I (waʼhehge:haʼ)
find
gets·hę́:nyeʼs, gets·hę́:nyǫhs I am a finder of things
[(N+) stem: -tsęi, tsęny$_{V}$- find]
a:yet·sę́i:ʼ she might find it
a·gét·sęn·yǫ: I have found it
haʼǫ·dag·yaʼdat·sę́·i:ʼ she found her over there
[TR+ stem: -yaʼdatsęi- find s.o.; consists of: -yaʼd(a)$_{N}$- body -tsęi, tsęny$_{V}$- find]

fine see: healthy, think
a·ga·da·gá·i:deʼ I am well, fine, healthy
sgę:nǫ́: ge·nǫ́h·dǫn·yǫh I am fine, healthy
finest see: best, greatest
gwáhs gyo·yá:nreʼ the best
néʼ gya·ǫ·hę́:ʼęh the greatest
finger
oʼnyaʼ fingers
[o+ stem: -(ʼ)ny(ahsra)$_{N}$- finger, hand]
oʼnyahs·rǫ́:dǫʼ it has fingers
[o+ consists of: -(ʼ)ny(ahsra)$_{N}$- finger, hand -ǫdǫʼ$_{V}$- several attached objects]
fingernail
o·jí·ʼeh·daʼ, o·jí·ʼoh·daʼ fingernails; toenails; animal nails; claws
[o+ stem: -jiʼohd(a), jiʼehd(a)$_{N}$- fingernail, toenail, claw, nail]
ge·jiʼoh·dáʼgeh on my nail
swa·jiʼoh·dáʼgeh on your (p) nails
ga·jiʼoh·dáʼgeh on its claws, nails
finish
a·wah·yę́:daʼ the berry season is over
[stem: -(a)hy(a)$_{N}$- fruit, berry -ędaʼ$_{V}$- finish]
a·ga·wę·hę́:daʼ flowers that have finished blooming
[stem: -(a)węh(ę)$_{N}$- flower -ędaʼ$_{V}$- finish]
a·ga·ta·háh·sa:ʼ I finished a road
[stem: -(h)ah(a)$_{N}$- road -(i)hsʼ$_{V}$- finish]
dwa·tę́·di̱hsʼahs we are finishing the field
[stem: -(h)ęd(a)$_{N}$- field -(i)hsʼ$_{V}$- finish]
ed·wa·tę·díhsʼa:ʼ we all (incl.) finished the field (said after thrashing it)
ǫg·wa·tę·díhsʼǫh we finished the field
a·ga·ha·hók·dęʼ I finished one row
[stem: -(h)ah(a)$_{N}$- road -oʼkd(ę,ani)$_{V}$- finish s.t.]
hę·sóʼkdęʼ you will finish s.t.

Cayuga pronunciation guide: /a/ father /e/ weigh /ę/ men (nasalized) /i/ police /o/ hole /ǫ/ home (nasalized) /u/ blue. Underlined vowels are voiceless or whispered. /ʹ/ high pitch. /t/ too /d/ do /k/ king /g/ good (never soft g) /j/ judge or adze /s/ soon /sh/ less heat (never the sh in shirt) /sr/ shrine /sy/ sure /hw/ which (the sound made when you blow out a candle) /h/ hi /ts/ cats hide /ʼ/ (the sound before the first vowel in 'uh-uh') /n/ noon /r/ round /w/ way /y/ yes.

finish (continued)
  a·wa·da̲h·yóʼkdęʼ the berries have run out; they are no more
  [ad+ stem: -(a)hy(a)$_{N}$- fruit, berry -oʼkd(ę,ani)$_{V}$- finish s.t.]
  haʼga·ha·hók·dęʼ I finished a row
  [stem: -(h)ah(a)$_{N}$- road -oʼkd(ę,ani)$_{V}$- finish s.t.]
finish see: accomplish, complete, stop
  ęhs·rih·wag·wę́:niʼ you will accomplish
  ha·wa·yę·nę́:daʼs he finishes
  a·tá:dahs he stopped it, prevented it
fir
  ots·góʼdaʼ balsam fir
  [o+ stem: -tsgoʼd$_{N}$- balsam fir]
fir see: pine
  o·nę́ʼdaʼ evergreen; conifer
fire
  o·dé:kaʼ fire; it is burning
  [o+ stem: -(a)dekaʼ- fire; consists of: -(a)deg$_{V}$- burn up]
  oʼga·hoʼjáde·kaʼ a grass fire is burning
  [o+ stem: -gahoʼj(a)$_{N}$- grass -(a)deg$_{V}$- burn up]
  sga·ję́·ha:t one fire
  [s+ga+ stem: -jęh(a)$_{N}$- fire -d$_{V}$- stand]
  sa·de·ję·hí·yohs make a good fire
  [ade+ stem: -jęhiyohsd- make a good fire; consists of: -jęh(a)$_{N}$- fire -iyohsd$_{V}$- make nice, good]
  ę·sa·de·ję·hę·né:dahk you will prepare your fire
  [ade+ stem: -jęhęnedahgw- prepare a fire; consists of: -jęh(a)$_{N}$- fire -nedahgw$_{V}$- kindle]
  ę·ga·de·ję·hǫ́:niʼ I will start a fire (old word)
  [ade+ stem: -jęhǫni- start a fire; consists of: -jęh(a)$_{N}$- fire -ǫni, ǫny$_{V}$- make]
  sa·de·ję·hǫ́:nih make a fire

fire (continued)
  de·se·ji̲hs·dá·węn·ye: stoke the fire
  [stem: -jihsdawęnye(:)- stir, poke a fire; consists of: -jihsd(a)$_{N}$- light -(a)węnye(:)$_{V}$- stir, mix]
  sgá:t sha·yę́·dǫ·toʼ he put one more piece of wood on the fire
  [(s+)... stem: -yędǫto- stoke a fire; consists of: -yęd(a)$_{N}$- wood -ǫtw$_{V}$- be unattached]
fire see: burn, release
  ę·ga:dé:gaʼt I will start a fire
  sa·ga·e·sáht·gaʼ they released you (s), fired you, let you go
fire arms see: rifle
  ga̲·hóʼde:s rifle
fire hydrant see: fountain
  tgah·né·go·taʼ fire hydrant; fountain
firefly
  jihs·dę: firefly
  [stem: -jihsdę:- firefly; consists of: -jihsd(a)$_{N}$- light -ę$_{V}$- lie on the ground]
firehall
  hę·nahs·wah·táʼgeh firehall
  [A+ stem: -(a)hswahtaʼgeh- firehall; consists of: -(a)hswahd, -(a)hstwahd$_{V}$- extinguish, dim]
firemen
  hę·náʼswa̲h·taʼ they (m) are firemen
  [A+ stem: -(a)hswahtaʼ- firemen; consists of: -(a)hswahd, -(a)hstwahd $_{V}$- extinguish, dim]
firewood see: wood
  o·yę́:daʼ wood; firewood
firm see: hard
  oh·ní:yǫh it is hard
first see: begin, lead, B (da·wa:gyę:t gyog·yęh·dǫh), I (hya:ʼ)
  da·wá:gyę:t the first one; the beginner
  ęhs·rę:t you will be the lead
First Nations see: C (Aboriginal, Ǫg·we·hǫ:weh)

fish
o·jǫ́ˀdaˀ fish
[o+ stem: -(i)jǫˀd(a)$_N$- fish]
o·jǫˀdo·wá:nęh big fish
[o+ stem: -(i)jǫˀd(a)$_N$- fish -owanęh$_V$- be big]
ga·dáhn·yoˀs I fish continually
[ad+ stem: -(a)hnyo- fish; consists of: -(a)hny(a)$_N$- hook -o(:)$_V$- submerge]
hę·ná·dahn·yoh they (m) are fishing over there
a·hę·na·dáhn·yo:ˀ they (m) fished
hę·gá·dahn·yo:ˀ I will fish over there
ga·dáhn·yǫh·neˀs I fish continuously
ag·ya·dahn·yóh·neˀ we two (incl.) did go fishing
Fish and Wildlife see: G (ga·na·dad·wę:ni:yoˀ ga·di:nyo:ˀ)
fish hook
gę·jǫˀda·yę́:nahs fish hook
[ga+ stem: -(i)jǫˀdayęnahs- fish hook; consists of: -(i)jǫˀd(a)$_N$- fish -yena(w), yenaǫ, yena(:)$_V$- catch, receive, accept]
e·ji·nǫ·wa·heˀda·ni·yǫ́·dahk·waˀ fish hook
[stem: -jinǫwahedaniyǫdahkwaˀ- fish hook; consists of: -jiˀnǫwaheˀd(a)- fishworm -niyǫdahkwaˀ$_V$- s.t. that hangs]
fish tail
ga·yóh·go:t fish tail
[ga+ stem: -(ˀ)yohg(wa)$_N$- tail, skirt -d$_V$- stand]
fisherman
ha·dáhn·yoˀ he is a fisherman
[ad+ stem: -(a)hnyo- fish; consists of: -(a)hny(a)$_N$- hook -o(:)$_V$- submerge]
fishworm
o·jiˀnǫ·wá·heˀdaˀ fishworm
[o+ stem: -jiˀnǫwaheˀdaˀ- fishworm; consists of: -jiˀnǫw(a), jiˀnǫh$_N$- insect, bug -(h)e:ˀ$_V$- sitting up on top of s.t.]
fist
se·gǫ́·hek·taˀ what you use to hit with
[stem: -gǫh(a)$_N$- fist -(ˀ)ekd$_V$- use for hitting]
fist see: hand
oh·sóh·daˀ hand; paw
fit see: healthy
a·ga·da·gá·i:deˀ I am well, fine, healthy
fitting see: right
tga:yéi: it is right, correct
five see: B (hwihs)
fix
ęh·sehs·rǫ́:niˀ you will create, make s.t.
[(N+) stem: -hsr$_N$- noun, -(h)srǫni$_V$- fix, repair]
ǫt·ge·hahs·rǫ́:niˀ she fixes her own hair
[at+ stem: -geˀ(a:), geh(a)$_N$- hair -(h)srǫni$_V$- fix, repair]
ǫ·de·kahs·rǫ́:nih she is fixing skirts
[ade+ stem: -(ˀ)k(a:)$_N$- skirt, slip -(h)srǫni$_V$- fix, repair]
sa·sęh·nihs·gahs·rǫ́:nih fix the wheel
[stem: -ęˀnihsg(a)$_N$- wheel -(h)srǫni$_V$- fix, repair]
fix s.o. (that is, get even) see: cure
a·hé:jęˀt I fixed (lit. cured) him; I got even with him
flag
ga·yęhs·ro:t flag
[ga+ stem: -yęhsrod- flag; consists of: -yęhsr(a)$_N$- blanket -od$_V$- stand]
flame
o·dǫ́hg·waˀ flame
[o+ stem: -idǫhg(wa)$_N$- flame]
o·dǫ́h·go:t flame
[o+ stem: -idǫhg(wa)$_N$- flame -od$_V$- stand]
de·wa·de·jíhs·dog·wahs a burst of flames
[de+w+ade+ stem: -jihsd(a)$_N$- light -ogw$_V$- scatter]
flame see: fire
o·dé:kaˀ fire; it is burning

Cayuga pronunciation guide: /a/ father /e/ weigh /ę/ men (nasalized) /i/ police /o/ hole /ǫ/ home (nasalized) /u/ blue. Underlined vowels are voiceless or whispered. /ˊ/ high pitch. /t/ too /d/ do /k/ king /g/ good (never soft g) /j/ judge or adze /s/ soon /sh/ less heat (never the sh in shirt) /sr/ shrine /sy/ sure /hw/ which (the sound made when you blow out a candle) /h/ hi /ts/ cats hide /ˀ/ (the sound before the first vowel in 'uh-uh') /n/ noon /r/ round /w/ way /y/ yes.

flash
ad·wa·tahs·ró:go' a flash of light
[de+...w+at+ stem: -(h)ahsr(a)$_N$- flash -ogw$_V$- scatter]
a·wát·gę'ę:k a flash; a glimpse
[at+ stem: -gahęgę- glance, glimpse, flash; consists of: -gę$_V$- see]
flashlight see: lantern, torch
ǫ·tahs·rǫ·dáhk·wa' flashlight; torch
a·hę·na·tahs·rǫ́:dę' they (m) carried a torch, lantern, flashlight
flat
ad·wa·dag·wę́h·dę: it became dented
[de+...ad/N+ stem: -(a)gwęhdę$_V$- flat, dented]
de·yo·dag·wę́h·dę:, de·wa·dag·wę́h·dę: it is flat
ad·ya·go·de·wa·né:ga:'s she got a flat tire
[de+P+ade+ stem: -wanega- get a flat tire; consists of: -w(a:)$_N$- air -(wa)negaǫ, (wa)nega(:)$_V$- explode, split]
de·yo·de·wa·ne:gá·ǫ: a flat tire
flatten see: knock down, iron
ęhs·ya'g·yé:nęht you will knock it down
ęhs·ríhs·da: you will iron s.t.
flatter see: praise
ęhs·he·ho·wá:naht you will praise her, uplift her spirits, flatter her
flavoring see: herb
ga·ga'ǫhs·rǫ́:nih it makes it taste good (for example, herbs, spices)
flaxen see: fair-haired
go·nǫ́h·gę:t she is fair haired; she has light hair
fleas
de·wát·sot·wahs fleas (lit.: it jumps, hops)
[de+wa+at+ stem: -(h)sotwahs- fleas; consists of: -(a)hsi('da), (ę)hs(a)$_N$- foot -otw$_V$- jump, hop]
flee see: escape, run away
go·di'nya'gę́'ǫh they (f/m) ran away
ę·gę·na·dé'go' they (z) will flee, run away
fleece see: wool
de·yo·di·na·ga·ǫ:dǫ́' o·hę́h·da:' wool
flesh see: meat, muscle
o'wá·hǫh meat
o'wa·ha·dé:nyǫ' muscles
flinch
da·wá:tgri:k it pulled back, flinched, shrank
[(d+)... at+ stem: -gri$_V$- wrinkle, flinch]
fling see: throw
he·hó:gyǫ: he has thrown it
flint
ot·rág·w'ę·da' flint
[o+ stem: -tragwę'd(a)$_N$- flint]
flip see: knock over, turn over, turn upside down
a·wa·d'ed·reh·da·gá·ha·to' a vehicle was turned over
dę·gǫ·nǫh·wét·s'o·dę' I am going to turn you upside down, upend you (said in anger)
ęhs·he·ya·dę́h·yęht you will flip s.o. over; knock s.o. over
flirt
ęh·sat·ga·hǫ́:nyǫ' you will flirt, bat your eyes
[P+at+ stem: -gahǫnyǫ'- flirt, bat one's eyes; consists of: -gah(a)$_N$- eye -(a)tgahǫ(:), (a)tgaha(:)$_V$- pay attention, watch]
float
og·ye' it is floating along (in the water)
[P+ stem: -ogye'- float; consists of: -gye$_V$- fly]
dá·o:gye' it is coming, floating along (in the water)
og·ye's it floats all the time (without sinking); it throws it away

float (continued)
ga·dig·ye·nǫ́·gye' they (z) are flying, floating about in the air (for example,seeds, etc.)
[A+ stem: -gyenogye'(s)- fly along, float along; consists of: -gye$_V$- fly]
gahs·gó·gye' it (s.t. alive) is floating
[A+ stem: -(h)sgogye'- float; consists of: -gye$_V$- fly]
wa·dá'grah·ta' it resurfaccs continually
[ad+ stem: -(a)'gr(ahd)$_V$- float]
dǫ·da·wa·dá'grahk it resurfaced
o·dá'grah·dǫh it is floating
o·da'grah·dǫ́·hǫg·ye' it is surfacing

flock
ji'dę:'ę́h gę·nád·rǫ·he:s a flock of birds
[consists of: jidę:'ęh bird; gęnadrǫhe:s they (z) are flocking, gathering]

flock see: congregate
gę·nád·rǫ·he:s they (z) are flocking

flood
ę·węh·nó:dǫ:' it will flood
[stem: -(i)hnod- flood; consists of: -(i)hn(a)$_N$- material, skin -od$_V$- stand]
a·węh·nó:dǫ' a flood; it flooded
oh·nó:dǫ' it is flooded

floor
ga·nehs·dá:'geh on the floor
[ga+ stem: -nehsd(a:)$_N$- floor, board]
ga·nehs·dá:dęh·da:' a floor
[ga+ stem: -nehsda:dęhda'- floor; consists of: -nehsd(a:)$_N$- floor, board -dęhda:'$_V$- lie spread out on the ground]

flour
o·té'tra' flour; powder
[o+ stem: -te'tr(a)$_N$- flour, powder]

flourish see: grow
ę·wáh·do:k it will multiply, grow

flow
wat·na·wí:ne' flowing liquid
[at+ stem: -(h)naw(a)$_N$- running water -ine$_V$- go]

flow (continued)
ot·ne·gah·dę́:gyǫ:, oh·ne·gah·dę́:gyǫ: flowing water
[o+(at)+ N+ stem: -(a)hdęgyǫ:- flow; consists of: -(h)neg(a)$_N$- water, liquid -(a)hdędi, (a)hdęgy$_V$- leave, go away]

flower
a·wę́·hę' flower
[stem: -(a)węh(ę)$_N$- flower]
a·wę·hę'shǫ́:'ǫh a variety of flowers, plants

flower bed
ga·wę·hę·yę́t·wah·sǫ' a flower bed; planted flowers
[ga+ stem: -węhęyętwahsǫ'- flower bed; consists of: -(a)węh(ę)$_N$- flower -yętw, yęto$_V$- plant]

flu see: fever, sickness
ak·dǫhg·wá·hǫh I have a fever
o·nǫh·so·dá·ę:' sickness

fluid see: dance, water
a·hah·si·ya·ǫ:nyáh·nǫ:' he is a fluid dancer
oh·né·ga·nohs water

fluke see: err, fin
a·hó:n·hi'k he made a mistake
o·wá:ya' fin of a fish; wings

flute
hę·na·ǫ'da:tkwá' wad·rę́·no·ta' a flute
[consists of: hęnaǫdatkwa' they use it for blowing; wadręnota' s.t. that makes music]
ga·ná:ga:t traditional flute (made of wood)
[ga+ stem: -na'gad- flute; consists of: -na'g(a)$_N$- horn, antler -d$_V$- stand]

fly
ot·rę́'da' housefly; fly
[o+ stem: -trę'd(a)$_N$- fly]
ot·rę'da·gó:wah horsefly
[stem: -trę'd(a)$_N$- fly -gowah- big]
hagye:' he is flying
[A+ stem: -gye(:)$_V$- fly]

Cayuga pronunciation guide: /a/ father /e/ weigh /ę/ men (nasalized) /i/ police /o/ hole /ǫ/ home (nasalized) /u/ blue. Underlined vowels are voiceless or whispered. /'/ high pitch. /t/ too /d/ do /k/ king /g/ good (never soft g) /j/ judge or adze /s/ soon /sh/ less heat (never the sh in shirt) /sr/ shrine /sy/ sure /hw/ which (the sound made when you blow out a candle) /h/ hi /ts/ cats hide /'/ (the sound before the first vowel in 'uh-uh') /n/ noon /r/ round /w/ way /y/ yes.

fly (continued)
gag·yeʼ it is flying along
de·gá:dęhs it flies, goes up in the air
[de+... stem: -dę$_{V}$- fly, take off]
a·tá:dęʼ he took off (from the ground)
heh·da·gẹ̲h·jíh ni·ga:gyéʼ de·gá:dęhs it is flying low
[consists of: hehdagẹ̲hjih low to the ground niga:gyę how it is flying; degadẹ̲hs it flies]

fly see: float
ga·dig·ye·nǫ́:gyeʼ they (z) are flying, floating about in the air (for example,seeds, etc.)

foam
oh·wę́ʼs·daʼ foam
[o+ stem: -(h)węʼsd(a)$_{N}$- foam]
ga̲h·wę́ʼs·doʼ foam
[stem: -(h)węʼsd(a)$_{N}$- foam -oʼ- boiled, stewed]

focus see: pay attention
ę·sáhs·di:s you will pay attention

fog
ot·sá:daʼ fog, steam, mist
[o+ at+ stem: -(h)sad(a)$_{N}$- fog]
ot·sá:do:t there is fog
[o+at+ stem: -(h)sad(a)$_{N}$- fog -od$_{V}$- stand]
de·yot·sa·dá·ęʼ it is foggy
[de+yo+at+ stem: -(h)sadaęʼ- foggy; consists of: -(h)sad(a)$_{N}$- fog -ę$_{V}$- lie on the ground]

foliage
on·rah·dáʼęt·ra·gǫ: foliage (lit.: under the dark green)
[o+ stem: -nrahdaętragǫ:- foliage; consists of: -nrahdaʼętr(a)$_{N}$- green; -agǫ: under]

foliage see: leaf
on·rah·da·shǫ́:ʼǫh variety of leaves

fold
de·séh·saʼge:t you will fold it once, bend it
[de+...stem: -shaʼged, shaʼkdǫ$_{V}$- bend, fold]
dę·seh·sak·da:nyǫ́:goʼ you will fold s.t.up
[de+... stem: -shaʼkdǫnyǫgw- fold s.t.up; consists of: -shaʼged, shaʼkdǫ$_{V}$- bend]

follow
a·gá·kehs·re:ʼ I chased them, followed them
[TR+ stem: -(i)hsre(:)$_{V}$- follow, chase]
hǫ·wá·di̲hs·reʼs they follow him around all the time
hǫ·wa·di̲hs·réhs·rǫh they are chasing him around
hǫ·wa·di̲hs·ré:gyeʼ they are following him along
hehs·nǫ́:dręʼ you follow him
[TR+ stem: -(h)nǫdr(e,ę)$_{V}$- follow]
hǫ·wáh·nǫd·reʼ s.o. is following him
ę·héhs·nǫd·ręʼ you will follow him
dǫ·da·hehs·nǫ́:dręh you follow him back
hǫ·wah·nǫd·rá:gyeʼ, hǫ·wah·nǫd·rá:gyeʼs s.o. is following him along wherever he goes
[TR+ stem: -(h)nǫdragyeʼ(s)- follow along; consists of: -(h)nǫdr(e,ę)$_{V}$- follow]

fondle see: caress, grope
ę·hes·yʼa·dahd·rǫ́:gǫʼ you will caress him
hęhs·yáh·nǫ:ʼ you will grope, touch, pick at s.t.

fond see: like
he·nǫ́h·weʼs I like him

food
gak·waʼ food
[ga+ stem: -k(wa)$_{N}$- food]

food (continued)
gak·wí·yo: good, nice food
[ga+ stem: -k(wa)$_N$- food -iyo:$_V$- be nice, good]
gak·wá·no:ʼ cold food
[ga+ stem: -k(wa)$_N$- food -no:ʼ$_V$- cold, cool]

food processor
de·gak·wa·híh·taʼ food processor
[de+ga+ stem: kwahihtaʼ food processor- consists of: -k(wa)$_N$- food -(hr)ihd$_V$- cause s.t. to break up]

fool see: deceive, trick
ęhs·he·ya·dǫ́·gǫh·dęʼ you will outdo s.o.; you will go right over her, go right past her; deceive her
se·sa·heht·só:goʼ you got fooled (like the frog)

foot
oh·síʼdaʼ feet
[o+ stem: -(a)hsi(ʼda), (ę)hs(a)$_N$- foot]
gah·síʼdʼa·geh on my foot
sah·síʼdʼa·geh on your foot
swah·síʼdʼa·geh on your (p) feet
de·yoh·sʼi·dá:ge: two feet (a measurement or body part)
[de+yo+ stem: -(a)hsi(ʼda), (ę)hs(a)$_N$- foot -(a)ge:$_V$- two or more]

foot stool
de·yǫh·siʼda·hahk·waʼ foot stool
[de+yǫ+ stem: -(a)hsiʼdahahkwaʼ- foot stool; consists of: -(a)hsi(ʼda), (ę)hs(a)$_N$- foot -(h)ahkwaʼ$_V$- s.t. that supports]

football
ę́·sę·twahs a football game
[(w)+ stem: -ę(h)sętwahs- football; consists of: -(a)hsi(ʼda), (ę)hs(a)$_N$- foot -ętw, ęto$_V$- kick]
węʼnhó:tre:s football (lit.: long ball)
[w+ stem: -ęʼnhotres- football; consists of: -ęʼnh(otra)$_N$- ball -es$_V$- long]

football (continued)
ǫ·wę:sęh·twáhs węʼnhó:tre:s football
[consists of: ǫwę:sęhtwahs s.o.'s football game; węʼnho:tre:s a football]

forage see: eat
ę·ji·sa·de·kǫ·ní·hag·yeʼ you will eat while you are going along

forbid see: stop
dęhs·dahs, dęhs·dęhs you will prevent it, stop it, stand it up

forbidden
o·nǫ́ʼne:ʼ it is forbidden, sacred, holy
[P+(N+) stem: -noʼne:ʼ$_V$- forbidden, sacred, holy]

forbidding see: evil power
go·ná:tgǫh they (f/m) are a force to be reckoned with; they (f/m) are ominous: they are bad medicine people

force
tgas·he·yę·nǫ́h·twahs you force people all the time
[de+TR+ stem: -nǫhtwahsd$_V$- force, rape]
dahs·ha·go·nǫ́h·twahs he forced (that is, raped) her

force see: power
gahs·háhs·dęhs·raʼ, ohs·háhs·dęhs·raʼ power; strength

forceful see: strong
gahs·há:sdeʼ it is strong, tough, powerful

forefather see: ancestor
ha·di·gęh·jih·sǫʼgę́·hę:ʼ they (m) are our grandfathers, our ancestors

forefoot see: hand
oh·sóh·daʼ hand; paw

forego see: forfeit, remove
a·sa:dwę́:deht you forfeited
de·se·nęt·sǫ́ʼne:k remove your arms (that is,retract them); remove your support

forehead see: hairline
ge·gę'ˀs·dá:ˀgeh on my forehead, hairline, upper brow
foreign see: different
o·yáˀ ní:yoht different
foremost see: begin
da·wa:gyę:t the first one; the beginner
foreshadowing see: omen
wat·sǫ́:nyǫ:s omen
forest
ga̱·há:daˀ forest
[ga+ stem: -(h)ad(a)$_N$- forest]
ga̱·ha·dak·dá:gyeˀ the edge of the bush
ga̱·há:gǫ: in the bush
ga̱·há:do:t forest
[ga+ stem: -(h)ad(a)$_N$- forest -od$_V$- stand]
ga̱·ha·dá·ę:dǫn·yǫˀ forests
Forest Industry see: G (ha·diˀnhahg·yaˀs ho·nah·dęg·yaˀdǫh)
foretell
o·hę:dǫ́: he·ha:dí:gęh they (m) look ahead, tell the future
[ohę:dǫ: ahead, in front he+... stem: -gę$_V$- see, look ahead, forsee]
foretell see: fortune teller
dę̱·ha·di·yaˀdo·wéh·taˀ they (m) are fortune tellers, thinkers; they (m) tell fortunes
forever see: always
haˀdę·wat·gǫ́:dęˀ always; forever
forfeit
sad·wę́·deh·taˀ you forfeit things all the time
[ad/adad+ stem: -wędehd$_V$- forfeit]
a·wa·dad·wę́:deht it (for example, a pet) forfeited (its life)
a·sa:dwę́:deht you forfeited
forget
sǫk·ni·gǫ́·hęh I forgot
[s+P+ stem: -(ˀ)nigǫhęh- forget; consists of: -(ˀ)nigǫh(a)$_N$- mind -(h)ęh$_V$- drop]

forget (continued)
ęh·saˀni·gǫ́·hęh you will forget
ęhs·heˀni·gǫ́·hęh·dęˀ you will make s.o. feel better, comfort s.o. (lit.: you will make s.o. forget s.t.)
[TR+ stem: -(ˀ)nigǫhęhdę- make s.o. forget consists of: -(ˀ)nigǫh(a)$_N$- mind -(h)ęhdę$_V$- cause to drop]
forgive see: mercy, pity
gę·dá·ǫhs·raˀ mercy
ęhs·hé:dę:ˀ you will pity her, show mercy, compassion
fork
ga̱h·só:gwa:ˀ a fork
[ga+ stem: -(h)sogwa:ˀ- fork; consists of: -(h)s(a)$_N$- mouth -ogw$_V$- scatter]
forlorn see: sad
de·saˀni·gǫ́·hęh·dǫh you are sad
form see: trunk
o·híˀyaˀ the body's trunk, form
former
ǫg·ya·dá·oˀgę̱·hę:ˀ my former ceremonial friend
[P+ad+ stem: -ao$_V$- ceremonial friend -gęhę:ˀ-former]
former
[-gęhę:ˀ decessive; denotes something that 'used to exist' or that 'existed formerly']
former see: past
oh·náˀgę·jih way back in the past; back then
formula
o·wi:ya:ˀáh go·nǫ́ˀgwaˀ baby's formula
[Consists of: owi:ya:ˀah baby; gonǫˀgwaˀ her milk]
forsake see: abandon, betray
a·hǫ·wag·yé:saht he abandoned her; he left her
ęh·sní·gǫ·haˀt you will betray
forsee see: foretell
o·hę:dǫ́: he·ha:dí:gęh they (m) look ahead, tell the future

forthright see: outspoken
he·ja·go·nę́·hęh they (f/m) are outspoken
fortify see: double
dęhs·náʼnetʼa:ʼ you will double it, reinforce it, line it
fortune see: luck, wealth
ad·ráʼswaʼ luck
ot·gah·nǫ·níhs·raʼ wealth
fortune teller
de̲·ha·di·ya·do·wéh·taʼ they (m) are fortune tellers, thinkers; they (m) tell fortunes
[de+A+ stem: -yaʼdowehtaʼ- fortune teller, seer; consists of: -yaʼdowehd$_{V}$- think about, consider]
de̲·ha·yʼa·dó·we̲h·taʼ he is a fortune teller, seer, thinker
de·ye·yʼa·dó·we̲h·taʼ she is a thinker, a seer
de·ga·e·yaʼdo·wéh·taʼ they (f/m) are thinkers (seers)
ę·gákya·dǫ:ʼ I will have a reading; I will have my fortune told
[ak+ stem: -(h)yadǫ(:)$_{V}$- write; have a reading]
ę·gak·ya·dǫ́h·naʼ I am going to go and have a reading
forward see: ahead
he·yo·dʼag·wá·is·hǫ: straight ahead
foster parent
ga·ǫ·da·dah·do·gáʼtaʼ foster parents
[TR+ stem: -(a)hdogaʼd, (a)hdogahd- raise s.o.; consists of: -(a)hdog$_{V}$- grow, mature]
foundation
de·gahs·dę́:dǫʼ foundation
[de+ga+ stem: -(h)sdędǫʼ- foundation consists of: -(h)sd(ęha)$_{N}$- stone -dǫʼ$_{V}$- several standing objects]

foundation (continued)
ga·nǫh·sa·gę́d·ra̲h·gǫh the foundation (of a building)
[ga+ stem: -nǫhsagędrahgǫh- foundation; consists of: -nǫhs(a)$_{N}$- house -gędrahgw$_{V}$- support]
foundation (an organization) see: G (ho·nad·rih·wahs·di:hs·dǫh)
foundling
ga·wi·yat·sę́:nyǫ: child born out of wedlock; foundling; illegitimate child
[ga+ stem: -wiyatsęnyǫ:- foundling, illegitimate; consists of: -wiy(a)$_{N}$- child, offspring -tsęi, tsęny$_{V}$- find]
fountain
tgah·né·go·taʼ fire hydrant; fountain
[t+ga+ / g+yo+ stem: -(h)negod- fountain; consists of: -(h)neg(a)$_{N}$- water, liquid -od$_{V}$- stand]
gyo̲h·né:go:t fountain
four see: B (ge·i:)
fourteen see: B (gei: sga·eʼ)
fourty see: B (gei: ni·wahs·hę:)
fox
héhs·ha·i: fox
[stem: -(h)ehshai$_{N}$- fox]
fraction
gyod·rá:gwęh fractions
[g+yo+ad+ stem: -(r)agwęh- fraction; consists of: -(r)agw$_{V}$- choose, take out]
fracture
de·yo·dehs·gyęʼdi·yáʼgǫh it (bone) is fractured
[de+yo+ade+ stem: -(h)sgyęʼdiyaʼg- fracture; consists of: -(h)sgyęʼd(a:)$_{N}$- bone -(i)yaʼg$_{V}$- cut, break]
fracture see: break
dę·gat·nęt·sí:yaʼk I will break my arm
fragile see: weak
ag·yaʼda·gę·hé:yǫ: I am physically weak, slow
fragment see: fraction, woodchip
o·wę́·ga:ʼ wood chips

Cayuga pronunciation guide: /a/ father /e/ weigh /ę/ men (nasalized) /i/ police /o/ hole /ǫ/ home (nasalized) /u/ blue. Underlined vowels are voiceless or whispered. /ʼ/ high pitch. /t/ too /d/ do /k/ king /g/ good (never soft g) /j/ judge or adze /s/ soon /sh/ less heat (never the sh in shirt) /sr/ shrine /sy/ sure /hw/ which (the sound made when you blow out a candle) /h/ hi /ts/ cats hide /ʼ/ (the sound before the first vowel in 'uh-uh') /n/ noon /r/ round /w/ way /y/ yes.

fragrance see: odour, perfume, smell
o·ded·rę·ná·i:ʼ an odour
gad·rę:ní:yoʼs perfume
gad·rę:ní:yo: a nice smell
frail see: weak
ag·yaʼda·gę·hé:yǫ: I am physically weak, slow
frame
de·wa·dę·níh·sa·dǫʼ frame
[de+wa+ stem: -(a)dęnihsadǫʼ- frame; consists of: -(a)dęnihs(a)- wall -dǫʼ$_{V}$- several standing objects]
frank see: outspoken
he·ja·go·nę́·hęh they (f/m) are outspoken
frankfurter see: hot dog
ga·yǫ·wa·wéʼta·hǫh hot dog; weiners; sausage on a bun
fray
a·wa·de̲h·si:yó:goʼ it frayed
[(de+)...ade+ stem: -(h)siyogw- fray; consists of: -(h)siy(a)$_{N}$- line, string -ogw$_{V}$- scatter]
de·yo·da̲h·si:yó:gwęh it is frayed
freckle
a·ge:gę́:na:ʼ I have a freckle
[P+ stem: -gęn(a)$_{N}$- mole, freckle -a:ʼ$_{V}$- hold, contain, include]
sa·gę́:na:ʼ you have moles
free see: inexpensive
tę́ʼ de·gá:nǫ:ʼ it is not costly
freeload see: beg
dę·gat·sá·i:de:ʼ I will freeload
freeway see: highway
o·ha·ho·wá·nʼę̲s·geh highway
freeze
ę·ga·nǫn·yá·ęʼ it will freeze
[stem: -nǫnyaę(:)- freeze; consists of: -nǫny(a)$_{N}$- ice -ę$_{V}$- lie on the ground]
o·nǫ́n·ya·ę:ʼ it is frozen
o·nǫn·yá·ę·dag·yeʼ it is freezing
freeze (continued)
ga·nǫn·yá·ę·da̲hs·dǫh it is made frozen
[stem: -nǫnyaędahsd- freeze s.t.; consists of: -nǫny(a)$_{N}$- ice -ędahsd$_{V}$- cause to lie on the ground]
freezer
ga·nǫn·yá·ę·da̲hs·taʼ freezer
[stem: -nǫnyaędahsd- freeze s.t.; consists of: -nǫny(a)$_{N}$- ice -ędahsd$_{V}$- cause to lie on the ground]
freight see: cargo
o·héh·naʼ, ga̲·héh·naʼ cargo; bundle; load
frenzied
o·dét·saʼdǫh it is frenzied
[ade+ stem: -tsaʼd$_{V}$- struggle, revolt]
fresh
a·se:ʼshǫ́:ʼǫh fresh (foods)
[(wa+) stem: -(a)se:(ʼ)$_{V}$- new]
oʼwá·ha·se:ʼ fresh meat
[o+ stem: -(ʼ)wah(a)$_{N}$- meat -(a)se:(ʼ)$_{V}$- new]
fresh see: new
á:se:ʼ it is fresh, new
fret see: worry
sʼę·ni·gǫ·hód·rǫh you are a worrier
Friday see: A (Hwihs ha·dǫʼt)
friend see: C (go·na:tsih, ǫg·ya:da·o:)
friendship
a·da·oʼtraʼ, o·da·oʼtraʼ friendship; also refers to a ceremonial friend
[P+ad+ stem: -(a)oʼtr(a)$_{N}$- friendship -ao$_{V}$- ceremonial friend]
frighten
ęh·sáhd·rǫ̲hg·węʼ it will frighten you
[TR+ stem: -(a)hdrǫ(h)gwęʼ- frighten s.o.; consists of: -(a)hdrǫʼ$_{V}$- scared, frightened]
eh·sáhd·rǫ̲hg·węʼ it did frighten you
frighten see: startle
ę·ke·yę·néʼwa̲h·dęʼ I will startle her

frightened, frightening
ę·sét·sa̱h·nihk you will be scared of it
[stem: -tsahnikd$_V$- frighten, scare]
a·sét·sa̱h·ni'k you are afraid
ot·sáh·nihk it is frightening, scary
frightened see: scared
a·gáhd·rǫ's I am scared, frightened
frigid see: cold, freeze
o·tó:we' it is cold
fringe
ga̱h·si·ya·ní:yǫ:t fringe
[ga+ stem: -(h)siyaniyǫd- fringe; consists of: -(h)siy(a)$_N$- line, string -niyǫd$_V$- hang]
ga̱h·si:yǫ́:ni: it is fringed
[stem: -(h)siyǫni:- fringed; consists of: -(h)siy(a)$_N$- line, string -ǫni, ǫny$_V$- make]
frog
sgwa'áh·da' frog
[stem: -(nęh)sg(wa'ahda), (nǫh)sg(wa'ahda)$_N$- frog]
sgwa'ah·da'gó:wah a species of bull frog
[stem: -sgwa'ahda'gowah- bullfrog; consists of: -(nęh)sg(wa'ahda), (nǫh)sg(wa'ahda)$_N$- frog -gowah- big]
frolic see: fun, play
a·gǫ́'we̱h·sahs I am having a good time, enjoying s.t.
o·nát·ga̱hn·ye' they (z) are playing
from see: come from, originate from, place, take
nǫ·dá:kne:' where we two (excl.) came from
dwa·gáh·dęg·yo: I come from
[-'geh, hneh external locative suffixes; denote a place]
ę·yók·wahk·wa' it will take the food from another animal

front
o·hę:dǫ́: ga·nǫ́h·so:t the house in front
o·hę:dǫ́: shę́h ga·nǫ́h·so:t in front of the house
[ohę:dǫ: ahead, in front; tsęh that A/P+N+ stem: -nǫhs(a)$_N$- house -od$_V$- stand]
front see: ahead, lead
o·hę́:dǫ: ahead; in front; the front
ęhs·rę:t you will be the lead
frontier see: boundary
de·ga·ihs·dí'dra̱·hǫh boundary
frost
oh·sę́·hę' frost
[o+ stem: -(h)sęh(ę)$_N$- frost]
frost (a cake) see: ice (a cake)
ęhs·ra·na·wę:dó:we:k you will ice, frost s.t. (for example, a cake)
froth see: foam
ga̱h·wę́'s·do' foam
frown
a·tát·gręg·ręht he frowned
[de+...at+ stem: -gręgręhd$_V$- frown, sneer]
dęh·sát·gręg·ręht you will sneer, frown
ag·yǫ́t·gręg·ręht she frowned
dę·yǫ́t·gręg·ręht she will frown
de·ya·got·grę́g·rę̱h·dǫh she is frowning
de̱·hot·gręg·rę́h·dǫh he is frowning
de·sát·gręg·ręht frown
frugal
de·ya·go·nǫ́hya·ni:s she is frugal
[de+P+ stem: -nǫhyani$_V$- frugal]
de·sa·nǫh·yá:ni:s you're stingy; you do not want to share
dę·ya·go·nǫh·ya·ní'se:k she will be frugal
frugal see: terrible
de·yo·nǫ̱h·yá:niht it is terrible, frugal, cheap

fruit
oh·ya' fruit, berry
[o+ stem: -(a)hy(a)$_N$- fruit, berry]
oh·ya'shǫ́:'ǫh a variety of fruits
wa̱h·ya·ni·yǫ́:ta' hanging fruit
[wa+ stem: -(a)hy(a)$_N$- fruit, berry -niyǫd$_V$- hang]
wah·yá·gę·hǫ' fruit lying around on the ground
[wa+ stem: -(a)hy(a)$_N$- fruit, berry -gehǫ'$_V$- lie about]
o·dah·yag·wá:sęh bruised fruit, fruit with brown spots
[o+ad+ stem: -(a)hy(a)$_N$- fruit, berry -(a)gwas$_V$- bruise]
oh·yá:tgę:' spoiled, rotten fruit
[o+ stem: -(a)hy(a)$_N$- fruit, berry -tgę$_V$- spoiled, rotten]
oh·yá:tgi' fruit that is not very good but still edible
[o+ stem: -(a)hy(a)$_N$- fruit, berry -tgi$_V$- dirty, ugly]
oh·yó·wa·neh big fruit
[o+ stem: -(a)hy(a)$_N$- fruit, berry -owanęh$_V$- be big]
hya·ík·hneh·geh berry-ripening time
[stem: -(h)yaiknehgeh- berry-ripening time; consists of: -(a)hy(a)$_N$- fruit, berry -(r)i, (w)i$_V$- ripe -(h)neh- at -(')geh- at]
fruit (sour, tart) see: crabapple
oh·ya·ji·wá:gę: crabapples; tart, sour fruit
frustrating see: maddening
o·ná'kwat it is irritating, maddening
fry see: roast
wa·dé's·gǫ:t it is roasting, frying
fulfill see: accomplish, earn (money)
ęhs·rih·wag·wę́:ni' you will accomplish
a·tad·ri̱h·wá:ts'a:' he earned it; he fulfilled it

full
d'e·yo·na·dǫhs·w'e·dá:nih they (z) are not hungry
[de'+ not P+ad+ stem: -ǫhswe'd(ę,ani)$_V$- be hungry, short of breath]
full of food
oh·da's it (z) gets full (finishes eating)
[P+ stem: -(a)hda'$_V$- get full of food]
a'óh·da' it (z) got full (finished eating)
ę·yóh·da' it (z) will get full (finish eating)
ǫ·gáh·da' I got full (finished eating)
oh·dá'ǫh it (z) got full (finished eating)
sa̱h·da' get full; finish eating
full-grown see: mature
ot·síh·s'ǫh it is done for the season; it has gone full cycle; it is mature; they (plants) have finished out
fumes see: fog
ot·sá:da' fog; steam
fun
o·dǫt·ga·dǫ́hs·ra' fun
[ad+ stem: -ǫtgadǫhsr(a)$_N$- fun -ǫtgad(ǫ:)$_V$- enjoy]
o·dǫt·ga·dǫhs·rí:yo: fun
[o+ad+ stem: -ǫtgadǫhsr(a)$_N$- fun -iyo:$_V$- be nice, good]
o·dǫ́tga·de' it is fun; a good feeling
[o+ad+ stem: -ǫtgade'- happy; consists of: -ǫtgad(ǫ:)$_V$- enjoy]
gá·ǫ·wę̱hs·hahs she is pleased; a good feeling
[P+ stem: -ǫ'wesahs- have a good time, enjoy oneself; consists of: -ǫ'wes$_V$- enjoy]
a·gǫ́'weh·sahs I am having a good time, enjoying s.t.
fun see: enjoy
ęhs·wa·dǫt·gá:dǫ:' you all will have a good time, enjoy yourselves, have fun
functional see: useful
o·í·hǫ:t it is useful

funeral director
dẹ·ha·he·yọ'dahsn·yé·ha' he is a funeral director
[de+A+ stem: -(h)eyọ'dahsnyeha'- funeral director; consists of: -(he)yọ('da)$_N$- corpse, cadaver -(h)snye$_V$- care for, look after]

funeral home
gyẹ·he·y'ọ·da·ẹ:dáhk·w'a·geh funeral home
[g+ye+ stem: -(h)e'yọhdaẹdahkwa'geh- funeral home; consists of: -(he)yọ('da)$_N$- corpse, cadaver -ẹdahkwa'$_V$- place where s.t. is put -(')geh- at]

fungus see: mushroom
on·ráhs·ra' mushroom

funny see: amusing, comical
o·yọ́:gya't it is amusing, laughable
o·yọ:g·yẹ́:ni: it is comical

fur
o·hẹ́h·da:' fur
[o+ stem: -(h)ẹhd(a:)$_N$- fur]
o·hẹ́h·da·i: fur on the animal
[o+ stem: -(h)ẹhd(a:)$_N$- fur -i:'$_V$- be stuck onto s.t.]
o·hẹ́h·da·ẹ:' it is furry
[o+ stem: -hẹhdaẹ:'- furry; consists of: -(h)ẹhd(a:)$_N$- fur -ẹ$_V$- lie on the ground]

furious see: angry
ak·ná'kwẹ'ọh I am angry

furnace
ga·nọh·sa·da·i·há'dahk·wa' it is used to heat up the house
[ga+ stem: -nọhs(a)$_N$- house -(')daiha'dahkwa'$_V$- s.t. that warms things up]

furrow see: row
o·tá·họ:t a row

fury see: anger
ohs·rọ́·hẹ'da' angry person; temper

fuzzy
ta'de·yo·ga·há·ẹ·daht it is fuzzy, out of focus, opaque, unclear
[ta'+de+yo+ stem: -gahaẹdahd- fuzzy, out-of-focus, unclear; consists of: -gah(a)$_N$- eye -ẹdahd$_V$- cause to lie on the ground]

G

gadget see: tool
ọd·ri·ho'dáhsta' tools; equipment

gain see: acquire, make
ẹ·sa:yẹ́·da' you will acquire, obtain
gọ́:nih I make, earn

gait see: slow
ho·ya·not·gẹ: he is a slow runner, walker; he has a slow gait

galaxy
o·ha·ha'dí·họh the Milky Way
[o+ stem: -(h)aha'dihọh- Galaxy, Milky Way; consists of: -(h)ah(a)$_N$- road -(adi)họh$_V$- lean against]

gale see: hurricane, wind
ga·wa·ẹ·hẹ́:wi' hurricane
ga·wa·o·wá:nẹh big wind

gallon
ge·í: ni·gat·se'dá:ge: one gallon (lit.: four quart jars)
[gei: four ni+ga stem: -(i)tse('da)$_N$- bottle -(a)ge:$_V$- two or more]

gamble
de·gá:yẹ' gambling; wagering
[de+(d)... stem: -ẹ$_V$- lie on the ground; gamble]
det·gá:yẹ' it is no longer laying there; they are betting over there
de·to·dí:yẹ' they (m) are gambling, betting

gamble (continued)

a·tę·nad·ra'·s·ró·i'·a:k they (m) tested, tried their luck
[de+...ad+ stem: -(r)a'sroiya'g- try one's luck, gamble; consists of: -ra'sro, ra'sw$_N$- luck -(i)ya'g$_V$- cut, break]

game

gan·yo'shǫ́:'ǫh wild game
[stem: -nyo:'$_N$- wild animal; consists of: -(r)iyo, nyo$_V$- kill someting]

at·gáhn·yeht·ra' sports, games
[at+ stem: -gahnyehtr(a)$_N$- games, sports; consists of: -gahnye$_V$- play]

de·ha·di·yęh·dahk·wa' they (m) are playing a game (dominoes, scrabble, etc.)
[de+... stem: -ęhdahkwa'$_V$- s.t. that hits]

game see: recreation

de·yǫ'ni·gǫ·ha·wę́n·y'e·ta' recreation; hobbies

gang see: crowd

gęg·yóh·go:t a crowd

gap

de·ya·ǫh·wę́:de' a gap; an opening
[de+ya+ stem: -(ǫh)węd(a)$_N$- hole, opening -e$_V$- go]

gape see: stare

sa·gahd·rǫ́:nihs you are staring at it

garage

sha·di'dręh·dǫ́·nihs·geh garage, auto shop
[(s+) A+ stem: -(')drehdǫnihsgeh- garage; consists of: -(')drehd(a)$_N$- vehicle, car -ǫni, ǫny$_V$- make, repair]

garbage see: junk

gat·gí'tra' junk

garbage can

gog·yé's e·yáhk·wa' garbage can
[consists of: gogye's to get rid of s.t.; eyahkwa' containers]

garbage man

gog·yé's ha·nęhg·wih garbage man
[consists of: gogye's to get rid of s.t.; hanęhgwih he is a courier]

garden

ga·yę́·twah·sǫ' garden; it is planted
[ga+ stem: -yętwahsǫ'- garden; consists of: -yętw, yęto$_V$- plant]

tga·yę́·twah·sǫ' garden; it is planted over there

garden see: tend

dę·se·heh·dá·wę:nye:' you will tend, till your garden

ęh·sa·tę·dǫ́:ni' you will make your garden

garfish

gahn·yę́:t·se:s garfish
[ga+ stem: -(h)nyętse:s- garfish; consists of: -(h)nyęts(a)$_N$- -es$_V$- long]

garment see: clothes, dress

at·rǫ́·n'i·da' clothes

ag·ya'da·wí'tra' coat; dress

garters

a·dah·d'it·rán·hahs·ta' garters (for holding up stockings)
[ad+ stem: -(a)hdahdi'tranhahsta'- garters; consists of: -(a)hdahdi'tr(a)$_N$- sock -nhahsd$_V$- encircle]

ǫt·sín·hahs·ta' garters; leg bands
[ǫ+at+ stem: -(h)sinhahsta'- garters; consists of: -(h)sin(a)$_N$- leg -nhahsd$_V$- encircle]

gas see: oil

oh·na' grease; oil; etc.

gas-burning

o·wa:dé:gahs it burns gas
[o+ stem: -wa:degahs- gas-burning; consists of: -w(a:)$_N$- air -(a)deg$_V$- burn up]

gas station
ǫt·nǫ·dahs·dáhk·wʼa·geh gas station [ǫ+at+ stem: -(h)nǫdasdahkwaʼgeh- gas station; consists of: -(h)n(a)$_N$- oil, gas -ǫdahsd$_V$- put in]

gas station attendant
hah·nǫ́:da:s he is a gas station attendant [stem: -(h)nǫda:s- gas station attendant; consists of: -(h)n(a)$_N$- oil, gas -ǫda:(h)$_V$- put in, attached]

gash see: cut, notch
a·hǫ́·wa·he:ʼ he slashed him with a sharp instrument
a·há·no̲hs·ga:ʼ he notched it (a tree, a casket)

gasp
ad·wák·sa·ga:ʼs you gasped, yawned [de+P+ stem: -(h)sag(a)$_N$- mouth -hsagaʼ(w)$_V$- gasp, yawn]
de·sah·sa·gá:węh yawn; gasp

gasp see: pant, wheeze
sha·ǫ:wi̲hs·hę́ʼǫh he is panting again; he is short of breath
oh·wę́hs·da·ga: it is wheezing

gate
gan·ho·ha·ní:yǫ:t gate; door [ga+ stem: -nhohaniyǫd- gate; consists of: -nho(ha)$_N$- door -niyǫd$_V$- hang]

gather
ga̲h·yá:gwahs I am picking fruit [stem: -(a)hy(a)$_N$- fruit, berry -gw$_V$- gather, pick, get]
haʼhá:goʼ he went and got it [stem: -gw$_V$- gather, pick, get]
a·gé:gwęh how much I have obtained, acquired
gá·e:yo·he:s they (f/m) are gathering [(N+) stem: -(r)oheg$_V$- gather]
ęhs·ró·he:k you will gather
ag·ro·hé:gǫh I have gathered
gá·o·hǫ:ʼ the act of gathering

gather see: accumulate, congregate, store
ęh·sa·dad·ro·hé:gęʼ you will accumulate (things, ideas, etc.) for yourself
ęd·wád·ro̲he:k we all (incl.) will gather together
ę·seh·sęnǫ́:niʼ you will store it

gathering see: crowd
gęg·yóh·go:t a crowd

gathering place see: meeting place
ǫd·ró·hek·taʼ meeting place; gathering place

gaunt see: thin
gohs·gyǫ́ʼwa·tę: she is thin

gauze see: sheer
o·jiʼá:deʼ sheer, lacy fabrics; lace

gawk see: stare
sa·gahd·rǫ́:nihs you are staring at it

gaze see: look
haʼsát·ga̲h·toʼ you looked

gear see: tools
ǫd·ri·hoʼdáhstaʼ tools; equipment

geld see: neuter
ę·hǫ·wa̲hs·gwá:da̲h·goʼ they will geld, neuter, fix him (lit.: they will remove his testicles)

generally see: I (gę:s)

generate see: produce
a·ha·i·hǫ́n·ya̲h·nǫ:ʼ he produced s.t.

generous
gog·yésʼa·geh she is generous, generous to a fault [P+ag+ stem: -yesaʼgeh- generous; consists of: -yes$_V$- be easy]

genitals
ga·jí:nah it is a male animal; the genitals of an animal [A+ stem: -jinah$_V$- strong, brave]
oʼn·héhg·yęʼ it is female animal; the genitals of a female animal [o+ stem: -(ʼ)nhehgyęʼ$_V$- female]
go̲h·séh·dǫh a woman's genitals [P+ stem: -(a)hsehdǫh- genitals; consists of: -(a)hsehd$_V$- hide s.t.]

Cayuga pronunciation guide: /a/ father /e/ weigh /ę/ men (nasalized) /i/ police /o/ hole /ǫ/ home (nasalized) /u/ blue. Underlined vowels are voiceless or whispered. /ˊ/ high pitch. /t/ too /d/ do /k/ king /g/ good (never soft g) /j/ judge or a̲d̲z̲e /s/ soon /sh/ le̲s̲s̲ h̲eat (never the sh in shirt) /sr/ s̲h̲r̲ine /sy/ s̲ure /hw/ w̲h̲ich (the sound made when you blow out a candle) /h/ hi /ts/ ca̲t̲s̲ h̲ide /ʼ/ (the sound before the first vowel in 'uh-uh') /n/ noon /r/ round /w/ way /y/ yes.

genitals see: penis, testicles, vagina
shęh ha·jí:nah penis; phallus
de·há'nhǫhs·tǫ:t his testicles
o'ya' female genitals; vagina
gentle see: humble
g'o·ni·gǫ·ha:ní:dęht she is gentle, nice, humble
genuine see: right
tga:yé·i: it is right, correct
geographer see: map maker
ho·nǫh·wę·jáhs·da̱h·nǫ' map makers; geographers
gesture see: beckon
gá:jih come here (used in the sense of, "it beckons")
get see: acquire, buy, catch
ę·sa:yę́:da' you will acquire, obtain
ęh·sní:nǫ' you will buy, purchase
ag·yé:na:' I caught it; I received it
get down see: descend
ę·sáhs·nęht you will get down
get into see: embark
ę·gát·nǫ̱h·da:' I will embark, get in s.t.
get off, get out see: disembark, descend
ę·gat·nǫ̱h·dáh·go' I will disembark, get out of a vehicle
get up
gat·gę́·hęhs I get up all the time
[at+ stem: -gęh$_V$- get up, awaken]
a·gá:tgęh I got up
ę·gá:tgęh I will get up
sat·gęh get up
dwat·gę́·hęh·sǫ: let us all (incl.) get up
get up see: stand up
a·tá:da' he stood up
geyser see: fountain
tgah·né·go·ta' fire hydrant; fountain
ghost
jihs·gę: a ghost
[stem: -jihsgę:- ghost; consists of: -jihs(a)$_n$- -(i)gę:$_V$- be white-coloured, light]
ghost see: vision (have a vision)
ad·wag·yá·ǫn·yo a haunted apparition
giant see: big
go·wá:nęh, ga·gó·wa·nęh it is big
Gibson Reserve, Ont. see: E (Wah·ta')
giddy see: dizzy
a·gah·sǫ·wá·den·ye's, a·gat·sǫ·wá·den·ye's I am dizzy
gift see: present
wa·dáwi̱·hǫ' presents
gigantic see: big
go·wá:nęh, ga·gó·wa·nęh it is big
giggle
ho·yǫ́g·y'ę·ni: he is a smiler, a giggler
[P+ stem: -yǫgye'ni:- have the giggles; consists of: -yǫdi, yǫgy$_V$- smile]
sa·yǫ́gy'e·ni: you have the giggles
ho·di·yǫgyę́'nih they (m) have the giggles
giggle see: laugh
gyǫg·yáh·ta' I am really laughing
gill
wa·dǫn·ye·dáhk·wa' gill
[stem: -(a)dǫnyedahk(wa)$_N$- gill; consists of: -ǫnyed$_V$- cause to breathe]
wa·dǫ́n·ye·ta' how it breathes; its a breather; the gill
[ad+ stem: -ǫnyed- cause s.t. to breathe; consists of: -ǫwi, ǫny$_V$- breathe]
ginger root, ginseng
ǫ:gwéh ok·dé·ha' ginger root; ginseng
[consists of: ǫ:gweh person; okdeha' edible roots]
giraffe
ga̱hn·ya'ses·gó:wah giraffe
[ga+ stem: -(h)nya'sesgowah- giraffe; consists of: -(h)nya('sa)$_N$- neck, throat -es$_V$- long -gowah- big]
girder see: beam, rafter
(de)·gahn·yǫhs·rá:de' iron beams
ga·nehs·dá:den·yǫ' rafters (made of board)

girdle

de·yǫg·y'a·dó·hak·ta' girdle
[de+yǫ+ag+ stem: -ya'dohakta'- girdle; consists of: -ya'd(a)$_N$- body -ohakd$_V$- be squeezed]

girl

ek·sa'dí:yo: she is a nice little girl
[e+ stem: -ksa('da)$_N$- child -iyo:$_V$- be nice, good]

de·gá·e:kęh twin girls; a twin boy and girl
[de+gae+ stem: -kęh$_V$- twins]

girl see: female, woman

je·yá'da:t one person (female)

a·gǫ́:gweh girl; woman; the female gender

girlfriend see: C

ǫg·yá:tsih my friend, my boyfriend, my girl friend

give

dę·hę·nę·dá·da·wihs trade; commerce; barter (lit.: they (m) give to each other)
[stem: -awi, ǫ$_V$- give]

ę·ye:tí:yǫ' presents; we will give her/them

shǫg·wá:wi: he has given us

dahs·gǫh give it to me

a·hǫ·wá·ę·nǫ' s.o. gave him a song
[stem: -(r)ęn(a)$_N$- song, music -awi, ǫ$_V$- give]

shǫg·wa·ę·ná·wi·hǫ' he has given each of us a song

shǫg·wa·ę·ná·wihs·hǫ' he has given us a song

give up

a·ge·wę·ná'ta', ag·wę́·n'a·ta' I give up (all the time)
[stem: -węna'd$_V$- give up]

ę·sa:wę́:na't you will give up

a·ge·wę·ná'dǫh I have given up

give up (continued)

ga·ǫ'ni·gǫ́·hǫ'k·ta' they (f/m) are giving up (in spirit)
[ę+ stem: -(')nigǫho'kd- give up; consists of: -(')nigǫh(a)$_N$- mind -o'kd$_V$- end]

a·hę'ni·gǫ́·ho'k·dę' he gave up (his will to live)

glad see: happy

a·gat·sę·nǫ́:ni' I got happy

glance

ǫ·gat·ga·hę́:gę' fleeting glance; she caught a glimpse (out of the corner of her eye)
[at+ stem: -gahęgę- glance, glimpse, flash; consists of: -gah(a)$_N$- eye -gę$_V$- see]

ęh·sat·ga·hę́:gę' you will glimpse it

glance see: look, peek

ha'sát·gah·to' you looked

se·ga·ha·nę́hsg·wahs you steal a peek

glare

a·ga·dehs·rę'dǫ́:ni: I am grouchy (glaring)
[ade+ stem: -(h)srę'dǫni- glare, be grouchy; consists of: -(a)hsrǫhę('da)$_N$- anger, temper -ǫni, ǫny$_V$- make]

sa·dehs·rę'dǫ́:ni: glare; make yourself look mad

glass tumbler see: glassy

glasses see: eye glasses

ga·gá·hihs·da' eye glasses

glassy

de·yo·wid·rá:teh it is glassy, icy; a glass tumbler
[de+yo+ stem: -widrateh- glassy, icy, glass tumbler; consists of: -widr(a)$_N$- ice -(a)te$_V$- bright, clear]

glazed see: glassy

gleam see: shimmer

de·wa·tá·ę·dǫn·yǫh it is twinkling; it is shimmering

Cayuga pronunciation guide: /a/ father /e/ weigh /ę/ men (nasalized) /i/ police /o/ hole /ǫ/ home (nasalized) /u/ blue. Underlined vowels are voiceless or whispered. /'/ high pitch. /t/ too /d/ do /k/ king /g/ good (never soft g) /j/ judge or adze /s/ soon /sh/ less heat (never the sh in shirt) /sr/ shrine /sy/ sure /hw/ which (the sound made when you blow out a candle) /h/ hi /ts/ cats hide /'/ (the sound before the first vowel in 'uh-uh') /n/ noon /r/ round /w/ way /y/ yes.

glide see: float
ga·dig·ye·nǫ́:gye' they (z) are flying, floating about in the air (for example, seeds, etc.)
glimpse see: glance, peek
ęh·sat·ga̱·hę́:gę' you will glimpse it
se·ga·ha·nę́hsg·wahs you steal a peek
gloat see: proud
ih·sé:hah you gloat
globe see: orb
gá:gwa:' a celestial body (for example, the sun, the moon)
gloomy see: dim
ga·jihs·da̱hk·wáh·dǫh, ga·jihs·da̱hk·wáh·twęh it is dim
glory
ga·i·ho·wá:nęh glory
[ga+ stem: -(r)ihowanęh- glory; consists of: -(r)ih(wa)$_N$- word -owanęh$_V$- be big]
gloss see: shine, smooth
dę·séhs·da·te't you are going to shine it
dę·yóhs·da·teh it is shiny, smooth (like silver)
glottal stop
de·gá·da̱hs·ta' glottal stop
[de+ga+ stem: -dahsta'- glottal stop; consists of: -dahsd$_V$- stop s.t.]
glove
o'n·yǫ́·dǫ', de·yo'nyǫ́:dǫ' gloves
[(de+)(y)o+ stem: -(')nyǫdǫ'- glove; consists of: -(')ny(a)$_N$- finger, hand -ǫdǫ'$_V$- several attached objects]
glow see: sunshine
o·dę́·ha·o:t sunshine
glue
et·séhs·da·ta' glue
[e+ stem: -tsehsdata'- glue; consists of: -tsehsd(a)$_N$- syrup, honey, gum, rubber; -ta'$_V$- dry]
glue see: resin, tape, sticky
ohs·da:'áh ot·séhs·da' pine pitch, resin
et·sehs·dá:ta' e·ya:nę·dák·da̱hk·wa' glue; scotch tape

glue (continued)
ot·séhs·da·ę:' it is sticky
glutton
a·gá·det·sę: I am a glutton
[ade+ stem: -tsę:- glutton; consists of: -tsę(:)$_V$- gobble, gorge]
ho·dé:tsę: he is a glutton
sa·dé:tsę: you're greedy for food; you are a glutton
ęh·sá·det·sęhs you will be a glutton; you will gobble, gorge yourself
[ade+ stem: -tsęhsd- make oneself a glutton; consists of: -tsę(:)$_V$- gobble, gorge]
a·gá·det·sęhs I made myself into a glutton
gluttonous see: greedy
hohs·gén·ha'seh he is greedy
gnarled see: bend
de·yót·sa'k·dǫh it is bent; a curve; a bend
gnat see: fly
ot·rę́'da' housefly; fly
gnaw see: chew
de·yóts·g'a·hǫ' it is chewing, it is a chewer (for example, a cow)
go
í:ge' I am walking, moving
[stem: -e$_V$- go]
ę́ tsǫ́: it·se' you are wandering (right now)
á:yak·ne:' we two (excl.) would go together
ęhs·ne:' you two will go together
go see: go across, go after, go ahead, go along doing s.t., go away, go back, go back inside, go back there, go down, go in, go in a direction, go out, go over, go over there, go somewhere, go under, go up
go across see: cross
a·ta·hę·dí:ya'k he went across the field

go after
sah·ga:gwá·ha' go get some wood chips
[stem: -gwah- go after; consists of: -(h)g(a:)$_N$- wood chip -gw$_V$- gather, pick, get]
a'ǫ·dę·na'trag·wá·ha' she went after groceries
[stem: -gwah- go after; consists of: -na'tr(a)$_N$- food, lunch -gw$_V$- gather, pick, get]
go ahead see: continue
hę·gá·dagye' it will continue on
go along doing s.t.
ga·ji'do·dá:gye' s.o. is going along crying
[A+(N+) stem: -ji'd(a)$_N$- cry -odagye'$_V$- go along doing s.t.]
go along doing s.t.
[-odagye'(s) the verb 'stand' in the progressive; denotes 'going along and doing something']
go away see: leave
he·sáh·dęg·yǫ: you went over there
go back
ihs·ge's I have returned home
[s+... stem: -e$_V$- go; go back]
go back see: return, turn
hes·gáh·gẹh·ta' I go back all the time
dǫ:sa·gat·ga·ha:dé:ni' I should turn around and go back; I should go home
go back inside
hǫ·sa·há:yǫ' he went back inside; he arrived back there
[he+s+... stem: -yǫ$_V$- arrive, go back inside]
go back there
hęs·géh·ta:k I will go again and again
[he'+s+... stem: -e$_V$- go back there]
hǫ·sá:kne:' we two (incl.) went back
hęs·ge' I am going back there
tó é: hęs·ge:' I will go again

go down see: descend
ę·sá:s·nęht you will get down (off of s.t.)
go in
ha'gyǫ' I went in
[he'+... stem: -yǫ$_V$- arrive, go in]
ha'ha:dí:yǫ' they (m) went in there, they arrived
hęd·wá:yǫ' we all (incl.) will go in together
hę·ya:gwá:yǫ' we all (excl.) will go in together
he·ho:dí:yǫ: they (m) arrived, they went in there
ha'jǫh, ha'syǫh go in; enter
go in a direction
tga·ęg·wá:dih they (f/m) are going in a direction
[d+A+ stem: -gwadih- go in a direction; consists of: -(a)dih$_V$- side]
go out
gyá:gę's I am going out
[stem: -yagę'$_V$- go out]
ęhs·yá:gę' you will go out
ęg·yá:gę' I will go out
he·yo·ya·gę́'ǫh that's where it went out
gyo·yá·gę'ǫh it comes out here; it is sticking out, protruding
go over see: climb
ęhs·rá:tę' you will climb
go over there
ha'se' you are going
[he'+... stem: -e$_V$- go; go over there]
to ha'ge' where I am going
ha'gę́:ne' they (z) are going
ha'á:kne:' we two (excl.) went
ha'gá·ę:' they (f/m) are going
hé:ge: let me go there
hǫ·ge'nhǫ́:gye' **(hǫ·ge'ǫ́·hǫ·gye')** while I am going there
[he'+... stem: -e'ǫhǫgye'$_V$- go along]
hęh·sé'sǫ' go on ahead, take the lead
[he'+... stem: -e'sǫ$_V$- go; go over there]

Cayuga pronunciation guide: /a/ father /e/ weigh /ę/ men (nasalized) /i/ police /o/ hole /ǫ/ home (nasalized) /u/ blue. Underlined vowels are voiceless or whispered. /'/ high pitch. /t/ too /d/ do /k/ king /g/ good (never soft g) /j/ judge or adze /s/ soon /sh/ less heat (never the sh in shirt) /sr/ shrine /sy/ sure /hw/ which (the sound made when you blow out a candle) /h/ hi /ts/ cats hide /'/ (the sound before the first vowel in 'uh-uh') /n/ noon /r/ round /w/ way /y/ yes.

go somewhere
ti·yo:né:no' where they have gone
[ti+P+ stem: -enǫ$_V$- originate from someplace, go somewhere]
go under
dęh·sa·d'ę·hę́:gǫht you will go under the fence
[de+...ad+N+ stem: -(a)dę'h(ę)$_N$- fence -ǫgohd$_V$- surpass, go under s.t.]
go up see: climb, fly
ęhs·rá:tę' you will climb
a·tá:dę' he took off (from the ground)
goal see: achieve
ę·sa·dad·rih·wag·wé:nyę's you will achieve s.t.
goat
ga·yá'dag·rahs goat
[ga+ stem: -ya'dagrahs- goat; consists of: -ya'd(a)$_N$- body -grahs$_V$- stink]
o·nǫ·da·geh·ká:' **ga·yá'dag·rahs** mountain goat
[consists of: onǫdagehgeha:' the hilly or mountainous type; gaya'dagrahs goat]
goat (get s.o.'s goat)
a'e·sa·hí:ya'k she got your goat
[TR+ stem: -(h)iya'g$_V$- hold a grudge, get s.o.'s goat]
goat shed
ga·ya'dag·ráhs ga·dí'drǫ' goat shed
[consists of: gaya'dagrahs goat; ga-di'drǫ' they (z) live (designates a shed, dog house; etc.)]
gobble see: glutton
ęh·sá·det·sęhs you will be a glutton; you will gobble, gorge yourself
godfather see: C
ha'ní:hah my godfather
gold
gah·wíhs·da·nǫ:' gold; anything expensive

gold (continued)
[ga+ stem: -(h)wihsdanǫ:'- gold; consists of: -(h)wihsd(a), (hr)ihsd(a)$_N$- metal, money -nǫ:'$_V$- costly, dear, expensive]
gę:gę́: gahwíhsdanǫ:' white gold
[consists of: gę'gę: it is white; it is light-coloured; gahwihsdanǫ:' gold]
goldenrod
gah·sę·hę·yę́h·ta' goldenrod (lit.: the frost hits it)
[ga+ stem: -(h)sęhęyęhta'- goldenrod; consists of: -(h)sęh(ę)$_N$- frost -(y)ęhd$_V$- hit, knock down, strike]
golf
ni·wę'n·hot·rus:'úh hę·nę'n·hot·rá'ehs golf
[consists of: niwę'nhotrus:'uh an amount of small balls; hęnę'nhotra'ehs they (m) hit balls]
o·ga·ho'jí·yo·geh golf
[o+ stem: -gaho'jiyo'geh- golf; consists of: -gaho'j(a)$_N$- grass; -iyo:$_V$- nice -(')geh- on]
gonorrhea
o·jíg·wę·da' gonorrhea
[o+ stem: -jigwęd(a)$_N$- gonorrhea]
good
o·yá:nre' it is nice, good, beautiful
[o+ stem: -yanre'$_V$- good, nice, beautiful]
shę́h ni·yó·yan·re' how good it is
good see: nice
sǫg·we'dí:yo: you are a nice person
good at s.t.
se·wá·i·hǫh you are good at s.t.
[A+(N+) stem: -waihǫh$_V$- be good at s.t.]
ha·nǫn·ya·wá·i·hǫh he is a good dancer
[A+(N+) stem: -nǫny(a)$_N$- dance -waihǫh$_V$- be good at s.t.]

good at s.t. (continued)
sa·yę́·dehs·gǫ: you are always really good at it
[P+(N+) stem: -(y)ęde(:,ʼ)V- recognize] -(h)sgǫ:V- easily]
ę·sa·yę·déʼǫ·hǫ:k you will be really good at it
sa·yę·dé:ʼǫh you are really good at s.t.
sak·wa·yę·déʼǫ: you are a good cook
[P+(N+) stem: -yęde:ʼ- be good at s.t.; consists of: -k(wa)N- food -(y)ęde(:,ʼ)V- recognize]
good-bye see: I (o:nęh gʼih·ya:ʼ), wave
de·sę·nęt·sá·ǫn·yǫ: wave your arms (goodbye)
good humored see: good-natured
good time (have a good time) see: enjoy
ęhs·wa·dǫt·gá:dǫ:ʼ you all will have a good time, enjoy yourselves, have fun
good-looking
ga·ya·ǫʼdí:yo: nice-looking body
[ga+ stem: -(he)yǫ(ʼda)N- corpse, cadaver -iyo:V- be nice, good]
good-natured
ga:gǫg·wʼe·dí:yo: they (f/m) are good natured people
[A+ stem: -ǫgwe(ʼda)N- person -iyo:V- be nice, good]
goodies
o·gaʼǫhs·hǫ́:ʼǫh goodies; dessert
[o+ stem: -gaʼǫhshǫ:ʼǫh- goodies, dessert; consists of: -gaʼV- like the taste of s.t.]
goose
hǫ́:ga:k goose
[stem: -(h)ǫga:kN- goose]
gooseberry
sa:nó:ʼ wa̲h·ya:s gooseberry
[consists of: sa:no:ʼ a raccoon; wa̲hya:s it eats the berries]
gopher see: ground hog
téh·tǫʼ ground hog; woodchuck; gopher

gore see: spear
a·to·waʼę́·naʼehs he speared him with a stick
gorge see: canyon, glutton
he·yo·heh·dę́ʼǫ·ge: canyon
ęh·sá·det·sęhs you will be a glutton; you will gobble, gorge yourself
gorilla
ga·jiʼnǫh·da:sgó:wah gorilla
[ga+ stem: -jiʼnǫhdasgowah- gorilla; consists of: -jiʼnǫw(a), jiʼnǫhN- insect, bug -(a)hdaʼV- get full of food -gowah- big]
gospel see: Bible
ga̲h·ya·dǫhs·ra·do·gę́h·diʼ, oh·ya·dǫhs·ra·do·gę́h·diʼ Bible
gospel singer see: choir
de̲·ha·dí:h·wa̲hk·waʼ a choir; they (m) are) gospel singers
gossamer see: sheer
o·jíʼa·deʼ sheer, lacy fabrics; lace
gossip
de·yǫd·ri̲h·wa·ę·dǫ́hk·waʼ a female gossiper
[de+...ad+ stem: -(r)ihwaędǫhkw- gossip; consists of: -(r)ih(wa)N- word -ędǫhV- shake s.t.]
dę·sad·ri̲h·wá·ę·dǫhk, dęh·sad·ri̲h·wá·ę·dǫh you will gossip
gouge see: scratch
de·sah·ji·yóhs·rǫ: really scratch it
gourmand see: glutton
a·gá·det·sę: I am a glutton
govern see: G (ǫg·wahs·ha·i·neʼ)
governor see: lead
ha·hę́:dǫʼ he is the front, leader
Governor General see: G (gwa:go:wah gon·haʼtraʼ)
grab
da·ję́:na: grab it
[d/heʼ+... stem: -yena(w), yenaǫ, yena(:)V- catch, receive, accept, grab s.t.]

grace see: mercy
gę·dá·ǫhs·ra' mercy
grain see: corn, rice
o·nę́·hę:' corn
o·ná·ja·gę:t rice
Grand River see: E (Gi·hę'go·wah·neh)
grand-child see: C (ga·ke·yad·re's·hǫ')
ga·ke·yad·ré'shǫ' my grand-children
grand-daughter see: C (ke·ya:dre')
ke·yá:dre' my grand-daughter
grand-father see: ancestor, C (heh·so:t)
ha·di·gęh·jih·sǫ'gę́·hę:' they (m) are our grandfathers, our ancestors
grand-mother see: C (ǫ·geh·so:t)
ǫ·géh·so:t my grand-mother
grand-son see: C (he·ya:dre')
he·yá:dre' my grand-son
grand-parent see: elder, old (person)
ga·e·gęh·jih·sǫ́:'ǫh they (f/m) are elderly
ga·e·gęh·jíhs·hǫ' they are old
grant see: G (hǫ·wa·di̲h·wihs·da·wihs), give, lend
dahs·gǫh give it to me
ęh·sa·dę·ní·hah·dę' you will lend
grape
ohn·yǫ́g·wid·ra' grapes
[o+ stem: -(h)nyǫgwidr(a)$_N$- grape]
grapefruit
ǫ·dehsg·yǫ·wa·ta'tá' oh·ya' grapefruit
[consists of: ǫdehsgyǫwata'ta' s.o. loses weight, diets; ohya' fruit]
ǫ·dehsg·yǫ·wa·ta'tá' oh·yá' gra̲he:t grapefruit tree
[consists of: ǫdesgyǫwata'ta' ohya' grapefruit; gra̲he:t living tree]
grasp see: catch, hold
ęg·yé:na:' I will accept it, catch it
e·ha:' she is holding s.t. right now
grass
o·gá·ho'ja' grass
[o+ stem: -gaho'j(a)$_N$- grass]
o·ga·ho'já'geh on the grass
o·ga·ho'já:gǫ: in the grass

grasshopper
jíhs·da: grasshopper
[stem: -jihsd(a:)$_N$- grasshopper]
grassland see: meadow
ga̲·hę́·da·ę' meadow; pasture; field
grate
se·gé·dahs you are scraping s.t. right now
[(N+) stem: -ged$_V$- grate, scrape, file]
sé:ge:t grate, scrape, file it
ęh·sé:ge:t you will grate, scrape, file
sa·gé·dǫh you are scraping s.t. right now
hę·nah·ga:gé·dahs they (m) are scraping the splints
[stem: -(a)hg(a:)$_N$- splint -ged$_V$- grate, scrape, file]
ha·di·ge·dá'ta' they (m) file it
[stem: -geda'd$_V$- grate, scrape, file s.t.]
gratefulness see: happiness
ot·sę́·nǫn·ya't a happy feeling; gratefulness, thankfulness, joy
gratification see: satisfaction
o'ni·gǫh·sí·yǫhs·de:' satisfaction
gratified see: happy
a·gat·sę·nǫ́:ni: I am glad, happy
gratitude see: happiness
ot·sę́·nǫn·ya't a happy feeling; gratefulness, thankfulness, joy
grave marker see: sign
ga·néhs·da·ot headboards; grave markers; billboards; signs
gravel
ni·gahs·gwa·ó:s'uh small gravel
[stem: -(h)sg(wa:)$_N$- stone, bullet, rock -u:s'uh$_V$- several small objects]
ga̲hs·wá·ǫg·yǫ: gravel has been put down
[stem: -(h)sg(wa:)$_N$- stone, bullet, rock -ǫdi, -ǫgy$_V$- throw]
ni·gahs·gwa·ǫ́:gyǫ: gravel thrown down somewhere

gravity
go·yaʼda·nę·da·gǫ́h·taʼ gravity (lit.: it keeps one down, holds one in place)
[go+ stem: -yaʼdanędagǫhtaʼ- gravity; consists of: -yaʼd(a)$_{N}$- body -(raʼ)nęd(aːʼg), (yaʼ)nęd(aːʼg)$_{V}$- stick, cling]

gray see: grey
de·yo·da·gę́hn·yʼa·gǫh grey

grease
sná·sǫː lubricate s.t.
[stem: -(h)nasǫ(ː)- oil oneself]
sna·sǫ́ː gad·réh·daʼ lubricate, grease the car

grease see: motor oil, oil
oh·ná·jiː motor oil; black grease
oh·naʼ grease; oil

greasy
ha·díh·naʼ they (m) are greasy people
[A+ stem: -(h)n(a)$_{N}$- oil, gas]

greasy see: oily
oh·ná·iːʼ it is oily, greasy

great
ha·do·wahs·góː·wah he is a great hunter
[stem: -(a)dowad$_{V}$- hunt; -gowah- great]

great
[-goːwah augmentative suffix; denotes 'largeness', 'greatness']

greatest
neʼ gya·ǫ·hę́ːʼęh the greatest
[neʼ g+ya+ stem: -(r)ǫhęːʼęh- greatest; consists of: -(r)ǫhę$_{V}$- alone]

greatest see: best
gwáhs gyo·yáː·nreʼ the best

greedy
hohs·gén·haʼseh he is greedy
[P+ stem: -(a)hsgęnhaʼseh$_{V}$- greedy]
sa̲hs·gę́n·haʼseh you are greedy

greedy see: stingy
sa·níʼǫh you are stingy, greedy, cheap

green
on·ráh·dʼa·ęːʼ green
[o+ stem: -nrahdʼaęːʼ- green; consists of: -nrahd(a)$_{N}$- leaf -ʼęːʼ$_{V}$- be coloured]
on·rah·dʼa·ęʼtra·jiːʼ dark green
[o+ stem: -nrahdaʼętr(a)$_{N}$- green -ji(ː,h)$_{V}$- dark]
o·géː·drǫːt hanging green fruit
[o+ stem: -gedr(a)$_{N}$- green, unripe -ǫd$_{V}$- attached]

green see: unripe
o·géː·draʼ it is green (not ripe); raw fruit

greenhouse
hę·nah·do·gáh·taʼgeh greenhouse (lit.: where they (m) grow things)
[A+ stem: -(a)hdogahtaʼgeh- greenhouse; consists of: -(a)hdogahd$_{V}$- raise s.t.]

greet see: thank
dęhs·he·nǫ·hǫ́ː·n·yǫːʼ you will welcome, greet, thank s.o.

greetings see: hello
sgę́ː·nǫʼ hello, how are you?

grey
de·yo·da·gę́hn·yʼa·gǫh grey
[de+yo+ad+ stem: -(a)gęhnyaʼgǫh- grey; consists of: -(a)ʼgęh(ęda)$_{N}$- ash, dust -(i)yaʼg$_{V}$- cut, break]

grey hair
ho·nǫ́h·raʼtęʼ he has grey hair
[P+ stem: -nǫʼ(aː), nǫh(a)$_{N}$- head -(r)aʼtęʼ$_{V}$- grey hair]
go·nǫ́h·raʼtęʼ she has grey hair

grieve
de·wak·ni·gǫ́hn·yʼa·gǫh I am broken-hearted, grieving
[de+P+ stem: -(ʼ)nigǫhnyaʼg- grieve, be broken-hearted; consists of: -(ʼ)nigǫh(a)$_{N}$- mind -(i)yaʼg$_{V}$- cut, break]

Cayuga pronunciation guide: /a/ father /e/ weigh /ę/ men (nasalized) /i/ police /o/ hole /ǫ/ home (nasalized) /u/ blue. Underlined vowels are voiceless or whispered. /ʹ/ high pitch. /t/ too /d/ do /k/ king /g/ good (never soft g) /j/ judge or adze /s/ soon /sh/ less heat (never the sh in shirt) /sr/ shrine /sy/ sure /hw/ which (the sound made when you blow out a candle) /h/ hi /ts/ cats hide /ʼ/ (the sound before the first vowel in 'uh-uh') /n/ noon /r/ round /w/ way /y/ yes.

grieve (continued)
de·gę'ni·gó·hog·wahs I am broken-hearted (lit.: my mind is scattered) [de+…ę+ stem: -(')nigǫhogw- grieve; consists of: -(')nigǫh(a)$_N$- mind -ogw$_V$- scatter]
ag·yǫ'ni·gǫ·hó:go' her mind is scattered
grieve see: mourn
ęh·sa·dę·nǫ́'nya:t you will mourn
grill see: barbecue
ǫ·de's·gǫ·dáhk·wa' barbecue equipment
grimace see: frown
dęh·sát·gręg·ręht you will sneer, frown
grime see: dirty
ot·gi' it is ugly, dirty, soiled
grin see: smile
a·ho:yǫ́:di' he smiled
grind see: grate, slice
sé:ge:t grate, scrape, file it
grind one's teeth
de·yo·n'o·já:ga: grinding, rattling teeth [de+…at+ stem: -no'jaga:- grind one's teeth; consists of: -no'j(a)$_N$- tooth -ga:$_V$- make a rattling or grinding noise]
de·sat·no'já:ga: grind your teeth
grinder
de·gá·hih·ta' grinder; cutter [de+ga+ stem: -(hr)ihta'- grinder; consists of: -(hr)ihd$_V$- cause to break up]
dehs·riht grind it
grip see: catch, hold
ęg·yé·na:' I will accept it, catch it
e·ha:' she is holding s.t. right now
gristle see: fat
o'dǫ́:dra' it is fat; gristle; rind
groan see: agony
sa·ǫ́h·ya·gę: groan
groceries see: lunch
a·dę́·n'at·ra' lunch; groceries
groin
o·há:na' groin [stem: -(h)an(a)$_N$- groin]
sha·ná'geh on your groin

groin (continued)
gę·há·n'a·geh on my groin
swa̲·há·n'a·geh on your (p) groins
ha·ná:ji: he has dark loins, a dark groin (can be a derogatory comment) [A+ stem: -(h)an(a)$_N$- groin, thigh -ji(:,h)$_V$- dark]
groom see: clean, husband, marry
de·sa·da·déhs·nyeh tidy up; groom yourself
he·gę́h·jih my husband
hon·yá:kd·re' he is getting married
grope
hehs·yáh·nǫ·ha' you are picking at s.t. (for example, your food); you are a groper [he'+… stem: -yahnǫ(:)$_V$- grope]
hęhs·yáh·nǫ:' you will grope, touch, pick at s.t.
hehs·yáh·nǫh you are touching here and there, groping
hehs·yáh·nǫn·yǫh you are going along groping, picking at things
gross see: twelve (dek·ni: sga·e'), unpleasant
de·a·ǫ·wé:saht it is unpleasant
grotesque see: evil
ga̲·hé:t·gę' it is ugly
grouchy see: grumpy
de·di·sa'ni·gǫ·hí:yo: you are grumpy, grouchy, not happy
ground see: earth, land, soil
oh·wę́·ja·gǫ: under the earth, ground
o·héh·da' dirt; earth
oh·né'dr'a·geh on the ground
ground hog
téh·tǫ' ground hog; woodchuck; gopher [stem: -tehtǫ'- ground hog, etc.; consists of: -(h)ehd(a)$_N$- land, dirt, earth, ground -(h)ǫ(:)$_V$- lie]

group
gęg·yóhg·wa·ęʼ a group
[ga+ stem: -(i)gyohgwaęʼ- association, group, agency, etc.; consists of: -(i)gyohg(wa)$_N$- crowd -ę$_V$- lie on the ground]
group see: association
gęg·yohg·wa·gé·hǫʼ associations; councils; agencies; groups
grout see: clay
oʼda:ʼ clay; mud; mortar
grove see: forest, orchard
ga·há:daʼ forest
wah·yá·yęt·węh orchard; berry field
grow
ǫh·dó:gahs she is prepubescent, she is maturing, she is reaching puberty
[stem: -(a)hdog$_V$- grow, mature]
ęh·sáh·do:k you will grow
ę·wáh·do:k it will multiply, grow
a·wáh·do:k it sprouted
o·nah·do·gé·hęg·yeʼ they (z) are growing (that is, plants, vegetation)
sah·do:k grow (not common)
o·tǫ·dǫn·yáh·nǫʼ growing bushes, saplings
[ad+N+ stem: -ǫnyahnǫʼ- grow; consists of: -(h)ǫd(a)$_N$- bush -ǫni, ǫny$_V$- make]
od·wę·nohg·rǫ́n·yah·nǫʼ the growing weeds
[ad+N+ stem: -ǫnyahnǫʼ- grow; consists of: -węnohgr(a)$_N$- weed -ǫni, ǫny$_V$- make]
gǫh·do·gʼa·dǫ́·hǫg·yeʼ she is growing s.t.
[P+ stem: -(a)hdogaʼd, (a)hdogahd- grow s.t., raise s.t., s.o.; consists of: -(a)hdog$_V$- grow, mature]
ę·ya·gǫh·do·ga·dǫ́·hǫg·yeʼ she will be continually growing it, them

grow see: raise
ęh·sah·dó:gaʼt you will grow s.t.
growth see: lump
og·wá·ǫt it has a lump, a bulge
grudge
sa·tíʼyahs·gǫ: you hold grudges; you get angry easily
[at+ stem: -(h)iyaʼg$_V$- hold a grudge -sgǫ:- easily]
ęh·sá:ti:yaʼk you will hold a grudge
a·sa:tí:yaʼk you held a grudge
sa·tí·yʼa·gǫh you are holding a grudge right now
grudging see: unwilling
de·wa·ge·gá·ę I do not want to do it; I am unwilling
grumpy
de·di·sʼa·ni·gǫ·hí:yo: you are grumpy, grouchy, unhappy
[de'+d+P+ -(ʼ)nigǫhiyo:- grumpy, grouchy, unhappy; consists of: -(ʼ)nigǫh(a)$_N$- mind -iyo:$_V$- be nice, good]
guard
dę·hó·nę·hę:ʼ he is a guard
[de+ stem: -nęhę(:)$_V$- guard, stand in a line]
dę·ha·di·nę·hę́:hęʼ they (m) are guards
haʼde·ho·di·nę·hę́·dag·yeʼ they (m) are guarding as they are on their way over, in transit
haʼde·ho·di·nę·hę́:deʼ they (m) are already guarding
ta·di·nę·hę́·da:s they (m) are guards; they are participants in a work-bee
guard see: protect, strikers
ho·na·dʼę·ní·gǫ·ha:ʼ they (m) are protecting, watching
dę·ho·di·nę́·hę:ʼ they (m) are guarding s.t. (for example, strikers); security guards

guardian
ǫ·gah·dǫ·gá'dǫh she raised me (that is, a guardian)
[TR+ stem: -(a)hdoga'd, (a)hdogahd- raise s.t., s.o.; consists of: -(a)hdog$_V$- grow, mature]
guess see: I (ǫh), think
ęh·sę·nǫh·dǫ́:nyǫ:' you will wonder, think
guffaw
ęs·yǫ́g·yat·ge: you will laugh loudly, guffaw
[stem: -yǫgyatge:- guffaw; consists of: -yǫgya'd$_V$- cause to smile -ge:- big]
guide see: lead, oversee, pattern, show
ęhs·rę:t you will be the lead
hod·rih·wat·gá·ha:' he is a supervisor, overseer
gyǫ·de'n·yę·dęhs·da̱hk·wa' pattern
gǫ·yǫh·wa·dá:nih I am showing you s.t.
guilty
a·ho·nǫ·dá:nha' he was found guilty
[P+ stem: -nǫdanh$_V$- guilty]
ęh·sat·nǫ·dá:nha' you will make yourself guilty
ho·nǫ́·dan·hęh he is guilty
o·nǫ́·dan·hęh it is guilty
go·nǫ́·dan·hęh she is guilty
sa·nǫ́·dan·hęh you are guilty
a·hod·ri̱h·wá'e:s he was found guilty
[P+ad+ stem: -(r)ihwa'ehsd- be found guilty, be blamed; consists of: -(r)ih(wa)$_N$- word -(')ehsd$_V$- cause to hit]
a·god·ri̱h·wá'ehs she got blamed
ǫ·gad·ri̱h·wá'ehs I was blamed
guilty see: condemn
ęhs·yé:saht you will condemn, slander, insult s.o.
guitar
ga·nó:wa' guitar; any string instrument
[ga+ stem: -nowa(gwa)$_N$- rounded back]
gulley
o·yá·dag·ye' gulley
[stem: -yadagye'- gulley; consists of: -yad(a)$_N$- hole, track, ditch; -agye'$_V$- be ongoing]
gullible see: believe
dih·séh·da̱h·gǫh you are credulous, gullible; you believe in s.t.
gulp
ha'gǫ́·nęht·ge: I took a big swallow, a gulp
[he'+... stem: -ǫnęhtge:- gulp; consists of: -ǫnęhd$_V$- swallow]
gum
sgat·sés·da:t one piece of gum
[s+ga+ stem: -tsehsd(a)$_N$- syrup, honey, gum, rubber -d$_V$- stand; be one]
gum see: resin
ohs·da:'áh ot·séhs·da' pine pitch; resin
gums
sy'ǫ·dá'geh on your gums
[stem: -yǫ'd(a)$_N$- gums]
gy'ǫ·dá'geh on my gums
gun see: machine gun, rifle
ę·ga·e'á:ksǫ:' a machine gun
ga̱·hó'de:s a rifle
guts
o·yǫ́:wa' guts; intestines
[o+ stem: -yǫw(a'da)$_N$- gut, intestine]
gut see: belly, eviscerate
ok·sé'da' a belly
ęhs·yǫ·wa·dáh·go' you will gut s.t.
gutter see: basement
o·yá:de' basement; track; ditch
guy see: male, man
de̱·ha·di·yáhs·he: two males; they (m) are two
hǫ́:gweh a man; a boy
gym
ot·gahn·ye̱·dahk·wá' o·nǫ́h·sǫt gym
[consists of: otgahnye̱dahkwa' a place where people play; a playground; onǫhsǫt a room]

gyrate see: turn
dęh·sat·ga·ha:dé:ni' you will turn yourself around

H

habit see: way
tsę́h ni·yǫg·wá·i·ho'dę: our ways
habit-forming see: addicted, helpless
hog·yá·na'ǫh he is possessed, addicted (with gambling, women, etc.)
tsa'hó:ya:t he can't help himself; it's become a habit with him
habitation see: house
ga·nǫ́h·sa' a house
hack see: chop
a·ge'ó:gǫh I did chop; I have chopped
Hagersville, Ont. see: E (Tga·nę·no·ga·he:')
haggle see: barter
dęhs·nǫ́·wa·yęht you will barter, bargain, affirm a deal
hail
o·wíd·rǫg·yǫ: it is hailing; sleet
[o+ stem: -widrǫdi- hail, sleet; consists of: -widr(a)$_N$- ice -(a)di, ogy, -ǫdi, -ǫgy$_V$- throw]
hail see: call
hęhs·hé·yah·sǫ:' you will be calling s.o.'s name
hail from see: come from
nǫ·dá:kne:' where we two (excl.) came from
hair
ǫt·ge' s.o.'s hair
[(at+) stem: -ge'(a:), geh(a)$_N$- hair]
o·gé'a:' hair; a rag; it is ragged, tattered
sa·gé'a:' your hair
sa·gé'a'geh on your hair
hair (continued)
go·gé'e:s she has long hair
[P+ stem: -ge'(a:), geh(a)$_N$- hair -es$_V$- be long]
hair see: grey hair, fair-haired
ho·nǫ́h·ra'tę' he has grey hair
go·nǫ́h·gę:t she is fair haired; she has light hair
hair dryer
ǫt·gé' a·tá'tkwa' hair dryer
[consists of: ǫtge' s.o.'s hair; ata'tkwa' dryer]
hair brush
ǫt·gé' ę·dé·dahk·wa' hair brush
[consists of: ǫtge' (having to do with hair); ędędahkwa' brush]
hair net
ot·ge:o·wé:kta' hair net
[o+at+ stem: -ge'owekta'- hair net; consists of: -ge'(a:), geh(a)$_N$- hair -(hr)owekd$_V$- cause to be covered]
ǫ·de·j'i·a·o:wé:kta' hair net
[ǫ+ade+ stem: -ji'aowekta'- hair net; consists of: -ji'(a:)$_N$- curtain, lace -(hr)owekd$_V$- cause to be covered]
hair salon
gyǫt·ge'ahs·rǫ́·nihs·geh hair salon
[g+yǫ+at+ stem: -ge'ahsrǫnihsgeh- hair salon; consists of: -ge'(a:), geh(a)$_N$- hair -ǫni, ǫny$_V$- make -(')geh- at]
hair tie
gat·ge'a·yę́n·hahs·ta' hair tie
[ga+at+ stem: -ge'aęnhahsta'- hair tie; consists of: -ge'(a:), geh(a)$_N$- hair -nhahsd$_V$- encircle]
hairdresser
e·ge·a's·rǫ́·ni: she is a hairdresser
[e+ stem: -ge'asrǫni:- hairdresser; consists of: -ge'(a:), geh(a)$_N$- hair -(h)srǫni$_V$- fix, repair]
hairless see: bald
tę' de·hó·ge'ot he has no hair; he is bald

Cayuga pronunciation guide: /a/ father /e/ weigh /ę/ men (nasalized) /i/ police /o/ hole /ǫ/ home (nasalized) /u/ blue. Underlined vowels are voiceless or whispered. /´/ high pitch. /t/ too /d/ do /k/ king /g/ good (never soft g) /j/ judge or adze /s/ soon /sh/ less heat (never the sh in shirt) /sr/ shrine /sy/ sure /hw/ which (the sound made when you blow out a candle) /h/ hi /ts/ cats hide /'/ (the sound before the first vowel in 'uh-uh') /n/ noon /r/ round /w/ way /y/ yes.

hairline
se.gę́'s.da.geh on your hairline, upper brow
[stem: -gę'sd(a:)$_N$- hairline, upper brow, forehead]
ge.gę́'sda:'geh on my forehead; on my hairline, upper brow
swa.gę́'ts'a.geh on your (p) hairline, upper brow; on your (p) foreheads
[stem: -gę'ts(a)$_N$- hairline, upper brow, forehead]
hairy see: fur
o.hę́h.da.e:' it is furry
half
tsa'de.yǫh.sę́:nǫh, tsa'de.wah.sę́:nǫh it is half; the middle
[tsa'de+A/P+(N+) stem: -(a)hsęnǫh$_V$- half]
tsa'de.ga.na'jǫhsg.wá.hęh one half cup
[tsa'+de+A+N+ consists of: -na'j(oh(s)gwa)$_N$- cup -(h)ęh$_V$- mid, half, middle]
half-past see: A (tsa'deyohsę:nǫ' niyodǫgohdǫh)
halfway see: middle
de.yó:gę: between; in the middle
hall see: meeting place
ǫd.ró.hek.ta' meeting place, gathering place
hallowed see: forbidden, sacred
o.nǫ́'ne:' it is forbidden, sacred, holy
o.ih.wá.ǫ:weh sacred idea
halve
de.só:wę: halve it
[de+(N+) stem: -owę(:)$_V$- split in two]
dę.sah.yó:wę' cut the fruit in half
[de+...(N+) stem: -(a)hy(a)$_N$- fruit -owę(:)$_V$- split in two]
hamburger
de.ga'wa.há.hih.dǫh hamburger
[de+ga+ stem: -(')wahahihdǫh- hamburger; consists of: -(')wah(a)$_N$- meat -(hr)ihd$_V$- be broken up]

Hamilton, Ont. see: E (Ga.hę.na.gǫ:)
hamlet see: village
ni.ga.na.dú:'uh village, small town
hammer
ga.jíh.wa' hammer
[ga+ stem: -jih(wa), jihy$_N$- hammer]
o.na'gá:' ga.jíh.wa' horn war club; club; hammer
[consists of: ona'ga:' horns, antlers; gajihwa' hammer]
hamper see: basket, clothes hamper, prevent
ga'áhd.ra' basket
es.dág.wahkwa' dirty clothes hamper; laundry basket
a.tá:dahs he stopped it, prevented it
hamstring
ohs.ná'da' hamstrings
[o+ stem: -(h)sna('da)$_N$- muscle, hamstring, calf]
hand
oh.sóh.da' hand; paw
[o+ stem: -(h)sohd(a)$_N$- hand, finger, paw]
seh.sóh.d'a.geh on your hand
geh.sóh.d'a.geh on my hand
swah.sóh.d'a.geh on your (p) hands
gah.sóh.dǫ:t hands on a clock
[ga+ stem: -(h)sohdǫd- clock hand; consists of: -(h)sohd(a)$_N$- hand -ǫd$_V$- attached]
ęgahjǫhai: I am going to wash my hands P
[-(a)hj(i'da)$_N$- hand -ohae$_V$- wash]
hand down
ęt.sá'sęht you will bring it down
[d+... stem: -(a')sęhd$_V$- hand down, bring down]
to'sę́h.dǫh he has handed down

handcuff

a·tǫ·wa·dihs·do·da:ʼ they handcuffed him, them (m)
[de+TR+ stem: -(h)sdoda:- handcuff; consists of: -hsd$_N$- tool, utensil -oda(:,h)$_V$- drape]

de·hǫ·wa·dihs·do·dáh·kwaʼ handcuffs
[de+hǫwadi+ stem: -(h)stodahkwaʼ- handcuff; consists of: : -hsd$_N$- tool, utensil -odahkwaʼ$_V$- s.t. draped]

handkerchief

ga̲h·nǫh handkerchief
[ga+ stem: -(h)nǫh- handkerchief]

handkerchief see: kerchief

ǫt·nǫʼá·o:wek·taʼ kerchief

handle

gat·gę́·het·saʼ a handle
[ga+ stem: -tgęhets(a)$_N$- handle]

gat·gę́·het·sǫ:t an attached handle
[ga+ stem: -tgęhets(a)$_N$- handle -ǫd$_V$- attached]

handle see: touch, pick up

haʼgye:ʼ I touched it

at·gehk I picked s.t. up

handsome

o·jí·nʼa·dǫ: it is handsome; s.t. / s.o. who is handsome, attractive
[P+ stem: -jinaʼdǫ:- consists of: -jinah$_V$- strong, brave]

ho·jí·nʼa·dǫ: he is a handsome man

a:gek·saʼgo·wá·gę̲·he:k I wish I were handsome
[A+ stem: -ksaʼgowah- pretty, handsome; consists of: -ksa(ʼda)$_N$- child -gowah- big, great]

hand span see: palm

ni·sesʼǫh·dá:dę:s how thick it is (measured by palms)

handstand

sa·dǫ·nǫ̲h·weʼt·só:taʼ you do handstands all the time
[(de+)…at+ stem: -nǫhweʼtsod$_V$- handstand]

handstand (continued)

dę·sat·nǫ̲h·weʼtsó:dǫʼ you will do a hand-stand, turn yourself upside down

de·sat·nǫ̲h·weʼt·so·dá:gyeʼ you are going along doing handstands

handy see: useful

o·í·hǫ:t it is useful

hang

ga·ní:yǫ:t it is hanging
[A+(N+) stem: -niyǫd$_V$- hang]

tga·ní:yǫ:t it is hanging over there

ga·ni:yǫ́:daʼk it hung there; it used to hang there

hǫ·wa·di̲hn·yáʼdręhs they hang him, them (m) all the time
[TR+ stem: -(h)nyaʼdr(ę:)$_V$- hang s.o.; consists of: -(h)nya(ʼsa)$_N$- neck -(aʼ)dręـ meet]

a·hǫ·wa·díhn·yʼad·rę:ʼ they hanged him, them (m)

hǫ·wa·di̲hn·yáʼd·ra·gǫh they have already hanged him (and his neck broke)

ak·ni:yǫ́:dęʼ I did hang it up
[stem: -niyǫd(ę)- hang s.t. up; consists of: -niyǫd$_V$- hang]

ak·ní:yǫ:t I hung it up

sa·ní:yǫ:t you hung it up

ę·yó·hęʼdǫ:ʼ it will be hanging over (an edge, a chair)
[P+ stem: -(h)ęʼdǫ:$_V$- hang over]

o·hę́ʼdǫh it is hanging over (an edge, a chair)

dę·sah·sʼi·dę́ʼdrǫ:ʼ you will hang your feet over the edge
[stem: -(a)hsi(ʼda), (ę)hs(a)$_N$- foot -ęʼdrǫ:$_V$- hang over]

hang see: drape, hang one's head

ę·gó:da:ʼ I will drape it

hanger see: clothes hanger

ga̲h·sǫh·dáʼ

ǫhg·wę̲n·ya·ni·yǫ·dáhk·waʼ wire clothes hangers

Cayuga pronunciation guide: /a/ father /e/ weigh /ę/ men (nasalized) /i/ police /o/ hole /ǫ/ home (nasalized) /u/ blue. Underlined vowels are voiceless or whispered. /´/ high pitch. /t/ too /d/ do /k/ king /g/ good (never soft g) /j/ judge or adze /s/ soon /sh/ less heat (never the sh in shirt) /sr/ shrine /sy/ sure /hw/ which (the sound made when you blow out a candle) /h/ hi /ts/ cats hide /ʼ/ (the sound before the first vowel in 'uh-uh') /n/ noon /r/ round /w/ way /y/ yes.

hang one's head
de·yo·nǫ·háʼkdǫ: it is hanging its head (for example, in sadness or shame)
[de+P+ stem: -nǫhakdǫ:- hang one's head, bow one's head; consists of: -nǫʼ(a:), nǫh(a)$_N$- head -(a)ʼkdǫ$_V$- be bent, crooked]

hang onto see: cling
sag·yé·na·waht cling to it; hang on

hangover
hoh·né·gan·yohs he has a hangover
[P+ stem: -(h)neganyohs- hangover; consists of: -(h)neg(a)$_N$- water, liquid -(r)iyo, nyo$_V$- kill someting]
ak·né·gan·yohs I have a hangover

hankie see: handkerchief
ga̱h·nǫh handkerchief

happen
ni·yá:węhs how it happens
[P+ stem: -ę(h,ʼ)$_V$- happen]
tsę́ haʼá:węh how it happened over there
dę·hoʼdę́ʼ naʼá:węh what happened?
ni·yá·wʼę·ǫh how it did happen

happen see: I (tęʼdaǫ, tęʼgiʼdaǫ)

happiness
ot·sę́·nǫn·yaʼt a happy feeling; gratefulness; thankfulness; joy
[o+at+ stem: -s(h)ęnǫnyaʼd- happiness; consists of: -s(h)ęnǫni$_V$- happy, glad]

happiness see: satisfaction
oʼni·gǫh·sí·yǫhs·de:ʼ satisfaction

happy
a·gę·nat·sę:nǫ́:niʼ they (z) got happy
[at+ stem: -s(h)ęnǫni$_V$- happy, glad]
a·gat·sę·nǫ́:niʼ I got happy
a·gat·sę·nǫ́:ni: I am glad, happy
go·nat·sę·nǫ́:ni: they (z) are happy, glad
hot·sę:nǫ́:ni: he is happy
ho·do·nǫ·há·he:ʼ he is happy
[P+ad+ stem: -ęnǫhahe:- be happy; consists of: -nǫʼ(a)/nǫh(a)$_N$- head; -(hr)e, (hr)ę$_V$- put, place]

happy-go-lucky
ho·dę·dǫn·yáʼda̱hs·gǫ: he is a joker, happy-go-lucky; he is obnoxious
[P+ad+ stem: -ędǫnyaʼdahsgǫ:- happy-go-lucky, joke, jest; consists of: -ędǫnyaʼd$_V$- be shaken up -(h)sgǫ:- easily]

harass see: bother
dęhs·ni·gǫ·há:haʼ you are annoying me, bothering me

hard
oh·ní:yǫh it is hard
[P+(N+) stem: -(h)niyǫh$_V$- hard, tough, solid]
ok·yę·da̱hk·wah·ní:yǫh it is a hard chair
[P+(N+) stem: -(a)kyędahkw(a)$_N$- chair -(h)niyǫh$_V$- hard, tough]

hard see: difficult
wę́:do:ʼ it is difficult

hard working see: work well
hot·sáh·niht he is a good worker, tireless, active, industrious, etc.

hard-on see: erection
ho·dáʼgę·ho:t he has an erection

harlot see: prostitute
wa·dat·gę·hǫ́·haʼ she (lit.: it) is a prostitute

harm see: hurt
ęhs·hé·nǫhn·yaʼk you will hurt s.o.

harmony
gʼa·ni·gǫ·hí:yo: harmony; to be of good mind
[ga+ stem: -(ʼ)nigǫh(a)$_N$- mind -iyo:$_V$- be nice, good]
dę·ga·ih·wá·ę·dʼad·reʼ harmony (lit.: every idea will always come together)
[de+ga+ stem: -(r)ihwaędadreʼ- harmony; consists of: -(r)ih(wa)$_N$- word -(aʼ)dre$_V$- go and meet]

harmony see: peace
sgę:nǫ́ʼ ge·nǫ́h·dǫn·yǫh I am at peace

harness
sen·heh·só:da: harness it (an animal)
[stem: -nhehsoda:- harness; consists of: -nhehs(a)$_N$- lace, ribbon, harness -oda(:,h)$_V$- drape]
wa·de'nheh·só·dahk·wa' a harness (for an animal)
[wa+(a)d+ stem: -nhehsodahkwa'- harness; consists of: -nhehs(a)$_N$- lace, ribbon, harness -odahkwa'$_V$- s.t. that stands]
harness see: lace
gan·héh·sa' harness; ribbon; laces
harry see: annoy
dęhs·ni·gǫ·há:ha' you are annoying me, bothering me
harrow see: hoe
at·keh·da·wę́:nye:' I hoed, tilled the earth
harrows
wa·de'dré's de·ga·heh·dá·hih·ta' drag harrows
[consists of: wade'dre's it is dragging itself; degahehdahihta' it breaks up the ground]
harsh see: demanding, rough
tgę·nǫ́h·dǫ·ha' I make the decisions; I am a strict person
á·o:ga't it is rough
harsh-speaking
sa·wę́·na·deht you are a harsh-speaking person; you are smark-alecky
[P+ stem: -węnadehd- harsh-speaking; consists of: -węn(a)$_N$- voice, word -dehd$_V$- bold, bright, strong]
o·wę́·na·deht harsh words
harvest
ha·yę́t·wag·wahs he is harvesting
[(N+) stem: -yętwagw- harvest; consists of: -yętw, yęto$_V$- plant]
ę·ha·yęt·wá:go' he will harvest
ho·yę́t·wag·węh he harvested it
ga·yę́t·wag·węh a harvest
harvester see: mower
ga̱hs·tǫ:drí:ya's mower (for hay)
hasten see: hurry, rush
dęh·sa'd·rá·i·hęh you will rush, hurry
deh·se'drá·i·ha't you rush s.t., hurry s.t. up
hat
a·na·há·ot·ra' hat
[stem: -anahaotr(a)$_N$- hat]
a·ga·na̱·há·o:tra' my hat
sa·na·há·o:tra' your hat
go̱hs·reh·ká:' a·na·há·ǫ:tra' winter hat
[consists of: go̱hsrehka:' winter kind; anahaotra' hat]
ohs·tǫd·rá' a·na·há·ǫ:tra' straw hat
[consists of: ohstǫ:dra' straw; anahaotra' hat]
hat see: cap
gatg·wę́h·do:t a cap
hatchet see: axe
a·dó:gę' axe; tomahawk
hate
gǫhs·wá·hęhs I hate you
[TR+ stem: -(h)swahęh$_V$- hate, dislike]
kehs·wá·hęhs I hate her
ęh·séhs·wa̱·hęh you will hate, dislike
hatred
ohs·wá·hęh·de:' hatred
[o+ stem: -(h)swahęhde:'- hatred; consists of: -(h)swahęhd$_V$- be hated, disliked]
ohs·wá·hęh·dǫ: hatred
[o+ stem: -(h)swahę'dǫ:- hatred; consists of: -(h)swahęhd$_V$- be hated, disliked]
haul
knęhg·wihs I carry it all the time
[(N+) stem: -nęhgwi$_V$- haul]
ga·nę́hg·wih it hauls things
ęk·nę́hg·wi' I will carry, move, tote it
ak·nę́hg·wi: I have moved it
e·nę́hg·w'it·a' what you haul with
[(N+) stem: -nęhgwi'd$_V$- be hauled]

Cayuga pronunciation guide: /a/ father /e/ weigh /ę/ men (nasalized) /i/ police /o/ hole /ǫ/ home (nasalized) /u/ blue. Underlined vowels are voiceless or whispered. /´/ high pitch. /t/ too /d/ do /k/ king /g/ good (never soft g) /j/ judge or adze /s/ soon /sh/ less heat (never the sh in shirt) /sr/ shrine /sy/ sure /hw/ which (the sound made when you blow out a candle) /h/ hi /ts/ cats hide /'/ (the sound before the first vowel in 'uh-uh') /n/ noon /r/ round /w/ way /y/ yes.

haunted
de·wag·yá·ǫn·yo·taʼ it is haunted
[de+wa+ stem: -(a)gyaǫnyod- be haunted; consists of: -(a)gyaǫʼ$_{V}$- tricked, fooled]

have
a·gá:węh it is mine
[P+ stem: -(a)węh$_{V}$- have]
sá:węh it is yours
ho·wę́·gę·hę:ʼ it used to be his
ho·wę́·hne:ʼ it used to be his
go·węhs·hǫ́:ʼǫh what she owns
ag·yęʼ I have, possess
[P+ stem: -(y)ęʼ- have s.t., own s.t.; consists of: -(y)ę$_{V}$- lie on the ground]
hó:yęʼ he has
ho·dí:yęʼ they (m) have; they are lying
a·gáh·ya·ę:ʼ I have fruit
[P+(N+) stem: -ęʼ- have s.t., own s.t.; consists of: -(a)hy(a)$_{N}$- fruit, berry +ę$_{V}$- lie on the ground]
sah·wíhs·da·ęʼ you have money
[P+(N+) stem: -ęʼ- have s.t., own s.t.; consists of: -(h)wihsd(a), (hr)ihsd(a)$_{N}$- metal, money -ę$_{V}$- lie on the ground]
ho·náhsg·wa·ę:ʼ he has a pet
[P+(N+) -ęʼ- have s.t., own s.t.; consists of: -nahsg(wa)$_{N}$- animal, domestic -ę$_{V}$- lie on the ground]
ho·nahs·gwá·ę·dǫʼ he has animals, pets
ak·nǫh·sá·ę·dǫʼ they (f/m) have several houses
[P+(N+) -ędǫʼ- have , own several things; consists of: -nǫhs(a)$_{N}$- house -ędǫʼ$_{V}$- several objects lying on the ground]
o·di·ę·na·ę·dǫ́:nyǫʼ they (z) have songs
[P+(N+) -ędǫnyǫʼ- have, own several things; consists of: -(r)ęn(a)$_{N}$- song, music -ędǫnyǫʼ$_{V}$- several things lying on the ground]
ho·i·hoʼdęhs·rí:yo: he has a good job
[P+ N+ stem: -(ri)hoʼdęhsr(a)$_{N}$- work -iyo:$_{V}$- be nice, good; have s.t. good]
sat·nat·rot·rá:se:ʼ you have new pants
[A/P+ad+N+ stem: -(a)tnaʼtsotr(a)$_{N}$- pants -(a)se$_{V}$- new; have s.t. new]

have see: keep
ę·sad·rǫ́:goʼ you will keep

hawk
gwę́:dihs night hawk
[stem: -gwę:dihs- night hawk]
gwi·yę́ʼgwi·yęʼ high soaring hawk
[stem: -gwiyęʼgwiyęʼ$_{N}$- high soaring hawk]
de·ga·yʼa·dáhk·waʼ hen hawk
[de+ga+ stem: -yaʼdahkwaʼ- hen hawk; consists of: -yaʼd(a)$_{N}$- body]
ga·wa·iʼyó:wiʼs pigeon hawk
[ga+ stem: -waiʼyowiʼs- pigeon hawk; consists of: -owi, ǫny$_{V}$- drive]
ga·jíh·węh·taʼ sparrow hawk
[ga+ stem: -jihwęhtaʼ- sparrow hawk]

Hawk Clan see: C (ho·dihs·węʼga·i·yoʼ)

hay see: straw
ohs·tǫ́:draʼ straw

haze see: fog
de·yot·sa·dá·ęʼ it is foggy

hazel see: witch hazel
ga·ahd·rǫ́:nih witch hazel

head
o·nǫ́ʼa:ʼ a head (owner unknown)
[o+ stem: -nǫʼ(a:), nǫh(a)$_{N}$- head]
sa·nǫʼá:ʼgeh on your head
ak·nǫʼá:ʼgeh on my head
swa·nǫʼá:ʼgeh on your (p) heads
oh·wę́ʼs·do:t a head (of foam on beer)
[o+ stem: -(h)węʼsdod- head (of foam); consists of: -(h)węʼsd(a)$_{N}$- foam -od$_{V}$- stand, attached]

head see: authority
dwę·nǫ́h·dǫ·haʼ it is the boss, the authority

head (lift one's head, have one's head up)
ga̲hn·yáh·do:t it's got its head up
[A+ stem: -(h)nyahdod- lift one's head; consists of: -(h)nya(ʼsa)$_N$- neck, throat -od$_V$- stand]
ehn·yáh·do:t she's got her head up (said of a child who is learning to lift her head herself)
hahn·yáh·do:t he's got his head up (said of a child who is learning to lift his head by himself)

head (put down one's head)
dęh·sa·nǫ̲·há:ge:t you will put your head down
[de+P+ stem: -nǫhaged- put down one's head; consists of: -nǫʼ(a:), nǫh(a)$_N$- head -ged$_V$- grate, scrape, file]

headache
ak·nǫʼá:nǫh·wa:s I have a headache
[P+N+ stem: -nǫʼ(a:), nǫh(a)$_N$- head -nǫhwag$_V$- sore, ache]

headband
de·yǫt·nʼa·ǫ́:nhahs·taʼ headband
[de+yǫ+at+ stem: -noʼanhahstaʼ- headband; consists of: -nǫʼ(a:), nǫh(a)$_N$- head -nhahsd$_V$- encircle]

headboard see: sign
ga·néhs·da·ot headboards; grave markers; billboards; signs

headdress
gahs·dó:waʼ headdress
[ga+ stem: -(h)sdow(a)$_N$- feather]

headlight
gʼad·reh·dáʼ ga·jís·do·taʼ a car's headlights
[consists of: gʼadrehdaʼ car, vehicle; gajihsdotaʼ light bulb]

headstone
gahsg·wá·o:t headstone
[ga+ stem: -(h)sg(wa:)$_N$- stone, bullet, rock -od$_V$- stand]

heal
tsih·sa:né:yǫhs when you are healing
[TR/...at+ stem: -neyǫ(:)$_V$- heal]
ę·ji·sa·né:yǫ:ʼ it will heal you
ęh·sa:tné:yǫ:ʼ you will heal yourself (with medicinal ointments)
ęhs·wad·rih·wá·ǫ·niʼ you will heal
[ad+ stem: -(r)ihwaǫni- heal; consists of: -(r)ih(wa)$_N$- word -ǫni, ǫny$_V$- make]
sa·wad·rih·wá·ǫ·niʼ it healed again

heal see: cure
a·gé:jęt it cured me

health
a·daʼgá·e·dę̲hs·raʼ health
[(wa)+ad+ stem: -(a)gaidehsr(a)$_N$- health -(a)gaideʼ$_V$- healthy, well, fine]

health see: G (A·daʼga·i·dę̲hs·raʼ O·ih·wa·geh)

Health Canada see: G (A·daʼga·e·dę̲hs·raʼ De·ho·di:h·wa̲h·ja:ʼ)

healthy
a·ga·da·gá·i:deʼ I am well, fine, healthy
[P+ad+ stem: -(a)gaideʼ$_V$- healthy, well, fine]
ho·da·gá·i·deʼ he is healthy
go·da·gá·i·deʼ she is healthy

healthy see: become, think
ęt·sá:dǫʼ you will become healthy again
jǫ·nǫ́h·dǫn·yǫh to be healthy; to have well being again
sgę:nǫ́: ge·nǫ́h·dǫn·yǫh I am fine, healthy

heap see: pile, stack
on·hóhs·ro:t a pile of things
dę·sa·dę·hó:dęʼ, dehs·rę́ʼho·dęʼ you will stack things, put one thing on top of the other

hear
a·ga:tǫ́:dęhs I hear it all the time (continually or off-and-on; for example, the sound of a regular train going by one's house)
[P+ stem: -(a)tǫdę(h,ʼ), (a)tǫdeʼ$_V$- hear]

Cayuga pronunciation guide: /a/ father /e/ weigh /ę/ men (nasalized) /i/ police /o/ hole /ǫ/ home (nasalized) /u/ blue. Underlined vowels are voiceless or whispered. /ʼ/ high pitch. /t/ too /d/ do /k/ king /g/ good (never soft g) /j/ judge or adze /s/ soon /sh/ less heat (never the sh in shirt) /sr/ shrine /sy/ sure /hw/ which (the sound made when you blow out a candle) /h/ hi /ts/ cats hide /ʼ/ (the sound before the first vowel in 'uh-uh') /n/ noon /r/ round /w/ way /y/ yes.

hear (continued)
ho·tǫ́:deʼ he hears
a·ga:tǫ́:deʼ I hear it (right now)
ę·sa:tǫ́:dęh you will hear it
a·ga·tǫ·dę́ʼǫh I have heard it before
a·tǫ́·dęʼǫ:ʼ the act of hearing
ga̲·hǫ́:kaʼ I understand (a language)
[stem: -(a)hǫg$_V$- hear, learn how to speak a language, understand]
sa̲·hǫ́:kahk you used to understand (and talk)
ę·gá·ǫ·hǫ:k they (f/m) will understand a language
ę·seʼgá:hǫ:k you will hear a story
[stem: -(ʼ)g(a:)$_N$- tale, story, legend, parable -(a)hǫg$_V$- hear, learn how to speak a language, understand]
a·ha·ę·ná·hǫ:k he heard music
[stem: -(r)ęn(a)$_N$- song, music -(a)hǫg$_V$- hear, learn how to speak a language, understand]

hearing aid
jǫ·hǫ́·gʼa·taʼ a hearing aid
[j+o+ stem: -(a)hǫgaʼtaʼ- hearing aid; consists of: -(a)hǫg$_V$- hear, learn how to speak a language, understand]
ǫ·da·hǫh·si·yǫ̲hs·dáhk·waʼ hearing aid
[ǫ+ad+ stem: -(a)hǫhsiyohsdahkwaʼ- hearing aid; consists of: -(a)hǫg$_V$- hear -iyohsdahkwaʼ$_V$- s.t. that makes things good]

hearsay see: rumour
ga·ih·wa·né·nǫg·yeʼs rumours

hearse
ga̲·he·yʼǫ·dá·nęhg·wih hearse
[ga+ stem: -(h)eyǫʼdanęhgwih- hearse; consists of: -(he)yǫ(ʼda)$_N$- corpse, cadaver -nęhgwi$_V$- haul]

heart
a·wę́·yǫ̲h·saʼ heart
[a+ stem: -węyǫhs(a)$_N$- heart, spirit]
sa·dǫ́n·heʼt·raʼ your soul, heart, spirit
[P+ad+ stem: -ǫnheʼtr(a)$_N$- heart, soul, spirit; consists of: -ǫnheʼ$_V$- alive]
o·dǫn·heht·rá:gǫ: in the heart

heart disease
o·nǫh·so·da·ę́:ʼ a·gǫ́n·heh·gǫh heart disease
[consists of: onǫhsodaę:ʼ sickness; agǫnhehgǫh s.o. is sustained by it]

heart operation
a·ga·ę·sa·węn·yáhs·ha: they gave you a heart operation
[TR+ stem: -węyǫhsha:- give s.o. a heart operation; consists of: -węyǫhs(a)$_N$- heart, spirit -(h)awi, (h)a:$_V$- hold, include, carry, bring]

heart problem
de·wa·ge·wa·yęh·síh·sǫhk·waʼ I have a heart problem
[de+P+ stem: -wayęhsihsǫhkwaʼ- heart problem; consists of: -wayę(n)$_N$- heart, spirit -(i)hsʼǫh$_V$- to have finished -(h)gw$_V$- lift up, pick up]

heart tremor
de·yo·wa·yęh·sis·hǫhk·wáʼ a·gǫ́n·heh·gǫh heart tremor
[consists of: deyowayęhsishǫhkwaʼ heart tremor; agǫnhehgǫh s.o. lives on it, is sustained by it]

hearty see: healthy
a·ga·da·gá·i:deʼ I am well, fine, healthy

heat see: hot, warm
oʼdá·i·hę:ʼ it is hot
wa·da·i·háʼtaʼ it heats things up

heater see: radiator
ga·naʼja·gę́ʼdo:ʼ radiator

heaven
ga·ǫ́:hya·deʼ in existing heaven
[ga+ stem: -(r)ǫhyadeʼ- heavens; consists of: -(r)ǫhy(a)$_N$- sky -deʼ$_V$- exist]
ha·di·ǫh·yaʼge̲·hó:nǫʼ they (m) are the heavenly kind
[stem: -(r)ǫhy(a)$_N$- sky]

heave see: throw
he·hó:gyǫ: he has thrown it
heaviness see: weight
tsę́h ni·yo·gǫt·rá:sdeʼ weight; pounds; poundage
heavy
ohs·deʼ it is heavy
[o+ stem: -(a)hsdeʼ$_{V}$- heavy]
go·di·yʼa·dáhs·deʼ they (f/m) are heavy
[P+ stem: -yaʼd(a)$_{N}$- body -(a)hsdeʼ$_{V}$- heavy]
go·yáʼdahs·deʼ she is heavy
hedge
o·hǫ:dáʼ ga·yę́t·wag·yeʼ hedge
[consists of: ohǫ:daʼ a bush, whip; gayętwagyeʼ it is planted along]
heed see: listen
ęh·sa·da·hǫh·si·yóhs·ta:k you will listen, obey
heel
gá:dʼa·geh a heel
[A+ stem: -(r)a(k)d(a)$_{N}$- heel]
sra·dáʼgeh on your heel
gra·dáʼgeh on my heel
hefty see: heavy
ohs·deʼ it is heavy
height
tsę́h nit·gaʼdręh·dá:deʼ the height of the car
[tsęh ni+t+ga+ -(ʼ)drehd(a)$_{N}$- car, vehicle; stem: -deʼ$_{V}$- exist; have a certain height]
nit·gá:deʼ how high it is (inanimate object); the height of s.t.
[ni+t+ga+ -deʼ$_{V}$- exist; have a certain height]
nit·ga:dé:nyǫʼ different levels of heights
ga·óʼ nit·gá:deʼ it is lower
[gaoʼ ni+t+ga+ stem: -deʼ$_{V}$- exist; be lower]
heh·da:géh nit·gá:deʼ it is low
[hehda:geh on the ground ni+t+ga+ -deʼ$_{V}$- exist;]
height see: same, top
tsaʼdétga·deh the same height
hé:t·gęh·jih the very top
helicopter
de·ga·wa·da:séhs de·gá:dęh helicopter
[consists of: degawada:sehs a tornado; dega:dęh it flies]
hello
sgę́:nǫʼ hello, how are you?
[stem: -ęnǫ$_{V}$- well]
hello see: I (haiʼ, gwe:)
gwé: well (used as a greeting)
haiʼ hello (a word attributed to Oneida or Tutelo)
help
ga·yę·na·wáhs·raʼ help
[ga+ stem: -yęnawahsr(a)$_{N}$- help]
ǫ·ki·ye·ná·wʼa·seh they are helpers (lit.: they help us)
[TR+ stem: -yenawaʼs- help, assist; consists of: -yena(w), yenaǫ, yena(:)$_{V}$- catch, receive, accept]
ha·de·yę·ná·wʼa·seh he is a helper, assistant
ę·gǫ·ye·ná:waʼs I will help you
dwa·yéna·wahs let us all (incl.) help it
ho·ye·na·wáʼs·gǫ: he is a willing helper
de·wa·dag·ye·na·wáʼse to be helpful to one other
a:hya·yaʼda·gé:n·haʼ he would help you
[TR+ stem: -yaʼdagenh- help; consists of: -yaʼd(a)$_{N}$- body -genh$_{V}$- argue for, advocate]
a:ye·sa·yʼa·dá·gen·haʼ she would help you
help see: benefit, support
ę·ya:gó:dǫʼs it will be for her benefit
a·héh·wa·waʼs I agree with him, support him

Cayuga pronunciation guide: /a/ father /e/ weigh /ę/ men (nasalized) /i/ police /o/ hole /ǫ/ home (nasalized) /u/ blue. Underlined vowels are voiceless or whispered. /ʼ/ high pitch. /t/ too /d/ do /k/ king /g/ good (never soft g) /j/ judge or adze /s/ soon /sh/ less heat (never the sh in shirt) /sr/ shrine /sy/ sure /hw/ which (the sound made when you blow out a candle) /h/ hi /ts/ cats hide /ʼ/ (the sound before the first vowel in ‘uh-uh’) /n/ noon /r/ round /w/ way /y/ yes.

helper see: assistant

gǫn·háʼtraʼ s.o.'s assistant

helpfulness

ga·yaʼda·gén·hahs·raʼ helpfulness [ga+ stem: -yaʼdagenhahsr(a)$_{N}$- helpfulness; consists of: -yaʼdagenh- help; consists of: -yaʼd(a)$_{N}$- body -genh$_{V}$- argue for, advocate]

helpless

tsaʼhóːyaːt he can't help himself; it's become a habit with him [tsaʼ+P+ stem: -(a)d$_{V}$- be contained, be in s.t.; be helpless]

hem

dęh·ség·wa·toʼ you will hem [de+... stem: -gwatw$_{V}$- hem]

de·gág·wat·węh a hem

dę·gag·wat·wę́·hęːk it will be hemmed

hemlock

saːnę·dah·taʼ hemlock [s+ stem: -anędahtaʼ- hemlock; consists of: -(raʼ)nęd(aːʼg), (yaʼ)nęd(aːʼg)$_{V}$- stick, cling]

hemlock see: poison

oʼnáʼsęː poison; water hemlock

hen

dó·gęːt guinea hen [stem: -dogęːt$_{N}$- guinea hen]

hen see: chicken

daks·há·eːʼdohs chicken

hen-pecked

ho·déʼkaːʼ he is hen-pecked [P+ade+ stem: -(ʼ)kaːʼ- hen-pecked; consists of: -(ʼ)k(aː)$_{N}$- skirt, slip -(h)awi, (h)aː$_{V}$- hold, include, carry, bring]

hǫ·waʼká·o·weːs he is hen-pecked [TR+ stem: -(ʼ)kaoweːs- hen-pecked; consists of: -(ʼ)k(aː)$_{N}$- skirt, slip -(hr)oweg$_{V}$- cover]

herb

de·ga·yehs·dáh·nǫʼ a mixture; it is mixed together to make it good (for example, herbs, spices, etc.) [de+ga+ stem: -yehsdahnǫʼ- herb, spice; consists of: -yehsd$_{V}$- add]

ga·gaʼǫhs·rǫ́ːnih it makes it taste good (for example, herbs, spices) [ga+ stem: -gaʼǫhsronih- herb, spice; consists of: -gaʼǫhsr(a)$_{N}$- good-tasting things -ǫni, ǫny$_{V}$- make]

herd

gahs·yá·oːt a standing herd [ga+ stem: -(h)sya$_{N}$- herd -od$_{V}$- stand]

gahs·yá·dagyeʼ a passing herd [stem: -(h)sya$_{N}$- herd -dagyeʼ- continue on, be ongoing]

herd see: drive

haʼsaːdóːwih drive it over there; herd the animals

here see: I (da...gwaːdih), be someplace

gę́ːneʼs they (z) are around; they are here; they are together

here and there see: all over

ti·gaːgwéːgǫh all over the place; here and there

hermaphrodite

on·roːt hermaphrodite [o+ stem: -nrod- hermaphrodite; consists of: -nr(a)$_{N}$- phallus, penis -od$_{V}$- stand]

hernia

de·wa·gag·yaʼda·né·ga·ǫː I have a hernia [de+P+ag+ stem: -yaʼdanega(ː,ǫ)- hernia; consists of: -yaʼd(a)$_{N}$- body -(wa)negaǫ, (wa)nega(ː)$_{V}$- explode, split]

heron

sgan·yaʼdíːgaːʼ heron [s+ga+ stem: -nyaʼdigaːʼ- heron; consists of: -nyad(aː)$_{N}$- lake, body of water, -ig(aːʼ)$_{V}$- be in water]

Heron clan see: C (De·ga·ǫh·ya·gah·neːʼ)

hesitant see: confused

de·wag·yad·ri·ho·dáh·seːʼ I am confused; I cannot make up my mind

hex see: bewitch, curse
ę·gǫ·yat·gǫ́ʼtra:s I will bewitch you
ęhs·he·yá·ę·na:ʼ you will curse, hex s.o.
hey see: I (hotgǫʼǫh)
hi see: hello, I (haiʼ, gwe:)
sgę́:nǫʼ hello, how are you?
hibernate see: sleep
o·dí:daʼs they (z) sleep, hibernate all the time
hiccough, hiccup
hohn·yáʼs·gaʼohs he is hiccupping, hiccoughing
[P+ stem: -(h)nyaʼsgaʼohsd$_{V}$- hiccough; consists of: -(h)nya(ʼsa)$_{N}$- neck, throat -ohsd$_{N}$- saturate]
ę·sahn·ya̲hs·gáʼohs you will hiccup, hiccough
hickory
o·nę́·no·ga:ʼ hickory wood; a hickory stick
[o+ stem: -nęnog(a:)$_{N}$- hickory]
hide
ga·dáh·se̲h·taʼ I hide
[ad+ stem: -(a)hsehd$_{V}$- hide s.t.; hide oneself]
ę·gę·na·dáh·seht they (z) will hide
ę·gá·dah·seht I will hide
a·ga·dah·séh·dǫh I am hiding now
ho·na·da̲h·seh·dǫ·hǫ́:gyeʼs they (m) are sneaking around
gah·séh·taʼ I hide s.t.
[stem: -(a)hsehd$_{V}$- hide s.t.]
ę·yǫ́h·seht there will be a burial (lit.: it will be hidden)
ę·gáh·seht I will hide s.t.
a·gáh·se̲h·dǫh I am hiding s.t.
ga̲h·séh·dǫh it is robbed, hidden
hide see: pelt, skin
o·hóh·wa:ʼ pelt
ga·néh·waʼ leather; hide
hideous see: ugly
e·hé:tgęʼ she is ugly, unruly

high see: height, tall
nit·gá:deʼ how high it is (inanimate object); the height of s.t.
hah·nę́:ye:s he is tall
highchair
o·wi:ya:ʼáh gok·yę́·da̲hk·waʼ baby's highchair
[consists of: owi:ya:ʼah baby; gokyędahkwaʼ her chair]
higher education see: G (he:t·gęh tga:deʼ hę·na·de·wa·yęhs·taʼ)
highway
o·ha·ho·wá:nęʼs big highways
[o+ stem: -(h)ah(a)$_{N}$- road -owanęʼs$_{V}$- several big objects]
o·ha·ho·wá·nę̲hs·geh on the highway
hike see: walk
dę·gá·ta·hahk I will walk
hill
o·nǫ́·da̲·he:ʼ hill
[o+ stem: -nǫd(a), ned(a)$_{N}$- hill -(h)e:ʼ$_{V}$- sitting up on top of s.t.]
o·nǫ·da̲·hǫ́:nyǫʼ hills
[o+ stem: -nǫd(a), ned(a)$_{N}$- hill -(h)ǫnyǫʼ$_{V}$- several things lying]
ę·hę·na·tohg·wá·ǫn·yǫʼ they (m) will make planting hills
[stem: -(a)tohgwaǫni- hill plants; consists of: -(a)tohg(wa)$_{N}$- bundle -ǫni, ǫny$_{V}$- make]
wa·tohg·wá·ǫn·yǫʼ planting hills (already made)
sna·gęhs·rǫ́·ni:ʼ make hills to plant in
[stem: -nagęhsrǫni- hill s.t.; consists of: -nagęhsr(a)$_{N}$- hill -ǫni, ǫny$_{V}$- make]
hilly
o·nǫ·da·géh·ge̲·ha:ʼ the on-the-hill type; s.t. belonging on the hills or mountains
[o+ stem: -nǫdagehgeha:ʼ- hill-type, mountain-type; consists of: -nǫd(a), ned(a)$_{N}$- hill -(ʼ)geh- on -geha:ʼ- kind]
hinder see: stop
a·tá:dahs he stopped it, prevented it

hip

se·jihs·gog·wá'geh on your hip
[stem: -jisgo'g(wa)$_N$- hip]
ge·jihs·g'og·wá'geh on my hip

hire

hę·ná·dęn·ha's they (m) hire it
[adę+ stem: -nha'$_V$- command, hire; order s.t]
ę·sá·dęn·ha' you will order s.t., hire s.t.
wa·dę́n·ha'ǫh it is chartered, hired

hire see: command

ęhs·he:n·ha' you will command, hire her

his

hó:węh it is his
[P+ stem: -(a)węh$_V$- have]

hit

ęhs·wá'e:k you will pound, tap
[stem: -(')e$_V$- hit]
he·nę'n·hot·rá'ehs they (m) hit balls
[stem: -ę'nh(otra)$_N$- ball -(')e$_V$- hit]
gah·ne·ga·yę́h·ta' the water is hitting against s.t.
[N+ stem: -(h)neg(a)$_N$- water, liquid -(y)ęhd$_V$- hit, knock down, strike]
a·wáh·yęht it knocked the fruit down
[N+ stem: -(a)hy(a)$_N$- fruit, berry -(y)ęhd$_V$- hit, knock down, strike]
ha'ga·nǫ'á·o:yęht the head hit suddenly
[N+ stem: -nǫ'(a:)$_N$- head -(y)ęhd$_V$- hit, knock down, strike]
ęhs·ya'g·yé:nęht you can knock it down
[N+ stem: -ya'd(a)$_N$- body -yenęhd$_V$- knock down]
a·te'd·rẹh·dá'ehs I hit his car
[de+TR+N+ stem: -(')drehd(a)$_N$- vehicle, car -(')ehsd- hit s.t. belonging to s.o.]
a·ta·g'ed·réh·da'ehs he hit my car

hit see: punch, pound, slap

a·há·gǫ·he:k he punched it
se·teht pound it (corn, etc.)
ęh·set·rag·wę́'da̱'e:k you will slap it (on the cheek)

hitch see: tie

de·se·ji̱hs·dǫg·wá·ǫ·dęh tie a knot

hives

go̱hǫ́:da:s she, s.o. has hives
[stem: -(h)ǫd(a)$_N$- bush -g$_V$- eat]
o'nah·gǫ·dǫ́:nyǫ:' to have hives all over; to be stung many times
[P+ stem: -(')nahgǫd- be inflamed, have a bee sting; consists of: -(')nahg(a)$_N$- sting -ǫdǫnyǫ$_V$- several attached objects]

hobbies see: recreation

de·yǫ'ni·gǫ·ha·wę́n·y'e·ta' recreation; hobbies

hobo see: tramp

a·ho·dẹh·té:'ah tramp; hobo; vagabond

hock see: pawn

ę·sat·gá·ę·dahk what you will pawn

hockey

o·wid·ra·géh de·ha·di·jíhg·wa̱'ehs hockey
[consists of: owidrageh on the ice; dehadijihgwa̱'ehs they (m) punch it]

hoe

at·só'k·dǫhs·ra' hoe
[a+ stem: -tsha'kdǫhsr(a)$_N$- hoe; consists of: sha'ged, sha'kdǫ- bend]
at·keh·da·wę́:nye:' I hoed, tilled the earth
[de+... stem: -(h)ehdawęnye(:)- hoe s.t., till s.t.; consists of: -(h)ehd(a)$_N$- land, dirt, earth, ground -(a)węnye(:)$_V$- stir, mix]
a·ta·heh·dá·wę·nye:' he hoed, tilled the earth

hoist see: jack

de·ga'drẹh·dáhk·wa' jack; tow truck; hoist

hold
ká:wi' I am carrying
[(N+) stem: -(h)awi, (h)a:$_V$- hold, include, carry, bring]
ha·di·há:wi's they (m) carry along
e·há:wi' she carried it here; she brought it here
dahs·ha: bring it here
e·ha:' she is holding s.t. right now
kreh·nę·hę́:wi' I am carrying a bundle, load
[(N+) stem: -(hr)ehn(a)$_N$- bundle -(h)awi, (h)a:$_V$- hold, include, carry, bring]
tsę́h ni·gá·ha:' all that is included
[ni+... stem: -(h)a:$_V$- hold, include, carry, bring; hold a certain amount]
ni·gá·ha:' how much it holds
hold see: keep, prison
í:ga:' it contains
ę·sa:drǫ́:go' you will keep
de·gahn·yǫhs·rá:de' prison
hole
a·ha·di·ga·hę́:dę' they (m) made a hole
[stem: -gahęd$_V$- drill, hole]
o·gá·hę:t it has a hole in it, an opening
ǫh·wę·ja·gá·hę·ta', gah·wę·ja·gá·hę·ta' a hole in the earth
[(ga+) stem: -(ǫh)węjagahęta'- hole; consists of: -ǫhwęj(a)$_N$- earth, land -gahęd$_V$- drill, hole]
ni·yah·wę·dú:'uh small hole, opening
[ni+A/P+N+ stem: -(h)węd(a)$_N$- hole, opening -u:'uh$_V$- small]
hole see: basement, cave
o·yá·da·gǫ: in the track; in the basement, ditch, hole
oh·wę·ja·gá·hęt·ge: cavern; cavity; big cave
hole punch see: drill
e·ga·hę·dáhk·wa' drill
holler see: yell
a·tó·he:t he hollered, yelled

hollow
ęh·sat·gá:dah·go' you will hollow out a canoe, a wooden bowl, etc. (take out the chips)
[at+ stem: -ga:dahgw- hollow out; consists of: -(h)g(a:)$_N$- chip -(h)gw$_V$- remove]
hollow see: cave, clearing
oh·wę·ja·gá·hęt·ge: cavern; cavity; big cave
de·yo·ha·da:g·wę́h·de' a clearing in the forest
holy see: forbidden
o·nǫ́'ne:' it is forbidden, sacred, holy
homage see: respect, honour
ga·gǫ́n·yǫhs·de:' respect
ahs·ha·go·dí·gǫn·yǫhs they honoured her
home
sgah·dę́:gye's I go home all the time
[s+... stem: -(a)hdędi, (a)hdęgy$_V$- leave, go away; go home]
ęhs·gah·dę́:di' I will go home
ęhs·gę·nah·dę́:di' they (z) will migrate
sa·sah·dę́:dih go home
sa·hoh·dęhg·yǫ́·hǫg·ye' he is on his way home
home see: house, live, turn
ga·nǫ́h·sa' a house
ha·dí'drǫ' they (m) are at home
dǫ:sa·gat·ga·ha:dé:ni' I should turn around and go back, I should go home
homeless see: stay
hot·wá'ehs·dǫh he is a boarder; he is homeless
homely see: ugly
ha·he:tgę́:s'ah he is unattractive
honest see: righteous
od·rih·wag·wá·ih·sǫ: it is believable, credible, righteous, fair, honest
honey see: syrup
ot·séhs·da' syrup; honey; gum

honeycomb

ga·nah·gǫ·tá' ga·dit·sehs·dǫ́·da·ta' honeycomb
[consists of: g'anahgǫta' bee; gadit-sehsdǫdata' where their (z) honey is contained]

honour

she·gǫ́n·yǫhs·tahk you used to honour her
[TR+ stem: -gǫnyǫhsd- honour; consists of: -gǫnyǫ$_V$- be clean, discriminating]

ahs·ha·go·dí·gǫn·yǫhs they honoured her

ęh·sé·gǫn·yǫhs you will honour s.t.

ęhs·hé·gǫn·yǫhs you will honour s.o.

honour see: revere

dęd·wa·dad·rih·wa·nǫ́hk·wa:k we all (incl.) will show respect for one another

honourable see: righteous

hod·rih·wag·wá·ih·sǫ: he is a noble person

hoof

wa̱h·sí'dǫ:t hoof
[w+ stem: -(a)hsi'dǫd- hoof; consists of: -(a)hsi('da), (ę)hs(a)$_N$- foot -ǫd$_V$- attached]

hook

e·ni·yǫ·dáhk·wa' hook
[e+ stem: -niyǫdahkwa'- hook; consists of: -niyǫd$_V$- hang]

de·gah·sǫ·wa̱h·dá:kdǫ: a hook
[de+ga+ stem: -(h)sǫwahdakdǫ:- hook; consists of: -(h)sǫwahd(a)$_N$- wire, nail, needle -(a)'kdǫ:$_V$- be bent, crooked]

hook see: fish hook

gę·jǫ'da·yę́·nahs fish hook

hoop

wę'nihs·gá·ǫ·ni: hoop
[w+ stem: -ę'nihsgaǫni- hoop; consists of: -ę'nihsg(a)$_N$- wheel -ǫni, ǫny$_V$- make]

hoop see: wheel

ę·níhs·ga:', wę·níhs·ga:' wheel; circle; hoop

hop see: jump, skip

dę·yǫ́·nahs·gwahk she will jump

de·ya·go·na'sg·wę·hę́:g·ye' she is skipping along

hope see: think, wish

í:wi: I want; I hope

a:yá:węh I wish, hope

hopeless see: desperate

de·yót·gan·yęh it is in dire need

horizon

de·yo·hag·węhdá:k'ah horizon
[de+yo+ stem: -ha$_N$- line, horizon -(a)gwęhd(ę)$_V$- be dented, flat -k'ah- beside]

horizon see: skyline

ga·ǫh·ya·dá:gye' skyline; horizon

horizontal see: flat

de·yo·dag·wę́h·dę:, de·wa·dag·wę́h·dę: it is flat

horn

o·ná'ga:' horns; antlers
[P+ stem: -na'g(a:)$_N$- horn, antler]

ho·ná'ga:' his horns

horny see: arouse

ho'deh he is horny

horrible see: terrible

de·yo·dę·nǫh·ya·níh·dǫh it is overwhelming, terrible

horse

ga·ǫ:da·nę́hg·wih horse
[ga+ stem: -(r)ǫdanęhgwih- horse; consists of: -(r)ǫd(a)$_N$- log -nęhgwi$_V$- haul]

goh·sá:dęhs horse (old word)
[go+ stem: -(h)sadęhs- horse; consists of: -(h)se'$_V$- ride horseback]

hose see: tube

ga̱·ho·we·dahs·hǫ́:'ǫh hoses; cylinders

hospital
ǫ·te·yʼǫ·da·ę:dáhk·waʼgeh hospital
[ǫ+at+ stem: -(h)eyǫʼdaędahkwaʼgeh- hospital; consists of: -(he)yǫ(ʼda)$_N$- corpse, cadaver -ędahkwaʼ$_V$- place where s.t. is put]

hospital see: clinic
ga·né:yǫhs a medical clinic; a healing place

hostile see: anger, grudge
ak·náʼkwęʼǫh I am angry
sa·tíʼyahs·gǫ: you hold grudges; you get angry easily

hot
oʼdá·i·hę:ʼ it is hot
[o+ stem: -(ʼ)daihę:$_V$- be hot]
ag·yaʼda·dá·i·hę: I am hot
[P+ stem: -yaʼdadaihę:- hot (person); consists of: -yaʼd(a)$_N$- body -(ʼ)daihę:$_V$- hot]
hoʼda·i·háʼseh he is too hot
[P+ stem: -(ʼ)daihaʼseh- too hot; consists of: -(ʼ)daih$_V$- be hot]

hot see: warm
o·da·i·há·dǫh it is really hot (weather)
o·né:nǫʼ it is mild, warm; a warm or hot day

hot dog
ga·yǫ·wa·wéʼta·hǫh hot dog; weiners; sausage on a bun
[ga+ stem: -yǫwaweʼdahǫh- hot dog; consists of: -yǫw(aʼda)$_N$- gut, intestine -(a)wiʼd$_V$- insert -(i)hǫh$_V$- lean against]

hothouse see: greenhouse
hę·nah·do·gáh·taʼgeh greenhouse

hot plate
oh·sǫ·wah·da·da·i:hé:ʼ ga·kǫ́:nihs hot plate
[consists of: ohsǫwahdadai:hę: electricity; gakǫ:nihs it cooks]
de·wę·ni·hóʼs gah·sǫ·wa·da:déʼ ga·kǫ́:nihs hot plate

hot plate (continued)
[consists of: dewęnihoʼs electricity; gahsǫwahda:deʼ existing wires; gakǫ:nihs it cooks]
de·wę·ni·hóʼs wa·da·i·háʼtaʼ hot plate
[consists of: dewęnihoʼs electricity; wadaihaʼtaʼ it warms things up]
gah·sǫh·da·dá·i·hę: hot plate
[ga+ stem: -(h)sǫhdadaihę:- hot plate; consists of: -(h)sǫhd(a)$_N$- plate -(ʼ)daihę:$_V$- be hot]
ga·nǫh·so·da·i·háʼda·he:ʼ hot plate (sitting on s.t.)
[ga+ stem: -nǫhsodaiha(ʼda)$_N$- hot plate -(h)e:ʼ$_V$- sitting up on top of s.t.]

hotel see: bar, motel
ǫt·ne·gah·ní:nǫh(geh) hotel; pub; bar; saloon
ǫ·nǫh·wehs·táʼgeh motel; inn; bed-and-breakfast; hotel

hound see: dog
só:wa:s dog

hour see: A (sga:t ę·gah·wihs·daʼe:k)

house
ga·nǫ́h·saʼ a house
[ga+ stem: -nǫhs(a)$_N$- house]
ga·nǫ́hs·gǫh·ka:ʼ s.t. used in a house
ga·nǫ́hs·gǫ: in the house
ga·nǫh·sá:kʼah beside the house
go·dí·nǫh·so:t their (f/m) home
[stem: -nǫhs(a)$_N$- house -od$_V$- stand]

house see: stay
a·hát·waʼehs he went to stay there; he was taken in

House of Commons see: G (hę·nag·yę·dahk·waʼ ha·di·ya·nęhs·rǫ:nih)

housecleaner see: clean, maid
de·gat·nǫh·sáhs·nyeʼs I am always cleaning my house; I'm a housecleaner
de·ga·ǫ·dóh·da:s they (f/m) tidy up; they are maids, housecleaners

Cayuga pronunciation guide: /a/ father /e/ weigh /ę/ men (nasalized) /i/ police /o/ hole /ǫ/ home (nasalized) /u/ blue. Underlined vowels are voiceless or whispered. /ʼ/ high pitch. /t/ too /d/ do /k/ king /g/ good (never soft g) /j/ judge or adze /s/ soon /sh/ less heat (never the sh in shirt) /sr/ shrine /sy/ sure /hw/ which (the sound made when you blow out a candle) /h/ hi /ts/ cats hide /ʼ/ (the sound before the first vowel in 'uh-uh') /n/ noon /r/ round /w/ way /y/ yes.

housecoat
ga·nǫhs·gǫ̱h·ká:ʼ ag·yaʼda·wíʼt·raʼ housecoat
[consists of: ganǫhsgǫ̱hka:ʼ household object; agyaʼdawiʼtraʼ coat, dress]

hover
od·ręʼ:deʼ it is hovering (for example, a hummingbird)
[P+ stem: -(r)ęd$_{V}$- hover]

how see: I (do:)

howl see: bay
a·wad·wę·nó:dęʼ it bayed, howled

hue see: colour, dye
oh·sohg·wa·dé:nyoʼ different kinds of colours
wa̱h·sá·hǫh it is dyed, coloured

huff see: pant
sha·ǫ:wi̱hs·hęʼʼǫh he is panting again; he is short of breath

huge
o·doʼdo·wá:nęh huge wave
[stem: -doʼd(a)$_{N}$- wave -owanęh- be big]

huge see: big
go·wá:nęh, ga·gó·wa·nęh it is big

hull see: stem
oʼníhs·daʼ a stem; berry hulls

hull berries
ę·se·ga̱·héhg·yaʼk you will hull berries
[stem: -gahehgyaʼk- hull; consists of: -gahehd(a)$_{N}$- eyelash, stem (of a berry), eye (of a corn kernel) -(i)yaʼg$_{V}$- cut, break]
ęhs·níhs·dęht you will hull strawberries
[stem: -(ʼ)nihsdęhd- hull; consists of: -(ʼ)nihsd(a)$_{N}$- stem, hull -(y)ęhd$_{V}$- hit, knock down, strike]
ęh·se·ga̱·hę́hdęht you will hull berries
[stem: -gahęhdęhd- hull; consists of: -gahehd(a)$_{N}$- eyelash, stem (of a berry), eye (of a corn kernel) -(y)ęhd$_{V}$- hit, knock down, strike]

hum
a·ha·ę·náhs·re:ʼ he followed the song; he sang along
[stem: -(r)ęnahsre:- hum; consists of: -(r)ęn(a)$_{N}$- song, music -(i)hsre(:)$_{V}$- follow, chase]

hum see: sing
god·ręʼ:no:t she is singing

human see: person
ǫ́:gweh person; human

human conditions
shęʼh dwa·yáʼda·deʼ human conditions
[tsęh d+wa+ stem: -yaʼdadeʼ- human conditions; consists of: -yaʼd(a)$_{N}$- body -deʼ$_{V}$- exist]

humane see: pity
ke·dę́·ǫhs I feel compassion for her

Human Resources Development see: G (Hę·na·dęn·haʼs De̱·hę·na·dǫg·weʼda·den·yeʼs)

Human Rights Commission see: G (He·yǫg·weʼda:gwe:gǫh Go·ya·nęhs·ra·ęʼ Gęg·yohg·wa·ęʼ)

humble
go·ni·gǫ̱·ha·ní:dęht she is gentle, nice, humble
[P+ stem: -(ʼ)nigǫhanidęhd- humble, gentle, nice; consists of: -(ʼ)nigǫh(a)$_{N}$- mind -nidęhd$_{V}$- cause to be kind]

humid see: damp, wet
ot·sá·dęʼǫh it is damp
o·nǫ́hg·wi·jaʼ it is soaking wet, saturated

humiliation see: shame
o·dé·haʼt a shame; an embarrassment

hummingbird
jiʼnhǫ·wę́:se: hummingbird
[stem: -jiʼnhǫwę:se:$_{N}$- hummingbird]

humorous see: amusing, comical
o·yǫ́:gyaʼt it is amusing, laughable
o·yǫ:gyę́:ni: it is comical

hunch see: squat
a·sęʼno·wá·ę:ʼ you are squatting

hunch-back
ho·no·wag·wá·ǫt he has a humped back
[P+ stem: -nowa(gwa)$_N$- rounded back -ǫd$_V$- attached]
hunch-back see: rounded back
ę·sa·no·wag·wá·ǫ·dę' you will get a rounded back
hundred see: B (sga:t de·wę'n·y'a·w'e:)
hunger see: famine
o·dǫ́hs·w' e·dęht famine; hunger
hungry
a·ga·dǫhs·wé'da·nih I am hungry
[stem: -ǫhswe'd(ę,ani)$_V$- hungry, short of breath]
a·ǫ·dǫhs·wé'dę' she got hungry
hungry see: crave
ak·nǫ́:wa:k I did get hungry for it
hunt
ha·dó:wa:s he is a hunter
[stem: -(a)dowad$_V$- hunt]
ę·ha:dó:wa:t he will hunt
a·do·wá:dǫ:' the hunt
sa·dó:wa:t hunt
ho·dó·wa·tǫ: he is gone hunting
ho·dó·wa·tǫhk he went hunting
sa·dó·wa·tah go and hunt
hurdle see: jump
dę·yǫ́·nahs·gwahk she will jump
hurl see: throw
ha'hó:di' he threw it
Huron people see: C (Oh·weh·na·ge·ho:nǫ')
hurricane
ga·wa·ę·hę́:wi' hurricane
[ga+ stem: -waęhęwi'- hurricane; consists of: -w(a:)$_N$- air -ęhę(:,w)$_V$- direct, convey]
hurry
de·wa·g'ed·rá·i·hęhs I am in a hurry
[de+P+ stem: -(')draihę$_V$- hurry]
de·ho'd·rá·i·hęhs he is in a hurry; he is impatient
ad·ya·go·di'd·rá·i·hę' they (f/m) hurried

hurry (continued)
dęhs·ni'd·rá·i·hę' you two will hurry up
de·sa'd·rá·i·hęh hurry
de·sa'd·ra·i·hęhs·dáh·ne' you are going along in a hurry
de·sa·dęh·snó:wa:t hurry up
[de+...ade+ stem: -(h)snowad- hurry up; consists of: -(h)snowe'$_V$- be fast]
hurry see: rush
deh·se'drá·i·ha't you rush s.t., hurry s.t. up
hurt
sa·dehs·tǫ·wís·ta' you hurt yourself all the time
[(ade+) stem: -(h)stǫwisd$_V$- hurt]
ę·ji·sahs·tǫ́:wi:s you will rehurt yourself
ę·wák·nǫh·ya'k I will get hurt
[P+ stem: -nǫhnya'g$_V$- hurt]
ho·nǫ́hn·ya·gǫh he is hurt
ęhs·hé·nǫhn·ya'k you will hurt s.o.
[TR+ stem: -nǫhnya'g$_V$- hurt s.o., s.t.]
o·nǫ́hn·ya't to hurt; the hurting
[o+ stem: -nǫhnya'd$_V$- hurt]
hurt see: ache, suffer
ag·ya'da·nǫ́h·wa:s I am sore; I ache
dęh·sa·dę·hǫ́·ga·i' you will suffer
husband
ha·gę́h·jih he is an old man (referring to one's husband)
[A/TR+ stem: -gęhjih$_V$- old person; spouse]
he·gę́h·jih my husband
husband see: C (spouse, he·gęh·jih)
he·gę́h·jih my husband
hush see: quiet
ta'dé·sag·yę: you are quiet
husk
o·hé'a: corn husk
[o+ stem: -(h)e'(a:)$_N$- husk]
o·nǫ́:nya' a husk
[o+ stem: -nǫny(a)$_N$- husk]
husk see: peelings
o·wá'wihs·da' a peeling

Cayuga pronunciation guide: /a/ father /e/ weigh /ę/ men (nasalized) /i/ police /o/ hole /ǫ/ home (nasalized) /u/ blue. Underlined vowels are voiceless or whispered. /'/ high pitch. /t/ too /d/ do /k/ king /g/ good (never soft g) /j/ judge or adze /s/ soon /sh/ less heat (never the sh in shirt) /sr/ shrine /sy/ sure /hw/ which (the sound made when you blow out a candle) /h/ hi /ts/ cats hide /'/ (the sound before the first vowel in 'uh-uh') /n/ noon /r/ round /w/ way /y/ yes.

husk corn
ęhs·nón·yot·si', **ęh·snę́n·yot·si'** you will husk the corn
[stem: -nǫnyotsi- husk corn; consists of: -nǫny(a)$_N$- husk -ots(i)$_V$- remove an outer covering]
snon·yó:tsih husk the corn
hustle see: hurry
de·sa·dęh·snó:wa:t hurry up
hutch see: buffet
gak·si:yó's ek·sa·ę:dáhk·wa' buffet, hutch
hydrant see: fountain
tgah·né·go·ta' fire hydrant; fountain
hymn see: pick up, song
to·díh·wahg·węh they (m) are raising hymns
gá·ę:na' song
hymn book
de·ye·ih·wahg·w'a·tá' ga·ę:ná·ǫ:nyǫ' hymn book
[consists of: deyeihwahgw'ata' s.o. lifts up words; gaę:naǫ:nyǫ' songs]
hypocritical see: two-faced
sa·gǫh·sah·ní:yǫh you are two-faced

I

I see: Appendix I (i:')
ice
o·wí:dra' ice
[o+ stem: -widr(a)$_N$- ice]
o·wíd·ra·geh on the ice
o·wid·ra·dę́h·da:' ice patch
[o+ stem: -widr(a)$_N$- ice -dęhda:'$_V$- lie spread out on the ground]

ice (a cake)
ęhs·ra·na·wę:dó:we:k you will ice, frost s.t. (for example, a cake)
[stem: -ranawę'doweg- ice (a cake), frost (a cake); consists of: -(rę)nawę'd(a)$_N$- sugar, candy -(hr)oweg$_V$- cover]
ice cream
o·wíd·ra·no: ice cream
[o+ stem: -widrano:- ice cream; consists of: -widr(a)$_N$- ice -no:$_V$- cold, cool]
ice cube
o·wí:dro' floating ice in the water; ice cubes
[o+ stem: -widro'- ice cube; consists of: -widr(a)$_N$- ice -o'$_V$- be submerged]
ice patch
o·wí:dre' ice patch
[o+ stem: -wi'dre'- ice patch; consists of: -widr(a)$_N$- ice -e$_V$- go]
icy see: glassy
de·yo·wid·rá:teh it is glassy, icy; a glass tumbler
idea
o·íh·wa·geh the reason; the idea for s.t.
[o+ stem: -(r)ih(wa)$_N$- word -(')geh- on]
o·ih·wa·nǫ́'ne:' a forbidden idea
[o+ stem: -(r)ih(wa)$_N$- word -no'ne:'$_V$- forbidden, sacred, holy]
identical see: same
tsa'dé:yoht they are (lit.: it is) the same
identify see: recognize
ęg·yę́:de:' I will recognize it
idiot see: stupid
de·sa'ni·gǫ́·ha:t you are stupid, foolish
idle see: lazy
sa·nǫ́'seh you are lazy
if see: I (gęh, gyę:gwa')
ignite see: burn
ęhs·rę́'da:' you will burn s.t.
ignore see: neglect
dehs·gahs·dí:s·ta' I no longer pay attention

ill see: nauseous, sick
ak·neʼdrʼa·dá:nih I am nauseated, nauseous
ak·nǫ·hǫk·dá:nih I am sick
illness see: sickness
o·nǫh·so·dá·i:yǫ:ʼ sickness; illness; epidemic; plague
illegitimate see: foundling
ga·wi·yat·sę́:nyǫ: child born out of wedlock; foundling; illegitimate child
ill-tempered see: cantankerous, grumpy
e·nǫ́·węhd·raʼ she is cantankerous
de·di·sʼa·ni·gǫ·hí:yo: you are grumpy, grouchy, unhappy
illumination see: light
ga·jís·do:t a light
imagine see: think
ęh·sę·nǫh·dǫ́:nyǫ:ʼ you will wonder, think
imitate
ęts·náʼgyę:ʼ you will imitate, mock, mimic s.t.
[(d+) TR+ stem: -naʼgyę(:,ni)$_V$- imitate, mock, mimic]
ę·di·sa·náʼgyę:ʼ it will mock, imitate you
imitate see: copy, similar
dah·sa·den·yę́:dęhs copy it; compare it
dehs·ga·yá·ǫ:da:ʼ it is an imitation of s.t.; it is similar; it is almost the same
immature
de·sat·ni·gǫ·hah·dó:gęh you are immature in mind
[deʼ+ not P+at+ stem: -(ʼ)nigǫhahdogęhd- immature; consists of: -(ʼ)nigǫh(a)$_N$- mind -dogę(:)$_V$- right, true]
immature see: childish, unripe
sa·dek·sʼa·dǫ́:nih you are immature, childish
o·gé:draʼ it is green, not ripe; raw fruit
immediately see: I (gǫ·dag·yeʼ)
immense see: big
go·wá:nęh, ga·gó·wa·nęh it is big
immerse
ęh·sá·dʼes·goh you will go into the water
[adade+/ade+ stem: -(ʼ)sgoh$_V$- immerse, drown; consists of: -o(:)$_V$- submerge]
immerse see: wet
a·e·nʼa·ná:węht she wet it
impale see: spear
a·to·waʼę́·naʼehs he speared him with a stick
impartial see: righteous
god·rih·wag·wá·eh·sǫh she is fair, righteous
impatient
ak·ni·gǫh·gá·hęhs I am running out of patience; I am impatiently waiting
[P+ stem: -(ʼ)nigǫhgahęhs- run out of patience, wait impatiently; consists of: -(ʼ)nigǫh(a)$_N$- mind -(ga)hey, (gę)hey, (i)hey, (ga)he:, (gę)he:, (i)he:$_V$- die, weak, exhausted]
impede see: stop
a·tá:dahs he stopped it, prevented it
impel see: force
tgas·he·yę·nǫ́h·twahs you force people all the time
impenetrable see: hard
oh·ní:yǫh it is hard
imperative see: necessity
tgá:gǫ:t a compelling must
implacable see: uncompromising
de·ya·gʼo·ni·gǫ·há:gǫ:t she cannot be swayed; she is uncompromising, distinguished
implied
a:wé:tʼah it is implied, pretend
[a:+w+ stem: -etʼah$_V$- pretend; consists of -d$_V$- stand -(ʼ)ah diminutive]
implore see: plead
ęh·sa·dę·ní:dęht you will plead

Cayuga pronunciation guide: /a/ father /e/ weigh /ę/ men (nasalized) /i/ police /o/ hole /ǫ/ home (nasalized) /u/ blue. Underlined vowels are voiceless or whispered. /ʹ/ high pitch. /t/ too /d/ do /k/ king /g/ good (never soft g) /j/ judge or adze /s/ soon /sh/ less heat (never the sh in shirt) /sr/ shrine /sy/ sure /hw/ which (the sound made when you blow out a candle) /h/ hi /ts/ cats hide /ʼ/ (the sound before the first vowel in ʻuh-uhʼ) /n/ noon /r/ round /w/ way /y/ yes.

important
ah·seh·sę·nó·wan·heʼ you became famous
[stem: -(h)sęnowanheʼ- become important, famous; consists of: -(h)sęn(a)$_N$- name -owanheʼ$_V$- become big]
hah·sę·no·wá:nęh he is an important person; he is famous, prominent (lit.: he has made a name for himself)
[A+ stem: -(h)sęnowanęh- be important, famous; consists of: -(h)sęn(a)$_N$- name -owanęh$_V$- be big]
seh·sę·no·wá:nęh you are famous
ga̱h·sę·no·wá:nęh it is famous

important see: special
o·i·ho·wá:nęh it is important; a great or worthy commendation; it is special

important
[-go:wah augmentative suffix; denotes 'largeness', 'greatness']

impoverished see: poor
a·gí:dęht I am poor, poverty-stricken, in poverty

impressionable see: sensitive
ni·wag·ri̱·hú:ʼuh I am sensitive

improper see: commit a crime
a·tad·ri̱h·wá·hęʼ he went afoul of the law; he did s.t. wrong

in
gʼa·nǫht it (usually an animal) is in s.t.
[A+ stem: -(ʼ)nǫhd$_V$- in]
heʼgáʼnǫht it is in there

in
[-agǫ: internal locative suffix; means 'in', 'on', or 'under']

in (get in) see: embark, water
ę·gát·nǫh·da:ʼ I will embark, get in s.t.
í:yoʼ it is in the water, submerged in liquid

in some place (be in some place)
gá·ǫ:nyǫʼ it included some; it is in there

in some place (continued)
[A+ stem: -ǫnyǫʼ- be in some place; consists of: -ǫni, ǫny$_V$- make, include some]

in s.t. (be in s.t.) see: contained
í:wa:t it is contained; it (inanimate) is in there; solid matter

in-between see: middle
de·yó:gę: between; in the middle

in-law see: C
hak·né:nhǫ:s my father-in-law
he·né:nhǫ:s my son-i̱n-law
ǫk·né:nhǫ:s my (a male's) mother-in-law
go·ná:gyoh their (f/m) or her in-laws
ho·ná:gyoh their (m) in-laws
ǫg·yá:gyoh my brother-in-law, sister-in-law

inactive see: lazy
ak·nǫ́ʼseh I am lazy

inane see: stupid
de·saʼni·gǫ́·ha:t you are stupid, foolish

incantation see: song
gá·ę:naʼ song

incapable see: unable
ak·nǫ́·haʼ I am unable

incest see: rape
ahs·ha·got·go·wa·nah·dę́ʼ
sha·go·há:wahk incest

inch
ja·wę́·yǫh·ga:t one inch
[j+a+węyǫhga:d inch+ consists of: -węʼyǫhg(a:)$_N$- thumb -d$_V$- stand, one]

incise
de·ha·di·ya·ǫʼdat·ręn·yáh·nǫʼ they (m) made an incision in a cadaver
[d+...(N+) stem: -yaǫʼdatre(n)- make an incision; consists of: -(he)yaǫ(ʼda)$_N$- corpse, cadaver -(hr)e(n)$_V$- cut]

incise see: cut
ęk·re:ʼ I will cut it

incisor see: tooth
o·nóʼjaʼ teeth

incite
ęt·ri·hǫ́:niʼ you will incite, be the cause of s.t.
[stem: -(r)ihǫni- incite, cause; consists of: -(r)ih(wa)$_{N}$- word -ǫni, ǫny$_{V}$- make]
incline see: lean
wa·dí·hǫh it is leaning against s.t.
inclined see: willing
ho·gá·ę:s he is willing
include
há·ǫ:nyah·nǫʼ he has included, designated s.t.
[(N+) stem: -ǫnyahnǫʼ- include, designate; consists of: -ǫni, ǫny$_{V}$- make]
include see: hold, in some place, insert
tsę́h ni·gá·ha:ʼ all that is included
gá·ǫ:nyǫʼ it included some; it is in there
he·sá·wit·aʼ you insert s.t. all the time
incorporate see: include
incorrect see: right
tę́ʼ de·dó:gęhs no, it is not right
increase see: big, grow, swell
a·ga·go·wá:nheʼ, **a·gó·wan·heʼ** it became big
ę·wáh·do:k it will multiply, grow
a·wáh·dę·goh it swelled up
indecisive see: undecided
de·saʼni·gǫ·ha·dó:gę: you cannot decide which way to go; you are flighty
indefatigable see: work well
hot·sáh·niht he is a good worker, tireless, active, industrious,etc.
indentation see: flat
ad·wa·dag·wę́h·dę: it became dented
Indian see: C, (Aboriginal, Ǫg·we·hǫ:weh; Indian from India O·ni·ga·hęhs·raʼ Ho·nǫt·noʼa:n·hah·węh)
indicate see: point, show
ęhs·hę́ʼnyʼa·da:t you will point s.o. out
gǫ·yǫh·wa·dá:nih I am showing you s.t.
indifferent see: unconcerned
taʼde·hoʼni·gǫ·há:nih he is unconcerned, indifferent
indiscriminate see: desperate
de·yǫ́t·gan·yahs she is desperate, desperately wanting s.t., in dire need; she will settle for just anyone (that is, a mate)
individual see: person, which
ǫ́:gweh person, human
ga·ę́ ní:ga:ʼ which one; a specific thing
individually
[-atsǫʼ the verb 'stand' with pluralizer; used in expressions meaning 'each' or 'individually' or 'one after another']
indolent see: lazy
sa·nǫ́ʼseh you are lazy
induce see: incite
ęt·ri·hǫ́:niʼ you will incite, be the cause of s.t.
industrious see: work well
got·sáh·niht she is a good worker, tireless, active, industrious,etc.
industry see: G (ha·diʼnhahg·yaʼs ho·nah·dęg·yaʼdǫh)
inevitable see: certain
o·ih·wí:yo: it is certain, for sure
inexhaustible see: work well
got·sáh·niht she is a good worker, tireless, active, industrious, etc.
inexpensive
tęʼ de·gá:nǫ:ʼ it is not costly
[tęʼ not stem: -nǫ:ʼ$_{V}$- costly, dear, expensive]
infant see: baby, new-born
o·wi:ya:ʼáh ek·sá:ʼah baby girl
o·wi:ya:ʼáh hak·sá:ʼah baby boy
gog·wę́·hęh·dǫh new born baby
go·dǫ:hǫ́:niʼ newborn child
infect
gʼo·nó:drahs she has open, weeping sores
[P+ stem: -(ʼ)nodra(h,ʼ)$_{V}$- be infected; have open, weeping sores]
oʼnó:drahs a skin rash

Cayuga pronunciation guide: /a/ father /e/ weigh /ę/ men (nasalized) /i/ police /o/ hole /ǫ/ home (nasalized) /u/ blue. Underlined vowels are voiceless or whispered. /ˊ/ high pitch. /t/ too /d/ do /k/ king /g/ good (never soft g) /j/ judge or adze /s/ soon /sh/ less heat (never the sh in shirt) /sr/ shrine /sy/ sure /hw/ which (the sound made when you blow out a candle) /h/ hi /ts/ cats hide /ʼ/ (the sound before the first vowel in 'uh-uh') /n/ noon /r/ round /w/ way /y/ yes.

infect (continued)
s'a·nó:drahs you have a skin rash, running sores, weeping sores
o'nó:dra' it is infected; an infection
ę·yó'nod·rahs it will become infected
[P+ stem: -(')nodrahsd- become infected; consists of: -(')nodra(h,')$_V$- infected]
a'a·go·nó:drahs she got chicken pox, a skin infection, allergic reactions; she became infected
s'a·nód·rahs·dǫh it has given you an infection, an allergic reaction; you have already had an allergic reaction
inferior see: bad
tę́' det·ga:yé·i' it is bad, false, wrong
inferno see: fire
o·dé:ka' fire; it is burning
infirmity see: sickness
o·nǫh·so·dá·ę:' sickness
inflame
o'náh·gǫ:t it (skin) is inflamed; a bee sting
[P+ stem: -(')nahgǫd- inflamed, bee sting; consists of: -(')nahg(a)$_N$- sting -ǫd$_V$- attached]
inflate
se·wá·ǫ:da:' inflate (a tire, balloon, etc.)
[stem: -waǫda:- inflate s.t.; consists of: -w(a:)$_N$- air -ǫda:(h)$_V$- put in]
ga·wa·ǫ:dá:hǫh it is inflated
gá:wa:t it is inflated
[ga+ stem: -wad- inflated; consists of: -w(a:)$_N$- air -d$_V$- stand]
inflexible see: demanding, hard, stiff
tgę·nǫ́h·dǫ·ha' I make the decisions; I am a strict person
oh·ní:yǫh it is hard
o·tǫ́·ga·i: it is stiff; rigor mortis
influence see: persuade
ęhs·he'ni·gǫ·hǫ́:ni' you will influence, persuade s.o.

inform see: tell
ahs·ha·gǫ·hó:wi' he told her
infuriating see: maddening
o·ná'kwat it is irritating, maddening
inhabit
ę·sat·na·dá·ę' you will inhabit
[at+ stem: -nadaę'- camp, inhabit; consists of: -nad(a)$_N$- town, community -ę$_V$- lie on the ground]
inhabit see: dwell, reside
tsę́h dwak·nǫ́h·so:t where I dwell (lit.: where my house is)
tsę́h tgi'drǫ' where I live, reside
inhale see: breathe
sa·dǫ́:nye's you are breathing
initial see: beginning
gyog·yę́h·dǫh the first one, the beginning
initiate see: begin
ęht·sáh·sa·wę' you will begin, start
injure see: hurt
ę·wák·nǫh·ya'k I will get hurt
inn see: motel
ǫ·nǫh·wehs·tá'geh motel; inn; bed-and-breakfast; hotel
innocent
de·ho·nǫ·dán·hęh he is innocent
[de'+ not P+ stem: -nǫdanh$_V$- guilty]
sga·ho'dę́' dę·ho·i·wá·ę' he is innocent
[sgaho'dę' nothing de'+ not P+ stem: -(r)ihwaę(:)- innocent; consists of: -(r)ih(wa)$_N$- word -ę$_V$- lie on the ground]
input see: put in
sǫ́:da:s you put s.t. in
inquire see: ask, investigate
ę·sa·da·hǫ́:dǫ' you will ask
ęhs·ríh·wih·sa:k you will investigate, inquire

inquisitive
sa·da·hǫh·dǫ́hs·gǫ: you are inquisitive [A+ad+ stem: -(a)hǫdǫsgǫ- inquisitive; consists of: -(a)hǫhd(a)$_N$- ear -(a)hǫdǫ(:)$_V$- ask -(h)sgǫ: easily]
insane see: crazy
de·ge·na̲·háwen·ye' I am crazy
inscribe see: write
ę̨k·yá:dǫ:' I will write
insect
o·ji'nǫ́:wa' bug, insect, worm [o+ stem: -ji'nǫw(a), ji'nǫh$_N$- insect, bug]
o·ji'nǫ·wa'shǫ́:'ǫh insects
insert
he·sá·w'i·ta' you insert s.t. all the time [stem: -(a)wi'd$_V$- insert]
insert see: put in
sǫ́:da:s you put s.t. in
inside see: in
gá·ǫ:nyǫ' it included some; it is in there
insignificant see: unimportant
ni·yo·i·hú:'uh it is of little importance
insincere see: two-faced
sa·gǫh·sa̲h·ní:yǫh you are two-faced
insist see: demand
ęt·ríh·wa̲·hek you will demand s.t., insist on s.t., force s.t.
insolvent see: poor
a·gí:dęht I am poor, poverty-stricken, in poverty
inspect see: examine
a·gat·ga̲·hí·yohs·dǫh I am staring at it, examining it closely
Inspector General see: G (Ha'k·do·ha'go:wah)
inspiration see: idea
o·íh·wa·geh the reason, idea for s.t.
instead see: I (gihne:)
instigate
ho·ih·wa·gę́:nya't he is an instigator [P+ stem: -(r)ihwagęnya'd- complain, instigate; consists of: -(r)ih(wa)$_N$- word -gęnya'd$_V$- cause to compete; be competitive]
instigate see: research
é·i:ho'gwa:s she is researching, instigating
instigator see: shit-disturber
de·ye'da·wę́:nye' she is a shit-disturber
institute, institution see: G (ho·nad·rih·wahs·di:hs·dǫh)
instruct see: teach
ha·i:hǫn·yá:nih he is a teacher
instruction see: education
ga·i:hǫn·yá:ni:' education
instrument see: tool
ehs·ta'shǫ́:'ǫh tools; utensils
instrument
[-hkwa' instrumental suffix; the object denoted is an 'instrument']
[-odahkwa' the verb 'stand' with instrumental; denotes a standing object]
[-ǫdahkwa' the verb 'attached' with instrumental; denotes an object which stands out from that to which it is attached]
[-ędahkwa' the verb 'be lying on the ground' with instrumental; denotes an object into which things are placed]
insufficient see: lack
da·wá·d'ok·dahs it lacks; it is not enough
insulation see: lining
de·yeh·na·néda̲hk·wa' insulation
insult see: condemn, jeer, offend
she·yéh·sa̲h·ta' you always condemn, insult, slander s.o.
ęh·sad·wę·ná:yęht you will jeer, jest, throw words at s.o.
ęhs·he'ni·gǫ́·ha'e:k you will offend s.o.

Cayuga pronunciation guide: /a/ father /e/ weigh /ę/ men (nasalized) /i/ police /o/ hole /ǫ/ home (nasalized) /u/ blue. Underlined vowels are voiceless or whispered. /'/ high pitch. /t/ too /d/ do /k/ king /g/ good (never soft g) /j/ judge or adze /s/ soon /sh/ less heat (never the sh in shirt) /sr/ shrine /sy/ sure /hw/ which (the sound made when you blow out a candle) /h/ hi /ts/ cats hide /'/ (the sound before the first vowel in 'uh-uh') /n/ noon /r/ round /w/ way /y/ yes.

insurance see: G (ad·rih·wag·ya·ǫhs·ra' ha·di·gan·ya's)
insurrection see: celebration
de·yog·yǫhg·wę́·dǫhs upheaval of a crowd of people; a celebration; a riot
integer see: number
ohs·hé:da' number
integrate see: add, mix
ęt·yehs you will add
dęs·yehs you will mix them all together
integrity see: honour
od·rih·wag·wá·ih·sǫ: it is believable, credible, righteous, fair, honest
intelligence agency see: G (de·ha·di·nę·hę·da:s ho·nad·rih·wah·sęh·dǫh oh·wę·ja·ę:dǫ:nyǫ')
intelligent see: smart, wise
sya·dǫhs·rá·ę·di' you are smart (educated)
ho·di'ni·gǫ·ho·wá·nę's they (m) are wise; they have the capacity for thinking
intend see: think
a·hi:' I thought, intended
intentional see: do on purpose
tsa'geht I did it on purpose
interchange see: expressway
de·wa·ta·há'drǫ' expressway; interchanges
intercourse
a·dá·i:sdǫ:' intercourse
[a+ stem: -(i)'daisdǫ:'- intercourse; consists of: -(ni)'d(a)$_N$- privates -(a)'ehsd pierce]
intercourse see: mate
s'a·dá'i:s you have intercourse
interested see: inquisitive
sa·da·hǫh·dǫ́hs·gǫh you are inquisitive
interesting see: enticing
ohs·gá:na't it is enticing, alluring, attractive, tempting
interpret see: translate
de·ye·wę·ná·den·ye's she is a translator; she is translating now
interpreter
ha·dę·wę·na:gá:da:s he is an interpreter
[A+adę+ stem: -węnagadad- interpreter; consists of: -węn(a)$_N$- voice, word -gadad$_V$- raise s.t. up]
interrogate see: ask
ę·sa·dą·hǫ́:dǫ' you will ask
interrupt see: quit
ta:gá·ǫ:nį·hę: they (f/m) suddenly quit
intersect see: cross
dę·ha·di·hę·dí:ya's they (m) cut across fields
intestine see: guts
o·yǫ́:wa' guts; intestines
intimidate see: corrupt, threaten
des·ha·g'o·ni·gǫ·há·gęn·yǫhs he intimidates people all the time
into see: in
[-agǫ: internal locative suffix; means 'in', 'on', or 'under']
into s.t. see: addicted
tsa'ho:ya:t he can't help himself; it has become a habit with him
[tsa'+P+...-ad$_V$- be unable to help oneself]
intrigue s.o. see: tempt s.o.
ęhs·he·yąhd·rǫ́hg·wę' you will threaten, scare s.o.
Inuit see: C (O·to·we·ge·ho:nǫ')
inundate see: flood
ę·węh·nó:dǫ:' it will flood
invert see: turn upside down
dę·gǫ·nǫh·wétso'dę' I am going to turn you upside down, upend you (said in anger)
investigate
ak·níh·sa:s we two (excl.) are looking for it
[(N+) stem: -(i)hsag$_V$- investigate, inquire, look for]

investigate (continued)
hih·sa:s he is looking for it
ę·gíh·sa:k I will seek, look for it
a·gíh·sa·gǫh I am looking for it
sih·sa:k look for it
sih·sá:kah go and look for it
a·ga·e·sá·keʼ they (f/m) are going to look for it
ęhs·ríh·wih·sa:k you will investigate, inquire
[(N+) stem: -(r)ih(wa)$_N$- word -(i)hsag$_V$- investigate, inquire, look for]
investigate see: examine
a·gat·ga·hí·yǫhs·dǫh I am staring at it, examining it closely
investment see: profit
wat·wihs·dǫn·yáʼdǫh profit; investment
invigorating see: cold
o·náʼno:ʼ it is cold, cool
invitation
a·dę·hę·gá·ǫhs·raʼ an invitation
[adę+ stem: -(ah)ęgaǫsr(a)$_N$- invitation -(ah)ǫgaǫ$_V$- invite]
invitation see: listen
ęh·sad·rę·na·tǫ·dáʼtaʼ you will go listen to the songs (said as an invitation)
invite
ę·gǫ·hǫ·gá·ǫʼ I will invite, request you
[TR+/adę+ stem: -(h)ǫgaǫ$_V$- invite; consists of: -(a)hǫg$_V$- hear, learn how to speak a language, understand]
ęh·sa·dę·hǫ́·ga·ǫʼ you will invite
ęh·sa·hǫ·gá·haʼ you will be invited, asked to go
invocation see: prayer
ga·ih·wa·né:gę:ʼ prayer, to pray
involuntary see: do unintentionally
taʼde·wa·géh·dǫ:ʼ I did not mean, intend it
ire see: anger
ohs·rǫ́·hęʼdaʼ an angry person; temper
irk see: annoy
as·gé·kęʼdęʼ you got sick of me; you are bored with me
iron
ęhs·ríhs·da: you will iron
[stem: -(r)ihsda:- iron; consists of: -(h)wihsd(a), (hr)ihsd(a)$_N$- metal -a:ʼ$_V$- hold, contain, include]
ęhs·ríhs·dah·sǫʼ you will iron (several things)
é·ihs·da·taʼ an iron
[e+ stem: -(r)ihsdataʼ- iron; consists of: -(h)wihsd(a), (hr)ihsd(a)$_N$- metal, money -taʼ- be dry]
gahn·yǫ́ʼǫhs·raʼ iron, steel
[ga+ stem: -(h)nyǫ(ʼǫ)hsr(a)$_N$- iron, steel]
ironing board
e·ihs·da·táʼ ga·nés·da:ʼ ironing board
[consists of: eihsdataʼ an iron; ganehsda:ʼ a board]
ironwood
te·ó:jiʼ iron wood (tree); red oak
[stem: -teojiʼ$_N$- ironwood, red oak]
ironworker
ha·dihn·yǫʼǫhs·rá:tęhs (**ha·dihn·yǫhs·rá:tęhs**) ironworkers, iron climbers
[A+ stem: -(h)nyǫhsratęhs- ironworker; consists of: -hnyǫ(ʼǫ)hsr(a)$_N$- iron, steel -(r)atę, (r)adeʼ$_V$- climb]
ha·dihn·yǫhs·ró:taʼ ironworkers
[A+ stem: -(h)nyǫhsrotaʼ- ironworker; consists of: -hnyǫ(ʼǫ)hsr(a)$_N$- iron, steel -od$_V$- stand]
irregular see: rough, unusual
a·ó:gaʼt it is rough
ti·yó:tah it is queer, unusual, odd
irritable see: cantankerous, grumpy, itchy, nervous
e·nǫ́·węhd·raʼ she is cantankerous
de·di·sʼa·ni·gǫ·hí:yo: you are grumpy, grouchy, not happy

Cayuga pronunciation guide: /a/ father /e/ weigh /ę/ men (nasalized) /i/ police /o/ hole /ǫ/ home (nasalized) /u/ blue. Underlined vowels are voiceless or whispered. /´/ high pitch. /t/ too /d/ do /k/ king /g/ good (never soft g) /j/ judge or adze /s/ soon /sh/ less heat (never the sh in shirt) /sr/ shrine /sy/ sure /hw/ which (the sound made when you blow out a candle) /h/ hi /ts/ cats hide /ʼ/ (the sound before the first vowel in ‘uh-uh’) /n/ noon /r/ round /w/ way /y/ yes.

irritable (continued)
á·ǫhk·wa:t it is itchy
wa·dón·yah·nǫ: it is nervous
irritating see: maddening
o·náʼkwa:t it is irritating, maddening
is see: I (be, gwatoh, ne:ʼ, ne:ʼgyę:ʼ, ne:ʼgyę:neʼ, ne:ʼhne:ne:ʼ, ne:neʼ)
island
oh·wéh·no:t island
[o+ stem: -(h)wehn(a)$_N$- island -od$_V$- stand]
Isn't it so? see: I (ę:ʼ)
issue see: go out, publish
gyo·yá·gęʼǫh it comes out here; it is sticking out, protruding
dęhs·ríhs·do·ha:k you will publish s.t.
it see: I (aǫhęʼ)
its see: I (o:węh)
itchy
á·ǫhk·wat it is itchy
[(y)a+ stem: -ǫhkwad$_V$- itchy]

J

jab see: poke, punch, spear
des·wáʼehs·taʼ you all are poking
a·há·gǫ·he:k he punched it
a·to·waʼę́·naʼehs he speared him with a stick
jack
de·gaʼdrẹh·dáhk·waʼ jack; tow truck; hoist
[de+ga+ stem: -(ʼ)drehdahkwaʼ- jack, tow truck; consists of: -(ʼ)drehd(a)$_N$- car, vehicle -(h)kwaʼ$_V$- s.t. that lifts things up]
jacket see: dress
ag·yaʼda·wíʼtraʼ coat; dress
jack-lighting see: night-fish
ę·hę·na·tahs·rǫ·dáh·naʼ they (m) will go jack-lighting, spear-fishing

jackass
de·wa·hǫh·dá·hǫʼ a jackass; a donkey (lit.: it has crossed ears)
[de+wa+ stem: -(a)hǫhdahǫʼ- jackass, donkey; consists of: -(a)hǫhd(a)$_N$- ear -(h)ǫ(:)$_V$- lie across]
jagged see: rough
á·o:gaʼt it is rough
jail
ǫ·da·dęn·ho·dǫhk·wáʼgeh jail; prison (lit.: place where s.o. is locked up)
[ǫ+ (a)dadę+ stem: -nhodǫhkwaʼgeh- jail, prison; consists of: -nhodǫ(:)$_V$- lock]
janitor
de·ga·ǫ:dóh·da:s they (f/m) are janitors
[de+A+ad+ stem: -ohda:s- janitor; consists of: -ohda(:,h)$_V$- tidy up, clean]
January see: A (Ga·yaʼda·go:wah)
jar see: bottle
gat·séʼdaʼ, gęt·séʼdaʼ bottle; jar
Jarvis, Ont. see: E (York, Ont., Tgag·wę:troʼ)
javex see: bleach
gahs·dag·wá:dahg·wahs bleach; javex
jaw see: chin, jowl
oʼyó:tsaʼ a chin
sgih·yóʼtsaʼ jowls
jealous
seʼnó:s·hahs you are envious
[A+ stem: -(ʼ)nosh$_V$- jealous, envious]
ak·nó:s·hę: I am envious
[P+ stem: -(ʼ)noshę$_V$- jealous, envious]
oʼnó:s·hę: it is jealous
oʼnó:s·haʼt it is jealous, envious
[o+ stem: -(ʼ)noshaʼd- jealous, envious; consists of: -(ʼ)nosh$_V$- jealous, envious]
gǫh·gá·hę: she is jealous
[P+ stem: -(a)hgahę:$_V$- jealous]
hoh·gá·hę: he is jealous

jealousy

ga·nóhs·hęhs·ra' jealousy
[ga+ stem: -(')noshęhsr(a)$_N$- jealousy -(')nosh$_V$- jealous, envious]

jeer

ęh·sad·wę·ná:yęht you will jeer, jest, throw words at s.o.
[ad+ stem: -węnayęhd- jeer, jest; consists of: -węn(a)$_N$- voice, word -(y)ęhd$_V$- hit, knock down, strike]

ahs·ha·god·wę́·na·yęht he lambasted, denigrated her / them

ahs·ha·god·wę·na·yę́h·da̱h·nǫ:' you (lit. he) really lambasted them, repeatedly hit them with words

jest see: jeer, tease

o·dę́·don·ya't a jest

jet

ot·sa:dó:t de·gá:dęh jet; plane
[consists of: otsa:do:t there is fog; dega:dęh airplane]

jittery see: fidgety

sat·nat·sa·gę́:nye' you are fidgety

job see: occupation

ni·sa·i·ho'dęhs·ró'dę: your occupation, your type of work

jock strap

hę·nat·na·johg·wa·ni·yǫ·dáh·kwa' jock strap
[hęn+ at+ stem: -na'johgwaniyǫdahkwa'- jock strap; consists of: -na'j(oh(s)gwa)$_N$- cup -niyǫdahkwa'$_V$- s.t. that hangs]

Joe Pye weed

ga̱h·no's Joe Pye weed
[ga+ stem: -(h)no's- Joe Pye weed; consists of: -(h)n(a)$_N$- oil, gas -o's- be submerged]

join

dęhs·nah·sǫ́:dę' you will join
[de+... stem: -nahsǫd- join; consists of: -nahs(a)- -ǫd$_V$- attached]

de·ga·na̱h·sǫ́:dǫ' many things are joined together (for example, cars in a train)

de·sah·sǫd·ré:ha' you join things together all the time; you do puzzles
[de+... stem: -(a)hsǫdrę, (a)hsǫdre$_V$- join together]

dęh·sáh·sǫd·rę' you will join two things together

de·yo·da̱h·sǫ́:dre:' it is joined

de·sáh·sǫd·ręh join it

join see: assemble, attach

dęh·sé·ga̱·hǫ' you will assemble, put together

ęh·só·ha·ę' you will attach s.t.

joint see: elbow, knee

kyoh·sá'geh on my elbow

ǫt·sa' knee

joist see: rafter

ga·nehs·dá:den·yǫ' rafters

joke see: happy-go-lucky, tease trick,

ho·dę·dǫn·yá'da̱hs·gǫ: he is a joker, happy-go-lucky; he is obnoxious

sa·dę·dǫn·yá'dǫh you are joking

a·ho·het·só:go' it tricked him

jolly jumper

wę·nits·gwa̱hs·ra:ní:yǫ:t jolly jumper
[w+ stem: -ęnitsgwahsraniyǫd- jolly jumper, hanging chair; consists of: -(ęn)itsg(wa)$_N$- lower body -niyǫd$_V$- hang]

Jordan, Ont. see: E (Dwa̱h·ya·yę·twęh)

journey see: travel

ni·ya·got·gę·ihs·dǫ́·hǫg·ye' she is travelling as she is moving

jowl

sgih·yó'tsa' jowls
[stem: -sgihyo'ts(a)$_N$- jowl]

joy see: happiness

ot·sę́·nǫn·ya't a happy feeling; gratefulness; thankfulness; joy

judge see: G (sha·go·dęn·yeh·ta'), send

a·hǫ·wa·dę́:nyeht he was sentenced

juice
oh·yá:gri' juice; fruit juice
[o+ stem: -(a)hy(a)$_N$- fruit, berry -gri'$_V$- juice, liquid]
July see: A (Hya·ik·neh·go:wah)
jump
de·yǫ·na̲hs·gwáhk·wa' she is jumping
[de+ stem: -(a)nahsgwahgw$_V$- jump; consists of: -na'sg(wa)$_N$- having to do with the lower body -(h)gw$_V$- lift, pick up]
dę·yǫ́·na̲hs·gwahk she will jump
de·ya·go·na'sgǫhǫ́:gye',
de·ya·go·na'sgwę̲·hę́:gye' she is going along jumping
de·há·nahs·gwe:s he jumps far horizontally
[de+A+ stem: -nahsgwes- jump far; consists of: -na'sg(wa)$_N$- -es$_V$- long]
de·ha·nahs·gwé:so's he jumps high
[de+A+ stem: -nahsgweso's- jump high; consists of: -na'sg(wa)$_N$- having to do with the lower body -esǫ's$_V$- several long objects]
jump see: pounce
hę·sag·y'a·dǫ́:di' you will pounce on it
jumpy see: fidgety
sat·nat·sa·gę́:nye' yǫu are fidgety
junction see: crossroad
de·yo·ha·hí'y'ak·sǫ' crossroads
June see: A (Hya·i:k·neh)
juneberry
ha'drohk juneberry
[stem: -(h)a'drohg$_N$- juneberry]
junk
gat·gí'tra' junk
[ga+ stem: -tgi'tr(a)$_N$- junk -tgi$_V$- dirty, ugly]
sat·gí'tra' your junk
jury see: G (des·ha·go·di·ya'do·weh·ta')
just see: I (gi'), right
tga:yé·i: it is right, correct
justice see: G (ga·ih·wa̲hs·rǫ·nih)
jut out see: attach, protrude
á·ǫ:t it is attached; it is sticking out
he·yá·ǫ:t it protrudes

K

Kahnawake, Que. see: E (Ga̲h·na·wa·geh)
Kanesatake, Que. see: E (Ga·neh·sa·da:geh)
kangaroo see: pocket
á·ǫ·gę̲hs·rǫ:t, á·ǫ·gǫ̲hs·rǫ:t a pocket; a kangaroo
keen see: quick-witted
ha'de·ho·íh·wa·ge: he is quick-witted; he has lots of business, different ideas, many ideas; he is into everything
keep
ę·sa:d·rǫ́:go' you will keep it
[ad+(N+) stem: -(r)ǫgw$_V$- keep]
keep see: preserve
sa·dah·ya̲h·sę:nǫ́:nih preserve fruit
kernel see: corn, nut
o·nę́·hę:' corn
ohn·yó'gwa' nut
kerchief
ǫt·nǫ'á·o:wek·ta' kerchief
[ǫ+at+ stem: -nǫ'aowekta'- kerchief; consists of: -nǫ'(a:), nǫh(a)$_N$- head -(hr)owekd$_V$- be covered]
kettle
de·gah·sí:nǫ:t a kettle
[de+ga+ stem: -(h)sinǫd- kettle; consists of: -(h)sin(a)$_N$- leg -ǫd$_V$- attached]
kettle see: tea kettle
eh·ne·ga·da·i·há'da̲hk·wa' a tea kettle
key
ęn·ho·dǫg·wáh·ta' key
[ę+ stem: -nhodǫgwahta'- key; consists of: -nhodǫgwahd$_V$- cause to open]

kick
gę́:sęt·wahs I am kicking
[stem: -ę(h)sętw, ę(h)sęto- kick; consists of: -(a)hsi(ʼda), (ę)hs(a)$_N$- foot -ętw, ęto$_V$- kick]
ę·gęh·sę́:to' I will kick it
a·gę́:sęt·węh I did kick it; I have kicked the ball
wę́:sęht·węh a kick
sę·toh kick it
kid see: child, goat
a·gék·s'a·da' my child
ga·yá'dag·rahs goat
kidnap
ha·wi·ya·nę́hsg·wahs he is a kidnapper
[stem: -wiyanęhsgw- kidnap a child; consists of: -wiy(a)$_N$- child, offspring -nęhsgw$_V$- steal]
a·ha·wi·yá·nęhs·go' he stole a child, kidnapped
ga·wi·ya·nę́hsg·węh a kidnapped child
a·hǫg·w'e·dá·nęhs·go' they stole him (for another group)
[stem: -ǫgwe'danęhsgw- kidnap a person; consists of: -ǫgwe('da)$_N$- person -nęhsgw$_V$- steal]
ęh·sǫg·w'e·dá·nęhs·go' you will kidnap s.o.
kill
han·yohs he kills s.t.
[TR+ stem: -(r)iyo, nyo$_V$- kill s.t.]
ęhs·rí:yo' you will kill s.t.
a·hǫ́·wan·yo' s.o. killed him
a·há:nyo' he killed it (an animal)
ahs·há·gon·yo' s.o. killed her
ho·dę́:nyo: he has killed s.o.
killdeer
du·wís·du·wi:' killdeer
[stem: -duwisduwi:'$_N$- killdeer]
kin see: C (ǫ·dę·nǫhk·sǫ')
ǫ·dę́·nǫhk·sǫ' relatives, kin, etc.

kind
a·wę·na·hó'dę: soft kind words
[a+stem: -węn(a)$_N$- voice, word -(ri)ho'dę:$_V$- worked, softened]
kind see: certain type, kind of thing; which
ni·ga·ę·nó'dę: a type of song
ga·ę́ ní:ga:' which one; a specific thing
kind
[-geha:', -ka:', -neha:' customary suffixes; denote a typical 'way' or 'kind' of thing]
kindness
a·dę·ni·dé·ǫ:sra' the act of kindness
[adęn+ stem: -(i)dęǫhsr(a)$_N$- kindness -(i)dęǫ, (i)dę(:)$_V$- pity]
kindred see: kin, family
gah·wa·ji·yá·gę·hǫ' families
king see: G (gwa:go:wah)
kingdom see: country
o·dǫh·wę·já:de' country
kingfisher
gę·nad·rę·nó·dahk·wa' kingfisher (bird)
[gęn+ad+ stem: -(r)ęnodahkwa'- kingfisher; consists of: -(r)ęn(a)$_N$- song, music -odahkwa'$_V$- s.t. that stands]
Kingston, Ont. see: E (Det·gahn·yǫhs·rah·dǫ')
kitten
da·gú:jih kitten
[stem: -dagu:s$_N$- cat -jih really]
klutz see: slow
sad·ri·hó:wi: you are a klutz; you're slow-moving; you are feeble, clumsy
knapsack
hohs·wę'na·géh ho·ya:géh·deh his knapsack
[consists of: hohswe'nageh on his upper back; hoya:gehdeh his knapsack]
hohs·we'na·geh·déh ga·yá:' his knapsack
[consists of: hohswe'nagehdeh he carries it on his upper back; gaya:' bag]

knapsack (continued)

hohs·we'na·géh·deh his knapsack [P+ stem: -(a)hswe'nagehdeh- knapsack; consists of: -(h)swa'n(a), (h)swe'n(a)$_N$- back, upper -gehdeh$_V$- have around one's neck, carry]

hag·ya:géh·dahk·wa' a man's knapsack [A+ag+ stem: -ya:gehdahkwa'- knapsack; consists of: -ya:$_N$- bag -gehdahkwa'$_V$- s.t. that is put around one's neck]

ǫg·ya:géh·dahk·wa' a woman's knapsack; a knapsack

ho·ya:géh·deh his knapsack [P+ stem: -ya:gehdeh- knapsack; consists of: -ya:$_N$- bag -gehd$_V$- have around one's neck]

knee

ǫt·sa' knee [stem: -ǫts(a)$_N$- knee]

sǫt·sá'geh on your knee

gǫts·há'geh on my knee

tsǫt·sá'geh on your (p) knee

kneel

dę·yǫ·dǫt·só:dę' she will become Christian; she will kneel in prayer [de+...ad+ stem: -ǫtsodę'- kneel; consists of: -ǫts(a)$_N$- knee -odę$_V$- stand]

kneel see: pray

dę·hę·na·dǫ́t·so·ta' they (m) pray on their knees

knife

e'wa·ha·isg·ya'k·tá' ga̱·hę́n'at·ra' butcher knife [Ccnsists of: e'wahai:sgyakta' butcher knife; ga̱hęn'atra' knife]

knife see: blade, paring knife

o·hę́·n'at·rǫ:t blade

e·ya:wi̱hs·dót·s'ata' paring knife

knob see: handle

gat·gę́·het·sǫ:t an attached handle

knock

sen·hó·ha'e:k knock on the door [stem: -nhoha'eg- knock (on a door); consists of: -nho(ha)$_N$- door -(')e$_V$- hit]

knock see: hit, noise, tap

ęhs·wá'e:k you will pound, tap

a·gan·ho·há:yęht noise made by banging a door

hoh·wá'e: he is tapping

knock down

da̱·hǫ·wag·yę·da̱hk·wá·hag·waht s.o. knocked him out of his chair [stem: -(a)kyędahkw(a)$_N$- chair -(h)agwahd$_V$- knock down]

knock down see: hit

ęhs·ya'g·yé:nęht you will knock it down

knock out see: punch

a·há·gǫ·he:k he punched it

knock over

sheh·déhn·yęh·ta' you are knocking her over right now [TR+ stem: -(a)hdehnyęhd$_V$- knock over; consists of: -yęhd$_V$- knock down]

ga̱hs·he·ya̱h·déhn·yę̱h·ta' I am going along knocking people over

ęhs·he·ya·dę́h·yęht you will flip s.o. over, knock s.o. over

ahs·héh·dehn·yęht you flipped s.o. over

knot

ok·jí:nǫ:t knot in a tree [o+ stem: -kjin(a)$_N$- stump -ǫd$_V$- attached]

o·jíhn·yo·go:t tree knot [o+ stem: -jihnyog(wa)$_N$- tree knot -od$_V$- stand]

o·jihn·yo·gó:dǫ' tree knots

de·ga·ji̱hs·dó'gwa·ǫt a tied knot [de+A+ stem: -jihsdo'gwaǫd- tie a knot; consists of: -jihsdǫg(wa)$_N$- knot -ǫd$_V$- attached]

knot see: stump, tie
ok·jí:na' a stump; knots in a tree
de·se·jihs·dog·wá·o·dęh tie a knot
knotted see: tangled
de·yót·gę'i: its hair is tangled; ideas and things are tangled
know
go·nǫ́h·dǫ' she knows
[P+ stem: -ęnǫhdǫ(:)$_V$- know]
sę·nǫ́h·dǫ' you know
a·gę́·nǫh·dǫ' I know
ho·nǫ́h·dǫ' he knows
o·nǫ́h·dǫ' it knows
ǫ·gę́·nǫh·dǫ:k I should know
ę·wa·gę·nǫ́h·dǫ:k I will know
ę·ya·wę·nǫ́h·dǫ' it will know
de·geh·sę·na·ę·dí: I do not know its name
[TR+ stem: -(h)sęn(a)$_N$- name -(y)ędei, (y)ędi$_V$- know]
gǫh·sę·na·ę·dí: I know your name
know see: I (c.f.: I don't know, do:ga')

L

label s.t. see: name s.t.
ho·dí·yahs·dǫh they (m) have named it
labour
a·hǫh·ya·gę́'dahk it made him work hard; he laboured
[stem: -(r)ǫhyagę'd- labour, make s.o. work hard; consists of: -(r)ǫhyagę$_V$- be in agony, groan]
ęh·sa·ǫh·yá·g'ę·dahk it's going to make you groan
labour see: pain, struggle
ęh·sá·det·sa't you will struggle, squirm to get loose, revolt
ęg·rǫ́h·ya·gę' I will be in pain; I will labour, be in agony

Labour Board see: G (Ga·i·ho'dęhs·ra' Ga·ya·nęhs·ra' Ha·dihs·re')
laborious see: difficult
wę́:do:' it is difficult
Labour Relations Board see: G (Ga·i·ho'dęhs·ra' Ga·ya·nęhs·ra' Ho·nahs·di:hs·dǫh)
lace
gan·héh·sa' harness: ribbon: laces
[ga+ stem: -nhehs(a)$_N$- lace, ribbon, harness]
lace see: curtain
o·jí'a:' curtains; lace
lacerate see: scratch, tear
dę·wa·gah·jí:yo:' it will scratch me (for example, a twig, a thorn)
ęhs·rá·drǫ:' you will tear, shred it
lack
da·wá·d'ok·dahs it lacks; it is not enough
[d+...ad+ stem: -o'kd(ę)$_V$- end; lack]
wa·dó:kta' it lacks; it is always ending (for example, a speech always ends at the same place)
da·wá·d'ok·dę' it lacked; it was not enough
gyo·dó'k·da'ǫh it is lacking
tę' dę·wá:gyę' it is not mine; I do not have
[de'+ not P+(N+) stem: -(y)ę$_V$- lie on the ground, have s.t.]
de·wag·wi·yá·ę' I do not have a child
[de'+ not P+(N+) stem: -wiy(a)$_N$- child, offspring -ę$_V$- lie on the ground, have s.t.]
ta'de·ga·wá:yǫ:t it has no wings
[ta'de'+not A+N+ stem: -way(a)$_N$- fin, wing -ǫd$_V$- be attached]

Cayuga pronunciation guide: /a/ father /e/ weigh /ę/ men (nasalized) /i/ police /o/ hole /ǫ/ home (nasalized) /u/ blue. Underlined vowels are voiceless or whispered. /'/ high pitch. /t/ too /d/ do /k/ king /g/ good (never soft g) /j/ judge or adze /s/ soon /sh/ less heat (never the sh in shirt) /sr/ shrine /sy/ sure /hw/ which (the sound made when you blow out a candle) /h/ hi /ts/ cats hide /'/ (the sound before the first vowel in 'uh-uh') /n/ noon /r/ round /w/ way /y/ yes.

lack a spirit
deʼo·di·naʼgó:wahs they (z) have lost their spirit of life (for example, dinosaurs)
[deʼ+(s/j+) P+ stem: -naʼgow$_V$- lack a spirit, be ominous]
de·jo·nʼa·gó:wahs it has no spirit of life
o:nę́h de·ja·go·naʼgó:wahs she is ominous

ladder see: stair
a·dǫ́h·nʼet·saʼ, o·dǫ́h·nʼet·saʼ a ladder; stairs

ladle
de·yo·wę·yéʼdahk·waʼ ladle
[de+yo+ stem: -(a)węnyeʼdahkwaʼ- ladle; consists of: -(a)węnye(:)$_V$- stir, mix]
gat·gę·het·sé:s a·go·jęh·dáhk·waʼ ladle
[consists of: gatgęhetse:s ladle, dipper; agojęhdahkwaʼ s.t. for dishes]
gat·gę́·het·se:s a ladle; a long-handled spoon, dipper
[ga+ stem: -tgęhetses- ladle, dipper; consists of: -tgęhets(a)$_N$- handle -es$_V$- long]

lady see: woman
a·gǫ́:gweh girl; woman; the female gender

lagoon see: pond
ga·ná·wa·gǫ: in the pond, swamp

lake
gan·ya·dá:ʼgeh to, at, on the lake
[stem: -nyad(a:)$_N$- lake, body of water]
gan·ya·dá:gę·ha:ʼ lake kind
gan·ya·dá:gǫ: in the lake
gan·ya·dak·dá:gyeʼ along the lake, shoreline

lake see: water
oh·né·ga·gǫ: under water; in the water; in the lake

lake people
gan·ya·da:ʼge·hó:nǫʼ lake people; cottagers

lake people (continued)
[ga+ stem: -nyadagehonǫʼ- cottager; consists of: -nyad(a:)$_N$- lake, body of water, water]

lake bed
haʼde·yo·nǫh·wa·ęʼdaʼǫ́h oh·né·ga·gǫ: lake bed
[consists of: haʼdeyonǫhwaęʼdaʼǫh; ohnegagǫ: in the water]

Lake Ontario see: E (Gan·ya·da·i·yoʼ)

lamb see: sheep
de·yo·na·gá·ǫt sheep; lamb; elk

lame see: crippled
go·jí:yoʼ she is crippled

lament see: grieve, mourn
de·wak·ni·gǫ́hn·yʼa·gǫh I am brokenhearted, grieving
ęh·sa·dę·nǫ́ʼnya:t you will mourn

lamp
ga·jíhs·daʼ a lamp; a light; etc.
[ga+ stem: -jihsd(a)$_N$- light]
ga·jíhs·do·taʼ a lamp
[ga+ stem: -jihsdotaʼ- lamp; consists of: -jihsd(a)$_N$- light -od$_V$- stand]

lampstand
e·jihs·da·háhk·waʼ s.t. that supports a light
[e+ stem: -jihsd(a)$_N$- light -(h)ahkwaʼ$_V$- s.t. that supports]
ǫ·de·jihs·dó·dahk·waʼ s.t. that holds lights
[ǫ+ade+ stem: -jihsdodahkwaʼ- light holder; consists of: -jihsd(a)$_N$- light -odahkwaʼ$_V$- s.t. that stands]

lance see: spear with a stick, stab, stick
a·to·waʼę́·naʼehs he speared him with a stick
dęhs·hę·naʼtráʼa:s you will stab s.t.
ganh·yaʼ stick

land
de·gę'drǫ́:da's it lands there all the time
[de+... stem: -(i)'drǫda'- land; consists of: -(i)'drǫ$_V$- live, dwell, be at home]
dę·gę'drǫ́:da' it will land
dę·ho'drǫ·dá'ǫh he has landed
o·héh·da' dirt; earth
[o+ stem: -(h)ehd(a)$_N$- land, dirt, earth, ground]
ga·héh·da·geh on the land
o·héh·da·gǫ: in the dirt, earth; under the ground
o·heh·dí:yo: good earth
[o+ stem: -(h)ehd(a)$_N$- land, dirt, earth, ground -iyo:$_V$- be nice, good]
o·heh·dah·ní:yǫh hard ground
[o+ stem: -(h)ehd(a)$_N$- land, dirt, earth, ground -(h)niyǫh$_V$- hard, tough]
o·héh·dǫhs·gǫ' barren land
[o+ stem: -(h)ehdohsga'(w)- barren land; consists of: -(h)ehd(a)$_N$- land, dirt, earth, ground -ohsga'(w)$_V$- clear]
land see: earth, loam
oh·wę́·ja·de' existing earth, land
ni·yo·heh·dó'dę: loam
land claim see: G (hę·nǫh·wę·jahs·gen·hahs)
landing see: dock
wa·tǫ·wa·ę:dahk·wá'geh a dock
land owner see: G (ho·nǫh·wę·ja·ę:dǫ')
land researcher
ha·ǫh·wę·jáhs·gen·hahs land researcher (lit.: he fights for land)
[stem: -ǫhwęj(a)$_N$- earth, land -genh$_V$- argue for, advocate]
land title see: G (ho·nǫh·wę·ja·ę:dǫ')
landscaper
ha·dǫh·ned·rǫ́:nihs he is a landscaper
[A+ad+ stem: -ǫhnedrǫnihs- landscaper; consists of: -ǫhnedr(a)$_N$- landscape -ǫni, ǫny$_V$- make, fix]

landslide
a·ǫ́h·wę·ję' landslide
[a+ stem: -ǫhwęję'- landslide, cave-in; consists of: -ǫhwęj(a)$_N$- earth, land -ę$_V$- lie on the ground]
ę·yǫ́h·wę·ję' it will cave in
laneway
ǫ·ta·há:gwah·ta' laneway
[ǫ+at+ stem: -(h)aha:gwahta'- laneway; consists of: -(h)ah(a)$_N$- road -(r)agwahd$_V$- be taken out, chosen]
language
ga·wę·nǫ·dáh·gǫh spoken language
[ga+ stem: -węnodahgw- language; consists of: -węn(a)$_N$- voice, word -ǫdahgw$_V$- unattach, lift up]
ni·ga·wę·nó:dę' language
[ni+ga+ stem: -węnodę'- language; consists of: -węn(a)$_N$- voice, word -odę$_V$- stand, put in]
nid·wa·wę·nó:dę: our language
o·wę·na·gá:yǫh high language; formal language
[o+ stem: -węnagayǫh- high, formal language; consists of: -węn(a)$_N$- voice, word -gayǫh$_V$- old (thing)]
o·íh·wat·gi' dirty, vulgar language
[o+ stem: -(r)ih(wa)$_N$- word -tgi$_V$- dirty, ugly]
o·ih·wat·gi'shǫ́:'ǫh smut; dirty language
lanky see: thin
gohsg·yǫ́'wa·tę: she is thin
lantern
ǫ·tahs·rǫ·dáhk·wa' flashlight; torch
[ǫ+at+ stem: -(h)ahsrǫdahkwa'- torch; consists of: -(h)ahsr(a)$_N$- flash -ǫd$_V$- attached]
e·jihs·dę·hę·wih·dáhk·wa' lantern; torch; flashlight
[e+ stem: -jihsdęhęwihdahkwa'- lantern; consists of: -jihsd(a)$_N$- light -(h)ęwihdahkwa'$_V$- s.t. used for carrying]

Cayuga pronunciation guide: /a/ father /e/ weigh /ę/ men (nasalized) /i/ police /o/ hole /ǫ/ home (nasalized) /u/ blue. Underlined vowels are voiceless or whispered. /´/ high pitch. /t/ too /d/ do /k/ king /g/ good (never soft g) /j/ judge or adze /s/ soon /sh/ less heat (never the sh in shirt) /sr/ shrine /sy/ sure /hw/ which (the sound made when you blow out a candle) /h/ hi /ts/ cats hide /'/ (the sound before the first vowel in 'uh-uh') /n/ noon /r/ round /w/ way /y/ yes.

lantern see: torch
a·hę·na·tahs·rǫ́·dę' they (m) carried a torch, lantern, flashlight
lard see: fat, oil
o'dróhs·ra' fat; pig rinds
oh·na' grease; oil
large see: big
go·wá:nęh, ga·gó·wa·nęh it is big
large
[-go:wah augmentative suffix; denotes 'largeness']
lark see: meadow lark
de·gahs·n'a·dó·wa·nę's meadow lark
larynx see: throat
o·há'da' quill; plume; feather; voice; throat; larynx; esophagus
lash see: eyelash, whip
o·gá·heh·da' eyelash; the stem of a berry; the eye of the corn kernel
o·hǫ́:da' a bush; a whip
last
hes·ga:gǫ:t the last
[he+s+ga+ stem: -gǫd$_V$- persevere, linger; be last]
last see: B (hes·ga:gǫ:t)
latch see: lock
e'no·wa·ni·yǫ·dáhk·wa' a lock
late
ę·wák·nihs·go' I will be late
[P+ stem: -nihsgo'$_V$- late]
ak·nihs·go'ǫ́·hǫg·ye' I am arriving late
oh·na'gę́:' ih·se' you are late again (said at the moment)
[ohna'gę:' behind A+stem: -e'(s)- be someplace; be late, behind; consists of: -e$_V$- go]
oh·na'gęh·jíh a·há:yǫ' he arrived late
[ohna'gęjih really behind stem: -yǫ$_V$- arrive; arrive late]
ǫg·yá'da̱hs·hę' I was late
[P+ stem: -ya'dahshę(:,')- be late, slow; consists of: -ya'd(a)$_N$- body -(a)hshę:$_V$- slow-moving]

late (continued)
ag·yá'da̱hs·hę:, ag·yá'da̱hs·hęh I am slow, I was late
sa·yá'da̱hs·hęh you are slow
ǫg·ya·da̱hs·hę'ǫ·hǫ́:gye' I am arriving late
[P+ stem: -ya'dahshę'ǫhǫgye'- be arriving late; consists of: -ya'd(a)$_N$- body -(a)hshę:$_V$- slow-moving]
sa·ya'da̱hs·hę'ǫ·hǫ́:gye' you are late
later see: I (wa'ji:hah)
lather see: foam
oh·wę́hs·da' foam
laugh
gyǫg·yáh·ta' I am really laughing
[stem: -yǫgya'd- laugh, smile; consists of: -yǫdi, yǫgy$_V$- smile]
ęhs·yǫ́:gya't you will smile
laugh see: guffaw
ęs·yǫ́g·y'at·ge: you will laugh loudly, guffaw
laughable see: amusing
o·yǫ́:gya't it is amusing, laughable
laundromat see: laundry room
e·no·ha·i:hǫ'dá'geh laundry room, laundromat
laundry
gahs·dag·wa:ni·yǫ́:dǫ' hanging laundry that is not clean
[stem: -(h)sdag(wa:)$_N$- dirt, dirty clothes -niyǫdǫ'$_V$- several hanging objects]
laundry room
e·no·ha·i:hǫ'dá'geh laundry room; laundromat
[e+ stem: -nohaihǫ'da'geh- laundry room, laundromat; consists of: -n$_N$- noun -ohaehǫ'd- be cleaned, washed]
lava flow
o'sg·wa:nya·hę́hs wat·na·wí:ne' lava flow
[consists of: o'sgwanyahęhs rocks are boiling; watnawi:ne' flowing water]

lavatory see: bathroom, toilet
o̜g·ya'do̲·ha·i'tá'geh bathroom
law see: G (ga·ya·ne̲hs·ra')
law (break the law) see: commit a crime
a·tad·ri̲h·wá·hę' he went afoul of the law; he did s.t. wrong
lawful see: righteous
od·rih·wag·wá·ih·so̜: it is believable, credible, righteous, fair, honest
lawmaker see: G (ga·i·ya·nehs·ro̜:ni)
lawn see: grass, sod
o·gá·ho'ja' grass
o'ǫ́hg·wa:' sod; moss
lawn chair
ahs·deh·ká:' ak·yę́·da̲hk·wa' lawn chair
[consists of: ahsdehka:' outside type; akyęda̲hkwa' chair]
lawn mower
wa·da·ded·ré's ga·ga·ho'jí:ya's riding lawn mower
[consists of: wadadedre's self-propelling; gagaho'ji:ya's lawn mower]
ga·ga·ho'jí:ya's lawn mower
[ga+ stem: -gaho'jiya's- lawn mower; consists of: -gaho'j(a)$_N$- grass -(i)ya'g$_V$- cut, break]
lawyer
de̲·ha·ih·wá·gen·hahs he is a lawyer
[de+A+ stem: -(r)ihwagenhahs- lawyer; consists of: -(r)ih(wa)$_N$- word -genh$_V$- argue for, advocate]
lay see: put, put down
he·wá:kre:' I put, placed it over there
i·ję: put it down; leave it alone
lay a floor
ęhs·ne·da:dęh·dá·ę' you will lay a floor
[stem: -neda:dęhdaę(:)- lay a floor; consists of: -neda:dęhd(a)$_N$- floor -ę(:)$_V$- lay s.t. down]

lazy
ak·nǫ́'seh I am lazy
[P+ stem: -no̜'seh- lazy, idle; consists of: -no̜'s$_V$- tire of s.t., get sick of s.t.]
sa·nǫ́'seh you are lazy
go·nǫ́'seh she is idle, lazy
lead
ha·hę́:do̜' he is the front, leader
[A+ stem: -(h)ędo̜'$_V$- lead]
ha·hę́·do̲h·ne:' he used to be a leader
ę·há·hę:t he will lead
[A+ stem: -(h)ęd$_V$- lead]
ęhs·rę:t you will be the lead
á:ha·hę:t he might, could lead
oh·ne·ga·ná:wę: lead, lukewarm water; also refers to a prepubescent boy
[o+ stem: -(h)neganawę:- lead, lukewarm water; consists of: -(h)neg(a)$_N$- water, liquid -nawę$_V$- wet]
lead see: arm (take s.o. by the arm), authority, go over there
ęt·go̜·nę:tsí:ne' I will take you by the arm
dwę·nǫ́h·do̲·ha' it is the boss, the authority
hęh·sé'so̜' go on ahead; take the lead
leader
de·gah·go̜nh·ní'go̜h
(**de·gah·go̜n·hí'go̜h**) the leader of equal standing
[de+ga+ contains: -o̜nhe'$_V$- be alive]
leader see: authority, G (go̜·wa·di·go·wa·nęh)
dwę·nǫ́h·do̲·ha' it is the boss, the authority
leading see: ahead
o·hę́:do̜: ahead; in front; the front
leaf
on·ráh·da' leaf
[o+ stem: -nrahd(a)$_N$- leaf]
on·ráh·da·go̜: in the leaves

leaf (continued)

on·ráh·dat·gę: rotten leaves
[o+ stem: -nrahd(a)$_N$- leaf -tgę$_V$- spoiled, rotten]
o·já·ǫ·sa' leaves of corn
[o+ stem: -jaǫs(a)$_N$- corn leaf]

leak

o·kahs it leaks
[o+ stem: -oka$_V$- leak, drip, trickle]
o·káhs·gę·hę:' it used to leak
ę·yó:ka' it will leak
oh·né·go·gahs (oh·né·go·kahs) dripping water (from a tap)
[o+ stem: -(h)neg(a)$_N$- water, liquid -oka$_V$- leak, drip, trickle]
ohs·dá·o·kahs one drop (at a time)
[o+ stem: -(h)sd(a:)$_N$- drop (of water) -oka$_V$- leak, drip, trickle]

lean

ę·sag·ya·dá'dih you will lean against s.t.
[ag+ stem: -ya'dadih- lean; consists of: -ya'd(a)$_N$- body -(a)dih$_V$- side]
wa·dí·hǫh it is leaning against s.t.
[A+(N+) stem: -(adi)hǫh$_V$- lean against]

lean see: thin

gohsg·yǫ́'wa·tę: she is thin

leap see: jump, pounce

dę·yǫ́·nahs·gwahk she will jump
hę·sag·y'a·dǫ́:di' you will pounce on it

learn

ǫ·de·wa·yę́hsta' she is a novice, learner, beginner
[ade+ stem: -wayę(n)$_N$- heart, spirit -wayę(h)sd$_V$- learn]
ga·ǫ·de·wá·yęhs·ta' they (f/m) are apprentices; they are learning together
hę·na·de·wá·yęhs·ta' they (m) are learning by reading
ęh·sa·de·wá:yęhs you will learn
sa·de·wa·yę́:sdǫh you are learning
wa·de·wa·yę́hs·dǫ:' the process of learning

learned see: wise

ho·di'ni·gǫ·ho·wá:nę's they (m) are wise; they have the capacity for thinking

learning see: education

ga·i:hǫn·yá:ni:' education

leather see: skin

ga·néh·wa' leather, hide

leave

sgah·dę́:gye's I am leaving again
[stem: -(a)hdędi, (a)hdęgy$_V$- leave, go away]
he·sáh·dęg·yǫ: you went over there
oh·dęg·yǫ·hǫ́:g·ye' it is on its way

leave see: come out, go out

ęhs·yá:gę' you will go out

lectern see: altar

ha·ji·hęhs·da:jí' had·rę·ná·ę:dahk·wa' an altar; a pulpit

leer see: smirk

de·sat·gǫh·sá:gri: wrinkle up your face; smirk

left

sgan·yę's·wa:dih to its left
[s+ga+ stem: -nyę'sw(a)$_N$- left -(a)dih$_V$- side; to the left side]

left over see: remainder

o·dá·da'ǫh, o·da:dá'ǫh remainder; it is left over

leg

oh·sí:na' leg
[stem: -(h)sin(a)$_N$- leg]
sęh·sín'a·geh on your leg

leg see: shin

gen·yę́d'a·geh on my shin, leg

legend see: tale

o'ga:' a parable, tale, story, legend

leggings

ga·í:sra' leggings
[stem: -(r)isr(a)$_N$- leggings]

Legislature see: G (hę·nag·yę·dahk·wa' ha·di·ya·nęhs·rǫ:nih)

legitimate see: right
tga:yéi: it is right, correct
leisurely see: slow
sgę.nǫ́:ʼǫh slowly
lemon
o.jitg.wáʼ oh.yaʼ lemon
[consists of: oji:tgwa:ʼ yellow; ohyaʼ fruit]
o.jitg.wáʼ oh.yáʼ grahe:t lemon tree
[consists of: ojitgwaʼ ohyaʼ lemon; grahe:t living tree]
lend
ǫ.ní.hahs.taʼ s.o. lends
[ę+ stem: -nihahsd- lend; consists of: -niha$_{V}$- borrow]
sa.dęh.wihs.da.ni.háh.danih you lend money; a lender
[adę+N+ stem: -nihahd(ę,ni)- lend; consists of: -niha$_{V}$- borrow]
ęh.sa.dę.ní.hah.dęʼ you will lend
sat.wihs.da.ní.hahs you lend money
[ad+ N+ stem: -nihahsd- lend; consists of: -(h)wihsd(a), (hr)ihsd(a)$_{N}$- metal, money -niha$_{V}$- borrow]
length see: be a certain length, depth
ni.yo:ya:de:s how deep the hole, trench, ditch is
lengthen see: stretch
de.ho:dí:yǫ:t he is stretching it
lengthy see: long
ǫ́:sʼǫhs lengthy objects
leniency see: mercy
gę.dá.ǫhs.raʼ mercy
lens
ga.gę́h ot.gǫ́hsg.wʼat.roʼ a lens
[consists of: ga:gęh it sees; otgǫhsgwʼatroʼ a window]
ga.gę́h wa.dę.nǫhsg.wáʼtroʼ a lens
[consists of: ga:gęh it sees; wadęnǫhsgwaʼtroʼ a window]
less
ga.óʼ ní:yǫ: less
less see: I (gao:ʼ)
lessen see: fall
da.wáʼsęʼ it dropped, reduced
let see: affirm
ęhs.rih.wah.ní:ya:t you will affirm it, agree
let see: I (do:ʼ i:ʼ)
let go see: release
a.wát.gaʼ it let go
lethargic see: sleepy
a.gíd.ręh.da:ʼs I am sleepy
letter see: paper
gah.yá.dǫhs.raʼ paper
lettuce
en.ráh.da:s lettuce
[e+ stem: -nrahda:s- lettuce; consists of: -nrahd(a)$_{N}$- leaf -g$_{V}$- eat]
leukemia
gat.gwę́h.sa:s leukemia
[ga+ stem: -tgwęhsa:s- leukemia; consists of: -tgwęhs(a)$_{N}$- blood -g$_{V}$- eat]
level
oh.naʼne.dá:nyǫʼ several levels
[o+ stem: -(h)naned- level; consists of: -(h)n(a)$_{N}$- oil, gas -ned$_{V}$- keep]
gah.né:ga:ʼ a level
[ga+ stem: -(h)nega:ʼ- level, solder; consists of: -(h)neg(a)$_{N}$- water, liquid -a:ʼ$_{V}$- hold, contain, include]
level see: flat
de.yo.dag.wę́h.dę:, de.wa.dag.wę́h.dę: it is flat
liability see: debt, responsibility
o.gá.ot a debt
sad.rih.wa.géh.deʼ your responsibility
liar
sę.nó:wę: you are a liar
[P+ę+ stem: -nowę(:)$_{V}$- liar]
a.gę.nó:wę: I am a liar
libel see: condemn
she.yéh.sah.taʼ you always condemn, insult, slander s.o.

Cayuga pronunciation guide: /a/ father /e/ weigh /ę/ men (nasalized) /i/ police /o/ hole /ǫ/ home (nasalized) /u/ blue. Underlined vowels are voiceless or whispered. /ʹ/ high pitch. /t/ too /d/ do /k/ king /g/ good (never soft g) /j/ judge or adze /s/ soon /sh/ less heat (never the sh in shirt) /sr/ shrine /sy/ sure /hw/ which (the sound made when you blow out a candle) /h/ hi /ts/ cats hide /ʼ/ (the sound before the first vowel in 'uh-uh') /n/ noon /r/ round /w/ way /y/ yes.

liberate see: release
a·kí·yaht·ga' we let them go, released them
libido see: sexuality
gę·déhs·ra' sexuality
librarian
eh·ya·dǫhs·ra·ni̱·hahs·ta'géh
gohs·díhs·dǫh she is a librarian
[consists of: ehyadǫhsrani̱hahsta'(geh) library; gohsdihsdǫh she is a director, principle, head, etc.]
gok·ya·dǫhs·ráhs·dis·dǫh she is a librarian
[P+ak+ stem: -(h)yadǫhsrahsdihsdǫh- librarian; consists of: -(h)yadǫhsr(a)$_N$- paper -(h)sdihsd$_V$- care for]
library
eh·ya·dǫhs·ra·ni̱·háhs·ta' library
[e+ stem: -(h)yadǫhsranihahsta'- library; consists of: -(h)yadǫhsr(a)$_N$- paper -nihahsd$_V$- lend]
lice see: louse
ohs·gé·ha' louse
license see: paper, permission
ga̱h·yá·dǫhs·ra' paper
ęhs·rih·wa̱h·ní:ya't you will affirm it, agree
Licensing and Control Board see: G (hǫ·wa·di̱h·ya·dǫhs·ra:wihs ga·ya·nę̱hs·ra'geh)
licensing body see: G (hǫ·wa·di̱h·ya·dǫhs·ra:wihs ga·ya·nę̱hs·ra'geh)
lick
se·gá:nę:s you are a licker; you are a brown-noser
[stem: -ganęd$_V$- lick]
ęh·sé·ga·nę:t you will lick it
se·gá:nę:t lick it
sa·ga·nę:tǫ:gye' (**sa·ga·nę·dǫ́·hǫg·ye'**) you are going along licking it

lie
o·nó·w'ę·da' a lie
[o+ stem: -nowę('da)$_N$- lie -nowę(:)$_V$- liar]
a·gę:nó:węht I lied
[ę+ stem: -nowęhd- lie; consists of: -nowę(:)$_V$- be a liar]
ga·gé·hǫ' things are lying about
[A+(N+) stem: -gehǫ'$_V$- lie about]
de·gá·hǫ' s.t. is lying across a path, a door, etc.
[de+A+ stem: -(h)ǫ(:,')$_V$- lie across]
ga·dí·dag·rǫ' they (z) are lying down
[A+ stem: -(i)dagrǫ'$_V$- lie around, be lying down]
ha·dí·dag·rǫ' they (m) are lying around
a·gę́na·tǫ:' they (z) lay down
[at+ stem: -(h)ǫ(:)$_V$- lie down]
sá:tǫ: lie down
ę·sę·ni·da:grę' you will lie down
[P+ęn+ stem: -(i)dagrę(:)$_V$- lay oneself down]
sę·ní·dag·ręh lie down
a·gę·ni·dá:gre:' I laid myself down
tę·dá:ge:' he is lying over there
[A+ stem: -(i)dage:'$_V$- be lying down]
si·dá:ge:' you are lying down, prostrate
gá:yę' it is lying on the ground
[A/P+(N+) stem: -(y)ę$_V$- lie on the ground]
tǫ́: hǫ:wéh gá:yę' where it is; it is lying
ga̱·he·yǫ·dá·ę' the body is lying (in state)
[A/P+(N+) consists of: -(he)yǫ('da)$_N$- corpse, cadaver -ę$_V$- lie on the ground]
ga·dęh·da:' it is lying spread out on the floor, the ground
[A/P+(N+) stem: -dęhda:'$_V$- lie spread out on the ground]

life expectancy
tsę̱h ni·sǫ́:nhi:s your life expectancy [ni+A+ stem: -ǫnhi:s- life expectancy; consists of: -ǫnhe'$_V$- be alive -is$_V$- be long]

lift see: elevator, pick up, uphold
at·gehk I picked s.t. up
dę·yehg·wa·dáh·nǫ:' she will raise, lift things up
de·ya·go·ya'da̱hk·wá' ǫ́:gweh elevator

lift bridge
wa·dahs·gwa·gá:da:s lift bridge [wa+ad+ stem: -(a)hsgwagada:s- lift bridge; consists of: -(a)hsg(wa)$_N$- roof, bridge -gadad$_V$- raise s.t. up]
wa·dahs·gwa·gé:ts·gwahs lift bridge [wa+ad+ stem: -(a)hsgwagetsgwahs- lift bridge; consists of: -(a)hsg(wa)$_N$- roof, bridge -getsgw$_V$- raise to a vertical position]

lift s.o.'s spirits see: praise s.o.
ęhs·he·ho·wá:naht you will praise her, uplift her spirits, flatter her

ligament see: tendon
o·jíhn·y'a·da' tendon; ligament; birth cord

light
ga·jíhs·do:t a light [ga+ stem: -jihsd(a)$_N$- light -od$_V$- stand]
tga·jihs·dǫ·dá:ha' the lights are there [ga+ stem: -jihsd(a)$_N$- light -oda(:)$_V$- be put someplace]
de·wa·da̱hg·wi'a·e:s (de·wat·gwi'á·e:s) flashing, blinking lights [de+wa+at+ stem: -gwi'a'e:s- flashing, blinking lights; consists of: -gwi'(a)$_N$- light -(')e$_V$- hit]
de·wat·gwi'a·ihs·dáh·ne' there were blinking lights [de+wa+at+ stem: -gwi'a'ehsdahne'- blinking lights; consists of: -gwi'(a)$_N$- light -(')e$_V$- hit]

light (continued)
de·wę·ni̱·hóks ga·jíhs·do·ta' electric light [consists of: dewęni̱hoks electricity; gajihsdota' light bulb]
de·wę·ni̱·hó's ga·jís·do:t electric light [consists of: dewęni̱ho's electricity; gajihsdo:t a light]

light bulb
ga·jíhs·do·ta' light bulb [ga+ stem: -jihsd(a)$_N$- light -od$_V$- stand]

light-coloured
ha'gę: he is light-skinned [A+ stem: -(i')gę:$_V$- be light-coloured, light-skinned, white]
e·yá'gę: she is light-skinned
gę'gę: it is white; it is light-skinned, it is light-coloured
gę'gęt·ró:sgǫ' it is all white [A+ stem: -(i')gętr(a)$_n$- s.t. light-coloured -o'$_V$- be saturated -sgǫ:- really]
wah·sí'da·gę:t white foot [A/P+N+ stem: -(a)hsi('da), (ę)hs(a)$_N$- foot -(i')gęd$_V$- be light-coloured, white]

lighten see: bright
dę·to·ha·té'dǫ·hǫk he will brighten from over there

light headed see: dizzy
a·gah·sǫ·wá·den·ye's, a·gat·sǫ·wá·den·ye's I am dizzy

lightning
de·wę·ni̱·hó'k·sǫh lightning [de+... stem: -ęniho'g$_V$- lightning -sǫ'- plural]

light-skinned see: light-coloured
e·yá'gę: she is light-skinned

like
ke·nǫ́h·wehs I like her [TR+ stem: -nǫhwe'$_V$- like]
e·nǫ́h·we's she likes it
knǫ̱h·we's I like, admire it
ę·yé·nǫ̱h·we' she will like it

Cayuga pronunciation guide: /a/ father /e/ weigh /ę/ men (nasalized) /i/ police /o/ hole /ǫ/ home (nasalized) /u/ blue. Underlined vowels are voiceless or whispered. /'/ high pitch. /t/ too /d/ do /k/ king /g/ good (never soft g) /j/ judge or adze /s/ soon /sh/ less heat (never the sh in shirt) /sr/ shrine /sy/ sure /hw/ which (the sound made when you blow out a candle) /h/ hi /ts/ cats hide /'/ (the sound before the first vowel in 'uh-uh') /n/ noon /r/ round /w/ way /y/ yes.

like (continued)
aʼé·nǫh·weʼ she has liked it
e·nǫh·wek·sǫ́:nyǫh she goes along liking things
ní:yoht what it is like (often preceded by a particle such as deʼ what, neʼ the)
[ni+yo+ stem: -(a)hd$_{V}$- like, resemble]
a·gé:gaʼs I like the taste of it
[P+ stem: -gaʼ$_{V}$- like the taste of s.t.]
sá:gaʼs you like the taste of it
dęʼó:gaʼs it does not like the taste
ǫ·géʼgaʼ I liked the taste of it
like see: enjoy, same, similar
a·gǫʼwe̲hs·gwá:nih I enjoy it
tsaʼdé:yoht they are (lit.: it is) the same
to:háh tsaʼdé:yoht it is similar
limb see: arm, branch, leg
snęt·sáʼgeh on your arm
og·wí:yaʼ a limb, twig, branch
se̲h·sínʼa·geh on your leg
limber see: agile, dance
ha·yaʼtgá·i·yeʼ he is agile
a·hah·si·ya·ǫ:nyáh·nǫ:ʼ he is a fluid dancer
limp
hoh·sóʼkaʼ he is limping
[P+ stem: -(h)soʼg$_{V}$- limp]
go̲h·sóʼkaʼ she is limping
go̲h·sóʼkahk she used to limp
ęh·sáh·soʼka:k you will limp
go̲h·sóʼga̲h·neʼ she limped as she arrived
wad·rág·wa·ęʼ it is limp
[w+ad+ stem: -(r)agwaęʼ- limp; consists of: -(r)ag(wa)$_{N}$- circle -ę$_{V}$- lie on the ground]
limp see: weak
ag·yaʼda·gę·hé:yǫ: I am physically weak, slow
line
ga̲h·sí·ya·deʼ a suspended line; a string

line (continued)
[stem: -(h)siy(a)$_{N}$- line, string -deʼ$_{V}$- exist]
oh·sí:yǫ:t attached cord, string; umbilical cord
[o+ stem: -(h)siy(a)$_{N}$- line, string -ǫd$_{V}$- attached]
ga·nę·hęhs·rǫ́·ni: a line formed
[stem: -nęhęsrǫni- stand in line; consists of: -nęhęsr(a)$_{N}$- line -ǫni, ǫny$_{V}$- make]
line see: clothesline, double, stand in a line
e·ha·da̲hk·wáʼ ga̲h·sí·ya·deʼ clothesline
dęhs·náʼnetʼa:ʼ you will double it, reinforce it, line it
swa·nę·hęs·rǫ́:nih you all stand in line, in a formation
lineage see: family
ga̲h·wa·ji·yá:deʼ a family (matrilineal)
liniment see: oil
oh·naʼ grease; oil
lining
de·gáh·na·ne:t a lining; an insulated wall
[de+ga+ stem: -(i)hnaned- lining, insulation; consists of: -(i)hn(a)$_{N}$- material, skin -ned$_{V}$- keep]
de·yeh·na·né:da̲hk·waʼ insulation
[de+ye+ stem: -(i)hnanedahkwaʼ- lining, insulation; consists of: -(i)hn(a)$_{N}$- material, skin -nedahkwaʼ$_{V}$- s.t. for keeping, preserving]
link see: join
dęhs·nah·sǫ́:dęʼ you will join
lion
ga̲·hahs·rǫg·yéh·taʼ lion
[ga+ stem: -(h)ahsrǫgyehtaʼ- lion; consists of: -(h)ahsr(a)$_{N}$- flash -ǫgyehd$_{V}$-]
lip
oh·sóhg·waʼ lips
[stem: -(h)sohg(wa)$_{N}$- lip]
se̲h·sóhg·wʼa·geh on your lip
e·sóhg·wʼa·geʼ on her lips

lip (upper)
se̱h·sǫh·gá:ˀgeh on your upper lip
[stem: -(h)sǫhg(a:)$_N$- upper lip]
ge̱h·sǫh·gá:ˀgeh on my upper lip
liquefy see: melt, thaw, wet
ga·naˀna·wę́ˀda·hǫh it has been melted
ęhs·ganˀa·ná:węˀ it will thaw, melt again
ęhs·náˀna·węˀt you will melt, liquefy s.t.
liquid see: water
oh·né·ga·nohs water
liquor
de·gaˀni·gǫ·ha·dé:nyǫhs alcoholic beverages (lit.: mind-altering substance)
[de+ga+ stem: -(ˀ)nigǫhadenyǫhs- liquor, spirits, alcohol; consists of: -(ˀ)nigǫh(a)$_N$- mind -deni, deny$_V$- change]
listen
a·ga·da·hǫh·sí:yohs I listen
[TR+ad+ stem: -(a)hǫhsiyohsd- listen to s.o., obey; consists of: -(a)hǫhd(a)$_N$- ear -iyohsd$_V$- make nice, good]
ę·jihs·wa·da·hǫh·sí:yohs you all will listen again
ęh·sa·da̱·hǫh·si·yóhs·ta:k you will listen, obey
ęhs·wa·da·hǫh·si·yóhs·dęˀ you all will listen to it
o·da·hǫh·sí·yǫ̱hs·de: the act of listening
ǫ·tǫ́:da:s she is obedient
[stem: -(a)tǫdaˀd- listen to s.t., be obedient; consists of: -(a)tǫdę(h,ˀ), (a)tǫdeˀ$_V$- hear]
ę·ga:tǫ́:daˀt I will consent
ęs·wad·rih·wa:tǫ́:dęˀ you will listen (to an idea)
[stem: -(r)ih(wa)$_n$- idea -(a)tǫdę(h,ˀ), (a)tǫdeˀ$_V$- hear]

listen (continued)
ęh·sad·rę·na·tǫ·dáˀtaˀ you will go listen to the songs (said as an invitation)
[stem: -(r)ęn(a)$_n$- song -(a)tǫdaˀd$_V$- listen to s.t.]
listen see: hear
ho·tǫ́:deˀ he hears
listless see: tired
a·gá·ǫt·sęht they (f/m) were tired, sleepy
little see: I (stǫ:hah), few, small
ni·yǫ́:hah few; a little bit
ni·wú:ˀuh it is small, little
live
ha·díˀdrǫˀ they (m) are at home
[A+ stem: -(i)ˀdrǫ$_V$- live, dwell, be at home]
shę́h tgiˀdrǫˀ where I live
gyˀed·rǫˀ she is at home
eˀdrǫˀ she is home
ga·díˀdrǫˀ they (z) live (designates a shed, dog house, etc.)
gá·e:nag·reˀ where they (f/m) live (that is, an area)
[A+ stem: -nagreˀ$_V$- live]
tga·e·ná:grehk they (f/m) used to live there
ę·yǫn·heh·gǫ́·hǫ:k it will live on
[P+ stem: -ǫnhehg- live on, be sustained; consists of: -ǫnheˀ$_V$- alive]
a·gǫ́n·heh·gǫh s.o. lives on it; she is sustained by it
live see: dwell, reside
nę·yak·nˀid·rǫ́:daˀk where we two (excl.) will dwell
tsę́h tgiˀdrǫˀ where I live, reside
lively see: active, quick
ha·yáˀt·ga·ǫ:ˀ he is quick to move; he is active, always moving around
gyaˀt·ga·hí:yeˀ I am quick

Cayuga pronunciation guide: /a/ father /e/ weigh /ę/ men (nasalized) /i/ police /o/ hole /ǫ/ home (nasalized) /u/ blue. Underlined vowels are voiceless or whispered. /ˊ/ high pitch. /t/ too /d/ do /k/ king /g/ good (never soft g) /j/ judge or adze /s/ soon /sh/ less heat (never the sh in shirt) /sr/ shrine /sy/ sure /hw/ which (the sound made when you blow out a candle) /h/ hi /ts/ cats hide /ˀ/ (the sound before the first vowel in 'uh-uh') /n/ noon /r/ round /w/ way /y/ yes.

live-in
des·ha·gʼo·ni·gǫ·ha:háʼ tsǫ: he is a live-in (lit.: he's just bothering her)
[de+TR+ … tsǫ: just stem: -(ʼ)nigǫha(:)$_V$- expect, bother s.o.]
hog·yǫʼsé: tsǫ: he is a live-in (lit.: he's just visiting, living with her)
[P+ag+ … tsǫ: just stem: -yǫʼse- visit; consists of: -yǫ$_V$- arrive]

liver
o·twę́h·saʼ liver
[o+ stem: -twęhs(a)$_N$- liver]

living see: alive
a·gá·dǫn·hi: I am alive; I am born; I am full of life

living room
ga·nǫh·si·yóhs·geh living room
[ga+ stem: -nǫhsiyohsgeh- living room; consists of: -nǫhs(a)$_N$- house -iyohsd$_V$- make nice, good]

load see: cargo, fill
o·héh·naʼ, ga·héh·naʼ cargo; bundle
ęhs·nǫ́:nheht, ęh·snę́:nheht you will fill in

loaf see: bread
o·náʼda:ʼ bread

loam
o·héh·da·ji: black loam
[o+ stem: -(h)ehd(a)$_N$- land, dirt, earth, ground; -ji(:,h)- dark]
ni·yo·heh·dóʼdę: loam (lit. some type of land)
[ni+yo+ stem: -(h)ehdoʼdę:- loam; consists of: -(h)ehd(a)$_N$- land, dirt, earth, ground -oʼdę:$_V$- type of]

loam see: soil
oh·néʼdrʼa·geh on the ground

loan see: lend
sa·dęh·wihs·da·ni·háh·da·nih you lend money; a lender

loathe see: hate
kehs·wá·hęhs I hate her

loathsome see: evil
ga·hét·gęʼ it is ugly

location see: live, place
gá·e:nag·reʼ where they (f/m) live (that is, an area)
tó: hǫ́:weh a place

lock
gen·hó·dǫ·haʼ I lock s.t.
[stem: -nhodǫ(:)$_V$- lock]
ę·ge:nhó:dǫ:ʼ I will lock it
ga·din·ho·dǫ́:nyǫʼ they (z) are locked up
ga·no·wa·ní:yǫ:t hanging lock
[ga+ stem: -now(a)$_N$- lock -niyǫd$_V$- hang]
eʼno·wa·ni·yǫ·dáhk·wa lock
[e+ stem: -(ʼ)nowaniyǫdahkwaʼ- lock; consists of: -now(a)$_N$- lock -niyǫdahkwaʼ$_V$- s.t. hanging]

lodge see: motel
ǫ·nǫh·wehs·táʼgeh motel; inn; bed-and-breakfast; hotel

loft see: upstairs
o·nák·da·he: loft

lofty see: height, tall
nit·gá:deʼ how high it is (inanimate object); the height of s.t.
hah·nę́:ye:s he is tall

log
gá·ǫ:daʼ log
[ga+ stem: -(r)ǫd(a)$_N$- log]
gá·ǫ·dʼa·geh on the log
ga·ǫ:dá:kʼah near the log
oʼnháhg·yaʼ, on·háh·daʼ lumber logs (large); timber
[o+ stem: -(ʼ)nhahgy(a), (ʼ)nhahd(a)$_N$- lumber, timber]
gaʼnhah·da·gé·hǫʼ timber, big logs lying around
[stem: -(ʼ)nhahgy(a), (ʼ)nhahd(a)$_N$- lumber, timber -gehǫʼ$_V$- lie about]

log (continued)
a·ha·d'in·háhg·ya'k they (m) cut the logs
[stem: -(')nhahgy(a), (')nhahd(a)$_N$- lumber, timber -(i)ya'g$_V$- cut, break]
log see: tree
gá·ǫ·da·ę' a dead tree; a log lying on the ground
o·héh·sa' decayed tree; log; etc.
log house
de·ga·ǫ·da·dǫ́' ga·nǫ́h·so·t log house
[consists of: degaǫda:dǫ' logs; ganǫhso:t standing house]
logger
ha·di'nhahg·yá's ho·nah·dęg·yá'dǫh loggers
[A+ stem: -(')nhahgya'(g)s- logger; consists of: -(')nhahgy(a), (')nhahd(a)$_N$- log (large), timber -(i)ya'g$_V$- cut, break]
lone see: I (it, aǫhę')
lonesome
o'ni·gǫh·sá:dǫhk it is lonesome
[o+ stem: -(')nigǫhsadǫhg- be lonesome; consists of: -(')nigǫh(a)$_N$- mind -(h)sadǫ$_V$- bury s.o., an animal]
ak'ni·gǫh·sá:dǫ's I am lonesome
[P+ stem: -(')nigǫhsadǫ- lonesome; consists of: -(')nigǫh(a)$_N$- mind -(h)sadǫ$_V$- bury s.o., an animal]
ǫk'ni·gǫh·sá:dǫ' I got lonesome
long
í:yǫ:s it is long
[(i)+y+ stem: -ǫs- be long (non-incorporating version); consists of: -es$_V$- long]
ǫ́:s'ǫhs lengthy objects
[stem: -ǫs'ǫ's, -e:s'ǫ's- several long objects; consists of: -es$_V$- long]
de·seh·si·né:s'ǫs you have long legs
[stem: -(h)sin(a)$_N$- leg -ǫs'ǫ's, -e:s'ǫ's- several long objects]

long (continued)
ho·gé'e:s he has long hair
[stem: -ge'(a:), geh(a)$_N$- hair -es$_V$- long]
o·hę́h·de:s it has long fur
[stem: -(h)ehd(a)$_N$- fur -es$_V$- long]
se·nę́:tse:s your arm is long
[stem: -nęts(a)$_N$- arm -es$_V$- long]
ho·íh·wi:s he has a long speech
[stem: -i:s- be long; consists of: -(r)ih(wa)$_N$- word -es$_V$- long]
a·há·ę·ni:s he made the song long
[stem: -(r)ęn(a)$_N$- song, music -i:s- be long]
ni·yǫ·háh dę' ne' just a little bit long
[ni+y+ ... dę' not ne' the stem: -ǫ:hah- be longish; consists of: -es$_V$- long]
long see: be a certain length, depth; I (wa'hehge:ha')
ni·yo:yá:de:s how deep the hole, trench, ditch is
long ago see: back then
swe·gé·ha' back then; long ago
Long Lake, N.Y. see: E (Sgan·ya·da·es)
Longhouse see: F (Ga·nǫh·se:s)
look
sat·gáht·wahs you look all the time
[at+ stem: -gahtw$_V$- look]
ha'sát·gah·to' you looked
sat·gáh·toh look
de·sat·gah·dǫ́:nyǫhs you are looking around
[de+...at+ stem: -gahdǫnyǫ- look around; consists of: -gahtw$_V$- look]
hęt·sáht·gah·to' you will look back
[ha'+...d+...at+ stem: -gahtw$_V$- look, look back]
de·ga·ǫ·géh·gah·ne:' they are looking at me
[TR+ stem: -gahne:'- look at s.o.; consists of: -gah(a)$_N$- eye]

Cayuga pronunciation guide: /a/ father /e/ weigh /ę/ men (nasalized) /i/ police /o/ hole /ǫ/ home (nasalized) /u/ blue. Underlined vowels are voiceless or whispered. /'/ high pitch. /t/ too /d/ do /k/ king /g/ good (never soft g) /j/ judge or adze /s/ soon /sh/ less heat (never the sh in shirt) /sr/ shrine /sy/ sure /hw/ which (the sound made when you blow out a candle) /h/ hi /ts/ cats hide /'/ (the sound before the first vowel in 'uh-uh') /n/ noon /r/ round /w/ way /y/ yes.

look (continued)
a·sat·ga̱·hát·giht you give dirty looks [at+ stem: -gahatgihd- give dirty looks; consists of: -gah(a)$_N$- eye -tgihd$_V$- cause to be dirty, ugly]
sat·ga·hat·gíh·dǫh you are always giving dirty looks, you are giving dirty looks (right now)
ha·dík·dǫ·ha' they (m) examine it [stem: -kdǫ(:)$_V$- taste, examine, look closely at s.t.]
a·gé:kdǫ:' I looked closely at it; I have examined it
dwak·dǫ: let us all (incl.) look
sek·dǫ: examine it
knik·dǫ́h·nah let's go look [stem: -kdǫhn$_V$- go and taste, examine, look closely at s.t.]
ed·wák·dǫ̱h·ne', ed·wák·dǫ̱h·na' we all (incl.) are going to see it
look see: examine, glance, I (nę:), look after, look ahead, look for, look like, look up to, see, stare
ę·sat·ga̱·hí:yohs you will look closely at s.t., peer at s.t.
ęh·sat·ga̱·hę́:gę: you will glimpse it
a·há:gę' he saw
sa·gahd·rǫ́:nihs you are staring at it
look after
deh·sę́'nya:' you are looking after it right now [de+TR+ stem: -(ę)'nya(ę,:)$_V$- govern, watch, look after]
dehsg·wę́'nya:' you who watch over us
at·sę́'nya:' you looked after it
dęh·sę́'nya·ę:', dęh·sę́'nya:' you will look after it
look after see: care for
ęhs·he·ya·de·wa·yę:nǫ́:ni' you will take care of them, care for them
look ahead see: foretell
o·hę:dǫ́: he·ha:dí:gęh they (m) look ahead, tell the future

look for
ded·wá·de̱h·sa:s we are looking for mates [de+ stem: -(i)hsag$_V$- investigate, inquire, look for; look for a mate]
ę·sá·yeh·wa' you will look for in vain; you will be unable to find s.t. [P+ stem: -yehw$_V$- look for in vain]
look for see: investigate
ę·gíh·sa:k I will seek, look for it
look like see: resemble
tsé:yę: you resemble
look up to see: revere
dęd·wa·dad·rih·wa·nǫ́hk·wa:k we all (incl.) will show respect for one another
loon
ha·hó:wę' loon [ha+ stem: -(h)owę'- loon; consists of: -(hr)owi, (hr)ǫny$_V$- tell]
loose see: soft
o·hó'dę:' it is soft, loose
loose (get loose) see: rescue
a·ha·do·dá·i·si: he got loose, escaped
lose (unintentionally)
e·sáh·dǫ:' you lost it [P+ stem: -(a)hdǫ(:)$_V$- lose s.t.]
ǫ·get·gw'ę·dáh·dǫ:' I lost my wallet [P+ stem: -tgwę('da)$_N$- wallet, suitcase, purse -(a)hdǫ(:)$_V$- lose, disappear]
e·sa·wi̱hs·dáhdǫ:' you lost money [P+ (N+) stem: -(h)wihsd(a), (hr)ihsd(a)$_N$- metal, money -(a)hdǫ(:)$_V$- lose, disappear]
lose (on purpose)
ęh·sáh·dǫ't you will lose it [(N+) stem: -(a)hdǫ'd- lose s.t.; consists of: -(a)hdǫ(:)$_V$- lose]
a·sáh·dǫ't you lost it
lose weight
ni·ja·go·di·ya·dá:sde' how much weight they (f/m) lost [ni+s+P+ stem: -ya'd(a)$_N$- body -(a)hsde'$_V$- heavy]

lose weight (continued)
dǫg·ya'dahgǫ' I lost weight
[d/g+P+ad+ stem: -ya'dahgw- lose weight; consists of: -ya'd(a)$_N$- body -(h)gw$_V$- remove]
dya·go·ya·dáhgwęh she has lost weight

lose weight see: diet
a·ga·ǫ:dehs·gyǫ·wá:ta't they (f/m) dieted, lost weight

loss
a·wáh·dǫ: a loss
[stem: -(a)hdǫ(:)$_V$- lose, disappear]
g'a·nǫ́' tsę́h na'á:węh it was a great loss
[consists of: g'anǫ' expensive; tsęh that; na'a:węh how it happened]

lots see: I (i:so'), often
ot·gá:de' often; many; lots

loud
o·dihs·do·wá:nęh they (z) are loud
[P+ stem: -(r)ihsdowanęh- be loud; consists of: -(h)wihsd(a), (hr)ihsd(a)$_N$- metal, money -owanęh$_V$- be big]
ag·rihs·do·wá:nęh I am loud, noisy
ga·ihs·do·wá:nęh it is noisy

loud see: noise
ot·gá·i'ni: it is noisy, loud

lounge
ǫ·dǫ·wi̱·sę·da̱hk·wá'geh lounge
[ǫ+ad+ stem: -owishędahkwageh- lounge; consists of: -owihshędahkwa'$_V$- place for resting, relaxing]

louse
ohs·gé·ha' louse
[o+ stem: -(h)sgeh(a)$_N$- louse]

love
ga·nǫ́hk·wahs·ra' love
[ga+ stem: -nǫhkwahsr(a)$_N$- love, respect -nǫhkw$_V$- love]
go·nǫ́hk·wa' I love you
[TR+ stem: -nǫhkw$_V$- love]
ke·nǫ́hk·wa' I love her
he·nǫ́hk·wa' I love him

lovely see: good, pretty
o·yá:nre' it is nice, good, beautiful
o·jí·n'a·dǫ: it is handsome; s.t. / s.o. handsome, attractive
ek·sa'gó:wah she is pretty

low
heh·dá:geh low
[stem: -hehd(a)$_N$- land, earth, dirt, ground]

Lower End see: C (Six Nations, Ga·ne·da·geh)

loyal
ha·dę·gǫn·yǫ́hs·ta' he is loyal (to the cause); he is respectful
[adę+ -gǫnyǫhsd- loyal, respectful; consists of: -gǫnyǫ$_V$- clean, discriminating]

lubricate see: grease
sná:sǫ: lubricate s.t.

Lucifer see: Devil
ga·jí·ha·ya' the devil

luck
ad·rá'swa' luck
[ad+ stem: -ra'sro, ra'sw$_N$- luck]
ad·ra'swa·hé:tgę' bad luck
[ad+ stem: -ra'swahe:tgę'- bad luck; consists of: -ra'sro, ra'sw$_N$- luck -(hr)etgę'$_V$- evil, bad, ugly]
wad·ra'swí:yo: good luck
[wa+ad+ stem: -(r)aswiyo:- good luck; consists of: -ra'sro, ra'sw$_N$- luck -iyo:$_V$- be nice, good]

lucky
go·dá·ǫ: she is lucky, fortunate
[P+ stem: -(i)daǫ$_V$- lucky, fortunate, chosen, special]
sę·dá·ǫ: you are chosen, special, fortunate
ǫ·gad·ras·wí·yo̱hs·dę' I got lucky
[P+ad+ stem: -(r)aswiyohsdę- get lucky; consists of: -ra'sro, ra'sw$_N$- luck -iyohsdę$_V$- become nice, good]

lug see: pull
ęt·gag·yę·hę́:to', ęt·gat·yę·hę́:to' I will pull
lumber see: log
o'nháhg·ya', on·háh·da' large lumber logs; timber
lump
og·wá·ǫt it has a lump; a bulge
[o+ stem: -g(wa)$_N$- lump, boil -ǫd$_V$- attached]
lunch
a·dę́·n'at·ra' lunch, groceries
[adę+ stem: -na'tr(a)$_N$- food, lunch]
sa·dę́n'at·ra' your lunch
ę·ga:dę́:na't I will take a lunch
[adę+ stem: -na'd$_V$- lunch]
lung
ǫ·dǫ́n·y'e·ta' lung
[ǫ+ad+ stem: -ǫnye'ta'- lung; consists of: -ǫnye'd$_V$- cause to breath]
lurch see: trip
de·sah·sig·yá'ks·gǫ: you are always stumbling, tripping, stubbing your toe; you are a klutz
lurk see: hide oneself, sneak around
ę·gá·dah·seht I will hide
sgę:nǫ:'ǫ́h hot·rihs·dǫhǫ́:gye' he is sneaking around slowly
lust see: crave, want
knǫ́:wa:s I crave s.t.
gahs·gá:ne:s I have longings for; I want; I desire
luster see: shine
dę·gahs·da·té'dǫh it is shined, waxed, polished
lustrous see: glassy, smooth
de·yo·wid·rá:teh it is glassy, icy; a glass tumbler
dę·yóhs·da·teh it is shiny, smooth (like silver)
lye corn
ge·gá·heh·dęht lye it (corn)
[ga+ stem: -gahehdęhd- lye corn; consists of: -gahehd(a)$_N$- eye (of a corn kernel) -(y)ęhd$_V$- hit, knock down, strike]
ga·ga·heh·dę́h·dǫh lyed corn
e·ga·heh·do·há·i'ta' s.o. washes, lyes corn
[stem: -gahehdohae'd- lye corn; consists of: -gahehd(a)$_N$- eye (of a corn kernel) -ohae'd$_V$- cause to be clean, washed]
lyric see: song
gá·ę:na' song

M

M.S. see: Multiple Sclerosis
wat·sihs·dęhs·rǫ́:nih Multiple Sclerosis
machine see: engine
ga·hǫ́'jihs·da' a motor; an engine
machine gun
ę·ga·e'á:ksǫ:' machine gun (lit.: it will shoot repetitively)
[ę+ga+ stem: -(i')aksǫ:'- machine gun, gun; consists of: -(i)ya'g$_V$- shoot -sǫ'- plural]
machinery
ga·heh·da·géh wad·ri·ho'dá:sta' farm machinery
[consists of: gahehdageh in the dirt, earth; wadriho'dahsta' machinery]
mad see: angry, cross
ak·ná'kwę'ǫh I am angry
es·ró·hę: she is habitually cross
maddening
o·ná'kwa:t it is irritating, maddening
[o+ stem: -na'kwad- maddening, irritating; consists of: -na'kwę(h,'), na'gǫ$_V$- angry]

magic see: witchcraft
ot·gǫt·ra·shǫ́:ʼǫh object used for witchcraft
magician see: evil power
go·ná:tgǫh they (f/m) are a force to be reckoned with; they (f/m) are ominous; they are bad medicine people
magnifying glass
ga·go·wa·nah·táʼ at·gǫ́hs·gwʼat·raʼ magnifying glass
[consists of: gagowanahtaʼ it makes things big; atgǫhsgwaʼtraʼ a window]
magnitude see: size
shę́h ní:waʼs sizes; how big they are (lit.: how big it is)
maid
de·ga·ǫ·dóh·da:s they (f/m) tidy up; they are maids, housecleaners
[de+gaǫ+ad+ stem: -ohda:s- janitor, etc.; consists of: -ohda(:,h)$_V$- tidy up, clean]
mailbox
ga̲·hǫhs·rót eh·ya·dǫhs·rǫ́·da̲hkwaʼ mailbox
[consists of: ga̲hǫhsrot box; ehyadǫ̲hsrǫdahkwaʼ receptacle for paper]
main see: begin, lead
da·wá:gyę·t the first one; the beginner
ęhs·rę:t you will be the lead
maintain see: keep, live on, uphold
ę·sa·d·rǫ́:goʼ you will keep
e·ya·gǫn·héh·gǫ·hǫ:k they (f/m) will live on; what will sustain them
de·yǫg·wa̲hg·wá·dǫh we all are upholding (some thing, idea)
majesty see: G (royalty, gwa:go:wah)
make
gǫ́:nih I make, earn
[(N+) stem: -ǫni, ǫny$_V$- make]
gǫ́:nihs I make, earn
a·gǫ́:niʼ I made, earned
make (continued)
hę·nah·gá·ǫ·ni: they (m) are making splints
[stem: -(a)hg(a:)$_N$- splint -ǫni, ǫny$_V$- make]
wa·toh·gǫ́·ni:ʼ it is made into a bundle
[stem: -(a)tohg(wa)$_N$- bundle -ǫni, ǫny$_V$- make]
ęk·ne·gag·riʼtrǫ́:niʼ I will make soup
[stem: -(h)negagriʼtr(a)$_N$- soup -ǫni, ǫny$_V$- make]
wa·dęh·sǫ́:nih it makes a nest
[adę+(N+) stem: -(a)dehs(a)$_N$- nest -ǫni, ǫny$_V$- make; make for one's benefit]
as·ha·go·nǫh·sǫ́:niʼ he built a house for her
[TR+(N+) stem: -nǫhs(a)$_N$- house -ǫni, ǫny$_V$- make; make for s.o.]
ho·nǫ·ni̲·há:gyeʼs they (m) are making, earning it (continually)
[(N+) stem: -ǫnihagyeʼ(s)- make continually; consists of: -ǫni, ǫny$_V$- make]
ak·nihs·rǫn·yáh·nǫh we two (incl.) are making several things
[stem: -(h)srǫnyahnǫʼ- make several things; consists of: -hsr$_N$- noun-ǫni, ǫny$_V$- make]
ę·yag·wa·dehs·rǫn·yáh·nǫ:ʼ we all (excl.) will prepare things
ga̲hs·rǫ́n·ya·dǫh it is made from
[stem: -(h)srǫnyaʼd- be made from; consists of: -hsr$_N$- noun -ǫni, ǫny$_V$- make]
make see: fix, produce
ęh·sehs·rǫ́:niʼ you will create, make s.t.
a·ha·i·hǫ́n·ya̲h·nǫ:ʼ he produced s.t.
make-believe
a:wetʼahs·hǫ́:ʼǫh make-believe; pretend
[a:+w+ stem: -etʼah$_V$- pretend]
make-believe see: pretend
a:we:tʼáh tsǫ́: dę·sáʼt·sǫhs pretend to sneeze

Cayuga pronunciation guide: /a/ father /e/ weigh /ę/ men (nasalized) /i/ police /o/ hole /ǫ/ home (nasalized) /u/ blue. Underlined vowels are voiceless or whispered. /ˊ/ high pitch. /t/ too /d/ do /k/ king /g/ good (never soft g) /j/ judge or adze /s/ soon /sh/ less heat (never the sh in shirt) /sr/ shrine /sy/ sure /hw/ which (the sound made when you blow out a candle) /h/ hi /ts/ cats hide /ʼ/ (the sound before the first vowel in 'uh-uh') /n/ noon /r/ round /w/ way /y/ yes.

make fun of see: tease
ho·dę·dǫn·yá'ta' it's making fun of him; s.t. turned on him
make good see: replace
o:yá' dęt·gǫ́:yǫ' I will give you a new one (that is, I will replace s.t.)
make oneself up
sat·go'jon·yáh·nǫ: beautify yourself; apply make-up
[at+ stem: -go'jonyahnǫ(:)- apply makeup; consists of: -go'j(a)$_{N}$- cheek -ǫnyahnǫ'$_{V}$- go and make several things]
make-up
ǫt·gǫh·sa̱h·soh·ta's·hǫ́:'ǫh make-up items
[ǫ+at+ stem: -gǫhsahsohd- apply make-up; consists of: -gǫhs(a)$_{N}$- face -(a)hsohd$_{V}$- colour]
ǫt·go'jon·yáh·ta' make-up; blush; rouge
[ǫ+at+ stem: -go'jonyahta'- make-up; consists of: -go'j(a)$_{N}$- cheek -ǫnyahd$_{V}$- cause to make]
make up see: reconcile
ę·ji·jad·ri̱h·wahs·rǫ́:ni' you two will reconcile
make-up bag
ǫt·gǫh·sa̱h·soh·ta'shǫ:'ǫ́h e·yáhk·wa' make-up bag
[consists of: ǫtgǫhsa̱hsohta'shǫ:'ǫh make-up items; eyahkwa' containers]
make love see: mate
sa·dá'i:s you have intercourse
male
de̱·ha·di·yáhs·he: two males (lit.: they (m) are two)
[de+A+ stem: -yahshe:$_{V}$- two or more living things]
male see: masculine, genitals
ha·jí:nah he is masculine, brave; his genitals
ga·jí:nah it is a male animal; the genitals of an animal

malevolence, malice see: hatred
ohs·wá·hę'dǫ: hatred
mall see: plaza
ǫt·ge·hǫ·dáhk·wa'geh plaza
mallet see: hammer
ga·jíh·wa' hammer
man
hǫ́:gweh a man; a boy
[A+ stem: -ǫgwe('da)$_{N}$- person]
man see: male
manage see: G (govern, ǫg·wahs·ha·i·ne')
mandate see: responsibility
sad·rih·wa·géh·de' your responsibility
mane
o·nǫ́·ha·he:' mane; scalp
[o+ stem: -nǫhahe:'- mane, scalp; consists of: -nǫh(a), nah(a)$_{N}$- scalp -(h)e:'$_{V}$- sitting up on top of s.t.]
manifestation see: ghost
jíhs·gę: a ghost
man-made
oh·wę·ja·geh·ge̱·há:' gá·ę·na' music made by man
[consists of: ohwęjagehge̱ha:' earthly things; resources; gaę:na' song]
man-made see: artificial
ti·gahs·rǫ́:ni' it is man-made, artificial
manner
ni·sa·i·hó'dę: your manner
[ni+P+ stem: -(r)iho'dę:- manner, way, belief; consists of: -(r)ih(wa)$_{N}$- word -o'dę:$_{V}$- type of]
tsę́h ni·yǫg·wá·i·ho'dę: our ways; our beliefs
manner see: attitude, way
tsę́h ni·sa'ni·gǫ́·ho'dę' your attitude, mood
mansion
ga·nǫh·so·wa·nęh·gó:wah mansion
[stem: -nǫhsowanęhgowah- mansion; consists of: -nǫhs(a)$_{N}$- house -owanęh$_{V}$- be big -gowah- big]

mantis see: praying mantis
wad·rę·ná·eh·nę' (**o·ji·nǫ́:wa'**) a praying mantis
manufacture see: make, produce
gǫ́:nihs I make, earn
a·ha·i·hǫ́n·yah·nǫ:' he produced s.t.
manure see: feces
o'da' feces; shit; excrement; manure
many
ni·yo·nat·gá'de' there are so many
[ni+...at+ stem: -ga'de'$_V$- be many]
hoh·wihs·da·gá'de' he has lots of money
[P+(ad+) N+ stem: -(h)wihsd(a), (hr)ihsd(a)$_N$- metal, money -ga'de'$_V$- many; have many, much]
ni·ga'ahd·rá:ge: that many baskets
[ni+A/P+N+ stem: -(')ahdr(a)$_N$- basket -(a)ge:$_V$- two or more, an amount]
ne·tóh ní:yǫ: that many
[ni+A+ stem: -ǫ$_V$- number (of things)]
ha'de·yoh·sóhg·wa·ge: all kinds of colours
[ha'+de+ stem: -(a)hsoh(gwa)$_N$- colour, paint, crayon -(a)ge:$_V$- two or more; many different types]
many see: I (i:so'), often
ot·gá'de' often; many; lots
map maker
ho·nǫh·wę·jáhs·dah·nǫ' map makers; geographers
[P+ stem: -ǫhwęjahsdahnǫ'- map maker, geographer; consists of: -ǫhwęj(a)$_N$- earth, land -(h)sdahnǫ'$_V$- go and use several things]
maple
oh·wáh·da' maple
[o+ stem: -(h)wahd(a)$_N$- maple]
gǫh·so:' soft maple
[stem: -gǫhso:'- soft maple]
maple syrup
oh·wah·dá' ot·séhs·da' maple syrup
[consists of: ohwahda' maple; otsehsda' syrup, honey, gum]
March see: A (Ga·nęsg·wa·ǫ·ta:'ah)
margin see: edge
tsę́h hǫ́ he·yo·d'ok·dá'ǫh the edge
mark
ęg·yá:na't I will mark s.t.
[ag+ stem: -yęna'd, yana'd$_V$- mark s.t.]
og·yá·n'a·dǫh it is marked
mark see: spot
o·wahg·wá·ǫn·yǫ' spots
market see: store
gyǫ·dęh·ní:nǫh grocery store
marriage
g'a·náhk·wa' a marriage; a wife
[ga+ stem: -(')nahk(wa)$_N$- wife, marriage]
de·ga'nahk·wáhs·hę: 20 wives, 20 marriages
g'a·náhk·wa·se: a new marriage
[stem: -(')nahk(wa)$_N$- wife, marriage -(a)se$_V$- new]
sg'a·náhg·wa:t one wife; one marriage
[s+ga+ stem: -(')nahk(wa)$_N$- wife, marriage -d$_V$- stand, be one]
marrow see: bone marrow, melon
ohsg·yę'da·gǫ́: gah·né:ga:t bone marrow
ohn·yǫ́h·sa' squash; melon; etc.
marry
gon·ya:s she's getting married
[P+ stem: -nyag$_V$- marry]
a·gé:nya:s I am getting married right now
ę·wá·gen·ya:k I will be married
a·ge:nyá:gǫh I am married
hon·yá:kdre' he is getting married
[P+ stem: -nyadre$_V$- go and get married]
marsh see: swamp
ga·ná·wa·ę:' swamp; pond

Cayuga pronunciation guide: /a/ father /e/ weigh /ę/ men (nasalized) /i/ police /o/ hole /ǫ/ home (nasalized) /u/ blue. Underlined vowels are voiceless or whispered. /'/ high pitch. /t/ too /d/ do /k/ king /g/ good (never soft g) /j/ judge or adze /s/ soon /sh/ less heat (never the sh in shirt) /sr/ shrine /sy/ sure /hw/ which (the sound made when you blow out a candle) /h/ hi /ts/ cats hide /'/ (the sound before the first vowel in 'uh-uh') /n/ noon /r/ round /w/ way /y/ yes.

masculine
ha·jí:nah he is masculine, brave; his genitals
[A+ stem: -jinah$_V$- strong, brave]
mash
dęh·se·j̱i̱hs·gǫ́:ni' you will mash it up
[de+... stem: -jihsgǫni- mash; consists of: -jihsg(wa)$_N$- mush -ǫni, ǫny$_V$- make]
ga·jih·gǫ́:ni: mashed food
dę·se·j̱i̱hsg·wá·hiht you will mash
[de+... stem: -jihsgwahihd- mash; consists of: -jihsg(wa)$_N$- mush -(hr)ihd$_V$- break s.t. up]
mash see: mush
on·yá·ha' native mush dishes made with corn
mask
ga·gǫ́h·sa' the mask
[ga+ stem: -gǫhs(a)$_N$- face, mask]
de̱·hot·ga̱·há·hęh he has masked eyes
[de+P+at+ stem: -gahahęh- masked eyes; consists of: -gah(a)$_N$- eye -(h)ęh$_V$- mid]
mass
tsę́h ni·yóhs·de' mass (lit.: how much it weighs; how heavy it is)
[tsęh ni+yo+ stem: -(a)hsde'$_V$- heavy; have mass]
mass see: weight
tsę́h ni·yo·gǫt·rá:sde' weight, pounds, poundage
massacre see: kill
a·hǫ́·wan·yo' s.o. killed him
massive see: big
go·wá:nęh, ga·gó·wa·nęh it is big
mass media see: movie
ga·yá'ta' movies, television
masticate see: chew
de·sáts·ga·hǫ: chew it

match
de·séh·ka·hǫ: match, pair things up (puzzle pieces, socks)
[de+... stem: -kahǫ:$_V$- match s.t. up, pair s.t. up; consists of: -kahǫ'$_V$- adjoin, abutt]
match see: resemble
tsé:yę: you resemble
matches
ǫ·de·g'a·dáhk·wa' fire-making tool; matches
[ǫ+ stem: -(a)dega'dąhkwa'- matches; consists of: -(a)dega'd- burn s.t. up]
e·jihs·do'á:sda̱hk·wa' matches (old word; lit.: s.o. torches the fire)
[e+ stem: -jihsdo'asdahkwa'- match; consists of: -jihsd(a)$_N$- light -o'as$_V$- torch]
mate
o·dih·weh·nǫ́:ni: they (z) are mating
[stem: -(h)wehnǫni- mate; consists of: -(h)wehn(a)$_N$- island -ǫni, ǫny$_V$- make]
sa·dá'i:s you have intercourse
[P+ stem: -(a')da'i:s- mate, have intercourse; consists of: -(ni)'d(a)$_N$- privates -(a)'ehsd pierce]
o·ná·da'i:s they (z) are mating
o·na·dá·is·dǫhs they (z) are mating
mate see: marry, pair
ę·wá·gen·ya:k I will be married
o·ná:tsih a pair (of shoes, socks)
material
ni·ga·hę́:hah it is thin (for example, material)
[ni+ga+ stem: -(h)ę:hah- material, cloth; consists of: -(h)ę:hah, hę:hęh$_V$- thin]
mathematics see: count
ęd·wáhs·he:t we all (incl.) will count
matriarch see: Queen
e·goh·gó:wah queen, the Queen
matrimony see: marriage, marry
g'a·náhk·wa' a marriage; a wife
ę·wá·gen·ya:k I will be married

matron see: woman
a·gǫ́:gweh girl; woman; the female gender
matter see: I (hę:gyeh), fault
o·íh·waʼ a message; it matters; it is its fault
mattress
gęts·ga:ʼ mattress; sleeping mat
[ga+ stem: -itsga:ʼ- mattress, sleeping mat; consists of: -(n)itsg(wa)$_N$- lower body -a:ʼ$_V$- hold, contain, include]
o·náʼsgwaʼ a mattress
[o+ stem: -naʼsg(wa)$_N$- mattress]
ga·na:kdáʼ o·ná:sgwaʼ mattress
[consists of: gana:kdaʼ bed; ona:sgwaʼ a mattress]
o·nǫ:nyáʼ gęts·ga:srǫn·yáʼdǫh corn husk mattress
[consists of: onǫ:nyaʼ husk; gętsgahsrǫnyaʼdǫh it is made for the body]
mattress see: bag
gá:ya:ʼ bag; mattress; etc.
mature
a·wát·sihsʼa:ʼ it (a plant) did mature; it completed its life-cycle
[stem: -(a)tsihsʼ$_V$- mature]
ot·síhsʼǫh it is done for the season; it has gone full cycle; it is mature; they (plants) have finished out
ot·sihsʼǫ̱·hǫ́:gyeʼ it is getting mature
ę·yǫg·yʼa·díh·sʼa:ʼ she has matured, completed her life cycle
[ag+ stem: -yaʼdihsʼ- mature; consists of: -yaʼd(a)$_N$- body -(i)hsʼ$_V$- finish]
mature see: puberty, ripen
de̱·had·wę·ná·dęn·yǫhs he is reaching puberty (lit.: his voice is changing)
ę·wáh·ya·iʼ it will ripen
may
ę·wá:dǫʼ yes, you may (lit.: it will become)
[ę+w(a)+ stem: -(a)dǫʼ$_V$- become]
May see: A (Ga·naʼgaht)
maybe
ę·wa:dǫ́ʼ gis·hęh maybe; a possibility
maybe see: I (gihshęh)
me see: Appendix I (i:ʼ)
meadow
ga̱·hę́·da·ęʼ meadow; pasture; field
[ga+ stem: -(h)ędaęʼ- meadow, pasture; consists of: -(h)ęd(a)$_N$- field -ę$_V$- lie on the ground]
ga̱·hę·dá·ę·dǫʼ meadows
meadow see: field
ga̱·hę́·da·gǫ: in the field; in the meadow
meadow lark
de·gahs·nʼa·dó·wa·nęʼs meadow lark
[de+ga+ stem: -(h)snaʼdowanęʼs- meadow lark; consists of: -(h)sna(ʼda)$_N$- muscle, hamstring, calf -owanęʼs$_V$- several big objects]
meal see: breakfast, flour, lunch, serve a meal, tea meeting
se·deh·ji·háh ni·yǫ·de·kǫ́:niʼ breakfast
o·téʼtraʼ flour; powder
a·dę́·nat·raʼ lunch; groceries
ę·yag·wa·dék·wa·hęʼ we all (excl.) will put on a meal, supper
gak·wá·he:ʼ tea meetings; supper
mealtime
ni·jǫ·de·kǫ́:nih the time to eat; mealtime
[ni+s+yǫ+ ade+ stem: -kǫnih- mealtime; consists of: -kǫni- cook]
mean (be mean)
ęh·se·gę·hęʼtrǫ́:nih you will be mean, abusive
[TR+ stem: -gęhęʼtrǫni- cruel, mean; consists of: -gęhęʼtr(a)$_N$- abuse -ǫni, ǫny$_V$- make]
a·gǫg·wʼe·dá·het·gęʼ she is a mean person
[P+ stem: -ǫgweʼdahetgęʼ- be cruel, mean; consists of: -ǫgwe(ʼda)$_N$- person -(hr)etgę$_V$- evil, bad, ugly]

Cayuga pronunciation guide: /a/ father /e/ weigh /ę/ men (nasalized) /i/ police /o/ hole /ǫ/ home (nasalized) /u/ blue. Underlined vowels are voiceless or whispered. /ˊ/ high pitch. /t/ too /d/ do /k/ king /g/ good (never soft g) /j/ judge or adze /s/ soon /sh/ less heat (never the sh in shirt) /sr/ shrine /sy/ sure /hw/ which (the sound made when you blow out a candle) /h/ hi /ts/ cats hide /ʼ/ (the sound before the first vowel in 'uh-uh') /n/ noon /r/ round /w/ way /y/ yes.

mean s.t.
e:dǫh she means s.o., s.t.
[A+ / TR+ stem: -(i)dǫh$_{N}$- mean s.t.]
gi:dǫh I mean s.t.
hę:dǫh he means s.t.
I:ʼ gęh sgi:dǫh? Do you mean me?
Neʼseʼ hǫwę:dǫh. He's the one she means.

mean see: abuse, do on purpose
se·gę́·hę·nih you abuse it, you are mean to it; you are an abuser
tsaʼgeht I did it on purpose

meander see: roam, stray, wander
ti·gę·ne·nǫ́g·yeʼs they (z) are roaming about
ę́ tsǫ́h ęt·seʼ you will wander

meaningful see: special
o·i·ho·wá:nęh it is important; a great or worthy commendation; it is special

measure
ę·ya·go·deʼnyę·dę́hs·dǫ·hǫ:k she will be measuring things
[ade+ stem: -(ʼ)nyędęhsd- measure; consists of: -(ʼ)nyędę$_{V}$- try]
wa·deʼnyę·dę́hs·dǫh the act of measuring

measure see: copy, scale
ęt·sa·den·yę́·dęhs you will copy, use as a model, a pattern
ga·gǫʼtra·hé:haʼ balance; weigh scale

measurement see: size
shę́h ní:waʼs sizes; how big they are

measuring cup
ǫ·deʼnyę·dęhs·da̱hk·wáʼ ga·náʼjo̱hsg·waʼ measuring cup
[consists of: ǫdeʼnyędęhsda̱hkwaʼ ruler, measuring tape; ganaʼjo̱hsgwaʼ cup]

measuring spoon
ǫ·deʼnyę·dęhs·da̱hk·wáʼ gan·yó:daʼ measuring spoon
[consists of: ǫdeʼnyędęhsda̱hkwaʼ ruler, measuring tape; ganyo:daʼ spoon]

measuring tape see: ruler
ǫ·deʼnyę·dę́hs·da̱hk·waʼ ruler; measuring tape

meat
oʼwá·hǫh meat
[o+ stem: -(ʼ)wah(a)$_{N}$- meat -(adi)hǫh$_{V}$- lean across]
waʼdeʼs·gǫ́:t oʼwá·hǫh fried meat
[consists of: wadeʼsgǫ:t it is roasting, frying; oʼwahǫh meat]
daks·ha·eʼdóhs oʼwá·hǫh chicken meat
[consists of: dakshae:ʼdohs chicken; oʼwahǫh meat]
gwihs·gwíhs oʼwá·hǫh pig meat; pork chop
[consists of: gwihsgwihs pig; oʼwahǫh meat]
oʼwa·hah·ní:yǫh tough meat
[stem: -(ʼ)wah(a)$_{N}$- meat -(h)niyǫh$_{V}$- hard, tough]
oʼwa·ha·gá:yǫh old meat
[stem: -(ʼ)wah(a)$_{N}$- meat -gayǫh$_{V}$- old (thing)]
oʼwá·hat·gę: spoiled meat
[stem: -(ʼ)wah(a)$_{N}$- meat -tgę$_{V}$- spoiled, rotten]
oʼwa·ha·gáh·deh raw meat
[stem: -(ʼ)wah(a)$_{N}$- meat -(a)gahdeh$_{V}$- raw]
gʼa·wá·hoʼ boiled meat
[stem: -(ʼ)wah(a)$_{N}$- meat -oʼ$_{V}$- boiled]
oʼwá·ha·tę: dry meat
[stem: -(ʼ)wah(a)$_{N}$- meat -tę(:)$_{V}$- be dry]

meat slicer
eʼwa·há·i:sgyʼak·taʼ meat slicer
[e+ stem: -(ʼ)wahaisgyaʼktaʼ- meat slicer; consists of: -(ʼ)wah(a)$_{N}$- meat -(h)wihsd(a), (hr)ihsd(a)$_{N}$- metal -(i)yaʼkd$_{V}$- cause to cut, break]

meat slicer (continued)
gˀa·wa·há·i:sgyaˀs meat slicer
[ga+ stem: -(ˀ)wahaisgyaˀs- meat slicer; consists of: -(ˀ)wah(a)$_N$- meat -(h)wihsd(a), (hr)ihsd(a)$_N$- metal -(i)yaˀg$_V$- cut, break]
mechanic
shaˀdreh·dǫ́:nihs he is a mechanic
[(s+) A+ stem: -(ˀ)drehdǫnihs- mechanic; consists of: -(ˀ)drehd(a)$_N$- vehicle, car -ǫni, ǫny$_V$- make, fix]
mechanism see: engine
ga̱·hǫ́ˀji̱hs·daˀ a motor; an engine
meddlesome see: mischievous
de·saˀnyǫ̱hs·wá·haˀt you can't keep your hands off; you're nosy
median see: middle
de·yó:gę: between; in the middle
medical clinic see: clinic
ga·né:yǫhs a medical clinic, etc.
medication see: pill
o·nę́n·yˀog·waˀ pills
medicine see: F (o·nǫh·gwˀat·raˀ), evil, weed
go·ná:tgǫh they (f/m) are a force to be reckoned with; they (f/m) are ominous; they are bad medicine people
a·wę́·nǫ̱hg·raˀ weeds
medicine cabinet
e·nǫhg·wat·ra·ę·dáhk·waˀ medicine cabinet
[e+ stem: -nǫhgwatraędahkwaˀ- medicine cabinet; consists of: -nǫhgwatr(a)$_N$- medicine -ędahkwaˀ$_V$- place where s.t. is put]
meditate see: think
sę·nǫ́h·dǫn·yǫh you are wondering, thinking
meet
swat·gę́·nihsˀahs you have meetings all the time
[at+ stem: -gęnihsˀ$_V$- meet]
meet (continued)
swat·gę·nihsˀáhs·gǫ: you are always having meetings (can be derogatory)
ęhs·wat·ge·níhsˀa:ˀ you all will have a meeting
swat·gę́·nihsˀǫh you are having a meeting right now
de·gá·ǫˀdraˀs they (f/m) meet all the time
[de+... stem: -(aˀ)draˀ$_V$- meet]
a·tę́·nˀad·raˀ they (m) met
de·ya·go·náˀd·raˀǫh they deserve each other (said in anger); they (f/m) are meeting right now
meet see: converge
de·yo·na·ta·hoˀdráˀǫh converging roads
meeting place
ǫd·ró·hek·taˀ meeting place; gathering place
[ǫ+ad+ stem: -(r)ohektaˀ- meeting place, gathering place; consists of: -(r)ohekd$_V$- cause to gather]
meeting room
ǫt·gę·ni̱hsˀáh·taˀgeh meeting room
[ǫ+at+ stem: -gęnihsˀahtaˀgeh- meeting room; consists of: -gęnihsˀahd$_V$- cause to meet]
melancholy see: mournful, sad
oˀni·gǫ̱h·sá:dǫhk it is mournful
de·saˀni·gǫ́·hęh·dǫh you are sad
mellow see: good-natured
ga:gǫg·wˀe·dí:yo: they (f/m) are good-natured people
melody see: music, song
gá·ę·no:t music that is playing
gá·ę·naˀ song
melon
ohn·yǫ́h·saˀ squash; melon
[o+ stem: -(h)nyǫhs(a)$_N$- melon, squash]
ohn·yǫh·sˀá·ǫ:weh squash (used for soup at the Longhouse; usually Hubbard squash)

melt
ga·naʼna·wę́ʼda·hǫh it has been melted [N+/naʼ+ stem: -nawęhdah- cause s.t. to melt, melt s.t., liquefy s.t.; consists of: -nawę$_{V}$- wet]
ga·náʼna·węht it is melted [N+/naʼ+ stem: -nawęhd- wet s.t., melt s.t., liquefy s.t.; consists of: -nawę$_{V}$- wet]
ga·naʼna·wę́h·dǫh it has melted; it is soaked

melt see: thaw, wet
ęhs·ga·nʼa·ná:wę ʼ it will thaw, melt again
ęhs·náʼna·węʼt you will melt, liquefy s.t.

Member of Parliament see: G (Han·haʼtraʼ)

memorandum see: fault
o·íh·waʼ a message; it matters; it is its fault

memorial see: monument
tgahs·dę́·ho:t monument

menace see: threaten
ęhs·he·yahd·rǫ́hg·węʼ you will threaten, scare s.o.

mend see: fix, repair, sew
ǫ·deʼkahs·rǫ́:nih she is fixing skirts
sa·sehs·rǫ́:niʼ you repaired it
á:kni·kǫ:ʼ I should, might sew

mentally challenged see: premature
to·dǫ́:nhoʼk he is mentally challenged; he was born premature
tega:yei:ʼ he's (lit.: it is) not all there; it's not right in the head

mentally ill see: crazy
de·sę·na·há·wę:nyeʼ you are crazy (not right in the mind)

merchant marine see: sailor
ha·di·hǫ·waʼge·hó:nǫʼ sailors; navy men; merchant marines

mercy
gę·dá·ǫhs·raʼ mercy [ga+ stem: -(i)dęǫhsr(a)$_{N}$- kindness -(i)dęǫ, (i)dę(:)$_{V}$- pity]

mercy see: pity
ęhs·hé:dę:ʼ you will pity her, show mercy, compassion

merge see: converge, mix
de·yo·na·ta·hoʼdráʼǫh converging roads
dęs·yehs you will mix them all together

merit see: earn (money)
de·sá·dęt·sʼǫh you've earned it; you deserve it; you've paid your dues

mesa see: plains
de·yǫh·wę·jág·węh·dę: flat land; prairies; plains

mesh see: web
o·dáʼa·ǫt web; net

message see: fault
o·íh·waʼ a message; it matters; it is its fault

message (charge s.o. with a message)
ę·hehs·rȩh·ná·gȩh·da:t you will put the bundle (that is, a load, a message) on him [stem: -(hr)ehnagehdad- charge s.o. with a message; consists of: -(hr)ehn(a)$_{N}$- cargo, bundle -gehdad$_{V}$- put around one's neck, carry]

message (convey a message)
he·ha·ih·wę́·hęhs he always takes the message; he is a messenger [haʼ+... stem: -(r)ihwęhę(:)- convey a message; consists of: -(r)ih(wa)$_{N}$- word -ęhę(:)$_{V}$- direct, convey]
hę·ha·ih·wę́·hę:ʼ he will take the message
he·ho·ih·wę́·hę: he has taken a message
ę·gǫ·ih·wę́h·dęʼ I will give you a significant message [TR+ stem: -(r)ihwęhdę- message (give s.o. a); consists of: -(r)ih(wa)$_{N}$- word -ęhdę(:)$_{V}$- cause to direct, convey]

message (deliver a message)
ǫ:nę́h tóh ha'gat·reh·n'a·geh·sí' dę'ho'dę' ehs·gwa·he'nǫ:nyę́' to·ha'grih·wá·ge·hǫ' I spread out the message in front of them
[consists of: ǫ:nęh now toh that ha'gatrehn'agehsi' I took the message apart dę'ho'dę' what ehsgwahe'nǫ:nyę' you made it for me to that ha'grihwagehǫ' I spread out the word]

messenger see: predict
né' hó:nę: predictors; messengers; etc.

metal
gá·i:sda' tin; metal
[ga+ stem: -(h)wihsd(a), (hr)ihsd(a)$_N$- metal, money]

metal see: iron
gahn·yǫ́'ǫhs·ra' iron; steel

meteor see: shooting star, star
o·jih·sǫ·dǫ́h·go:t shooting star
ga·jíhs·dǫg·ye' flaming star; meteor; comet

method see: manner
tsę́h ni·yǫ·gwá·ih·o'dę: our ways; our beliefs

Metis see: C (De·ho·na·detg·węh·sa·yehs·dǫh)

metropolis see: city
ga·na·do·wá:nęh city

Mexican see: C (hodihswe'danawę:, hodihswe'nanawę:)

microwave oven
gak·wahs·no:wé' ga·kǫ́:nihs microwave oven
[consists of: gakwahsno:we' fast-food cooker; gakǫ:nihs it cooks]

middle
de·yó:gę: between; in the middle
[de+yo+ stem: -gę:- middle, between, in-between; consists of: -gę$_V$- see]

middle see: half
tsa'de·yoh·sę́:nǫh, tsa'de·wah·sę́:nǫh half; the middle

middle-age
ni·ta·we:nǫ́:hah middle-aged male
[ni+d+P+ stem: -enǫ:hah- middle-aged; consists of: -enǫ$_V$- originate from someplace, come from someplace]
nig·ya·ga·we:nǫ́:hah middle-aged female
ha'de·ya·gǫg·w'e·dá·ę:' middle age
[ha'de+yag+ stem: -ǫgwe'daę'- middle age; consists of: -ǫgwe('da)$_N$- person -ę$_V$- lie on the ground]

middy see: blouse
a·déhs·wa' blouse; middy

mid-morning see: A (sedehjihahne:hah)

midnight see: A (tsa'dewahsǫ:tęh)

midpoint, midway see: middle

might see: power
gahs·háhs·dęhs·ra', ohs·háhs·dęhs·ra' power; strength

mighty see: strong
gahs·háhsde' it is strong, tough, powerful

migrate see: home
ęhs·gę·nah·dę́:di' they (z) will migrate

mild see: warm
o·né:nǫ' it is mild, warm; a warm or hot day

mile
sgá:t he·yót·gah·twęh one mile (lit.: how far you can see)
[he'+yo+at+ stem: -gahtwęh- mile; consists of: -gahtw$_V$- look]

milk
o·nǫ́'gwa' milk
[o+ stem: -nǫ'g(wa)$_N$- breast, milk]

milk see: skim milk
de·ga·wid·rá·gęd·rǫ: skimmed milk

milking machine
ga·nǫʼgwa·dáhg·wahs milking machine
[ga+ stem: -nǫʼgwadahgwahs- milking machine; consists of: -nǫʼg(wa)$_N$- breast, milk -(h)gw$_V$- remove]
milkman
ha·nǫʼgwa·nę́hg·wih milkman
[ha+ stem: -nǫʼgwanęhgwih- milkman; consists of: -nǫʼg(wa)$_N$- breast, milk -nęhgwi$_V$- haul]
milkweed
ga·nóʼgwą̱·hihs milkweed
[ga+ stem: -noʼgwahihs- milkweed; consists of: -nǫʼg(wa)$_N$- breast, milk -(hr)ihsd$_V$- bump s.o.]
Milky Way see: galaxy
o·ha·haʼdí·hǫh the Milky Way
millstone see: grinder
de·gá·hih·taʼ grinder; cutter
mimic see: imitate
ęts·náʼgyę:ʼ you will imitate, mock, mimic s.t.
mind
gʼa·ní·gǫ·haʼ the mind
[ga+ stem: -(ʼ)nigǫh(a)$_N$- mind]
ǫg·waʼni·gǫ́·haʼ our mind
gʼa·ni·gǫ·háʼgeh on the minds
sgʼa·ni·gǫ·há:t o·dǫ́ʼǫh one mind
[consists of: sgʼanigǫha:t on mind odǫʼǫh it has become]
mind see: strong
ak·ni·gǫ·hah·ní:yǫh I have a strong mind
mine
a·ga·wę·gę́·hę:ʼ it used to be mine
[P+ stem: -(a)węh$_V$- have]
mine see: have
a·gá:węh it is mine
miner
oh·wę·ja·gǫ́: hę·nad·rį̱·hóʼda:s miners
[consists of: ohwęjagǫ: under the earth; hęnadrį̱hoʼda:s they (m) are workers]

miniature see: small
ni·wú:ʼuh it is small, little
minister see: G (gon·haʼtraʼs·hǫʼ)
ministry see: G (hǫ·wa·dis·hahs·dęhs·ra:wi:)
mink
jǫʼdá·gaʼ mink
[(w)a+ stem: -jǫʼdagaʼ- mink; consists of: -(i)jǫʼd(a)$_N$- fish -gaʼ$_V$- like the taste of s.t.]
minute
a·węʼyǫh·gá:yęht one minute
[a+ stem: -węʼyǫhgayęhd- minute; consists of: -węʼyǫhg(a:)$_N$- thumb -(y)ęhd$_V$- hit, knock down, strike]
mire see: clay
oʼda:ʼ clay; mud; mortar
mirror
at·gǫh·sǫ̱hg·waʼtráʼ ǫt·gáh·twah·taʼ mirror
[consists of: atgǫhsgwaʼtraʼ a window; ǫtgahtwahtaʼ s.t. that causes the eye to see]
miscarriage
sǫg·wi:yǫ́:diʼ I had a miscarriage again
[P+ stem: -wiyǫdi- miscarriage, abandon a child, abort; consists of: -wiy(a)$_N$- child, offspring -ǫdi, -ǫgy$_V$- throw]
a·go·wi:yǫ́:diʼ she abandoned her child, had an abortion
wad·wí·yǫg·yǫ: an abandoned child
sǫg·wí:yeʼs I had a miscarriage
[P+ stem: -wiyęʼs- miscarry; consists of: -wiy(a)$_N$- child, offspring -(aʼs)ęʼ$_V$- fall, drop, reduce]
a·go:wí:yęhs she had a miscarriage
mischievous
de·saʼnyǫhs·wá·haʼt you can't keep your hands off; you're nosy
[de+P+ stem: -(ʼ)nyǫhswahaʼd- mischievous, nosy; consists of: -(ʼ)nyǫhs(a)$_N$- nose -swahaʼd$_V$- go and smell]

mischievous (continued)
de·yǫg·w'an·yǫ́hs·wa·ha't we are mischievous, nosy
de·wa·g'en·yǫ́hs·wa·ha't I am mischievous, nosy
mischievous see: bad, naughty
de·ta·dih·wa:yé·i: they (m) are corrupt, impish, bad
ek·sa'da̱·hé:tgę' a naughty child
miserly see: stingy
sa·ní'ǫh you are stingy, greedy, cheap
misery see: pain
ęg·rǫ́h·ya·gę' I will be in pain; I will labour, in agony
misfortune see: accident, disaster
a·wad·ri̱h·wág·ya·ǫ' there was an accident
ad·rih·wag·ya·ǫhs·ra' a disaster
mishap see: accident
a·wad·ri̱h·wág·ya·ǫ' there was an accident
mislay see: lose
e·sáh·dǫ:' you lost it
mislead see: deceive, fool
dęhs·hé·ga̱hg·we:k you will pull the wool over her eyes, outsmart her, deceive her
se·sa·het·só:go' you got fooled (like the frog)
misplace see: lose
e·sáh·dǫ:' you lost it
misrepresent see: deceive
dęhs·hé·ga̱hg·we:k you will pull the wool over her eyes, outsmart her, deceive her
miss
gad·wáh·ta' I miss it always
[stem: -(a)twahd, (a)dwahd$_V$- miss s.t.]
sa·gá:twaht I missed it (a ball, etc.)
a·gád·wa̱h·dǫh I have missed it

miss (continued)
sha·háhat·waht he missed the road again
[s+...(N+) stem: -(h)ah(a)$_N$- road -(a)twahd, (a)dwahd$_V$- miss s.t.]
sa·gę'nhot·rá:twaht I missed the ball
[s+...(N+) stem: -ę'nh(otra)$_N$- ball -(a)twahd, (a)dwahd$_V$- miss s.t.]
missile see: cannon
ga̱·ho'da·gó:wah cannon; missile
mist see: drizzle, fog
a·wá·yǫ:gyǫ: it is drizzling; misty rain; fine rain
ot·sá:da' fog; steam
mistake see: err
ęh·sá:nhi'k you will err, make a mistake
mistreat see: abuse
se·gę́·hę·nih you abuse it; you are mean to it; you are an abuser
misunderstand
tę́' de'ak'ni·gǫ·há·ę·da's I do not understand
[tę' de'+ not P+ stem: -(')nigǫhaęda'- misunderstand; consists of: -(')nigǫh(a)$_N$- mind -ęda'$_V$- finish]
misuse see: abuse
dehs·ha·god·rǫ́'we̱hs·ta' he abuses s.o.
mite see: tick
ohs·gé·ha' louse
mittens
ę'nyó:tra' mittens
[ę+ stem: -(')nyotr(a)- mittens; consists of: -(')ny(a)$_N$- finger, hand -od$_V$- stand]
mix
dęs·yehs you will mix them all together
[(de+)...(N+) stem: -yehsd$_V$- add; mix together]
de·gah·ne·gá·ye̱hs·dǫh water is mixed in it
[(de+)...(N+) stem: -(h)neg(a)$_N$- water, liquid -yehsd$_V$- add; mix together]

mix see: stir
deh·sá·wę̨n·ye:ʼ beat it; mix it; stir it
mixer
de·wá·wę̨n·yehs a mixer
[de+wa+ stem: -(a)wę̨nyehs- mixer; consists of: -(a)wę̨nye(:)$_V$- stir, mix]
MLA see: G (Han·haʼtraʼ)
moan see: pain, sigh
ę̨g·rǫ́h·ya·gę̨ʼ I will be in pain; I will labour; I will be in agony
de·yag·wi̱hs·ra·gę̱·hé:yǫ: she is sighing
mobile
ǫt·ga·hiʼdahk·wáʼ ga·ní:yǫ:t a mobile (a hanging toy)
[consists of: ǫtgahiʼdahkwaʼ toy; gani:yǫ:t it is hanging]
mock see: jeer
ę̨h·sad·wę̨·ná:yę̨ht you will jeer, jest, throw words at s.o.
mockingbird
saʼsaʼ mockingbird; chatterbox
[stem: -saʼsaʼ$_N$- mockingbird, chatterbox]
mode see: way
tsę̨́h ni·yǫg·wá·i·hoʼdę̨: our ways
model see: pattern
gyǫ·deʼnyę̨·dę̨́hs·da̱hk·waʼ pattern
moderate see: warm
o·né:nǫʼ it is mild, warm; a warm or hot day
modest see: humble
gʼo·ni·gǫ̱·ha:ní:dę̨ht she is gentle, nice, humble
modify see: change
dę̨hs·wíhs·da̱·hiht you will make change
Mohawk people see: C (Gan·yę̨ʼge̱·ho:nǫʼ)
Mohawk Territory see: E (Gan·yę̨ʼge·ho·nǫ·geh)
moiety see: C (ǫg·wat·nǫh·soh·dahg·wę̨h)
moist see: damp, wet
ot·sá·dę̨ʼǫh it is damp
o·nǫ́hg·wi·jaʼ it is soaking wet, saturated
mole see: freckle
sa·gę̨́:na:ʼ you have moles
molest see: rape
ahs·ha·got·go·ho·wá·na̱h·dę̨ʼ he raped her (lit.: he forced her in a big way)
monarch see: Queen, G (royalty, gwa:go:wah)
e·goh·gó:wah queen, the Queen
Monday see: A (A·wę̨·dę̨·daʼǫh)
money see: B (oh·wihs·daʼ, gwę̨·nihs·hǫ:ʼǫh)
monitor
ǫ·ki·yʼa·dę̨ʼni·gǫ́·ha:ʼ monitors (people)
[TR+adę̨+ stem: -(ʼ)nigǫh(a)$_N$- mind -(ʼ)nigǫha(:)$_V$- expect, watch]
monkey
ga·jíʼnǫh·da:s monkey
[ga+ stem: -jiʼnǫhda:s- monkey; consists of: -jiʼnǫw(a), jiʼnǫh$_N$- insect, bug -(a)hdaʼ$_V$- get full of food]
month see: A (ę̱hniʼda:ʼ)
monument
tgahs·dę̨́·ho:t monument
[(t+) ga+ stem: -(h)sdę̨hod- mountain; monument; consists of: -(h)sd(ę̨ha)$_N$- stone -od$_V$- stand]
monumental see: special
o·i·ho·wá·nę̨h it is important; a great or worthy commendation; it is special
mood see: attitude, nerves
tsę̨́h ni·saʼni·gǫ́·hoʼdę̨: your attitude, mood
shę̨́h dwa·nih·na·dó·gʼa·taʼ human emotions; feelings; nerves
moody
e·nǫ́·gʼę̨·daʼ she is moody
[stem: -nǫgę̨ʼdaʼ$_V$- moody]

moody see: ugly
á·ǫ·teht·gęht s.o. turned funny (moody, etc.)
ho·teht·gę·dǫ́:ni: he is in a funny, odd mood; he is moody
moon
sǫ·heh·ká:ʼ gá:gwa:ʼ moon
[consists of: (ah)sǫhehka:ʼ night kind; ga:gwa:ʼ the sun, the moon]
sǫ·heh·ká:ʼ ęh·níʼda:ʼ moon
[consists of: (ah)sǫhehka:ʼ night kind; ęhniʼda:ʼ a month, a moon]
ęh·niʼda·sé:ʼ sa·gáhg·wa:ʼ new moon
[consists of: ęhniʼdase:ʼ it is a new month; sagahgwa:ʼ it was a moon again]
ga:hgwa·náh·nǫh the full moon (which brings rain)
[ga+ stem: -(r)agwanahnǫh- full moon; consists of: -(r)ag(wa)$_N$- the sun, the moon -nahnǫh$_V$- full]
gahg·wá:se:ʼ new moon
[ga+ stem: -(r)agwase:- new moon; consists of: -(r)ag(wa)$_N$- the sun, the moon -(a)se:$_V$- new]
ad·wad·rihg·wag·we·nǫ́:ni: there was a full moon
[de+...ad+ stem: -(r)ihgwagwenǫni:- full moon; consists of: -(r)ihg(wa)$_N$- moon -gwenǫni$_V$- full]
de·yod·rih·wag·we·nǫ́:ni: there is a full moon
he·jo·gę́:ʼęh last quarter moon
[he+s+yo+ stem: -(ʼ)gę:ʼęh$_V$- younger sibling, last quarter moon, a waning moon]
moon see: A (sǫhehka:ʼ ga:gwa:ʼ), sun
ga:gwá:gyeʼs the sun and moon
moose
sgan·yǫ́h·saʼ moose
[s+ga+ stem: -(ʼ)nyǫhsaʼ- moose; consists of: -(ʼ)nyǫhs(a)$_N$- nose]

moose (continued)
haʼnyǫhs·gwá:ʼah he is a little moose
[A+ stem: -(ʼ)nyǫhsgwa:ʼah- moose; consists of: -(ʼ)nyǫhs(a)$_N$- nose -a:ʼah$_V$- small]
mop
e·nehs·da·o:há·iʼtaʼ mop
[e+ stem: -nehsdaohaiʼtaʼ- mop; consists of: -nehsd(a:)$_N$- floor, board -ohaeʼd- cause to clean, wash]
moral see: righteous
god·rih·wag·wá·ih·sǫh she is fair, righteous
more see: I (ahsǫh, i:soʼ), often
ot·gáʼdeʼ often; many; lots
morel
o·nég·rʼę·daʼ morel mushroom
[o+ stem: -negręʼd(a)$_N$- morel]
yah·gęh·daʼ morel, black type of mushroom
[stem: -yahgęhd(a)$_N$- morel]
moreover see: I (also, gwatoh)
morgue
de·ha·di·ya·ǫʼdahs·nye·háʼgeh a morgue (lit.: where they (m) take care of the cadaver)
[de+A+ stem: -yaǫʼdahsnyehaʼgeh- morgue; consists of: -(he)yǫ(ʼda)$_N$- corpse, cadaver -(h)snye$_V$- care for, look after -ʼgeh at]
morning
she·dęh·ji·háh·gę·ha:ʼ morning kind
[stem: -sehdehjihah$_N$- morning]
morning see: A (sedęhji:hah)
morning star
dwę·dę·hę́:wih·taʼ morning star (lit.: it brings the day)
[stem: -ęd(a)$_N$- day -(a)wiʼd- insert]
da·wę·dá·ę·taʼ morning star
[d+aʼ+w+ stem: -ędaętaʼ- morning star; consists of: -ęd(a)$_N$- day -ęd$_V$- cause to lie on the ground]

moron see: stupid
de·sa'ni·gǫ́·ha:t you are stupid, foolish
morose see: mournful, sad
o'ni·gǫh·sá:dǫhk it is mournful
de·sa'ni·gǫ́·hęh·dǫh you are sad
morsel see: food
gak·wa' food
mortal see: alive, person
a·gǫ́:nhe' she is alive
ǫ́:gweh a person; a human
mortar see: clay
o'da:' clay; mud; mortar
mortification see: shame
o·dé·ha't a shame; an embarrassment
mortify see: feel bad, offend
ga·dé·hęhs I am embarrassed, ashamed
ęhs·he'ni·gǫ́·ha'e:k you will offend s.o.
mosquito
ni·gǫ́·hęh mosquitoes
[stem: -(')nigǫhęh- forget; mosquito; consists of: (')nigǫh(a)- mind; -(h)ęh$_V$- mid]
moss see: sod
o'ǫ́hg·wa:' sod; moss
most see: I (aǫ:hę:'ęh)
motel
ǫ·nǫh·wehs·tá'geh motel; inn; bed-and-breakfast; hotel
[ǫ+ stem: -nǫhwehsta'- bedroom]
moth
ó:wa:' moth
[o+ stem: -w(a:)$_N$- moth]
ga·díhs·dihs·ra:s moth larvae
[A+ stem: -(r)ihsdihsra:s- moth; consists of: (r)ihsdihsr(a)- cloth; -g- eat]
mother see: C (e·ti·nǫ·ha')
e·tí·nǫ·ha' our mother; women
mother-in-law see: C (ǫk·ne:n·hǫ:s)
ǫk·né:nhǫ:s my (a male's) mother-in-law
motion see: move
ohę:dǫ́: he'sé·nǫg·ye' you're moving forward
motionless see: quiet
ta'déyog·yę: quietness; quiet; stillness
motive see: idea
o·íh·wa·geh the reason; the idea for s.t.
motor see: engine
ga·hǫ́'jihs·da' a motor; an engine
motorist see: drive
ha·dó:nye's he drives it; he is a driver
motor oil
oh·ná:ji: motor oil; black grease
[o+ stem: -(h)naji:- motor oil; consists of: -(h)n(a)$_N$- oil, gas -ji(:,h)$_V$- dark]
motorcycle
dek·ní: de·wę'nihs·ga:ǫ́t
wa·dá·de'dre's motorcycle
[consists of: dekni: dewę'nihsgaǫ:t it has two wheels; wadadedre's it drives itself]
mouldy
a·gahs·g'ęd·rǫ́:dę' it is rusty, mouldy
[stem: -(h)sgę'drǫd- mouldy, rusty; consists of: -(h)sgę'dr(a)$_N$- rust, mould -ǫd$_V$- attached]
a·wahs·g'ęd·rǫ́:dę:' it got mouldy; it got rusty
a·ga·wé·o·dę' it got mouldy
[N+ stem: -weodę- become mouldy; consists of: -we$_N$- mould -od$_V$- stand]
mouldy see: rust
ohs·gę́'dro:t it is rusting, mouldy
moult
a·wa·dehs·tó'dręht it moulted
[ade+ stem: -(h)sto'dręhd- moult; consists of: -(h)sto'dr(a)$_N$- feather -(y)ęhd$_V$- hit, knock down, strike]
mound see: pile, stack
on·hóhs·ro:t a pile of s.t.
wa·dę́·hi:' it is stacked
mount a horse
ę·wa·gęh·sá:dę' I will mount a horse
[P+ stem: -(h)sadę- mount a horse; consists of: -(h)se'$_V$- ride horseback]

mountain
de·gáhs·dę·he:s a high mountain
[de+ga+ stem: -(h)sdęhes- mountain; consists of: -(h)sd(ęha)$_{N}$- stone -es$_{V}$- long]
gahs·dę́·ho:t mountain
[ga+ stem: -(h)sdęhod- mountain; consists of: -(h)sd(ęha)$_{N}$- stone -od$_{V}$- stand]
gahs·dę·hó:dǫʼ mountains; a pile of boulders
he·gahs·dę́:doʼk the end of the mountain
[stem: -(h)sd(ęha)$_{N}$- stone -oʼkd$_{V}$- end]
de·gahs·dę·hó·dag·yeʼ a mountain range; the Rockies
[de+ ga+ stem: -(h)sdęhodagyeʼ- mountain range, Rockies; consists of: -(h)sd(ęha)$_{N}$- stone -odagyeʼ$_{V}$- stand along]
mourn
ęh·sa·dę·nǫ́ʼnya:t you will mourn
[P+adę+ stem: -nǫʼnyad$_{V}$- mourn]
a·ga·de·nǫ́ʼnya·dǫ:ʼ I am in mourning
mourn see: bereaved, depressed, grieve
sat·ga·ǫ·níʼǫh you are bereaved
dwak·ni·gǫ·hę́ʼǫh I am in sorrow, mourning; I am sad
de·wak·ni·gǫ́hnyʼa·gǫh I am brokenhearted, grieving
mournful
oʼni·gǫh·sá:dǫhk it is mournful
[o+stem: -(ʼ)nigǫhsadǫhk- mournful; consists of: -(ʼ)nigǫh(a)$_{N}$- mind -(h)sadǫ$_{V}$- bury s.o., an animal]
mouse
ji·nó:wę: mouse
[stem: -jinowę$_{N}$- mouse]
mouth
oh·sa:ʼ mouth
[stem: -(h)sa(:), (h)sag(a)$_{N}$- mouth]
gah·sá·gahę:t mouth
[ga+ stem: -(h)sa(:), (h)sag(a)$_{N}$- mouth -gahęd$_{V}$- drill, hole]

mouth (continued)
gęh·sá·ga·hę:t my mouth
swah·sá·ga·hę:t your (p) mouths
ho·nǫ́·hǫ:t he has s.t. in his mouth
[P+ stem: -nhǫd- have s.t. in one's mouth; consists of: -nh(a)$_{N}$- mouth -ǫd$_{V}$- attached]
hon·hǫ́·dag·yeʼ he has it in his mouth as he moves
[P+ stem: -nhǫd$_{N}$- have s.t. in one's mouth -agyeʼ$_{V}$- continue on, be ongoing]
move
se·gę́·ihs·taʼ you postpone it all the time; you move it all the time
[stem: -gęihsd$_{V}$- move, postpone]
ęd·wa:gę́·is we all (incl.) will postpone
ęh·se:gę́·is you will move it (for example, checkers)
sa·gę́·ihs·dǫh you have postponed it
ohę:dǫ́: heʼsé·nǫg·yeʼ you're moving forward
[ohę:dǫ: heʼ+... stem: -enǫgyeʼ- move; consists of: -enǫ$_{V}$- originate from someplace, come from someplace]
sa·dón·yah·nǫh you move all the time
[ad/N+ stem: -ǫnyahnǫ(:)- move; consists of: -ǫni, ǫny$_{V}$- make]
ę·sa·don·yáh·nǫ:ʼ you will make yourself move
gʼad·réh·taʼ it moves itself, it rides
[(N+) stem: -(i)ʼdrehd- move oneself, be self-propelled; consists of: -(i)ʼdre(:)$_{V}$- drag, drive]
move see: move away, move in, remove
ǫʼnǫ:ʼ it has been moved
move see: I (sigwa:dih)
move away
dwa·dǫ́ʼne:s it moves away all the time; it shrinks
[ad+ stem: -ǫʼn(eg)$_{V}$- remove, take away, move away, shrink]
ę·wá·dǫ·ne:k it (animal) will move away

Cayuga pronunciation guide: /a/ father /e/ weigh /ę/ men (nasalized) /i/ police /o/ hole /ǫ/ home (nasalized) /u/ blue. Underlined vowels are voiceless or whispered. /ʼ/ high pitch. /t/ too /d/ do /k/ king /g/ good (never soft g) /j/ judge or adze /s/ soon /sh/ less heat (never the sh in shirt) /sr/ shrine /sy/ sure /hw/ which (the sound made when you blow out a candle) /h/ hi /ts/ cats hide /ʼ/ (the sound before the first vowel in 'uh-uh') /n/ noon /r/ round /w/ way /y/ yes.

move away (continued)
sa·dǫ́ʼne:k get away; move away
move in
gę·na·din·yǫ́ʼtaʼ I am moving into a dwelling
[ę/ad+ stem: -nadinyǫ(ʼd)$_V$- move in; consists of: -nad(a)$_N$- town, community -inyǫ(ʼd)$_V$- put in]
ga·ǫ·na·díny ʼǫ·taʼ they (f/m) are moving into a dwelling
ę·gę·na·dí:nyǫʼ I will be moving into a dwelling
wat·na·din·yǫ́ʼdǫh it has moved in
go·nę·na·dínyʼǫ·dǫh they (f/m) have moved in
movie
ga·yáʼtaʼ movies; television
[A+ stem: -yaʼtaʼ- movie, television, photographer; consists of: -yaʼd(a)$_N$- body]
mower
gahs·tǫ:drí:yaʼs mower (for hay)
[ga+ stem: -(h)stǫdriyaʼs- mower; consists of: -(h)stǫdr(a)$_N$- straw, hay -(i)yaʼg$_V$- cut, break]
mower see: lawn mower
ga·ga·hoʼjí:yaʼs lawn mower
MP see: G (Member of Parliament, Han·haʼtraʼ)
much see: I (i:soʼ), many, often
ni·yo·nat·gáʼdeʼ there are so many
ot·gáʼdeʼ often; many; lots
mucus
o·jí·nǫhg·raʼ nasal mucus
[o+ stem: -jiʼgr(a), jinǫhgr(a), jinǫdagr(a)$_N$- mucus]
o·jíʼgraʼ mucus
mud see: clay
oʼda:ʼ clay; mud; mortar
mud puppy
nǫh·so·dá·i:yǫ: mud puppies; dogfish
[stem: -nǫhsodaiyǫ:- mud puppy, dogfish; consists of: -nǫhsod(a)$_N$- sickness -iyǫ:$_V$-]
mud slide
da·wa·da·jíhs·dęht there was a mud slide
[d+...ad+ stem: -jihsdęhd- mud slide; consists of: -jihsd(a)$_N$- -(y)ęhd$_V$- hit, knock down, strike]
muddy
oʼdá:griʼ muddy water
[o+ stem: -(ʼ)dagriʼ- muddy; consists of: -(i)ʼd(a:)$_N$- clay, mud, mortar -griʼ$_V$- juice, liquid]
muddy see: dirty
a·gaʼdá·ǫ·niʼ it got muddy
mullet
sga·i:sdó:wa:ʼ mullet
[s+ga+ stem: -(r)ihsdowa:ʼ- mullet; consists of: -(h)wihsd(a), (hr)ihsd(a)$_N$- metal -owa:ʼ$_V$- bitter]
multiply see: grow
ę·wáh·do:k it will multiply, grow
multilingualism see: G (taʼde·ga·wę·na·ge:)
Multiple Sclerosis
wat·sihs·tęhs·rǫ́:nih Multiple Sclerosis
[wa+ stem: -(a)tsihstęhsrǫ:nih- Multiple Sclerosis, M.S.; consists of: -(a)tsihstęhsr(a)$_N$- -ǫni, ǫny$_V$- make]
munch see: chew
de·sáts·ga·hǫ: chew
municipal see: G (ha·di·hahs·hę·hęʼ)
municipality see: G (he·ga·nęt·sa:deʼ), city
ga·na·do·wá:nęh city
murder see: kill
a·hǫ́·wan·yoʼ s.o. killed him
murky
oh·né:kę: it is murky water
[o+ stem: -(h)neg(a)$_N$- water - (h)ę:$_V$- dry]

murky see: muddy
o'dá:gri' muddy water
murmur see: whisper
ęh.sa.ję.hǫ́hsg.wa.ę:' you will whisper
muscular see: strong
ęd.wag.y'a.dah.ní:ya:t we all (incl.) will be strong in body
muscle
o'wa.ha.dé:nyǫ' muscles
[o+ stem: -(')wahadenyǫ'- muscle; consists of: -(')wah(a)$_{N}$- meat -denyǫ'$_{V}$- several existing objects]
Muscular Dystrophy
gahs.ná'da:s Muscular Dystrophy
[ga+ stem: -(h)sna'da:s- Muscular Dystrophy; consists of: -(h)sna('da)$_{N}$- muscle, hamstring, calf -g$_{V}$- eat]
museum
ek.dǫ.dahk.wá'geh museum
[e+ stem: -kdǫdahkwa'geh- museum; consists of: -kdǫd$_{V}$- cause to taste, examine, look closely at s.t. -ahkwa'geh- place]
mush
on.yá.ha' native mush dishes made with corn
[o+ stem: -nyah(a)$_{N}$- mush]
wa.dęh.sǫ́' o.jíhg.wa' roasted corn mush
[consists of: wadęhsǫ' it is roasted; ojihgwa' porridge, mush]
o.nę.hę'ǫ:wéh on.yá.ha' flint corn mush (native dish)
[consists of: onęhę'ǫ:weh flint corn; onyaha' native mush dishes made with corn]
mush see: porridge, sweetmilk pop
o.jíhg.wa' porridge; mush
de.wę'nya.gá:nye:' flour mush; sweetmilk pop
mushroom
on.ráhs.ra' mushroom
[o+ stem: -nrahsr(a)$_{N}$- mushroom]
mushroom see: morel
o.nég.r'ę.da' a morel mushroom
music
ni.ga.e:nó'dę's a kind of music
[ni+ga+ stem: -(r)ęn(a)$_{N}$- song, music -o'dę:$_{V}$- type of]
gá.ę:no:t music playing
[stem: -(r)ęnod- play music; consists of: -(r)ęn(a)$_{N}$- song, music -od$_{V}$- stand]
gá.ę.not.ge: loud, amplified music
[stem: -(r)ęnod- play music; consists of: -(r)ęn(a)$_{N}$- song, music -od$_{V}$- stand, -ge:- big]
ga.ę.no.wá:nęh loud music
[stem: -(r)ęn(a)$_{N}$- song, music -owanęh$_{V}$- be big]
music see: song
gá.ę:na' song
musical group see: band
hę.nad.rę.nó:ta' male singers; a band; a musical group
musk melon see: cantaloupe
wah.yá.is a musk melon; a cantaloupe
muskrat
te.á:ǫt muskrat
[stem: -teaǫd$_{V}$- consists of: -ǫd$_{V}$- attached]
muslin
os.ge.há.i:'ah muslin
[o+ stem: -sgehai:'ah- muslin; consists of: -(h)sgeh(a)$_{N}$- louse -i:'$_{V}$- stuck onto s.t. -'ah diminutive]
mutiny see: revolt
ęt.sę'ni.gǫ́.ho'ne:k you will revolt, remove yourself (bodily and in spirit)
mysterious see: secret
od.rih.wa.séh.dǫh it is secret
myth see: tale
o'ga:' a parable; tale; story; legend

Cayuga pronunciation guide: /a/ father /e/ weigh /ę/ men (nasalized) /i/ police /o/ hole /ǫ/ home (nasalized) /u/ blue. Underlined vowels are voiceless or whispered. /´/ high pitch. /t/ too /d/ do /k/ king /g/ good (never soft g) /j/ judge or adze /s/ soon /sh/ less heat (never the sh in shirt) /sr/ shrine /sy/ sure /hw/ which (the sound made when you blow out a candle) /h/ hi /ts/ cats hide /'/ (the sound before the first vowel in 'uh-uh') /n/ noon /r/ round /w/ way /y/ yes.

N

nag see: hen-pecked
ho·dé'ka:' he is hen-pecked
nail see: fingernail, wire
o·jí'eh·da', **o·jí'oh·da'** fingernails; toenails; animal nails; claws
ga̲h·sǫ́·wa̲h·da' nails; wire; needle
nail clippers
ǫ·de·ji̲'óhg·ya'k·ta' nail clippers
[ǫ+ade+ stem: -ji'ohgya'kta'- nail clippers; consists of: -ji'ohd(a), ji'ehd(a)$_{N}$- fingernail, toenail -(i)ya'kd$_{V}$- cause to cut, break]
nail polish
ǫ·de·j'i·o·da̲h·sóh·ta' nail polish
[ǫ+ade+ stem: -ji'odahsohta'- nail polish; consists of: -ji'ohd(a), ji'ehd(a)$_{N}$- fingernail, toenail -(a)hsohd$_{V}$- colour]
nail puller
eh·sǫ·wa̲h·do·dag·wáh·ta' nail puller
[e+ stem: -(h)sǫwahdodagwahta'- nail puller; consists of: -(h)sǫwahd(a)$_{N}$- wire, nail, needle -odagw$_{V}$- remove, detach]
naked
ga·jí'gwa', **o·jí'gwa'** nakedness; nudity
[ga/o+ stem: -ji'g(wa)$_{N}$- naked]
ga·ji'go·dá:gye' she (lit.: it) is going along nude
[stem: -ji'g(wa)$_{N}$- naked -odagye'$_{V}$- go along doing s.t.]
o'né:sta', **o'nó:sta'** nudity
[o+ stem: -(')no:sd(a)$_{N}$- naked]
name
ga̲h·sę́:na' a name
[ga+ stem: -(h)sęn(a)$_{N}$- name]
ga·díya̲h·sǫh they (z) are called, named
[A+ stem: -yahsǫ(:)$_{V}$- named]
ha·yá:sǫh his name
swa·ya·sǫ·hǫ́:nyǫ' your (p) names
ga·di·yah·sǫ́·hǫn·yǫ' their (z) names

name (continued)
ho·dí·ya̲hs·dǫh they (m) have named it
[stem: -yahsd- name s.o., s.t.; consists of: -yahsǫ(:)$_{V}$- named]
a:yag·wah·sę́:nǫ' we all (excl.) should give it a name
[stem: -(h)sęn(a)$_{N}$- name -awi, ǫ$_{V}$- give]
name see: know
gǫh·sę·ná·ę·di: I know your name
nap see: sleep
ǫ·gí:da' I am sleeping; I slept
nape of neck
o·séh·da' willow; nape of neck
[o+ stem: -sehd(a)$_{N}$- nape, willow]
se·séh·da·gǫ: on the nape of your neck
napkin see: serviette
ǫ·dek·wa·gé·wa̲h·ta' serviettes; napkins
narcissism see: conceited, self-important
ha·dá:ta:' he is conceited
ǫ·dat·go·wá:nęh she is a legend in her own mind, self-important
narrate see: recount, tell
ęt·sa:tró:wi' you will recount, retell
ęd·wa:tró:wi' we all (incl.) will tell
narrative see: tale
o'ga:' a parable; tale; story; legend
narrow
ni·wu'd·rug·yé:'ah it is narrow
[ni+w+ stem: -u'drugye:'ah$_{V}$- narrow]
nation see: country, G
o·dǫh·wę·já:de' country
national see: G (he·yǫh·wę·ja:gwe:gǫh)
Native see: C (Aboriginal, Ǫg·we·hǫ:weh)
nature see: G (na·ha·wa·yę·nan·he'), same
tsa'ó:ya:t it has always been that way; nature
naughty
ek·sa'da̲·hé:tgę' a naughty child
[e+ stem: -ksa('da)$_{N}$- child -(hr)etgę$_{V}$- evil, bad, ugly]

naughty see: bad
de·ta·dih·wa:yé·i: they (m) are corrupt, impish, bad
nauseous
ak·neʼdrʼa·dá:nih I am nauseated, nauseous
[P+ stem: -neʼdraʼdanih$_{V}$- nauseous, nauseated]
navel
get·séʼdo:t my navel
[A+ stem: -(i)tseʼdod- belly button, navel; consists of: -(i)tse(ʼda)$_{N}$- bottle -od$_{V}$- stand]
gik·séʼdo:t my navel
[A+ stem: -kseʼdod- belly button, navel; consists of: -kseʼd(a)$_{N}$- belly -od$_{V}$- stand]
ek·séʼdo:t her belly button
navy see: sailor
ha·di·hǫ·waʼgę·hó:nǫʼ sailors; navy men; merchant marines
near
i·wá:kʼah near
[i+w+ stem: -a:kʼah$_{V}$- near]
dęhs·gę́:hęh near here
[d+s+ga+ stem: -ęhęh- near; consists of: -ęhę(:)$_{V}$- direct, convey]
near see: along, approach, beside, next in line
o·ha·hak·dá:gyeʼ along the edge of the road
ęh·sad·rʼa·nę́:da:k you will get close to s.t., approach it
ak·dá:gyeʼ the edge; beside
sho·nǫ́ʼne:t he is behind him; he is next in line
nearby see: be someplace, I (gaęgwaʼ nhǫ:weh)
gę́:neʼs they (z) are around; they are here; they are together
neat see: tidy
dwa·de·wa·yęhs·dǫ́h ga·gé·hǫʼ it is tidy, neatly placed

necessity
de·yot·wę·jó·hǫh a necessity
[de+yo+at+ stem: -(ǫh)węjohǫh- necessity; consists of: -ǫhwęjoni, ǫhwęjoh$_{V}$- want, need]
ad·wát·wę·johs it became a necessity
[de+...at+ stem: -(ǫh)węjohsd- become necessary; consists of: -ǫhwęjoni, ǫhwęjoh$_{V}$- want, need]
tgá:gǫ:t a compelling must
[t+ga+stem: -gǫd$_{V}$- persevere, linger; necessity, duty]
neck
ohn·yaʼ the neck; the throat
[o+stem: -(h)nya(ʼsa)$_{N}$- neck, throat]
ohn·yáʼsaʼ neck
ohn·yáʼsa·gǫ: in the throat
sęhn·yáʼsʼa·geh on your neck
gęhn·yáʼsʼa·geh on my neck (front of neck)
gahn·yáʼse:s it has a long neck
[stem: -(h)nya(ʼsa)$_{N}$- neck, throat -es$_{V}$- long]
neck (have around one's neck)
sat·géh·dǫh you have it around your neck
[at+ stem: -gehd$_{V}$- have around one's neck]
neck (put around one's neck)
sat·géh·da:s you put it around your neck all the time
[at+ stem: -gehdad- put around one's neck; consists of: -gehd$_{V}$- have around one's neck]
ęh·sá·gęh·da:t you will put s.t. around your neck
se·géh·da:t put it around your neck
a·sáht·gęh·da:t you put it on now
ęh·sat·re·ná·gęh·da:t you will put it (a load) around your neck
[at+ stem: -(hr)ehn(a)$_{N}$- cargo, -gehdad- put around one's neck]

Cayuga pronunciation guide: /a/ father /e/ weigh /ę/ men (nasalized) /i/ police /o/ hole /ǫ/ home (nasalized) /u/ blue. Underlined vowels are voiceless or whispered. /ˊ/ high pitch. /t/ too /d/ do /k/ king /g/ good (never soft g) /j/ judge or adze /s/ soon /sh/ less heat (never the sh in shirt) /sr/ shrine /sy/ sure /hw/ which (the sound made when you blow out a candle) /h/ hi /ts/ cats hide /ʼ/ (the sound before the first vowel in 'uh-uh') /n/ noon /r/ round /w/ way /y/ yes.

necklace
os·dá·oʼgwaʼ necklace
[o+ stem: -(h)sdaoʼg(wa)- necklace; consists of: -(h)sd(a:)$_{N}$- drop (of water) -oʼ$_{V}$- be submerged -g(wa)$_{N}$- a lump]
need see: lack, necessity, want
da·wá·dʼok·dęʼ it lacked; it was not enough
dęh·sa·do̱h·wę:jǫ́:niʼ you will want s.t.
needle
eʼni·kǫhk·wáʼ ga̱h·sǫ́·wa̱h·daʼ needle
[consists of: eʼnikǫhkwaʼ sewing item; ga̱hsǫwa̱hdaʼ nails, wire, needle]
needle see: wire
ga̱h·sǫ́·wa̱h·daʼ nails; wire; needle
neglect
dehs·gáhs·dis·taʼ I no longer pay attention
[deʼ+ not stem: -(a)hsdisd$_{V}$- pay attention, bother with; neglect, ignore]
negotiate see: barter
dęhs·nǫ́·wa·yęht you will barter, bargain, affirm a deal
Negro see: C (African-American Ha·hǫʼjiʼ)
neighbour see: C (des·wę·no̱h·sa·ka·hǫʼ)
nephew see: C (he·yǫ·hwa:dęʼ, he·ya·daʼwęʼ)
nerve
sa·gǫh·sa̱h·ní:yǫh you've got nerve! (lit.: you've got a hard face)
[P+ stem: -gǫhs(a)$_{N}$- face -(h)niyǫh$_{V}$- hard, tough]
nerves
gę·nih·na·dó·ga·taʼ nerve
[ga+ stem: -ęnihnadogataʼ- nerves, emotions, feelings; consists of: -ęnihnadog$_{V}$- perceive]
shę́h dwa·nih·na·dógʼa·taʼ human emotions; feelings; nerves
o·nih·na·dók·da̱hk·waʼ nerves; sensations

nerves (continued)
[o+ stem: -ęnihnadokdahkwaʼ- nerves, sensations; consists of: -ęnihnadog$_{V}$- perceive -dahkwaʼ instrument]
gę·nih·na·dók·da̱hk·waʼ my nerves
nervous
wa·dǫ́n·ya̱h·nǫ: it is nervous
[A+ad+ stem: -ǫnyahnǫ(:)- move around, be nervous; consists of: -ǫnyahn$_{V}$- go and move around]
nervous see: fidgety, shake
sat·naʼt·sa·gę́:nyeʼ you are fidgety
sa·yaʼdǫ·dáʼtaʼ you are nervous, shaking, shivering
nest
o·déhs·hęʼ cocoon; nest; hive; bee-hive
[o+ stem: -(a)dehs(a)$_{N}$- nest -ę$_{V}$- lie on the ground]
o·ná·de̱h·sęʼ they (z) (bees, etc.) have a nest
wa·déhs·hęʼ it made its nest
net see: hair net, web
ot·ge:o·wé:k·taʼ a hair net
o·dáʼa·ǫt a web; a net
neuter
ę·hǫ·waʼsgwá:da̱h·goʼ they will geld, neuter, fix him
[TR+ stem: -(h)sgwadahgw- neuter, geld; consists of: -(h)sg(wa:)$_{N}$- stone, bullet, rock -(h)gw$_{V}$- remove]
gahs·gwá:da̱hg·węh a neutered animal; a gelding
never see: I (tęʼ hwę:dǫh)
never mind
hę́:gyeʼ never mind
[h+ę+g+ stem: -ye(:)$_{V}$- do]
new
á:se:ʼ it is fresh, new
[(wa+) stem: -(a)se:$_{V}$- new]
sha·yáhk·wa:se: you have new pants
[A/P+N+ stem: -yahk(wa)$_{N}$- pants -(a)se:$_{V}$- new]

newborn
gog·wę́·hęh·dǫh a new-born baby
[(ya)go+ stem: -ǫgwęhęhdǫh- new-born; consists of: -ǫgweh$_{N}$- person -(y)ęhd- hit, knock down, strike]
go·dǫ:hǫ́:niʼ newborn child
[(ya)go+ stem: -(a)dǫhǫniʼ- toddler]
newborn see: child
o·wi·yá:ʼah baby
newcomer see: stranger
ti·yǫg·wʼe·dá:deʼ a stranger
newspaper
de·ga·ihs·dó·ha·gǫh a newspaper
[de+ga+stem: -(r)ihsdohagǫh- newspaper; consists of: -(r)ihsdohag- publish]
New York, N.Y. see: E (Ga·nǫ:nyoʼ)
next
haʼdehsg·ya·dǫ·dá·i:ʼ next week
[haʼde+s+g+ stem: -yadǫd(a)$_{N}$- week -i:ʼ$_{V}$- stuck onto s.t.; be next]
néʼ hwáʼ he·jó·nǫh·sǫ:t the room after the next room
[neʼ hwaʼ heʼ+s+A/P+N stem: -nǫhs(a)$_{N}$- house -ǫd$_{V}$- attached]
sho·nǫ́ʼne:t he is behind him, he is next in line
[s+P+ stem: -nǫʼned- be next in line, behind; consists of: -nǫʼ(a:), nǫh(a)$_{N}$- head -ned$_{V}$- keep]
next see: I, alongside
Niagara Falls see: E (Tga̲h·na·wę̲h·taʼ, Ga̲h·na·we̲h·taʼ)
Niagara-On-The-Lake, Ont. see: E (Tga·na̲h·wai:ʼ)
nibble see: chew
de·sáts·ga·hǫ: chew it
nice
saʼni·gǫ·hí:yo: you have a good mind
[P+ stem: -(ʼ)nigǫh(a)$_{N}$- mind -iyo:$_{V}$- be nice, good]
hes·hoʼni·gǫ·hí:yo: his mind is good over there
nice (continued)
sǫg·weʼdí:yo: you are a nice person
[A+ stem: -ǫgwe(ʼda)$_{N}$- person -iyo:$_{V}$- be nice, good]
gǫg·weʼdí:yo: I am a nice person
a·gǫg·wʼe·dí:yo: she/s.o. is a nice person
hǫg·weʼdí:yo: he is a charming, polite, nice person
sa·węh·ni̲hs·rí:yohs, a·węh·ni̲hs·rí:yohs it became a nice day again
[A/P+N+ stem: -iyohsd- become nice, good; consists of: -ęhnihsr(a)$_{N}$- day -iyo:$_{V}$- be nice, good]
nice see: good, humble
o·yá:nreʼ it is nice, good, beautiful
go·ni·gǫ̲·ha:ní:dęht she is gentle, nice, humble
nick see: notch
a·há·nohs·ga:ʼ he notched it (a tree, a casket)
nickel see: B (hwihsg·wę·nihs)
niece see: C (ke·ha·wa:kʼah, ga·ge·he·yǫh·wa:dęʼ)
night
ah·sǫ́·heh·ka:ʼ night kind
[stem: -(a)hsǫ(da)$_{N}$- night, blackness]
night see: A (ahsǫheh)
nightfall see: sunset
haʼgáhg·węʼ sunset; the sun went down
night stand
e·jihs·da̲·hahk·wáʼ a·dek·wa·háhs·raʼ night stand
[consists of: ejihsda̲hahkwaʼ s.t. that supports a light; adekwahahsraʼ table]
night-fish
a·hę·na·tahs·rǫ·dáhnaʼ they (m) went night-fishing
[at+ stem: -(h)ahsrǫd- night-fish, spear-fish, jack-light; consists of: -(h)ahsr(a)$_{N}$- flash -ǫd$_{V}$- attached]
ę·hę·na·tahs·rǫ·dáh·naʼ they (m) will go jack-lighting, spear-fishing

Cayuga pronunciation guide: /a/ father /e/ weigh /ę/ men (nasalized) /i/ police /o/ hole /ǫ/ home (nasalized) /u/ blue. Underlined vowels are voiceless or whispered. /ʹ/ high pitch. /t/ too /d/ do /k/ king /g/ good (never soft g) /j/ judge or adze /s/ soon /sh/ less heat (never the sh in shirt) /sr/ shrine /sy/ sure /hw/ which (the sound made when you blow out a candle) /h/ hi /ts/ cats hide /ʼ/ (the sound before the first vowel in 'uh-uh') /n/ noon /r/ round /w/ way /y/ yes.

nightgown
go·dá'sta' a nightgown; her / s.o.'s pyjamas
[(ya)go+ stem: -(i)da'sta'- nightgown, pyjamas; consists of: -(i)da'sd - cause to sleep]
nightgown see: sleeper
o·wi:ya:'áh go·dá'sta' baby's sleeper, night gown
nightmare
a·ga·ded·rę̨h·dat·gih·da·níhs·gę̨·hę̨:' I used to have bad dreams
[P+ (a)de+ stem: -(')drę̨hdatgihd(ę̨, ani)$_V$- have a nightmare]
ǫ·ga·ded·rę̨·dat·gí·dę̨' I had a bad dream
go·yá'dit·gę̨'s she is having a nightmare; she is sleepwalking
[P+ stem: -ya'ditgę̨'s- nightmare; consists of: -ya'd(a)$_N$- body -itgę̨'$_V$- rise]
ǫg·ya'dit·gę̨́h·sǫ:' nightmares
nimble see: agile, quick
ha·ya'tgá·i·ye' he is agile
gya't·ga·hí:ye' I am quick
nine see: B (gyǫh·dǫ:)
nineteen see: B (gyǫh·dǫ: sga·e')
ninety see: B (gyǫh·dǫ: ni·wahs·hę̨:)
nip see: bite
got·só·hi·hǫh I have bit it
nipple
o·nǫ́n·he'dra' soother; pacifier; nipple
[o+ stem: -nǫnhe'dr(a)$_N$- nipple]
sa'nǫn·he'drá'geh on your nipples
knǫ·he'drá'geh on my nipples
swa·nǫn·he'drá'geh on your (p) nipples
no see: I (tę̨', hę̨'ę̨h)
nobility see: G (royalty, gwa:go:wah)
noble see: righteous
hod·rih·wag·wá·ih·sǫh he is a noble person

nod one's head
de·sat·nǫ'á·ę̨·dǫh nod; shake your head
[de+...at+ stem: -nǫ'aę̨dǫ- nod one's head, shake one's head; consists of: -nǫ'(a:), nǫh(a)$_N$- head -ę̨dǫh$_V$- shake s.t.]
noise
ot·ga:' noise
[P+at+ stem: -ga:$_V$- make a rattling or grinding noise, be loud]
ot·gá·i'ni: it is noisy, loud
[(y)o+at+ stem: -gai(ni:)$_V$- make a rattling or grinding noise, loud]
a'ót·ga·i: it made a noise
de·yohs·da·wę̨́'dra·ga: a rattling noise (from a rattle)
[de+yo+ stem: -(h)sdawę̨'dr(a)$_N$- rattle -ga:$_V$- make a rattling or grinding noise]
de·yohs·gę̨·drá:ga: a tinny, metallic rattling noise
[de+yo+ stem: -(h)sgę̨'dr(a)$_N$- rust, mould -ga:$_V$- make a rattling or grinding noise]
ag·yoh·sa·gá·e: there was the sound of smacking lips
[de+yo+ stem: -(h)sa(:), (h)sag(a)$_N$- mouth -ga:, gae$_V$- make a rattling or grinding noise]
ohs·dá:ga: the sound of the rain
[o+ stem: -(h)sdaga(:)- the sound of rain; consists of: -(h)sd(a:)$_N$- drop (of water) -ga:$_V$- make a rattling or grinding noise]
a·gan·ho·há:yę̨ht there was a noise made by banging a door
[stem: -nhohayę̨hd- bang a door; consists of: -nho(ha)$_N$- door -(y)ę̨hd$_V$- hit, knock down, strike]
o·hǫ́:ga't a clear sound
[o+ stem: -(a)hǫga'd- sound; consists of: -(a)hǫg$_V$- hear, learn how to speak a language, understand]

noise (continued)
ho·wę́:sęh·dǫh he is keeping a beat with his feet
[P+ stem: -ęhsędǫh- tap one's foot repetitively; consists of: -(a)hsi(ʼda), (ę)hs(a)$_N$- foot -ędǫh$_V$- shake s.t.]
sęh·sę:dǫh you are tapping your foot
de·sęh·sę́:dǫh you are stamping your feet (moving them up and down)
[de+ P+ stem: -ęhsędǫh- stamp one's feet up and down; consists of: -(a)hsi(ʼda), (ę)hs(a)$_N$- foot -ędǫh$_V$- shake s.t.]
de·yoh·sʼi·dá:ga: to stamp one's feet (lit.: it stamped its feet)
[de+... stem: -(a)hsiʼdaga:- stamp one's feet; consists of: -(a)hsi(ʼda), (ę)hs(a)$_N$- foot -ga:$_V$- make a rattling or grinding noise]
de·ga·noʼjá:ga: grinding teeth
[de+ ga+ stem: -noʼj(a)$_N$- tooth -ga:$_V$- make a rattling or grinding noise]
ę·sná·ga·i: you will whistle
[stem: -naʼg(a)$_N$- horn, antler -naga:, nagai$_V$- whistle]
nominate see: appoint, elect, include
a·hǫ·wa·i·hǫ́:dęʼ they delegated him a duty
a·hǫ·wa·díʼd·rǫʼ they placed him, elected him
há·ǫ·nyah·nǫʼ he has included, designated it
none
dehs·gá:yęʼ there is none
[(tęʼ) deʼ+ not (s+)ga+ stem: -(y)ęʼ$_V$- lie on the ground; exist]
tę́ʼ de·gá:yęʼ there is not any
none see: I (nothing, tęʼ, sgahoʼdęʼ)
noon see: A (gaǫ:hyahęh)
north
o·tó·wʼe·geh north
[o+ stem: -(a)toweʼgeh- north; consists of: -(a)tow(eʼ)$_V$- cold (weather), -ʼgeh at -(h)neh at]
o·to·wʼe·géh·neh North place
nose
oʼn·yǫ́h·saʼ a nose
[o+ stem: -(ʼ)nyǫhs(a)$_N$- nose]
sʼen·yǫ́h·sʼa·geh on your nose
gʼan·yǫ́ʼse:s a long nose
[stem: -(ʼ)nyǫhs(a)$_N$- nose -es$_V$- long]
nose see: runny
a·ge·jʼin·yǫ́hg·ro:t I have a runny nose
nosy see: mischievous
de·saʼnyǫhs·wá·haʼt you can't keep your hands off; you're nosy
not see: I (o: tęʼǫh, tęʼ)
notable see: greatest, special
néʼ gya·ǫ·hę́:ʼęh the greatest
o·i·ho·wá:nęh it is important; a great or worthy commendation; it is special
notch
gah·węʼgaʼó:ʼo: it is notched
[A+ hwęʼga/N+ stem: -(hwęʼga)ʼoh$_V$- notch]
gah·węʼga:tgwęh it is notched (that is, a casket)
a·há·noh·sga:ʼ he notched it (a tree, a casket)
[stem: -nohsga:$_V$- notch s.t.]
note see: fault, paper
o·íh·waʼ a message; it matters; it is its fault
gah·yá·dǫhs·raʼ paper
nothing see: I, (tęʼ) sgahoʼdęʼ
notice see: see
a·gé:gęʼ I saw
notion see: idea
o·íh·wa·geh the reason; the idea for s.t.
nourish see: feed, live on
ęk·nǫ:t I will give it s.t.to eat
ę·yǫn·heh·gǫ́·hǫk it will live on

Cayuga pronunciation guide: /a/ father /e/ weigh /ę/ men (nasalized) /i/ police /o/ hole /ǫ/ home (nasalized) /u/ blue. Underlined vowels are voiceless or whispered. /ʹ/ high pitch. /t/ too /d/ do /k/ king /g/ good (never soft g) /j/ judge or adze /s/ soon /sh/ less heat (never the sh in shirt) /sr/ shrine /sy/ sure /hw/ which (the sound made when you blow out a candle) /h/ hi /ts/ cats hide /ʼ/ (the sound before the first vowel in 'uh-uh') /n/ noon /r/ round /w/ way /y/ yes.

nourishment see: food
gak·wa' food
November see: A (Jo:to:')
novice see: learn
ǫ·de·wa·yę́·s·ta' she is a novice, a learner, a beginner
now see: I (o:nęh, gǫdagye')
now and again, now and then see: I (ogwęhę:gye')
nowhere see: I (tę' ga'toh)
nozzle see: tube, water spout
ga̲·ho·w'e·dahs·hǫ́:'ǫh hoses; cylinders
de·gah·ne·gáhk·wa' water spout
nude see: naked
ga·ji'go·dá:gye' she (lit.: it) is going along nude
nudge see: poke, touch
des·wá'ehs·ta' you all are poking
ha'gye:' I touched it
nuisance
des·ha·y'a·da'ni·gǫ́·ha:t you are a nuisance
[de'+not ...TR/adę+ stem: -(')nigǫhad- be a nuisance; consists of: -(')nigǫha(:)$_V$- expect, watch]
dę̲·ha'ni·gǫ·há:ha' he is a nuisance, a bother
[de+... stem: -(')nigǫha(ę,nih)- bother s.o., annoy; consists of: -(')nigǫh(a)$_N$- mind -(')nigǫha(:)$_V$- expect, watch]
numb
a'ót·sihs·dęh it got numb
[(y)o+ stem: -tsihsdę(h,')$_V$- become numb]
ot·sís·da̲'ǫh it is numb
ot·sís·hę'ǫh it is numb
[o+ stem: -tsihshę(h,')$_V$- be numb]
number
ohs·hé:da' number
[o+ stem: -(a)hshed$_V$- count]
ní:yǫ: an amount of things
[ni+A+ stem: -ǫ$_V$- number (of things)]

number (continued)
ni·gę́:nǫ: that many animals
dó: ní:yǫ: how many
number see: count, same
ęd·was·hé:dǫh we all (incl.) will give a number; we all will number
tsa'de·yohs·hé:dęh it is the same number of things
numeral see: number
ohs·hé:da' number
nun see: Catholic
dę̲·ga·e·yáh·sǫ·ta' Catholics; nuns
nuptials see: marriage
ga·náhk·wa' a marriage; a wife
nurse
de·yǫ·te·yǫ'da̲hs·nyé·ha' nurse
[de+A+at+ stem: -(h)eyǫ'dahsnyeha'- nurse; consists of: -(he)yǫ(’da)$_N$- corpse, cadaver -(h)snye$_V$- care for, look after]
nursing home
ga·e·gę̲h·jihs·hǫ́'
sha·go·di·nǫh·son·yá:ni: nursing home
[consists of: gaegę̲hjihshǫh they are old; shagodinǫhsonya:ni: nursing home]
ga·e·gę̲h·jihs·hǫ́' he·ya·go·na·da·dá·ǫ: nursing home
[consists of: gaegę̲hjihshǫh they are old; heyagonadadaǫ: they (f/m) are a remainder]
nurture see: live on
ę·yǫn·heh·gǫ́·hǫk it will live on
nut
ohn·yó'gwa' nut
[o+ stem: -(h)nyo'g(wa)$_N$- nut]
te·o:jí' ohn·yó'gwa' acorn
[consists of: teo:ji' iron wood (tree); ohnyo'gwa' nut]
nutmeat
ohn·ya:' nutmeat
[o+ stem: -(h)ny(a:)$_N$- nutmeat]

nuts and bolts
ga̲hn·yǫ'srá' ga·di·yé:nahs nuts and bolts
[consists of: ga̲hnyǫ'sra' a bar; gadiye:-nahs they (z) catch s.t.]
nutshell
ok·da' a nutshell
[o+ stem: -kd(a)$_N$- nutshell]
nylons
gan·heh·sa·ga:hę:háh a·dáh·d'it·ra' nylons
[consists of: ganhehsaga:hę:hah nylons; adahd'itra' socks]
gan·heh·sa·ga:hę́:hah nylons
[ga+ stem: -nhehsaga:hę:hah- nylons; consists of: -nhehsag(a)$_N$- silk -(h)ę:hah, hę:hęh$_V$- thin]
nylons see: panty hose
o·dah·d'it·rǫ́:t at·ná'tsot·ra' panty hose

O

o.k. see: I (hao')
o'clock see: A (ohwihsda'e:)
oak
gó:wih red oak
[stem: -gowih- red oak]
ga·gá'da' white oak
[ga+ stem: -ga'd(a)$_N$- white oak]
oak see: ironwood
te·ó:ji' iron wood (tree); red oak
obedient see: listen to s.t.
ęh·sa·da̲·hǫh·si·yóhs·ta:k you will listen, obey
obese see: fat
hoh·sę: he is fat
obey see: listen to s.o., serve
ęh·sa·da̲·hǫh·si·yóhs·ta:k you will listen, obey
ahs·he:hahs you did serve her
object see: disagree
ta'deg·ri̲h·wáhs·nye' I oppose it; I do not agree
objective see: righteous
god·rih·wag·wá·eh·sǫh she is fair, righteous
obligation see: responsibility
ga·ih·wa·géh·de' responsibility
obliging see: help
ho·ye·na·wá'sgǫ: he is a willing helper
oblong see: rectangle
dek·nihs·hó' tsa'dé:yǫ:s rectangle, oblong
obnoxious see: happy-go-lucky
ho·dę·dǫn·yá'da̲hs·gǫ: he is a joker; he is happy-go-lucky; he is obnoxious
obscure see: hide oneself, fuzzy
ę·gá·da̲h·seht I will hide
ta'de·yo·ga·há·ę·daht it is fuzzy, out of focus, opaque, unclear
observable see: visible
ó:gę't it is visible
observance see: celebration, ceremony
o·dǫt·ga·déhs·ra' celebration
od·rih·wa̲h·dę́:gyǫ: the ceremony
observant see: quick-witted
ha'de·ho·íh·wa·ge: he is quick-witted; he has lots of business, different ideas, many ideas; he is into everything
observe see: see
a·há:gę' he saw
obsolete see: old (thing)
o·gá:yǫh it is old
obstruct see: quit
a:hę·ní:hę:' he would stop (himself)
a·tá:dahs he stopped it, prevented it
obtain see: acquire, purchase, catch
ę·sa·yę́:da' you will acquire, obtain
ęh·sní:nǫ' you will buy, purchase
ag·yé:na:' I caught it; I received it
obtrude see: protrude
he·yá·ǫ:t it protrudes

Cayuga pronunciation guide: /a/ father /e/ weigh /ę/ men (nasalized) /i/ police /o/ hole /ǫ/ home (nasalized) /u/ blue. Underlined vowels are voiceless or whispered. /'/ high pitch. /t/ too /d/ do /k/ king /g/ good (never soft g) /j/ judge or adze /s/ soon /sh/ less heat (never the sh in shirt) /sr/ shrine /sy/ sure /hw/ which (the sound made when you blow out a candle) /h/ hi /ts/ cats hide /'/ (the sound before the first vowel in 'uh-uh') /n/ noon /r/ round /w/ way /y/ yes.

obvious see: recognizable
o·yę́:deht it is recognizable, plain to be seen, conspicuous
occupation
ni·sa·i·hoʼdęhs·róʼdę: your occupation; your type of work
[ni+P+ stem: -(ri)hoʼdęhsr(a)$_{N}$- work -oʼdę:$_{V}$- type of]
occupy see: dwell, inhabit
o·dí·nǫh·so:t they (z) dwell
ę·sat·na·dá·ęʼ you will inhabit
occur see: emerge unintentionally, happen, start from
a·ǫ·yę·déh·teʼ it emerged unintentionally
ni·yá:węhs how it happens
tę·wa·da·dǫ́:niʼ it will emerge or appear unintentionally; it will do it by itself
ocean
o·ji·keʼ·dág·riʼgeh oceans
[o+ stem: -jikeʼdagriʼgeh- ocean; consists of: -jikeʼd(a)$_{N}$- salt -griʼ$_{V}$- juice, liquid -(ʼ)geh at]
ocean liner
ga̲·hǫ·waʼgó:wah ocean liner
[ga+ stem: -(h)ǫwagowah- ocean liner; consists of: -(h)ǫw(a)$_{N}$- boat -gowah- big]
October see: A (Saʼge̲h·neh·go:wah)
odd
og·ya·nǫh·sá:nǫht a weird, odd, spooky house
[P+N+ stem: -nǫhs(a)$_{N}$- house -nǫhd$_{V}$- spooky]
ti·yo·ye̲hs·rá·deʼ it is an odd-ball blanket
[ti+A/P+N+ stem: -yęhsr(a)$_{N}$- blanket -deʼ$_{V}$- exist; be different, unusual]
odd see: different, strange, unusual
de·sáh·di̲·hęh you are different
og·yá:nǫhk it is strange, bizarre
ti·yó:tʼah it is queer, unusual, odd
odour
o·ded·rę·ná·i:ʼ an odour
[o+(a)de+ stem: -dręn(a)$_{N}$- smell -i:ʼ$_{V}$- stuck onto s.t.]
od·rę́·na·deht a strong odour; a smell
[P+N+ stem: -dręn(a)$_{N}$- smell -dehd$_{V}$- bold, bright, strong]
gad·rę·no·wá:nęh a big smell, odour, scent
[stem: -dręn(a)$_{N}$- smell -owanęh$_{V}$- be big]
odiferous see: strong-smelling
gad·rę·na̲hs·há:sdeʼ it is a strong smell; it is strong-smelling
of see: I (shęh, tsęh)
offend
ęhs·heʼni·gǫ́·haʼe:k you will offend s.o.
[TR+ stem: -(ʼ)nigǫhaʼeg- offend; consists of: -(ʼ)nigǫh(a)$_{N}$- mind -(ʼ)e$_{V}$- hit]
offend see: condemn
she·yéh·sa̲h·taʼ you always condemn, insult, slander s.o.
offensive see: bother, happy-go-lucky, unpleasant
dęhs·ni·gǫ·há:haʼ you are annoying me, bothering me
ho·dę·dǫn·yáʼda̲hs·gǫ: he is a joker; he is happy-go-lucky; he is obnoxious
de·a·ǫ·wé:saht it is unpleasant
offer see: give, present
shǫg·wá:wi: he has given us
ęh·sá:dǫʼ you will present, offer s.t.; you will become s.t.
office see: G (ho·nad·rih·wahs·di:hs·dǫh), room
o·nǫ́h·sǫ:t a room; a vault
offspring see: child, tadpole
a·géksʼa·daʼ my child
ohs·twá:sah a young animal; a little animal; a tadpole
often
ot·gáʼdeʼ often; many; lots
[o+at+stem: -gaʼdeʼ$_{V}$- many, lots, often]

Ohsweken, Ont. see: E (Os·we:gę', Gyę·hahs·hę·dahk·wa')

oil

oh·na' grease, oil

[o+ stem: -(h)n(a)$_N$- oil, gas, grease]

oh·na'shǫ́:'ǫh a variety of oils; greasy materials

oh·ná·de·ka: burning oil

[P+(N+) stem: -(h)n(a)$_N$- oil, gas -(a)deg$_V$- burn up]

ǫt·náh·ta' oil (for the bath)

[ǫ+at+ stem: -nahta'- oil; consists of: -(h)n(a)$_N$- oil, gas]

o·wi:ya:'áh ǫt·náh·ta' baby oil

[consists of: owi:ya:'ah baby; ǫtnahta' oil (for the bath)]

a·hat·na:sǫ' he did oil himself

[(a)t+ stem: -(h)nasǫ(:)- oil oneself; consists of: -(h)n(a)$_N$- oil, gas -sǫ$_V$- stir]

sat·ná:sǫ: oil yourself

oil see: grease

sna:sǫ́: g'ad·réh·da' lubricate, grease the car

oily

oh·ná·i:' it is oily, greasy

[o+ stem: -(h)n(a)$_N$- oil, gas -i:'$_V$- stuck onto s.t.]

ointment see: heal

ęh·sa:tné:yǫ:' you will heal yourself (with medicinal ointments)

Oka, Que. see: E (Ga·neh·sa·da:geh)

Oklahoma see: E (Ga̲h·na·wi·yo'geh)

old (in years)

dó: ni·sohs·ri·yá'gǫh how old are you

[ni+P+ stem: -ohsriya'gǫh- be a certain age; consists of: -(o)hsr(a)$_N$- year, winter -(i)ya'g$_V$- cut, break, cross]

dó: ni·ya·go·nohs·ri·yá'gǫh how old are they (f/m)

old (living thing)

go̲hs·dę́:'ęh she is old

[P+ stem: -(a)sdę:'ęh$_V$- old (living thing)]

old (continued)

hohs·dę́:'ęh he is old; he is an old man

ohs·dę́:'ęh it is old (for example, an old dog or cat)

gohs·dę́h·ya·i she is an older woman

old (person)

ha·gęh·jí:hah he is an old man; he is getting old, getting on

[A+ stem: -gęhjih$_V$- old (person)]

ga·e·gęh·jíhs·hǫh they are old

old (thing)

o·gá:yǫh it is old

[o+ stem: -gayǫh$_V$- old (thing)]

o·gá·yǫh·sǫ' old things

ga·ę·na·gá·yǫh·sǫ' old songs

[A/P+(N+) stem: -gayohsǫ'- several old things; consists of: -(r)ęn(a)$_N$- song, music -gayǫhsǫ'$_V$- old (things)]

old see: age, elder

ni·sohs·ri·yá'gǫh you are a certain number ofyears old.

ha·di·gęh·ji·sǫ́:'ǫh they (m) are old men, male elders

ombudsman

en·há'tra' ombudsman, etc.

[A+ stem: -nha'tr(a)$_N$- employee, civil servant, minister -nha'$_V$- command, hire]

ombudsman see: G (En·ha'tra')

omen

wat·sǫ́:nyǫ:s omen

[w+ at+ stem: -sǫnyǫs$_V$- omen]

ominous see: evil power, lack a spirit

go·ná:tgǫh they (f/m) are a force to be reckoned with; they (f/m) are ominous; they are bad medicine people

o:nę́h de·ja·go·na'gó:wahs she is ominous

omit see: forget, neglect

sǫk·ní·gǫ·hęh I forgot

dehs·gáhs·dis·ta' I no longer pay attention

Cayuga pronunciation guide: /a/ father /e/ weigh /ę/ men (nasalized) /i/ police /o/ hole /ǫ/ home (nasalized) /u/ blue. Underlined vowels are voiceless or whispered. /'/ high pitch. /t/ too /d/ do /k/ king /g/ good (never soft g) /j/ judge or adze /s/ soon /sh/ less heat (never the sh in shirt) /sr/ shrine /sy/ sure /hw/ which (the sound made when you blow out a candle) /h/ hi /ts/ cats hide /'/ (the sound before the first vowel in 'uh-uh') /n/ noon /r/ round /w/ way /y/ yes.

on
[-agǫ: internal locative suffix; means 'in', 'on', or 'under']
[-ʼgeh external locative suffixes; denote a place]
once more see: I (e:ʼ)
once see: B (sga:t hę.wa:dra:s)
one
sga.yáʼda:t one animal; one living thing
[s+A/P+N+ stem: -yaʼd(a)$_N$- body -d$_V$- stand; be one item]
sgats.hǫ́:ʼǫh one by one
[stem: sga:t one]
one see: I (sga:t), B (neʼgiʼgyę:ʼ)
one after another, one apart, one at a time, each
jǫh.síʼdat.sǫʼ one foot apart
[s+A/P+N+ stem: -ts(h)ǫʼ- one after another, one at a time; consists of: -(a)hsi(ʼda), (ę)hs(a)$_N$- foot -tsǫʼ$_V$- several standing objects]
sgad.réh.dat.sǫʼ each car
[s+A/P+N+ stem: -ts(h)ǫʼ- one after another, one at a time; consists of: -(ʼ)drehd(a)$_N$- vehicle, car -tsǫʼ$_V$- several standing objects]
jo.yę́hs.rat.sǫʼ one blanket at a time
[s+A/P+N+ stem: -ts(h)ǫʼ- one after another, one at a time; consists of: -yęhsr(a)$_N$- blanket -tsǫʼ$_V$- several standing objects]
one after another
[-atsǫʼ the verb 'stand' with pluralizer; used in expressions meaning 'each' or 'individually' or 'one after another']
one more see: another
he.jo:yáʼ tsǫ: another thing again; elsewhere; on a tangent
one-night stand
hot.sínah.dǫʼ a one-night stand (lit.: he's got his leg buried someplace)
[P+(a)t+ stem: -(h)sinahdǫ- one-night stand; consists of: -(h)sin(a)$_N$- leg -(a)hdǫ$_V$- hide]
Oneida see: C (Ohn.ya.hę.ho:nǫʼ)
Oneida, N.Y. see: E (O.nę.yot.ga:ʼ)
Oneida, Ont. see: E (Ohn.ya.hęh)
ongoing
[-dagyeʼ the verb 'stand' with progressive; meaning 'to continue on', 'to be ongoing']
onion
oʼnǫ́h.saʼ onions
[o+ stem: -(ʼ)nǫhs(a)$_N$- onion]
onlooker see: witness
ęhs.rih.wag.wá.ih.siʼ you will be a witness
only see: I (tsǫ:)
Onondaga, Ont. see: E (O.nǫn.da.geh)
Onondaga people see: C (O.nǫ.da.ge.ho:nǫʼ)
Ontario see: E (Gan.ya.da.i.yoʼ)
onward see: ahead
he.yo.daʼgwá.is.hǫ: straight ahead
opaque see: fuzzy
taʼde.yo.ga.há.ę.daht it is fuzzy, out of focus, opaque, unclear
open
gen.hó.dǫg.wahs I open it, unlock it
[stem: -nhodǫgw$_V$- open]
a.gen.ho.dǫ́:gwęh I have opened, unlocked it
gan.hó.dǫ.gwęh it is open
sen.ho:dǫ́:goh open the door
ę.ha.ih.wan.ho.dǫ́:goʼ he will open the gathering
[stem: -(r)ihwanhodǫgw- open a gathering; consists of: -(r)ih(wa)$_N$- word -nhodǫgw$_V$- open]
se.ji.ho.dá:goh open it
[stem: -jihodagw- open, turn on; consists of: -jihod$_V$- close, turn off]

opener see: can opener
e.ji.ho.dág.wah.ta' a can opener; a bottle opener
opening see: door, gap
gan.hó.ha' door
de.ya.ǫh.wę́:de' a gap; an opening
operate
hǫ.wa.di.ya'da.hé:neh they operate on him
[TR+ stem: -ya'dahe(n)- operate; consists of: -ya'd(a)$_N$- body -(hr)e(n)$_V$- cut]
a.hǫ.wa.di.y'a.dá.he:' they gave him an operation
operator see: telephone operator
ǫd.wę.nǫ.dah.tá' gohs.díhs.dǫh telephone operator
opinion see: idea, think
o.íh.wa.geh the reason; the idea for s.t.
ga.ya'do.wéh.dǫ:' the idea of thinking
opinionated see: self-centred
sa.dág.ya.da's you are opinionated
opossum
o.yǫ́.dih opossum
[o+ stem: -yǫdih - opossum; consists of: -yǫdi, yǫgy$_V$- smile]
oppose see: disapprove, denounce, disagree
des.rih.wa.nǫ́h.we's you disapprove
dęhs.ríh.wa.ya:'k you will denounce it, disapprove of it
ta'deg.rih.wáhs.nye' I oppose it; I do not agree
opposite see: other
o.yá:jih another type
optimism see: happiness
ot.sę́.nǫn.ya't a happy feeling; gratefulness; thankfulness; joy
option see: choose
ęhs.rá:go' you will choose it, take it out
or see: I (nigę'ǫh)
orange
o.jít.gwa:ji: orange colour
[o+ stem: -jitgwaji:- orange; consists of: -jitgw(a:)$_N$- yellow -ji(:,h)$_V$- dark]
o.jit.gwa:jí: oh.ya' oranges
[consists of: ojitgwa:ji: orange; ohya' fruit]
o.jitg.wa.jí: oh.yá' grahe:t orange tree
[consists of: ojitgwa:ji: ohya' oranges; grahe:t living tree]
orb
gá:gwa:' the sun; the moon
[ga+ stem: -(r)ag(wa)$_N$- s.t. circular in shape]
orb see: ball, moon, sun
ę'n.hó:tra' ball
sǫ.heh.ká:' gá:gwa:' the moon
ga:gwá:gye's the sun and moon
orchard
wah.yá.yęt.węh orchard; berry field
[wa+ stem: -(a)hyayętwęh- orchard; consists of: -(a)hy(a)$_N$- fruit, berry -yętw, yęto$_V$- plant]
orchestra see: band
hę.nad.rę.nó:ta' male singers; a band; a musical group
order see: hire
ę.sá.dęn.ha' you will order s.t., hire s.t.
orderly see: janitor, tidy
de.ga.ǫ:dóh.da:s they (f/m) are janitors
dwa.de.wa.yę.s.dǫ́h ga.gé.hǫ' it is tidy, neatly placed
organ
ga.wá:t wad.rę́.no.ta' organ
[consists of: gawa:t it is inflated; wadrenota' stereo, radio]
organ see: guts, heart, liver, lung
o.yǫ́:wa' guts; intestines
a.wę́.yǫh.sa' the heart
ot.węh.sa' the liver
ǫ.dǫ́n.ye'ta' a lung

Cayuga pronunciation guide: /a/ father /e/ weigh /ę/ men (nasalized) /i/ police /o/ hole /ǫ/ home (nasalized) /u/ blue. Underlined vowels are voiceless or whispered. /'/ high pitch. /t/ too /d/ do /k/ king /g/ good (never soft g) /j/ judge or adze /s/ soon /sh/ less heat (never the sh in shirt) /sr/ shrine /sy/ sure /hw/ which (the sound made when you blow out a candle) /h/ hi /ts/ cats hide /'/ (the sound before the first vowel in 'uh-uh') /n/ noon /r/ round /w/ way /y/ yes.

organize
had·rih·wa̱hs·dí:hs·ta' he takes care of the event all the time; he pays attention to what is going on
[ad+(N+/(r)ih(wa)+) stem: -(r)ih(wa)$_{N}$- word -(h)sdihsd$_{V}$- care]
had·rih·wahs·díhs·tahk he used to take care of the event
ę·had·ri̱h·wáhs·dihs he will take care of the event
organize (continued)
ę·há:s·di:s he will be chosen to look after the event or ceremony
organize see: arrange, raise to a vertical position
ęhs·dó:gęhs you will arrange things (flowers, etc.)
se·gé:ts·gwahs you are lifting it to a vertical position; you give parties
Oriental see: C (De̱·ho·di·ga·ha·di:yo:t)
orifice see: mouth
oh·sa:' mouth
origin see: begin
gyo̱h·sa:' the beginning of s.t.
original see: new
á:se:' it is fresh, new
originate
dwa·gáh·dęg·yo: I come from
[d+ … stem: -(a)hdędi, (a)hdęgy$_{V}$- leave, go away; originate from, come from]
nig·ya:wé:nǫ: where it came from
[ni+d/g+P+ stem: -enǫ$_{V}$- originate from someplace, come from someplace]
nig·yo:né:nǫ: where they (z) came from
nig·ya·go·né:no: they (f/m) come from
nig·ya:wé:no: it comes from
tę·wa·da·dǫ́:ni' it will emerge or appear unintentionally; it will do it by itself
[d+(h+) A+adad+ stem: -ǫni, ǫny$_{V}$- make; start from, originate, emerge]
dwa·da:dǫ́:nih where it starts from

oriole
gyó:gyo:' Baltimore oriole
[stem: -gyo:gyo:'$_{N}$- Baltimore oriole]
orphan
go·yéhs·ha'ǫh she is an orphan
[P+ stem: -yehsha'ǫh$_{V}$- orphan]
orphan see: foundling
ga·wi·yat·sę́:nyǫ: child born out of wedlock; foundling; illegitimate child
Osage see: C (Wa·sah·se̱·ho:nǫ')
other
ó:ya' the other; another
[o+ stem: -y(a)$_{N}$- other, different]
o·yá:jih another type
ha'de·jo·yá's·hǫ' one thing to another
[ha'de+s+yo+ stem: -y(a)$_{N}$- other, different -shǫ' pluralizer]
Ottawa, Ont. see: E (Tga·ya'dag·wę:ni:yo'geh)
otter
jo·dé'drǫ:' otter
[s+yo+(a)de+ stem: -(')drǫ:'- otter; consists of: -(')dr(a)$_{N}$- case, quiver -ǫ:$_{V}$- resemble]
sgwá:yęh otter
[stem: -sgwayęh- otter; consists of: -(h)sg(wa:)$_{N}$- stone, bullet, rock -ę$_{V}$- lie on the ground]
ouch see: I (agi:, aju!)
outburst see: scream
dęh·sad·rihs·da:né:ga:' you will burst out screaming, crying; you will make a loud outburst
outdoor
ahs·déh·ge̱·ha:' outside type
[stem: -(a)hsdeh- outside]
outdoor see: outside
outfit see: dress
ag·ya'da·wí'tra' coat; dress
at·rǫ́·n'i·da' clothes
ahg·wę́:nya' clothing; clothes
outline see: shadow
o·dah·sǫ́:da:' shadow

outmaneuver see: out-think
ęhs·he'ni·gǫ·hag·wé:ni' you will out-think her
out-of-focus see: fuzzy
ta'de·yo·ga·há·ę·daht it is fuzzy, out of focus, opaque, unclear
outside
ahs·deh outside
[stem: -(a)hsdeh- outside]
outsmart see: deceive, out-think
dęhs·hé·gahg·we:k you will pull the wool over her eyes, outsmart her, deceive her
ęhs·he'ni·gǫ·hag·wé:ni' you will out-think her
outspoken
he·ja·go·nę́·hęh they (f/m) are outspoken
[he'+s/j+P+ stem: -ęhęh- be outspoken; consists of: -ęhę(:)$_V$- direct, convey]
out-think
ęhs·he'ni·gǫ·hag·wé:ni' you will out-think her
[TR+ stem: -(')nigǫha'gweni- out-think s.o.; consists of: -(')nigǫh(a)$_N$- mind -gweni, gweny$_V$- able to do s.t., succeed]
outward see: outside
outwit see: deceive, out-think
dęhs·hé·gahg·we:k you will pull the wool over her eyes, outsmart her, deceive her
ęhs·he'ni·gǫ·hag·wé:ni' you will out-think her
oven
gak·wa·dá·i:ha'ta' toaster oven
[ga+ stem: -kwadaiha'ta'- toaster oven; consists of: -k(wa)$_N$- food -(')daiha'd$_V$- heat up]
oven see: microwave oven, stove
gak·wah·sno:wé' ga·kǫ́:nihs microwave oven
hǫ́h·ji stove

over see: I (again, e:')
over-estimate see: overdo
e·sá'dra·hehs you are exaggerating
overcast see: cloudy, dreary
ga·góh·dah·sǫhs cloudy intervals
de·yot·gręg·rę́h·dǫh the sky is dreary, grey
overcome see: overpower
ęhs·he's·hę́:ni' you will overpower s.o. (physically)
overcooked
o·wíh·jih it is overcooked
[o+ stem: -wihjih- overcooked; consists of: -(r)i, (w)i$_V$- ripe]
overdo
sad·rá·hehs·ta' you are always going overboard; you are excessive
[P+ stem: -(')drahehsd$_V$- overdo, exaggerate]
e·sá'dra·hehs you are exaggerating
ęh·sá'dra·hehs you will go overboard, above and beyond;, you will exceed
o'drá·hehs it is overdone, exaggerated
over here see: I (da...gwa:dih)
over there see: I (sigwa:dih)
overpass
de·wa·dahs·gǫ·gǫh·tá' o·há:de' overpass
[consists of: dewadahsgǫgǫhta' overpass; oha:de' an existing road]
de·wa·dahs·gǫ́·gǫh·ta' overpass
[de+wa+(a)d+ stem: -(a)hsgǫgohta'-overpass; consists of: -(a)hsg(wa)$_N$-roof, bridge -ǫgohd$_V$- surpass]
overpower
she's·hę́:nyǫhs you are always overpowering s.o.; you are overpowering s.o. right not
[TR+ stem: -(')shęni, (')shęny$_V$- overpower]
ęhs·he's·hę́:ni' you will overpower s.o. (physically)

overpower (continued)
she'sʼs·hę́n·yǫg·wę̨h you have overpowered s.o. (before; a long time ago)
gas·he'ʼs·hę̨n·yǫ́:gwę̨h you have overpowered them
overpowering see: strong
ga̱hs·há:sde' it is strong, tough, powerful
over-reach see: overdo
ę̨h·sá'dra̱·hehs you will go overboard, above and beyond; you will exceed
oversee
hod·rih·wat·gá·ha:',
hod·rih·wat·ga̱·ha:' he is a supervisor, overseer
[P+ (a)d+ stem: -(r)ihwatgaha:- oversee, supervise; consists of: -(r)ih(wa)$_N$- word -(a)tgahǫ(:), (a)tgaha(:)$_V$- pay attention, watch]
ę̨h·sad·ri̱h·wát·ga̱·hǫ:' you will oversee, supervise
overshoe
de·yǫ·da̱hg·wa·ne·dáhs·ta' overshoes
[de+yǫ+ stem: -(a)hdahgwanedahsta'- overshoe; consists of: -(a)hdahg(wa)$_N$- shoe -nedahsd$_V$- protect s.t.]
oversight see: neglect
dehs·gáhs·di̱hs·ta' I no longer pay attention
overstate see: exaggerate, overdo
hę̨h·só:goht you will exaggerate, go above and beyond
e·sá'dra̱·hehs you are exaggerating
overthrow see: revolt
ę̨t·sę̨'ni·gǫ́·ho'ne:k you will revolt, remove yourself (bodily and in spirit)
ę̨h·sá·det·sa't you will struggle, squirm to get loose, revolt
overturn see: turn upside down
dę̨·gǫ·nǫh·wétso'dę̨' I am going to turn you upside down, upend you! (said in anger)
overwhelm see: overpower
ę̨hs·he's·hę́:ni' you will overpower s.o. (physically)
overwhelming see: amazing, terrible
o·né·hag·waht it is amazing, awesome
de·yo·dę̨·nǫh·ya·níh·dǫh it is overwhelming, terrible
owl
hi·hi: great horned owl
[stem: -(h)ihi:$_N$- great horned owl]
own see: have
a·gá:wę̨h it is mine
ag·yę̨' I have, possess
own (a business)
hoh·dę́g·y'a·dǫh he is an owner
[stem: -(a)hdę̨gya'd- start s.t., own (a business), having to do with business; consists of: -(a)hdę̨di, (a)hdę̨gy$_V$- leave, go away]
oyster see: bass
o'nó:ksa' bass (fish); oysters; shellfish; sea shells
oxidize see: rust
ohs·gę́'dra̱·he:' it is rusting, rusty

P

pacify see: console, forget
ę̨hs·he'ni·gǫ́·ho'drǫ:' you will console s.o. (lit.: you will caress s.o.'s mind)
ę̨hs·he'ni·gǫ́·hę̨h·dę̨' you will make s.o. feel better, comfort s.o.
pack
sat·reh·nǫ́:nih you pack
[at+ stem: -(h)rehnǫni- pack; consists of: -(hr)ehn(a)$_N$- cargo, bundle -ǫni, ǫny$_V$- make]
pack see: herd, knapsack
gahs·yá·o:t a standing herd
hohs·wę̨'n'a·géh ho·ya:géh·deh his knapsack

package
ga·hó:tra' a package
[ga+ stem: -(h)otr(a)$_N$- package]
pad see: pillow
ga·gǫ́'dra' pillow; cushion
paddle
ga·gá·wẹh·sa' paddle
[ga+ stem: -gawehs(a)$_N$- paddle]
gat·gwẹ́n·y'at·ra', gat·gǫ́n·y'at·ra' corn bread paddles; corn soup paddles
[ga+ stem: -(a)tgwẹnya'tr(a), (a)tgǫnya'tr(a)$_N$- corn bread paddle]
paddle see: row
ẹh·sé·ga·we:' you will row
pail
ga·ná'ja' pail
[ga+ stem: -na'j(a)$_N$- pail, drum]
ga·na'jas·hǫ́:'ǫh cooking pots
ga·na'j'á·ǫ·weh cooking pots with the feet; iron kettle
pain
grǫh·yá:gẹhs I am always in pain
[stem: -(r)ǫhyagẹ$_V$- be in agony, groan]
ẹg·rǫ́h·ya·gẹ' I will be in pain; I will labour, in agony
sá·ǫh·ya·gẹ: groan
pain see: ache
ǫg·ya'da·nǫh·wa:k I ached
painful
o·nó·hǫk·de' it is painful
[o+ stem: -nǫhǫkde'- painful; consists of: -nǫhǫkd(ẹ,anih)$_V$- sick]
o·no·hǫk·dé:nyǫ' there is pain all over
painful see: sore
a·gah·s'i·dá·nǫh·wa:s I have a sore foot
paint see: colour, water colours
ǫh·sóh·ta' colour; paints; crayons
de·gah·ne·ga·yẹhs·dǫ́h ǫh·sǫ́h·ta' water colours; paint
paintbrush
oh·soh·dahk·wá' e·yá:ta' paintbrush
[consists of: ǫhsohdahkwa' s.t. that colours; eya:ta' s.o. spreads it]

pair
o·ná:tsih a pair (of shoes, socks)
[o+ stem: -(a)tsih$_V$- friend]
sga:dí:hah one side (for example, one of a pair of shoes)
[s+ga+ stem: -(a)dih$_V$- side]
pair see: match
de·séh·ka·hǫ: match things; pair things up (for example, puzzle pieces, socks)
palatable see: taste good
o·gá'ǫh it tastes good
pale
de·wa·gẹhs·gyẹ·nag·y'á·gǫh I am pale
[de+P+ stem: -(h)sgyẹna'gyagǫh- pale; consists of: -(h)sgyǫ'w(a), (h)sgyẹ'w(a)$_N$- bone -(i)ya'g$_V$- cut, break]
de·yohs·gyẹ·ná'gy'a·gǫh it is pale
dẹ·hohs·gyẹ·ná'gy'a·gǫh he is pale
de·sahs·gyẹ·ná'gy'a·gǫh you are pale, ashen
pale, pallid see: light-coloured
gẹ'gẹ: it is white; it is light-skinned, it is light-coloured
palm
ni·ses'ǫh·dá:dẹ:s how thick (measured by palms)
[(ni+) A+(N+) stem: -s'ǫhd(a)$_N$- palm -(a)dẹs$_V$- thick]
palm see: hand
oh·sóh·da' hand; paw
pan see: bread pan, cake pan, pot, utensils
ǫt·na'dá·ǫ:dahk·wa' a bread pan; a cake pan
de·ga'nhǫh·sá·yẹhs·dǫ́h ǫt·na'dá·ǫ:dahk·wa' a cake pan
e·kǫn·ya'tá' ga·na'jas·hǫ́:'ǫh cooking pots
e·kǫn·ya·ta·géh ehs·ta·shǫ́:ǫh kitchen items; utensils

Cayuga pronunciation guide: /a/ father /e/ weigh /ẹ/ men (nasalized) /i/ police /o/ hole /ǫ/ home (nasalized) /u/ blue. Underlined vowels are voiceless or whispered. /ˊ/ high pitch. /t/ too /d/ do /k/ king /g/ good (never soft g) /j/ judge or adze /s/ soon /sh/ less heat (never the sh in shirt) /sr/ shrine /sy/ sure /hw/ which (the sound made when you blow out a candle) /h/ hi /ts/ cats hide /'/ (the sound before the first vowel in 'uh-uh') /n/ noon /r/ round /w/ way /y/ yes.

pane
wat·gǫ́hs·gwa'tro' window pane
[wa /o+ (a)t+ stem: -gǫhsgwa'tro'- pane of glass; consists of: -gǫhsgwa'tr(a)$_N$- window -o'$_V$- be submerged]
ge·í ni·yot·gǫhs·gwá'tro' four panes of glass
panic see: frightened, frightening
a·sét·sah·ni'k you are afraid
pannier see: basket
ga'áhd·ra' basket
pant
ha·ǫ:wihs·hę́'ǫh he is panting
[P+ stem: -(r)ǫwihshę'$_V$- pant]
sha·ǫ:wihs·hę́'ǫh he is panting again; he is short of breath
ga·ǫ:wihs·hę́'ǫh she is panting
ga·ǫ:wihs·hę'ǫ·hǫ́:gye' breathing in a state of panic
pant see: gasp, wheeze
ad·wák·sa·ga:'s you gasped, yawned
oh·wę́hs·da·ga: it is wheezing
panther
gaho'jíh da·gus·gó:wah panther
[consists of: gahǫ'ji: it is dark-coloured; dagu:sgo:wah big cat; tiger]
panties see: underwear
hná·gǫh·ka:' underwear
pantry
ek·wa·ę·dahk·wa'géh o·nǫ́h·sǫ:t pantry
[consists of: ekwaędahkwa' cupboard, pantry; onǫhsǫ:t a room; a vault]
pantry see: cupboard
ek·wa·ę·dáhk·wa' cupboard; pantry
pants
at·nát·sot·ra' pants
[at+ stem: -(h)na'tsotra'- pants, trousers; consists of: -(h)na'ts(a)$_N$- buttock -od$_V$- stand]
o·yáhk·wa' pants
[o+ stem: -yahk(wa)$_N$- pants]

pants (continued)
o·gá'da', o·ga'da's·hǫ́:'ǫh pants; underpants
[o+ stem: -ga'd(a)$_N$- pants, underpants]
panty hose
o·dáh·d'it·rǫ:t panty hose
[o+ stem: -(a)dahdi'trǫd- panty hose; consists of: -(a)hdahdi'tr(a)$_N$- sock -ǫd$_V$- attached]
o·dah·dit·rǫ́:t at·ná'tsot·ra' panty hose
[consists of: odahditrǫ:t panty hose; atna'tsotra' pants]
paper
gah·yá·dǫhs·ra' paper
[ga+ stem: -(h)yadǫhsr(a)$_N$- paper]
oh·ya·dǫhs·ra:gwé:gǫh all the paper
[stem: -(h)yadǫhsr(a)$_N$- paper -gwegǫh$_V$- all]
paper clip
de·yeh·ya·dǫhs·ra·ę·dahk·wá'
gah·sǫ́·wah·da' paper clip
[consists of: deyehyadǫhsraędahkwa' s.t. used to collate paper; gahsǫwahda' nails, wires, needles, etc.]
gah·ya·dǫhs·ra:yé:nahs paper clip
[ga+ stem: -(h)yadǫhsrayenahs- paper clip; consists of: -(h)yadǫhsr(a)$_N$- paper -yena(w), yenaǫ, yena(:)$_V$- catch, receive, accept]
paper punch
gah·ya·dǫhs·ra·ga·hę́:ta' paper punch
[ga+ stem: -(h)yadǫhsragahęta'- paper punch; consists of: -(h)yadǫhsr(a)$_N$- paper -gahęd$_V$- drill, hole]
paper towel
gah·ya·dǫhs·rá' ǫh·ja·ge·wáh·ta' paper towels
[consists of: gahyadǫhsra' paper; ǫhjagewahta' towel]
paper towel see: serviette
ǫ·dek·wa·gé·wah·ta' serviettes; napkins
parable see: tale
o'ga:' a parable; a tale; a story; a legend

paradise see: heaven
ga·ǫ́:hya·deʼ in existing heaven
parallel see: equal, resemble
tsaʼdé:yǫ: of equal number or amount
sgá:yę: it resembles
paralyze see: numb
ot·sís·daʼǫh it is numb
paramount see: special
o·i·ho·wá:nęh it is important; a great or worthy commendation; it is special
paraphrase see: recount, translate
ęt·sa:tró:wiʼ you will recount, retell
de·ye·wę·ná·den·yeʼs she is a translator; she is translating now
paratroopers see: sky-dive
de·tę·nahsg·wáhk·waʼ they (m) are sky-diving; paratroopers
parcel see: bundle, package
swa·tóhg·wa:t one bundle
ga·hó:traʼ a package
parched see: dry, thirsty
o·hę: it is dry
kaʼdá:tęhs I am thirsty
pardon see: mercy, pity
gę·dá·ǫhs·raʼ mercy
ęhs·hé:dę:ʼ you will pity her, show mercy, compassion
pare see: peel
ęhs·ra·wihs·dó:tsiʼ you will peel
parent see: C, (father, haʼnih; mother, e·ti·nǫ·haʼ), foster parent
haʼnih my father
knó:haʼ my mother
ga·ǫ·da·dah·do·gáʼtaʼ foster parents
paring knife
e·ya·wihs·dót·sʼa·taʼ paring knife
[e+ stem: -yawihsdotsaʼtaʼ- paring knife, peeler; consists of: -rawihsd(a)$_N$- peel -otsaʼd$_V$- cause to remove an outer covering]

park
ǫg·yaʼda·nohs·dahk·wáʼgeh a park
[ǫ+(a)g+ stem: -yaʼdanohsdahkwaʼgeh- recreation area; consists of: -yaʼd(a)$_N$- body -nohsdahkwaʼ$_V$- place for cooling off -(ʼ)geh at]
gyǫg·ya·dʼed·réh·da·ę:ʼ we all parked our car over there
[(a)de+ stem: -(ʼ)drehdaę- park one's vehicle; consists of: -(ʼ)drehd(a)$_N$- car, vehicle -ę$_V$- lie on the ground]
gad·réh·da·ę: one parked car
gad·reh·dá·ę·dǫʼ the cars are parked
parking lot, garage
ǫ·deʼdręh·da·ę·dáhk·waʼ parking lot or garage
[ǫ+(a)de+ stem: -(ʼ)drehdaędahkwaʼ- parking lot; consists of: -(ʼ)drehd(a)$_N$- vehicle, car -ędahkwaʼ$_V$- place where s.t. is put]
Parkinson's disease
Go·yaʼdǫ·dáʼtaʼ Parkinson's disease
[(ya)go+ stem: -yaʼdǫdaʼtaʼ- Parkinson's disease; consists of: -yaʼd(a)$_N$- body -ǫdaʼd$_V$- shake, shiver]
Parks and Wildlife Federation see: G
(De·ga·na·da·węn·yeʼtaʼgeh Ga·di:nyo:ʼ)
Parliament see: G
(Ga·nǫh·so·wa·nęh·go:wah)
parlour see: lounge
ǫ·dǫ·wih·sę·dahk·wáʼgeh lounge
parrot
de·gá:gyaʼs parrot
[de+ga+(a)k+ stem: -yaʼs- parrot; consists of: -(i)yaʼg$_V$- cut, break]
part see: divide, fraction
dęh·se·kah·sǫ́:goʼ you will divide it into parts
gyod·rá:gwęh fractions

participate
dę·ya·goʼnyaʼgwę·hę́:gyeʼ she will have a hand in it
[de+P+ stem: -(ʼ)nyagw- participate; consists of: -(ʼ)ny(a)$_N$- finger, hand -gw$_V$- gather, pick, get]
hed·wa·ih·wag·yę·hę́:tohs, hed·wa·ih·wag·yę·hę́:twahs we all partake; we all (incl.) pull forth the words or ideas all the time
[heʼ+... stem: -(r)ihwagyęhętw- participate, partake; consists of: -(r)ih(wa)$_N$- word -yęhętw, yęhęto$_V$- pull]
hę·jid·wa·ih·wag·yę́·hę·toʼ we all (incl.) will bring the idea back again
hęd·wa·ih·wag·yę·hę́:toʼ we all (incl.) will pull forth the words or ideas (said by a speaker during a ceremony)
he·yǫhg·wa·ih·wa·dí·hę·twęh, he·yǫhg·wa·ih·wag·yę́·hę·twęh we have pulled forth the ideas; we are participating right now
participation
gan·héhs·raʼ to take s.o.'s part
particle see: stapler, fraction
de·ga·nǫh·sǫ́:taʼ particle (lit.: joiners); stapler
gyod·rá:gwęh fractions
particular see: which
ga·ę́ ní:ga:ʼ which one; a specific thing
partition
wa·dę·nǫh·sa·we·tá·hǫh a partition
[(w)a+adę+ stem: -nǫhs(a)$_N$- house -(a)wiʼd$_V$- insert -(adi)hǫh$_V$- lean]
partition see: wall
o·dę́·nih·saʼ a wall
partridge
gwé:sęʼ partridge
[stem: -gwes$_N$- partridge]
partridge see: quail
gǫh·gó:wi:ʼ a quail; a partridge
parturition see: birth
a·dǫ́n·hehs·raʼ birth
party see: celebrate, raise to a vertical position
wa·dę́ʼnyo:t a celebration; a party
se·gé:ts·gwahs you are lifting it to a vertical position; you give parties
pass by
wa·dǫ́·gǫh·taʼ it passes by
[ad+ stem: -ǫgohd$_V$- surpass; pass by]
a·ha:dǫ́:goht he went past
a:ga·dǫ́:goht I should go on
ho·dǫ́·gǫh·dǫh he has gone past
o·dǫ́·gǫh·dǫh it has passed by; the past
pass out see: faint
ǫk·ni·gǫ·háh·dǫʼ I fainted
pass wind
a·gon·ya:gę́ʼs I am passing wind
[P+ stem: -nyagęʼs$_V$- pass wind]
pass wind see: fart
aʼǫ·nʼi·dé:niʼ she farted
passage see: doorway, gate, path
gan·hó·ga·hę:t doorway
gan·ho·ha·ní:yǫ:t gate, door
ęh·dáhk·waʼ path; hallway
passion see: love, want
ga·nǫ́hk·wahs·raʼ love
gahs·gá:ne:s I have longings for; I want; I desire
past
oh·náʼgę·jih way back in the past; back then
[o+ stem: -(h)naʼg$_V$- bottom]
o·dóʼk·dǫh it is past
[o+ (a)d+ stem: -oʼkd$_V$- end]
past see: pass by, bring up the past
o·dǫ́·gǫh·dǫh it has passed by; the past
go·i·hó:gaʼt she is always bringing up the past, looking for information
paste see: attach, glue
ęh·só·ha·ęʼ you will attach s.t.
et·séhs·da·taʼ glue

pasture
ga·di:tse:nę́ʼ ha·diʼdrǫ·dáhk·waʼ pasture
[consists of: gadi:tse:nęʼ farm animals; hadiʼdrǫdahkwaʼ a place where they (m) live]
pasture see: meadow
ga·hę́·da·ęʼ a meadow; a pasture; a field
pat see: touch
haʼga·ké:ye:ʼ I touched them
patch see: fix, material
ǫ·de·kahs·rǫ́:nih she is fixing skirts
ni·ga·hę́:hah it is thin (for example, material)
path
ǫ·dǫh·gǫh·dáhk·waʼ path
[ǫ+(a)d+ stem: -ǫgęhdahkwaʼ, ǫgohdahkwaʼ- path; consists of: -ǫgohd$_V$- surpass; pass by]
he·yǫ·do·gę́h·dahk·waʼ a path; a shortcut
[he+yo+(a)d+ stem: -ǫgęhdahkwaʼ, ǫgohdahkwaʼ- path; consists of -ǫgohd$_V$- surpass; pass by]
ęh·dáhk·waʼ path; hallway (lit. where they walk)
[stem: -ęhdahkwaʼ- path, hallway; consists of: -ęhd$_V$- walk]
path see: trail
de·yǫ·do·gę́h·dahk·waʼ trail
pathetic see: sadness
ok·ni·gǫh·sá:dǫh sadness
patience
ga·dęʼni·gǫ·hah·ní·yahs·taʼ I have patience
[adę+ stem: -(ʼ)nigǫhahniyahsd- have patience; consists of: -(ʼ)nigǫh(a)$_N$- mind -(h)niyahsd$_V$- harden, toughen]
pattern
gyǫ·deʼnyę·dę́hs·dahk·waʼ pattern
[g+yǫ+(a)de+ stem: -(ʼ)nyędęhsdahkwaʼ- ruler, pattern; consists of: -(ʼ)nyędę$_V$- try]

paw see: hand
oh·sóh·daʼ hand; paw
pawn
ǫt·ga·ę:dáhk·waʼ an item that is to be pawned
[at+ stem: -gaędahgw$_V$- pawn]
wat·ga·ę:dáhk·waʼ an item that has been pawned
ę·sat·gá·ę·dahk you will pawn s.t.
ę·gǫ·yat·ga·ę·dahg·węʼ I will pawn on you
[TR+ at+ stem: -gaędahgwę$_V$- pawn]
wat·ga·ę:dáhg·węh an item that has been pawned
a·hat·gá·ę·daʼ he pawned
[at+ stem: -gaędaʼ- pawn; consists of: -ga$_N$- price -ędaʼ$_V$- lay down]
a·ha·ga·dahg·wá·ę·hęhs he did pawn
[ad+ stem: -(a)hgwaęhęhsd- pawn s.t.; consists of: -(a)hgwaę$_V$- store]
a·hǫ·wa·dahg·wá·ę·hęhs they pawned on him, them (m)
ęhs·he·ya·dahg·wá·ę·hęhs you will pawn s.t.
pawn shop
ǫt·ga·ę:dáhk·wʼa·geh a pawn shop
[at+ stem: -gaędahgw$_V$- pawn]
pay
e·gá:nyaʼs she pays all the time
[stem: -ganyaʼg$_V$- pay]
aʼé·gan·yaʼk she paid
ga·gán·yʼa·gǫh payment
e·gán·yaʼktaʼ what one pays with; barter
[stem: -ganyaʼkd- pay with; consists of: -ganyaʼg$_V$- pay]
e·gán·yaʼktahk what she used to pay with
go·gan·yaʼkdǫ́hǫg·yeʼ she is paying as the goes along
pay see: buy
ęh·sní:nǫʼ you will buy, purchase

Cayuga pronunciation guide: /a/ father /e/ weigh /ę/ men (nasalized) /i/ police /o/ hole /ǫ/ home (nasalized) /u/ blue. Underlined vowels are voiceless or whispered. /ʹ/ high pitch. /t/ too /d/ do /k/ king /g/ good (never soft g) /j/ judge or adze /s/ soon /sh/ less heat (never the sh in shirt) /sr/ shrine /sy/ sure /hw/ which (the sound made when you blow out a candle) /h/ hi /ts/ cats hide /ʼ/ (the sound before the first vowel in 'uh-uh') /n/ noon /r/ round /w/ way /y/ yes.

pay attention
ę·sáhs·di:s you will pay attention
[stem: -(a)hsdisd$_{V}$- pay attention, bother with]
a·sá:sdi:s you did pay attention
sahs·dí:sdǫh you are paying attention (right now)
sahs·di:s pay attention

payment
ga·gán·y'a·gǫh payment
[ga+ stem: -ganya'gǫh- payment; consists of: -ga$_{N}$- price -ganya'g$_{V}$- pay]

payment see: price
ga·gá·he:' the price of s.t.

pea
o·né:gwa' peas
[o+ stem: -neg(wa)$_{N}$- pea]
de·yo:do:wę́' **o·né:gwa'** split peas
[consists of: deyo:do:wę' it is split; one:gwa' peas]

peace
od·ri·yǫhs·rę́·da'ǫh peace (lit.: the war has ended)
[o+(a)d+ stem: -(r)iyohsręda'ǫh- peace; consists of: -(r)iyohsr(a)$_{N}$- war -ęda'$_{V}$- lay down, finish]

peace see: just, think
wad·rih·wahs·rǫ́:ni: peace; to make peace with s.o.
sgę:nǫ́: **se·nǫ́h·dǫn·yǫh** you are safe; you are feeling well; you are at peace with yourself

peach
o·hęh·dá·e:' **oh·ya'** peach
[consists of: ohęhdaę:' it is furry; ohya' fruit]
o·hęh·dá·e:' **oh·yá'** **grahe:t** peach tree
[consists of: ohęhdae:' ohya' peaches; grahe:t living tree]

peacock
ga·ná·i'da' a peacock; pride; boastfulness
[ga+ stem: -nai'd(a)$_{N}$- peacock; consists of: -nai'd$_{V}$- cause to be proud]

peak see: top
hé:tgęh·jih the very top

pear
ot·se'dá' **oh·ya'** pear
[consists of: otse'da' bottle, jar; ohya' fruit]
ot·se'dá' **oh·yá'** **grahe:t** pear tree
[consists of: otse'da' ohya' pear; grahe:t living tree]

peasant see: farmer
ha·hę·da·ge·hó:nǫ' farmer

pebble
ni·gahs·gwa·ó:s'uh pebbles
[ni+ ga+ stem: -(h)sgwao:(s)'uh- pebble; consists of: -(h)sg(wa:)$_{N}$- stone, bullet, rock -u:s'uh$_{V}$- several small items]

peck
ęh·sák·da'e:k it will peck you
[stem: -kda'e- peck s.t.; consists of: -kd(a)$_{N}$- nutshell -(')e$_{V}$- hit]

peculiar see: strange, unusual
og·yá:nǫhk it is strange, bizarre
ti·yó:t'ah it is queer, unusual, odd

pee see: urinate
a·ga·ǫ·níhsg·ya·ge' they (f/m) urinated

peek
se·ga·ha·nę́hsg·wahs you steal a peek
[stem: -gahanęhsgwah- peek; consists of: -gah(a)$_{N}$- eye -nęhsgwah$_{V}$- go and steal]
ęh·se·ga·hę·nęhsg·wá·hǫ:' you will peek (lit.: steal a look)

peel
ęhs·ra·wihs·dó:tsi' you will peel
[stem: -(r)awihsdotsi- peel s.t.; consists of: -rawihsd(a)$_{N}$- peel -ots(i)$_{V}$- remove an outer covering]

peel (continued)
sra·wíhs·dot·sih peel it
peel see: peelings
peeler
ok·de·há' e·ya'wihs·dóts'a·ta' a vegetable peeler
[consists of: okdeha' edible roots; eya:wihsdotsa'ta' paring knife]
peeler see: paring knife
e·ya:wihs·dóts'a·ta' a paring knife
peelings
o·wá'wihs·da' a peeling
[o+ stem: -(r,w)awihsd(a)$_N$- peel]
o·wá·jihs·da' peelings; the bark of a tree
[o+ stem: -wajihsd(a)$_N$- peelings, bark, rind]
o·wa·jihs·dá:gǫ: inner bark
[o+ stem: -wajihsdagǫ- inner bark; consists of: -wajihsd(a)$_N$- peelings, bark, rind]
peep see: noise
ot·ga:' a noise
peer see: examine, peek
a·gat·ga·hí·yohs·dǫh I am staring at it, examining it closely
se·ga·ha·nę́hsg·wahs you steal a peek
peg see: clothespin
ga·wáhs·da' clothespin
pelican
o·jíh·yo·ha:' pelican (refers to a bag hanging from its beak)
[o+ stem: -jihyoha:'- pelican; consists of: -jih(wa), jihy$_N$- hammer -oha:'$_V$- be attached]
pelt
o·hóh·wa:' pelt
[o+ stem: -hoh(wa:)$_N$-]
pelt see: skin
ga·néh·wa' leather, hide
pen
gah·ne:gá:' eh·yá·dǫhk·wa' a pen
[consists of: gahne:ga:' it contains liquid; ehyadǫhkwa' pencil]
pen see: chicken coop, duck pen, goat shed, pig pen
daks·ha·e'dóhs o·dí·nǫh·so:t chicken coop
twę:twę́:t de·wa·tę·hę:dǫ́'
ha·dí'drǫ·ta' duck pen
ga·ya'dag·ráhs ga·dí'drǫ' goat shed
gwihs·gwíhs ga·dí'drǫ' pig pen
penalize see: punish
ę·sa:tré:waht you will be punished
pencil
eh·yá·dǫhk·wa' pencil
[e+ stem: -(h)yadǫhkwa'- pencil; consists of: -(h)yadǫ(:)$_V$- write]
ha'de·yǫh·sohg·wa·gé: eh·yá·dǫhk·wa' coloured pencils
[consists of: ha'deyǫhsohgwage: all kinds of colours; ehyadǫhkwa' pencil]
ha·nǫh·sǫ:níh hoh·yá·dǫhk·wa' carpenter's pencil
[consists of: hanǫhsǫ:nih he is a carpenter; ehyadǫhkwa' pencil]
pencil sharpener
eh·ya·dǫhk·wá' gah·yo'tí:yǫhs pencil sharpener
[consists of: ehyadǫhkwa' pencil; gahyo'ti:yǫhs it sharpens s.t.]
penetrate see: come in, go in, poke, stab
da·ha:dí:yǫ' they (m) came in
ha'jǫh, ha'syǫh go in; enter
des·wá'ehs·ta' you all are poking
dęhs·hę·n'atrá'a:s you will stab s.t.
peninsula
he·yoh·wę·já:de' a peninsula
[he+yo+ stem: -ǫhwęjade'- country; peninsula; consists of: -ǫhwęj(a)$_N$- earth, land -de'- exist]
peninsula see: point
he·yo·dǫh·wę'ok·dá'ǫh a point of land; a cape; a peninsula
penis
shę́h ha·jí:nah a penis; a phallus
[shęh ha+ stem: -jinah$_V$- strong, brave]

penis see: phallus
on·ra' phallus
pennant see: flag
ga·yę́hs·ro:t flag
penny see: B (sgag·we·ni'da:t)
people see: person
ǫ́:gweh a person; a human
people
[-(a')geho:nǫ' external locative plus populative; denotes 'people who live on or near a place']
[-(h)onǫ' populative suffix; denotes 'people who live on or near a place']
People's Council see: G (Ǫg·weh He·ye·ih·wa̱h·win·yǫ'ta'geh)
pepper
de·yóh·sa·it pepper
[de+yo+ stem: -(a)hsait- pepper, cause to cough; consists of: -(')a)hsa(w)$_N$- chest, cough]
na·wę'da·wéht de·yóh·sa·it sweet peppers
[consists of: nawę'daweht it is sweet; rich; deyohsait pepper]
peppery see: spicy
ga·wę·na̱h·sa·dá·i·ha'ta' it is hot and peppery (lit.: it heats up the tongue)
perceive
sę·nih·na·dó:ka' you are perceiving s.t. right now
[stem: -ęnihnadog$_V$- perceive]
ęh·sę·ni̱h·ná:do:k you will perceive s.t.
a·wę·ni̱h·ná:do:k it sensed s.t.
perceive see: hear, know, recognize, see, understand
ę·sa:tǫ́:dęh you will hear it
ga̱·hǫ́:ka' I understand
ho·nǫ́h·dǫ' he knows
ęg·yę́:de:' I will recognize it
a·gé:gę' I saw
a·ho'ni·gǫ·há·ę·da' he understood
perch see: sit up on s.t.
gits·gwá·he:' I am perched up on s.t.; I am sitting on s.t.
perchance see: maybe
ę·wa:dǫ́' g'is·hęh maybe; a possibility
perform see: do
hę·nág·ye̱·hę' they (m) do it
performer see: actor
hag·yę́n'a·ta' he is an actor, a clown, etc.
perfume
gad·rę:ní:yo's perfume
[ga+ stem: -dręniyo's- perfume; consists of: -dręn(a)$_N$- smell -iyo's$_V$- several nice objects]
perhaps see: I, (gat)gi'shęhwa', gyę:gwa'
perimeter see: edge
tsę́h hǫ́ he·yo·d'ok·dá'ǫh the edge
permit see: agree, willing
ęhs·rih·wa̱h·ní:ya:t you will affirm it, agree
ęh·sá·ga·ę: you will allow, give permission
pernicious see: evil
wa̱·hé:tgęh evil (in mind); bad
perplexed see: confused
de·wa·ga·da·węn·yá'seh I am confused, doubtful
persevere
ge·já:gǫhs I persevere all the time
[stem: -jagǫ(:)$_V$- persevere, try]
a·gé·ja·gǫ:' I persevered
ęh·sé:ja:gǫ:' you will persevere
se·já:gǫh persevere; keep it up
swa·já:gǫh you all persevere; keep it up (a word of encouragement)
sa·ja·gǫ̱'ǫ́h·ne:' you have persevered (in the past)
[stem: -jagǫ'$_V$- persevere, try]
a·ge·ja·gǫ́'ǫh I persevere (all the time)
persist see: endure, persevere
ęh·sę'ni·gǫ·hah·ní:ya:t you will endure

person
ǫ:gweh person, human
[stem: -ǫgwe(ʼda)$_N$- person]
ǫg·weʼdag·wé:gǫh all the people
[stem: -ǫgwe(ʼda)$_N$- person -gwegǫh$_V$- all]
perspire see: sweat
hoʼda·i·hę́hd·ro:t he is sweating
persuade
ęhs·heʼni·gǫ·hǫ́:niʼ you will influence, persuade s.o.
[TR+ stem: -(ʼ)nigǫhǫni- persuade, influence; consists of: -(ʼ)nigǫh(a)$_N$- mind -ǫni, ǫny$_V$- make]
ęh·seʼni·gǫ·ho·dá:goʼ you will persuade her, overcome her mind
[TR+ stem: -(ʼ)nigǫhodagw- persuade, influence; consists of: -(ʼ)nigǫh(a)$_N$- mind -odagw$_V$- remove, detach]
aʼe·sʼani·gǫ·hóda·goʼ she bested your mind, bewitched you
ęs·hǫg·wʼa·ni·gǫ·hó·da·goʼ he will influence, bribe us / s.o.
peruse see: read
ga·dad·ri·hǫ́n·ya:nih I am reading
pest see: insect, nuisance
o·jiʼnǫ́:waʼ a bug; an insect; a worm
des·ha·yaʼdaʼni·gǫ́·ha:t you are a nuisance
pester see: bother
dęhs·ni·gǫ·há:haʼ you are annoying me, bothering me
pet
a·ge:tsé:nęʼ my pet
[stem: -tsenę$_N$- tame animal]
sat·sé:nęʼ your pet
pet see: animal (tame)
ga·náhs·gwaʼ a tame animal; a pet; a domestic animal
petite see: small
ni·wú:ʼuh it is small, little
pew see: bench
wak·yę·da̱hk·wé:sǫʼs benches; pews
phallus
on·raʼ phallus
[o+ stem: -nr(a)$_N$- phallus, penis]
han·ráʼgeh on his penis, phallus
phallus see: penis
shę́h ha·jí:nah his penis, phallus
phantom see: ghost
jihs·gę: a ghost
phantom see: vision (have a vision)
ad·wag·yá·ǫn·yo:ʼ a haunted apparition
phase
ęh·níʼdag·yeʼs phases of the moon
[stem: consists of: -ęhniʼd(a)$_N$- month -dagyeʼ(s) $_V$- continue on, be ongoing]
pheasant
daks·ha·eʼdóhs gan·yo:ʼ pheasant
[consists of: dakshaeʼdohs chicken; ganyo:ʼ wild game]
Philadelphia, PA see: E (Tga·na·da·ęʼgo:wah)
philosophy see: belief
tsę́h hǫ:wéh gyǫg·wéh·da̱h·gǫh our belief; religion
phlegm see: mucus
o·jí·nǫhg·raʼ nasal mucus
photographer
ha·yáʼtaʼ he is a photographer
[A+ stem: -yaʼtaʼ- movie, television, photographer; consists of: -yaʼd(a)$_N$- body]
physician see: doctor
ha·dé:jęʼs he is a doctor
pick see: gather, pick s.o. up, pick s.t. up, pluck
ęhs·ró·he:k you will gather
ę·séhs·toʼdręht you will pluck feathers
pick at see: grope, pinch
hehs·yáh·nǫ·haʼ you are picking at s.t. (for example, your food); you are a groper
de·saʼji·dó·ha:k pinch, squeeze it

Cayuga pronunciation guide: /a/ father /e/ weigh /ę/ men (nasalized) /i/ police /o/ hole /ǫ/ home (nasalized) /u/ blue. Underlined vowels are voiceless or whispered. /ʹ/ high pitch. /t/ too /d/ do /k/ king /g/ good (never soft g) /j/ judge or adze /s/ soon /sh/ less heat (never the sh in shirt) /sr/ shrine /sy/ sure /hw/ which (the sound made when you blow out a candle) /h/ hi /ts/ cats hide /ʼ/ (the sound before the first vowel in 'uh-uh') /n/ noon /r/ round /w/ way /y/ yes.

pick axe
e·hehg·y'ak·tá' a·dó:gę' a pick axe
[consists of: ehehgya'kta' spade; ado:gę' axe, tomahawk]
pick one's nose
ǫ·de·ji·nǫ·dag·ráhg·wahs she is picking her nose
[(a)de+ stem: -jinǫdagrahgw- pick one's nose; consists of: -jinǫdagr(a)$_N$- mucus -(h)gw$_V$- lift, pick up s.t.]
pick up
at·ga·ke·yá'dahk I picked them up
[de+...TR+ stem: -ya'd(a)$_N$- body -(h)gw$_V$- lift, pick up; pick up s.o., s.t. (living)]
dę·ho·y'a·dáhg·węh it picked him up
de·yǫg·wa̱hg·wę́·hęg·ye's we all are continually picking it up
at·gehk I picked s.t. up
[de+...(N+) stem: -(h)gw$_V$- lift, pick up s.t.]
a·táh·yahk he picked up the fruit
[de+...(N+) stem: -(a)hy(a)$_N$- fruit, berry -(h)gw$_V$- lift, pick up; pick up s.t.]
to·díh·wa̱hg·węh they (m) are raising hymns
[de+...(N+) stem: -(r)ih(wa)$_N$- word -(h)gw$_V$- lift, pick up; pick up s.t.]
picnic table
ahs·deh·ge̱·há:' a·dek·wa·háhs·ra' picnic table
[consists of: ahsdehka:' outside type; adekwahahsra' table]
picture
ga·yá'da:' picture
[ga+ stem: -ya'da:'- picture; consists of: -ya'd(a)$_N$- body -a:'$_V$- hold, contain, include]
ga·ya'dá·ǫ:nyǫ' pictures
ha·yá'da:' his picture

pie
de·gáhs·wa'ne:t pie
[de+ga+ stem: -(h)swa'ned- pie; consists of: -(h)swa'n(a), (h)swe'n(a)$_N$- upper back -(h)swa'ned$_V$- support s.o., s.t., agree with s.o., back s.o.]
piece see: fraction
gyod·rá:gwęh fractions
pie plate
de·gahs·w'a·né:t ǫt·na'dá·ǫ:da̱hk·wa' pie plate
[consists of: degahswa'ne:t pie; ǫtna'daǫ:da̱hkwa' bread pan]
pierce see: poke, spear with a stick, stab
dę·gá'e:s I will pierce s.t.
a·to·wa'ę́·na'ehs he speared him with a stick
dęhs·hę·n'at·rá'a:s you will stab s.t.
piercing see: sharp
oh·yu'tí:yeht it is sharp
pig
gwíhs·gwihs pig
[stem: -gwihsgwihs$_N$- pig]
pig pen
gwihs·gwíhs ga·dí'drǫ' pig pen
[consists of: gwihsgwihs pig; gadi'drǫ' they (z) live (designates a shed)]
pigeon
tsah·gó:wah pigeon
[stem: -tsah$_N$- pigeon; -gowah- big]
piggy-back see: carry
ęhs·héh·sa·dę' you will carry s.o. on your back
pigment see: colour
ǫh·sóh·ta' colour; paints; crayons
pigs feet
gwihs·gwíhs oh·sí'da' pigs feet
[consists of: gwihsgwihs pig; ohsi'da' feet]
pike
ji·gǫ́h·se:s pike
[ji+ stem: -gǫhses- pike; consists of: -gǫhs(a)$_N$- face -es$_V$- long]

pile

ę·yag·wʼag·ran·hohs·ró:dęʼ we all (excl.) will pile the snow
[stem: -(a)ʼgr(a)$_N$- snow -nhohsrod(ę)$_V$- pile]

dwʼag·ran·hohs·ró:dęh let's pile the snow here

on·hóhs·ro:t a pile of s.t.
[o+ stem: -nhohsr(a)$_N$- pile -od$_V$- stand]

oʼgrán·hohs·ro:t a pile of snow
[o+ stem: -(a)ʼgr(a)$_N$- snow -nhohsrod$_V$- pile]

pile see: mountain, stack

gahs·dę·hó:dǫʼ mountains; a pile of boulders

dehs·ręʼho·dęʼ you stack things up

pilgrim see: pioneer

a·ta·di·hę́·dohs·ga:ʼ they (m) were pioneers

pill

o·nę́n·yʼog·waʼ pills
[o+ stem: -nęnyoʼg(wa)$_N$- pill]

pillage see: rob

a·hǫ́·wah·seht he robbed him

pillow

ga·gǫ́ʼdraʼ a pillow; a cushion
[ga+ stem: -gǫʼdr(a)$_N$- pillow, cushion, cotton batting]

pillow case

e·gǫʼdro·wé:ktaʼ pillow cases
[e+ stem: -gǫʼdrowektaʼ- pillow case; consists of: -gǫʼdr(a)$_N$- pillow, etc. +oweg$_V$- cover s.t.]

se·gǫʼdró:we:k you put the pillowcase on

pin

ga·jí·ho·ha:ʼ, **o·jí·ho·ha:**ʼ straight pin; pin; brooch; safety pin
[ga/o+ stem: -jihoh(a:)$_N$- pin]

pin see: needle, wire

eh·ni·kǫhk·wá gah·sǫ́·wah·daʼ needle

gah·sǫ́·wah·daʼ nails; wire; needle

pinch

de·sah·jʼi·dó·ha:k pinch it; squeeze it
[de+... stem: -(a)hjiʼdohag- pinch; consists of: -(a)hj(iʼda)$_N$- hand -ohag$_V$- squeeze]

pincushion

ehn·yó·dahk·waʼ a pincushion
[e+ stem: -(h)nyodahkwaʼ- pincushion; consists of: -(h)ny(a)$_N$- stick -odahkwaʼ$_V$- s.t. used for standing things up]

eh·sǫ·wah·dó·dahk·waʼ s.t. used for holding pins
[e+ stem: -(h)sǫwahdodahkwaʼ- pin cushion; consists of: -(h)sǫwahd(a)$_N$- wire, nail, needle -odahkwaʼ$_V$- s.t. used for standing things up]

ęʼni·kǫhk·wáʼ eh·nyó·dahk·waʼ pin cushion
[consists of: eʼnikǫhkwaʼ s.t. used for sewing; ehnyodahkwaʼ pincushion]

e·sǫ·wah·do·dahk·wáʼ eʼníh·kǫhk·waʼ pin cushion
[consists of: esǫwahdodahkwaʼ pincushion; eʼnihkǫkwaʼ s.t. used for sewing]

pine

os·dáʼa:ʼ pine tree
[o+ stem: -(h)sda:ʼah$_N$- pine pitch, pine tree]

o·nę́ʼdaʼ evergreen; conifer
[o+ stem: -nęʼd(a)$_N$- evergreen, conifer]

o·nęʼda·gá:yǫh white pine
[o+ stem: -nęʼdagayǫh- white pine; consists of: -nęʼd(a)$_N$- pine -gayǫh$_V$- old (thing)]

pine cone

o·nę́ʼdǫ:t pine cone
[o+ stem: -nęʼd(a)$_N$- conifer -ǫd$_V$- attached]

Cayuga pronunciation guide: /a/ father /e/ weigh /ę/ men (nasalized) /i/ police /o/ hole /ǫ/ home (nasalized) /u/ blue. Underlined vowels are voiceless or whispered. /ʹ/ high pitch. /t/ too /d/ do /k/ king /g/ good (never soft g) /j/ judge or adze /s/ soon /sh/ less heat (never the sh in shirt) /sr/ shrine /sy/ sure /hw/ which (the sound made when you blow out a candle) /h/ hi /ts/ cats hide /ʼ/ (the sound before the first vowel in 'uh-uh') /n/ noon /r/ round /w/ way /y/ yes.

pine cone (continued)
ga·nę́ˀdęˀs pine cones
[ga+ stem: -nęˀdęˀs- pine cone; consists of: -nęˀd(a)$_N$- pine; -(aˀs)ęˀ$_V$- fall, drop, reduce]

pine pitch see: resin
ohs·da:ˀáh ot·séhs·daˀ pine pitch; pine resin

pineapple
o·nęˀdó:t oh·yaˀ pineapple
[consists of: onęˀdǫ:t pine cone; ohyaˀ fruit]

pinnacle see: top
hé:t·gęh·jih the very top

pint
tsaˀde·gat·séˀda·hęh one pint
[tsaˀ+de+ga+ stem: -tseˀdahęh- pint; consists of: -(i)tse(ˀda)$_N$- bottle -(h)ęh$_V$- mid; half, middle]

pioneer
a·ta·di·hę́·dohs·ga:ˀ they (m) were pioneers
[de+... stem: -(h)ędohsga:ˀ- pioneer; consists of: -(h)ęd(a)$_N$- field -ohsgaˀ(w)$_V$- clear]

pipe
ot·sóg·wah·daˀ pipe (for tobacco)
[o+at+ stem: -(h)sohgwahdaˀ- pipe; consists of: -(h)sohg(wa)$_N$- lip -(a)hd$_V$- be like, resemble]

pipe see: tube, water spout
ga·hó·wˀe·daˀ tube; cylinder
de·gah·ne·gáhk·waˀ water spout

piquant see: spicy
ga·wę·nah·sa·dá·i·haˀtaˀ it is hot and peppery (lit.: it heats up the tongue); hot peppers

pit
ots·gę́ˀęˀ peach pit
[o+ stem: -tsgęˀę(da)$_N$- pit]
de·yots·gęˀę́·gęh·dę: flat pits
[de+yo+ stem: - tsgęˀę(da)$_N$- pit -(a)gwęhdę$_V$- flat, dented]

pit see: deseed
ęh·sets·gęˀę́·dah·goˀ you will remove seeds

pitch see: resin, throw
ohs·da:ˀáh ot·séhs·daˀ pine pitch; pine resin
he·hó:gyǫ: he has thrown it

pitcher
he·hó:gyeˀs he throws it (all the time); he is a pitcher
[he+P+ stem: -ogyeˀs- pitcher; consists of: -(a)di, ogy, -ǫdi, -ǫgy$_V$- throw]
gah·sóh·gǫ:t pitcher
[ga+ stem: -(h)sohgǫd- pitcher; consists of: -(h)sohg(wa)$_N$- lip -ǫd$_V$- attached]
gah·soh·gǫ́:t e·yáhk·waˀ pitcher
[consists of: gahsohgǫ:t pitcher; eyahkwaˀ containers]

pitchfork
de·yes·tǫd·raˀehs·dáhk·waˀ pitchfork
[de+ye+ stem: -(h)stǫdraˀehsdahkwaˀ- pitchfork; consists of: -(h)stǫdr(a)$_N$- straw, hay -(ˀ)ehsdahkwaˀ$_V$- hitting implement]
e·hǫ·nˀa·dóˀgwahs·taˀ potato digging fork
[e+ stem: -(h)ǫˀnadoˀgwahstaˀ- pitchfork; consists of: -(h)ǫnaˀd(a)$_N$- potato -oˀgwahsd$_V$- dig]

pitiful see: poor
ó:dęht poverty; it is poor, pitiful

Pittsburg, PA see: E (De·yo·ha·teh·sǫˀ)

pity
gę·dę́·ǫˀ to help each other; compassion; helpfulness
[ga+ stem: -(i)dęǫ, (i)dę(:)$_V$- pity]
ke·dę́·ǫhs I feel compassion for her
[TR+ stem: -(i)dęǫ, (i)dę(:)$_V$- pity]
a·ké:dę:ˀ I felt sorry for her
ęhs·hé:dę:ˀ you will pity her, show mercy, compassion
a·ga:ké:dę:ˀ I felt compassion for them
a·ké:dę: I feel sorry for her

pity (continued)
dahs·gí:dę: pity me
placate see: forget
ęhs·he'ni·gǫ́·hęh·dę' you will make s.o. feel better, comfort s.o.
place
tó: hǫ́:weh a place
o·nak·da·gǫ́n·yǫhs(geh) an important or higher place
[o+(at) stem: -nakd(a)$_N$- bed, seat -gǫnyǫhsd$_V$- honour]
ot·nak·da·gǫ́:nyǫhs an important, prestigious seat, place
place see: dwell, put, put down
nę·yak·n'id·rǫ́:da'k where we two (excl.) will dwell
ę·yé·hę' she will place it
ha·yę́·hę' he puts, places it there
place
[-'geh, hneh external locative suffixes; denote a place]
[-(a)ędahkwa' the verb 'lie' with instrumental; denotes 'a place where certain objects are put']
placenta see: uterus
e·wi·ya:hk·wa' uterus; placenta
placid see: peace, quiet
sgę:nǫ́' ge·nǫ́h·dǫn·yǫh I am at peace
ta'déyog·yę: quietness; quiet; stillness
plague see: sickness
o·nǫh·so·dá·i:yǫ:' sickness; illness; epidemic; plague
plainly see: I (gwa' ti:gę:)
plains
de·yǫh·wę·jág·węh·dę: flat land; prairies; plains
[de+yo+ stem: -ǫhwęjagwęhdę:- plains, prairie; consists of: -ǫhwęj(a)$_N$- earth, land -(a)gwęhdę:$_V$- be flat, dented]
plait see: braid
gan·ya:tsǫ́:ni: it is braided
plan
srih·wáhs'ahs you promise, make an agreement all the time
[stem: -(r)ihwahs'- plan; consists of: -(r)ih(wa)$_N$- word -(h)s'$_V$- plan, promise]
ha·íh·wi̱h·s'ahs he is making promises, making agreements
ę·jad·rih·wáhs'a:' you two will plan, make a plan
ęd·wad·ri̱h·wáh·s'a:' we all (incl.) will plan s.t.
ęhs·ríh·wa̱h·s'a:' you will plan an idea; you will promise, make an agreement
ha·ih·wih·s'ǫ́·hǫg·ye' he is going along making promises, making agreements
ęd·wę'ni·gǫ·hó:dę' we all (incl.) will come up with an idea, plan s.t.
[stem: -(')nigǫh(a)$_N$- mind -odę$_V$- put]
plan see: do on purpose
tsi·wéh·dǫh it was planned on purpose
plane see: airplane, jet
de·gá:dęhs an airplane (lit.: it flies)
ot·sa:dó:t de·gá:dęh a jet; a plane
planet see: orb
gá:gwa:' a heavenly body (for example, the sun, the moon)
plank see: board
ga·néhs·da:' a board
plant
tę́' de·há·yę·twahs he is not a planter
[(N+) stem: -yętw, yęto$_V$- plant]
ęk'nǫh·sa·yę́:to' I will plant onions
[(N+) stem: -(')nǫhs(a)$_N$- onion -yętw, yęto$_V$- plant]
ga·yę́:twęh a seeded field; it is planted
ho·yę́:twęh he planted
plant see: flower, tree, weed
a·wę·hę'shǫ́:'ǫh a variety of flowers, plants
gra̱·hé:dǫ' many trees
a·wę́·no̱hg·ra' weeds

plantain
de·yó·ha·hǫ: common plantain
[de+yo+ stem: -(h)ahǫ:- plantain; consists of: -(h)ah(a)$_N$- road -(h)ǫ(:)$_V$- lie across]
planting tool
e·yę́t·wahk·waʼ planting tool
[e+ stem: -yętwahkwaʼ- planting tool; consists of: -yętw, yęto$_V$- plant]
plaster see: clay
o·ná·wa·daʼ clay; plaster; white-wash
plate see: dish
ga·jęʼ, gadseʼ a dish; a plate; a bowl
plateau see: plains
de·yǫh·wę·jág·węh·dę: flat land; prairies; plains
play
hot·gáhn·yeʼ he is playing
[at+ stem: -gahnye$_V$- play]
sat·gáhn·yeʼ play
a·wát·g̱a̱·hiʼt it played with it
[at+ stem: -gahiʼd$_V$- play with s.t.]
got·gá·hiʼdǫh she is playing with it now
ę·sa·da̱ẖ·yó·ji̱ẖ·dęht you will play in the playground
[ad+ stem: -(a)hyojihdęhd$_V$- play]
ga·ę·no·dá:gyeʼ they (f/m) are making music as they travel
[stem: -(r)ęnod- play music; consists of: -(r)ęn(a)$_N$- song, music -odagyeʼ$_V$- stand along]
play see: fun, gamble, game, play dead
a·gǫ́ʼwę̱ẖ·sahs I am having a good time, enjoying s.t.
de·to·dí:yęʼ they (m) are gambling, betting
de·ha·di·yę́h·da̱ẖk·waʼ they (m) are playing a game (dominoes, scrabble, etc.)
play dead
ę·sa·dę·ni·hé:yaʼt you will play dead, pretend to be dead
[P+ (a)dęn+ stem: -(i)heyaʼd- play dead; consists of: -(ga)hey, (gę)hey, (i)hey, (ga)he:, (gę)he:, (i)he:$_V$- die, weak, exhausted]
plaything see: toy
ǫt·ga·hiʼdáhk·waʼ a toy
playground
ot·gahn·yʼe̱·dáhk·waʼ a place where people play; a playground
[o+at+ stem: -gahnyeʼdahkwaʼ- playground; consists of: -gahnye$_V$- play]
plaza
ǫt·ge·hǫ·dáhk·waʼgeh plaza
[ǫ+ stem: -(a)tgehǫdahkwaʼgeh- plaza; consists of: -(a)tgehǫ$_V$- sell]
gyǫ·dęh·ni·nǫ́:nyǫh plaza
[g+yǫ+(a)dę+ stem: -(h)ninǫnyǫh- plaza; consists of: -(h)ninǫ$_V$- buy; sell]
plead
sa·dę·ni·dę́h·taʼ you plead all the time
[(a)dę+ stem: -nidęhd- plead; consists of: -nidę$_V$- be kind]
ęh·sa·dę·ní:dęht you will plead
go·na·dę·ní·dę̱ẖ·dǫh they (f/m) are pleading
pleasant see: enjoyable, nice
a·ǫʼwé:sęh(t), a·ǫʼwé:sah(t) it is enjoyable; a good feeling
o·yá:nreʼ it is nice, good, beautiful
please see: I (waʼgyęh)
please see: fun, enjoyable
a·gǫ́ʼwę̱ẖ·sahs I am having a good time, enjoying s.t.
pleasing see: enjoyable, nice
a·ǫʼwé:sęh(t), a·ǫʼwé:sah(t) it is enjoyable; a good feeling
o·yá:nreʼ it is nice, good, beautiful
pleat see: fold
dę·seh·sʼak·da:nyǫ́:goʼ you will fold s.t. up

pledge see: plan
ha·íh·wih·sʼahs he is making promises, making agreements
plentiful
o·dah·yǫ́:ni: plentiful fruit
[A/P+ad+(N+) stem: consists of: -(a)hy(a)$_N$- fruit, berry -ǫni, ǫny$_V$- make; be plentiful]
plot see: field, garden, plan, yard
ga·hę́·da·gǫ: in the field; in the meadow
ga·yę́·twah·sǫʼ a garden; it is planted
ha·íh·wih·sʼahs he is making promises, making agreements
wa·dę·hę́:gǫ:, a·dę·hę́·gǫ: in the yard
plow see: harrows, hoe, turn over
wa·déʼdreʼs de·ga·heh·dá·hih·taʼ drag harrows
ats·hóʼkdǫhs·raʼ a hoe
at·keh·da·wę́:n·ye:ʼ I hoed, tilled the earth
ga·heh·da·gá·hat·węh a ploughed field
pluck
ę·séhs·toʼdręht you will pluck feathers
[stem: -(h)stoʼdręhd- pluck; consists of: -(h)stoʼdr(a)$_N$- feather -(y)ęhd$_V$- hit, knock down, strike]
sehs·tóʼdręht pluck it
plum
de·yots·gęʼę·gęh·dę́: oh·yaʼ plums
[consists of: deyotsgęʼęgęhdę: flat pits; ohyaʼ fruit]
plumber
oh·ne·ga·nóhs ga·hǫ·we·da·den·yǫ́ʼ shahs·rǫ́:nihs a plumber
[consists of: ohneganohs water; gahǫwedadenyǫʼ plumber; shahsrǫ:nihs repairman]
ga·hǫ·we·dá·den·yǫʼ a plumber
[ga+ stem: -(h)oweʼdadenyǫʼ- plumber; consists of: -(h)oweʼd(a)$_N$- tube, cylinder, hose -deni, deny$_V$- change]
plume see: feather, pen, throat
gahs·doʼdro·wá:nęh a big feather
gah·ne:gá:ʼ eh·yá·dǫhk·waʼ a pen
o·háʼdaʼ a quill; a plume; a feather; the voice; the throat; the larynx; the esophagus
plunder
ga·nę́hsg·węh stolen property; plunder; s.t. robbed
[ga+ stem: -nęhsgwęh- plunder, stolen property; consists of: -nęhsgw$_V$- steal]
plunge see: dive, swim
ę·háh·do:ʼ he will dive
ę·há·da·wę:ʼ he will swim
plural see: many
ni·yo·nat·gáʼdeʼ there are so many
plural
[-dǫʼ the verb 'stand' with distributive; denotes 'a group of similar standing objects']
[-odǫʼ the verb 'stand' with distributive; denotes 'a group of objects or actions']
[-odǫnyǫʼ the verb 'stand' with distributives; denotes many objects or actions]
[-ǫʼ distributive suffix; denotes 'several objects or actions']
[-ǫdǫʼ the verb 'attached' with distributive; denotes 'several attached objects']
[-ǫdǫnyǫʼ the verb 'attached' with distributives; denotes 'several (attached) objects']
[-ǫnyahnǫʼ the verb 'make' plus dislocative plus plural; denotes 'growing' or 'several objects']
[-ǫnyǫʼ distributive suffixes; denote 'several objects or actions']
[-(h)sǫʼ pluralizer; denotes several objects]
[-(h)sǫ:ʼa, (h)sǫ:ʼǫh pluralizer; denotes 'several objects']

plural (continued)
[-ʼs pluralizer suffix; denotes ‘several objects’]
[-adenyǫʼ the verb ‘exist’ with distributive; denotes ‘several existing objects’]
[-agehagyeʼ the verb ‘be more than one’ in the progressive; denotes ‘several objects at a time’]
plus see: I (also, gwatoh)
pocket
á·ǫ·gęhs·rǫ:t, á·ǫ·gǫhs·rǫ:t a pocket; a kangaroo
[a+ǫ+ stem: -gęhsr(a)$_N$- pouch, pocket -ǫd$_V$- attached]
pocket see: pouch
ga·ya:ʼ pouch
pocketbook see: wallet
gatgwę́·daʼ a wallet; a purse; a pocketbook; a suitcase
point
ęhs·hę́ʼnyʼa·da:t you will point s.o. out
[TR+ stem: -(ʼ)nyaʼdad- point out s.o.; consists of: -(ʼ)ny(a)$_N$- finger, hand -dad$_V$- cause to stand]
he·yo·dǫh·wę·joʼk·dáʼǫh a point of land; a cape; a peninsula
[he+yo+(a)d+ stem: -ǫhwęjokdaʼǫh- point, peninsula, cape; consists of: -ǫhwęj(a)$_N$- earth, land -oʼkdaʼ$_V$- come to an end]
point see: decimal point
o·jihs·da·nóhg·waʼ a decimal point; a point; a dot
pointed see: sharp
oh·yuʼtí:yeht it is sharp
poise see: erect, patience
ę·wa·dʼa·yó:dęʼ it will be erect (poised to strike)
ga·dęʼni·gǫ·hah·ní·yahs·taʼ I have patience

poison
o·náʼsę: poison; water hemlock
[o+ stem: -(h)naʼsę:- poison, water hemlock; consists of: -(h)n(a)$_N$- oil, gas -(aʼs)ęʼ$_V$- fall, drop, reduce]
poison ivy see: weed
go·wę́·nǫhg·ra:ʼs poison ivy; any plant that causes a skin infection
poke
des·wáʼehs·taʼ you all are poking
[de+... stem: -(a)ʼehsd- poke, pierce; consists of: -(ʼ)e$_V$- hit]
dę·gáʼe:s I will pierce s.t.
ats·wáʼehs you all pierce
dęh·sáʼehs you will spear s.t.
polar see: North
o·tó·wʼe·geh north
polar bear
gę:ʼgę́: ni·ga·yʼa·doʼdę́: hnyag·wá·iʼ a polar bear
[consists of: gęʼgę: it is white; nigayʼadoʼdę: it has a certain kind of body; hnyagwaiʼ bear]
gahn·yag·wá·iʼda·gę:t polar bear
[ga+ stem: -(h)nyagwai(ʼda)$_N$- bear -gęʼd$_V$- light-coloured, white]
pole see: stick
oʼę́:naʼ a snowsnake; a pole
police
sha·go·di·yé:nahs a policemen
[TR+ stem: -yenahs- police; consists of: -yena(w), yenaǫ, yena(:)$_V$- catch, receive, accept]
sha·go:yé:nahs a policeman
ǫ·dę:yé:nahs a policewoman
ga·ǫ·dę·yé:nahs a policewomen
police station
sha·go·di·yé·nahs·geh a police station
[TR+ stem: -yenahsgeh- police station; consists of: -yena(w), yenaǫ, yena(:)$_V$- catch, receive, accept -(ʼ)geh at]

polish see: nail polish, shine
ǫ·de·j'i·o·dah·sóh·ta' nail polish
dę·gahs·da·té'dǫh it is shined, waxed, polished
pollution
o·ji'nǫ·wahs·hǫ:'ǫ́h ot·gǫhs·hǫ:'ǫ́h hní' ę·gę·na·déhs·goh pollution from the cultural aspect
[consists of: oji'nǫwa'shǫ:'ǫh insects; otgǫ'shǫ:ǫh things with evil power; hni' and; ęgęnadehsgoh they (z) will drown]
ę·wá:tno:' there will be pollution
[at+ stem: -(h)no:- pollution; consists of: -(h)n(a)$_N$- oil, gas -o(:)$_V$- submerge]
pond
ga·ná·wa·gǫ: in the pond, swamp
[ga+ stem: -naw(a)$_N$- pond, swamp]
pond see: puddle, swamp
oh·né:go' a puddle; any type of water
ga·ná·wa·ę:' a swamp; a pond
ponder see: think
a·hi:' I thought, intended
pool see: pond, puddle, swimming pool
ga·ná·wa·gǫ: in the pond, swamp
oh·né:go' a puddle; any type of water
ahs·deh·ká:' ǫ·dah·w'ę·dáhk·wa' an outdoor swimming pool
poor
a·gí:dęht I am poor, poverty-stricken, in poverty
[P+ stem: -(i)dęhd- be poor; consists of: -(i)dęǫ, (i)dę(:)$_V$- pity s.o.]
ó:dęht poverty; it is poor, pitiful
ǫ·gí·dęh·te' I am poor at s.t., I am not rich
[P+ stem: -(i)dęhte'- poor; consists of: -(i)dęǫ, (i)dę(:)$_V$- pity]
pop
oh·ne·ga·gá'ǫh pop; soda
[o+ stem: -(h)negaga'ǫh- pop, soda; consists of: -(h)neg(a)$_N$- water, liquid -ga'ǫh$_V$- be tasty, delicious]
poplar
on·rah·dǫ·dáhs·ra' a poplar tree
[o+ stem: -nrahdǫdahsr(a)$_N$- a poplar; consists of: -nrahd(a)$_N$- leaf -ǫdah$_V$- put in]
porch
ohs·gǫ:t a porch
[o+ stem: -(a)hsgǫd- porch; consists of: -(a)hsg(wa)$_N$- roof, bridge -ǫd$_V$- attached]
ohsg·wá:gǫ: in the porch
[stem: -(a)hsg(wa)$_N$- roof, bridge]
porcupine
gan·hé'da' a porcupine
[ga+ stem: -nhe'd(a)$_N$- porcupine]
pork
ga·jik·he'da·hǫ́h gwihs·gwíhs o'wá·hǫh salt pork
[consists of: gajikhe'dahǫh s.t. with salty striations; gwihsgwihs pig; o'wahǫh meat]
gwihs·gwíhs o'wá·hah·se:' fresh pork
[consists of: gwihsgwihs pig; o'wahahse:' fresh meat]
porkchop
gwihs·gwihs o'wá·hǫh pig meat; pork chops
[consists of: gwihsgwihs pig; o'wahǫh meat]
porridge
o·jíhg·wa' porridge; mush
[o+ stem: -jih(s)g(wa)$_N$- porridge, mush]
o·jíhsg·wa' mush
portable
wat·gę́·ihs·ta' it is portable
[at+ stem: -gęihsd$_V$- move; be portable]
portal see: doorway, gate
gan·hó·ga·hę:t a doorway
gan·ho·ha·ní:yǫ:t a gate; a door
portrayal see: description
tsę́h ni·yóh·dǫ's descriptions

Cayuga pronunciation guide: /a/ father /e/ weigh /ę/ men (nasalized) /i/ police /o/ hole /ǫ/ home (nasalized) /u/ blue. Underlined vowels are voiceless or whispered. /′/ high pitch. /t/ too /d/ do /k/ king /g/ good (never soft g) /j/ judge or adze /s/ soon /sh/ less heat (never the sh in shirt) /sr/ shrine /sy/ sure /hw/ which (the sound made when you blow out a candle) /h/ hi /ts/ cats hide /'/ (the sound before the first vowel in 'uh-uh') /n/ noon /r/ round /w/ way /y/ yes.

positive see: certain
o·ih·wí:yo' it is certain, for sure
possessed see: addicted, haunted
hog·yá·na'ǫh he is possessed, addicted (with gambling, women, etc.)
de·wag·yá·ǫn·yo·ta' it is haunted
possession see: have
a·gá:węh it is mine
ag·yę' I have, possess
possessive see: jealous, treasure
go̱h·gá·hę: she is jealous
o·nǫ́hs·da't, o·nǫ́hs·deht it is a treasure; it is precious, valuable; it is possessive
possibility see: maybe
ę·wa:dǫ́' gis·hęh maybe; a possibility
posterior see: anus, behind
o·hét·ga'a:' rear end; posterior
ga̱h·ná'tso:t its attached ass; a bare ass (said of children with no clothes on, etc.)
post office
ga̱h·ya·dǫhs·ra·nęhg·wíh gęg·yóhg·wa·ę' a post office
[consists of: ga̱hyadǫhsranęhgwih it hauls paper; post office; gęgyohgwaę' corporation]
eh·ya·dǫ̱hs·ra·ę:dáhk·wa'geh post office
[e+ stem: -(h)yadǫhsraędahkwa'geh- post office; consists of: -(h)yadǫhsr(a)$_N$- paper -ędahkwa'$_V$- place where s.t. is put -(')geh at]
postpone see: move
se·gę́·ihs·ta' you postpone it all the time; you move it all the time
postponement
ga·gę́·ihs·dǫh a postponement
[ga+ stem: -gęihsdǫh- postponement; consists of: -gęihsd$_V$- move, postpone]
postsecondary education see: G (education, postsecondary, he:t·gęh tga:deh hę·na·de·wa·yęhs·ta')
pot
e·kǫn·ya'tá' ga·na'jas·hǫ́:'ǫh cooking pots
[consists of: ekǫnya'ta' what one cooks with; gana'jashǫ:'ǫh cooking pots]
ge·í: ga̱h·sí:na:t an iron pot
[consists of: gei: four; ga̱hsi:na:t it has standing legs]
pot see: kettle
de·gah·sí:nǫ:t a kettle
pot cleaner
e·na'jo̱·há·i'ta' a pot cleaner
[e+ stem: -na'johai'ta'- pot cleaner; consists of: -na'j(a)$_N$- pail, drum -ohai'd$_V$- cause to clean, wash]
potato
o·hǫ́n'a·da' a potato
[o+ stem: -(h)ǫna'd(a)$_N$- potato]
ga̱·hǫ́n'a·do' boiled potatoes
[stem: -(h)ǫna'd(a)$_N$- potato -o'$_V$- boiled, stewed]
o·hǫn'a·dó·wane's big potatoes
[stem: -(h)ǫna'd(a)$_N$- potato -owanę's$_V$- big objects]
potato masher
de·ye·hǫ·na'da̱·híh·da̱hk·wa' a potato masher
[de+ye+ stem: -(h)ǫna'dahihdahkwa'- potato masher; consists of: -(h)ǫna'd(a)$_N$- potato -(hr)ihd$_V$- break up s.t.]
potency see: power
ga̱hs·háhs·dę̱hs·ra', ohs·háhs·dę̱hs·ra' power; strength
potty chair
o·wi:ya:'áh ǫ·nin·hę·hę́hk·wa' baby's potty chair
[consists of: owi:ya:'ah baby; ǫninhęhęhkwa' potty chair]
pouch
ga·ya:' a pouch
[ga+ stem: -ya:$_N$- bag]

pouch see: pocket
á·ǫ·gęhs·rǫ:t, á·ǫ·gohs·rǫ:t a pocket; a kangaroo
pounce
hę·sag·y’a·dǫ́:di’ you will pounce on it
[he+P+ag+ stem: -ya’dǫdi- pounce; consists of: -ya’d(a)$_{N}$- body -(a)di, ogy, -ǫdi, -ǫgy$_{V}$- throw]
hęh·sag·ya·dó·i·ya’k you will pounce on it
[he+P+ag+ stem: -ya’doiya’g- pounce; consists of: -ya’d(a)$_{N}$- body -(i)ya’g$_{V}$- cut, break]
pound
ge·té’ta’ I am a pounder
[(N+) stem: -te’d$_{V}$- pound]
ęh·sé:te’t you will pound corn
ę·gé:te’t I will pound
a·gé·te’dǫh I did pound
se·te’t pound it (corn, etc.)
o·gǫ́:tra’ a pound (measurement)
[o+ stem: -gǫ’tr(a)$_{N}$- weight]
de·ga·g’ǫt·rá:ge: two pounds
[de+ga+ stem: -gǫ’tr(a)$_{N}$- weight -(a)ge:$_{V}$- two or more]
ni·ga·g’ǫt·rá:ge: that many pounds
[ni+ga+ stem: -gǫ’tr(a)$_{N}$- weight -(a)ge:$_{V}$- two or more]
pound see: hit, knock, weight
ęhs·wá’e:k you will pound, tap
sen·hó·ha’e:k knock on the door
tsę́h ni·yo·gǫt·rá:s·de’ weight; pounds; poundage
pour see: flow, rain, sprinkle
ot·ne·gah·dę́:gyǫ:, oh·ne·gah·dę́:gyǫ: flowing water
a·gas·dá·o:wa·naht it rained hard
ę·hę́·nod·rahs they (m) will sprinkle on
poverty see: poor
a·gí:dęht I am poor, poverty-stricken, in poverty
pow wow
ha·dihs·do·wá·he·ha’ a pow wow (lit.: they (m) put on their headdresses and perform)
[A+ stem: -(h)sdowaheha’- pow wow; consists of: -(h)sdow(a)$_{N}$- feather -(hr)e, (hr)ę$_{V}$- put, place]
dę·hę·nat·nǫn·ya·gę́:nye’s a pow-wow (lit: they (m) perform competition dancing)
[de+...at+ stem: -nǫyagęnye’s- pow-wow; consists of: -nǫny(a)$_{N}$- dance -gęni, gęny$_{V}$- compete]
o·ih·wa·ga:yǫ́h hę·had·rǫ·hé:s dę·hę́nat·kwa’ a pow-wow (the traditional type)
[consists of: oihwaga:yǫh traditional hęhadrǫhe:s they (m) will gather over there; dęhęnatkwa’ they dance]
powder
ǫ·de·te’tráh·ta’ powder
[ǫ+ade+ stem: -te’trahta’- powder; consists of: -te’tr(a)$_{N}$- flour, powder -te’trahd$_{V}$- powder oneself]
wa·de·te’tráh·ta’ it powders itself
[ade+ stem: consists of: -te’tr(a)$_{N}$- flour, powder -te’trahd$_{V}$- powder oneself]
ga·te’trǫ́:ni: it has been pounded into powder (for example, corn)
[stem: -te’tr(a)$_{N}$- flour, powder -ǫni, ǫny$_{V}$- make]
ga·dé·te’tra:s I am powdering myself
[(a)de+ stem: -te’tra:’- powder oneself; consists of: -te’tr(a)$_{N}$- flour, powder -a:’$_{V}$- hold, contain, include]
ę·ga·de·té’tra:’ I am going to powder myself
o·wi:ya:’áh ǫ·de·te’tráh·ta’ baby powder
[consists of: owi:ya:’ah baby; ǫdete’trahta’ powder]

Cayuga pronunciation guide: /a/ father /e/ weigh /ę/ men (nasalized) /i/ police /o/ hole /ǫ/ home (nasalized) /u/ blue. Underlined vowels are voiceless or whispered. /´/ high pitch. /t/ too /d/ do /k/ king /g/ good (never soft g) /j/ judge or adze /s/ soon /sh/ less heat (never the sh in shirt) /sr/ shrine /sy/ sure /hw/ which (the sound made when you blow out a candle) /h/ hi /ts/ cats hide /’/ (the sound before the first vowel in ‘uh-uh’) /n/ noon /r/ round /w/ way /y/ yes.

powder see: bath powder, flour
ǫ·de·te'tro·há:ta' bath powder
o·té'tra' flour; powder
power
gahs·háhs·dęhs·ra', ohs·háhs·dęhs·ra' power; strength
[ga/o+ stem: -shasdęhsr(a)$_N$- power, strength]
gahs·hahs·dęt·rá:t·gǫ' evil power
[ga+ stem: -shasdęhsr(a)$_N$- power, strength -(a)tgǫ'$_V$- have evil power, bad medicine; be a witch, a warlock; be ominous]
powerful see: strong
gahs·há:sde' it is strong, tough, powerful
powerless see: weak
a·gę́·da·gę: I am a wimp; I am weak (mentally or physically); I am cowardly
practical see: useful
o·í·hǫ:t it is useful
practice medicine see: cure
a·gé:ję't it cured me
prairie see: plains
de·yǫh·wę·jág·węh·dę: flat land; prairies; plains
praise
ęhs·he·ho·wá:naht you will praise her, uplift her spirits, flatter her
[TR+ stem: -(r)ihowanahd- proclaim, announce; praise s.o., uplift s.o.; consists of: -owanahd$_V$- enlarge]
praise see: revere
dęd·wa·dad·rih·wa·nǫ́hk·wa:k we all (incl.) will show respect for one another
prank see: trick
og·yá·ǫhs·ra', ag·yá·ǫhs·ra' a trick
pray
ho·nad·rę·ná·ę:' they (m) (Christians) are praying
[(a)d+ stem: -(r)ęnaę(:)- pray; consists of: -(r)ęn(a)$_N$- song, music -ę:$_V$- lay s.t. down]

pray (continued)
tę·nad·rę·ná·i·ha' they (m) are praying
dę·hę·na·dǫ́t·so·ta' they (m) pray on their knees
[de+...(a)d+ stem: -ǫtsod- pray on one's knees; consists of: -ǫts(a)$_N$- knee -od$_V$- stand]
srih·wá·n'e·ka' you are always praying
[-(r)ih(wa)$_N$- word, matter, affair -(')neg$_V$- pray]
ęhs·ríh·w'a·ne:k you will pray P
sa·ih·w'a·né:gęh you are praying S
prayer
ga·ih·wa·né:gę:' prayer; to pray
[ga+ stem: -(r)ihwanegę:'- prayer; consists of: -(r)ih(wa)$_N$- word -(')negę$_V$- pray for oneself; hope]
praying mantis
ǫg·wéh o·ji'nǫ́:wa' a praying mantis
[consists of: ǫ:gweh person; oji'nǫ:wa' a bug; an insect]
wad·rę·ná·eh·nę' (o·ji'nǫ́:wa') a praying mantis
[consists of: wadręnaehnę' it prays; oji'nǫ:wa' a bug, an insect]
precede
jǫ·ki·hę·dǫ́'se:' she has gone on before us
[s/j+TR+ stem: -(h)ędǫ'se:'- precede s.o.; consists of: -(h)ęd$_V$- lead]
precede see: go over there, lead
hęh·sé'sǫ' you will go on ahead, take the lead
ę·há·hę:t he will lead
precious see: costly, prosperity, treasure
ga·nǫ:' it is expensive, dear, precious
ot·ga:nǫ́:ni: prosperity; it is precious
o·nǫ́hs·da't, o·nǫ́hs·deht it is a treasure; it is precious, valuable; it is possessive
predecessor see: ancestor
ha·di·gęh·jih·sǫ'gę́·hę:' they (m) are our grandfathers, our ancestors

predict
né' hó:nę: predictors, messengers (lit.: what they (m) said); proverb; a prediction; a saying; a prophesy
[ne' P+ stem: -ę:- predictor, messenger; consists of: -i, ę$_{V}$- say]
predict see: foretell, omen
o.hę:dǫ́: he.ha:dí:gęh they (m) look ahead, tell the future
wat.sǫ́:nyǫ:s an omen
predominant see: special
o.i.ho.wá:nęh it is important; a great or worthy commendation; it is special
prefer see: like, want
he.nǫ́h.we's I like him
dęh.sa.dǫh.wę:jǫ́:ni' you will want s.t.
prefix
dwa.sá.wahk.wa' a prefix
[d+wa+ stem: -(a)hsawahkwa'- prefix; consists of: -(a)hsawę, (a)hsa:$_{V}$- begin, start]
pregnant
wa.dé'dǫh.ne' a pregnant animal
[wa+(a)de+ stem: -(')dǫ(:)$_{V}$- be due]
e.gó.wa.nęh she is big, pregnant
[e+ stem: -gowanęh$_{V}$- be big, pregnant]
go.wí:ya:t she is pregnant, has a baby in her
[P+ stem: -wiyad- be pregnant; consists of: -wiy(a)$_{N}$- child, offspring -d$_{V}$- stand]
go.wi.yá.ę.d'ad.re' she is with child
[P+ stem: -wiyaęda'(dre')- be pregnant, expecting; consists of: -wiy(a)$_{N}$- child, offspring -ędadre'$_{V}$- cause to go and lie down]
swahs.gwá.węn.yǫ' you all are carrying babies
[P+ stem: -(h)sg(wa)$_{N}$- stone; -(a)węnye(:)$_{V}$- stir, mix]
swa.dę.hę.wá.ǫ:nyǫ' you all are carrying babies
[P+ (a)dę+ stem: -(h)ęwaǫnyǫ'$_{V}$- be holding, carrying several things]

prehistoric see: dinosaur, old (thing), past, previously
de.ga'ni.gǫh.dę́:dǫhs dinosaurs
o.gá.yǫh.sǫ' old things
oh.ná'gę.jih way back in the past; back then
ga.ó' na.wá:dih previously
premature
to.dǫ́:nho'k he is mentally challenged; he was born premature
[d+P+ad+ stem: -ǫnho'g- be premature, mentally challenged; consists of: -ǫnhe'$_{V}$- be alive]
gyo.dǫ́:nho'k it is mentally challenged
dya.gó.dǫn.ho'k she is not full term; she is mentally challenged
Premier see: G (O.hę.dǫh.go:wah)
premium see: special
o.i.ho.wá:nęh it is important; it is special
premonition see: foretell, omen
o.hę:dǫ́: he.ha:dí:gęh they (m) look ahead, tell the future
wat.sǫ́:nyǫ:s an omen
preoccupation see: burden
o.íh.wahs.de' a mental burden; a preoccupation
prepare see: cook, make
go.kǫ́:ni: she is cooking
gǫ́:nihs I make, earn
prepronominal prefix
o.hę.dǫ́: dwa.sá.wahk.wa' a prepronominal prefix
[consists of: ohę:dǫ: ahead, in front, the front; dwasawahkwa' prefix]
prepubescent see: grow, teenager
ǫh.dó:gahs she is prepubescent; she is maturing; she is reaching puberty
ho.gá'das.wahs he smells (or sniffs) pants (said of prepubescent teenagers)
ho'ká:swahs he smells (or sniffs) skirts (said of prepubescent teenagers)

present
ęh·sá:dǫ' you will present, offer s.t.; you will become s.t.
[ad+ stem: -awi, ǫ$_V$- give; present, offer]
wa·dá·wi̱hǫ' presents
[wa+ad+ stem: -awihǫ'- presents; consists of: -awih$_V$- go and give]
gá·ǫ·hǫ·ta' a wedding present (lit.: they (f/m) are asking)
[gaǫ+ stem: -(a)hǫta'- wedding; consists of: -(a)hǫdǫ(:)$_V$- ask]
ęhs·ríh·wa̱·hę' you will present an idea
[stem: -(r)ihwahę- present an idea, submit an idea; consists of: -(r)ih(wa)$_N$- word -(hr)e, (hr)ę$_V$- put, place]
present see: give
shǫg·wá:wi: he has given us
presentation
ga·íh·wa̱·he:' a presentation
[stem: -(r)ihwahe:'- presentation; consists of: -(r)ih(wa)$_N$- word -(hr)e, (hr)ę$_V$- put, place]
presentation see: sing
ho·no:dré̜:not they (m) are making a presentation
presently see: I (wa'ji:hah)
preservation see: G (de·hę·nǫh·wę·jahsn·ye')
preserve
sa·dah·ya̱h·sę:nǫ́:nih preserve fruit
[ad+N+ stem: -(a)hy(a)$_N$- fruit, berry -(h)sęnǫni$_V$- store, put away; preserve]
president see: G (sha·go·hę:dǫ: gyoh·wę·ja:de')
press see: iron, squeeze
ęhs·ríhs·da:' you will iron
de·wak·dǫ̱·há:gǫh I am squeezing it
pressure see: explode
de·wad·ra·né·ga·ǫ:s it is exploding
presume see: believe, suppose
ta·wéh·da̱h·gǫh he believes
gǫ·dǫ́h·ne:' I suppose

pretend
a:we:t'áh tsǫ́: dę·sá'tsǫhs pretend to sneeze
[a:+ w+ stem: -et'ah$_V$- pretend]
[consists of: a:we:t'ah pretend; tsǫ: just, only dęsa'tsǫhs you (s) will sneeze]
pretend see: implied, make-believe
a:wé:t'ah implied; pretend
a:wet'ahs·hǫ́:'ǫh make-believe; pretend
pretty
ek·sa'gó:wah she is pretty
[A+ stem: -ksa'gowah- pretty, handsome; consists of: -ksa('da)$_N$- child -gowah- big, great]
ga·ek·s'a·gó:wah they (f/m) are pretty
a:gek·sa'go·wá·gę̱·he:k I wish I were handsome
pretty see: enticing, good, handsome
ohs·gá:na't it is enticing, alluring, attractive, tempting
o·yá:n·re' it is nice, good, beautiful
o·jín'a·dǫ: it is handsome; s.t. / s.o. handsome, attractive
prevail see: able, accomplish, win
ęh·se:gwé:ni' you will succeed
ęhs·rih·wag·wé̜:ni' you will accomplish s.t.
a·e·tig·wé:ni' we won a competition
prevalent see: special
o·i·ho·wá:nęh it is important, etc.
prevent see: quit, stop
a·gé̜·ni̱·hę' I stopped, quit
dęhs·dahs, dęhs·dęhs you will prevent it, stop it, stand it up
previous
ga·ó' na·wá:dih previously
[gao' na'+ w+ stem: -(a)dih$_V$- side; previously]
previous see: former, past
ǫg·ya·dá·o'gę̱·hę:' my former ceremonial friend
oh·ná'gę·jih way back in the past; back then

price
ga·gá·he:ʼ the price of s.t.
[ga+ stem: -ga:$_N$- price -(h)e:ʼ$_V$- sitting up on top of s.t.]
ó:ga:ʼ a price (is on it)
[o+ stem: -ga:$_N$- price]
o·gá:gǫ: in debt
[o+ stem: -ga:$_N$- price -(a)gǫ: in]
price see: cost, debt
ǫ·gé·ga̱h·dę̨ʼ that's how much it cost me
wat·gá·ot a debt; a price
prickly see: sharp, thorn bush
oh·yuʼtí:yeht it is sharp
o·hí:k·da·i:ʼ a thorn bush
pride
ga·ná·i: pride; boastfulness
[ga+ stem: -nai$_V$- proud]
gahs·he·go·wá·nęh·taʼ you have pride in them
[TR+ stem: -gowanęhd- have pride in s.o.; consists of: -(g)owanęhd$_V$- enlarge]
pride see: peacock
ga·ná·iʼdaʼ a peacock; pride; boastfulness
primary see: begin, lead, special, B (da·wa:gyę:t gyog·yęh·dǫh), I (hya:ʼ)
da·wá:gyę:t the first one; the beginner
ęhs·rę:t you will be the lead
o·i·ho·wá:nęh it is important; a great or worthy commendation it is special
primate see: gorilla, monkey
ga·jiʼnǫ̱h·da:sgó:wah a gorilla
ga·jíʼnǫ̱h·da:s a monkey
Prime Minister see: G (gwa:go:wah gon·haʼtraʼ)
primogenitor see: ancestor
ha·di·gę̱h·jih·sǫʼgę́·hę:ʼ they (m) are our grandfathers, our ancestors
principal
ǫ·dad·ri̱·hǫn·ya·niʼtáʼ hohs·díhs·dǫh a male principal

principal (continued)
[consists of: ǫdadri̱hǫnyaniʼtaʼ school; hohsdihsdǫh he is a director, principal, head, etc.]
ǫ·dad·ri̱·hǫn·ya·niʼtáʼ gohs·díhs·dǫh a female principal
[consists of: ǫdadri̱hǫnyaniʼtaʼ school; gohsdihsdǫh she is a director, principal, head, etc.]
print see: publish, write
dęhs·ríhs·dǫ̱·ha:k you will publish s.t.
ęk·yá:dǫ:ʼ I will write
printed fabrics
og·yę·nʼa·dáh·nǫʼ printed fabrics
[o+ag+ stem: -yęnaʼdahnǫʼ- printed fabrics; consists of: -yęnaʼd, yanaʼd$_V$- mark s.t.]
prior see: former, past, previously
ǫg·ya·dá·oʼgę·hę:ʼ my former ceremonial friend
oh·náʼgę·jih way back in the past; back then
ga·óʼ na·wá:dih previously
prison
de·gahn·yǫhs·rá:deʼ a prison
[de+ga+ stem: -(h)nyǫhsradeʼ- prison; consists of: -hnyǫ(ʼǫ)hsr(a)$_N$- iron, steel -deʼ$_V$- exist]
prison see: jail
ǫ·da·dęn·ho·dǫ̱hk·wáʼgeh a jail; a prison
private
go·nǫ́·hę·jih they are private people
[P+ stem: -ǫhęʼjih- private; consists of: -(r)ǫhę$_V$- alone -jih really]
private see: secret
od·rih·wa̱h·séh·dǫh it is secret
Privy Council see: G (Gwa:go:wah Hǫ·wa·di̱hn·yaʼso·da·hǫh)
probably see: I (ne:ʼgiʼshęh)

Cayuga pronunciation guide: /a/ father /e/ weigh /ę/ men (nasalized) /i/ police /o/ hole /ǫ/ home (nasalized) /u/ blue. Underlined vowels are voiceless or whispered. /ʼ/ high pitch. /t/ too /d/ do /k/ king /g/ good (never soft g) /j/ judge or adze /s/ soon /sh/ less heat (never the sh in shirt) /sr/ shrine /sy/ sure /hw/ which (the sound made when you blow out a candle) /h/ hi /ts/ cats hide /ʼ/ (the sound before the first vowel in 'uh-uh') /n/ noon /r/ round /w/ way /y/ yes.

probe see: examine, poke
ę-sat-ga̱-hí:yohs you will look closely at s.t., peer at s.t.
des-wá'ehs-ta' you all are poking
proceed see: continue, go, move, pass by, persevere
hę-gá-dag-ye' it will continue on
ęhs-ne:' you two will go together
ohę:dǫ́: he'sé-nǫ̱hg-ye' you're moving forward
a:ga-dǫ́:goht I should go on
se-já:gǫh persevere; keep it up
proclaim
ęt-ri-ho-wá:naht you will proclaim, announce s.t.
[stem: -(r)ihowanahd- proclaim, announce; consists of: -owanahd$_V$- enlarge]
procure see: acquire, buy, catch
ę-sa:yę́:da' you will acquire, obtain
ęhs-ní:nǫ' you will buy, purchase
ag-yé:na:' I caught it; I received it
produce
a-ha-i-hǫ́n-ya̱h-nǫ:' he produced s.t. (lit.: he made or started the idea)
[stem: -(r)ihǫnyahnǫ(:)- produce s.t.; consists of: -(r)ih(wa)$_N$- word -ǫnyahnǫ(:)- go and make several things]
ga-yęt-wah-sǫ́' a-sé's-hǫ:' produce (lit.: new vegetables, fruit)
[consists of: gayętwahsǫ' it is planted; ase'shǫ:' vegetables]
produce see: make
gǫ́:nihs I make, earn
product see: make
ga̱hs-rǫ́n-y'a-dǫh it is made from s.t.
profanity see: swear
ęhs-rih-wa-né'ak-sǫ:' you will swear, use profane language

profit
ęh-sat-wihs-dǫ́:ni' you will profit
[at+ stem: -(h)wihsdǫni- profit; consists of: -(h)wihsd(a), (hr)ihsd(a)$_N$- metal, money -ǫni, ǫny$_V$- make]
wat-wihs-dǫ́:ni: profit
ot-wíhs-don-ya't profit
[at+ stem: -(h)wihsdǫnya'd- profit; consists of: -(h)wihsd(a), (hr)ihsd(a)$_N$- metal, money -ǫnya'd- be made]
sat-wíhs-do:nya't you profit
wat-wihs-dǫ-nyá'dǫh profit; investment
prohibited see: forbidden
o-nǫ́'ne:' it is forbidden, sacred, holy
project see: protrude
he-yá-ǫ:t it protrudes
projectile see: arrow, ash, stone, throw
g'a-nǫh an arrow
o'gę́-hę' ashes; bullets; dust
gahsg-wa:' a stone; a rock; a boulder; a bullet
wag-yǫ: s.t. thrown away; discards
prolonged see: take time
tó na'ǫ́-nis-he' it took that long
prominent see: special
o-i-ho-wá:nęh it is important; a great or worthy commendation; it is special
promise
ga-ih-wi̱h-s'á-hǫh a promise
[ga+ stem: -(r)ihwahs'ahǫh- a promise; consists of: -(r)ih(wa)$_N$- word -(h)s'$_V$- plan, promise]
promise see: plan
ęhs-ríh-wa̱h-s'a:' you will plan an idea; you will promise, make an agreement
proper see: right
tga:yé-i: it is right, correct
property see: belongings
sa-wę́h-sǫ' your belongings; your property
prophet see: fortune teller
dę̱-ha-di-ya-do-wéh-ta' they (m) are fortune tellers, thinkers

proportion see: size
shę́h ní:waʼs sizes; how big they are
propose see: suggest
ęt·sęʼni·go·hó:dęʼ you will suggest, present an idea
prosper see: able
ęh·se:gwé:niʼ you will succeed
prosperity
got·ga·nǫ·ní·hag·yeʼ prosperity; s.o. is prospering
[at+ stem: -ganǫni- rich, wealthy; consists of: -ga$_N$- price -ǫni, ǫny$_V$- make]
ot·ga:nǫ́:ni: prosperity; it is precious
prostitute
wa·dat·ge·hǫ́·haʼ she (lit.: it) is a prostitute
[wa+(a)d+ stem: -(a)tgehǫhaʼ- prostitute; consists of: -(a)tgehǫ$_V$- sell]
wa·daʼyat·gé·hǫ·haʼ a prostitute (lit.: it sells its private parts)
[wa+(a)d+ stem: -(a)ʼyatgehǫhaʼ- prostitute; consists of: -(a)ʼy(a)$_N$- female genitals -(a)tgehǫ$_V$- sell]
protect
ho·na·dʼę·ní·gǫ·ha:ʼ they (m) are protecting, watching
[TR+adę+ (ʼ)nigǫha(:)$_V$- expect, watch]
de·yǫ·ki·yęʼnya·dǫ́·haʼ they protect us; they are protectors
[de+TR+ę+ stem: -(ʼ)ny(a)$_N$- finger, hand -(ʼ)nyadǫ(:)$_V$- protect, embrace]
dęh·sę́ʼnya·dǫ:ʼ you will protect, embrace
protect see: guard
dę·hó·nę·hę:ʼ he is a guard
protest see: argue, complain
dęhs·rih·wa·gé:nhaʼ you will argue, debate, protest
sa·eh·wa·gę́:nyaʼt you will complain; you are a complainer
prototype see: pattern
gyǫ·den·yę·dę́hs·dahk·waʼ pattern

protrude
he·yá·ǫ:t it protrudes
[heʼ+ ya+ stem: -ǫd$_V$- attached]
protrude see: go out
gyo·yá·gʼę·ǫh it comes out here; it is sticking out, protruding
protrusion see: lump
og·wá·ǫt it has a lump, a bulge
proud
se·ná·i: you are proud
[A+ stem: -nai$_V$- be proud]
e·ná·i: she is proud in a boastful manner
ha·ná·i: he is proud, boastful, bragging, conceited
gę:né:hah they (z) are proud
[(i+) A+ stem: -e:hah- be proud, gloat; consists of: -i:, ę:, e:$_V$- think, hope, want -hah diminutive]
i·hé:hah he thinks highly of himself; his thoughts
ih·sé:hah you gloat
i·gé:hah I am gloating, boastful
proverb see: predict
néʼ hó:nę: predictors; messengers (lit.: what they (m) said); a proverb; a prediction; a saying; a prophesy
provide see: give
shǫg·wá:wi: he has given us
province see: G
(de·yoh·wę·jah·kah·sǫ:gwęh)
provincial see: G (ha·di:go:wahs)
provoke see: incite
ęt·ri·hǫ́:niʼ you will incite, be the cause of s.t.
prowl see: sneak around
sgę:nǫ:ʼǫ́h hod·rihs·dǫ·hǫ́:gyeʼ he is sneaking around slowly
proximate see: near
dęhs·gę́:hęh near here
proxy see: appoint
a·hǫ·wa·i·hǫ́:dęʼ they delegated him a duty

prune
a·hę·na·tǫ·dahs·rǫ́:ni' they (m) pruned the trees
[at+ stem: -(h)ǫdahsrǫni- prune; consists of: -(h)ǫd(a)$_N$- bush -(h)srǫni$_V$- fix, repair]

prune see: wrinkle
ohs·gwí'dra' a prune; wrinkles

pruning shears
ha·di·hǫ·dahs·rǫn·yá'ta' they (m) are using pruning shears
[A+ stem: -(h)ǫdahsrǫnya'ta'- pruning shears; consists of: -(h)ǫd(a)$_N$- bush -(h)srǫnya'd$_V$- cause to fix, repair]
e·hǫ·da̱hs·rǫ́n·y'a·ta' pruning shears
[e+ stem: -(h)ǫdahsrǫnya'ta'- pruning shears; consists of: -(h)ǫd(a)$_N$- bush -(h)srǫnya'd$_V$- cause to fix, repair]

pry see: uphold
dę·yehg·wa·dáh·nǫ:' she will raise or lift things up

prying see: inquisitive, mischievous
sa·da·hǫh·dǫ́hs·gǫh you are inquisitive
de·sa'nyǫ̱hs·wá·ha't you can't keep your hands off; you're nosy

pub see: bar
ǫt·ne·ga̱h·ní:nǫh(geh) hotel; pub; bar; saloon

puberty
dę̱·had·wę·ná·dęn·yǫhs he is reaching puberty (lit.: his voice is changing)
[de+A+ad+ stem: -węnadęnyǫhs- puberty (reach); consists of: -węn(a)$_N$- voice, word -deni, deny$_V$- change]

public see: G (gęgyohgwagǫ:, gęgyohgwa')

publication see: book
oh·ya·dǫ̱hs·rǫ́:dǫ' a book

publish
dęhs·ríhs·do·ha:k you will publish s.t.
[de+... stem: -(r)ihsdohag- publish; consists of: -(h)wihsd(a), (hr)ihsd(a)$_N$- metal, money -ohag$_V$- squeeze]

puddle
oh·né:go' a puddle; any type of water
[o+ stem: -(h)nego'- puddle; consists of: -(h)neg(a)$_N$- water, liquid -o'$_V$- be submerged]
oh·né·gǫn·yǫ' lots of puddles

puff see: air, pant
ó:wa:' air; wind
sha·ǫ:wi̱hs·hę́'ǫh he is panting again; he is short of breath

puffball
de·wag·yęg·wá·og·wahs small puffballs (already gone to seed)
[de+wa+ag+ stem: -yęgwaogwahs- puffball; consists of: -yę'g(wa)$_N$- tobacco, smoke, cigarettes -ogw$_V$- scatter]

puff up see: inflate
ga·wa·ǫ:dá:hǫh it is inflated

pull
tgag·yę́·hęt·wahs I am a puller
[he+/d+ stem: -yęhętw, yęhęto$_V$- pull]
dwag·yę́·hęt·wahs, dwa·dí·hęt·wahs it pulls
ęt·gag·yę̱·hę́:to', ęt·gat·yę̱·hę́:to' I will pull
gya·gog·yę·hę́:twęh, gya·got·yę·hę́:twęh, dya·got·yę·hę́:twęh she is pulling it

pull back see: flinch
da·wá:tgri:k it pulled back, flinched, shrank

pull by the arm see: arm (take s.o. by the arm)
ęt·gǫ·nę:tsí:ne' I will take you by the arm

pulp see: mash
ga·jih·gǫ́:ni: mashed food

pulpit see: altar
ha·ji·hęhs·da:jí' had·rę·ná·ę·da̱hk·wa' an altar; a pulpit

pulverize see: pound
ę·gé:te't I will pound

pummel see: beat up, hit
a·hǫ·wę·dá:nyo' s.o. beat him up, broke his spirit
ęhs·wá'e:k you will pound, tap

pump
ga·wá·ǫ·da:s an air pump
[ga+ stem: -waǫda:- inflate s.t.; consists of: -w(a:)$_N$- air -ǫda:(h)$_V$- put in, attached]

pump see: water pump
gah·ne·ga·dáhg·wahs a water pump

pumpkin
ohn·yǫh·so·wá:nęh a pumpkin
[o+ stem: -(h)nyǫhsowanęh- pumpkin; consists of: -(h)nyǫhs(a)$_N$- melon, squash -owanęh$_V$- be big]

punch
se·gǫ́·he:s you hit it all the time
[TR+ stem: -gǫhe- punch; consists of: -gǫh(a)$_N$- fist -(')e$_V$- hit]
a·há·gǫ·he:k he punched it
de·ha·di·jíhg·wa'ehs they (m) punch it
[stem: -jihgwa'ehsd- punch; consists of: -jihg(wa)$_N$- porridge, mush -(')e$_V$- hit]
a·ha·jihg·wá'e:k he punched it
ga·jíhg·wa'e:' it punches

punch see: drill
e·ga·hę·dáhk·wa' a drill

puncture see: hole
ni·yah·wę·dú:'uh a small hole; an opening

pungent see: strong-smelling
gad·rę·nahs·há:sde' it is a strong smell; it is strong-smelling

punish
sat·ré·wah·ta' you are being punished right now
[TR/...at+ stem: -(hr)ewahd$_V$- punish]
ęhs·he·hé:waht you will punish her
e·sa·hé:waht you have been punished
sat·ré·wah·dǫh you have been punished

punish (continued)
a·hǫ·wa·di·y'a·dá·gęn·ye:' they raked him over the coals (lit. they dragged him around)
[TR+ stem: -ya'dagęni- rake s.o. over the coals; consists of: -ya'd(a)$_N$- body -gęni, gęny$_V$- compete]

purchase
gah·ní:nǫ' s.t. that is bought
[ga+ stem: -(h)ninǫ$_V$- buy]
ga·nǫ·wa·yę́h·dǫ: a purchase
[ga+ stem: -nǫwayęhdǫ:- purchase; consists of: -nǫwayęhd$_V$- barter]

puppy see: dog
só:wa:s dog

purchase see: buy
ęh·sní:nǫ' you will buy, purchase it

pure-bred
gat·gwęh·sa·náh·nǫh pure-bred (lit.: full of the same blood)
[ga+ stem: -tgwęhsanahnǫh- pure-bred; consists of: -tgwęhs(a)$_N$- blood -nahnǫh$_V$- be full]

purple
oh·sohg·wa·gá:nyǫ: purple
[o+ stem: -(a)hsohgwaganyǫh- purple; consists of: -(a)hsoh(gwa)$_N$- colour, paint, crayon -ganyǫ:$_V$-]
drę́·na'ę:' purple
[stem: -dręnaę:'- purple; consists of: -dręn(a)$_N$- smell -'ę:'$_V$- be coloured]
a·ǫh·ya·ęt·rá:ji: dark blue; purple
[a+ stem: -(r)ǫhyaętr(a)$_N$- blue -ji(:,h)$_V$- dark]

purpose see: idea
o·íh·wa·geh the reason; the idea for s.t.

purposeful see: come for a purpose
sen·yę́'de' you came for a purpose

purr see: sing
od·rę́:no:t it is singing, purring

purse see: wallet
gat·gwę́·da' a wallet; a purse; a pocketbook; suitcasa e

pursue see: follow
a·gá·kehs·re:ʼ I chased them, followed them
ę·ha·dó·wa·t he will hunt

push see: uphold
de·séhg·waʼt lift it up; push it up

push ups
de·ga·ǫ·dag·yʼa·dáhg·wa·taʼ they (f/m) are doing push ups
[de+…(a)dag+ stem: -yaʼdahgwaʼd- push ups; consists of: -yaʼd(a)$_N$- body -(h)gwaʼd$_V$- cause to lift, pick up]
dę·ha·dag·yáʼdahg·waʼt he will do push ups

put
ha·hé·haʼ he sets it up; he puts it somewhere
[(N+) stem: -(hr)e:, (hr)ę$_V$- put, place]
kré·haʼ I am setting it on s.t.
ęk·ręʼ I will place it into s.t.
ęhs·ręʼ you will put s.t. on a surface; you will set it on s.t.
he·wá·kre:ʼ I put, placed it over there
it·ręh place it; put it down
tóh it·ręh put it down there
tóh haʼtręh put it up on there (that is, up off the floor somehow)
dę·saʼę·ná·hęʼ you will put on the stick
[de+…stem: -(a)ʼęn(a)$_N$- stick, pole, rod -(hr)e, (hr)ę$_V$- put, place]
ha·diʼǫh·gwá·e·hęʼ they (m) are laying sod
[stem: -(ʼ)ǫhg(wa:)$_N$- sod -(hr)e, (hr)ę$_V$- put, place]
set·seʼdó·dęh stand the bottles up
[stem: -(i)tse(ʼda)$_N$- bottle -odę$_V$- put]
as·nę·tsó·dęʼ you put on its arm (for example, on a doll)
[stem: -nęts(a)$_N$- arm -odę$_V$- put]

put see: put away, put back, put down, put in, put on, put s.o. down, put things side by side, put together

put away see: store
ę·seh·sę·nǫ́·niʼ you will store it

put back
hęts·yę:ʼ you will put it back in its place
[heʼ+…d+…stem: -(y)ę(:)$_V$- put back; consists of: -(y)ę(:)$_V$- lay s.t. down]

put down
ha·yę́·hęʼ he puts, places it there
[stem: -(y)ę(:)$_V$- put down, place, set down; consists of: -(y)ę$_V$- lie on the ground]
ęd·wá·yę:ʼ we all (incl.) will set forth; we all will set down
ęhs·wá·yę:ʼ you all will set down, lay down
heh·sá·yęʼ put it there
ni·gá·yęʼ where it is at; where it is placed
ni·sá·yęʼ where you placed it
i·ję: put it down; leave it alone
swá·yę: you all set it down
a·ha·diʼǫ́hg·wa·ę:ʼ they (m) laid sod
[stem: -(ʼ)ǫhg(wa:)$_N$- sod -(y)ę(:)$_V$- put down, place, set]
ę·seʼǫhg·wá·ę: you are going to lay sod

put in
sǫ́·da·s you put s.t. in
[(N+) stem: -ǫda:(h)$_V$- put in, be attached]
aʼa·gǫ́·da:ʼ she put it in a container
ęh·sǫ́·da:ʼ you will put an object in there
a·gǫ·dá·hǫh I have put it in
ęhs·nǫ́·da:ʼ you will put gas in
[stem: -(h)n(a)$_N$- oil, gas -ǫda:(h)$_V$- put in, be attached]
a·ha·dah·diʼtrǫ́·da:ʼ he put his socks on
[ad+ stem: -(a)hdahdiʼtr(a)$_N$- sock -ǫda:(h)$_V$- put in; put in/on for oneself]
hę·nǫ́·da·staʼ they (m) put it in there all the time
[at+ stem: -ǫdahsd- put in; consists of: -ǫda:(h)$_V$- put in, attached]

put in (continued)
ǫt·nǫ́·dahs·ta' she, s.o. is put in there all the time
she·no'jan·hǫ́:dęh put her teeth in
[TR/at+ N+ stem: -no'j(a)$_N$- tooth -nhǫd(a:,ę)$_V$- put in]
sat·no'jan·hǫ́:dęh put your teeth in

put in see: insert
he·sá·w'it·a' you insert s.t. all the time

put on
ahadahdi'trǫda:' he put his socks on
[-(a)dahdi'tr(a)$_N$- sock -ǫda:(',h)$_V$- put in, on]

put on see: clothe, wear
ę·sát·rǫn·ya't you will wear s.t.
ę·sag·y'a·dá:wi:t you will put on (clothes)

put out see: extinguish, publish
sahs·waht put the light out
dęhs·ríhs·dǫ·ha:k you will publish s.t.

putrefy see: bad, decomposition, spoiled
ę·wá·het·gę' it (an idea) will spoil, go bad
o·ya·ǫ'dá:t·gę: a state of decomposition
ot·gę: it is rotten, decayed; spoilage

put s.o. down
ha·dá'sęh·ta' he puts people down; he discriminates
[TR+ad+ stem: -(a')sęhd$_V$- hand down, bring down; put s.o. down]
she·ya·d'a·sę́h·ta' you put s.o. down all the time
she·ya·d'a·sę́h·dǫh you have already put s.o. down; you discriminated against her

put things side by side
tsa'dę́hs·yę:' you will put, lay them side by side
[tsa'+de+...stem: -(y)ę(:)$_V$- put down, place, set down; put things side by side]

put together
dęhs·wat·nęt·sá'drǫ:' you all will cross your arms
[de+...ad+ stem: -nęts(a)$_N$- arm -(')drǫ(:)$_V$- put several things together]
des·wat·si·ná'drǫ' you all have your legs crossed
[de+...ad+ stem: -(h)sin(a)$_N$- leg -(')drǫ'$_V$- have several things put together]
des·wat·nęt·sá'drǫ' you all have your arms crossed
[de+...ad+ stem: -nęts(a)$_N$- arm -(')drǫ'$_V$- have several things put together]
de·sat·si·ná'drę' put your legs together
[de+...ad+ stem: -(h)sin(a)$_N$- leg -(')drę'$_V$- put several things together]
de·sat·nęt·sá'drę' put your arms together

put together see: add, assemble
ha'dę́:syehs you will put them all together
dęh·sé·ka·hǫ' you will assemble, put together

puzzle see: join, match
de·sah·sǫd·ré:ha' you join things together all the time; you do puzzles
de·séh·ka·hǫ: you match things, pair things up (puzzle pieces, socks)

pyjamas
go·da'stá' ahg·wę́:nya' pyjamas
[consists of: goda'sta' her / s.o.'s pyjamas; ahgwę:nya' clothing, clothes]

pyjamas see: nightgown
go·dá'sta' a nightgown

Q

q-tip see: cotton batting
o·gǫ́:dra' cotton batting; q-tips
quail
go̱h·gó:wi:' quail; partridge
[go+ stem: -(a)hgowi:'- quail; consists of: -(a)hg(a:)$_N$- splint -owi, ǫny$_V$- drive]
quake see: earthquake, quiver, shake
ag·yǫh·węh·jẹ́:dǫh an earthquake
ę·sa·y'a·dahd·rǫ́:gǫ' you will quiver, shudder
sa·ya'dǫ·dá'ta' you are nervous, shaking, shivering
qualify see: win
a·hǫ·wa·di:gwé:ni' they won a competition (lit.: they beat him, them (m))
quantity see: amount, mass, volume
shę́h ní:yǫ: the amount of
tsę́h ni·yó:sde' mass (lit.: how much it weighs, how heavy it is)
tsę́h ni·gá:dę:s volume; density; how thick it is; mass
quarrel see: argue
dęh·sá·dats'a:' you will quarrel
de·wá·dats'ǫh a quarrel; an argument
quart
sgat·sé'da:t one bottle; a quart
[s+ga+ stem: -(i)tse('da)$_N$- bottle -d$_V$- stand; one]
quarter see: B (de·gah·si·ǫ'tra:ge:)
quarter moon
a·wa·dęh·ní·d'ok·dę' the end of the moon; the last quarter
[a+wa+ad+ stem: -ęhni'd(a)$_N$- month -o'kd(ę,ani)$_V$- finish s.t.]
queasy see: nauseous
ak·ne'dr'a·dá:nih I am nauseated, nauseous
queen
e·goh·gó:wah a queen; the Queen
[e+ stem: -gohgowah$_V$- royalty]
sha·go·di·goh·gó:wah their queen
queer see: unusual
ti·yó:t'ah it is queer, unusual, odd
quench one's thirst
ę·ye·ha'dá·na·wę:' they (lit.: she) will wet their cores, throat
[stem: -(h)a'danawę- quench one's thirst; consists of: -(h)a'd(a)$_N$- throat, voice, feather -nawę(:)$_V$- wet s.t.]
ę·ka'da·ná:wę:' I will quench my thirst, wet my throat
ę·ga·ha'dá·na·wę:' it will quench its thirst, wet its throat
ga̱·ha'da·ná·wę̱h·dǫh it is quenched
[stem: -(h)a'danawęhd- be quenched; consists of: -(h)a'd(a)$_N$- throat, voice, feather -nawęhd$_V$- wet s.t.]
query see: ask, investigate, wonder
ę·sa·da̱·hǫ́:dǫ' you will ask
ęhs·ríh·wi̱h·sa:k you will investigate, inquire
ęh·sę·nǫh·dǫ́:nyǫ:' you will wonder, think
question see: I (gęh), query
quick
gya'tga·hí:ye' I am quick
[A+ stem: -ya'tgahiye'- be quick; consists of: -ya'd(a)$_N$- body -gahiye'$_V$- be quick]
quick see: active, agile, fast
ag·yá'da·deht I am nimble, active, energetic
ha·ya'tgá·i·ye' he is agile
oh·snó:we' it is fast, quick
quick thinker
ha'ni·gǫ̱·hahs·nó:we' he is a quick thinker
[A+ stem: -(')nigǫhahsnowe'- quick thinker; consists of: -(')nigǫh(a)$_N$- mind -(h)snowe'$_V$- be fast]

quick-witted
ha'de·ho·íh·wa·ge: he is quick-witted; he has lots of business, different ideas, many ideas; he is into everything
[ha'+de+P+ stem: -(r)ihwage:- quick-witted; consists of: -(r)ih(wa)$_N$- word -(a)ge:$_V$- two or more; all sorts of, all kinds of]
quiet
ta'de:yó:gyę: quietness; quiet; stillness
[ta'+de+P+ag+ stem: -ye(:)$_V$- do; be quiet, still]
ta'dé·sag·yę: you are quiet
quill see: pen, throat
gah·ne:gá:' **eh·yá·dǫhk·wa'** a pen
o·há'da' a quill; a plume; a feather; the voice; the throat; the larynx; the esophagus
quilt
de·gęh·na·ká·hǫ' a quilt
[de+ga+ stem: -(i)hnakahǫ'- quilt; consists of: -(i)hn(a)$_N$- material, skin -kahǫ'$_V$- adjoin]
quilt see: bedspread
e·nak·do·wé:kta' a bedspread
quit
gę·ní·hę·ha', **ga·ní·hę·ha'** I always quit
[stem: -ęnihę(:)$_V$- quit, prevent, stop s.t.]
a·gę́·nį·hę' I stopped, quit
a:hę·ní·hę:' he would stop (himself)
ta:gá·ǫ:nį·hę: they (f/m) suddenly quit
sę·ní:hę: quit
sę·ni:hę́: **tó:gyęh** quit that
a·ga·ǫ·ní·hę'dahk they (f/m) suddenly quit
[stem: -ęnihę'd$_V$- quit suddenly]
quiver
g'a·dá:tra' a quiver
[ga+ stem: -(')dr(a), (')datr(a)$_N$- case, quiver]

quiver (continued)
ę·sa·y'a·dahd·rǫ́:gǫ' you will quiver, shudder
[P+ stem: -ya'd(a)$_N$- body -(a)hdrǫgǫ$_V$- quiver, shudder consists of: -(a)hdrǫgw$_V$- caress]
quiz see: test
ęg·wá:kdǫ:' I will test you all

R

rabbit
gwa'yǫ' a rabbit
[stem: -gwa'yǫ$_N$- rabbit]
gw'a·yǫ́:'ah a cottontail rabbit
[stem: -gwa'yǫ$_N$- rabbit -'ah diminutive]
gwa'yǫ·gó:wah jackrabbit
[stem: -gwa'yǫgo:wah- jackrabbit; consists of: -gwa'yǫ$_N$- rabbit -gowah big]
tǫ·dá·ęht a snowshoe rabbit
[t+ stem: -(h)ǫdaęhd- snowshoe rabbit; consists of: -(h)ǫd(a)$_N$- bush -(y)ęhd$_V$- hit, knock down, strike]
raccoon
sá:no:' a raccoon
[stem: -sano:'$_N$- raccoon]
race
dę·hę·ná·ǫ·ha' they (m) race; they are racing (right now)
[de+… stem: -aǫ, ęǫ$_V$- race]
a·tę:né·ǫ' they (m) raced
race see: cross-country meet
dę·ha·di·hę:di:yá's **dę·hę·ná·ǫ:ha'** a cross-country meet
rack see: shelf
wę·níhs·rǫ' shelves; shelving
radiance see: sunshine
od·rǫ́h·yo:t sunbeam; a ray of light; sunshine

radiator
ga·naʼja·gę́ʼdo:ʼ a radiator
[ga+ stem: -naʼjagęʼdo:ʼ- radiator; consists of: -naʼj(a)$_{N}$- pail, drum -gęʼdo:ʼ$_{V}$- be stuck under s.t. but removable]
radio see: clock radio, stereo
go·yeh·táʼ wad·rę́·no·taʼ a clock radio
wad·rę́·no·taʼ a stereo; a radio
raffle
de·wadrʼas·róyʼa·gǫh a raffle
[de+…ad+ stem: -(r)aʼsroiyaʼg- test one's luck, gamble; a raffle; consists of: -raʼsro, raʼsw$_{N}$- luck -(i)yaʼg$_{V}$- cut, break]
rafter
ga·nehs·dá:den·yǫʼ rafters (made of board)
[ga+ stem: -nesda:denyǫʼ- rafter; consists of: -nehsd(a:)$_{N}$- floor, board -denyǫʼ$_{V}$- several existing things]
ga·ǫ·da·dé:nyǫʼ log rafters
[ga+ stem: -(r)ǫdadenyǫʼ- rafter; consists of: -(r)ǫd(a)$_{N}$- log -deʼ$_{V}$- exist]
rafter see: beam
gá·ǫ·da·deʼ a beam
rag
ga·geʼa·ni:yǫ́:dǫʼ hanging rags
[stem: -geʼ(a:), geh(a)$_{N}$- hair -niyǫdǫʼ$_{V}$- several hanging objects]
de·yot·geʼó:gwęh clothes; rags scattered all over
[de+yo+at+ stem: -geʼ(a:), geh(a)$_{N}$- hair -ogw$_{V}$- scatter]
rag see: hair
o·géʼa:ʼ hair, a rag; it is ragged, tattered
rage see: anger
ak·náʼkwʼęǫh I am angry
ragged
ge·géʼa:ʼ I am raggedy, ragged
[A+ stem: -geʼa:ʼ- ragged, tattered; consists of: -geʼ(a:), geh(a)$_{N}$- hair -a:ʼ$_{V}$- hold, contain, include]
se·géʼa:ʼ you are raggedy, ragged

ragged (continued)
de·wa·ge·géʼǫ:t I am raggedy, ragged
[de+P+ stem: -geʼǫd- ragged; consists of: -geʼ(a:), geh(a)$_{N}$- hair -ǫd$_{V}$- attached]
railing
ǫg·ye·na·wáh·taʼgeh a hand railing
[ǫ+ag+ stem: -yenawahtaʼgeh- railing; consists of: -yena(w), yenaǫ, yena(:)$_{V}$- catch, receive, accept]
rain
ohs·da:ʼ rain
[o+ stem: -(h)sda:ʼ- rain; consists of: -(h)sd(a:)$_{N}$- drop of water]
o·nǫn·ya·ę:dag·yéʼ os·dá·ǫ:gyǫ: freezing rain
[consists of: onǫnyaę:dagyeʼ it goes along freezing; osdaǫ:gyǫ: it is raining]
ohs·dá:ga: the sound of the rain
[o+ stem: -(h)sdaga(:)- rain (the sound of rain); consists of: -(h)sd(a:)$_{N}$- drop (of water) -ga:$_{V}$- make a rattling or grinding noise]
ę·yohs·dá·ǫ·diʼ it is going to rain
[(y)o+ stem: -(h)sdaǫdi- rain; consists of: -(h)sd(a:)$_{N}$- drop (of water) -ǫdi, -ǫgy$_{V}$- throw]
aʼos·dá·ǫ·diʼ it rained
os·dá·ǫ:gyǫ: it is raining
a·gas·dá·o:wa·naht it rained hard
[stem: -(h)sdaowanahd- rain hard; consists of: -(h)sd(a:)$_{N}$- drop (of water) -gowanahd$_{V}$- get big]
gahs·da·o·wá:nęh it is raining hard
[stem: -(h)sdaowanę- rain hard; consists of: -(h)sd(a:)$_{N}$- drop of water -owanęh$_{V}$- be big]
a·gahs·dá·ę:daʼ it stopped raining
[stem: -(a)hsdaędaʼ- stop raining; consists of: -(h)sd(a:)$_{N}$- drop of water -ędaʼ$_{V}$- finish, stop]

rain see: drizzle, hail
a·wá·yǫ:gyǫ: it is drizzling; misty rain; fine rain
o·wíd·rǫg·yǫ: it is hailing; sleet
rain water
os·dá:griʼ rain water
[o+ stem: -(h)sdagriʼ- rain water; consists of: -(h)sd(a:)$_{N}$- drop (of water) -griʼ$_{V}$- juice, liquid]
rain wear
ohs·da·ǫ:gyǫ́·gęha:ʼ s.t. used when it is raining
[(y)o+ stem: -(h)sdaǫgyǫgeha:ʼ- rain wear consists of: -(h)sdaǫdi$_{V}$- rain]
rainbow
oʼhnyo:t there is a rainbow
[o+ stem: -(rǫ)ʼnih(a)$_{N}$- rainbow, sunbeam, ray -od$_{V}$- stand]
raise
gahs·he·yah·dó·gʼa·taʼ you raise children; foster parents
[TR+ stem: -(a)hdogaʼd- grow s.t., raise s.t., s.o.; consists of: -(a)hdog$_{V}$- grow, mature]
ęh·sah·dó:gaʼt you will grow s.t.
ęhs·he·yah·dó:gaʼt you will raise s.o.
raise see: grow, raise up, raise to a vertical position
goh·do·ga·dǫ́·hǫg·yeʼ she is growing s.t.
raise up
wad·wę·na·gá:da:s it raises up words
[ad+N+ stem: -węn(a)$_{N}$- voice, word -gadad$_{V}$- raise s.t. up]
raise up see: uphold
dę·yehg·wa·dáh·nǫ:ʼ she will raise things, lift things up
raise to a vertical position
se·gé:ts·gwahs you are lifting it to a vertical position; you give parties
[(N+) stem: -getsgw$_{V}$- raise to a vertical position]
ęh·sé·gets·goʼ you will lift things to a vertical position
gya·gó·gets·gwęh she's having a gathering over there; she is lifting s.t. into a vertical position
ga·gé:ts·gwęh it is raised to a vertical position
se·gé:ts·goh raise s.t. to a vertical position
sa·nęt·sa·gé:ts·goh raise your arm
[(N+) stem: -nęts(a)$_{N}$- arm -getsgw$_{V}$- raise to a vertical position]
dǫ·da·ha·ę·na·gé:tsgoʼ he brings the song back up
[(N+) stem: -(r)ęn(a)$_{N}$- song, music -getsgw$_{V}$- raise to a vertical position]
raisin
gahn·yǫg·wid·rá·taʼdǫh raisins
[ga+ stem: -(h)nyǫgwidrataʼdǫh- raisins; consists of: -(h)nyǫgwidr(a)$_{N}$- grape; -taʼd$_{V}$- dry]
rake
gahs·tǫd·rá·o:he:s a hay rake
[ga+ stem: -(h)stǫdraohes- hay rake, rake; consists of: -(h)stǫdr(a)$_{N}$- straw, hay -(r)oheg$_{V}$- gather]
ę·yag·wan·rah·dá·ohe:k we all will rake leaves
[stem: -nrahd(a)$_{N}$- leaf -(r)oheg$_{V}$- gather]
en·rah·dá·o:hek·taʼ a rake
[e+ stem: -nrahdaohektaʼ- rake; consists of: -nrahd(a)$_{N}$- leaf -(r)oheg$_{V}$- gather]
rake see: harrows
wa·deʼd·réʼs de·ga·heh·dá·hih·taʼ drag harrows
rake s.o. over the coals see: punish
a·hǫ·wa·di·yʼa·dá·gęn·ye:ʼ they raked him over the coals
ram
ga·ji:náh de·yo·na·gá·ǫt ram (lit.: male sheep)
[consists of: gaji:nah he is a male; genitals (of an animal); deyonagaǫt sheep, lamb, elk]

Cayuga pronunciation guide: /a/ father /e/ weigh /ę/ men (nasalized) /i/ police /o/ hole /ǫ/ home (nasalized) /u/ blue. Underlined vowels are voiceless or whispered. /ˊ/ high pitch. /t/ too /d/ do /k/ king /g/ good (never soft g) /j/ judge or adze /s/ soon /sh/ less heat (never the sh in shirt) /sr/ shrine /sy/ sure /hw/ which (the sound made when you blow out a candle) /h/ hi /ts/ cats hide /ʼ/ (the sound before the first vowel in 'uh-uh') /n/ noon /r/ round /w/ way /y/ yes.

ramble see: roam, wander
ti·gę·ne·nǫ́g·yeʼs they (z) are roaming about
ti·gá·ęʼs they (f/m) are roaming about
rancher see: farmer
ha·hę·da·ge·hó:nǫʼ a farmer
random see: err
aʼón·hiʼk it was a mistake, accidental
range see: mountain
de·gahs·dę·hó·dag·yeʼ a mountain range; the Rockies
rap see: knock, hit, tap
sen·hó·haʼe:k knock on the door
ęhs·wáʼe:k you will pound, tap it
hoh·wáʼe: he is tapping
rape
sha·got·go·wáh·da·nih he is a rapist; he is raping s.o. now
[TR+at+ stem: -gowanahdę, gowanęhd(ę,ani) - rape, molest; consists of: -gowanęh$_V$- be big]
ahs·ha·got·go·ho·wá·na̲h·dęʼ he raped her (lit.: he forced her in a big way)
a·hǫ·wat·go·ho·wá·na̲h·dęʼ she raped, molested him
ahs·ha·got·go·wa·na̲h·dę́ʼ
sha·go·há:wahk incest
[consists of: ahshagotgowanahdęʼ he raped her; shagohawahk his daughter]
rape see: force
dahs·ha·go·nǫ́h·twahs he forced (or raped) her
rapid see: fast
oh·snó:weʼ it is fast, quick
rapids
ga̲h·na·wahs·háhs·deʼ fast flowing currents, rapids
[ga+ stem: -(h)nawahsha(h)sdeʼ- rapids, current; consists of: -(h)naw(a)$_N$- water, running -sha(h)sd$_V$- strong]
rapids see: current
oh·ná·wa·deht strong currents

rare
dehs·gá·nag·reʼ it is rare
[deʼ+ not s+ga+ stem: -nagreʼ, nagrad$_V$- live, be rare]
rare see: raw
o·gáh·deh it is raw
rash see: self-important
wa·dat·go·wá:nęh it is rash, unwise, self-important, egotistical
raspberry
joʼdá·e:ya:ʼ raspberries
[stem: -jǫʼdeya:ʼ$_N$- raspberry]
rat
ji·no·wę·gó:wah rat
[stem: -jinowę$_N$- mouse -gowah big]
ratify see: rectify
sga·ih·wa̲hs·rǫ́:nih ratification
rattle
o·wi:ya:ʼáh go̲hs·dá·wʼęd·raʼ baby's rattle
[consists of: owi:ya:ʼah baby; gohsdawʼędraʼ her rattle; a horn rattle]
de·yohsg·yę·dá:ga: bones are rattling
[de+(s+) A/P+N+ stem: -(h)sgyęʼd(a:)$_N$- bone -ga:, gae:$_V$- make a rattling or grinding noise]
dęhs·ga·nǫʼá:ga·e: there will be heads banging
[de+(s+)A/P+N+ stem: -nǫʼ(a:), nǫh(a)$_N$- head -ga:$_V$- make a rattling or grinding noise]
des·ga·nǫʼá:ga: the noise of a head banging
rattle see: grind one's teeth, F, noise
de·yo·nʼo·já:ga: grinding or rattling teeth
de·yohs·da·wę́ʼdraga: a rattling noise (from a rattle)
rattle snake
ohs·hóʼgwa·ǫ:t a rattle snake
[o+ stem: -(h)shoʼgwaǫd- rattle snake; consists of: -(h)shoʼg(wa)$_N$- -ǫd$_V$- attached]

ravage see: rape
ahs·ha·got·go·ho·wá·na̱h·dę' he raped her
raven see: crow
ga'ga:' crow; raven
ravine see: canyon
he·yo·heh·dę́'ǫ·ge: a canyon
raw
o·gáh·deh it is raw
[o+(N+) stem: -(a)gahdeh$_V$- raw]
o·jǫ'da·gáh·deh raw fish
[o+(N+) stem: -(i)jǫ'd(a)$_N$- fish -(a)gahdeh$_V$- raw]
raw see: unripe
o·gé:dra' it is green (not ripe); raw fruit
rawhide see: skin
ga·néh·wa' leather; hide
razor
ǫt·gǫhs·tǫ'ę́h·da̱hk·wa' a razor
[ǫ+at+ stem: -gǫhstǫ'ęhdahkwa'- razor; consists of: -gǫhstǫ'(a)$_N$- whiskers -ęhdahkwa'$_V$- s.t. that hits]
razor blade
ǫt·gǫhs·tǫ'ęh·da̱hk·wá' o·hę́n'at·ra' a razor blade
[consists of: ǫtgǫhstǫ'ęhda̱hkwa' a razor; ohęn'atra' a blade]
RCMP see: G, (Royal Canadian Mounted Police, Sha·go·di·ye·na̱hs·go:wah)
re-elect see: G (hǫ·sa'hǫ·wa·di·ya'din·yǫ:t)
reach
de·sé·nęt·se:s stretch out your arms; reach
[(ha')+de+A+ stem: -nętses- reach, stretch out; consists of: -nęts(a)$_N$- arm -es$_V$- long]
ha'de·sa·nę́:tse:s reach away from your body (using your arm)
ha't·sę́·nęt·se:s reach out
reach see: arrive
ę·ga·e:yǫ́·hǫ:' they (f/m) will arrive

read
ǫ·dad·ri̱·hǫ́n·ya·nih she is reading
[adad+ stem: -(r)ihǫnyanih, rihǫnyę- read; consists of: -(r)ih(wa)$_N$- word -ǫni, ǫny(ę,ani)$_V$- make for one's benefit]
ga·dad·ri·hǫ́n·ya:nih I am reading
wa·dad·ri̱·hǫ́n·ya·ni: reading material (lit.: it has been read)
sa·dad·ri̱·hǫ́:nyęh read
reading (have a reading) see: fortune-teller
ę·gák·ya·dǫ:' I will have a reading; I will have my fortune told
ready
a·ga·de̱hs·rǫ́·ni̱hs'ǫh I am ready
[P+ade+ stem: -(h)srǫnihs'ǫh$_V$- be ready; consists of: -hsr$_N$- noun -ǫnih$_V$- make -(i)hs'$_V$- finish]
sa·dehs·rǫ·níhs'ǫh you are ready
ę·sa·de̱hs·rǫ·ni̱hs'ǫ́·hǫ:k you will be ready
sa·déhs'ǫh? Are you ready? (this word may come from Onondaga)
[P+ade+ stem: -(i)hs'ǫh- be ready; consists of: -(i)hs'$_V$- finish]
ready see: complete, willing
ga·wa·ya·nę́·da̱'ǫh it is ready, prepared
sa·gá·ę:s you are willing
real see: right
dó:gęhs sure; truly; right; it is a fact
real
[-ǫ:weh typicalizer suffix; denotes something that is typically 'Indian, ceremonial, or traditional']
real estate see: G (sa̱h·wę:ja')
realize see: understand
a·ho'ni·gǫ·há·ę·da' he understood
really see: I (gwahs ǫ:weh)
really
[-(h)sgǫ: facilitative suffix; means 'prone to,' 'easily' or 'really']
[-jih intensifier suffix; means 'really' or 'even more so']

rear see: behind, next in line
a·hǫ·wę·no·wa̱h·sǫ́:drę' he's right behind him
sho·nǫ́'ne:t he is behind him; he is next in line
rearrange see: adjust
ęt·sa:dó:gęhs you will adjust s.t.
rearward see: behind
(oh·)na'gę́:' shę́h ga·nǫ́h·so:t behind the house
[consists of: ohna'gę:' behind; shęh that, etc.; ganǫhso:t a standing house]
reason see: idea
o·íh·wa·geh the reason; the idea for s.t.
rebel see: revolt
ęt·sę'ni·gǫ́·ho'ne:k you will revolt, remove yourself
recall see: remember
swa·gahs·ha'drǫ́:nyǫh I am recalling, remembering
receive see: catch
a·ga·e·yé:na:' they (f/m) caught, received, accepted it
receive a name
ę·yǫ:tsę:nǫ́: ga̱h·sę·ná·ǫ:weh she will receive her name
[consists of: ęyǫtsęnǫ: she will be given a name; gahsęnaǫweh an Indian (lit.: real) name]
receptacle
wat·né·gǫh·da:s water receptacle; it holds liquid
[w+at+ stem: -(h)negǫhdas- receptacle for water; consists of: -(h)neg(a)$_N$- water, liquid -ohda(:,h)$_V$- tidy up, clean]
receptacle see: container
wad·rá'kwa' a container
recess see: cavity
oh·wę·ja·gá·hęt·ge: a cavern; a cavity; a big cave
recline see: lie
ę·sę·ni·dá:grę' you will lie down

recognizable
o·yę́:deht it is recognizable, plain to be seen, conspicuous
[o+ stem: -yędehd- recognizable, obvious, conspicuous; consists of: -(y)ęde(:,')$_V$- recognize]
recognize
ęg·yę́:de:' I will recognize it
[TR+ stem: -(y)ęde(:,')$_V$- recognize]
ta:ga·e·sa·yę́·de: they will not recognize you (that is, a disguise)
recollect see: remember
swa·gahs·ha'drǫ́:nyǫh I am recalling, remembering
recommence see: restart
dǫ·da·hah·sá:wę' he restarted it
recommend see: counsel, refer, suggest
ho·ha·hah·sę́·hęg·ye' he is counselling
hę·gǫ·ya·dę́:nyeht I will refer you to s.o. else
ęt·se·y'ę·ni·gǫ·hó:tahs you will suggest to her, advise her
reconcile
ę·ji·jad·rih·wa̱hs·rǫ́:ni' you two will reconcile
[s+... stem: -(r)ihwahsrǫni- reconcile; consists of: -(r)ihwahsr(a)$_N$- agreement -ǫni, ǫny$_V$- make]
record songs
a·ha·ę·nǫ́·da̱h·sǫ:' he recorded many songs
[stem: -(r)ęnǫda:(h)- record songs; consists of: -(r)ęn(a)$_N$- song, music -ǫda:(h)$_V$- put in, attached -sǫ' plural]
a·ha·ę·nǫ́:da: he recorded songs or taped
recorder
ga·wę·na·yé:na:s recorder (lit.: it catches the voice)
[ga+ stem: -węnayenahs- recorder; consists of: -węn(a)$_N$- voice, word -yena(w), yenaǫ, yena(:)$_V$- catch, receive, accept]

recount
ę̨t·sa:tró:wi' you will recount, retell [s+TR/at+ stem: -(hr)owi, (hr)ǫny$_V$- tell; recount, retell]
recourse (without recourse)
a·to·da·níh·sa'e:k he got cornered, put up against the wall with no recourse [de+TR+ stem: -(a)dęnihsa'e- corner s.o.; consists of: -(a)dęnihs(a)$_N$- wall -(')e$_V$- hit]
recover see: acquire
ę·sa:yę́:da' you will acquire, obtain
recreation
de·yǫ'ni·gǫ·ha·wę́ny'e·ta' recreation; hobbies [de+yǫ+ stem: -(')nigǫhawęnye'd- entertain, recreation, hobbies; consists of: -(')nigǫh(a)$_N$- mind -(a)węnye'd$_V$- cause to stir, mix]
rectangle
dek·nihs·hó' tsa'dé:yǫ:s rectangle, oblong (lit.: it has two long sides of equal length) [consists of: deknihsho' two-ish; tsa'de:yǫ's they are two of equal length]
rectify
sga·ih·wa̱hs·rǫ́:nih to rectify; ratification [s+…stem: -(r)ihwahsrǫni- reconcile, agree; consists of: -(r)ih(wa)$_N$- word -(h)srǫni$_V$- fix, repair]
rectify see: repair
sa·sehs·rǫ́:ni' you repaired it
red
ot·gwę́h·j'i·a:' red [o+ stem: -tgwęhj'ia:'- red; consists of: -tgwęhji'(a)$_N$- red -a:'$_V$- hold, contain, include]
ot·gwęh·j'i·á:ji: maroon; dark red [o+ stem: -tgwęhj'ia:ji:- dark red, maroon; consists of: -tgwęhji'(a)$_N$- red -jih$_V$- dark]
reduce see: fall, shrink
da·wá'sę' it dropped, reduced
ohs·twá'ǫh it has shrunk
red whip
ga̱·hę·deh·ge̱·há:' otg·węh·j'i·á:' o·hǫ́:da' red whip (the plant that grows in the field) [consists of: gahędehgeha:' the field type; otgwęhj'ia:' red; ohǫ:da' whip]
ga·na·wa·géh·ge̱·ha:' red whip (the plant that grows in the water, pond) [ga+ stem: -nawagehgeha:'- red whip; consists of: -(h)naw(a)$_N$- running water -'geh at -geha:' type of]
reed
tsa'gę́:da' common reed [stem: -tsa'gę:da'- common reed; consists of: -(i)da'$_V$- sleep]
reek see: stink
gag·rahs it stinks
refer
hę·gǫ·ya·dę́:nyeht I will refer you to s.o. else [he'+TR+adę+ stem: -nyehd$_V$- send; refer s.o.]
refrain see: remove
de·se·nęt·sǫ́'ne:k remove your arms (that is, retract them); remove your support
refreshed see: rest
a·ga·ǫ:dǫ́h·wi̱hs·hę:' they (f/m) rested
refreshment see: drink
ę·yeh·ne·gé·ha' she will drink
refrigerator
ga·ná'no̱hs·ta' refrigerator (lit.: it cools things off) [ga+ stem: -na'nohsta'- refrigerator; consists of: -(na')nohsd$_V$- cool s.t. off]
gak·wá' ga·ná'no̱hs·ta' refrigerator [consists of: gakwa' food; gana'no̱hsta' refrigerator]
refund see: repay
ę̨t·sé·gan·ya'k you will repay, refund

Cayuga pronunciation guide: /a/ father /e/ weigh /ę/ men (nasalized) /i/ police /o/ hole /ǫ/ home (nasalized) /u/ blue. Underlined vowels are voiceless or whispered. /'/ high pitch. /t/ too /d/ do /k/ king /g/ good (never soft g) /j/ judge or adze /s/ soon /sh/ less heat (never the sh in shirt) /sr/ shrine /sy/ sure /hw/ which (the sound made when you blow out a candle) /h/ hi /ts/ cats hide /'/ (the sound before the first vowel in 'uh-uh') /n/ noon /r/ round /w/ way /y/ yes.

refuse see: balk, unwilling
a·had·rǫh·yá'dahk he balked at the suggestion
de·wa·ge·gá·ę I do not want to do it; I am unwilling
region see: area, place
og·ye·na·wáh·dǫh an area
tó: hǫ́:weh a place
register see: perceive, put in
ęh·sę·nih·ná:do:k you will perceive s.t.
sǫ́:da:s you put s.t. in
regret
sah·sę́h·tahk you used to regret it
[P+ stem: -(a)hsę(hd)$_V$- regret s.t.]
ęh·sáh·sęhs you will regret
[P+ stem: -(a)hsęhsd$_V$- regret s.t.]
ǫ·gáh·sęhs I regret it, I did regret it
e·sah·sę́hs gęh Do you regret it? Did you regret it? Are you satisfied now?
regretful
o·sę́hs·de:' it is regretful
[o+ stem: -(a)hsęhsde:'- regretful; consists of: -(a)hsę(hsd)$_V$- regret s.t.]
regurgitate see: vomit
ǫ·gény'a·go' I vomited
reign
ha·dag·ye's·gę́·hę:' a reign (lit.: he was standing there)
[A+ stem: -dagye'(s)- continue on, be ongoing; consists of: -d$_V$- stand]
e·dá:gye's a reign (lit.: she is still standing; that is, a queen)
reign see: G, (govern, ǫg·wahs·ha·i·ne')
reimburse
ę·ji·sat·gán·y'a·gę' you will be reimbursed, refunded
[s+…at+ stem: -ganya'gę'- be reimbursed, refunded; consists of: -ga:$_N$- price -(i)ya'g$_V$- cut, break]
reimburse see: repay
ęt·sé·gan·ya'k you will repay, refund

reinforce
ęt·ríh·wa·wa's you will back up the idea (that is, reinforce it)
[TR+ stem: -(r)ihwawa's- reinforce an idea, back up an idea; consists of: -(r)ih(wa)$_N$- word -(h)wawa's$_V$- support s.t.]
reinforce see: double
dęhs·ná'net'a:' you will double it, reinforce it, line it
reinforcement
gahs·wá'ne:t reinforçement; backing
[ga+ stem: -(h)swa'ned- support s.o., s.t., agree with s.o., back s.o.; reinforcement, backing; consists of: -(h)swa'n(a), (h)swe'n(a)$_N$- upper back -d$_V$- stand]
reiterate see: recount
ęt·sa:tró:wi' you will recount, retell
reject see: throw
gog·ye's to get rid of s.t., throw it away
rejoin see: come back, meet
na'dé:tge:' I will come back over here, return
a·díg·y'a·dra' we two (incl.) met
relate see: recount, say, tell
ęt·sa:tró:wi' you will recount, retell
ę·hę' he will say
ahs·ha·gǫ·hó:wi' he told her
relative see: C
sa·dę·ni·hó:nǫ' relatives on your (s) father's side
ǫ·dę́·nǫhk·sǫ' relatives; kin
relax see: rest
a·ha·dǫh·wíhs·hę:' he rested
relaxation see: recreation
de·yǫ'ni·gǫ·ha·wę́ny'e·ta' recreation; hobbies
relaxed see: comfortable
ęh·sa·nak·dí:yohs you will become physically comfortable

relay see: send
hęh·sad·ri̱h·wá:nyeht you will send a message
release
saht·gaʼs you forfeit, you let go of things all the time
[stem: -(a)htga(w)$_V$- release, let go]
saht·gaʼwa̱hs·gę́·hę:ʼ you used to let go, you used to give up
a·wáht·ga:ʼ it let go
sa·ga·e·sáht·ga:ʼ they released you (s), fired you, let you go
a·kí·ya̱ht·ga:ʼ we let them go, released them
haʼhé·ya̱ht·ga:ʼ I left him there; I took him over there
a·ho·wę·náht·ga:ʼ they released him, them (m)
a·gáht·gaʼ I gave it up (right now)
di·saht·gʼa·wę́·hęg·yeʼ you are going along giving things up
reliable
ho·yaʼda·dá:ni: he is reliable, dependable
[P+ stem: -(a)ʼdadani- reliable, dependable; consists of: -(a)ʼda(ni)$_V$- rely on]
o·yaʼda·dá:ni: to rely (on s.o., s.t.)
ho·ih·wa·dó:gę: he is a reliable person
[P+ stem: -(r)ihwadogę:- reliable; consists of: -(r)ih(wa)$_N$- word -dogę(:)$_V$- right, true]
o·ih·wa·dó:gę: it is a certainty
reliance see: reliable
relief see: help
ga·yę·na·wáhs·raʼ help
religion
ga·ih·wi·yóhs·dęhs·raʼ religion; the Christian faith
[ga+ stem: -rihwiyohsdęhsr(a)$_N$- religion, faith consists of: -(r)ih(wa)$_N$- word -iyohsd$_V$- make good]
religion see: belief
tsęh hǫ:wéh gyǫg·wéh·da̱h·gǫh our belief; our religion
relinquish see: forfeit
a·sa:dwę́:deht you forfeited
reluctant see: balk, unwilling
a·had·rǫh·yáʼdahk he balked at the suggestion
de·wa·ge·gá·ę: I do not want to do it; I am unwilling
rely on
she·yáʼdaʼs you rely on s.o.
[TR+ stem: -(a)ʼda(:,ni)$_V$- rely on]
ke·yáʼdaʼs I rely on her
ę·kéyʼa·da:ʼ I will rely on her
remain see: stay
he·ya·got·wáʼehs·dǫh she is there for an extended stay
remainder
he·yo·da·dá·ǫ: a remainder; a residue
[heʼ+yo+adad+ stem: -aʼǫ:- remainder, residue; consists of: -ǫ$_V$- a number (of things)]
o·dá·daʼǫh a remainder; it is left over
remainder see: surplus
he·yó·gǫh·so:t it is a surplus
remains see: corpse
o·yǫ́ʼdaʼ a dead body; a cadaver
remark see: say
a·hęʼ he said
remarkable see: exceptional
á·ǫ·gǫh·dǫh exceptional; above average; too much
remedy see: cure, heal
a·gé:jęʼt it cured me
ę·ji·sa·né:yǫ:ʼ it will heal you
remember
ęh·sáh·saʼse:k you will remember
[(heʼ+)(s/j+) P+ stem: -(a)hshaʼe:k$_V$- remember, recall]

remember (continued)
hę·jí·sas·ha:ʼ you will remember back in time
[(heʼ+)(s/j+) P+ stem: -(a)hsha(:)$_{V}$- remember, recall]
a·gahs·haʼdrǫ́:nyǫh I am reminiscing, remembering
[(heʼ+)(s/j+) P+ stem: -(a)hsʼdrǫnyǫh$_{V}$- remember, recall]
hehs·hohs·haʼdrǫ́:nyǫh he is remembering back then
swa·gahs·haʼdrǫ́:nyǫh I am recalling, remembering
shohs·háʼdrǫh he is remembering (right now)
[(heʼ+)(s/j+) P+ stem: -(a)hsʼdrǫh$_{V}$- remember, recall]
ęt·sa·da·dáhs·ha:gwęʼ you will remind yourself, make yourself remember
[de+...P+ stem: -(a)hshagwę, (a)hshagwani- make oneself remember; consists of: -(a)hsha(:)$_{V}$- remember, recall]

remembrance
ohs·há:gwaht remembrance
[o+ stem: -(a)hshagwahd- rememberance; consists of: -(a)hs(h)a(:)$_{V}$- remember, recall]
ohs·há:gwa·ni: remembrance; to remember
[stem: -(a)hsha:gwę, (a)hsha:gwani- remember for oneself; consists of: -(a)hs(h)a(:)$_{V}$- remember, recall]

remind see: remember
ęt·sa·da·dahs·há:gwęʼ you will remind yourself, make yourself remember

remorseful see: feel bad, regret
ga·dé·hęhs I am embarrassed, ashamed
ǫ·gáh·sęhs I regret it; I did regret it

remote see: distance
tó: ni·yó:weʼ that far

remove
ę·sǫ́·da·goʼ you will remove, detach s.t.
[stem: -odagw$_{V}$- remove, detach]
a·gat·nʼo·jó·da·goʼ I had my tooth pulled
[(at+)(N+) stem: -noʼj(a)$_{N}$- tooth -odagw$_{V}$- remove, detach]
sʼǫne:k remove s.t.
[stem: -ǫʼn(eg)$_{V}$- remove, take away]
ę·sá·dʼǫ·ne:k you will move away
sʼǫ·né:ksǫ: you remove several things
[stem: -ǫʼneksǫʼ- remove several things; consists of: -ǫʼn(eg)$_{V}$- remove, take away]
gyʼo·nǫ: it has been removed
[g+yo+ stem: -(ʼ)nǫ:- removed; consists of: -ǫʼn(eg)$_{V}$- remove, take away]
ǫʼnǫ:ʼ it has been moved
ęt·sá·dǫʼne:k you will remove yourself
[de+...ad+ stem: -ǫʼn(eg)$_{V}$- remove, take away; remove oneself]
de·se·nęt·sǫ́ʼne:k remove your arms (that is, retract them); remove your support
[de+...ad+ stem: -nęts(ha)$_{N}$- arm -ǫʼn(eg)$_{V}$- remove, take away]
da·ge·nęt·sǫ́ʼne:k I withdrew my arm; I withdrew my support
ęhsetsgęʼęda̱hgoʼ you will remove seeds
[-tsgęʼęd(a)$_{N}$- pit -(h)gw, (h)go$_{V}$- remove]
gahsgwa:da̱hgwęh a neutered animal, a gelding
[-(h)sg(wa:)$_{N}$- stone, bullet, rock -(h)gw, (h)go$_{V}$- remove]

remove see: throw
gog·yeʼs to get rid of s.t., throw it away

renounce see: forfeit, remove
a·sa:dwę́:deht you forfeited
de·se·nęt·sǫ́ʼne:k remove your arms (that is, retract them); also, remove your support

rent see: borrow
ęh·sę́·ni̲·ha' you will borrow, rent s.t.
repair
sa·sehs·rǫ́:ni' you repaired it
[s+...stem: -hsr$_N$- noun -(h)srǫni$_V$- fix, repair]
repair see: fix
ęh·sehs·rǫ́:ni' you will create, make s.t.
repairman
shahs·rǫ́:nihs repairman
[s+A+ stem: -(h)srǫnihs- repairman; consists of: -(h)srǫni$_V$- fix, repair]
repairman see: mechanic, telephone repairman
sha'dreh·dǫ́:nihs he is a mechanic
ǫd·wę·nǫ·dah·tá' shahs·rǫ́:nihs telephone repairman
repay
ęt·sé·gan·ya'k you will repay, refund
[s+ stem: -ga:$_N$- price -ganya'g$_V$- pay; repay, refund;]
ęhs·gǫ·gan·yá'gę' I will repay you for your actions
[s+ TR+ stem: -ga:$_N$- price -ganya'gę$_V$- pay; repay, refund]
repent
ęt·sa·dat·ré:waht you will repent, redeem yourself, apologize
[d...TR/...adat+ stem: -(hr)ewahd$_V$- punish; repent, apologize]
repent see: apologize
ęs·ga·dat·ré:waht I will apologize, repent
repentance
a·dat·re·wáh·dǫ:' repentance; punishment
[adat+ stem: -(hr)ewahdǫ:'- repentance, punishment; consists of: -(hr)ewahd$_V$- punish]
replace
o:yá' dęt·gǫ́:yǫ' I will give you a new one (that is, replace s.t.)

replace (continued)
[consists of: oya' another; dętgǫ:yǫ' I will replace it for you]
[de+d+...TR+ stem: -awi, ǫ$_V$- give; replace;]
o:yá' dęts·gǫ' you will give me another (that is, replace)
[consists of: oya' another; dętsgǫ' you will replace it for me]
ded·wáht·ga·węh to replace (lit.: it has been re-given)
[de+d+... stem: -(a)htga(w)$_V$- release, let go; replace]
ti·gǫ́:nihs I use s.t. in place of s.t. else
[ti+... stem: -ǫni, ǫny$_V$- make; replace, substitute]
ta'gǫ́:ni' I made it in place of s.t. else, replaced it
ti·wa:gǫ́:ni: I have made it in place of s.t. else, replaced it
replace see: change
ęhs·na:dé:ni' you will change the oil, fluid
replenish see: fill, replace
á:knǫn·heht I would fill
reply see: answer
dęhs·rih·wad·rá:go' you will answer, reply
report
ęt·rih·wa̲h·wí:nyǫ't you will report
[stem: -(r)ihwinyǫ'd- report; consists of: -(r)ih(wa)$_N$- word -inyǫ'd$_V$- put in]
ga·ih·wa'éhs·dǫ:' a report
[stem: -(r)ihwa'ehsd- demand a report, an account; consists of: -(r)ih(wa)$_N$- word -(')ehsd$_V$- cause to hit]
represent
ęhs·ha·gog·ya'dǫ́:dahk he will be an ambassador, represent s.o. (lit.: they will put his body in)
[TR+ag+ stem: -ya'dǫda:- represent, be an ambassador; consists of: -ya'd(a)$_N$- body -ǫda:(h)$_V$- put in, attached]

Cayuga pronunciation guide: /a/ father /e/ weigh /ę/ men (nasalized) /i/ police /o/ hole /ǫ/ home (nasalized) /u/ blue. Underlined vowels are voiceless or whispered. /'/ high pitch. /t/ too /d/ do /k/ king /g/ good (never soft g) /j/ judge or adze /s/ soon /sh/ less heat (never the sh in shirt) /sr/ shrine /sy/ sure /hw/ which (the sound made when you blow out a candle) /h/ hi /ts/ cats hide /'/ (the sound before the first vowel in 'uh-uh') /n/ noon /r/ round /w/ way /y/ yes.

representative see: appoint
a·hǫ·wa·i·hǫ́:dę' they delegated him a duty
reprimand see: scold
ęhs·he·da̱hs·wá·hęd·rǫ:' you will scold her, s.o.
reproach see: blame, scold
ęhs·héh·wa'ehs you will blame s.o.
ęhs·he·da̱hs·wá·hęd·rǫ:' you will scold her, s.o.
reproduce see: grow
ę·wáh·do:k it will multiply, grow
reptile see: snake
os·há·ihs·da' a snake
repulsion see: hatred
ohs·wá·hęh·de:' hatred
repulsive see: evil
ga̱·hé:tgę' it is ugly
request see: ask, invite
ę·sa·da̱·hǫ́:dǫ' you will ask
ę·gǫ·hǫ·gá·ǫ' I will invite, request you
requirement see: necessity
de·yot·wę·jó·hǫh a necessity
requisition see: command, hire
ęhs·hé:nha' you will command, hire her
wa·dę́n·ha'ǫh it is chartered, hired
rescue
a·ha·do·dá·i·si: he got loose, escaped
[TR+ad+ stem: -odais(i)$_V$- comb; rescue s.o., help s.o. escape]
ęt·seya·do·dá·ih·si' you will rescue s.o.
ęhs·heya·do·dá·i·si' you will help her escape; you will save her
research
é·i:ho'gwa:s she is researching, instigating
[A+ stem: -(r)iho'gwad- research, instigate; consists of: -(r)ih(wa)$_N$- word -o'gwad$_V$- dig]
há·i:ho'gwa:s he is researching, instigating

research (continued)
e·ih·wá·o·he:s she is a researcher
[stem: -(r)ihwaoheg- research; consists of: -(r)ih(wa)$_N$- word -(r)oheg$_V$- gather]
ha·ih·wá·o·he:s he is a researcher
ęhs·rih·wá·o·he:k you will gather ideas, news
resemble
sgá:yę: it resembles
[s+A+ stem: -ye(:)$_V$- do; resemble]
tsé:yę: you resemble
o'grǫ: it looks like snow
[o+(N+) stem: -(a)'gr(a)$_N$- snow -ǫ:$_V$- resemble]
os·dá·ǫ: it looks like rain
[o+(N+) stem: -(h)sd(a:)$_N$- drop (of water) -ǫ:$_V$- resemble]
tsa'de·g'ad·réh·d'o·dę: the cars look the same
[tsa'+de+A/P+N+ stem: -(')drehd(a)$_N$- vehicle, car -o'dę:$_V$- type of; resemble, be similar, look the same]
resemble see: like, same, similar
ní:yoht what it is like (preceded by a particle such as de', ne')
tsa'dé:yoht they are (lit.: it is) the same
to:háh tsa'dé:yoht it is similar
resent see: grudge, testy
ęh·sá·ti·ya'k you will hold a grudge
ho·tí·ya̱'sgǫ: he's testy; he has a short fuse
reserve
ęh·sat·wi̱hs·dá·ę' you will economize
[at+ stem: -(h)wihsdaę(:)- reserve, economize; consists of: -(h)wihsd(a), (hr)ihsd(a)$_N$- metal, money -ę:$_V$- lie down]
sat·wíhs·da·ę' reserve it

reserve (continued)
wag·ye·na·wáh·dǫh a reserved or booked venue
[ag+ stem: -yenawahd- cling; book a venue, reserve a room, retain a room; consists of: -yena(w), yenaǫ, yena(꞉)$_V$- catch, receive, accept]
reserve see: keep
ę·sa꞉drǫ́꞉goʼ you will keep it
reserve a venue see: reserve
wag·ye·na·wáh·dǫh a reserved or booked venue
reserved see: shy
go·díʼgrǫʼ she is shy
reside
tsę́h tgiʼdrǫʼ where I live, reside
[tsęh that t+A+ stem: -(i)ʼdrǫ$_V$- live, dwell, be at home]
reside see: dwell, inhabit, truth
tsę́h dwak·nǫ́h·so꞉t where I dwell
ę·sat·na·dá·ęʼ you will inhabit
grih·wag·wę·ní꞉yoʼ where I reside, dwell
residence see: house
ga·nǫ́h·saʼ a house
residue see: remainder, surplus
he·yo·da·dá·ǫ꞉ a remainder; a residue
he·yó·gǫh·so꞉t it is a surplus
resin
ohs·da꞉ʼáh ot·séhs·daʼ pine pitch; pine resin
[consists of: ohsda꞉ʼah pine tree; otsehsdaʼ syrup, honey, gum]
resin see: syrup
ot·séhs·daʼ syrup; honey; gum; rubber
resist see: balk, disagree, unwilling
a·had·rǫh·yáʼdahk he balked at the suggestion
taʼdeg·rih·wáhs·nyeʼ I oppose it; I do not agree
de·wa·ge·gá·ę꞉ I do not want to do it; I am unwilling
resistant see: hard
oh·ní꞉yǫh it is hard
resolve see: decide, uncompromising
ad·wag·rih·wá·ę꞉daʼs I came to a decision
de·hoʼni·gǫ́·hagǫ꞉t he is set in his ways; his mind is set
resources see: G (oh·wę·ja·geh·ge·ha꞉ʼ), wealth
ot·ga·nǫ·níhs·raʼ wealth
respect
ga·gǫ́n·yǫhs·de꞉ʼ respect
[ga+ stem: -gǫnyǫhsde꞉ʼ- respect; consists of: -gǫnyǫ$_V$- be clean, discriminating]
respect see: honour, revere
ahs·ha·go·dí·gǫn·yǫhs they honoured her
dęd·wa·dad·rih·wa·nǫ́hk·wa꞉k we all (incl.) will show respect for one another
respond see: answer
dęhs·rih·wad·rá꞉goʼ you will answer, reply
responsibility
ga·ih·wa·géh·deʼ responsibility
[ga+ stem: -(r)ihwagehdeʼ- responsibility; consists of: -(r)ih(wa)$_N$- word -gehd$_V$- have around one's neck]
sad·rih·wa·géh·deʼ your responsibility (lit.: it is hanging on you)
ę·ga·ih·wá·ę·dahk it will become s.o.'s responsibility
[stem: -(r)ihwaędahgw- responsibility; consists of: -(r)ih(wa)$_N$- word -ędahgw$_V$- raise from the ground]
ga·ih·wá·ę·dah·gǫh their (lit.: it is a) collective responsibility
ga·ih·wa·ę·dahg·wáh·nǫʼ their (f/m) collective responsibility; delegations
[stem: -(r)ihwaędahgw- responsibility; consists of: -(r)ih(wa)$_N$- word -ędahgwahnǫʼ$_V$- several objects raised from the ground]

Cayuga pronunciation guide: /a/ father /e/ weigh /ę/ men (nasalized) /i/ police /o/ hole /ǫ/ home (nasalized) /u/ blue. Underlined vowels are voiceless or whispered. /ˊ/ high pitch. /t/ too /d/ do /k/ king /g/ good (never soft g) /j/ judge or adze /s/ soon /sh/ less heat (never the sh in shirt) /sr/ shrine /sy/ sure /hw/ which (the sound made when you blow out a candle) /h/ hi /ts/ cats hide /ʼ/ (the sound before the first vowel in 'uh-uh') /n/ noon /r/ round /w/ way /y/ yes.

responsibility see: necessity
de·yot·wę·jó·hǫh a necessity
rest
ga·dǫh·wihs·hę́·hę' I rest all the time
[ad+ stem: -ǫhwihshę(:)$_V$- rest, relax]
ę·ga·ǫ:dǫ́h·wihs·hę:' they (f/m) will rest
a·ga·dǫ·wihs·hę́:da'k I did have a rest
[ad+ stem: -ǫhwihshęda'$_V$- rest, relax]
restart
ded·wah·sa·wé:ha' to restart
[de+d+... stem: -(a)hsawę, (a)hsawe:, (a)hsa:$_V$- begin, start; restart, resume]
dǫ·da·hah·sá:wę' he restarted
deg·yóh·sa:' it has resumed
restaurant
ǫ·de·kǫn·yá'ta'geh a restaurant; a cafeteria; a dining room; a dining hall
[ǫ+ade+ stem: -kǫnya'ta'geh- kitchen; restaurant, cafeteria, dining room; consists of: -k(wa)$_N$- food -ǫnya'd$_V$- cause to make -'geh at]
restful
a·dǫh·wih·sę́h·de:' it is restful
[ad+ stem: -ǫwihshęhde:'- restful; consists of: -owihshę(:)$_V$- rest, relax]
restless see: fidgety, nervous
sat·na't·sa·gę́:nye' you are fidgety
wa·dón·yah·nǫ: it is nervous
restore see: cure, give, repair
a·gé:ję't it cured me
dahs·gǫh give it to me
sa·sehs·rǫ́·ni' you repaired it
restrain see: tie up
gęhs·há·ǫ:t I am tied up
resume
hęt·sáh·sǫd·rę' you will resume, add on
[he+s+... stem: -(a)hsǫdrę, (a)hsǫdre$_V$- join together; resume, add on]
resume see: restart
deg·yóh·sa:' it has resumed
resurface
sga·dę́h·da:' to resurface s.t.
[s+... stem: -dęhda:'$_V$- lie spread out on the ground; resurface s.t.]
resurface see: float
dǫ·da·wa·dá'grahk it resurfaced
retain see: have, keep
ag·yę' I have, possess s.t.
ę·sa:drǫ́:go' you will keep ut
retaliate see: cure, goat (get s.o.'s goat), retribution (receive retribution)
a·hé:ję't I fixed (lit. cured) him; I got even with him
a'e·sa·hí:ya'k she got your goat
ęh·sa·wę·ná·hǫ:k your words will come back on you; you will be revenged, repaid for your words
retch see: vomit
e·san·yag·wá·hǫ' you vomited
retell see: recount
ęt·sa:tró:wi' you will recount, retell
reticent see: shy, timid
go·dí'grǫ' she is shy
tot·gri: he's a wimp; he pulls back
retort see: answer
dęhs·rih·wad·rá:go' you will answer, reply
retract
hehs·wag·yę·hę́:twęh you retracted
[he'+...ag+ stem: -yęhętw, yęhęto$_V$- pull; retract]
retribution (receive retribution)
ęh·sa·wę·ná·hǫ:k your words will come back on you; you will be revenged, repaid for your words
[stem: -węnahǫg- receive retribution; consists of: -węn(a)$_N$- voice, word -(h)ǫ(:)$_V$- lie]
return
het·séh·ta' you go back (all the time)
[(he')+ s+... stem: -(a)hge(h)d$_V$- return, go back]
hes·gáh·gęh·ta' I go back all the time

return (continued)
swa̱h·gé·dahs you return, regress
ęt·sáh·ge:t you will go back, regress
shá:yǫʼ he returned
[s+… stem: -yǫ$_V$- arrive; return, come back]
ęhs·gyǫʼ I will come back
de·ja:gó:yǫ: she did not return
shó:yǫ: he returned
return see: come back, double back, go back, go back inside, go back there
ǫ́·da̱·heʼ, **á·ǫ·da̱·heʼ** he would come this way
ǫ:sa·gat·ga·ę:hę́:goʼ I should turn around and go back the way I came
ihs·geʼs I have returned home
hǫ·sá·ha·yǫʼ he went back inside; he arrived back there
hęs·geʼ I am going back there
reveal see: find
a·gét·sęn·yǫ: I have found it
revelry see: celebration
o·dǫt·ga·déhs·raʼ a celebration
revenge see: cure, repay, retribution (receive retribution)
a·hé:jęʼt I fixed (lit. cured) him; I got even with him
ęhs·gǫ·gan·yáʼgęʼ I will repay you for your actions
ęh·sa·wę·ná·hǫ:k your words will come back on you; you will be revenged, repaid for your words
revere
de·ke·nǫ·hǫk·waʼ (**de·ké·nǫk·waʼ**) she who I revere as…
[de+TR+ stem: -nǫhkw$_V$- love; revere, show respect]
dęd·wa·dad·rih·wa·nǫ́hk·wa:k we all (incl.) will show respect for one another
revered see: forbidden
o·nǫ́ʼne:ʼ it is forbidden, sacred, holy

reverence see: honour, respect
ahs·ha·go·dí·gǫn·yǫhs they honoured her
ga·gǫ́n·yǫhs·de:ʼ respect
reverse see: double back
ǫ:sa·gat·ga·ę:hę́:goʼ I should turn around and go back the way I came
revolt
ęt·sęʼni·gǫ́·hoʼne:k you will revolt, remove yourself (bodily and in spirit)
[de+…ę+ stem: -(ʼ)nigǫhoʼneg- revolt, rebel; consists of: -(ʼ)nigǫh(a)$_N$- mind -ǫʼn(eg)$_V$- remove, take away]
revolt see: struggle
ęh·sá·det·saʼt you will struggle, squirm to get loose, revolt
revolting see: evil
ga̱·hé:tgęʼ it is ugly
revolve see: roll, turn around, twirl
sat·gá·ha·toh roll over
de·sat·ga̱·ha:dé:nih turn around
de·sat·ga̱·ha·den·yǫ́g·wa̱·hǫ: twirl
reward see: pay, repay
ga·gán·yʼa·gǫh a payment
ęhs·gǫ·gan·yáʼgęʼ I will repay you for your actions
reword see: recount, say, tell, translate
ęt·sa:tró:wiʼ you will recount, retell
ę·hęʼ he will say
ahs·ha·go̱·hó:wiʼ he told her
de·ye·wę·ná·den·yeʼs she is a translator; she is translating now
rhetoric see: language
o·wę·na·gá:yǫh high language; formal language
rhythm
de·yóhk·waʼ a steady rhythm, beat; a throbbing noise
ni·gáhn·yoʼdę: the rhythm; the beat of a piece of music
[ni+ ga+ stem: -(h)ny(a)$_N$- stick -oʼdę:$_V$- type of]

rib
oh·dé:ga:ˀ ribs
[o+ stem: -(h)deg(a:)$_N$- rib]
sẹh·de·gá:ˀgeh on your ribs
swạh·de·gá:ˀgeh on your (p) ribs
rib cage
oh·de:gá:ˀ ohsg·yẹˀdǫ́:dǫˀ the rib cage
[consists of: ohdega:ˀ ribs; ohsgyẹˀdǫ:dǫˀ bones]
oh·de·gá:ˀ ohsg·yẹ́ˀdǫ:t the rib cage
ribbon see: lace
gan·héh·saˀ a harness; ribbon; laces
rice
o·ná·ja·gẹ:t rice
[o+ stem: -naˀjagẹd- rice; consists of: -na(ˀ)ja(da)$_N$- wheat, grain -(ˀ)gẹd$_V$- light-coloured, white]
rich
ot·ga:nǫ́:nih it is rich; prosperity; it is precious
[at+ stem: -ganǫni- rich, wealthy; consists of: -ga:$_N$- price -ǫni, ǫny$_V$- make]
got·ga·nǫ·ní·hag·yeˀ prosperity; s.o. is prospering
oh·ná·i:ˀ it is rich, fatty food
[o+ stem: -(h)nai:ˀ- rich, fatty; consists of: -(h)n(a)$_N$- oil, gas -i:ˀ$_V$- stuck onto s.t.]
richness
ot·ga·nǫ·níhs·raˀ richness; wealth
[o+at+ stem: -(a)tganǫnihsr(a)$_N$- richness, wealth consists of:-ganǫni$_V$- be rich, wealthy]
rid see: throw
gog·yeˀs to get rid of s.t., throw it away
ride see: drag
ǫk·níˀdre:ˀ we two are riding along in s.t.
ride (give s.o. a ride)
ẹhs·héˀnǫh·da:ˀ you will put s.o. in s.t., you will give him a ride
ride (continued)
[TR+ stem: -(ˀ)nǫhda(:,h)- get into a vehicle, embark; give s.o. a ride, put s.o., s.t. in; consists of: -(ˀ)nǫhd$_V$- in]
ride horseback
hoh·seˀ he is riding a horse
[P+ stem: -(h)seˀ$_V$- ride horseback]
gǫh·seˀ she is riding a horse
ẹ·tóh·seˀ he is coming by horseback
ridicule see: jeer
ẹh·sad·wẹ·ná:yẹht you will jeer, jest, throw words at s.o.
rifle
gạ·hóˀde:s rifle
[ga+ stem: -(h)oˀde:s- rifle; consists of: -(h)oˀd(a)$_N$- gun -es$_V$- long]
rigging see: line, rope
gạh·sí·ya·deˀ a suspended line; a string
gá:tsgˀẹ·daˀ a rope
right
dó:gẹhs sure; truly; right; it is a fact
[stem: -dogẹ(:)$_V$- right, true]
tẹ́ˀ de·dó:gẹhs no, it is not right
ga·dó:gẹ: a certain way; together; a certain thing
ga·ih·wa·dó:gẹ: it is the main idea
[stem: -(r)ih(wa)$_N$- word -dogẹ(:)$_V$- be right, true]
tga:yé·i: it is right, correct
[t+ga+ stem: -yei, (y)í$_V$- right, correct]
ga·wa·i·hǫhs·dǫ́h gwá·i / gwá:dih to the right (side)
[consists of: gawayẹhǫhsdǫh it is right-handed; gwai, gwa:dih to one side]
right see: do right, arrange, G (dwa·ga:wi:)
dẹhs·yí:dahs you do things right
ẹh·sad·ri̲h·wa:dó:gẹhs you will right a wrong
right away see: I (gǫdagyeˀ)

right-handed

ha·wa·yę·hǫ́hs·dǫh he is right-handed
[A+ stem: -wayęhǫhsdǫh- right-handed; consists of: -wayę(n)$_N$- heart, spirit -(h)ǫhsd$_V$- be lying across]

righteous

o·ya'da·wá:dǫh a righteous person
[o+ stem: -ya'dawadǫh- righteous; consists of: -ya'd(a)$_N$- body -wadǫh$_V$-]
god·rih·wag·wá·ih·sǫh she is fair, righteous
[P+ad+ stem: -(r)ihwagwaihs(h)ǫ- be a witness; be fair, noble, righteous, etc.; consists of: -(r)ih(wa)$_N$- word -gwaihs(i)$_V$- straight]
od·rih·wag·wá·ih·sǫ: it is believable, credible, righteous, fair, honest
hod·rih·wag·wá·ih·sǫ he is a noble person

rigid see: stiff

o·tǫ́·ga·i: it is stiff; rigor mortis

rigor mortis see: stiff

o·tǫ́·ga·i: it is stiff; rigor mortis

rim see: brim, edge

de·yo'nihs·gá:de' the brim of a hat
o·dó'kdag·ye' a rim; the outer and inner rim splint; along the edge

rind see: fat, peelings

o'dǫ́:dra' it is fat; gristle; rind
o'dróhs·ra' fat; pig rinds
o·wá'wihs·da' a peeling

ring see: circle, wheel

de·wę'nyahs·gá·ǫni: (**de·wę'nihs·gá·ǫni:**) a circle
ę'níhs·ga:', **wę'níhs·ga:'** a wheel; a circle; a hoop

rink see: arena

de·ta·di·jihg·w'a·éhs·ta' an arena

riot

ha·di·nǫhs·gá:nyahs they (m) are rioting
[stem: -nǫhsgany- riot; consists of: -nǫhs(a)$_N$- house -gany, gai$_V$- be desperate]
a·ha·di·nǫ́hs·ga·i' they (m) made a riot
a·ha·nǫhs·gá·i:' he raised cain, had a tantrum
ga·nǫ́hs·gan·yęh a riot

riot see: celebration

de·yog·yǫhg·wę́:dǫhs an upheaval of a crowd of people; a celebration; a riot

rip see: tear

a·wád·rat·sǫ: it got torn, ripped

ripe

ę·wáh·ya·i' it will ripen
[stem: -(a)hyai- ripen; consists of: -(a)hy(a)$_N$- fruit, berry -(r)i, (w)i$_V$- ripe]
oh·yá·ih ripe fruit
a·wát·sih·sę:' it ripened for harvesting
[stem: -(a)tsihsę:- ripe; consists of: -(a)tsihs'$_V$- mature]
ot·síhs·hę: it is at a mature state

ripe see: mature

a·wát·sihs'a:' it (a plant) matured; it completed its life-cycle

rise

wa·tá:da:s it rises up
[at+ stem: -(h)adad$_V$- rise up]
ę·wa:tá:da:t it will rise up
o·ta·da·dǫ́·hǫg·ye' it is going along rising up
de·yog·wit·gę́'ǫh, gya:gwit·gę́'ǫh the sun or moon has risen
[(d+)... stem: -(r)ag(wa)$_N$- sun, moon -itgę'$_V$- rise]

rise early

syeh·wa:t you are an early riser
[stem: -yehwad- rise early; consists of: -ye(h,:)$_V$- wake up, awaken]

rise up see: revolt, struggle

ęt·sę'ni·gǫ́·ho'ne:k you will revolt, remove yourself (bodily and in spirit)
ęh·sá·det·sa't you will struggle, squirm to get loose, revolt

Cayuga pronunciation guide: /a/ father /e/ weigh /ę/ men (nasalized) /i/ police /o/ hole /ǫ/ home (nasalized) /u/ blue. Underlined vowels are voiceless or whispered. /´/ high pitch. /t/ too /d/ do /k/ king /g/ good (never soft g) /j/ judge or adze /s/ soon /sh/ less heat (never the sh in shirt) /sr/ shrine /sy/ sure /hw/ which (the sound made when you blow out a candle) /h/ hi /ts/ cats hide /'/ (the sound before the first vowel in 'uh-uh') /n/ noon /r/ round /w/ way /y/ yes.

risk see: gamble
a·tę·nad·ra' s·ró·i' a:k they (m) tested or tried their luck
ritual see: ceremony
od·rih·wa̱h·dę́:gyo̜: the ceremony
river
gi̱·hę:k river
[stem: -gihę(k)$_N$- river, stream, creek]
gi·hę́:de' a creek; a river; a stream
[stem: -gihę(k)$_N$- river, stream, creek -de'$_V$- exist]
gi·hę́:go̜: it is in the stream, creek, river
gi̱·hęk·dak·dá:gye' along the river, stream, creek, shoreline
gi·hę́:k' ah the riverside; along the river
ni·gi·hú:' uh a small stream
[stem: -gihę(k)$_N$- river, stream, creek; -u:'uh-$_V$ small]
river flats
o̜hn·yá' geh on the river flats
[stem: -(r)o̜hny(a)$_N$- river flats]
á·o̜hn·ya·go̜: in the river flats
rivet see: nuts and bolts
ga̱hn·yo̜' srá' ga·di:yé:nahs nuts and bolts
rivulet see: river
gi·hę́:de' creek; river; stream
road
o·há·ha' road
[o+ stem: -(h)ah(a)$_N$- road]
o·há·ha' geh on the road
o·há:de' an existing road
[o+ stem: -(h)ah(a)$_N$- road -de'$_V$- exist]
o·há·den·yo̜' roads, highways
[o+ stem: -(h)ah(a)$_N$- road -denyo̜'$_V$- several existing things]
o·ha·hó:ga' t a rough road
[o+ stem: -(h)ah(a)$_N$- road -(r)oga'd$_V$- rough]
ni·yo·ha·hú:' uh a small road
[ni+yo+ stem: -(h)ah(a)$_N$- road -u:'uh$_V$- small]
ga̱hs·wa·o̜g·yó̜: o·há:de' gravel roads
road (continued)
[consists of: ga̱hswao̜gyo̜:' gravel has been put down; oha:de' an existing road]
o·no̜·da̱·ha·o̜:nyó̜' o̱·há·ha' geh hilly roads
[consists of: ono̜da̱ho̜:nyo̜' hills; o̱haha'geh on the road]
ga·di' dre̱h·dáhk·wa' vehicular pathways; roads
[stem: -(i)'drehdahkwa'- road; consists of: -(i)'dre(:)$_V$- drag, drive]
road see: highway, laneway
o·ha·ho·wá·nęhs·geh a highway
o̜·ta·ha:gwa̱h·ta' a laneway
road scraper
de·wa·ha·há·gęd·ro̜hs a road scraper; a grader
[de+wa+ stem: -(h)ahagędro̜hs- road scraper, road grader; consists of: -(h)ah(a)$_N$- road -gędro̜(:)$_V$- separate]
road sign
o·ha·hak·da' géh ga·nes·dá·o·do̜' a road sign
[consists of: ohahakda'geh on the road; ganesdaodo̜' boards]
roadside weed cutter
ga·wę·no̱hg·ri·ya' s·gó:wah a roadside weed cutter; a brush cutter
[ga+ stem: -węnohgriya'sgowah- roadside weed cutter; consists of: -węnohgr(a)$_N$- weed -(i)ya'g$_V$- cut, break -gowah- big]
roam
ga·di·dak·sé·no̜g·ye' s they (z) are running about, roaming
[A+ stem: -daksenǫgye'- roam, run about; consists of: -dakse$_V$- run all over]
ti·gę·ne·nó̜g·ye' s they (z) are roaming about
[ti+ stem: -eno̜gye's- roam; consists of: -eno̜:$_V$- originate from someplace, come from someplace]

roam (continued)
gęg·yóh·gǫg·ye's people roaming about [stem: -(i)gyohg(wa)$_N$- crowd -ǫgye's$_V$- roam]
roam see: stray, wander
a·gę·na·tá·ha:go' they (z) turned off the road
ti·gá·ę's they (f/m) are roaming about
roast
wad·wá·hǫ:t it is roasting (on a spit) [wa+ad+ stem: -(')wahǫd- roast; consists of: -(')wah(a)$_N$- meat -ǫd$_V$- attached]
wad·wa·hǫ́:da'k it was roasted meat
wa·dé'sgǫ:t it is roasting, frying [ade+ stem: -(')sgǫd- roast, fry; consists of: -'sg$_N$- roast -ǫd$_V$- attached]
ęh·sa·d'es·gǫ́:dę' you will roast it
sa·de'sgǫ́:dęh fry it
roasting pan
ǫd·wa·hǫ·dáhk·wa' a roasting pan [ǫ+ad+ stem: -(')wahǫdahkwa'- roasting pan; consists of: -(')wah(a)$_N$- meat -ǫdahkwa'$_V$- container]
rob
sha·góh·se̲h·ta' he is a robber, a stealer [TR+ stem: -(a)hsehd$_V$- hide s.t.; rob s.o.]
a·hǫ́·wa̲h·seht he robbed him
rob see: steal
ęhs·nę́hs·go' you will steal
robin
jíhs·go·go', **jíhs·gu·gu'** robin [stem: -jihsgogo', jihsgugu'$_N$- robin]
robot
ti·ga·y'a·do:ní: wa·dǫ́n·ya̲h·nǫ:' a robot [consists of: tigay'ado:ni: a robot, a puppet; wadǫnya̲hnǫ:' it moves along]
ti·ga·y'a·do:ní: wa·dé'drehs a robot (lit.: it moves) [consists of: tigay'ado:ni: a robot, puppet; wade'dre's self-propelled]

robot (continued)
ti·ga·y'a·dó:ni: a robot; a puppet, etc. [ti+ga+ stem: -ya'dǫni:- robot, puppet; consists of: -ya'd(a)$_N$- body -ǫni, ǫny$_V$- make; man-made, artificial]
robust see: healthy
a·ga·da·gá·i:de' I am well, fine, healthy
rock see: boulder, gravel, pebble, stone
gahsg·wa·o·wá:nęh a boulder
ni·gahsg·wa·ó:s'uh small gravel; pebbles
gahsg·wa:' a stone; a rock; a boulder; a bullet
rock a child see: babysit
ęh·sa·dę·gáhn·ye' you will comfort, rock a child; you are babysitting
rock formation
de·gahsg·wa:dǫ' rocks piled in an arrangement [de+ga+ stem: -(h)sgwadǫ'- rock formation; consists of: -(h)sg(wa:)$_N$- stone, bullet, rock -dǫ'$_V$- several standing objects]
rock slide
a·gahs·den·yę́'ge: a rock slide [stem: -(h)sdenyę'ge:- rock slide; consists of: -(h)sd(ęha)$_N$- stone]
rock-pile
ohsg·wán·hohs·ro:t a pile of rocks [o+ stem: -(h)sg(wa:)$_N$- stone, bullet, rock -nhohsrod$_V$- pile]
Rockies see: mountain
de·gahs·dę·hó·dag·ye' mountain range, the Rockies
rocking chair
de·yǫt·gá:hǫhk·wa' rocking chair [de+yǫ+at+ stem: -gahǫhkwa'- rocking chair; consists of: -kahǫ$_V$- adjoin, abutt]
rod see: bar, stick
ga̲hn·yǫ́'sra' a bar; a stick-like object
o'ę́:na' a snowsnake; a pole

rodent see: mouse, rat
ji·nó:wę: a mouse
ji·no·wę·gó:wah a rat
roe
o·né'da: roe (fish eggs)
[o+ stem: -ne'd(a:)$_N$- roe]
role see: occupation, responsibility
ni·sa·i·ho'dęhs·ró'dę: your occupation; your type of work
sad·rih·wa·géh·de' your responsibility
roll
wat·gá·ha·dǫhs it rolls
[at+ stem: -gahadǫ- roll; consists of: -gah(a)$_N$- eye -dǫh$_V$- go and stand up several things]
sat·gá·ha·toh roll over
roll one's eyes
ęh·sat·ga·hǫ́:di' you will roll your eyes (in disgust); you will snub s.o.
[at+ stem: -gahǫdi- roll one's eyes, snub s.o.; consists of: -gah(a)$_N$- eye -ǫdi, -ǫgy$_V$- throw]
roller skate
wę'nihs·ga·ǫ:dǫ́' a·do'jí:na' roller skates; roller blades
[consists of: wę'nihsgaǫ:dǫ' wheels; ado'jina' skate]
wę'nihs·ga·ǫ:dǫ́' dę·hę·na·do'ji·néh·ta' they (m) are roller skating, roller blading
[consists of: wę'nihsgaǫ:dǫ' wheels; dęhęnado'jinehta' they (m) are skating]
rolling pin
de·yehs·he'ag·węh·dę́hs·ta' a rolling pin
[de+ye+ stem: -(h)she'agwęhdęhsta'- rolling pin; consists of: -(h)she'(a)$_N$- dough -(a)gwęhdęhsd$_V$- flatten, dent s.t.]
romp see: play
o·nát·gahn·ye' they (z) are playing
roof
ahsg·wa' a roof
[stem: -(a)hsg(wa)$_N$- roof, bridge]
ahsg·wá'geh on top of the house, roof
room
o·nǫ́h·sǫ:t a room; a vault
[o+ stem: -nǫhsǫd- room; consists of: -nǫhs(a)$_N$- house -ǫd$_V$- attached]
o·nǫh·sǫ·dǫ́:nyǫ' rooms
[o+ stem: -nǫhsǫd- room; consists of: -nǫhs(a)$_N$- house -ǫdǫnyǫ'$_V$- several attached objects]
he·yó·nǫh·sǫ:t the next room
[he'+ yo+ stem: -nǫhsǫd- room; consists of: -nǫhs(a)$_N$- house -ǫd$_V$- attached]
he·jó·nǫh·sǫ:t the room after the next room
[he'+ s/j+ yo+ stem: -nǫhsǫd- room; consists of: -nǫhs(a)$_N$- house -ǫd$_V$- attached]
roost see: sit up on s.t.
gits·gwá·he:' I am perched up on s.t.; I am sitting on s.t.
root
ok·dé·ha' a root; edible roots (pepper roots, turnips, carrots)
[o+ stem: -kdeh(a)$_N$- edible root]
ek·dé·ha:s edible roots (pepper roots, turnips, carrots)
[e+ stem: -kdeh(a)$_N$- edible root -g$_V$- eat]
ok·dé·hǫ:t it has roots
[o+ stem: -kdeh(a)$_N$- edible root -ǫd$_V$- attached]
gak·de·hag·wę:ní:yo',
ok·de·hag·wę:ní:yo' the Main Root (refers to a special plant)
[ga/o+ stem: -kdehagwęniyo'- main root; consists of: -kdeh(a)$_N$- edible root -gwęniyo'$_V$- main]
rope
gá:ts·g'ę·da' a rope
[ga+ stem: -tsgę('da)$_N$- rope]
os·há·i:s a long string, rope, etc.
[o+ stem: -sh(a)$_N$- string -is$_V$- be long]

rope see: line, thread
ga̱h·sí·ya·de' a suspended line; a string
oh·sí:ya' a thread; a string; a cord
rose
gǫ·het·gá·ǫg·wę·nih wild roses
[go+ stem: -(h)etgaǫgwęnih- rose]
o·hik·da·déht a·wę·hę́' o·hǫ́:da' rose bushes
[consists of: ohikdadeht rose bushes; awęhę' flower ohǫda' bush]
rot
a'ó:tgęh it became spoiled, rotten
[P+(N+) stem: -tgęh- become rotten; spoil; consists of: -tgę$_V$- spoiled, rotten]
ę·yó:tgęh it will spoil
a'on·ra̱h·dá:tgęh rotted leaves
[P+(N+) stem: -nrahd(a)$_N$- leaf -tgęh$_V$- become rotten, spoil]
rot see: bad, spoil
da·wá·teht·gęht it went bad
ę·yóh·yat·gę' the fruit will spoil
rotate see: roll, turn around, twirl
sat·gá·ha·toh roll over
de·sat·ga̱·ha:dé:nih turn around
de·sat·ga̱·ha·den·yǫ́g·wa̱·hǫ: twirl
rototiller
wat·ga·ha·dǫ́hs de·ga·heh·dá·hih·ta' a rototiller
[consists of: watgahadǫhs it rolls; degahehdahihta' disc]
rotten see: bad, rot, spoil
da·wá·teht·gęht it went bad
ę·yóh·yat·gę' the fruit will spoil
rouge see: make-up
ǫt·go'jon·yáh·ta' make-up; blush; rouge
rough
á·o·ga't it is rough
[a+ (N+) stem: -(r)oga'd$_V$- rough]
round
de·sat·w'ę·nǫ́:nihs you make it round
[de+…at+ stem: -(h)wę'nǫni- wrap s.t.; make s.t. round; be round; consists of: -(h)wę'n(a)$_N$- round, circle -ǫni, ǫny$_V$- make]
de·yo·twę'nǫ́:nih it is round
rove see: roam, stray, wander
ti·ga·e·né·nǫg·ye's they (f) are roaming about
a·gę·na·tá·ha·go' they (z) turned off the road
ti·gá·ę's they (f/m) are roaming about
row
se·gá·wę̱·ha'k you used to paddle
[stem: -gawe(:)$_V$- row, paddle]
ęh·sé·ga·we:' you will row
ga·gá:we: the act of rowing
sa·ga·wę̱·há:gye' you are paddling along
o·tá·hǫ:t a row
[o+at+ stem: -(h)ahǫd- row; consists of: -(h)ah(a)$_N$- road -ǫd$_V$- attached]
o·ta·há·ǫ:nyǫ' rows
[o+at+ stem: -(h)ahǫd- row; consists of: -(h)ah(a)$_N$- road -ǫnyǫ'- several objects]
Royal Canadian Mounted Police see: G (Sha·go·di·ye·na̱hs·go:wah)
royalty see: G (gwa:go:wah)
rub see: grate
ęh·sé:ge:t you will grate, scrape, file it
ha'gye:' I touched it
rubber see: syrup
ot·séhs·da' syrup; honey; gum; rubber
rubber band
de·wa·di·yǫ́:ta' it stretches (shortened form of 'rubber band'); balloon; elastic
[de+w+ad/N+ stem: -(i)yǫd$_V$- stretch]
de·wa·di·yǫ:tá' oh·ná:gri' rubber band, elastic
[consists of: dewadiyǫ:ta' rubber band; ohna:gri' rubber]
rubber pants
gat·sehs·da:hǫ́h at·ná'tsot·ra' rubber pants
[consists of: gatsehsda:hǫh rubber leaning against s.t.; atna'tsotra' pants]

Cayuga pronunciation guide: /a/ father /e/ weigh /ę/ men (nasalized) /i/ police /o/ hole /ǫ/ home (nasalized) /u/ blue. Underlined vowels are voiceless or whispered. /´/ high pitch. /t/ too /d/ do /k/ king /g/ good (never soft g) /j/ judge or adze /s/ soon /sh/ less heat (never the sh in shirt) /sr/ shrine /sy/ sure /hw/ which (the sound made when you blow out a candle) /h/ hi /ts/ cats hide /'/ (the sound before the first vowel in 'uh-uh') /n/ noon /r/ round /w/ way /y/ yes.

ruby see: red
otg·węh·j'i·á:ji: maroon; dark red
rueful see: regretful, sad
o·sę́hs·de:' it is regretful
de·sa'ni·gǫ́·hęh·dǫh you are sad
ruffle see: rumple
de·sat·ge'ó:gwęh you have rumpled hair, ruffled hair
rug
ga·nehs·da:géh e·dę́h·dahkwa' a rug [consists of: ganehsda:geh on the floor; edęhdahkwa' rug]
e·dę́h·dahk·wa' a rug
[e+ stem: -dęhdahkwa'- rug; consists of: -dęhda:'$_V$- lie spread out on the ground]
rugged see: rough
á·o:ga't it is rough
ruin
ęhs·hé:tgęht you will damage, ruin, wreck s.t.
[stem: -(hr)etgęhd- ruin, wreck, damage; consists of: -(hr)etgę$_V$- evil, bad, ugly]
ga·hét·gęh·dǫh it is ruined, wrecked by s.o.
ruin see: bad
o·hét·gę'ǫh it is wrecked, ruined
rule see: G (govern, ǫg·wahs·ha·i·ne')
ruler
ǫ·de'nyę·dę́hs·dahk·wa' a ruler; a measuring tape
[ǫ+ade+ stem: -(')nyędęhsdahkwa'- ruler; consists of: -(')nyędę$_V$- try]
rules see: G (ga·ih·wahs·rǫ·nih)
rumour
ga·ih·wa·né·nǫg·ye's rumours
[stem: -(r)ihwanenǫgye's- rumour; consists of: -(r)ih(wa)$_N$- word -nęnogye's$_V$- go along being warm]
rumour see: gossip, scandal
dę·sad·rih·wá·ę·dǫhk,
dęh·sad·rih·wá·ę·dǫh you will gossip
o·ih·wat·gí:nyǫ' scandalous news; rumours
rumple
de·sat·ge'ó:gwęh you have rumpled hair, ruffled hair
[de+P+at+ stem: -ge'ogw- have rumpled hair; consists of: -ge'(a:), geh(a)$_N$- hair -ogw$_V$- scatter]
rumple see: wrinkle
ęh·sé:gri:k you will wrinkle, fan-fold it
run
de·ga·ǫ:wę́h·da:s they (f/m) run
[de+... stem: -(w)ęhdad$_V$- run]
dę·ga·ǫ:wę́h·da:t they (f/m) will run
de·wa·gęh·dá:dǫh I have run
dę·gę·nęh·dá:tǫ:' they (z) will run all over
[de+... stem: -(w)ęhdatǫ(:)- run all over; consists of: -(w)ęhdad$_V$- run]
run see: race, run about, run all over, run away, stampede
a·tę:nę́·ǫ' they (m) raced
ag·yo·nęh·dáhs·dę' a stampede
run about see: roam, stray, wander
ti·ga·e·né·nǫ:gye's they (f) are roaming about
a·gę·na·tá·ha:go' they (z) turned off the road
ti·gá·ę's they (f/m) are roaming about
run all over
ga·dí·dak·se' they (z) are running all over
[A+ stem: -dakse'$_V$- run all over]
kdak·se' I am running
ga·dá:kse' it is running; to run
run away
a·gę·na·dé'go' they (z) ran away
[ade+ stem: -(')gw$_V$- run away, flee]
ęh·sá·d'e·go' you will flee, run away
a·gad'eg·wę́·hęg·ye' I am running away again

run away see: elope, escape
a·ga·e'nya:gę' **a'a·go·dí:nya'k** they eloped
go·di'ny'a·gę́'ǫh they (f/m) ran away
run out of see: lack
da·wa·d'ok·dę' it lacked; it was not enough
rung see: stair
a·dǫ́h·n'et·sa', **o·dǫ́h·n'et·sa'** a ladder; stairs
runny
a·ge·ji·nyǫ́hg·ro:t I have a runny nose
[P+ stem: -jinyǫhgrot- have a runny nose consists of: -ji'gr(a), jinǫhgr(a), jinǫdagr(a)$_{N}$- mucus -od$_{V}$- stand]
rural see: field, forest
ga̲·há:gǫ: in the bush
ga̲·hę́·da·gǫ: in the field; in the meadow
rush
de·yo'drá·i·ha't hurried, immediate attention; an urgent matter; urgency; a rush
[de+... stem: -(')draiha'd- rush s.t., hurry s.t. up; consists of: -(')draihę$_{V}$- hurry]
deh·se'drá·i·ha't you rush s.t., hurry s.t. up
rust
ohs·gę́'dra' rust
[o+ stem: -(h)sgę'dr(a)$_{N}$- rust, mould]
ohs·gę́'dro:t it is rusting, mouldy
[o+ stem: -(h)sgę'dr(a)$_{N}$- rust, mould -od$_{V}$- stand]
ohs·gę́'dra̲·he:' it is rusting, rusty
[o+ stem: -(h)sgę'dr(a)$_{N}$- rust, mould -(h)e:'$_{V}$- sitting up on top of s.t.]
rusty see: mouldy
a·gahs·g'ęd·rǫ́:dę' it is rusty, mouldy
ruthless see: demanding
tgę·nǫ́h·dǫ·ha' I make the decisions; I am a strict person

rye see: liquor
de·ga'ni·gǫ·ha·dé:nyǫhs alcoholic beverages (lit.: mind-altering substances)

S

sabotage see: ruin
ęhs·hé:tgęht you will damage, ruin, wreck s.t.
sack see: bag
gá:ya:' a bag; a mattress; etc.
sacred
o·ih·wá·ǫ:weh a sacred idea
[o+ stem: -(r)ih(wa)$_{N}$- word -ǫweh- real]
sacred see: forbidden
o·nǫ́'ne:' it is forbidden, sacred, holy
sad
de·sa'ni·gǫ́·hęh·dǫh you are sad
[de+P+ stem: -(')nigǫhęhdǫh- sad; consists of: -(')nigǫh(a)$_{N}$- mind -(a)hdǫ(:)$_{V}$- lose, disappear]
sad see: depressed, unhappy
dwak·ni·gǫ·hę́'ǫh I am in sorrow, in mourning; I am sad
de·sa·dǫt·gá:de' you are unhappy
sadness
ok·ni·gǫh·sá:dǫh sadness
[ǫ+ak+ stem: -(')nigǫhsadǫh- sadness; consists of: -(')nigǫh(a)$_{N}$- mind -(h)sadǫ$_{V}$- bury s.t.]
o'ni·gǫh·sa·dǫhk·gé·ha:' the sad kind
safe see: think, vault
sgę:nǫ́: **se·nóh·dǫn·yǫh** you are safe; you are feeling well; you are at peace with yourself
eh·wihs·da·ę·da̲hk·wá' **o·nǫ́h·sǫ:t** a bank vault; a safe
safeguard see: protect
ho·na·d'ę·ní·gǫ·ha:' they (m) are protecting, watching

Cayuga pronunciation guide: /a/ father /e/ weigh /ę/ men (nasalized) /i/ police /o/ hole /ǫ/ home (nasalized) /u/ blue. Underlined vowels are voiceless or whispered. /'/ high pitch. /t/ too /d/ do /k/ king /g/ good (never soft g) /j/ judge or adze /s/ soon /sh/ less heat (never the sh in shirt) /sr/ shrine /sy/ sure /hw/ which (the sound made when you blow out a candle) /h/ hi /ts/ cats hide /'/ (the sound before the first vowel in 'uh-uh') /n/ noon /r/ round /w/ way /y/ yes.

safety pin
de·wa·do·dá:s ga·jí·ho·ha:ʼ safety pins [consists of: dewadoda:s it drapes itself; gajihoha:ʼ straight pin, pin, brooch, safety pin]
safety pin see: pin
ga·jí·ho·ha:ʼ, o·jí·ho·ha:ʼ a straight pin; a pin; a brooch; a safety pin
sage see: wise
ho·diʼni·gǫ·ho·wá:nę'ʼs they (m) are wise; they have the capacity for thinking
Sahara see: desert
Gyo·neh·sa·da·i:hę·go·wáh·neh the Sahara Desert
sailor
ha·di·hǫ·waʼgę·hó:nǫʼ sailors; navy men; merchant marines
[A+ stem: -(h)ǫwaʼgehonǫʼ- sailor; consists of: -(h)ǫw(a)$_N$- boat]
salamander
dó:dihs a salamander
[stem: -dodihs$_N$- salamander]
salary
de·sá·dęts'ahs your salary; what you make
[de+...adę+ stem: -(a)tsʼahs- salary; consists of: -(a)tsʼ$_V$- use up; earn (money)]
sale
wat·gé·hǫʼ sales
[wa+ stem: -(a)tgehǫ$_V$- sell]
wag·yé·sahs·dǫh sales; bargains
[w+ag+ stem: -yesahsdǫh- sale; consists of: -yesahsd$_V$- make easy]
sales tax see: G (ha·di·ga:he·haʼ)
saline see: salty
o·ji·keʼdá:weht it is salty
saliva
otsg·raʼ saliva, spit, sputum
[o+ stem: -(ni)tsgr(a)$_N$- saliva]
salivate see: drool
sętsg·ro:t you are drooling
salon see: hair salon, lounge
gyǫt·geʼahs·rǫ́·nihs·geh a hair salon
ǫ·dǫ·wi·sę·dahk·wáʼgeh a lounge
saloon see: bar
ǫt·ne·gah·ní:nǫh(geh) a hotel; a pub; a bar; a saloon
salt
o·jí·keʼdaʼ salt
[o+ stem: -jikeʼd(a)$_N$- salt]
salt and pepper shakers
o·jik·eʼdáʼ de·yoh·sa·ít hníʼ wad·ráhk·waʼ salt and pepper shakers [consists of: ojikeʼdaʼ salt; deyohsait pepper; hniʼ and; wadrahkwaʼ container]
salty
o·ji·keʼdá:weht it is salty
[o+ stem: -jikeʼdawehd- salty; consists of: -jikeʼd(a)$_N$- salt -wehd$_V$-]
salty see: sour
o·jí·wa·gę: it is sour, salty, bitter
same
tsaʼdé:yoht they are (lit.: it is) the same
[tsaʼde+yo+ stem: -(a)hd$_V$- be like, resemble, be the same]
tsaʼde·yo·yę́hs·ra·ge: they are (lit. it is) two of the same kind of blanket
[tsaʼde+A/P+N+ stem: -yęhsr(a)$_N$- blanket -(a)ge:$_V$- two or more; two of the same kind]
tsaʼó:ya:t it has always been that way; nature
[tsaʼ+ stem: -oyad- nature; consists of: -y(a)$_N$- other, another -d$_V$- stand]
tsaʼdę:ya:węh they (lit.: it) will be the same
[tsaʼde+yaw+ stem: -ę(h,ʼ)$_V$- happen; be the same]
tsaʼgáʼdręh·da:t the same kind of car
[tsaʼ+A/P+N+stem: -(ʼ)drehd(a)$_N$- vehicle, car -d$_V$- stand; be the same]

same (continued)

tsa'gá·nǫ'a:t they deserve each other (lit.: it is the same kind of head)
[tsa'+A/P+N+ stem: -nǫ'(a:), nǫh(a)$_N$- head -d$_V$- stand; be the same]

tsa'détga·deh the same height
[tsa'de+t+ga+ stem: -de'$_V$- exist; be the same height]

tsa'de·yohs·hé:dęh it is the same number (of things)
[tsa'de+yo+ stem: -(a)hshed$_V$- count; be the same number of things]

tsa'de·yǫhs·yá:de' they come from (lit. it comes from) the same line, family
[tsa'de+P+N+ stem: -(h)siy(a)$_N$- line, string -de'$_V$- exist; be the same type of]

same see: similar, size

tsa'de·ga·e·y'a·dó'dę: they (f/m) are similar; they look the same

tsa'dé:wa's they are (lit. it is) the same size

sanction

ęhs·rih·wag·wę:ní:yohs you will sanction, charter, give authority to s.o.
[stem: -(r)ihwagwęniyohsd- sanction, charter, give authority; consists of: -(r)ih(wa)$_N$- word -gwęniyohsd$_V$- cause to be the main thing]

sanction see: agree

ęhs·rih·wa̱h·ní:ya:t you will affirm it, agree

sand

o'néh·sa' sand
[o+ stem: -(')nehs(a)$_N$- sand]

o'néh·sa·i:' it is sandy
[o+ stem: -(')nehs(a)$_N$- sand -i:'$_V$- stuck onto s.t.]

sand see: gravel

ni·gahsg·wa·ó:s'uh small gravel

sand pile

o'neh·san·hóhs·ro:t a sand pile
[o+ stem: -'nehs(a)$_N$- sand nhohsrod$_V$- pile up]

sand storm

o'neh·sa·dá:se: sand storm
[o+ stem: -(')nehsadase:- sand storm; consists of: -(')nehs(a)$_N$- sand -dase:$_V$- whirl]

sander

de·wat·nęh·sóg·wa̱h·ta' a sander
[de+wa+at+ stem: -nehsogwahta'- sander; consists of: -(')nehs(a)$_N$- sand -ogwahd$_V$- cause to scatter; spread out, distribute]

sandpiper

o'neh·sí:yo: a sandpiper
[o+ stem: -(')nęhsiyo- sandpiper; consists of: -(')nehs(a)$_N$- sand -iyo:$_V$- be nice, good]

Sandpiper clan see: C (O'neh·si:yo')

Sandy's Road see: E (De·yo·yęg·wa:kęh)

sap see: resin

ohs·da:'áh ot·séhs·da' pine pitch; pine resin

sapling

wa'ę:nó:dǫ' saplings; young trees
[w+ stem: -(a)'ęn(a)$_N$- stick, pole, rod -odǫ'$_V$- several standing objects]

o·hǫ́·dase:' sapling
[o+ stem: -(h)ǫdase:'- sapling; consists of: -(h)ǫd(a)$_N$- bush -(a)se:$_V$- new]

sash see: belt

at·na'ga·wíhd·ra' a belt

Satan see: Devil

ga·jí·ha·ya' the devil

satiated see: full

a·'óh·da' it (z) got full, finished eating

satisfaction

o'ni·gǫh·sí·yǫhs·de:' satisfaction
[o+ stem: -(')nigǫhsiyohsde:'- satisfaction; consists of: -(')nigǫh(a)$_N$- mind -iyohsd$_V$- make nice, good]

Cayuga pronunciation guide: /a/ father /e/ weigh /ę/ men (nasalized) /i/ police /o/ hole /ǫ/ home (nasalized) /u/ blue. Underlined vowels are voiceless or whispered. /'/ high pitch. /t/ too /d/ do /k/ king /g/ good (never soft g) /j/ judge or adze /s/ soon /sh/ less heat (never the sh in shirt) /sr/ shrine /sy/ sure /hw/ which (the sound made when you blow out a candle) /h/ hi /ts/ cats hide /'/ (the sound before the first vowel in 'uh-uh') /n/ noon /r/ round /w/ way /y/ yes.

satisfied
ęh·sa'ni·gǫ·hí:yoh you will be satisfied
[(d+) P+ stem: -(')nigǫhiyoh- become satisfied; consists of: -(')nigǫh(a)$_N$- mind -iyoh$_V$- become nice, good]
ę·di·sa'ni·gǫ·hí:yoh your mind will become satisfied
dwak·ni·gǫ·hí:yo: I am satisfied, peaceful
[d+ P+ stem: -(')nigǫhiyo:- be satisfied; consists of: -(')nigǫh(a)$_N$- mind -iyo:$_V$- be nice, good]
di·sa'ni·gǫ·hí:yo: you are satisfied
satisfied see: regret
e·sah·sę́hs gęh? Do you regret it? Did you regret it? Are you satisfied now?
saturated see: wet
o·nǫ́hg·wi·ja' it is soaking wet, saturated
Saturday see: A (Nak·do·ha·ehs)
saucer see: dish
ga·ję' a dish; a plate; a bowl
sausage
o·hé:ts·ha' raw sausage; bologna; wieners
[o+ stem: -(h)ets(ha)$_N$- sausage, wiener, bologna]
o·hé:tsa·i: (cooked) wieners, bologna
[o+ stem: -(h)ets(a)$_N$- sausage, wiener, bologna -i:'$_V$- stuck onto s.t.]
o·hets·ha·gáh·deh uncooked sausage
[o+ stem: -(h)ets(a)$_N$- sausage, wiener, bologna -(a)gahdeh$_V$- raw]
save see: accumulate, gather, rescue, store
ęh·sa·dad·ro·hé:gę' you will accumulate (things, ideas, etc.) for yourself
ęhs·ró·he:k you will gather
ęhs·hey'a·do·dá·i·si' you will help her escape; you will save her
sęh·sę:nǫ́:nih store it; put it away
savour see: like
a·gé:ga's I like the taste of it
savoury see: taste good
o·gá'ǫh it tastes good
saw
e·nehs·dá·i·ya'kta', e·nehs·dan·yá'kta' a hand saw
[e+ stem: -nehsdaiya'kta', nehsdanya'kta'- saw; consists of: -nehsd(a:)$_N$- floor, board -(i)ya'gd$_V$- cause to cut, break]
de·ya·ǫg·yá'kta', de·yǫ́g·ya'kta' buzz saw (lit.: it cuts logs)
[de+ya+ stem: -(r)ǫgya'kta'- saw; consists of: -(r)ǫd(a)$_N$- log -(i)ya'gd$_V$- cause to cut, break]
saw see: chain saw, cut
wat·ga·ha·dǫ́hs de·gá·yęg·ya's a chainsaw
ękre:' I will cut it
say
ǫ́:dǫh she is saying it (all the time, now)
[A+ stem: -(a)dǫh$_V$- say]
wá:dǫh it is said
gá:dǫh I am saying it all the time
wa·dǫ́h·nǫn·yǫ' what the song says; it says s.t.; a song that speaks
[A+ stem: -(a)dǫhnǫnyǫ'$_V$- say several things]
a'á:gę' she did say
[stem: -i, ę$_V$- say]
ęhs·ni' you two will say
ę·hę' he will say
a·hę́:ni' they (m) said
ed·wę' we all (incl.) said
ęh·si' you will say
ihs·nę: you two have said
í:sę: you have said it
á:gę: I have said it
say see: I, awę', speak, talk
a·gad·wę́nǫ·dahk I should use that language
ę·géh·ta·ę' I will talk

scale
ǫt·gǫʼtra·háhk·waʼ, e·gǫʼtra·háhk·waʼ a weigh scale
[e+ / ǫ+at+ stem: -gǫʼtrahahkwaʼ- scale; consists of: -gǫʼtr(a)$_{N}$- weight -(h)ahkwaʼ$_{V}$- s.t. that supports]
ga·gǫʼtra·héːhaʼ a balance; a weigh scale
[ga+ stem: -gǫʼtraheːhaʼ- scale, balance; consists of: -gǫʼtr(a)$_{N}$- weight -(hr)e, (hr)ę$_{V}$- put, place]
ǫt·gǫʼtra·ni·yǫ·dáhk·waʼ a weigh scale (with weights used to balance one side)
[ǫ+at+ stem: -gǫʼtraniyǫdahkwaʼ- scale; consists of: -gǫʼtr(a)$_{N}$- weight -niyǫdahkwaʼ$_{V}$- s.t. that hangs]
ohs·daːʼ, ohs·dá·iʼ a scale (of a fish)
[o+ stem: -(ih)sd(aː)$_{N}$- scale -iːʼ$_{V}$- be stuck onto s.t.]
ę·séhs·dęht you will take the scales off (the fish)
[stem: -(ih)sdęhd- scale fish; consists of: -(ih)sd(aː)$_{N}$- scale -(y)ęhd$_{V}$- hit, knock down, strike]
a·séhsdęht you did take the scales off (the fish)
scale see: climb
ęhs·ráːtęʼ you will climb
scalp see: mane
o·nǫ́·ha·heːʼ a mane; a scalp
scalpel see: blade
o·hę́nʼat·rǫːt a blade
scandal
o·ih·wat·gíːnyǫʼ scandalous news, rumours
[o+ stem: -(r)ihwatginyǫʼ- scandal, rumour; consists of: -(r)ih(wa)$_{N}$- word -tginyǫʼ$_{V}$- several dirty, ugly objects]
scanty see: lack
da·wá·dʼok·dahs it lacks; it is not enough

scare see: frighten, startle, threaten
ęh·sáhd·rǫhg·węʼ it will frighten you
ę·ke·yę·néʼwa̲h·dęʼ I will startle her
she·yad·rǫhg·wáːnih you are threatening, scaring s.o.
scare see: scared
scarecrow
wa·tęːdóːwih a scarecrow
[wa+at+ stem: -(h)ędowih- scarecrow; consists of: -(h)ęd(a)$_{N}$- field -owi, ǫny$_{V}$- drive]
scared
a·gáhd·rǫʼs I am scared, frightened
[P+ stem: -(a)hdrǫʼ$_{V}$- scared, frightened]
ǫ·gáhd·rǫʼk it frightened me; I got frightened
ę·wá·ga̲hd·rǫʼk I will be frightened
ęh·sáhd·rǫʼk you will be afraid of s.t.; it will frighten you
sa̲hd·rǫʼk be afraid
a·gáhd·rǫʼniːʼ I am scared all the time, a fraidy-cat
[P+ stem: -(a)hdrǫʼniː$_{V}$- be scared, frightened]
sahd·rǫ́ʼniː you are a 'fraidy cat'
ohd·rǫhk it is frightening, fierce, scary; danger
[o+ stem: -(a)hdrǫhg$_{V}$- be frightening]
a·ǫ·gǫ̱h·dǫ́ʼ ohd·rǫhk it is extremely dangerous
[aǫgǫhdǫʼ extremely P+ stem: -(a)hdrǫhg$_{V}$- be frightening]
scarf
ǫt·géh·da̲hs·taʼ a scarf; a bib
[ǫ+at+ stem: -gehdastaʼ- scarf; consists of: -geʼ(aː), geh(a)$_{N}$- hair -dahsd$_{V}$- cause to stand]
scarf see: tie
ga·géh·daʼ a tie; a scarf
scarlet see: red
otg·wę́hjʼi·aːʼ red

Cayuga pronunciation guide: /a/ father /e/ weigh /ę/ men (nasalized) /i/ police /o/ hole /ǫ/ home (nasalized) /u/ blue. Underlined vowels are voiceless or whispered. /ˊ/ high pitch. /t/ too /d/ do /k/ king /g/ good (never soft g) /j/ judge or adze /s/ soon /sh/ less heat (never the sh in shirt) /sr/ shrine /sy/ sure /hw/ which (the sound made when you blow out a candle) /h/ hi /ts/ cats hide /ʼ/ (the sound before the first vowel in 'uh-uh') /n/ noon /r/ round /w/ way /y/ yes.

scatter
ad·wa:dó:go' it scattered
[de+... stem: -ogw$_V$- be scattered]
de·ga·dog·wáh·ta' I scatter s.t.
[de+...ad+ stem: -ogwahd- scatter s.t., distribute s.t.; consists of: -ogw$_V$- scatter]
de·sa·dog·wáh·dǫh you have distributed it
de·wa·dog·wáh·dǫh it has been spread out, distributed, scattered
dę·sat·neh·só:gwaht you will distribute sand
[de+...N+ ad+ stem: -nehs(a) $_N$- sand -ogwahd$_V$- scatter s.t.]
de·sat·ne·gó:g·waht you spread water around
[de+...N+ ad+ stem: -(h)neg(a)$_N$- water, liquid -ogwahd$_V$- scatter s.t.]
scent see: odour, perfume
o·ded·rę·ná·i:' an odour
gad·rę:ní:yo's perfume
scheme see: plan, secret
ę·jad·ri̱h·wáhs'a:' you two will plan, make a plan
a·hę·nad·ríh·wa̱h·seht they (m) hid their idea (that is, they schemed)
school
ǫ·dad·ri̱·hǫn·ya·ní'ta' a school
[ǫ+adad+ stem: -(r)ihǫnyani'ta'- school; consists of: -(r)ihǫnyanih, rihǫnyę $_V$- read]
school bus
gak·sa'da·nę́hg·wih a school bus
[ga+ stem: -ksa'danęhgwih school bus; consists of: ksa'd(a)-$_N$ child; -nęhgwi$_V$- haul]
schooling see: education
ga·i:hǫn·yá:ni:' education

scissors
de·ga·hę·ná'tr'ase:' scissors
[de+ga+ stem: -(hr)ęna'tra'se:'- scissors; consists of: -(hr)ena'tr(a)$_N$- knife -(a)'se:' $_V$- cousin; be double]
scoff see: jeer
ęh·sad·wę·ná:yęht you will jeer, jest, throw words at s.o.
scold
she'dáhs·wa̱·hęhs you scold people all the time
[TR+ stem: -(ni)'d(a)$_N$- feces, privates -(a)hswahę(hdrǫ)$_V$- scold]
ęhs·he'da̱hs·wá·hęd·rǫ:' you will scold her or s.o.
a·ha·d'i·dahs·wa·hę́hd·rǫ:' they (m) scolded, reprimanded
a·gę·n'i·dahs·wa·hę́hd·rǫ:' I got scolded
ga·ke'dahs·wa·hę·hę́hdrǫh I am going along scolding people
gę·dahs·wa·hę́hd·rǫ:' a scolding
scoop see: dig, shovel
ę·yó'gwa:t it will dig
ga·gáh·wẹh·sa' a shovel
score see: bring
a·há:yǫ:t he scored; he brought it
scorch see: burn, overcooked
ęhs·rę́'da:' you will burn s.t.
o·wíh·jih it is overcooked
scour see: clean, grate
gek·so·há·i·hǫh I am washing dishes
ęh·sé:ge:t you will grate, scrape, file
scowl see: frown
dęh·sát·gręg·ręht you will sneer, frown
scrap see: hair
o·gé'a:' hair; a rag; it is ragged, tattered
scrape see: grate, scratch
ęh·sé:ge:t you will grate, scrape, file it
scratch
de·gah·jí:yohs, de·gah·ji·yó·ha' I am scratching
[de+... stem: -(a)hjiyo(:)$_V$- scratch]

scratch (continued)
dę·wa·gah·jí:yo:ʼ it will scratch me (for example, a twig or thorn)
de·wa·gah·jí:yoʼ I am digging in my nails; I am scratching
de·sah·jí:yo: scratch
de·sah·ji·yóhs·rǫ: really scratch
[de+... stem: -(a)hjiyohsrǫ:- really scratch; consists of: -(a)hjiyo(:)$_V$- scratch -hsrǫ:- really]
ęh·sá:tge:t you will scratch (yourself)
[at+ stem: -ged$_V$- grate, scrape, file; scratch oneself]
sat·gé:dǫh you are scratching yourself
sah·naʼt·sa·gé:dahs you are scratching your behind
[ad+(N+) stem: -(h)naʼts(a)$_N$- buttock -ged$_V$- grate, scrape, file; scratch s.t.]
dahs·gehs·wʼe·ná:ge:t scratch my back
[de+TR+N+ stem: -(h)swaʼn(a), (h)sweʼn(a)$_N$- upper back -ged$_V$- grate, scrape, file; scratch s.t. for s.o.]
scrawl see: write
ęk·yá:dǫ:ʼ I will write
scrawny see: thin
hohs·gyę́ʼwa·tę:, hohs·gyǫ́ʼwa·tę: he is skinny
scream
ǫ·dę·ná·i:kǫn·yǫh she is screaming
[adę+ stem: naikǫnyǫ$_V$- scream]
deh·sad·rihs·dá·ne·gahs you burst out screaming or crying all the time
[de+...ad+ stem: -(r)ihsdanega(ǫ,:)- scream; consists of: -(h)wihsd(a), (hr)ihsd(a)$_N$- metal, money -(wa)negaǫ, (wa)nega(:)$_V$- explode, split]
deh·sad·rihs·da·ne·gá·ǫhs you are bursting out screaming or crying right now
dęh·sad·rihs·da:né:ga:ʼ you will burst out screaming, crying; you will make a loud outburst
de·sad·rihs·da:né:ga:ʼ scream (lit.: split your voice)
scream see: yell
haʼdęh·sa·he:t you will scream, yell over there
screech see: scream
screech owl
gwá·oh a screech owl
[stem: -gwaoh$_N$- screech owl]
screwdriver
ga·jiʼdrǫ·wá·da·sehs a screwdriver
[ga+ stem: -jiʼdrǫwadasehs- screwdriver; consists of: -jiʼdrǫw(ę:)$_N$- seashell -dase$_V$- whirl]
scripture see: Bible
gah·ya·dǫhs·ra·do·gęh·diʼ, oh·ya·dǫhs·ra·do·gęh·diʼ the Bible
scrub see: clean
ę·sah·yǫ·há·i:ʼ you will wash fruit
scuff see: scratch
dę·gah·jí:yo:ʼ I will scratch
scum see: water
oh·né·gat·giʼ scum; dirty water
scurry see: run, sneak
dę·ga·ǫ·węh·da:t they (f/m) will run
sgę·nǫ:ʼǫ́h hod·rihs·dǫ·hǫ́:gyeʼ he is sneaking around slowly
scythe
de·yo·tę·naʼtrʼak·dǫ́: e·wę·nǫhg·ríʼyak·taʼ a scythe
[consists of: deyotęnaʼtraʼkdǫ: it has a crooked blade; ewęnǫhgriʼyaktaʼ it cuts weeds]
sea see: ocean
o·ji·keʼdág·riʼgeh oceans
sear see: burn, roast
ęhs·rę́ʼda:ʼ you will burn s.t.
wa·déʼsgǫ:t it is roasting, frying
search see: investigate
ę·gíh·sa:k I will seek, look for it
seagull
jǫh·wę́ʼs·da·gaʼ a seagull
[stem: -johwęʼsdagaʼ$_N$- seagull]

Cayuga pronunciation guide: /a/ father /e/ weigh /ę/ men (nasalized) /i/ police /o/ hole /ǫ/ home (nasalized) /u/ blue. Underlined vowels are voiceless or whispered. /ʹ/ high pitch. /t/ too /d/ do /k/ king /g/ good (never soft g) /j/ judge or adze /s/ soon /sh/ less heat (never the sh in shirt) /sr/ shrine /sy/ sure /hw/ which (the sound made when you blow out a candle) /h/ hi /ts/ cats hide /ʼ/ (the sound before the first vowel in 'uh-uh') /n/ noon /r/ round /w/ way /y/ yes.

seal

gan·yaʼkwa·i: a seal (the word refers to its lack of a neck)
[ga+ stem: -nyaʼkwai:- seal; consists of: -(h)nya(ʼsa)- neck -k(wa)$_N$- lump -i:ʼ$_V$- stuck onto s.t.]

seam

gʼa·ní:kǫʼ seam
[ga+ stem: -(ʼ)nikǫʼ- seam; consists of: -(ʼ)nikǫ(:)$_V$- sew]

seam ripper

gʼa·ní·kǫg·wahs a stitch ripper; a seam ripper
[ga+ stem: -(ʼ)nikǫgwahs- seam ripper; consists of: -(ʼ)nikǫgw$_V$- unsew]

seamstress

eʼní:kǫhs a seamstress
[e+ stem: -(ʼ)nikǫhs- seamstress; consists of: -(ʼ)nikǫ(:)$_V$- sew]

sea shell

jiʼdrǫ́:wę: a sea shell
[stem: -jiʼdrǫwę:$_N$- sea shell]

sea shell see: bass

oʼnó:ksaʼ bass (fish); oysters; shellfish; sea shells

season see: A (shęh niyotgęihsdǫhǫ:gyeʼ deyowa:węnyeʼ)

seasoning see: herb, pepper, salt, vanilla

de·ga·yehs·dáh·nǫʼ a mixture; it is mixed together to make it good (for example, herbs, spices, etc.)

de·yóh·sa·it pepper

o·jí·keʼdaʼ salt

de·yehs·ta·sǫ́:ʼǫh vanilla, etc.

seat

ga·nak·di·yóhs·geh a good seat; one that is good for s.o. to be there
[ga+ stem: -nakdiyǫhsgeh- consists of: -nakd(a)$_N$- bed, seat -iyohs$_V$- make nice, good -ʼgeh on]

seat see: buttock, chair, place

oh·náʼtsaʼ buttock; ass; the behind; the posterior

ak·yę́·da̲hk·waʼ, ag·yę́·da̲hk·waʼ a chair

ot·nak·da·gǫ́:nyǫhs an important, prestigious seat, place

secluded see: secret, hide.

od·rih·wa·séh·dǫh it is secret

ę·yǫ́h·seht there will be a burial (lit.: it will be hidden)

second

dek·ní wa·dǫ́ʼtaʼ second

second see: B (dek·ni wa·dǫʼtaʼ)

second-rate see: unimportant

o·gaʼos·hǫ́:ʼǫh s.t. unimportant, second-rate

secret

a·hę·nad·ríh·wa̲h·seht they (m) hid their idea (that is, they schemed)
[(ad)+ stem: -(r)ihwahsehd- have a secret; consists of: -(r)ih(wa)$_N$- word -(a)hsehd$_V$- hide s.t.]

ęhs·níh·wa̲h·seht, ę·jad·ri̲h·wáh·seht you two will have a secret

od·rih·wa·séh·dǫh it is secret

ad·rih·wa̲h·séh·dǫ:ʼ a secret

secretary

eh·yá·dǫ̲·haʼ she is a secretary, stenographer, court recorder, transcriber
[e+ stem: -(h)yadǫhaʼ- secretary; consists of: -(h)yadǫ(:)$_V$- write]

Secretary of State see: G (Sha·goh·ya·dǫh·seh·go:wah)

section see: area, divide

og·ye·na·wáh·dǫh an area

dęh·se·kah·sǫ́:goʼ you will divide it into parts

secure see: lock, think

ę·ge·nhó:dǫ:ʼ I will lock it

sgę·nǫ́: se·nóh·dǫn·yǫh you are safe; you are feeling well; you are at peace with yourself

sediment see: sand

oʼnéh·saʼ sand

seductive see: enticing
ohs·gá:na'·t it is enticing, alluring, attractive, tempting
see
gé:gęh I see (regularly, but perhaps at irregular intervals)
[stem: -gę$_V$- see]
gé:gęhs I see (for example, I see apple trees, orange trees... and sometimes, I also see cherry trees)
a·há:gę' he saw
a·gé:gę: I have seen it
á:gę·hę:k it should be
ę·kék·dǫh·na' I am going to see her
[TR+ stem: -kdǫhn- go and see s.o.; consists of: -kdǫ(:)$_V$- taste, examine, look closely at s.t.]
see see: visit
ę·gag·yǫ·sé·ha' I am going to go and visit
seed
ga·na·há·ǫg·wę' seeds; seed corn
[ga+ stem: -nahaǫgwę('tra)$_N$- seed corn consists of: -nęh(ę)$_N$- corn -ogw$_V$- scatter]
seemly see: right
tga:yé·i: it is right, correct
seep see: leak
o·kahs it leaks
seer see: fortune teller
dę·ha·di·ya'do·wéh·ta' they (m) are fortune tellers, thinkers; they (m) tell fortunes
see-through see: sheer, transparent
o·jí'a·de' sheer, lacy fabrics; lace
he·yó:gę't it is transparent
seize see: catch, grab
ah·sa·go·di:yé·na:' they arrested, caught her
da·ję́:na: grab it
seizure see: convulse
go·yé·nah·sǫhs a convulsion

select see: appoint, choose
a·hǫ·wa·i·hǫ́:dę' they delegated him a duty
ęhs·rá:go' you will choose, take out
self-centred
sa·dág·y'a·da's you are opinionated
[A+adag+ stem: -ya'da:s- self-centred, bold, opinionated; consists of: -(a)'da(ni)$_V$- rely on]
ha·dágy'a·da:s he has a high opinion of himself, he is self-centred, he is bold; he is conceited, boastful, bragging
wa·dágy'a·da:s it is bold; a snob; she (lit.: it) has a high opinion of herself; she (lit.: it) is boastful
self-centred see: self-important
self esteem see: pride, proud, self-important
ga·ná·i: pride; boastfulness
i·hé:hah he thinks highly of himself; his thoughts
self-important
ǫ·dat·go·wá:nęh she is a legend in her own mind; she is self-important
[A+adat+ stem: -gowanęh- self-important, rash, unwise; consists of: -gowanęh$_V$- be big]
wa·dat·go·wá:nęh it is rash, unwise, self-important, egotistical
selfish see: self-centered
ha·dágy'a·da:s he has a high opinion of himself; he is self-centred, he is bold; he is conceited, boastful, bragging
self-propelled
wa·dá·d'ed·re's it drives itself; it is self-propelled
[wa+adade+ stem: -(i)'dre's- self-propelled; consists of: -(i)'dre(:)$_V$- drag, drive]
self respect see: self esteem
self satisfied see: proud
ha·ná·i: he is proud, boastful, bragging, conceited

sell
ho·nát·ge̱·hǫʼ they (m) are selling s.t.
[(ade+N+) stem: -(a)tgehǫ$_V$- sell]
to·nát·ge̱·hǫʼ where they (m) are selling
ęh·sát·ge·hǫʼ you will sell

Senate see: G (Gwa:go:wah Hǫ·wa·di̱hn·yaʼso·da·hǫh)

send
wa·dę́n·ye̱h·dǫh it is sent
[adę+ stem: -nyehd$_V$- send]
he·wa·ga·dę́n·ye̱h·dǫh I sent it
[he+...adę+N+ stem: -nyehd$_V$- send s.t.]
a·hǫ·wa·dę́:nyeht he was sentenced (lit.: they sent him)
[TR+adę+ stem: -nyehd$_V$- send s.o., sentence s.o.]
hęh·sad·ri̱h·wá:nyeht you will send a message
[heʼ+...ad+N+ stem: -(r)ih(wa)$_N$- word -nyehd$_V$- send s.t.]

Seneca people see: C (O·nǫ·do·waʼga:ʼ)

senior citizen see: elder
ga·e·gę̱h·jih·sǫ́:ʼǫh they (f/m) are elderly

sense see: perceive
a·wę·ni̱h·ná:do:k it sensed s.t.

senseless see: stupid
de·saʼni·gǫ́·ha:t you are stupid, foolish

sensitive
ni·wag·ri̱·hú:ʼuh I am sensitive
[ni+P+ stem: -(r)ihu:ʼuh- sensitive, unimportant; consists of: -(r)ih(wa)$_N$- word -u:ʼuh$_V$- small]
ni·ya·go·i·hú:ʼuh she has a small mind

sensuality see: enjoyable
a·ǫʼwé:sęh(t), a·ǫʼwé:sah(t) it is enjoyable; a good feeling

sentence
jo·íh·wa:t one written sentence
[s/j+o+ stem: -(r)ihwad- sentence; consists of: -(r)ih(wa)$_N$- word -d$_V$- stand, be one]

sentence see: send
a·hǫ·wa·dę́:nyeht he was sentenced (lit.: they sent him)

separate see: divide, other, scatter
dęh·se·kah·sǫ́:goʼ you will divide it into parts
ó:yaʼ the other; another
de·wa·dog·wáh·dǫh it has been spread out, distributed, scattered

September see: A (Saʼge̱h·neh)

serenity see: peace
sgę:nǫ́ʼ ge·nǫ́h·dǫn·yǫh I am at peace

series see: one after another
jo·yę́hs·rat·sǫʼ one blanket at a time

serpent see: snake
os·há·ihs·daʼ a snake

serve
she·háh·seh you serve her/them all the time
[TR+(N+) stem: -(h)ahs$_V$- serve]
ęhs·hé:hahs you will serve s.o.
ęh·sné:kahs you will give it s.t. to drink
[TR+(N+) stem: -(h)neg(a)$_N$- water, liquid -(h)ahs$_V$- serve]

serve a meal
a·ga·ǫ:dék·wa̱·hęʼ they (f/m) put on a meal
[TR+ade+ stem: -kwahę- serve a meal; consists of: -k(wa)$_N$- food -(hr)e, (hr)ę$_V$- put, place]
ę·yag·wa·dék·wa̱·hęʼ we all (excl.) will put on a meal, supper
ęh·sa·da·dék·wa·nǫ:t you will serve yourself a meal
[stem: -kwanǫd- serve a meal; consists of: -k(wa)$_N$- food -nǫd$_V$- feed]

service see: G (hǫ·wa·di·ye·na·waʼseh)

serviette
ǫ·dek·wa·gé·wa̱h·taʼ serviettes, napkins
[ǫ+ade+ stem: -kwagewahtaʼ- serviette; consists of: -k(wa)$_N$- food -(r)agewahd$_V$- wipe up]

set
haʼgáhg·węʼ sunset; the sun went down
[heʼ+ga+ stem: -(h)gwę$_V$- set]
a·wah·yǫ́:dęʼ the fruit is coming on, setting
[stem: -(a)hy(a)$_N$- fruit, berry -ǫdę(:)$_V$- put in]

set see: put, put down, sit up on
kré:haʼ I am setting it on s.t.
ęd·wá:yę:ʼ we all (incl.) will set forth; we all will set down

set free see: release, rescue
a·kí·yaht·gaʼ we let them go, released them
ęt·se·yʼa·do·dá·ih·siʼ you will rescue s.o.

settle
hat·ga:yę́:daʼ it is settled
[heʼ+d+... stem: -(y)ędaʼ- become, acquire, finish; settle (a matter); consists of: -(y)ę$_V$- lie on the ground]
haʼhoʼni·gó·haʼehs his mind settled on
[heʼ+P+ stem: -(ʼ)nigǫhaʼehsd- decide; consists of: -(ʼ)nigǫh(a)$_N$- mind -(ʼ)ehsd$_V$- be hit]

settle see: decide, land, reconcile
a·to·ih·wá·ę:daʼs he came to a decision, a conclusion
dę·gęʼdrǫ́:daʼ it will land
ę·ji·jad·rih·wa̱hs·rǫ́:niʼ you two will reconcile

seven see: B (ja:dahk)

seventeen see: B (ja:dahk sgaeʼ)

seventy see: B (ja:dahk ni·wahs·hę:)

several see: amount
shę́ ní:yǫ: the amount of s.t.

several
[-dǫʼ the verb 'stand' with distributive; denotes 'a group of similar standing objects']
[-odǫʼ the verb 'stand' with distributive; denotes 'a group of objects or actions']

several (continued)
[-odǫnyǫʼ the verb 'stand' with distributives; denote many objects or actions]
[-ǫʼ distributive suffix; denotes 'several objects or actions']
[-ǫdǫʼ the verb 'attached' with distributive; denotes 'several attached objects']
[-ǫdǫnyǫʼ the verb 'attached' with distributives; denote 'several (attached) objects']
[-ǫnyahnǫʼ the verb 'make' plus dislocative plus plural; denotes 'growing' or 'several objects']
[-ǫnyǫʼ distributive suffixes; denote 'several objects or actions']
[-(h)sǫʼ pluralizer; denotes several objects]
[-(h)sǫ:ʼah, (h)sǫ:ʼǫh pluralizer; denotes several objects]
[-ʼs pluralizer suffix; denotes 'several objects']
[-adenyǫʼ the verb 'exist' with distributive; denotes 'several existing objects']
[-agehagyeʼ the verb 'be more than one' in the progressive; denotes 'several objects at a time']

severe see: demanding
tgę·nǫ́h·dǫ·haʼ I make the decisions; I am a strict person

sew
á:kni·kǫ:ʼ I should, might sew
[stem: -(ʼ)nikǫ(:)$_V$- sew]
ę·gáʼni·kǫhk it will be sewn

sewing box
eʼni·kǫhk·wáʼ ga̱·hǫ́hs·raʼ a sewing box
[consists of: eʼnikǫhkwaʼ sewing item; ga̱hǫhsraʼ a box]

Cayuga pronunciation guide: /a/ father /e/ weigh /ę/ men (nasalized) /i/ police /o/ hole /ǫ/ home (nasalized) /u/ blue. Underlined vowels are voiceless or whispered. /´/ high pitch. /t/ too /d/ do /k/ king /g/ good (never soft g) /j/ judge or adze /s/ soon /sh/ less heat (never the sh in shirt) /sr/ shrine /sy/ sure /hw/ which (the sound made when you blow out a candle) /h/ hi /ts/ cats hide /ʼ/ (the sound before the first vowel in 'uh-uh') /n/ noon /r/ round /w/ way /y/ yes.

sewing item
e'níh.kǫhk.wa' a sewing item
[e+ stem: -(')nikǫhkwa'- sewing item; consists of: -(')nikǫ(:)$_V$- sew]
ę'ni.kǫhk.wa'shǫ́:'ǫh sewing room items

sewing machine
g'a.ní.kǫ.ha' a sewing machine
[ga+ stem: -(')nikǫha'- sewing machine; consists of: -(')nikǫ(:)$_V$- sew]

sewing room
ę'ni.kǫhk.wá'geh a sewing room
[ę+ stem: -(')nikǫhkwa'geh- sewing room; consists of: -(')nikǫ(:)$_V$- sew -'geh on]

sex (have sex) see: mate
sa.dá'i:s you have intercourse

sexuality
gę.déhs.ra' sexuality
[ga+ stem: -(i)dehsr(a)$_N$- sexuality]

shabby see: ragged
ge.gé'a:' I am raggedy

shadow
o.dah.sǫ́.da:' a shadow
[o+ad+ stem: -(a)hsǫda:'- shadow; consists of: -(a)hsǫd(a:)$_N$- night, blackness]

shaft see: bar, stick
gahn.yǫ́'sra' a bar (for example, a stick-like object)
gan.hya' a stick

shake
sa.ya'dǫ.dá'ta' you are nervous, shaking, shivering
[P+ stem: -ya'dǫda'd- be nervous, shake, shiver; consists of: -ya'd(a)$_N$- body -ǫda'd$_V$- shake, shiver]
ę.sa.y'a.dǫ́:da't you will shiver, shake
ag.ya'dǫ.dá'dǫh I shiver
de.ya:wę́:dǫh it shakes
[de+P+(N+) stem: -ędǫh$_V$- shake s.t.]
dę.ya:wę́:dǫh it will sway
de.sa.y'a.dę́:dǫh you will shake your body
[de+P+(N+) stem: -ya'd(a)$_N$- body -ędǫh$_V$- shake s.t.]
dęh.sat.na't.sę́:dǫ' you will shake your behind
[de+...at+ stem: -(h)na'tsędǫ- shake one's behind; consists of: -(h)na'ts(a)$_N$- buttock -ędǫh$_V$- shake s.t.]

shake see: quiver, winnow
ę.sa.y'a.dahd.rǫ́:gǫ' you will quiver, shudder
ęh.sá:wa:k you will winnow, shake out, sift s.t.

shake one's head see: nod one's head
de.sat.nǫ'á.ę.dǫh nod, shake your head

shallow
ni.yoh.no.dá:k'ah it is shallow
[ni+yo+ stem: -(h)noda:k'ah- shallow; consists of: -(h)nod(a)$_N$- water -a:k'ah$_V$- short]
dę'oh.nó:de:s it is not deep
[de'+ not o+ stem: -(h)nodes- deep; shallow; consists of: -(h)nod(a)$_N$- water -es$_V$- long]

shame
o.dé.ha't a shame; an embarrassment
[o+ade+ stem: -(h)a'd- shame, embarassment; consists of: -(h)ę(h,')$_V$- feel bad]

shame see: feel bad
a.há.dę.hęh he felt shame

shampoo
ǫt.nǫ'a.o:há.i'ta' shampoo
[ǫ+at+ stem: -nǫ'aohai'ta'- shampoo; consists of: -nǫ'(a:), nǫh(a)$_N$- head -ohai'd$_V$- cause to clean, wash]
o.wi:ya:'áh ot.nǫ'a.o:há:'ta' baby's shampoo
[consists of: owi:ya:'ah baby; ǫtnǫ'ao:hai'ta' shampoo]

shank see: leg
oh.sí:na' an (unattached) leg

share
de·gé·kah·sǫhs I divide it
[de+...(N+) stem: -kahs(i)$_{V}$- share, divide]
dęh·sé·kah·si' you will share, divide
de·wa·ge·káhs·hǫ: I have taken one object apart

share see: participate
dę·ya·go'nya:gwę́·hęg·ye' she will have a hand in it

sharp
oh·yu'tí:yeht it is sharp
[o+ stem: -(h)yo'tiyehd, (h)yu'tiyehd- be sharpened; consists of: -(h)y(a)$_{N}$- blade -o'tiy$_{V}$- be sharp]

sharpen
gah·yo'tí:yǫhs it sharpens
[stem: -(h)yo'tiy- sharpen; consists of: -(h)y(a)$_{N}$- blade -o'tiy$_{V}$- sharp]

sharpener see: pencil sharpener
eh·ya·dǫhk·wá' gah·yo'tí:yǫhs pencil sharpener

shave
hat·gǫhs·tǫ'ę́h·ta' he is shaving
[at+ stem: -gǫhstǫ'ęhd- shave; consists of: -gǫhstǫ'(a)$_{N}$- whiskers -(y)ęhd$_{V}$- hit, knock down, strike]
a·hat·gǫhs·tǫ́'ęht he shaved
sat·gǫ́hs·tǫ'ęht shave
ęhs·ré·nah·nǫ:' you will shave (with a draw knife)
[stem: -(hr)enahnǫ(:)- shave; consists of: -(hr)enahnǫ(:)$_{V}$- go and make several cuts]

shawl see: kerchief
ǫt·nǫ'á·o:wek·ta' a kerchief

shear see: shave
ęhs·ré·nah·nǫ:' you will shave (with a draw knife)

shed see: goat shed, shed fur, shed skin, shed tears
ga·ya'dag·ráhs ga·dí'drǫ' a goat shed

shed fur
wa·tęh·dá·ę·hę' it is shedding fur
[wa+at+ stem: -(h)ęhdaę:- shed fur; consists of: -(h)ęhd(a:)$_{N}$- fur -ę:$_{V}$- lay s.t. down]
wa·tęh·dá·ę·ta' it is shedding fur
[at+ stem: -(h)ęhdaęhd- shed fur; consists of: -(h)ęhd(a:)$_{N}$- fur -ęd$_{V}$- cause to lie down]
a·wa·tęh·dá·ę't they shed their fur

shed skin
a·wag·y'a·dá·wih·si' it (a snake) shed its skin
[ag+ stem: -ya'dawihs(i)- shed skin; consists of: -ya'd(a)$_{N}$- body -(r)i, (w)i$_{V}$- ripe -hsi- undo]

shed tears
ęh·sa·gahd·rá·hi' you will shed tears
[P+ stem: -gahdrahi- shed tears, cry; consists of: -gahdr(a)$_{N}$- tear -(hr)i'$_{V}$- break up]
ę·sa·gahd·rę́:dǫ:' you will shed tears
[P+ stem: -gahdrędǫ'- shed tears, cry; consists of: -gahdr(a)$_{N}$- tear -(r)ęd$_{V}$- hover]

shed tears see: drip sweat
ęh·sa·gahd·ró:dę' you will drip tears, shed tears

sheep
de·yo·n'a·gá·ǫt sheep; lamb; elk
[de+P+ stem: -na'gaǫd- sheep, lamb; consists of: -na'g(a)$_{N}$- horn, antler -ǫd$_{V}$- attached]
de·yo·di·ná'ga·ǫt a horned animal
de·yo·di·na'gá·ǫ:dǫ' a herd of sheep; a horned animal; the Billy Goat Dance

sheep see: ram
ga·ji:náh de·yo·na·gá·ǫt a ram

sheep fold
de·yo·di·na'ga·ǫ·dǫ́' ga·dí'drǫ' a sheep fold
[consists of: deyodina'gaǫ:dǫ' sheep, etc.; gadi'drǫ' they (z) live]

Cayuga pronunciation guide: /a/ father /e/ weigh /ę/ men (nasalized) /i/ police /o/ hole /ǫ/ home (nasalized) /u/ blue. Underlined vowels are voiceless or whispered. /'/ high pitch. /t/ too /d/ do /k/ king /g/ good (never soft g) /j/ judge or adze /s/ soon /sh/ less heat (never the sh in shirt) /sr/ shrine /sy/ sure /hw/ which (the sound made when you blow out a candle) /h/ hi /ts/ cats hide /'/ (the sound before the first vowel in 'uh-uh') /n/ noon /r/ round /w/ way /y/ yes.

sheer
o·jí'a·de' sheer, lacy fabrics; lace
[o+ stem: -ji'(a:)$_N$- curtain, lace -de'$_V$- exist]

sheet
ǫ·nits·gá:kwa' sheets
[ǫ+ stem: -(ę)nitsgahkwa'- sheet; consists of: -(n)itsg(wa)$_N$- lower body]
o·wi:ya:'áh ǫ·nits·gá:kwa' a baby's crib sheet
[consists of: owi:ya:'ah baby; ǫnitsga:kwa' sheets]

sheets see: bedding
gęts·ga'shǫ́:'ǫh bedding

shelf
wę·níhs·rǫ' shelves; shelving
[w+ stem: -ęnihsr(a)$_N$- shelf]

shell
deh·sék·da'e:k shell (them); hit the shell
[de+... stem: -kda'e- peck s.t.; shell s.t.; consists of: -kd(a)$_N$- nutshell -(')e$_V$- hit]
ęh·sék·dot·sih you will shell (eggs, coconuts, etc.)
[stem: -kdotsi- shell s.t.; consists of: -kd(a)$_N$- nutshell -ots(i)$_V$- remove an outer covering]

shellfish see: bass
o'nó:ksa' bass (fish); oysters; shellfish; sea shells

shelter see: preserve s.t., protect
dęh·sę́'nya·dǫ:' you will protect, embrace

sherrif see: police
sha·go·di·yé:nahs policemen

shield see: protect
dęh·sę́'nya·dǫ:' you will protect, embrace

shimmer
ad·wa·tá·ę·dǫn·yǫh it shimmered
[de+...at+ stem: -(h)aędǫnyǫh- shimmer; consists of: -ha$_N$- line, horizon -ędǫnyǫ'$_V$- lay down several things]
de·wa·tá·ę·dǫn·yǫh it is twinkling; it is shimmering
dǫ·da·wa·ta·ę·dǫ́n·yǫh·ne' it is shimmering and coming towards you
[de+...at+ stem: -(h)aędǫnyǫh- shimmer; consists of: -ha$_N$- line, horizon -ędǫnyǫhne'$_V$- go and lay down several things]

shin
sen·yę́·d'a·geh on your shin
[stem: -nyęd(a)$_N$- shin, leg]
gen·yę́·d'a·geh on my shin, leg

shine
dę·gehs·dá:te't I am going to shine it
[de+... stem: -(h)sda:te'd- shine s.t.; consists of: -(h)sd(a:)$_N$- drop (of water) -te'd$_V$- pound]
dę·gahs·da·té'dǫh it is shined, waxed, polished

shiny see: smooth
dę·yohs·dá:teh it is shiny, smooth (like silver)

ship see: boat, haul, ocean liner
ga·hǫ́:wa' a boat
ęk·nę́hg·wi' I will carry, move, tote it
ga·hǫ·wa'gó:wah an ocean liner

shipment see: cargo
o·héh·na', ga·héh·na' cargo; a bundle; a load

shirt see: blouse, dress
a·déhs·wa' a blouse; a middy
ag·ya'da·wí'tra' a coat; a dress

shit see: feces
o'da' feces; shit; excrement; manure

shit on s.o.
ta·ha·gę·ni'da·hęh he won't shit on me
[ę+ stem: -ni'dahęh- shit on s.o.; consists of: -(ni)'d(a)$_N$- feces -(hr)e, (hr)ę$_V$- put, place]

shit-disturber

de·ye'da·wę́:nye' she is a shit-disturber [de+A+ stem: -(i)'dawęnye'- shit-disturber; consists of: -(ni)'d(a)$_N$- feces -(a)węnye(:)$_V$- stir, mix]

de·hę'da·wę́:nye' he is a shit-disturber

shiver

sa·ya'dod·rǫhg·wá·ǫ·hǫ·ha' you are twitching (right now) [(de+)... stem: -ya'd(a)$_N$- body -odrǫhgwa(ǫhǫ)$_V$- shiver, twitch]

de·sa·ya'dod·rǫhg·wá·ǫ·hǫ' you twitch all the time; you are a twitcher

a·ho·ya'da·did·rǫ́g·wa·hǫ:' it made him twitch

sa·ya'dod·rǫhg·wá·ǫ·nihs·gǫ: you are always shivering [(de+)... stem: -ya'd(a)$_N$- body -odrǫhgwaǫni$_V$- shiver, twitch -hsgǫ: easily]

shiver see: quiver, shake

ę·sa·y'a·dahd·rǫ́:gǫ' you will quiver, shudder

sa·ya'dǫ·dá'ta' you are nervous, shaking, shivering

shoe

ah·dáhg·wa' shoes [stem: -(a)hdahg(wa)$_N$- shoe]

ah·dahg·w'á·ǫ:weh moccasins; shoes (the ceremonial type, put on a corpse at a funeral) [stem: -(a)hdahgwa'ǫweh- moccasin; consists of: -(a)hdahg(wa)$_N$- shoe -ǫweh- real, Aboriginal]

de·ga:dé:s ah·dáhg·wa' high-heel shoes [consists of: dega:de:s two high things; ahdahgwa' shoes]

de·yohs·há·og·we:s high-top shoes [de+yo+ stem: -(a)hsaogwe's- high-top shoe; consists of: -(ę)hs(a)$_N$- foot -ogwe$_V$- go and scatter]

shoe (have shoes on, put on one's shoes, remove one's shoes)

de·sęh·só:tsih take your shoes off [de+... stem: -ęhsotsi- take off one's shoes; consists of: -(ę)hs(a)$_N$- foot -ots(i)$_V$- remove an outer covering]

de·sęh·so·wé:ksih take your shoes off [de+... stem: -ęhsoweksi- take off one's shoes; consists of: -(ę)hs(a)$_N$- foot -(hr)oweksi$_V$- uncover]

a·tę·nah·só:we:k they put shoes on a horse [de+... stem: -ęhsoweg- put on shoes; consists of: -(a)hsi('da), (ę)hs(a)$_N$- foot -(hr)oweg$_V$- cover]

de·sęh·só:we:k put your shoes on

de·ya·go·nę·so·wé:ksǫ' they (f/m) have their shoes on [de+P+ stem: -ęhsoweksǫ- have on one's shoes; consists of: -(a)hsi('da), (ę)hs(a)$_N$- foot -(hr)oweksǫ'$_V$- cover several things]

dẹ·ho·nęh·só·wek·sǫ' they (m) have their shoes on

dẹ·ho:wę́:sǫ: he has the shoes on [de+P+ stem: -(a)hsi('da), (ę)hs(a)$_N$- foot -(w)ęsǫ:$_V$- be shod]

shoot

ha·dí:y'a:s they (m) are shooting [stem: -(i)ya'g, i:'a:k$_V$- shoot]

a·ha·da·dí:ya'k he shot himself

ęhsí:'a'k you will shoot

a·ha·da·di:y'ák ha'hǫ́n·yọh·dahk he shot himself [consists of: ahadadi:y'a:k he shot himself; ha'hǫnyọhdahk he shot himeself there]

ha·dí·y'ak·ta' ammunition (lit. they (m) shoot it) [stem: -(i)ya'kd$_V$- cause to shoot s.t.]

hah·sí:sahs he shoots all the time [stem: -(h)sis$_V$- shoot]

a·hǫ́·wạh·si:s he was shot by s.o.

shoot (continued)
a·hóh·si:s he was shot
hoh·sí:sęh he has been shot
hǫ·wah·sí:sęh he got shot by s.o.
shoot see: branch
og·wí:ya' a limb; a twig; a branch
shooting star
o·jih·sǫ·dóh·go:t a shooting star
[o+ stem: -jihsǫdǫgohd- shooting star; consists of: -jihsǫd(a)$_N$- star -ohgod-]
o·jih·sǫ·doh·go·dá:gye' a shooting star
shop see: buy, store
ęh·sní:nǫ' you will buy, purchase
ǫ·dęh·ní:nǫh a store; a storekeeper
short
tę́' d'e·yǫ:s it is not long
[(tę') not de'+y+ stem: -ǫ:s- be long]
ni·yo:há:kah it is short in height (vertically)
[ni+yo+ stem: -(h)a:k'ah- short in height; consists of: -ha$_N$- line, horizon -a:k'ah$_V$- short]
nik·nę:yá:k'ah I am short
[ni+A+ stem: -(h)nęya:k'ah$_V$- short of stature]
de·seh·si·ná:k'ah you have short legs
[ni/de+A/P+N+ stem: -(h)sin(a)$_N$- leg -a:k'ah$_V$- short]
ni·ya·go·ge'á:k'ah she has short hair
[ni/de+P+N+ stem: -ge'(a)$_N$- hair -a:k'ah$_V$- have s.t. short]
tsǫ́: ni·wa·tǫ·ná'de:s they are (lit. it is) just short spuds; they are short people
[tsǫ: just ni+A+(at+) N+ stem: -(h)ǫna'd(a)$_N$- potato -es$_V$- long]
short of breath
ha·dǫ́hs·w'e·ta' he is short of breath
[A+ad+ stem: -ǫhswe'd(ę,ani)$_V$- be hungry, be short of breath]
a·ha·dǫhs·wé'dę' he will be short of breath
shorts
na'de·ga̱h·si·nag·wa:s'áh
at·ná'tsot·ra' shorts
[consists of: na'dega̱hsinagwa:s'ah shorts; atna'tsotra' pants]
na'de·ga̱h·si·nag·wá:s'ah shorts
[na'+de+ga+ stem: -(h)sinagwa:s'ah- shorts; consists of: -(h)sin(a)$_N$- leg -g(wa)- lump -a:s'ah$_V$- several small objects]
short-tempered see: grumpy
de·di·s'a·ni·gǫ·hí:yo: you are grumpy, grouchy, not happy
shot see: ash
o'gę́·hę' ashes; a bullet; dust
shot see: shoot
a·hóh·si:s he was shot
shot (be a good shot)
ni·se'drí:yo: how good a shot you are
[(ni+) A+ stem: -(')driyo- be a good shot; consists of: -(')dr(a)$_N$- case, quiver -iyo:$_V$- be nice, good]
ha'drí:yo: he's a good, accurate shot
shoulder
oh·nę́h·sa' a shoulder
[o+ stem: -(h)nęs(a)$_N$- shoulder]
snęh·sá'geh on your shoulders
swa̱h·nę́h·s'a·geh on your (p) shoulders
shout see: scream, yell
dęh·sad·ri̱hs·da·né:ga:' you will burst out screaming, crying; you will make a loud outburst
ha·dę́h·sa̱·he:t you will scream, yell over there
shovel
ga·gáh·wę̱h·sa' a shovel
[ga+ stem: -gahwehs(a)$_N$- shovel]
e·hehg·ya'k·tá' ga·gá·wę̱h·sa' a shovel
[consists of: ehehgya'kta' spade; gagawę̱hsa' paddle]

shovel (continued)
o'gę·hǫh·dáhk·wah·ta' an ashes shovel [o+ stem: -(')gęhǫdahkwahta'- ashes shovel; consists of: -(a)'gęh(ęda)$_{N}$- ash, dust -(h)gwahd$_{V}$- cause to lift, pick up]
shovel see: snow shovel, spade
de·yǫ·d'ag·roh·da:stá' ga·gáh·węh·sa' a snow shovel
e·héhg·ya'k·ta' a spade
show
gǫ·yǫh·wa·dá:nih I am showing you s.t. [TR+ stem: -ǫhwad(ę,ani)$_{V}$- show]
a·gǫh·wa·dá:nih it has shown me s.t.
ę·sa·yǫh·wá:dahs it will show you s.t. [TR+ stem: -ǫhwadahsd$_{V}$- show s.o. s.t.]
shower see: rain
a'os·dá·ǫ·di' it rained
shower curtain
tgah·ne·go·y'á:s o·jí'a:' a shower curtain [consists of: tgahne'goy'a:s shower; oji'a:' curtains, lace]
show up see: appear unintentionally, arrive
ta'sa·do·dáh·si' you appeared unintentionally
a'é:yǫ' she arrived
shred see: tear
ęhs·rá:drǫ:' you will tear, shred
shrink
wahs·twahs it shrinks [stem: -(a)hstwa(h,')$_{V}$- shrink]
ę·wáhs·twa' it will shrink (for example, wool)
ohs·twá'ǫh it has shrunk
wahs·twáh·ta' it shrinks (for example, wool) [stem: -(a)hstwahd- cause to shrink; consists of: -(a)hstwa(h,')$_{V}$- shrink]
a·wáhs·twaht it shrank
wahs·twáh·dah·nǫh it goes around shrinking; its a shrinker [stem: -(a)hstwahdahn$_{V}$- go along and shrink]
shrink see: flinch, move away
da·wá:tgri:k it pulled back, flinched, shrank
dwa·dǫ́'ne:s it moves away all the time; it shrinks
shrug
a·tat·nęh·sę́:dǫh he shrugged [de+...at+ stem: -(h)nęhsędǫh- shrug; consists of: -(h)nęs(a)$_{N}$- shoulder -(w)ędǫh$_{V}$- shake s.t.]
shrivel see: shrink
dwa·dǫ́'ne:s it moves away all the time; it shrinks
shrub see: bush
o·hǫ́·da·ę:' a bush; a shrub
shuck see: husk corn, shell s.t.
ęhs·nón·yot·si', ęh·snę́n·yot·si' you will husk the corn
ęh·sék·dot·sih you will shell (eggs, coconuts, etc.)
shudder see: quiver
ę·sa·y'a·dahd·rǫ́:gǫ' you will quiver, shudder
shuffle
ǫhs·gán·ye·hahk she used to shuffle [(de+)... stem: -(a)hsganye(:)- shuffle; consists of: -(a)hsi('da), (ę)hs(a)$_{N}$- foot -ganye(:)$_{V}$- chant, trill]
ę·yǫ́hs·ga:nye:' she will shuffle
gohs·gá:nye:' she has shuffled
de·sáhs·ga:nye: shuffle
gohs·gan·ye·há:gye' she is shuffling along
shut up
ęhs·hé:sgwe:k you will shut her up [TR/ad+ stem: -(h)sgweg- shut s.o. up; consists of: -(h)s(a)$_{N}$- mouth -gweg$_{V}$- close]
a·gǫ́·nahs·gwe:k I shut you up
sats·gwe:k shut up

Cayuga pronunciation guide: /a/ father /e/ weigh /ę/ men (nasalized) /i/ police /o/ hole /ǫ/ home (nasalized) /u/ blue. Underlined vowels are voiceless or whispered. /'/ high pitch. /t/ too /d/ do /k/ king /g/ good (never soft g) /j/ judge or adze /s/ soon /sh/ less heat (never the sh in shirt) /sr/ shrine /sy/ sure /hw/ which (the sound made when you blow out a candle) /h/ hi /ts/ cats hide /'/ (the sound before the first vowel in 'uh-uh') /n/ noon /r/ round /w/ way /y/ yes.

shy
go·dí'grǫ' she is shy
[P+ stem: -(i)'grǫ'$_V$- shy]
shyness
adí'grǫhs·ra' shyness
[ad+ stem: -(i')grǫhsr(a)$_N$- shyness -(i)'grǫ'$_V$- shy]
sibling see: C
de·yag·ya·dęh·nǫ́:de:' my brother; my sister (my nearest sibling)
heh·jí'ah my older brother
keh·jí'ah my older sister
he'gę́:'ęh my younger brother
ke'gę́:'ęh my younger sister
ǫg·yá:gyoh my brother-in-law; my sister-in-law
sick
ak·nǫ·hǫk·dá:nih I am sick
[P+ stem: -nǫhǫkd(ę,anih)$_V$- sick]
tę́' de·sa·da·gá·i·de' you feel sick
[tę' not de'+P+ad+ stem: -(a)gaide'$_V$- feel healthy; feel sick]
ę·sahs·dǫ́:wi' it will disrupt your physical system
[P+ stem: -hsd$_N$- tool, utensil -(h)sdǫwi$_V$- sicken]
sick see: cold, nauseous, sickness
a·ga·to·wín·y'ǫ·se: I have a cold
ak·ne'dr'a·dá:nih I am nauseated, nauseous
o·nǫh·so·dá·i:yǫ:' a sickness; an illness; an epidemic; a plague
sick of s.t. see: annoyed
sge·gę·hę'dá:nih you are sick of me, annoyed wih me, bored with me
sickle
ni·ga·hę·na'tru:'úh
de·yǫ·te·na'tra'k·dǫ́:
e·wę·nǫhg·rí·y'ak·ta' a sickle
[consists of: nigahęna'tru:'uh it has a small blade; deyotęna'tra'kdǫ: it has a crooked blade; ewęnǫhgriya'kta' weed-cutter]
sickle see: scythe
de·yo·tę·na'tra'k·dǫ́:
e·wę·nǫhg·rí·y'ak·ta' a scythe
sickness
o·nǫh·so·dá·ę:' sickness
[o+ consists of: -nǫhsod(a)$_N$- sickness -ę$_V$- lie on the ground]
o·nǫh·so·da'shǫ́:'oh human sicknesses
o·nǫh·so·dá·i:yǫ:' a sickness; an illness; an epidemic; a plague
[stem: -nǫhsod(a)$_N$- sickness]
ga·nǫh·so·dá·ęn·ye's human sicknesses
[stem: -nǫhsod(a)$_N$- sickness -ęnye's several objects lying on the ground]
ga·no·hǫk·déhs·ra' sickness
[ga+ stem: -nohǫkdehsr(a)$_N$- sickness -nǫhǫkd(ę,anih)$_V$- be sick]
side
jǫ·há·ha:dih, swa·há·ha·dih the other side of the road
[s+ A/P+ stem: -(h)ah(a)$_N$- road -(a)dih$_V$- side]
ę́: na·há·ha·dih on the other side of the road
[ę: na'+ A+ stem: -(h)ah(a)$_N$- road -(a)dih$_V$- side; other side of s.t.]
ę́: n'a·ga·nǫh·sá:dih on the other side of the house
[ę: na'+ stem: -nǫhs(a)$_N$- house -(a)dih$_V$- side; other side of s.t.]
ę́: na·gan·ya·dá:dih the other side of the lake
[ę: na'+ stem: -nyad(a:)$_N$- lake, body of water, water -(a)dih$_V$- side; other side of s.t.]
side see: I (gwa:dih, gwai)
sideboard see: cupboard
ek·wa·ę·dáhk·wa' a cupboard; a pantry
side road
o·há·hǫ:t side road
[o+ stem: -(h)ahǫd- side road; consists of: -(h)ah(a)$_N$- road -ǫd$_V$- attached]

side road (continued)
o·ha·ho·dǫ́:nyǫ' side roads
[o+ stem: -(h)ahǫd- side road; consists of: -(h)ah(a)$_N$- road -ǫdǫnyǫ'$_V$- several attached objects]

sieve
ǫ·wá:kta' a sifter; a sieve
[ǫ+ stem: -(a)wakta'- sieve; consists of: -(a)wagd$_V$- cause to winnow, shake out, sift]

sift see: winnow
ęh·sá:wa:k you will winnow, shake out, sift s.t.

sigh
de·yag·wihs·ra·gę·hé:yǫ: (**de·yag·ǫ·wihs·ra·gę·hé:yǫ:**) she is sighing
[de+P+ stem: -ǫhwihsragęheyǫ- sigh; consists of: -ǫhwihsr(a)$_N$- breath -(ga)hey, (gę)hey, (i)hey, (ga)he:, (gę)he:, (i)he:$_V$- die, be weak, exhausted]

sightless see: blind
de·ha·gahg·wé:gǫh he is blind

sign
ga·néhs·da·ot headboards; grave markers; billboards; signs
[ga+ stem: -nehsdaod- sign; consists of: -nehsd(a:)$_N$- floor, board -od$_V$- stand]

significant see: special
o·i·ho·wá:nęh it is important; a great or worthy commendation; it is special

silent see: quiet
ta'dé·sag·yę: you are quiet

silhouette see: shadow
o·dah·sǫ́:da:' a shadow

silk
gan·heh·sa·ga:hę́:hęh silk
[ga+ stem: -nhehsagahę:hęh- silk; consists of: -nhehsag(a)$_N$- silk -(h)ę:hah, hę:hęh$_V$- thin]

silk see: cotton
ga·nih·ga:hęhs·rí:yo: cotton, silk

silt see: land, sand
o·héh·da' dirt; earth
o'néh·sa' sand

silver
de·yohs·da:téh gah·wíhs·da·nǫ:' silver
[consists of: deyohsda:teh it is shiny, smooth (like silver); gahwihsdanǫ:' gold]

similar
to:háh tsa'dé:yoht it is similar
[to:hah there tsa'de+yo+ stem: -(a)hd$_V$- be like, resemble]
dehs·ga·yá·ǫ:da:' it is an imitation of s.t.; it is similar; it is almost the same
[de+s+ga+ stem: -yaǫda:- similar, imitation; consists of: -y(a)$_N$- other, different -ǫda:(h)$_V$- put in, attached]
tsa'de·ga·e·y'a·dó'dę: they (f/m) are similar; they look the same
[tsa'de+ A+ stem: -ya'd(a)$_N$- body -o'dę:$_V$- type of; resemble, be similar, look the same]
tsa'de·ga·di·y'a·dó'dę: they (z) look the same

similar see: like, same
ní:yoht what it is like (preceded by a particle such as de', ne')
tsa'dé:yoht they are (lit.: it is) the same

simmer see: boil
ęg·yǫ́n·ya·hęh it will boil

sin
grih·wá·ne'a:s I am a sinner
[stem: -(r)ihwane'ag- sin; consists of: -(r)ih(wa)$_N$- word -ne'ag$_V$- sin]
ęg·rih·wa·né'a:k I will sin
ag·rih·wa·né'a·gǫh I have sinned
ga·ih·wa·né'aks·ra' sin
[stem: -(r)ihwane'aksr(a)$_N$- sin]

since see: I (because gi' gyę:', shęh)

sincere see: righteous
od·rih·wag·wá·ih·sǫ: it is believable, credible, righteous, fair, honest

Cayuga pronunciation guide: /a/ father /e/ weigh /ę/ men (nasalized) /i/ police /o/ hole /ǫ/ home (nasalized) /u/ blue. Underlined vowels are voiceless or whispered. /'/ high pitch. /t/ too /d/ do /k/ king /g/ good (never soft g) /j/ judge or adze /s/ soon /sh/ less heat (never the sh in shirt) /sr/ shrine /sy/ sure /hw/ which (the sound made when you blow out a candle) /h/ hi /ts/ cats hide /'/ (the sound before the first vowel in 'uh-uh') /n/ noon /r/ round /w/ way /y/ yes.

sing
ga·ǫd·rę·nó:ta' they (f/m) are singers [ad+ stem: -(r)ęnod- play music; sing; consists of: -(r)ęn(a)$_N$- song, music -od$_V$- stand]
a:gad·rę́·no·ta:k I would be a singer
god·rę́:no:t she is singing
od·rę́:no:t it is singing, purring
ho·na:d·rę́:not they (m) are making a presentation
go·nad·rę·nó:dahk they (f/m) did sing
da̱·ho·nad·rę·no·dá:gye' they (m) are singing as they are approaching [ad+ stem: -(r)ęnodagye'$_V$- go along playing music, singing]
god·rę·no·dá:gye' she is singing as she travels
ęd·wa·ę·na·gá:da:t we all (incl.) will raise the song [stem: -(r)ęnagadad- sing; consists of: -(r)ęn(a)$_N$- song, music -gadad$_V$- raise s.t. up]
go̱·ha'dí:yo: she is a good singer; she has a good voice [P+ stem: -(h)a'diyo- be a good singer; have a good voice; consists of: -(h)a'd(a)$_N$- throat, voice, feather -iyo:$_V$- be nice, good]
o·ha'dí:yo: a good voice
hǫ·ha'dí:yo: he is a good singer, he has a good voice

sing see: chant
ęhs·wa·ę·ná·gan·ye:' you all will yodel, chant

single see: alone
né' a·ǫ·hę́:'ęh all alone; the most

sinister see: bad, evil, evil power
tę́' det·ga·yé·i' it is bad, false, wrong
wa̱·hé:tgęh it is evil (in mind), bad
go·ná:tgǫh they (f/m) are a force to be reckoned with; they (f/m) are ominous; they are bad medicine people

sink
wę·nǫ·wá·ę·hę' it sinks (all the time) [stem: -ęnǫwaę$_V$- sink]
a·wę·no·wá·ę:' it sank
ę·wę·nǫ·wá·ę:' it will sink
o·ná·wa·ę' it has sunk in liquid
o·wę·no·wa·ę·dá:gye' it is sinking [P+ stem: -ęnǫwaędagye'$_V$- go along sinking]
a·ga·ǫ·nǫ·wá·ę·dahk they (f/m) made it sink [stem: -ęnǫwaęd- sink s.t.; consists of: -ęnǫwaę$_V$- sink]
a·gę·no·wá·ę·dahk I made it sink
ǫh·jo·ha·i:'tá'geh a sink; a wash basin [ǫ+ stem: -(a)hjohai:'ta'geh- sink; consists of: -(a)hj(a)$_N$- hand -ohai'd$_V$- cause to clean, wash]
ek·so·ha·i·hǫ'dáhk·wa' kitchen sink or dish pan [e+ stem: -ksohaihǫ'dahkwa'- kitchen sink; consists of: -ks(a)$_N$- dish -ohaihǫ'dahkwa'$_V$- s.t. used for cleaning, washing]

sink see: submerge
ę·sáh·do:' you will submerge s.t.

sinless
de·ho·i:hwa·né'a·gǫh he is sinless [de'+not P+ stem: -(r)ihwane'ag- sin; be sinless, blameless; consists of: -(r)ih(wa)$_N$- word -ne'ag$_V$- sin]

sip
ęts·ne·gag·yę́·hę·to' you will sip (through a straw) [d+... stem: -(h)negagyęhętw- sip; consists of: -(h)neg(a)$_N$- water, liquid -yęhętw, yęhęto$_V$- pull]

sister see: C
de·yag·ya·dęh·nǫ́:de:' my brother; my sister
keh·jí'ah my older sister
ke'gę́:'ęh my younger sister

sister (continued)
ǫg·yá:gyoh my brother-in-law; my sister-in-law

sit
ga·dí:tsgo:t they (z) are all sitting
[A+ stem: -(i)tsgod- be sitting; consists of: -(n)itsg(wa)$_N$- lower body -od$_V$- stand]
gęts·go:t it is sitting
ets·go:t she is sitting
gits·go:t I am sitting
ga·di:tsgó:dǫʼ they (z) are sitting
[A+ stem: -(i)tsgodǫʼ- be sitting; consists of: -(n)itsg(wa)$_N$- lower body -odǫʼ$_V$- several standing objects]

sit see: sit down, sit up on

sit down
ęhs·wá:g·yę:ʼ you all will sit
[ag+ stem: -yę(:)- sit down; consists of: -(y)ę$_V$- lie on the ground]
haʼgę́·nag·yę:ʼ they (z) went and sat over there
sag·yę: sit down

sit up on
gits·gwá·he:ʼ I am perched up on s.t.; I am sitting on s.t.
[A+ stem: -(i)tsgwahe:ʼ- sit on s.t., perch on s.t.; consists of: -(n)itsg(wa)$_N$- lower body -(h)e:ʼ$_V$- sitting up on top of s.t.]
ga·haʼk it did sit on s.t.
[A+ stem: -(h)e:ʼ, (h)aʼk$_V$- be sitting up on top of s.t.]
ga·he:ʼ it is sitting up on top of s.t.; it is sitting here
ga·hǫ́:nyǫʼ things are setting there
[A+ stem: -(h)ǫnyǫʼ- several things sitting there; consists of: -(h)e:ʼ$_V$- sitting up on top of s.t.]

sit ups
ga·ǫ:nits·gó:taʼ they (f/m) do sit ups
[ę+ stem: -nitsgod(ǫnyǫ:)- do sit ups; consists of: -(n)itsg(wa)$_N$- lower body -od$_V$- stand -ǫnyǫʼ several]
ę·ga·ǫ:nits·go·dǫ́:nyǫ:ʼ they (f/m) will do sit ups
ę·yǫ·nits·gó·dǫn·yǫ:ʼ she will do sit ups

site see: place
tó: hǫ́:weh a place

six see: B (hye·iʼ)

Six Nations Reserve, Ont. see: E (Hye·i Ni·yǫh·wę·ja:ge:)

sixteen see: B (hye·iʼ sga·eʼ)

sixty see: B (hye·iʼ ni·wahs·hę:)

size
shęh ní:waʼs sizes; how big they are (lit. how big it is)
[(shęh) that ni+w+ stem: -aʼs$_V$- be a certain size]
tsaʼdé:waʼs they are (lit. it is) the same size
[tsaʼde+w+ stem: -aʼs$_V$- be a certain size; be the same size]

size see: volume
ę·ya·go·deʼnyę·dęhs·dǫ·hǫ:k she will be measuring things
tsęh ni·gá:dę:s volume; density; how thick it is; mass

Skaneateles, N.Y. see: E (Long Lake, N.Y., Sgan·ya·da·es)

skate
a·doʼjí:naʼ skates
[ad+ stem: -oʼjin(a)$_N$- skate]
ga·ǫ:gya·naʼtáʼ de·ga·ǫ:doʼji·néh·taʼ figure skating
[consists of: gaǫ:gyanaʼtaʼ they (f/m) are performers (for example, figure skaters, actors, etc.); degaǫ:doʼjinehtaʼ they (f/m) figure-skate]

Cayuga pronunciation guide: /a/ father /e/ weigh /ę/ men (nasalized) /i/ police /o/ hole /ǫ/ home (nasalized) /u/ blue. Underlined vowels are voiceless or whispered. /ʹ/ high pitch. /t/ too /d/ do /k/ king /g/ good (never soft g) /j/ judge or adze /s/ soon /sh/ less heat (never the sh in shirt) /sr/ shrine /sy/ sure /hw/ which (the sound made when you blow out a candle) /h/ hi /ts/ cats hide /ʼ/ (the sound before the first vowel in ‘uh-uh’) /n/ noon /r/ round /w/ way /y/ yes.

skate (continued)
de·ga·ọ:do'ji·néh·ta' they (f/m) figure-skate
[de+...ad+ stem: -o'jinehd- skate; consists of: -o'jin(a)$_N$- skate -ehd$_V$- do on purpose]
dẹ·hẹ·na·do'ji·néh·ta' they (m) are skating
a·do'ji·néh·dọ:' the act of skating
skeleton
ohs·gyẹ́'dohs·gọ' skeleton
[o+ stem: -(h)sgyẹ'dohsgọ'- skeleton; consists of: -(h)sgyẹ'd(a:)$_N$- bone -ohsga'(w)$_V$- clear (of matter)]
skeptical see: believe
ta·wéh·da̱h·gọh he believes
skewed see: slanted
ga·gá·ẹ:he' it is slanted
ski
de·yọg·ya·nọ́·da̱hk·wa' the act of skiing
[de+yọ+ag+ stem: -yanọdahkwa'- ski; consists of: -yan(a)$_N$- tire, track -ọdahkwa'$_V$- attached objects]
skill see: good at s.t.
se·wá·i·họh you are good at s.t.
skim see: hover
od·rẹ́:de' it is hovering (for example, a hummingbird)
skim milk
dẹ·se·wid·rá·gẹd·rọ:' you will take the cream off, skim the milk
[de+... stem: -widragẹdr- milk (skim); consists of: -widr(a)$_N$- ice -gẹdrọ(:)$_V$- scrape]
de·ga·wid·rá·gẹd·rọ: skimmed milk
skin
ge̱h·ná'geh, gi̱h·ná'geh (on) my skin
[stem: -(i)hn(a)$_N$- material, skin]
gi̱h·ná'gehs·họ' all over my skin
[stem: -(i)hn(a)$_N$- material, skin -'geh on -sọ' several]
eh·ná:dẹ:s she has thick skin
[stem: -(i)hn(a)$_N$- material, skin -(a)dẹs$_V$- thick]
ni·yéh·n'o·dẹ: the type of skin she has
[ni+A+ stem: -(i)hn(a)$_N$- material, skin -o'dẹ:$_V$- type of]
tsẹ́h ni·síh·n'o·dẹ: your skin type
se̱h·ná:tẹ:, si̱h·ná:tẹ: you have dry skin
[A+ stem: -(i)hnatẹ:- have dry skin; consists of: -(i)hn(a)$_N$- material, skin -tẹ(:)$_V$- be dry]
ge̱h·ná:tẹ:, gi̱h·ná:tẹ: I have dry skin
ga·néh·wa' leather, hide
[ga+ stem: -neh(wa)$_N$- skin, hide, leather, rawhide]
o·neh·ní:yọh tough hide
[o+ stem: -neh(wa)$_N$- skin, hide, leather, rawhide -(h)niyọh$_V$- hard, tough]
syẹ́:sehs you skin animals all the time
[stem: -yẹse(:)$_V$- skin s.t.]
ẹhs·yẹ́·se:' you will skin (s.t.)
sa·yẹ́:se: you are skinning it right now
skin see: husk, peel
o·nọ́:nya' a husk
o·wá'wi̱hs·da' a peeling
skin cream
ọt·na·sọ·dáhk·wa' skin cream
[ọ+at+ stem: -(h)nasọdahkwa'- skin cream; consists of: -(h)n(a)$_N$- oil, gas -ọdahkwa'$_V$- s.t. attached]
skinny see: thin
gohs·gyọ́'wa·tẹ: she is thin
skip
de·ya·go·na's·gwẹ·hẹ́:gye' she is skipping along
[de+... stem: -na'sgw- skip; consists of: -na'sg(wa)$_N$- lower body -(h)gwẹhẹgye'$_V$- go along lifting, picking up]
skipping rope
de·yọ·nahsg·wahg·w'a·tá' gá:tsg'ẹ·da' a skipping rope
[consists of: deyọnahsgwahgwata' s.t. used for skipping; ga:tsg'ẹda' a rope]

skirt, slip
ga'ka:' a slip
[ga+ stem: -(')k(a:)$_N$- skirt, slip]
he.jo'ká.o:gye's flaring, swaying skirts
[he+s+yo+ stem: -(')k(a:)$_N$- skirt, slip -ǫgye's$_V$- flare]
o'yóh.go:t attached skirt
[o+ stem: -(')yohg(wa)$_N$- tail, skirt -od$_V$- attached]
skirt see: tail
o'yóhg.wa' a skirt; a tail; a feather
skis
oh.wę'gá:' o.yá:na' skis
[consists of: ohwę'ga:' a splint; oya:na' a tire; a track; anything that leaves long tracks]
skulk see: sneak around
sgę.nǫ:'ǫ́h hod.rihs.dǫ.hǫ́:gye' he is sneaking around slowly
skunk
drę́:na: skunk
[stem: -dręna:- skunk; consists of: -dręn(a)$_N$- smell -a:'$_V$- hold, contain, include]
sky
gá.ǫh.y'a.geh in the heavens; in the sky
[ga+ stem: -(r)ǫhy(a)$_N$- sky -'geh on]
ga.ǫ:hya.dá:gye' on-going skies, heavens
[stem: -(r)ǫhy(a)$_N$- sky -dagye'$_V$- continue on, be ongoing]
od.rǫh.yo.gé:węh clear sky
[o+ad+ stem: -(r)ǫhy(a)$_N$- sky -ogewęh$_V$- be clear]
ǫh.y'a.ę́' ni.yǫh.sǫh.go'dę́:
gá.ǫh.y'a.geh blue sky
[consists of: ǫhyaę:' blue; dę' niyohsǫhgo'dę: what colour it is; gaǫhya'geh in the heavens, in the sky]
sky-dive
de.tę.nahsg.wáhk.wa' they (m) are sky-diving; paratroopers
[de+d+ stem: -(a)nahsgwahgw$_V$- jump; sky-dive]
skyline
ga.ǫh.ya.dá:gye' the skyline; the horizon
[ga+ stem: -(r)ǫhyadagye'- skyline, horizon; consists of: -(r)ǫhy(a)$_N$- sky -dagye'$_V$- continue on, be ongoing]
slack see: soft
o.hó'dę:' it is soft, loose
slander see: condemn, gossip, scandal
ęhs.yé:saht you will condemn, slander, insult s.o.
dę.sad.rih.wá.ę.dǫhk,
dęh.sad.rih.wá.ę.dǫh you will gossip
o.ih.wat.gí:nyǫ' scandalous news, rumours
slanted
ga.gá.ę:he' it is slanted
[ga+ stem: -gaęhe'$_V$- slanted]
wahsg.wa.gá.ę.he' a slanted roof
[w+ stem: -(a)hsg(wa)$_N$- roof, bridge -gaęhe'$_V$- slanted]
slap
ęh.set.rag.wę́'da'e:k you will slap it on the cheek
[TR+ stem: -tragwę'da'eg- slap; consists of: -tragwę'd(a)$_N$- flint -(')e$_V$- hit]
slap see: hit
ęhs.wá'e:k you will pound, tap
slave
set.sé:nę' you are tied up (as in: you are a slave to your work; lit.: you are an animal)
[A+ stem: -tsenę$_N$- tame animal]
ha.di:tsé:nę' they (m) are slaves (lit.: they (m) are animals)
sled
ǫ.de'dręh.dę́h.dahk.wa' a sled; a sleigh
[ǫ+ade+ stem: -(')drehdęhdahkwa'- sled; consists of: -(')drehd(a)$_N$- vehicle, car -ęhdahkwa'$_V$- s.t. that hits, knocks down, strikes]

sled, sledge see: toboggan
hę·na·d'ed·réh·dęh·ta' they (m) are tobogganing
sledgehammer
ga·jih·yo·wá:nęh a sledgehammer; a big hammer
[ga+ stem: -jihyowanęh- sledgehammer; consists of: -jih(wa), jihy$_N$- hammer -owanęh$_V$- be big]
sleep
a·gí:da's I'm a (good) sleeper
[P+ stem: -(i)da'$_V$- sleep]
o·dí:da's they (z) sleep, hibernate all the time
ę·sę́:da' you will sleep
ǫ·gí:da' I am sleeping; I slept
sǫ·gí:da' I went back to sleep
a·gí·da'ǫh I was asleep; I am sleeping
o·dá'ǫh it is asleep
sę́:da' you sleep
sę·dá'drah you go to bed; you go to sleep
[P+ stem: -(i)da'drah$_V$- go to sleep]
o·wíd·ręh·da', gá·id·ręh·da' sleep; the act of sleeping
[o/ga+ stem: -(w)idręhd(a)$_N$- sleep -(w)idręhd(a:)$_V$- be sleepy]
o·wid·ręh·dá:gǫ: it came through a dream
[o+ stem: -widręhdagǫ:- dream; consists of: -widręhd(a)$_N$- sleep -agǫ: in]
ę·sa·id·ręh·dí:yo:s you will have a nice sleep
[P+ stem: -(w)idręhdiyohsd- sleep well; consists of: -(w)idręhd(a:)$_V$- be sleepy, -iyohsd$_V$- make good, nice]
ęgęnǫhwe:t I will sleep over
[ę+ stem: -nǫhwed$_V$- sleep over]
sleeper
o·wi:ya:'áh go·da'stá'
ag·ya'da·wí'tra' a baby's sleeper; a nightgown
[consists of: owi:ya:'ah baby; goda'sta' her pyjamas agya'dawi'tra' nightgown]
sleepy
a·gíd·ręh·da:'s I am sleepy
[P+ stem: -(w)idręhd(a:)$_V$- sleepy]
ę·sa·id·rę́h·da:' you will get sleepy
e·sa·id·rę́h·da:' you got sleepy
sid·ręhg·yé:nyę's you are nodding off, falling asleep
[P+ stem: -(w)idręgyenyę's$_V$- be nodding off, falling asleep]
sleepy see: tired
a·gá·ǫ:tsęht they (f/m) were tired, sleepy
sleet see: hail
o·wíd·rǫg·yǫ: it is hailing; sleet
sleeve
ga·nę́:tsǫ:t sleeve
[ga+ stem: -nętsǫd- sleeve; consists of: -nęts(a)$_N$- arm -ǫd$_V$- attached]
slender see: thin
gohs·gyǫ́'wa·tę: she is thin
slice
dęhs·riht you will break s.t.
[de+...(N+) stem: -(hr)ihd- slice, mash, grind; consists of: -(hr)i'$_V$- break up]
de·gá·hih·dǫh to smash s.t. into tiny pieces
dehs·riht grind it
deh·sáh·ya̱·hiht dice, cut, mash, etc. the fruit
[de+...(N+) stem: -(a)hya)$_N$- berry, fruit -(hr)ihd$_V$- slice, mash, grind]
de·ga·heh·dá·hih·dǫh land that has been disced, worked
[de+...(N+) stem: -(h)ehd(a)$_N$- land, dirt, earth, ground -(hr)ihd$_V$- slice, mash, grind]

slice (continued)
at·ga·da·deh·sʼoh·dá·hiht I smashed my finger
[de+...(N+) stem: -(h)sʼohd(a)$_N$- hand, finger, paw -(hr)ihd$_V$- slice, mash, grind]
dęh·snę́·hę·hiht you will grind corn
[de+...(N+) stem: -nęh(ę)$_N$- corn -(hr)ihd$_V$- slice, mash, grind]
de·ga·jihs·gwá·hih·dǫh it is smashed up, mashed
[de+...(N+) stem: -jihsgwahihd- mash, smash; consists of: -jihsg(wa)$_N$- mush -(hr)ihd$_V$- slice, mash, grind]
jó·wihs·da:t, sga·íh·wihs·da:t one slice
[s+(y)o/ga stem: -(raʼ)wisd(a)$_N$- slice -d$_V$- stand, be one]
swad·ráʼwihs·da:t one slice
[s+wa+ad+ stem: -(raʼ)wisd(a)$_N$- peel -d$_V$- stand, be one]
ni·wad·rʼa·wíhs·da·dę:s paper-thin slices (for example, of pie)
[ni+wa+ad+ stem: -(raʼ)wisd(a)$_N$- slice -(a)dęs$_V$- be a certain thickness]

slice see: chop, cut
a·geʼó:gǫh I did chop; I have chopped
ak·ré:nęh I did cut it

slide
o·deh·yo·jih·dęh·dáhk·waʼ a slide
[o+ade+ stem: -(h)yojihdęhdahkwaʼ- slide; consists of: -(h)yojihdęhd$_V$- play]

slip see: skirt, trip
gaʼka:ʼ a slip
ę·dih·sah·síʼgyaʼk you will stumble, stub your toe

slippers
ga·nǫhs·gǫh·ká:ʼ ah·dáhg·waʼ house slippers
[consists of: ganǫhsgǫhka:ʼ s.t. used in the house; ahdahgwaʼ shoes]

slobber see: drool, saliva
sęts·gro:t you are drooling
ots·graʼ saliva; spit; sputum

slope see: hill, slanted
o·nǫ́·da·he:ʼ a hill
ga·gá·ę:heʼ it is slanted

slow
sgę·nǫ́:ʼǫh slowly
[s+g+ stem: -ęnǫ$_V$- be slow]
sgę·nǫ·go·wá:hah slowly, fairly slow
[s+g+ stem: -ęnǫ$_V$- be slow -gowahah fairly big]
hohs·hę: he is slow-moving
[P+ stem: -(a)hshę:$_V$- be slow-moving]
a·gáhs·hę: I am slow to act
ohs·hę: it is slow-moving
sad·ri·hó:wi: you are a klutz; you're slow-moving; you are feeble, clumsy
[P+ad+ stem: -(r)ihowi- slow, feeble; consists of: -(r)ih(wa)$_N$- word -owi, ǫny$_V$- drive]
hod·ri·hó:wi: he is clumsy
ho·yá·no:tgę: he is a slow runner, walker; he has a slow gait
[P+ stem: -yanotgę:$_V$- slow runner]
dę·ho·wa·yę́n·heʼs·gǫ: he has difficulty learning
[deʼ+ not P+ stem: -wayę(n)$_N$- heart, spirit -wayęnheʼsgǫ:$_V$- be clever, educated; be a slow learner]

slow see: late, weak
ag·yáʼdahs·hę:, ag·yáʼdahs·hęh I am slow; I was late
ag·yaʼda·gę·hé:yǫ: I am physically weak, slow

slow marker (glottal stop)
ga·wę́·nihs·taʼ a slow marker; a glottal stop
[ga+ stem: -węnistaʼ- slow marker; consists of: -węn(a)$_N$- voice, word -isd$_V$- make long]

sluggish see: lazy, slow
sa·nǫ́ʼseh you are lazy
hohs·hę: he is slow-moving

slumber see: sleep
ę·sę́:daʼ you will sleep

Cayuga pronunciation guide: /a/ father /e/ weigh /ę/ men (nasalized) /i/ police /o/ hole /ǫ/ home (nasalized) /u/ blue. Underlined vowels are voiceless or whispered. /ˊ/ high pitch. /t/ too /d/ do /k/ king /g/ good (never soft g) /j/ judge or adze /s/ soon /sh/ less heat (never the sh in shirt) /sr/ shrine /sy/ sure /hw/ which (the sound made when you blow out a candle) /h/ hi /ts/ cats hide /ʼ/ (the sound before the first vowel in 'uh-uh') /n/ noon /r/ round /w/ way /y/ yes.

slush see: rain, snow
o·nǫn·ya·ę·dag·yé' **os·dá·ǫ:gyǫ:** freezing rain
o'gra' snow; a snowflake
smack see: slap, spank
ęh·set·rag·wę́'da̱'e:k you will slap it on the cheek
ęh·ya·n'at·sá'e:k he will spank you
small
ni·ya:gú:'uh she is small; a little female; a small girl
[ni+A+ stem: -u:'uh$_V$- small]
ni·wú:'uh it is small, little
ni·ga:gú:s'uh they (f/m) are small
[ni+A+ stem: -u:s'uh$_V$- several small objects]
ni·hah·wa·ji·yú:'uh his family is small
[ni+A/P+N+ stem: -(h)wajiy(a)$_N$- family -u:'uh$_V$- small]
small
[-'ah diminutive suffix; can denote smallness; present in many kinship terms]
[-hah diminutive suffix; often means 'fairly']
smaller
ga·ó' ní:wa' it is smaller (than s.t. else)
[gao' ni+...(N)+ stem: -a:'(ah)$_V$- small]
ga·ó' ni·wak·yę·dáhk·wa' a smaller chair
[gao' ni+...(N)+ stem: -(a)kyędahkw(a)$_N$- chair -a:'(ah)$_V$- small]
smart
sya·dǫhs·rá·ę·di' you are smart (educated)
[A+ stem: -(h)yadǫhsraędi'- smart, educated; consists of: -(h)yadǫhsr(a)$_N$- paper -(y)ędei, (y)ędi$_V$- know]
s'a·ní·gǫ·ha:t you are smart, brilliant
[P+ stem: -(')nigǫhad- smart; consists of: -(')nigǫh(a)$_N$- mind -d$_V$- stand]
ho·di'ni·gǫ́·ha:t they (m) have wisdom; male elders
Smart Weed
go·wę·na̱h·sá·is Smart Weed (a special plant)
[go+ stem: -węnahsais- Smart Weed; consists of: -(a)wę'nahs(a), (a)wę'nohs(a)$_N$- tongue -is$_V$- long]
go·ta:dá:dih Smart Weed
[go+at+ stem: -(h)adadih- Smart Weed; consists of: -(h)ad(a)$_N$- forest -(a)dih$_V$- side]
smash see: mash
dę·se·ji̱hsg·wá·hiht you will mash it
smell
a·gé:swahs I smell it (right now)
[P+(N+) stem: -sw, sho$_V$- smell]
a·ges·wahs·gę́·hę:' I used to be able to smell (but my nose quit working)
ę·wá·ges·ho' I will smell it
ǫ·gé:s·ho' I did smell it
ę·wá·des·waht it will smell it
[TR+ade+ stem: -swahd- smell s.t. on purpose; consists of: -sw, sho$_V$- smell]
de·sá·des·waht smell it
sa·dé:swaht smell it
sa·dehs·wah·dáh·nǫ: sniff it
[TR+ade+ stem: -swahdahnǫ(:)- sniff s.t.; consists of: -sw, sho$_V$- smell]
o·ded·rę·ná:', o·ded·rę·ná·i:' a smell
[o+ade+ stem: -dręn(a)$_N$- smell -a:'$_V$- hold, contain, include]
gad·rę:ní:yo: a nice smell
[ga+ stem: -dręn(a)$_N$- smell -iyo:$_V$- be nice, good]
ged·rę:ní:yo: I smell nice
[A+ stem: -dręniyo:- smell nice; consists of: -dręn(a)$_N$- smell -iyo:$_V$- be nice, good]
sed·rę:ní:yo: you smell nice

smell (continued)
ed·rę·no·wá:ne' she has a big smell, odour, scent
[A+ stem: -drę̨n(a)$_N$- smell -owanęh$_V$- be big]
had·rę·no·wá:ne' he has a big smell, odour, scent; he has been drinking
gad·rę·na·gá'ǫh it smells good, sweet, appetizing
[ga+ stem: -dręnaga'ǫh- sweet-smelling; consists of: -dręn(a)$_N$- smell -ga'$_V$- like the taste of s.t.]

smell bad, smelly see: stink, strong-smelling
gag·rahs it stinks
gad·rę·nahs·há:sde' it is a strong smell; it is strong-smelling

smelts
gan·yá·dah·ka:' smelts
[ga+ stem: -nyad(a:)$_N$- lake, body of water, water -ka:'- typical of]

smile
ag·yǫ́:dih I am smiling
[P+ stem: -yǫdi, yǫgy$_V$- smile]
ho·yǫ́:dih he is smiling
ę·ho:yǫ́:di' he will smile
ho·yǫ́g·yǫh·ne:' he has already smiled; he did smile
ag·yǫ·di·há:gye' I am going along smiling
[P+ stem: -yǫdihagye'$_V$- go along smiling]

smile see: giggle, laugh
ho·yǫg·yę́:ni: he is a smiler, a giggler
ęhs·yǫ́:gya't you will smile

smirk
de·sat·gǫh·sá:gri: wrinkle up your face; smirk
[de+...at+ stem: -gǫhsagri- smirk; consists of: -gǫhs(a)$_N$- face -gri$_V$- wrinkle]

smite see: hit
ęhs·wá'e:k you will pound, tap

smoke
ęh·se·já·o·dę' you will smoke
[stem: -jaodę- smoke; consists of: -j(a)$_N$- smoke -odę$_V$- put in]
tę́' ta:wa:dǫ́h a:se·já·o·dę' No Smoking
[consists of: tę' not; ta:wa:dǫh it's not said a:sejaodę' you (s) should smoke]
dęh·sa·y'ęg·wá·ohs the smoke will get in your eyes
[de+ ...stem: -yę'gwaohsd- get smoke in one's eyes; consists of: -yę'g(wa)$_N$- tobacco, smoke, cigarettes -ohsd$_V$- immerse s.t.]

smoke see: stink, tan, tobacco
ha·yę́'gwag·rahs he smells like smoke
ęhs·yę́'gw'a·e:k you will smoke it (meat, etc.); you will tan it
o·yę́'gwa' tobacco; cigarettes

smokestack see: chimney
gan·yę́·ho:t a (standing) chimney

smoky
o·yę́'gwa:' it is smoky
[o+ stem: -yę'gwa:'- smoky; consists of: -yę'g(wa)$_N$- tobacco, smoke, cigarettes -a:'$_V$- hold, contain, include]
de·yo·yęg·wá·ę:' it is a smoky, hazy day
[de+yo+ stem: -yęgwaę:'- smoky, hazy; consists of: -yę'g(wa)$_N$- tobacco, smoke, cigarettes -ę$_V$- lie on the ground]

smooth
dę·yohs·dá:teh it is shiny, smooth (like silver)
[de+yo+ stem: -hsd$_N$- tool, utensil -(h)sdateh$_V$- smooth, shiny]

smother see: choke
dę·héhs·hǫn·ya'k you will strangle him

smudge see: burn, soot
ęhs·rę́'da:' you will burn s.t.
o·há'kda' soot

Cayuga pronunciation guide: /a/ father /e/ weigh /ę/ men (nasalized) /i/ police /o/ hole /ǫ/ home (nasalized) /u/ blue. Underlined vowels are voiceless or whispered. /'/ high pitch. /t/ too /d/ do /k/ king /g/ good (never soft g) /j/ judge or adze /s/ soon /sh/ less heat (never the sh in shirt) /sr/ shrine /sy/ sure /hw/ which (the sound made when you blow out a candle) /h/ hi /ts/ cats hide /'/ (the sound before the first vowel in 'uh-uh') /n/ noon /r/ round /w/ way /y/ yes.

smut
o·jíhg·wę’s corn smut; black corn fungus
[o+ stem: -jihgwę’s- corn smut; consists of: -jihg(wa)$_N$- porridge, mush]
smut see: language
o·ih·wat·gi’shǫ́:’ǫh smut; dirty language
snack
ę·jid·wa·ná’da:k we all (incl.) will snack
[stem: -na’dag- snack; consists of: -na’d(a:)$_N$- bread -g$_V$- eat]
ę·jid·wa·na’dá·ik·sǫ:’ we all (incl.) will snack
[stem: -na’daiksǫ:’- snack; consists of: -na’d(a:)$_N$- bread -(sho)hih$_V$- bite]
snail
ga·nǫ́h·s’id·re’ a snail
[ga+ stem: -nǫhsi’dre’- snail; consists of: -nǫhs(a)$_N$- house -(i)’dre(:)$_V$- drag, drive]
snake
os·há·ihs·da’ a snake
[o+ stem: -(h)saihsd(a)$_N$- snake, serpent]
(o)h·wíh·sǫ:t a milk snake
[o+ stem: -(h)wihsǫd- milk snake; consists of: -(h)wihs(a)$_N$- -ǫd$_V$- attached]
ha·ná:dǫh a black snake
[ha+ stem: -nadǫh- black snake]
ji·nǫh·ya̱·há·e: a garter snake
[stem: -jinǫhyahae:- garter snake]
sga·yá’de:s a water snake
[s+ga+ stem: -ya’de:s- water snake; consists of: -ya’d(a)$_N$- body -es$_V$- long]
snare see: trap
ǫd·rihs·dá·ę·dahk·wa’ a trap
snatch see: grab
da·ję́:na: grab it
sneak around
sgę:nǫ:’ǫ́h hod·rihs·dǫ·hǫ́:gye’ he is sneaking around slowly
[sgę:nǫ:’ǫh slowly P+ at+ stem: -(hr)ihsdǫhǫgye’- sneak around; consists of: -(hr)ihsd$_V$- bump s.o.]
sneer see: frown, smirk
dęh·sát·gręg·ręht you will sneer, frown
de·sat·gǫh·sá:gri: wrinkle up your face; smirk
sneeze
de·sá’tsǫhs·tahk you have sneezed; you were sneezing
[de+P+ stem: -(’)tsǫhsd$_V$- sneeze]
dę·sá’tsǫhs you will sneeze
a·dí·s’at·sǫhs you did sneeze
snicker see: giggle
sa·yǫ’gyé:ni:, sa·yǫ’gyę́:ni: you have the giggles
sniffle see: sneeze
sniff see: smell
sa·dehs·wah·dáh·nǫ: sniff it
snob see: conceited, self-centred, stuck up
wa·dá:ta:’ a snob
wa·dág·y’a·da:s it is bold; a snob; she (lit.: it) has a high opinion of herself; she (lit.: it) is boastful
wa·dat·gǫn·yǫ́hs·ta’ she (lit.: it) is stuck up
snooze see: sleep
ę·sę́:da’ you will sleep
snore
o·hǫ́’gwa·ga: a snoring noise
[o+ stem: -(h)ǫ’gwaga:- snore; consists of: -(h)ǫ’g(wa)$_N$- snore -ga:$_V$- make a rattling or grinding noise]
snort see: sneeze
dę·sá’tsǫhs you will sneeze
snot see: mucus
o·jí·nǫhg·ra’ nasal mucus
snow
ę·yo’grǫ́:di’ it will snow
[(y)o+ stem: -(’)grǫdi- snow; consists of: -(a)’gr(a)$_N$- snow -ǫdi, -ǫgy$_V$- throw]
o’grǫ́:gyǫ: it is snowing

snow (continued)
o'gra' snow; a snowflake
[o+ stem: -(a)'gr(a)$_N$- snow]
o'grá'geh on the snow
[stem: -(a)'gr(a)$_N$- snow -'geh on]
o'grá·ę' there is snow on the ground
[o+ stem: -(a)'gr(a)$_N$- snow -ę'$_V$- lie on the ground]
a'o·gahg·wę'drǫ́:di' it snowed
[o+ stem: -(')gahwgę'drǫdi- snow, ice pellet; consists of: -gahgwę'dr(a)$_N$- granular snow -ǫdi, -ǫgy$_V$- throw]
o·gahg·wę·dǫ́:gyǫ: it is snowing; ice pellets
o·há'gęd·re' crusty snow
[o+ -ha'$_N$- -gędr$_V$- scrape -e$_V$- go]
on·yę'gwá·o·hǫh drifted snow
[o+ stem: -nyę'g(wa)$_N$- drifting snow -(h)ǫ(:)$_V$- lie]
o'gro·wa·náh·dǫh it is snowing hard
[(y)o+ stem: -(a)'growanahd- snow hard; consists of: -(a)'gr(a)$_N$- snow -owanahd$_V$- make big]
o·da'gra·dé:nyǫ: there are snow flurries
[o+ad+ stem: -(a)'gradenyǫ:- snow flurry; consists of: -(a)'gr(a)$_N$- snow -denyǫ'$_V$- several existing things]
snow plough
de·wa·d'ag·róh·da:s a snow plough
[de+wa+ad+ stem: -(a)'grohda:s- snow plough; consists of: -(a)'gr(a)$_N$- snow -ohda(:,h)$_V$- tidy up, clean]
snow shovel
de·yǫ·d'ag·roh·da:stá' ga·gáh·wẹh·sa' a snow shovel
[consists of: deyǫd'agrohda:sta' it cleans up snow; gagahwẹhsa' a shovel]
snow suit
o·wi:ya:'áh gọhs·re·ká: gọhg·wę́:nya' a baby's snowsuit
[consists of: owiya:'ah baby gọhsrehka:' winter kind; ahgwę:nya' clothing, clothes]

snowflake see: snow
o'gra' snow; a snowflake
snowshoe
de·yǫt·wę'ga·ǫ:dáhk·wa' snowshoes
[de+yǫ+at+ stem: -(h)wę'gaǫdahkwa'- snowshoe; consists of: -(h)wę'g(a)$_N$- splint -ǫdahkwa'$_V$- s.t. attached]
snowsnake see: stick
o'ę́:na' a snowsnake pole; a pole
snub see: offend, roll one's eyes
ęhs·he'ni·gǫ́·ha'e:k you will offend s.o.
ęh·sat·gạ·hǫ́:di' you will roll your eyes (in disgust); you will snub s.o.
so see: I (di')
soak see: bathe, submerge, wet
ǫg·ya'dọ·há·i: she is bathing
í:yo' it is in the water, submerged in liquid
o·nǫ́hg·wi·ja' it is soaking wet, saturated
soap
e·no·há:'ta' soap; what one washes with
[e+ / o+ stem: -noha'ta'- soap; consists of: -n$_N$- noun -oha:'d$_V$- cause to clean, wash]
o·wi:ya:'áh go·no·há:'tra' baby's soap
[consists of: owi:ya:'ah baby; gonoha'tra' s.o.'s soap]
e·no·ha·i:hǫ'dahk·wá' e·no·há:'ta' laundry soap
[consists of: enohai:hǫ'dahkwa' s.t. that is used for laundering; enoha:'ta' soap; what one washes with]
soar
od·rę́·dag·ye's it is soaring (for example, a bird)
[(de+)...ad+ stem: -(r)ędagye'- soar; consists of: -(r)ęd$_V$- hover]
de·yo·ded·rę́·dag·ye' it is soaring
soar see: float, fly
ga·dig·ye·nǫ́:gye' they (z) are flying, floating about in the air (for example, seeds, etc.)

Cayuga pronunciation guide: /a/ father /e/ weigh /ę/ men (nasalized) /i/ police /o/ hole /ǫ/ home (nasalized) /u/ blue. Underlined vowels are voiceless or whispered. /´/ high pitch. /t/ too /d/ do /k/ king /g/ good (never soft g) /j/ judge or adze /s/ soon /sh/ less heat (never the sh in shirt) /sr/ shrine /sy/ sure /hw/ which (the sound made when you blow out a candle) /h/ hi /ts/ cats hide /'/ (the sound before the first vowel in 'uh-uh') /n/ noon /r/ round /w/ way /y/ yes.

soar (continued)
de·gá:dęhs it flies, goes up in the air
sob
ǫhs·tá·ha'ge: s.o. is sobbing (lit.: s.o. is doing a big cry)
[stem: -(a)hsda:ha', (a)hsdaę'$_V$- cry -ge:- big]
ak·ni·gǫ·há·het·gę's I am crying uncontrollably
[P+ stem: -(')nigǫhahetgę's- sob; consists of: -(')nigǫh(a)$_N$- mind -(hr)etgę's$_V$- evil, bad, ugly things]
g'o·ni·gǫ·há·het·gę's she is sobbing
sob see: cry
ǫhs·dá:ha' she is crying
so be it see: I (netogyę:')
social work(ers) see: G (ga·ih·wa·ji·ya't·ga·ha:')
society see: association, group
gęg·yohg·wa·gé·hǫ' associations; councils; agencies; groups; lit.: crowds lying about
gęg·yóhg·wa·ę' a group
sock
a·dáh·d'it·ra' socks
[stem: -(a)dahdi'tr(a)$_N$- sock]
sock see: booties
o·wi:ya:'áh go·dáh·d'it·ra' a baby's booties, socks
sod
o'ǫ́hg·wa:' sod; moss
[o+ stem: -(')ǫ(h)g(wa:)$_N$- sod]
soda see: pop
oh·ne·ga·gá'ǫh pop; soda
sofa see: couch
ǫg·ya'gye·nę́·da̱hk·wa' a couch
soft
o·hó'dę:' it is soft, loose
[o+ stem: -(ri)ho'dę:- soft, loose; consists of: -(ri)ho'd$_V$- worked]
o·heh·da̱·hó'dę: soft ground
[P+(N+) stem: consists of: -(h)ehd(a)$_N$- land, dirt, earth, ground -(ri)ho'dę:$_V$- soft, loose, worked]
soft drink see: pop
oh·ne·ga·gá'ǫh pop; soda
soil
oh·né'dr'a·geh on the ground
[o+ stem: -(h)ne'dr(a)$_N$- soil, ground]
soil see: earth, land
oh·wę́·ja·gǫ: under the earth, ground
o·héh·da' dirt; earth
soiled
de·ya·ǫ·góh·dǫh it is soiled (lit. penetrated, permeated)
[de+... stem: -ǫgohd$_V$- surpass; filter, strain, penetrate]
soiled see: dirty,undergarment
ot·gi' it is ugly, dirty, soiled
de·yó'da·gę:t dirty undergarments; soil; fecal matter
[de+yo+ stem: -(')dagęd- undergarment; consists of: -(ni)'d(a)$_N$- feces, privates -(')gęd$_V$- light-coloured, white]
solder
ęh·sné·ga:' you will solder
[A+ stem: -(h)nega:'- level, solder; consists of: -(h)neg(a)$_N$- water, liquid -a:'$_V$- hold, contain, include]
soldier
ha·dih·só:da: they (m) are military (referring to putting the gun over their shoulders)
[A+ stem: -(h)soda:'- soldier; consists of: -hs$_N$- tool, utensil -oda(:,h)$_V$- drape]
hah·só:da:' a soldier (lit.: he drapes it)
sole see: alone, ball of foot, I (one), sga:t
né' a·ǫ·hę́:'ęh all alone; the most
á:gwa̱h·da', og·wáh·da' the sole; the ball of the foot
solicit see: ask
ę·sa·da̱·hǫ́·dǫ' you will ask
solicitor see: lawyer
dę̱·ha·ih·wá·gen·hahs he is a lawyer

solid see: contained, hard
í:wa:t it is contained; it (z) is in there; solid matter
oh·ní:yǫh it is hard
solitary see: alone, I (one sga:t)
néʼ a·ǫ·hę́:ʼęh all alone; the most
somber see: sad
de·saʼni·gǫ́·hęh·dǫh you are sad
someone see: I (sǫga:ʼah)
someplace see: be someplace, I (somewhere, gʼatoh)
gę́:neʼs they (z) are around; they are here; they are together
s.t. see: I (sgahoʼdęʼ)
sometime see: I (hwędǫgwaʼ)
somewhere see: I (gʼatoh)
son see: C
he·há:wahk my son
he·né:nhǫ:s my son-in-law
song, music
gá·ę:naʼ a song
[ga+ stem: -(r)ęn(a)$_N$- song, music]
ga·ę·ná·ǫ:nyǫʼ songs
gá·ę·na·gǫ: in the song
ga·ę·na·séʼs·hǫʼ new songs
[ga+ stem: -(r)ęn(a)$_N$- song, music -(a)se:$_V$- new]
ga·ę·na·gá:yǫh old song
[ga+ stem: -(r)ęn(a)$_N$- song, music -gayǫh$_V$- old (thing)]
ga·ę·ní:yo: nice song
[ga+ stem: -(r)ęn(a)$_N$- song, music -iyo:$_V$- nice, good]
hehs·ga·ę·ná:gǫ:t the last song
[he+s+ga+(N+) stem: -(r)ęn(a)$_N$- song, music -gǫd$_V$- persevere, linger; be last]
gá·ę·ni:s a long song
[ga+ stem: -(r)ęn(a)$_N$- song, music -is$_V$- long]
oh·wę·ja·geh·gę·há:ʼ
haʼde·gá·ę·na·ge: all kinds of earth songs
[consists of: ohwęjagehgęha:ʼ earthly things; resources; haʼdegaęnage: all kinds of songs]
soon see: I (waʼjihtsǫ:)
soot
o·háʼkdaʼ soot
[o+ stem: -(h)akd(a)$_N$- soot]
soot see: ash
oʼgę́·hęʼ ashes; a bullet; dust
soothe see: babysit, console, forget
ęh·sa·dę·gáhn·yeʼ you will comfort, rock a child; you are babysitting
ęhs·heʼni·gǫ́·hoʼdrǫ:ʼ you will console s.o. (lit.: you will caress s.o.'s mind)
ęhs·heʼni·gǫ́·hęh·dęʼ you will make s.o. feel better, comfort s.o. (lit.: you will make s.o. forget s.t.)
sorcerer see: evil power, witch
go·ná:tgǫh they (f/m) are a force to be reckoned with; they (f/m) are ominous; they are bad medicine people
de·ga·hęh·jí·da·hǫh a Hallowe'en witch
sorcery see: witchcraft
ot·gǫt·ras·hǫ́:ʼǫh an object used for witchcraft
sore
ęh·saʼno:dráʼ seh·sóhg·wʼa·geh you will have sores on your lips
[P+ stem: -(ʼ)nodra(h,ʼ)$_V$- infected; consists of ęhsaʼno:draʼ you will get infected sehsohgwʼageh on your lips]
a·gah·sʼi·dá·nǫh·wa:s I have a sore foot
[P+N+ stem: -(a)hsi(ʼda), (ę)hs(a)$_N$- foot -nǫhwag$_V$- be sore, ache]
a·ge·ga·há·nǫh·wa:s I have a sore eye
[P+N+ stem: -gah(a)$_N$- eye -nǫhwag$_V$- sore, ache]
a·geh·si·ná·nǫh·wa:s I have a sore leg
[P+N+ stem: -(h)sin(a)$_N$- leg -nǫhwag$_V$- sore, ache]

Cayuga pronunciation guide: /a/ father /e/ weigh /ę/ men (nasalized) /i/ police /o/ hole /ǫ/ home (nasalized) /u/ blue. Underlined vowels are voiceless or whispered. /ˊ/ high pitch. /t/ too /d/ do /k/ king /g/ good (never soft g) /j/ judge or adze /s/ soon /sh/ less heat (never the sh in shirt) /sr/ shrine /sy/ sure /hw/ which (the sound made when you blow out a candle) /h/ hi /ts/ cats hide /ʼ/ (the sound before the first vowel in 'uh-uh') /n/ noon /r/ round /w/ way /y/ yes.

sore (continued)
a·geh·s'oh·dá·nọh·wa:s I have a sore hand
[P+N+ stem: -(h)s'ohd(a)$_N$- hand, finger, paw -nọhwag$_V$- sore, ache]
a·gehs·w'e·ná·nọh·wa:s I have a sore back
[P+N+ stem: -(h)swa'n(a), (h)swe'n(a)$_N$- upper back -nọhwag$_V$- sore, ache]
a·gọt·sa·nọ́h·wa:s I have a sore knee
[P+N+ stem: -ọts(a)$_N$- knee -nọhwag$_V$- sore, ache]
ag·ra·da·nọ́h·wa:s I have a sore heel
[P+N+ stem: -(r)a(k)d(a)$_N$- heel -nọhwag$_V$- sore, ache]
ag·ya'da·nọ́h·wa'ksọh I am going along aching
[P+N+ stem: -ya'd(a)$_N$- body -nọhwag$_V$- sore, ache -sọ' plural]
sore see: ache
ag·ya'da·nọ́h·wa:s I am sore; I ache
sorrow see: depressed, mournful
dwak·ni·gọ·hę́'ọh I am in sorrow, in mourning; I am sad
o'ni·gọh·sá:dọhk it is mournful
sort
dę·só:nyahs you will sort
[de+... stem: -ọnyahsd- sort; consists of: -ọni, ọny$_V$- make]
sort see: divide into parts
de·seh·kah·sọ́·gwa̧·họ: divide them (several objects) up into categories
sotto voce see: whisper
a·ja·họhs·gwá:gọ: in a whisper
sound
o·họ́:ga'·t a clear sound
[o+ stem: -(a)họga'd- sound; consists of: -(a)họg$_V$- hear, learn how to speak a language, understand]
sound see: noise
otga:' noise

soup
oh·né·gag·ri' soup; rubber
[o+ stem: -(h)negagri'- soup; consists of: -(h)neg(a)$_N$- water, liquid -gri'$_V$- juice, liquid]
o·họ·na·dá' oh·né·gag·ri' potato soup
[consists of: (o)họn'ada' potato; ohnegagri' soup]
o·họn'a·dá:gri' potato soup; potato water
[o+ stem: -(h)ọna'd(a)$_N$- potato -gri'$_V$- juice, liquid]
ohn·yé:ha' flint corn soup
[o+ stem: -(h)nye:h(a)$_N$- flint corn soup]
o·gę́:nye:' roasted green corn; dried corn soup (made with roasted green corn)
[o+ stem: -gęnye:'- dried corn soup]
o·nę́·hohg·wa' lyed corn soup
[o+ stem: -nęhohgwa'- lyed corn soup; consists of: -nęh(ę)$_N$- corn -ohgw$_V$- remove from liquid]
soup see: coffee
oh·sa·he'dá:gri' bean soup; coffee
sour
o·jí·wa·gę: it is sour, salty, bitter
[o+(N+) stem: -jiwagę:$_V$- sour, bitter, salty]
de·yóh·yo·jihs it is sour; salty water
[de+yo+ stem: -(a)hyojihs$_V$- sour, salty; consists of: -(a)hy(a)$_N$- fruit, berry -jiwagę:$_V$- sour, bitter, salty, salty]
Sour Spring see: E (Six Nations Reserve, Ont., Ga·nọhg·w'at·ro')
sovereign see: queen, G (crown, king)
e·goh·gó:wah a queen; the Queen
gwa:gó:wah a king; the Crown
space see: galaxy, place
o·ha·ha'dí·họh the Milky Way
tó: hó:weh a place

spade
e·héhg·y'ak·ta' a spade
[e+ stem: -(h)ehgya'kta'- spade; consists of: -(h)ehd(a)$_N$- land, dirt, earth, ground -(i)ya'g$_V$- cut, break]
spade see: shovel
ga·gáh·wẹh·sa' a shovel
span
tsa'de·ha·nẹ:t·sé:s·họ' his arm span
[tsa'de+A+ stem: -nẹtse:sọ'- span; consists of: -nẹts(a)$_N$- arm -esọ'$_V$- several long objects]
tsa'de·ha·wá:ye:s his wing span
[tsa'de+A+ stem: -waye:s- span; consists of: -way(a)$_N$- fin, wing -es$_V$- long]
tsa'de·ga·wá:ye:s its wing span
span see: bridge
wahs·gó·họh a bridge
spank
ẹh·ya·n'at·sá'e:k he will spank you
[TR+ stem: -(h)na'tsa'eg- spank; consists of: -(h)na'ts(a)$_N$- buttock -(')e$_V$- hit]
ẹhs·ná'tsa'e:k you will spank s.o.
spark see: coal
de·yohs·wẹ·da:nẹ́:yọ:t coals; embers
sparkle
de·yo·jihs·dọ́:nyọ' it is sparkling (eg. like a light in the cat's eyes when it's dark)
[de+yo+ stem: -jihsdọnyọ'- sparkle; consists of: -jihsd(a)$_N$- light -ọnyọ' plural]
sparkle see: shimmer
de·wa·tá·ẹ·dọn·yọh it is twinkling; it is shimmering
spasm see: convulse, cramp
ọg·yéh·nah·sọ:' I had convulsions
ọ·géhs·nag·ri:k I had muscle cramps; I got a cramp

spatula
o·he·nat·ra·ho'dẹ́: de·gak·sa·gẹ́:drọhs a spatula
[consists of: ohenatraho'dẹ: spatula; degaksagẹ:drọhs it scrapes dishes]
o·he·nat·rá·ho'dẹ: a spatula
[o+ stem: -(hr)ẹna'tro'dẹ:- spatula; consists of: -(hr)ena'tr(a)$_N$- knife -o'dẹ:$_V$- type of]
speak
a:gad·wẹ:nọ́:dahk I should use that language
[ad+ stem: -wẹnọda:- speak; consists of: -wẹn(a)$_N$- voice, word -ọda:(h)$_V$- put in, be attached]
speak see: say, speak carelessly, speak sharp words, talk, tell
ẹh·si' you will say
ẹ·géh·ta·ẹ' I will talk
ẹd·wa:tró:wi' we all (incl.) will tell
speak carelessly
he·ji:sẹ:hẹ́h tsọ́: you speak without thinking, spout off
[he+s/j+A+ ... tsọ: just stem: -(w)ẹ:hẹh- speak carelessly; consists of: -(w)ẹhẹh, i, ẹ$_V$- say]
hes·ha·wẹ·hẹ́h tsọ́: he speaks without thinking
hehs·ha·wẹ·hẹ́h gwá'e:' he is speaking without thinking again as usual
[he+s+A+ ... gwa' e:' again stem: -(w)ẹ:hẹh- speak carelessly; consists of: -(w)ẹhẹh, i, ẹ$_V$- say]
speak sharp words
ho·i·hó:ga't he speaks sharp words
[P+ stem: -(r)ihoga'd- speak sharp words; consists of: -(r)ih(wa)$_N$- word -ga'd$_V$- sharp]
o·i·hó:ga't sharp words; harsh words
go·i·hó:ga't she is always bringing up the past, looking for information

Cayuga pronunciation guide: /a/ father /e/ weigh /ẹ/ men (nasalized) /i/ police /o/ hole /ọ/ home (nasalized) /u/ blue. Underlined vowels are voiceless or whispered. /'/ high pitch. /t/ too /d/ do /k/ king /g/ good (never soft g) /j/ judge or adze /s/ soon /sh/ less heat (never the sh in shirt) /sr/ shrine /sy/ sure /hw/ which (the sound made when you blow out a candle) /h/ hi /ts/ cats hide /'/ (the sound before the first vowel in 'uh-uh') /n/ noon /r/ round /w/ way /y/ yes.

spear
a·to·wa'ę́·na'ehs he speared him with a stick
[de+TR+ stem: -(a)'ęna'ehsd- spear with a stick; consists of: -(a)'ęn(a)$_N$- stick, pole, rod -(')ehsd$_V$- hit with an instrument]
dęh·sa'ę·ná'ehs you will spear s.t.

spear see: stab, stick
dęhs·hę·n'at·rá'a:s you will stab s.t.
o'ę́:na' a snowsnake; a pole

spear-fish see: night-fish
ę·hę·na·tahs·rǫ·dáh·na' they (m) will go jack-lighting, spear-fishing

special
gyo·i·ho·wá:nęh the most important
[(g)+(y)o+ stem: -(r)ihowanęh- special, important; consists of: -(r)ih(wa)$_N$- word -owanęh$_V$- be big]
o·i·ho·wá:nęh it is important; a great or worthy commendation; it is special

special see: lucky
sę·dá·ǫ: you are chosen, special, fortunate

specific see: which
ga·ę́ ní:ga:' which one; a specific thing

speck see: decimal point
o·jihs·da·nóhg·wa' decimal point; point; dot

spectator see: witness
ęhs·rih·wag·wá·ih·si' you will be a witness

spectre see: ghost, vision (have a vision)
jíhs·gę: a ghost
ad·wag·yá·ǫn·yo:' a haunted apparition

speculate see: think
ęh·sę·nǫh·dǫ́:nyǫ:' you will wonder, think

speech
ga·wę·nit·gę'ǫ:' a speech
[ga+ stem: -węnitgę'ǫ:'- speech; consists of: -węn(a)$_N$- voice, word -itgę'$_V$- rise]

spell see: write
ęk·yá:dǫ:' I will write

spell (cast a spell) see: bewitch
ę·gǫ·yat·gǫ́'tra:s I will bewitch you

spendthrift
oh·wihs·da·ná'go:' a big spender; a spendthrift
[(o+) stem: -(h)wihsdana'go:'- spendthrift; consists of: -(h)wihsd(a), (hr)ihsd(a)$_N$- metal, money -na'go(w)$_V$- lack a spirit, be ominous]

sperm
de·há'nhǫhs·dǫ:t his testicles
[de+ha+ stem: -(')nhǫhsdǫd- testicles; consists of: -(')nhǫhsd(a)$_N$- sperm -ǫd$_V$- attached]

spew see: flow
wat·na·wí:ne' flowing liquid

sphere see: ball, circle
ę'n·hó:tra' a ball
de·wę'nyahs·gá·ǫni:
(**de·wę'nihs·gá·ǫni:**) a circle

spherical see: round
de·yo·tw'ę·nǫ́:nih it is round

spice see: herb, pepper, salt
de·ga·yehs·dáh·nǫ' a mixture; it is mixed together to make it good (for example, herbs, spices, etc.)
de·yóh·sa·it pepper
o·jí·ke'da' salt

spicy
ga·wę·nah·sa·dá·i·ha'ta' it is hot and peppery (lit.: it heats up your tongue); hot peppers
[ga+ stem: -węnahsadaiha'ta'- spicy, peppery; consists of: -(a)wę'nahs(a), (a)wę'nohs(a)$_N$- tongue -(')daiha'd$_V$- heat up]

spider
ji'á·o:yę: a spider
[stem: -ji'(a:)$_N$- curtain, lace -oyę:$_V$-]

spill
ga·hí·hǫh it is spilled
[stem: -(h)ih$_V$- spill]
spike see: stick
gan·hya' a stick
spiked see: sharp, thorn
oh·yu'tí:yeht it is sharp
o·hí:kda·i:' a thorn bush
spin see: turn around, twirl
dęh·sat·ga̱·ha:de:ni' you will turn yourself around
de·sat·ga̱·ha·den·yǫ́g·wa̱·hǫ: twirl
spin out see: take off
sa·wę́hs·ga:' it spun out
spine see: backbone
ses·hǫh·néh sehs·wę'n'a·géh
ohsg·yę́'da·geh the backbone; the spine
spiral see: curl
de·yó·jitsg·rǫ:t flat curls; flat curls on a basket
spirit
tsę́h sǫn·hé:gye's your spirit
[tsęh that P+ stem: -ǫnhegye's- spirit; consists of: -ǫnhe'$_V$- alive]
spirit see: ghost
jíhs·gę: a ghost
spiritual see: belief
tsę́h hǫ:wéh gyǫg·wéh·da̱h·gǫh our belief; religion
spirits see: liquor
de·ga'ni·gǫ·ha·dé:nyǫhs alcoholic beverages (lit.: mind-altering substance)
spit
sę·ni:tsg·rǫ́:dih spit
[ę+ stem: -nitsgrǫdi- spit; consists of: -(n)itsgr(a)$_N$- saliva -ǫdi, -ǫgy$_V$- throw]
spit see: saliva
otsg·ra' saliva; spit; sputum
splash, splatter
ad·wa·dehs·dá·o:go' it splashed
[de+...ade+ stem: -(h)sdaogw- splash; consists of: -(h)sd(a:)$_N$- drop of water -ogw$_V$- scatter]
de·yo·dehs·dá·o:gwęh it is splashing
ot·ne·go·dá:gwęh splashing water
[o+ at+ stem: -(h)neg(a)$_N$- water, liquid -odagw$_V$- remove, detach]
splint
oh·wę́'ga:' a splint
[o+ stem: -(h)wę'g(a:)$_N$- splint]
ga̱h·wę'ga·ǫ·ní: o·wę́h·ga:' a splint
[consists of: ga̱hwę'gaǫni: it is made into a splint; ohwę'ga:' a splint]
splint see: edge (along the edge)
o·dó'kdag·ye' the rim; the outer and inner rim splint; along the edge
split
ad·wa:dó:wę:' it split
[de+...ad+(N+) stem: -owę(:)$_V$- split in two (from within)]
de·yo:dó:wę' it is split
de·só:wę: halve it
ad·wa·da̱h·yó:wę:' the fruit did split
[de+ad+(N+) stem: -(a)hy(a)$_N$- berry, fruit -owę(:)$_V$- split in two (from within)]
de·yo·da̱h·yó:wę' the fruit is split
at·gó:wę:' I split it open
[de+...N+ stem: -owę(:)$_V$- split in two, cut s.t. in half]
split see: halve, tear
de·só:wę: halve it
ęhs·rá:drǫ:' you will tear, shred it
spoil
ot·gęh it is rotten, decayed; spoilage
[(y)o+(N+) stem: -tgęh$_V$- spoiled, rotten]
ę·yóh·yat·gę' the fruit will spoil
[(y)o+(N+) stem: -(a)hy(a)$_N$- fruit, berry -tgę'$_V$- spoil, go rotten]
ok·sa'da̱hé:tgę' a spoiled child
[o+ stem: -ksa('da)$_N$- child -(hr)etgę'$_V$- evil, bad, ugly]
spoil see: bad
da·wá·teht·gęht it went bad

Cayuga pronunciation guide: /a/ father /e/ weigh /ę/ men (nasalized) /i/ police /o/ hole /ǫ/ home (nasalized) /u/ blue. Underlined vowels are voiceless or whispered. /'/ high pitch. /t/ too /d/ do /k/ king /g/ good (never soft g) /j/ judge or adze /s/ soon /sh/ less heat (never the sh in shirt) /sr/ shrine /sy/ sure /hw/ which (the sound made when you blow out a candle) /h/ hi /ts/ cats hide /'/ (the sound before the first vowel in 'uh-uh') /n/ noon /r/ round /w/ way /y/ yes.

spooked (get spooked) see: vision (have a vision)
ad·wa·gag·yá·ǫ:nyǫ'ˀs I had a vision; I got spooked
spooky see: evil power, haunted
o:nę́h de·ja·go·naˀgó:wahs she is ominous
de·wag·ya·ǫn·yó:taˀ it is haunted
spoon
gan·yó:daˀ a spoon; a canoe; a birch bark canoe
[ga+ stem: -nyod(a)$_N$- spoon, canoe]
sport see: game
at·gáhn·yeht·raˀ sports; games
spot
o·wahg·wá·ǫn·yǫˀ spots
[o+ stem: -(wah)g(wa)$_N$- lump, boil -ǫnyǫˀ plural]
o·jihs·da·nohg·wá·ǫn·yǫˀ spots
[o+ stem: -jihsdanohg(wa)$_N$- spot -ǫnyǫˀ plural]
o·jihn·yo·wá·ǫt it is spotty
[o+ stem: -jihnyowaǫd- spotty; consists of: -jihnyow(a)$_N$- spot -ǫd$_V$- attached]
spot see: decimal point, place
o·jihs·da·nóhg·waˀ a decimal point; a point; a dot
tó: hǫ́:weh a place
spouse see: husband, wife
he·gę́h·jih my husband
ke·gę́h·jih my wife
spout see: water spout
de·gah·ne·gáhk·waˀ a water spout
spray see: fog, sprinkle
ot·sá:daˀ mist; steam
ho·nód·ra̲hs·dǫh they (m) are going along sprinkling; they (m) have sprinkled
spread
ihs·ra:s you spread it on all the time
[stem: -(r)a(:,h)$_V$- spread]
ęhs·ra:ˀ you will spread it
ag·rá·hǫh I did spread it already
ga·hǫh it has been spread on
í:drah spread it on
e·yá:taˀ s.o. spreads it
[stem: -(r)ad, yad, wad- spread s.t.; consists of: -(r)a(:,h)$_V$- spread]
spread news see: broadcast
dę·ha·ih·wá·ęt·wahs he brings forth the message all the time
spring see: A (tsigadehgwideh)
spring see: fountain
tgah·né·go·taˀ a fire hydrant; a fountain
spring water
gyoh·ne·ga·hí·hǫh spring water
[g+yo+ stem: -(h)negahihǫh- spring water; consists of: -(h)neg(a)$_N$- water, liquid -hihǫh$_V$- spill]
sprinkle
ę·hę́·nod·rahs they (m) will sprinkle on
[stem: -odrah$_V$- sprinkle]
hę·nód·ra̲hs·taˀ they (m) sprinkle on
[stem: -odrahsd- sprinkle on; consists of: -odrah$_V$- sprinkle]
ho·nód·ra̲hs·dǫh they (m) are going along sprinkling; they (m) have sprinkled
o·dehs·dá:den·yǫ: it is sprinkling
[o+ (a)de+ stem: -(h)sda:denyǫ:- sprinkle; consists of: -(h)sd(a:)$_N$- drop of water -denyǫˀ$_V$- several existing objects]
sprinkle see: scatter, spread
de·wa·dog·wáh·dǫh it has been spread out, distributed, scattered
e·yá:taˀ s.o. spreads it
sprout
da·o:do·gę́heg·yęˀ it sprouted
[de+... P+ stem: -dogęhegyęˀ- sprout; consists of: -dogę(:)$_V$- right, true]
a·gag·wi·yǫ́:dęˀ it got buds
[stem: -gwiy(a)$_N$- branch, limb, twig -ǫdę$_V$- be attached; sprout]

sprout (continued)
ę·gah·sa̱·he'dǫ́:dę' beans will sprout
[A/P+N+ stem: -(h)sahe'd(a)$_N$- bean -ǫdę$_V$- be attached; sprout]
dǫ·dat·gę·na·teh·dǫ́:goht they (z) sprouted
[dǫda+t+… stem: -(h)ehdǫgohd- sprout; consists of: -(h)ehd(a)$_N$- land, dirt, earth, ground -ǫgohd$_V$- surpass]
sprout see: grow, potato
a·wáh·do:k it sprouted
a·ga'ęh·gó:dę' potato sprouts
sputum see: saliva
ots·gra' saliva; spit; sputum
spy see: G (ho·natk·wę·hę:gye's)
square
ge·í: n'a·de·yo·da·gá·ǫ:de' a square
square see: plaza, town square
tsa'de·ga·ná·da̱·hęh a village square; a village centre; a town square
ǫt·ge·hǫ·dáhk·wa'geh a plaza
squash
ot·sé'do:t hubbard squash
[o+ stem: -(i)tse'dod- belly button, navel, squash; consists of: -(i)tse('da)$_N$- bottle -od$_V$- stand]
gahn·yǫ́h·so' boiled squash
[ga+ stem: -(h)nyǫhs(a)$_N$- melon, squash -o'$_V$- boiled, stewed]
squash see: melon
ohn·yǫ́h·sa' squash; melons
squat
a·ge'no·wá·ę:' I am squatting
[stem: -(ę')nowaę(:)$_V$- squat]
a·sę'no·wá·ę:' you are squatting
sę·ni'jǫ̱hs·gwá·ę·hę' you squat all the time
[stem: -ęni'jǫhsgwaę(:)$_V$- squat]
ę·sę·n'i·jǫ́hs·gwa·ę: you will squat
sę·ni'jǫ̱hs·gwá·ę: squat
squat see: sit
gits·go:t I am sitting
squeal see: scream
dęh·sad·ri̱hs·da:né:ga:' you will burst out screaming, crying; you will make a loud outburst
squeeze
dęhs·dó·ha:k you will squeeze
[de+ad/N/(h)sd+ stem: -hsd$_N$- tool, utensil -ohag$_V$- squeeze]
de·wak·do̱·há:gǫh I am squeezing it
de·ga·do̱·há:gǫh it has been squeezed
dehs·dó·ha:k squeeze it
a·tǫ·wan·yá·o·ha:k s.o. squeezed his neck
[de+TR+ stem: -nyaohag- squeeze s.o.'s neck; consists of: -(h)nya('sa)$_N$- neck, throat -ohag$_V$- squeeze]
squeeze see: pinch
de·sa'ji·dó·ha:k pinch it; squeeze it
squirm see: struggle
ęh·sá·det·sa't you will struggle, squirm to get loose, revolt
squirrel
jo·ní:ts·grǫ:t a squirrel
[j+o+ stem: -nitsgrǫd- squirrel; consists of: -(n)itsgr(a)$_N$- saliva -ǫd$_V$- attached]
kdá:gǫ' grey squirrel, black squirrel
[stem: -kdagǫ'$_N$- black squirrel, grey squirrel; consists of: -kdeh(a)$_N$ - edible root -agǫ: in]
gwa'da: flying squirrel
[stem: -gwa'da:- flying squirrel]
St. Catharines, Ont. see: E (Deg·yot·nǫh·sa:k·dǫ:)
St. Regis see: E (Ahkwesahsne, Gwe·sa̱hs·neh, Og·we·sa̱hs·neh)
stab
deh·se·he·na'tr'aéhs·ta' you stab it repeatedly
[de+TR+ stem: -(hr)ęna'tra'ehsd - stab; consists of: -(hr)ena'tr(a)$_N$- knife -(')ehsd$_V$- hit with an instrument]
de·wa·ge·hę·n'at·ra'ehs·dǫ́·hǫg·ye' I am going along stabbing things

Cayuga pronunciation guide: /a/ father /e/ weigh /ę/ men (nasalized) /i/ police /o/ hole /ǫ/ home (nasalized) /u/ blue. Underlined vowels are voiceless or whispered. /'/ high pitch. /t/ too /d/ do /k/ king /g/ good (never soft g) /j/ judge or adze /s/ soon /sh/ less heat (never the sh in shirt) /sr/ shrine /sy/ sure /hw/ which (the sound made when you blow out a candle) /h/ hi /ts/ cats hide /'/ (the sound before the first vowel in 'uh-uh') /n/ noon /r/ round /w/ way /y/ yes.

stab (continued)
dęhs·he·hę·ná'tra'a:s you will stab s.o. [de+TR+ stem: -(hr)ęna'tra'a:s- stab; consists of: -(hr)ena'tr(a)$_N$- knife -(')a:s, (')i:s$_V$- pierce]
dęhs·hę·n'at·rá'a:s you will stab s.t.
dę·gǫ·hę·ná'tra'ehs I will stab you
stab see: spear
a·tǫ·wa'ę́·na'ehs he speared him with a stick
stable
de·ga·di·dáhs·ta' a stable; a barn; a bus stop
[de+... gadi+ stem: -dahsta'- stable, etc. consists of: -dahsd, dęhsd$_V$- stop s.t., stand s.t. up, prevent s.t.]
de·ga·di·dę́hs·da̱hk·wa' a stable
[de+A+ stem: -dęhsdahkwa'- stable; consists of: -dahsd, dęhsd$_V$- stop s.t., stand s.t. up, prevent s.t.]
stable see: barn
ha·di'drǫ·dáhk·wa' a place where they (m) live; a stable, a barn
stack
dę·sa·d'ę·hó·dę', dęhs·rę'hó:dę' you will stack things, put one thing on top of the other
[de+...(ad+) stem: -(r)ę'hodę- stack things; consists of: -(r)ę'h(a)$_N$- bundle -odę$_V$- stand things up]
dehs·rę́'ho·dę' you stack things up
de·ga·i'ę́·ho:t it is piled up
wa·dę́·hi:' it is stacked
[A+ad+ stem: -ęhi:'- be stacked up; consists of: -(r)ę'h(a)$_N$- bundle -i:'$_V$- stuck onto s.t.]
stack see: pile
on·hóhs·ro:t a pile of s.t.
stadium see: arena
de·ta·di·jihg·w'a̱·éhs·ta' an arena

stagger
hehs·hohs·hę·dá'ǫh tsǫ: he is staggering
[he+... tsǫ: just stem: -(a)hshęda'- step on s.t., stagger consists of: -(a)hsi('da), (ę)hs(a)$_N$- foot -(h)ęda'$_V$- come to lead]
stain see: coloured, dirty, spot
wa̱h·só·hǫ:t it is coloured, dyed
ot·gi' it is ugly, dirty, soiled
o·wahg·wá·ǫn·yǫ' spots
stair
a·dǫ́hn'et·sa', o·dǫ́hn'et·sa' a ladder; stairs
[(a)/o+ stem: -ǫhne'ts(a)$_N$- stair, ladder]
a·dǫhn'ets·há'geh on the stairs
ǫhs·nę́h·ta'geh a thing to descend by; stairs, ladder
[(o+) ad+ stem: -(a)hsnęhta'geh- stairs, ladder; consists of: -(ah)snęhd$_V$- descend]
e·snę́h·da̱hk·wa' you descended or climbed down the stairs, ladder
[o+ stem: -(a)hsnęhdahgw- descend, climb down; consists of: -(ah)snęhd$_V$- descend]
stair
wa·dǫ́h·net·so:t stairs; a ladder
[wa+ad+ stem: -ǫhnetsod- stairs, ladder; consists of: -ǫhne'ts(a)$_N$- ladder -od$_V$- stand]
stake see: gamble, stick
gan·hya' a stick
de·to·dí·yę' they (m) are gambling, betting
stalk see: corn stalk, hunt
o·hé:ya' a corn stalk
ę·ha:dó:wa:t he will hunt
stall see: goat shed, pig pen, stand up
ga·ya'dag·ráhs ga·dí'drǫ' a goat shed
gwihs·gwíhs ga·dí'drǫ' a pig pen
dehs·da' stand up; stop
stammer see: stutter
sa·wę·n'aéhs·ta' you stutter

stamp
ho·wę́:sęh·dǫh (ho·węh·sę́:dǫh) he is keeping a beat with his feet
[(de+) P+ stem: -ęhsędǫh- stamp one's foot; consists of: -(a)hsi(ʼda), (ę)hs(a)$_{N}$- foot -(w)ędǫh$_{V}$- shake s.t.]
de·sęh·sę́:dǫh you are stamping your feet (moving them up and down)
sęh·sę́:dǫh you are tapping your foot
de·yoh·sʼi·dá:ga: to stamp one's feet (lit.: it stamped its feet)
[de+... stem: -(a)hsiʼdaga:- stamp one's feet; consists of: -(a)hsi(ʼda), (ę)hs(a)$_{N}$- foot -ga:$_{V}$- make a rattling or grinding noise]
stampede
de·yot·ji̲ʼéh·ta:ʼ a stampede
[de+yo+at+ stem: -jiʼehta:ʼ- stampede; consists of: -ji$_{N}$- hoof -(ʼ)ehd$_{V}$- hit with s.t.]
de·yo·ęh·dá:staʼ s.t. that makes one run
[de+... stem: -(w)ęhdahsd- stampede, make s.o. run; consists of: -(a)hsi(ʼda), (ę)hs(a)$_{N}$- foot -(w)ęhdahsd$_{V}$- make s.o. run]
ag·yo·nę:dáhs·dęʼ a stampede (lit.: s.t. made them run)
stand
gá:di:t they (z) are standing
[A+ stem: -d$_{V}$- stand]
í:gye:t she is standing over there
í:ga:t it is standing
gahn·yo:t it is standing
[ga+ stem: -(h)nyod- stand; consists of: -(h)ny(a)$_{N}$- stick -od$_{V}$- stand]
stand see: stand in a bunch or group, stand in a line, stand up
stand in a bunch or group
ga·díh·si̲·ha:ʼ they (z) are congregated
[A+ stem: -(h)siha:ʼ$_{V}$- stand in a bunch or group, congregate]
ha·díh·si̲·ha:ʼ they (m) are standing in a group, a clump
gá·eh·si̲·ha:ʼ they (f/m) are standing in a group, a clump
stand in a line
to·di·nę·hę́:deʼ they are standing there (in a line formation); they are guarding
[(de)+d+P+ stem: -nęhędeʼ$_{V}$- go and guard, go stand in a line]
de·to·di·nę·hę́:deʼ they (m) are standing
swa·nę·hęs·rǫ́:nih you all stand in line, a formation
[stem: -nęhęsrǫni- stand in line; consists of: -nęhęsr(a)$_{N}$- line -ǫni, ǫny$_{V}$- make]
stand up, stop
dek·daʼs I stop here (whenever...)
[de+... stem: -daʼ- stand up, stop; consists of: -d$_{V}$- stand]
a·tá:daʼ he stood up
dehs·daʼ stand up; stop
dę·ya·go·daʼǫ·hǫ́:gyeʼ they (f/m) will be standing along (to be born)
[de+... stem: -daʼǫhǫgyeʼ- stand along; consists of: -daʼ$_{V}$- stand up, stop]
stand up see: stop
dęhs·dahs, dęhs·dęhs you will prevent it, stop it, stand it up
standards (have high standards) see: clean
got·gǫ́:nyohs (got·gǫ́:nyǫhs) she has high standards
stapler
de·ga·na̲h·sǫ:taʼ particle (lit.: joiners); stapler
[de+ga+ stem: -nahsǫtaʼ- particle; stapler; consists of: -nahsǫd$_{V}$- join]
ga̲h·ya·dǫhs·ráʼ de·ga·na̲h·sǫ́:taʼ stapler
[consists of: ga̲hyadǫhsraʼ paper; deganǫhsǫ:taʼ stapler]
star
o·jih·sǫ́:da:ʼ a cluster of stars; a star
[o+ stem: -jihsǫd(a)$_{N}$- star]

Cayuga pronunciation guide: /a/ father /e/ weigh /ę/ men (nasalized) /i/ police /o/ hole /ǫ/ home (nasalized) /u/ blue. Underlined vowels are voiceless or whispered. /´/ high pitch. /t/ too /d/ do /k/ king /g/ good (never soft g) /j/ judge or adze /s/ soon /sh/ less heat (never the sh in shirt) /sr/ shrine /sy/ sure /hw/ which (the sound made when you blow out a candle) /h/ hi /ts/ cats hide /ʼ/ (the sound before the first vowel in 'uh-uh') /n/ noon /r/ round /w/ way /y/ yes.

star (continued)

o·jih·sǫ·dáh·si·ha꞉ʼ a group of stars showing
[stem: -jihsǫd(a)$_N$- star, -(h)siha꞉ʼ$_V$- stand in a bunch or group, congregate]

ga·jíhs·dǫg·yeʼ a flaming star; a meteor; a comet
[stem: -jihsd(a)$_N$- light -ǫgyeʼ$_V$- attached]

star see: evening star, morning star

o·jihs·da·nóhg·wa꞉ʼ the evening star; a star

ga·jihs·dǫ·dá꞉haʼ the evening star; the morning star; Venus

starch

wa·tǫ·gá·i꞉staʼ starch
[wa+at+ stem: -(h)ǫgaistaʼ- starch; consists of: -(h)ǫgaihsd$_V$- stiffen]

stare

sat·gahd·rǫ́꞉nihs you are staring at it; examining it closely
[(at+) stem: -gahdrǫni$_V$- stare, gape; consists of: -gah(a)$_N$- eye -ǫny, ǫni$_V$- make]

sa·gahd·rǫ́꞉nihs you are staring at it

sa·gahd·rǫ·níh·ne꞉ʼ you used to stare all the time

sa·gahd·rǫ́꞉ni꞉ you are 'nosy' with your eyes (always looking); gape; stare

stare see: look

haʼsát·gah·toʼ you looked

start see: begin, originate, restart

deh·sáh·sa·węh begin; start

dwa·da꞉dǫ́꞉nih where it starts from

dǫ·da·hah·sá꞉węʼ he restarted

startle

ę·he·yę·neʼwá꞉dęʼ I will startle him
[TR+ ę+ stem: -neʼwa(h)dę- startle s.o., surprise s.o.; consists of: -neʼwaǫ, neʼwa(꞉)$_V$- startled]

ę·ke·yę·neʼwá꞉dęʼ I will startle her

ę·sęʼni·gǫ·ha·néʼwa꞉ you will be mentally startled
[P+ę+ stem: -(ʼ)nigǫha)neʼwa꞉ʼ- be surprised; consists of: -(ʼ)nigǫh(a)$_N$- mind -neʼwaǫ, neʼwa(꞉)$_V$- be startled]

ę·sag·yaʼdá·neʼwa꞉ you will be physically startled
[P+ag+ stem: -yaʼdaneʼwa꞉ʼ- surprised; consists of: -yaʼd(a)$_N$- body -neʼwaǫ, neʼwa(꞉)$_V$- startled]

startle see: frighten

eh·sáhd·rǫhg·węʼ it did frighten you

stash see: store

ę·seh·sę·nǫ́꞉niʼ you will store it

state see: E (province, de·yoh·wę·jah·kah·sǫ꞉gwęh), say

ę·hęʼ he will say

static

de·wa·de·jíhs·do·yʼa꞉s static
[de+wa+ade+ stem: -jihsdoyaʼs- static; consists of: -jihsd(a)$_N$- light -oiʼa꞉s$_V$- torch]

station see: gas station, stereo

ǫt·nǫ·da꞉s·dahk·wáʼgeh a gas station

wad·rę́·no·taʼ a stereo; a radio

statistics see: G (hę·nahs·he꞉dahs o·ih·wa·geh·sǫʼ)

Statistics Canada see: G (Hę·nahs·he꞉dahs O·ih·wa·geh·sǫʼ)

statue see: monument

tgahs·dę́·ho꞉t a monument

stay

a·hát·waʼehs he went to stay there; he was taken in (he had no place else to stay)
[at+ stem: -(h)waʼehsd$_V$- stay somewhere, board somewhere, be homeless]

a·wát·waʼehs it stayed there (for example, a stray dog)

aʼǫ́t·waʼehs she is a transient

he·ya·got·wáʼehs·dǫh she is there for an extended stay

hot·wáʼehs·dǫh he is a boarder, homeless

stay (continued)
got·wáʼehs·do̜h she is a boarder, homeless, a transient
stay see: dwell
nę·yak·nʼid·ró̜:daʼk where we two (excl.) will dwell
steadfast see: uncompromising
de·ya·gʼo·ni·go̜·há:go̜:t she cannot be swayed; she is uncompromising, distinguished
steal
ęhs·nę́hs·goʼ you will steal s.t.
[(N+) stem: -nęhsgw$_{V}$- steal]
steal see: rob
ah·sa·go·náh·seht they robbed her
steam see: fog
ot·sá:daʼ fog; steam; mist
steamer see: boat, bread steamer
ga̲·hó̜:waʼ a boat
e·naʼda:na·wę́h·da̲hk·waʼ a bread steamer
steel see: iron
ga̲hn·yó̜ʼo̜hs·raʼ iron; steel
stem
oʼníhs·daʼ a stem; a berry hull
[o+ stem: -(ʼ)nihsd(a)$_{N}$- stem, hull]
on·yę́:daʼ a stem
[o+ stem: -nyęd(a)$_{N}$- stem]
stench see: smell, stink
ed·rę·no·wá:nęh she has a big smell, odour, scent
gag·rahs it stinks
stenographer see: secretary
eh·yá·do̜·haʼ she is a secretary, stenographer, court recorder, transcriber
step
ęh·sahs·hę́:daʼ you will step on s.t.
[stem: -(a)hshędaʼ- step on s.t.; consists of: -(a)hsi(ʼda), (ę)hs(a)$_{N}$- foot -(h)ędaʼ$_{V}$- come to lead]
step see: doorstep, stair
o̜hs·hę́·da̲hk·waʼ a doorstep
a·dó̜hnʼet·saʼ, o·dó̜hnʼet·saʼ a ladder; stairs
step-relative see: C
hak·no:ʼ my step-father
hehs·no:ʼ your step-son
ho·wá:no:ʼ her step-son
o̜·dá:tno:ʼ her step-daughter
o̜k·no:ʼ my step-mother
shé:no:ʼ your step-daughter
stereo
wad·rę́·no·taʼ a stereo; a radio
[wa+ad+ stem: -ręnotaʼ- stereo, radio consists of: -(r)ęnod$_{V}$- play music]
sterling see: silver
de·yohs·da:téh ga̲h·wíhs·da·no̜:ʼ silver
stern see: demanding, uncompromising
tgę·nó̜h·do̜·haʼ I make the decisions; I am a strict person
de·ya·gʼo·ni·go̜·há:go̜:t she cannot be swayed; she is uncompromising, distinguished
stew see: boil, water
sęn·yá·haʼt boil s.t.
ęhs·naʼjó:dęʼ you will boil
wa̲h·yoʼ cooked fruit; stewed fruit
í:yoʼ it is in the water, submerged in liquid
steward see: waiter
hak·wá·he·haʼ he is a waiter
stick
gan·hyaʼ a stick
[ga+ stem: -(h)ny(a)$_{N}$- stick]
oʼę́:naʼ a snowsnake; a pole
[o+ stem: -(a)ʼęn(a)$_{N}$- stick, pole, rod]
o·waʼnę́:da:s it sticks to it; it adheres to it
[P+waʼ/raʼ/yaʼ/N+ stem: -(raʼ)nęd(a:ʼg), (yaʼ)nęd(a:ʼg)$_{V}$- stick, cling]
a·o·waʼnę́:da:ʼk it is stuck

Cayuga pronunciation guide: /a/ father /e/ weigh /ę/ men (nasalized) /i/ police /o/ hole /o̜/ home (nasalized) /u/ blue. Underlined vowels are voiceless or whispered. /ʼ/ high pitch. /t/ too /d/ do /k/ king /g/ good (never soft g) /j/ judge or adze /s/ soon /sh/ less heat (never the sh in shirt) /sr/ shrine /sy/ sure /hw/ which (the sound made when you blow out a candle) /h/ hi /ts/ cats hide /ʼ/ (the sound before the first vowel in 'uh-uh') /n/ noon /r/ round /w/ way /y/ yes.

stick (continued)
sa·ya'da·nę́·d'a·gǫh your body is stuck to s.t.
[stem: -ya'd(a)$_N$- body -(ra')nęd(a:'g), (ya')nęd(a:'g)$_V$- stick, cling]
sag·ya'da·nę́·da·gǫh cling to it
[ag+ stem: -ya'd(a)$_N$- body -(ra')nęd(a:'g), (ya')nęd(a:'g)$_V$- stick, cling]
stick see: drumstick
eh·wá'es·ta' a drumstick; a baseball bat
stick out see: attach, go out, protrude
á·ǫ:t it is attached; it is sticking out
gyo·yá·g'ęǫh it comes out here; it is sticking out, protruding
he·yá·ǫ:t it protrudes
sticky
ot·séhs·da·e:' it is sticky
[stem: -tsesdaę:'- be sticky; consists of: -tsehsd(a)$_N$- syrup, honey, gum, rubber -ę$_V$- lie on the ground]
et·séhs·d'a·ta' s.t. that sticks
[e+ stem: -tsehsda'd- stick; consists of: -tsehsd(a)$_N$- syrup, honey, gum, rubber -d$_V$- stand]
e·ya:nę·dák·dahk·wa' s.t. that makes things stick
[P+wa'/ra'/ya'/N+ stem: -(ra')nęd(a:'g), (ya')nęd(a:'g)$_V$- stick, cling]
stiff
wa·tǫ́·ga·i:s it stiffens up all the time
[at+ stem: -(h)ǫgai$_V$- stiff]
a·wa·tǫ·gá·i: it did stiffen up
o·tǫ́·ga·i: it is stiff; rigor mortis
still see: I, ahsǫh, quiet
ta'de·yó:gyę: quietness; quiet; stillness
stillborn
de·a·gǫn·hé:gye' she was stillborn; she came to be not living
[de'+ not P+ stem: -ǫnhegye'- be stillborn; consists of: -ǫnhe'$_V$- be alive]

sting see: inflamed
o'náh·gǫ:t it (skin) is inflamed; a bee sting
stingy
sa·ní'ǫh you are stingy, greedy, cheap
[P+ stem: -ni'ǫh$_V$- stingy, greedy, cheap]
o·ní'ǫh it is stingy
go·ní'ǫh she is stingy
sa·ní'ǫh·ne:' you used to be stingy
stingy see: frugal, value
de·sa·nǫh·yá:ni:s you're stingy; you do not want to share
sa·nǫ́hs·de' you value it; you are stingy
stink
gag·rahs it stinks
[A+(N+) stem: -grahs$_V$- stink]
gya̱h·sí'dag·rahs we two (incl.) have smelly feet
[stem: -(a)hsi('da), (ę)hs(a)$_N$- foot -grahs$_V$- stink]
ga̱h·náht·sag·rahs a bum smells
[stem: -(h)na'ts(a)$_N$- buttock -grahs$_V$- stink]
ga·di·j'ǫ·dá:grahs they (z) smell like fish
[stem: -(i)jǫ'd(a)$_N$- fish -grahs$_V$- stink]
g'en·hǫ́hs·dag·rahs my armpits smell
[stem: -(')nhǫh(s)d(a)$_N$- armpit -grahs$_V$- stink]
ha·yáhk·wag·rahs he has smelly pants
[stem: -yahk(wa)$_N$- pants -grahs$_V$- stink]
gy'a·dá:grahs my body smells
[stem: -ya'd(a)$_N$- body -grahs$_V$- stink]
ha·yę́'gwag·rahs he smells like smoke
[stem: -yę'g(wa)$_N$- tobacco, smoke, cigarettes -grahs$_V$- stink]
stir
de·gá·węn·yeh I stir all the time
[de+... stem: -(a)wenye(:)$_V$- stir, mix]
dę·gá·węn·ye:' I will stir

stir (continued)
de·wa·ga·wę́:nyeˀ I am stirring
deh·sá·węn·ye:ˀ beat, mix, stir it
stock exchange, stock market see: G (dẹ·hẹ·nat·wihs·da·de:nyọhs)
stockpile see: store
ę·seh·sę·nọ́:niˀ you will store it
stoke a fire see: fire
de·se·jihs·dá·węn·ye: stoke the fire
stomach
gek·wá:hk·waˀ my stomach (lit.: where I put the food)
[A+ stem: -kwahkwaˀ- stomach; consists of: -k(wa)$_N$- food -(h)gw$_V$- lift, pick up]
ek·wá:hk·waˀ a stomach
stomach see: belly, guts
ok·séˀdaˀ a belly
o·yọ́:waˀ guts; intestines
stomach ache
a·gek·sˀe·dá·nọh·wa:s I have a stomach ache
[P+N+ stem: -kseˀd(a)$_N$- belly -nọhwag$_V$- sore, ache]
stone
gahs·gwa:ˀ a stone; a rock; a boulder; a bullet
[ga+ stem: -(h)sg(wa:)$_N$- stone, bullet, rock]
stone see: gravel
ni·gahs·gwa·ó:sˀuh small gravel; pebbles
stool see: chair, foot stool
ak·yẹ́·dahk·waˀ, ag·yẹ́·dahk·waˀ a chair
de·yọh·sˀi·dá·hahk·waˀ a foot stool
stoop see: bend
de·sát·saˀge:t bend forwards
stop
a·tá:dahs he stopped it, prevented it
[de+… stem: -dahsd, dẹhsd- stop s.t., stand s.t. up, prevent s.t. consists of: -d$_V$- stand]
dá:ha·dahs he would try and stop s.t.
dẹhs·dahs, dẹhs·dẹhs you will prevent, stop it; stand it up
dehs·dahs stop it
a·gahs·dá·ę·daˀ it stopped raining
[stem: -(a)hsdaędaˀ- stop raining; consists of: -(h)sd(a:)$_N$- drop of water -ędaˀ$_V$- finish]
stop see: quit, stand up, visit
a·gẹ́·ni·hẹˀ I stopped, quit
dehs·daˀ stand up; stop
ę·gag·yọ·sé·haˀ I am going to go and visit
store
sẹh·sę:nọ́:nih you are storing it right now
[stem: -(h)sęnọni$_V$- store, put away]
ę·seh·sę·nọ́:niˀ you will store it
gah·sę:nọ́:ni: stored items
gah·sę·nọn·yáh·nọˀ stored items; it is put away
sẹh·sę:nọ́:nih store it; put it away
sa·dahg·wá·ę:hęˀ you store things all the time
[ad+ stem: -(a)hgwaę:$_V$- store]
a·sa·dahg·wá·ę:ˀ you did store it
sa·dáhg·wa·ę:ˀ store it; hold on to it temporarily
ga·ọ·ga·dahg·wá·ę:nih they (f/m) always leave it for me to store temporarily
[ad+ stem: -(a)hgwaęni$_V$- store for s.o.]
ọ·dẹh·ní:nọh a store; a storekeeper
[(g+y)ọ+adẹ+ stem: -(h)ninọh- store, grocery store; storekeeper; consists of: -(h)ninọ$_V$- buy]
gyọ·dẹh·ní:nọh a grocery store
store see: accumulate
ęh·sa·dad·ro·hé:gęˀ you will accumulate (things, ideas, etc.) for yourself

Cayuga pronunciation guide: /a/ father /e/ weigh /ę/ men (nasalized) /i/ police /o/ hole /ọ/ home (nasalized) /u/ blue. Underlined vowels are voiceless or whispered. /´/ high pitch. /t/ too /d/ do /k/ king /g/ good (never soft g) /j/ judge or adze /s/ soon /sh/ less heat (never the sh in shirt) /sr/ shrine /sy/ sure /hw/ which (the sound made when you blow out a candle) /h/ hi /ts/ cats hide /ˀ/ (the sound before the first vowel in 'uh-uh') /n/ noon /r/ round /w/ way /y/ yes.

storekeeper

ha·dęh·ní:nǫh he is a storekeeper
[A+adę+ stem: -(h)ninǫh- store, grocery store; storekeeper; consists of: -(h)ninǫ$_V$- buy]

storm

a·wá·det·giht it was bad weather, stormy
[ade+ stem: -tgihd- turn ugly, bad, dirty; consists of: -tgi$_V$- dirty, ugly]
o·dét·gih·dǫh it is storming right now

story see: tale, hear a story

o'ga:' a parable; a tale; a story; a legend
ę·se·gá:hǫ:k you will hear a story

stout see: fat

ho·hsę:' he is fat

stove

hǫh·ji a stove
[stem: -hǫhji- stove; consists of: -ji(:,h)$_V$- dark]
oh·sǫ·wa̱h·da·da·i:hę́:
ga·nǫh·sa·da·i·há'tra' an electric stove
[consists of: ohsǫwa̱hdadai:hę: electricity; ganǫhsadaiha'tra' stove]
o·wa:de:gáhs ga·nǫh·sa·da·i·há'tra' a gas stove
[consists of: owa:de:gahs it burns gas; ganǫhsadaiha'tra' stove]
e·kǫn·ya'tá'
ga·nǫh·sa·da·i·há'da̱hk·wa' a cook stove
[consists of: ekǫnya'ta' what one cooks with; ganǫhsadaiha'da̱hkwa' it is used to warm up the house]
ga·nǫh·sa·da·i·há'ta' a stove
[ga+ stem: -nǫhsadaiha'ta'- stove; consists of: -nǫhs(a)$_N$- house -(')daih$_V$- hot]
o·yę:dá' ga·nǫh·sa·da·i·hát·ra' a wood stove
[consists of: oyę:da' wood, firewood; ganǫhsadaiha'tra' stove]
o·yę:dá' wa·dǫ́:twahs a wood stove
[consists of: oyę:da' wood, firewood; wadǫ:twahs it is used up]

straight

o·de·dag·wá·ih·sǫ: it is straight
[o+ade+ stem: -d(a)$_N$- way -gwaihs(i)$_V$- be straight]
hęh·sa·dag·wá·ih·saht you will go straight
[he+P+ stem: -dagwaihsahd- go straight; consists of: -d(a)$_N$- way -gwaihs(i)$_V$- straight]

straight pin see: pin

ga·jí·ho·ha:', o·jí·ho·ha:' a straight pin; a pin; a brooch; a safety pin

straighten

ęhs·dag·wá·ih·si' you will straighten
[da/N+ stem: -d(a)$_N$- way -gwaihs(i)$_V$- straighten]
ho·di·dag·wá·ihs·hǫ: they (m) keep straight the ways
hę·nah·ga:gwá·ihs·hǫhs they (m) are straightening out the splint
[da/N+ stem: -(a)hg(a:)$_N$- splint -gwaihs(i)$_V$- straight]
ha·di·nehs·da:gwá·ihs·hǫhs they (m) are straightening out the board
[da/N+ stem: -nehsd(a:)$_N$- floor, board -gwaihs(i)$_V$- straight]

strain

ęhs·nǫ·wa·dé·ni' you will strain
[stem: -(h)nawadeni- strain; consists of: -(h)naw(a), (h)nǫw(a)$_N$- running water -deni, deny$_V$- change]
ga·nǫ·wa·dé:nyǫ: it is being strained

strain see: filter

dęh·sne:gǫ́:goht you will filter, strain liquid

strand see: thread

oh·sí:ya' a thread; a string; a cord

strange

og·yá:nǫhk it is strange, bizarre
[o+ag+ stem: -yanǫhg- strange, bizarre; consists of: -yanǫ'$_V$- dream]

strange see: unusual
ti·yó·tʼah it is queer, unusual, odd
stranger
ni·ta·wé·nọh a male stranger; he's that age (lit.: where he comes from)
[ni+d+P stem: -enọh- stranger; consists of: -enọ$_V$- originate from someplace, come from someplace]
ni·ja·go·wé·nọh a female stranger (lit.: where she comes from)
ti·yọg·wʼe·dá·deʼ a stranger
[ti+yọ+ stem: -ọgweʼdadeʼ- stranger; consists of: -ọgwe(ʼda)$_N$- person -deʼ$_V$- exist; be different]
strangle see: choke
dẹ·héhs·họn·yaʼk you will strangle him
strap see: burden strap, harness, rope
dẹ·sat·noʼá·nhaʼ you will have a burden strap
wa·deʼnheh·só·dahk·waʼ a harness (for an animal)
gá·ts·gʼẹ·daʼ a rope
strategize see: plan
ẹ·jad·rih·wáh·sʼa:ʼ you two will plan, make a plan
straw
ohs·tọ́·draʼ straw
[o+ stem: -(h)stọdr(a)$_N$- straw, hay]
straw hat see: hat
ohs·tọd·ráʼ a·na·há·ọ·traʼ a straw hat
strawberry
jih·sọ́·dahk strawberry
[stem: -jihsọdahk$_N$- strawberry]
stray
a·gẹ·na·tá·ha·goʼ they (z) turned off the road
[at+ stem: -(h)ahagw- stray, turn off; consists of: -(h)ah(a)$_N$- road -(r)agw$_V$- choose, take out]
ẹh·sa·ta·há·goʼ you will stray, go off the road, turn into your driveway
tí·wehs a stray (animal)
[ti+w+ stem: -eʼs- stray animal; consists of: -e$_V$- go; go astray]
stray see: roam, wander, wild
ti·ga·e·né·nọg·yeʼs they (f) are roaming about
ẹ́: tsọ́h ẹt·seʼ you will wander
wa·dad·wẹ·ní·yoʼ a wild animal
stream
gi·hẹ́·den·yọʼ streams; rivers; creeks
[consists of: -gihẹ(k)$_N$- river, stream, creek -denyọʼ$_V$- several existing things]
ẹ·gi·hẹ·dé·nyọk there will be streams, rivers
stream see: river
gi·hẹ́·deʼ a creek; a river; a stream
street see: road
o·há·deʼ an existing road
street car
o·daʼẹ·ná·he:ʼ a street car
[o+ad+ stem: -(a)ʼẹnahe:ʼ- street car; consists of: -(a)ʼẹn(a)$_N$- stick, pole, rod -(h)e:ʼ$_V$- sitting up on top of s.t.]
strength (use one's strength)
ga·des·hahs·dọ́·haʼ I use my strength
[ade+ stem: -sha(h)sdọh- use one's strength; consists of: -sha(h)sdọh$_V$- become strong]
ẹh·sadʼes·há·s·dọh you will use your strength
strength see: power
gahs·háhs·dẹhs·raʼ, ohs·háhs·dẹhs·raʼ power; strength
strengthen see: double
dẹhs·náʼnetʼa:ʼ you will double it, reinforce it, line it
strenuous see: difficult
wẹ́·do:ʼ it is difficult
stretch
de·ya·go·dí·yọ·t she is stretching it
[de+ad/N+ stem: -(i)yọd$_V$- stretch]
de·ho·dí·yọ·t he is stretching it
de·yo·dí·yọ·t it is stretched

Cayuga pronunciation guide: /a/ father /e/ weigh /ẹ/ men (nasalized) /i/ police /o/ hole /ọ/ home (nasalized) /u/ blue. Underlined vowels are voiceless or whispered. /ʹ/ high pitch. /t/ too /d/ do /k/ king /g/ good (never soft g) /j/ judge or adze /s/ soon /sh/ less heat (never the sh in shirt) /sr/ shrine /sy/ sure /hw/ which (the sound made when you blow out a candle) /h/ hi /ts/ cats hide /ʼ/ (the sound before the first vowel in 'uh-uh') /n/ noon /r/ round /w/ way /y/ yes.

stretch see: reach
de·sé·nęt·se:s stretch out your arms; reach
strew see: scatter
de·wa·dog·wáh·dǫh it has been spread out, distributed, scattered
strict see: demanding
tgę·nǫ́h·dǫ·ha' I make the decisions; I am a strict person
stride see: walk
dę·gá·ta·hahk I will walk
strike see: hit, punch, pound, slap
ęhs·wá'e:k you will pound, tap it
a·há·gǫ·he:k he punched it
se·teht pound it (corn, etc.)
ęh·set·rag·wę́'da̲'e:k you will slap it on the cheek
strikers
de̲·ho·di·nę́·hę:' they (m) are guarding s.t. (for example, strikers); security guards
[de+P+ stem: -nęhę:'- strikers; consists of: -nęhę(:)$_V$- guard, stand in a line]
string
e·ni·há·ǫ·ha' she is stringing
[stem: -nihaǫ- string s.t.; consists of: -niha$_N$- -(r)ǫ$_V$- bead s.t.]
ha·ni·há·ǫ·ha' he is stringing
ga·ní·ha·ǫ:' it is strung
string see: line, thread
oh·sí:yǫ:t an attached cord, string; an umbilical cord
oh·sí:ya' a thread; a string; a cord
string bean see: bean
oh·sa·he'dá:se: string beans (yellow, green)
string instrument see: guitar
ga·nó:wa' guitar; any string instrument
string up
ik·da:s I am stringing it, draping it
[stem: -dahsd, dęhsd- string s.t. up, drape s.t.; consists of: -d$_V$- stand]

stripe
o·ha·hęh·dáh·nǫh stripes; it is patterned
[o+ stem: -(h)ahęhdahnǫh$_V$- be striped, patterned]
o·jih·ne·wá·ǫn·yǫ', o·jih·no·wá·ǫn·yǫ' stripes
[o+ stem: -jihnew(a)$_N$- stripe -ǫnyǫ' plural]
o·jih·ne·wá·e' it has stripes
[o+ stem: -jihnew(a)$_N$- stripe -ę$_V$- lie on the ground]
strive see: struggle, try
ęh·sá·det·sa't you will struggle, squirm to get loose, revolt
a:ga·de'nyę́:dę' I might try, attempt it
stroke see: caress
ęs·ya'da̲hd·rǫ́:go' you will caress a pet
stroke (have a stroke)
ǫ·gehs·gę́·na:' I had a stroke
[P+ stem: -(h)sgęna:'- have a stroke; consists of: -(h)sgęn(a)$_N$- stroke -a:'$_V$- hold, contain, include]
a·gohs·gę́:na:' she had a stroke
a·hohs·gę́:na:' he had a stroke
stroll see: walk
dę·gá·ta·hahk I will walk
stroller see: carriage
o·wi:ya:'áh ǫt·nǫ́·da̲hs·ta' a baby carriage; a stroller
strong
ge·jí:nah I am strong
[A+ stem: -jinah$_V$- strong, brave]
gahs·há:sde' it is strong, tough, powerful
[A+(N+) stem: -sha(h)sde'$_V$- be strong, tough, powerful]
ęd·wag·ya·dah·ní:ya:t we all will be strong in body
[ag+ stem: -ya'dahniya'd- strong; consists of: -ya'd(a)$_N$- body -(h)niya'd$_V$- harden, toughen]

strong (continued)
ak·ni·gǫ·hah·níːyǫh I have a strong mind
[P+ stem: -(ʼ)nigǫhahniyǫh- have a strong mind; consists of: -(ʼ)nigǫh(a)$_N$- mind -(h)niyǫh$_V$- be hard, tough]

strong-smelling
gad·rę·nahs·háːsdeʼ it is a strong smell; it is strong-smelling
[ga+ stem: -drę n(a)$_N$- smell -sha(h)sdeʼ$_V$- strong, etc.]

strong-willed see: strong
ak·ni·gǫ·hah·níːyǫh I have a strong mind

struggle
sa·dét·saʼtaʼ you struggle all the time
[ade+ stem: -tsaʼd$_V$- struggle, revolt]
ęh·sá·det·saʼt you will struggle, squirm to get loose, revolt
sa·déʼtsaʼdǫh you are going along struggling

stub see: trip
de·sah·sʼig·yáʼks·gǫː you are always stumbling, tripping, stubbing your toe; you are a klutz

stubborn see: balk
god·rǫ́h·yaʼt she is unwilling, stubborn

stuck
o·waʼnę·dáːgoː it is stuck on s.t.
[o+waʼ/raʼ/yaʼ/N+ stem: -nędagoː$_V$- be stuck on s.t.; consists of: -(raʼ)nęd(aːʼg), (yaʼ)nęd(aːʼg)$_V$- stick, cling]
o·héh·da·iːʼ earth is stuck to it
[o+ stem: -(h)ehd(a)$_N$- land, dirt, earth, ground -iːʼ$_V$- stuck onto s.t.]
ga·gę́ʼdǫːʼ it is stuck under s.t. but it is removable (for example, a piece of gum under a table); it is stuck on s.t. else (for example, on a wall)
[ga+ stem: -gęʼdoːʼ$_V$- be stuck onto s.t.]

stuck up
wa·dat·gǫn·yǫ́hs·taʼ she (lit.: it) is stuck up
[adat+ stem: -gǫnyǫhstaʼ- stuck up, snobbish; consists of: -gǫnyǫhsd$_V$- honour s.o.]

stud see: beam
gá·ǫ·da·deʼ a beam

study see: investigate, learn
ęhs·ríh·wih·saːk you will investigate, inquire
ęh·sa·de·wáːyęːs you will learn

stuff see: fill up
ę·gá·nǫn·heʼ it will fill up

stumble see: trip
de·sah·sʼig·yáʼks·gǫː you are always stumbling, tripping, stubbing your toe; you are a klutz

stump
ok·jíːnaʼ a stump; knots in a tree
[o+ stem: -kjin(a)$_N$- stump]
ok·jiːnóːdǫʼ stumps; knots in a tree
[o+ stem: -kjin(a)$_N$- stump -odǫʼ$_V$- several standing objects]

stun see: numb
aʼót·sihs·dęh it got numb

stupefy see: startle
ę·he·yę·neʼwáːdęʼ I will startle him

stupid
de·saʼni·gǫ́·haːt you are stupid, foolish
[deʼ+ not P+ stem: -(ʼ)nigǫhad- smart; stupid, foolish, ignorant; consists of: -(ʼ)nigǫh(a)$_N$- mind -d$_V$- stand]
de·hoʼni·gǫ́·haːt he is ignorant, unthinkingly foolish

sturdy see: strong
gahs·háːsdeʼ it is strong, tough, powerful

sturgeon
sgat·séhs·daʼ sturgeon
[s+ga+ stem: -tsehsdaʼ- sturgeon; consists of: -tsehsd(a)$_N$- syrup, honey, gum, rubber]

Cayuga pronunciation guide: /a/ father /e/ weigh /ę/ men (nasalized) /i/ police /o/ hole /ǫ/ home (nasalized) /u/ blue. Underlined vowels are voiceless or whispered. /ʹ/ high pitch. /t/ too /d/ do /k/ king /g/ good (never soft g) /j/ judge or adze /s/ soon /sh/ less heat (never the sh in shirt) /sr/ shrine /sy/ sure /hw/ which (the sound made when you blow out a candle) /h/ hi /ts/ cats hide /ʼ/ (the sound before the first vowel in 'uh-uh') /n/ noon /r/ round /w/ way /y/ yes.

stutter
sa·wę·n'aéhs·ta' you stutter
[P+ stem: -węna'ehsd- stutter; consists of: -węn(a)$_N$- voice, word -(')ehsd$_V$- hit with an instrument]
sty (have a sty)
a·ge·ga·hág·wa·ǫ:t I have a sty
[P+ stem: -gahagwaǫd- have a sty; consists of: -gahag(wa)$_N$- sty -ǫd$_V$- be attached]
stylus see: pen
gah·ne:gá:' eh·yá·dǫhk·wa' a pen
subdue see: overpower
ęhs·he's·hę́:ni' you will overpower s.o. (physically)
submerge
ę·sáh·do:' you will submerge s.t.
[TR+ stem: -(a)hdo(:)$_V$- dive; submerge s.t.]
ę·wáh·do:' it will submerge s.t.
submerge see: dip, flood, immerse, water
he·wá·gǫ·hǫh I have already dipped, submerged it
a·węh·nó:dǫ' a flood; it flooded
ęh·sád'es·goh you will go into the water
í:yo' it is in the water, submerged in liquid
subordinate see: assistant
gǫn·há'tra' s.o.'s assistant
subsidy see: G (hǫ·wa·dih·wihs·da·wihs)
substance see: contained
í:wa:t it is contained; it (z) is in there; solid matter
substantial see: special
o·i·ho·wá:nęh it is important; a great or worthy commendation; it is special
substitute see: replace
ti·gǫ́:nihs I use s.t. in place of s.t. else
substructure see: foundation
ga·nǫh·sa·gę́d·rah·gǫh the foundation (of a building)

subtract
tsǫ'nehs you subtract, take away all the time
[de+(N+) stem: -ǫ'n(eg)$_V$- remove, take away; subtract s.t.]
ęt·sǫ́'ne:k you will subtract
di·sǫ́'nǫ: you have taken away
dah·sǫ́'ne:k subtract it
succeed see: able
ęh·se:gwé:ni' you will succeed
sucker
ohs·wá:tgęhs a black sucker (fish)
[o+ stem: -(a)hswatgęhs- black sucker; consists of: -(a)hs(t)wahd$_V$- extinguish, dim]
ga·di's·gwá·o:he:s a Stonegather sucker (fish)
[gadi+ stem: -(h)sgwaohes- Stonegather sucker; consists of: -(h)sg(wa:)$_N$- stone, bullet, rock -(r)oheg$_V$- gather]
at·sók·wah·da' a big-headed sucker
[at+ stem: -(h)sohg(wa)$_N$- lip -d$_V$- stand]
o·nǫ·há·i:yoh a white sucker (fish)
[o+ stem: -nǫhaiyoh- white sucker; consists of: -nǫh(a)$_N$- scalp -iyo$_V$- be nice, good]
sudden see: unexpected
o·né·wa·ǫ: s.t. unexpected, surprising
suddenly
da·wę́:nǫhk sudden; all of a sudden
[d+a+w+ stem: -nǫhg$_V$- be sudden]
tó: hé:yoht suddenly
[to: there he'+yo+ stem: -(a)hd$_V$- like, resemble; suddenly]
tóh tga·nǫ́h·sa·de' suddenly the house appeared
[toh there t+ga+ stem: -nǫhs(a)$_N$- house -de'- exist; suddenly appear]
suddenly see: I (o:nęgwa')
suds see: head
oh·wę́'sdo:t a head (of foam on beer)

suffer

de·sa·dę·hǫ́·ga·i:s you suffer all the time [de+P+adę+ stem: -(h)ǫgai, (h)ǫgany$_V$- suffer]

dęh·sa·dę·hǫ́·ga·i' you will suffer

dę·sa·dę·hǫ́·gan·yęh you are suffering right now

de·sę'ni·gǫ́h·ga·e' you suffer [de'+ not ...ę+ stem: -(')nigǫhgaę- suffer; consists of: -(')nigǫh(a)$_N$- mind -gaę$_V$- willing]

suffer see: ache, pain

ag·ya'da·nǫ́h·wa:s I am sore; I ache

ęg·rǫ́h·ya·gę' I will be in pain; I will labour; I will be in agony

sufficient see: able, I (To tsǫ:), enough

ę·ga:gwé:ni' it can be; that is enough

a·ság·ye·niht you got enough

suffocate see: choke

de·sáh·si̱·ha's you are choking

sugar

na·wę́'da' sugar [stem: -(rę)nawę'd(a)$_N$- sugar, candy]

sugar bowl

e·ya:na·w'ę·dáhkwa' a sugar bowl [e+ stem: -ya:nawę'dahkwa' - sugar bowl; consists of: -(rę)nawę'd(a)$_N$- sugar, candy]

suggest

ęt·sę'ni·go·hó:dę' you will suggest, present an idea [de+...ę+ stem: -(')nigǫhod- suggest, advise; consists of: -(')nigǫh(a)$_N$- mind -od$_V$- stand]

ęt·se·y'ę·ni·gǫ̱·hó:tahs you will suggest to her, advise her [de+TR+ę+ stem: -(')nigǫhotahsd- suggest, advise; consists of: -(')nigǫh(a)$_N$- mind -odahsd$_V$- cause to stand]

suggest see: counsel, present

ho·ha·hah·sę́·hęg·ye' he is counselling

ęhs·ríh·wa̱·hę' you will present an idea

suicide

a·wa·dad·ríh·wa̱h·dǫ't suicide (lit.: s.o. did away with himself, herself) [adad+ stem: -(r)ihwahdǫ'd- suicide; consists of: -(r)ih(wa)$_N$- word -(a)hdǫ'd$_V$- cause to lose, disappear]

a·wa·dad·rí:yo' it killed itself; suicide [adad+ stem: -(r)iyo, nyo$_V$- kill s.t.; commit suicide]

a·ha·dad·rí:yo' he killed himself (on purpose)

suitable see: right

tga:yé:i: it is right, correct

suitcase see: wallet

gatg·wę́'da' a wallet; a purse; a pocketbook; a suitcase

sulk see: grudge, testy

sa·tíy'a·gǫh you are holding a grudge right now

sa·tí·y'as·gǫ: you hold grudges; you get angry easily

sum

ę·gá:go' a sum; a total [ę+ga+ stem: -gw$_V$- gather, pick, get]

sum see: add, count

hęt·yehs you will add

ęd·wáhs·he:t we all (incl.) will count

sumac

ot·gó'da' sumac [o+ stem: -tgo'd(a)$_N$- sumac]

ot·gwęh·j'i·á' **ot·gó'da'** red sumac [consists of: otgwęhj'ia:' red; otgo'da' sumac]

summer

gęn·héh·ge̱·ha:' the summer type [stem: -gęnh(a)$_N$- summer -geha:'- type]

gęn·hag·wé:gǫh all summer [stem: -gęnh(a)$_N$- summer -gwegǫh$_V$- all]

gagę·nhí:s ǫhne: it was a long summer [consists of: gagęnhis a long summer; ǫhne:' maybe][ga+ stem: -gęnh(a)$_N$- summer -is$_V$- long]

summer see: A (gęnhehneh)
summit see: top
hé:tgęh.jih the very top
summon see: command, invite
ęhs.hé:nha' you will command, hire her
ęhs.he.hǫ.gá.ǫ' you will invite her, them
sun
ga:gwá:gye's the sun and moon
[ga+ stem: -(r)agwagye's- sun, moon; consists of: -(r)ag(wa)$_N$- sun, moon -gye$_V$- fly]
sun dog
od.ráhg.wa:' a sun dog
[o+ad+ stem: -(r)ahg(wa:)$_N$- sun dog]
de.yod.rahg.wá:dǫ' a sun dog; a circle around the moon or sun (indicating bad weather)
[de+yo+ad+ stem: -rahgwa:dǫ'- sun dog; consists of: -(r)ahg(wa:)$_N$- sun dog -dǫ'$_V$- several standing objects]
Sunday see: A (A.wę.da.do.gę:dǫh)
Sunday best see: clothes
ǫg.ya'dahs.rǫn.y'a.tá' ahg.wę́:nya' dress clothes; Sunday best
sundown
he.gáhg.wę's towards the setting sun, the direction of the sunset, west
[he'+ga+ stem: -(h)gwę$_V$- set]
sundown see: set
ha'gáhg.wę' sunset; the sun went down
sunlight see: sunshine
o.dę́.ha.o:t sunshine
sunrise
tgá:gwit.gę's east (direction); the sun rises there
[(t+)... stem: -(r)agwitgę'(s)- sunrise, east; consists of: -(r)ag(wa)$_N$- sun, moon -itgę'$_V$- rise]
da.ga:gwi:tgę' sunrise; the sun did rise
tga:gwit.gę́'s.geh the east (where the sun rises)
[(d+)... stem: -(r)agwitgę'(s)- sunrise, east; consists of: -(r)ag(wa)$_N$- heavenly body -itgę'$_V$- rise -'geh on]
ha.de.wat.só:twahs towards the sunset (a direction)
[ha'de+w+at+ stem: -(h)sotw$_V$- jump, hop; sunset]
sunset see: set
ha'gáhg.wę' sunset; the sun went down
sunshine
o.dę́.ha.o:t sunshine
[o+ stem: -dęh(a)$_N$- sunshine -od$_V$- stand]
o.dę.há.i:yo: nice sunshine
[o+ stem: -dęh(a)$_N$- sunshine -iyo:$_V$- be nice, good]
od.rǫ́h.yo:t a sunbeam; a ray of light; sunshine
[o+ ad+ stem: -(rǫ)'nih(a)$_N$- rainbow, sunbeam, ray -od$_V$- stand]
sun-tan
sa.dę́.hę:k you are getting a sun tan
[A+adę+ stem: -(h)ę:g- sun-tan; consists of: -hę(:)$_V$- dry]
e.sá.dę.hę:k you got a tan
superficial see: shallow, unimportant
ni.yoh.no.dá:k'ah it is shallow
ni.yo.i.hú:'uh it is of little importance
superintendant see: oversee
hod.rih.wat.gá.ha:',
hod.rih.wát.ga.ha:' he is a supervisor, overseer
superior
he:tgę́' tgá:de' it is superior
[consists of: he:tgę' above; tga:de' it is sticking out]
superior see: exceptional
á.ǫ.gǫh.dǫh exceptional; above average; too much
supervise see: oversee
hod.rih.wat.gá.ha:' he is a supervisor, overseer

supper see: tea meeting, serve a meal
gak·wá·he:ʼ tea meetings; supper
ę·yag·wa·dék·wa·hęʼ we all (excl.) will put on a meal, supper

support
a·héh·wa·waʼs I agree with him, support him
[TR+ stem: -(h)wawaʼs_V- support]
heh·wá·wʼa·sehk I used to support him, agree with him
heh·wa·wʼa·seh I did agree with him, support him
ę·hehs·rih·wá:waʼs you will back up his ideas
[TR+ stem: -(r)ihwawaʼs- support s.o., back s.o.; consists of: -(r)ih$(wa)_N$- word -(h)wawaʼs_V- support]
ęhs·héh·wa·waʼs you will back her up
ęh·sehs·waʼné:dęʼ you will back up s.t. (that is, reinforce it)
[TR+ stem: -(h)swaʼned(ę)- support s.o., s.t., agree with s.o., back s.o.; consists of: -(h)swaʼn(a), (h)sweʼ$n(a)_N$- back, upper -d_V- stand]
ęhs·hes·wʼa·né:dęʼ you will back her up
a·hehs·wʼa·né:dęʼ I supported him
sehs·wáʼne:t you are supporting, backing them
hehs·wáʼne:t I support, back him
a·hehs·waʼné:tʼa:ʼ I supported him
[TR+ stem: -(h)swaʼnetʼa:ʼ- support s.o., s.t., agree with s.o., back s.o.; consists of: -(h)swaʼn(a), (h)sweʼ$n(a)_N$- back, upper -d_V- stand]
hǫ·wa·dihs·wáʼne·taʼ they support them
a·ga·ǫ·gehs·waʼné:tʼa:ʼ they supported me

support see: advocate, help
ha·dihs·waʼné:tʼa:ʼ they (m) are advocates, backers, supporters
ga·ǫ·dag·ye·na·wáʼseh they help her

suppose
gǫ·dǫ́h·ne:ʼ I suppose

sure see: certain
o·ih·wí:yoʼ it is certain, for sure

surface see: area, float
og·ye·na·wáh·dǫh an area
o·daʼgrah·dǫ́·hǫg·yeʼ it is surfacing

surmount see: climb
ęhs·rá:tęʼ you will climb it

surname
dehs·wah·sę·náʼse:ʼ your (p) surname; your family name (lit.: your (p) double name or joiner name)
[de+A+ stem: -(h)sęnaʼse:ʼ- surname; consists of: -(h)sę$n(a)_N$- name -(a)ʼse:$ʼ_V$- cousin; double]
de·hah·sę·náʼse:ʼ his surname
de·gah·sę·náʼse:ʼ a surname

surplus
he·yó·gǫh·so:t it is a surplus
[heʼ+yo+ stem: -gohsod- surplus; consists of: -ǫgohd_V- surpass]

surprise see: startle
ę·ke·yę·neʼwá:dęʼ I will startle her

surprised
ak·né·hag·wahs I'm always amazed
[P+ stem: -nehagwa(h,ʼ), nehago_V- be surprised, amazed]
a·ho·nę·há:goʼ he was amazed, surprised
ak·ne·hag·wáʼǫh I am amazed
a·génʼe·wa:ʼ I was surprised
[P+ (ę+) stem: -neʼwa:ʼ- be surprised; consists of: -neʼwaǫ, neʼ$wa(:)_V$- be startled]
a·sęnʼe·wáʼge: you are really surprised, shocked
[P+ (ę+) stem: -neʼwa:ʼ- get surprised; consists of: -neʼwaǫ, neʼ$wa(:)_V$- be startled -ge: big]

surprised see: unexpected
gę·néʼwa·ǫ:s I get surprised

surprising see: unexpected
o·né·wa·ǫ: s.t. unexpected, surprising

Cayuga pronunciation guide: /a/ father /e/ weigh /ę/ men (nasalized) /i/ police /o/ hole /ǫ/ home (nasalized) /u/ blue. Underlined vowels are voiceless or whispered. /ʹ/ high pitch. /t/ too /d/ do /k/ king /g/ good (never soft g) /j/ judge or adze /s/ soon /sh/ less heat (never the sh in shirt) /sr/ shrine /sy/ sure /hw/ which (the sound made when you blow out a candle) /h/ hi /ts/ cats hide /ʼ/ (the sound before the first vowel in 'uh-uh') /n/ noon /r/ round /w/ way /y/ yes.

survey
ha·díhs·d'id·rehs they (m) are surveying the land; surveyors
[stem: -(r)ihsdi'dr(e)- survey; consists of: -(h)wihsd(a), (hr)ihsd(a)$_N$- metal, money -(i)'dre(:)$_V$- drag, drive]
gá·ihs·d'id·rǫ: it has been surveyed
survive see: endure, live
ęh·sę'ni·gǫ·hah·ní:ya:t you will endure
e·ya·gǫn·héh·gǫ·hǫk they (f/m) will live on; what will sustain them
survivor
go·ya'da·gǫ́h·sǫh·ta' human survivors
[P+ stem: -ya'dagǫhsohta'- survivor; consists of: -ya'd(a)$_N$- body -gǫhsohd$_V$-]
suspend see: hang
ga·ní:yǫ:t it is hanging
suspenders
at·na'gwihd·rá' ǫ·do·dá:ta' suspenders
[consists of: atna'gwihdra' belt; ǫdoda:ta' s.o. drapes it on herself]
suspect see: wonder
ęh·sę·nǫh·dǫ́:nyǫ:' you will wonder, think
suspension see: postponement
ga·gę́·ihs·dǫh a postponement
sustain see: live
e·ya·gǫn·héh·gǫ·hǫk they (f/m) will live on; what will sustain them
swallow
he·gǫ́·nęh·ta' I swallow
[he'+... stem: -ǫnęhd$_V$- swallow]
hę·gǫ́:nęht I will swallow
he·wa·gǫ·nę́h·dǫh I have swallowed
ha'sǫ́:nęht swallow it
de·gan·rę'ó:gę' a swallow (bird)
[de+ga+ stem: -nre'ogę'- swallow; consists of: -nre'(a)$_N$- -ogę$_V$- together, between]
swallow see: gulp, barn swallow
ha'gǫ́·nęht·ge: I took a big swallow, a gulp
gwi·yó:gę' a barn swallow
swamp
ga·ná·wa·ę:' a swamp; a pond
[ga+ consists of: -naw(a)$_N$- pond, swamp -ę$_V$- lie on the ground]
swan
ohn·ya'sag·wá·ǫ:t a swan
[o+ stem: -(h)nya'sagwa:ǫt- swan; consists of: -(h)nya('sa)$_N$- neck, throat -g(wa)$_N$- lump -ǫd$_V$- attached]
swap see: trade
dę·sá·da·dǫ' you will trade, exchange
swarm see: group
gęg·yóhg·wa·ę' a group
sway see: shake
dę·ya:wę́:dǫh it will sway
swear
ęhs·rih·wa·né'ak·sǫ:' you will swear, use profane language
[stem: -(r)ihwane'aksǫ(:)- swear; consists of: -(r)ih(wa)$_N$- word -ne'ag$_V$- sin -sǫ(:) plural]
sweat
o'da·i·hęhd·ra' sweat
[o+ stem: -(i')daihęhdr(a)$_N$- sweat -(')daihę$_V$- hot]
ęt·se'da·i·hęhd·rá·hi' you will sweat profusely, perspire
[d+... stem: -(')daihęhdrahi- sweat, perspire; consists of: : -(i')daihęhdr(a)$_N$- sweat -(')daihę$_V$- hot]
ho'da·i·hę́hd·ro:t he is sweating
[P+ stem: -(i')daihęhdrod- sweat; consists of: -(i')daihęhdr(a)$_N$- sweat -od$_V$- stand]
a·ge'dá·i·hęhd·ro:t I am sweating
sweater see: dress
ag·ya'da·wí'tra' a coat; a dress
sweep
de·gó·n'os·gwihs I am sweeping
[de+...(ę)+ stem: -(o)no'sgwi$_V$- sweep]
de·wa·gę·nó'sg·wi: I have swept

sweet-smelling see: smell
gad·rę·na·gáʼǫh it smells good, sweet, appetizing
sweet flag
a·wę́·hoʼdaʼ sweet flag (a plant)
[a+ stem: -węhoʼdaʼ- sweet flag; consists of: -(a)węh(ę)$_N$- flower -oʼ be submerged -daʼ$_V$- stand up]
sweeten
ęhs·ra·na·wę́ʼdoh you will sweeten
[stem: -(r)anawęʼdoh- sweeten; consists of: -(rę)nawęʼd(a)$_N$- sugar, candy -oh$_V$- dip in liquid]
sweetmilk pop
de·węʼnya·gá:nye:ʼ flour mush; sweetmilk pop
[de+w+ę+ stem: -(ʼ)nyaganye:- sweetmilk pop; consists of: -(ʼ)ny(a)$_N$- finger, hand -ganye(:)$_V$- chant, trill]
sweets see: dessert, goodies
na·węʼda·wets·hǫ́:ʼǫh dessert
o·gaʼǫhs·hǫ́:ʼǫh goodies; dessert
swell
wa̲h·dę́ʼgwahs it swells up
[stem: -(a)hdęʼgw- ; consists of: -ęʼgw, -(a)hdęʼgw$_V$- swell up]
a·wáh·dʼę·goh it swelled up
oh·dę́ʼgwęh it is swollen
a·wat·ne·gę́ʼgoʼ water rose up, swelled
[ad+N+ stem: -(h)neg(a)$_N$- water, liquid -ęʼgw$_V$- swell up]
ę·hag·yaʼdę́ʼgoʼ his body will swell up
[ad+N+ stem: -yaʼd(a)$_N$- body -ęʼgw$_V$- swell up]
o·dóʼdo:t swells (waves)
[o+ stem: -doʼd(a)$_N$- wave -od$_V$- stand]
swelling see: lump
og·wá·ǫt it has a lump, a bulge
swift see: fast
gyʼa·dahs·nó:weʼ I am fast, quick
swim
hę·ná·da·węhs they (m) are swimming
[ad+ stem: -(a)wę(:)$_V$- swim]
ę·há·da·wę:ʼ he will swim
ho·dá:węh he did swim
haʼsá·da·wę: swim over there
aʼǫ·da·wę́ʼneʼ she is / is she going swimming
[ad+ stem: -(a)węʼne$_V$- go and swim]
swimming pool
ahs·deh·ká:ʼ ǫ·dah·wʼę·dáhk·waʼ outdoor swimming pool
[consists of: ahsdehka:ʼ outside typc; ǫdawʼędahkwaʼ bathing suit]
swimsuit see: bathing suit
ǫ·da·wʼę·dáhk·waʼ a bathing suit; s.t. used for swimming
swindle see: cheat
ęhs·ni·gǫ·háʼdęʼ you will cheat
swing
sa·dǫh·wi·dáʼtaʼ you swing (all the time); you're a swinger
[ad+ stem: -ǫhwidaʼd$_V$- swing]
a:sa·dǫh·wí:daʼt you will swing
sa·dǫh·wi·dáʼdǫh you are swinging
sa·dǫh·wí:daʼt swing
wa·dǫh·wi·daʼtra·ní:yǫ:t a swing
[wa+ ad+ stem: -ǫhwidaʼtr(a)$_N$- swing -niyǫd$_V$- hang]
switch see: trade
dę·sá·da·dǫʼ you will trade, exchange it
switch off see: extinguish
sa̲hs·waht put the light out
switch on see: turn on
se·jihs·dó:dęh turn on the light
de·se·ga̲·ha·dé:nih turn it on
swoop
da·wádʼa·sęht it swooped down
[d+...ad+ stem: -(aʼ)sęhd$_V$- hand down, bring down; swoop down]
symbol see: number
ohs·hé:daʼ a number
symmetry see: equality, same
tsaʼde·ga·yaʼdag·wę:ní:yoʼ equality
tsaʼdé:yoht they are (lit.: it is) the same

Cayuga pronunciation guide: /a/ father /e/ weigh /ę/ men (nasalized) /i/ police /o/ hole /ǫ/ home (nasalized) /u/ blue. Underlined vowels are voiceless or whispered. /ʹ/ high pitch. /t/ too /d/ do /k/ king /g/ good (never soft g) /j/ judge or adze /s/ soon /sh/ less heat (never the sh in shirt) /sr/ shrine /sy/ sure /hw/ which (the sound made when you blow out a candle) /h/ hi /ts/ cats hide /ʼ/ (the sound before the first vowel in 'uh-uh') /n/ noon /r/ round /w/ way /y/ yes.

symphony see: music
tgá·ę·no:t music playing over there
synthetic see: man-made
oh·wę·ja·geh·gę·há:ʼ gá·ę·naʼ music made by man
syrup
ot·séhs·daʼ syrup; honey; gum; rubber
[o+ stem: -tsehsd(a)$_N$- syrup, honey, gum, rubber]
syrup see: maple syrup
oh·wah·dáʼ ot·séhs·daʼ maple syrup

T

t.v. see: movie
ga·yáʼtaʼ movies; television
table
a·dek·wa·háhs·raʼ table
[stem: -(a)dekwahahsr(a)$_N$- table]
de·yeh·na·hih·da̱hk·wáʼ a·dek·wa·háhs·raʼ a cut-out table
[consists of: deyehnahihda̱hkwaʼ s.t. used for cutting fabric; adekwahahsraʼ table]
table cloth
ǫ·dek·wa·hahs·ro·wé:ktaʼ a table cloth
[ǫ+ade+ stem: -kwahahsrowektaʼ- table cloth; consists of: -(a)dekwahahsr(a)$_N$- table -(hr)oweg$_V$- cover]
tablespoon
gan·yo·do·wá:nęh a tablespoon
[ga+ stem: -nyodowanęh- tablespoon; consists of: -nyod(a)$_N$- spoon, canoe -owanę$_V$- be big]
tsaʼde·gan·yo·da̱·hę́h gan·yo·do·wá:nęh one half tablespoon
[consists of: tsaʼdeganyoda̱hęh one half teaspoon; ganyodowa:nęh tablespoon]
tack see: line, rope
ga̱h·sí·ya·deʼ a suspended line; a string
gá:tsgʼę·daʼ a rope

tackle see: fish hook
gę·jǫʼda·yę́:nahs a fish hook
tadpole
ohs·twá:sʼah a young animal; a little animal; a tadpole
[o+ stem: -(a)hstwa:sʼah- tadpole, young animal; consists of: -(a)hstwa(h,ʼ)$_V$- shrink]
tag see: mark
ęg·yá:naʼt I will mark s.t.
tail
gan·hę́h·jo:t its tail; it has a tail
[ga+ stem: -(ʼ)nhęhts(a)$_N$- tail -od$_V$- stand]
oʼnhę́ht·saʼ, oʼnhwę́ht·saʼ the tail of an animal
[o+ stem: -(ʼ)nhęhts(a)$_N$- tail]
oʼyóhg·waʼ a skirt; a tail; a feather
[o+ stem: -(ʼ)yohg(wa)$_N$- tail, skirt, feather]
gʼa·yóhg·wʼa·geh on its (a bird's) tail
tail see: fish tail
ga·yóh·go:t a fish tail
tailor
hahg·wę:nyǫ́:nihs he is a tailor
[A+ stem: -(a)hgwęnyǫnihs- tailor; consists of: -(a)hgwęny(a)$_N$- clothes -ǫni, ǫny$_V$- make]
tailor see: seamstress
eʼní:kǫhs a seamstress
take apart
de·wa·ge·káhs·hǫ: I have taken one object apart
[de+...(N+) stem: -kahs(i)$_V$- share, divide; take s.t apart.]
take
ha·há:wiʼ he is carrying it
[haʼ+... stem: -(h)awi, (h)a:$_V$- hold, include, carry, bring; take s.t.]
haʼák·hni̱·ha:ʼ we two (excl.) took it
haʼs·ha: take it over there

take (continued)
ę·yók·wahk·waʼ it will take the food from another animal
[N+ stem: -k(wa)$_{N}$- food -(h)kw$_{V}$- take s.t. from s.o.]
ah·sa·gok·wáhk·waʼ he grabbed the food from her

take see: release, take away, take down, take in, take off, take apart, take one's time, take out, take over, take place, take time
haʼhé·yaht·gaʼ I left him there; I took him over there

take away see: remove
sǫ́ːneːk you remove s.t.

take down see: unhang
ęts·ni·yǫ·dáːgoʼ you will unhang it

take in see: adopt
ęh·sa·dǫg·weʼdá·ǫ·goʼ you will adopt a person

take off
da·hę́hs·gaːʼ he squealed out; took off abruptly
[(d+)… stem: -ęhsgaːʼ- take off; consists of: -(a)hsi(ʼda), (ę)hs(a)$_{N}$- foot -gaː$_{V}$- make a rattling or grinding noise]
ęt·sę́hs·gaːʼ you (will) take off abruptly, quickly, suddenly
sa·wę́hs·gaːʼ it spun out
a·wę́hs·gaːʼ it (a car, a dog) took off fast

take off see: fly
a·táːdęʼ he took off (from the ground)

take one's time
sgę·nǫːʼǫ́h nęt·syeː you will take your time
[sgęnǫːʼǫh slowly ni+…d+ A+ stem: -ye(ː)$_{V}$- do]

take out see: choose
ęhs·ráːgoʼ you will choose, take out

take over
a·hǫ·wa·ę·nan·hǫ́·daːgoʼ he took over the song
[TR+ stem: -(r)ęn(a)$_{N}$- song, music -nhodagw$_{V}$- open]

take place see: happen
ni·yáːwęhs how it happens

take time
tó ę naʼǫ́·nis·heʼ it took that long
[to ęː even that naʼ+ o+ stem: -nihsheʼ$_{V}$- take time]

tale
oʼgaːʼ a parable; a tale; a story; a legend
[o+ stem: -(ʼ)g(aː)$_{N}$- tale, story, legend, parable]

talk
gęh·táːhaʼ I talk
[stem: -(h)taː$_{V}$- talk, speak]
ę·géh·ta·ęʼ I will talk
goh·taːʼ she is speaking
a·géh·taːʼk I did talk
hoh·táh·gǫh·neːʼ he used to talk about it
a·géh·taːgyeʼ I am talking as I go along
[P+ stem: -(h)tagyeʼ$_{V}$- go along talking]
a·géh·taːkneːʼ what I did talk about
ęhs·hé·ta·hahs you talk to her
[TR+ stem: -(h)tahahsd- talk to s.o.; consists of: -(h)taː$_{V}$- talk, speak]
hod·rih·wat·gíh·dǫh he is talking dirty
[ad+ stem: -(r)ihwatgihd- talk dirty; consists of: -(r)ih(wa)$_{N}$- word -tgihd$_{V}$- make dirty, ugly]

talk see: say, tell
ęh·siʼ you will say
ęd·waːtróːwiʼ we all (incl.) will tell

talkative see: chatterbox
goːih·wa·gáʼdeʼ she is a chatterbox

tall
hah·nę́ːyeːs he is tall
[A+ stem: -(h)nęyeːs$_{V}$- tall]
knę́ːyeːs I am tall

talon see: claw
de·ga·jiʼéh·deːs a claw

Cayuga pronunciation guide: /a/ father /e/ weigh /ę/ men (nasalized) /i/ police /o/ hole /ǫ/ home (nasalized) /u/ blue. Underlined vowels are voiceless or whispered. /ˊ/ high pitch. /t/ too /d/ do /k/ king /g/ good (never soft g) /j/ judge or adze /s/ soon /sh/ less heat (never the sh in shirt) /sr/ shrine /sy/ sure /hw/ which (the sound made when you blow out a candle) /h/ hi /ts/ cats hide /ʼ/ (the sound before the first vowel in 'uh-uh') /n/ noon /r/ round /w/ way /y/ yes.

tame
a·hat·na̲hs·gǫ́:niʼ he raised a pet
[at+ stem: -nahsgǫni- tame s.t.; consists of: -nahsg(wa)$_N$- animal, domestic -ǫni, ǫny$_V$- make]
wat·nahs·gǫ́:ni: it has been made into a pet
hot·sé·nęh·sǫʼ his many pets (a variety)
[stem: -tsenę$_N$- tame animal -sǫʼ plural]
tan
ę·sat·gǫ·waʼdǫ́:niʼ you will tan a hide
[at+ stem: -gǫwaʼdǫni- tan; consists of: -gǫwa(ʼda)$_N$- hide -ǫni, ǫny$_V$- make]
ęhs·yę́ʼgwʼa·e:k you will smoke it (meat, etc.); you will tan it
[stem: -yęʼgwaeg- tan, dry; consists of: -yęʼg(wa)$_N$- tobacco, smoke, cigarettes -(ʼ)e$_V$- hit]
tan see: brown, dark
héhsʼa·ę:ʼ brown
a·kǫ́ʼji̲h·neʼ I got dark, black, really tanned
tangent see: another
he·jó:yaʼ tsǫ: another thing again; elsewhere; on a tangent
tangled
de·wa·gat·géʼi:ʼ my hair is tangled
[de+P+at+ stem: -geʼi:ʼ- be tangled; consists of: -geʼ(a:), geh(a)$_N$- hair -i:ʼ$_V$- stuck onto s.t.]
de·yót·ge̲ʼi: its hair is tangled; ideas and things are tangled
tantrum (have a tantrum) see: riot
a·ha·nǫ̲hs·gá·i:ʼ he raised cain, had a tantrum
tangy see: sour
o·jí·wa·gę: it is sour, salty, bitter
tap
hoh·wáʼe: he is tapping
[stem: -(h)waʼe- tap; consists of: -(h)w(a)$_N$- -(ʼ)e$_V$- hit]
ę·yag·wa̲h·ga·o·dǫ́:nyǫ:ʼ we all (excl.) will tap trees
[stem: -(a)hgaodǫnyǫ:ʼ- tap trees; consists of: -(a)hg(a:)$_N$- splint -odǫnyǫ(:)$_V$- stand up several objects]
tap see: stamp
sęh·sę́:dǫh you are tapping your foot
tape
et·sehs·da:táʼ e·ya:nę·dak·dáhk·waʼ glue; scotch tape
[consists of: etsehsda:taʼ s.t. that sticks; eya:nędakdahkwaʼ s.t. that causes things to stick]
tape recorder
ga·wę·na·yé:nahs a tape recorder; a transcriber
[ga+ stem: -węnayenahs- tape recorder, transcriber; consists of: -węn(a)$_N$- voice, word -yena(w), yenaǫ, yena(:)$_V$- catch, receive, accept]
ga·wę:nǫ́:da:s a tape recorder
[ga+ stem: -węnǫdas- tape recorder; consists of: -węn(a)$_N$- voice, word -ǫda:(h)$_V$- put in, attached]
ga·wę·no·dá:taʼ a tape recorder
[ga+ stem: -węnǫdataʼ- tape recorder; consists of: -węn(a)$_N$- voice, word -ǫdad$_V$- put in]
tapeworm
on·rę́·hęʼ a tapeworm
[o+ stem: -nręh(ę)$_N$- tapeworm]
tardy see: late
ę·wák·ni̲hs·goʼ I will be late
target
de·yǫ·dʼed·rat·gęn·yá·da̲hk·waʼ (a) target
[de+yǫ+ade+ stem: -(ʼ)dratgęnyadahkwaʼ- target; consists of: -(ʼ)dr(a)$_N$- case, quiver -tgęnyadahkwaʼ$_V$- s.t. used for competition]
tariff see: price
ga·gá·he:ʼ the price of s.t.
tarnish see: rust
ohs·gę́ʼdra̲·he:ʼ it is rusting, rusty

tart see: sour
o·jí·wa·gę: it is sour, salty, bitter
tassel see: corn tassel
tsa'gę́:da' a corn tassel
taste
ni·yo·ga'ǫ́hs·r'o·dę: what it tastes like
[ni+yo+ stem: -ga'ǫhsr(a)$_N$- taste -o'dę:$_V$- type of]
taste see: eat, try
a·ha:k he ate it
sa·de'nyę́:dęh sample it; try it
taste good
o·gá'ǫh it tastes good
[o+ stem: -ga'ǫh- tasty, delicious; consists of: -ga'$_V$- like the taste of s.t.]
o·ga'ǫhs·rí:yo: it tastes good
[o+ stem: -ga'ǫhsriyo:- taste good; consists of: -ga'ǫhsr(a)$_N$- taste -iyo:$_V$- be nice, good]
oh·yá·ga'ǫh good-tasting fruit
[A/P+(N+) stem: -(a)hy(a)$_N$- fruit, berry -ga'ǫh$_V$- tasty, delicious]
o'wa·ha·gá'ǫh the meat is delicious
[A/P+(N+) stem: -(')wah(a)$_N$- meat -ga'ǫh$_V$- tasty, delicious]
tasteless
de'o·ga'ǫ́hs·ra·e' it is tasteless
[de'+ not (y)o+ stem: -ga'ǫhsrae'- tasty; tastless; consists of: -ga'ǫhsr(a)$_N$- taste -ę$_V$- lie on the ground]
tattered see: hair, ragged
o·gé'a:' hair, a rag; it is ragged, tattered
se·gé'a:' you are raggedy, ragged
tavern see: bar
ǫt·ne·gah·ní:nǫh(geh) a hotel; a pub; a bar; a saloon
tax
ę·yǫ·ki·gá·hę' they will tax us
[TR+ stem: -gahę- tax s.o.; consists of: -ga:$_N$- price -(hr)e, (hr)ę$_V$- put, place]
tax see: G (ǫ·ki·ga:gwahs), bother
dęhs·ni·gǫ·há:ha' you are annoying me, bothering me

Taxation Department see: G (Ha·di·ga:he·ha'geh)
taxi
wa·dǫg·we·dá·nęhg·wih taxi
[wa+ad+ stem: -ǫgwe'danehgwih- taxi; consists of: -ǫgwe('da)$_N$- person -nęhgwi$_V$- haul]
tea
o·di: tea
[o+ stem: -di('tra)$_N$- tea]
edi'trǫnya'ta' a teapot
[e+ stem: -di'trǫnya'ta'- teapot; consists of: -di('tra)$_N$- tea -ǫnya'd$_V$- cause to make]
tea kettle
oh·sǫ·wah·da·da·i:hę́:
eh·ne·ga·da·i·há'dahk·wa' an electric tea-kettle
[consists of: ohsǫwahdadai:hę: electricity; ehnegadaiha'dahkwa' tea kettle]
eh·ne·ga·da·i·há'dahk·wa' a tea kettle
[e+ stem: -(h)negadaiha'dahkwa'- tea kettle; consists of: -(h)neg(a)$_N$- water, liquid -(')daiha'dahkwa'$_V$- s.t. that heats things up]
tea meeting
go·dih·ne·ga·dá·i:ha'dǫh they (f/m) do tea meetings, supper
[P+ stem: -(h)nega'daiha'dǫh- tea meeting; consists of: -(h)neg(a)$_N$- water, liquid -(')daiha'd$_V$- heat up]
gak·wá·he:' tea meetings; supper
[ga+ stem: -kwahe:'- tea meeting; consists of: -k(wa)$_N$- food -(h)e:'$_V$- sitting up on top of s.t.]
teach
ha·i:hǫn·yá:nih he is a teacher
[A+(adę+) stem: -(r)ihǫnyanih- teach; consists of: -(r)ih(wa)$_N$- word -ǫnyani$_V$- make for oneself]
ha·dę·i·hǫ́n·ya·nih he is a teacher
ǫ·dę·i·hǫ́n·ya·nih she is a teacher

Cayuga pronunciation guide: /a/ father /e/ weigh /ę/ men (nasalized) /i/ police /o/ hole /ǫ/ home (nasalized) /u/ blue. Underlined vowels are voiceless or whispered. /´/ high pitch. /t/ too /d/ do /k/ king /g/ good (never soft g) /j/ judge or adze /s/ soon /sh/ less heat (never the sh in shirt) /sr/ shrine /sy/ sure /hw/ which (the sound made when you blow out a candle) /h/ hi /ts/ cats hide /'/ (the sound before the first vowel in 'uh-uh') /n/ noon /r/ round /w/ way /y/ yes.

teaching assistant
ǫ·dę·i·hǫn·ya·níh gǫn·háʼtraʼ teaching assistant
[consists of: ǫdęihǫnyanih she is a teacher; gǫnhaʼtraʼ s.o.'s assistant]
teapot
e·diʼtrǫn·yáʼtaʼ a teapot
[e+ stem: -diʼtrǫnyaʼtaʼ- teapot; consists of: -di(ʼtra)$_{N}$- tea -ǫnyaʼd$_{V}$- cause to make]
tear
o·gáhd·raʼ a tear (in one's eye)
[o+ stem: -gahdr(a)$_{N}$- tear]
ęhs·rá:drǫ:ʼ you will tear it, shred it
[stem: -(r)adrǫ(:)- consists of: -(r)adrǫ(:), (r)atsǫ(:)$_{V}$- tear s.t., shred s.t.]
wad·rá:tsǫhs it gets torn all the time
[ad+ stem: -(r)atsǫ(:)- ; consists of: -(r)adrǫ(:), (r)atsǫ(:)$_{V}$- tear s.t., shred s.t.]
a·wád·rat·sǫ: it got torn, ripped
od·rá:tsǫh it is torn
tear see: drip sweat
o·gáhd·ro:t it is tearing, producing teardrops
tease
ha·dę·dǫn·yáʼtaʼ he is a joker
[TR+ad+ stem: -ędǫnyaʼd- tease, joke, jest; consists of: -(w)ędǫh$_{V}$- shake s.t.]
ho·dę·dǫn·yáʼtaʼ it is making fun of him; s.t. turned on him
ęhs·heyʼa·dę́·dǫn·yaʼt you will make fun of it; s.t. will make fun of you, messing with your head or mind (refers to reliving your sins before death); you will joke
sa·dę·dǫn·yáʼdǫh you are joking
o·dę́dǫn·yaʼt a jest
tease (continued)
tę·nat·na̱hs·gǫ́:nih they (m) are teasing the animal(s)
[d+…at+(N+) stem: -nahsg(wa)$_{N}$- animal, domestic -ǫni, ǫny$_{V}$- make; tease s.o., s.t.]
teaspoon
sgan·yó:da:t one teaspoon
[s+ ga+ stem: -nyod(a)$_{N}$- spoon, canoe -d$_{V}$- stand; be one]
tsaʼde·gan·yó·da̱·hęh one half teaspoon
[tsaʼ+de+ga+ stem: -nyod(a)$_{N}$- spoon, canoe -(h)ęh$_{V}$- mid; half, middle]
teat see: nipple
o·nǫ́n·heʼdraʼ a soother; a pacifier; a nipple
teenager
hak·saʼda·sé:ʼah he is a teenage boy
[A+ stem: -ksaʼdase:ʼah- teenager; consists of: -ksa(ʼda)$_{N}$- child -(a)se$_{V}$- new -ʼah- diminutive]
ek·saʼda·sé:ʼah a teenage girl
ho·gáʼdas·wahs he smells (or sniffs) pants (said of pubescent teenagers)
[P+ stem: -gaʼdasw- teenager; consists of: -gaʼd(a)$_{N}$- pants, underpants -sw, sho$_{V}$- smell]
a·go·gʼa·dáhs·hoʼ she smells the pants (said of prepubescent girls)
hoʼká:swahs he smells (or sniffs) skirts (said of pubescent teenagers)
[P+ stem: -(ʼ)kaswahs- teenager; consists of: -(ʼ)k(a:)$_{N}$- skirt, slip -sw, sho$_{V}$- smell]
teenager see: puberty
dę·had·wę·ná·dęn·yǫhs he is reaching puberty (lit.: his voice is changing)
teeter-totter
de·wat·nehs·da·gá·i:hǫhs a teeter-totter
[de+wa+at+ stem: -nehsadagaihǫhs- teeter-totter; consists of: -(ʼ)nehs(a)$_{N}$- sand -dagaihǫhs$_{V}$-]

teething ring
ǫt·no'jon·yá'ta' a teething ring
[ǫ+at+ stem: -no'jonya'ta'- teething ring; consists of: -no'j(a)$_N$- tooth -ǫnya'd$_V$- cause to make]

telephone operator
ǫd·wę·nǫ·dah·tá' gohs·díhs·dǫh a telephone operator
[consists of: ǫdwęnǫdahta' telephone; gohsdihsdǫh she is a director, principle, head, etc.]

telephone repairman
ǫd·wę·nǫ·dah·tá' shahs·rǫ́:nihs a telephone repairman
[consists of: ǫdwęnǫdahta' telephone; shahsrǫ:nihs repairman]

telescope
i:nó' he'gá:gęh a telescope
[consists of: i:no' far; hega:gęh it sees]

television see: movie
ga·yá'ta' movies; television

tell
gat·ró:wih, gat·ró:wihs I tell all the time
[TR/…at+ stem: -(hr)owi, (hr)ǫny$_V$- tell]
ahs·ha·go·hó:wi' he told her
ęd·wa:tró:wi' we all (incl.) will tell
a·ga:tró:wi: I have told
she·hó:wih tell her
se·gá:dǫ: tell a story
[stem: -(')ga:dǫh- tell a story; consists of: -(')g(a:)$_N$- tale, story, legend, parable -(a)dǫh$_V$- say]

tell see: recount
ęt·sa:tró:wi' you will recount, retell

teller see: cashier
e·gá:gwahs a cashier

temper see: anger
ohs·rǫ́·hę'da' an angry person; temper

temperament see: attitude, nerves
tsę́h ni·sa'ni·gǫ́·ho'dę: your attitude, mood
shę́h dwa·nih·na·dó·g'a·ta' human emotions; feelings; nerves

temperate see: warm
o·né:nǫ' it is mild, warm; a warm or hot day

tempt
ęhs·he·yahs·gá·nek·dę',
ęhs·hehs·ga·né:k·dę' you will tempt s.o.
[TR+ stem: -(a)hsganekd- tempt s.o.; consists of: -(ahs)gan(eg)$_V$- want, desire, long for]
ęhs·gá:neht you will tempt
[stem: -(a)hsganehd- be tempting; consists of: -(ahs)gan(eg)$_V$- want, desire, long for]
os·gá:neht it is enticing, alluring, attractive, tempting

tempt see: want
ęh·sáhs·ga·ne:k you will be tempted, you will long for s.t.

tempting see: enticing
ohs·gá:na't it is enticing, alluring, attractive, tempting

ten see: B (wahs·hę:)

tend
dę·se·heh·dá·węn·ye:' you will tend, till your garden
[de+… stem: -(h)ehdawęnye(:)- consists of: -(h)ehd(a)$_N$- land, etc. -(a)węnye(:)$_V$- stir, mix]
ęh·sa·tę·dǫ́:ni' you will make your garden
[at+ stem: -(h)ędǫni- make a garden; consists of: -(h)ęd(a)$_N$- field -ǫni, ǫny$_V$- make]

tend see: care for
ęhs·he·ya·de·wa·yę·nǫ́:ni' you will take care of them, care for them

tendency see: attitude
tsę́h ni·sa'ni·gǫ́·ho'dę: your attitude, mood

Cayuga pronunciation guide: /a/ father /e/ weigh /ę/ men (nasalized) /i/ police /o/ hole /ǫ/ home (nasalized) /u/ blue. Underlined vowels are voiceless or whispered. /'/ high pitch. /t/ too /d/ do /k/ king /g/ good (never soft g) /j/ judge or adze /s/ soon /sh/ less heat (never the sh in shirt) /sr/ shrine /sy/ sure /hw/ which (the sound made when you blow out a candle) /h/ hi /ts/ cats hide /'/ (the sound before the first vowel in 'uh-uh') /n/ noon /r/ round /w/ way /y/ yes.

tender
o'wa·hí:yo: good (tender) meat
[o+ stem: -(')wah(a)$_N$- meat -iyo:$_V$- be nice, good]
tender see: sore
a·gah·s'i·dá·nǫh·wa:s I have a sore foot
tendon
o·jíhn·y'a·da' a tendon; a ligament; a birth cord
[o+stem: -jihnya('da)$_N$- tendon, ligament, birth cord]
o·jihn·y'a·dá·den·yǫ' tendons
[o+stem: -jihnya'dadenyǫ'- tendon; consists of: -jihnya('da)$_N$- tendon, ligament, birth cord -denyǫ'$_V$- several changing things]
ohs·ha:dé:nyo' tendons
[o+ stem: -(h)shadenyoh- tendons; consists of: -sh(a)$_N$- string -denyǫ'$_V$- several existing things]
tense see: nervous
wa·dón·yah·nǫ: it is nervous
tent
ga·ya·o:wá:nęh big bag; big tent
[ga+ stem: -ya:$_N$- bag -owanęh$_V$- be big]
hog·yá·o:t he has put up a tent
[P+ag+ stem: -yaod- put up a tent; consists of: -ya:$_N$- bag -od$_V$- stand]
tepid see: warm
o·né:nǫ' it is mild, warm; a warm or hot day
terminate see: finish, stop
hę·só'kdę' you will finish s.t.
a·tá:dahs he stopped it, prevented it
terminology see: language, word
ni·ga·wę·nó:dę's language words
o·wę·na·gá:yǫh high language; formal language
o·wę·nas·hó:'ǫh words
terra cotta see: clay
o'da:' clay; mud; mortar
terrible
de·yo·dę·nǫh·ya·níh·dǫh it is overwhelming, terrible
[de+yo+(adę+) stem: -nǫhyanihd- be terrible, overwhelming; consists of: -nǫhyani$_V$- be frugal]
de·yo·nǫh·yá:niht it is terrible, frugal, cheap
terrify see: frighten, startle
eh·sáhd·rǫhg·wę' it did frighten you
ę·ke·yę·ne'wá:dę' I will startle her
territory see: area, G (province), de·yoh·wę·jah·kah·sǫ:gwęh
og·ye·na·wáh·dǫh an area
terrorize see: frighten, startle, threaten
eh·sáhd·rǫhg·wę' it did frighten you
ę·ke·yę·ne'wá:dę' I will startle her
she·yad·rǫhg·wá:nih you are threatening, scaring s.o.
testament see: Bible, message (convey a message)
gah·ya·dǫhs·ra·do·gę́h·di', **oh·ya·dǫhs·ra·do·gę́h·di'** the Bible
hę·ha·ih·wę́·hę:' he will take the message
testify see: message (convey a message)
hę·ha·ih·wę́·hę:' he will take the message
test
ęg·wá:kdǫ:' I will test you all
[TR+ stem: -kdǫ(:)$_V$- taste, examine, look closely at s.t.; test s.o.]
testicles
hahs·gwá'geh his testicles
[ha+ stem: -(h)sg(wa:)$_N$- stone, bullet, rock -(a')geh- on]
de·há'nhǫhs·dǫ:t his testicles
[de+ha+ stem: -(')nhǫhsdǫd- testicles; consists of: -(')nhǫhsd(a)$_N$- sperm -ǫd$_V$- attached]

testy

ho·ti·y'as·gǫ: he's testy; he has a short fuse

[P+at+ stem: -(h)iya'sgǫ:- be testy, hold a grudge; consists of: -(h)iya'g$_V$- -sgǫ: easily]

sa·tíy'as·gǫ: you hold grudges; you get angry easily

testy see: grumpy

de·di·s'a·ni·gǫ·hí:yo: you are grumpy, grouchy, unhappy

textile see: cloth, fabric

ni·gęh·ne:s a length of cloth, material

o·ni·gá:hęhs·ra' material; cloth

thank

dę·ke·nǫ·hǫ́:nyǫ' I will greet her

[de+TR+ stem: -nǫhǫnyǫ(:)$_V$- thank, greet]

dęd·wa·nǫ·hǫ́:nyǫ:' we all (incl.) will thank s.o.

dęhs·he·nǫ·hǫ́:nyǫ: you will welcome, greet, thank s.o.

dęh·sa·dę·nǫ́·hǫn·yǫhk what you will give thanks with

[de+adę+ stem: -nǫhǫnyǫ(:)$_V$- thank, greet; give thanks]

thank you see: I (nya:węh)

that see: I (shęh, tsęh, toh, etc.)

thaw

ga·ná'na·wę's it melts

[ga+ N+/na'+ stem: -nawę'- thaw, melt down; consists of: - na'- noun -nawę$_V$- be wet, saturated]

ęhs·gan'a·ná:wę' it will thaw again, melt again

o·na'na·wę́'ǫh it has thawed, melted

a·wa'gra·ná:wę' the snow melted

[N+/na'+ consists of: -(a)'gr(a)$_N$- snow -nawę'$_V$- thaw, melt]

the see: I (ne')

theft see: plunder

ga·nę́hsg·węh stolen property; plunder; s.t. robbed

then see: I (di', toh geh)

their see: I (gona:węh, hona:węh, on-a:węh)

there see: I (sigwa:dih, etc.)

thereabouts see: I (gaęgwa' nhǫ:weh)

thick

gá:dę:s it is thick, dense

[(ni+) ga+(N+) stem: -dęs$_V$- thick]

ni·gá:dę:s how thick it is

ni·gíh·na·dę:s how thick my skin is

[(ni+) A+(N+) stem: -(i)hn(a)$_N$- material, skin -dęs$_V$- thick]

thickener see: flour, starch

o·té'tra' flour; powder

wa·tǫ·gá·i:sta' starch

thicket see: bush, hedge

o·hǫ́·da·gǫ: in the bushes

o·hǫ:dá' ga·yę́t·wag·ye' a hedge

thick-headed

ho·nǫ'á:dę:s he is thick-headed

[P+ stem: -nǫ'(a:), nǫh(a)$_N$- head -(a)dęs$_V$- thick]

thickness see: thick

ni·gá:dę:s how thick it is

thief

knęhs·gwahs I am a thief

[A+ stem: -nęhsgwah- thief; consists of: -nęhsgw$_V$- steal]

thief see: rob

sha·góh·sę̱h·ta' he is a robber, a stealer

thigh (inner)

sen·hǫhs·gá:'geh on your inner thigh

[stem: -(')nhǫhsg(a:)$_N$- inner thigh]

g'en·hǫhs·gá:'geh on my inner thigh

sw'an·hǫhs·gá:'geh on your (p) thighs

thigh (outer)

sehs·ná'da·geh on your outer thighs

[P+ stem: -(h)sna('da)$_N$- muscle, hamstring, calf (body part)]

thimble
ǫ·dehs'oh·dó·hahk·wa' a thimble
[ǫ+ade+ stem: -(h)s'ohdohahkwa'- thimble; consists of: -(h)s'ohd(a)$_N$- hand, finger, paw; -(h)ahkwa'$_V$- s.t. that supports]

thimble berry
nę́:nǫ' thimble berries
[stem: -nęnǫ'- thimble berry; consists of: -nenǫ(:)$_V$- warm (weather), mild (weather)]
shah·ye:s thimble berries
[s+ha+ stem: -(a)hyes- thimble berry; consists of: -(a)hy(a)$_N$- fruit, berry -es$_V$- long]

thin
tę́' de·gá:dę:s it is not thick
[tę' not de'+ga+ stem: -dęs$_V$- thick, thin]
hohs·gyę́'wa·tę:, hohs·gyǫ́'wa·tę: he is skinny
[P+ stem: -(h)sgyǫ'watę, (h)sgyę'watę- thin; consists of: -(h)sgyǫ'w(a), (h)sgyę'w(a)$_N$- bone -tę(:)$_V$- dry]
gohs·gyǫ́'wa·tę: she is thin
sgyę́'wa·tę: it is skinny

thing see: I (something, sgaho'dę'), right, which
ga·dó:gę: a certain way; together; a certain thing
ga·ę́ ní:ga:' which one; a specific thing

think
es·we:' you all thought
[(i+) A+ stem: -i:, ę:, e:$_V$- think, hope, want]
a·hę:' he thought
ehs·ne:' you two thought
ęd·wé:he:k we all (incl.) will in thought
a·hę́:ne' they (m) thought; they left together
a·hi:' I thought, intended
i·he: he wants
ihs·ne: you two want

think (continued)
ag·we: we all (excl.) want
í:wi: I want, I hope
í:yę: she wants
ih·se: you want
ęh·sę·nǫh·dǫ́:nyǫ:' you will wonder, think
[stem: -ęnǫhdǫnyǫ(:)- think, wonder, feel well; consists of: -ęnǫhdǫ(:)$_V$- know]
sę·nǫ́h·dǫn·yǫh you are wondering, thinking
jǫ·nǫ́h·dǫn·yǫh to be healthy; to have well being again
sgę:nǫ́: se·nǫ́h·dǫn·yǫh you are safe; you are feeling well; you are at peace with yourself
sgę:nǫ́: ge·nǫ́h·dǫn·yǫh I am fine, healthy
[sgę:nǫ: well, fine stem: -ęnǫhdǫnyǫ- think, wonder, feel well; consists of: -ęnǫhdǫ(:)$_V$- know]
í:hs a·gǫ́·yahs·ha:' I thought of you
[TR+ stem: -(a)hs(h)a(:)$_V$- remember, recall; think of s.o.]
de·wag·ya'dó·weh·dǫh I have already thought about it; I am thinking about it
[de+ stem: -ya'dowehd$_V$- think about, consider]
ga·ya'do·wéh·dǫ:' the idea of thinking
[ga+ stem: -ya'dowehdǫ:'- thinking; consists of: -ya'dowehd$_V$- think about, consider]
ga·ya'do·wéh·dahs·ra' the ability to think; thinking skills
[stem: -ya'dowehdahsr(a)$_N$- thinking ability]
ęt·sę'ni·gǫ́·ho'dę' you will come up with an idea
[de...ę+ stem: -(')nigǫho'dę'- think of an idea, come up with an idea; consists of: -(')nigǫh(a)$_N$- mind -o'dę:$_V$- type of]

thinker see: fortune teller
dę.ha.yʼa.dó.we̲h.taʼ he is a fortune teller, seer, thinker

thinner
ga.óʼ ni.gá:dę:s it is thinner
[gaoʼ less ni+ ga+ stem: -dęs$_V$- thick; thinner]

third
ah.sę́h wa.dǫ́ʼtaʼ third

thirsty
kaʼdá:tęhs I am thirsty
[A+ stem: -(h)aʼdatęhs- be thirsty; consists of: -(h)aʼd(a)$_N$- throat, voice, feather -tęhsd$_V$- dry out]
shaʼdá:tęhs you are thirsty
ga̲.háʼda.tęhs it is thirsty

thirteen see: B (ah.sęh sga.eʼ)
thirty see: B (ah.sęh ni.wahs.hę:)
this see: I (nę:dah, nę:gyęh)

thistle
o.híʼk.dat.giʼ Scottish thistle (a big type of thistle)
[o+ stem: -(h)iʼkdatgiʼ- Scottish thistle; consists of: -(h)iʼkd(a)$_N$- thorn, thistle -tgiʼ$_V$- be dirty, ugly]

thistle see: thorn

thorn
o.híʼkdaʼ a thorn; a thistle
[o+ stem: -(h)iʼkd(a)$_N$- thorn, thistle]
o.híʼk.da.i:ʼ a thorn bush
[o+ stem: -(h)iʼkdai:ʼ- thorn bush; consists of: -(h)iʼkd(a)$_N$- thorn, thistle -i:ʼ$_V$- stuck onto s.t.]

thorn berry
haʼdrǫhk thornberry
[ha+ stem: -(ʼ)drǫhg- thorn berry; consists of: -(ʼ)dr(a)$_N$- case, quiver]

thoughtfulness see: pity
gę.dę́.ǫʼ to help each other; compassion; helpfulness

thousand see: B (wa̲hs.hę naʼde.wʼęn.ya:wʼe:)

thrash see: convulse, pound
ǫg.yéh.na̲h.sǫ:ʼ I had convulsions
ęh.sé:teht you will pound corn

thread
oh.sí:yaʼ a thread; a string; a cord
[o+ stem: -(h)siy(a)$_N$- line, string]
eʼni.kǫhk.wáʼ oh.sí:yaʼ a thread
[consists of: eʼnikǫhkwaʼ sewing item; ohsi:yaʼ thread, string, cord]

threaten
she.yad.rǫ̲hg.wá:nih you are threatening, scaring s.o.
[TR+(ad+) stem: -(r)ǫhgw(ę, anih)$_V$- threaten]
ęhs.he.ya̲hd.rǫ́hg.węʼ you will threaten, scare s.o.

three see: B (ah.sęh)
three times see: B (ah.sęh hę.wa:dra:s)

thresher
ga.ná.jʼa.ehs a grain threshing machine
[ga+ stem: -najʼaehs- thresher; consists of: -na(ʼ)ja(da)$_N$- wheat, grain -(ʼ)e$_V$- hit]

thrice see: B (ah.sęh hę.wa:dra:s)
thrifty see: frugal
de.ya.go.nǫ́h.yani:s she is frugal

thrive see: grow
ę.wáh.do:k it will multiply, grow

throat
o.háʼdaʼ a quill; a plume; a feather; the voice; the throat; the larynx; the esophagus
[o+ stem: -(h)aʼd(a)$_N$- throat, voice, feather]
ga̲.háʼdʼa.geh on its throat

throb see: ache, noise
ga.nǫ.hǫk.déhs.raʼ an ache
otga:ʼ a noise

throng see: crowd
ni.gęg.yǫh.góʼdę: an assembled crowd; a kind of crowd

Cayuga pronunciation guide: /a/ father /e/ weigh /ę/ men (nasalized) /i/ police /o/ hole /ǫ/ home (nasalized) /u/ blue. Underlined vowels are voiceless or whispered. /ˊ/ high pitch. /t/ too /d/ do /k/ king /g/ good (never soft g) /j/ judge or adze /s/ soon /sh/ less heat (never the sh in shirt) /sr/ shrine /sy/ sure /hw/ which (the sound made when you blow out a candle) /h/ hi /ts/ cats hide /ʼ/ (the sound before the first vowel in ‘uh-uh’) /n/ noon /r/ round /w/ way /y/ yes.

throttle see: squeeze
a·tǫ·wan·yá·o·ha:k s.o. squeezed his neck

through see: along, beside
wa·dę·hę́:k'ah alongside the fence
[-a:'k'ah locative suffix; means 'beside' or 'alongside']
[-akdagye' locative; means 'beside' or 'alongside']

throw
gog·ye's to get rid of s.t., throw it away
[P+(N+) stem: -(a)di, ogy, -ǫdi, -ǫgy$_V$- throw]
ha'hó:di' he threw it
he·hó:gyǫ: he has thrown it
wag·yǫ: s.t. thrown away; discards
he'sá:dih throw it away from me
hǫ'gehn·yǫ́:di' I threw a stick
[he'+ P+(N+) stem: -(h)ny(a)$_V$ stick -(a)di, ogy, -ǫdi, -ǫgy$_V$- throw]

throw see: scatter
de·sa·dog·wáh·dǫh you have distributed it

throw one's voice see: ventriloquist
hęh·sad·wę·nǫ́:di' you will throw your voice (as a ventriloquist)

throw up see: vomit
ǫ·gén·y'a·go' I vomited

thud see: noise
otga:' a noise

thumb
a·wę́'yǫh·ga:' thumb
[a+ stem: -wę'yǫhg(a:)$_N$- thumb]
gw'ę·yǫh·gá:'geh on my thumb
swa·wę'yǫh·gá:'geh on your (p) thumbs

thump see: noise
otga:' a noise

thunder
de·wa·de·wa·yę·dá·ǫ·ha' it is thundering
[de+w(a)+ade+ stem: -wayędaǫha'$_V$- thunder; consists of: -wayę(da)$_N$- heart, spirit -(r)ǫ$_V$- string s.t.]

Thursday see: A (Gei: Ha̲dǫ't)

tick
ǫg·yá:gwah a tick mattress
[ǫ+ag+ stem: -ya:gwah- tick mattress; consists of: -ya:$_N$- bag -gw$_V$- gather, pick, get]

tick see: bag
gá:ya:' bag, mattress, tick (that is, a mattress bag into which straw is stuffed)

ticket
ho·na·des·he·dat·géhǫ' they (m) are selling tickets
[(ade+N+) stem: -sheda(da)$_N$- ticket -(a)tgehǫ$_V$- sell]

tickle
dęhs·he'nǫhs·gá'dę' you will tickle her
[de+TR+ stem: -'nohsga'dę$_V$- tickle]
dęhs·nóhs·g'a·dę' you will tickle it

tidal wave
da·wat·ne·gę́'gwaht there was a tidal wave
[de+...at+ stem: -(h)negę'gwahd- tidal wave; consists of: -(h)neg(a)$_N$- water, liquid -ę'gwa'd$_V$- be swelled up]

tide
ęt·gah·ne·gá·he:k it will be high tide
[d+ stem: -(h)negaheg- high tide; consists of: -(h)neg(a)$_N$- water, liquid -(h)e:'$_V$- sitting up on top of s.t.]
ęd·wat·ne·gę́'go' it will be high tide
[d+wa+at+ stem: -(h)negę'gw- high tide; consists of: -(h)neg(a)$_N$- water, liquid -ę'gw$_V$- swell up]
gyot·ne:gę́:gwęh high tide
dęt·gah·ne·gák·yę·to' it will be low tide
[de+...t+ga+ stem: -(h)negakyęto'- low tide; consists of: -(h)neg(a)$_N$- water, liquid -kyętw$_V$- be seated]

tidy
dwa·de·wa·yę:sdǫ́h ga·gé·hǫʼ it is tidy, neatly placed
[consists of: dwadewayę:sdǫh it is tidy, neat; gagehǫʼ it is lying there]
[d+wa+ade+ stem: -wayęsdǫh- tidy, neat; consists of: -wayę(n)$_N$- heart, spirit -wayę(h)sd$_V$- learn]
dwa·de·wa·yę:sdǫ́h gah·sę·nǫn·yáh·nǫʼ it is neatly put away
[consists of: dwadewayę:sdǫh it is tidy, neat; gahsęnǫnyahnǫʼ stored items; it is put away]

tidy up
dę·sá·doh·da:ʼ you will tidy it up, clean it
[de+...ad+ stem: -ohda(:,h)$_V$- tidy up, clean]
de·yo·doh·dá·hǫh it is tidy, neat
de·sá·doh·da: clean up
de·sa·doh·dáh·sǫ: clean up your surroundings
[de+...ad+ stem: -ohda(:,h)$_V$- tidy up, clean -sǫʼ plural]

tidy up see: clean
de·gat·nǫh·sáhs·nyeh I am cleaning up the house

tie
ga·géh·daʼ a tie; a scarf
[ga+ stem: -gehd(a)- tie, scarf; consists of: -geʼ(a:), geh(a)$_N$- hair -daʼ$_V$- stand up, stop]
de·se·jihs·dǫg·wá·ǫ·dęh tie a knot
[de+ stem: -jihsdoʼgwaǫd- tie a knot; consists of: -jihsdǫg(wa)$_N$- knot -ǫdę$_V$- put in]

tie see: hair tie, rope
gat·geʼa·yę́n·hahs·taʼ a hair tie
gá:ts·gʼę·daʼ a rope

tied up
gęhs·há·ǫ:t I am tied up
[A+ stem: -(h)shaǫd- be tied up; consists of: -sh(a)$_N$- string -ǫd$_V$- attached]
sehs·há·ǫ:t you are tied up

tied up see: tangled
de·yót·geʼi: its hair is tangled; ideas and things are tangled

tiger
da·gu:s·gó:wah a big cat; a tiger
[stem: -dagusgowah- tiger, big cat; consists of: -dagu:s$_N$- cat -gowah big]
o·jih·ne·waéʼ da·gu:s·gó:wah tiger
[consists of: ojihnewa:eʼ it has stripes; dagu:sgo:wah big cat; tiger]

tight
gah·níy·ʼa·dǫh it is tight, tightened
[ga+ stem: -(h)niyaʼd- tighten; consists of: -(h)niyaʼd$_V$- harden, toughen]

till see: hoe
at·keh·da·wę́:nye:ʼ I hoed, tilled the earth

tilt see: lean, slanted
wa·dí·hǫh it is leaning against s.t.
ga·gá·ę:heʼ it is slanted

timber see: log
oʼnháhg·yaʼ, on·háh·daʼ large lumber logs; timber

time
aʼǫ·nihs·hé:ʼah a short duration
[aʼ+ǫ+ stem: -nihshe:ʼah- a short length of time; consists of: -nihsheʼ$_V$- take time -ʼah diminutive]
tsaʼó·nihs·heʼ a long time; for that length of time
[tshaʼ+ǫ+ stem: consists of: -nihsheʼ$_V$- take time]
ni·ga·i·hóʼdęhs·ri:s a length of time working
[ni+ga+ stem: -(ri)hoʼdęhsr(a)$_N$- work -is$_V$- long; be a certain length, depth]

time see: A (nigahawiʼ), I (ne:ʼ gwahs hwaʼ)

time see: take one's time
sgę·nǫ:ʼǫ́h nęt·sye: you will take your time

Cayuga pronunciation guide: /a/ father /e/ weigh /ę/ men (nasalized) /i/ police /o/ hole /ǫ/ home (nasalized) /u/ blue. Underlined vowels are voiceless or whispered. /ʼ/ high pitch. /t/ too /d/ do /k/ king /g/ good (never soft g) /j/ judge or adze /s/ soon /sh/ less heat (never the sh in shirt) /sr/ shrine /sy/ sure /hw/ which (the sound made when you blow out a candle) /h/ hi /ts/ cats hide /ʼ/ (the sound before the first vowel in 'uh-uh') /n/ noon /r/ round /w/ way /y/ yes.

time piece see: clock
gah̲·wíhs·d'a̲·ehs a clock
timid
totg·ri: he's a wimp; he pulls back
[de+P+at+ stem: -gri:- be a wimp; consists of: -gri$_V$- wrinkle]
timid see: shy, weak
go·dí'grǫ' she is shy
ha·wę́·da·gę: he is weak (mentally or physically); he is a wimp; he is a coward
tin see: metal
gá·i:s·da' tin; metal
tint see: coloured, dyed
wa̲h·só·hǫ:t it is coloured, dyed
wa̲h·sá·hǫh it is dyed, coloured
tiny see: littl
ni·wú:'uh it is small, little
tip see: turn upside down, top
dę·gǫ·nǫh·wétso'dę' I am going to turn you upside down, upend you (said in anger)
hé:t·gęh·jih the very top
tipsy see: drunk
dih·sa:t·né:ga:t you are not level; you are tipsy
tire
o·yá:na' a tire; a tire track; anything that leaves tracks
[o+ stem: -yan(a)$_N$- tire, track]
tire see: flat
ad·ya·go·de·wa·né:ga:'s she got a flat tire
tired
a·gá·ǫ:t·sęht they (f/m) were tired, sleepy
[(N+) stem: -(a)tsę(hd)$_V$- get tired, sleepy]
ǫ'ni·gǫ·hát·sęh·ta' s.o. has a tired mind
[(N+) stem: -(')nigǫh(a)$_N$- mind -(a)tsę(hd)$_V$- be tired]
g'a·ni·gǫ·hát·sęh·ta' a tired mind

tired (continued)
a·ga·dat·sę́h·se: I am tired
[P+ad+ stem: -atsęhse:- be tired]
tired see: exhausted
ęk·ni·gǫ·há·ga̲·he:' I will be mentally exhausted
tireless see: active
ha·yá'tga·ǫ:' he is quick to move; he is active, always moving around
tire c.f.: annoyed, bother
ǫ'k·nǫ's I am sick of it, bored, fed up; I got sick of it
dęhs·ni·gǫ·há:ha' you are annoying me, bothering me
tiring
ot·sę́h·de:' it is tiring
[(N+) stem: -(a)tsę(hd)$_V$- tired]
tiring see: boring
o·nó's·hes·de:' it is boring, tiring
tissue see: handkerchief
ga̲h·nǫh a handkerchief
tit see: breast
e·nǫ́'gw'a·geh on her breast
title see: G (de·yǫ·ki·yah·węh·jah·snye'), D (chief title, ga·ya:ne:da')
title holder see: D (clan mother, Go·ya:neh)
titter see: giggle
sa·yǫ'gyé:ni:, sa·yǫ'gyę́:ni: you have the giggles
toad
sgwa:gwá·ǫ:dǫ' a toad
[stem: -sgwagwaǫdǫ'- consists of: -(nę)sgw(a)$_N$- frog -ǫdǫ'$_V$- several attached objects]
o·nǫhsg·wá·ǫ:dǫ' a toad
[o+ stem: -nǫhsgwaǫdǫ'- toad; consists of: -(nęh)sg(wa), (nǫh)sg(wa)$_N$- frog -ǫdǫ'$_V$- several attached objects]
sgwag·wa·ǫ·da·gó:wah a big, fat toad
[stem: -sgwagwaodagǫwah- toad; consists of: -(nęh)sg(wa), (nǫh)sg(wa)$_N$- frog -gowah big]

toaster
ga·naʼdá·ę:ʼdahs a toaster
[ga+ stem: -naʼdaę:ʼdahs- toaster; consists of: -naʼd(a:)$_{N}$- bread -(hr)ęʼda:$_{V}$- burn s.t.]

tobacco
o·yę́ʼgwaʼ tobacco; cigarettes
[o+ stem: -yęʼg(wa)$_{N}$- tobacco, smoke, cigarettes]
o·yęʼgwʼá·ǫ·weh Indian tobacco (ceremonial, home-grown, not processed)
[o+ stem: -yęʼg(wa)$_{N}$- tobacco, cigarettes -ǫweh- real, Aboriginal]

tobacco pipe see: pipe
ot·sóg·wah·daʼ a pipe (for tobacco)

tobacco pouch
o·yęʼgwáʼ wa·dǫ·dá:taʼ a tobacco pouch
[consists of: oyęʼgwaʼ tobacco, cigarettes; wadǫda:taʼ a container]
e·yęʼgwa·dǫ·da:táʼ ga·ya:ʼ a tobacco pouch
[consists of: eyęʼgwadǫda:taʼ s.t. that holds tobacco; gaya:ʼ bag, etc.]
e·yęʼgwa·dǫ·dá:taʼ s.t. that holds tobacco
[e+ stem: -yęʼgwadǫdataʼ- tobacco holder; consists of: -yęʼg(wa)$_{N}$- tobacco, smoke, cigarettes -ǫdad$_{V}$- hold s.t.]

tobacco worm
ga·yęʼgwa:sgó:wah a tobacco worm
[ga+ stem: -yęʼgwasgowah- tobacco worm; consists of: -yęʼg(wa)$_{N}$- tobacco, smoke, cigarettes -g$_{V}$- eat -gowah big]

toboggan
hę·na·ded·réh·dęh·taʼ they (m) are tobogganing
[ade+ stem: -(ʼ)drehdęhd- toboggan consists of: -(ʼ)drehd(a)$_{N}$- car, vehicle -(y)ęhd$_{V}$- hit]

today see: I (waʼne:ʼ)

toe
oh·ya:gwí:yaʼ a toe; toes
[o+ stem: -(a)hyagwiy(a)$_{N}$- toe]
gah·yag·wi·yáʼgeh on my toes
swah·yag·wi·yáʼgeh on your (p) toes

together see: add, assemble, be someplace, escort, put together
haʼdę́:syehs you will put them all together
dęh·sé·ga·hǫʼ you will assemble, put together
gę́:neʼs they (z) are around; they are here; they are together
hęhs·he·ha·wíh·dahk you will escort her, take her with you
de·sat·si·náʼdręʼ you put your legs together

toilet
ahs·déh he·yę́h·dahk·waʼ a toilet
[consists of: ahsdeh outside; heyęhdahkwaʼ it removes feces]

toilet bowl
ahs·déh ǫ·dǫ́ʼdahk·waʼ a toilet bowl
[consists of: ahsdeh outside; ǫdǫʼdahkwaʼ toilet bowl]
ǫ·dǫ́ʼdahk·waʼ a toilet bowl
[ǫ+ad+ stem: -(i)ʼdǫdahkwaʼ- toilet; consists of: -(ni)ʼd(a)$_{N}$- feces -ǫdahkwaʼ$_{V}$- container]

toilet paper
ahs·déh ǫ·dǫʼdahk·wáʼ oh·yá·dǫhs·raʼ toilet paper
[consists of: ahsdeh ǫdǫʼdahkwaʼ toilet bowl; ohyadǫhsraʼ paper]

tomahawk see: axe
a·dó:gęʼ an axe; a tomahawk

tomato
oh·yá·ka·hǫʼ tomatoes
[o+ stem: -(a)hyakahǫʼ- tomato; consists of: -(a)hy(a)$_{N}$- fruit, berry -kahǫ$_{V}$- adjoin, abutt]

Cayuga pronunciation guide: /a/ father /e/ weigh /ę/ men (nasalized) /i/ police /o/ hole /ǫ/ home (nasalized) /u/ blue. Underlined vowels are voiceless or whispered. /ʹ/ high pitch. /t/ too /d/ do /k/ king /g/ good (never soft g) /j/ judge or adze /s/ soon /sh/ less heat (never the sh in shirt) /sr/ shrine /sy/ sure /hw/ which (the sound made when you blow out a candle) /h/ hi /ts/ cats hide /ʼ/ (the sound before the first vowel in 'uh-uh') /n/ noon /r/ round /w/ way /y/ yes.

tomb-stone see: sign
ga·néhs·da·ot headboards; grave markers; billboards; signs
tomorrow see: A (ęyo:hę')
Tonawanda, N.Y. see: E (Tah·na·wa:de')
tongue
a·wę́'nah·sa' a tongue
[(a+) stem: -(a)wę'nahs(a), (a)wę'nohs(a)$_N$- tongue]
sw'ę·nóh·s'a·geh on your tongue
gw'ę·nóh·s'a·geh on my tongue
swa·wę'noh·sá'geh on your (p) tongues
tonic see: F (various plant names), weed
a·wę́·nohg·ra' weeds
tonight see: A (ęyo'ga:)
too see: I (hni'), exceptional
á·o·goh·doh exceptional; above average; too much
tool
ehs·ta'shó:'oh tools; utensils
[e+ stem: -(h)sta'- tool consists of: -hsd$_N$- tool, utensil -(h)s(d)$_V$- use -so:'oh plural]
od·ri·ho'dá:sta' tools, equipment
[o+ad+ stem: -(r)iho'dahsta'- tool; consists of: -(ri)ho'dahsd$_V$- cause to work]
had·ri·ho'dáhs·ta' his tools
ha'dreh·do:níhs had·ri·ho'dá:sta' a mechanic's working tools
[consists of: (s)ha'drehdo:nihs he is a mechanic; hadriho'da:sta' his tools]
too much see: exceptional
á·o·goh·doh exceptional, above average; too much
tooth
o·nó'ja' teeth
[o+ stem: -no'j(a)$_N$- tooth]
sa·nó'ja' your teeth
sn'o·já'geh on your teeth
kn'o·já'geh on my teeth
swa·nó'j'a·geh on your (p) teeth
e·nó'jo:t she has teeth
[A+ stem: -no'j(a)$_N$- tooth -od$_V$- stand]
de·ga·no'já:ga: grinding teeth
[de+ ga+ stem: -no'j(a)$_N$- tooth -ga:$_V$- make a rattling or grinding noise]
toothache
ak·no'ja·nóh·wa:s I have a toothache
[P+ stem: -no'j(a)$_N$- tooth -nohwag$_V$- sore, ache]
toothbrush
ot·no'jo·há·i'ta' a toothbrush
[o+at+ stem: -no'johai'ta'- toothbrush; consists of: -no'j(a)$_N$- tooth -ohai'd$_V$- cause to be clean]
toothpaste
ot·no'jo·ha·i·dáhk·wa' toothpaste
[o+at+ stem: -no'johai'dahkwa'- toothpaste; consists of: -no'j(a)$_N$- tooth -ohai'dahkwa'$_V$- s.t. that cleans]
top
hé:tgęh·jih the very top
toque
ga·jihn·yog·wa·hé:' a·na·há·o:tra' a toque
[consists of: gajihnyogwahe:' toque; anahaotra' hat]
ga·jihn·yog·wá·he:' a toque
[ga+ stem: -jihnyogwahe:'- toque; consists of: -jihnyog(wa)$_N$- tree knot -(h)e:'$_V$- sitting up on top of s.t.]
torch
a·hę·na·tahs·ró·dę' they (m) carried a torch, lantern, flashlight
[at+ stem: -(h)ahsrod- night-fish, spearfish, go jack-lighting; consists of: -(h)ahsr(a)$_N$- flash -od$_V$- be attached]
torch see: lantern
o·tahs·ro·dáhk·wa' a flashlight; a torch
torment see: agony, tease
groh·yá:gęhs I am always in pain
ęhs·hey'a·dę́·don·ya't you will make fun of it; s.t. will make fun of you, messing with your head or mind (refers to reliving your sins before death); you will joke

tornado
de·ga·wa:dá:sehs a tornado
[de+ga+ stem: -wadasehs- tornado; consists of: -w(a:)$_N$- air -dase$_V$- whirl]
Toronto, Ont. see: E (Tga·ǫ:do')
torso see: body, trunk
o·yá'da' a body
o·hí'ya' the body's trunk, form
toss see: throw
ha'hó:di' he threw it
total see: sum
ę·gá:go' a sum; a total
tote see: haul, hold, wallet
ęk·nęhg·wi' I will carry, move, tote it
e·há:wi' she carried it here
gat·gwę·da' wallet, purse, pocketbook, suitcase
totter see: stagger
hehs·hohs·hę·dá'ǫh tsǫ: he is staggering
touch
hehs·yé:ha' you are a toucher
[he'+... stem: -ye:, yę:$_V$- touch]
ha:ga·ké:ye:' I touched them
heh·sá:yę: you did touch s.t.
touch see: caress, grope
ę·hes·y'a·dahd·rǫ́:gǫ' you will caress him
hęhs·yáh·nǫ:' you will grope, touch, pick at s.t.
touchy see: cantankerous, grumpy, nervous
e·nǫ́·wę̱hd·ra' she is cantankerous
de·di·s'a·ni·gǫ·hí:yo: you are grumpy, grouchy, unhappy
wa·dón·ya̱h·nǫ: it is nervous
ni·wag·ri̱·hú:'uh I am sensitive
tough see: hard
oh·ní:yǫh it is hard
tow see: drag
ak·ní'dre' we two (excl.) are dragging s.t.; we are riding along
tow truck
g'ad·reh·da·nęhg·wi̱h·ta' a tow truck
[ga+ stem: -(')drehdanęhgwihta'- tow truck; consists of: -(')drehd(a)$_N$- vehicle, car -nęhgwihd$_V$- haul with s.t.]
towel
ǫh·ja·ge·wáh·ta' a towel
[ǫ+ stem: -(a)hjagewahta'- towel; consists of: -(a)hj(a)$_N$- hand -(r)agewahd$_V$- wipe with s.t.]
towel see: paper towel
ga̱h·ya·dǫhs·rá' ǫh·ja·ge·wáh·ta' paper towels
town
ga·ná:da' town
[ga+ stem: -nad(a)$_N$- town, community]
ga·ná·da·gǫ: in the town, community
[ga+ stem: -nad(a)$_N$- town, community -agǫ: in]
ga·na·da·gǫ́h·ge̱·ha:' urban
[ga+ stem: -nad(a)$_N$- town, community -agǫ: in -geha:' type]
ǫg·wa:ná:da' our community
ǫg·wa·na·dá:gǫ: in our community
ga·ná·da·ę' a town
[ga+ consists of: -nad(a)$_N$- town, community -ę$_V$- lie on the ground]
tga·na·dá·ę:dǫ' the towns are over there
[ga+ consists of: -nad(a)$_N$- town, community -ędǫ'$_V$- several objects lying on the ground]
town see: village
ni·ga·na·dú:'uh a village; a small town
town square
tsa'de·ga·ná·da̱·hęh a village square; a village centre; a town square
[tsa'+de+ga+ stem: -nadahęh- town square, village square; consists of: -nad(a)$_N$- town, community -(h)ęh$_V$- mid, half, middle]
towtruck see: jack
de·ga'drę̱h·dáhk·wa' a jack; a tow truck; a hoist

Cayuga pronunciation guide: /a/ father /e/ weigh /ę/ men (nasalized) /i/ police /o/ hole /ǫ/ home (nasalized) /u/ blue. Underlined vowels are voiceless or whispered. /'/ high pitch. /t/ too /d/ do /k/ king /g/ good (never soft g) /j/ judge or adze /s/ soon /sh/ less heat (never the sh in shirt) /sr/ shrine /sy/ sure /hw/ which (the sound made when you blow out a candle) /h/ hi /ts/ cats hide /'/ (the sound before the first vowel in 'uh-uh') /n/ noon /r/ round /w/ way /y/ yes.

toxin see: poison
o'ná'sę: poison
toy
ǫt·gá·hi'ta' what she plays with; a toy
[ǫ+at+ stem: -gahi'd$_V$- play with s.t.]
ǫt·ga·hi'dáhk·wa' a toy (lit.: children play with it)
[ǫ+at+ stem: -gahi'dahkwa'- toy; consists of: -gahi'd$_V$- play with s.t.]
o·wi:ya:'áh ǫt·ga·hi'dáhk·wa' a baby's toys
[consists of: owi:ya:'ah baby; ǫtgahi'dahkwa' toy]
trace see: mark, write
ęg·yá:na't I will mark s.t.
eh·yá:dǫh she writes
track see: basement, hunt, path, tire, trail
o·yá:de' a basement; a track; a ditch
hę·na:dó:wa:s they (m) are hunting
ǫ·dǫh·gǫh·dáhk·wa' a path
o·yá:na' a tire; a tire track; anything that leaves tracks
de·yǫ·do·gę́h·dahk·wa' a trail
tractor
ga·heh·da·geh·ká:' g'ad·réh·da' a tractor
[consists of: gahehdagehka:' dirt or earth kind; g'adrehda' vehicle]
trade
dę·hę·nę·dá·da·wihs trades; commerce; barter
[(de+)...adad+ stem: -awi, ǫ$_V$- give; trade, exchange]
dę·sá·da·dǫ' you will trade, exchange it
trade see: sell
ęh·sát·gę·hǫ' you will sell it
trade cloth
ohs·di:s trade cloth
[o+ stem: -(h)sdi:s- trade cloth; consists of: -hsd$_N$- tool, utensil -es$_V$- long]
tradition
o·ih·wa·gá:yǫh it is traditional
[o+ stem: -(r)ih(wa) $_N$- matter, etc. -gayǫh$_V$- old (thing)]
tragedy
ga·nǫ́:' tsę́ nǫ'ǫg·wa·yá'da·węh tragedy has befallen us
[consists of: ganǫ:' it is costly; tsę how nǫ'ǫgwaya'dawęh it happened to us]
trail
de·yǫ·do·gę́h·dahk·wa' a trail
[de+yǫ++ad+ stem: -ǫgęhdahkwa'- path; consists of: -ǫgohd$_V$- surpass; pass by]
trail see: path
ǫ·dǫh·gǫh·dáhk·wa' a path
train
ęhs·he·wa·yę́·sdę' you will train, educate, teach s.o.
[TR+ stem: -waye(h)sd(ę, ani)- train, educate, teach; consists of: -wayę(n)$_N$- heart, spirit -wayę(h)sd$_V$- learn]
ga·wa·yęhs·dá:ni: it has been taught
g'ad·reh·da·ya:nó:we' train; a fast car
[ga+ stem: -(')drehdayanowe'- train; consists of: -(')drehd(a)$_N$- vehicle, car -yanowe'$_V$- fast]
traitor
de·ho·ih·wa·dó:gę: he is a traitor
[de'+ not P+ stem: -(r)ihwadogę:- be reliable; be a traitor; consists of: -(r)ih(wa)$_N$- word -dogę(:)$_V$- right, true]
tramp
a·ho·dęh·té:'ah a tramp; a hobo; a vagabond
[P+ad+ stem: -ęhte:'ah- tramp, vagabond; consists of: -ęhte$_V$- go and hit, strike, knock -'ah diminutive]
transaction see: agreement
ga·íh·wih·sa' an agreement
Trans-Canada Highway see: G (De·yoh·wę·ji·ya'gǫh)

transcriber see: secretary, tape recorder
eh·yá·dọ·haʼ she is a secretary, stenographer, court recorder, transcriber
ga·wẹ·na·yé:nahs a tape recorder; a transcriber
transgress see: sin
ẹg·rih·wa·néʼa:s I will sin
transient see: stay
got·wáʼehs·dọh she is a boarder, homeless, a transient
transit see: across (go)
at·sa:dǫ́:goht you went across; you have completed s.t.
translate
de·ye·wẹ·ná·den·yeʼs she is a translator; she is translating now
[de+ stem: -wẹnadeni- translate; consists of: -wẹn(a)$_N$- voice, word -deni, deny$_V$- change]
dẹ·ha·wẹ·ná·den·yeʼs he is a translator
translator see: interpreter
ha·dẹ·wẹ·ná·ga·da:s he is an interpreter
translucent see: transparent
transmit see: send
he·wa·ga·dẹ́n·yeh·dọh I sent it
transparent
he·yó:gẹʼt it is transparent
[heʼ+ yo+ stem: -gẹʼd- be visible; be transparent; consists of: -(ʼ)gẹd$_V$- be light-coloured, white]
transpire see: happen
ni·yá·wʼẹọh how it did happen
transportation
go·yaʼda·nẹ́hg·wih transportation; a bus; an elevator (lit.: people mover)
[go+ stem: -yaʼdanẹhgwih- transportation, bus, elevator; consists of: -yaʼd(a)$_N$- body -nẹhgwi$_V$- haul]
trap
hẹ·nad·rihs·dá·ẹ·hẹʼ they (m) are trappers
[ad+ stem: -(r)ihsdaẹ(:)- trap; consists of: -(h)wihsd(a), (h)rihsd(a)$_N$- metal, money -ẹ$_V$- lie on the ground]
ọd·rihs·dá·ẹ·dahk·waʼ a trap
[ọ+ad+stem: -rihsdaẹdahkwaʼ- trap; consists of: -(h)wihsd(a), (hr)ihsd(a)$_N$- metal, money -ẹdahkwaʼ$_V$- place where s.t. is put]
travel
ni·ya·got·gẹ·ihs·dǫ́·hǫg·yeʼ she is travelling as she is moving
[ni+P+at+ stem: -gẹihsdọhọgyeʼ- travel along; consists of: -gẹihsd$_V$- move, postpone]
ni·yot·gẹ·i:s·dọ·hǫ́:gyeʼ it is travelling along
ẹt·ga·ọ:tǫ́:yo:ʼ they (f/m) will come by boat
[d+...at+ stem: -(h)ọyo(:)- travel by boat; consists of: -(h)ọw(a)$_N$- boat -o(:)$_V$- submerge, boil, cook]
traverse see: across (go across)
at·sa:dǫ́:goht you went across; you have completed s.t.
tray
ga·jẹʼe·ha·wʼi·dáhk·waʼ a tray
[ga+ stem: -jẹʼehawiʼdahkwaʼ- tray; consists of: -jẹʼ$_N$- dish, plate, bowl -(h)awiʼdahkwaʼ$_V$- s.t. that holds, carries s.t.]
tread see: step on s.t., tire, walk
ẹh·sahs·hẹ́:daʼ you will step on s.t.
o·yá:naʼ a tire; a tire track; anything that leaves tracks
dẹ·gá·ta·hahk I will walk
treasure
o·nǫ́hs·daʼt, o·nǫ́hs·deht it is a treasure; it is precious, valuable; it is possessive
[o+ stem: -nọhsdaʼd, nọhsdehd- treasure, precious, valuable; consists of: -nọ:ʼ$_V$- be costly, dear, expensive]

Cayuga pronunciation guide: /a/ father /e/ weigh /ẹ/ men (nasalized) /i/ police /o/ hole /ọ/ home (nasalized) /u/ blue. Underlined vowels are voiceless or whispered. /ˊ/ high pitch. /t/ too /d/ do /k/ king /g/ good (never soft g) /j/ judge or adze /s/ soon /sh/ less heat (never the sh in shirt) /sr/ shrine /sy/ sure /hw/ which (the sound made when you blow out a candle) /h/ hi /ts/ cats hide /ʼ/ (the sound before the first vowel in 'uh-uh') /n/ noon /r/ round /w/ way /y/ yes.

treat see: dessert, goodies
na·wę’da·wehts·hǫ́ː’ǫh dessert (lit. sweet things)
o·ga’ǫhs·hǫ́ː’ǫh goodies, dessert

tree
gra̲·heːt living tree
[stem: -grahe’d(a)$_{N}$- tree -d$_{V}$- stand]
gra̲·héːdǫ’ many trees
[stem: -grahe’d(a)$_{N}$- tree -dǫ’$_{V}$- several standing objects]
gra̲·hé·dǫn·yǫ’ variety of trees
[stem: -grahe’d(a)$_{N}$- tree -dǫnyǫ’$_{V}$- several standing objects]
gra̲·hé·da’geh on the tree
[stem: -grahe’d(a)$_{N}$- tree -’geh- on]
nig·ra·he·dó’dęː what type of tree
[ni+ stem: -grahe’d(a)$_{N}$- tree -o’dęː$_{V}$- type of]
gra̲·he·do·wáːnęh a big tree
[stem: -grahe’d(a)$_{N}$- tree -owanęh$_{V}$- be big]
o·héh·sa’ a decayed tree; a log; wood; a board
[o+ stem: -(h)ehs(a)$_{N}$- decayed tree]
gá·ǫ·da̲’oː a notched tree
[ga+ stem: -(r)ǫd(a)$_{N}$- log -(hwę’ga)’oh$_{V}$- notch]
gá·ǫ·da·ę’ a dead tree; a log lying on the ground
[ga+stem: -(r)ǫd(a)$_{N}$- log -ę$_{V}$- lie on the ground]
á·ǫ·dat·gęː a dead tree
[a+ stem: -(r)ǫd(a)$_{N}$- log -tgęː$_{V}$- be spoiled, rotten]

tree see: sapling
wa’ęːnóːdǫ’ saplings’ young trees

tree sap see: resin
ohs·daː’áh ot·séhs·da’ pine pitch; pine resin

trek see: walk
dę·gá·ta·hahk I will walk

tremble see: quiver, shake, shiver
ę·sa·y’a·dahd·rǫ́ːgǫ’ you will quiver, shudder
ę·sa·y’a·dǫ́ːda’t you will shiver, shake
sa·ya’dod·rǫhg·wá·ǫ·ni̲hs·gǫː you are always shivering

tremor see: heart tremor, earthquake
de·yo·wa·yęh·sis·hǫhk·wá’
a·gǫ́n·heh·gǫh a heart tremor
ag·yǫh·węh·ję́ːdǫh an earthquake

trench see: basement
o·yáːde’ basement, track, ditch

triangle
ah·sę́h na’de·yo·do·gá·ǫ·de’ triangle
[consists of: ahsęh three; na’deyodogaǫde’ it has a certain number of sides]

trick
tso·hét·sog·wahs it tricks him all the time
[(s+) P+ stem: -(h)etsogw$_{V}$- trick, fool]
se·sa·heht·sóːgo’ you got fooled (like the frog)
a’o·di·heːt·sóːgo’ it tricked them (for example, frogs)
sa’o·di·heːt·sóːgo’ they (frogs) were fooled (that is, they came out in the spring too early)
a·ho·het·sóːgo’ it tricked him (like the frog)
sa·go̲·het·sóːgo’ it tricked her (like the frog)
sha·o·het·sóːgo’ it has tricked him; he got fooled (like the frog)
sho·het·sog·węh he was fooled (like the frog)
og·yá·ǫhs·ra’, ag·yá·ǫhs·ra’ a trick
[(o+) stem: -(a)gyaǫhsr(a)$_{N}$- trick -(a)gyaǫ’$_{V}$- be tricked, fooled]
eh·saːgyá·ǫ’ you were tricked, fooled
[P+ stem: -(a)gyaǫ’$_{V}$- be tricked, fooled]

trick see: deceive
ęh·se·ya·dó·goh·dę' you will outdo s.o.; you will go right over her, go right past her; deceive her

trickle see: leak
oh·né·go·gahs dripping water (from a tap)

trifling see: unimportant
o·ga·os·hǫ́:'ǫh s.t. not important, second-rate

trim
ęt·só·ha·go' you will cut down, trim s.t. [d+...(N+) stem: -ohagw$_{V}$- trim, cut down, unattach; consists of: -oha(:,ę)$_{V}$- attach]

trinket see: toy
ǫt·ga·hi'dáhk·wa' a toy

trip
de·de·sa·do·dah·dá:nih it trips you all the time
[de+...+ad+ stem: -odahd(ę, ani)$_{V}$- trip]
dęh·sa·do·dáh·dę' it will trip you
de·sah·sig·yá'ksgǫ: you are always stumbling, tripping, stubbing your toe; you are a klutz
[de+... stem: -(a)hsigya'g- trip, stumble, stub one's toe; consists of: -(a)hsi('da), (ę)hs(a)$_{N}$- foot -(i)ya'g$_{V}$- cut, break -sgǫ: easily]
ę·dih·sah·sí'gya'k you will stumble, stub your toe
ę·ga·ǫ:gi·dag·ráh·dę' they are going to trip me, make me fall
[TR+ stem: -(i)dagrahd- trip s.o., make s.o. fall; consists of: -(i)dagra'$_{V}$- fall down]

trip see: bar
ęts·he·yah·si·no·dáh·dę', **dęhs·he·yah·si·no·dáh·dę'** you will trip s.o., bar s.o.'s way with your leg

tripe
on·ré·g'ę·da' tripe (cow stomach lining); an animal stomach
[P+ stem: -nregę'd(a)$_{N}$- tripe, stomach (animal)]

triumph see: win
a·hǫ·wa·di:gwé:ni' they won a competition

trivial see: unimportant
o·ga·os·hǫ́:'ǫh s.t. not important, second-rate

trouble see: nuisance
des·hay'ada'ni·gǫ́·ha:t you are a nuisance

trough
gat·se:nę́' **ga·dih·ne·ga·he'dáhk·wa'** a trough
[consists of: gatse:nę' tame animal; gadihnegahe'dahkwa' watering trough]
ha·dih·ne·gáhk·wa' a trough
[hadi+ stem: -(h)negahkwa'- water spout; water trough; consists of: -(h)neg(a)$_{N}$- water, liquid -hkwa' an instrument]

trout
o·nǫ́'seh a trout
[o+ stem: -nǫ'seh- trout; consists of: -nǫ'seh$_{V}$- be lazy, idle]

trowel see: spade
e·héhg·y'ak·ta' a spade

truck
deg·rǫ'sga·é' **ni·wę'nihs·ga·ǫ́:t** **ga·nę́hg·wih** a transport truck
[consists of: degrǫ'sgae' niwę'nihsgaǫ:t it has eighteen wheels; ganęhgwih it hauls things]
gah·wihs·da·nęhg·wíh **g'ad·réh·da'** an armoured truck (for example, a Brink's truck)
[consists of: gahwihsdanęhgwih it hauls money; g'adrehda' vehicle]
hye·í' **ni·wę·nihs·ga·ǫ́:t** **g'ad·réh·da'** a stake truck
[consists of: hyei' niwęnihsgaǫ:t it has six wheels; g'adrehda' vehicle]

Cayuga pronunciation guide: /a/ father /e/ weigh /ę/ men (nasalized) /i/ police /o/ hole /ǫ/ home (nasalized) /u/ blue. Underlined vowels are voiceless or whispered. /´/ high pitch. /t/ too /d/ do /k/ king /g/ good (never soft g) /j/ judge or adze /s/ soon /sh/ less heat (never the sh in shirt) /sr/ shrine /sy/ sure /hw/ which (the sound made when you blow out a candle) /h/ hi /ts/ cats hide /'/ (the sound before the first vowel in 'uh-uh') /n/ noon /r/ round /w/ way /y/ yes.

truck see: car
gʼad·réh·daʼ a car; a vehicle
truck driver
hye·íʼ ni·wę̨ʼni̲hs·ga·ǫ́·t ha·dó:nyeʼs a truck driver
[consists of: hyeiʼ niwę̨ʼni̲hsgaǫ:t it has six wheels; hadonyeʼs he is a driver]
true see: right
dó:gęhs sure; truly; right; it is a fact
trunk
o·híʼyaʼ the body's trunk, form
[o+ stem: -(h)iʼy(a)$_N$- trunk, form]
trunk see: wallet
gat·gwę́ʼdaʼ a wallet; a purse; a pocketbook; a suitcase
trust see: rely
ke·yáʼdaʼs I rely on her
trustworthy see: reliable
ho·ih·wa·dó:gę: he is a reliable person
truth
ga·ih·wag·wę:ní:yoʼ the truth
[ga+ stem: -(r)ihwagwęniyoʼ- truth, leader; consists of: -(r)ih(wa)$_N$- word -gwęniyoʼ$_V$- main]
grih·wag·wę·ní:yoʼ where I reside, dwell (lit.: where I'm the boss)
truthful see: righteous
od·rih·wag·wá·ih·sǫ: it is believable, credible, righteous, fair, honest
try
ga·deʼnyę́:dęhs I try all the time
[ade+ stem: -(ʼ)nyędę$_V$- try]
ęh·sa·dʼen·yę́:dęʼ you will try
a:ga·deʼnyę́:dęʼ I might try or attempt
sa·deʼnyę́:dęh sample it; try it
sa·deʼnyę·dęhs·dǫ·hǫ́:gyeʼ you are trying as you go
[ade+ stem: -(ʼ)nyędęhsdǫhǫgyeʼ- measure, go along trying; consists of: -(ʼ)nyędę$_V$- try]
try see: persevere
swa·já:gǫh you all persevere; keep it up (a word of encouragement)

tub see: bath tub, sink
ǫg·yaʼdǫ·há·iʼtaʼ, ǫg·yaʼdǫ·háʼtaʼ bath tub
ǫh·jo·há·i:ʼtaʼgeh a sink; a wash basin
tube
ga̲·hó·wʼe·daʼ a tube; a cylinder
[ga+ stem: -(h)oweʼd(a)$_N$- tube, cylinder, hose]
ga̲·ho·we·dahs·hǫ́:ʼǫh hoses; cylinders
tuber see: root
ok·dé·haʼ root; edible roots (pepper roots, turnips, carrots)
tuck in see: cover
ęh·se·hó:we:k you will cover s.t.
tumbler
de·yo·wid·ra·téh ga·náʼjo̲hsg·waʼ a glass tumbler
[consists of: deyowiʼdra:teh it is icy, glassy; ganaʼjo̲hsgwaʼ cup]
tumor see: cancer
gaʼwá·ha:s, goʼwáha:s cancer
tumultuous see: loud, noise
ga·iʼs·do·wá:nęh it is noisy
ot·gá·iʼni: it is noisy, loud
turf see: sod
oʼǫ́hg·wa:ʼ sod; moss
turkey
so·hǫ:t turkey
[stem: -sohǫ:t$_N$- turkey]
turn
dęh·sat·ga̲·ha:dé:niʼ you will turn yourself around
[de+...at+ stem: -gahadeni- turn around; consists of: -gah(a)$_N$- eye -deni, deny$_V$- change]
dę·gat·ga̲·ha:dé:niʼ I am going to turn around (and go home)
dǫ:sa·gat·ga·ha:dé:niʼ I should turn around and go back; I should go home
de·sat·ga̲·ha:dé:nih turn around
turn see: roll, turn off, turn on, turn over, turn upside down
sat·gá·ha·toh roll over

turn off see: extinguish
sahs·waht put the light out
turn on
ga·jíhs·do:t the light is on
[ga+ stem: -jihsdod- turn on; consists of: -jihsd(a)$_N$- light -od$_V$- stand]
se·jihs·dó:dęh turn on the light
[stem: -jihsdod- turn on; consists of: -jihsd(a)$_N$- light -odę$_V$- put in]
de·se·ga·ha:dé:nih turn it on (involves movement)
[de+... stem: -gahadeni- turn around; turn s.t. on, switch s.t. on; consists of: -gah(a)$_N$- eye -deni, deny$_V$- change]
a·há·ha·ha:ʼ he went onto the road here
[stem: -(h)ah(a)$_N$- road -(h)awi, (h)a:$_V$- hold, include, carry, bring]
turn over
a·wa·dʼed·reh·da·gá·ha·toʼ a vehicle was turned over
[ade+N+ stem: -(ʼ)drehd(a)$_N$- vehicle, car -gahatw$_V$- turn over]
ga·heh·da·gá·hat·węh a ploughed field
[stem: -(h)ehd(a)$_N$- land, dirt, earth, ground -gahatw$_V$- turn over]
turn upside down
dę·gǫ·nǫh·wétsoʼdęʼ I am going to turn you upside down, upend you (said in anger)
[de+TR+ stem: -nǫhwetsoʼdę- turn s.o. upside down; consists of: -nǫhwetsoʼd(ǫ, ę)$_V$- do a handstand, turn s.o. upside down]
turn upside down see: handstand
dę·sat·nǫh·wétsoʼdǫʼ you will do a hand stand, turn yourself upside down
turnip see: root (edible)
ok·dé·haʼ a root; edible roots (pepper roots, turnips, carrots)
turtle
ha·no·wa·he:t·gę́:sʼah a mischievous turtle; a mud turtle
[ha+ stem: -nowahetgę:sʼah- mischievous turtle, mud turtle; consists of: -nowa(gwa)$_N$- rounded back -(hr)etgęsʼah$_V$- unattractive]
od·ręʼí:ga:ʼ painted turtle
[o+ stem: -dręʼiga:ʼ$_N$- painted turtle]
gan·yáh·dę: a turtle
[ga+ stem: -nyahdę:$_N$- turtle]
ga·no·wa·ga·hé:ʼah a box turtle
[ga+ stem: -nowagahe:ʼah- box turtle; consists of: -nowa(gwa)$_N$- rounded back -(h)e:ʼ$_V$- sitting up on top of s.t. -ʼah diminutive]
gan·yah·dę·gó:wah a snapping turtle
[stem: -nyahdęgowah$_N$- snapping turtle; consists of: -nyahdę$_N$- turtle -gowah big]
Turtle clan see: C (gen·yah·dę:)
Tuscarora, N.Y. see: E (Dahs·gao·węʼgeh)
Tuscarora people see: C (Dahs·ga·o:węʼ)
tusk
ga·nóʼje:s a tusk
[ga+ stem: -noʼjes- tusk; consists of: -noʼj(a)$_N$- tooth -es$_V$- long]
o·nóʼje:s a fang
[o+ stem: -noʼjes- fang; consists of: -noʼj(a)$_N$- tooth -es$_V$- long]
ga·gǫ́n·yǫh·se:s a rhino tusk
[ga+ stem: -(ʼ)nyǫhses- tusk; consists of: -gǫnyǫhs(a)$_N$- tusk -es$_V$- long]
Tutelo people see: C (Ho·nǫh·wę·ja:do:gę, De·yo·di:ho:nǫʼ)
t.v. see: movie
ga·yáʼtaʼ movies; television
twelve see: B (dek·ni: sga·eʼ)
twenty see: B (de·wahs·hę:)
twice
dek·ní hę·wá:dra:s twice
[dekni two heʼ+ wa+ ad+ stem: -(r)ahs(d)$_V$- times]
twilight see: A (węda:jihs)

twin
dę̱·há·di·kęh twin boys
[de+A+(N+) stem: -kęh$_V$- twins]
twine see: line, thread
oh·sí:yǫ:t an attached cord; a string; an umbilical cord
oh·sí:ya' a thread; a string; a cord
twirl
de·sat·ga̱·ha·den·yǫ́g·wa̱·hǫ: twirl
[de+...at+ stem: -gahadenyǫgwahǫ:- twirl; consists of: -gah(a)$_N$- eye -deni, deny$_V$- change]
twist see: twirl
twister see: tornado
de·ga·wa:dá:sehs a tornado
twitch see: shiver
de·sa·y'a·dod·rǫhg·wá·ǫ·hǫ' you twitch all the time; you are a twitcher
two
de·ga·di·yáhs·he: two of them; they (z) are two
[de+A+ stem: -yahshe:$_V$- two or more living things]
dę̱·ha·di·yáhs·he: two males; they (m) are two
two see: B (dek·ni:)
two-faced
sa·gǫh·sa̱h·ní:yǫh you are two-faced
[P+ stem: -gǫhsahniyǫh- two-faced; consists of: -gǫhs(a)$_N$- face -(h)niyǫh$_V$- be hard, tough]
Tyendinaga, N.Y. see: E (Det·ga·yę:da:ne·gę', Ta·yę·da:ne:gę')
type see: certain type, kind of thing
ni·ga·ę·nó'dę: a type of song
type
[-geha:', -ka:', -neha:' customary suffixes; denote a typical 'way' or 'kind' of thing]
typewriter
de·ga·ihs·dó:ha:s a typewriter
[de+ga+ stem: -(r)ihsdohas:- typewriter; consists of: -(r)ihsdohag$_V$- publish]
typist see: secretary
eh·yá·dǫ·ha' she is a secretary, stenographer, court recorder, transcriber

U

udder
e·nǫ́'go:t udders
[e+ stem: -nǫ'g(wa)$_N$- breast, milk -od$_V$- stand]
ugly
a·ǫ́·teht·gęht s.o. turned funny (moody, etc.)
[at+ stem: -(hr)etgęhd- ruin, wreck, damage; turn moody; consists of: -(hr)etgę$_V$- be evil, bad, ugly]
ho·teht·gę·dǫ́:ni: he is in a funny, odd mood; he is moody
[P+ad+ stem: -(hr)etgędǫni- be in a bad mood; consists of: -(hr)etgęd$_V$- turn dirty, ugly -ǫni, ǫny$_V$- make]
ęh·sé:tgiht you will dirty it up
[(ad+)(N+) stem: -tgihd- turn ugly; turn bad; get dirty; consists of: -tgi$_V$- dirty, ugly]
ę·wá·det·giht it will be bad weather
o·dét·gih·dǫh it is storming right now
ę·wa·dę̱hs·rá:tgiht it will be a bad winter
[ade+ stem: -(o)hsr(a)$_N$- year, winter -tgihd$_V$- turn ugly]
ugly see: evil, unattractive
e·hé:tgę' she is ugly, unruly
ha·he:tgę́:s'ah he is unattractive
uh-oh see: I (hoho:)
ultimately see: I (finally, wa'hehge:ha')
umbilical cord see: tendon
o·jíhn·y'a·da' a tendon; a ligament; a birth cord

umbrella
ọt·nọh·so·dáhk·wa' an umbrella
[ọ+at+ stem: -nọhsodahkwa'- umbrella; consists of: -nọhs(a)$_N$- house -odahkwa'$_V$- container]
unable
ak·nǫ́·ha' I am unable
[P+ stem: -nọ$_V$- be unable]
ęh·sá·nọ:' you will fail P
ę·wá:knọ:' I will fail P
ho·nǫ́'ọh he is unable S
unable see: look for
ę·sá·yeh·wa' you will look for in vain; you will be unable to find s.t.
unaccustomed see: unusual
ti·yó:t'ah it is queer, unusual, odd
unadorned see: naked
ga·jí'gwa' it is naked
unattractive
ha·he:tgę́:s'ah he is unattractive
[A+ stem: -(hr)etgęs'ah- unattractive; consists of: -(hr)etgęs$_V$- evil, bad, ugly things; -'ah diminutive]
unbelievable see: absurd
o·nó:węht it is absurd, unbelievable
uncanny see: strange, unusual
og·yá:nọhk it is strange, bizarre
ti·yó:t'ah it is queer, unusual, odd
uncle see: C
hak·nó'sęh he is my uncle
unclean see: dirty, filthy
ho·yá'dat·gi' he is dirty; he has dirty ways
de·wá·ge·jọ:t I am filthy
unclear see: fuzzy
ta'de·yo·ga·há·ę·daht it is fuzzy, out of focus, opaque, unclear
uncompromising
de·ya·g'o·ni·gọ·há:gọ:t she cannot be swayed; she is uncompromising, distinguished
[de+P+ stem: -(')nigọhagọd- uncompromising, steadfast; consists of: -(')nigọh(a)$_N$- mind -gọd$_V$- persevere, linger]
de·ho'ni·gǫ́ha·gọ:t he is set in his ways; his mind is set
de·sa'ni·gǫ́ha·gọ:t you persevere; your mind is set (and cannot be swayed)
unconcerned
ta'de·ho'ni·gọ·há:nih he is unconcerned, indifferent
[ta'de+P+ stem: -(')nigọha(ę,nih)- bother s.o., annoy s.o.; be unconcerned, indifferent; consists of: -(')nigọh(a)$_N$- mind -(')nigọha(:)$_V$- expect, watch]
unconcerned see: happy-go-lucky
ho·dę·dọn·yá'dahs·gọ: he is a joker, happy-go-lucky; he is obnoxious
unconscious see: consciousness (lose consciousness)
hęh·sah·dǫ́:' **ęh·sa'ni·gǫ́·hah·dọ'** you will lose consciousness
uncooked see: raw
o·gáh·deh it is raw
uncover
ęhs·nahs·go·wé:ksih you will uncover the bed
[(N+) stem: -(hr)oweksi- uncover; consists of: -na'sg(wa)$_N$- mattress -(hr)oweg$_V$- cover]
uncover see: dig, find
ę·yó'gwa:t it will dig
a·gét·sęn·yọ: I have found it
undecided
d'e·sa'ni·gọ·ha·dó:gę: you cannot decide which way to go, you are flighty
[de'+not P+ stem: -(')nigọhadogę:- undecided, indecisive; consists of: -(')nigọh(a)$_N$- mind -dogę(:)$_V$- right, true]
under
oh·ná'gọ: under
[o+ stem: -(h)na'gọ:$_V$- under]

under
[-agǫ: internal locative suffix; means 'in', 'on', or 'under']
underarm see: armpit
sen·hǫ́h·da:gǫ: your underarm, armpit
undercooked, underdone
de·yó:wi:h it is undercooked
[deˀ+ not yo+ stem: -(r)i, (w)i$_V$- ripe; undercooked]
undergarment see: girdle, slip, soiled, underwear
de·yǫg·yˀa·do·ha:ktaˀ a girdle
gaˀka:ˀ a slip
de·yó·da·gę:t dirty undergarments; soil; fecal matter
hná·gǫh·ka:ˀ underwear
undergo see: feel, happen
shę́h ni·wa·ga·déˀdroˀdę: how I feel about s.t., s.o.
ni·yá·wˀęǫh how it did happen
underneath
oh·naˀgǫ́h tgá:yęh it lies underneath, below
[o+ stem: -(h)naˀg$_V$- under; consists of: ohnagǫh underneath; tgagyęˀ it lies there]
underpants see: underwear
hná·gǫh·ka:ˀ underwear
undershirt
o·wi:ya:ˀáh o·hnaˀgǫh·ká:ˀ gog·yaˀda·wít·raˀ a baby's undershirt
[consists of: owiya:ˀah baby hnaˀgǫhka:ˀ underwear; gogyaˀdawiˀtraˀ her coat, dress]
underside see: bottom
heh·dáˀ geg·wá·i where it starts; the bottom
understand
ak·ni·gǫ·há·ę·daˀs I understand
[P+ stem: -(ˀ)nigǫhaęda'- understand; consists of: -(ˀ)nigǫh(a)$_N$- mind -ęda'$_V$- finish, settle]

understand (continued)
a·hoˀni·gǫ·há·ę·daˀ he understood
oˀni·gǫ·há·ę·dahk, oˀni·gǫ·há·ę·daht it is clearly understood
[stem: -(ˀ)nigǫhaędahd- understood; consists of: -(ˀ)nigǫh(a)$_N$- mind -ędahd$_V$- cause to lie down]
understand see: hear, know
ga·hǫ́·kaˀ I understand
ho·nǫ́h·dǫˀ he knows
undertaker
ha·he·yˀǫ·dahs·rǫ́:ni: an undertaker
[A+ stem: -(h)eyǫˀdahsrǫnih- undertaker; consists of: -(he)yǫ(ˀda)$_N$- corpse, cadaver -(h)srǫni$_V$- fix, repair]
ha·he·yˀǫ·dá·nęhg·wih an undertaker
[A+ stem: -(h)eyǫˀdanęhgwih- undertaker; consists of: -(he)yǫ(ˀda)$_N$- corpse, cadaver -nęhgwi$_V$- haul]
underwear
hná·gǫh·ka:ˀ underwear
underwear see: girdle, pants, slip, soiled, underwear
de·yǫg·yˀa·do·ha:ktaˀ a girdle
o·gáˀdaˀ, o·gaˀdaˀshǫ́:ˀǫh pants; underpants
gaˀka:ˀ a slip
de·yóˀda·gę:t dirty undergarments; soil; fecal matter
undrape
ęt·so·dá·ih·siˀ you will undrape s.t.
[d+... stem: -odaihsi- undrape; consists of: -oda(:,h)$_V$- drape]
undress
ę·sat·rǫn·yáh·siˀ you will take your clothes off
[at+ stem: -(h)rǫnyahsi- undress; consists of: -(a)trǫni, (a)trǫny$_V$- dress]
ę·gat·rǫn·yáh·siˀ I will undress
a·gat·rǫn·yáh·si·hǫh I finished undressing; I got fully undressed

unearth
ę̱t·sat·sa·dǫ́·goʼ you will unearth it
[d+…at+ stem: -(h)sadǫgw- unearth; consists of: -(h)sadǫ$_V$- bury s.o., an animal]
unequivocal see: certain
o·ih·wí:yoʼ it is certain, for sure
unethical see: bad
de·ta·dih·wa:yé·i: they (m) are corrupt, impish, bad
uneven see: rough
á·o:gaʼt it is rough
unexpected
gę·né·wa·ǫ:s I get surprised
[ę+ stem: -neʼwaǫ- be unexpected, be surprised; consists of: -neʼwaǫ, neʼwa(:)$_V$- be startled]
o·né·wa·ǫ: s.t. unexpected, surprising
[o+ stem: -neʼwaǫ- be unexpected, be surprised; consists of: -neʼwaǫ, neʼwa(:)$_V$- be startled]
unfamiliar see: strange
og·yá:nǫhk it is strange, bizarre
unfavorable see: bad
tę́ʼ det·ga:yéiʼ it is bad, false, wrong
unfortunate see: regretful
o·sę́hs·de:ʼ it is regretful
unhang
ę̱t·sni·yǫ·dá:goʼ you will unhang it
[d+… stem: -niyǫdagw- unhang; consists of: -niyǫd$_V$- hang]
unhappy
de·a·ga·dǫ́t·ga·deʼ, de·wa·ga·dǫ́t·ga·dǫʼ I am not happy
[deʼ+not P+…ad+ stem: -ǫtgadeʼ- be happy; be unhappy; consists of: -ǫtgad(ǫ:)$_V$- enjoy]
de·sa·dǫt·gá:deʼ you are not happy
unhappy see: sad
de·saʼni·gǫ́·hęh·dǫh you are sad
unhurried see: slow
hohs·hę: he is slow-moving
unimportant
o·ga·os·hǫ́:ʼǫh s.t. not important, second-rate
[o+ stem: -gao$_N$- unimportant -sǫ:ʼǫh plural]
ni·yo·i·hú:ʼuh it is of little importance
[ni+yo+ stem: -(r)ihu:ʼuh- sensitive, unimportant; consists of: -(r)ih(wa)$_N$- word -u:ʼuh$_V$- small]
unintentional see: appear unintentionally, do unintentionally, err
taʼsa·do·dáh·siʼ you appeared unintentionally
taʼde·wa·géh·dǫ:ʼ I did not mean it, intend it
aʼón·hiʼk it was a mistake; it was accidental
uninteresting see: boring
o·nóʼs·hes·de:ʼ it is boring, tiring
unique see: special
o·i·ho·wá:nęh it is important; a great or worthy commendation; it is special
unit see: fraction
gyod·rá:gwęh fractions
unite see: join
dęh·sáh·sǫd·ręʼ you will join two things together
United States see: E (Gwahs·dǫ·ho·nǫh·geh)
unjoin
de·wa·da̱h·sǫ́d·ra:gwahs they come apart (lit.: it comes apart)
[de+…ad+ stem: -(a)hsǫdragw$_V$- unjoin, come apart; consists of: -(a)hsǫdrę, (a)hsǫdre$_V$- join]
dę·gę·na·dah·sǫd·rá:goʼ they (z) will be unjoined (for example, a train, a chain); they will come apart
de·yo·da̱h·sǫ́d·rag·węh it is disjointed
unknown see: secret
od·rih·wa·séh·dǫh it is secret

Cayuga pronunciation guide: /a/ father /e/ weigh /ę/ men (nasalized) /i/ police /o/ hole /ǫ/ home (nasalized) /u/ blue. Underlined vowels are voiceless or whispered. /ʹ/ high pitch. /t/ too /d/ do /k/ king /g/ good (never soft g) /j/ judge or a<u>dz</u>e /s/ soon /sh/ le<u>ss h</u>eat (never the sh in shirt) /sr/ <u>shr</u>ine /sy/ <u>s</u>ure /hw/ <u>wh</u>ich (the sound made when you blow out a candle) /h/ hi /ts/ ca<u>ts h</u>ide /ʼ/ (the sound before the first vowel in 'uh-uh') /n/ noon /r/ round /w/ way /y/ yes.

unlike see: different
de·wáh·di·hęh the difference; it is different
unlit see: dim
ga·jihs·da̱hk·wáh·dǫh,
ga·jihs·da̱hk·wáh·twęh it is dim
unlock see: open
a·gen·ho·dǫ́:gwęh I have opened it; unlocked it
unnatural see: unusual
ti·yó:t'ah it is queer, unusual, odd
unpleasant
de·a·ǫ·wé:saht it is unpleasant
[de'+(y)a+ stem: -ǫ'wesahd, ǫ'wesęh(d)- be enjoyable; be unpleasant; consists of: -ǫ'wes$_V$- enjoy]
unprecedented see: exceptional
á·ǫ·go̱h·dǫh exceptional; above average; too much
unravel see: take s.t. apart
de·wa·ge·káhs·hǫ: I have taken one object apart
unreal see: make-believe
a:wet'ahs·hǫ́:'ǫh make-believe; pretend
unrelenting see: uncompromising
de·ya·g'o·ni·gǫ·há:gǫ:t she cannot be swayed; she is uncompromising, distinguished
unripe
o·gé:dra' it is green (not ripe); raw fruit
[o+ stem: -gedra'$_V$- unripe, raw, green]
unruly see: evil
e·hé:tgę' she is ugly or unruly
unsatisfied see: dissatisfied
dǫ·gá·d'ok·tahs I was not satisfied with s.t.; I didn't get enough
unselfish see: generous
gog·yés'a·geh she is generous, generous to a fault
unsightly see: evil, unattractive
e·hé:tgę' she is ugly, unruly
ha·he:tgę́:s'ah he is unattractive

untamed see: wild
wa·dad·wę·ní:yo' a wild animal
until see: I, shęniyo:(we'), distance
shę́ ni·yó:we' up to there; until
untroubled see: happy-go-lucky
ho·dę·dǫn·yá'da̱hs·gǫ: he is a joker, happy-go-lucky; he is obnoxious
untruth see: lie
o·nó·w'ę·da' a lie
unusual
ti·yó:t'ah it is queer, unusual, odd
[ti+yo+ stem: -t'ah- unusual, queer; consists of: -d$_V$- stand -'ah diminutive]
unusual see: strange
og·yá:nǫhk it is strange, bizarre
unwell see: sick
ak·nǫ·hǫk·dá:nih I am sick
unwilling
de·wa·ge·gá·ęhs I am always unwilling
[de'+ not P+ stem: -gaę$_V$- be willing; be unwilling]
de·wa·ge·gá·ę I do not want to do it; I am unwilling
tę́' te:sá·ga·ę: you are not willing
od·rǫ́h·ya't it is unwilling, stubborn
[ad+ stem: -(r)ǫhya'd(ahkw)$_V$- balk, be reluctant]
unwilling see: balk
god·rǫ́h·ya't she is unwilling, stubborn
unwise see: self-important
wa·dat·go·wá:nęh it is rash, unwise, self-important, egotistical
unyielding see: hard, stiff, uncompromising
oh·ní:yǫh it is hard
o·tǫ́·ga·i: it is stiff; rigor mortis
de·ya·g'o·ni·gǫ·há:gǫ:t she cannot be swayed; she is uncompromising, distinguished
up (be up)
a·gát·gę·hǫh I am up now
[P+ at+ stem: -gęhǫh- up; consists of: -gęh$_V$- get up, awaken]

up see: I (he:tgęh)
upend see: turn upside down
dę.gǫ.nǫh.wétso'dę' I am going to turn you upside down, upend you (said in anger)
uphill (go uphill)
ęh.se.ne.dá.wę.hę:t you will go uphill
[stem: -nedawęhęd- go uphill; consists of: -nǫd(a), ned(a)$_N$- hill -węhę(h)d$_V$- climb s.t.]
uphold
de.gáhg.w'a.ta' it upholds things, raises things up
[de+... (ade+) stem: -(h)gwa'd- uphold s.t., raise up s.t.; consists of: -(h)gw$_V$- lift, pick up]
de.wa.dęhg.wá'ta' it raises (s.t.)
de.yǫg.wahg.wá'dǫh we all are upholding (some thing or idea)
de.hóhg.w'a.dǫh he is lifting it up
dę.yehg.w'a.dáh.nǫ:' she will raise, lift things up
upper
de.yó.ihs.re:s upper (part of a shoe)
[de+yo+ stem: -(r)ihsres- upper; consists of: -(r)ihsr(a)$_N$- leggings -es$_V$- long]
Upper End see: C (Da.gęh.ya.t)
upright see: righteous
god.rih.wag.wá.eh.sǫh she is fair, righteous
uproar see: riot
a.ha.di.nǫ́hs.ga.i' they (m) made a riot
upset see: feel bad, turn upside down
ęh.sá.dę.hęh you will become embarrassed, ashamed
dę.gǫ.nǫh.wétso'dę' I am going to turn you upside down, upend you (said in anger)
upstairs
gyo.nák.da.he: upstairs
[g+yo+ stem: -nakdahe:- upstairs, loft; consists of: -nakd(a)$_N$- bed, seat -(h)e:'$_V$- sitting up on top of s.t.]
o.nák.da.he: a loft
[o+ stem: -nakdahe:- upstairs, loft; consists of: -nakd(a)$_N$- bed, seat -(h)e:'$_V$- sitting up on top of s.t.]
upward see: I (up, he:tgęh)
upwind
o.hę́.da.gǫ: upwind
[o+ stem: -(h)ęd$_V$- lead -agǫ: in]
urban
e.nag.rehs.rá.ę' s.t. is urban
[e+ stem: -nagrehsraę'- urban; consists of: -nagrehsr(a)$_N$- living -ę$_V$- lie on the ground]
ga.na.da.ge.hó:nǫ' urban dwellers; city people; urbanites
[ga+ stem: -nadagehonǫ'- urban dwellers, city dwellers; consists of: -nad(a)$_N$- town, community -'geh on -ho:nǫ' people]
urban see: city
ga.na.da.gǫ́h.ge.ha:' urban
Urban Design and Development see: G (E.nag.rehs.ra.ę' Ho.dis.rǫ.ni.hag.ye')
urge see: encourage, walk fast
ęh.sasg.yá.ǫn.yǫ' you will encourage
ęh.sáhsg.ya.ǫ:' you will walk fast; you will encourage
urinate
ga.ǫ.nihsg.yá:gehs they (f/m) urinate
[ę+stem: -nihsgyage$_V$- urinate]
a.gę.nihsg.yá:ge' I am urinating
ę.ga.ǫ.níhsg.yage' they (f/m) will urinate
urine
ǫn.hę́.hę' urine
[ǫ+ stem: -(a)nhęhę'$_N$- urine]
USA see: E (United States, Gwahs.dǫ.ho.nǫh.geh)

Cayuga pronunciation guide: /a/ father /e/ weigh /ę/ men (nasalized) /i/ police /o/ hole /ǫ/ home (nasalized) /u/ blue. Underlined vowels are voiceless or whispered. /´/ high pitch. /t/ too /d/ do /k/ king /g/ good (never soft g) /j/ judge or adze /s/ soon /sh/ less heat (never the sh in shirt) /sr/ shrine /sy/ sure /hw/ which (the sound made when you blow out a candle) /h/ hi /ts/ cats hide /'/ (the sound before the first vowel in 'uh-uh') /n/ noon /r/ round /w/ way /y/ yes.

use
ehs·ta' she uses it; people use it
[stem: -(h)s(d)$_V$- use]
hahs·tahk he used to use it
ę·hahs he will use it
ęh·sehs you will use it
ih·sehs use it
gǫhs·dǫ́·hǫg·ye' she is arriving wearing that
[stem: -(h)sdǫhǫgye'$_V$- go along using s.t.]

use up
a·wá:ts'a:' it is worn out, all gone, burnt up; it went down to nothing
[(N+) stem: -(a)ts'a:'$_V$- use up]
ha·wat·ne·gáts·aht water is all gone
[he'+...at+ stem: -(h)neg(a)$_N$- water, liquid -(a)ts'ahd$_V$- be used up]

useful
o·í·hǫ:t it is useful
[o+ stem: -(r)ihǫd- be useful; consists of: -(r)ih(wa)$_N$- word -ǫd$_V$- attached]

useless
sga·ho·dę́' de·yó·i·hǫ:t it is useless
[consists of: sgaho'dę' nothing; deyoihǫ:t it is not useful]
de·yó·i·hǫ:t it is useless
[de'+ not yo+ stem: -(r)ihǫd- useful; useless; consists of: -(r)ih(wa)$_N$- word -ǫd$_V$- attached]

utensils
e·kǫn·ya·ta'géh ehs·ta·shǫ́:'ǫh kitchen items; utensils
[consists of: ekǫnyata'geh kitchen; ehsta'shǫ:'ǫh tools, utensils]

uterus
e·wi·ya:hk·wa' the uterus; the placenta
[e+ stem: -wiyahkwa'- uterus, placenta; consists of: -wiy(a)$_N$- child, offspring -(h)gw$_V$- lift, pick up]

utilize see: use
ęh·sehs you will use it

utterance see: language, speech, word
ga·wę·nǫ·dáh·gǫh spoken language
ga·wę·nit·gę́'ǫ:' a speech
ga·wę́·na·gǫ:' in the words, voice; in the speech

V

vacant see: empty
gadé:nyǫ: it is empty

vacate see: go out
ęhs·yá:gę' you will go out

vagabond see: tramp
a·ho·dęh·té:'ah a tramp; a hobo; a vagabond

vagina
o'ya' female genitals; the vagina
[o+ stem: -(a)'y(a)$_N$- female genitals]

vague see: fuzzy
ta'de·yo·ga·há·ę·daht it is fuzzy, out of focus, opaque, unclear

vain see: proud
ha·ná·i: he is proud, boastful, bragging, conceited

vain (in vain) see: look
ę·sá·yęh·wa' you will look for in vain; you will be unable to find s.t.

valet see: waiter
hak·wá·he·ha' he is a waiter

valley
o·nǫ́·da·gǫ: a valley
[o+ stem: -nǫdagǫ:, nedagǫ:- valley; consists of: -nǫd(a), ned(a)$_N$- hill -agǫ: in]
ga·né·da·gǫ: in, under the valley

valuable see: cost, treasure
ga·nǫ:' it is expensive, dear, precious
o·nǫ́hs·da't, o·nǫ́hs·deht it is a treasure; it is precious, valuable; it is possessive

value
ak·nǫ́hs·de’ I value it
[P+ stem: -nǫhsde’- value s.t., cherish s.t.; consists of: -nǫ:’$_{V}$- costly, dear, expensive]
sa·nǫ́hs·de’ you value it; you are stingy
value see: equity, price
tsę̄h ni·yó·ga:’ equity; capital; value; worth
ga·gá·he:’ the price of s.t.
vandalize see: ruin
ęhs·hé:tgęht you will damage, ruin, wreck s.t.
vanilla
de·yehs·ta·sǫ́:’ǫh vanilla, etc.
[de+ye+ stem: -(h)sda’sǫ:’ǫh- vanilla, seasoning, etc.; consists of: -(h)s(d)$_{V}$- use -sǫ:’ǫh plural]
vanish see: lose
ęh·sáh·dǫ’ you will disappear
vanishing point
he·yo·ta·hi·nǫk·dá’ǫh the vanishing point of the road
[he+yo+at+ stem: -hahinǫkda’ǫh- vanishing point; consists of: -(h)ah(a)$_{N}$- road -in(e)$_{V}$- go -o’kda’$_{V}$- come to an end]
vanity see: proud
ha·ná·i: he is proud, boastful, bragging, conceited
vanquish see: able, win
ęh·se:gwé:ni’ you will succeed
a·hę·nat·gwę́·n’i·ge: the big win, victory
vapour see: fog
ot·sá:da’ mist; steam
vapourize see: evaporate
wahs·déhs·ta’ it is evaporating; it evaporates
variety
wa̲h·yá’ ni·yǫ́:ta’ different hanging fruits; a variety of hanging fruits
[consists of: wa̲hya’ it is fruit; niyǫ:ta’ an amount of attached objects]
ha’de·yo̲h·yá:ge: a variety of fruit
[ha’de+A/P+N+ stem: -(a)hy(a)$_{N}$- fruit, berry -(a)ge:$_{V}$- two or more; many different types of, all sorts of, all kinds of]
various see: many
ha’de·yo̲h·sóhg·wa·ge: all kinds of colours
vault
eh·wihs·da·ę·da̲hk·wá’ o·nǫ́h·sǫ:t a bank vault; a safe
[consists of: ehwihsdaędа̲hkwa’ bank; onǫhsǫ:t a room; a vault]
vegetable
a·se·shǫ́:ǫh vegetables
[stem: -(a)se’$_{N}$- vegetable]
vehicle
g’ad·réh·da’ a vehicle; a car; a truck
[ga+ stem: -(’)drehd(a)$_{N}$- vehicle, etc.]
g’ad·reh·d’as·hǫ́:’ǫh a variety of cars, trucks, vehicles
g’ad·réh·da·se: a new car
[ga+ stem: -(’)drehd(a)$_{N}$- vehicle, car -(a)se:$_{V}$- new]
vend see: sell
ęh·sát·ge·hǫ’ you will sell s.t.
venerate see: revere
dęd·wa·dad·rih·wa·nǫ́hk·wa:k we all (incl.) will show respect for one another
venison
de·wa·hǫh·dé:s o’wá·hǫh deer meat; venison
[consists of: dewahǫhde:s deer; o’wahǫh meat]
venom see: poison
o’ná’sę: poison
ventriloquist see: throw one’s voice
hęh·sad·wę·nǫ́:di’ you will throw your voice (as a ventriloquist)
Venus see: evening star, morning star
ga·jihs·dǫ·dá:ha’ the evening star; the morning star; Venus

verbalize see: speak, talk
a:gad·wę:nǫ́:dahk I should use that language
ę·géh·ta·ę' I will talk
verify see: certain, decide
o·ih·wí:yo' it is certain, for sure
a·to·ih·wá·ę:da's he came to a decision, a conclusion
vertebrae see: backbone
ses·hǫh·néh sehs·wę'na·géh
ohsg·yę́'da·geh the backbone; the spine
vessel see: boat, dish
ga̱·hǫ́:wa' a boat
ga·ję' a dish; a plate; a bowl
vestige see: remainder
he·yo·da·dá·ǫ: a remainder; a residue
vibrate see: quiver
ę·sa·ya·dahd·rǫ́:gǫ' you will quiver, shudder
victuals see: food, lunch
gak·wa' food
a·dę́·n'at·ra' lunch; groceries
video see: movie
ga·yá'ta' movies; television
video store
ga·ya·tá' ǫ·ní·hahs·ta' a video store
[consists of: gaya'ta' movies, television; ǫnihahsta' s.o. lends s.t.]
vie see: compete
dę·ho·nat·gę́:nyǫ: they (m) compete
view
ok·dǫ't a good view
[o+ stem: -kdǫ'd- good view; consists of: -kdǫ(:)$_V$- taste, examine, look closely at s.t.]
vile see: evil
wa̱·hé:t·gęh evil (in mind); bad
village
ni·ga·na·dú:'uh a village; a small town
[ni+ga+ stem: -nadu:'uh- village; consists of: -nad(a)$_N$- town, community -u:'uh$_V$- small]
village see: town
ga·ná·da·ę' a town
vindicate see: uphold
de·yǫg·wa̱hg·wá'dǫh we all are upholding (a thing or idea)
vine
o·ǫ́h·sa' vines
[o+ stem: -(')ǫhs(a)$_N$- vine]
violate see: rape
ahs·ha·got·go·ho·wá·na̱h·dę' he raped her
viper see: snake
os·há·ihs·da' a snake
virtuous see: good, righteous
o·yá:nre' it is nice, good, beautiful
god·rih·wag·wá·eh·sǫh she is fair, righteous
virus see: cold, sickness
a·ga·to·wín·y'ǫ·se: I have a cold
o·nǫh·so·dá·i:yǫ:' a sickness; an illness; an epidemic; a plague
visible
ó:gę't it is visible
[o+ stem: -gę'd- be visible; consists of: -(')gęd$_V$- be light-coloured, white]
vision see: blurred vision
at·gat·ga̱·há·węn·ye:' I had blurred vision
vision (have a vision)
ad·wag·yá·ǫn·yo:' a haunted apparition
[de+... stem: -(a)gyaǫnyǫ'(s)- have a vision, get spooked; consists of: -y(a)$_N$- other, different -(a)gyaǫ'$_V$- be tricked, fooled]
ad·wa·gag·yá·ǫ:nyǫ's I had a vision; I got spooked
de·wag·yá·ǫn·yǫh it (a haunted vision) is happening right now

visit
ę·gag·yǫ·sé·haʼ I am going to go and visit
[ag+ stem: -yǫʼseh- go and visit; consists of:
-yǫ$_{V}$- arrive]
a·gag·yʼǫ·sé·heʼ I am going to go visit

visor see: hat
a·na·há·ot·raʼ a hat

vocalize see: sing
god·rę́:no:t she is singing

vocation see: occupation
ni·sa·i·hoʼdęhs·róʼdę: your occupation; your type of work

voice see: say, sing, throat, word
ęhs·niʼ you two will say
o·haʼdí:yo: a good voice
o·háʼdaʼ a quill; a plume; a feather; the voice; the throat; the larynx; the esophagus
ga·wę́·na·gǫ:ʼ in the words, voice; in the speech

voiceless syllable
tę́ʼ de·ga:wę́:na:t a voiceless syllable
[tęʼ not deʼ+ga+ stem: -węnad- voiceless syllable; consists of: -węn(a)$_{N}$- voice, word -d$_{V}$- stand]

void see: cave, empty
oh·wę·ja·gá·hęt·ge: a cavern; a cavity; a big cave
ga·dé:nyǫ: it is empty

volcano
ad·wa·dehs·dę·hó:węʼ there was a volcano
[a+d+wa+ade+ stem: -(h)sdęhowęʼ- volcano; consists of: -(h)sd(ęha)$_{N}$- stone -owę(:)$_{V}$- split in two]

volume
tsę́h ni·gá:dę:s volume; density; how thick it is; mass
[tsęh that (ni+)A+(N+) stem: -(a)dęs$_{V}$- thick]

vomit
a·gén·yʼag·wahs I am vomiting; I am a vomiter; I vomit all the time
[P+ stem: -nyaʼgw, nyaʼgo$_{V}$- vomit]
ǫ·gén·yʼa·goʼ I vomited
a·gen·yʼag·wá·hǫh I am vomiting (right now)
[P+ stem: -nyaʼgwah$_{V}$- vomit]
ǫ·gen·yʼag·wá·hǫ: I vomited
on·yáʼgwaʼ vomit; vomitus
[o+ stem: -nyaʼg(wa)$_{N}$- vomit]
ga·den·yʼag·wáh·taʼ I make myself vomit; I am bulemic
[ade+ stem: -nyaʼgwahd- make oneself vomit, be bulemic; consists of:
-nyaʼgw$_{V}$- vomit]
ha·den·yag·wáh·taʼ he makes himself vomit (for example, in a cleansing ritual)
ęh·sa·den·yág·waht you will make yourself vomit
sa·dén·yag·waht make yourself vomit

vote
dęh·sę·nig·yohg·wa·gę́:niʼ you will vote, cast lots
[de+…ęn+ stem: -(i)gyohgwagęni- vote, elect; consists of: -(i)gyohg(wa)$_{N}$- crowd -gęni, gęny$_{V}$- compete]
dę·hę·nę·nig·yohg·wa:gę́:niʼ they (m) will have an election; they will have a voting to do

vow see: plan
ęhs·ríh·wah·sʼa:ʼ you will plan an idea; you will promise, make an agreement

voyage see: travel
ni·ya·got·gę·ihs·dǫ́·hǫg·yeʼ she is travelling as she is moving

vulture see: buzzard
ga·ję́·hęh·da:s buzzards; vultures

Cayuga pronunciation guide: /a/ father /e/ weigh /ę/ men (nasalized) /i/ police /o/ hole /ǫ/ home (nasalized) /u/ blue. Underlined vowels are voiceless or whispered. /ˊ/ high pitch. /t/ too /d/ do /k/ king /g/ good (never soft g) /j/ judge or adze /s/ soon /sh/ less heat (never the sh in shirt) /sr/ shrine /sy/ sure /hw/ which (the sound made when you blow out a candle) /h/ hi /ts/ cats hide /ʼ/ (the sound before the first vowel in 'uh-uh') /n/ noon /r/ round /w/ way /y/ yes.

W

wad see: pile
on·hóhs·ro:t a pile
wag
de·yoʼnhęht·sę́·dǫ·hǫh it is wagging its tail
[de+P+ stem: -(ʼ)nhęhtsędǫh- wag a tail; consists of: -(ʼ)nhęhts(a)$_N$- tail -ędǫh$_V$- shake s.t.]
wager see: gamble
de·to:dí:yęʼ they (m) are gambling, betting
wages see: salary
de·sá·dęts'ahs your salary; what you make
wagon
ehs·tǫd·ra·nęhg·wi·taʼ a hay wagon
[e+ stem: -(h)stǫdranęhgwihtaʼ- hay wagon; consists of: -(h)stǫdr(a)$_N$- straw, hay -nęhgwihd$_V$- cause to haul]
e·na·ja·nę́hg·wi·taʼ grain wagon
[e+ stem: -naʼjanęhgwihtaʼ- grain wagon; consists of: -na(ʼ)ja(da)$_N$- wheat, grain -nęhgwihd$_V$- cause to haul]
wail see: cry
ohs·tá·haʼge: it is really crying
waist
o·yáʼga:ʼ a waist
[o+ stem: -yaʼg(a:)$_N$- waist]
syʼa·gá:ʼgeh on your waist
gyʼa·gá:ʼgeh on my waist
swa·yáʼgʼa·geh on your (p) waist
wait
ę·gǫ́·hǫh·waʼs you will wait for me
[TR+ stem: -(hr)ǫhwaʼs- wait for s.o.; consists of: -(hr)ǫhw$_V$- wait]
dahs·krǫ́h·waʼs wait for me
wait see: I (waʼjih, waʼjihya:ʼ), impatient
ak·ni·gǫh·gá·hęhs I am running out of patience; I am impatiently waiting

waiter
hak·wá·he·haʼ he is a waiter
[A+ stem: -kwahehaʼ- waiter, waitress; consists of: -k(wa)$_N$- food -(hr)e, (hr)ę$_V$- put, place]
ek·wá·he·haʼ she is a waitress
waitress see: waiter
wake up
ig·yehs I wake up (all the time)
[stem: -ye(h,:)$_V$- wake up, awaken]
ęhs·yeh you will wake up
sá:ye: you are awake
í:jeh wake up
ęhs·yeht you will wake up s.t.
[TR+ stem: -yehd- wake up s.o.; consists of: -ye(h,:)$_V$- wake up, awaken]
a·hé:yeht I woke him up
hehs·yeht wake him up
wake up see: get up
ę·gá:tgęh I will get up
a·gat·gę·hǫh I am up now
walk
de·hę·na·tá·hahk·wah they (m) are ironworkers
[de+...at+ stem: -(h)ahahgw$_V$- walk; consists of: -(h)ah(a)$_N$- road -(h)gw$_V$- lift, pick up]
dę·sá·ta·hahk you will walk
ta·dę·ja·tá·hahk you two will walk side by side
[taʼde+...at+ stem: -(h)ahahgw$_V$- walk; walk side by side; consists of: -(h)ah(a)$_N$- road -(h)gw$_V$- lift, pick up]
ga·ta·hí:neʼ I am walking
[A+at+ stem: -(h)ahineʼ- walk; consists of: -(h)ah(a)$_N$- road -ineʼ$_V$- go]
walk see: go, walk about, walk fast, walk on one's hands
í:geʼ I am walking, moving

walk about

de·ya·go·dá·wę̨n·ye' she is walking about

[de+P+ad+ stem: -(a)wę̨nye(:)$_V$- stir, mix; walk about]

de·sa·da·wę́:nye' you are walking about

walk along

ti·hé:'ah he is just walking along

[ti+A+ (tsǫ: just) stem: -e:'ah- walk along; consists of: -e$_V$- go 'ah diminutive]

ti·hé:'ah tsǫ: he is just walking along

walk fast

hahs·gyá·ǫ·ha' he walks quickly; he gives s.o. encouragement

[stem: -(a)hsi('da), (ę)hs(a)$_N$- foot -(ah)sgyaǫ$_V$- walk fast]

ęh·sáhs·gya·ǫ:' you will walk fast; you will encourage s.o.

hohs·gyá·ǫ:gye' he is going along walking quickly

ga·ke·yahs·gyá·ǫn·yǫh I am giving them words of encouragement

[stem: -(a)hsgyaǫnyǫ- encourage; consists of: -(ah)sgyaǫ$_V$- walk fast]

walk on one's hands

ę·hag·y'a·dó:dę' he will stand his body up, walk on his hands

[ag+ stem: -ya'd(a)$_N$- body -odę$_V$- put in]

wall

o·dę́·nih·sa' a wall

[(o+) stem: -(a)dęnihs(a)$_N$- wall]

a·dę·nih·sá'geh on the wall

[(o+) stem: -(a)dęnihs(a)$_N$- wall -'geh on]

wallet

gat·gwę́'da' a wallet; a purse; pocketbook; a suitcase

[ga+ stem: -tgwę('da)$_N$- wallet, suitcase, purse]

a·gét·gw'ę·da' my wallet

sat·gwę́'da' your wallet, purse

walnut

gahn·yó'g·wa·ji: walnuts

[ga+ stem: -(h)nyo'gwaji:- walnut; consists of: -(h)nyo'g(wa)$_N$- nut -ji(:,h)$_V$- dark]

tsihn·yó'g·wak wild walnuts

[stem: -tsinyo'gwag$_N$- wild walnut; consists of: -(h)nyo'g(wa)$_N$- nut -g$_V$- eat]

walrus

gan·ya'k·wa·i:gó:wah a walrus

[ga+ stem: -nya'kwaigowah- walrus; consists of: -(h)nyakwai('da)$_N$- seal -gowah big]

wander

ti·gá·ę's they (f/m) are roaming about

[ti+A+ stem: -e$_V$- go; wander, roam, loiter]

ę́: tsǫ́: it·se's you wander (all the time); you are over there

[ę again tsǫ: just d+ stem: -e$_V$- go; wander]

ę́: tsǫ́: ęt·se' you will wander

ti·héh·sǫ' he is a wanderer, loiterer

[ti+A+ stem: -ehsǫ'-wander, roam, loiter; consists of: -e$_V$- go -sǫ' plural]

wander see: go, roam, stray

ę́: tsǫ́: it·se' you are wandering (right now)

ti·gę·ne·nǫ́:g·ye's they (z) are roaming about

ęh·sa·ta·há:go' you will stray, go off the road, turn into your driveway

want

de·sa·dǫh·wę·jo·níhs·gǫ: you always want s.t.

[de+P+ad+ stem: -ǫhwęjoni, ǫhwęjoh$_V$- want, need]

dęh·sa·dǫh·wę:jó:ni' you will want s.t.

de·wa·ga·dǫh·wę·jó:nih I want s.t.

de·wa·ga·dǫh·wę·jó·nih·ne:' I wanted s.t. in the past

Cayuga pronunciation guide: /a/ father /e/ weigh /ę/ men (nasalized) /i/ police /o/ hole /ǫ/ home (nasalized) /u/ blue. Underlined vowels are voiceless or whispered. /'/ high pitch. /t/ too /d/ do /k/ king /g/ good (never soft g) /j/ judge or adze /s/ soon /sh/ less heat (never the sh in shirt) /sr/ shrine /sy/ sure /hw/ which (the sound made when you blow out a candle) /h/ hi /ts/ cats hide /'/ (the sound before the first vowel in 'uh-uh') /n/ noon /r/ round /w/ way /y/ yes.

want (continued)
ad·wa·ga·dǫ́h·wę·johs I did want s.t.
[de+P+ad+ stem: -ǫhwęjohsd- want s.t.; consists of: -ǫhwęjoni, ǫhwęjoh$_V$- want, need]
ga̱hs·gá:ne:s I have longings for; I want; I desire
[stem: -(ahs)gan(eg)$_V$- want, desire, long for]
gǫhs·gá:ne:s I desire you
ęh·sáhs·ga·ne:k you will be tempted, you will long for s.t.
ę·gáhs·ga·ne:k I will long for s.t.
sa̱hs·gá·nek·sǫh you are longing for s.t.
[stem: -(ahs)gan(eg)$_V$- want, desire, long for -sǫ' plural]
want see: crave, lack, will, wish
ęk·nǫ́:wa:k I will crave s.t.
da·wá·d'ok·dę' it lacked; it was not enough
sé:ǫ:' you wanted; you believed
a:yá:węh I wish, hope
war
od·ri·yo̱h·dę́·d'a·ǫh a war
[o+ad+ stem: -(r)iyohdęda'ǫh- war; consists of: -(r)iyo, nyo$_V$- kill s.t. -ęda'$_V$- finish]
war see: fight, world war
wad·rí:yo: a war; a fight
tsi·yoh·wę·ja:gwe:gǫ́h wad·rí:yo: a world war (lit: there is fighting all over the world)
warbler
tgwęh·ji·á·gę̱·ha:' warbler
[stem: -tgwęhjia'geha:'- warbler; consists of: -tgwęhji'(a)$_N$- red -geha:' type]
ward see: child
a·gék·s'a·da' my child
warlock see: evil power (have evil power)
go·ná:tgǫh they (f/m) are a force to be reckoned with; they (f/m) are ominous; they are bad medicine people

warm
owa:dá·i:hę: a warm wind
[o+ stem: -w(a:)$_N$- air -(')daihę$_V$- hot]
w'a·da·i·há·ta' it heats things up
[(de+) stem: -(')daiha'd- warm (s.t.) up; consists of: -(')daih$_V$- hot]
ęt·s'a·dá·i·ha't you will heat it up; you will make it hot
o'da·i·há'dǫh it is really hot (weather)
ę·ho'da·i·ha'dǫ́·hǫk he will be heating up s.t.
o·né:nǫ' it is mild, warm; a warm or hot day
[o+ stem: -nenǫ(:)$_V$- warm (weather), mild (weather)]
a·ǫ·gǫ̱h·dǫ́h o·né:nǫ' it is exceptionally hot (weather)
dę̱'o:tó:we' it is not cold (pertaining to weather)
[de'+ not o+at+ stem: -(a)tow(e')$_V$- cold (weather); not cold]
Warren, PA see: E (Ga̱h·na·wa·gǫ:)
wary
wa·dat·ni·gǫ́·ha:' it is wary, cautious
[A+adat+ stem: -(')nigǫha:'- wary, cautious; consists of: -(')nigǫh(a)$_N$- mind -(')nigǫha(:)$_V$- expect, watch]
wash see: clean
o·dę́·no̱·ha·i:' it is washed, clean
wash basin see: sink
ǫh·jo·há·i:'ta'geh a sink; a wash basin
washing machine
ga·nó·ha·ihs a washing machine
[ga+ stem: -nohaehs- washing machine; consists of: -n$_N$- noun -ohae$_V$- clean, wash]
Washington D.C. see: E (Ha·na·da·gan·ya̱hs·geh)

washroom
hę.nǫ́g.wẹh.neh men use it; just for men; a men's washroom
[A+ stem: -ǫgwehneh- men's washroom; consists of: -ǫgwe(ʼda)$_N$- person -hneh at]
washroom see: bathroom
ǫg.yaʼdǫ.ha.iʼtáʼgeh a bathroom
waste
sag.yéh.sạh.taʼ you are wasteful
[P+ag+ stem: -yesahd- waste, be wasteful; consists of: -yes$_V$- easy]
ęh.sa:gyé:saht you will waste
waste see: junk, throw, waste money
gat.gíʼtraʼ junk
wag.yǫ: s.t. thrown away; discards
wasteland see: desert
o.neh.sʼa.dá.i.hę: a desert
waste money
sat.wíhs.dʼę.da:s you burn your money
[at+ stem: -(h)wihsdęʼda:- waste money; consists of: -(h)wihsd(a), (hr)ihsd(a)$_N$- metal, money : -(hr)ęʼda:$_V$- burn s.t.]
a.gat.wịhs.dę́ʼda:ʼ I wasted my money
ahg.wíh ęh.sat.wịhs.dę́ʼda:ʼ do not waste your money
wasteful see: extravagant
gog.yéh.sạhs.dǫ: she is extravagant, wasteful
watch
há.ǫtgʼę.se:ʼ she is watching over there
[TR+at+ stem: -gęʼse- watch s.o.; consists of: -gę$_V$- see]
a:ga.ke.yat.gę́ʼse:ʼ I should watch them
ga.ǫ́t.gʼę.seh they (f/m) are watching s.t. going on
watch see: attention (pay), expect, protect, stare
sat.gá.hǫ.haʼ you are paying attention, watching right now
kni.gǫ́:ha:ʼ I am expecting, watching
ho.na.dʼę.ní.gǫ.ha:ʼ they (m) are protecting, watching
sat.gahd.rǫ́:nihs you are staring at it, examining it closely
watchful see: stare
sat.gahd.rǫ́:nihs you are staring at it, examining it closely
watch over see: care for, look after, protect
dẹ.ha.dịhs.nyé:gyeʼs they (m) look after all
dehsg.wę́ʼnya:ʼ you (who) watch over us
ho.na.dʼę.ní.gǫ.ha:ʼ they (m) are protecting, watching
water
oh.né.ga.nohs water
[o+ stem: -(h)neganohs- water; consists of: -(h)neg(a)$_N$- water, liquid -nohsd$_V$- make cold, cool]
oh.né.gʼa.geh on the water
oh.né.ga.gǫ: under water; in the water; in the lake
oh.ne:gí:yo: good water
[o+ stem: -(h)neg(a)$_N$- water, liquid -iyo:$_V$- be nice, good]
oh.ne.gʼa.dá.i.hę: hot water
[o+ stem: -(h)neg(a)$_N$- water, liquid -(ʼ)daihę:$_V$- hot]
oh.né.ga.no: cold water
[o+ stem: -(h)neg(a)$_N$- water, liquid -no:$_V$- cold, cool]
oh.ne.gan.yá.hęhs boiling water
[o+ stem: -(h)neg(a)$_N$- water, liquid -nyahę(h,ʼ)$_V$- boil]
oh.né.gat.giʼ scum; dirty water
[o+ stem: -(h)neg(a)$_N$- water, liquid -tgiʼ$_V$- dirty, ugly]
í:yoʼ it is in the water, submerged in liquid
[y+ stem: -oʼ- boiled, stewed; consists of: -o(:)$_V$- submerge, boil, cook]

water (continued)
oh·né:go' a puddle; any type of water [o+ (h)neg(a) water -o' submerged]

water see: lake, lead, well water
gan·ya·dá:'geh to, at, on the lake
oh·ne·ga·ná:wę: lead, lukewarm water; also refers to a prepubescent boy
oh·na·wá·o:tge̲·ha:' well water

water colours
de·gah·ne·ga·ye̲hs·dǫ́h ǫh·sǫ́h·ta' water colours; paint
[consists of: degahnegaye̲hsdǫh water is mixed in it; ǫhsohta' colour, paints, crayons]

water fountain
oh·ne·ga·nóhs gyo̲h·né:go:t a water fountain
[consists of: ohneganohs water; gyo̲hne:go:t fountain]

water jug see: pitcher
ga̲h·soh·gǫ́:t e·yáhk·wa' a pitcher

watering hole
ha·dih·ne·gá:kwa' an animal watering place; a watering hole; a trough
[A+ stem: -(h)negahkwa'- water spout; watering hole; consists of: -(h)neg(a)$_{N}$- water, liquid -(h)gw$_{V}$- lift, pick up]
ga·dih·ne·ga·he·dáhk·wa' animal watering place; watering hole; trough
[gadi+ stem: -(h)negahedahkwa'- trough consists of: -(h)neg(a)$_{N}$- water, liquid -(hr)edahkwa'$_{V}$- receptacle into which s.t. is placed]

water pump
ga̲h·ne·ga·dáhg·wahs a water pump
[stem: -(h)negodawahs- water pump; consists of: -(h)neg(a)$_{N}$- water, liquid -odagw$_{V}$- remove, detach]

water root
de·ga·gǫ·dǫ́·dǫh·gǫh water root (a medicine)
[de+ga+ stem: -gǫdǫdǫhgǫh- water root]

water spout
de·gah·ne·gáhk·wa' a water spout
[de+ga+ stem: -(h)negahkwa'- water spout; consists of: -(h)neg(a)$_{N}$- water, liquid -(h)gw$_{V}$- lift, pick up]

watermelon
ohn·yǫh·sa·gáh·deh a watermelon
[o+ stem: -(h)nyǫhsagahdeh- watermelon; consists of: -(h)nyǫhs(a)$_{N}$- melon, squash -(a)gahdeh$_{V}$- raw]

waterway see: river, stream
gi·hę́:de' a creek; a river; a stream
gi·hę́·den·yǫ' streams; rivers; creeks

watery
ga̲h·né:ga:t it is watery
[ga+ stem: -(h)negad- watery; consists of: -(h)neg(a)$_{N}$- water, liquid -d$_{V}$- stand]

wave
at·gę·nęt·sá·ǫ:nyǫ:' I waved my arms
[de+...ę+ stem: -nętsaǫnyǫ:- wave one's arms; consists of: -nęts(a)$_{N}$- arm -ǫnyǫ(:)$_{V}$- make several things]
de·sę·nęt·sá·ǫn·yǫ: wave your arms (goodbye)
o·do'dó:dǫ' little waves
[o+ stem: -do'd(a)$_{N}$- wave -odǫ'$_{V}$- several standing objects]
o·dó'da̲·hǫ' little waves
[o+ stem: -do'd(a)$_{N}$- wave -(h)ǫ(:)$_{V}$- lie]
o·do'do·wá:nę's big waves
[o+ stem: -do'd(a)$_{N}$- wave -owanę's$_{V}$- several big objects]
o·do'do·wa·n'ęs·gó:wah a big ocean wave
[o+ stem: -do'd(a)$_{N}$- wave -owanę's$_{V}$- several big objects -gowah big]

wave see: swell
o·dó'do:t swells; waves

waver see: stagger
hehs·hohs·hę·dá'ǫh tsǫ: he is staggering

wax see: shine
dę·gahs·da·té'dǫh it is shined, waxed, polished
way
tsę́h ni·yǫg·wá·i·ho'dę: our ways
[tsęh ni+P+ stem: -(r)iho'dę:- ways, beliefs -(r)ih(wa)$_N$- word -o'dę:$_V$- type of]
way see: I (gao:', ne'gi'ę:')
weak
ha·wę́·da·gę: he is weak (mentally or physically); he is a wimp; he is a coward
[P+ stem: -ędagę:$_V$- wimp, timid, weak, cowardly]
tę́' de·gáhs·hahs·de' no, it is not strong
[tę' not de'+ga+ stem: -sha(h)sde'- be strong; be weak]
ag·ya'da·gę́·he:' I got limp, weak
[stem: -ya'dagęhe(y)- weak (physically), slow (physically); consists of: -ya'd(a)$_N$- body -(ga)hey, (gę)hey, (i)hey, (ga)he:, (gę)he:, (i)he:$_V$- die, be weak, exhausted]
ag·ya'da·gę·hé:yǫ: I am physically weak, slow
wealth
ot·ga·nǫ·níhs·ra' richness; wealth
[o+ stem: -(a)tgahnǫnihsr(a)$_N$- wealth]
ot·gá·nǫn·ya't wealth; it is rich
[o+at+ stem: -ganǫnya'd- wealth; consists of: -ga(n)$_N$- price -ǫnya'd$_V$- cause to make]
a·gat·ga·nǫ́:nih I am wealthy
[P+ at+(N+) stem: -ga(n)$_N$- price -ganǫni$_V$- wealthy]
wealthy see: rich
ot·ga:nǫ́:nih it is rich
wean
ęhs·he·nǫg·wáh·kwa' you will take the milk from the child, wean it
[TR+ stem: -nǫgwahkgw- wean; consists of: -nǫ'g(wa)$_N$- breast, milk -(h)kw$_V$- take s.t. from s.o.]
weapon
ǫd·ri·yǫh·dáh·kwa' a weapon
[ǫ+ad+ stem: -(r)iyohdahkwa'- weapon; consists of: -(r)iyohd$_V$- use s.t. to kill s.t.]
wear
a·ga·ih·wę́:da' it wore out (for example, clothing)
[stem: -(r)ihwęda'- wear out; consists of: -(r)ih(wa)$_N$- word -ęda'$_V$- finish]
ę·sát·rǫn·ya't you will wear s.t.
[at+ stem: -(h)rǫnya'd- wear s.t.; consists of: -(a)trǫni, (a)trǫny$_V$- dress]
wear see: erode, tiring, use, use up
ę·wáh·tehg·ya'k it will erode
ot·sę́h·de:' it is tiring
gohs·dǫ́·hǫg·ye' she is arriving wearing that
a·wá:ts'a:' it is worn out, all gone, burnt up; it went down to nothing
weary see: annoyed, bother
ǫ'k·nǫ's I am sick of it, bored, fed up; I got sick of it
dęhs·ni·gǫ·há:ha' you are annoying me, bothering me
weasel
sgad·rí·yǫ·de:s weasel
[s+ga+ad+ stem: -(r)iyǫde:s- weasel; consists of: -(r)iyǫd(a)$_N$- -es$_V$- long]
weather
shę́h ni·węh·nihs·ró·dę's seasonal weather conditions
[tsęh ni+w+ stem: -ęhnihsr(a)$_N$- day -o'dę:$_V$- type of]
weather see: storm, ugly
a·wá·det·giht it was bad weather, stormy
ę·wá·det·giht it will be bad weather

Cayuga pronunciation guide: /a/ father /e/ weigh /ę/ men (nasalized) /i/ police /o/ hole /ǫ/ home (nasalized) /u/ blue. Underlined vowels are voiceless or whispered. /´/ high pitch. /t/ too /d/ do /k/ king /g/ good (never soft g) /j/ judge or adze /s/ soon /sh/ less heat (never the sh in shirt) /sr/ shrine /sy/ sure /hw/ which (the sound made when you blow out a candle) /h/ hi /ts/ cats hide /'/ (the sound before the first vowel in 'uh-uh') /n/ noon /r/ round /w/ way /y/ yes.

weave
  ę·sát·gwa·dǫ: you will zig-zag
  [at+ stem: -gwadǫ- weave, zig-zag; consists of: -g(wa)$_N$- lump, boil -dǫ'$_V$- several standing objects]
  hat·gwá:dǫh he is zig-zagging
  ot·gwá:dǫ' it is woven, in and out
web
  o·dá'a·ǫt a web; a net
  [o+ stem: -da'(a)$_N$- web -ǫd$_V$- attached]
wed see: marry
  ę·wá·gen·ya:k I will be married
wedlock see: marriage
  ga·náhk·wa' a marriage; a wife
Wednesday see: A (Ah·sęh ha·dǫ't)
wee see: small
  ni·wú:'uh it is small, little
weed
  a·wę́·nǫhg·ra' weeds
  [a+ stem: -węnohgr(a)$_N$- weed]
  o·wę́·nǫhg·re:s tall weeds
  [o+ stem: -węnohgr(a)$_N$- weed -es$_V$- long]
  go·wę́·nǫhg·ra:'s poison ivy; any plant that causes a skin infection
  [stem: -węnohgr(a)$_N$- weed -węnohgra:$_V$- cause an allergic reaction]
weed cutter
  e·wę·nǫhg·ríy'ak·ta' s.t. that cuts weeds
  [e+ stem: -węnohgr(a)$_N$- weed -(i)ya'gd$_V$- cause to cut, break]
week see: A (sga:t ęyaǫ:dadogehte')
week before last see: A (tsa'degyadǫdadrehk)
weep see: cry
  gahs·dá:ha' I am crying
weigh
  a·ga·ǫ:t·gǫt·ra·ni:yǫ́:dę' they (f/m) weighed themselves
  [at+ stem: -gǫ'traniyǫdę- weigh; consists of: -gǫ'tr(a)$_N$- weight -niyǫdę$_V$- hang for oneself]
  ęhs·ga·ǫ:t·gǫt·ra·ni:yǫ́:dę' they (f/m) will weigh themselves again
weigh consequences see: consequences
  de·yo·y'a·dó·węh·de:' to weigh the consequences; it is brain-wracking
weight
  tsę́h ni·yo·gǫt·rá:s·de' weight; pounds; poundage
  [tsęh ni+yo+ stem: -gǫtrahsde'- weight, etc.; consists of: -gǫ'tr(a)$_N$- weight -(a)hsde'$_V$- heavy]
weird see: odd, strange, unusual
  og·ya·nǫh·sá:nǫht a weird, odd, spooky house
  og·yá:nǫhk it is strange, bizarre
  ti·yó:t'ah it is queer, unusual, odd
welcome see: I, nyoh, thank, hello
  sgę́:nǫ' hello, how are you?
  dęhs·he·nǫ·hǫ́:n·yǫ:' you will welcome, greet, thank s.o.
welding machine
  gah·né:gohs a welding machine
  [ga+ stem: -(h)negohs- welding machine; consists of: -(h)neg(a)$_N$- water, liquid -oh$_V$- dip in liquid]
Welfare Office see: G (To·na·dę·ni·dę·ǫh)
well
  a:s·gę·nǫ́h·gę·hęk I hope you (all) will be well
  [A+ stem: -ęnǫ$_V$- be well]
  oh·na·wá·ǫ:dǫn·yǫ' many wells, springs
  [o+ stem: -(h)nawaod- well, spring; consists of: -(h)naw(a)$_N$- water, running -odǫnyǫ'$_V$- several standing objects]
well see: healthy, I, gwe:, think
  a·ga·da·gá·i:de' I am well, fine, healthy
  jǫ·nǫ́h·dǫn·yǫh to be healthy; to have well being again
well water
  oh·na·wá·o:tgę·ha:' well water
  [o+ stem: -(h)nawaotgeha:'- well water; consists of: -(h)naw(a)$_N$- water, running -od$_V$- stand -geha:' type, kind]

well-endowed

de·hahs·gwá·o·wa·nę'ʼs he has big rocks (that is, he is well-endowed)

[de+ha+ stem: -(h)sgwaowanęʼs- well-endowed; consists of: -(h)sg(wa:)$_N$- stone, bullet, rock -owanęʼs$_V$- several big things]

welt

oʼwá·o·ni: welts

[o+ stem: -(iʼ)waǫni:- welt; consists of: -(iʼ)w(a)$_N$- -ǫni, ǫny$_V$- make]

ga·i·wá·o·ni: welts

[stem: -(iʼ)waǫni:- welt; consists of: -(iʼ)w(a)$_N$- welt -ǫni, ǫny$_V$- make]

west see: sun-down

he·gahg·węʼs towards the setting sun; the direction of the sunset; west

wet

o·nǫ́hg·wi·jaʼ it is soaking wet, saturated

[o+ stem: -nǫhgwijaʼ$_V$- be soaking wet]

sga·nǫhg·wi.jǫ́:gyeʼ they (lit. it) came back all wet

[o+ stem: -nǫhgwijǫhǫgyeʼ$_V$- go along being soaking wet]

a·wę·dę·ná:wę (a·wę·dę·ná:wę:ʼ) it got wet

[stem: -wędęnawę:ʼ- get wet; consists of: -węd(a)$_N$- day -nawę:$_V$- be wet]

ahs·náʼna·węht you wet it

[N+/naʼ+ stem: -nawęhd- wet s.t., melt s.t., liquefy s.t.; consists of: -nawę:$_V$- be wet]

ęhs·náʼna·węʼt you will melt, liquefy s.t.

o·naʼna·wę́h·dǫh it has been melted

wet see: damp

ot·sá·dęʼǫh it is damp

what see: I (deʼhoʼdęʼ, neʼgiʼgyę:ʼ)

what the...? see: I (hoh)

whatever see: I (shęhoʼdęʼ)

wheel

ęʼníhs·ga:ʼ, węʼníhs·ga:ʼ a wheel; a circle; a hoop

[stem: -ęʼnihsg(a:)$_N$- wheel]

wheelbarrow

sgá:t wʼę·nihs·ga·ǫ́:t e·nę́hg·wi·taʼ a wheelbarrow

[consists of: sga:t wʼęnihsgaǫ:t it has one wheel; enęhgwitaʼ s.t. that is used for hauling]

wheeze

oh·wę́hs·da·ga: it is wheezing

[o+ stem: -ǫhwęhsdaga:- wheeze; consists of: -(h)węhsd(a)$_N$- -ga:$_V$- make a rattling or grinding noise]

when see: I (hwę:dǫh, nęh, o:nęh)

where see: I (danhǫweh, etc.)

whereas see: I (because, giʼ gyę:ʼ, shęh)

which

ga·ę́ ní:ga:ʼ which one; a specific thing

[gaę which ni+ga+ stem: -a:ʼ$_V$- hold, contain, include; be a specific object]

which see: I (gaę, sǫ ʼǫ naht)

while see: I (waʼjihtsǫ:, waʼjihya:)

whine

at·ga.ji·dá·ga·i: there was whining, crying, repetitive complaining

[de+... stem: -jiʼdaga:- whine, cry, complain; consists of: -jiʼd(a)$_N$- cry -ga:$_V$- make a rattling or grinding noise]

de·ga.ji·dá:ga: a whiner; a cryer

whip

ęhs·węʼs·dǫ́:niʼ you will whip (for example, meringue)

[stem: -(h)węʼsdǫni- whip; consists of: -(h)węʼsd(a)$_N$- foam -ǫni, ǫny$_V$- make]

ni·yo·hǫ·dú:sʼuh little whips

[ni+yo+ stem: -(h)ǫd(a)$_N$- bush -u:sʼuh$_V$- several small objects]

ę·ke·hǫ·dá:yęht I will whip her

[TR+ stem: -(h)ǫdayęhd- whip s.o.; consists of: -(h)ǫd(a)$_N$- bush, whip -(y)ęhd$_V$- hit, knock down, strike]

Cayuga pronunciation guide: /a/ father /e/ weigh /ę/ men (nasalized) /i/ police /o/ hole /ǫ/ home (nasalized) /u/ blue. Underlined vowels are voiceless or whispered. /ʹ/ high pitch. /t/ too /d/ do /k/ king /g/ good (never soft g) /j/ judge or adze /s/ soon /sh/ less heat (never the sh in shirt) /sr/ shrine /sy/ sure /hw/ which (the sound made when you blow out a candle) /h/ hi /ts/ cats hide /ʼ/ (the sound before the first vowel in 'uh-uh') /n/ noon /r/ round /w/ way /y/ yes.

whip see: bush
o·hǫ́:da' a bush; a whip
whip-poor-will
gwę́'gohnyę' whip-poor-will
[stem: -gwę'gohnyę'$_N$- whip-poor-will]
whirl see: twirl, whirlpool
de·sat·ga·ha·den·yǫ́g·wa·hǫ: twirl
whirlpool
oh·na·wa·dá:se: a whirlpool
[o+ stem: -(h)nawadase:- whirlpool; consists of: -(h)naw(a)$_N$- water, running -dase:$_V$- whirl]
ot·ne·ga·dá:se: a whirlpool
[o+at+ stem: -(h)negadase:- whirlpool; consists of: -(h)neg(a)$_N$- water, liquid -dase:$_V$- whirl]
whisk see: broom, sweep
ga·nóhs·gw'i·ta:' broom
de·gó·nohs·gwihs I am sweeping
whiskers
o·gǫhs·twę́:'ę:' a beard
[o+ stem: -gǫhstǫ'(a), gǫhstwę'(ę:)$_N$- whiskers, beard]
ga·gǫhs·tǫ·á'geh on its whiskers
de·yo·di·no·gę́:dǫ:t whiskers on a catfish
[de+yodi+ stem: -nogędǫd- whiskers; consists of: -nogęd(a)$_N$- -ǫd$_V$- attached]
whisper
a·ja·hǫhs·gwá:gǫ: in a whisper
[stem: -(a)jahǫhsg(wa),(a)jęhǫhsg(wa)$_N$- whisper -ag:ǫ in]
ęh·sa·ję·hǫ́hs·gwa·ę:' you will whisper
[stem: -(a)jęhǫhsgwaę(:)- whisper; consists of: -(a)jahǫhsg(wa), (a)jęhǫhsg(wa)$_N$- whisper -ę$_V$- lie on the ground]
sa·ję·hǫhs·gwá·ę' whisper
whistle
ę·sná·ga·i: you will whistle
[stem: -na'g(a)$_N$- horn, antler -na'ga:, na'gai$_V$- whistle]
ha·ná·ga: he is whistling
sna·gá·i: whistle
ga·na·gá·i·dahk·wa' a whistle
[stem: -na'gidahkwa'$_N$- whistle; consits of: -naga:, nagai$_V$- whistle]
white
hnyǫ́·ǫh white
[(A)+ stem: -(h)nyǫ'ǫh$_V$- white]
gahn·yǫ́'ǫh it is white
[ga+ stem: -(h)nyǫ'ǫh$_V$- white]
white see: C (Caucasian, hnyǫ'ǫhneha:', gahnyǫ'ǫhgeha:'), light-coloured
gę'gę: it is white; it is light-skinned; it is light-coloured
white-wash see: clay
o·ná·wa·da' clay; plaster; white-wash
whitener see: bleach
gahs·dag·wá:dahg·wahs bleach; javex
who see: I (sǫ'ǫ naht)
whole
o·nę·hęg·wé:gǫh whole corn; all of the corn
[o+ stem: -nęhęgwegǫh- whole corn; consists of: -nęh(ę)$_N$- corn -gwegǫh$_V$- all]
whole see: complete
ga·wa·ya·nę́·da'ǫh it is ready, prepared
whore see: prostitute
wa·dat·ge·hǫ́·ha' she (lit.: it) is a prostitute
whose see: I (sǫ: go:węh)
why see: I (dę' hne:', ne:'hǫ:ni')
wicked see: bad, evil
de·ta·dih·wa·yé·i: they (m) are corrupt, impish, bad
wa·hé:tgęh evil (in mind); bad
wide
de·yóh·se:s it has a wide mouth
[de+ yo+ N+ stem: -(h)s(a)$_N$- mouth -es$_V$- long]
widen see: stretch
de·ho:dí:yǫ:t he is stretching it

widow
a·ǫ·de̲·hę́·ǫhs, a·go·de̲·hę́·ǫhs she became a widow
[P+ade+ stem: -(h)ęʼǫhsd- become a widow, widower; consists of: -(h)ę(h,ʼ)$_{V}$- feel bad]
ho·de·hę·ǫ́hs·dǫh he is a widower
go·de·hę·ǫ́hs·dǫh she is a widow

wiener see: sausage
o·hé:tsa·i: cooked wieners; bologna

wife
ke·gę́h·jih my wife
[TR+ stem: -gęhjih$_{V}$- old (person); spouse]
ak·náhg·waʼ my wife
[stem: -(ʼ)nahg(wa)$_{N}$- wife, marriage]

wig
ǫt·nǫ·ha·háhk·waʼ wig
[ǫ+at+ stem: -nǫhahahkwaʼ- wig; consists of: -nǫʼ(a:), nǫh(a)$_{N}$- head -(h)ahahkwaʼ$_{V}$- s.t. that supports]
ot·nǫ́·ha·he:ʼ it has a wig on
[P+…at+ stem: -nǫhahe:ʼ- mane; have a wig on; consists of: -nǫh(a), nah(a)$_{N}$- scalp -(h)e:ʼ$_{V}$- sitting up on top of s.t.]

wild
wa·dad·wę:ní:yoʼ a wild animal
[adad+ stem: -węniyoʼ$_{V}$- wild]
gan·yo:ʼsó:ʼah wild animals
[ga+ stem: -nyo:ʼ- animal; consists of: -nyo:ʼ$_{N}$- wild animal -(r)iyo, nyo$_{V}$- kill s.t.]

wild see: animal (wild)
gan·yo:ʼ wild animals

wild cat see: lion
ga̲·hahs·rǫg·yéh·taʼ a lion

willing
ho·gá·ęs he is willing
[P+ stem: -gaę$_{V}$- be willing]
sa·gá·ęs you are willing
ęh·sá·ga·ę: you will allow, give permission
ę·wa·ge·gá·ęʼ I will consent
ęhs·wa·gá·ę:se:k you all will be willing

willow see: nape of neck
o·séh·daʼ a willow; the nape of the neck

will
ha·wé:ǫ: he has willed
[P+ stem: -e:ʼǫ:- will s.t.; consists of: -i:, ę:, e:$_{V}$- think, hope, want]
sé:ǫ:ʼ you wanted, believed

wimp see: timid
tot·gri: he's a wimp; he pulls back

win
a·gę·na·dę́hn·ye̲·ha:ʼ they (z) won a bet
[adę+ stem: -(h)nyaha:- win (a bet); consists of: -(h)ny(a)$_{N}$- stick -(h)awi, (h)a:$_{V}$- hold, include, carry, bring]
a·hǫ·wa·di:gwé:niʼ they won a competition (lit.: they beat him, them (m))
[TR+/…at+ stem: -gweni, gweny$_{V}$- be able to do s.t., succeed; win a competition]
a·e·tig·wé:niʼ we won a competition
a·hę·nat·gwę́·nʼi·ge: the big win; the victory (lit.: they (m) won big)

wind
de·yo·wá:węn·ye: stirring winds
[de+yo+ stem: -w(a:)$_{N}$- air -(a)węnye(:)$_{V}$- stir, mix]
ga·wa·o·wá:nęh a big wind
[ga+ stem: -w(a:)$_{N}$- air -owanęh$_{V}$- be big]
ga·was·há:sdeʼ strong wind
[ga+ stem: -w(a:)$_{N}$- air -sha(h)sdeʼ$_{V}$- strong]

wind see: air
ó:wa:ʼ air; wind

winding
de·yot·saʼkdǫ́n·yǫg·węh it is twisted
[de+yo+at+N/sha+ stem: -(sha)ʼkdǫnyǫgwęh- winding, twisted; consists of: -shaʼged, shaʼkdǫ$_{V}$- bent, crooked]

Cayuga pronunciation guide: /a/ father /e/ weigh /ę/ men (nasalized) /i/ police /o/ hole /ǫ/ home (nasalized) /u/ blue. Underlined vowels are voiceless or whispered. /ʼ/ high pitch. /t/ too /d/ do /k/ king /g/ good (never soft g) /j/ judge or adze /s/ soon /sh/ less heat (never the sh in shirt) /sr/ shrine /sy/ sure /hw/ which (the sound made when you blow out a candle) /h/ hi /ts/ cats hide /ʼ/ (the sound before the first vowel in 'uh-uh') /n/ noon /r/ round /w/ way /y/ yes.

winding (continued)

de·yo·ta·ha'k·dǫn·yǫ́:gwęh winding roads
[de+yo+at+$_N$/sha+ stem: -(h)ah(a)$_N$- road -(sha)'kdǫnyǫgwęh$_V$- winding, twisted]

window

at·gǫ́hs·gwat·ra' a window
[at+ stem: -gǫhsgwa'tr(a)$_N$- window]

ot·gǫ́hs·gwat·ro' a window
[o+ at+ stem: -gǫhsgwa'tro'- pane of glass; consists of: -gǫhsgwa'tr(a)$_N$- window -o'$_V$- be submerged]

wa·dę·nǫhs·gwát·ro' a window
[wa+ adę+ stem: -nǫhsgwa'tro'- window; consists of: -nǫhsgwa'tr(a)$_N$- window -o'$_V$- be submerged]

o·noh·sa·gá·hęt a window
[o+ stem: -nǫhsagahęd- window; consists of: -nǫhs(a)$_N$- house -gahęd$_V$- drill, hole]

o·nǫh·sa·ga·hę́:dǫ' windows
[o+ stem: -nǫhsagahęd- window; consists of: -nǫhs(a)$_N$- house -gahęd$_V$- drill, hole -ǫ' plural]

oh·sohg·wi:yó's wat·gǫhs·gwat·ró' o·nǫh·sa·ga·hę́:dǫ' stained glass windows
[consists of: ohsohgwi:yo's beautiful colours; onǫhsagahę:dǫ' windows; watgǫhsgwa'tro' window pane]

window blind see: blind

(o·nǫh·sa·ga·hę́t) eh·si·há·ǫ:kwa' a window blind

windward

nig·yo·wá·ę·hę: the direction of the wind
[ni+g+yo+ stem: -waęhę:- wind direction; consists of: -w(a:)$_N$- air -ęhę(:)$_V$- direct, convey]

windy

o·wá:de' it is windy; wind; it is a breeze
[o+ stem: -wade'- windy; consists of: -w(a:)$_N$- air -de'$_V$- exist]

wing see: fin

o·wá:ya' fin of a fish, wings

wink

de·sat·gwi'á'ek a wink
[de+...at+ stem: -gwi'a'eg- wink; consists of: -gwi'(a)$_N$- -(')e$_V$- hit]

winnow

sá:wa:s you are a winnower, shaker, sifter
[stem: -(a)wag$_V$- winnow, shake out, sift]

ęh·sá:wa:k you will winnow, shake out, sift s.t.

sa·wá:gǫh I am sifting right now

sawá:ksǫh you are winnowing, shaking, sifting right now

ęh·sa·gę·hę́:wa:k you will winnow the chaff (corn or beans)
[stem: -(a)'gęh(ęda)$_N$- ash, dust -(a)wag$_V$- winnow, shake out, sift]

sa·wá:kta' you are a sifter
[stem: -(a)wakd$_V$- winnow, shake out, sift]

winter

gǫhs·réh·ka:' winter kind
[g+ stem: -(o)hsr(a)$_N$- year, winter -e$_V$- go -ka:' type]

winter see: A, gǫhsrehneh, ugly

ę·wa·dehs·rá:tgiht it will be a bad winter

wipe

gra·gé:wahs I am erasing it, wiping it
[stem: -(r)age(:,w)$_V$- wipe]

ęg·rá:ge:' I will erase, wipe it

ag·ra:gé:węh I have erased,wiped it

ę·gę·ni·dá:ge:' I will wipe myself clean of fecal matter
[ęn+ stem: -i'dage(w)- wipe one's behind; consists of: -(ni)'d(a)$_N$- feces, privates -(r)age(:,w)$_V$- wipe]

wire
ga̱h·só̜·wa̱h·da' nails; wire; a needle
[ga+ stem: -(h)so̜wahd(a)$_N$- wire, nail, needle]
ga̱h·so̜·wa̱h·dá:de' it has wires that stand out
[stem: -(h)so̜wahd(a)$_N$- wire, nail, needle -de'$_V$- exist]
de·gah·so·wá:ke̜h two wires
[de+A+(N+) stem: -(h)so̜w(ahda)$_N$- wire, nail, needle -ke̜h$_V$- twins]
wise
ho·di'ni·go̜·ho·wá:ne̜'s they (m) are wise; they have the capacity for thinking
[P+ stem: -(')nigo̜howane̜- wise; consists of: -(')nigo̜h(a)$_N$- mind -owane̜'s$_V$- several big objects]
wish
a:yá:we̜h I wish, hope (lit.: it should happen)
[a;+yaw+ stem: -e̜(h,')$_V$- happen]
wish see: want
de̜h·sa·do̱h·we̜:jó̜:ni' you will want s.t.
witch
de·ga·he̜h·jí'da·ho̜h a Hallowe'en witch
[de+ga+ stem: -(h)e̜hji'dahǫh- witch; consists of: -(h)e̜hji(')da)- dried out -(adi)ho̜h$_V$- lean against]
witch see: divine, evil power
ha·dih·ne·gát·se̜n·yo̜hs they (m) divine, witch for water
go·ná:tgo̜h they (f/m) are a force to be reckoned with; they (f/m) are ominous; they are bad medicine people
witchcraft see: fetish
ot·go̜t·ras·hó̜:'o̜h an object used for witchcraft
witch doctor see: evil power
go·ná:tgo̜h they (f/m) are a force to be reckoned with; they (f/m) are ominous; they are bad medicine people
witch hazel
ga̱'ahd·ró̜:nih witch hazel
[ga+ stem: -(')ahdro̜nih- witch hazel; consists of: -(')ahdr(a)$_N$- basket -o̜ni, o̜ny$_V$- make]
witch light
de·wa·tahs·ró:gwahs a witch light
[de+wa+at+ stem: -(h)ahsrogwahs- phantom light, witch light; consists of: -(h)ahsr(a)$_N$- flash -ogw$_V$- scatter]
with see: bring, escort
sha·há:wi' he brought it with him
he̜hs·he·ha·wíh·dahk you will escort her, take her with you
withdraw see: flinch
da·wá:tgri:k it pulled back, flinched, shrank
withdrawn see: shy
go·dí'gro̜' she is shy
within see: in
g'a·no̜ht it (usually an animal) is in s.t.
within
[-ago̜: internal locative suffix; means 'in', 'on', or 'under']
withstand see: endure
e̜h·se̜'ni·go̜·hah·ní:ya:t you will endure (lit. toughen or strengthen your mind)
witness
e̜hs·rih·wag·wá·ih·si' you will be a witness
[stem: -(r)ihwagwaihsi- witness; consists of: -(r)ih(wa)$_N$- word -gwaihs(i)$_V$- straight]
witness see: see
a·há:ge̜' he saw
wizard see: evil power
go·ná:tgo̜h they (f/m) are a force to be reckoned with; they (f/m) are ominous; they are bad medicine people
wolf
o·tah·yó̜:ni: a wolf
[(o+) stem: -tahyo̜ni:$_N$- wolf]
Wolf clan see: C (Ho·tah·yo̜:ni:)

Cayuga pronunciation guide: /a/ father /e/ weigh /e̜/ men (nasalized) /i/ police /o/ hole /o̜/ home (nasalized) /u/ blue. Underlined vowels are voiceless or whispered. /'/ high pitch. /t/ too /d/ do /k/ king /g/ good (never soft g) /j/ judge or adze /s/ soon /sh/ less heat (never the sh in shirt) /sr/ shrine /sy/ sure /hw/ which (the sound made when you blow out a candle) /h/ hi /ts/ cats hide /'/ (the sound before the first vowel in 'uh-uh') /n/ noon /r/ round /w/ way /y/ yes.

woman
a·gó̧:gweh a girl; a woman; the female gender
[A+ stem: -ǫgwe(ʼda)$_N$- person]
gá:gǫg·weh women
e·gę́h·jih she is old; an old woman
[A+ stem: -gęhjih$_V$- old (person)]
a·gǫg·wʼe·dá:se: a young woman
[A+ stem: -ǫgweʼdase:- young; consists of: -ǫgwe(ʼda)$_N$- person -(a)se:$_V$- new]
woman see: female
je·yáʼda:t one person (female)
wonder see: think
ęh·sę·nǫh·dó̧:nyǫ:ʼ you will wonder, think
wood
o·yę́:daʼ wood; firewood
[o+ stem: -yęd(a)$_N$- wood]
wood see: log, tree
gá·ǫ:daʼ a log
o·héh·saʼ a decayed tree; a log; wood; a board
wood chip
oh·wę́ʼga:ʼ wood chips
[o+ stem: -(h)węʼg(a:)$_N$- chip]
woodchuck see: ground hog
téh·tǫʼ a ground hog; a woodchuck; a gopher
woodland see: forest
ga·há:daʼ a forest
woodpecker
díhs·dihs a house woodpecker
[stem: -dihsdihs$_N$- house woodpecker]
gá·ǫ·daʼehs a woodpecker
[ga+ stem: -(r)ǫdaʼehs- woodpecker; consists of: -(r)ǫd(a)$_N$- log -(ʼ)e$_V$- hit]
gwi·dóʼgwi·doʼ black breasted woodpecker
[stem: -gwidoʼgwidoʼ$_N$- black breasted woodpecker]
wood pile
de·wá·tę·ho:t a pile of wood
[de+wa+at+ stem: -(h)ęhod- wood pile; consists of: -hęh(a)$_N$- wood -od$_V$- stand]
woodstove see: stove
o·yę·dáʼ ga·nǫh·sa·da·i·hát·raʼ a wood stove
o·yę·dáʼ wa·dó̧:twahs a woodstove
wood tick
o·séh·dǫk a wood tick
[o+ stem: -sehdǫg- wood tick]
wood worker see: carpenter
ha·nǫh·só̧:nih he is a carpenter
wool
de·yo·di·naʼga·ǫ:dó̧ʼ o·hę́h·da:ʼ wool
[consists of: deyodinaʼgaǫ:dǫʼ sheep, horned animal; ohęhda:ʼ fur]
wool see: fur
o·hę́h·da·i: fur on the animal
word
o·wę́:naʼ a word
[o+ stem: -węn(a)$_N$- voice, word]
o·węnas·hó̧:ʼǫh words
[o+ stem: -węn(a)$_N$- voice, word -sǫ:ʼǫh plural]
ga·wę́·na·gǫ:ʼ in the words, voice; in the speech
[o+ stem: -węn(a)$_N$- voice, word -agǫ: in]
o·wę́·nah·sęht harsh words
[o+ stem: -węnaʼsęhd- harsh words; consists of: -węn(a)$_N$- voice, word -(aʼ)sęhd$_V$- hand down, bring down]
ga·wę·nag·wę:ní:yoʼ the main word
[ga+ stem: -węn(a)$_N$- voice, word -gwęniyoʼ$_V$- main]
o·wę́·nat·giʼ an ugly sounding voice
[o+ stem: -węn(a)$_N$- voice, word -tgiʼ$_V$- dirty, ugly]
word, idea, matter, affair, message, etc.
o·íh·waʼ a message; it matters; it is its fault; a word; an affair; business
[o+ stem: -(r)ih(wa)$_N$- word]

word, etc. (continued)
o·ih·wá·ǫ:weh sacred idea
[o+ stem: -(r)ih(wa)$_N$- word -ǫweh real, Aboriginal]
o·íh·w'a·geh the reason or idea for s.t.; an affair
work
hę·nad·ri̲·hó'da:s they (m) work; they are workers
[ad+ stem: -(ri)ho'dad- work; consists of: -(ri)ho'd$_V$- work]
a·gad·ri̲·hó'da:t I worked
sad·rí·ho'da:t work
ho·í·ho'de' he is working
[P+ stem: -(ri)ho'de'- be working; consists of: -(ri)ho'd$_V$- work]
sa·i·ho'dę́hs·ra' your work
[stem: -(ri)ho'dęhsr(a)$_N$- work]
ga·i:ho'dęhs·ras·hǫ́:'ǫh occupations; jobs
ga·i·ho'dę́s·rahs·de',
o·i·ho'dę́s·rahs·de' heavy work; hard work
[ga/o+ stem: -(ri)ho'dęhsr(a)$_N$- work -(a)hsde'$_V$- heavy]
ga·i·ho'dęhs·rí:yo: it is nice work
[ga+ stem: -(ri)ho'dęhsr(a)$_N$- work -iyo:$_V$- be nice, good]
ga·i·ho'dęhs·ro·wá:nęh a lot of work; big work; it is a big job
[ga+ stem: -(ri)ho'dęhsr(a)$_N$- work -owanęh$_V$- be big]
a·hǫh·ya·gę́'dahk it made him work hard; he laboured
[A/TR+ stem: -(r)ǫhyagę'd- labour, make s.o. work hard; consists of: -(r)ǫhyagę$_V$- be in agony, groan]
work see: work together, work well
working bee
dę·ha·di·nę́·hę·da:s a working bee; a barn raising
[de+A+ stem: -nęhę'das- working bee, barn raising; consists of: -nęhę(:)$_V$- guard, stand in a line]
work together
a·ta·di·yé:na' they (m) did it together (for example, accomplices)
[de+... stem: -yena(w), yenaǫ, yena(:)$_V$- catch, receive, accept; work together]
ded·wa:yé:na: let's work together, help each other
ded·wa·ye·ná·w'a·kǫ' we all (incl.) are working united for one cause
[de+... stem: -yenawa'kǫ(:)$_V$- work together]
de·yag·wa·ye·na·wá'kǫ' we all (excl.) are working together
ded·wa·ye·ná·w'a·kǫ: let's work together
work well
ot·sáh·niht it is a smart worker
[P+at+ stem: -sahnihd$_V$- be ambitious, tireless, zealous]
got·sáh·niht she is a good worker, tireless, active, industrious, etc.
hot·sáh·niht he is a good worker, tireless, active, industrious, etc.
sat·sáh·niht you are overzealous, ambitious
wat·sáh·niht it works diligently
world
o·ih·wa·gę́h·yat·geh to the edge of the world (that is, in the last days)
[o+ stem: -(r)ih(wa)$_N$- word -gęhyad$_V$- beside -'geh on]
world see: earth
oh·wę́·ja·de' existing earth; land
World War
tsi·yoh·wę·ja:gwe:gǫ́h wad·rí:yo: a world war (lit: there is fighting all over the world)
[tsiyohwęja:gwe:gǫh all over the earth wadri:yo: war, fight]

worm see: fishworm, insect
o·ji'nǫ·wá·he'da' a fishworm
o·ji'nǫ́:wa' a bug; an insect; a worm
worn out
o·déhs·da̱h·sǫ: it is worn out
[o+ade+ stem: -(h)sdahsǫ:- worn out; consists of: -(h)s(d)$_V$- use -sǫ' plural]
worn out see: hair, use up
o·gé'a:' hair; a rag; it is ragged, tattered
a·wá:ts'a:' it is worn out, all gone, burnt up; it went down to nothing
worry
ęh·sę'ni·gǫ́·ho'drǫ:' you will worry, despair; you will be desperate
[ę+ stem: -(')nigǫho'drǫ- console s.o.; worry, despair, be desparate; consists of: -(')nigǫh(a)$_N$- mind -o'drǫ(:)$_V$- caress]
s'ę·ni·gǫ·hó'd·rǫh you are a worrier
worth see: equity
tsę́h ni·yó'ga:' equity; capital; value; worth
worthless see: unimportant, useless
o·ga·os·hǫ́:'ǫh s.t. not important, second-rate
de·yó·i·hǫ:t it is useless
worthy
od·rih·wa·ga:nǫ́:ni: a worthy idea; it is excellent
[ad+(N+) stem: -(r)ih(wa)$_N$- word -ganǫni$_V$- wealthy]
wound see: hurt, punch, slap
ęhs·hé·nǫhn·ya'k you will hurt s.o.
a·há·gǫ·he:k he punched it
ęh·set·rag·wę́'da̱'e:k you will slap it(on the cheek
wow see: I (hotgǫ'ǫh)
wrap
swe·nǫ́:nih wrap it
[stem: -(h)we'nǫni- wrap s.t.; consists of: -(h)we'n(a)$_N$- round, circle -ǫni, ǫny$_V$- make]
wrath see: anger
ohs·rǫ́·hę'da' an angry person; temper
wreck
ęhs·ré:tgęh you will wreck it
[stem: -(hr)etgęh- wreck s.t.; consists of: -(hr)etgę$_V$- be evil, bad, ugly]
wreck see: bad, ruin
o·hét·gę'ǫh it is wrecked, ruined
ęhs·hé:tgęht you will damage, ruin, wreck s.t.
wren
sgá·i:s·gęd·ri: a marsh wren
[s+ga+ stem: -(r)i:sgędri:- marsh wren]
ga·nǫh·sak·dá:gye' a brown wren; around the house; alongside the house (that is, a yard that isn't fenced in)
[stem: -nǫhs(a)$_N$- house ; -akdagye'- beside]
wrestle
de̱·hę·na·da:gyé:nahs wrestlers; they (m) are wrestling
[de+...adag+ stem: -yena(w)- wrestle; consists of: -yena(w), yenaǫ, yena(:)$_V$- catch, receive, accept]
ęh·sa·dag·yé:na:' you will wrestle
de·sa·dag·yé:na: wrestle
wriggle see: struggle
ęh·sá·det·sa't you will struggle, squirm to get loose, revolt
wrinkle
ęh·sé:gri:k you will wrinkle, fan-fold it
[(d+)... stem: -gri$_V$- wrinkle]
ah·sé:gri:k you wrinkled, fan-folded it; you made it smaller, shrank it
dah·sé:gri:k wrinkle, fan-fold it
sę·nín·yǫg·ri: you wrinkle up your nose (in disgust)
[ęni+ stem: -(')nyǫgri- wrinkle up one's nose; consists of: -(')nyǫ(hsa)$_N$- nose -gri$_V$- wrinkle]
ohsg·wí'dra' a prune; wrinkles
[o+ stem: -(h)sgwi'dr(a)$_N$- wrinkle]

wrinkle (continued)
otg·ríhs·rǫ' wrinkled clothes; it is wrinkled up
[P+at+ stem: -grihsrǫ'$_V$- several wrinkled items]

wrinkly
de·yóhsg·w'id·rǫ·t it is wrinkly
[de+yo+ stem: -(h)sgwi'dr(a)$_N$- wrinkle -ǫd$_V$- attached]
sgahs·gwi'd·ra̱·hé·' **t·sǫ:** you are (lit.: it is) pruny, wrinkly
[s+ga+ tsǫ: just stem: -(h)sgwi'drahe:'- wrinkly; consists of: -(h)sgwi'dr(a)$_N$- wrinkle -(h)e:'$_V$- sitting up on top of s.t.]
ad·wa·dehs·gwi'd·rǫ́·dę' you (lit.: it) became wrinkly, pruny
[de+... stem: -(h)sgwi'drǫd(ę)- be wrinkly; consists of: -(h)sgwi'dr(a)$_N$- wrinkle -ǫd(ę)$_V$- be attached; put in]

wristband
ǫn·yę́n·hahs·ta' a wristband
[ǫ+ stem: -(')nyęnhahsta'- wristband; consists of: -(')ny(a)$_N$- finger, hand -(ę)nhahsd$_V$- encircle]

write
eh·yá:dǫh she writes
[stem: -(h)yadǫ(:)$_V$- write]
ęk·yá:dǫ:' I will write

wrong see: bad; commit a crime; right
tę́' **det·ga:yé·i'** it is bad, false, wrong
a·tad·ri̱h·wá·hę' he went afoul of the law; he did s.t. wrong
tega:yé·i: it is wrong; s.o. who isn't right in the head
[t+ga+ stem: -yei, (y)í$_V$- right, correct]

Y

yank see: grab, pull
da·ję́:na: grab it
ęt·gag·yę·hę́:to', ęt·gat·yę·hę́:to' I will pull it

yard
wa·dę·hę́:gǫ:, a·dę·hę́:gǫ: in the yard
[(wa+) stem: -(a)dę'h(ę)$_N$- fence]
jo̱·ę́·na:t one yard (measurement)
[j+yo+ stem: -(a)'ęn(a)$_N$- stick, pole, rod -d$_V$- stand; one]

yarn see: thread, wool
oh·sí:ya' a thread; a string; a cord
de·yo·di·na'ga·ǫ·dǫ́' **o·hę́h·da:'** wool

yawn
de·sah·sag·wáh·ta' you are yawning
[de+P+ stem: -(h)sag(a)$_N$- mouth -(h)sagwahd$_V$- yawn]

yawn see: gasp
ad·wák·sa·ga:'s you gasped, yawned

year see: A (ohsre:dahs, niyohsrage:)

yearling
o·gęn·hi·yá'gǫ' a yearling
[o+ stem: -gęnhiya'gǫ'- yearling; consists of: -(gę)nh(a)$_N$- summer -(i)ya'g$_V$- cut, break]

yearn see: crave, want
ęk·nǫ́:wa·k I will crave s.t.
ga̱hs·gá:ne:s I have longings for; I want; I desire

yell
de̱·hó·he·ta' he is hollering
[de+P+ stem: -(h)ed$_V$- yell, scream]
a·tó·he:t he hollered or yelled
de̱·ho·he·dáh·ne' he is going along hollering
[de+P+ stem: -(h)edahne(')$_V$- go along yelling, screaming]

Cayuga pronunciation guide: /a/ father /e/ weigh /ę/ men (nasalized) /i/ police /o/ hole /ǫ/ home (nasalized) /u/ blue. Underlined vowels are voiceless or whispered. /´/ high pitch. /t/ too /d/ do /k/ king /g/ good (never soft g) /j/ judge or adze /s/ soon /sh/ less heat (never the sh in shirt) /sr/ shrine /sy/ sure /hw/ which (the sound made when you blow out a candle) /h/ hi /ts/ cats hide /'/ (the sound before the first vowel in 'uh-uh') /n/ noon /r/ round /w/ way /y/ yes.

yellow
o·jí:tgwa:ʼ yellow
[o+ stem: -jitgw(a:)$_N$- yellow]
o·jit·gwá·i:yo: yellow
[o+ stem: -jitgwaiyo- yellow; consists of: -jitgw(a:)$_N$- yellow -iyo:$_V$- be nice, good]
yes see: I (ęhęʼ)
yesterday see: A (te:dę:ʼ)
yet see: I (ahsǫh)
yield see: forfeit, give up, harvest
a·sa:dwę́:deht you forfeited
ę·sa:wę́:naʼt you will give up
ga·yę́t·wag·węh a harvest
yodel see: chant
ęhs·wa·ę·ná·ga·nye:ʼ you all will yodel, chant
yoke
ǫt·nę·hęhs·dáhk·waʼ a yoke
[ǫ+at+ stem: -nęhęhsdahkwaʼ- yoke; consists of: -nęhę(:)$_V$- guard, stand in a line]
York, Ont. see: E (Tgag·wę:troʼ)
you see: I (i:s)
young
a·gǫg·wʼe·dá:se: she is a young woman
[A+ stem: -ǫgweʼdase:- be young; consists of: -ǫgwe(ʼda)$_N$- person -(a)se:$_V$- new]
hǫg·wéʼda·se: he is a young man
gǫg·wéʼda·se: I am a young person
hok·se·dá·i·hah he is a young tender belly (that is, nine-to-thirteen-ish and not really tough)
[P+ stem: -kseʼdaihah- young; consists of: -kseʼd(a)$_N$- belly -(r)i, (w)i$_V$- ripe -hah diminutive]
young (continued)
tsi·yǫg·wak·se·dá·i·hah when we all were young tender bellies (that is, nine-to-thirteen-ish)
young see: child, tadpole
o·wí:ya:ʼah a baby
ohs·twá:sʼah a young animal; a little animal; a tadpole
yours see: I (sa:węh)
youth see: teenager
hak·saʼda·sé:ʼah he is a teenage boy
ek·saʼda·sé:ʼah teenage girl

Z

zig-zag see: weave
ę·sát·gwa·dǫ: you will zig zag
zipper
de·wę́h·da:s a zipper
[de+w+ stem: -ęhdas- zipper; consists of: -(w)ęhdad$_V$- run]
de·węh·dá:s de·yǫt·na̱h·sǫ́·da̱hk·waʼ a zipper
[consists of: dewęhda:s zipper; deyǫtna̱hsǫda̱hkwaʼ zipper lit.: s.t. that has a tongue]
de·yǫt·na̱h·sǫ́·da̱hk·waʼ a zipper
[de+yo+at+ stem: -(ʼ)nahsǫdahkwaʼ- zipper; consists of: -(a)węʼnahs(a), (a)węʼnohs(a)$_N$- tongue -ǫdahkwaʼ$_V$- attached instrument]
zoo animal
ga·din·ho·dǫ:nyǫ́ʼ ga·dí:nyo:ʼ zoo animals
[consists of: gadinhodǫ:nyǫʼ they (z) are locked up; gadi:nyo:ʼ wild animals]

Cayuga-English Dictionary

ˀ (Glottal Stop)

•(ˀ)ahdr(a) basket
[ga+]
gaˀahdraˀ a basket
•(ˀ)ahdrǫnih witch hazel
[ga+ -(ˀ)ahdr(a)$_N$- basket -ǫni, ǫny$_V$- make, grow]
ga̱ˀahdrǫ:nih witch hazel
•(ˀ)gęhohkwaˀ ammunition
[ǫ+ -(a)ˀgęh(ęda)$_N$- ash, dust -(h)gw$_V$- lift, pick up]
ǫˀgęhohkwaˀ ammunition
•(ˀ)aksǫ:ˀ machine gun
[ę+gae+ -iˀag$_V$- shoot -sǫˀ plural]
ęgaeˀa:ksǫ:ˀ a machine gun
•(ˀa)hsa(w) chest, cough
oˀahsˀaˀ a chest
sˀahsaˀgeh on your chest
•(ˀa)hsawˀe have asthma
[de+P+ -(ˀa)hsa(w)$_N$- chest, cough -(ˀ)e$_V$- hit]
toˀahsawˀehs (he has) asthma H
•(ˀ)d(a:) clay, mortar
cf: (i)ˀd(a:) clay, mortar
oˀda:ˀ clay; mud; mortar
•(ˀ)d(a) feces, shit, excrement
cf: (ni)ˀd(a) feces, shit, excrement
oˀdaˀ feces; shit; excrement
•(ˀ)dagęd undergarment, soil, feces
cf: (iˀ)dagęd undergarment, soil, feces
deyoˀdagę:t dirty undergarments; soil; fecal matter
•(ˀ)dai:ˀ dirty
cf: (iˀ)dai:ˀ [de+P+] dirty
de̱hoˀdai:ˀ he got dirty (that is, covered with manure) S
•(ˀ)dai:ˀ brick
cf: (iˀ)dai:ˀ brick
oˀda:iˀ a brick
•(ˀ)daihaˀd warm up, heat up
[(d+) A/P+(N+); contains: -(ˀ)daih$_V$- hot]
wadaihaˀtaˀ it heats things up H
ętsaˀdaihaˀt you will heat it up; you will make it hot P
oˀdaihaˀdǫh it (weather) is really hot S
•(ˀ)daihaˀseh be too hot
[P+ contains: -(ˀ)daih$_V$- hot]
hoˀdaihaˀseh he is too hot H
•(ˀ)daihę: hot
[o+ contains: -(ˀ)daih$_V$- hot]
oˀdaihę:ˀ it is hot S
•(ˀ)daihę: hot
[A/P+(N+) contains: -(h)neg(a)$_N$- water -(ˀ)daih$_V$- hot]
ohnegadaihę: hot water S
•(ˀ)daihęhdrahi sweat, perspire
[d+ contains -(ˀ)daih$_V$- hot]
ętseˀdaihęhdrahiˀ you will sweat profusely, perspire P

Legend: H habitual, P punctual, S stative, I imperative, PURP purposive, PURP-H purposive habitual, PURP-PAST purposive past, PURP-P purposive punctual, PURP-I purposive imperative; see §8.6, §8.11 in Appendix J. Alphabetization in stems ignores length (:), and any h's or glottal stops (ˀ) that are not between vowels. See §2.2 of the User Guide for explanation.

•(ʼ)daihęhdrod sweat
[P+ -(iʼ)daihęhdr(a)$_N$- sweat -od$_V$- stand]
hoʼdaihęhdro:t he is sweating S

•(ʼ)daisdǫ:ʼ intercourse
cf: (i)ʼdaisdǫ:ʼ intercourse
adai:sdǫ:ʼ intercourse

•(ʼ)danyo beat up
see: (i)ʼdanyo [TR+] beat up
ahǫwęda:nyoʼ s.o. beat him up, broke his spirit P

•(ʼ)daǫni dirty, muddy
see: (iʼ)daǫni [(ade+)] dirty, muddy
agaʼdaǫniʼ it got muddy P

•(ʼ)dahswahę(drǫ) scold
see: (i)ʼdahswahę(drǫ) [TR+] scold
ahadiʼdahswahęhdrǫ:ʼ they (m) scolded, reprimanded P

•(ʼ)dawęnyeʼ shit-disturber
see: (i)ʼdawęnyeʼ [de+A+] shit-disturber
deyeʼdawę:nyeʼ she is a shit-disturber H

•(ʼ)dǫ(:) be due, be child-bearing, give birth
[ade+]
ǫdeʼdǫhaʼ she is child-bearing; she is giving birth right now H
ęyǫdʼedǫ:ʼ when she will be due P

•(ʼ)dǫdr(a) fat, gristle, rind
[o+]
oʼdǫ:draʼ it is fat; gristle; rind

•(ʼ)dǫhneʼ pregnant animal
[w+ade+ contains: -(ʼ)dǫ(:)$_V$- be due]
wadeʼdǫhneʼ pregnant animal

•(ʼ)dr(a) case, quiver
[ga+ad+]
gʼada:traʼ (gadaʼdraʼ) a case; a quiver

•(ʼ)dragęnyǫhs archery
[de+...ade+ -(ʼ)dr(a)$_N$- case, quiver -gęni, gęny$_V$- compete]
dęhęnadeʼdragę:nyǫhs archery

•(ʼ)drahehsd overdo, exaggerate
[P+]
sadrahehstaʼ you are always going overboard; you are excessive H
ęhsaʼdra̱hehs you will go overboard, above and beyond; you will exceed P

•(ʼ)drahehsdǫh be extreme
[heʼ+yo+ -(ʼ)drahehsd$_V$- overdo, exaggerate]
heyoʼdra̱hehsdǫh it is extreme S

•(ʼ)drahaʼd rush s.t., hurry s.t. up
[de+... contains: -(ʼ)draih$_V$- hurry]
deyoʼdraihaʼt hurried or immediate attention; an urgent matter; urgency; a rush S
dehseʼdraihaʼt you rush s.t., hurry s.t. up I

•(ʼ)draihę hurry
[de+P+ contains: -(ʼ)draih$_V$- hurry]
deyagʼodraihęhs she is in a hurry H
adyǫknʼidraihęʼ we two hurried P
haoʼ desaʼdrai:hęh o.k., hurry up I

•(ʼ)dre(:) drag, drive
see: (i)ʼdre(:) [(N+)] drag, drive
haʼdreʼ he is dragging it PURP

•(ʼ)drehd move oneself
see: (i)ʼdrehd [(N+)] move oneself
gadrehtaʼ it moves itself; it rides H

•(ʼ)drehd(a) vehicle, car, truck
[ga+]
gʼadrehdaʼ a car; a truck; a vehicle

•(ʼ)drehdaę(:) park oneʼs vehicle
[ade+ -(ʼ)drehd(a)$_N$- car, vehicle -ę$_V$- lie]
gyǫgyadʼedrehdaę:ʼ we all parked our car over there S

•(ʼ)drehdahkwaʼ jack, tow truck, hoist
[de+ga+ -(ʼ)drehd(a)$_N$- car, vehicle -(h)gw$_V$- lift, pick up]
degaʼdrȩhdahkwaʼ a jack; a tow truck; a hoist

•(ʼ)drehdǫnihs mechanic
[(s+)A+ -(ʼ)drehd(a)$_N$- vehicle, car -ǫni, ǫny$_V$- make, repair]
shaʼdrehdǫ:nihs he is a mechanic

•(ʼ)dreʼs car
[w+ade+ -(i)ʼdre(:)$_V$- drag, drive]
wadeʼdreʼs a drag; a car (old word) (lit.: it is dragging itself)

•(ʼ)dręː(:), (ʼ)drǫ(:) put together
[de+...ad+N+]
desatnętsaʼdręʼ you put your arms together I

•(ʼ)driyo: be a good shot
[(ni+)A+ -(ʼ)dr(a)$_N$- case, quiver -iyo:$_V$- be nice, good]
haʼdri:yo: he's a good, accurate shot S

•(ʼ)drǫ live, dwell, be at home
see: (i)ʼdrǫ [A+] live, dwell, be at home
hadiʼdrǫʼ they (m) are at home S

•(ʼ)drǫ elect
see: (i)ʼdrǫ [TR+] elect
ahǫwadiʼdrǫʼ they placed, elected him P

•(ʼ)drǫ:ʼ otter
[j+o+ade+ -(ʼ)dr(a)$_N$- case, quiver -ǫ:$_V$- resemble]
jodeʼdrǫ:ʼ an otter

•(ʼ)drǫ(:), (ʼ)dręː(:) put together, be crossed
[de+...ad+N]
dęhswatnętsaʼdrǫ:ʼ you all will cross your arms P
deswatnętsaʼdrǫʼ you all have your arms crossed S

•(ʼ)drǫdaʼ be placed, live, stay at home
see: (i)ʼdrǫdaʼ [A+] be placed, live, stay at home
tgidrǫ:daʼk where I lived S

•(ʼ)drǫdaʼ land
see: (i)ʼdrǫdaʼ [de+...] land
dęgęʼdrǫ:daʼ it will land P

•(ʼ)drǫda:ʼdiaper
cf: (i)ʼdrǫda:ʼdiaper
gʼadro:da:ʼ a diaper

•(ʼ)droʼdę: experience
[ni+wa+ade+ -(ʼ)dr(a)$_N$- case, quiver -oʼdę:$_V$- type of experience]
niwadʼedroʼdę: an experience

•(ʼ)drǫdǫʼ several things, etc. placed somewhere
see: (i)ʼdrǫdǫʼ [A+] several things, etc. placed somewhere
hadiʼdrǫ:dǫʼ how they (m) are placed S

•(ʼ)drohsr(a) fat, rind
[o+]
oʼdrohsraʼ fat; pig rinds

•(ʼ)drǫhg thorn berry
[ha+ -(ʼ)dr(a)$_N$- case, quiver]
haʼdrǫhk a thornberry

•(ʼ)e hit
[N+ occurs in:]
g̲ahwihsdʼa̲ehs a clock H
ahaʼnǫhgwaʼe:k he beat the drum, barrel P
hohwaʼe: he is tapping it S
desatgwʼiaʼek wink I

•(ʼ)ehsd hit s.t. belonging to s.o.
[de+TR+N+ -(ʼ)drehd(a)$_N$- vehicle, car -(ʼ)ehsd$_V$- hit with s.t.]
ateʼdre̲hdaʼehs I hit his car P

•(ʼ)g(a:) tale, legend, parable, story
[o+]
oʼga:ʼ a parable; a tale; a story; a legend

•(ʼ)ga:dǫh tell a story
sʼega:dǫ: tell a story I

•(ʼ)gęd light-coloured, white
[A/P+N+ occurs in:]
onęhęgęːt, onęhęgę: white corn S

•(ʼ)gęd transparent
[he+yo+]
heyo:gęʼt it is transparent S

•(ʼ)gęd visible
[o+]
o:gęʼt it is visible S

Legend: H habitual, P punctual, S stative, I imperative, PURP purposive, PURP-H purposive habitual, PURP-PAST purposive past, PURP-P purposive punctual, PURP-I purposive imperative; see §8.6, §8.11 in Appendix J. Alphabetization in stems ignores length (:), and any h's or glottal stops (ʼ) that are not between vowels. See §2.2 of the User Guide for explanation.

•(ʼ)gę:ʼęh younger sibling
[TR+]
keʼgę:ʼęh my younger sister S
•(ʼ)gęʼęh last quarter moon
[he+j+o+ -(ʼ)gę:ʼęh_V- younger sibling]
hejogę:ʼęh the last quarter moon
•(ʼ)gęhędahkwaʼ a clothes brush
[e+ -(a)ʼgęh(ęda$)_N$- ash, dust -(h)gw_V- lift, pick up]
egęhędahkwaʼ a clothes brush
•(ʼ)gęhękwaʼ ashtray
[ǫ+ -(a)ʼgęh(ęda$)_N$- ash, dust -(h)gw_V- lift, pick up]
ǫʼgęhę:kwaʼ an ashtray
•(ʼ)grǫdi, (ʼ)grǫgy snow
[P+ -(a)ʼgr(a$)_N$- snow -ǫdi, -ǫgy_V- throw]
ęyoʼgrǫ:diʼ it will snow P
oʼgrǫ:gyǫ: it is snowing S
•(ʼ)gw run away, flee
[ade+]
ęgęnadeʼgoʼ they (z) will flee, run away P
•(ʼ)gwęhęgyeʼs avoid
[P+ade+ contains: -(ʼ)gw_V- run away, flee]
sadeʼgwęhę:gyeʼs you are avoiding S
•(ʼ)howeg cover
see also: oweg [TR+(N+)] cover [TR+(N+)]
geʼho:we:s I am covering s.t. H
ęhseʼho:we:k you will cover s.t. P
ageʼhowe:gǫh I did cover s.t. S
segǫʼdro:we:k you put the pillowcase on I
•(ʼ)howeks(i) uncover
see: oweks(i) uncover
ęhsnaʼsgowe:ksih you will uncover the bed P
•(ʼ)k(a:) slip
[ga+]
gaʼka:ʼ a slip

•(ʼ)ka:ʼ be hen-pecked
[P+ade+ -(ʼ)k(a:$)_N$- skirt slip -(h)awi, (h)a:$_V$- hold, include, carry, bring]
hodeʼka:ʼ he is hen-pecked S
•(ʼ)kaowe:s hen-pecked
[TR+ -(ʼ)k(a:$)_N$- skirt slip -oweg_V- cover]
hǫwaʼkaowe:s he is hen-pecked H
•(ʼ)kaǫdahkwaʼ breech cloth
[ǫ++ade+ -(ʼ)k(a:$)_N$- skirt, slip -ǫdahkwaʼ$_V$- s.t. attached]
ǫdeʼkaǫ:da̱hkwaʼ a breech cloth
•(ʼ)nahgǫd bee swarm, bee sting
[P+ -(ʼ)nahg(a$)_N$- sting -ǫd_V- attached]
ęsaʼna̱hgǫ:dęʼ you will get a bee sting P
oʼnahgǫ:t it (skin) is inflamed; a bee sting S
•(ʼ)nahgǫtaʼ bee
[ga+ -(ʼ)nahg(a$)_N$- bee sting -ǫd_V- attached]
gʼanahgǫtaʼ a bee
•(ʼ)nahg(wa), (ʼ)nahk(wa) wife, marriage
cf: (ʼ)nahk(wa) wife, marriage
gʼanahkwaʼ a marriage
aknaʼgwaʼ my wife
•(ʼ)naʼsę: poison
[o+ -(h)n(a$)_N$- oil, gas -(aʼs)ęʼ$_V$- fall, reduce]
oʼnaʼsę: poison
onahsę: water hemlock
•(ʼ)neg pray, hope
sri̱hwaʼnekaʼ you are always praying H
ęhsrihwane:k you will pray P
saihwʼane:gęh, you are praying S
•(ʼ)nehs(a) sand
[o+]
oʼnehsaʼ sand
•(ʼ)nehsadaihę: desert
[o+ -(ʼ)nehs(a$)_N$- sand -(ʼ)daihę:$_V$- hot]
oʼnehsʼadaihę: desert
•(ʼ)nehsadase: sand storm
[o+ -(ʼ)nehs(a$)_N$- sand -dase$_V$- whirl]
oʼnehsada:se: a sand storm

•(ʼ)nesd(a), (ʼ)nosd(a) nudity
[o+]
oʼne:staʼ, oʼno:staʼ nudity
•(ʼ)nehsiyo: sandpiper
[o+ -(ʼ)nehs(a)$_N$- sand -iyo:$_V$- be nice, good]
oʼnehsi:yo: sandpiper
•(ʼ)nehsogwahtaʼ sander
[de+at+ -(ʼ)nehs(a)$_N$- sand -ogwahd$_V$- dig with s.t.]
dewatnęhsogwahtaʼ sander H
•(ʼ)nhahgy(a), (ʼ)nhahd(a) large log, timber
[o+]
oʼnhahgyaʼ, onhahdaʼ large lumber logs; timber
•(ʼ)nhahgyaʼs logger
[A+ -(ʼ)nhahgy(a), (ʼ)nhahd(a)$_N$- log (large) timber -(i)yaʼg$_V$- cut, break, cross]
hadiʼnhahgyaʼs loggers H
•(ʼ)nhehgyęʼ female, genitals
[o+ -(ʼ)nhehgyęʼ$_V$- female]
oʼnhehgyęʼ female genitals (animals only); a female animal
•(ʼ)nhęhts(a), (ʼ)nhwęhts(a), tail
[o+]
oʼnhęhtsaʼ, oʼnhwęhtsaʼ the tail of an animal
•(ʼ)nhęhtsędǫh wag
[de+P+ -(ʼ)nhęhts(a)$_N$- tail -ędǫh$_V$- shake s.t.]
deyoʼnhęhtsędǫhǫh it is wagging its tail S
•(ʼ)nhǫhd(a) armpit
onhǫhdaʼ an armpit
senhǫhda:gǫ: your underarm, armpit
•(ʼ)nhǫhs(a) egg
[o+]
oʼnhǫhsaʼ egg(s)
•(ʼ)nhǫhsg(a:) inner thigh
sʼenhǫhsga:ʼgeh on your inner thigh

•(ʼ)nhǫhsdǫd testicles
[de+ha+ -(ʼ)nhǫhsd(a)$_N$- sperm -ǫd$_V$- attached]
dehaʼnhǫhsdǫ:t his testicles
•(ʼ)nih father
[TR+]
haʼnih my father S
•(ʼ)nigǫh(a) mind
[ga+]
gʼanigǫhaʼ the mind
ǫgwaʼnigǫhaʼ our mind
gʼanihgǫhaʼgeh on the minds
•(ʼ)nigǫhgaę suffer
[(tęʼ) deʼ+ not ...ę+ -(ʼ)nigǫh(a)$_N$- mind -gaę:$_V$- be willing]
desęʼnigǫhgaeʼ you suffer S
•(ʼ)nigǫhgahęhs run out of patience, wait impatiently
[P+]
aknigǫhgahęhs I am running out of patience; I am impatiently waiting H
•(ʼ)nigǫha(:,ʼ) expect, watch
knigǫ:ha:ʼ I am expecting, watching H
ęknigǫhaʼk I will expect it, be watching out for s.t. P
snigǫhaʼk watch out for yourself I
•(ʼ)nigǫha:ʼ be wary, cautious
[A+adat+ -(ʼ)nigǫha(:)$_V$- expect, watch]
wadatnigǫha:ʼ it is wary, cautious H
•(ʼ)nigǫha(:) monitor
[TR+adę+ -(ʼ)nigǫha(:)$_V$- expect, watch]
ǫkiyaʼdęʼnigǫha:ʼ monitors (people) H
•(ʼ)nigǫhad elder
[P+ -(ʼ)nigǫh(a)$_N$- mind -d$_V$- stand]
hodiʼnigǫha:t they (m) have wisdom; male elders
•(ʼ)nigǫhad stupid, foolish, ignorant
[de+P+ not -(ʼ)nigǫh(a)$_N$- mind -d$_V$- stand]
dehoʼnigǫha:t he is ignorant, unthinkingly foolish S

•(ʼ)nigǫhad be a nuisance
[de+ not ...TR+ -yaʼd(a)$_N$- body -(ʼ)nigǫhd$_V$- be wise]
deshayʼadaʼnigǫha:t you are a nuisance S

•(ʼ)nigǫhad be smart
[P+ -(ʼ)nigǫh(a)$_N$- mind -d$_V$- stand]
sʼanigǫha:t you are smart, brilliant S

•(ʼ)nigǫhaʼd(ę, ani) cheat, betray
[TR/adę+ -(ʼ)nigǫh(a)$_N$- mind -dę$_V$- stand for s.o.'s benefit]
gasheʼnigǫhaʼda:nih you betray them continually H
ęhsheʼnigǫhaʼdęʼ you will cheat her, betray her P

•(ʼ)nigǫhaʼd cheat, betray
[TR/adę+ -(ʼ)nigǫh(a)$_N$- mind -d$_V$- stand]
gasheʼnigǫhaʼtaʼ you betray them continually H
ęhsheʼnigǫhaʼt you will cheat s.o. P

•(ʼ)nigǫhadogę undecided, indecisive
[(tęʼ) deʼ+P+ -(ʼ)nigǫh(a)$_N$- mind -dogę(:)$_V$- right, true]
desaʼnigǫhado:gę: you cannot decide which way to go, you are flighty S

•(ʼ)nigǫhahdogęh immature
[(tęʼ) deʼ+P+at+ -(ʼ)nigǫh(a)$_N$- mind -dogę(:)$_V$- right, true]
desathnigǫhahdo:gęh you are immature in mind S

•(ʼ)nigǫhahdǫ(ʼ) faint
[P+ -(ʼ)nigǫh(a)$_N$- mind -(a)hdǫ(:)$_V$- lose, disappear]
ǫknigǫhahdǫʼ I fainted P

•(ʼ)nigǫhaʼe offend
[TR+ -(ʼ)nigǫh(a)$_N$- mind -(ʼ)e$_V$- hit]
ęhsheʼnigǫhaʼe:k you will offend s.o. P

•(ʼ)nigǫhaʼehsd decide
[he+P+ -(ʼ)nigǫh(a)$_N$- mind -(ʼ)ehsd$_V$- hit with s.t.]
haʼhoʼnigohaʼehs his mind settled on s.t., decided on s.t. P

•(ʼ)nigǫha(:,ę) bother s.o., annoy
[de+not TR+ -(ʼ)nigǫh(a)$_N$- mind -(ʼ)nigǫha(:,ę)$_V$- expect, watch]
dehsknigǫha:haʼ you are annoying me H
dęhsnigǫhaę:ʼ you will be annoying P

•(ʼ)nigǫha(ę,nih) unconcerned, indifferent
[taʼde+P+ -(ʼ)nigǫha(ę,nih)$_V$- expect, watch for s.o.'s benefit]
taʼdehoʼnigǫha:nih he is unconcerned, indifferent S

•(ʼ)nigǫhaęda' understand
[P+ -(ʼ)nigǫh(a)$_N$- mind -ędaʼ$_V$- finish]
hoʼnigǫhaędaʼs he understands H
ahoʼnigǫhaędaʼ he understood P

•(ʼ)nigǫhaędaʼ misunderstand
[(tęʼ) de+not P+ -(ʼ)nigǫh(a)$_N$- mind -ędaʼ$_V$- finish]
tęʼ dʼehoʼnigǫhaędaʼs he does not understand H

•(ʼ)nigǫhagahe(y) be mentally exhausted
[P+ -(ʼ)nigǫh(a)$_N$- mind -gahe(y)$_V$- be weak, die]
aknigǫhagahe:ʼ my mind got beat; I'm mentally exhausted P
aknigǫhagahe:yǫh I am mentally exhausted S

•(ʼ)nigǫhagęni, (ʼ)nigǫhagęny corrupt, intimidate s.o.
[de+TR+ -(ʼ)nigǫh(a)$_N$- mind -gęni, gęny$_V$- compete]
deshagonigǫhagęnyǫhs he intimidates people all the time H
dęhsheʼnigǫhagę:niʼ you will corrupt s.o.'s mind P

•(ʼ)nigǫhagǫd be uncompromising, steadfast
[(tęʼ) de+ not P+ -(ʼ)nigǫh(a)$_N$- mind -gǫd$_V$- persevere, linger]
deyagʼonigǫha:gǫ:t she cannot be swayed; she is uncompromising, distinguished S

•(ʼ)nigǫhaʼgweni, (ʼ)nigǫhaʼgweny out-think s.o.
[TR+ -(ʼ)nigǫh(a)$_N$- mind -gweni, gweny$_V$- be able to do s.t., succeed]
ęhsheʼnigǫhagwe:niʼ you will out-think her P

•(ʼ)nigǫhahetgęʼ sob, cry uncontrollably
[P+ -(ʼ)nigǫh(a)$_N$- mind -(hr)etgęʼ$_V$- be evil, bad, ugly]
aknigǫhahetgęʼs I am crying, uncontrollably H

•(ʼ)nigǫhaneʼwa(:,ǫ) be mentally surprised, startled
[P+ę+ -(ʼ)nigǫh(a)$_N$- mind -neʼwaǫ, neʼwa(:)$_V$- be startled]
ęsęʼnigǫhaneʼwa: you will be mentally startled P

•(ʼ)nigǫhanidęhd humble, gentle, nice
[P+ -(ʼ)nigǫh(a)$_N$- mind -nidęhd$_V$- cause to be kind]
gʼonigǫha:ni:dęht she is gentle, nice, humble S

•(ʼ)nigǫhahniyaʼd endure
[adę+ -(ʼ)nigǫh(a)$_N$- mind -(h)niyaʼd$_V$- harden, toughen]
ęhsaʼnigǫhahni:yaʼt you will endure P
sadęʼnigǫhahni:yaʼt keep your mind strong I

•(ʼ)nigǫhahniyǫh be stubborn
[P+ -(ʼ)nigǫh(a)$_N$- mind -(h)niyǫh$_V$- be hard, tough]
aknigǫhahni:yǫh I have a strong mind S

•(ʼ)nigǫhahsnoweʼ quick thinker
[A+ -(ʼ)nigǫh(a)$_N$- mind -(h)snoweʼ$_V$- be fast]
haʼnigǫhahsno:weʼ he is a quick thinker S

•(ʼ)nigǫhawęnyaʼd be entertaining
[de+...ę+ -(ʼ)nigǫh(a)$_N$- mind -(a)węnyaʼd$_V$- cause to stir, mix]
deyoʼnigǫhawę:nyaʼt it is enter -taining S

•(ʼ)nigǫhawęnye(:) entertain
[de+...TR+ -(ʼ)nigǫh(a)$_N$- mind -(a)węnye(:)$_V$- stir, mix]
desheʼnigǫhawę:nye:ʼ entertain her / them I

•(ʼ)nigǫhayei: crazy, mentally ill
[(tęʼ) deʼ+ not heʼ+A+ -(ʼ)nigǫh(a)$_N$- mind -yei, (y)í$_V$- be right, correct]
tehaʼnigǫhayei: he is not right in the mind S

•(ʼ)nigǫhęh mosquito
[-(ʼ)nigǫh(a)$_V$- mind -(h)ęh$_V$- be in the middle]
nigǫhęh mosquitoes

•(ʼ)nigǫhęʼ be depressed, sad
[d+... -(ʼ)nigǫh(a)$_N$- mind -(h)ę(h,ʼ)$_V$- feel bad]
ętsnigǫhęʼ you will be depressed P
dwaknigǫhęʼǫh I am in sorrow, in mourning; I am sad S

•(ʼ)nigǫhęhd(ę,ani) make s.o. forget
[TR+ -(ʼ)nigǫh(a)$_N$- mind -(a)hdę,ani$_V$- lose for s.o.'s benefit]
ęhsheʼnigǫhęhdęʼ you will make s.o. feel better, comfort s.o. (lit.: you will make s.o. forget s.t.) P

•(ʼ)nigǫhęhdǫh be sad
[de+P+ -(ʼ)nigǫh(a)$_N$- mind -(a)hdǫ(:)$_V$- lose, disappear]
desaʼnigǫhęhdǫh you are sad S

•(ʼ)nigǫhiyo: be satisfied, peaceful
[d+P+ -(ʼ)nigǫh(a)$_N$- mind -iyo:$_V$- be nice, good]
dwaknigǫhi:yo: I am satisfied, peaceful S

•(ʼ)nigǫhiyo: harmony
[ga+ -(ʼ)nigǫh(a)$_N$- mind -iyo:$_V$- be nice, good]
gʼaniʼgǫhi:yo: harmony; to be of good mind

Legend: H habitual, P punctual, S stative, I imperative, PURP purposive, PURP-H purposive habitual, PURP-PAST purposive past, PURP-P purposive punctual, PURP-I purposive imperative; see §8.6, §8.11 in Appendix J. Alphabetization in stems ignores length (:), and any h's or glottal stops (ʼ) that are not between vowels. See §2.2 of the User Guide for explanation.

•(ˀ)nigǫhiyoh become satisfied
[(d+)P+ -(ˀ)nigǫh(a)$_N$- mind -iyoh$_V$- become nice, good]
ęhsaˀnigǫhi:yoh you will be satisfied P

•(ˀ)nigǫhiyohsd become comfortable, be at ease
[P+ -(ˀ)nigǫh(a)$_N$- mind -iyohsd$_V$- become nice, good]
ęhsaˀnigǫhi:yohs your mind will adjust (that is, become comfortable) P

•(ˀ)nigǫhiyohsdę:ˀ be discontent
[(tęˀ) deˀ+ not d/g+P+ -(ˀ)nigǫh(a)$_N$- mind -iyohsdę$_V$- become nice, good for one's benefit]
degyoˀnigǫhiyohsdę:ˀ it is discontent S

•(ˀ)nigǫhod suggest, advise
[d+...ę+ -(ˀ)nigǫh(a)$_N$- mind -odę$_V$- stand for s.o.'s benefit]
ętsęˀnigoho:dęˀ you will suggest, present an idea P

•(ˀ)nigǫhodagw persuade, influence
[TR+ -(ˀ)nigǫh(a)$_N$- mind -odagw$_V$- remove, take away]
ęhseˀnigǫhoda:goˀ you will persuade her, overcome her mind P

•(ˀ)nigǫhoˀdę: think a certain way, have an attitude, a mood
[tsęh that ni+P+ -(ˀ)nigǫh(a)$_N$- mind -oˀdę:$_V$- type of]
tsęh nisaˀnigǫhoˀdę: your attitude, mood S

•(ˀ)nigǫhoˀdrǫ(:) console s.o.
[TR+ -(ˀ)nigǫh(a)$_N$- mind -(a)hdrǫ:(gw)$_V$- caress]
ęhsheˀnigǫhoˀdrǫ:ˀ you will console s.o. (lit.: you will caress s.o.'s mind) P

•(ˀ)nigǫhoˀdrǫ(:) worry, despair, desparate
[ę+ -(ˀ)nigǫh(a)$_N$- mind -(a)hdrǫ:(gw)$_V$- caress]
ęhsęˀnigǫhoˀdrǫ:ˀ you will worry, despair; you will be desparate P
sęˀnigo̱hoˀdrǫh you are a worrier S

•(ˀ)nigǫhogw grieve
[de+...ę+ -(ˀ)nigǫh(a)$_N$- mind -ogw$_V$- scatter]
degęˀnigohogwahs I am broken-hearted (lit.: my mind is scattered) H
agyǫˀnigǫho:goˀ her mind is scattered P

•(ˀ)nigǫhoˀkd(ę) give up
[ę+ -(ˀ)nigǫh(a)$_N$- mind -oˀkd$_V$- end]
gaǫˀnigǫhǫˀktaˀ they (f/m) are giving up (in spirit) H
ahęˀnigǫhoˀkdęˀ he gave up (his will to live) P

•(ˀ)nigǫhoˀneg revolt, rebel
[d+...ę+ -(ˀ)nigǫh(a)$_N$- mind -(ˀ)neg$_V$- pray, hope]
ętsęˀnigǫhoˀne:k you will revolt, remove yourself (bodily and in spirit) P

•(ˀ)nigǫhotahsd suggest, advise
[de+TR+ę+ -(ˀ)nigǫh(a)$_N$- mind +otahsd$_V$- go and cause s.o. to stand]
ętseyęˀnigo̱hotahs you will suggest to her, advise her P

•(ˀ)nigǫhowanę wise
[P+ -(ˀ)nigǫh(a)$_N$- mind -owanęh$_V$- be big -ˀs plural]
hodiˀnigǫhowa:nęˀs they (m) are wise; they have the capacity for thinking S

•(ˀ)nigǫhowanęh broad-minded
[A+ -(ˀ)nigǫh(a)$_N$- mind -owanęh$_V$- be big]
snigǫhowa:nęh you have a broad mind S

•(ˀ)nigǫhǫni persuade, influence s.o.
[TR+ -(ˀ)nigǫh(a)$_N$- mind -ǫni, ǫny$_V$- make]
ęhsheˀnigǫhǫ:niˀ you will influence, persuade s.o. P

•(ˀ)nigǫhnyaˀg grieve, be broken-hearted
[de+P+ -(ˀ)nigǫh(a)$_N$- mind -(ni)yaˀg$_V$- cut, break, cross]
dewaknigǫhnyaˀgǫh I am broken-hearted, grieving S

•(ʼ)nigǫhnyaʼg discourage s.o.
[de+TR+ -(ʼ)nigǫh(a)$_N$- mind -(ni)yaʼg$_V$- cut, break, cross]
dęhsheʼnigǫhnyaʼk you will discourage s.o. P

•(ʼ)nigǫhsadǫ be lonesome
[P+ -(ʼ)nigǫh(a)$_N$- mind -(h)sadǫ$_V$- bury s.o., an animal]
akʼnigǫhsa:dǫʼs I am lonesome H
ǫkʼnigǫhsa:dǫʼ I got lonesome P
oʼnigǫhsadǫhk it is lonesome S

•(ʼ)nigǫhsadǫh sadness
[o+ak+ -(ʼ)nigǫh(a)$_N$- mind -(h)sadǫ$_V$- bury s.t.]
oknigǫhsa:dǫh sadness

•(ʼ)nigǫhsadǫhg be mournful
[o+ -(ʼ)nigǫh(a)$_N$- mind -(h)sadǫ$_V$- bury s.t.]
oʼnigǫhsadǫhk it is mournful S

•(ʼ)nikǫ(:) sew
eʼni:kǫhs seamstress H
a:knikǫ:ʼ I should, might sew P
akni:kǫʼ I have sewn S

•(ʼ)nikǫʼ seam
[ga+ contains: -(ʼ)nikǫ(:)$_V$- sew]
gani:kǫʼ a seam

•(ʼ)nikǫgwahs seam ripper, stitch ripper
[ga+ contains: -(ʼ)nikǫgw$_V$- unsew]
gʼanikǫgwahs stitch ripper

•(ʼ)nikǫhaʼ sewing machine
[ga+ contains: -(ʼ)nikǫ(:)$_V$- sew]
ganikǫhaʼ a sewing machine

•(ʼ)nikǫhkwaʼ sewing item
[e+ contains: -(ʼ)nikǫ(:)$_V$- sew -shǫ:ʼǫh several objects]
ęʼnikǫhkwaʼshǫ:ʼǫh sewing room items

•(ʼ)nikǫhs seamstress
[e+ contains: -(ʼ)nikǫ(:)$_V$- sew]
eʼni:kǫhs seamstress

•(ʼ)nihsd(a) stem, hull
[o+]
oʼnihsdaʼ the stem or hull of a berry

•(ʼ)nihsdęhd hull
[-(ʼ)nihsd(a)$_N$- stem, hull -(y)ęhd$_V$- hit, knock down, strike]
ęhsnihsdęht you will hull strawberries P

•(ʼ)nihsgadeʼ brim
[de+yo+ -(ʼ)nihsg(a)$_N$- brim -deʼ$_V$- exist]
deyoʼnihsga:deʼ the brim of a hat

•(ʼ)nodra(h,ʼ) be infected
[P+]
gʼono:drahs she has open, weeping sores H
ęhsʼano:draʼ sehsohgwʼageh you will have sores on your lips P
oʼno:draʼ it is infected; an infection S

•(ʼ)nodrahs skin rash
[o+ contains: -(ʼ)nodra(h,ʼ)$_V$- be infected]
oʼno:drahs skin rash

•(ʼ)nodrahsd become infected, have an allergic reaction
[P+ contains: -(ʼ)nodra(h,ʼ)$_V$- be infected]
aʼagono:drahs s.o. got chicken pox, a skin infection, allergic reactions; s.o. became infected P
sʼanodrahsdǫh it has given you an infection, an allergic reaction; you have already had an allergic reaction S

•(ʼ)noshę: be envious
[P+]
akno:shę: I am envious S

•(ʼ)noshahs be jealous
[o+ contains: -(ʼ)nosh$_V$- be jealous, envious]
seʼno:shahs you are envious H

•(ʼ)noshaʼd jealous, envious
[o+ contains: -(ʼ)nosh$_V$- be jealous, envious]
oʼno:shaʼt it is jealous, envious S

Legend: H habitual, P punctual, S stative, I imperative, PURP purposive, PURP-H purposive habitual, PURP-PAST purposive past, PURP-P purposive punctual, PURP-I purposive imperative; see §8.6, §8.11 in Appendix J. Alphabetization in stems ignores length (:), and any h's or glottal stops (ʼ) that are not between vowels. See §2.2 of the User Guide for explanation.

•(ʼ)noshęhsr(a) jealousy
[ga+ contains: -(ʼ)nohs$_V$- be jealous, envious]
ganohshęhsraʼ jealousy
•(ʼ)nǫhd be in s.t.
[ga+]
gʼanǫht it (usually an animal) is in s.t. S
•(ʼ)nǫdǫd alligator
[de+ga+ -(ʼ)nǫd(a)$_N$- alligator -ǫd$_V$- attached]
degaʼnǫ:dǫ:t an alligator
•(ʼ)ny(a) finger, hand
oʼnyaʼ fingers
•(ʼ)nya(ę,:) look after
[de+...ę+ -(ʼ)ny(a)$_N$- finger, hand -a:ʼ$_V$- hold, contain, include]
dehseʼnya:ʼ you look after it (all the time) H
dęhsęʼnyaę:ʼ, dęhsęʼnya:ʼ you will look after it P
•(ʼ)nyaʼdad point out s.o.
[TR+ -(ʼ)ny(a)$_N$- finger, hand -d$_V$- stand]
ęhshęʼnyʼada:t you will point s.o. out P
•(ʼ)nyagę escape, run away
geʼnya:gęʼs I'm an escaper H
shaʼnya:gęʼ he escaped P
godiʼnyaʼgęʼǫh they (f/m) ran away S
•(ʼ)nyagęhd help s.o. escape
[TR+ contains: -(ʼ)nyagęʼ$_V$- escape, run away]
ęhsheʼnya:gęht you will help s.o. escape P
•(ʼ)nyędeʼ come for a purpose
[A+ contains: -(ʼ)nyędę$_V$- try]
senyęʼdeʼ you came for a purpose P
•(ʼ)nyędę try, sample, attempt
[ade+]
gadeʼnyę:dęhs I try all the time H
a:gadeʼnyę:dęʼ I might try, attempt it P
sadeʼnyę:dęh sample it; try it I

•(ʼ)nyędęhsd measure
[ade+ contains: -(ʼ)nyędę$_V$- try]
wadeʼnyędęhsdǫh the act of measuring S
•(ʼ)nyędęhsd copy, compare
[d+...ade+ contains: -(ʼ)nyędę$_V$- try]
ętsadenyę:dęhs you will copy, use as a model or pattern P
dahsadenyę:dęhs copy compare I
•(ʼ)nyędęhsdǫh measurement
[w+ade+ contains: -(ʼ)nyędę$_V$- try]
wadeʼnyędęhsdǫh the act of measuring
•(ʼ)nyod celebrate, party
[adę+ -(ʼ)ny(a)$_N$- finger, hand -od$_V$- stand]
sadęʼnyotaʼ you celebrate all the time; you are celebrating H
ęhsadęʼnyo:dęʼ you will celebrate P
wadęʼnyo:t a celebration, party S
•(ʼ)nyod celebration, party
[w+adę+ -(ʼ)ny(a)$_N$- finger, hand -od$_V$- stand]
wadęʼnyo:t a celebration; a party
•(ʼ)hnyod rainbow
[o+ -(rǫ)ʼnih(a)$_N$- rainbow, sunbeam, ray -od$_V$- stand]
oʼhnyo:t there is a rainbow
•(ʼ)nyotraʼ mittens
[ę+ contains: -(ʼ)ny(a)$_N$- finger, hand -od$_V$- stand]
ęʼnyo:traʼ mittens
•(ʼ)nyǫdǫʼ glove
[(de+y)o+ -(ʼ)ny(a)$_N$- finger, hand -ǫdǫʼ$_V$- several attached objects]
oʼnyǫdo gloves
deyonyǫ:dǫh gloves
•(ʼ)nyǫhs(a) nose
oʼnyǫhsaʼ a nose
sʼenyǫhsʼageh on your nose
•(ʼ)nyǫhsaʼ moose
[s+ga+ -(ʼ)nyǫhs(a)$_N$- nose]
sganyǫhsaʼ a moose

•(ʼ)nyǫhswahaʼd mischievous, nosy
[de+P+ -(ʼ)nyǫhs(a)$_N$- nose -swahaʼd$_V$- go and sniff s.t.]
dewagʼenyǫhswahaʼt I am mischievous, nosy S

•(ʼ)og axe, chop
ge̱ʼohs I am a chopper H
ęhsaʼo:k it will chop you P
ageʼo:gǫh I did chop; I have chopped S

•(ʼ)ǫhg(wa:) sod
[o+]
oʼǫhgwa:ʼ sod; moss

•(ʼ)ǫhs(a) vine
[o+]
oʼǫhsaʼ vines

•(ʼ)sgoh immerse, drown s.o.
[ade+]
ęhsadʼesgoh you will go into the water P

•(ʼ)sgoh baptize s.o.
[TR+]
hǫwadʼihsgohs baptism (lit.: s.o. baptizes them) H
ahǫwadiʼsgoʼ they (m) have baptized him, them (m) P

•(ʼ)sgǫd(ę) roast, fry
[ade+ -ʼsg$_N$- roast -ǫd(ę)$_V$- attached]
ęhsadʼesgǫ:dęʼ you will roast P
wadeʼsgǫ:t it is roasting, frying S
sadeʼsgǫ:dęh fry it I

•(ʼ)sgohs baptism
[TR+ -(ʼ)sgoh$_V$- immerse, drown]
hǫwadʼihsgohs baptism (lit.: s.o. baptizes them)

•(ʼ)sgǫdahkwaʼ barbecue equipment
[ǫ+ade+ -ʼsg$_N$- roast -ǫdahkwaʼ$_V$- attached object]
ǫdeʼsgǫdahkwaʼ barbecue equipment

•(ʼ)shahsdeʼ be strong tough, powerful
[A+(N+) contains: -(ʼ)shahsd$_V$- be strong]
gahsha:sdeʼ it is strong, tough, powerful S

•(ʼ)sha(h)sdeʼ weak
[(tęʼ) deʼ+ not A+(N+) contains: -(ʼ)shahsd$_V$- be strong]
tęʼ degahshahsdeʼ no, it is not strong S

•(ʼ)sha(h)sdeʼ exponents
[tsęh that ni+ga+ contains: -(ʼ)shahsd$_V$- be strong]
tsęh nigaʼshahsdeʼ exponents

•(ʼ)shahsdǫh use one's strength
[ade+ contains: -(ʼ)shahsd$_V$- be strong]
gadeshahsdǫhaʼ I use my strength H
ęhsadesha:sdǫh you will use your strength P

•(ʼ)shęny(ǫgw), (ʼ)shęni overpower s.o. physically
[TR+]
sheʼshę:nyǫhs you are always overpowering s.o.; you are overpowering s.o. right now H
ęhsheʼshę:niʼ you will overpower s.o. (physically) P
sheʼshęnyǫgwęh you have overpowered s.o. S

•(ʼ)syade clan
oʼsya:de:nyǫʼ clans S

•(ʼ)tsǫhsd sneeze
[de+P+]
desaʼtsǫhstahk you have sneezed, you were sneezing H
dęsaʼtsǫhs you will sneeze P

•(ʼ)wah(a) meat
[o+ present in]
oʼwahǫh meat
oʼwahase:ʼ fresh meat

•(ʼ)wahadenyǫʼ muscle
[o+ -(ʼ)wah(a)$_N$- meat -deni, deny$_V$- change -ǫʼ plural]
oʼwahade:nyǫʼ muscles

•(ʼ)wahahihdǫh hamburger
[de+ga+ -(ʼ)wah(a)$_N$- meat -(hr)ihd$_V$- break s.t. up]
degaʼwa̱hahihdǫh hamburger

Legend: H habitual, P punctual, S stative, I imperative, PURP purposive, PURP-H purposive habitual, PURP-PAST purposive past, PURP-P purposive punctual, PURP-I purposive imperative; see §8.6, §8.11 in Appendix J. Alphabetization in stems ignores length (:), and any h's or glottal stops (ʼ) that are not between vowels. See §2.2 of the User Guide for explanation.

•(ˀ)wahaisgyaˀs meat slicer
[ga+ -(ˀ)wah(a)$_N$- meat -(hr)ihsd(a)- metal -(i)yaˀg$_V$- cut, break]
gˀawahai:sgyaˀs a meat slicer

•(ˀ)wahaˀ butcher
[A+ad+ -(ˀ)wah(a)$_N$- meat]
hadwahaˀ he is a butcher

•(ˀ)wahahninǫh butcher
[A+ad+ -(ˀ)wah(a)$_N$- meat -(h)ninǫ$_V$- sell]
hadwahahni:nǫh he is a butcher, a seller of meat

•(ˀ)waha:s cancer
[ga+ -(ˀ)wah(a)$_N$- meat -g$_V$- eat]
gaˀwaha:s cancer

•(ˀ)wahǫdahkwaˀ roasting pan
[ǫ+at+ -(ˀ)wah(a)$_N$- meat -ǫdahkwaˀ$_V$- container]
ǫtwahǫdahkwaˀ a roasting pan

•(ˀ)wahǫh meat
[o+ -(ˀ)wah(a)$_N$- meat -(h)ǫ(:)$_V$- lie]
oˀwahǫh meat

•(ˀ)wahsh(a:,aǫ) earrings
[ga+]
gˀawahsha:ˀ earrings

•(ˀ)wahsaǫhkwaˀ earring
[de+yǫ+at+ -(ˀ)wahs(a:,aǫ)$_N$- earring -hkwaˀ instrument]
deyǫtwahsaǫ:kwaˀ earrings

•(ˀ)wahsd(a) pin
[ga/o+]
gˀawahsdaˀ, oˀwahsdaˀ a clothespin

•(ˀ)waǫni: welt
cf: (iˀ)waǫni:welt
gaiˀwao:ni: welts
oˀwao:ni: welts

•(ˀ)wi: corner
[he+yo+ -(iˀ)w(a)$_N$- welt -i:ˀ$_V$- stuck onto s.t.]
heyoˀwi: a corner

•(ˀ)yohgod tail (of a fish)
[ga+ -(ˀ)yohg(wa)$_N$- tail, skirt -d$_V$- stand]
gˀayohgo:t a fish tail

•(ˀ)yohg(wa) skirt, tail, feather
oˀyohgwaˀ a skirt; a tail; a feather
gˀayǫhgwˀageh on its (a bird's) tail

•(ˀ)yohg(wa) Avocet blue stocking
[ga+]
gˀayohgwaˀ Avocet blue stocking (a bird)

A

•aˀ be small
[A+ (N+)]
gaoˀ ni:waˀ it is smaller than s.t. else S
do: niya:gaˀ how big is it / she? S
niyesgyę̱daˀ she is a small person (lit: she has small bones) S
[-(h)sgyę̱ˀd(a:)$_N$- bone -aˀ$_V$- be small]

•a:ˀ contain (liquid)
[i+ga+]
i:ga:ˀ it contains (liquid) S

•a(:,h) spread
see: (r)a(:,h) spread
ę̱hsra:ˀ you will spread P

•a:ˀah be small
[ni+ A+ (N+)]
niwa:ˀah it is small S
niganǫhsa:ˀah a small house S
[-nǫhs(a)$_N$- house -a:ˀah$_V$- be small]

•(a)ˀawayeˀ dew
[o+ -(a)ˀaw(a)$_N$- dew -yeˀ$_V$-]
oˀawayeˀ dew on s.t.

•(a)ˀawayǫdi drizzle
[-(a)ˀaw(a)$_N$- dew -ǫdi, ǫgy- throw]
awayǫ:gyǫ: it is drizzling; misty rain, fine rain S

•ad be contained in s.t.; be in s.t.
[A+]
i:wa:t it is contained; it (inanimate) is in there; solid matter S

•ad be unable to help oneself
[tsa'+P+]
tsa'ho:ya:t he can't help himself; it's become a habit with him S

•ad spread s.t.
see: (r)ad, yad, wad spread s.t.
eya:ta' s.o. spreads it H

•(a)hd be like, resemble
[ni+yo+]
ni:yoht what it is like (preceded by a particle such as de', ne') S

•(a)hd be similar
[to:hah almost tsa'de+yo+-ahd $_V$- be similar]
to:hah tsa'de:yoht it is similar S

•(a)hd suddenly
[to: that he'+yo+-ahd $_V$- be similar]
to: he:yoht suddenly S

•(a)hd abruptly
[tsa'+d+wa+ -ahd $_V$- be similar -ge: big]
tsa'dwahtge: abruptly P

•(a)hd be the same
[tsa'de+yo+-ahd $_V$- be similar]
tsa'de:yoht they are (lit.: it is) the same S

•(a)hda' get full of food
[P+]
ohda's it gets full, finishes eating H
a'ohda' it got full, finished eating P
ohda'ọh it got full, finished eating S
sahda' get full; finish eating I

•(a)hdahd be filling
[o+ contains: -(a)hda' $_V$- get full of food]
ohdaht it is filling S

•(a)'da:dani be reliable, dependable
[P+]
hoya'da:dani: he is reliable, dependable S

•(a)dadawi, (a)dadọ trade, redeem, exchange
see: awi, ọ [(de+)...adad+]
dęsadadọ' you will trade, exchange it P

•(a)dade'dre's be self-propelled
see: (i)'dre's [wa+adade+] be self-propelled
wadad'edre's it drives itself H

•(a)dadehsnyeh groom onself
see: (h)snye(h,') [de+TR+/adad+] groom onself
desadadehsnyeh tidy up; groom yourself I

•(a)dahdi'tr(a) sock
adahd'itra' socks

•(a)dahdi'trọd panty hose
[o+ -(a)dahdi'tr(a) $_N$- sock -ọd $_V$- attached]
odahd'itrọ:t panty hose

•(a)dadogę between
see: ogę [de+A+adad+] between
detniy'ada:do:gę: between you and me, between our bodies S

•(a)dahdọ'd corrupt s.o.
see: (a)hdọ'd [TR+ad+] corrupt s.o.
ęhshey'adahdọ't you will corrupt her / them P

•(a)dadọhwęja'eg be buried
see: (a)dọhwęja'eg [de+P+ad+] bury
deyodọhwęja'e:k she is going into the earth (that is, being buried) P

•(a)dadrihọny(ę,ani) read
see: (r)ihọny(ę,ani) [adad+] read
ọdadrihọnyanih she is reading H

•(a)dadriyo commit suicide
see: (r)iyo, nyo [adad+] commit suicide
awadadri:yo' it killed itself; suicide P

•(a)dadrohegę accumulate for oneself
see: (r)ohegę [adad+] accumulate for oneself
ęhsadadrohe:gę' you will accumulate (things, ideas, etc.) for yourself P

Legend: H habitual, P punctual, S stative, I imperative, PURP purposive, PURP-H purposive habitual, PURP-PAST purposive past, PURP-P purposive punctual, PURP-I purposive imperative; see §8.6, §8.11 in Appendix J. Alphabetization in stems ignores length (:), and any h's or glottal stops (') that are not between vowels. See §2.2 of the User Guide for explanation.

•(a)dadwędehd forfeit
see: wędehd [ad/adad+] forfeit
awadadwę:deht it (for example, a pet) forfeited (its life) P

•(a)dagaideʼ be healthy, well, fine
see: (a)gaideʼ [P+ad+] healthy, well, fine
agadagai:deʼ I am well, fine, healthy S

•(a)dagaideʼ feel sick
see: (a)gaideʼ [tęʼ deʼ+ not P+ad+] feel sick
tęʼ desadagaideʼ you feel sick S

•(a)dahgahsd(ǫ) endure
see: (a)hgahsd(ǫ) [ad+] endure
sadahgahstaʼ you do endure H

•(a)daʼgehod have an erection
see: (a)ʼgehod [ad+] have an erection
sadaʼge̱ho:t you have an erection S

•(a)daʼgr(ahd) float, resurface
see: (a)ʼgr(ahd) [ad+] float
odaʼgra̱hdǫh it is floating S

•(a)daʼgradenyǫ: snow flurries
see: (a)ʼgradenyǫ: [P+ad+] snow flurries
odaʼgrade:nyǫ: there are snow flurries S

•(a)hdahg(wa) shoe
ahdahgwaʼ shoes

•(a)dahgwaę store s.t
see: (a)hgwaę [ad+] store s.t.
asada̱hgwaę:ʼ you stored it P

•(a)dahgwaęhęhsd pawn s.t.
see: (a)hgwaęhęhsd [ad+] pawn s.t.
ahagadahgwaęhęhs he pawned s.t. to me P

•(a)dagwas bruise
see: (a)gwas [ad(e)+(N/da)+] bruise
odagwasęh, odedagwa:sęh it is bruised S

•(a)dagwasd get bruised
see: (a)gwasd [ad(e)+(N/da)+] get bruised
ęwadagwa:s it will get bruised P

•(a)dagwęhdę flat, dented
see: (a)gwęhdę [de+...ad/N+] be flat, dented
deyodagwęhdę:, dewadagwęhdę: it is flat S

•(a)dagyaʼda:s self-centred, bold
see: yaʼda:s [A+adag+] self-centred, bold
hadagyʼada:s he has a high opinion of himself; he is self-centred; he is bold H

•(a)dagyena(w) wrestle
see: yena(w) [de+...adag+] wrestle
ęhsadagye:na:ʼ you will wrestle P

•(a)dahǫdǫ(:) ask
see: (a)hǫdǫ(:) [ad+] ask
sadahǫ:dǫ: ask; inquire I

•(a)dahǫdǫsgǫ be inquisitive
see: (a)hǫdǫsgǫ [A+ad+] inquisitive
sadahǫhdǫhsgǫ: you are inquisitive H

•(a)dahǫhsiyohsd listen to s.o., obey
see: (a)hǫhsiyohsd [TR+ad+] listen to s.o., obey
agada̱hǫhsi:yohs I listen S

•(a)daʼi:s mate, have intercourse
[P+ -(ni)ʼd(a)$_N$- privates -(ʼ)a:s, (ʼ)i:s$_V$- pierce]
sadaʼi:s you have intercourse H
onadaʼi:sęh they (z) are mating S

•(a)dakdǫ: blackcap
[d+he+ǫ+(a)d+ -(a)ʼkdǫ:$_V$- be bent, crooked]
tǫda:kdǫ: blackcaps

•(a)daʼkędahs ladies' fern
[wa+ (a)d+ -(ʼ)k(a:)$_N$- skirt, slip -ędahsd$_V$- cause s.t. to lie on the ground]
wadaʼkędahs ladies' fern

•(a)ʼda:ʼ rely on
[TR+]
hǫwadiyaʼda:ʼs they rely on him, them (m) H
ękeyʼada:ʼ I will rely on her P

•(a)dahnyo: fish
see: (a)hnyo: [ad+] fish
ahęnadahnyo:ʼ they (m) fished P
•(a)dao ceremonial friend
see: ao [P+ad+] ceremonial friend
agaǫ:daoʼtsę:ʼ they (f/m) became ceremonial friends P
•(a)dahsehd hide oneself
see: (a)hsehd [ad+] hide oneself
gadahsehtaʼ I hide H
ęgęnadahseht they (z) will hide P
agadahsehdǫh I am hiding now S
•(a)dahsehdǫhǫgyeʼs hide oneself, sneak around
see: (a)hsehdǫhǫgyeʼs [P+ad+] hide oneself
honadahsehdǫhǫ:gyeʼs they (m) are sneaking around S
•(a)daʼsęhd swoop
see: (aʼ)sęhd [d+...ad+] swoop
dawadʼasęht it swooped down P
•(a)daʼsęhd put s.o. down
see: (aʼ)sęhd [TR+ad+] put s.o. down
hadaʼsęhtaʼ he puts people down; he discriminates H
•(a)dahsogw fade
see: (a)hsogw [ad+] fade
odahsogwęh it is faded S
•(a)dahsǫdragw unjoin, come apart
see: (a)hsǫdragw [de+...ad+] unjoin, come apart
dewadahsǫdragwahs they come apart (lit.: it comes apart) H
•(a)daʼstaʼ nightgown, pyjamas
[(ya)go+ stem: -(i)daʼstaʼ- nightgown, pyjamas; consists of: -(i)daʼsd - cause to sleep]
godaʼstaʼ s.o.'s pyjamas, nightgown
•(a)da:ta:ʼ be conceited, be a snob
see: (a)ta:ʼ [A+ad+] be conceited, be a snob
hada:ta:ʼ he is conceited H
•(a)datgowa:nęh be self-important, rash, unwise, egotistical
see: gowanęh [A+adat+] be self-important, rash, unwise
wadatgowa:nęh it is rash, unwise, self-important, egotistical S
•(a)datgǫhe box
see: gǫhe [de+adat] box
dehęnadatgǫhe:s boxers; they (m) are boxing H
•(a)datgǫnyǫhsd be stuck up, snobbish
see: gǫnyǫhsd [adat+] stuck up, snobbish
wadatgǫnyǫhstaʼ she (lit.: it) is stuck up H
•(a)datnigǫha:ʼ wary, cautious
see: (ʼ)nigǫha:ʼ [A+adat+] wary, cautious
wadatnigǫha:ʼ it is wary, cautious H
•(a)datrewahd apologize, repent
see: (hr)ewahd [s+...adat+] apologize, repent
sahęnada:tre:waht they (m) repented P
•(a)datsʼ be empty, burnt up, used up
see: (a)tsʼ [heʼ+...ad+(N+)] empty, burnt up, used up
haʼwadatsʼǫh it is empty, burnt up, used up S
•(a)datsęhse: be tired
see: atsęhse: [P+ad+] tired
agadatsęhse: I am tired S
•(a)dawę(:) swim
see: (a)wę(:) [ad+] swim
hęnadawęhs they (m) are swimming H
•(a)dawęhęd climb s.t.
see: węhęd [de+...ad/N+] climb s.t.
deyodawęhędǫh it went over the fence; it is going over the fence S

Legend: H habitual, P punctual, S stative, I imperative, PURP purposive, PURP-H purposive habitual, PURP-PAST purposive past, PURP-P purposive punctual, PURP-I purposive imperative; see §8.6, §8.11 in Appendix J. Alphabetization in stems ignores length (:), and any h's or glottal stops (ʼ) that are not between vowels. See §2.2 of the User Guide for explanation.

•(a)dawęnya'seh be confused, doubtful
see: (a)węnya'seh [de+P+ad+] be confused, doubtful
dewagadawęnya'seh I am confused and doubtful; my thinking is going around in circles H

•(a)dawęnye(:) walk about
see: (a)węnye(:) [de+...P+ad+] walk about
deyagodawęnye' she is walking about S

•(a)dawi. (a)dǫ present, offer s.t.
see: awi, ǫ [ad+] present, offer
wadawihǫ' presents H

•(a)da'yod be erect
see: (a)'yod [ad+] be erect
ęwad'ayo:dę' it will be erect, poised to strike P

ade' climb
see: (r)ade' climb
sra:de' you are climbing S

•(a)de'dǫ(:) be due
see: (')dǫ(:) [ade+] be due
ęyǫd'edǫ:' when she will be due P

•(a)de'drehdaę park one's vehicle
see: (')drehdaę [ade+] park one's vehicle
gyǫgyad'edrehdaę:' we all parked our car over there S

•(a)de'dre's [wa+(a)dade+] car
see: (i)'dre's [wa+(a)dade+] car
wade'dre's a drag; a car (old word) (lit.: it is dragging itself) H

•(a)dedręhdatgihd (ę, ani) nightmare
see: (i)dręhdatgihd(ę, ani) [P+(a)de+] nightmare
ǫgadedręhdatgihdę' I had a bad dream P

•(a)de'drǫ, (a)de'drę put together, be crossed
see: (')drǫ, (')drę [de+...ad+] put together, be crossed
dęhswatnętsa'drǫ:' you all will cross your arms P

•(a)deg burn
[P+(N+)]
ode:ka' a fire; it is burning H
a'o:de:k it did burn P
ode:gęh it is burnt S

•(a)dega'd burn s.t. up, start a fire
[P+(N+) contains: -(a)deg$_V$- burn]
ǫdeg'ata' s.o. burns up s.t. H
ęga:de:ga't I will start a fire P

•(a)dega'dahkwa' fire-making tool; matches
[ǫ+ -(a)dega'dahkwa'$_V$- s.t. that burns]
ǫdega'dahkwa' a fire-making tool; matches

•(a)de'gw run away, flee
see: (')gw [ade+] run away, flee
ęgęnade'go' they (z) will flee, run away P

•(a)de'gwęhęgye's avoid
see: (')gwęhęgye's [P+ade+] avoid
sade'gwęhę:gye's you are avoiding S

•(a)dehę'ǫhsd widow, widower
see: (h)ę'ǫhsd [P+ade+] widow, widower
hodehę'ǫhsdǫh he is a widower S

•(a)dę'hęgǫ: yard
[(w)a+ -(a)dę'h(ę)$_N$- fence -gǫ:- in]
wadę'hę:gǫ:, **adę'hę:gǫ:** in the yard

•(a)dejęhiyohsd make a good fire
see: jęhiyohsd [ade+] make a good fire
sadejęhi:yohs make a good fire I

•(a)dejęhǫni start a fire
see: jęhǫni [ade+] start a fire
ęgadejęhǫ:ni' I will start a fire (an old word) P

•(a)dejinǫdagrahgw pick one's nose
see: jinǫdagrahgw [ade+] pick one's nose
ǫdejinǫdagrahgwahs she is picking her nose H

•(a)deji'ohgya'g cut one's nails
see: ji'ohgya'g [ad+(N+)] cut one's nails
ęgadeji'ohgya'k I am going to cut my nails P

•(a)deka' fire
[o+ -(a)deg$_V$- burn up]
ode:ka' a fire; it is burning

•(a)de'ka:' be hen-pecked
see: (')ka:' [P+ade+] be hen-pecked
hode'ka:' he is hen-pecked S

•(a)dekǫni eat
see: kǫni [ade+] eat
agęnade:kǫ:ni' they (z) ate P

•(a)dekǫnige: feast
see: kǫnige: [ade+] feast
ęhsadekǫnige: you will feast P

•(a)deksa'dǫni be childish, immature
see: ksa'dǫni [A+ade+] be childish, immature
ǫdeks'adǫ:nih she is childish H

•(a)dekwahę serve a meal
see: kwahę' [TR+ade+] serve a meal
agaǫ:dekwahę' they (f/m) put on a meal P

•(a)hdeny be a shape-shifter
[de+...]
deyǫhdenyǫhs she undergoes a magical transformation (generally for an evil purpose) H
deyohdenyǫhǫgye' it is changing as it goes (for example, a shape-shifter) S

•(a)denya'gwahd make oneself vomit, be bulemic
see: nya'gwahd [ade+] make oneself vomit, be bulemic
agadenya'gwaht I made myself throw up P

•(a)hdeh(n)yęhd knock over
[TR+]
gahsheyahdehnyęhta' I am going along knocking people over H
ęhsheyadęhyęht you will flip s.o. over; knock s.o. over P

•(a)de'nyędę try
see: (')nyędę [ade+] try
a:gade'nyę:dę' I might try, attempt it P

•(a)de'nyędęhsd copy, compare
see: (')nyędęhsd [de+...ade+] copy, compare
ętsad'enyę:dęhs you will copy, use as a model or pattern P

•(a)de'nyod celebrate, party
see: (')nyod [adę+] celebrate, party
ęhsad'ęnyo:dę' you will celebrate P

•(a)dehs(a) nest
[o+ -(a)dehs(a)$_N$- nest -ę$_V$- lie on the ground]
odehshę' a cocoon; a nest; a hive; a bee-hive

•(a)desha(h)sdǫh use one's strength
see: sha(h)sdǫh [ade+] use one's strength
ęhsadesha:sdǫh you will use your strength P

•(a)de'sgo immerse, drown
see: (')sgo [adade+/ade+] immerse, drown
ęhsad'esgoh you will go into the water P

•(a)de'sgǫd roast, fry
see: (')sgǫd [ad+N+] roast, fry
ęhsad'esgǫ:dę' you will roast it P

•(a)dehsgyę'diya'g fracture
see: (h)sgyę'diya'g [de+yo+ade+] fracture
deyodehsgyę'diya'gǫh it (bone) is fractured S

•(a)dehsgyǫ'wata'd diet, lose weight
see: (h)sgyǫ'wata'd [ade+] diet, lose weight
agaǫ:dehsgy'ǫwa:ta't they (f/m) dieted P

Legend: H habitual, P punctual, S stative, I imperative, PURP purposive, PURP-H purposive habitual, PURP-PAST purposive past, PURP-P purposive punctual, PURP-I purposive imperative; see §8.6, §8.11 in Appendix J. Alphabetization in stems ignores length (:), and any h's or glottal stops (') that are not between vowels. See §2.2 of the User Guide for explanation.

•(a)dehsiyogw fray
see: (h)siyogw [(de+)...ade+] fray
awadẹ̱hsi:yo:goʼ it frayed P
•(a)dehsnowad hurry up
see: (h)snowad [de+...ade+] hurry up
desadẹ̱hsno:wa:t hurry up I
•(a)dehsʼǫh ready
see: (i)hsʼǫh [P+ade+] ready
sadehsʼǫh? Are you ready? (this phrase may come from Onondaga) S
•(a)dehsw(a) blouse
adehswaʼ a blouse; a middy
•(a)dehsręʼdǫni glare, be grouchy
see: (h)sręʼdǫni [ade+] glare, be grouchy
agadẹ̱hsręʼdǫ:ni: I am grouchy, glaring S
•(a)dehsrǫnihsʼǫh be ready
see: (h)srǫnihsʼǫh [P+ade+] be ready
agadẹ̱hsrǫni̱hsʼǫh I am ready S
•(a)dehstoʼdręhd moult
see: (h)stoʼdręhd [ade+] moult
awadẹ̱hstoʼdręht it moulted P
•(a)dehstǫwisd hurt
see: (h)stǫwisd [(ade+)] hurt
sadehstǫwi:staʼ you hurt yourself all the time H
•(a)deswahd smell s.t. on purpose
see: swahd [TR+ade+] smell s.t. on purpose
ęwadehswaht it will smell it P
•(a)deswahdahnǫ(:) sniff s.t.
see: swahdahnǫ(:) [TR+ade+] sniff s.t.
sadehswa̱hdahnǫ: sniff it I
•(a)deteʼtra: powder oneself
see: teʼtra:ʼ [ade+] powder oneself
gadeteʼtra:s I am powdering myself H
•(a)detsaʼd struggle, revolt
see: tsaʼd [ade+] struggle, revolt
ęhsadetsaʼt you will struggle, squirm to get loose, revolt P
•(a)detsę: glutton
see: tsę [P+ade+] glutton
hode:tsę: he is a glutton S
•(a)detsęhsd gobble, gorge oneself
see: tsęhsd [ade+] gobble, gorge oneself
ęhsadetsęhs you will be a glutton; you will gobble, gorge yourself P
•(a)dewa:dahgw deflate
see: wa:dahgw [(ade+)] deflate
awadewa:dahgoʼ it deflated P
•(a)dewanega(:,ǫ) get a flat tire
see: (wa)nega(:,ǫ) [de+P+ade+] get a flat tire
adyagodewane:ga:ʼs she got a flat tire P
•(a)dewayęnǫni care for, do carefully
see: wayęnǫni [ade+] care for, do carefully
ęhsheyadewayę:nǫ:niʼ you will take care of them, care for them P
•(a)dewayęhsd learn s.t.
see: wayę(h)sd [ade+] learn s.t.
ęhsadewa:yę:s you will learn s.t. P
•(a)dewayęsdǫh be tidy, neat
see: wayęsdǫh [d+wa+ade+] be tidy, neat
dwadewayę:sdǫh gagehǫʼ it is tidy; it is neatly placed S
•(a)dewayęstaʼ learner, novice
see: wayęstaʼ [A+ade+] learner, novice
ǫdewayę:staʼ she is a novice, learner, beginner H
•(a)hdędi, (a)hdęgy leave, go away
gahdę:gyeʼs I am leaving H
ęgahdę:diʼ I will leave P
hohdęhgyǫhǫgyeʼ he is leaving S
sahdę:dih leave I
•(a)hdędi, (a)hdęgy originate from, come from somewhere
[d+]
dwagahdęgyǫ: I come from there S

•(a)hdędi, (a)hdęgy go home, leave again [s+...]
sgahdę:gye's I am leaving again H
ęhsgahdę:di' I will go home P
sahohdęgyǫhǫgye' he is on his way home S
sasahdę:dih go home I

•(a)dędǫnya'd tease, joke, jest
see: ędǫnya'd [TR+ad+] tease, joke, jest
hadędǫnya'ta' he is a joker H

•(a)dędǫnya'dahsgǫ: be happy-go-lucky, joke, jest
see: ędǫnya'dahsgǫ: [P+ad+] e happy-go-lucky, joke, jest
hodędǫnya'dahsgǫ: he is a joker, happy-go-lucky; he is obnoxious H

•(a)dęgahnye comfort a child, babysit
see: gahnye [adę+] comfort a child, babysit
ęhsadęgahnye' you will comfort, rock a child; you are babysitting P

•(a)dęgǫnyǫhsd be loyal, respectful
see: gǫnyǫhsd [adę+] be loyal
hadęgǫnyǫhsta' he is loyal (to the cause); he is respectful H

•(a)hdę'gw, -ę'gw swell up
wahdę'gwahs it swells up H
awahdęgoh it swelled up P
ohdę'gwęh it is swollen S

•(a)hdę'gw swell up
cf: ę'gw, (a)hdę'gw [ad+N+] swell up
awatnegę'go' the water rose up, swelled P

•(a)dę'h(ę) fence
adę'hę' a fence

•(a)dęhę(:) sun-tan
see: (h)ę: [A+adę+] sun-tan
esadęhę:k you got a tan P

•(a)dęhi:' be stacked
see: ęhi:' [A+ad+] be stacked
wadęhi:' it is stacked S

•(a)dęhǫgaǫ invite
see: (h)ǫgaǫ [TR+/adę+] invite
ęhshehǫgaǫ' you will invite her/them P

•(a)dęnha' order s.t.
see: nha' [adę+] order s.t.
ęsadęnha' you will order s.t., hire s.t. P

•(a)dęna'd lunch
see: na'd [adę+] lunch
ęga:dę:na't I will take a lunch P

•(a)dęnahsgwahgw jump
see: (ę)nahsgwahgw, (ę)na'sgwahgw, [de+] jump
deyǫnahsgwahkwa' she is jumping H

•(a)dęnahsgwahgw sky-dive
see: (ę)nahsgwahgw [de+d+] sky-dive
detęnahsgwahkwa' they (m) are sky-diving; paratroopers H

•(a)dęna'traęni feed
see: na'traęni [TR+adę+] feed
shǫgwadęna'traę:ni: the food he has given us S

•(a)dęnidęhd plead
see: nidęhd [adę+] plead
ęhsadęni:dęht you will plead P

•(a)dę'nigǫha(:) monitor
see: (')nigǫha(:) [TR+adę+] monitor
ǫkiy'adę'nigǫha:' monitors (people) H

•(a)dęnihahd(ę,ani) lend
see: nihahd(ę,ni) [adę+N+] lend
sadęhwihsdanihahda:nih you lend money; a lender H

•(a)dęnihs(a) wall
[o+]
odęnihsa' a wall

•(a)dęnihsadǫ' frame
[de+wa+ -(a)dęnihs(a)$_N$- wall -dǫ'$_V$- several standing objects]
dewadęnihsadǫ' a frame

•(a)dęnihsa'e corner s.o.
[de+... -(a)dęnihs(a)$_N$- wall -(')e$_V$- hit]
atodanihsa'e:k he was cornered, put up against the wall with no recourse P

•(a)dęnowęhd deny
see: nowęhd [adę+] deny
agadęno:węht I denied it P
•(a)denǫhahe:' happy
see: nǫhahe:' [P+ad+] happy
hodonǫhahe:' he is happy S
•(a)dęnǫhǫnyǫ(:) give thanks
see: nǫhǫnyǫ(:) [de+adę+] give thanks
dędwadęnǫhǫnyǫ:' we all (incl.) will give thanks P
•(a)dęnǫ'nyad mourn
see: nǫ'nyad [P+adę+] mourn
ęhsadęnǫ'nya:t you will mourn P
•(a)dęnǫhyanihd be terrible, overwhelming
see: nǫhyanihd [de+yo+(adę+)] be terrible, overwhelming
deyodęnǫhyanihdǫh it is overwhelming, terrible S
•(a)dęnyeha: win (a bet)
see: (h)nyeha: [adę+] win (a bet)
agęnadęhnyęha:' they (z) won (a bet) P
•(a)dęnyehd send s.o., sentence s.o.
see: nyehd [TR+adę+] send s.o., sentence s.o.
ahǫwadę:nyeht he was sentenced (lit.: they sent him) P
•(a)di, ogy, -ǫdi, -ǫgy throw
heho:gye's he throws it (all the time); he is a pitcher H
ęhsa:di' you will get rid of s.t., abandon it, throw it out P
heho:gyǫ: he has thrown it S
he'sa:dih throw it away from me I
•(a)di, ogy, -ǫdi, -ǫgy abandon, let go [TR+/ad+N+]
ęhshe:ya:di' you will abandon s.o., let them go P
hotwajiyǫ:gyǫ: he has abandoned the family; he threw his family aside S
[ad+N+ -(h)wajiy(a)$_N$- family -ǫdi, ǫgy$_V$- throw]

•(a)dih be on a certain side; go in a direction, lean against s.t.
[(ad)+N+]
tgaęgwadih they (f/m) are going in a direction H
ęsagyada'dih you will lean against s.t. P
[ag+N+ -ya'd(a)$_N$- body -adih$_V$- lean against, etc.]
jo̱haha:dih, swaha:dih the other side of the road S
[j+ o+ -hah(a)$_N$- road -adih$_V$- lean against, etc.]
•(a)di'grǫ' shy
see: (i)'grǫ' [P+ad+] shy
godi'grǫ' she is shy S
•(a)di'grǫhsr(a) shyness
see: (i')grǫhsr(a) shyness
adi'grǫhsra' shyness
•(a)dihah a side; a member of a pair
[s+ga+ -(a)dih$_V$- side]
sga:di:hah one side (for example, one of a pair of shoes)
•(a)didręhdaho'drǫ stay awake
see: (i)dręhdaho'drǫ [ad+] stay awake
agadidręhdaho'drǫ: I had to stay awake P
•(a)hdihęh be different
[de+wa+]
dewahdihęh the difference; it is different S
•(adi)hǫh lean against s.t.
[A+(N+)]
wadihǫh it is leaning against s.t. s
ga̱hǫwadihǫh a leaning boat s
•(a)'ditr(a) cane
[ad+]
ada'ditra' a cane
•(a)diyǫd stretch
see: (i)yǫd [de+ad/N+] stretch
dewadiyǫ:ta' it stretches (shortened form of 'rubber band'); a balloon; an elastic H

•(a)hdo(:) dive
hahdohsgęhę:ʼ he used to dive H
ęsahdo:ʼ you will submerge s.t. P
sa̲hdo: dive I
•(a)dod(a:) bow
ado:da:ʼ a bow (as in bow and arrow)
•(a)dohda(:,h) tidy up, clean s.t.
see: ohda(:,h) [de+...ad+] tidy up, clean
dęsado̲hda:ʼ you will tidy it up, clean it P
•(a)dodais(i) escape
see: odais(i) [ad+] rescue s.o., help someone escape
ahadodaisiʼ he got loose, escaped P
•(a)dodais(i) comb one's own hair
see: odais(i) [de+ad+] comb one's own hair
dęgadodai:siʼ I am going to comb my hair P
•(a)dodais(i) rescue s.o.
see: odais(i) [TR+ad+] rescue s.o.
ęhsheyadodaisiʼ you will help her escape; you will save her P
•(a)dodahs(i) appear unintentionally
see: odahsi [taʼ+...ad+] appear unintentionally
taʼsadodahsiʼ you appeared unintentionally P
•(a)hdog grow, mature
ǫhdo:gahs she is prepubescent; she is maturing; she is reaching puberty H
ęhsahdo:k you will grow P
sa̲hdo:k grow (not common) I
•(a)hdogaʼd grow s.t., raise s.t., s.o.
ga̲hsheya̲hdogʼataʼ you raise children; foster parents H
ęhsahdo:gaʼt you will grow s.t. P
ǫgahdǫgaʼdǫh she raised me (for example, a guardian) S
•(a)hdogaʼtaʼ foster parents
[TR+ -(a)hdogaʼd_V- raise s.o.]
gaǫdadahdogaʼtaʼ they (f/m) are foster parents
•(a)dogęʼ axe
ado:gęʼ an axe; a tomahawk
•(a)dogę between
see: ogę [de+...ad+] between
deyodogęʼǫh it is in between; a duel between two people S
•(a)dogwahd distribute s.t., scatter s.t.
see: ogwahd [de+...ad+(N+)] distribute s.t., scatter s.t.
degadogwahtaʼ I scatter s.t. H
•(a)dohahd(ę,ani) trip s.o.
see: odahd(ę, ani) [de+...+ad+] trip s.o.
dęhsadodahdęʼ it will trip you P
•(a)doʼjinehd skate
see: oʼjinehd [de+...ad+] skate
degaǫ:doʼjinehtaʼ they (f/m) figure-skate H
•(a)doʼkd be the end of s.t., edge of s.t.
see: oʼkd [ad+(N)+] end of s.t., edge of s.t.
heyotahoʼk the end of the trail, path, row S
[ad+ -hah(a)$_N$- body -oʼkd_V- be the end]
•(a)doʼkd lack s.t.
see: oʼkd [d+...ad+] lack
dawadʼokdęʼ it lacked; it was not enough P
•(a)doʼkdaʼ lack, be dissatisfied with
see: oʼkdaʼ [d+...ad+] lack, be dissatisfied with
gyodoʼkda̲ʼǫh it is lacking S
•(a)doʼkdagyeʼs times, end times
see: oʼkdagyeʼs [ni+yo+ad+] times, end times
niyodʼokda:gyeʼs up to these (end) times H

•(a)do'kdahsd lack, be dissatisfied with
see: o'kdahsd [d+...ad+] lack, be dissatisfied with
dawad'okdahs it lacks; it is not enough H

•(a)do'kd(ę,ani) be dissatisfied, lack
see: o'kd(ę,ani) [d+...+ad+] be dissatisfied, lack
dawad'okdę' it lacked; it was not enough P

•(a)donye's driver
see: onye's [ad+] driver
hadonye's he drives it; he is a driver H

•(a)dowad hunt
hado:wa:s he is a hunter H
ęha:do:wa:t he will hunt P
sado:wa:t hunt I

•(a)dowadǫ:' hunt
adowa:dǫ:' the hunt

•(a)dowas be a hunter
[A+ -(a)dowad$_V$- hunt]
hado:wa:s he is a hunter

•(a)do:wę(:) split in two from within
see: owę(:) [de+ad+(N+)] split in two from within
adwa:do:wę:' it split P

•(a)do:wi, (a)dǫny drive
see: owi, ǫny [ad+] drive
hęhsa:do:wih you will drive over there P

•(a)dowihshę(:) rest, relax
see: owihshę(:) [ad+] rest, relax
a'ǫdowihshę:' she rested P

•(a)hdǫ:' loss
[a+w+ -(a)hdǫ(:)$_V$- lose, disappear]
awahdǫ: a loss

•(a)hdǫ lose, disappear
wa̱hdǫhs it disappears H
ęhsahdǫ' you will disappear P
oihwahdǫ'ǫh it is extinct S
[o+ -(r)ih(wa)$_N$- affair, matter, word -(a)hdǫ'$_V$- come to lose]

•(a)dǫ' become
awa:dǫ' it has become; it became P
odǫ'ǫh it has become S

•(a)dǫh say
[A+]
ǫ:dǫh she is saying it (all the time, now) H

•(a)hdǫ's descriptions
[tsęh that ni+yo+ -(a)hdǫ's$_V$- several things that are like, that resemble one another]
tsęh niyohdǫ's descriptions

•(a)hdǫ'd lose s.t.
ęhsahdǫ't you will lose it P

•(a)hdǫ'd corrupt s.o.
[TR+ad+ -(a)hdǫ(:)$_V$- lose, disappear]
ęhsheyadahdǫ't you will corrupt her/them P

•(a)dǫdata' contain s.t.
see: ǫdata' [wa+ad+] contain
wadǫdata' it contains s.t.; a container H

•(a)dǫgohd go under s.t.
see: ǫgohd [de+...ad+N+] go under s.t.
dęhsad'ęhę:gǫht you will go under the fence P
[de+ -adę'h(ę)$_N$- fence -ǫgohd$_V$- go under s.t., surpass]

•(a)dǫgohdę deceive
see: ǫgohdę [TR+ad+] deceive
ęhseyadǫgo̱hdę' you will outdo s.o.; you will go right over her, go right past her, deceive her P

•(a)dǫgwe'dagǫnyǫhsd be choosy, discriminate
see: ǫgwe'dagǫnyǫhsd [P+ad+] be choosy, discriminate
hodǫgw'edagǫnyǫhs he is choosy about who he associates with; he discriminates H

•(a)dǫgwe'diyohsd compose oneself
see: ǫgwe'diyohsd [ad+] compose oneself
agadǫgwe'di:yohs I made myself nice (put on my public face or facade) P

•(a)dǫhǫni' be a newborn
[P+]
godǫ:hǫ:ni' she is a newborn child

•(a)dǫ'n(eg) move away
see: ǫ'n(eg) [ad+] move away
ęwad'one:k it (an animal) will move away P

•(a)dǫ'n(eg) remove oneself
see: ǫ'n(eg) [de+...ad+] remove oneself
ętsad'ǫne:k you will remove yourself P

•(a)dǫnhed be born
see: ǫnhed [ad+] be born
sadǫ:nhe:dǫh you were born S

•(a)dǫnhi:(') enjoy life, be born
see: ǫnhi:(') [P+ad+] enjoy life
agadǫnhi: I am alive; I am born; I am full of life S

•(a)dǫni start from, originate, emerge
see: ǫni [d+...+adad+] start from, originate, emerge
tęwadadǫ:ni' it will emerge, appear unintentionally P

•(a)dǫni: little, few
see: ǫni: [de'+ not ad+(N+)] little, few
de'odahyǫ:ni: not much fruit on the trees S
[de'+ not yo+ ad+ -(a)hy(a)$_N$- fruit -ǫni, ǫny$_V$- make]

•(a)dǫni, (a)dǫny start from, originate, emerge
see: ǫni, ǫny [d+A+adad+] start from, originate, emerge
dwada:dǫ:nih where it starts from H

•(a)dǫnho'g be premature, mentally challenged
see: ǫnho'g [d+P+ad+] be premature, mentally challenged
todǫ:nho'k he is mentally challenged; he was born premature S

•(a)dǫnyahnǫ(:) move
see: ǫnyahnǫ(:) [ad+] move
ęsadonyahnǫ:' you will make yourself move P

•(a)dǫnye'd cause s.t. to breathe; be a gill
see: ǫnye'd [ad+] cause s.t. to breathe
wadǫnyeta' how it breathes; it is a breather; the gill H

•(a)dǫ'se benefit s.o.
see: ǫ's [P+ad+] benefit s.o.
godǫ'se:' it did benefit her S

•(a)dǫ'sd benefit s.o.
see: ǫ'sd [P+ad+] benefit s.o.
godǫ'sta' it always benefits her H

•(a)dǫhswe'd(ę,ani) be short of breath
see: ǫhswe'd(ę,ani) [A+ad+] be short of breath
hadǫhswęhta' he is short of breath H

•(a)dǫhswe'd(ę,ani) be hungry, short of breath
see: ǫhswe'd(ę,ani) [P+ad+] be hungry, short of breath
agadǫhswe'danih I am hungry H

•(a)dǫtgade' be happy, be fun
see: ǫtgade' [ad+] be happy, be fun
odǫtga:de' it is fun; a good feeling S

•(a)dǫtgade' be unhappy
see: ǫtgade' [de'+ not ...ad+] be unhappy
de'agadǫtgade', dewagadǫtgadǫ' I am not happy S

•(a)dǫtgadǫ(:) enjoy s.t.
see: ǫtgadǫ [ad+] enjoy
ędwadǫtga:dǫ:' we all (incl.) will have a good time, enjoy ourselves P

•(a)dǫtsod(ę) pray on one's knees; become a Christian
see: ǫtsod [de+...ad+] pray on one's knees; become a Christian
dęyǫdǫtso:dę' she will become Christian; she will kneel in prayer P

Legend: H habitual, P punctual, S stative, I imperative, PURP purposive, PURP-H purposive habitual, PURP-PAST purposive past, PURP-P purposive punctual, PURP-I purposive imperative; see §8.6, §8.11 in Appendix J. Alphabetization in stems ignores length (:), and any h's or glottal stops (') that are not between vowels. See §2.2 of the User Guide for explanation.

•(a)dǫtw burn
see: ǫtw [ad+] burn
wadǫ:twahs what it burns (in the way of fuel) H
•(a)dǫhwęjaʼeg [de+P+ad+] bury s.o.
deyodǫhwęjaʼe:k she is going into the earth (that is, being buried) P
(a)dǫhwęjoni, (a)dǫhwęjoh want, need s.t.
see: ǫhwęjoni, ǫhwęjoh [de+P+ad+] want, need
dęhsadǫhwę:jǫ:niʼ you will want s.t. P
•(a)dǫhwęjohsd want, need
see: ǫhwęjohsd [de+P+ad+] want, need
adwagadǫhwę:johs I did want s.t. P
•(a)dǫwi, (a)dǫny breathe
see: ǫwi, ǫny [ad+] breathe
sadǫ:nyeʼs you are breathing H
•(a)dǫhwidaʼd swing
see: ǫhwidaʼd [ad+] swing
a:sadǫhwi:daʼt you will swing P
•(a)dǫwihsręhd breathe
see: ǫwihsręhd [ad+] breathe
ęyǫdowihsręht she will breathe P
•(a)dǫwihsriyaʼs be breathless, be dying
see: ǫwihsriyaʼs [A+ ad+] be breathless, be dying
hadǫwi̱hsri:yaʼs he is out of breath; he is dying H
•(a)dǫhwihsroʼkd be breathless
see: ǫhwihsroʼkd [ad+] be breathless
hadǫhwi̱hsroʼktaʼ he is out of breath H
•(ʼ)ahdr(a) basket
[ga+]
gaʼahdraʼ a basket
•(a)ʼdraʼ meet
[de+...]
degaǫ:draʼs they (f/m) meet all the time H
atgaǫ:draʼ they (m) met P
deyagonaʼdra̱ʼǫh they deserve each other (said in anger); they (f/m) are meeting right now S

•(a)dragwaęʼ be limp
see: (r)agwaęʼ [A+ad+] be limp
wadragwaęʼ it is limp S
•(a)dranega(:,ǫ) explode, split
see: (ra)nega(:,ǫ) [de+...ad+N+] explode, split
dewadranegaǫ:s it is exploding H
•(a)draʼswiyohsdę be lucky
see: (r)aʼswiyohsdęʼ [P+ad+] be lucky
ǫgadrʼaswiyo̱hsdęʼ I got lucky P
•(a)dratsǫ(:) tear s.t., shred s.t.
see: (r)atsǫ(:) [ad+] tear s.t., shred s.t.
wadra:tsǫhs it gets torn all the time H
•(a)drędagyeʼs soar
see: (r)ędagyeʼ [(de+)...ad+] soar
odrędagyeʼs it is soaring (for example, a bird) S
•(a)dęhod stack s.t.
see: (r)ęhod [de+...ad+] stack s.t.
dęsadęhodęʼ you will stack things, put one thing on top of the other P
•(a)dręnaę(:) pray
see: (r)ęnaę(:) [ad+] pray
honadręnaę:ʼ they (m) (Christians) are praying S
•(a)dręnod sing
see: (r)ęnod [ad+] sing
gęnadręno:taʼ they (z) are singers H
•(a)dręnǫni compose
see: (r)ęnǫni [ad+] compose
ahadręnǫ:niʼ he made a song P
•(a)drihoʼdad work
see: (ri)hoʼdad [ad+] work
ęgaǫ:drihoʼda:t they (f/m) are going to work P
•(a)drihodahǫh be confused, mixed up
see: (r)ihodahǫh [de+P+ad+] be confused, mixed up
dewagadrihodahǫh I am confused, mixed up; s.t. is blocking my thinking S

•(a)drihodahse:ʼ be confused, indecisive
see: (r)ihodahse:ʼ [de+P+ad+] be confused, indecisive
dewagadrihodahse:ʼ I am confused; I cannot make up my mind S

•(a)driho:wi: be slow, feeble, clumsy
see: (r)ihowi [P+ad+] be slow, feeble, clumsy
hodriho:wi: he is clumsy S

•(a)drihsdane:ga(:,ǫ) scream
see: (r)ihsdanega(:,ǫ) [de+...ad+] scream
dęhsadrihsda:ne:ga:ʼ you will burst out screaming, crying; you will make a loud outburst P

•(a)drihwahdędi, (a)drihwahdęgy start a ceremony
see: (r)ihwahdędi, (r)ihwahdęgy [ad+] start a ceremony
ęwadrihwahdę:diʼ the ceremony will start P

•(a)drihwahdęgyaʼd do a ceremony
see: (r)ihwahdęgyaʼd [ad+] do a ceremony
edwadrihwahdęgyaʼt we all (incl.) did the ceremony P

•(a)drihwaʼehsd accuse s.o.
see: (r)ihwaʼehsd [P+ad+] accuse s.o.
ahodrihwaʼe:s he was accused P

•(a)drihwaędǫhkw gossip
see: (r)ihwaędǫhkw [de+...ad+] gossip
dęsadrihwaędǫhk you will gossip P

•(a)drihwagwaihshǫ be righteous
see: (r)ihwagwaihshǫ [P+ad+] be righteous
godrihwagwaihsǫh she is fair, righteous S

•(a)drihwahę commit a crime, do wrong
see: (r)ihwahę [de+...ad+] commit a crime, do wrong
atadrihwahęʼ he went afoul of the law; he did s.t. wrong P

•(a)drihwanyehd send s.t.
see: nyehd [he+...ad+N+] send s.t.
hęswadrihwanyeht you all will send a message P
[heʼ+ ... ad+ -(r)ih(wa)$_N$- message, etc. -nyęhd- send s.t.]

•(a)drihwaǫni heal
see: (r)ihwaǫni [ad+] heal
ęhswadriwaǫniʼ you will heal P

•(a)drihwahsehd have a secret, scheme
see: (r)ihwahsehd [ad+] have a secret, scheme
ahęnadrihwahseht they (m) hid their idea (that is, they schemed) P

•(a)drihwahsrǫni be in charge, come to an arrangement
see: (r)ihwahsrǫni [(ad+)] be in charge, come to an arrangement
ęhsrihwahsrǫ:niʼ you will come to an arrangement P

•(a)drihwahsrǫni reconcile
see: (r)ihwahsrǫni [s/j+...(ad+)] reconcile
ęjijadrihwahsrǫ:niʼ you two will reconcile P

•(a)drihwahsrǫni make peace with s.o.
see: (r)ihwahsrǫni [(a)d+] make peace with s.o.
wadrihwahsrǫ:ni: peace; to make peace with s.o. S

•(a)drihwatgaha(:,ǫ) oversee, supervise [(a)d+]
hodrihwatgaha:ʼ he is a supervisor, overseer H
ęhsadrihwatgahǫ:ʼ you will oversee, supervise P

•(a)drihwatgihd talk dirty
see: (r)ihwatgihd [ad+] talk dirty
hodrihwatgihdǫh he is talking dirty S

•(a)drihwatsʼa: earn s.t., fulfill s.t.
see: (r)ihwatsʼa: [de+...(ad+)] earn s.t., fulfill s.t.
atadrihwa:tsʼa:ʼ he earned it; he fulfilled it P

Legend: H habitual, P punctual, S stative, I imperative, PURP purposive, PURP-H purposive habitual, PURP-PAST purposive past, PURP-P purposive punctual, PURP-I purposive imperative; see §8.6, §8.11 in Appendix J. Alphabetization in stems ignores length (:), and any h's or glottal stops (ʼ) that are not between vowels. See §2.2 of the User Guide for explanation.

•(a)driyohsd(ę,ani) make s.o. fight
see: (r)iyohsd(ę,ani) [TR+ad+] make s.o. fight
ęgasheyadriyohsdęʼ you will make them fight P

•(a)droheg congregate, gather together
see: (r)oheg [ad+] congregate, gather together
ędwadro̱he:k we all (incl.) will gather together P

•(ʼ)ahdrowanęh a big basket
[ga+ -(ʼ)ahdr(a)$_N$- basket -owanęh$_V$ be big]
gaʼahdrowa:nęh a bushel basket

•adrǫ(:) tear s.t., shred s.t.
see: (r)adrǫ(:) tear s.t., shred s.t.
ęhsra:drǫ:ʼ you will tear, shred P

•(a)hdrǫʼ be scared, frightened
[P+]
agahdrǫʼs I am scared, frightened H
ęwaga̱hdrǫʼk I will be frightened P
agahdrǫʼ ni:ʼ I am scared all the time; I'm a fraidy-cat S
sa̱hdrǫʼk be afraid (non-sensical) I

•(a)hdrǫgw caress
see: yaʼdahdrǫgw [P+] caress
hehsyaʼda̱hdrǫ:gwahs you are caressing him now H
ęhesyʼadahdrǫ:gǫʼ you will caress him P
hehsyaʼda̱hdrǫ:gwęh you did caress him S

•(a)hdrǫgwęʼ frighten s.o.
[TR+ contains: -(a)hdrǫʼ$_V$- be scared, frightened]
ęhsahdrǫgwęʼ it will frighten you P

•(ʼ)ahdrǫnih witch hazel
[ga+ -(ʼ)ahdr(a)$_N$- basket -ǫni, ǫny$_V$- make, grow]
ga̱ʼahdrǫ:nih witch hazel

•(a)drǫʼwęsd abuse s.o.
see: (r)ǫʼwęsd [ad+] abuse s.o.
dehshagodrǫʼwe̱hstaʼ he abuses s.o. H

•(a)drǫhyaʼd be unwilling, stubborn
see: (r)ǫhyaʼd [P+ad+] be unwilling, stubborn
godrǫhyaʼt she is unwilling, stubborn S

•(a)drǫhyaʼdahgw balk, be reluctant
see: (r)ǫhyaʼdahgw [ad+] balk, be reluctant
ahadrǫhyaʼdahk he balked at the suggestion P

•(a)dwęnadęnyǫhs reach puberty
see: węnadęnyǫhs [de+A+ad+] reach puberty
dehadwęnadęnyǫhs he is reaching puberty (lit.: his voice is changing) H

•(a)dwęnayęhd jeer, jest
see: węnayęhd [ad+] jeer, jest
ęhsadwęna:yęht you will jeer, jest, throw words at s.o. P

•(a)dwęnod bay, howl
see: węnod [ad+] bay, howl
odwę:no:t it is baying S

•(a)dwęnǫda: speak, use a language
see: węnǫda: [ad+] speak, use a language
a:gadwę:nǫ:dahk I should use that language P

•(a)dwęnǫdi be a ventriloquist
see: węnǫdi [he+P+ad+] be a ventriloquist
hę:sadwęnǫ:diʼ you will throw your voice (as a ventriloquist) P

•(a)dwiyanǫ: babysit
see: wiyanǫ [ad+] babysit
ęgadwiya:nǫ:ʼ I will babysit P

•(a)dwiyaǫgw, (a)dwiyaǫgo adopt babies
[ad+ -wiy(a)$_N$- baby -(r)ǫgw$_V$- keep]
sadwiyaǫ:gwahs you adopt babies H
ęhsadwiyaǫgoʼ you will adopt a baby P
agadwiyaǫ:gwęh I have adopted a baby S

•(a)dwiyǫdi abandon one's child
see: wiyǫdi [P+ad+] abandon one's child
ęhsadwiyǫ·diʼ you will abandon your baby, child P
•(a)ʼehsd poke, pierce
[de+... -aʼ$_N$- -(ʼ)ehsd$_V$- hit with s.t.]
deswaʼehstaʼ you all are poking H
dęhsaʼehs you will spear s.t. P
•(a)ʼęn(a) stick, rod, pole
[o+]
oʼę·naʼ a snowsnake; a pole
•(a)ʼęn(a) yard
[j+o+ -(a)ʼęn(a)$_N$- stick, rod -d$_V$- stand, be one]
jǫʼę·na·t one yard
•(a)ʼęnahe·ʼ street car
[o+ad+ -(a)ʼęn(a)$_N$- stick, rod -(h)e·ʼ$_V$- be sitting up on top of s.t.]
odaʼęnahe·ʼ a street car
•(a)ʼęnaʼehsd spear with a stick
[de+TR+ -(a)ʼęn(a)$_N$- stick, pole, rod -(ʼ)ehsd$_V$- hit with s.t.]
atǫwaʼęnaʼehs he speared him with a stick P
•(a)ʼęnaę(·) play snowsnake
[de+ -(a)ʼęn(a)$_N$- stick, pole, rod -ę$_V$- lie on the ground]
dęhęnʼęnaę·hęʼ they (m) are snowsnake players H
da·yagwaʼęnaę·ʼ we all (excl.) would play snowsnake P
•(a)ʼęnod sapling
[w+ -(a)ʼęn(a)$_N$- stick, rod -odǫʼ$_V$- several standing objects]
waʼę·no·dǫʼ saplings; young trees
•(a)gahdeh be raw
[o+(N+)]
ogahdeh it is raw S
ohetsagahdeh uncooked sausage
[o+ stem: -(h)ets(a)$_N$- sausage, wiener, bologna -(a)gahdeh$_V$- be raw]
•(a)gahdeh celery
[ǫ+(a)d+ -(a)gahdeh$_V$- raw]
ǫ·dagahdeh celery
•(a)hgahę· be jealous
[P+]
go̱hgahę· she is jealous S
•(a)gaideʼ be healthy, well, fine
[P+ad+]
agadagai·deʼ I am well, fine, healthy S
•(a)gaideʼ feel sick
[tęʼ deʼ+ not P+ad+]
tęʼ desadagaideʼ you feel sick S
•(a)hgaodǫnyǫ(·) tap trees
[-(a)hg(a·)$_N$- splint -odǫnyǫ(·)$_V$- several standing objects]
ęyagwa̱hgaodǫ·nyǫ·ʼ we all (excl.) will tap trees P
•(a)hgahsd(ǫ) endure
[ad+]
sadahgahstaʼ you do endure H
ęsadahga·sdǫʼ you will tough it out, endure P
sadahgahsdǫ· endure (a phrase which in context means, "go and cook in the cookhouse") I
•(a)ge· two
[de+A/P+N+]
degaʼahdra·ge· two baskets S
[de+ ga+ -(ʼ)ahdr(a)$_N$- basket -age·- be a certain number]
•(a)ge· three or more
[ni+A/P+N+]
niganaʼja·ge· an amount of pails S
[ni+ ga+ -naʼj(a)$_N$- pail -age·- be a certain number]
•(a)ʼged bend (forwards)
see: shaʼged, shaʼkdǫ [de+...at+] bend (forwards)
dęwatsaʼge·t it will bend P
•(a)hge(h)d come back
[de+d+...]
dǫdasa̱hge·t you should come back P

Legend: H habitual, P punctual, S stative, I imperative, PURP purposive, PURP-H purposive habitual, PURP-PAST purposive past, PURP-P purposive punctual, PURP-I purposive imperative; see §8.6, §8.11 in Appendix J. Alphabetization in stems ignores length (·), and any h's or glottal stops (ʼ) that are not between vowels. See §2.2 of the User Guide for explanation.

•(a)hge(h)d return, go back
[s+...]
hesgahge̱htaʼ I go back all the time H
ętsahge:t you will go back, regress P
sasahge:t go back I
•(a)ʼgehod(ę) have, get an erection
[ad+]
ęhadage̱ho:dęʼ he will get an erection P
sadaʼge̱ho:t you have an erection S
•(a)ʼgęh(ęda) ash, dust, bullet
[o+]
oʼgęhęʼ ashes; a bullet; dust
•(aʼ)gęhędahkwaʼ brush (for clothes)
[e+ -(a)ʼgęh(ęda)$_N$- ash, dust -(h)gwaʼ$_V$- s.t. that lifts or picks things up]
egęhędahkwaʼ a clothes brush
•(aʼ)gęhę(h)kwaʼ ashtray
[ǫ+ -(a)ʼgęh(ęda)$_N$- ash, dust -(h)gwaʼ$_V$- s.t. that lifts or picks things up]
ǫʼgęhę:kwaʼ an ashtray
(ʼ)gęhohkwaʼ ammunition
[ǫ+ -(a)ʼgęh(ęda)$_N$- ash, dust -(h)gwaʼ$_V$- s.t. that lifts or picks things up]
ǫʼgęhohkwaʼ ammunition
•(a)gęhnyaʼgǫh grey
[de+yo+ad+ -(a)ʼgęh(ęda)$_N$- ash, dust -(i)yaʼg$_V$- cut, break]
deyodagęhnyʼagǫh grey
•age(:,w) wipe
see: (r)age(:,w) wipe
ęgra:ge:ʼ I will erase, wipe it P
•agi: ouch
see: Appendix I
•(a)hgowi:ʼ quail, partridge
[go+ -(a)hg(a:)$_N$- splint -owi, ǫny$_V$- drive]
go̱hgo:wi:ʼ quail; partridge
•(a)ʼgr(a) snow, snowflake
[o+]
oʼgraʼ snow; a snowflake
•(a)ʼgr(ahd) float, resurface
[ad+]
wadaʼgrahtaʼ it resurfaces continually H
dǫdawadaʼgrahk it resurfaced P
odaʼgrahdǫh it is floating S
•(a)ʼgradenyǫ: snow flurries
[o+ ad+ -(a)ʼgr(a)$_N$- snow -deʼnyǫ$_V$- several existing things]
odaʼgrade:nyǫ: there are snow flurries S
•(a)ʼgrohda:s snow plough
[de+wa+ad+ -(a)ʼgr(a)$_N$- snow -ohda(:,h)$_V$- tidy up, clean]
dewadaʼgrohda:s a snow plough
•(a)ʼgrowanahd snow hard
[-(a)ʼgr(a)$_N$- snow -owanahd$_V$- enlarge]
oʼgrowanahdǫh it is snowing hard S
•agw, ago choose, take out
see: (r)agw, (r)ago choose, take out
ęhsra:goʼ you will choose, take out P
•ag(wa:) celestial body, s.t. circular in shape
see: (r)ag(wa:) celestial body, s.t. circular in shape
ga:gwa:ʼ a celestial body (for example, the sun, the moon)
•a:gwahd(a) ball of foot, sole
see: (r)agwahd(a) ball of foot, sole
a:gwa̱hdaʼ, ogwahdaʼ the sole; the ball of the foot
•(a)hgwaę(:) store
[ad+]
sadahgwaę:hęʼ you store things all the time H
asada̱hgwaę:ʼ you did store it P
sadahgwaę:ʼ store it; hold on to it temporarily I
•(a)hgwaęhęhsd pawn s.t.
[ad+ contains: -(a)hg(wa)$_N$- -(a)hgwaę$_V$- store]
ahagadahgwaęhęhs he pawned s.t. to me P

•a:gwagye's sun, moon
see: (r)agwagye's sun, moon
ga:gwa:gye's the sun; the moon
•(a)gwasd get bruised
[ad(e)+(N/da)+ -(a)gwas$_V$- bruise]
ęwadagwa:s it will get bruised P
odedagwa:sdǫh it is bruised S
•(a)gwasęh be bruise
[ad(e)+(N/da)+]
odagwa:sęh, odedagwa:sęh it is bruised S
•ahgwase: new moon
see: (r)ahgwase: [ga+] new moon
ga̱hgwase:' a new moon
•(a)gwęhdę: be flat, dented
[de+...ad/N+]
adwadagwęhdę: it became dented P
deyodagwęhdę:, dewadagwęhdę: it is flat S
•(a)hgwęny(a) clothes
ahgwę:nya' clothing; clothes
•ahgwę:nya' ga̱ha'ta' clothes dryer
ahgwę:nya' clothing, clothes
ga̱ha'ta' it dries
•ahgwih don't...
see: Appendix I
•(a)gya'dadih
see: ya'dadih [ag+] lean
ęsagy'ada:dih you will lean against s.t. P
•(a)gya'dagw lose weight
see: ya'dagw [d/g+P+ad+] lose weight
dǫgya'da:go' I lost weight (lit.: lost part of my body) P
•(a)gya'dahgwa'd push ups
see: ya'dahgwa'd [adad+] push ups
dęgaǫ:dagy'adahgwa't they (f/m) will do push ups P
•(a)gya'dagweg constipate
see: ya'dagweg [ag+] constipate
ęsagy'ada:gwe:k you will get constipated P
•(a)gya'danega(:,ǫ) hernia
see: ya'danega(:,ǫ) [de+P+ag+] hernia
dewagagya'danegaǫ: I have a hernia S
•(a)gya'dahniya'd strong
see: ya'dahniya'd [ag+] strong
ędwagy'adahni:ya:t we all will be strong in body P
•(a)dagya'da:s be self-centred, bold
see: ya'da:s [A+adag+] self-centred, bold
hadagy'ada:s he has a high opinion of himself; he is self-centred; he is bold H
•(a)gya'dahsrǫnya'd dress up
see: ya'dahsrǫnya'd [ag+] dress up
ǫgya'da̱hsrǫny'ata' s.o. dresses up H
•(a)gya'dawi'd put on clothes, clothe oneself
see: ya'dawi'd [ag+] put on clothes, clothe oneself
ęsagy'ada:wi:t you will put on clothes P
•(a)gya'dohai bathe s.o.
see: ya'dohae [ag+] bathe
ęwagy'adohai: it is going to give me a bath P
•(a)gya'dǫda: represent s.o., be an ambassador
see: ya'dǫda: [TR+ag+] represent s.o., be an ambassador
ęhshagogya'dǫ:dahk he will be an ambassador, represent s.o. (lit.: they will put his body in) P
•(a)gya'dǫdi pounce
see: ya'dǫdi [he+P+ag+] pounce
hęsagy'adǫ:di' you will pounce on it P
•(a)gyana', (a)gyanǫ' be addicted
see: yana', yanǫ' [P+ag+] be addicted
agagyanǫ'ǫh I am addicted S
•(a)gyana'dahnǫ', (a)gyęna'dahnǫ' calico, printed fabrics
see: yana'dahnǫ', yęna'dahnǫ' [o+ag+] calico, printed fabrics
ogyan'adahnǫ', ogyęn'adahnǫ' patterned material; calico; printed fabric S

Legend: H habitual, P punctual, S stative, I imperative, PURP purposive, PURP-H purposive habitual, PURP-PAST purposive past, PURP-P purposive punctual, PURP-I purposive imperative; see §8.6, §8.11 in Appendix J. Alphabetization in stems ignores length (:), and any h's or glottal stops (') that are not between vowels. See §2.2 of the User Guide for explanation.

•(a)gyanǫʼ dream
see: yanǫʼ [P+ag+] dream
ęyogyanǫʼk it will dream P
•(a)gyanǫhg be strange, bizarre
see: yanǫhg [o+ag+] be strange, bizarre
ogya:nǫhk it is strange, bizarre S
•(a)gyaod put up a tent
see: yaod [ag+] put up a tent
hogyaot he has put up a tent S
•(a)gyaǫʼ be tricked, fooled
[P+]
ehsa:gyaǫʼ you were tricked, fooled P
•(a)gyaǫnyod haunted
[de+P+ contains -(a)gyaǫʼ$_V$- be tricked, fooled -ǫny- plural -od- stand]
dewagyaǫnyotaʼ it is haunted H
•(a)gyaǫnyǫʼ apparition
[de+P+ contains: -(a)gyaǫʼ$_V$- tricked, fooled -ǫnyǫʼ- plural]
adwagyaǫnyo:ʼ there was a haunted apparition
•(a)gyaǫhsr(a) trick
[(o+)]
ogyaǫhsraʼ, agyaǫhsraʼ a trick
•(a)gyenawahd cling
see: yenawahd [ag+] cling
ęhsagyena:waht you will retain, book a venue, hold onto s.t., cling to s.t. P
•(a)gyesahd waste, be wasteful
see: yesahd [P+ag+] waste, be wasteful
ęhsa:gye:saht you will waste P
•(a)gyesaʼgeh be generous
see: yesaʼgeh [P+ag+] be generous
gogyesʼageh she is generous to a fault S
•(a)gyesahsdǫ: be extravagant, wasteful
see: yesahsdǫ: [P+ag+] be extravagant, wasteful
gogyehsa̱hsdǫ: she is extravagant, wasteful S
•(a)gyesęh be easy
see: yes [w+ag+] be easy
wagye:sęh it is easy S

•(a)dagyeʼshǫʼ continue on
see: yeʼshǫʼ [haʼ+...adag+] continue on
haʼgadagyeʼshǫʼ it continues on endlessly H
•(a)gyę(:) sit down
see: yę(:) [ag+] sit down
ęhswa:gyę:ʼ you all will sit down P
•(a)gyęʼ be quiet, still
see: (y)ęʼ [taʼ+de+P+ag+] be quiet, still
taʼdesagyę: you are quiet S
•(a)gyęhd begin, be first
see: yęhd [d/g+...ag+] begin, be first
dawa:gyę:t the first one; the beginner P
•(a)gyęhętw, (a)gyęhęto retract s.t.
see: yęhętw, yęhęto [heʼ+...ag+] retract s.t.
hehswagyęhęhtwęh you retracted s.t. S
•(a)gyęnaʼd, (a)gyanaʼd mark s.t.
see: yęnaʼd, yanaʼd [(ag+)] mark s.t.
ęgya:naʼt I will mark s.t. P
•(a)gyęnaʼtaʼ, (a)gyanaʼtaʼ act
see: yęnaʼtaʼ, yanaʼtaʼ [(ag+)] act
ǫgyanʼataʼ an actress H
•(a)gyęhsaǫ bandage (oneself)
see: yęhsaǫ [ag+] bandage (oneself)
sagyęhsaǫ: bandage yourself I
•(a)gyǫʼseh visit
see: yǫʼse [ag+] visit
ęgagyʼǫsehaʼ I am going to go and visit P
•(a)hǫhd(a) ear
ohǫhdaʼ ears
sa̱hǫhdʼageh on your ears
•(a)hǫhdahǫʼ jackass, donkey
[de+wa+ -(a)hǫhd(a)$_N$- ear -(h)ǫ(:)$_V$- lie across]
dewahǫhdahǫʼ a jackass; a donkey (lit.: it has crossed ears)
•(a)hǫhde:s deer
[de+wa+ -(a)hǫhd(a)$_N$- ear -es$_V$- long]
dewahǫhde:s a deer

•(a)hǫdǫ(:) ask
[ad+]
gaǫdahǫdǫhaʼ they (f/m) are asking H
aʼǫdadahǫdǫ:ʼ she asked her P
sadahǫdǫ: ask; inquire I
•(a)hǫdǫ(:) ask for s.t.
[N+]
agakwa̱hǫ:dǫ:ʼ it asked for food P
•(a)hǫdǫ(:) ask s.o.
[TR+]
aʼǫdadahǫdǫ:ʼ she asked her P
hesahǫ:dǫ: ask him I
•(a)hǫdǫsgǫ: inquisitive
[A+ad+ -(a)hǫhd(a)$_N$- ear -(a)hǫdǫ(:)$_V$- ask -sgǫ: easily]
sadahǫdǫhsgǫ: you are inquisitive H
•(a)hǫg hear, learn how to speak a language, understand
gaǫhǫkaʼ they (f/m) understand a language H
agaǫhǫ:k they (f/m) heard; they learned how to understand a language P
•(a)hǫgahaʼ be invited
[P+]
ęhsahǫgahaʼ you will be invited, asked to go P
•(a)hǫgaʼtaʼ hearing aid
[j+o+ -(a)hǫgaʼd$_V$- hear with s.t.]
jǫhǫgataʼ a hearing aid
•(a)hǫgaʼd a clear sound
[o+ contains: -(a)hǫg$_V$- hear, learn how to speak a language, understand]
ohǫ:gaʼt a clear sound
•(a)hǫhsiyohsd listen to s.o., obey
[TR+ad+ contains: -(a)hǫhd(a)$_N$- ear -iyohsd$_V$- make nice, good]
ęjihswadahǫhsi:yohs you all will listen again P
•(a)hǫtaʼ wedding present
[gaǫ+ contains: -(a)hǫdǫ(:)$_V$- ask]
gaǫhǫtaʼ a wedding present (lit.: they (f/m) are asking)
•(a)jęhǫhsgwaę(:) whisper
ęhsajęhǫhsgwaę:ʼ you will whisper P
sajęhǫhsgwaęʼ whisper I
•(a)hj(iʼda) hand
[present in:]
ęgahjǫhai: I am going to wash my hands P
[-(a)hj(iʼda)$_N$- hand -ohae$_V$- wash]
desahjʼidoha:k pinch it; squeeze it I
[de+... -(a)hj(iʼda)$_N$- hand -ohag$_V$- squeeze]
•(a)hjiʼdohag pinch
[de+... -(a)hj(iʼda)$_N$- hand -ohag$_V$- squeeze]
desahjʼidoha:k pinch it; squeeze it I
•(a)hjiʼgr(a) cloud
[o+]
ohjiʼgraʼ a cloud
•(a)hjiʼgreʼ cloudy
[o+ -(a)hjiʼgr(a)$_N$- cloud -e$_V$- go]
ohjiʼgreʼ it is cloudy S
•(a)hjiyo(:) scratch, dig in one's nails
[de+]
degahji:yohs, degahjiyohaʼ I am scratching H
dęwaga̱hji:yo:ʼ it will scratch me (for example, a twig or thorn) P
dewagahji:yoʼ I am digging in my nails; I am scratching S
desahji:yo: scratch I
•(a)hjiyohsrǫ(:) scratch forcefully
[de+... -(a)hjiyo(:)$_V$- scratch -srǫ(:) really]
desahjiyohsrǫ: scratch really hard I
•aju exclamation; said when you touch something cold or hot
see: Appendix I
•a:kʼah be near
[i+wa+]
iwa:kʼah it is near S
•a:kʼah be short
[ni/de+A/P+N+]
dehanętsa:kʼah his arm is short S
[de+... -nęts(a)$_N$- arm -a:kʼah$_V$- be short]

Legend: H habitual, P punctual, S stative, I imperative, PURP purposive, PURP-H purposive habitual, PURP-PAST purposive past, PURP-P purposive punctual, PURP-I purposive imperative; see §8.6, §8.11 in Appendix J. Alphabetization in stems ignores length (:), and any h's or glottal stops (ʼ) that are not between vowels. See §2.2 of the User Guide for explanation.

•a(k)d(a) heel
see: (r)a(k)d(a) heel
ga:dageh a heel
•(a)kdagyeʼ edge, beside s.t.
[-(a)kdagyeʼ$_{V}$- edge]
akda:gyeʼ the edge; beside s.t.
•(a)ʼkdǫ, (a)ʼged bend (forwards)
see: shaʼged, shaʼkdǫ [de+...at+] bend (forwards)
dęwatsaʼge:t it will bend P
•(a)ʼkdǫnyǫgwęh be winding, twisted
[de+yo+at+N+ contains: -(h)ah(a)$_{N}$- road -(a)ʼkdǫ$_{V}$- be bent, crooked -ǫnyǫ- plural -gw- reversive]
deyotahaʼkdǫnyǫgwęh winding roads S
•(a)ʼkdǫnyǫgw, (a)ʼkdǫnyǫgo fold s.t. up
see: shaʼkdǫnyǫgw, shaʼkdǫnyǫgo [de+...] fold s.t. up
dęsehsaʼkda:nyǫ:goʼ you will fold s.t. up P
•(ʼ)aksǫ:ʼ machine gun
[ę+gae+ -iʼaʼg$_{V}$- shoot -sǫʼ plural]
ęgaeʼa:ksǫ:ʼ a machine gun (lit.: it shoots repetitively)
•(a)kyadǫ(:) have a reading; have one's fortune told
see: (h)yadǫ(:) [ak+] have a reading
ęgakyadǫ:ʼ I will have a reading; I will have my fortune told P
•(a)kyohsgwi(n) crawl
see: (h)yohsgwi(n) [de+...ak+] crawl
desahkyohsgwi: crawl I
•(a)nahaotr(a) hat
anahaotraʼ a hat
•anawęʼdoh sweeten s.t.
see: (r)anawęʼdoh sweeten s.t.
ęhsranawęʼdoh you will sweeten s.t. P
•(a)nhęhęʼ urine
[o+]
ǫnhęhęʼ urine
•anoʼsgwita:ʼ broom
see: onoʼsgwita:ʼ broom
deyaganoʼsgwita:ʼ a broom
•(a)hnyo(:) fish
[ad+ -(a)hny(a)$_{N}$- hook -o(:)$_{V}$- submerge]
gaǫdahnyoh they (f/m) are fishing H
ahęnadahnyo:ʼ they (m) fished P
•ao ceremonial friend
[P+ad+]
ǫgya:dao:ʼ my ceremonial friend; Friend (term of address)
agaǫ:daoʼtsę:ʼ they (f/m) became ceremonial friends P
•(a)oʼtr(a) friendship
[ad+]
adaoʼtraʼ friendship; also refers to a ceremonial friend
•aʼǫ remainder, residue
[heʼ+yo+adad+ -aʼ$_{N}$- -ǫ$_{V}$- a number (of things)]
heyodadaǫ: a remainder; a residue
•aǫ, ęǫ race
[de+...]
degęnaǫ:haʼ they (z) are racers H
atę:nęǫʼ they (m) raced P
dehonaǫhǫgyeʼ they (m) are racing along S
•aǫʼdad blow
gaǫʼda:s I blow H
hęhsaǫʼda:t you will blow P
agaǫʼda:dǫh I am blowing now; I have blown S
•(a)ǫhaʼ racer
[de+A+ -aǫ, ęǫ$_{V}$- race]
degęnaǫ:haʼ they (z) are racers
•aǫ:hę:ʼęh the most
see: Appendix I
•aʼs be a certain size
[shęh ni+w(a)+]
shęh ni:waʼs sizes; how big they are (lit. how big it is) S

•a'ʼs be the same size
[tsaʼde+w(a)+]
tsaʼde:waʼs they are (lit. it is) the same size S

•(a)hsa:ʼ beginning
[g+yo+ -(a)hsawę, (a)hsa:$_V$- begin, start]
gyǫhsa:ʼ the beginning of s.t.

•(a)hsaʼg cough
gahsaʼkaʼ I have a cough; I am coughing H
ęsahsaʼk you will cough P
agahsʼagǫh I am coughing right now S

•(a)hsahǫh dyed, coloured
[wa+]
wahsahǫh, wahsohǫh it is dyed, coloured S

•(a)hsait pepper
[de+yo+ contains: -(ʼa)hsa(w)$_N$- chest, cough]
deyohsait pepper

•(a)hsaogweʼs high-top shoes
[de+yo+ -(a)hsi(ʼda), (ę)hs(a)$_N$- foot -ogw$_V$- scatter]
deyohsaogwe:s high-top shoes

•(ʼa)hsa(w) chest, cough
sʼahsaʼgeh on your chest

•(a)hsawʼe have asthma
[de+P+ -(ʼa)hsa(w)$_N$- chest, cough -(ʼ)e$_V$- hit]
toʼahsawʼehs he has asthma H

•(a)hsawę, (a)hsa: begin, start
[d+]
ędyagwahsa:węʼ we all (excl.) will begin, start P
tohsa:ʼ he has begun S
dehsahsawęh begin; start I

•(a)hsawę, (a)hsa: restart, resume
[de+d+…]
dedwahsawe:haʼ to restart H
dǫdahahsa:węʼ he restarted P
degyohsa:ʼ it has resumed S

•(a)hsdaędaʼ stop raining
[-(h)sd(a:)$_N$- drop of water -ędaʼ$_V$- stop]
agahsdaę:daʼ it stopped raining P

•(a)hsda:haʼ, (a)hsdaęʼ cry
ǫhsda:haʼ she is crying H
a:sahsdaę:ʼ you might cry P

•(a)hsda:haʼge: sob
[-(a)hsda:haʼ, (a)hsdaęʼ$_V$- cry -ge: big]
ǫhstahaʼge: s.o. is sobbing (lit.: s.o. is doing a big cry) H

•(a)hsdeʼ heavy
[o+(N+)]
ohsdeʼ it is heavy S
tsęh niyogǫtrahsdeʼ weight; pounds; poundage
[-tsęh that ni+ yo+ gǫtr(a)$_N$- weight -(a)hsdeʼ$_V$- be heavy]

•(a)hsdeʼ mass
[tsęh ni+yo+ -(a)hsdeʼ$_V$- heavy mass]
tsęh niyo:sdeʼ mass (lit.: how much it weighs; how heavy it is)

•(a)hsdeh outside
[-ahsdeh-$_N$ outside -gęha:ʼ type, kind]
ahsdehgęha:ʼ the outside type

•(a)hsdehsd evaporate, boil down
wahsdehstaʼ it is evaporating; it evaporates H
ęwa:stehs it will evaporate P
ohsdehsdǫh it has evaporated; it is all dried up S

•(a)hsdęh(a) chalk
[o+]
ohsdęhęʼgeh on the chalk

•(a)sdę:ʼęh old (living thing)
[P+]
gǫhsdę:ʼęh she is old S

•(a)hsdisd pay attention, bother with s.t.
dehsgahsdi:staʼ I no longer pay attention H
ęsa:sdi:s you will pay attention P
sahsdi:sdǫh you are paying attention (right now) S
sahsdi:s pay attention I

Legend: H habitual, P punctual, S stative, I imperative, PURP purposive, PURP-H purposive habitual, PURP-PAST purposive past, PURP-P purposive punctual, PURP-I purposive imperative; see §8.6, §8.11 in Appendix J. Alphabetization in stems ignores length (:), and any h's or glottal stops (ʼ) that are not between vowels. See §2.2 of the User Guide for explanation.

•(a)hsdisd neglect
[(tęʼ) deʼ+ not -(a)hsdisd$_{V}$- pay attention]
dehsgahsdi:staʼ I no longer pay attention H

•(a)ʼse:ʼ cousin
[TR+]
ǫgyaʼse:ʼ my cousin (lit. we two are cousins) S

•(a)ʼse:ʼ be double
[de+ga+ -y$_{N}$ - -(a)ʼse:ʼ$_{V}$- be double]
degayʼase:ʼ it is doubled S

•(a)se:ʼ be fresh, new
[A/P+(N+)]
a:se:ʼ it is fresh, new S
oʼwahase:ʼ fresh meat S
[-(ʼ)wah(a)$_{N}$- meat -(a)se:ʼ$_{V}$- new]

•(a)se:ʼ have s.t. new
[A/P+ad+N+]
satnatsotra:se:ʼ you have new pants S
[-(h)naʼtsotr(a)$_{N}$- pants -(a)se:ʼ$_{V}$- new]

•(a)hsehd hide s.t.
shagohse̱htaʼ he is a robber, stealer H
ęgahseht I will hide s.t. P
agahsehdǫh I am hiding s.t. S

•(a)hsehd hide oneself
[ad+]
gadahse̱htaʼ I hide H
ęgęnadahseht they (z) will hide P
agadahsehdǫh I am hiding now S

•(a)hsehd rob s.o.
[TR+ contains: -(a)hsehd$_{V}$- hide s.t.]
shagohse̱htaʼ he is a robber, stealer H
ahǫwanahseht they robbed him, them (m) P
ga̱hsehdǫh it is robbed, hidden S

•(a)hsehdǫh female genitals
[go+ contains: -(a)hsehd$_{V}$- hide s.t.]
go̱hsehdǫh a woman's genitals

•(a)hsehdǫhǫgyeʼs sneak around
[P+ad+ contains: -(a)hsehd$_{V}$- hide s.t. -ǫhǫgyeʼs progressive]
honadahsehdǫhǫgyeʼs they (m) are sneaking around S

•(a)seʼshǫ:ʼǫh vegetable
aseʼshǫ:ʼǫh vegetables

•(a)hsehtaʼ robber, stealer
[TR+ -(a)hsehd$_{V}$- hide s.t. rob]
shagohse̱htaʼ he is a robber, stealer

•(aʼs)ęʼ fall, drop, reduce
[d/g+...(a)ʼs/N+]
dwasęʼs it falls, it's a dropper H
dawaʼsęʼ it dropped, reduced P
gyosęʼǫh it has fallen off s.t. S
heyohnegęʼǫh falling water
[heʼ/g+yo+ stem: -(h)neg(a)$_{N}$- water, liquid -(aʼs)ęʼ$_{V}$- fall, drop, reduce]

•(aʼs)ęʼ fall in
[heʼ+...(a)ʼs/N+]
hewaʼsęʼs it falls in (all the time) H
hęwaʼsęʼ it will fall in P
heyoʼsę̱ʼǫh it has fallen in S

•(a)hsę: be fat
[P+(N+)]
agahsę: I am fat S

•(aʼ)sęhd hand down, bring down
[d+...]
ętsaʼsęht you will bring it down P
toʼsęhdǫh he has handed down S

•(aʼ)sęhd swoop
[d+...ad+]
dawadʼasęht it swooped down P

•(aʼ)sęhd put s.o. down, discriminate
[TR+ad+]
hadaʼsę̱htaʼ he puts people down; he discriminates H
sheyadʼasęhdǫh you have already put s.o. down; you discriminated against her S

•(a)hsęhd regret s.t.
[P+]
sa̱hsęhtahk you used to regret it H

•(a)hsęhsd regret s.t.
[P+]
ǫgahsęhs I regret it; I did regret it P

•(a)hsęhsde:ʼ be regretful
[o+]
osęhsde:ʼ it is regretful S

•(a)hsęnọh be half, be in the middle
[tsaʼde+A/P+]
tsaʼdeyohsę:nọʼ, tsaʼdewahsę:nọh half; the middle S

•(a)hsganaʼd enticing, attractive
[o+ contains: -(ahs)gan(eg)$_V$- want, desire, long for]
ohsga:naʼt it is enticing, alluring, attractive, tempting S

•(ahs)ganehd tempt s.o., s.t.
[TR+ contains: -(ahs)gan(eg)$_V$- want, desire, long for]
ęhsga:neht you will tempt P

•(ahs)ganehd be enticing, etc.
[o+]
osga:neht it is enticing, alluring, attractive, tempting S

•(ahs)ganeg want, desire, long for
[TR+]
ọhsga:ne:s she has longings for H
ęhsahsgane:k you will be tempted; you will long for s.t. P

•(a)hsganekd(ę,ani) tempt s.o.
[TR+ contains: -(ahs)gan(eg)$_V$- want, desire, long for]
ęhsheyahsganekdęʼ, ęhshehsgane:kdęʼ you will tempt s.o. P

•(a)hsgohọh bridge
[w+ -(a)hsg(wa)$_N$- roof, bridge -(adi)họh$_V$- lean against]
wahsgohọh a bridge

•(a)hsgọd porch
[o+ -(a)hsg(wa)$_N$- roof, bridge -ọd$_V$- attached]
ohsgọ:t a porch

•(a)hsgọgohtaʼ overpass
[de+wa+ad+ -(a)hsg(wa)$_N$- roof, bridge -ọgohd$_V$- surpass]
dewadahsgọgohtaʼ an overpass

•(a)hsg(wa) roof
ahsgwaʼ a roof

•(a)hsgwadeʼ ceiling
[o+ad+ -(a)hsg(wa)$_N$- roof, bridge -deʼ$_V$- exist]
odahsgwa:deʼ a ceiling

•(a)hsgwagọ: porch
[o+ -(a)hsg(wa)$_N$- roof -gọ: in]
ohsgwa:gọ: in the porch

•(ah)sgyaọ(:) walk fast, encourage s.o.
hahsgyaọhaʼ he walks quickly; he gives s.o. encouragement H
ęhsahsgyaọ:ʼ you will walk fast; you will encourage s.o. P
hohsgyaọhọ:gyeʼ he is going along walking quickly S

•(a)hsgyaọnyọ:ʼ encouragement
[ga+ -(ah)sgyaọ$_V$- walk fast, encourage -ọnyọ- plural]
gahsgyaọ:nyọ:ʼ words of encouragement

•(a)hs(h)a(:) remember, recall
[(heʼ+)(s/j+)...]
hęjihsasha:ʼ you will remember back in time P
shohshaʼdrọh he is remembering (right now) S

•(a)hs(h)a(:) think of s.o.
[TR+]
i:hs agọyahsha:ʼ I thought of you P

•(a)hshaʼdrọnyọ(:) remember, reminisce
[(heʼ+) (s/j+) P+]
agahshaʼdrọ:nyọh I am reminiscing, remembering S

•(a)hsha:gwahd rememberance
[o+ -(a)hs(h)a(:)$_V$- remember, recall]
ohsha:gwaht a rememberance

•(a)hsha:gw(ę,ani) make oneself remember
ętsadadahsha:gwęʼ you will remind yourself, make yourself remember P
ohsha:gwani: a rememberance; to remember S

•(a)hshed count
hę̨nahshe:dahs they (m) count things H
ę̨dwahshe:t we all (incl.) will count P
tsaʼdeyohshe:dę̨h it is the same number of things S
jidwahshe:t let us all (incl.) count again I

•(a)hshed be the same number of things
[tsaʼde+yo+]
tsaʼdeyo̱hshe:dę̨h it is the same number of things S

•(a)hshed(a) number
[o+]
ohshe:daʼ a number

•(a)hshę: be slow-moving
[P+(N+)]
agahshę: I am slow to act S
ohn·yáhs·hę: a slow beat
[o+ stem: -(h)ny(a)$_N$- stick -(a)hshę:$_V$- be slow-moving]

•(a)hshę̨daʼ step on s.t.
[he+ -(a)hsi(ʼda), (ę̨)hs(a)$_N$- foot -(hr)ę̨daʼ$_V$- come to lead]
ę̨hsahshę̨:daʼ you will step on s.t. P

•(a)hshę̨daʼ stagger
[he+ -(a)hsi(ʼda), (ę̨)hs(a)$_N$- foot -(hr)ę̨daʼ$_V$- come to lead (tsǫ: just)]
hehshohshę̨daʼǫh tsǫ: he is staggering S

•(a)hshę̨htw cry
[de+]
degahsę̨htwahs I am crying H
dę̨gahsę̨htoʼ I will cry P
o:nę̨h ni: dewagahshę̨htwę̨h I've already cried S

•(a)hsi(ʼda), (ę̨)hs(a) foot
ohsiʼdaʼ feet
sa̱hsiʼdʼageh on your foot

•(a)hsiʼdaga: stamp one's feet
[de+... -(a)hsi(ʼda), (ę̨)hs(a)$_N$- foot -ga:$_V$- make a rattling or grinding noise]
deyohsida:ga: to stamp one's feet (lit.: it stamped its feet) S

•(a)hsiʼgyaʼg trip, stumble, stub one's toe
[(de+)... -(a)hsi(ʼda), (ę̨)hs(a)$_N$- foot -(i)yaʼg$_V$- cut, break (-sgǫ: easily)]
desahsʼigyaʼksgǫ: you are always stumbling, tripping, stubbing your toe; you are a klutz H
ę̨dihsa̱hsiʼgyaʼk you will stumble, stub your toe P

•(a)hsihaʼs choke
[de+P+]
dewage̱hsihaʼs I choke all the time H
adwaga̱hsiha:ʼs I choked P
atohsi̱ha:ʼs he choked P

•(a)hsnę̨hd descend, get down
ǫhsnę̨htaʼgeh a thing to descend by; stairs; a ladder H
ę̨sahsnę̨ht you will get down off of s.t. P
sahsnę̨hdo̱hǫgyeʼ you are getting down from there right now S
sahsnę̨ht get down from there I

•(a)hsogw fade
[ad+ -(a)hsoh(gwa)$_N$- colour, paint, crayon -ogw$_V$- scatter]
ę̨wada̱hso:goʼ it loses its colour (for example, old paint) P
odahsogwę̨h it is faded S

•(a)hsohǫd be coloured, dyed
[wa+ -(a)hsoh(gwa)$_N$- colour, paint, crayon -ǫd$_V$- attached]
wa̱hsohǫ:t it is dyed S

•(a)hsohtaʼ colour, paint, crayon
[ǫ+ -(a)hsohd$_V$- colour s.t.]
ǫhsohtaʼ colour; paints; crayons

•ahsǫh still, yet, some more; More (Said when you want someone to pour a drink.)
see: Appendix I

•(a)hsǫ(da) night, blackness
[o+ad+ -(a)hsǫd(a)$_N$- night, blackness -hę̨h$_V$- be in the middle of]
ahsǫheh night

•(a)hsǫ(da) night, blackness (continued)
ęhsahsǫdǫ:ni' you will mark the night (that is, set a time) P
[-(a)hsǫd(a)$_N$- night, blackness -ǫni, ǫny$_V$- make]

•(a)hsǫda:' shadow
[o+ad+ -(a)hsǫd(a)$_N$- night, blackness -a:'$_V$- hold, contain, include]
odahsǫ:da:' shadow

•(a)hsǫdǫni mark the night, set a time
[-(a)hsǫd(a)$_N$- night, blackness -ǫni, ǫny$_V$- make]
ęhsahsǫdǫ:ni' you will mark the night (that is, set a time) P
wa̱hsǫdǫ:ni: the night is marked (that is, a time has been designated) S

•(a)hsǫdragw unjoin, come apart, be disjointed
[de+...ad+ contains: -(a)hsǫdr$_V$- join together -gw- reversive, undo]
dewadahsǫdra:gwahs they come apart (lit.: it comes apart) H
dęgęnadahsǫdra:go' they (z) will be unjoined (for example, a train, a chain); they will come apart P
deyoda̱hsǫdragwęh it is disjointed S

•(a)hsǫdr(ę,e:) join together
[de+...]
desahsǫdre:ha' you join things together all the time; you do puzzles H
dęhsahsǫdrę' you will join two things together P
deyoda̱hsǫ:dre:' it is joined S
desahsǫdręh join it I

•(a)hsǫdr(ę,e:) resume, add on
[he+d+...]
hętsahsǫdrę' you will resume, add on P

•(a)hsǫwadenye's be dizzy
[P+ -(a)hsǫw(a)$_N$- -deni, deny$_V$- change]
agahsǫwade:nye's, agatsǫwadenye's I am dizzy H

•(a)hsrǫhę('da) anger, temper
[o+]
ohsrǫhę'da' an angry person; temper

•(a)hstwa(h,') shrink
wahstwahs it shrinks H
ęwahstwa' it will shrink (for example, wool) P
ohstwa'ǫh it has shrunk S

•(a)hstwahd shrink s.t.
wahstwahta' it shrinks (for example, wool) H
awahstwaht it shrank P

•(a)hswahd extinguish, dim s.t.
hęnahswa̱hta' they (m) are firemen H
sahswaht put the light out I

•(a)hstwahd extinguish, dim
[N+ -(a)hstwahd$_V$- extinguish, dim s.t.]
ęhsi'dǫhgwahstwaht you will dim the lights P
[P+ -i'dǫg(wa)$_N$- flame -(a)hstwahd$_V$- change]
gędǫ'gwa̱hstwahdǫh the flame is turned down S

•(a)hstwa:s'ah tadpole, young animal
[o+ -(a)hstwa(h,')$_V$- shrink -'ah little]
ohstwa:s'ah a young animal; a little animal; a tadpole

•(a)hswahta' firemen
[A+ -(a)hswahd$_V$- extinguish, dim]
hęnahswa̱hta' they (m) are firemen

•(a)hswatgęhs black sucker
[o+ -(a)hswahd$_V$- extinguish, dim -gę-]
ohswa:tgęhs black sucker (fish)

•(a)'sweg be deaf
[de+A+]
deyǫ'swe:gǫh she is deaf S

•(a)'sweg go deaf
[de+...]
dega'swe:s I am getting deaf H
dęga'swe:k I will be deaf P

•(a)ta:' conceited, snobbish
[A+ad+ -(a)d$_V$- be contained; be in s.t. -ha:$_V$- hold]
hada:ta:' he is conceited H

Legend: H habitual, P punctual, S stative, I imperative, PURP purposive, PURP-H purposive habitual, PURP-PAST purposive past, PURP-P purposive punctual, PURP-I purposive imperative; see §8.6, §8.11 in Appendix J. Alphabetization in stems ignores length (:), and any h's or glottal stops (') that are not between vowels. See §2.2 of the User Guide for explanation.

•(a)ta:dad rise up
see: (h)a(:)dad [at+] rise up
ęwata:da:t it will rise up P
•(a)tahagw stray, turn off
see: (h)ahagw [at+] stray, turn off
agęnataha:goʼ they (z) turned off the road P
•(a)tahahgw walk
see: (h)ahahgw [de+...at+] walk
dęgatahahk I will walk P
•(a)tahahgwaʼdę corrupt s.o.
see: (h)ahahgwaʼdę [TR+at+] corrupt s.o.
ęhsheyatahagwaʼdęʼ you will corrupt her/them; (lit.: you will take her off the path) (high language)P
•(a)tahineʼ walk
see: (h)ahineʼ [A+at+] walk
gatahineʼ I am walking PURP
•(a)tahitʼa:ʼ take the heavenly road, come to a concensus
see: (h)ahitʼa:ʼ [at+] take the heavenly road, come to a concensus
ahęnatahiʼta:ʼ they (m) came to a consensus; they followed their idea; now they are ready to go (referring to the Confederacy Council) P
•(a)tahsrǫd night-fish, spear-fish, jack-lighting
see: (h)ahsrǫd [at+] night-fish, spear-fish, jack-lighting
ahęnatahsrǫ:dęʼ they (m) carried a torch, lantern, flashlight P
•(a)teʼ be bright, clear
[de+yo+]
deyohateʼ it is bright (for example, sunlight) S
•(a)teʼd brighten up
[de+d+P+]
dętohateʼdǫhǫk he will brighten from over there S
•(a)tehgyaʼg erode
see: (h)ehgyaʼg [at+] erode
ęwahtehgyaʼk it will erode P
•(a)tetgęhd become moody
see: (hr)etgęhd [ad+] become moody
aʼǫtehtgęht s.o. turned funny, moody, etc. P
•(a)tehtgędǫni: be in a funny, odd mood
see: (hr)etgędǫni [P+ad+] be in a funny, odd mood
hotehtgędǫ:ni: he is in a funny or odd mood; he is moody S
•atę climb
see: (r)atę climb
ęhsra:tęʼ you will climb P
•(a)tędǫni tend (a garden)
see: (h)ędǫni [at+] tend (a garden)
ęhsatędǫ:niʼ you will make your garden P
•(a)tga:dahgw hollow out
see: ga:dahgw [at+] hollow out
ęhsatga:da̱hgoʼ you will hollow out a canoe, a wooden bowl, etc. (lit.: take out the chips) P
•(a)tgaʼdeʼ be so many
see: gaʼdeʼ [ni+...ad+] so many
niyonatgaʼdeʼ there are so many S
•(a)tgaʼdeʼ often, many, lots
see: gaʼdeʼ [o+at+] often, many, lots
otgadeʼ often; many; lots S
•(a)tgahdǫnyǫ look around
see: gahdǫnyǫ [de+...at+] look around
desatga̱hdǫ:nyǫhs you are looking around H
•(a)tgahdrǫni examine closely
see: gahdrǫni [at+] examine closely
sagahdrǫni: you are 'nosy' with your eyes; always looking; gape; stare S
•(a)tgaęhęgw double back, re
see: gaęhęgw [s+...at+] double back, return
ǫsagatgaę:hę:goʼ I should turn around and go back the way I came P

•(a)tgahgweg close one's eyes, outsmart
see: gahgweg [de+...at+] close one's eyes, outsmart
dęsatgahgwe:k you will close your eyes P

•(a)tgahadeni turn around
see: gahadeni [de+...at+] turn around
dęhsatgaha:de:ni' you will turn yourself around P

•(a)tgahadenyǫgwahǫ: twirl
see: gahadenyǫgwahǫ: [de+...at+] twirl
desatgahadenyǫgwahǫ: twirl I

•(a)tahadǫh roll
see: gahadǫh [at+] roll
watgahadǫhs it rolls H

•(a)tgahatgihd give s.o. dirty looks
see: gahatgihd [at+] give s.o. dirty looks
asatgahatgiht you give dirty looks P

•(a)tgahatw roll over
see: gahato [at+] roll
satgahatoh roll over I

•(a)tgahawęnye(:) have blurred vision
see: gahawęnye(:) [de+...at+] blurred vision
atgatgahawęnye:' I had blurred vision P

•(a)tgahi'd play with s.t.
see: gahi'd [at+] play with s.t.
ǫtgahi'ta' what she plays with; a toy H

•(a)tgahiyohsd look at closely, stare, peer
see: gahiyohsd [at+] look at closely, stare, peer
ęsatgahiyohs you will look closely at s.t., peer at s.t. P

•(a)tgah(:,ǫ) pay attention, watch
[P+(N+)]
satgahǫha' you are paying attention, watching right now H
ęhsatgahǫ:' you will pay attention, keep a close eye on s.t. P
satgahǫ: pay attention I

•(a)tgahǫdi roll one's eyes, snub s.o.
see: gahǫdi [at+] roll one's eyes, snub s.o.
ęhsatgahǫ:di' you will roll your eyes (in disgust); you will snub s.o. P

•(a)tgahǫnyǫ
see: gahǫnyǫ' [P+at+] flirt, bat one's eyes
ęhsatgahǫ:nyǫ' you will flirt, bat your eyes P

•(a)tga:nǫni be rich, wealthy, precious
see: ga:nǫni [at+] be rich, wealthy, precious
otga:nǫ:nih it is rich H

•(a)tgany be desperate
see: gany [de+...at+] be desperate
dehotganyęh he is really desperate S

•(a)tganya'gę be reimbursed, refunded
see: ganya'gę' [s/j+...at+] be reimbursed, refunded
ęjisatgany'agę' you will be reimbursed, refunded P

•(a)tgahnye play
see: gahnye [P+ at+] play
hotgahnye' he is playing S

•(a)tgahtw look
see: gahtw [at+] look
hętsahtgahto' you will look back P

•(a)htga(w) release, let go
sahtga's you forfeit, you let go of things all the time H
awahtga' it let go P
disatga'węhęgye' you are going along giving things up S

•(a)htga(w) replace
[de+d+...]
dedwatgawęh to replace (lit.: it has been re-given) S

•(a)tgehd have around one's neck
see: gehd [at+(N+)] have around one's neck
satgehdǫh you have it around your neck S

Legend: H habitual, P punctual, S stative, I imperative, PURP purposive, PURP-H purposive habitual, PURP-PAST purposive past, PURP-P purposive punctual, PURP-I purposive imperative; see §8.6, §8.11 in Appendix J. Alphabetization in stems ignores length (:), and any h's or glottal stops (') that are not between vowels. See §2.2 of the User Guide for explanation.

•(a)tged scratch oneself
see: ged [at+/N+] scratch oneself
ęhsa:tge:t you will scratch yourself P
sahna'tsage:dahs you are scratching your behind
[ad+(N+) stem: -(h)na'ts(a)$_N$- buttock -ged$_V$- grate, scrape, file; scratch s.t.]

•(a)tgehdad put around one's neck
see: gehdad [at+] put around one's neck
ęhsatge̱hda:t you will put s.t. around your neck P

•(a)tgehǫ sell
[(ade+N+)]
hatgehǫha' he is an auctioneer (lit.: he is a seller) H
ęhsatgehǫ' you will sell P
honatge̱hǫ' they (m) are selling s.t. S
honadeshedatgehǫ' they (m) are selling tickets
[(ade+N+) stem: -sheda(da)$_N$- ticket -(a)tgehǫ$_V$- sell]

•(a)tgehǫ' sales
[w+ -(a)tgehǫ$_V$- sell]
watgehǫ' sales

•(a)datgehǫha' be a prostitute
[wa+adad+ -(a)tgehǫ$_V$- sell]
wadatgehǫha' she (lit.: it) is a prostitute

•(a)tgeh get up, awaken
see: gęh [at+] get up, awaken
aga:tgęh I got up P

•(a)tge'i:' have tangled hair
see: ge'i:' [de+P+at+] tangled hair
dewagatge'i:' my hair is tangled S

•(a)tge'ogw have rumpled hair
see: ge'ogw [de+P+at+] have rumpled hair
desatge'o:gwęh you have rumpled hair, ruffled hair S

•(a)tgęhǫh be up
see: gęhǫh [at+] be up
agatgęhǫh I am up now S

•(a)tgęihsd be portable
see: gęihsd [at+] be portable
watgęihsta' it is portable H

•(a)tgęihsdǫhǫgye' travel
see: gęihsdǫhǫgye' [ni+P+at+] travel
niyagotgęihsdǫhǫgye' she is travelling as she is moving S

•(a)tgęhjih(s)d age, grow old
see: gęhjih(s)d [at+] age, grow old
hatgęji̱hta' he is getting old H
otgęhjihsdǫhǫgye' it is getting old, aging S

•(a)tgęni, (a)tgęny compete
see: gęni, gęny [de+...ad/N+] compete
de̱honatgę:nyǫ: they (m) compete S

•(a)tgęnihs'a: meet
see: gęnihs' [at+] meet
ęhswatgenihs'a:' you all will have a meeting P

•(a)tgę'se watch s.o.
see: gę'se [TR+at+] watch s.o.
gaǫtg'ęseh they (f/m) are watching s.t. going on H

•(a)tgo'jonyahnǫ(:) make oneself up
see: go'jonyahnǫ: [at+] make oneself up
satgo'jonyahnǫ: beautify yourself; apply make-up I

•(a)tgowanahdę, (a)tgowanęhdę rape, molest s.o.
see: gowanahdę, gowanęhdę [TR+at+] rape, molest s.o.
ahshagotgowanahdę', ahshagotgowanęhdę' he raped her (lit.: he forced her in a big way) P

•(a)tgǫ' have evil power, have bad medicine; be a witch, warlock; be ominous
[P+]
gotgǫ' she is a witch S

•(a)tgǫd always
see: gǫd [g+yo+at+] always
gyo'tgǫ:t always S

•(a)tgǫnyǫ be clean, be discriminating, have high standards
see: gǫnyǫ [P+at+] be clean, be discriminating, have high standards
gotgǫ:nyohs she has high standards H
•(a)tgǫnyǫ be important
see: gǫnyǫ [P+at+] be important
otnakdagǫ:nyǫhs an important or prestigious seat, place H
•(a)tgǫhsagri smirk
see: gǫhsagri [de+...at+] smirk
desatgǫhsa:gri: wrinkle up your face; smirk I
•(a)tgǫhsǫhae clean, wash s.t.
see: ohae [(ad+)n/N+] clean, wash
agatgǫhsǫhai: I did wash my face P
o·dę́·nǫ·ha·i:ʼ it is washed, clean S
•(a)tgǫhstǫʼęhd shave
see: gǫhstǫʼęhd [at+] shave
ahatgǫhstǫʼęht he shaved P
•(a)tgǫʼtra: bewitch s.o.
[TR+ -(a)tgǫʼtr(a)$_N$- ominous medicine -a:ʼ$_V$- hold, contain, include]
ęgǫyatgǫʼtra:ʼ I will bewitch you P
•(a)tgǫʼtraniyǫd weigh
see: gǫʼtraniyǫd [at+] weigh
agaǫ:tgǫʼtrani:yǫ:dęʼ they (f/m) weighed themselves P
•(a)tgǫʼtra:sd bewitch s.o.
[TR+ -(a)tgǫʼtr(a)$_N$- ominous medicine -a:hsd$_V$- cause to include]
ęgǫyatgǫʼtra:s I will bewitch you P
•(a)tgǫwaʼdǫni tan s.t.
see: gǫwaʼdǫni [at+] tan
ęsatgǫwaʼdǫ:niʼ you will tan a hide P
[at+ -gǫwa(ʼda)$_N$- hide -ǫni, ǫny$_V$- make]
•(a)tgręgręhd frown, sneer
see: gręgręhd [de+...at+] frown, sneer
agyǫtgręgręht she frowned P
•(a)tgręgręhdǫh be dreary, overcast
see: gręgręhdǫh [de+yo+at+] be dreary, overcast
deyotgręgręhdǫh the sky is dreary, grey S
•(a)tgri flinch, shrink, pull back
see: gri [(d+)...at+] flinch
dawa:tgri:k it pulled back, flinched, shrank
•(a)tgrihsrǫ(:) several wrinkled items
see: grihsrǫʼ [P+at+] several wrinkled items
otgrihsrǫʼ wrinkled clothes; it is wrinkled up S
•(a)tgw dance
see: gw [de+at+] dance
dęhęna:t they (m) will dance P
•(a)tgwadǫ weave, zig-zag
see: gwadǫ [at+] weave, zig-zag
hatgwa:dǫh he is zig-zagging H
•(a)tgweni, (a)tgweny do to best of one's ability
see: gweni, gweny [naʼ+A+at+] do to the best of one's ability
naʼga:tgwe:niʼ the best I could do P
•(a)tgwęnige: win a competition
see: gwęnige: [TR+/...at+] win a competition
ahęnatgwęnige: the big win; the victory P
•(a)tgwiʼaʼe wink
see: gwiʼaʼe [de+...at+] wink
desatgwiʼaʼe:k wink I
•(a)tiyaʼg hold a grudge; get mad, disgusted
see: (h)i(ʼ)yaʼg [at+] hold a grudge; get mad, disgusted
ęhsa:ti:yaʼk you will hold a grudge P
•(a)tnadaę inhabit
see: nadaę [at+] inhabit
ęsatnadaęʼ you will inhabit a town P
•atnaʼgwi̱hdraʼ ǫdoda:taʼ suspenders
atnaʼgwi̱hdraʼ a belt
ǫdoda:taʼ s.o. drapes it

Legend: H habitual, P punctual, S stative, I imperative, PURP purposive, PURP-H purposive habitual, PURP-PAST purposive past, PURP-P purposive punctual, PURP-I purposive imperative; see §8.6, §8.11 in Appendix J. Alphabetization in stems ignores length (:), and any h's or glottal stops (ʼ) that are not between vowels. See §2.2 of the User Guide for explanation.

•(a)tnakdiyohsd make oneself comfortable
see: nakdiyohsd [(at+)] make oneself comfortable
agatnakdi:yohs I made myself comfortable P

•(a)tnahsgǫni tame
see: nahsgǫni [at+] tame
ahatna̱hsgǫni' he raised a pet P

•(a)tnahsgǫni tease s.o.,s.t.
see: ǫni, ǫny [d+A+at+(N+)] tease s.o., s.t.
tęnatna̱hsgǫ:nih they (m) are teasing the animal(s) H

•(a)tnahsgǫni make oneself comfortable
see: nahsgǫni [at+] make oneself comfortable
ęsatna̱hsgǫ:ni' you will get comfortable in bed P

•(a)tnasǫ(:) oil oneself
see: (h)nasǫ(:) [at+] oil oneself
ahatnasǫ' he oiled himself P

•(a)tna'tsagęnye' be fidgety
see: (h)na'tsagęnye' [P+at+] be fidgety
satna'tsagę:nye' you are fidgety H

•(a)tna'tsędǫ shake one's behind
see: (h)na'tsędǫ [de+...at+] shake one's behind
dęhsatna'tsę:dǫh you will shake your behind P

•(a)tnegad drunk, tipsy
see: (h)negad [de'+P+at+] drunk, tipsy
dihsa:tne:ga:t you are not level; you are tipsy S

•(a)tnegǫni ferment, brew s.t.
ęhsatnegǫ:ni' you will ferment s.t. P

•(a)tnehsogwahd spread out
see: nehsogwahd [de+at+] spread out
dewatnęhsogwa̱hta' a sander H

•(a)tnęhsędǫh shrug
see: (h)nęhsędǫh [de+...at+] shrug
atatnęhsę:dǫh he shrugged P

•(a)tnętsadahgw dislocate one's shoulder
see: nętsadahgw [at+] dislocate
asatnętsadahgo' your arm came out of its socket p

•(a)tnętsiya'g break one's arm in two
see: nętsiya'g [de+...ad+N+] break one's arm in two
dęgatnętsi:ya'k I will break my arm p

•(a)tnigǫhahdo:gęh be immature
see: (')nigǫhahdogęh [de'+ not P+at+] be immature
desatnigǫhahdo:gęh you are immature in mind S

•(a)tno: pollution
see: (h)no: [at+] pollution
ęwa:tno:' there will be pollution P

•(a)tnǫ'aędǫh nod one's head, shake one's head
see: nǫ'aędǫh [de+...at+] nod one's head, shake one's head
desatnǫ'aędǫh nod; shake your head I

•(a)tnǫhda(:,h) get into a vehicle, embark
see: (')nǫhda(:,h) [at+] get into a vehicle, embark
ęgatnǫhda:' I will embark, get in s.t. P

•(a)tnǫhdahgw disembark
see: nǫhdahgw [at+] disembark
ęgatnǫhdahgo' I will disembark, get out of a vehicle P

•(a)tnǫhahe:' have a wig on
see: nǫhahe:' [P+...at+] have a wig on
otnǫhahe:' it has a wig on S

•(a)tnǫhga(:,ǫ) cut hair
see: nǫhga(:,ǫ) [at+] cut hair
ęgatnǫhga:' I am going to cut my hair P

•(a)tnǫhwetso'd(ǫ) do a handstand, turn oneself upside down
see: nǫhwetso'd(ǫ) [de+...at+] do a handstand, turn oneself upside down
dęsatnǫhwe:tso'dǫ' you (s) will do a hand stand, turn yourself upside down P

•(a)tohgwaǫnyǫ(:) hill (plants)
[-(a)tohg(wa)$_N$- bundle -ǫnyǫ(:)$_V$- make several things]
ęhęnatohgwaǫnyǫʼ they (m) will make planting hills P
watohgwaǫnyǫʼ planting hills that have already been made S

•(a)towahsd cold
see: (h)owahsd [P+at+] cold
agatowahstaʼ I am cold H

•(a)toweʼ cold (weather)
[o+]
oto:weʼ it is cold S

•(a)towinyǫʼse: have a cold
see: (h)owinyǫʼse: [P+at+] have a cold
gotowinyǫʼse: she has a cold S

•(a)tǫ(:) lie down
see: (h)ǫ(:) [at+] lie down
agęna:tǫ:ʼ they (z) laid themselves down P

•(a)tǫdaʼd listen to s.o., s.t., be obedient, consent
[contains: -(a)tǫdę(h,ʼ), (a)tǫdeʼ$_V$- hear]
ǫtǫ:da:s she is obedient H
ęgatǫ:da:t I will consent P

•(a)tǫdaʼd be disobedient
[(tęʼ) deʼ not A+ -(a)tǫdę(h,ʼ), (a)tǫdeʼ$_V$- hear]
desa:tǫ:da:s you are disobedient

•(a)tǫdahsrǫni prune
see: (h)ǫdahsrǫni [at+] prune
ahęnatǫdahsro:niʼ they (m) pruned (lit.: fixed) the trees P

•(a)tǫdeʼ hear
[P+]
hotǫ:deʼ he hears S

•(a)tǫdę(h,ʼ) hear s.t.
[P+]
aga:tǫ:dęhs I hear it all the time (continually or off-and-on; for example, the sound of a regular train going by one's house) H
ǫga:tǫ:dęh I heard it P
agatǫdęʼǫh I have heard it before S

•(a)tǫdęʼǫ:ʼ hearing
[a+ contains: -(a)tǫdę(h,ʼ), (a)tǫdeʼ$_V$- hear]
atǫdęʼǫ:ʼ the act of hearing

•(a)tǫgai stiffen
see: (h)ǫgai [at+] stiffen
awatǫgai: it did stiffen up P

•(a)tǫgai, (a)tǫgany suffer
see: (h)ǫgai, (h)ǫgany [de+P+adę+] suffer
dęhsadęhǫgaiʼ you will suffer P

•(a)tǫwanędag dock a boat
see: (h)ǫwanędag [at+] dock a boat
ahęnatǫwanę:da:k they (m) docked a boat P

•(a)tǫwis be a woman; sing seed songs
gatǫ:wi:sahs I sing seed songs; I am a woman H
ęga:tǫ:wi:s I will sing seed songs P
agatǫwi:sęh I am singing seed songs S

•(a)tǫyo(:) travel by boat
see: (h)ǫyo(:) [de+...at+] travel by boat
ętgaǫ:tǫ:yo:ʼ they (f/m) will come by boat P

•(a)trehnǫni pack
see: (h)rehnǫni [at+] pack
satrehnǫ:nih pack I

•(a)trewahd punish
see: (hr)ewahd [TR/...at+] punish
satrewahdǫh you have been punished S

•(a)trihsd come together, gather around
see: (hr)ihsd [at+] come together, gather around
ędihswatrihs you all will come closer, gather around P

•(a)trowi, (a)trǫny tell
see: (hr)owi, (hr)ǫny [TR/...at+] tell
ędwa:tro:wiʼ we all (incl.) will tell P

Legend: H habitual, P punctual, S stative, I imperative, PURP purposive, PURP-H purposive habitual, PURP-PAST purposive past, PURP-P purposive punctual, PURP-I purposive imperative; see §8.6, §8.11 in Appendix J. Alphabetization in stems ignores length (:), and any h's or glottal stops (ʼ) that are not between vowels. See §2.2 of the User Guide for explanation.

•(a)trǫhgw(ę,ani) threaten s.o.
see: (r)ǫhgw(ę,ani) [TR+(ad+)] threaten s.o.
sheyadro̱hgwa:nih you are threatening, scaring s.o. H

•(a)trǫni, (a)trǫny dress
satrǫ:nih get dressed I

•(a)trǫniʼd(a) clothes
atrǫniʼdaʼ clothes

•(a)trǫnyaʼd wear s.t.
[-(a)trǫni, (a)trǫny$_V$- dress]
ęsatrǫnyaʼt you will wear s.t. P

•(a)trǫnyahsi undress
[at+ contains: -(a)trǫni, (a)trǫny$_V$- dress -hsi- undo]
ęsatrǫnyahsiʼ you will take your clothes off P
agatrǫnyahsi̱hǫh I finished undressing; I got fully undressed S

•(a)trǫnyahsih get fully undressed
[at+ contains: -(a)trǫni, (a)trǫny$_V$- dress -hsi- undo -h cause]
agatrǫnyahsi̱hǫh I finished undressing; I got fully undressed S

•(a)tsʼ quarrel, argue
[de+ad+]
dęhsadatsʼa:ʼ you will quarrel P
dewadatsʼǫh a quarrel; an argument S

•(a)tsʼ be empty, burnt up, used up
[heʼ+…ad+(N+)]
haʼwadatsʼǫh it is empty, burnt up, used up S

•(a)tsʼahd all gone
[heʼ+...(N+) contains: -(a)tsʼ$_V$- use up]
haʼwa:tsʼaht it is all gone P
heyotsʼahdǫh it is all gone S

•(a)tsadaęʼ be foggy
see: (h)sadaęʼ [de+yo+at+] be foggy
deyotsadaęʼ it is foggy S

•(a)tsadǫ(:) bury an object
see: (h)sadǫ [at+] bury an object
ęgatsadǫ:ʼ I will bury s.t. over there P

•(a)tsadǫgw unearth s.t.
see: (h)sadǫgw [d+…at+] unearth s.t.
ętsatsadǫ:goʼ you will unearth it P

•(a)tsaʼged, (a)tsaʼkdǫ bend (forwards)
see: shaʼged, shaʼkdǫ [de+…at+] bend (forwards)
dęwatsaʼge:t it will bend (forwards) P

•(a)tsaide(:) beg, freeload
see: saide(:) [de+…at+] beg, freeload
desatsai:deʼs you are a freeloader H

•(a)tsahnihd be ambitious, tireless, zealous
see: sahnihd [P+at+] be ambitious, tireless, zealous, etc.
gotsahniht she is a good worker, tireless, active, industrious, etc. S

•(a)tsʼahs salary
[de+...adę+ contains: -(a)tsʼ$_V$- use up]
desadętsʼahs your salary; what you make

•(a)tsęhd be tired
[P+ad/N+]
gʼanigo̱hatsęhtaʼ a tired mind H
agaǫ:tsęht they (f/m) were tired, sleepy P

•atsęhse: be tired
[P+ad+]
agadatsęhse: I am tired S

•(a)tsga(ʼ)hǫ chew
[de+P+]
deyotsgʼahǫʼ it is chewing, it is a chewer (for example, a cow) H
dewagatsgaʼhǫ: I am chewing right now S
desatsgʼahǫ: chew I

•(a)tsęnǫni: be happy, glad
see: s(h)ęnǫni: [at+] be happy, glad
agatsęnǫ:ni: I am glad, happy S

•(a)tsohih bite
see: (sho)hih [at+] bite
ęyǫtsohih she will bite it P

•(a)tsih friend
[A+]
gona:tsih they (z) are friends S

•(a)tsih pair (of shoes, socks)
[on+ contains: -(a)tsih$_V$- friend]
ona:tsih a pair (of shoes, socks)
•(a)tsihs' mature
awatsihs'a:' it (a plant) matured; it completed its life-cycle P
otsihs'ǫh it is done for the season; it has gone full cycle; it is mature; they (plants) have finished out S
•(a)tsihsę(:) ripen, be mature
awatsihsę:' it ripened for harvesting P
otsihshę: it is at a mature state S
•(a)tsogę' calendar
[a+]
atso:gę' calendar
•(a)tsotw sunset
see: (h)sotw [ha'+de+w+at+] sunset
ha'dewatsotwahs the sunset H
•(a)ts'ǫh quarrel, argument
[de+wa+ad+ -(a)ts'$_V$- use up, quarrel]
dewadats'ǫh a quarrel; an argument
•(a)tsǫnyǫs omen
see: sǫnyǫs [wa+at+] omen
watsǫ:nyǫ:s omen H
•(a)twahd, (a)dwahd miss s.t.
gadwahta' I miss it always H
saga:twaht I missed it (a ball, etc.) P
agadwahdǫh I have missed it S
•(a)twadased encircle
see: (h)wadased [de+...at+] encircle
dęwatwadahsedahk it will encircle it P
•(a)twe'nǫni round
see: (h)we'nǫni [de+yo+at+] round
deyotw'eno:ni: it is round S
•(a)twe'nǫnihsd make s.t. round
see: (h)we'nǫnihsd [de+...at+] make s.t. round
desatw'enǫ:nihs make it round I
•(a)twihsdaę(:) reserve, economize
see: (h)wihsdaę(:) [at+] reserve, economize
ęhsatwihsdaę' you will economize P
•(a)twihsdani'ǫhsd economize
see: (h)wihsdani'ǫhsd [at+] economize
ęhsatwihsdani'ǫhs you will economize P
•(a)twihsdanǫ(:) guard
see: nǫ(:) [at+N+] guard
hęnatwihsdanǫh they (m) guard the money H
•(a)twihsdęda(:) waste money
see: (h)wihsdęda:' [at+] waste money
aga'twihsdę'da:' I wasted my money P
•(a)wag winnow, shake out, sift
sa:wa:s you are a winnower, shaker, sifter H
ęhsa:wa:k you will winnow, shake out, sift s.t. P
sawa:gǫh you are sifting right now S
•(a)wakta' sifter, sieve
[ǫ+ -(a)wagd$_V$- winnow, shake out, sift with s.t.]
ǫwa:kta' a sifter; a sieve
•(a)wę(:) [ad+] swim
hęnadawęhs they (m) are swimming H
a:yǫda:wę:' she might swim P
hoda:węh he did swim S
ha'sadawę: swim over there I
•(a)wę'dahkwa' bathing suit, swimming pool
[ǫ+ad+ -(a)wędahkwa'$_V$- s.t. to swim with]
ǫdaw'ędahkwa' a bathing suit; s.t. used for swimming
•awę' it is said
see: Appendix I
•(a)węh have
[P+]
aga:węh it is mine S
•(a)węh(ę) flower
[a+]
awęhę' flower
•(a)węhe'go:wah eagle
[a+]
awęhe'go:wah an eagle

Legend: H habitual, P punctual, S stative, I imperative, PURP purposive, PURP-H purposive habitual, PURP-PAST purposive past, PURP-P purposive punctual, PURP-I purposive imperative; see §8.6, §8.11 in Appendix J. Alphabetization in stems ignores length (:), and any h's or glottal stops (') that are not between vowels. See §2.2 of the User Guide for explanation.

•awę̨ˀhę̨:gyeh let it go, release it (short form of hę̨gyeh tsǫ:)
see: Appendix I
•(a)wę̨ˀnahs(a), (a)wę̨ˀnohs(a) tongue
awę̨ˀna̱hsaˀ a tongue
swę̨ˀnohsˀageh on your tongue
•(a)wę̨nyaˀseh [de+P+ad+] confused, doubtful
[de+P+ad+ contains: -(a)wę̨nye(:)$_V$- stir, mix]
dewagadawę̨nyaˀseh I am confused and doubtful (lit: my thinking is going around in circles) H
•(a)wę̨nye(:) [de+...] stir, mix, beat
degawę̨nyeh I stir all the time H
dę̨gawę̨nye:ˀ I will stir P
dewagawę̨:nyeˀ I am stirring S
dehsawę̨nye:ˀ beat, mix, stir it I
•(a)wę̨nye(:) [de+...P+ ad+] walk about
deyagodawę̨nyeˀ she is walking about S
•(a)wę̨nyehs mixer
[de+wa+ contains: -(a)wę̨nye(:)$_V$- stir, mix]
dewawę̨nyehs a mixer
•(a)wę̨hsǫˀ belongings, property
[P+ -(a)wę̨h$_V$- have -sǫˀ plural]
sawę̨hsǫˀ your belongings; your property
•awi, ǫ give
de̱hę̨nę̨dadawihs trades; commerce; barter H
ę̨:gǫˀ I will give it to it P
shǫgwa:wi: he has given us s.t. S
dahsgǫh give it to me I
•awi, ǫ present, offer
[ad+]
wadawi̱hǫˀ presents H
•awi, ǫ trade, redeem, exchange
[(de+)...adad+]
dę̨sadadǫˀ you will trade, exchange P
•awi, ǫ replace
[o:yaˀ other de+d+...]
o:yaˀ dę̨tsgǫˀ you will give me another (that is, you will replace s.t.) P
•(a)wiˀd insert
[(N+)]
hesawˀitaˀ you insert s.t. all the time H
ę̨hsa:wiˀt you will insert it P
ę̨sagyaˀda:wi:t you will put on (clothes) P
[ag+ -yaˀd(a)$_N$- body -awiˀd$_V$- insert]
•(a)wihs trade, commerce, barter
[de+A+adad+ -awi, ǫ$_V$- give]
de̱hę̨nę̨dadawihs tradesl commercel barter
•aˀwisd(a) slice, peeling
see: (raˀ)wisd(a) slice, peeling
owaˀwi̱hsdaˀ a slice; a peeling
•aˀwisdots(i) peel
see: (raˀ)wisdots(i) peel
ę̨hsrawi̱hsdo:tsiˀ you will peel s.t. P
•(a)hy(a) fruit, berry
[o+]
ohyaˀ fruit
•(a)ˀy(a) female genitals, vagina
[o+]
oˀyaˀ female genitals; the vagina
•(a)hyagwiy(a) toe
ohya:gwi:yaˀ toe(s)
ga̱hyagwiyaˀgeh on my toes
•(a)hyai ripen
[-(a)hy(a)- fruit, berry -(r)i, wi$_V$- ripen]
wa̱hyais a musk melon; a cantaloupe (lit: fruit is beginning to ripen) H
ę̨wahyaiˀ it (fruit) will ripen P
ohyaih ripe fruit S
•(a)hyais cantaloupe, musk melon
[wa+ -(a)hy(a)$_N$- fruit, berry -(r)i, (w)i$_V$- ripe]
wa̱hyais a musk melon; a cantaloupe (lit: fruit is beginning to ripen)

•(a)hyajih blueberry, blackberry
[o+ -(a)hy(a)$_N$- fruit, berry -ji(:,h)$_V$- dark]
ohya:jih dark fruit; blueberries, blackberries
•(a)hyajiwagę: crabapples, etc.
[o+ -(a)hy(a)$_N$- fruit, berry -jiwagę:$_V$- sour, bitter, salty]
ohyajiwa:gę: crabapples; tart, sour fruit
•(a)hyakahǫ' tomato
[o+ -(a)hy(a)$_N$- fruit, berry -kahǫ$_V$- adjoin, abutt]
ohyakahǫ' tomatoes
•(a)hyakdǫ: banana
[de+yo+ad+ -(a)hy(a)$_N$- fruit, berry -(a)'kdǫ$_V$- be bent, crooked]
deyodahya'kdǫ: banana
•(a)'yatgehǫha' prostitute
[wa+ad+ -(a)'y(a)$_N$- female genitals -(a)tgehǫ$_V$- sell]
wada'yatgehǫha' a prostitute (lit.: it sells its private parts)
•(a)hyayętwęh orchard, berry field
[wa+ -(a)hy(a)$_N$- fruit, berry -yętw, yęto$_V$- plant]
wahyayętwęh an orchard; a berry field
•(a)hyes thimble berry
[s+ha+ -(a)hy(a)$_N$- fruit, berry -es$_V$- long]
shahye:s thimbleberries
•(a)'yod [ad+] be erect
ęwad'ayo:dę' it will be erect (poised to strike) P
•(a)hyojihs be sour, salty
[de'+P+ -(a)hy(a)$_N$- fruit, berry -jiwagę:$_V$- sour, salty]
deyohyojihs it is sour; salty water H
•(a)hyowa:' apple
[s+wa+ -(a)hy(a)$_N$- fruit, berry -owa:'-$_V$ bitter]
swahyo:wa:' apples; crabapples

D

•d stand
[A+]
ga:di:t they (z) are standing S
i:gye:t she is standing over there
ihswa:t you all are standing
i:ga:t it is standing
ita:t he is standing over there
he:ye:t she is standing over there
i:ye:t she is standing over here
i:ge:t I am standing
•d one object
[s+A/P+N+]
sg'anigǫha:t one mind S
[s+ga+ -(')nigǫh(a)$_N$- mind -d$_V$- stand]
swęhni'da:t one month S
[s+w+ -ęhni'd(a)$_N$- month -d$_V$- stand]
jǫhsi'da:t one foot S
[s/j+o+ -(a)hsi'd(a)$_N$- foot -d$_V$- stand]
•d be the same
[tsa'+A/P+N+]
tsa'ga'drehda:t the same kind of car S
[tsa'+ga+ -(')drehd(a)$_N$- mind -d$_V$- stand]
•da' stand up, stop
[de+ contains: -d$_V$- stand]
dekda's I stop here (whenever...) H
ata:da' he stood up P
dęyagoda'ǫhǫ:gye' they (f/m) will be standing along (to be born) S
dehsda' stand up; stop I
•da' sleep
see: (i)da' [P+] sleep
ęwagi:da' I will sleep P
•(')d(a:) clay, mortar
see: (i)'d(a:) clay, mortar
o'da:' clay; mud; mortar
•(')d(a) feces, shit, excrement
see: (ni)'d(a) feces, shit, excrement
o'da' feces; shit; excrement

Legend: H habitual, P punctual, S stative, I imperative, PURP purposive, PURP-H purposive habitual, PURP-PAST purposive past, PURP-P purposive punctual, PURP-I purposive imperative; see §8.6, §8.11 in Appendix J. Alphabetization in stems ignores length (:), and any h's or glottal stops (') that are not between vowels. See §2.2 of the User Guide for explanation.

•daʼaǫd web, net
[o+ -daʼ(a)$_N$- web -ǫd$_V$- attached]
odaʼaǫt a web; a net
•dad create
[N+ -ǫhwęj(a)$_N$- earth, land -dad$_V$- create]
tsaʼhǫhwęja:da:t when he made the earth P
hǫhwęjada:dǫh he has created the earth S
•daʼdr(e) go to bed
see: (i)daʼdr(e) [a+P+] go to bed
ehsęd'adre' you are going to bed PURP
•dage:ʼ lie
see: (i)dage:ʼ lie
sida:ge:ʼ you are lying down, prostrate S
•(ʼ)dagęd undergarment, soil, feces
see: (iʼ)dagęd undergarment, soil, feces
deyoʼdagę:t dirty undergarments; soil; fecal matter
•dago:s, da:gu:s cat
[-dagu:s$_N$- cat]
dago:s, dagu:s a cat
•dagǫh dark
[o+N+ -(a)hsohg(wa)$_N$- colour]
ohsohgwada:gǫh dark colour S
•dagraʼ fall
see: (i)dagraʼ fall
ęyedagraʼ she will fall down P
•dagrahd(ę,ani) [TR+] trip s.o.
see: (i)dagrahd(ę,ani) [TR+] trip s.o.
ęgaǫ:gidagrahdęʼ they are going to trip me, make me fall P
•dagrǫʼ several living things lying down
see: (i)dagrǫʼ [A+] several living things lying down
gadidagrǫʼ they (z) are lying down S
•dagyeʼ continue on, be ongoing
[-d$_V$- stand -agyeʼ go along doing s.t.]
hęgadagyeʼ it will continue on S
gaǫhyada:gyeʼ on-going skies, heavens S
[-(r)ǫhy(a)$_N$- sky -dagyeʼ$_V$- continue on, be ongoing]
•dagujih kitten
[-dagu:s$_N$- cat -jih little]
dagu:jih a kitten
•dahgw remove
see: (o)da(h)gw remove, take away
sagęhędahgoh remove the ashes out of it I
•dagwa:dih, da...gwa:dih over here, this side here
see: Appendix I
•dagwaihsahd go straight
[heʼ+P+ contains: -d(a)$_N$- way -gwaihs(i)$_V$- straight]
hęhsadagwaihsaht you will go straight P
•dagwais(i) straighten
see: gwahs(i) straighten
ęhsdagwaihsiʼ you will straighten P
•dagwaihshǫ: straight ahead
see: gwaihshǫ: straight ahead
heyodaʼgwaishǫ: straight ahead
•dagyeʼ(s) continue on, be ongoing
[ad/N+ contains: -(r)ǫhy(a)$_N$- sky -d$_V$- stand]
gaǫ:hyada:gyeʼ on-going skies; the heavens H
•dagyeʼs reign
[A+ contains: -d$_V$- stand]
eda:gyeʼs a reign (lit.: she is still standing; that is, a queen)
hadagyeʼsgęhę:ʼ a reign (lit.: he was standing there)
•(ʼ)dai:ʼ dirty
see: (iʼ)dai:ʼ [de+P+] dirty
dęhoʼdai:ʼ he got dirty (that is, covered with manure) S
•(ʼ)dai:ʼ brick
see: (iʼ)dai:ʼ brick
oʼda:iʼ a brick (lit.: there is mud on it)

•(ʼ)daihaʼd warm up
[(d+) A/P+(N+) contains: -(ʼ)daih$_V$- hot]
wadaihaʼtaʼ it heats things up H
ętsaʼdaihaʼt you will heat it up; you will make it hot P
oʼdaihaʼdǫh it (weather) is really hot S

•(ʼ)daihaʼseh be too hot
[P+ contains: -(ʼ)daih$_V$- hot]
hoʼdaihaʼseh he is too hot H

•(ʼ)daihę: be hot
[o+ contains: -(ʼ)daih$_V$- hot]
oʼdaihę:ʼ it is hot S

•(ʼ)daihę: be hot
[A/P+(N+) contains: -(h)neg(a)$_N$- water -(ʼ)daih$_V$- hot]
ohnegadaihę: hot water S

•(ʼ)daihęhdrahi sweat, perspire
[d+ contains: -(ʼ)daih$_V$- hot]
ętseʼdaihęhdrahiʼ you will sweat profusely, perspire P

•(ʼ)daihęhdrod sweat
[P+ -(iʼ)daihęhdr(a)$_N$- sweat -od$_V$- stand]
hoʼdaihęhdro:t he is sweating S

•(ʼ)daisdǫ:ʼ intercourse
see: (i)ʼdaisdǫ:ʼ intercourse
adai:sdǫ:ʼ intercourse

•dakse run all over
[A+]
kdakseʼ I am running PURP

•daksenǫgyeʼ(s) roam, run about
[A+ contains: -dakse$_V$- run all over]
gadidaksenǫgyeʼ(s) they (z) are running about, roaming H

•dane:ʼ that it
see: Appendix I

•dane:ʼhniʼ that also
see: Appendix I

•dane:onęh and now that
see: Appendix I

•da:netoh that is all
see: Appendix I

•da:nę:dah now this also
see: Appendix I

•danhǫweh this is where
see: Appendix I

•(ʼ)danyo beat up
see: (i)ʼdanyo [TR+] beat up
ahǫwęda:nyoʼ s.o. beat him up, broke his spirit P

•da:onęh and now
see: Appendix I

•daǫ be lucky, fortunate, chosen, special
see: (i)daǫ [P+] be lucky, fortunate, chosen, special
sędaǫ: you are chosen, special, fortunate S

•(ʼ)daǫni be dirty, muddy
see: (iʼ)daǫni [(ade+)] be dirty, muddy
agaʼdaǫniʼ it got muddy P

•dahsd, dęhsd string s.t. up, drape s.t.
[de+ contains: -d$_V$- stand]
ikda:s I am stringing it; draping it H

•dahsd, dęhsd stop s.t., stand s.t. up, prevent s.t.
[de+ contains: -d$_V$- stand]
degadidahstaʼ a stable; barn; a bus stop H
ata:dahs he stopped it, prevented it P

•dase whirl
[N+]
degawa:da:sehs a tornado H
[-w(a:)$_N$- wind, air -dase$_V$- whirl]
ohnawada:se: whirlpool S
[-(h)naw(a)$_N$- running water -dase$_V$- whirl]

•dahstaʼ stable, barn, bus stop
[de+gadi+ contains: -dahsd$_V$- stop s.t., stand s.t. up, prevent s.t.]
degadidahstaʼ a stable; a barn; a bus stop

•dahstaʼ glottal stop
[de+ga+ contains: -d$_V$- stand]
degadahstaʼ a glottal stop

Legend: H habitual, P punctual, S stative, I imperative, PURP purposive, PURP-H purposive habitual, PURP-PAST purposive past, PURP-P purposive punctual, PURP-I purposive imperative; see §8.6, §8.11 in Appendix J. Alphabetization in stems ignores length (:), and any h's or glottal stops (ʼ) that are not between vowels. See §2.2 of the User Guide for explanation.

•(ʼ)dahswahę(drǫ) scold
see: (i)ʼdahswahę(drǫ) [TR+] scold
ahadiʼdahswahęhdrǫ:ʼ they (m) scolded, reprimanded P
•(ʼ)dawęnyeʼ be a shit-disturber
see: (i)ʼdawęnyeʼ [de+A+] be a shit-disturber
deyeʼdawę:nyeʼ she is a shit-disturber H
•deʼ exist
[N+]
ęyǫhwęja:de:k the earth will exist P
[-ǫhwęj(a)$_N$- earth -deʼ$_V$- exist]
oha:deʼ an existing road S
[-(h)ah(a)$_N$- earth -deʼ$_V$- exist]
•deʼ be low, lower
[gaoʼ less ni+t+ga+ -deʼ$_V$- exist]
gaoʼ nitga:deʼ it is lower S
•deʼ have a certain height
[ni+t+A/P+(N+) -deʼ$_V$- exist]
nitga:deʼ how high it is (inanimate object); the height of s.t. S
•deʼ be the same height
[tsaʼde+t+ga+ -deʼ$_V$- exist]
tsaʼde:tga:deʼ the same height S
•deʼ be the same type of
[tsaʼde+N+-deʼ$_V$- exist]
tsaʼdeyahsyadeʼ (**tsaʼdeyo̱hsiyadeʼ**) they come from (lit. it comes from) the same line, family S
[tsaʼde+ yo+ -(h)siy(a)$_N$- line -deʼ$_V$- exist]
•dehd be bold, bright, strong
[o+N+]
ohsohgwadeht vibrant colours, florescent, neon S
[o+ -(a)hsohg(wa)$_N$- colour -dehd$_V$- bold]
•(h)deg(a:) rib
ohde:ga:ʼ ribs
se̱hdega:ʼgeh on your ribs
•degahnegaye̱hsdǫh ǫhsǫhtaʼ water colours, paint
degahnegaye̱hsdǫh water is mixed in it
ǫhsohtaʼ colour; paints; crayons
•degawada:sehs dega:dęh helicopter
degawada:sehs it stirs the air
dega:dęh it flies
•dehęnatwihsdagę:nyǫhs watgehǫʼ an auction
dehęnaʼtwihsdagę:nyǫhs they compete for money
watgehǫʼ sales
•dejaǫ: both (of you two)
see: Appendix I
•deni, deny change
[de+...(N+)]
dęhęnadǫgweʼdadenyeʼs they change people H
[-ǫgwe(ʼda)$_N$- people -deny$_V$- change]
aha:de:niʼ he emptied s.t. (lit.: he changed it) P
gade:nyǫ: it is empty S
•deni, deny change for oneself
[at+(N+)]
ęhsatgwęnya:de:niʼ you will change your clothes P
[-(a)hgwęny(a)$_N$- clothes -deni$_V$- change]
•denyǫʼ be several existing things
[A/P+N+ contains: -deʼ$_V$- exist -nyǫʼ plural]
ohadenyǫʼ roads; highways S
[o+ -(h)ah(a)$_N$- road -denyǫʼ$_V$- several existing things]
węhniʼdade:nyǫʼ months S
[w+ -ęhniʼd(a)$_N$- month -denyǫʼ$_V$- several existing things]
•dehsr(a) sexuality
see: (i)dehsr(a) sexuality
gędehsraʼ sexuality
•dewada̱hsgǫgo̱htaʼ oha:deʼ overpass
dewada̱hsgǫgo̱htaʼ an overpass
oha:deʼ an existing road
•dewadiyǫ:taʼ ohna:griʼ rubber band, elastic
dewadiyǫ:taʼ it stretches
ohna:griʼ rubber

•dewahǫhde:s o'wahǫh venison
dewahǫhde:s deer
o'wahǫh meat
•deyagoya'dahkwa' ǫ:gweh elevator
deyagoya'dahkwa' s.t. that lifts
ǫ:gweh' a person
•deyodina'gaǫ:dǫ' gadi'drǫ' sheep fold
deyodina'gaǫ:dǫ' a horned animal
gadi'drǫ' they (z) live (designates a shed, dog house; etc.)
•deyodina'gaǫ:dǫ' ohęhda:' wool
deyodina'gaǫ:dǫ' a horned animal
ohęhda:' fur
•deyo:do:wę' one:gwa' split peas
deyo:do:wę' it is split
one:gwa' peas
•deyohse:s gaję' bowl
deyohse:s it has a wide mouth
gaję' a dish; a plate; a bowl
•deyotsgę'ęgęhdę: ohya' plums
deyotsgę'ęgęhdę: flat pits
ohya' fruit
•deyowidra:teh ganǫ:' diamonds
deyowi'dra:teh it is icy, glassy
ganǫ:' it is expensive, dear
•dę [de+...] fly, take off
dega:dęhs it flies, goes up in the air H
ata:dę' he took off (from the ground) P
•dę' what (short form)
see: Appendix I
•dę' hne:' why?; what is that? why me?
see: Appendix I
•dę' ho' dę' what
see: Appendix I
•dęhd poverty; be poor, pitiful
see: (i)dęhd poverty; be poor, pitiful
o:dęht poverty; it is poor, pitiful
•dęhd be poor
cf: (i)dęhd [P+] be poor
agi:dęht I am poor, poverty-stricken, in poverty S
•dęhda:' lie spread out on the ground [A/P+(N+)]
gadęhda:' it is lying spread out on the floor or the ground S
ganehsda:dęhda:' a floor
[ga+ stem: -nehsda:dęhda'- floor; consists of: -nehsd(a:)$_N$- floor, board -dęhda:'$_V$- lie spread out on the ground]
•dęhda:' resurface s.t.
[s+...]
sgadęhda:' to resurface s.t. S
•dęǫ, dę(:) pity s.o., feel compassion
see: (i)dęǫ, (i)dę(:) [(d+)...TR+] pity s.o., feel compassion for s.o.
kedęǫhs I feel compassion for her H
•dęs be thick, dense
[ga+]
ga:dę:s it is thick, dense S
•dęs be thin
[(tę') de'+ not A+]
tę' dega:dę:s it is not thick S
•dęhsdahkwa' a stable
[de+gadi+ contains: -dahsdahkwa'$_V$- stopping place]
degadidęhsdahkwa' a stable
•dęhs plane, airplane
[de+ga+ -dę$_V$- fly, take off]
dega:dęhs an airplane (lit.: it flies)
•dęhsd, dahsd stop s.t., stand s.t. up, prevent s.t.
[de+ contains: -d$_V$- stand]
degadidahsta' a stable; a barn; a bus stop H
ata:dahs he stopped it, prevented it P
•di' so, then
see: Appendix I
•di'di:' blue jay
di'di:' a blue jay
•dihsdihs house woodpecker
dihsdihs a house woodpecker
•(h)disoda: cardinal
[ga+ -(h)dis(a)$_N$- -oda(:,h)$_V$- drape]
gahdiso:da: a cardinal (bird)

Legend: H habitual, P punctual, S stative, I imperative, PURP purposive, PURP-H purposive habitual, PURP-PAST purposive past, PURP-P purposive punctual, PURP-I purposive imperative; see §8.6, §8.11 in Appendix J. Alphabetization in stems ignores length (:), and any h's or glottal stops (') that are not between vowels. See §2.2 of the User Guide for explanation.

•di(ʼtra) tea
[o+]
odi: tea
ediʼtrǫnyaʼtaʼ a teapot
[e+ stem: -diʼtrǫnyaʼtaʼ- teapot; consists of: -di(ʼtra)$_N$- tea -ǫnyaʼd$_V$- cause to make]
•diʼtrǫnyaʼtaʼ teapot
[e+ -di(ʼtra)$_N$- tea -ǫnyaʼd$_V$- cause to make]
ediʼtrǫnyaʼtaʼ a teapot
•do: how (much)
see: Appendix I
•do:ʼ i:ʼ let me
see: Appendix I
•do:gaʼ I do not know
see: Appendix I
•dodihs salamander
do:dihs a salamander
•doʼdod swells
[o+ -doʼd(a)$_N$- wave -od$_V$- stand attached object]
odoʼdo:t swells (waves)
•dogę(:) be right, true, factual
[(A/P+) (N+)]
do:gęhs sure, truly; right; it is a fact H
gado:gę: a certain way; together; a certain thing S
gaihwado:gę: it is the main idea S
[stem: -(r)ih(wa)$_N$- word -dogę(:)$_V$- be right, true]
•dogęhsd arrange things, right s.t.
[(ad+rihwa+) -dogę(:)$_V$- right, true]
ęhsdo:gęhs you will arrange (things, flowers, etc.) P
ęhsadri̲hwa:do:gęhs you will right a wrong P
•dogęhsd adjust s.t.
[d+ contains -dogę(:)$_V$- right, true]
ętsa:do:gęhs you will adjust s.t. P
•dogę:t guinea hen
dogę:t a guinea hen
•do:gwaʼ how; a certain amount, a measure
see: Appendix I
•dǫʼ be a group of similar objects standing in a line or in an arrangement
[de+ A+ N+ contains: -d$_V$- stand -ǫʼ plural]
deganehsda:dǫʼ a board fence S
[-nehsd(a:)$_N$- board -dǫʼ$_V$- several standing objects]
degahsgwa:dǫʼ rocks piled in an arrangement S
[-(h)sg(wa)$_N$- rock -dǫʼ$_V$- several standing objects]
degahnyo̲hsra:dǫʼ bars on a window S
[-(h)nyǫhsr(a)$_N$- bar -dǫʼ$_V$- several standing objects]
•dǫh mean s.t.
see: (i)dǫh [A+ / TR+]
hę:dǫh he means s.t. S
•(ʼ)dǫ(:) be due, be child-bearing
[ade+]
ǫdeʼdǫhaʼ child-bearing; she is giving birth right now H
ęyǫdʼedǫ:ʼ when she will be due P
•(ʼ)dǫdr(a) fat, gristle, rind
[o+]
oʼdǫ:draʼ it is fat; gristle; rind
•dǫhgoia:s dragon
cf: (i)dǫhgoia:s dragon
hegęʼdǫhgoiʼa:s a dragon (lit.: a flame thrower)
•dǫhg(wa:) fever
[o+]
odǫhgwa: a fever
•dǫhgwa: have, get a fever
[P+]
ǫgiʼdǫhgwa: I got a fever P
akdǫhgwa:hǫh I have a fever S
•dǫhg(wa) flame
cf: (i)dǫhg(wa) flame
odǫhgwaʼ a flame
•(ʼ)dǫhneʼ pregnant animal
[w+ade+ contains -(ʼ)dǫ(:)$_V$- due -hneʼ- go and be]
wadeʼdo̲hneʼ a pregnant animal

•(ʼ)dr(a) case, quiver
[ga+ad+]
gʼada:traʼ (**gʼada:draʼ**) a case; a quiver
dę̱hęnadeʼdragę:nyǫhs archery (lit. they (m) are competing)
[de+...ade+ -(ʼ)dr(a)$_N$- case, quiver -gęni, gęny$_V$- compete]

•(ʼ)dragęnyǫhs archery
[de+...ade+ -(ʼ)dr(a)$_N$- case, quiver -gęni, gęny$_V$- compete]
dę̱hęnadeʼdragę:nyǫhs archery (lit. they (m) are competing)

•(ʼ)drahehsd overdo, exaggerate
[P+]
sʼadrahehstaʼ you are always going overboard; you are excessive H
ęhsaʼdra̱hehs you will go overboard, above and beyond; you will exceed P

•(ʼ)drahehsdǫh be extreme
[heʼ+yo+ -(ʼ)drahehsd$_V$- overdo, exaggerate]
heyoʼdra̱hehsdǫh it is extreme S

•(ʼ)draihaʼd rush s.t., hurry s.t. up
[de+ contains: -(ʼ)draih$_V$- hurry]
deyoʼdraihaʼt hurried or immediate attention, urgent matter, urgency; a rush S
dehseʼdraihaʼt rush s.t.; hurry it up I

•(ʼ)draihę hurry
[de+P+ contains: -(ʼ)draih$_V$- hurry]
deyagʼodraihęhs she is in a hurry H
adyǫknʼidraihęʼ we two hurried P
haoʼ desaʼdrai:hęh o.k., hurry up I

•(ʼ)dre(:) drag, drive
see: (i)ʼdre(:) [(N+)] drag, drive
haʼdreʼ he is dragging PURP

•(ʼ)drehd move oneself
see: (i)ʼdrehd [(N+)] move oneself
gʼadrehtaʼ it moves itself, it rides H

•(ʼ)drehd(a) vehicie, car, truck
[ga+]
gʼadrehdaʼ a car; a truck; a vehicle

•(ʼ)drehdaę(:) park one's vehicle
[ade+ -(ʼ)drehd(a)$_N$- car, vehicle -ę$_V$- lie]
gyǫgyadedrehdaę:ʼ we all parked our car over there S

•(ʼ)drehdahkwaʼ jack, tow truck, hoist
[de+ga+ -(ʼ)drehd(a)$_N$- car, vehicle -(h)kwaʼ$_V$- s.t. that lifts, picks up]
degaʼdre̱hdahkwaʼ a jack; a tow truck; a hoist

•(ʼ)drehdǫnihs mechanic
[(s+) A+ -(ʼ)drehd(a)$_N$- vehicle, car -ǫni, ǫny$_V$- make, repair]
shaʼdrehdǫ:nihs he is a mechanic H

•dręhdahoʼdrǫ(:) stay awake
see: (i)dręhdahoʼdrǫ(:) [ad+] stay awake
agadidręhtaodrǫ: (**agadidręhda̱hoʼdrǫ:**) I had to stay awake P

•dręhgyenyęʼs nod off, fall asleep
see: idręhgyenyęʼs [A+] nod off, fall asleep
sidręhgyenyęʼs you are nodding off, falling asleep H

•dręnagaʼǫh be sweet-smelling
[ga+ -dręn(a)$_N$- smell -gaʼ$_V$- like the taste of s.t.]
gadręnagaʼǫh it smells good, sweet, appetizing S

•dręniyo: smell nice
[A+ -dręn(a)$_N$- smell -iyo:$_V$- be nice, good]
gedrę:ni:yo: I smell nice S

•(ʼ)dreʼs car
[w+ade+ -(i)ʼdre(:)$_V$- drag, drive]
wadeʼdreʼs a drag; car (old word) (lit.: it is dragging itself)

•(ʼ)dręę(:) put together
[de+...ad+ N+]
desatnętsaʼdręʼ you put your arms together I
[A+ -nęts(a)$_N$- arm -(ʼ)dręę(:)$_V$- put together]

Legend: H habitual, P punctual, S stative, I imperative, PURP purposive, PURP-H purposive habitual, PURP-PAST purposive past, PURP-P purposive punctual, PURP-I purposive imperative; see §8.6, §8.11 in Appendix J. Alphabetization in stems ignores length (:), and any h's or glottal stops (ʼ) that are not between vowels. See §2.2 of the User Guide for explanation.

•drę'iga:' painted turtle
[o+]
odrę'i:ga:' a painted turtle
•dręna:, dręnai:' smell
[o+ade+ -dręn(a:)$_N$- smell -a:'$_V$- hold, contain, include]
odedręna:', odedręnai:' a smell
•dręnaę:' purple
[-dręn(a)$_N$- purple -'ę:'$_V$- be coloured]
dręnaę:' purple
•dręna: skunk
[contains: -dręn(a:)$_N$- smell]
drę:na: a skunk
•dręniyo's perfume
[ga+ -dręn(a:)$_N$- smell -iyo's$_V$ be nice, good things]
gadrę:ni:yo's perfume
•(')driyo: be a good shot
[(ni+) A+ -(')dr(a)$_N$- case, quiver -iyo:$_V$- be nice, good]
ha'dri:yo: he's a good, accurate shot S
•(')drǫ live, dwell, be at home
see: (i)'drǫ [A+] live, dwell, be at home
hadi'drǫ' they (m) are at home S
•(')drǫ elect
see: (i)'drǫ [TR+] elect
ahǫwadi'drǫ' they placed or elected him P
•(')drǫ:' otter
[j+o+ade+ -(')dr(a)$_N$- case, quiver -ǫ:$_V$- resemble]
jode'drǫ:' an otter
•(')drǫ(:), (')drę(:) put together, be crossed
[de+...ad+N]
dęhswatnętsa'drǫ:' you all will cross your arms P
[-nęts(a)$_N$- arm -(')drǫ(:)$_V$- put together]
deswatnętsa'drǫ' you all have your arms crossed S
•(')drǫda' be placed, live, stay at home
see: (i)'drǫda' [A+] be placed, live, stay at home
tgidrǫ:da'k where I lived S
•(')drǫda' land
see: (i)'drǫda' [de+...] land
dęgę'drǫ:da' it will land P
•(')drǫda:'diaper
see: (i)'drǫda:'diaper
g'adro:da:' a diaper
•(')dro'dę: experience
[ni+wa+ade+ -(')dr(a)$_N$- case, quiver -o'dę:$_V$- type of experience]
niwadedro'dę: an experience
•(')drǫdǫ' several things, people placed somewhere
see: (i)'drǫdǫ' [A+] several things, people placed somewhere
hadi'drǫ:dǫ' how they (m) are placed S
•(')drohsr(a) fat, rind
[o+]
o'drohsra' fat; pig rinds
•(')drǫhg thorn berry
[ha+ contains: -(')dr(a)$_N$- case, quiver]
ha'drǫhk a thornberry

E

•e go
a:yakhne' we two (excl.) would go together PURP-P
he:ge: let me go there PURP-I
•e come this way
[d+]
dagę:ne' they (z) are coming PURP
ęte' he will come this way PURP-P
•e come back this way
[de+d+]
dǫdahe' he is coming back PURP
dętge' I will come this way; I will come back; I am coming back PURP-P
•e go back there
[ha'+s+]
hęhsge' I am going back there PURP-P

•e come from somewhere
[ni+d+]
nǫda꞉ge꞉ʼ I come from somewhere; I came from somewhere PURP-PAST
gaoʼ nǫdahse꞉ come this way PURP-I
•e come back here, return
[ni+de+d+]
naʼdǫ꞉da̱heʼ he would come this way PURP-P
•e wander; be someplace
[ę tsǫ꞉ just d+]
ę tsǫ꞉ itseʼs you wander (all the time); you are over there PURP-H
ę tsǫ꞉ ętseʼ you will wander PURP-P
•e꞉ʼah walk along
[ti+A+ contains: -e$_V$- go -ʼah diminutive]
tihe꞉ʼah he is just walking along H
•(ʼ)e hit
[N+ present in:]
ga̱hwihsdʼa̱ehs a clock H
[ga+ stem: -(h)wihsdʼaehs- clock; consists of: -(h)wihsd(a), (h)rihsd(a)$_N$- metal, money -(ʼ)e$_V$- hit]
ahaʼnǫhgwaʼe꞉k he beat the drum (barrel) P
[stem: -(ʼ)nǫhgwaʼe- beat a drum; consists of: -nahg(wa)$_N$- drum, barrel -(ʼ)eg$_V$- hit]
hohwaʼe꞉ he is tapping S
[stem: -(h)waʼe- tap; consists of: -(h)w(a)$_N$- -(ʼ)e$_V$- hit]
desatgwiaʼek wink I
[de+…at+ stem: -gwiʼaʼeg- wink; consists of: -gwiʼ(a)$_N$- -(ʼ)eg$_V$- hit]
•e꞉, i꞉, ę꞉ think, hope, want
[A+]
i꞉wi꞉ he wants H
i꞉wi꞉ I want H
i꞉yę꞉ she wants H
ihse꞉ you want H
ihsne꞉ you two want H
agwe꞉ we all (excl.) want H
ahi꞉ʼ I thought, I intended P
ehswe꞉ʼ you all thought P
ahe꞉ʼ he thought P
ehsne꞉ʼ you two thought P
ehswe꞉ʼ you all thought P
ędwe꞉he꞉k we all (incl.) will in thought P
ahę꞉ne꞉ʼ they (m) thought; they left together P
hawe꞉ʼǫ꞉ he has willed S
se꞉ǫ꞉ʼ you wanted, believed S
•ed stand; also see -d stand
[N+]
gra̱·he꞉t living tree
[stem: -graheʼd(a)$_N$- tree -ed$_V$- stand]
gra̱·hé꞉dǫʼ many trees
[stem: -graheʼd(a)$_N$- tree -edǫʼ$_V$- several standing objects]
gra̱·hé·dǫn·yǫʼ va ariety of trees
[stem: -graheʼd(a)$_N$- tree -edǫnyǫʼ$_V$- several standing objects]
•ehd do unintentionally
[(teʼ) not taʼ+de+]
taʼdewagehdǫ꞉ I did not mean it, intend it I
•ehd do on purpose
[tsi+…]
tsigehtaʼ I do it on purpose all the time H
tsaʼgeht I did it on purpose P
tsiwage̱hdǫh I did it on purpose S
•ehdahgǫhsgǫ꞉ be gullible
[d+A+ contains: -ehdahgw$_V$- escort s.o., believe s.t. -sgǫ꞉ easily]
dihsehda̱hgǫhsgǫh you are really gullible H
•ehdahgw believe s.t.
[d+A+ contains: -ehdahgw$_V$- escort s.o.]
dihsehda̱hgǫh you are credulous, gullible; you believe in s.t. S

Legend: H habitual, P punctual, S stative, I imperative, PURP purposive, PURP-H purposive habitual, PURP-PAST purposive past, PURP-P purposive punctual, PURP-I purposive imperative; see §8.6, §8.11 in Appendix J. Alphabetization in stems ignores length (꞉), and any h's or glottal stops (ʼ) that are not between vowels. See §2.2 of the User Guide for explanation.

•edahkw come from
[d+ contains: -e$_V$- go]
tęneda̱hkwaʼ where they (m) come from H
•egaʼgwao:sʼageh ǫhsohtaʼ eyebrow pencil
ogahgwaohsaʼ eyebrow
ǫhsohtaʼ colour, paints, crayons
•ega:gwahtaʼ gajęʼ collection plate
ega:gwahtaʼ (s.o. collects money)
gajęʼ dish, plate, bowl
•egahehdohaiʼtaʼ gaʼahdraʼ lyed corn basket (for washing corn)
egahehdohaiʼtaʼ s.o. washes or lyes corn
gaʼahdraʼ basket
•e:hah be proud, gloat
[(i+) A+ contains: -i:, ę:, e:$_V$- think, hope, want -hah diminutive]
gęne:hah they (z) are proud H
ihse:hah you gloat
•ehehgyaktaʼ ado:gęʼ a pick axe
ehehgyaktaʼ a spade
ado:gęʼ an axe; a tomahawk
•eho... spelling variant; look under stems beginning with (r)ih(wa)...
•eiʼgo:wah gra̱he:t a cherry tree
eiʼgo:wah cherries
gra̱he:t a living tree
•eiʼgo:wah cherry
eiʼgo:wah cherries
•ekwaędahkwaʼgeh onǫhsǫ:t a pantry
ekwaędahkwaʼ a cupboard; a pantry
onǫhsǫ:t a room; a vault
•eʼnikǫhkwaʼ ohsi:yaʼ thread
eʼnikǫhkwaʼ s.t. used for sewing
ohsi:yaʼ thread; string; cord
•enohai:hǫʼdahkwaʼ enoha:ʼtaʼ laundry soap
enohai:hǫʼdahkwaʼ s.t. used for laundering
enoha:ʼtaʼ soap
•enǫʼge̱haʼda̱hkwaʼ gatseʼdaʼ a nursing bottle
enǫʼge̱haʼda̱hkwaʼ a nursing bottle
gatseʼdaʼ a bottle; a jar
•enǫ be a stranger, be a certain age
[ni+d+P]
nita:we:nǫh a male stranger; he's that age (lit.: where he comes from) H
nigyawe:nǫ: where it came from S
•enǫ go somewhere
[ti+P+]
tiyo:ne:nǫ: where they have gone S
•enǫgyeʼ move forward
[ohę:dǫ: ahead heʼ+ contains: -enǫ$_V$- originate from someplace, come from someplace]
ohę:dǫ: heʼsenǫgyeʼ you're moving forward H
•enǫgyeʼs roam
[ti+... -enǫ$_V$- originate from someplace, come from someplace]
tigęnenǫgyeʼs they (z) are roaming about H
•enǫh be a stranger
[ni+d+P contains: -enǫ$_V$- originate from someplace, come from someplace]
nita:we:nǫh a male stranger; he's that age (lit.: where he comes from)
nijagowe:nǫh a female stranger (lit.: where she comes from)
•enǫhah be middle-aged
[ni+d+P+ -enǫ$_V$- originate from someplace, come from someplace -hah diminutive]
nitawe:nǫ:hah a middle-aged male
nigyagawe:nǫ:hah a middle-aged female
•e:ʼǫ: will s.t.
[P+ contains: -i:, ę:, e:$_V$- think, hope, want]
hawe:ʼǫ: he has willed S

•e'(s) be someplace
[A+ contains: -e$_V$- go]
gę:ne's they (z) are around; they are here; they are together H
•e's be a stray (animal)
[ti+w+ contains: -e$_V$- go]
ti:wehs a stray animal
•e'(s) wander; be someplace
[ę tsǫ: just d+ contains: -e$_V$- go]
ę tsǫ: itse's you wander (all the time); you are over there PURP-H
ę tsǫ: ętse' you will wander PURP-P
•es be long
[A/P+(N+)]
degenętse:s my arms are long S
[-nęts(a)$_N$- arm -es$_V$- be long]
•es be two long objects
[de+A/P+(N+)]
degenętse:s my arms are long S
[-nęts(a)$_N$- arm -es$_V$- be long]
•e:s'ah be short in length
[ni+A/P+N+ contains: -es$_V$- be long -'ah diminutive]
nigęhne:s'ah a short length of cloth S
[-(i)hn(a)$_N$- cloth -es$_V$- be long]
•e:s'ah be longish
see: ǫ:s'ah, e:s'ah [ni+y+] be longish
niyǫ:s'ah just a little bit long S
•(')ehsd hit s.t. belonging to s.o.
[de+TR+N+ -(')drehd(a)$_N$- vehicle, car -(')ehsd$_V$- hit with s.t.]
ate'drehda'ehs I hit his car P
•e:sǫ's several long objects
[A/P+N+]
onrahde:sǫ's long leaves S
[-nrahd(a)$_N$- leaf -esǫ's$_V$- several long objects]
•ehsǫ' be a wanderer, a loiterer
[ti+A+ contains: -e$_V$- go -sǫ' plural]
tihehsǫ' he is a wanderer, a loiterer
•et'ah pretend
[a:+ w+]
a:we:t'ah it is implied; pretend P
•et'ahshǫ:'ǫh make-believe, pretend
[a:+w+ -et'ah$_V$- pretend -sǫ:'ǫh plural]
a:wet'ahshǫ:'ǫh make-believe; pretend
•ehwa... look for stems beginning with (r)ih(wa)...
•ehwihsdaędahkwa' onǫhsǫ:t a bank vault; a safe
ehwihsdaędahkwa' bank
onǫhsǫ:t a room; a vault
•eyę'gwadǫda:ta' gaya:' a tobacco pouch
eyę'gwadǫda:ta' s.t. that holds tobacco
gaya:' a bag

Ę

•ę' fall, drop, reduce
see: (a's)ę' fall in
goge'ę:s her hair is falling out H
•ę:' coloured
[N+]
ǫhya'ę:' S
•i:, ę:, e: think, hope, want
[A+]
i:wi: he wants H
i:wi: I want H
i:yę: she wants H
ihse: you want H
ihsne: you two want H
agwe: we all (excl.) want H
ahi:' I thought, I intended P
ehswe:' you all thought P
ahe:' he thought P
ehsne:' you two thought P
ehswe:' you all thought P
ędwe:he:k we all (incl.) will in thought P
ahęne:' they (m) thought; they left together P
hawe:'ǫ: he has willed S
se:ǫ:' you wanted or believed S

Legend: H habitual, P punctual, S stative, I imperative, PURP purposive, PURP-H purposive habitual, PURP-PAST purposive past, PURP-P purposive punctual, PURP-I purposive imperative; see §8.6, §8.11 in Appendix J. Alphabetization in stems ignores length (:), and any h's or glottal stops (') that are not between vowels. See §2.2 of the User Guide for explanation.

•ę: predictor, messenger, proverb, prediction, saying, prophesy
[neʼ P+ -ę$_{V}$- say]
neʼ ho:nę: predictors, messengers (lit.: what they (m) said); proverb, prediction, saying, prophesy

•ę:, e:, i: think, hope, want
[A+]
i:wi: he wants H
i:wi: I want H
i:yę: she wants H
ihse: you want H
ihsne: you two want H
agwe: we all (excl.) want H
ahi:ʼ I thought, I intended P
ehswe:ʼ you all thought P
ahe:ʼ he thought P
ehsne:ʼ you two thought P
ehswe:ʼ you all thought P
ędwe:he:k we all (incl.) will in thought P
ahę:ne:ʼ they (m) thought; they left together P
hawe:ʼǫ: he has willed S
se:ǫ:ʼ you wanted or believed S

•ęʼ lie on the ground
see: (y)ęʼ [ga+] lie on the ground
ga:yęʼ it is lying on the ground S

•ę(:) put down, place, set down
see: (y)ę(:) [A+(N+)] put down, place, set down
ęhsyę:ʼ you will put it there P
niga:yęʼ where it is at; where it is placed S

•ęʼ a group of things lying on the ground, be lying on the ground covering a large area
ganawaę:ʼ a swamp; a pond S
[ga+ -naw(a)$_{N}$- pond, swamp -ę$_{V}$- lie on the ground]
gayęhsraę:ʼ a blanket lying on the ground S
[ga+ -yęhsr(a)$_{N}$- blanket -ę$_{V}$- lie on the ground]
ohǫdaę:ʼ a bush; a shrub S
[o+ -(h)ǫd(a)$_{N}$- bush, shrub -ę$_{V}$- lie on the ground]
węʼnihsgaę:ʼ a hoop (lying down) S
[w+ -ęʼnihsg(a)$_{N}$- wheel -ę$_{V}$- lie on the ground]

•ę: predictor, messenger, proverb, prediction, saying, prophesy
[neʼ P+ -ę$_{V}$- say]
neʼ ho:nę: predictors, messengers (lit.: what they (m) said); proverb, prediction, saying, prophesy

•ę:, e:, i: think, hope, want
[A+]
i:wi: he wants H
i:wi: I want H
i:yę: she wants H
ihse: you want H
ihsne: you two want H
agwe: we all (excl.) want H
ahi:ʼ I thought, I intended P
ehswe:ʼ you all thought P
ahe:ʼ he thought P
ehsne:ʼ you two thought P
ehswe:ʼ you all thought P
ędwe:he:k we all (incl.) will in thought P
ahę:ne:ʼ they (m) thought; they left together P
hawe:ʼǫ: he has willed S
se:ǫ:ʼ you wanted or believed S

•ęʼ lie on the ground
see: (y)ęʼ [ga+] lie on the ground
ga:yęʼ it is lying on the ground S

•ę(:) put down, place, set down
see: (y)ę(:) [A+(N+)] put down, place, set down
ęhsyę:ʼ you will put it there P
niga:yęʼ where it is at; where it is placed S

•ęʼ a group of things lying on the ground, be lying on the ground covering a large area
ganawaę:ʼ a swamp; a pond S
[ga+ -naw(a)$_N$- pond, swamp -ę$_V$- lie on the ground]
gayęhsraę:ʼ a blanket lying on the ground S
[ga+ -yęhsr(a)$_N$- blanket -ę$_V$- lie on the ground]
ohǫdaę:ʼ a bush; a shrub S
[o+ -(h)ǫd(a)$_N$- bush, shrub -ę$_V$- lie on the ground]
węʼnihsgaę:ʼ a hoop (lying down) S
[w+ -ęʼnihsg(a)$_N$- wheel -ę$_V$- lie on the ground]

•ęʼ gamble, bet, play a game
see: (y)ęʼ [de+A+(N+)] gamble, bet, play a game
dęhodi:yęʼ, detodi:yęʼ they (m) are gambling, betting S

•ęʼ lack s.t.
see: (y)ęʼ [(tęʼ) deʼ+ not P+(N+)] lack s.t.
tęʼ dewa:gyęʼ it is not mine; I do not have S

•ęʼ have s.t.
see: (y)ęʼ [P+(N+)] have s.t.
hodi:yęʼ they (m) have; they have laid S
agahyaę:ʼ I have fruit
[-(a)hy(a)$_N$- fruit, berry -ę$_V$- lie]

•ę(:) be quiet, still
see: (y)ę(:) [taʼ+de+P+ag+] be quiet, still
taʼdesagyę: you are quiet S

•ę(:) put things side by side, lie side by side, be lying side by side
see: (y)ę(:) [tsaʼde+] put things side by side, lie side by side, be lying side by side
tsaʼdęhsyę:ʼ you will put, lay them side by side P

•ędaʼ become, acquire, finish
see: (y)ędaʼ [A/P+(N+)] become, acquire, finish
ęsayę:daʼ you will acquire, obtain s.t. P

•ędaʼ settle
see: (y)ędaʼ [ha+d+ga+] settle
hatga:yę:daʼ it is settled P

•ęʼda(:,h) burn s.t.
see: (hr)ęʼda(:,h) [(N+)] burn s.t.
ęhsręʼda:ʼ you will burn s.t. P

•ęhdad run
see: (w)ęhdad [de+…] run
da:gaǫ:węhda:t they (f/m) might run P

•ęhdatǫ(:) run all over
[de+... -(w)ęhdad$_V$- run]
dęgęnę:datǫ:ʼ they (z) will run all over P

•ędaętaʼ morning star
[d+aʼ+w+ -ęd(a)$_N$- day -ęd$_V$- cause to lie on the ground]
dawędaętaʼ the morning star

•ędagę: be a wimp, be timid, weak, cowardly
see: (w)ędagę: [P+] be a wimp, be timid, weak, cowardly
gowędagę:, agawęda:gę: she is a wimp, timid S

•ędahkwaʼ a place where s.t. is put
[contains: -(y)ę$_V$- lie on the ground]
hadihstǫdraędahkwaʼ a barn (lit.: where they (m) put the hay)
[hadi+ -(h)stǫdr(a)$_N$- straw, hay -ędahkwaʼ- place where s.t. is put]
ehwihsdaędahkwaʼ a bank
[e+ -(h)wihsd(a)$_N$- money -ędahkwaʼ- place where s.t. is put]

•ęhdahkwaʼ path, hallway
[contains: -ęhd$_V$- walk]
ęhdahkwaʼ a path; a hallway (lit. where they walk)

•ęhdas zipper
[de+w+ contains: -(w)ęhdad$_V$- run]
dewęhda:s a zipper (lit.: it runs)

Legend: H habitual, P punctual, S stative, I imperative, PURP purposive, PURP-H purposive habitual, PURP-PAST purposive past, PURP-P purposive punctual, PURP-I purposive imperative; see §8.6, §8.11 in Appendix J. Alphabetization in stems ignores length (:), and any h's or glottal stops (ʼ) that are not between vowels. See §2.2 of the User Guide for explanation.

•ędei, ędí know
see: (y)ędei, (y)ędí [(N+)] know
dejidwayę:dí: we all (incl.) do not know any longer S
•ędehsr(a) arousal
[ę+]
ędehsraʼ sexual arousal
•ędędahkwaʼ brush
ędęda̱hkwaʼ a brush
•ędęhęwihtaʼ morning star
[d+w+ -ęd(a)$_N$- day -ęhęwihd$_V$- cause to convey]
dwędęhę:wihtaʼ the morning star (lit.: it brings the day)
•ędǫʼ several things lying on the ground; have several things
[contains: -(y)ę$_V$- lie on the ground]
gʼadrehdaędǫʼ parked cars S
[ga+ -(ʼ)drehd(a)$_N$- vehicle -ędǫʼ$_V$- several objects lying on the ground]
ageʼdre̱hdaędǫʼ I have several cars S
[P+ -(ʼ)drehd(a)$_N$- vehicle -ędǫʼ$_V$- several objects lying on the ground]
•ędo:ʼ be difficult
[w+]
wę:do:ʼ it is difficult S
•ędǫh shake, sway
[de+A/P+(N+)]
deya:wę:dǫh it shakes H
dęya:wę:dǫh it will sway P
•ędǫh shake s.t., etc.
[de+P+(N+)]
deyogyo̱hgwę:dǫhs upheaval of a crowd of people (celebration, riot) H
[de+yo+ stem: -(i)gyohgwędǫhs- celebration, riot; consists of: -(i)gyohg(wa)$_N$- crowd -ędǫh$_V$- shake s.t.]
deyoʼnhęhtsędǫhǫh it is wagging its tail S
de·yoʼnhęht·sę́·dǫ·hǫh it is wagging its tail
[de+P+ stem: -(ʼ)nhęhtsędǫh- wag a tail; consists of: -(ʼ)nhęhts(a)$_N$- tail -ędǫh$_V$- shake s.t.]
desayaʼdę:dǫh you will shake (your body) I
[de+P+(N+) stem: -yaʼd(a)$_N$- body -ędǫh$_V$- shake s.t.]
•ędǫnyaʼd tease, joke, jest
[TR+ad+ contains: -ędǫh- $_V$ shake s.t.]
hadędǫnyaʼtaʼ he is a joker H
ęhsheyʼadędǫnyaʼt you will make fun of it; s.t. will make fun of you, messing with your head or mind (refers to reliving your sins before death); you will joke P
sadędǫnyaʼdǫh you are joking S
•ędǫnyaʼd jest
[o+ad+]
odędo:nyaʼt a jest
•ędǫnyaʼdahsgǫ: happy-go-lucky, joke, jest, be obnoxious
[P+ad+ - ędǫnyaʼd- $_V$ tease, joke, jest -hsgǫ: easily]
hodędǫnyaʼda̱hsgǫ: he is a joker, happy-go-lucky; he is obnoxious H
•ędǫnyaʼtaʼ convulsions
[go+ad+ contains: -ędǫh$_V$- shake s.t.]
godędǫnyaʼtaʼ convulsions
•ędǫnyǫʼ many things lying on the ground
[contains: -(y)ę$_V$- lie on the ground]
ga̱hędaędǫnyǫʼ fields S
[ga+ -(h)ęd(a)$_N$- field -ędǫnyǫʼ$_V$- several objects lying on the ground]
ohwęjaędǫnyǫʼ lands S
[o+ -(ǫ)hwęj(a)$_N$- land -ędǫnyǫʼ$_V$- several objects lying on the ground]
•ęgohd go under s.t.
see: ǫgohd [de+...ad+N+] go under s.t.
dęhsadʼęhę:gǫht you will go under the fence P
[de+...ad+N+ stem: -(a)dęʼh(ę)$_N$- fence -ǫgohd$_V$- surpass, go under s.t.]

•ę'gw, (a)hdę'gw swell up
[ad+N+]
awatnegę'go' water rose or swelled P
[-(h)neg(a)$_N$- water, liquid -ę'gw$_V$- swell up]

•ę(h,') happen
[P+]
niya:węhs how it happens H
a:ya:węh I wish, hope P
niyawę'ǫh how it did happen S

•ęhę(:,w) direct, convey
see: (r)ihwęhę(:)
hehoihwęhę: he has taken a message S

•ęhęh be outspoken
[he'+s+P+ contains: -ęhę(:,w)- $_V$ direct, convey tsǫ: just; gwa'e:' again]
heji:sę:hęh tsǫ: you speak without thinking, spout off H
heshawęhęh tsǫ: he speaks without thinking H
heshawęhęh tsǫ: he speaks without thinking H
hehshawęhęh gwa'e:' he is speaking without thinking again, as usual H
hejagonęhęh they (f/m) are outspoken H

•ęhęh be near here
[d+s+ga+ -ęhę(:)$_V$- direct, convey]
dęhsgę:hęh near here

•ęhi:' be stacked
[A+ad+ -(r)ęh(a)$_N$- bundle -i:'- $_V$ be stuck onto s.t.]
wadęhi:' it is stacked S

•ęhod(ę) stack s.t.
see: (r)ęhod [de+...ad+] stack
dęsad'ęhodę', dęhsrę'ho:dę' you will stack things, put one thing on top of the other

•ęhod stack things
see: (r)ęhod [de+...N+] stack things
degai'ęho:t it is piled up S

•ęn(a) song, music
see: (r)ęn(a) song, music
gaę:na' a song

•ęnadaę
see: nadaę' [ę+] camp
ęhsęnadaę:' you will camp P

•ęnadinyǫ('d)
see: nadinyǫ('d) [ę+] move in
ęgęnadi:nyǫ' I will be moving into a dwelling P

•ęnagrad
see: nagrad [ę+] be born
a'ǫnagra:t birth (lit.: s.o. was born) P

•ęnanhǫdagw take over a song from s.o.
see: (r)ęnanhǫdagw [TR+] take over a song from s.o.
ahǫwaęnanhǫda:go' he took over the song P

•(ę)nahsgwahgw jump
[de+]
deyǫnahsgwahkwa' she is jumping H
dęyǫnahsgwahk she will jump P
desęnahsgwahgwęh you are jumping S

•(ę)nahsgwahgw sky-dive
[de+d+]
detęnahsgwahkwa' they (m) are sky-diving; paratroopers H

•ęnahsre: sing
see: (r)ęnahsre: sing
ahaęnahsre:' he followed the song; he sang along P

•ęne'waǫ, ęne'wa(:) be unexpected, become surprised
see: ne'waǫ, ne'wa(:) [ę+] be unexpected, become surprised
gęne'waǫ:s I get surprised H

•ę'nhe:ga:' ball deer
[de+w+ contains: -ę'nh(otra)$_N$- ball]
dewę'nhe:ga:' a ball deer (so-called because they roll up in a ball)

•ę'nho: baseball game
[de+w+ contains: -ę'nh(otra)$_N$- ball]
dewę'nho: a baseball game

Legend: H habitual, P punctual, S stative, I imperative, PURP purposive, PURP-H purposive habitual, PURP-PAST purposive past, PURP-P purposive punctual, PURP-I purposive imperative; see §8.6, §8.11 in Appendix J. Alphabetization in stems ignores length (:), and any h's or glottal stops (') that are not between vowels. See §2.2 of the User Guide for explanation.

•(ę)nhoktaʼgeh ball diamond
[de+yǫ+ contains:-ęʼnh(otra)$_N$- ball -oʼkd$_V$- end -ʼgeh on, at]
deyǫʼnhoktaʼgeh ball diamond

•ęʼnh(otra) ball
ęʼnho:traʼ a ball

•ęʼnhotre:s football
[w+ -ęʼnh(otra)$_N$- ball -es$_V$- long]
węʼnho:tre:s a football

•ęʼnhotroiʼa:s play basketball
hęnęʼhotroiʼa:s they (m) play basketball H
[-ęʼnh(otra)$_N$- ball -oiʼa:$_V$- torch]

•ęniʼdage(w)
see: iʼdage(w) [ęn+] wipe one's behind
ęgęnida:ge:ʼ I will wipe myself clean of fecal matter P

•ęnidagrę
see: (i)dagrę [P+ęn+] lay oneself down
agęnida:gre:ʼ I laid myself down S

•ęhniʼdagyeʼs moon phases, phases
[-ęhniʼd(a)$_N$- month -dagyeʼ$_V$- be ongoing]
ęhniʼdagyeʼs phases of the moon

•ęniʼdeni, ęniʼdeny
see: niʼdeni, niʼdeny [ę+] fart
agęniʼdenyǫ: I have farted S

•ęhniʼdoʼkdę last quarter moon
[a+wa+ad+ -ęhniʼd(a)$_N$- month -oʼkd$_V$- end]
awadę̱hnidoʼkdęʼ the was the end of the moon, the last quarter

•ęʼnigǫhgaę suffer
see: (ʼ)nigǫhgaę [deʼ+ not …ę+] suffer
desęʼnigǫhgaeʼ you suffer S

•ęʼnigǫhawęnyaʼd be entertaining
see: (ʼ)nigǫhawęnyaʼd [de+…ę+] be entertaining
deyoʼnigǫhawę:nyaʼt it is entertaining S

•ęʼnigǫhod suggest, advise
see: (ʼ)nigǫhod [de+…ę+] suggest, advise
ętsęʼnigǫho:dęʼ you will suggest, present an idea P

•ęʼnigǫhoʼdrǫ worry, despair, be desperate
see: (ʼ)nigǫhoʼdrǫ [ę+] worry, despair, desperate
ęhsęʼnigǫhoʼdrǫ:ʼ you will worry, despair; you will be desperate P

•ęʼnigǫhogw grieve
see: (ʼ)nigǫhogw [de+…ę+] grieve
degęʼnigǫhogwahs I am brokenhearted (lit.: my mind is scattered) H

•ęʼnigǫhoʼkd give up
see: (ʼ)nigǫhoʼkd [ę+] give up
ahęʼnigǫhoʼkdęʼ he gave up (his will to live) P

•ęʼnigǫhoʼneg revolt, rebel
see: (ʼ)nigǫhoʼneg [de+…ę+] revolt, rebel
ętsęʼnigǫhoʼne:k you will revolt, remove yourself (bodily and in spirit) P

•ęʼnigǫhotahsd suggest, advise
see: (ʼ)nigǫhotahsd [de+TR+ę+] suggest, advise
ętseyʼęnigǫho:tahs you will suggest to her, advise her P

•ęʼnihsg(a) wheel, circle, hoop
[(w)+]
ęnihsga:ʼ, węʼnihsga:ʼ a wheel; a circle; a hoop

•ęʼnihsg(a) button
see: (h)nyahsg(a:) button
ęhnyahsga:ʼ a button

•ęʼnihsgaǫni: circle
[de+w+ -ęʼnihsg(a)$_N$- wheel -ǫni, ǫny$_V$- make circle]
dewęʼnya̱hsgaǫni: a circle

•ęʼnihsgaǫni: hoop
[w+ -ęʼnihsg(a)$_N$- wheel -ǫni, ǫny$_V$- make circle]
węʼnihsgaǫ:ni: hoop

•ęnihsr(a) shelf
[w+]
węnihsrǫ' shelves; shelving
•ęnigyohgwagęni vote, elect
see: (i)gyohgwagęni [de+...ę(n)+] vote, elect
dęhsęnigyohgwagę:ni' you will vote, cast lots P
•ęniha borrow, rent
see: niha [ę+] borrow, rent
ęhsęniha' you will borrow, rent P
•ęnihę(:) quit, prevent, stop
gęnihęha', ganihęha' I always quit H
a:hęni:hę:' he would stop (himself) P
agęnihę' I stopped or quit S
sęni:hę: quit I
•ęniho'g electricity
[de+w+ contains: -'s plural, -sǫ' plural]
dewęnihoks, dewęniho's electricity H
dewęniho'ksǫh lightning S
•ęni'jǫhsgwaę(:) squat
sęnijǫhsgwaęhę' you squat all the time H
ęsęnijǫhsgwaę: you will squat P
sęni'jǫhsgwaę: squat I
•ęnihnadog perceive
sęnihnado:ka' you are perceiving s.t. right now H
ęhsęnihna:do:k you will perceive s.t. P
•ęnihsgyage urinate
see: nihsgyage [ę] urinate
agęnihsgya:ge: I am urinating S
•ęnitsgod(ǫnyǫ) sit ups
see: nitsgod(ǫnyǫ) [ę+] sit ups
ęgaǫ:nitsgodǫ:nyǫ:' they (f/m) will do sit ups P
•ęnitsgrǫdi spit
see: nitsgrǫdi [ę+] spit
sęni:tsgrǫ:dih spit I
•ęniya'gya'g burp, belch
see: niya'gya'g [ę+] burp, belch
atgęninya'gya'k I burped, belched P
•ęno'sgwi sweep
see: ono'sgwi [de+...ę+] sweep
dęgęn'osgwi' I will sweep P
•(ę')nowaę(:) squat
asę'nowaę:' you are squatting P
•ęno:wę:
see: nowę(:) [P+ę+] liar
sęno:wę: you are a liar S
•ęnowęhd
see: nowęhd [ę+] lie
agę:no:węht I lied P
•ęnǫ:'ǫh be slow
[s+ga+ -inǫ:'ǫh$_v$-]
sgęnǫ:'ǫh slowly S
•ęnǫ' be well; hello
[s+ga+ -inǫ:'ǫh$_v$-]
sgę:nǫ' it is well; hello S
•ęnǫda:(h) record songs
see: (r)ęnǫda:(h) record songs
ahaę:nǫ:da: he recorded songs, he taped s.t. P
•ęnǫhdǫ(:) know
[P+]
ęwagęnǫhdǫ:k I will know P
agęnǫhdǫ' I know S
•ęnǫhdǫha' boss, authority
[d+w+ contains: -ęnǫhdǫ(:)$_V$- know]
dwęnǫhdǫha' it is the boss, the authority
•ęnǫhdǫnyǫ(:) think, wonder, feel well
[contains: -ęnǫhdǫ(:)$_V$- know -nyǫ plural]
sęnǫhdǫnyǫh you are wondering, thinking H
ęhsęnǫhdǫ:nyǫ:' you will wonder, think P
jǫnǫhdǫnyǫh to be healthy; to have well being again
•ęnotge: loud music
see: (r)ęnotge: loud music
gaęnotge: loud, amplified music
•ęnǫhtwahsd force, rape
see: nǫhtwahsd [de+TR+ę+] force, rape
dahshagonǫhtwahs he forced her P

Legend: H habitual, P punctual, S stative, I imperative, PURP purposive, PURP-H purposive habitual, PURP-PAST purposive past, PURP-P purposive punctual, PURP-I purposive imperative; see §8.6, §8.11 in Appendix J. Alphabetization in stems ignores length (:), and any h's or glottal stops (') that are not between vowels. See §2.2 of the User Guide for explanation.

•ęnǫwaę(:) sink
[P+]
węnǫwaęhę' it sinks (all the time) H
awęnowaę:' it sank P
onawaę:' it has sunk in liquid; it sank S

•ęnǫwaęd sink s.t.
agęnowaędahk I made it sink P

•ęnǫhwed sleep over
see: nǫhwed [ę+…] sleep over
ęgęnǫhwe:t I will sleep over P

•ę'nyadǫ' angel
[de+yǫkiy+ę+ -(')ny(a)$_N$- finger, hand -(')nyadǫ(:)$_V$- protect, embrace]
deyǫkiyę'nyadǫ' angels (lit.: they protect us with their hands)

•ę'nya(ę,:) govern, watch, look after
[contains: ę+ -(')ny(a)$_N$- finger, hand -a:'$_V$- hold, contain, include]
atsę'nya:' you looked after it P
dehsę'nya:' you are looking after it right now S

•ęnyaha'd boil s.t.
see: nyaha'd [ę+] boil s.t.
sęnyaha't boil it I

•ę'nyawe, ę'nya'o clap
see: (')nyawe [de+…ę+] clap
desę'nya'we:k, desę'nya'o:k clap I

•ę'nyotra' mittens
see: (')nyotra' mittens
ę'nyo:tra' mittens

•ęhsędǫh stamp one's foot, tap one's foot
[(de+) P+ -(a)hsi('da), (ę)hs(a)$_N$- foot -ędǫh- $_V$ shake s.t.]
howęhsę:dǫh he is keeping a beat with his feet H
desęhsę:dǫh you (s) are stamping your feet (moving them up and down) H

•ę(h)sętw, ę(h)sęto kick
gęsętwahs I am kicking H
ęgęhsę:to' I will kick it P
wę:sę:twęh a kick S
sę:sętoh kick it I

•ęhsga: take off
[(d+)... -(a)hsi('da), (ę)hs(a)$_N$- foot -ga:- $_V$ make a rattling or grinding noise]
dahęhsga:' he squealed out; took off abruptly P

•(ę)hshǫ lower back
[contains: -hneh on, at]
sęhshǫhneh on your lower back

•ęhsots(i) take off one's shoes
[de+... -(a)hsi('da), (ę)hs(a)$_N$- foot -ots(i)- $_V$ remove an outer covering]
desęhso:tsih take your shoes off I

•ęhsoweg put on one's shoes
[de+... -(a)hsi('da), (ę)hs(a)$_N$- foot +oweg- $_V$ cover s.t.]
desęhso:we:k put your shoes on P

•ęhsoweks(i) take off one's shoes
[de+... -(a)hsi('da), (ę)hs(a)$_N$- foot +oweg- $_V$ cover -s(i) undo]
desęhsowe:ksih take your shoes off I

•ęhsoweksǫ(:) be shod
[de+P+ -(a)hsi('da), (ę)hs(a)$_N$- foot +oweg- $_V$ cover -sǫ' plural]
dęhonęhsoweksǫ' they (m) have their shoes on S

•ęsǫ: be shod
[de+P+ contains: -(a)hsi('da), (ę)hs(a)$_N$- foot]
dęhowę:sǫ: he has the shoes on S

•ęhte:'ah tramp, vagabond, hobo
[P+ad+ contains: -ęhte$_V$- go and hit, strike, knock -'ah diminutive]
ahodęhte:'ah tramp, hobo, vagabond

•ętsga:' mattress, sleeping mat
[ga+ contains: -(n)itsg(wa)$_N$- lower body -a:'$_V$- hold, contain, include]
gętsga:' a mattress; a sleeping mat

•ę'tsigahgya'g cartwheel
[de+…ę+ contains: -(')tsigahd(a)- -(i)ya'g$_V$- cut, break]
desę'tsihgahgya'ks you do cartwheels H
dęsę'tsigahgya'k you will do a cartwheel P

•ętw(ahd) broadcast s.t.
see: (y)ętw(ahd) broadcast s.t.
dęshaihwaętwaht he will bring forth a message P

G

•g eat
i:ge:s I eat H
ęge:k I will eat P
agahyagǫh I am eating fruit S
[stem: -(a)hy(a)$_N$- fruit, berry -g$_V$- eat]

•ga: make a rattling or grinding noise
[de+(s+) A/P+N+ present in:]
ętsęhsga:ˀ you take off abruptly, quickly, suddenly P
[(d+)… stem: -ęhsga:ˀ- take off; consists of: -(a)hsi(ˀda), (ę)hs(a)$_N$- foot -ga:$_V$- make a rattling or grinding noise]
deyohsgyęda:ga: bones are rattling S
[de+(s+) A/P+N+ stem: -(h)sgyęˀd(a:)$_N$- bone -ga:, gae:$_V$- make a rattling or grinding noise]
desatnoˀja:ga: (you (s)) grind your teeth! I
[de+…at+ stem: -noˀjaga:- grind one's teeth; consists of: -noˀj(a)$_N$- tooth -ga:$_V$- make a rattling or grinding noise]

•ga:ˀ noise
[o+at+ -ga:$_V$- make a rattling or grinding noise, loud noise]
otga:ˀ a noise

•gaˀ like the taste of s.t.
[P+]
age:gaˀs I like the taste of it H
ǫge:gaˀ I liked the taste of it P
ogaˀǫh it tastes good S

•ga: price
[o+]
o:ga:ˀ a price on s.t.

•ga: debt
[o+ -ga$_N$- price -gǫ: in]
oga:gǫ: in debt

•ga:ˀ equity, capital, value, worth
[tsęh what ni+yo+ -ga:$_N$- price]
tsęh niyoga:ˀ equity; capital; value; worth

•(ˀ)g(a:) tale, legend, parable, story
[o+]
oˀga:ˀ a parable; a tale; a story; a legend

•gaˀd(a) white oak
[ga+]
gagaˀdaˀ white oak

•gaˀd(a) pants, underpants
[o+]
ogaˀdaˀ, ogaˀdaˀshǫ:ˀǫh pants; underpants

•gadad raise s.t.
[N+ present in:]
hadęwęnaga:da:s he is an interpreter H
[A+adę+ contains: -węn(a)$_N$- voice, word -gadad$_V$- raise s.t. up]
ędwaęnagada:t we all (incl.) will raise the song P
[A+adę+ contains: -(r)ęn(a)$_N$- song -gadad$_V$- raise s.t. up]

•gadahgw hollow out
[at+ contains: -(h)g(a:)$_N$- chip -(h)gw$_V$- remove]
ęhsatga:dahgoˀ you will hollow out a canoe, a wooden bowl, etc. (take out the chips) P

•gaˀdeˀ be many, lots
[A/P+(N+)]
ęyǫgwadęnˀatragaˀdeˀ we all will have lots of food P
[contains: -naˀtr(a)$_N$- food, lunch -gaˀdeˀ$_V$- many, lots]

•gaˀdeˀ be so many
[ni+yon+ at+]
niyonatgaˀdeˀ there are so many S

•gaˀdeˀ often, many, lots
[o+at+]
otgadeˀ often; many; lots S

Legend: H habitual, P punctual, S stative, I imperative, PURP purposive, PURP-H purposive habitual, PURP-PAST purposive past, PURP-P purposive punctual, PURP-I purposive imperative; see §8.6, §8.11 in Appendix J. Alphabetization in stems ignores length (:), and any h's or glottal stops (ˀ) that are not between vowels. See §2.2 of the User Guide for explanation.

•ga'de' have much, many, lots
[P+(ad+) N+]
aknǫhsaga'de' I have many houses S
[contains: -nǫhs(a)$_N$- house
-ga'de'$_V$- many, lots]
•gadinhodǫ:nyǫ' gadi:nyo:' zoo animals
gadinhodǫ:nyǫ' they (z) are locked up
gadi:nyo:' wild animals
•gaditse:nę' hanyohs a butcher (lit.: he kills the animals)
gadi:tse:nę' farm animals (lit.: they (z) are domesticated, tame)
hanyohs he kills s.t.
•gahd(ę,ani) cost s.o.
[P+ -ga:$_N$- price -(a)hd$_V$- be like, resemble]
ǫge:gahdę' that's how much it cost me P
•(')ga:dǫh tell a story
s'ega:dǫ: tell a story I
•gahdǫnyǫ look around
[de+...at+ -gahtw$_V$- look -ǫnyǫ plural]
desatga̱hdǫ:nyǫhs you are looking around H
•gahdr(a) tear
[o+]
ogahdra' a tear (in one's eye)
•gahdrahi shed tears, cry
[P+ -gahdr(a)$_N$- tear -(hr)i'$_V$- break up]
ęhsaga̱hdrahi' you will shed tears P
•gahdrod drip sweat, tears
[P+ -gahdr(a)$_N$- tear -od$_V$- stand]
ęhsagahdro:dę' you will drip tears P
sagahdro:t you are tearing, shedding tear-drops S
•gahdrǫni, gahdrǫny examine closely
[at+]
satgahdrǫnihs you are staring at it; examining it closely H
sagahdrǫni: you are 'nosy' with your eyes (always looking); gape; stare S

•gaę be willing, consent
[P+]
ęwagegaę' I will consent P
•gaę be unwilling
[(tę') de'+ not P+ contains: -gaę$_V$- be willing]
dewagegaęhs I am always unwilling H
dewagegaę: I do not want to do it; I am unwilling S
•gaędahkwa' pawned item
[ǫ+at+ -gaędahgw$_V$- pawn -hkwa' instrument]
ǫtgaędahkwa' the item to be pawned
•gaęhęgw double back, return
[s+...at+ -n$_N$- noun-gaęh(e')$_V$- cross -gw undo, reverse]
ǫsagatgaę:hę:go' I should turn around and go back the way I came P
•ga'ga:' crow, raven
ga'ga:' a crow; a raven
•ga:gwahd collect money
[-ga:$_N$- price -gwahd$_V$- cause to gather, choose, pick]
ega:gwahta' s.o. collects money H
•gahgwaos(a) eyebrow
ogahgwaohsa' eyebrow(s)
segahgwao:s'ageh on your eyebrow
•ga:gwahs cashier
[e+ -ga:$_N$- price -gw$_V$- gather, choose, pick]
ega:gwahs a cashier
•gahgweg close one's eyes
[de+TR+ -gah(a)$_N$- eye -gweg$_V$- close]
dęsatga̱hgwe:k you will close your eyes P
•gahgweg deceive
[de+TR+ -gah(a)$_N$- eye -gweg$_V$- close]
dęhshega̱hgwe:k you will pull the wool over her eyes, outsmart her, deceive her P
•gahgwegǫh be blind
[de+A+ -gah(a)$_N$- eye -gwegǫh$_V$- all]
dehaga̱hgwe:gǫh he is blind S

•ga:gweni, ga:gweny afford s.t.
ęgega:gwe:niʼ I will afford it P
[-ga:$_N$- price -gweni, gweny$_V$- able to do s.t., succeed]

•gah(a) eye
ogahaʼ an eye
segahaʼgeh on your eyes

•gahadeni, gahadeny turn s.t. on
[de+... -gah(a)$_N$- eye -deni, deny$_V$- change]
desegaha:de:nih turn it on (involves movement) I

•gahadeni, gahadeny turn around
[de+...at+ -gah(a)$_N$- eye -deni, deny$_V$- change]
dęhsatgaha:de:niʼ you will turn yourself around P
desatgaha:de:nih turn around I

•gahadenyǫgwahǫ(:) twirl
[de+...at+ -gah(a)$_N$- eye -deni, deny$_V$- change -gw- undo, reverse -ǫh go and do several things]
desatgahadenyǫgwahǫ: twirl I

•gahadǫh roll
[at+ -gah(a)$_N$- eye -ędǫh$_V$- shake s.t.]
watgahadǫhs it rolls H

•gahaędahd fuzzy, out-of-focus, unclear
[taʼ+de+yo+ contains: -gah(a)$_N$- eye -ędahd$_V$- cause to lie on the ground]
taʼdeyogahaędaht it is fuzzy, out of focus, opaque, unclear S

•gahagaęheh be cross-eyed
[A+ -gah(a)$_N$- eye -gaęh(eʼ)$_V$- cross]
hagahgaęheh he is cross-eyed S

•gahagwaǫd have a sty
[P+ -gah(a)- eye -gw(a)$_N$- lump -ǫd$_V$- attached]
agegahagwaǫ:t I have a sty S

•gahahęh have masked eyes
[de+P+at+ -gah(a)$_N$- eye -(h)ęh$_V$- mid]
dęhotgahahęh he has masked eyes

•gahahsohtaʼ eyeliner
[ǫ+at+ -gah(a)$_N$- eye -(a)hsohd$_V$- colour]
ǫtgahahsohtaʼ eyeliner

•gahatgihd give dirty looks
[at+ -gah(a)$_N$- eye -tgihd$_V$- make dirty, ugly]
asatgahatgiht you give dirty looks P
satgahatgihdǫh you are always giving dirty looks; you are giving dirty looks (right now) S

•gahatw, gahato roll, turn over
[at+ -gah(a)$_N$- eye -to, tw$_V$- go and stand several things]
satgahatoh roll over I

•gahatw, gahato turn over
[N+ present in:]
gahehdagahatwęh a ploughed field S
[-hehd(a)$_N$- earth - gahatw, gahato$_V$- go turn over]

•gahawęnye(:) blurred vision
[de+...at+ -gah(a)$_N$- eye -(a)węnye(:)$_V$- stir, mix]
atgatgahawęnye:ʼ I had blurred vision P

•gahe:ʼ price
[ga+ -ga:$_N$- price -(h)e:ʼ$_V$- sitting up on top of s.t.]
gagahe:ʼ the price of s.t.

•gahehd(a) eyelash, stem (of a berry), eye (of a corn kernel)
ogahehdaʼ eyelash; the stem of a berry; the eye of the corn kernel
segahehdaʼgeh on your eyelashes

•gahehdaę:ʼ have dandruff
[P+ -gahehd(a)$_N$- eyelash, stem (of a berry), eye (of a corn kernel) -ę$_V$- lie, have]
sagahehdaę:ʼ you have dandruff S

•gahehdęhd hull
ęhsegahehdęht you will hull berries P
[-gahehd(a)$_N$- eyelash, stem (of a berry), eye (of a corn kernel) ; -(y)ęhd$_V$- hit, knock down, strike]

Legend: H habitual, P punctual, S stative, I imperative, PURP purposive, PURP-H purposive habitual, PURP-PAST purposive past, PURP-P purposive punctual, PURP-I purposive imperative; see §8.6, §8.11 in Appendix J. Alphabetization in stems ignores length (:), and any h's or glottal stops (ʼ) that are not between vowels. See §2.2 of the User Guide for explanation.

•gahehgyaʼg hull
ęsega̱hehgyaʼk you will hull berries P
[P+ -gahehd(a)$_N$- eyelash, stem (of a berry), eye (of a corn kernel) -iyaʼg$_V$- cut]

•(ga)hey, (gę)hey, (i)hey, (ga)he:, (gę)he:, (i)he: die, be weak, be exhausted
hęhe:yǫhs he is dying H
ęgihe:ʼ I will die P
awe:tʼa:ʼ agihe:yǫ: I'm pretending I am dead S
a.go.wi.ya.ge.hé:yaʼs her baby died
[-wiy(a)$_N$- child, offspring -(ga)hey, (gę)hey, (i)hey, (ga)he:, (gę)he:, (i)he:$_V$- die, be weak, exhausted]

•(ga)heyaʼd die suddenly, play dead, pretend to be dead
hahęhe:yaʼt he died suddenly
[haʼ+...contains: -(ga)hey, (gę)hey, (i)hey, (ga)he:, (gę)he:, (i)he:$_V$- die, weak, exhausted]

•gaheyaʼs die
[P+N+ -wiy(a)$_N$- child, offspring -(ga)hey, (gę)hey, (i)hey, (ga)he:, (gę)he:, (i)he:$_V$- die, be weak, be exhausted]
agowiyagehe:yaʼs her baby died P

•gahęd drill, make a hole
gagahętaʼ a drill bit H
ahadigahę:dęʼ they (m) made a hole P
segahę:dęʼ drill it I

•gahęd have a hole, opening
[o+]
ogahę:t it has a hole in it, an opening S

•ga̱hędehge̱ha:ʼ otgwęhjʼia:ʼ ohǫ:daʼ red whip (a specaial plant that grows in the field)
gahędehge̱ha:ʼ the field kind
otgwęhjʼia:ʼ red
ohǫ:daʼ whip

•gahędahkwaʼ drill, awl
[e+ contains: -gahęd$_V$- drill, hole]
egahędahkwaʼ a drill; an awl

•gahęgę glance, glimpse, flash
[ǫg+at+ -gah(a)$_N$- eye -gę$_V$- see]
ǫgatga̱hę:gęʼ a fleeting glance; she caught a glimpse (out of the corner of her eye)

•gahętaʼ drill bit
[ga+ contains: -gahęd$_V$- drill, hole]
gagahętaʼ a drill bit

•gahiʼd play with s.t.
[at+]
ǫtgahiʼtaʼ what she plays with; a toy H
awatga̱hiʼt it played with it P
gotgahiʼdǫh she is playing with it S

•gahiʼdahkwaʼ toy
[ǫ+at+ contains: -gahiʼd$_V$- play with s.t.]
ǫtgahiʼdahkwaʼ a toy (lit.: children play with it)

•gahihsd(a) eye glasses
[ga+ gah(a)$_N$- eye -(h)wihsd(a), (hr)ihsd(a)$_N$- metal]
gagahihsdaʼ eye glasses

•gahiʼtaʼ toy
[ǫ+at+ -contains: gahiʼd$_V$- play with s.t.]
ǫtgahiʼtaʼ what she plays with; a toy

•gahiyohsd look at closely, stare, peer
[at+ -gah(a)$_N$- eye -iyohsd$_V$- make nice, good]
ęsatga̱hiyohs you will look closely at s.t., peer at s.t. P
agatga̱hiyo̱hsdǫh I am staring at it, examining it closely S

•gahoʼj(a) grass
[o+]
ogahoʼjaʼ grass

•gahoʼjiyaʼs lawn mower
[ga+ -gahoʼj(a)$_N$- grass -(i)yaʼg$_V$- cut, break]
gagahoʼji:yaʼs a lawn mower

•gahoʼsd have an eyelash in one's eye
[de+P+ -gah(a)$_{N}$- eye -ohsd- $_{V}$ immerse with s.t.]
adwagegahoʼs I got an eyelash in my eye P

•gahowektaʼ eye patch
[ǫ+at+ -gah(a)$_{N}$- eye -owegd$_{V}$- cover up]
ǫtgahowe꞉ktaʼ an eye patch

•gahǫ(꞉) assemble, put together
see: kahǫ(꞉) [de+...(N+)] assemble, put together
dęhsega̲hǫʼ you will assemble, put together P

•gahǫʼ adjoin, abutt
see: kahǫʼ [N+] adjoin, abutt
degaihwakahǫʼ an alliance S

•gahǫdi roll one's eyes, snub s.o.
[at+ -gah(a)$_{N}$- eye -ǫdi, -ǫgy$_{V}$- throw]
ęhsatga̲hǫ꞉diʼ you will roll your eyes (in disgust); you will snub s.o. P

•gahǫʼji꞉ have a black eye
[de+A+ -gah(a)$_{N}$- eye -hǫʼji(꞉,h)$_{V}$- be dark]
desega̲hǫʼji꞉ you have a black eye S

•gahǫhkwaʼ rocking chair
[de+yǫ+at+ -kahǫ$_{V}$- adjoin, abutt -hkwaʼ instrument]
deyǫtga꞉hǫhkwaʼ a rocking chair

•gahǫnyǫʼ flirt, bat one's eyes
[P+at+ -gah(a)$_{N}$- eye -ǫnyǫ$_{V}$- make several things]
ęhsatga̲hǫ꞉nyǫʼ you will flirt, bat your eyes P

•gai, gany bite s.o.
[TR+]
ęsa꞉gai꞉ʼ it will bite P
dahsge꞉gai꞉ bite me, take a bite I

•gajikheʼdahǫh gwihsgwihs oʼwahǫh salt pork
gajikheʼdahǫh it has salty streaks
gwihsgwihs pig
oʼwahǫh meat

•gakshaeʼdohs oʼwahǫh chicken meat
dakshae꞉ʼdohs chicken
oʼwahǫh meat

•ganaʼjǫ̲hgwaʼshǫ꞉ʼǫh eyahkwaʼ canisters
ganaʼjǫ̲hsgwaʼ cup
eyahkwaʼ containers

•gana꞉kdaʼ ona꞉sgwaʼ a mattress
gana꞉kdaʼ bed
ona꞉sgwaʼ a mattress

•ganehd tempt s.o., s.t.
[TR+ contains: -(ahs)gan(eg)$_{V}$- want, desire, long for]
ęhsga꞉neht you will tempt P

•ganęd lick s.t.
sega꞉nę꞉s you are a licker; you are a brown-noser H
ęhseganę꞉t you will lick it P
saganętǫ꞉gyeʼ (**saganędǫhǫgyeʼ**) you are going along licking it S
sega꞉nę꞉t lick it I

•ganǫni be rich, wealthy, precious
[at+ -g(an)$_{N}$- price -ǫni, ǫny$_{V}$- make]
otga꞉nǫ꞉nih it is rich H
ǫtga꞉nǫ꞉ni꞉ it is precious S

•ganǫni꞉ prosperity
[o+at+ -gan$_{N}$- price -ǫni, ǫny$_{V}$- make]
otga꞉nǫ꞉ni꞉ prosperity

•ganǫnihagyeʼ prosperity
[go+ at+ -gan$_{N}$- price -ǫnihagyeʼ$_{V}$- go along making s.t.]
gotganǫnihagyeʼ prosperity; s.o. is prospering

•ganǫnihsr(a) richness, wealth
[o+at+ -ganǫnihsr(a)$_{N}$- richness, wealth; contains: -gan$_{N}$- price -ǫni, ǫny$_{V}$- make]
otganǫnihsraʼ richness; wealth

•ganǫnyaʼd wealth, rich
[o+at+ -gan$_{N}$- price -ǫnyaʼd$_{V}$- cause to make]
otganǫnyaʼt wealth; it is rich

Legend: H habitual, P punctual, S stative, I imperative, PURP purposive, PURP-H purposive habitual, PURP-PAST purposive past, PURP-P purposive punctual, PURP-I purposive imperative; see §8.6, §8.11 in Appendix J. Alphabetization in stems ignores length (꞉), and any h's or glottal stops (ʼ) that are not between vowels. See §2.2 of the User Guide for explanation.

•gany be desperate
[de+…at+]
deyǫtganyahs she is desperate, desperately wanting s.t.; in dire need; she will settle for just anyone (that is, a mate) H
dęhatganyahse:k he will be desperate P
dehotganyęh he is really desperate S

•ganyaʼg pay
ega:nyaʼs she pays all the time H
aʼeganyaʼk she paid P
ganganyʼagǫh a payment S

•ganyaʼg repay, refund
[s+]
ętseganyaʼk you will repay, refund P

•ganyaʼg(ę,ani) be reimbursed, refunded
[s+...at+ -gan$_N$- price -(i)yaʼg$_V$- cut, break, cross]
ęjisatganyʼagęʼ you will be reimbursed, refunded P

•ganyaʼgǫh payment
[ga+ -gan$_N$- price -(i)yaʼg$_V$- cut, break, cross]
gaganyʼagǫh payment

•ganyaʼkd pay with s.t.
eganyaʼktaʼ what one pays with; barter H
goganyaʼkdǫhǫgyeʼ she is paying as she goes along S

•ganye(:) shuffle
ǫhsganyehahk she used to shuffle H
ęyǫhsga:nye:ʼ she will shuffle P
gohsga:nye:ʼ she has shuffled S
desahsga:nye: shuffle I

•gahnye play
[at+]
hotgahnyeʼ he is playing S
satgahnyeʼ play I

•gahnye comfort a child, babysit
[adę+]
gadęga̱hnyeh I am babysitting H
ęhsadęgahnyeʼ you will comfort, rock a child; you are babysitting P

•ganyęʼd(a) cadaver
[o+]
oganyʼędaʼ a cadaver

•ganyo:so:ʼah ganyoʼ wild animal meat
ganyo:so:ʼah wild animals
ganyo:ʼ wild animals

•ga̱hnyǫʼǫh ohyaʼ apples
ga̱hnyǫʼǫh it is white
ohyaʼ fruit

•gaod debt
[o+ -ga:$_N$- price -od$_V$- stand]
ogaot a debt

•gaoʼshǫ:ʼǫh unimportant
[o+ contains: -gao$_N$- unimportant -sǫ:ʼǫh plural]
ogaoshǫ:ʼǫh s.t. not important, second-rate

•gaǫ active, quick
[A+ contains: -yaʼd(a)- body]
hayaʼtgaǫ:ʼ he is quick to move; he is active, always moving around S

•gaʼǫhshǫ:ʼǫh goodies, dessert
[o+ contains: -gaʼ$_V$- like the taste of s.t. -shǫ:ʼǫh several things]
ogaʼǫhshǫ:ʼǫh goodies, dessert

•gaʼǫhsraęʼ tasteless
[deʼ+ not (y)o+ -gaʼǫhsr(a)$_N$- taste -ę$_V$- lie, have]
deʼogaʼǫhsraeʼ it is tasteless S

•gaǫhsronih herb, spice
[ga+ -gaǫhsr(a)$_N$- good-tasting things -ǫni, ǫny$_V$- make]
gagaʼǫhsro:nih it makes it taste good (for example, herbs, spices)

•gaʼǫhsriyo: taste good
[o+ -gaʼǫhsr(a)$_N$- taste -iyo:$_V$- be nice, good]
ogaʼǫhsri:yo: it tastes good S

•ga̱hsohgǫ:t eyahkwaʼ a pitcher
ga̱hsohgǫ:t pitcher
eyahkwaʼ containers

•ga̲hswaǫgyǫ: oha:de' gravel roads
ga̲hswaǫgyǫ:' gravel has been thrown down
oha:de' an existing road
•gatse:nę' gadi'drǫ' farm yard buildings
gatse:nę' an animal; a pet
gadi'drǫ' they (z) live (designates a shed, dog house; etc.)
•gahtw look
[at+ contains: -gah(a)$_{N}$- eye]
satgahtwahs you look all the time H
hętsahtga̲hto' you will look back P
sga:t heyotga̲htwęh one mile (lit.: one of how far you can see) S
satgahtoh look I
•ga̲hwajiya:do:gę: jidę'ęshǫ:'ǫh ga'ga:' the crow family or species
ga̲hwajiya:do:gę: a certain family, dynasty; a species
jidę'shǫ:'ǫh birds
ga'ga:' crows
•gawahsda' eyahkwa' clothespin bag
gawahsda' clothespin
eyahkwa' containers
•gawe(:) row, paddle
segawe̲ha'k you used to paddle H
ęhsegawe:' you will row P
gaga:we: the act of rowing S
•gawehs(a) paddle, shovel
[ga+ contains: -gawe(:)$_{V}$- paddle]
gagawe̲hsa' paddle, shovel
•ga̲hwę'gaǫni: owęhga:' a splint
ga̲hwę'gaǫni: it is made into a splint
ohwę'ga:' a splint
•gaya'dagrahs gadi'drǫ' goat shed
gaya'dagrahs a goat
gadi'drǫ' they (z) live (designates a shed, dog house, etc.)
•gahyę'gwai:dǫh o'wahǫh bacon
gayę'gwaikdǫh it is smoked
o'wahǫh meat

•gayętwahsǫ' ase'shǫ:' produce (lit.: new vegetables, fruit)
gayętwahsǫ' garden it is planted (here)
ase'shǫ:' vegetables
•gayǫh old thing
[o+]
oga:yǫh it is old S
ga·ę·na·gá·yǫh·sǫ' old songs
[A/P+(N+) stem: -gayohsǫ'- several old things; consists of: -(r)ęn(a)$_{N}$- song, music -gayǫhsǫ'$_{V}$- old (things)]
•ge'(a:), geh(a) hair, rag, s.t. tattered
[o+]
oge'a:' hair; a rag; it is ragged, tattered
sage'a'geh on your hair
•ge'a:' be ragged, tattered
[A+ -ge'(a:), geh(a)$_{N}$- hair -a:'$_{V}$- hold, contain, include]
gege'a:' I am raggedy, ragged S
•ge'asrǫni:' hairdresser
[-ge'(a:), geh(a)$_{N}$- hair -(h)srǫni$_{V}$- fix, repair]
egea'srǫni:' she is a hairdresser
•ge'aęnhahsta' hair tie
[ga+at+ -ge'(a:), geh(a)$_{N}$- hair -nhahsd$_{V}$- encircle]
gatge'ayęnhahsta' a hair tie
•ged grate, scrape, file
sege:dahs you are scraping s.t. right now H
ęhse:ge:t you will grate, scrape, file P
sage:dǫh you are scraping s.t. right now S
se:ge:t grate, scrape, file it I
•ged scratch oneself
[at+/N+]
sahnatsage:dahs you are scratching your behind H
[ad+(N+) stem: -(h)na'ts(a)$_{N}$- buttock -ged$_{V}$- grate, scrape, file; scratch s.t.]
ęhsa:tge:t you will scratch yourself P
satge:dǫh you are scratching yourself S

Legend: H habitual, P punctual, S stative, I imperative, PURP purposive, PURP-H purposive habitual, PURP-PAST purposive past, PURP-P purposive punctual, PURP-I purposive imperative; see §8.6, §8.11 in Appendix J. Alphabetization in stems ignores length (:), and any h's or glottal stops (') that are not between vowels. See §2.2 of the User Guide for explanation.

•ged scratch s.t. for s.o.
[de+TR+N+]
dahsgehsweʼna:ge:t scratch my back I
[de+TR+N+ stem: -(h)swaʼn(a), (h)sweʼn(a)$_N$- upper back -ged$_V$- grate, scrape, file; scratch s.t. for s.o.]

•gehd put, have s.t. around one's neck
[at+(N+)]
satgehda:s you put it around your neck all the time H
sahtgehdataʼ you put it around your neck all the time H
satgehdǫh you have it around your neck S

•gehd(a) tie, scarf
[ga+]
gagehdaʼ a tie; a scarf

•gehdad put around one's neck
[(at+) contains: -gehd$_V$- have around one's neck]
sahtgehdataʼ you put it around your neck all the time H
ęhsatge̱hda:t you will put s.t. around your neck P
segehda:t put it around your neck I

•gehdastaʼscarf, bib
[ǫ+at+ -gehdahsd$_V$- tie around one's neck with s.t.]
ǫtgehdastaʼ a scarf; a bib

•gedraʼ unripe, raw, green
[o+]
oge:draʼ it is green (not ripe); raw fruit S

•gedrǫd fruit (green)
[o+ -gedr(a)$_N$- green fruit -ǫd$_V$- attached]
oge:drǫ:t hanging green fruit

•geʼęhdahkwaʼ brush
[ǫ+at+ -geʼ(a:), geh(a)$_N$- hair -ęhdahkwaʼ$_V$- s.t. that hits]
ǫtgeʼęhdahkwaʼ hair brush

•gehǫʼ be several things lying about
[ga+]
gagehǫʼ things are lying about S

•gehǫʼ lie about
[A+(N+)]
gęgyohgwagehǫʼ associations; councils; agencies; groups (lit.: crowds lying about) S

•gehǫhaʼ auctioneer
[A+at+ -(a)tgehǫ$_V$- sell]
hatgehǫhaʼ he is an auctioneer (lit.: he is a seller)

•geʼi:ʼ tangled
[de+P+at+ -geʼ(a:), geh(a)$_N$- hair -i:ʼ$_V$- be stuck onto s.t.]
dewagatgeʼi:ʼ my hair is tangled S

•gei: gahsi:na:t an iron pot (with four legs)
gei: four
gahsi:na:t it has standing legs

•genh argue for, advocate
[de+ -(r)ihwa/N+]
de̱haihwagenhahs he is a lawyer H
dęhsrihwage:nhaʼ you will argue, debate, protest P
deyagodihwage:nhęh they (f/m) are arguing S

•geʼod be bald
[tęʼ deʼ+ not P+ -geʼ(a:), geh(a)$_N$- hair -od$_V$- stand]
tęʼ dʼehogeʼo:t he has no hair; he is bald S

•geʼogw rumpled hair
[de+P+at+ -geʼ(a:), geh(a)$_N$- hair -ogw$_V$- scatter]
desatgeʼo:gwęh you have rumpled hair, ruffled hair S

•geʼǫd be ragged
[de+P+ -geʼ(a:), geh(a)$_N$- hair -ǫd$_V$- attached]
dewagegeʼǫ:t I am raggedy, ragged S

•geʼowektaʼ hair net
[o+at+ -geʼ(a:), geh(a)$_N$- hair -(hr)owegd$_V$- cause to cover]
otge:owe:ktaʼ a hair net

•getsgw raise to a vertical position, give parties
[(N+)]
sege:tsgwahs you are lifting it to a vertical position; you give parties H
ęhsegetsgo' you will lift things to a vertical position P
gyagogetsgwęh she's having a gathering over there; she is lifting s.t. into a vertical position S
sege:tsgoh you raise s.t. to a vertical position I
sanętsagétsgoh raise your arm I
[-nęts(a)$_N$- arm -getsgw$_V$- raise to a vertical position]

•gę see
ge:gęh I see (regularly, but perhaps at irregular intervals) H
ge:gęhs I see (for example, I see apple trees, orange trees,... and sometimes, I also see cherry trees) H
ęge:gę' I will see P
age:gę: I have seen it S

•gę: be in the middle, between, in-between
[de+yo+ contains: -gę$_V$- see]
deyo:gę: between, in the middle S

•gę look ahead, forsee
[ohę:dǫ: ahead he+ contains: -gę$_V$- see]
ohę:dǫ: heha:di:gęh they (m) look ahead, tell the future H

•gę' glance, glimpse
[at+ contains: -gę$_V$- see]
awatgę'ę:k there was a flash, a glimpse

•(')gę: be light-coloured, white
[A/P+N+]
onęhęgę:t, onęhęgę: white corn S
[o+ stem: -nęh(ę)$_N$- corn -(')gę:$_V$- light-coloured, white]

•gę'd be transparent
[he+yo+ contains: -gęd$_V$- cause to see]
heyo:gę't it is transparent S

•(')gę'd be visible
[o+ contains: -gęd$_V$- cause to see]
o:gę't it is visible S

•(')gęd be light-coloured, white
[A/P+N+]
onęhęgę:t, onęhęgę: white corn S
[o+ stem: -nęh(ę)$_N$- corn -(')gęd$_V$- light-coloured, white]

•gę'do:' be stuck
[ga+]
gagę'do:' it is stuck under s.t. but it is removable (for example, a piece of gum under a table); it is stuck on s.t. else (for example, on a wall) S

•gę'do:'aę:' attached
[A+ contains: -gę'do:'$_V$- be stuck]
gagę'do:aę:' it is attached to s.t. S

•gędrahgw support, be a foundation for s.t.
[N+ present in:]
ganǫhsagędrahgǫh a foundation (of a building) S
[ga+ stem: -nǫhsagędrahgǫh- foundation; consists of: -nǫhs(a)$_N$- house -gędrahgw$_V$- support]

•gędrǫ(:) scrape
[de+ N+ present in:]
degawidragędrǫhs cream separator H
[de+... stem: -widragędr- skim milk; consists of: -widr(a)$_N$- ice -gędrǫ(:)$_V$- scrape]
dęsewidragędrǫ:' you will take the cream off, skim the milk P
degawidragędrǫ: skimmed milk S

•(')gę:'ęh younger sibling
[TR+]
ke'gę:'ęh my younger sister S

•(')gę'ęh last quarter moon
[he+j+o+ -(')gę:'ęh$_V$- younger sibling]
hejogę:'ęh last quarter moon

•gęh get up, awaken
[at+]
gatgęhęhs I get up all the time H
aga:tgęh I got up P
agatgęhǫh I am up now S

Legend: H habitual, P punctual, S stative, I imperative, PURP purposive, PURP-H purposive habitual, PURP-PAST purposive past, PURP-P purposive punctual, PURP-I purposive imperative; see §8.6, §8.11 in Appendix J. Alphabetization in stems ignores length (:), and any h's or glottal stops (') that are not between vowels. See §2.2 of the User Guide for explanation.

•gęh get up, awaken (continued)
satgęh get up I
•gęhęnih abuse s.o., be mean to s.o., annoy s.o.
[TR+]
segęhęnih you abuse it; you are mean to it; you are an abuser H
•gęhęʼd(ę,ani) be annoyed, disgusted, sick of s.t.
[TR+ contains: -gęhę$_V$- abuse s.o., be mean to s.o., annoy s.o.]
gǫgęhęʼda:nih I am sick of you H
ahsgegęhęʼdęʼ you got sick of me; you are bored with me P
•(ʼ)gęhędahkwaʼ brush (for clothes)
[e+ -(a)ʼgęh(ęda)$_N$- ash, dust -(h)kwaʼ$_V$- s.t. that lifts, picks up]
egęhędahkwaʼ a clothes brush
•(ʼ)gęhękwaʼ ashtray
[ǫ+ -(a)ʼgęh(ęda)$_N$- ash, dust -(h)gw$_V$- lift, pick up]
ǫʼgęhę:kwaʼ an ashtray
•gęhęʼtrǫni be cruel, mean
[contains: -gęhętr(a)$_N$- abuse, annoyance -ǫni, ǫny$_V$- make]
ęhsegęhęʼtrǫ:niʼ you will be mean, abusive P
gagęhętrǫ:niʼ it has been abused S
•gęhjih be old (person)
[A+]
egęhjih she is old; an old woman S
•gęhjih husband, wife
[A+ -gęhjih$_V$- old (person)]
hagęhjih he is an old man (referring to one's husband)
egęhjih she is an old woman (referring to one's wife)
•gęhjih(s)d age, get old
[at+ contains: -gęhjih$_V$- old (person)]
hatgęji̱htaʼ he is getting old H
otgęhjihsdǫhǫgyeʼ it is getting old, aging S
[at+ contains: -gęhjihsdǫhǫgyeʼ$_V$- go along getting old (a person)]
•gęhǫh up
[at+ contains: -gęh$_V$- get up, awaken]
agatgęhǫh I am up now S
•gęihsd move, postpone s.t.
segęihstaʼ you postpone it all the time; you move it all the time H
ędwa:gęis we all (incl.) will postpone s.t. P
gagęihsdǫh a postponement (lit.: it has been moved) S
•gęihsd be portable
[wa+ at+ contains: -gęihsd$_V$- move, postpone s.t.]
watgęihstaʼ it is portable H
•gęihsdǫh postponement
[ga+ -gęihsd$_V$- move, postpone]
gagęihsdǫh a postponement (lit.: it has been moved)
•gęihsdǫhǫgyeʼ travel along
[ni+P+at+ contains: -gęihsd$_V$- move, postpone]
niyagotgęihsdǫhǫgyeʼ she is travelling as she is moving S
•(gę)nh(a), (i)nh(a) summer
[-hneh on]
gęnhehneh summer
•gęnh [de+...(r)ihwa/N+] argue for, advocate
see: (hs)gęnh [de+...(r)ihwa/N+] argue for, advocate
saǫhwęjahsgęnhęh you are fighting over the land right now S
[stem: consists of: -ǫhwęj(a)$_N$- earth, land -(h)sgenh$_V$- argue for, advocate]
•gęnhiyaʼgǫʼ yearling
[o+ -(gę)nh(a)$_N$- summer -(i)yaʼg$_V$- cut across, cross]
ogęnhiyaʼgǫʼ yearling

•gęni, gęny compete
[de+...ad/N+ present in:]
dęhęnatnǫnyagę:nye's a pow wow (lit: they (m) perform competition dancing) H
[de+...at+ stem: -nǫyagęnye's- pow-wow; consists of: -nǫny(a)$_N$- dance -gęni, gęny$_V$- compete]
dęhęnatgę:nyǫhs a fair (lit. they (m) compete there)
dęshagoni'gǫha:gę:ni' he will overcome their mind, intimidate s.o. P
[de+TR+ stem: -(')nigǫhagęni- corrupt, intimidate; consists of: -(')nigǫh(a)$_N$- mind -gęni, gęny$_V$- compete]
dęhonatgę:nyǫ: they (m) compete S

•gęnihs' meet
[at+]
swatgęnihs'ahs you have meetings all the time H
ęhswatgenihs'a:' you all will have a meeting P
swatgęnihs'ǫh you are having a meeting right now S

•gęnya'ta'geh fairgrounds
[de+g+yǫ+at+ -gęnya'd$_V$- cause to compete -'geh on, at]
degyǫtgęnya'ta'geh fairgrounds

•gęnye:' roasted green corn; dried corn soup
[o+]
ogę:nye:' roasted green corn; dried corn soup (made with roasted green corn)

•gęnyǫ: competition
[de+wa+at+ contains: -gęni, gęny$_V$- compete]
dewatgęnyǫ: a competition

•gęnyǫhs fair
[de+A+at+ contains: -gęni, gęny$_V$- compete]
dęhęnatgę:nyǫhs a fair (lit. they (m) compete there)

•gę'sd(a:) hairline, upper brow, forehead
gegę'sda:'geh on my forehead; on my hairline, upper brow

•gę'se watch s.o.
[TR+at+ contains: -gę$_V$- see]
gaǫtgę'seh they (f/m) are watching s.t. going on H
a:gakeyatgę'se:' I should watch them P

•gęhsrǫd pocket, kangaroo
[a+ǫ+ -gęhsr(a)$_N$- pouch, pocket -ǫd$_V$- attached]
aǫgęhsrǫ:t, aǫgohsrǫ:t a pocket; a kangaroo

•gęhyad be at the edge, be at the end, be above
ohnegagęhya:t just above the water S
[o+ stem: -(h)negagęhyad- above the water; consists of: -(h)neg(a)$_N$- water, liquid -gęhyad$_V$- beside]

•gihę:k river, stream, creek
gihę:k a river; a stream; a creek
gihę:k'ah the riverside; along the river
[-k'ah$_V$- beside]

•go' sum, total
[ę+ga+ -gw$_V$- gather, choose, pick]
ęga:go' it will be a sum, a total

•gohdahsǫhs cloudy intervals
[ga+]
gagohdahsǫhs cloudy intervals

•godrihwagyaǫ'ǫh goya'danęhgwih hado:wih an ambulance driver
godrihwagyaǫ'ǫh s.o. had an accident
goya'danęhgwih transportation (lit.: people-mover)
hado:wih he is a driver

•gohgowah royalty
[A+ contains: -gowah big]
(e)gohgo:wah a queen; the Queen S

•gogye's eyahkwa' a garbage can
gogye's to get rid of s.t., throw it away
eyahkwa' containers

•gogye's g'adroda:' disposable diapers
gogye's to get rid of s.t., throw it away
g'adroda:' a diaper

Legend: H habitual, P punctual, S stative, I imperative, PURP purposive, PURP-H purposive habitual, PURP-PAST purposive past, PURP-P purposive punctual, PURP-I purposive imperative; see §8.6, §8.11 in Appendix J. Alphabetization in stems ignores length (:), and any h's or glottal stops (') that are not between vowels. See §2.2 of the User Guide for explanation.

•goʼjonyahnǫ(:) make oneself up
[at+ -goʼj(a)$_N$- cheek -ǫnyahnǫ$_V$- go and make]
satgoʼjonyahnǫ: beautify yourself, apply make-up I

•goʼjonyahtaʼ make-up, blush, rouge
[ǫ+at+ -goʼj(a)$_N$- cheek -ǫnyahd$_V$- cause to make]
ǫtgoʼjonyahtaʼ make-up; blush; rouge

•gowanahd, gowanęhd enlarge s.t.
[A/P+N+ contains: -(g)owan$_V$- be big]
gagowanahtaʼ it makes things big H
ęsehsgo̱haowa:neht you will branch it out (that is, add particles, etc. to 'dress up' speech) P
[A/P+N+ -(h)sgoh(a)$_N$- branch -gowanęh$_V$- be big]

•gowanahd(ę, ani), gowanęhd(ę, ani) rape s.o.
[TR+at+ contains: -(g)owanahd$_V$- enlarge s.t.]
ahshagotgowanahdęʼ, ahshagotgowanęhdęʼ he raped her (lit.: he forced her in a big way) P

•gowanęh be big
[(ga+)]
gowa:nęh, gagowanęh it is big S

•gowanęh be big
[A/P+(N+) -owanęh$_V$- be big]
ga̱hwajiyowanęh a large family S
[ga+ stem: -(h)wajiy(a)$_N$- family -owanęh$_V$- be big]

•gowanęhd have pride in s.o.
[TR+ -gowanęhd$_V$- enlarge]
gahshegowanęhtaʼ you have pride in them H

•gowanęhgowah be really big
[A+ -gowanęh$_V$- be big -gowah big]
egowanęhgo:wah she is really big S

•gowanęh self-important, rash, unwise
[A+adat+ -gowanęh$_V$- be big]
wadatgowa:nęh it is rash, unwise, self-important, egotistical S

•gowanęh be pregnant
[e+ -gowanęh$_V$- be big]
egowanęh she is big, pregnant S

•gowanęhah be fairly big
[A+ -gowanęh$_V$- be big -hah fairly]
gowa:nę:hah it is fairly big S

•gowanheʼ become big
[(A+) contains: -gowanęh$_V$- be big]
agagowa:nheʼ it became big P

•gowih red oak
go:wih red oak

•gǫd persevere, linger, be last
[he+s+ga+(N+)]
hesga:gǫ:t the last S
hehsgaęna:gǫ:t the last song
[-(r)ęn(a)$_N$- song, music -gǫd$_V$- persevere, linger, be last]

•gǫd always
[g+yo+at+]
gyotgǫ:t always S

•gǫd necessity, duty
[d+ga+]
tga:gǫ:t a compelling must S

•gǫʼd(a) bridge of nose
ogǫʼdaʼ the bridge of one's nose
gegǫʼdʼageh on the bridge of my nose

•gǫdeh eel
gǫ:deh an eel

•gǫdǫdǫhgǫh water root
[de+ga+]
degagǫdǫdǫ̱hgǫh water root (a medicine plant)

•gǫʼdr(a) pillow, cushion
[ga+]
gagǫʼdraʼ a pillow; a cushion

•gǫʼdr(a) cotton batting, q-tips
[o+ contains: -gǫʼdr(a)$_N$- pillow, cushion]
ogǫʼdraʼ cotton batting, q-tips

•gǫ'drahkwa' body pad
[A+at+ contains: -gǫ'dr(a)$_N$- pillow, cushion, cotton batting]
hęnatg'ǫdrahkwa' body pads, body protectors
•gǫ'drowekta' pillow case
[e+ -gǫ'dr(a)$_N$- pillow, cushion, cotton batting -owekd$_V$- cause to cover]
egǫ'drowe:kta' pillow cases
•gǫhe box
[de+adat -gǫh(a)$_N$- fist -(')eg$_V$- hit]
dęhęnadatgǫhe:s boxers; they (m) are boxing H
•gǫhe punch s.t., hit s.t.
[TR+ -gǫh(a)$_N$- fist -(')eg$_V$- hit]
segǫhe:s you hit it all the time H
ahagǫhe:k he punched it P
•gǫhekta' hitting implement
[A+ -gǫh(a)$_N$- fist -(')ekd$_V$- cause to hit; contains: -(')eg$_V$- hit]
segǫhekta' what you use to hit with
•(h)gǫnhni'gǫh leader
[de+ga+ contains: -ǫnhe'$_V$- be alive]
degahgǫnhni'gǫh (**degahgǫnhi'gǫh**) the leader of equal standing
•gǫnyǫ be clean, discriminating; have high standards
[P+at+]
gotgǫ:nyohs she has high standards H
•gǫnyǫ be choosy, discriminate against s.o.
see: ǫgwe'dagǫnyǫ [P+ad -ǫgwe'd(a) person] be choosy, discriminate against s.o.
hodǫgw'edagǫnyǫhs he is choosy about who he associates with; he discriminates H
•gǫnyǫhsd be important
[P+at+ contains: -gǫnyǫ$_V$- be clean, discriminating; have high standards]
otnakdagǫ:nyǫhs an important, prestigious seat, place H
[o+(at) stem: -nakd(a)$_N$- bed, seat -gǫnyǫhsd$_V$- honour]
•gǫnyǫhsd be stuck up, snobbish
[adat+ contains: -gǫnyǫ$_V$- be clean, discriminating; have high standards]
wadatgǫnyǫhsta' she (lit.: it) is stuck up H
•gǫnyǫhsd be loyal, respectful
[adę+ contains: -gǫnyǫ$_V$- be clean, discriminating; have high standards]
hadęgǫnyǫhsta' he is loyal (to the cause); he is respectful H
•gǫnyǫhsd honour s.o.
[TR+ contains: -gǫnyǫ$_V$- be clean, discriminating; have high standards]
ahshagodigǫnyǫhs they honoured her P
•gǫnyǫhsde:' respect
[ga+ contains: -gǫnyǫhsd$_V$- be respectful, loyal]
gagǫnyǫhsde:' respect
•gǫnyǫhses rhino tusk
[ga+ -gǫnyǫhs(a)$_N$- tusk -es$_V$- long]
gagǫnyǫhse:s a rhino tusk
•gǫhs(a) face
ogǫhsa' a face
segǫhs'ageh on your face
•gǫhs(a) mask
[ga+]
gagǫhsa' a mask
•gǫhsagri smirk
[de+...at+ -gǫhs(a)$_N$- face -gri$_V$- wrinkle]
desatgǫhsagri: wrinkle up your face; smirk I
•gǫhsahniyǫh be two-faced
[P+ -gǫhs(a)$_N$- face -(h)niyǫh$_V$- be hard, tough]
sagǫhsahni:yǫh you are two-faced S
•gǫhsgwa'tro' window (pane)
[wa / o+ at+ -gǫhsgwa'tr(a)$_N$- window -o'$_V$- be submerged]
watgǫhsgwa'tro', **otgǫhsgwa'tro'** a window pane

Legend: H habitual, P punctual, S stative, I imperative, PURP purposive, PURP-H purposive habitual, PURP-PAST purposive past, PURP-P purposive punctual, PURP-I purposive imperative; see §8.6, §8.11 in Appendix J. Alphabetization in stems ignores length (:), and any h's or glottal stops (') that are not between vowels. See §2.2 of the User Guide for explanation.

•gǫhsohaiʼtaʼ face cloth
[ǫ+at+ -gǫhs(a)$_N$- face -ohaiʼd$_V$- cause to clean, wash]
ǫtgǫhsǫhaiʼtaʼ a face cloth
•gǫhso:ʼ soft maple
gǫhso:ʼ a soft maple
•gǫhstǫʼ(a), gǫhstwę(ʼę) whiskers
ogǫhstwę:ʼę:ʼ a beard
gagǫhstǫʼaʼgeh on its whiskers
•gǫhstǫʼęʼǫd, gǫhstwęʼǫd have a beard
[de+A+ -gǫhstǫʼ(a)$_N$- whiskers -ǫd$_V$- attached]
dehagǫhstwęʼo:t he has a beard S
•gǫhstǫʼęhd shave
[at+ -gǫhstǫʼ(a)$_N$- whiskers -ęhd$_V$- hit, knock down, strike]
hatgǫhstǫʼęhtaʼ he is shaving H
ahatgǫhstǫʼęht he shaved P
satgǫhstǫʼęht, satgǫhstwęʼęht shave I
•gǫʼ(tra) weight, pound, powerful medecine
[o+]
ogǫʼtraʼ a pound (measurement)
ęgǫyatgǫʼtra:s I will bewitch you
[TR+ at+ stem: -gǫʼtra:- bewitch; consists of: -gǫʼtr(a)$_N$- ominous medicine -a:ʼ$_V$- hold, contain, include]
•gǫʼ(tra:) bewitch s.o.
[TR+ at+ stem: -gǫʼtra:- bewitch; consists of: -gǫʼtr(a)$_N$- ominous medicine -a:ʼ$_V$- hold, contain, include]
ęgǫyatgǫʼtra:s I will bewitch you
•gǫʼtrahe:haʼ balance, weigh scale
[ga+ -gǫʼtr(a)$_N$- weight -(hr)e, (hr)ę$_V$- put, place]
gagǫʼtrahe:haʼ a balance; a weigh scale
•gǫʼtraniyǫd weigh
[at+ -gǫʼtr(a)$_N$- weight -niyǫd$_V$- hang]
agaǫ:tgǫʼtrani:yǫ:dęʼ they (f/m) weighed themselves P
•gǫtrahsdeʼ weight
[tsęh that, what ni+yo+ -gǫʼtr(a)$_N$- weight -(a)hsdeʼ$_V$- be heavy]
tsęh niyogǫtra:sdeʼ weight; pounds; poundage
•gǫw(aʼd) hide
[present in:]
ęsatgǫwaʼdǫ:niʼ you will tan a hide P
[at+ -gǫwa(ʼda)$_N$- hide -ǫni, ǫny$_V$- make]
•gǫwaʼdǫni tan
[at+ -gǫwa(ʼda)$_N$- hide -ǫni, ǫny$_V$- make]
ęsatgǫwaʼdǫ:niʼ you will tan a hide P
•graheʼd(a) tree
gra̱he:t a living tree
gra̱heʼdʼageh on the tree
•grahs stink
[A+(N+)]
gagrahs it stinks H
gya̱h·síʼdag·rahs we two (incl.) have smelly feet
[-(a)hsi(ʼda), (ę)hs(a)$_N$- foot -grahs$_V$- stink]
•gręgręhd frown, sneer
[de+...at+]
agyǫtgręgręht she frowned P
deyagotgręgręhdǫh she is frowning S
•gręgręhdǫh dreary, overcast
[de+yo+at+ contains: -gręgręhd$_V$- frown, sneer]
deyotgręgręhdǫh the sky is dreary, grey S
•gri wrinkle, fan-fold
[(d+)...]
ęhse:gri:k you will wrinkle, fan-fold P
dahse:gri:k wrinkle it; fan-fold it I
•gri flinch, pull back, shrink, be a wimp
[(d+)...at+]
dawa:tgri:k it pulled back, flinched, shrank P
totgri: heʼs a wimp; he pulls back S

•gri' juice, liquid
[o+N+]
ohya:gri' juice, fruit juice S
[o+ stem: -(a)hy(a)$_N$- fruit, berry -gri'$_V$- juice, liquid]
•grihsrǫ' several wrinkled items
[o+at+ -gri$_V$- wrinkle]
otgrihsrǫ' wrinkled clothes; it is wrinkled up S
•griya'gǫ' buffalo
[de+ contains: -gr(a)$_N$- -(i)ya'g$_V$- cut, break]
degriya'gǫ' buffalo
•(')grǫdi, (')grǫgy snow
[(y)o+ -(a)'gr(a)$_N$- snow -ǫdi, -ǫgy$_V$- throw]
ęyo'grǫ:di' it will snow P
o'grǫ:gyǫ: it is snowing S
•gw,go gather, pick, get
ga̱hya:gwahs I am picking fruit H
[stem: -(a)hy(a)$_N$- fruit, berry -gw$_V$- gather, pick, get]
ha'ha:go' he went and got it P
age:gwęh I have obtained, acquired it S
•(')gw run away, flee
[ade+]
ęgęnade'go' they (z) will flee, run away P
•(h)gw lift, pick up
[de+...(N+)]
atgehk I picked s.t. up P
de̱hoya'dahgwęh it picked him up S
•(h)gw dance
[de+at+ contains: -(h)gw$_V$- lift, pick up]
de̱hęnatkwa' they dance H
de̱hęna:t they (m) will dance P
dewa:tgwęh (the act of) dancing S
•(h)gw(ę,ani) take s.t. back from s.o.
[s+ contains: -(h)gw$_V$- lift, pick up]
shǫwadihkwę' (**sa̱hǫwadihgwę'**) they took it back from him again P
•(h)gw, (h)go remove s.t.
[N+ present in:]
ęhsetsgę'ęda̱hgo' you will remove seeds P
[de+ contains: -tsgę'ęd(a)$_N$- -(h)gw, (h)go$_V$- remove s.t.]
gahsgwa:da̱hgwęh a neutered animal, a gelding S
[-(h)sg(wa:)$_N$- stone, bullet, rock -(h)gw$_V$- remove]
•(h)gwa'd uphold s.t., raise up s.t., lift up, pick up
[de+ contains: -(h)gw$_V$- lift, pick up]
degahgwata' it upholds, raises things up H
dehohgwadǫh he is lifting it up S
deyǫdesehgwa't lift it up; push it up I
•gwa'da: flying squirrel
[contains: -(h)gwa'd$_V$- raise s.t. up, etc.]
gwa'da: flying squirrel
•gwadih go in a direction
[d+A+ contains: -(a)dih$_V$- side]
tgaęgwadih they (f/m) are going in a direction H
•gwadih be a direction
see: Appendix I sigwa:dih over there
•gwadǫ weave, zig-zag, go in several directions
[at+ contains: -gwadǫ$_V$- be several directions]
hatgwa:dǫh he is zig-zagging H
•gwadre:' grandchild
gwadre:' grandchild (term of address said by any old person to a young child) S
•gwah go after
[N+ -na'tr(a)$_N$- food, lunch -gw$_V$- gather, choose]
a'ǫdęna'tragwaha' she went after groceries P

Legend: H habitual, P punctual, S stative, I imperative, PURP purposive, PURP-H purposive habitual, PURP-PAST purposive past, PURP-P purposive punctual, PURP-I purposive imperative; see §8.6, §8.11 in Appendix J. Alphabetization in stems ignores length (:), and any h's or glottal stops (') that are not between vowels. See §2.2 of the User Guide for explanation.

•gwaihs(i) be straight, straighten
[d(a)$_{N}$- way / N+]
hadinehsda:gwaihshǫhs they (m) are straightening out the board H
stem: -nehsd(a:)$_{N}$- floor, board -gwaihs(i)$_{V}$- straight]
ęhsdagwaihsiʼ you will straighten it P
heyodagwaishǫ: straight ahead S
•dagwaihshǫ: straight ahead
[heʼ+yo+ -d(a)$_{N}$- way -gwaihs(i)$_{V}$- straight straight ahead]
heyodaʼgwaishǫ: straight ahead
•gwaoh screech owl
gwaoh a screech owl
•gwaǫd abcess, bulge
[P+ -g(wa)$_{N}$- lump, boil -ǫd$_{V}$- attached]
agegwaǫ:t I have an abscess, a boil S
•gwaʼtaʼ community hall
[de+d+A+at+ -gwaʼd$_{V}$- cause to gather]
detęnatgwaʼtaʼ a community hall
•gwatw, gwato hem s.t.
[de+…]
dęhsegwatoʼ you will hem s.t. P
degagwatwęh hem it S
•gwatwęh hem
[de+ga -gwatw$_{V}$- hem]
degagwatwęh a hem
•gwaʼyǫʼ rabbit
gwaʼyǫʼ a rabbit
•gwaʼyǫ:ʼah, gwaʼyę:ʼah cottontail rabbit
[-gwaʼyǫ$_{N}$- rabbit -ʼah diminutive]
gwʼayǫ:ʼah, gwaʼyę:ʼah a cottontail rabbit
•gwaʼyǫgowah jackrabbit
[-gwaʼyǫ$_{N}$- rabbit -gowah big]
gwaʼyǫgo:wah a jackrabbit
•gweg close s.t.
[N+]
ǫgyaʼdagwe:s she gets bound up; constipated H
[ag+ -yaʼd(a)$_{N}$- body -gweg$_{V}$- close]
ęhshe:sgwe:k you will shut her up P
[-(h)s(a)$_{N}$- mouth -gweg$_{V}$- close]
gogyaʼdagwe:gǫh she is constipated S
•gwegǫh all
[A/P+N+]
oihwagwe:gǫh everything; the whole idea S
[o+ stem: -(r)ih(wa)$_{N}$- word -gwegǫh$_{V}$- all]
•gwegǫh all over, here and there
[ti+ga+]
tiga:gwe:gǫh all over the place; here and there S
•gwegǫh all
[ti+yo+]
tiyogwe:gǫh all of it S
•gweni, gweny be able to do s.t., succeed
[ad+/N+]
ahsadadrihwagwe:nyaʼs you are a success H
[-(r)ih(wa)$_{N}$- word, affair, matter -gweni, gweny$_{V}$- be able to do s.t., succeed]
agatgwe:niʼ I won a competition P
saihwagwe:nyǫ: you are able to perform (i.e run, dance, orate, etc.) S
•gweni, gweny the best (of one's ability)
[naʼ+A+at+ contains: -gweni, gweny$_{V}$- be able to do s.t., succeed]
naʼga:tgwe:niʼ the best I could do P
•gweni, gweny win a competition
[TR+/...at+ contains: -gweni, gweny$_{V}$- be able to do s.t., succeed]
ahǫwadigwe:niʼ they won a competition P
•gwenǫni be full
[present in:]
adwadri̱hgwagwenǫ:ni: there was a full moon P
[de+…ad+ -(r)ihg(wa)$_{N}$- moon -gwenǫni$_{V}$- be full]
deyodri̱hwagwenǫ:ni: there is a full moon S
•gwesęʼ partridge
gwe:sęʼ a partridge

•(h)gwę sunset
hegahgwę'̨s to the setting sun; the direction of the sunset; the west H
[he'+ga+ stem: -(h)gwę$_V$- set]
ha'gahgwę' sunset; the sun went down P

•(h)gwę's west
[ha'+ga+ contains: -(h)gwę$_V$- set]
hegahgwę's to the setting sun; the direction of the sunset; the west H

•gwę:dihs night hawk
gwę:dihs a night hawk

•gwę'gohnyę' whip-poor-will
gwę'gǫhnyę' a whip-poor-will

•(')gwęhęgye's avoid
[P+ade+ contains: -(')gw$_V$- run away, flee]
sade'gwęhę:gye's you are avoiding S

•gwęnige: win a competition
[TR+/...at+...-gweni, gweni- win -ge: big]
ahęnatgwęnige: the big win; the victory (lit.: they (m) won big) P

•gwi'a'eg wink
[de+...at+ -gwi'(a)$_N$- eyelid -(')eg$_V$- hit]
desatgwi'aek wink I

•gwihsgwihs pig
gwihsgwihs a pig

•gwihsgwihs gadi'drǫ' pig pen
gwihsgwihs pig
gadi'drǫ' they (z) live (designates a shed, dog house; etc.)

•gwihsgwihs ohsi'da' pig's foot
gwihsgwihs a pig
ohsi'da' feet

•gwihsgwihs o'wahǫh pig meat; pork chop, bacon
gwihsgwihs a pig
o'wahǫh meat

•gwitgę' rise
see: itgę' [(d+)...] rise
daga:gwi:tgę' sunrise; the sun did rise P

•gwiy(a) branch, twig, limb
[o+]
ogwi:ya' a limb; a twig; a branch

•gwiyo:gę' barn swallow
[-gwiy(a)$_N$- branch, twig -ogę$_V$- be together, between]
gwiyo:gę' a barn swallow

•gwiyogę' catfish
[t+ -gwiy(a)$_N$- branch, twig -ogę$_V$- be together, between]
tgwiyo:gę' a channel catfish

•gye fly
[A+]
gagye' it is flying along PURP

•gyenǫhǫgye'(s) fly along, float along, float about
[A+ contains: -gye$_V$- fly]
gadigyenǫhǫgye'(s) they (z) are flying, floating about in the air (for example, seeds, etc.) H

•gyohgǫgye's roam
see: (i)gyohgǫgye's roam
gęgyohgǫgye's people roaming about H

•gyohg(wa) crowd
see: (i)gyohg(wa) crowd
sgęgyohgwa:t one crowd; one body of people

•gyohgwaę' association, agency, group, crowd
see: (i)gyohgwaę' association, agency, group, crowd
gęgyohgwaę' an association; an agency; a group; a crowd

•gyogyo:' Baltimore oriole
gyo:gyo:' a Baltimore oriole

•gyǫnhohsgwa:ǫt o'wahǫh beef
gyonhohsgwaǫ:t a cow
o'wahǫh meat

Legend: H habitual, P punctual, S stative, I imperative, PURP purposive, PURP-H purposive habitual, PURP-PAST purposive past, PURP-P purposive punctual, PURP-I purposive imperative; see §8.6, §8.11 in Appendix J. Alphabetization in stems ignores length (:), and any h's or glottal stops (') that are not between vowels. See §2.2 of the User Guide for explanation.

H

•(h)aʼd dry out, dry s.t.
gahaʼtaʼ it dries H
ęhse:haʼt you will dry s.t. P
ohaʼdǫh it is dry (for example, fields, weather); a drought S

•(h)ad(a) forest
[ga+]
gaha:daʼ a forest; a bush

•(h)aʼd(a) quill, plume, feather, voice, throat, larynx, esophagus
[o+]
ohaʼdaʼ a quill; a plume; a feather; the voice; the throat; the larynx; the esophagus
gahaʼdʼageh on its throat

•(h)a(:)dad rise up
[at+]
wata:da:s it rises up H
ęwata:da:t it will rise up P
ota:dadǫhǫgyeʼ it is going along rising up S

•(h)adadih Smart weed
[go+at+ -(h)ad(a)$_N$- forest -(a)dih$_V$- side]
gota:da:dih Smart weed (a medicinal plant)

•(h)adagwęhdeʼclearing
[de+yo+ -(h)ad(a)$_N$- forest -(a)gwęhdę$_V$- be flat, dented]
deyohada:gwęhdeʼ a clearing in the forest

•(h)aʼdanawę(:) quench one's thirst
ęyehaʼdanawę:ʼ they (lit.: she, someone) will wet their cores, their throats P
[-(h)aʼd(a)$_N$- throat, voice, feather -nawę(:)$_V$- wet s.t.]

•(h)aʼdatęh thirsty
[A+ -(h)aʼd(a)$_N$- throat, voice, feather -tę(:)$_V$- be dry]
shaʼda:tęhs you are thirsty H

•(h)aʼdiyo: be a good singer
[P+ -(h)aʼd(a)$_N$- throat, voice, feather -iyo:$_V$- be nice, good]
gohaʼdi:yo: she is a good singer; she has a good voice S

•(h)aʼdǫhnǫʼ clothesline
[ga+ contains: -(h)aʼd$_V$- be dry]
gahaʼdǫhnǫʼ clothesline; it is hanging up to dry

•(h)aʼdrohg juneberry
haʼdrohk a juneberry

•(h)aędǫnyǫh shimmer
[de+...at+ -ha$_N$- line, horizon -ędǫnyǫ(:)$_V$- lay down several things]
adwataędǫ:nyǫh it shimmered P
dewataędǫnyǫh it is twinkling; it is shimmering S

•(h)aʼg aunt
age:haʼk my aunt (old word) S

•(h)aʼgędreʼ crusty snow
[o+ -haʼ$_N$- -gędr$_V$- scrape -e$_V$- go]
ohaʼgędreʼ crusty snow

•(h)agwędakʼah horizon
[de+yo+ contains: -ha$_N$- horizon -(a)gwęhdę$_V$- be flat, dented]
deyohagwęda:kʼah the horizon

•(h)ah support
[present in:]
deyǫhsʼidahahkwaʼ a foot stool H
[de+yǫ+ stem: -(a)hsiʼdahahkwaʼ- foot stool; consists of: -(a)hsi(ʼda), (ę)hs(a)$_N$- foot -(h)ahkwaʼ$_V$- s.t. that supports]

•(h)ah(a) road
[o+]
ohahaʼ a road
oha:deʼ an existing road
[o+ -(h)ah(a)$_N$- road -deʼ$_V$- exist]

•(h)ahaʼdihǫh Galaxy, Milky Way
[o+ -(h)ah(a)$_N$- road -(adi)hǫh$_V$- lean against]
ohahaʼdihǫh the Milky Way

•(h)aha'drǫ' expressway, interchange
[de+wa+at+ -(h)ah(a)$_N$- road -(a)drǫ'$_V$- several things a certain distance apart]
dewataha'drǫ' an expressway; interchanges

•(h)ahagw stray, turn off
[at+ -(h)ah(a)$_N$- road -(h)gw$_V$- lift, pick up]
agęnataha:go' they (z) turned off the road P

•(h)ahahgw walk
[de+...at+ -(h)ah(a)$_N$- road -(h)gw$_V$- lift, pick up]
dehęnatahahkwa' ga̱hnyǫ'ǫhsra'geh they (m) are ironworkers (lit. they walk on the iron) H
dęgatahahk I will walk P

•(h)ahahgwa'd(ę, ani) corrupt s.o.
[TR+at+-(h)ah(a)$_N$- road -(h)gwa'dę$_V$- cause to lift or pick up for someone]
ęhsheyataha:gwa'dę' you will corrupt her/them (lit.: you will take her off the path; high language) P

•(h)ahagwahta' laneway
[ǫ+at+ -(h)ah(a)$_N$- road -(h)gwahd$_V$- cause to lift or pick up]
ǫtaha:gwahta' a laneway

•(h)ahakdǫ: curve in the road
[de+yo+at+ -(h)ah(a)$_N$- road -(a)'kdǫ$_V$- be bent, crooked]
deyotaha'kdǫ: a curve in the road

•(h)ahahiya'kd(ę,ani) escort s.o.
[TR+ -(h)ah(a)$_N$- road -(i)ya'gę$_V$- cut, break, cross for one's benefit]
dęhsheya̱hahiya'kdę' you will escort her across the road P

•(h)ahęhdahnǫh stripe, pattern
[o+]
ohahęhdahnǫh stripes; it is patterned S

•(h)ahin(e') walk
[A+at+ -(h)ah(a)$_N$- road -in(e')$_V$- go]
gatahine' I am walking PURP

•(h)ahinǫ: concession
[sga:t one he+yo+at+ -(h)ah(a)$_N$- road -inǫ$_V$- to have gone]
sga:t heyotahinǫ: one concession (a measurement)

•(h)ahit'a:' take the heavenly road, come to a consensus
[at+ -(h)ah(a)$_N$- road -(hr)i'd$_V$- cause to break]
ahęnatahi'ta:' they (m) came to a consensus; they followed their idea; now they are ready to go (referring to the Confederacy Council) P

•(h)ahiya'g crossroad
[de+yo+ -(h)ah(a)$_N$- road -(i)ya'g$_V$- cut, break, cross]
deyohahiy'agǫh a crossroad
deyohahi'y'aksǫ' crossroads

•(h)aho(k)da'ǫh dead end
[(he')+(y)o+ -(h)ah(a)$_N$- road -o'kda'$_V$- come to an end]
ohahoda'ǫh a dead end (lit.: where the road goes onto another road) S
otaho'kda'ǫh a dead end
heyotaho'kda'ǫh dead end S

•(h)ahowanę highway
[o+ -(h)ah(a)$_N$- road -owanęh$_V$- be big]
ohahowa:nę's big highways

•(h)ahǫ: common plantain
[de+yo+ -(h)ah(a)$_N$- road -(h)ǫ(:)$_V$- lie across]
deyohahǫ: common plantain

•(h)ahǫd, (h)ahǫnyǫ' row
[o+at+ -(h)ah(a)$_N$- road -ǫd$_V$- attached -ǫnyǫ$_V$- plural]
otahǫ:t a row
otahaǫ:nyǫ' rows

•(h)ahǫd side road
[o+ -(h)ah(a)$_N$- road -ǫd$_V$- attached -ǫnyǫ$_V$- plural]
ohahǫ:t a side road
ohahodǫ:nyǫ' side roads

Legend: H habitual, P punctual, S stative, I imperative, PURP purposive, PURP-H purposive habitual, PURP-PAST purposive past, PURP-P purposive punctual, PURP-I purposive imperative; see §8.6, §8.11 in Appendix J. Alphabetization in stems ignores length (:), and any h's or glottal stops (') that are not between vowels. See §2.2 of the User Guide for explanation.

•(h)aʼg sitting up on top of s.t.
see: (h)e:ʼ [A+] sitting up on top of s.t.
g̱ahaʼk it did sit on s.t. S
•(h)a:kʼah be short in height
[ni+yo+ -ha$_{N}$- line, horizon -a:kʼah$_{V}$- be short]
niyo:ha:kah it is short in height (vertically) S
•(h)aʼkd(a) soot
[o+]
ohaʼkdaʼ soot
•(h)an(a) groin, thigh
oha:naʼ groin
shanaʼgeh on your groin
•haoʼ o.k.; come on
see: Appendix I
•haoʼ dʼęnyoh. o.k. then
see: Appendix I
•(h)ahs serve s.o.
[TR+(N+)]
shehahseh you serve her/them all the time H
ęhshe:hahs you will serve s.o. P
ęh-sné:kahs you will give it s.t. to drink P
[TR+(N+) stem: -(h)neg(a)$_{N}$- water, liquid -(h)ahs$_{V}$- serve]
•(h)ahshę counsel
hahahshęhęʼ he is a counsellor H
ęhahahsęhę:k he will be a counsellor P
hohahahsęhęgyeʼ he is going along counselling S
•(h)ahsrǫd night-fish, spear-fish, jack-lighting
[at+ -(h)ahsr(a)$_{N}$- flash -ǫd(ę)$_{V}$- be attached, put in]
ahęnatahsrǫ:dęʼ they (m) carried a torch, lantern, flashlight P
•(h)aʼtge: drought
[-(h)aʼd$_{V}$- be dry -ge: big]
agahaʼtge: there was a big drought

•(h)awahg son, daughter
[TR+]
keha:wahk my daughter S
heha:wahk my son S
•(h)awa:kʼah maternal niece
kehawa:kʼah my maternal niece S
•(h)awi, (h)a: hold, include, carry, bring s.t.
[(de+)...(N+)]
haha:wiʼ he is carrying it H
ętaha:wiʼ he is going to bring s.t. P
nigaha:ʼ how much it holds S
dahsha: bring it here I
•(h)awi, (h)a: bring s.t.
[d+...(N+)]
dahsha: bring it here I
•(h)awi, (h)a: bring s.t. back
[de+d+...(N+)]
dę:taha:wiʼ he will bring it back P
•(h)awi, (h)a: hold a certain amount
[ni+...]
nigaha:ʼ how much it holds S
•(h)awi, (h)a: bring s.t. with oneself
[s+...]
shaha:wiʼ he brought it with him P
•(h)awihsǫ(:) carry around
[contains: -(h)awi, (h)a:- bring, etc. -sǫʼ- several items, events]
ęhahawihsǫ:ʼ he will carry s.t. around P
•(h)deg(a:) rib
ohde:ga:ʼ ribs
se̱hdega:ʼgeh on your ribs
•(h)disoda: cardinal
[ga+ contains: -(h)dis(a)$_{N}$- -oda(:,h)$_{V}$- drape]
g̱ahdiso:da: a cardinal (a bird)
•(h)e(:) be a birthday
[he+s+]
hejehehs her birth date H
hęjehe:ʼ it will be her birthday (lit.: she will come to her birth time) P

•(h)e:ʼ be sitting up on top of s.t.
[A/P+(N+)]
ga̱he:ʼ it is sitting up on top of s.t.; it is sitting here S
gana'ja̱he:ʼ a pail setting on s.t. S
[ga+ stem: -na'j(a)$_N$- pail, drum-(h)e:ʼ$_V$- be sitting up on top of s.t.]

•he: put, place s.t.
see: (hr)e, (hr)ę [(N+)] put, place s.t.
ęhshręʼ you will set it on s.t. P

•(h)e'(a:) husk
[o+]
ohe'a:ʼ a corn husk

•(h)ed yell, scream
[de+P+]
de̱hohetaʼ he is hollering H
atohe:t he hollered, yelled P

•(h)ehd(a) land, ground
[o+]
ohehdaʼ dirt; earth; ground; land

•(h)ehdagahatw, (h)ehdagahato plough a field
[contains: -(h)ehd(a)$_N$- land, dirt, earth, ground -gahatw$_V$- turn over]
ga̱hehdagahatwęh a ploughed field S

•(h)ehdę'ǫge: canyon
[he+yo+ -(h)ehd(a)$_N$- land, ground -(a's)ę'$_V$- fall, reduce -ge: big]
heyohehdę'ǫge: canyon

•(h)ehdo'dę: loam
[ni+yo+ -(h)ehd(a)$_N$- land, ground -o'dę:$_V$- type of]
niyohehdo'dę: loam (lit.: some type of land)

•(h)ehdohsgǫʼ barren land
[o+ -(h)ehd(a)$_N$- land, ground -ohsga'(w)$_V$- clear]
ohehdǫhsgǫʼ barren land

•(h)ehdǫne:s bulldozer
[ga+ -(h)ehd(a)$_N$- land, ground -ǫ'n(eg)$_V$- remove, take away]
ga̱hehdǫ:ne:s a bulldozer

•he:gę: just, only
see: Appendix I

•(h)ehgya'g erode
[at+ -(h)ehd(a)$_N$- land, dirt, earth, ground -(i)ya'g$_V$- cut, break, cross]
watehgya's it is eroding H
ęwahtehgya'k it will erode P

•(h)ehgya'ktaʼ spade
[e+ -(h)ehd(a)$_N$- land, ground -(i)ya'gd$_V$- cut, break with s.t.]
ehehgya'ktaʼ a spade

•he(n) cut
see: (hr)e(n) [(N+)] cut
a·hǫ́·wa̱·he:ʼ he slashed him with a sharp instrument

•hehn(a) cargo, bundle, load
see: (hr)ehn(a) cargo, bundle, load
ohehnaʼ, ga̱hehnaʼ a cargo; a bundle; a load

•hehnǫni pack s.t.
see: (h)rehnǫni [at+] pack
satrehnǫ:nih pack it I

•hena'tr(a) blade, knife
see: (hr)ena'tr(a) blade, knife
ohęn'atraʼ a blade

•hena'tra'se:ʼ scissors
see: (hr)ena'tra'se:ʼ scissors
degahęna'tra'se:ʼ scissors

•hena'trǫd blade
see: (hr)ena'trǫd blade
ohęn'atrǫ:t blade

•hena'traho'dę: spatula
see: (hr)ena'traho'dę: spatula
ohenatraho'dę: a spatula

•(h)ehnawęhę:s bail elevator
[ga+ -(hr)ehn(a)$_N$- cargo, bundle -węhę(h)d$_V$- climb s.t.]
ga̱hehnawęhę:s a bail elevator

•(h)ehnoha:s bailer
[de+ga+ -(hr)ehn(a)$_N$- bundle -(r)oh(eg)$_V$- gather]
degahehnoha:s a bailer

Legend: H habitual, P punctual, S stative, I imperative, PURP purposive, PURP-H purposive habitual, PURP-PAST purposive past, PURP-P purposive punctual, PURP-I purposive imperative; see §8.6, §8.11 in Appendix J. Alphabetization in stems ignores length (:), and any h's or glottal stops (ʼ) that are not between vowels. See §2.2 of the User Guide for explanation.

•(h)ehs(a) decayed tree, log, wood, board [o+]
ohehsa' a decayed tree; a log; wood; a board

•(h)ehsa'ę:' brown
[-(h)ehs(a)$_N$- decayed tree -'ę:'$_V$- be coloured]
hehs'ae̜:' brown

•(h)ehshai fox
[-(h)ehs(a)$_N$- decayed tree -i:'$_V$- be stuck onto s.t.]
hehshai: a fox

•(h)etga(a) anus
se̱hetga'a'geh on your anus

•(h)etga'a:' rear end, posterior, anus
[-(h)etg(a)$_N$- anus -a:'$_V$- hold, contain, include]
ohetga'a:' the rear end; the posterior; an anus

•(h)etgahęd anus
[o+ -(h)etg(a)$_N$- anus -(ga)hęd$_V$- drill, hole]
ohetga̱hę:t an anus

•hetgę evil, bad, ugly
see: (hr)etgę [A+(N+)] evil, bad, ugly
ga̱he:tgę' it is ugly S

•hetgę' go bad, get wrecked
see: (hr)etgę' [P+(N+)] go bad, get wrecked
ǫge'dre̱hdahe:tgę' my car broke down P
[-(')drehd(a)$_N$- car, etc. -(hr)etgę'$_V$- go bad, get wrecked]

•he:tgęh up, above
see: Appendix I
he:tgęh up; above

•hetgęh wreck s.t.
see: (hr)etgęh wreck s.t.
ęhsre:tgęh you will wreck it P

•hetgęhd ruin, wreck, damage s.t.
see: (hr)etgęhd ruin, wreck, damage
ęhshe:tgęht you will damage, ruin, wreck s.t. P

•hetgęhd become moody
see: (hr)etgęhd [at+] become moody
a'ǫtehtgęht s.o. turned funny, moody, etc. P

•hetgęhd go bad
see: (hr)etgęhd [d+...at+] go bad
dawatehtgęht it went bad P

•hetgędǫni be in a funny mood; be moody
see: (hr)etgędǫni [P+at+] be in a funny mood; be moody
hotehtgędǫ:ni: he is in a funny or odd mood; he is moody S

•(h)etge̱hjih the very top
[he:tgęh up, above -jih really]
he:tge̱hjih the very top

•hetgęs'ah be unattractive
see: (hr)etgęs'ah [A+] be unattractive
hahe:tgę:s'ah he is unattractive S

•(h)ehtǫ' ground hog, woodchuck, gopher
[t+ -(h)ehd(a)$_N$- land, ground -(h)ǫ(:)$_V$- lie across]
tehtǫ' a ground hog; a woodchuck; a gopher

•(h)ets(a) sausage, wiener, bologna [o+]
ohe:tsa' raw sausage; bologna; wieners

•(h)etsogw trick, fool s.o.
tsohetsogwahs it tricks him all the time H
ahohetso:go' it tricked him (like the frog) P
shohetsogwęh he was fooled (like the frog) S

•hewahd apologize, repent
see: (hr)ewahd [s+...adat+] apologize, repent
sa̱hęnada:tre:waht they (m) repented P

•hewahd punish s.o.
see: (hr)ewahd [TR/...at+] punish
ęhshehe:waht you will punish her P

•(h)ey(a) corn stalk [o+]
ohe:ya' a corn stalk

•(h)eyǫ:ʼ death
[ga+ -(ga)hey, (gę)hey, (i)hey, (ga)he:, (gę)he:, (i)he:$_V$- die, exhausted]
g̲aheyǫ:ʼ death

•(he)yǫʼd(a) dead body, cadaver
[o+ -(he)yǫ(ʼda)-$_N$ corpse, cadaver]
oyǫʼdaʼ a dead body; a cadaver
gye̲.he.yʼǫ.da.ę:dáhk.wʼa.geh a funeral home
[g+ye+ stem: -(h)eʼyǫhdaędahkwaʼgeh- funeral home; consists of: -(he)yǫ(ʼda)$_N$- corpse, cadaver -ędahkwaʼ$_V$- place where s.t. is put -(ʼ)geh- at]

•hęʼ (a particle that occurs in particle combinations)
see: Appendix I

•(h)ę: dry
[o+ -tę(:), hę(:)$_V$- be dry]
ohę: it is dry S

•(h)ę: sun-tan
[A+adę+]
esadę̲hę:k you got a tan P
sadę̲hę:k you are getting a tan S

•hę be a day
see: (r)hę be a day
ęyo:hęʼ it will be tomorrow P

•hę put, place
see: (hr)e, (hr)ę [(N+)] put, place
ęhshręʼ you will set it on s.t. P

•(h)ę(h,ʼ) feel bad, be embarrassed, ashamed, etc.
[ade+]
gadehęhs I am embarrassed, ashamed H
ęgadę̲hęh I will be embarrassed P
hodehęʼǫh he is embarrassed right now S

•(h)ęh be in the middle, be halved
[tsaʼde+...N+ occurs in:]
tsaʼdewa̲hsǫ:tęh at midnight (lit.: in the middle of the night)
[tsaʼ+de+wa+ -(a)hsǫd(a)$_N$- evening, night -(h)ęh$_V$- be in the middle, be halved]
tsaʼdeganada̲hęh village square, village centre, town square S
[tsaʼ+de+ga+ stem: -nadahęh- town square, village square; consists of: -nad(a)$_N$- town, community -(h)ęh$_V$- be in the middle, be halved]

•(h)ęd lead
see: (hr)ęd lead
ęhsrę:t you will be the lead P

•hęʼda(:,h) burn s.t.
see: (hr)ęʼda(:,h) [(N+)] burn s.t.
ęhsręʼda:ʼ you will burn s.t. P

•(h)ęd(a) field, meadow
[ga+ ... -(a)gǫ: in]
g̲ahędagǫ: in the field; in the meadow

•(h)ęhd(a:) fur
[o+]
ohęhda:ʼ fur

•(h)ędaęʼ meadow, pasture, field
[ga+ -(h)ęd(a)$_N$- field -ę$_V$- lie on the ground]
g̲ahędaęʼ a meadow; a pasture; a field
g̲ahędaędǫʼ meadows

•(h)ęhdaę:ʼ be furry
[o+ -(h)ęhd(a:)$_N$- fur -ę$_V$- lie on the ground, have s.t.]
ohęhdaę:ʼ it is furry S

•(h)ędagǫ: upwind
[o+ -(hr)ęd$_V$- lead -(a)gǫ: in]
ohędagǫ: upwind

•(h)ędohsga:ʼ pioneer
[de+... -(h)ęd(a)$_N$- field -ohsgaʼ(w)$_V$- clear]
atadihędosga:ʼ they (m) were pioneers P

•(h)ędowih scarecrow
[wa+at+ -(h)ęd(a)$_N$- field -owi, ǫny$_V$- drive]
watę:do:wih a scarecrow

Legend: H habitual, P punctual, S stative, I imperative, PURP purposive, PURP-H purposive habitual, PURP-PAST purposive past, PURP-P purposive punctual, PURP-I purposive imperative; see §8.6, §8.11 in Appendix J. Alphabetization in stems ignores length (:), and any h's or glottal stops (ʼ) that are not between vowels. See §2.2 of the User Guide for explanation.

•(h)ędǫ: ahead, front
[o+ -(hr)ęd$_V$- lead]
ohę:dǫ: ahead; in front; the front
•(h)ęʼdǫ(:) hang over
[P+]
ęyohęʼdǫ:ʼ it will be hanging over (an edge, a chair) P
ohęʼdǫh it is hanging over (an edge, a chair) S
•(h)ędǫni tend (a garden)
[at+ -(h)ęd(a)$_N$- field -ǫni, ǫny$_V$- make]
ęhsatędǫ:niʼ you will make your garden P
•(h)ędǫʼse:ʼ precede s.o.
[s/j+TR+ contains: -(hr)ęd$_V$- lead]
jǫkihędǫʼse:ʼ she has gone on before us S
(h)ęhjihwęh be really dried out
[o+ contains: -hę(:)$_V$- be dry -jih really]
ohęhji̱hwęh it is really dried out S
•hęʼęh no
see: Appendix I
•(h)ęgaǫsr(a) invitation
[adę+]
adęhęgaǫhsraʼ an invitation
•hę:gyeh it does not matter; does not make any difference
see: Appendix I
•(h)ę:hah, (h)ę:hęh be thin, be a material
[ni+ga+ -(h)ę:hah, hę:hęh$_V$- be thin]
nigahę:hah it is thin (for example, material)
•(h)ęhod wood pile
[de+wa+at+ -hęh(a)$_N$- wood -od$_V$- stand]
dewatęho:t a pile of wood
•hęnaʼtraʼa:s stab s.o.
see: (hr)ęnaʼtraʼa:s [de+TR+] stab s.o.
dęhshehęnaʼtraʼa:s you will stab s.o. P
•hęnaʼtraʼehsd stab s.o.
see: (hr)ęnaʼtraʼehsd [de+TR+] stab s.o.
dęgǫhęnaʼtraʼehs I will stab you P

•hęʼhne:ʼ too, also, and
see: Appendix I
•hęʼni:ʼ me too
see: Appendix I
•(h)ęʼǫhsd widow, widower
[P+ade+ contains: -(h)ę(h,ʼ)$_V$- feel bad]
aʼǫdȩ̱hęʼǫhs she became a widow P
hodehęʼǫhsdǫh he is a widower S
•(h)ęhsd dry out, evaporate
ga̱hęhstaʼ it is drying out H
•(h)gǫnhniʼgǫh be a leader
[de+ga+ contains: -ǫnheʼ$_V$- be alive]
degahgǫnhniʼgǫh the leader of equal standing
•(h)gw lift, pick up
[de+...(N+)]
atgehk I picked s.t. up P
dȩ̱hoyaʼdahgwęh it picked him up S
[de+...TR+ stem: -yaʼd(a)$_N$- body -(h)gw$_V$- lift, pick up]
•(h)gw(ę, ani) take s.t. back from s.o.
[s+ contains: -(h)gw$_V$- lift, pick up]
shǫwadihkwęʼ they took it back from him again P
•(h)gw, (h)go remove s.t.
[N+ occurs in:]
ęhsetsgęʼęda̱hgoʼ you will remove seeds P
[-tsgęʼęd(a)$_N$- pit -(h)gw, (h)go$_V$- remove]
gahsgwa:da̱hgwęh a neutered animal, a gelding S
[-(h)sg(wa:)$_N$- stone, bullet, rock -dahgw, dahgo$_V$- remove]
•(h)gwaʼd uphold s.t., raise up s.t., lift up, pick up
[de+ contains: -(h)gw$_V$- lift, pick up]
degahgwʼataʼ it upholds s.t., raises things up H
dehohgwaʼdǫh he is lifting it up S

•(h)gwę set
hegahgwę's to the setting sun; the direction of the sunset; west H
ha'gahgwę' sunset; the sun went down P

•(h)gwę' sunset
[ha'+ga+ contains: -(h)gwę$_V$- set]
ha'gahgwę' sunset; the sun went down

•(h)gwę's west
[he'+ga+ contains: -(h)gwę$_V$- set]
hegahgwę's to the setting sun; the direction of the sunset; west H

•hi' break up
see: (hr)i' [de+...(N+)] break up
dęgahi' it will break P

•(h)ih spill
[ga+]
gahihǫh it is spilled S

•hihd slice, mash, grind, break s.t. up
see: (hr)ihd [de+...(N+)] slice, mash, grind, break s.t. up
dęhsriht you will break s.t. P

•(h)ihi: great horned owl
hihi: a great horned owl

•(h)i'kd(a) thorn, thistle
[o+]
ohi'kda' a thorn; a thistle

•(h)i'kdai:' thorn bush
[o+ -(h)i'kd(a)$_N$- thorn, thistle -i:'$_V$- be stuck onto s.t.]
ohi'kdai:' a thorn bush

•(h)i'kdatgi' Scottish thistle
[o+ -(h)i'kd(a)$_N$- thorn, thistle -tgi'$_V$- be dirty, ugly]
ohi'kdatgi' Scottish thistle

•hihta' grinder, cutter
see: (hr)ihta' grinder, cutter
degahihta' a grinder; a cutter

•(h)i'y(a) trunk, form
ohi'ya' the body's trunk, form

•(h)i'ya'g hold a grudge; get mad, disgusted
[at+]
hoti'ya̱'hsgǫ: he's testy; he has a short fuse H
ęhsati'ya'k you will hold a grudge P
satiy'agǫh you are holding a grudge right now S

•(h)i'yagaęhe' be bent over
[A+ -(h)i'y(a)$_N$- trunk, form -gaęh(e')$_V$- cross]
ha'hi'yagaę:he' his body trunk is crooked; he is bent over S

•(h)ji'ah older sibling
[TR+]
hehji'ah my older brother S
kehji'ah my older sister S

•(h)kw take s.t. from s.o.
[N+]
ęhshenǫgwahkwa' you will take the milk from the child (that is, wean the child) P
[-nǫ'g(wa)$_N$- breast, milk -(h)kw$_V$- take s.t. from s.o.]

•(h)kwa' rhythm, beat, throbbing noise
[de+yo+ contains: -(h)gw$_V$- lift, pick up]
deyohkwa' a steady rhythm, beat; a throbbing

•(h)n(a) oily substance
[o+]
ohna' grease; oil; gas; gravy

•(h)n(a) material, skin
see: (i)hn(a) material, skin
gi̱hna'geh on my skin

•(h)na'gǫ: under, beneath, below, on the bottom
[o+ -(h)na'g$_V$- bottom]
ohna:gǫ: under
ohna'gǫh tga:yęh it lies underneath, below S

•(h)na'gǫhka:' underwear
[-(h)na'gǫh$_V$- bottom -ka:' type of]
hna'gǫ̱hka:' underwear

Legend: H habitual, P punctual, S stative, I imperative, PURP purposive, PURP-H purposive habitual, PURP-PAST purposive past, PURP-P purposive punctual, PURP-I purposive imperative; see §8.6, §8.11 in Appendix J. Alphabetization in stems ignores length (:), and any h's or glottal stops (') that are not between vowels. See §2.2 of the User Guide for explanation.

•(h)nai:ʼ oily, greasy
[o+ -(h)n(a)$_N$- oil, gas -i:ʼ$_V$- be stuck onto s.t.]
ohnai:ʼ it is oily, greasy S

•(h)naji: motor oil, black grease
[o+ -(h)n(a)$_N$- oil, gas -ji(:,h)$_V$- be dark]
ohna:ji: motor oil; black grease

•(h)naned level
[o+ -(h)n(a)$_N$- oil, gas -ned$_V$- keep -nyǫʼ several items]
ohnaʼneda:nyǫʼ several levels

•(h)naned lining, insulated wall
see: (i)hnaned lining, insulated wall
degahnane:t lining; an insulated wall

•(h)nasǫ(:) oil oneself
[at+ -(h)n(a)$_N$- oil, gas -sǫ$_V$- several items, events]
hatna:sǫʼ he is oiling himself H
ahatna:sǫʼ he did oil himself P
satna:sǫ: oil yourself I

•(h)natę: have dry skin
see: (i)hnatę: [A+] have dry skin
se̱hna:tę:, si̱hna:tę: you have dry skin S

•(h)natęhsdǫh be a cradle-robber
see: (i)hnatęhsdǫh be a cradle-robber
ohnahtęhsdǫh 'dried-up skin' (a derogatory term referring to s.o. with a younger woman or man)

•(h)naʼts(a) buttock, behind, ass
ohnaʼtsaʼ a buttock; an ass
snʼatsaʼgeh on your buttocks

•(h)naʼtsaʼe spank
[TR+ -(h)naʼts(a)$_N$- buttock -(ʼ)e$_V$- hit]
ęhyahnʼatsaʼe:k he will spank you P

•(h)naʼtsagęnyeʼ be fidgety
[P+at+ -(h)naʼts(a)$_N$- buttock -gęni, gęny$_V$- compete]
satnaʼtsagę:nyeʼ you are fidgety H

•(h)naʼtsędǫh shake one's behind
[de+...at+ -(h)naʼts(a)$_N$- buttock -ędǫh$_V$- shake s.t.]
dęhsatnaʼtsę:dǫʼ you will shake your behind P

•(h)naw(a), (h)nǫw(a) running water
[occurs in:]
ohnawada:se: whirlpool
[-(h)naw(a)$_N$- running water -dase:$_V$- whirl]
ohnawadeht strong currents
[o+ stem: -(h)nawadehd- strong current; consists of: -(h)naw(a)$_N$- running water -dehd$_V$- bold, bright, strong]

•(h)nawadase: whirlpool
ohnawada:se: a whirlpool
[o+-(h)naw(a)$_N$- water, running -dase:$_V$- whirl]

•(h)nawadehd strong currents
[o+ -(h)naw(a)$_N$- flowing water -dehd$_V$- bold, bright, strong]
ohnawadeht strong currents

•(h)nawadeni, (h)nawadeny strain s.t.
[N+ -(h)naw(a)$_N$- running water -deni, deny$_V$- change]
ęhsnǫwade:niʼ you will strain P
ganǫwade:nyǫ: it is being strained S

•(h)nawaędahgw filter water
[contains: -(h)naw(a)$_N$- water, running -ędahgw$_V$- raise from the ground]
ęhsnǫwaęhdahk you will filter the water P

•(h)nawaǫd well, spring
[o+ -(h)naw(a)$_N$- water, running -ǫd$_V$- stand -ǫnyǫʼ several items, events]
ohnawaǫ:dǫnyǫʼ many wells, springs

•(h)neʼdr(a) soil, ground
[o+ -(h)neʼdr(a)$_N$- soil, ground -(a)ʼgeh on]
ohneʼdrʼageh on the ground

•(h)neg(a) water, liquid
[o+ -(h)neg(a)$_N$- water, liquid -ʼgeh- on, at]
ohnegʼageh on the water

•(h)nega:ʼ level
[ga+ -(h)neg(a)$_N$- water, liquid -a:ʼ$_V$- hold, contain, include]
ga̱hne:ga:ʼ a level

•(h)negad be drunk, tipsy
[(tęʼ) not deʼ+ not P+at+ -(h)neg(a)$_{N}$- water, liquid -d$_{V}$- stand]
dihsa:tne:ga:t you are not level; you are tipsy S

•(h)negad be watery
[ga+ -(h)neg(a)$_{N}$- water, liquid -d$_{V}$- stand]
gahne:ga:t it is watery S

•(h)negadase: whirlpool
[o+at+ -(h)neg(a)$_{N}$- water, liquid -dase$_{V}$- whirl]
otnegada:se: a whirlpool

•(h)negadeni, (h)negadeny drain s.t.
[N+ -(h)neg(a)$_{N}$- water, liquid -deni, deny$_{V}$- change]
snegade:nih drain it (potatoes, etc.) I

•(h)negagaʼǫh pop, soda
[o+ -(h)neg(a)$_{N}$- water, liquid -gaʼǫh$_{V}$- be good-tasting]
ohnegagaʼǫh pop; soda

•(h)negagęhyad above the water
[o+ -(h)neg(a)$_{N}$- water, liquid -gęhyad$_{V}$- be at the edge of]
ohnegagęhya:t just above the water S

•(h)negagreʼ rubber coat
[o+ -(h)neg(a)$_{N}$- water, liquid -griʼ$_{V}$- juice, liquid -e$_{V}$- go]
ohnegagreʼ a rubber coat

•(h)negagriʼ soup, rubber
[o+ -(h)neg(a)$_{N}$- water, liquid -griʼ$_{V}$- juice, liquid]
ohnegagriʼ soup; rubber

•(h)negagyęhętw sip
[d+... -(h)neg(a)$_{N}$- water, liquid -yęhętw, yęhęto$_{V}$- pull]
ęhtsnegagyęhętoʼ you will sip through a straw P

•(h)negaheʼdahkwaʼ animal watering place, watering hole, trough
[A+ -(h)neg(a)$_{N}$- water, liquid -(hr)eʼdahkwaʼ$_{V}$- place where s.t. is put]
gadihnegaheʼdahkwaʼ an animal watering place; a watering hole; a trough

•(h)negahe be high tide
[de+... -(h)neg(a)$_{N}$- water, liquid -(h)e:ʼ$_{V}$- sitting up on top of s.t.]
ętgahnegahe:k it will be high tide

•(h)negahihǫh spring water
[g+yo+ -(h)neg(a)$_{N}$- water, liquid -(adi)hǫh$_{V}$- lean against s.t.]
gyohnegahihǫh spring water

•(h)negahkwaʼ water spout
[de+ga+ -(h)neg(a)$_{N}$- water, liquid -(h)gw$_{V}$- lift, pick up]
degahnegahkwaʼ a water spout

•(h)negahkwaʼ animal watering place, watering hole, trough
[hadi+ -(h)neg(a)$_{N}$- water, liquid -(h)gw$_{V}$- lift, pick up]
hadihnegahkwaʼ an animal watering place; a watering hole; a trough

•(h)neganawę: lead, lukewarm water, prepubescent boy
[o+ -(h)neg(a)$_{N}$- water, liquid -nawę:$_{V}$- be wet]
ohnegana:wę: lead; lukewarm water; a word referring to a prepubescent boy

•(h)neganyo hangover
[P+ -(h)neg(a)$_{N}$- water, liquid -(r)iyo, nyo$_{V}$- kill s.t.]
hohneganyohs he has a hangover H

•(h)negatgiʼ scum
[o+ -(h)neg(a)$_{N}$- water, liquid -tgiʼ$_{V}$- be dirty, ugly]
ohnegatgiʼ scum; dirty water

•(h)negatsęi, (h)negatsęny divine, witch for water
[-(h)neg(a)$_{N}$- water, liquid -tsęi, tsęny$_{V}$- find]
hadihnegatsęnyǫhs they (m) divine, witch for water H

Legend: H habitual, P punctual, S stative, I imperative, PURP purposive, PURP-H purposive habitual, PURP-PAST purposive past, PURP-P purposive punctual, PURP-I purposive imperative; see §8.6, §8.11 in Appendix J. Alphabetization in stems ignores length (:), and any h's or glottal stops (ʼ) that are not between vowels. See §2.2 of the User Guide for explanation.

•(h)negayehsd dilute
[de+... -(h)neg(a)$_N$- water, liquid -yehsd$_V$- add]
dehsnegayehs dilute it I

•(h)negeha drink
gahnege̱haʼ it is drinking H
ęyehnegehaʼ she will drink P
snegehah drink I

•(h)negęʼgwahd tidal wave
[de+...at+ -(h)neg(a)$_N$- water, liquid -ęʼgw, (a)hdęʼgw$_V$- swell up]
dawatnegęʼgwaht a tidal wave

•(h)negoʼ puddle, water
[o+ -(h)neg(a)$_N$- water, liquid -oʼ$_V$- submerged -nyǫʼ several items]
ohne:goʼ a puddle; any type of water S
ohnegǫnyǫʼ lots of puddles

•(h)negod fire hydrant, fountain
[t+ga -(h)neg(a)$_N$- water, liquid -od$_V$- stand]
tgahnegotaʼ a fire hydrant; a fountain

•(h)negod fountain
[g+yo+ -(h)neg(a)$_N$- water, liquid -od$_V$- stand]
gyo̱hne:go:t fountain

•(h)negoni ferment, brew
[at+ -(h)neg(a)$_N$- water, liquid -ǫni, ǫny$_V$- make]
ęhsatnegǫ:niʼ you will ferment s.t. P

•(h)negohs welding machine
[ga+ -(h)neg(a)$_N$- water, liquid -oh$_V$- dip in liquid]
ga̱hne:gohs a welding machine

•(h)negǫgohd filter liquid, strain liquid
[de+...(at+) -(h)neg(a)$_N$- water, liquid -ǫgohd$_V$- surpass]
dęhsne:gǫ:goht you will filter, strain liquid P
deyotnegǫgo̱hdǫh strained water S

•(h)neka:ʼdam
[de+ga+ -(h)neg(a)$_N$- water, liquid -(h)awi, (h)a:$_V$- hold, include, bring]
degahneʼka:ʼ a dam

•(h)nekaʼ bartender
[A+ contains: -(h)neg(a)$_N$- water, liquid]
hahne:kaʼ bartender

•(h)nekę: murky water
[o+ -(h)neg(a)$_N$- water, liquid -(h)ę(:)$_V$- dry]
ohne:kę: it is murky water

•(h)nęhs(a) shoulder
ohnęhsaʼ shoulder
snęhsaʼgeh on your shoulders

•(h)nęhsędǫh shrug
[de+...at+ -(h)nęs(a)$_N$- shoulder -ędǫh$_V$- shake s.t.]
atatnęhsę:dǫh he shrugged P

•(h)nęye:s be tall
[A+]
ehnę:ye:s she is tall S

•(h)nodǫ flood
see: (i)hnodǫ flood
ohno:dǫʼ it is flooded S

•(h)ni bark
ga̱hnih(s) it is barking H

•(h)ninǫ buy s.t.
aʼehni:nǫʼ she purchased s.t. P
tęʼ dewa:kni:nǫh tęʼ de̱ʼa:kni:nǫh I did not buy it S

•(h)ninǫh store, storekeeper
[A+adę+ -(h)ninǫ$_V$- sell]
ǫdęhni:nǫh a store; she is a storekeeper
hadęhni:nǫh he is a storekeeper

•(h)ninǫh grocery store
[g+yǫ+adę+ -(h)ninǫ$_V$- store, grocery store]
gyǫdęhni:nǫh a grocery store

•(h)ninǫnyǫʼ consumption
[ga+ -(h)ninǫ$_V$- buy -nyǫʼ several objects]
ga̱hninǫnyǫʼ consumption (lit.: things which are bought)

•(h)ninǫnyǫʼ plaza
[g+yǫ+adę+ -(h)ninǫ$_V$- sell -nyǫʼ several objects]
gyǫdęhninǫ:nyǫh a plaza
•(h)niyǫh be hard, tough
[o+(N+)]
ohni:yǫh it is hard S
okyędahkwahni:yǫh it is a hard chair
[P+(N+) stem: -(a)kyędahkw(a)$_N$- chair -(h)niyǫh$_V$- hard, tough]
•(h)niyaʼd tighten
[ga+ contains: -(h)niy$_V$- hard, tough]
gahniyʼadǫh it is tight, tightened S
•(h)no(:) pollution
[at+ -(h)n(a)$_N$- oil, gas -o(:)$_V$- be submerged]
ęwa:tno:ʼ there will be pollution P
•(h)noda:kʼah shallow
[ni+yo+ -(h)nod(a)$_N$- water -a:kʼah$_V$- short]
niyohnoda:kʼah it is shallow S
•(h)nodes deep
[o+ -(h)nod(a)$_N$- water -es$_V$- long]
ohno:de:s deep water
•(h)noʼs Joe Pye weed
[ga+ contains: -(h)n(a)$_N$- oily substance -oʼs$_V$- several submerged objects]
gahnoʼs Joe Pye weed
•(h)nǫh handkerchief
see: (i)hnǫh handkerchief
gahnǫh a handkerchief
•(h)nǫda:s gas station attendant
[A+ -(h)n(a)$_N$- oil, gas -ǫda:(h)$_V$- put in, be attached]
hahnǫ:da:s he is a gas station attendant
•(h)nǫde:ʼ sibling
[de+ TR+ adę+]
deyagyadęhnǫ:de:ʼ my brother; my sister (lit.: the one nearest to me in age and gender) S
•(h)nǫdragyehsǫ(:) follow around
[TR+ contains: -(h)nǫdragyeʼ$_V$- follow along -sǫʼ several objects, events]
ęhshehnǫdragehsǫ:ʼ (**ęhshehnǫdragyęhsǫ:ʼ**) you will follow s.o. around P
•(h)nǫdragyeʼ follow along
[TR+ contains: -(h)nǫdr$_V$- follow]
hǫwahnǫdra:gyeʼ s.o. is following him along H
•(h)nǫdre follow
[TR+ contains: -(h)nǫdr$_V$- follow -e- go]
hǫwahnǫdreʼ s.o. is following him PURP
ęhehsnǫdręʼ you will follow him PURP-P
dǫdahehsnǫ:dręh you follow him back
•(h)nǫg call
see: (i)hnǫg [heʼ/d+TR+] call
tagihnǫ:s he is calling me H
•(h)ny(a) stick
[ga+]
ganhyaʼ (**gahnyaʼ**) a stick
•(h)ny(a:) nutmeat
[o+]
ohnya:ʼ nutmeat
•(h)nyahdod lift one's head
[A+ -(h)nya(ʼsa)$_N$- neck, throat -od$_V$- stand]
ehnyahdo:t she's got her head up (said of a child who is learning to lift its head by itself) S
•(h)nyaʼdr(ę:) hang s.o.
[TR+ contains: -(h)nya(ʼsa)$_N$- neck, throat]
hǫwadihnyaʼdręhs they hang him, them (m) all the time H
ahǫwadihnyadrę:ʼ they hanged him, them (m) P
hǫwadihnyaʼdragǫh they have already hanged him (and his neck broke) S
•(h)nyaha: win (a bet)
[adę+ -(h)ny(a)$_N$- stick -(h)awi, (h)a:$_V$- hold, include, carry, bring]
agęnadęhnyęha:ʼ they (z) won (a bet) P

Legend: H habitual, P punctual, S stative, I imperative, PURP purposive, PURP-H purposive habitual, PURP-PAST purposive past, PURP-P purposive punctual, PURP-I purposive imperative; see §8.6, §8.11 in Appendix J. Alphabetization in stems ignores length (:), and any h's or glottal stops (ʼ) that are not between vowels. See §2.2 of the User Guide for explanation.

•(h)nya(ˀsa) neck, throat
ohnyaˀsaˀ a neck
ohnyaˀ the neck; the throat
se̱hnyaˀsˀageh on your neck (the front of the neck)
ohnyaˀsaˀgǫ: in the throat
•(h)nyahsg(a:) button
[contains: -ęˀnihsg(a)$_N$- circle]
ęhnyahsga:ˀ a button
•(h)nyaˀsgaˀohsd hiccough, hiccup
[P+ contains: -(h)nya(ˀsa)$_N$- neck, throat]
hohnyaˀsgˀaohs he is hiccupping, hiccoughing H
ęsahnyˀasgaˀohs you will hiccup, hiccough P
•(h)nyahshę: slow beat
[o+ -(h)ny(a)$_N$- stick -(a)hshę:$_V$- be slow-moving]
ohnyahshę: a slow beat
•(h)nyahsnoweˀ fast beat
[o+ -(h)ny(a)$_N$- stick -(h)snoweˀ$_V$- be fast]
ohnyahsno:weˀ a fast beat
•(h)nye:h(a) flint corn soup
[o+]
ohnye:haˀ flint corn soup
•(h)nyędahs(a) beak
[ga/o+]
gahnyęda̱hsaˀ, ohnyęda̱hsaˀ a beak
ga̱hnyęda̱hsaˀgeh on its beak
•(h)nyętse:s garfish
[ga+ -(h)nyęts(a)$_N$- -es$_V$- long]
ga̱hnyętse:s garfish
•(h)nyod stand
[A+ -(h)ny(a)$_N$- stick -od$_V$- stand]
gahnyo:t it is standing S
•(h)nyoˀdę: rhythm, beat
[ni+ga+ -(h)ny(a)$_N$- stick -oˀdę:$_V$- be a certain type, kind of thing]
nigahnyoˀdę: the rhythm; the beat of a piece of music

•(h)nyoˀg(wa) nut
[o+]
ohnyoˀgwaˀ a nut
•(h)nyˀogęˀ chipmunk
[ji+ -(h)ny(a)$_N$- stick -ogę$_V$- be together, between, double]
jihnyˀogęˀ chipmunk (this word refers to the stripe on the chipmunk's back)
•(h)nyoˀgwaji: walnut
[ga+ -(h)nyoˀg(wa)$_N$- nut -ji(:,h)$_V$- dark]
ga̱hnyoˀgwaji: a walnut
•(h)nyǫ(ˀǫ)hsr(a) iron, steel, bar
[ga+]
ga̱hnyǫˀǫhsraˀ iron; steel
ga̱hnyǫˀsraˀ a bar of iron, steel
•(h)nyǫˀǫh white
[ga+]
ga̱hnyǫˀǫh it is white S
•(h)nyǫhs(a) melon, squash
[o+]
ohnyǫhsaˀ a melon; a squash
•(h)nyǫhsaǫweh hubbard squash
[o+ -(h)nyǫhs(a)$_N$- squash -ǫweh- traditional]
ohnyǫhsˀaǫ:weh squash (used for soup at the Longhouse; usually Hubbard squash)
•(h)nyǫhsgwaeˀ cucumber
[o+ contains: -(h)nyǫhs(a)$_N$- melon, squash -g(wa)$_N$- lump]
ohnyǫhsgwa:eˀ a cucumber
•(h)nyǫhsr(a) bar
[ga+].
ga̱hnyǫˀsraˀ a bar of iron, steel
•(h)nyǫhsradeˀ prison, iron beams
[de+ga+ -hnyǫ(ˀǫ)hsr(a)$_N$- iron, steel -deˀ$_V$- exist]
degahnyǫhsra:deˀ prison; iron beams
•hoh what the...?
see: Appendix I
•(h)oˀde:s rifle
[ga+ -(h)oˀd(a)$_N$- gun -es$_V$- long]
ga̱hoˀde:s a rifle

•hoʼdęʼ what (shortened form)
see: Appendix I

•(h)odr(a) basswood
[o+]
oho:draʼ basswood

•hoho: exclamation, said in anticipation of something bad or good (that is, someone's about to win at bingo, or have a fight)
see: Appendix I

•(h)ohsgr(a) slippery elm
[o+]
ohohsgraʼ slippery elm

•hohsweʼnagehdeh gaya:ʼ his knapsack
hohsweʼnagehdeh he carries it on his upper back
gaya:ʼ a bag

•(h)otr(a) bundle, package
[ga+]
gaho:traʼ a package; a bundle

•hotgǫʼǫh exclamation; said when something is out of the ordinary.
see: Appendix I

•(h)oh(wa) pelt
[o+]
ohohwa:ʼ a pelt

•(h)owahsd cold
[P+at+ contains: -(a)tow(eʼ)$_{V}$- be cold (weather)]
agatowahstaʼ I am cold H

•(h)oweʼd(a) tube, cylinder, hose
[ga+]
gahoweʼdaʼ a tube; a cylinder; a hose

•(h)oweʼgeh North
[o+at+ -(a)tow(eʼ)$_{V}$- cold (weather) -ʼgeh on, at -hneh at]
otowʼegeh North
otoweʼgehneh a northern place

•(ʼ)howeg cover
see also: oweg [TR+(N+)] cover [TR+(N+)]
geʼho:we:s I am covering s.t. H
ęhseʼho:we:k you will cover s.t. P
ageʼhowe:gǫh I did cover s.t. S
segǫʼdro:we:k you put the pillowcase on I

•(ʼ)howeks(i) uncover
see: oweks(i) uncover
ęhsnaʼsgowe:ksih you will uncover the bed P

•(h)owęʼ loon
[ha+ contains: -(hr)owi, (hr)ǫny$_{V}$- tell]
haho:węʼ a loon

•howi tell
see: (hr)owi, (hr)ǫny [TR/...at+] tell
sheho:wih tell her I

•(h)owinyǫʼse: have a cold
[P+at+]
gotowinyǫʼse: she has a cold S

•(h)ǫʼ several objects lying across
[A/P+N+ present in:]
odoʼdahǫʼ little waves S
[o+ stem: -doʼd(a)$_{N}$- wave -(h)ǫ(:)$_{V}$- lie]

•(h)ǫʼ lie across
[de+ga+]
degahǫʼ s.t. is lying across a path, a door, etc. S

•(h)ǫ(:) lie down
[at+]
agęna:tǫ:ʼ they (z) lay down P
sa:tǫ: lie down I

•(h)ǫh crane, barrier, bar
[de+ga+ -(adi)hǫh$_{V}$- lean against]
degahǫh a marsh crane (lit.: it leans; referring to its legs); a bar; a barrier

•(h)ǫd(a) bush
[o+]
ohǫ:daʼ a bush; a whip

•(h)ǫdaęhd snowshoe rabbit
[t+ -(h)ǫd(a)$_{N}$- bush -(y)ęhd$_{V}$- hit, knock down, strike]
tǫdaęht a snowshoe rabbit

•(h)ǫdase:ʼ sapling
[o+ -(h)ǫd(a)$_{N}$- bush -(a)se:$_{V}$- be new]
ohǫda:se:ʼ a sapling

•(h)ǫdahsrǫni prune
[at+ -(h)ǫd(a)$_{N}$- bush -(h)srǫni$_{V}$- fix, repair]
ahęnatǫdahsro:niʼ they (m) pruned s.t.

•(h)ǫdayęhd whip s.o.
[TR+ -(h)ǫd(a)$_{N}$- bush -(y)ęhd$_{V}$- hit, knock down, strike]
ękehǫda:yęht I will whip her P

•(h)ǫgai be stiff, stiffen up; rigor mortis
[at+]
watǫgai:s it stiffens up all the time H
awatǫgai: it did stiffen up P
otǫgai: it is stiff; rigor mortis S

•(h)ǫgai, (h)ǫgany suffer
[de+P+adę+]
desadęhǫgai:s you suffer all the time H
dęhsadęhǫgaiʼ you will suffer P
dęsadęhǫganyęh you are suffering right now S

•(h)ǫgaistaʼ starch
[wa+at+ -(h)ǫgaihsd$_{V}$- stiffen with s.t.]
watǫgai:staʼ starch

•(h)ǫg(a:) elm
[ga+]
g̲ahǫ:ga:ʼ an elm tree

•(h)ǫga:g goose
hǫ:ga:k a goose

•(h)ǫgaǫ invite
[TR+/adę+]
ęhshehǫgaǫʼ you will invite her/them P

•(h)ǫʼgwaga: snore
[o+ -(h)ǫʼg(wa)$_{N}$- -ga:$_{V}$- make a rattling or grinding noise]
ohǫʼgwaga: a snore

•(h)ǫʼji(:,h) be dark
[A/P+N/(hǫʼ)+ occurs in:]
węda:jihs dusk; twilight H
[-ęd(a)$_{N}$- day -ji$_{V}$- be dark]
ękǫʼjihneʼ I am going to get dark P
[-(h)ǫʼ- -jihneʼ$_{V}$- go and get dark]
g̲ahǫʼji: it is dark-coloured S

•hǫhji stove
[contains: -(h)ǫʼji(:,h)$_{V}$- be dark]
hǫhji stove

•(h)ǫjihsd(a) motor, engine
[ga+ contains: -(h)ǫʼjihsd$_{V}$- make dark]
g̲ahǫʼji̲hsdaʼ a motor; an engine

•(h)ǫnaʼd(a) potato
[(o+)]
ohǫnʼadaʼ, **hǫnʼadaʼ** a potato

•(h)ǫnaʼdǫd baked potatoes
[wa+at+ -(h)ǫnaʼd(a)$_{N}$- potato -ǫd$_{V}$- roasted]
watǫnʼadǫ:t baked potatoes

•hǫny tell
see: (hr)owi, (hr)ǫny [TR/…at+] tell
sheho:wih tell her I

•(h)ǫnyaʼg choke s.o.
[de+…TR+]
dęhehshǫnyaʼk you will strangle him P

•(h)ǫnyǫʼ several things sitting up on top of something
see: (h)e:ʼ [A+] sitting up on top of s.t.
g̲ahǫ:nyǫʼ things are sitting up on top S

•(h)ǫhsr(a) box
[ga+]
g̲ahǫhsraʼ a box

•(h)ǫhsrod mailbox
[ga+ -(h)ǫhsr(a)$_{N}$- box -od$_{V}$- stand]
g̲ahǫhsrot a mailbox

•(h)ǫhsrǫdǫʼ dresser
[o+ -(h)ǫhsr(a)$_{N}$- box -ǫdǫʼ$_{V}$- several attached objects]
ohǫhsrǫ:dǫʼ a dresser

•(h)ǫw(a) boat
[ga+]
g̲ahǫ:waʼ a boat

•hǫhwaʼs wait for s.o.
see: (hr)ǫhwaʼs [TR+] wait for s.o.
ęgǫhǫhwaʼs you will wait for me P

•(h)ǫwanęda(h)g dock a boat
[at+ -(h)ǫw(a)$_{N}$- boat -(raʼ)nęd(a:ʼg), (yaʼ)nęd(a:ʼg)$_{V}$- stick, cling to s.t.]
ahęnatǫwanę:da:k they (m) docked a boat P

•hǫ(weh), nhǫ:(weh) somewhere
see: Appendix I

•hǫhw(ę, ani) bar a pathway
see: (hr)ǫhw(ę, ani) [de+…] bar a pathway
dęhsrǫhwęˀ you will bar s.t., put up a barrier P

•(h)ǫyo(:) travel by boat
[de+...at+ -(h)ǫw(a)$_{N}$- boat -o(:)$_{V}$- submerge in liquid]
ętgaǫ:tǫ:yo:ˀ they (f/m) will come by boat P

•(hr)e, (hr)ę put, place s.t.
kre:haˀ I am setting it on s.t. H
ęhshręˀ you will set it on s.t. P
hewa:kre:ˀ I put, placed it over there S
itręh place it I

•(hr)e(n) cut s.t.
kre:nahs I cut it all the time H
ękre:ˀ I will cut it P
akre:nęh I have cut it S

•(hr)etgęˀ to be ugly
[A+ (N+)]
ga̲he:tgęˀ it is ugly P
ehsinahe:tgęˀ she has a bad leg P
[A+ stem: -(h)sin(a)$_{N}$- leg -(hr)etgęˀ$_{V}$- be evil, bad, ugly]

•(hr)etgęh to damage, ruin, wreck s.t.
ęhshe:tgęh you will wreck it P

•(hr)etgęhd to damage, ruin, wreck s.t.
[contains: -(hr)etgęˀ$_{V}$- be evil, bad, ugly]
ęhshe:tgęht you will damage, ruin, wreck s.t. P
ga̲hetgęhdǫh it has been ruined, wrecked P

•(hr)etgęhd to go bad
[at+ contains: -(hr)etgęˀ$_{V}$- be evil, bad, ugly]
dawatehtgęht it went bad P
aˀǫtehtgęht someone turned funny, moody, etc. P

•(hr)etgęhdǫni to be moody
[P+…at+ contains: -(hr)etgęˀ$_{V}$- be evil, bad, ugly -ǫni, ǫny$_{V}$- make]
hotehtgędǫ:ni: he is in a funny or odd mood; he is moody S

•(hr)etgęsˀah to be unattractive
[A+ contains: -(hr)etgęˀ$_{V}$- be evil, bad, ugly -ˀs plural -ˀah diminutive]
hahe:tgę:sˀah he is unattractive P

•(hr)cwahd punish
[at+ / TR+]
satrewa̲htaˀ you are being punished right now H
ęhshehe:waht you will punish her P
satrewa̲hdǫh you have been punished S

•(hr)ewahd repent
[s+…adat+]
tsadatrewahtaˀ you are repenting right now; you repent all the time H
sa̲hęnada:tre:waht they (m) repented P

•(hr)ęd lead, be the leader
ęhsrę:t you will be the lead P
ohę:dǫ: ahead; in front; the front S

•(hr)ęˀda: burn s.t.
[(N+)]
kręˀda:s I always burn s.t. H
ęhsręˀda:ˀ you will burn s.t. P
a·hǫ·wa·di·yˀa·dęˀda:ˀ they burned the body, cremated him P
[-yaˀd(a)$_{N}$- body -(hr)ęˀda:$_{V}$- burn s.t.]

•(hr)ędǫˀse:ˀ precede s.o.
[s+ TR+ contains: -(hr)ęd $_{V}$- lead, be the leader]
jǫkihędǫˀse:ˀ she has gone on before us P

•(hr)iˀ break up; be breakable
[de+ …(N+)]
dęgahihs it breaks; it is breakable H
dęgahiˀ it will break P
deyohiˀǫh it is broken S

Legend: H habitual, P punctual, S stative, I imperative, PURP purposive, PURP-H purposive habitual, PURP-PAST purposive past, PURP-P purposive punctual, PURP-I purposive imperative; see §8.6, §8.11 in Appendix J. Alphabetization in stems ignores length (:), and any h's or glottal stops (ˀ) that are not between vowels. See §2.2 of the User Guide for explanation.

•(hr)iʼ break up, etc. (continued)
deyohgwę̱nyahiʼǫh torn clothes S
[de+yo+ stem: -(a)hgwę̱ny(a)$_N$- clothes -(hr)iʼ$_V$- break up]

•(hr)ihd break s.t. up
[de+ …(N+)]
dę̱hsriht you will break s.t. P
degahehdahihdǫh land that is disced, worked S
[de+ -(h)ehd(a)$_N$- land -hrihd$_V$- break up]

•(hr)ihsd bump s.o.
[TR+]
ahehihs I bumped him (for example, with a car) P

•(hr)ihsd come together, gather around
[at+]
ę̱dihswatrihs you all will come closer, gather around P
sgę̱:nǫ:ʼǫh hotrihsdǫ̱hǫ:gyeʼ he is sneaking around slowly P
I:wa:kʼah dǫdahotrihsdǫ̱hǫgyeʼ he's getting nearer and nearer again P

•(hr)owi, (hr)ǫny tell s.o.
[TR+ / at+]
gatro:wihs, gatro:wih I tell all the time H
ę̱dwa:tro:wiʼ we all (incl.) will tell P
aga:tro:wi: I have told S
agatrǫnyahnǫh I am telling right now S
sheho:wi: tell her I

•(hr)owi, (hr)ǫny recount
[s+…TR+ / (a)t+]
ę̱tsa:tro:wiʼ you will recount, retell P

•(hr)ǫhwaʼs wait for s.o.
[TR+]
ę̱gǫhǫhwaʼs you will wait for me P

•(hr)ǫhwę̱ bar a pathway
[de+]
dę̱hsrǫhwę̱ʼ you will bar s.t., put up a barrier P

•(h)sadaę̱ʼ foggy
[de+…at+ -(h)sad(a)$_N$- fog -ę̱$_V$- lie on the ground]
deyotsadaę̱ʼ it is foggy S

•(h)sadę̱ come by horseback
[d+...P+ contains: -(h)seʼ$_V$- ride horseback]
ę̱dyago̱hsa:dę̱ʼ she will come by horseback P

•(h)sadę̱ mount a horse
[P+ contains: -(h)seʼ$_V$- ride horseback]
ę̱wage̱hsa:dę̱ʼ I will mount a horse P

•(h)sadę̱ carry s.o. on one's back
[TR+ contains: -(h)seʼ$_V$- ride horseback]
gohsa:dę̱hs a horse (old word)
ę̱hshehsa:dę̱ʼ you will carry s.o. on your back P

•(h)sadę̱hs horse
[go+ contains: -(h)seʼ$_V$- ride horseback]
gohsa:dę̱hs a horse (old word)

•(h)sadǫ(:) bury s.o., an animal
ę̱gehsadǫ:ʼ I will bury it (an animal) P

•(h)sadǫ(:) bury an object
[at+]
ę̱gatsadǫ:ʼ I will bury s.t. over there P

•(h)sadǫgw, (h)sadǫgo unearth s.t.
[s+...at+ contains: -(h)sadǫ$_V$- bury s.t.]
ę̱tsatsadǫ:goʼ you will unearth it P

•(h)sag investigate, inquire, look for
see: (i)hsag [(N+)] investigate, inquire, look for
ę̱gihsa:k I will seek it, look for it P

•(h)sag look for a mate
see: (i)hsag [de+] look for a mate
dedwade̱hsa:s we are looking for mates H

•(h)sa:, (h)sag(a) mouth
[o+]
ohsa:ʼ a mouth
ga̱hsaga̱hę̱:t a mouth
[ga+ -(h)sag(a)$_N$- mouth -gahę̱d$_V$- drill, hole]

•(h)sagahǫ:ʼ large-mouthed bass
[s+ga+ -(h)sag(a)$_N$- mouth -kahǫ$_V$- adjoin, abutt]
sga̲hsaga̲hǫ:ʼ a large-mouthed bass

•(h)sagahę̱d mouth
[ga+ -(h)sag(a)$_N$- mouth -gahęd$_V$- drill, hole]
ga̲hsaga̲hę:t mouth
gę̱hsaga̲hę:t my mouth
swahsagahę:t your (p) mouths

•(h)saheʼd(a) bean
[o+]
ohsaheʼdaʼ beans

•(h)saheʼdagriʼ coffee, bean soup
[o+ -(h)saheʼd(a)$_N$- bean -griʼ$_V$- juice, liquid]
ohsaheʼda:griʼ bean soup; coffee

•(h)saheʼdase: string bean, yellow bean, green bean
[o+ -(h)saheʼd(a)$_N$- bean -(a)se:$_V$- new]
ohsaheʼda:se: string beans; yellow beans; green beans

•(h)saihsd(a) snake, serpent
[o+]
oshaihsdaʼ a snake; a serpent

•(h)s(d) use
ehstaʼ she uses it; people use it H
ę:yehs she will use s.t. P
go̲hsdǫhǫgyeʼ she is arriving wearing that S
ihsehs use it I

•(h)sd(a:) drop of water, raindrop
[o+]
ohsda:ʼ rain

•(h)sd(a:) scale
see: (ih)sd(a:) scale
ohsda:ʼ, ohsdaiʼ the scale (of a fish)

•(h)sdaʼa:ʼ pine tree
[o+ -(h)sd(a:)$_N$- drop of water -a:ʼ$_V$- hold, include]
osdaʼa:ʼ a pine tree

•(h)sdadenyǫ sprinkle
[o+ -(h)sd(a:)$_N$- drop (of water) -denyǫ$_V$- several existing objects]
odesda:denyǫ: it is sprinkling S

•(h)sdae:ʼ scale
see: (ih)sdae:ʼ scale
osdae:ʼ scales

•(h)sdaga(:) the sound of rain
[o+ -(h)sd(a:)$_N$- drop (of water) -ga:$_V$- make a rattling or grinding noise]
osda:ga: the sound of the rain S

•(h)sdagriʼ rain water
[o+ -(h)sd(a:)$_N$- drop (of water) -griʼ$_V$- juice, liquid]
osda:griʼ rain water

•(h)sdag(wa) dirt, dirty clothes
[ga/o+]
gahsda:gwaʼ, ohsda:gwaʼ dirt; dirty clothes

•(h)sdagwaę(:) be dirty, soiled
[P+ -(h)sdag(wa)$_N$- dirt, dirty -ę$_V$- lie]
aʼohsdagwaę: it got dirty, soiled P
ohsdagwaę: it is soiled, dirty, stained S

•(h)sdaowanęh rain hard
[ga+ -(h)sd(a:)$_N$- drop (of water) -owanęh$_V$- be big]
gahsdaowa:nęh it is raining hard S

•(h)sdaowanahd rain hard
[ga+ -(h)sd(a:)$_N$- drop (of water) -owanahd$_V$- make big]
agasdao:wanaht it rained hard P

•(h)sdaǫdi, (h)sdaǫgy rain
[(y)o+ -(h)sd(a:)$_N$- drop (of water) -ǫdi, -ǫgy$_V$- throw]
ęyohsdaǫdiʼ it is going to rain P
osdaǫ:gyǫ: it is raining S

•(h)sdahsǫ be worn out
[o+ade+ -(h)sdahsǫ$_V$- several used objects]
odehsdahsǫ: it is worn out S

•(h)sdaʼsǫ:ʼǫh vanilla, seasoning, etc.
[de+ye+ -hsd$_N$- tool, utensil -shǫ:ʼǫh several things]
deyehstaʼsǫ:ʼǫh vanilla; seasoning; etc.

Legend: H habitual, P punctual, S stative, I imperative, PURP purposive, PURP-H purposive habitual, PURP-PAST purposive past, PURP-P purposive punctual, PURP-I purposive imperative; see §8.6, §8.11 in Appendix J. Alphabetization in stems ignores length (:), and any h's or glottal stops (ʼ) that are not between vowels. See §2.2 of the User Guide for explanation.

•(h)sdateʼd shine s.t.
[de+... -(h)sd(a:)$_N$- drop (of water) -teʼd$_V$- pound]
dęgehsda:teʼt I am going to shine it P
dęgahsdatęʼdǫh it is shined, waxed, polished S

•(h)sdateh shiny, smooth, silver
[de+yo+ -hsd$_N$- tool, utensil -(a)te$_V$- be bright, clear]
deyohsda:teh it is shiny, smooth (like silver); silver S

•(h)sdenyęʼge: rock slide, avalanche
[contains: -(h)sd(ęha)$_N$- stone -(aʼs)ęʼ$_V$- fall, reduce -ge: big]
agahstenyęʼge: rock slide, falling rocks, avalanche

•(h)sdęhd scale fish
see: (ih)sdęhd scale fish
ęsehsdęht you will take the scales off (the fish) P

•(h)sdędoʼ foundation
[de+ga+ -(h)sd(ęha)$_N$- stone -dǫʼ$_V$- several standing objects]
degahstę:doʼ a foundation

•(h)sdęhes mountain
[de+ga+ -(h)sd(ęha)-$_N$ stone -es$_V$- long]
degahsdęhe:s a high mountain

•(h)sdęhod monument
[t+ga+ -(h)sd(ęha)-$_N$ stone -od$_V$- stand]
tgahsdęho:t a monument

•(h)sdęhod mountain, etc.
[ga+ -(h)sd(ęha)-$_N$ stone -od$_V$- stand]
gahsdęho:t a mountain
gahsdęho:dǫʼ mountains; a pile of boulders

•(h)sdęhyai old person
[P+]
gohsdęhyai she is an older woman S

•(h)sdęhowęʼ volcano
[a+d+wa+ade+ -(h)sd(ęha)$_N$- stone -owę(:)$_V$- split in two]
adwadesdęho:węʼ a volcano

•(h)sdi:s trade cloth
[o+ -hsd$_N$- tool, utensil -is$_V$- long]
ohsdi:s trade cloth

•(h)sdihsd care
[ad+(N+/(r)ih(wa)+)]
hadrihwahsdi:hstaʼ he takes care of the event all the time; he pays attention to what is going on H
ęhadri̱hwahsdihs he will take care of the event P

•(h)sdihsra:s moth
see: (ih)sdihsra:s moth
gadihsdihsra:s moth

•(h)sdohag squeeze
see: ohag [de+ad/N/(h)sd+] squeeze
dęhsdǫ̱ha:k you will squeeze P

•(h)sdow(a) headdress
[ga+]
gahsdo:waʼ a headdress

•(h)sdowahehaʼ pow wow
[A+ -(h)sdow(a)$_N$- feather -(hr)e, (hr)ę$_V$- put, place]
hadihsdowahehaʼ a pow wow (lit.: they (m) put on their headdresses and perform)

•(h)seʼ ride horseback
[P+]
hohseʼ he is riding a horse S

•(h)sęh(ę) frost
[o+]
ohsęhęʼ frost

•(h)sęhęyęhtaʼ goldenrod
[ga+ -(h)sęh(ę)$_N$- frost -(y)ęhd$_V$- hit, knock down, strike]
ga̱hsęhęyęhtaʼ goldenrod

•(h)sęn(a) name
[ga+]
ga̱hsę:naʼ a name

•(h)sęnaʼse:ʼ surname, family name
[de+A+ -(h)sęn(a)$_N$- name -(a)ʼse:ʼ$_V$- be double]
degahsęnaʼse:ʼ a surname

•(h)sęna'se:' surname (continued)
dehswahsęna'se:' your (p) surname, family name (lit.: your (p) double name, joiner name)
dehahsęna'se:' his surname

•(h)sęniyohsd compliment, flatter
[TR+ -(h)sęn(a)$_N$- name -iyohsd$_V$- make nice]
gǫwahsęniyǫhsta' it is complimentary, flattering H

•(h)sęnowanhę' become famous
[A+ -(h)sęn(a)$_N$- name -owanhę$_V$- become big]
ahsehsęnowanhe' you became famous P

•(h)sęnowanęh be important, famous
[A+ -(h)sęn(a)$_N$- name -owanęh$_V$- be big]
hahsęnowa:nęh he is an important person; he is famous, prominent S

•(h)sęnǫni store, put away
[-(h)sęn(a)$_N$- name -ǫni,ǫny$_V$- make]
sęhsę:nǫ:nih you are storing it right now H
asehsęnǫ:ni' you did store it P
gahsę:nǫ:ni: stored items S
sęhsę:no:nih store it; put it away I

•(h)sęnǫni preserve, can s.t.
[ad+N+]
sadahyahsęnǫnih you preserve fruit I
[-(a)hy(a)$_N$- fruit, berry -(h)sęnǫni$_V$- store, put away]

•(h)sętrǫni fatten
[TR+ -(h)sętr(a)$_N$- fat -ǫni, ǫny$_V$- make]
ęhsahsętrǫ:ni' it will make you fat P

•(h)sgeh(a) louse
[o+]
ohsgeha' a louse

•(h)sgehai:'ah muslin
[o+ -(h)sgeh(a)$_N$- louse -i:'$_V$- stuck onto s.t. -'ah diminutive]
osgehai:'ah muslin

•(h)sgę'dr(a) rust
[o+]
ohsgę'dra' rust

•(h)sgę'draga: rattling noise
[de+yo+ -(h)sgę'dr(a)$_N$- rust -ga:$_V$- make a rattling or grinding noise]
deyohsg'ędra:ga: a tinny, metallic rattling noise

•(h)sgę'drod mouldy, rusty
[-(h)sgę'dr(a)$_N$- rust -od$_V$- be attached]
awahsg'ędro:dę:' it got mouldy; it got rusty P

•(h)sgęna:' have a stroke
[P+ -(h)sgęn(a)$_N$- stroke -a:'$_V$- hold, contain, include]
ahohsgęna:' he had a stroke P

•(h)sgęnh fight over s.t.
[de+...(r)ihwa/N+]
saǫhwęjahsgęnhęh you are fighting over the land right now S
[-ǫhwęj(a)$_N$- earth, land -genh$_V$- argue for, advocate]

•(h)sgogye' float
[A+ -(h)sg$_N$- -ogye$_V$- float]
gahsgo:gye' it (s.t. alive) is floating PURP

•(h)sgoh(a) branch
[o+]
ohsgoha' a branch

•(h)sg(wa:) stone, rock, boulder, bullet
[ga+]
gahsgwa:' a stone; a rock; a boulder; a bullet

•(h)sg(wa:) testicles
[A+ contains: -(h)sg(wa:)$_N$- stone, bullet, rock -'geh on, at]
hahsgwa'geh his testicles

•(h)sgwadahgw neuter, geld
[TR+ -(h)sg(wa:)$_N$- stone, bullet, rock -dahgw$_V$- remove]
ęhǫwa'sgwa:dahgo' they will geld, neuter, fix him (lit.: they will remove his testicles) P

Legend: H habitual, P punctual, S stative, I imperative, PURP purposive, PURP-H purposive habitual, PURP-PAST purposive past, PURP-P purposive punctual, PURP-I purposive imperative; see §8.6, §8.11 in Appendix J. Alphabetization in stems ignores length (:), and any h's or glottal stops (') that are not between vowels. See §2.2 of the User Guide for explanation.

•(h)sgwadahgw neuter, geld (continued)
gahsgwa:da̱hgwęh a neutered animal; a gelding S

•(h)sgwadǫʼ rock formation
[de+ga+ -(h)sg(wa:)$_N$- stone, bullet, rock -dǫʼ$_V$- several standing objects]
degahsgwa**:dǫʼ** rocks piled in an arrangement

•(h)sgwaę(ʼda) coltsfoot
[(o+)]
ohsgwaęʼdaʼ, sgwaęʼdaʼ coltsfoot (a plant)

•(h)sgwaohes stonegather sucker
[gadi+ -(h)sg(wa:)$_N$- stone, bullet, rock -oheg$_V$- gather]
gadiʼsgwao:he:s a stonegather sucker (a fish)

•(h)sgwaowanęʼs be well-endowed
[de+A+ -(h)sg(wa:)$_N$- stone, bullet, rock -owanęʼs$_V$- several big objects]
dehahsgwaowanęʼs he has big rocks; he is well-endowed S

•(h)sgwaǫd cliff, outcropping
[he+yo+ -(h)sg(wa:)$_N$- stone, bullet, rock -ǫd$_V$- attached]
heyoʼsgwaǫ:t a rock formation that protrudes; a cliff

•(h)sgwaǫd headstone
[ga+ -(h)sg(wa:)$_N$- stone, bullet, rock -od$_V$- stand]
gahsgwao:t a headstone

•(h)sgwaǫdi, (h)sgwaǫgy gravel
[ga+ -(h)sg(wa:)$_N$- stone, bullet, rock -ǫdi, -ǫgy$_V$- throw]
ga̱hswaǫgyǫ: gravel has been put down
nigahsgwaǫgyǫ: gravel somewhere

•(h)sgweg shut s.o. up
[TR+ -(h)s(a)$_N$- mouth -gweg$_V$- close]
ęhshe:sgwe:k you will shut her up P

•(h)sgwiʼdr(a) wrinkle
[o+]
ohsgwiʼdraʼ wrinkles

•(h)sgwiʼdrahe:ʼ be wrinkly
[s+ga+N+ -(h)sgwiʼdr(a)$_N$- wrinkle -(h)e:ʼ$_V$- sitting up on top of s.t ts:ǫ just]
sgahsgwʼidra̱he:ʼ tsǫ: you are pruny, wrinkly S

•(h)sgyęʼd(a:) bone
[o+]
ohsgyęʼda:ʼ bone; bare bones

•(h)sgyęʼdiyaʼg fracture
[de+…ade+ -(h)sgyęʼd(a:)$_N$- bone -(i)yaʼg$_V$- cut, break, cross]
deyodehsgyęʼdiyaʼgǫh it (bone) is fractured S

•(h)sgyęnaʼgyagǫh pale
[de+P+ -(h)sgyęnaʼd(a)$_N$- -(i)yaʼg$_V$- cut, break, cross]
dehohsgyęnaʼgyʼagǫh he is pale S

•(h)sgyęʼwatę, (h)sgyǫʼwatę thin
[P+ contains: -(h)sgyǫʼw(a), (h)sgyęʼw(a)$_N$- bone -tę(:)$_V$- dry]
hohsgyęʼwatę:, hohsgyǫʼwatę: he is skinny S

•(h)sgyǫʼ(wa) blue beech
[o+ contains: -(h)sgyǫʼw(a), (h)sgyęʼw(a)$_N$- bone]
ohsgyǫʼwaʼ blue beech (a tree)

•(h)sgyǫʼwataʼd diet, lose weight
[ade+ -(h)sgyǫʼw(a), (h)sgyęʼw(a)$_N$- bone -taʼd$_V$- dry out]
ǫdehsgyǫwataʼtaʼ s.o. loses weight, diets H
agaǫ:dehsgyǫwa:taʼt they (f/m) dieted P

•(h)sgyǫʼwatę, (h)sgyęʼwatę be thin, skinny
[P+ -(h)sgyǫʼw(a), (h)sgyęʼw(a)$_N$- bone -tę(:)$_V$- be dry]
hohsgyęʼwatę:, hohsgyǫʼwatę: he is skinny S

•(h)sh(a) string
[occurs in:]
ohshai:s a long string; a rope
[o+ -sh(a)$_N$- string -is$_V$- be long]

•(h)shadenyoh tendons
[o+ -sh(a)$_N$- string -denyǫʼ$_V$- several existing objects]
ohsha:de:nyoh tendons

•(h)shaǫd be tied up
[A+ -sh(a)$_N$- string -ǫd$_V$- attached]
ge̱hshaǫ:t I am tied up S

•(h)sheʼ(a) dough
[o+]
ohsheʼaʼ dough

•(h)shoʼgwaǫd rattle snake
[o+ -(h)shoʼg(wa)$_N$- -ǫd$_V$- attached]
ohshoʼgwaǫ:t a rattle snake

•(h)siha:ʼ stand in a bunch or group, congregate
[A+]
gadihsi̱ha:ʼ they (z) are congregated S

•(h)siha:ʼ stand in a bunch or group, congregate
[A/P+N+]
ojihsǫdahsiha:ʼ stars showing S
[-jihsǫd(a)$_N$- star, -(h)siha:ʼ$_V$- stand in a bunch or group, congregate]

•(h)sin(a) leg
ohsi:naʼ leg
se̱hsinʼageh on your leg

•(h)sinhahstaʼ garters
[ǫ+at+ -(h)sin(a)$_N$- leg -nhahsd$_V$- encircle]
ǫtsinhahstaʼ garters; leg bands

•hsinodahd(ę,ani) bar s.o.'s way
[de+TR+ -(h)sin(a)$_N$- leg -odahd(ę, ani)$_V$- trip]
ętsheya̱hsinodahdęʼ you will trip s.o., bar s.o.'s way with your leg P

•(h)sinǫd kettle
[de+ga+ -(h)sin(a)$_N$- leg -ǫd$_V$- attached]
degahsi:nǫ:t kettle (lit.: it has legs attached)

•(h)sis shoot
hǫwahsi:sahs he is always getting shot by s.o. H
ahohsi:s he was shot P
hohsi:sęh he has been shot S

•(h)siy(a) thread, string, cord, line
[o+]
ohsi:yaʼ a thread; a string; a cord
ohsi:yǫ:t an attached cord; a string; an umbilical cord
[-(h)siy(a)$_N$- line, string -od$_V$- attached]

•(h)siyaniyǫd fringe
[ga+ -(h)siy(a)$_N$- line, string -niyǫd$_V$- hang]
ga̱hsiyani:yǫ:t a fringe

•(h)siyaǫnyahnǫ:ʼ be a fluid dancer
[-(h)siy(a)$_N$- line, string -ǫnyahnǫ$_V$- go along making several things]
ahahsiyaǫ:nyahnǫ:ʼ he is a fluid dancer P

•(h)siyogw, (h)siyogo fray
[(de+)...ade+ -(h)siy(a)$_N$- line, string -ogw$_V$- scatter]
awade̱hsiyo:goʼ it frayed P
deyoda̱hsiyo:gwęh it is frayed S

•(h)siyǫni: be fringed
[-(h)siy(a)$_N$- line, string -ǫni, ǫny$_V$- make]
ga̱hsi:yǫ:ni: it is fringed S

•(h)siyǫd thread, string, cord, line, umbilical cord
[o+ -(h)siy(a)$_N$- line, string -ǫd$_V$- attached]
ohsi:yǫ:t an attached cord; a string; an umbilical cord

•(h)sna(ʼda) muscle, hamstring, calf, outer thigh
[o+]
ohsnaʼdaʼ hamstrings; calves (of the legs); outer thighs
se̱hsnaʼdʼageh on your calf

•(h)snaʼda:s Muscular Dystrophy
[ga+ -(h)sna(ʼda)$_N$- muscle, hamstring, calf -g$_V$- eat]
ga̱hsnaʼda:s Muscular Dystrophy

•(h)snagri have muscle cramps
[P+ -(h)sna(ʼda)$_N$- muscle, hamstring, calf -gri$_V$- wrinkle]
ǫgehsnagri꞉k I had muscle cramps; I got a cramp P

•(h)snagriksǫ(꞉) cramp
[P+ -(h)sna(ʼda)$_N$- muscle, hamstring, calf -gri$_V$- wrinkle -sǫʼ plural]
ǫgehsnagrihksǫ꞉ʼ I got cramps P

•(h)snowad hurry up
[de+...ade+ contains: -(h)snow$_V$- fast]
desade̲hsno꞉wa꞉t hurry up I

•(h)snoweʼ be fast
[o+]
ohsno꞉weʼ it is fast, quick S

•(h)snoweʼ fast
[A/P+N+]
ohnyasnoweʼ a fast beat S
[o+ stem: -(h)ny(a)$_N$- stick -(h)snoweʼ$_V$- fast]

•(h)snye care for, look after
[de+TR+ occurs in:]
de̲haheyǫʼda̲hsnyehaʼ he is a funeral director H
[de+… -(he)yǫ(ʼda)$_N$- corpse, cadaver -(h)snye$_V$- care for, look after]
de̲hǫwadihsnyeʼ they care for them S

•(h)snye(h,ʼ) clean s.t. up
[de+…at+N+ occurs in:]
degatnǫhsahsnyeh I am cleaning up the house H
[de+…at+ stem: -nǫhs(a)$_N$- house -(h)snye(h,ʼ)$_V$- clean s.t. up]
dęgatnǫ̲hsahsnyeʼ I will clean up the house P
degahsnyeʼǫ꞉ʼ it cleans up S

•(h)snye(h,ʼ) groom onself
[de+TR+/adad+ contains: -(h)snye$_V$- care for, look after]
desadadehsnyeh tidy up; groom yourself I

•(h)sod grandparent
hehso꞉t my grandfather S
ge̲hso꞉t my grandmother S

•(h)sohd(a) hand, paw
ohsohdaʼ a hand; a paw
se̲hsohdʼageh on your hand

•(h)soda꞉ʼ soldier
[A+ -hs(a)$_N$- -oda(꞉,h)$_V$- drape]
hadihso꞉da꞉ they (m) are military (the word refers to putting the gun over their shoulders)
hahso꞉da꞉ʼ a soldier (lit.: he drapes it)

•(h)sohdǫd hand (of a clock)
[ga+ -(h)sohd(a)$_N$- hand, finger, paw -ǫd$_V$- attached]
ga̲hsohdǫ꞉t hands on a clock

•(h)soʼg limp
[P+]
gǫhsoʼkaʼ she is limping H

•(h)sohgae꞉ smacking sound
[a+g+yo+ -(h)s(a꞉)$_N$- mouth -ga꞉, gae$_V$- make a rattling or grinding noise]
agyohsagae꞉ the sound of smacking lips

•(h)sohgǫd pitcher
[ga+ -(h)sohg(wa)$_N$- lip -ǫd$_V$- attached]
ga̲hsohgǫ꞉t a pitcher

•(h)sohg(wa) lip
ohsohgwaʼ lips
se̲hsǫhgwʼageh on your lip
ge̲hsohgwʼageh on my lip

•(h)sogwa꞉ʼ fork
[ga+ -(h)sohg(wa)$_N$- lip -a꞉ʼ$_V$- contain]
ga̲hsogwa꞉ʼ a fork

•(h)sohgwahd(a) big-headed sucker
[at+ -(h)sohg(wa)$_N$- lip -(a)hd$_V$- resemble]
atsokwa̲hdaʼ (**atsogwa̲hdaʼ**) a big-headed sucker

•(h)sohgwahs west
[de+wa+at+ -(ę)hs(a)$_N$- foot -ogw$_V$- scatter]
dewatsohgwahs the west

•(h)sotwahs sunset
[haʼde+w+at+ -(ę)hs(a)$_{N}$- foot -otw$_{V}$- burn as fuel]
haʼdewatso:twahs towards the sunset; a direction
•(h)sotwahs fleas
[de+wa+at+ -(ę)hs(a)$_{N}$- foot -(h)sotw$_{V}$- jump, hop]
dewatsotwahs fleas (lit.: it jumps, hops)
•(h)sǫhg(a:) upper lip
se̲hsǫhga:ʼgeh on your upper lip
•(h)sʼǫh be ready
see: (i)hsʼǫh [P+ade+] ready
sadehsʼǫh? Are you ready? (used by Cayuga speakers, but may be an Onondaga phrase) S
•(h)sǫwahd(a) nail, wire, needle
[ga+]
ga̲hsǫwa̲hdaʼ nails; wire; a needle
•(h)sre(:) follow, chase
see: (i)hsre(:) [TR+] follow, chase
ahǫwadihsre:ʼ they chased him, followed him PURP-P
•(h)srędǫni glare, grouchy
[ade+ contains: -(a)hsrǫhę(ʼda)$_{N}$- anger, temper -ǫni, ǫny$_{V}$- make]
agade̲hsręʼdǫ:ni: I am grouchy, glaring S
sadehsręʼdǫ:ni: glare; make yourself look mad I
•(h)srǫhę: cross, angry
[A+]
ehsrohę: she is habitually cross, cantankerous S
•(h)srǫni fix, repair
[(N+) contains: -hsr$_{N}$- noun -(h)srǫni$_{V}$- fix, repair]
sasehsrǫ:nih deyodewane:gaǫ: fix the flat tire I
•(h)srǫnihs repairman
[s+A+ -(h)srǫni$_{V}$- fix, repair]
shahsrǫ:nihs repairman
•(h)srǫnihsʼǫh ready
[P+ade+ contains: -(h)srǫni$_{V}$- fix, repair]
agade̲hsrǫni̲hsʼǫh I am ready S
•(h)srǫnyaʼd made from
[contains: -(h)srǫni, (h)srǫny$_{V}$- fix, repair]
ga̲hsrǫnyadǫh it is made from s.t. S
•(h)srǫnyahnǫ(:) make several things
[contains: -(h)srǫni, (h)srǫny$_{V}$- fix, repair -ahnǫʼ go and do several things]
aknihsrǫnyahnǫh we two (incl.) are making several things H
ęyagwadehsrǫnyahnǫ:ʼ we all (excl.) will prepare things P
•(h)staʼ tool, utensil
[e+ contains -hsd$_{N}$- tool, utensil]
ehstaʼshǫ:ʼǫh tools; utensils; what one uses)
•(h)sdoda: handcuff s.o.
[de+TR+ -hsd$_{N}$- tool, utensil -oda(:,h)$_{V}$- drape]
atǫwadihstoda:ʼ they handcuffed him, them (m) P
•(h)sdoʼdr(a), (h)stoʼdr(a) feather
[o+]
ohsdoʼdrʼageh on its feathers
•(h)stoʼdręhd pluck
[-(h)stoʼdr(a)$_{N}$- feather -(y)ęhd$_{V}$- hit, knock down, strike]
ęsehstoʼdręht you will pluck feathers P
sehstoʼdręht pluck it I
•(h)stoʼdręhd moult
[ade+ -(h)stoʼdr(a)$_{N}$- feather -(y)ęhd$_{V}$- hit, knock down, strike]
awadehstoʼdręht it moulted P
•(h)stǫdr(a) straw, hay
[o+]
ohstǫ:draʼ straw; hay
•(h)stǫdriyaʼs mower
[ga+ -(h)stǫdr(a)$_{N}$- straw, hay -(i)yaʼg$_{V}$- cut, break]
ga̲hstǫ:dri:yaʼs a hay mower

Legend: H habitual, P punctual, S stative, I imperative, PURP purposive, PURP-H purposive habitual, PURP-PAST purposive past, PURP-P purposive punctual, PURP-I purposive imperative; see §8.6, §8.11 in Appendix J. Alphabetization in stems ignores length (:), and any h's or glottal stops (ʼ) that are not between vowels. See §2.2 of the User Guide for explanation.

•(h)stǫdroha:s bailer
[de+ga+ -(h)stǫdr(a)$_N$- straw, hay -ohag$_V$- squeeze]
degastǫdroha:s a hay bailer

•(h)stǫwisd hurt
[P+ (ade+)]
sadehstǫwi:staʼ you hurt yourself all the time H
ęjisahstǫ:wi:s you will rehurt yourself P

•(h)swahęh hate, dislike
go̱hswahęhs I hate you H
ęhsehswa̱hęh you will hate, dislike P

•(h)swahęhde:ʼ hatred
[o+ contains: -(h)swahęhd$_V$- cause to hate, dislike]
ohswahęhde:ʼ hatred

•(h)swahęʼdǫ: hatred
[o+ contains: -(h)swahęʼd$_V$- cause to hate]
ohswahęʼdǫ: hatred

•(h)swaʼn(a), (h)sweʼn(a) upper back
ohsweʼnaʼ the upper back
se̱hsweʼnʼageh on your upper back
degahswʼane:t a pie
[de+ga+ -(h)swaʼn(a), (h)sweʼn(a)$_N$- reinforced, backed -d$_V$- stand]

•(h)swaʼned pie
[de+ga+ -(h)swaʼn(a), (h)sweʼn(a)$_N$- reinforced, backed -d$_V$- stand]
degahswaʼne:t pie

•(h)swaʼned reinforce, back
[ga+ -(h)swaʼn(a), (h)sweʼn(a)$_N$- upper back -d$_V$- stand]
ga̱hswaʼne:t reinforcement; backing

•(h)swaʼned support s.o., s.t., agree with s.o., back s.o.
[TR+ -(h)swaʼn(a), (h)sweʼn(a)$_N$- upper back -d$_V$- stand]
hadihswʼane:taʼ they (m) are advocates, backers, supporters H
ęhsehswʼane:dęʼ you will back up s.t. (that is, reinforce it) P
shehswaʼne:t you are supporting, backing them S

•(h)sweʼn(a), (h)swaʼn(a) upper back
ohsweʼnaʼ upper back
se̱hsweʼnʼageh on your upper back

•(h)swęʼd(a) coal, ember
[o+]
ohswędaʼ coal; a ember

•(h)swęʼdaę:ʼ black
[-(h)swęʼd(a)$_N$- coal, ember -ʼę:ʼ$_V$- be coloured]
swęʼdʼaę:ʼ black

•(h)sy(a:) herd
[present in:]
gahsyadagyeʼ a passing herd
[ga+ -(h)sy(a)$_N$- herd -dagyeʼ$_V$- be ongoing]
ga̱hsyao:t a standing herd
[ga+ -(h)sy(a)$_N$- herd -od$_V$- stand]

•(h)ta(:,ę) talk, speak
gęhta:haʼ I talk H
agehtaę:ʼ, agehta:ʼk I did talk P
gohta:ʼ she is speaking S

•(h)tagw, (h)tago discuss
[de+ contains: -(h)ta:$_V$- talk, speak -gw- undo]
dędwahta:goʼ we all (incl.) will discuss P

•(h)tahahsd talk to s.o.
[TR+ contains: -(h)ta:$_V$- talk, speak]
ęhshetahahs you will talk to her P

•(h)wahd(a) maple
[o+]
ohwahdaʼ a maple tree

•(h)wadased encircle
[de+...at+ -(h)wad(a)$_N$- year -(a)hsehd$_V$- whirl]
dęwatwadahsedahk it will encircle it; one year will go around P

•(h)waʼe tap
[-(h)w(a)$_N$- -(ʼ)e$_V$- hit]
hohwaʼe: he is tapping S

•(h)wajiy(a) family
[ga+]
gahwa:ji:ya' a family
•(h)wajiyade' family line, lineage
[A+ -(h)wajiy(a)$_N$- family -de'$_V$- exist]
gaehwajiyade' their (f/m) family line
•(h)wajiyǫnih be barren
[(tę') not de'+A+ -(h)wajiy(a)$_N$- family -ǫni, ǫny$_V$- make]
tę' deyǫtwaji:yǫ:nih she is barren H
•(h)węhd(a:) ear of corn
[o+]
ohwęhda: corn ears
•(h)we'nǫni wrap s.t.
[-(h)we'n(a)$_N$- round, circle -ǫni, ǫny$_V$- make]
sw'enǫ:nih wrap I
•(h)we'nǫni be round
[de+yo+at+ -(h)we'n(a)$_N$- round, circle -ǫni, ǫny$_V$- make]
deyotwe'no:ni: it is round S
•(h)we'nǫnihsd make s.t. round
[de+...at+ -(h)we'n(a)$_N$- round, circle -ǫni, ǫny$_V$- make]
desatw'enǫ:nihs make it round I
•(h)wędahd clear out
[de+... -(h)węd(a)$_N$- hole, opening -(a)hd$_V$- be like, resemble]
dęhsehwędaht you will make a clearing P
•(h)węde' gap, opening
[de+ya(ǫ)+ -(h)węd(a)$_N$- hole, opening -de'$_V$- exist]
deyaǫhwę:de' a gap; an opening
•hwę:dǫh ever, when
cf: Appendix I
•hwędǫgwa' sometime
cf: Appendix I
•(h)wę'g(a:) wood chip, splint
[o+]
ohwę'ga:' a splint; a wood chip
•(hwę'ga)'oh notch s.t.
[A+hwę'ga/N+]
ga̱hwę'ga̱'o:'o: it is notched S
•(h)węj(a) earth, land
[o+ -(h)węj(a)$_N$- land, earth -'geh at, on]
ohwęj'ageh on the earth, land
•(h)węjagahęd cave
[o+ -ǫhwęj(a)$_N$- earth, land -gahęd$_V$- drill, hole]
ohwęjagahę:t a cave
•(h)węjohǫh be a necessity
[de+yo+at+ contains: -ǫhwęjoni, ǫhwęjoh$_V$- want, need]
deyotwęjohǫh a necessity
•(h)węjohsd become a necessity
[de+yo+at+ contains: -ǫhwęjoni, ǫhwęjoh$_V$- want, need]
adwatwęjohs it became a necessity
•(h)wę'sd(a) foam
[ga+ -(h)wę'sd(a)$_N$- foam -o'$_V$- be submerged]
ga̱hwę'sdo' foam
•(h)wę'sdod head of foam
[o+ -(h)wę'sd(a)$_N$- foam -od$_V$- attached]
ohwę'sdo:t a head of foam (on a beer)
•(h)wę'sdǫni whip
[-(h)wę'sd(a)$_N$- foam -ǫni, ǫny$_V$- make]
ęhswę'sdo:ni' you will whip (for example, meringue) P
•(h)wę'sdota' beer
[ga+ -(h)wę'sd(a)$_N$- foam -od$_V$- stand]
ga̱hwę'sdota' beer (lit.: it has a head on it)
•(h)wihsd(a), (hr)ihsd(a) tin, metal, money
[ga+]
gai:sda' tin; metal
hęnatwi̱hsda:nǫh they (m) guard the money
[at+ -(h)wihsd(a), (h)rihsd(a)$_N$- metal, money -nǫ(:)$_V$- guard]
•(h)wihsd'aehs clock
[ga+ -(h)wihsd(a), (h)rihsd(a)$_N$- metal, money -(')e$_V$- hit]
ga̱hwihsd'a̱ehs a clock

Legend: H habitual, P punctual, S stative, I imperative, PURP purposive, PURP-H purposive habitual, PURP-PAST purposive past, PURP-P purposive punctual, PURP-I purposive imperative; see §8.6, §8.11 in Appendix J. Alphabetization in stems ignores length (:), and any h's or glottal stops (') that are not between vowels. See §2.2 of the User Guide for explanation.

•(h)wihsdanǫ:ʼ gold, expensive item
[ga+ -(h)wihsd(a), (hr)ihsd(a)$_N$- metal, money -nǫ:ʼ$_V$- be costly, expensive]
ga̱hwihsdanǫ:ʼ gold; anything expensive

•(h)wihsdaę(:) reserve, economize
[at+ -(h)wihsd(a), (hr)ihsd(a)$_N$- metal, money -ę$_V$- lie]
ęhsatwi̱hsdaęʼ you will economize P
satwihsdaęʼ you will reserve (money) S

•(h)wihsdahihd make change
[de+... -(h)wihsd(a), (hr)ihsd(a)$_N$- metal, money -(hr)ihd$_V$- cause to break up]
dęhswihsda̱hiht you will make change P

•(h)wihsdaniʼǫhsd economize
[at+ -(h)wihsd(a), (hr)ihsd(a)$_N$- metal, money -niʼǫhsd$_V$- be stingy, greedy, cheap with s.t.]
satwihsdaniʼǫhs you economize H
ęhsatwihsdaniʼǫhs you will economize P

•(h)wihsdęda:ʼ waste money
[at+ -(h)wihsd(a), (hr)ihsd(a)$_N$- metal, money -(hr)ęʼda(:,h) $_V$- burn]
satwihsdʼęda:s you burn your money H
agatwi̱hsdęʼda:ʼ I wasted my money P

•(h)wihsdǫni: profit
[w+at+ -(h)wihsd(a), (hr)ihsd(a)$_N$- metal, money -ǫni, ǫny$_V$- make]
watwihsdǫ:ni: profit

•(h)wihsǫd milk snake
[(o+) -(h)wihs(a)- -ǫd$_V$- attached]
(o)hwihsǫ:t a milk snake

•(h)ya:ʼ refers to a period of time
see: Appendix I

•(h)yadǫ(:) write
ehyado̱haʼ she is a secretary, stenographer, court recorder, transcriber H
ehya:dǫh she writes H
ękya:dǫ:ʼ I will write P

•(h)yadǫ(:) have a reading
[ak+ contains: -(h)yadǫ(:)$_V$- write]
ęgakyadǫ:ʼ I will have a reading; I will have my fortune told P

•(h)yadǫhaʼ be a secretary, stenographer, transcriber, etc.
[e+ contains: -(h)yadǫ(:)$_V$- write]
ehyado̱haʼ she is a secretary, stenographer, court recorder, transcriber

•(h)yadǫhkw(a) pencil, pen
[e+ contains: -(h)yadǫ(:)$_V$- write -hkwaʼ instrument]
ehyado̱hkwaʼ pencil, pen
ehyado̱hkwaʼgeh on s.o.'s pencil

•(h)yadǫhsr(a) paper
[ga+ contains: -(h)yadǫ(:)$_V$- write]
ga̱hyado̱hsraʼ paper

•(h)yadǫhsraędiʼ be smart, educated
[A+ -(h)yadǫhsr(a)$_N$- paper -(y)ędei, (y)ędí$_V$- know]
syado̱hsraędiʼ you are smart (educated) H

•(h)yagwaǫd blighted fruit
[o+ -(a)hy(a)$_N$- fruit -g(wa)$_N$- bump -ǫd$_V$- attached]
ohya:gwaǫt fruit with bumps, blight

•(h)yohs(a) elbow
swahyohsʼageh on your (p) elbows

•(h)yohsgwi(n) crawl
[de+…ak+ contains: -(h)yohs(a)$_N$- elbow -in(e)$_V$- go]
desakyo̱hsgwi:neʼ you are crawling H
agyǫkyo̱hsgwi:ʼ she crawled (that is, she learned how to crawl) P
desakyo̱hsgwi: crawl I

•(h)yoʼtiyehd, (h)yuʼtiyehd be sharp
[o+ contains: -(h)y(a)$_N$- blade -oʼtiy$_V$- sharp]
ohyuʼti:yeht, ohyoʼti:yeht it is sharp S

I

•i:ʼ me, I
see: Appendix I
•i:ʼ be stuck onto s.t.
[A/P+N+ present in:]
ohehdai:ʼ earth is stuck to it S
[o+ stem: -(h)ehd(a)$_N$- land, dirt, earth, ground -i:ʼ$_V$- stuck onto s.t.]
•i, ę say
[A+]
ęhsniʼ you two will say P
ahę:niʼ they (m) said P
ęhsiʼ you will say P
ahsiʼ you said P
ęhęʼ he will say P
edwęʼ we all (incl.) said P
aʼa:gęʼ she did say P
ihsnę: you two have said S
i:sę: you have said it S
a:gę: (that's what) I did say S
•i:, ę:, e: think, hope, want
[A+]
i:wi: I want H
i:yę: she wants H
ihse: you want H
i:he: he wants H
ihsne: you two want H
agwe: we all (excl.) want H
ahi:ʼ I thought, I intended P
ehswe:ʼ you all thought P
ahe:ʼ he thought P
ehsne:ʼ you two thought P
ehswe:ʼ you all thought P
ahę:ne:ʼ they (m) thought; they left together P
ędwe:he:k we all (incl.) will in thought P
hawe:ʼǫ: he has willed S
se:ʼǫ:ʼ you wanted, believed S
•i:ʼ hya:ʼ me first
see: Appendix I
•í be right, correct
see: yei, (y)í [t+ga+] be right, correct
tga:yei:, tgayi: it is right, correct S
•í be bad, false, wrong
see: yei, (y)í [(tęʼ) deʼ+ not d+A+] be bad, false, wrong
tęʼ detga:yeiʼ, tęʼ detga:yi:ʼ it is bad, false, wrong S
•í be enough
see: yei, (y)í [toh that haʼde+] be enough
toh haʼdegayei:ʼ you get enough S
•ih undercooked
see: (w)ih [de+yo+] undercooked
deyo:wi:h it is undercooked S
•(i)ʼaʼg shoot
hadiyʼa:s they (m) are shooting H
•(i)daʼ sleep
[P+]
odidaʼs they (z) sleep, hibernate all the time H
ęwa:gi:daʼ I will sleep P
agidaʼǫh I was asleep, I am sleeping S
•(i)daʼ common reed
[tsaʼ+ga+ -(i)daʼ$_V$- sleep]
tsaʼgę:daʼ the common reed
•(i)ʼd(a:) clay, mortar
[o+]
oʼda:ʼ clay; mud; mortar
•(iʼ)d(a) feces, shit, excrement
[o+]
oʼdaʼ feces; shit; excrement
•(i)ʼdahswahę(hdrǫ) scold s.o.
[TR+]
sheʼdahswahęhs you scold people all the time H
ahadiʼdahswahęhdrǫ:ʼ they (m) scolded, reprimanded P
•(i)daʼdr(e) go to bed
[a+P+ contains: -(i)daʼ$_V$- sleep]
ehsędʼadreʼ you are going to bed PURP
sędaʼdrah go to bed; go to sleep I

Legend: H habitual, P punctual, S stative, I imperative, PURP purposive, PURP-H purposive habitual, PURP-PAST purposive past, PURP-P purposive punctual, PURP-I purposive imperative; see §8.6, §8.11 in Appendix J. Alphabetization in stems ignores length (:), and any h's or glottal stops (ʼ) that are not between vowels. See §2.2 of the User Guide for explanation.

•(i)dage:ʼ be prostrate
sida:ge:ʼ you are lying down, prostrate S
•(i)ʼdage(w) wipe one's behind
[ęn+ -(i)ʼd(a)$_N$- feces, privates -(r)age(:,w)$_V$- wipe]
ęgęnida:ge:ʼ I will wipe myself clean of fecal matter P
•(iʼ)dagęd undergarment, soil, feces
[de+yo+ -(i)ʼd(a)$_N$- feces -(ʼ)gęd$_V$- light-coloured, white]
deyoʼdagę:t dirty undergarments; soil; fecal matter
•(i)dagraʼ fall
eda:graʼs she is forever falling (for example, an old person) H
ęyedagraʼ she will fall down P
agidagraʼǫh I have fallen S
•(i)dagrahd(ę,ani) trip s.o.
[TR+ contains: -(i)dagraʼ$_V$- fall]
ęgaǫ:gidagrahdęʼ they are going to trip me, make me fall P
•(i)dagr(e:, ę) lay oneself down
[P+ęn+ contains: -idage:ʼ$_V$- lie]
ęsęnida:gręʼ you will lie down P
agęnida:gre:ʼ I laid myself down S
sęnidagręh lie down I
•(i)dagrǫʼ several living things lying down
[A+ contains: -idage:ʼ$_V$- lie]
gadidagrǫʼ they (z) are lying down S
•(iʼ)dai:ʼ dirty
[de+P+ -(i)ʼd(a:)$_N$- clay, mud, mortar -i:ʼ$_V$- be stuck onto s.t.]
dęhoʼdai:ʼ he got dirty (that is, covered with manure) S
•(iʼ)dai:ʼ brick
[o+ -(i)ʼd(a:)$_N$- clay, mortar -i:ʼ$_V$- stuck onto s.t.]
oʼda:iʼ brick (lit.: there is mud on it)
•(i)ʼdaisdǫ:ʼ intercourse
[a+ -(i)ʼd(a)$_N$- privates - (ʼ)a:sd, (ʼ)i:sd$_V$- pierce with s.t.]
adai:sdǫ:ʼ intercourse
•(i)ʼdanyo beat up
[TR+ -(i)ʼd(a)$_N$- feces -(r)iyo, nyo$_V$- kill s.t.]
ahǫwęda:nyoʼ s.o. beat him up, broke his spirit P
hǫwęʼdanyohsrǫh he is beating him up S
•(i)daǫ: lucky, fortunate, chosen, special
[P+]
sędaǫ: you are chosen, special, fortunate S
•(iʼ)daǫni dirty, muddy
[(ade+) -(i)ʼd(a:)$_N$- clay, mud, mortar -ǫni, ǫny$_V$- make]
agaʼdaǫniʼ it got muddy P
•(iʼ)dawęnyeʼ shit-disturber
[de+A+ -(i)ʼd(a)$_N$- feces -(a)węnye(:)$_V$- stir, mix]
deyeʼdawę:nyeʼ she is a shit-disturber H
•(iʼ)deni, (iʼ)deny fart
[ęn+ -(i)ʼd(a)$_N$- feces -deni, deny$_V$- change]
ǫniʼdenyǫhs she farts H
ęyǫniʼde:niʼ she will fart P
agęniʼdenyǫ: I have farted S
•(iʼ)dehsr(a) sexuality
[ga+]
gʼędehsraʼ sexuality
•(i)dęhd poverty
[o+ contains: -(i)dęǫ, (i)dę(:)$_V$- pity]
o:dęht poverty; it is poor, pitiful
•(i)dęhd be poor
[P+ contains: -(i)dęǫ, (i)dę(:)$_V$- pity]
ǫgidęhteʼ I am poor at s.t., I am not rich P
agi:dęht I am poor, poverty-stricken, in poverty S
•idęhd plead
[adęn+ contains: -(i)dęǫ, (i)dę(:)$_V$- pity]
sadęnidęhtaʼ you plead all the time H
ęhsadęni:dęht you will plead P

•idęhd plead (continued)
gonadęnidęhdǫh they (f/m) are pleading S
•(i)dęǫ, (i)dę(:) pity s.o., feel compassion for s.o.
[(d+)...TR+]
kedęǫhs I feel compassion for her H
ęhshe:dę:ʼ you will pity her; you will show mercy, compassion P
dahsgi:dę: pity me I
•(i)dęǫhsr(a) kindness
[adęn+ contains: -(i)dęǫ, (i)dę(:)$_V$- pity]
adęnideǫ:sraʼ the act of kindness
•(i)dęǫhsr(a) mercy
[ga+ contains: -(i)dęǫ, (i)dę(:)$_V$- pity]
gędaǫhsraʼ mercy
•(iʼ)dodaehsę fart
[P+ -(i)ʼd(a)$_N$- feces, privates -odaihsę$_V$- remove for oneself]
ahonʼidodaehsęʼ he farted P
•(i)dǫh mean s.t.
[A+ / TR+]
e:dǫh she means s.t. S
gi:dǫh I mean s.t. S
hę:dǫh he means s.t. S
i:ʼ gęh sgi:dǫh? do you mean me? S
Neʼ seʼ hǫwę:dǫh. He's the one she means.
•(i)dǫhg(wa) flame
[o+]
odǫhgwaʼ a flame
•(i)dǫhgoia:s dragon
[he+ga+ -idǫhg(wa)$_N$- flame -oiʼas$_V$- torch s.t.]
hegęʼdǫhgoiʼa:s a dragon (lit.: flame thrower)
•(i)ʼdre(:) drag, drive
[(N+)]
haʼdreʼ he is dragging PURP
ageʼdre:ʼ I dragged it PURP-PAST
gaihsdʼidrǫ: it has been surveyed S
[-(h)wihsd(a), (hr)ihsd(a)$_N$- metal, money -(i)ʼdre(:)$_V$- drag, drive]
desaʼdre: drive over here PURP-I
•(i)ʼdreʼs car
[wa+ade+]
wadeʼdreʼs a drag; a car (old word) (lit.: it is dragging itself) H
•(i)ʼdrehd move oneself
[(N+) contains: -(i)ʼdre(:)$_V$- drag, drive]
gʼadrehtaʼ it moves itself, it rides H
•(i)ʼdreʼs be self-propelled
[wa+adade+ -(i)ʼdre(:)$_V$- drag, drive]
wadadedreʼs it drives itself H
•(i)dręhd(a:) be sleepy
[P+]
agidręhda:ʼs I am sleepy H
ęsaidręhda:ʼ you will get sleepy P
•(i)dręhdiyohsd sleep well
[P+ contains: -(i)dręhd(a:)$_V$- sleepy -iyohsd$_V$- make good]
ęsaidręhdi:yohs you will have a nice sleep P
•(i)drędatgihd(ę, ani) nightmare
[P+ade+ contains: -(i)dręhd(a:)$_V$- sleepy -tgihdę$_V$- make bad for oneself]
agadedręhdatgihdanihsgęhę:ʼ I used to have bad dreams H
ǫgadedrędatgi:dęʼ I had a bad dream P
•(i)dręhdahoʼdrǫ(:) stay awake
[ad+ contains: -(i)dręhd(a:)$_V$- be sleepy]
agadidręhtaodrǫ:
(**agadidręhdahoʼdrǫ:**) I had to stay awake P
•idręhgyenyęʼs nod off, fall asleep
[A+ contains: -(i)dręhd(a:)$_V$- be sleepy]
sidręhgye:nyęʼs you are nodding off, falling asleep H
•(i)ʼdrǫ live, dwell, be at home
[A+]
hadiʼdrǫʼ they (m) are at home S
•(i)ʼdrǫ place s.o., elect s.o.
[TR+]
ahǫwadiʼdrǫʼ they placed him, elected him P

Legend: H habitual, P punctual, S stative, I imperative, PURP purposive, PURP-H purposive habitual, PURP-PAST purposive past, PURP-P purposive punctual, PURP-I purposive imperative; see §8.6, §8.11 in Appendix J. Alphabetization in stems ignores length (:), and any h's or glottal stops (ʼ) that are not between vowels. See §2.2 of the User Guide for explanation.

•(i)ʼdrǫdaʼ be placed, live, stay at home
[A+ contains: -(i)ʼdrǫ$_V$- live, dwell, be at home]
ęhsniʼdrǫ:daʼk you two will stay home P
tgidrǫ:daʼk where I lived S
•(i)ʼdrǫdaʼ land
[de+ contains: -(i)ʼdrǫ$_V$- live, dwell, be at home]
degęʼdrǫ:daʼs it lands there all the time H
dęgęʼdrǫ:daʼ it will land P
dęhoʼdrǫdaʼǫh he has landed S
•(i)ʼdrǫda:ʼ diaper
[ga+ -(i)ʼd(a)$_N$- feces -oda:$_V$- put in]
gʼadro:da:ʼ a diaper
•(i)ʼdrǫdǫʼ several things, etc. placed somewhere
[A+ contains: -(i)ʼdrǫ$_V$- live, dwell, be at home]
hadiʼdrǫ:dǫʼ how they (m) are placed S
•(i)g(a:ʼ) be in water
[N+ present in:]
sganyaʼdi:ga:ʼ heron
[s+ga+ stem: -nyaʼdiga:ʼ- heron; consists of: -nyad(a:)$_N$- lake, body of water, -ig(a:ʼ)$_V$- be in water]
•iʼgeh as for me
see: Appendix I
•iʼgeh gwadih on my side; referring to a matrilineage
see: Appendix I
•(i)ʼgrǫʼ be shy
[P+ad+]
godiʼgrǫʼ she is shy S
•(iʼ)grǫhsr(a) shyness
[ad+ contains: -(i)ʼgrǫʼ$_V$- be shy]
adiʼgrǫhsraʼ shyness
•(i)gyohgǫgyeʼs roam
[-(i)gyohg(wa)$_N$- crowd -ǫgyeʼs$_V$- stand along]
gęgyohgǫgyeʼs people roaming about H

•(i)gyohg(wa) crowd
sgęgyohgwa:t one crowd; one body
[s+ga+ -(i)gyohg(wa)$_N$- crowd -d$_V$- stand]
•(i)gyohgwaęʼ association, agency, group, crowd
[ga+ -(i)gyohg(wa)$_N$- crowd -ę$_V$- lie on the ground]
gęgyohgwaęʼ an association; an agency; a group; ą crowd
•(i)gyohgwagęni, (i)gyohgwagęny vote, elect
[de+...ęn+ -(i)gyohg(wa)$_N$- crowd -gęni, gęny$_V$- compete]
dęhsęnigyohgwagę:niʼ you will vote, cast lots P
•iho... look for stems beginning with (ri)h(wa)...
•iho word, affair, business, message, matter, idea, reason
see: (r)ih(wa) word, affair, business, message, matter, idea, reason
oihwaʼ message; it matters; it is its fault; a word; an affair; business
oihwʼageh the reason; the idea for s.t.
oihwaǫ:weh a sacred idea
•ihoʼdahǫh disagree
see: (ri)hoʼdahǫh [(tęʼ) deʼ+ not P+] disagree
dewagrihoʼdahǫh I am not in complete agreement S
•ihoʼdeʼ be working
see: (ri)hoʼdeʼ [P+] be working
hoihoʼdeʼ he is working S
•ihoʼdę: be soft, loose
see: (ri)hoʼdę: [P+(N+)] be soft, loose
ohehda̱hoʼdę: soft ground S
•ihoʼdę: way, manner, belief
see: (r)ihoʼdę: way, manner, belief
nisaihoʼdę: your manner
•ihoʼgaʼd speak sharp words
see: (r)ihoʼgaʼd [P+] speak sharp words
hoihoʼgaʼt he speaks sharp words S

•ihowanahd praise, flatter s.o.
(r)ihowanahd [TR+] praise, flatter s.o.
ęhshehowa:naht you will praise her, uplift her spirits, flatter her P
•ihowanęh be special, important
see: (r)ihowanęh [(g)+(y)o+] be special, important
gyoihowa:nęh the most important S
•ihowęhs computer
see: (r)ihowęhs [de+ga+] computer
degaiho:węhs a computer
•ihǫd appoint, delegate
see: (r)ihǫd [TR+] appoint, delegate
ahǫwaihǫdę' they delegated him a duty P
•ihǫni incite, cause
see: (r)ihǫni incite, cause
ętrihǫ:ni', ęsrihǫ:ni' you will incite, be the cause of s.t. P
•ihǫnyanih teacher
see: (r)ihǫnyanih teacher
hadęihǫnyanih he is a teacher
ǫdęihǫnyanih she is a teacher
hai:hǫnya:nih he is a teacher
•ihǫnyani:' education
see: (r)ihǫnyani:' [ga+] education
gai:hǫnya:ni:' education
•ihu:'uh be sensitive, unimportant
see: (r)ihu:'uh [ni+P+] be sensitive, unimportant
niwagri̱hu:'uh I am sensitive S
•(i)jǫd be filthy
[de+P+]
dewagejǫ:t, dewagijǫ:t I am filthy S
•(i)jǫ'd(a) fish
[o+]
ojǫ'da' a fish
•(i)hn(a) material, skin
gi̱hna'geh on my skin
degęhnakahǫ' a quilt
[de+ga+ -(i)hn(a)$_N$- material, skin -kahǫ$_V$- adjoin, abutt assemble, put together]
•(i)hnakahǫ' quilt
[de+ga+ -(i)hn(a)$_N$- material, skin -kahǫ$_V$- adjoin, abutt assemble, put together]
degęhnakahǫ' a quilt
•(i)hnaned lining, insulated wall
[de+ga+ -(i)hn(a)$_N$- material, skin -ned$_V$- keep]
degahnane:t a lining; an insulated wall
•(i)hnatę: have dry skin
[A+ -(i)hn(a)$_N$- material, skin -tę(:)$_V$- be dry]
se̱hna:tę:, si̱hna:tę: you have dry skin S
•(i)hnatęhsdǫh cradle-robber
[o+ -(i)hn(a)$_N$- material, skin -tęhsd$_V$- dry out]
ohnahtęhsdǫh dried-up skin (a derogatory term referring to s.o. with a younger woman or man)
•in(e) go
[N+]
gatahine' I am walking PURP
ętgǫnę:tsi:ne' I will take you by the arm PURP-P
[d+TR+ stem: -nętsine'- take s.o. by the arm, lead by the arm; consists of: -nęts(a)$_N$- arm; -ine$_V$- go]
sga:t heyotahinǫ: one concession (measurement) PURP-S
[sga:t one he+yo+at+ stem: -(h)ahinǫ:- concession; consists of: -(h)ah(a)$_N$- road -ine$_V$- go]
•ines extinct
[(tę') de'+ not s+A+ contains: -ine$_V$- go]
dehsgę:ne:s it is extinct PURP-H
•(i)hnodǫ flood
awęhnodǫ' flood; it flooded P
[-(i)hn(a)$_N$- material, skin -odǫ'$_V$- several standing objects]
ohno:dǫ' it is flooded S

Legend: H habitual, P punctual, S stative, I imperative, PURP purposive, PURP-H purposive habitual, PURP-PAST purposive past, PURP-P purposive punctual, PURP-I purposive imperative; see §8.6, §8.11 in Appendix J. Alphabetization in stems ignores length (:), and any h's or glottal stops (') that are not between vowels. See §2.2 of the User Guide for explanation.

•inǫʔ be well; hello
[s+ga+ -inǫʔ$_V$- be well]
sgę:nǫʔ it is well; hello S
•inǫʔǫh be slow
[s+ga+ -inǫ:ʔǫh$_V$- be slow]
sgęnǫ:ʔǫh slowly S
•i:nǫh far
see: Appendix I
•i:nǫh heʔga:gęh a telescope
i:nǫh it is far
heʔga:gęh it sees over there
•(i)hnǫh handkerchief
[ga+]
ga̱hnǫh a handkerchief
•(i)hnǫg call s.o.
[heʔ/d+TR+]
tagihnǫ:s he is calling me H
hęgihnǫ:k I will call P
hewagi̱hnǫ:gǫh I have called it; it has called me S
haʔsihnǫ:k call it I
•i:s long
[A/P+N+ occurs in:]
oshai:s long string, rope, etc. S
[-sh(a)$_N$- song, music -is$_V$- long]
•i:s you
see: Appendix I
•i:s tsǫ: only you; you'll do.
see: Appendix I
•(i)hsʔ finish
[(N+) occurs in:]
dwatędihsʔahs we are finishing the field H
[stem: -(h)ęd(a)$_N$- field -(i)hsʔ$_V$- finish]
edwatędihsʔa:ʔ we all (incl.) finished the field (said after thrashing it) P
ǫgwatędihsʔǫh we finished the field S
•(i)hsag investigate, inquire, look for
[(N+)]
gi̱hsa:s I am looking for it H
ęgihsa:k I will seek or look for it P
agihsagǫh I am looking for it S
si̱hsa:k look for it I
ęhs-ríh-wi̱h-sa:k you will investigate, inquire P
[-(r)ih(wa)$_N$- word -(i)hsag$_V$- investigate, inquire, look for]
•(i)hsag look for a mate
[de+]
dedwade̱hsa:s we are looking (for mates) H
•(ih)sd(a:, ai) scale
[o+]
ohsda:ʔ, ohsdaiʔ a scale (on a fish)
•ihsd(a) tin, metal, money
see: (h)wihsd(a), (hr)ihsd(a) [ga+] tin, metal, money
gai:sdaʔ tin; metal
•ihsdataʔ iron
see: (r)ihsdataʔ iron
ei:sda:taʔ s.t. to iron with; an iron
•(ih)sdęhd scale fish
[-(ih)sd(a:)$_N$- scale -(y)ęhd$_V$- hit, knock down, strike]
ęsehsdęht you will take the scales off (the fish) P
•ihsdiʔdr survey
see: (r)ihsdiʔdr survey
hadihsdʔidrehs they (m) are surveying the land; they (m) are surveyors H
•(ih)sdihsra:s moth
[ga+ ad+ -(ih)sdihsr(a)$_N$- trade cloth -g$_V$- eat]
gadihsdihsra:s a moth
•ihsdowanęh be loud
see: (r)ihsdowanęh [P+] be loud
odiʔsdowanęh they (z) are loud S
•ihsdohas typewriter
see: (r)ihsdohas typewriter
degaihsdo:ha:s a typewriter
•ihsdowa:ʔ mullet
see: (r)ihsdowa:ʔ mullet
sgai:sdo:wa:ʔ a mullet
•i:sgędri: wren
see: (r)i:sgędri: wren
sgai:sgędri: a marsh wren

•ihsgya'ksǫ' cut up s.t.
see: (r)ihsgya'ksǫ' cut up s.t.
ęhsrihsgya'ksǫ' you will slice s.t. up P
•i:so' much, many, lots
see: Appendix I
•(i)hs'ǫh ready
[P+ade+ contains: -(i)hs'$_V$- finish]
sadehs'ǫh? Are you ready? (this expression is used by Cayuga speakers, but may come from Onondaga) S
•isr(a) leggings
see: (r)isr(a) leggings
gai:sra' leggings
•(i)hsre(:) follow, chase
[TR+]
hǫwadihsre's they follow him around all the time PURP-H
ahǫwadihsre:' they chased, followed him PURP-P
hǫwadihsrehsrǫh they are chasing him around S
•ihsres shoe upper
see: (r)ihsres shoe upper
deyoihsre:s an upper (part of a shoe)
•itgę' rise
[(d+) occurs in:]
tga:gwitgę's east; the sun rises there H
[(t+)... stem: -(r)agwitgę'(s)- sunrise, east; consists of: -(r)ag(wa)$_N$- sun, moon -itgę'$_V$- rise]
daga:gwi:tgę' sunrise; the sun did rise P
deyogwitgę'ǫh, gya:gwitgę'ǫh the sun, moon has risen S
•(i)tse('da) bottle, jar
[ga+]
gatse'da', gętse'da' a bottle; a jar
•(i)tse'dahęh pint
[tsa'de+ga+ -(i)tse('da)$_N$- bottle -(h)ęh$_V$- be mid, be half]
tsa'degatse'dahęh one pint
•(i)tse'do' cold packing
[ga+ -(i)tse('da)$_N$- bottle -o'$_V$- be submerged]
gętse'do' cold packing (part of the process of canning)
•(i)tse'dod standing bottle
[ga+ -(i)tse('da)$_N$- bottle -od$_V$- stand]
gatse'do:t a standing bottle; a belly button
•(i)tse'dod belly button, navel
[A+ -(i)tse('da)$_N$- bottle -od$_V$- stand]
getse'do:t my navel
swętse'do:t your (p) navels
•(i)tse'dod hubbard squash
[o+ -(i)tse('da)$_N$- bottle -od$_V$- stand squash]
otse'do:t hubbard squash
•itsg(a) having to do with the lower body
[occurs in:]
gadi:tsgo:t they (z) are all sitting
[A+ stem: -(i)tsgod- be sitting; consists of: -(i)tsg(wa)$_N$- lower body -od$_V$- stand]
gaǫ:nitsgo:ta' they (f/m) do sit ups H
[A+ ęn+ stem: -(i)tsgod- be sitting; consists of: -(i)tsg(wa)$_N$- lower body -od$_V$- stand -ǫnyǫ' several]
ęyǫnitsgodǫnyǫ:' she will do sit ups
•(i)tsga'shǫ:'ǫh bedding
[ga+ contains: -(i)tsg(wa)$_N$- lower body -shǫ:'ǫh plural]
gętsga'shǫ:'ǫh bedding
•(i)tsgod be sitting
[A+ -(i)tsg(wa)$_N$- lower body -od$_V$- stand]
etsgo:t she is sitting S
•(i)tsgodę' re-elect
[TR+ -(i)tsg(wa)$_N$- lower body -odę$_V$- stand, put in]
ahǫwaditsgo:dę' they elected him, them (m) P
•(i)tsgodǫ' several living things sitting
[A+ contains: -(i)tsg(wa)$_N$- lower body -odǫ'$_V$- several standing objects]
gadi:tsgo:dǫ' they (z) are sitting S

Legend: H habitual, P punctual, S stative, I imperative, PURP purposive, PURP-H purposive habitual, PURP-PAST purposive past, PURP-P purposive punctual, PURP-I purposive imperative; see §8.6, §8.11 in Appendix J. Alphabetization in stems ignores length (:), and any h's or glottal stops (') that are not between vowels. See §2.2 of the User Guide for explanation.

•itsgod(ǫnyǫ(:)) sit ups
[ęn+ -itsg(wa)$_N$- lower body -od$_V$- stand -ǫnyǫʼ several]
gaǫ:nitsgo:taʼ they (f/m) do sit ups H
ęgaǫ:nitsgodǫ:nyǫ:ʼ they (f/m) will do sit ups P

•(i)tsgr(a) saliva, spit, sputum
[o+]
otsgraʼ saliva; spit; sputum

•(i)tsgrod drool
[P+ -(i)tsgr(a)$_N$- saliva -od$_V$- stand]
sętsgro:t you are drooling S

•(i)tsgrǫdi spit
[ę+ -(i)tsgr(a)$_N$- saliva -ǫdi, -ǫgy$_V$- throw]
sęni:tsgrǫ:dih spit I

•(i)tsgwahe:ʼ sit on s.t., perch on s.t.
[A+ -(i)tsg(wa)$_N$- lower body -(h)e:ʼ$_V$- sitting up on top of s.t.]
gitsgwahe:ʼ I am perched up on s.t.; I am sitting on s.t. S

•ih(wa), iho word, affair, business, message, matter, idea, reason
see: (r)ih(wa) word, affair, business, message, matter, idea, reason
oihwaʼ message; it matters; it is its fault; a word; an affair; business
oihwageh the reason; the idea for s.t.
oihwaǫ:weh a sacred idea

•ihwad sentence
see: (r)ihwad sentence
joihwa:t one written sentence

•ihwadogę be reliable
see: (r)ihwadogę [P+] reliable
hoihwado:gę: he is a reliable person S

•ihwadogę traitor
see: (r)ihwadogę [(tęʼ) deʼ+ not P+] traitor
dehoihwado:gę: he is a traitor S

•ihwahdǫ(ʼ) be extinct
see: (r)ihwahdǫ(ʼ) [o+] be extinct
oihwahdǫʼǫh it is extinct S

•ihwaʼe demand s.t., insist on s.t.
see: (r)ihwaʼe [d+...] demand s.t., insist on s.t.
ętrihwa̱he:k you will demand s.t., insist, force s.t. P

•ihwaʼehsd demand a report, an account
see: (r)ihwaʼehsd [de+TR+] demand a report, an account
atgaǫgrihwaʼehs they wanted a report P

•ihwaʼehsd blame s.o.
see: (r)ihwaʼehsd [TR+] blame s.o.
ęhshehwaʼehs you will blame s.o. P

•ihwaʼehsd(ę, ani) demand an audience from s.o.
see: (r)ihwaʼehsd(ę, ani) [TR+] demand an audience from s.o.
ęhǫwadihwaʼehsdęʼ they will unravel his message, demand an audience from him P

•ihwaʼehsdǫ:ʼ report
see: (r)ihwaʼehsdǫ:ʼ report
gaihwaʼehsdǫ:ʼ a report

•ihwaę(:) innocent
see: (r)ihwaę(:) [sgahoʼdęʼ nothing deʼ+not P+] innocent
sgahoʼdęʼ dehoiwaęʼ he is innocent S

•ihwaędahgw responsibility
see: (r)ihwaędahgw responsibility
ęgaihwaędahk it will become s.o.'s responsibility P

•ihwaędaʼs decide, agree, conclude
see: (r)ihwaędaʼs [de+P+] decide, agree, conclude
atoihwaę:daʼs he came to a decision, a conclusion P

•ihwaędǫhgw gossip
see: (r)ihwaędǫhgw [de+...ad+] gossip
deyǫdri̱hwaędǫhkwaʼ a female gossiper H
dęsadri̱hwaędǫhk you will gossip P

•ihwaętwa(hd) spread the news, bring forth a message
see: (r)ihwaętwa(hd) [de+s+...] spread the news, bring forth a message
dęshaihwaętwaht he will bring forth a message P

•ihwaga'de' be a chatterbox, be talkative
see: (r)ihwaga'de' [P+] be a chatterbox, be talkative
goihwaga'de' she is a chatterbox S

•ihwage: be quick-witted
see: (r)ihwage: [ha'de+P+ -(r)ih(wa)$_N$-word] be quick-witted
ha'dehoihwage: he is quick-witted; he has lots of business, different ideas, many ideas; he is into everything S

•ihwagehde' responsibility
see: (r)ihwagehde' responsibility
gaihwagehde' a responsibility

•ihwagęnya'd complain, instigate
see: (r)ihwagęnya'd [P+] complain, instigate
hoihwagę:nya't he is an instigator S

•ihwagenh argue for, advocate
(r)ihwagenh [de+...(r)ihwa/N+] argue for, advocate
dęhsrihwage:nha' you will argue, debate, protest P

•ihwagwaihs(i) be a witness
see: (r)ihwagwaihs(i) be a witness
ęhsrihwagwaihsi' you will be a witness P

•ihwagweny accomplish, achieve, lead
see: (r)ihwagweny accomplish, achieve, lead
ęhsrihwagwę:ni' you will accomplish P

•ihwagwęniyo' be a boss, reside, dwell
see: (r)ihwagwęniyo' [A+] be a boss, reside, dwell
grihwagwęni:yo' where I reside, dwell (lit.: where I'm the boss) S

•ihwagwęniyohsd sanction, charter, give authority
see: (r)ihwagwęniyohsd sanction, charter, give authority
ęhsrihwagwę:ni:yohs you will sanction, charter, give authority to s.o. P

•ihwagyęhętw, ihwagyęhęto participate, partake
see: (r)ihwagyęhętw [he'+...] participate, partake
hęjidwaihwagyęhęto' we all (incl.) will bring the idea back again P

•ihwahe:' presentation
see: (r)ihwahe:' presentation
gaihwahe:' a presentation

•ihwahę, ihwahe present an idea, submit an idea
see: (r)ihwahę, (r)ihwahe present an idea, submit an idea
ęhsrihwahę' you will present an idea P

•ihwahę, ihwahe commit a crime, do wrong
(r)ihwahę, (r)ihwahe [de+...ad+] commit a crime, wrong (do)
atadrihwahę' he went afoul of the law; he did s.t. wrong P

•i:wa:k'ah nearby
see: Appendix I

•ihwakahǫ' alliance
see: (r)ihwakahǫ' alliance
degaihwakahǫ' an alliance

•ihwahkwa' choir
see: (r)ihwahkwa' choir
dęhadi:hwahkwa' a choir

•ihwane'aksrǫ(:) swear
see: (r)ihwane'aksrǫ(:) swear
ęhsrihwane'aksrǫ:' you will swear, use profane language P

•ihwanegę:' prayer
see: (r)ihwanegę:' prayer
gaihwane:gę:' a prayer; to pray

Legend: H habitual, P punctual, S stative, I imperative, PURP purposive, PURP-H purposive habitual, PURP-PAST purposive past, PURP-P purposive punctual, PURP-I purposive imperative; see §8.6, §8.11 in Appendix J. Alphabetization in stems ignores length (:), and any h's or glottal stops (') that are not between vowels. See §2.2 of the User Guide for explanation.

•ihwanhodǫgw, ihwanhodǫgo open a gathering
see: (r)ihwanhodǫgw, (r)ihwanhodǫgo open a gathering
ęhaihwanhodǫ:go' he will open the gathering P

•ihwahniya'd affirm, agree
see: (r)ihwahniya'd affirm, agree
ęhsrihwa̱hni:ya:t you will affirm it, agree P

•ihwahniya'd marry s.o. off
see: (r)ihwahniya'd [TR+] marry s.o.
shagodi:hwahniy'adǫh they got married by the Chiefs; a marriage ceremony usually sanctioned by the Chiefs S

•ihwanǫhwe' disapprove
see: (r)ihwanǫhwe' [(tę') de'+ not] disapprove
desrihwanǫhwe's you disapprove H

•ihwanǫhkw care for, respect
see: (r)ihwanǫhkw [TR+] care for, respect
a:goi:hwanǫhkwa:k I should care for, respect your ideas P

•ihwaohes be a researcher
see: (r)ihwaohes be a researcher
eihwaohe:s she is a researcher
haihwaohe:s he is a researcher

•(i')waǫni: welt
[ga/o+ -(i')w(a)$_N$- welt -ǫni, ǫny$_V$- make]
gai'wao:ni: welts
o'wao:ni: welts

•ihwahs' plan
see: (r)ihwahs' plan
ęhsrihwa̱hs'a:' you will plan an idea; you will promise, make an agreement P

•ihwahs'(a) plan
see: (r)ihwahs'(a) plan
gaihwi̱hsa' an agreement

•ihwahsde' burden, preoccupation
see: (r)ihwahsde' burden, preoccupation
oihwahsde' a mental burden; a preoccupation

•ihwahsgęnh fight over
see: (hs)gęnh [de+...(r)ihwa/N+] fight over
saǫhwęjahsgęnhęh you are fighting over the land right now S
[-ǫhwęj(a)$_N$- earth, land -genh$_V$- argue for, advocate]

•ihwate'd explain
see: (r)ihwate'd [de+] explain
dęhsrihwate't you will explain P

•ihwate'ta' dictionary
see: (r)ihwate'ta' [de+ga+] dictionary
degaihwate'ta' a dictionary

•ihwats' earn s.t., fulfill s.t.
see: (r)ihwats' [de+...ad+] earn s.t., fulfill s.t.
dehodi:hwa̱hts'a:' they are earning, fulfilling it S

•ihwahtsęnyahsgǫ: find fault
see: (r)ihwahtsęnyahsgǫ: [P+] find fault
saihwahtsęnya̱hsgǫ: you find faults H

•ihwawa's support s.o., back s.o.
see: (r)ihwawa's [TR+] support s.o., back s.o.
hehwaw'aseh I did agree with him, support him H
ęhehsrihwa:wa's you will back up his ideas P

•ihwahwinyǫ'd report
see: (r)ihwahwinyǫ'd report
ętrihwa̱hwi:nyǫ't you will report P

•ihwaya'g denounce, disapprove
see: (r)ihwaya'g [de+...] denounce, disapprove
dęhsrihwaya:'k you will denounce it, disapprove of it P

•ihwayena(w) accept advice
see: (r)ihwayena(w) accept advice
ęhsri:hwaye:na:' you will accept advice, a suggestion, etc. P

•ihwaętw(ahd) broadcast s.t.
see: (y)ętw(ahd) broadcast s.t.
dęshaihwaętwaht he will bring forth a message P
[de+(s+)... stem: -(r)ihwaętwahd- spread the news, bring forth a message; consists of: -(r)ih(wa)$_N$- word -(y)ętw(ahd)$_V$- spread (seeds), seed s.t.]
•ihwęhd bring down an idea
see: (r)ihwęhd bring down an idea
ętrihwęht you will bring the idea down P
•ihwęda' wear out
see: (r)ihwęda' wear out
agaihwę:da' it wore out (for example, clothing) P
•ihwęhd(ę, ani) give s.o. a message
see: (r)ihwęhd(ę, ani) [TR+] give s.o. a message
ęgǫihwęhdę' I will give you a significant message P
•ihwęhę(:) convey a message
see: (r)ihwęhę(:) [ha'+...] convey a message
hęhaihwęhę:' he will take the message P
•ihwiyo' certain, sure
see: (r)ihwiyo' [o+] certain, sure
oihwi:yo' it is certain, for sure S
•ihwiyohsd become Christian, convert to Christianity
see: (r)ihwiyohsd become Christian, convert to Christianity
ahsrihwi:yohs you became a Christian; you converted to Christianity P
•(i)ya'g cut, break, cross
[(N+) occurs in:]
enehsdanya's, enehsdaiya's she is sawing a board H
[-nehsd(a:)$_N$- floor, board -(i)ya'g$_V$- cut, break]
awatehgya'k it did erode P
[at+ stem: -(h)ehgya'g- erode; consists of: -(h)ehd(a)$_N$- land, dirt, earth, ground -(i)ya'g$_V$- cut, break]
swaǫ:gya'gǫh you all have cut the log S
[-(r)ǫd(a)$_N$- log -(i)ya'g$_V$- cut, break]
sadeji'ohgyak cut your nails I
[ade+ stem: -ji'ohd(a), ji'ehd(a)$_N$- fingernail, toenail, claw, nail -(i)ya'g$_V$- cut, break, cut for oneself]
•(i)ya'g, (i)'a'g shoot
hadiy'a:s they (m) are shooting H
•iya'gya'g burp, belch
[ęn+ contains: -(i)ya'g$_V$- cut, break, cross -(i)ya'g$_V$- cut, break, cross]
degęniya'gya's, deganiya'gya's I always burp, I'm a burper H
atgęninya'gya'k I burped, belched P
dewagęniya'gya'gǫh I am burping S
•(i)ya'ksǫ' several broken pieces
[(N+) occurs in:]
degay'aksǫ' it is broken S
[de+... -(h)sgoh(a)$_N$- branch -(i)ya'g$_V$- cut, break, cross]
•(i)ya'ksǫ' broken up in different ways
[occurs in:]
ęsehsgwiy'aksǫ:' you will cut the twigs off P
[-(h)sgoh(a)$_N$- branch -(i)ya'g$_V$- cut, break, cross]
ha'degaya'ksǫ' it is broken up in different ways S
•(i)ya'kta' ammunition
[hadi+ -(i)ya'kd$_V$- shoot with s.t.]
hadiy'akta' ammunition (lit. they (m) shoot it)
•iyo: be nice, good
[A/P+N+ occurs in:]
gahę:di:yo: good ground S
[ga+ stem: -(h)ed(a)$_N$- field -iyo:$_V$- be nice, good]

Legend: H habitual, P punctual, S stative, I imperative, PURP purposive, PURP-H purposive habitual, PURP-PAST purposive past, PURP-P purposive punctual, PURP-I purposive imperative; see §8.6, §8.11 in Appendix J. Alphabetization in stems ignores length (:), and any h's or glottal stops (') that are not between vowels. See §2.2 of the User Guide for explanation.

•iyo: be nice, good (continued)
ohehdi:yo: good earth
[o+ stem: -(h)ehd(a)$_N$- land, dirt, earth, ground -iyo:$_V$- be nice, good]
•iyo: have s.t. good
[P+ occurs in:]
hoiho'dęhsri:yo: he has a good job S
[P+ stem: -(ri)ho'dęhsr(a)$_N$- work -iyo:$_V$- be nice, good]
•iyo: be bad
[de'+ not A/P+N+ occurs in:]
deyohnegi:yo: it is not good water S
[de'+ not yo+ stem: -(h)neg(a)$_N$- water, liquid -iyo:$_V$- be nice, good]
•iyo: be grumpy, grouchy, unhappy
[de'+ not d+P+]
dedis'anigo̱hi:yo: you are grumpy, grouchy, not happy S
•iyo kill someting
see: (r)iyo, nyo [TR+] kill someting
aha:nyo' he killed an animal P
•iyo's several good things
[A/P+N+ occurs in:]
gaksi:yo's good dishes S
[-ks(a)$_N$- dish -iyo:$_V$- be nice, good]
•iyohsd become nice, good
[A/P+N+ occurs in:]
sawęhni̱hsri:yohs it became a nice day again P
[-ęhnihsr(a)$_N$- day -iyohsd$_V$- become nice, good]
•(i)yǫd stretch
[de+ad/N+]
dewadiyǫ:ta' it stretches (shortened form of 'rubber band'); a balloon; an elastic H
deyagodi:yǫ:t she is stretching it S

J

•jagǫ(',:) persevere, try
geja:gǫhs I persevere all the time H
agejagǫ:' I persevered P
agejagǫ'ǫh I persevere (all the time) S
seja:gǫh persevere; keep it up I
•jagwahdihs blood sucker
jagwa̱dihs blood suckers
•jaoho'g(wa) ankle
ojaho'gwa' an ankle
sejao:ho'gw'ageh on your ankle
•jaod smoke
[-j(a)$_N$- smoke -odę$_V$- put in]
ęhsejaodę' you will smoke P
•jaǫs(a) corn leaf
[o+]
ojaǫsa' leaves of corn
•jaǫ: both
[de+A+]
degae:jaǫ: both of them (f/m) S
•ję' dish, plate, bowl
[ga+]
gaję' a dish; a plate; a bowl
•ję'd cure, practice medicine
skeję'ta' you cure me (all the time) H
ęjisaję't it will cure you again P
swagej'ędǫh it cured me again S
•jęhęhdas buzzard, vulture
[ga+ -jęhęhd(a)$_N$- flesh -g$_V$- eat]
gajęhęhda:s buzzards; vultures
•jęhiyohsd make a good fire
[ade+ -jęh(a)$_N$- fire -iyohsd$_V$- make nice, good]
sadejęhiyohs make a good fire I
•jęhǫni start a fire
[ade+ -jęh(a)$_N$- fire -ǫni, ǫny$_V$- make]
ęgadejęhǫ:ni' I will start a fire (old word) P
sadejęhǫ:nih make a fire I

•jęʼs doctor
[A+ade+ contains: -jęʼd$_V$- cure, practice medicine]
hade:jęʼs he is a doctor

•jęʼsgeh doctor's office, clinic
[A+ade+ contains: -jęʼd$_V$- cure, practice medicine -ʼgeh on, at]
hadejęhsgeh a doctor's office; a clinic

•ji(:,h) dark
see: (hǫʼ)ji(:,h) [A/P+N/(hǫʼ)+] dark
gahǫʼji: it is dark-coloured S

•jiʼ(a:) curtain, lace
[o+]
ojiʼa:ʼ curtains; lace

•jiʼadeʼ lace, sheer fabric
[o+ -jiʼ(a:)$_N$- curtain, lace -deʼ$_V$- exist]
ojiʼa:deʼ sheer, lacy fabrics; lace

•jianęʼdǫt stag deer
[de+yo+ -jiʼanę(ʼda)$_N$- -ǫd$_V$- attached]
deyojia:nʼędǫ:t a stag deer

•jiʼaowektaʼ hair net
[ǫ+ade+ -jiʼ(a:)$_N$- curtain, lace -(hr)owekd$_V$- cover with s.t.]
ǫdejʼiao:we:ktaʼ a hair net

•jiʼaʼoyę: spider
[-jiʼ(a:)$_N$- curtain, lace -oyę:$_V$-]
jiʼao:yę: spider

•jiʼd(a) cry
[occurs in:]
degajiʼda:ga: a whiner, cryer
[de+ ga+ -jiʼd(a)$_N$- cry -ga:$_V$- make a rattling or grinding noise]
gajiʼdoda:gyeʼ someone is going along crying
[-jiʼd(a)$_N$- cry -odagyeʼ$_V$- go standing along]

•jiʼdaga(:,i) whine, cry, complain
[de+... -jiʼd(a)$_N$- cry -ga:$_V$- make a rattling or grinding noise]
degajiʼda:ga: a whiner, cryer H
atgajiʼdagai: there was whining, crying, repetitive complaining P

•jiʼdana:wę: butterfly
[-jiʼd(a)- cry -nawę:$_V$- wet]
jiʼdana:wę: butterfly (lit.: s.t. is wet, referring to the transformation)

•jiʼdędaʼ stop crying
[-jiʼd(a)$_N$- cry -(y)ędaʼ$_V$- finish]
sejiʼdę:daʼ stop crying I

•jidęʼęh bird
[ji+]
jidę:ʼęh bird

•jidęhtras evening bird
[ga+ contains: -jidęʼęh$_N$- bird]
gajidęhtra:s evening bird

•jiʼdowanęh be a big cry-baby
[P+ -jiʼd(a)$_N$- cry -owanęh$_V$- be big]
gojiʼdowanęh she's a great big cry-baby

•jiʼdrǫwę: sea shell
jiʼdrǫ:wę: a sea shell

•jiʼehd(a), jiʼohd(a) fingernail, toenail, nail
ojiʼehdaʼ, ojiʼohdaʼ fingernails; toenails; animal nails; claws
swajiʼohdaʼgeh on your (p) nails

•jiʼehde:s, jiʼohde:s claw
[de+ga+ -jiʼohd(a), jiʼehd(a)$_N$- fingernail, toenail, nail -es$_V$- long]
degajiʼehde:s a claw

•jiʼohgyaʼg, jiʼehgyaʼg cut one's nails
[ad+(N+)]
ęgadejiʼohgyak I am going to cut my nails P

•jiʼehta:ʼstampede
[de+yo+at+ -ji$_N$- hoof -(ʼ)ehd$_V$- hit with s.t.]
deyotjiʼehta:ʼ a stampede

•jihgǫni: mashed food
[ga+ -jihg(wa)$_N$- porridge, mush -ǫni, ǫny$_V$- make]
gajihgǫ:ni: mashed food

•jigǫhses pike
[ji+ -gǫhs(a)$_N$- face -es$_V$- long]
jigǫhse:s pike (a fish)

Legend: H habitual, P punctual, S stative, I imperative, PURP purposive, PURP-H purposive habitual, PURP-PAST purposive past, PURP-P purposive punctual, PURP-I purposive imperative; see §8.6, §8.11 in Appendix J. Alphabetization in stems ignores length (:), and any h's or glottal stops (ʼ) that are not between vowels. See §2.2 of the User Guide for explanation.

•jihg(wa) porridge, mush
[o+]
ojihgwaʼ porridge; mush
•jiʼg(wa) nakedness, nudity
[ga/o+]
gajiʼgwaʼ nakedness
ojiʼgwaʼ nudity
•jihgwaʼe punch
[(de+)... -jih(s)g(wa)$_N$- porridge, mush -(ʼ)e$_V$- hit]
dehadijihgwaʼehs they (m) punch it H
ahaji̱hgwaʼe:k he punched it P
gajihgwaʼe:ʼ it punches S
•jigwę̨daʼ gonorrhea
[o+ -jigwę̨d(a)$_N$- gonorrhea]
ojigwę̨daʼ gonorrhea
•jihgwę̨ʼs corn smut
[o+ contains: -jihg(wa)$_N$- porridge, mush]
ojihgwę̨ʼs corn smut; black corn fungus
•jihayaʼ
[ga+]
gajihayaʼ the devil
•jihod close, turn off
sejiho:dę̨hs you close it all the time H
gejihohtaʼ I am closing it right now; I am going along closing things H
ę̨geji̱ho:dę̨ʼ I will close it P
sejiho:dę̨h close it I
•jihodagw open, turn on
[contains: -jihod$_V$- close]
sejihoda:goh open it I
•jihoh(a:) pin
[ga/o+]
gajihoha:ʼ, ojihoha:ʼ a straight pin; a pin; a brooch; a safety pin
•jikeʼd(a) salt
[o+]
ojikeʼdaʼ salt
•jikeʼdawehd be salty
[o+ -jikeʼd(a)$_N$- salt -(na)wę̨hd$_V$- be saturated with s.t.]
ojikeʼda:weht it is salty S

•jikjiye:ʼ chickadee
[ji+]
jikji:ye:ʼ a chickadee
•jinaʼdǫ: be handsome, good-looking
[P+ contains: -jinah$_V$- be strong, brave]
hojinʼadǫ: he is a handsome man S
•jinah be strong, be brave, male genitals
[A+]
haji:nah he is masculine, brave; his genitals S
•jinah penis, phallus
[shę̨h that ha+ -jinah$_V$- strong, brave]
shę̨h haji:nah a penis; a phallus
•jinah genitals, a male
[ga+ contains: -jinah$_V$- strong, brave]
gaji:nah it is a male; the genitals of an animal
•jihnew(a) stripe
[o+…-ǫnyǫʼ several]
ojihnewaǫnyǫʼ, ojihnowaǫnyǫʼ stripes
•jinowę̨ mouse
[ji+]
jino:wę̨: a mouse
•jinowę̨go:wah rat
[-jiʼnǫwę̨:$_N$- mouse -go:wah- big]
jinowę̨go:wah a rat
•jiʼnǫhda:s monkey
[ga+ -jiʼnǫw(a), jiʼnǫh$_N$- insect, bug -(a)hdaʼ$_V$- get full of food]
gajiʼnǫ̱hda:s monkey (lit.: it eats bugs)
•jinǫdagragw pick one's nose
[(a)de+ -jinǫ(dagra)$_N$- mucus -(h)gw$_V$- lift, pick up s.t.]
ǫdejinǫdagrahgwahs she is picking her nose H
•jiʼnǫhdoy(a) bed bug
[ji+]
jiʼnǫ̱hdo:yaʼ a bed bug

•ji'nǫge(w) blow one's nose
[P+ contains: -jinǫ(dagra)$_N$- mucus -(r)age(:,w)$_V$- wipe]
saji'nǫge:wahs you are blowing your nose H

•jinǫhgr(a) mucus
[o+]
ojinǫhgra' nasal mucus

•ji'nǫw(a), ji'nǫh bug, insect, worm
[o+]
oji'nǫ:wa' a bug; an insect; a worm

•ji'nǫwahe'da' fishworm
[o+ -ji'nǫw(a), ji'nǫh$_N$- insect, bug, worm -(h)e:'d$_V$- cause to sit up on top of s.t.]
oji'nǫwahe'da' a fishworm

•jinǫhyahae: garter snake
[ji+ -nǫhy(a)$_N$- -ohae$_V$- clean, wash]
jinǫhyahae: a garter snake

•jihnya('da) tendon, ligament, birth cord
ojihnya'da' a tendon; a ligament; a birth cord

•jihnyogod tree knot
[o+ -jihnyog(wa)$_N$- tree knot -od$_V$- stand attached object]
ojihnyogo:t a tree knot

•jihnyowaǫd be spotty
[o+ -jihnyow(a)$_N$- spot -ǫd$_V$- attached]
ojihnyowaǫt it is spotty S

•ji'ohgya'g cut one's nails
see: ji'ehgya'g [ad+(N+)] cut one's nails
ęgadeji'ohgya'k I am going to cut my nails P

•ji'o: crab
[-ji'(a)$_N$- crab -o(:)$_V$- submerge]
ji'o: a crab

•ji'ohd(a) fingernail, toenail, nail
see: ji'ehd(a) fingernail, toenail, nail
oji'ehda' **oji'ohda'** fingernails; toenails; animal nails; claws

•jiohde:s claw
see: jiehde:s, jiohde:s claw
degaji'ehde:s a claw

•ji'ohgyakta' nail clippers
[ǫ+ade+ -ji'ohd(a), ji'ehd(a)$_N$- fingernail, toenail, nail -(i)ya'gd$_V$- cut, break with s.t.]
ǫdeji'ohgya'kta' nail clippers

•ji:s cheese
[o+]
o:ji:s cheese

•jihsd(a) lamp, light, fire
[ga+]
gajihsda' a lamp
dęsejihsdawęnye:' you will poke the fire P
[de+... -jihsd(a)$_N$- light -(a)węnye(:)$_V$- stir, mix]

•jihsd(a:) grasshopper
[ji+ contains: -jihsd(a)$_N$- light]
jihsda: a grasshopper

•jihsdawęnye(:) stir, poke the fire
[de+... -jihsd(a)$_N$- light -(a)węnye(:)$_V$- stir, mix]
dęsejihsdawęnye:' you will poke the fire P
desejihsdawę:nye: stoke the fire I

•jihsdod turn on
[-jihsd(a)$_N$- light -od$_V$- stand]
shęh niyejihsdo:ta' the time when you turn the lights on H
gajihsdo:t the light is on S
sejihsdo:dęh turn on the light I

•jihsdoi'as static
[de+wa+ade+ -jihsd(a)$_N$- light, -oi'as$_V$- torch s.t.]
dewadejihsdoy'a:s static

•jihsdoi'asdahkwa' matches
[e+ -jihsd(a)$_N$- light, -oi'as$_V$- torch s.t.]
ejihsdo'a:sdahkwa' matches (an old word) (lit.: someone torches the fire) H

•jihsdota' light bulb, lamp
[ga+ -jihsd(a)$_N$- light, -od$_V$- stand]
gajihsdota' a light bulb; a lamp

Legend: H habitual, P punctual, S stative, I imperative, PURP purposive, PURP-H purposive habitual, PURP-PAST purposive past, PURP-P purposive punctual, PURP-I purposive imperative; see §8.6, §8.11 in Appendix J. Alphabetization in stems ignores length (:), and any h's or glottal stops (') that are not between vowels. See §2.2 of the User Guide for explanation.

•jihsdǫda:haʼ Venus, evening star
[ga+ -jihsd(a)$_N$- light -ǫda:(h)$_V$- put in, attached]
gajihsdǫda:haʼ the evening star; the morning star; Venus
•jihsdǫgyeʼ falling star, meteor, comet
[ga+ -jihsd(a)$_N$- light, -ǫgyeʼ$_V$- be ongoing]
gajihsdǫgyeʼ a flaming star; a meteor; a comet
•jihsgę: ghost
[-jihs(a)$_n$- -(i)gę:$_V$- be white-coloured, light]
jihsgę: a ghost
•jihsgogoʼ robin
[ji+]
jihsgogoʼ a robin
•jisgoʼg(wa) hip
sejihsgʼogwaʼgeh on your hip
•jihsgǫni mash
[de+... -jihsg(wa)$_N$- mush -ǫni, ǫny$_V$- make]
dęhseji̱hsgǫ:niʼ you will mash it up P
•jihsg(wa) porridge, mush
[o+]
ojihsgwaʼ porridge; mush
•jihsgwahihd mash
[de+... -jihsg(wa)$_N$- mush -(hr)ihd$_V$- break up with s.t.]
dęseji̱hsgwahiht you will mash it P
degaji̱hsgwahihdǫh it is smashed, mashed S
•jihsǫd(a:) cluster of stars; star
[o+]
ojihsǫda:ʼ a cluster of stars; a star
•jihsǫdahg strawberry
[ji+]
jihsǫ:dahk a strawberry
•jitgw(a:) yellow
[o+]
oji:tgwa:ʼ yellow

•jitgwa:ʼę:ʼ yellow corn
[o+ -jitgw(a:)$_N$- yellow -ʼę:ʼ$_V$- be coloured]
ojiʼtgwa:ʼę:ʼ yellow corn
•jitgwaiyo: yellow
[o+ -jitgw(a:)$_N$- yellow -iyo:$_V$- nice]
ojiʼtgwai:yo: yellow
•jitgwaji: orange
[o+ -jitgw(a:)$_N$- yellow -ji(:,h)$_V$- dark]
ojitgwa:ji: orange
•jitgwaogo:ʼ diabetes
[a+de+w+ade+ -jitgw(a:)$_N$- yellow -ogw$_V$- scatter]
adwadejitgwaogo:ʼ diabetes
•jitrehs too much
see: Appendix I
•jitsgri: have curly hair
[de+P+ -jitsgr(a)$_N$- curl -i:ʼ$_V$- be stuck onto s.t.]
deyojitsgri: it has curly hair S
•jih(wa), jihy hammer
[ga+]
gajihwaʼ hammer
gajihyowa:nęh sledgehammer, big hammer
•jiwagę: sour, bitter, salty, salty
[o+(N+)]
ojiwagę: it is sour, salty, bitter S
•jihwęd(a) bell
[o+]
ojihwędaʼ bell
•jihwęhtaʼ sparrow hawk
[ga+ -jih(wa), jihy$_N$- hammer -(y)ęhd$_V$- hit, knock down, strike]
gajihwęhtaʼ sparrow hawk
•jiyoʼ crippled, lame
[P+(N+)]
goji:yoʼ she is crippled S

•jihyod pan bread, oven bread
[ga+ -jihnyow(a)$_N$- spot -od$_V$- stand attached object]
gajihyo:t type of bread baked in a shallow pan; pan bread (it has bumps like porridge); oven bread

•jihyoha:ʼ pelican
[o+]
ojihyǫha:ʼ pelican (refers to a bag hanging from its beak)

•jihyowanęh sledgehammer
[ga+ -jih(wa), jihy$_N$- hammer -owanęh$_V$- be big]
gajihyowa:nęh sledgehammer, big hammer

•jogrihs blackbird
[j+o+ stem: -grihs$_V$- be dark]
jogrihs blackbird

•joni:tsgrǫ:t squirrel
[jo+ -(ni)tsgr(a)$_N$- saliva -ǫd$_V$- attached]
joni:tsgrǫ:t a squirrel

•jǫd filthy
see: (i)jǫd [de+P+] filthy
dewagejǫ:t, dewagijǫ:t I am filthy S

•jǫʼd(a) fish
see: (i)jǫʼd(a) fish
ojǫʼdaʼ a fish

•jǫʼdaeya: raspberry
[j+o+]
joʼdae:ya:ʼ raspberries

•jǫʼdagaʼ mink
[j+o+]
jǫʼdagaʼ a mink

•jǫnyǫ:ʼ bluebird
[j+]
jǫ:nyǫ:ʼ a bluebird

K

•ka leak, drip, trickle
[(N+)]
okahs it leaks H
ęyo:kaʼ it will leak P

•(ʼ)k(a:) slip
[ga+]
gaʼka:ʼ a slip

•(ʼ)ka:ʼ be hen-pecked
[P+ade+ -(ʼ)k(a:)$_N$- skirt slip -(h)awi, (h)a:$_V$- hold, include, carry, bring]
hodeʼka:ʼ he is hen-pecked S

•kahǫ(:) assemble, put together
[de+...(N+)]
dęhsegahǫʼ (**dęhsekahǫʼ**) you will assemble, put things together P
desekahǫ: you match or pair things up (puzzle pieces, socks) I

•kahǫʼ adjoin, abutt
[N+ occurs in:]
degaihwakahǫʼ alliance S
[de+ga+ stem: -(r)ihwakahǫʼ- alliance consists of: -(r)ih(wa)$_N$- word -kahǫ$_V$- adjoin, assemble, put together]

•(ʼ)kaowe:s be hen-pecked
[TR+ -(ʼ)k(a:)$_N$- skirt, slip -oweg$_V$- cover]
hǫwaʼkaowe:s he is hen-pecked H

•(ʼ)kaǫdahkwaʼ breech cloth
[ǫ+ade+ -(ʼ)k(a:)$_N$- skirt, slip -ǫdahkwaʼ$_V$- attached implement]
ǫdeʼkaǫ:dahkwaʼ a breech cloth

•kahs(i) share, divide, take apart
[de+...(N+)]
degekahsǫhs I divide it H
dęhsekahsiʼ you will share, divide P
dewagekahshǫ: I have taken one object apart S

•kahsǫ: division
[de+ga+ -kahs(i)$_V$- share, divide]
degakahsǫ: a division; it is separated

Legend: H habitual, P punctual, S stative, I imperative, PURP purposive, PURP-H purposive habitual, PURP-PAST purposive past, PURP-P purposive punctual, PURP-I purposive imperative; see §8.6, §8.11 in Appendix J. Alphabetization in stems ignores length (:), and any h's or glottal stops (ʼ) that are not between vowels. See §2.2 of the User Guide for explanation.

•kahsǫgw divide into parts
[(de+)...(N+) contains: -kahs(i)$_V$- share, divide]
dęhsekahsǫ꞉goʼ you will divide it into parts P
hoihwakahshǫgweh he has divided into parts or duties S
[(de+)...(N+) -(r)ih(wa)$_N$- word -kahsǫgw$_V$- divide into parts]

•kahsǫgwahǫ divide into parts
[de+...(N+) contains: -kahs(i)$_V$- share, divide]
dęsehkahsǫgwa̱hǫʼ you will divide them (several objects) up into categories P
desehkahsǫgwa̱hǫ꞉ divide them (several objects) up into categories I

•kd(a) nutshell
[o+]
okdaʼ a nutshell

•kdaʼe(g) shell s.t.
[de+... -kd(a)$_N$- nutshell -(ʼ)e(g)$_V$- hit]
dehsekdaʼe꞉k shell them; hit the shell I

•kdaʼe(g) peck s.t.
[TR+ -kd(a)$_N$- nutshell -(ʼ)e(g)$_V$- hit]
ęhsaʼkdaʼe꞉k it will peck you P

•kdagǫʼ black squirrel, grey squirrel
[-kdeh(a)$_N$ - edible root -agǫ꞉ in]
kda꞉gǫʼ grey squirrel; black squirrel

•kdeh(a) root (edible)
[o+]
okdehaʼ edible roots (pepper roots, turnips, carrots, etc.)

•kdeha꞉s edible roots
[e+ -kdeh(a)$_N$- root (edible) -g$_V$- eat]
ekdeha꞉s edible roots (pepper roots, turnips, carrots, etc.)

•kdots(i) shell s.t.
[-kd(a)$_N$- nutshell -ots(i)$_V$- remove an outer covering]
ęhsekdo꞉tsih you will shell (eggs, coconuts, etc.) P

•kdǫ(꞉) taste, examine, look closely at s.t.
hadikdo̱haʼ they (m) examine it H
age꞉kdǫ꞉ʼ I looked closely at it; I have examined it P
sekdǫ꞉ examine it I

•kdǫ(꞉) test s.o.
[TR+]
ęgwa꞉kdǫ꞉ʼ I will test you all P

•kdǫʼd a good view
[o+ contains: -kdǫ(꞉)$_V$- taste, examine, look closely at s.t.]
okdǫʼt a good view

•kdǫhn go visit s.o., go look
[TR+ contains: -kdǫ(꞉)$_V$- taste, examine, look closely at s.t.]
ękekdo̱hnaʼ I am going to see her P
knikdǫhnah let's go look I

•kdǫnyǫ(꞉) examine fully
[contains: -kdǫ(꞉)$_V$- taste, examine, look closely at s.t. -nyǫʼ several]
ęhsekdǫnyǫʼ you will fully examine it P
dwakdǫ꞉nyǫ꞉ let's examine it I

•kęh be twins
[de+ A+]
dęhadikęh twin boys S

•kjin(a) stump, knots in a tree
[o+]
okji꞉naʼ a stump; knots in a tree

•kjinǫd tree knot
[o+ -kjin(a)$_N$- stump -ǫd$_V$- attached]
okji꞉nǫ꞉t knot in a tree

•kǫni cook
[-k(wa)$_N$- food -ǫni, ǫny$_V$- make]
gakǫ꞉nihs it cooks H
age꞉kǫ꞉niʼ I cooked a meal P
gokǫ꞉ni꞉ she is cooking S
sekǫ꞉nih cook I

•kǫni eat
[ade+ -k(wa)$_N$- food -ǫni, ǫny$_V$- make]
gaǫ꞉dekǫ꞉nih they (f/m) eat H
agęnadekǫ꞉niʼ they (z) ate P
hode꞉kǫ꞉ni꞉ he is eating S

•kǫni: cooking
[ga+ -k(wa)$_N$- food -ǫni, ǫny$_V$- make]
gakǫ:ni: (the act of) cooking
•kǫnige: feast
[ade+ -k(wa)$_N$- food -ǫni, ǫny$_V$- make -ge: big]
ęhsadekǫnige: you will feast P
•kǫnya'ta' dining hall
[(a)de+ -kǫnya'd$_V$- cause to eat]
dekǫny'ata' a dining hall
•kǫnya'ta'geh restaurant, cafeteria, dining room, dining hall
[ǫ+ade+-kǫnya'd$_V$- cause to eat -'geh on, at]
ǫdekǫnya'ta'geh a restaurant; a cafeteria; a dining room; a dining hall
•ksa:'ah child, boy, girl
haksa:'ah he is a child; a boy
eksa:'ah she is a child (under 12); a girl
•ksa('da) child, boy, girl
ageks'ada' my child
oksa'da̱he:tgę' a spoiled child
[o+ stem: -ksa('da)$_N$- child -(hr)etgę'$_V$- evil, bad, ugly].
•ksa'dase:'ah teenager
[A+ -ksa('da)$_N$- child -(a)se:$_V$- be new -'ah diminutive]
haksa'dase:'ah he is a teenage boy
eksa'dase:'ah she is a teenage girl
•ksa'dǫni be childish, immature
[ade+ -ksa('da)$_N$- child -ǫni, ǫny$_V$- make]
ǫdeks'adǫ:nih she is childish H
•kse'd(a) belly
okse'da' a belly
sekse'da'geh on your belly
•kse'dod belly button, navel
[A+ -(i)kse'd(a)$_N$- belly -od$_V$- stand]
gikse'do:t my navel
ekse'do:t her belly button
•ksohaehs dish washer
[ga+ -ks(a)$_N$- dish -ohae$_V$- clean, wash]
gaksohaehs a dish washer
•k(wa) food
[ga+]
gakwa' food
•(h)kw take s.t. from s.o.
[N+]
ęhshenǫgwahkwa' you will take the milk from the child (that is, wean the child) P
[TR+ stem: -nǫgwahkgw- wean; consists of: -nǫ'g(wa)$_N$- breast, milk -(h)kw$_V$- take s.t. from s.o.]
•(h)kwa' rhythm, beat
[de+yo+ -(h)gw$_V$- lift, pick up]
deyohkwa' a steady rhythm, beat; a throbbing
•kwadaiha'ta' toaster oven
[ga+ -k(wa)$_N$- food -(')daiha'd$_V$- heat up]
gakwadaiha'ta' a toaster oven
•kwaędahkwa' cupboard, pantry
[e+ -k(wa)$_N$- food -ędahkwa'$_V$- container]
ekwaędahkwa' a cupboard; a pantry
•kwagewahta' serviette, napkin
[ǫ+ ade+ -k(wa)$_N$- food -(r)age(:,w)$_V$- wipe]
ǫdekwagewa̱hta' serviettes; napkins
•kwaheha' waiter, waitress
[A+ -k(wa)$_N$- food -(hr)e, (hr)ę$_V$- put, place]
hakwaheha' he is a waiter
ekwaheha' she is a waitress
•kwahe:' tea meeting, supper
[ga+ -k(wa)$_N$- food -(h)e:'$_V$- sitting up on top of s.t.]
gakwahe:' tea meetings; supper
•kwahę' serve a meal
[TR+ade+ -k(wa)$_N$- food -(hr)e, (hr)ę$_V$- put, place]
agaǫ:dekwahę' they (f/m) put on a meal P

Legend: H habitual, P punctual, S stative, I imperative, PURP purposive, PURP-H purposive habitual, PURP-PAST purposive past, PURP-P purposive punctual, PURP-I purposive imperative; see §8.6, §8.11 in Appendix J. Alphabetization in stems ignores length (:), and any h's or glottal stops (') that are not between vowels. See §2.2 of the User Guide for explanation.

•kwahihtaʼ food processor
[de+ga+ -k(wa)$_N$- food -(hr)ihd$_V$- break up]
degakwahihtaʼ a food processor
•kwa:hkwaʼ stomach
[A+ -k(wa)$_N$- food -(h)gw$_V$- lift, pick up]
ekwa:hkwaʼ a stomach
gekwa:hkwaʼ my stomach (lit.: where I put the food)
•kwanǫd serve a meal
[-k(wa)$_N$- food -nǫd$_V$- feed]
ęhsadadekwanǫ:t you will serve yourself a meal P
•kwahsnoweʼ fast-food cooker
[ga+ -k(wa)$_N$- food -(h)snoweʼ$_V$- fast]
gakwahsno:weʼ a fast-food cooker
•kwatgehǫ auction s.t.
[A+ade+ -k(wa)$_N$- food - (a)tgehǫ$_V$- sell]
honadekwatgehǫʼ they (m) are auctioning off the food
•kwędaʼ finish eating
[-k(wa)$_N$- food -ędaʼ$_V$- finish]
ęga:kwę:daʼ it is going to finish eating P
agekwędaʼǫh I have finished eating S
•kyętw be seated
[occurs in:]
dętgahnegakyętoʼ it will be low tide P
[-(h)neg(a)$_N$- water -kyętw$_V$- be seated]

N

•(h)n(a) oil, gas
[o+]
ohnaʼ grease; oil; gas; gravy, etc.
•(h)n(a) material, skin
see: (i)hn(a) material, skin
gihnaʼgeh on my skin

•naʼd lunch
[adę+]
ęga:dę:naʼt I will take a lunch P
agadęnaʼdǫh I have taken a lunch S
•nahd(a) comb
[ga+]
ganahdaʼ a comb
•naʼd(a:) bread
[o+]
onaʼda:ʼ bread
•nad(a) town, community
[ga+]
gana:daʼ a town; a community
•nadaę(:) inhabit
[at+ -nad(a)$_N$- town, community -ę$_V$- lie]
ęsatnadaęʼ you will inhabit P
•nadaę(:) camp
[ę+ -nad(a)$_N$- town, community -ę$_V$- lie]
ęhsęnadaę:ʼ you will camp P
•naʼdaę:ʼdahs toaster
[ga+ -naʼd(a:)$_N$- bread -(hr)ęʼda:$_V$- burn s.t.]
ganaʼdaę:ʼdahs a toaster
•naʼdag snack
[stem: -naʼdag- snack; consists of: -naʼd(a:)$_N$- bread -g$_V$- eat]
ęjidwanaʼda:k we all (incl.) will snack (lit.: we all (incl.) will eat bread) P
•nadagehonǫʼ urban dwellers, city dwellers
[ga+ -nad(a)$_N$- town, community -ʼge- on -hǫ:nǫʼ dwellers]
ganadagehо:nǫʼ urban dwellers; city people; urbanites
•naʼdagidaǫ fried bread
[ga+ stem: -naʼd(a:)$_N$- bread -gidaǫ$_V$- fry]
ganaʼda:gi:daǫ fried bread

•nadahęh village square, village centre, town square
[tsa'de+ga+ -nad(a)$_N$- town, community -(h)ęh$_V$- be mid, be in the middle]
tsa'deganadahęh a village square; a village centre; a town square

•na'daiksǫ:' snack
ęjidwana'daiksǫ:' we all (incl.) will snack (lit.: we all (incl.) will bite the bread) P

•na'dahkwa' bread container
[e+ -na'd(a:)$_N$- bread -(h)gw$_V$- lift, pick up]
ena'da:kwa' a bread container

•na'daos'uh cookies
[ni+yo+ -na'd(a:)$_N$- bread -u:'suh$_V$- several small objects]
niyon'adao:s'uh cookies

•na'daǫd bannock
[ti+wa+at+ -na'd(a:)$_N$- bread -ǫd$_V$- roasted]
tiwatna'daǫt coal-baked bannock

•na'daǫnihs baker
[A+ -na'd(a:)$_N$- bread -ǫni, ǫny$_V$- make]
hana'daǫnihs he is a baker

•na'da:'tę: cracker
[o+ -na'd(a:)$_N$- bread -tę(:)$_V$- be dry]
ona'da:'tę: crackers

•nadinyǫ('d) move in
[ę/ad+ -nad(a)$_N$- town, community -inyǫ('d)$_V$- put in]
gęnadinyǫ'ta' I am moving into a dwelling H
ęgęnadi:nyǫ' I will be moving into a dwelling P
gonęnadinyǫ'dǫh they (f/m) have moved in S

•nadowanęh city
[ga+ -nad(a)$_N$- town, community -owanęh$_V$- be big]
ganadowa:nęh a city

•nadǫh black snake
[ha+]
hana:dǫh a black snake

•nadu:'uh village, small town
[ni+ga+ -nad(a)$_N$- town, community -u:'uh$_V$- small]
niganadu:'uh a village; a small town

•na'ehs step-mother
sana'ehs your step-mother S

•naga:, nagai whistle
[contains: -na'g(a)$_N$- horn, antler]
hana:ga: he is whistling H
ęsnagai: you will whistle P
snagai: whistle I

•na'g(a:) horn, antler
[o+]
ona'ga:' horns; antlers

•na'gad flute
[ga+ -na'g(a)$_N$- horn, antler -d$_V$- stand]
gana:ga:t a traditional flute (made of wood)

•na'gaǫd sheep, ram, horned animal
[de+P+ -na'g(a)$_N$- horn, antler -ǫd$_V$- attached]
deyodina'gaǫt horned animals
deyon'agaǫt sheep; lambs; elk

•na'gaǫdǫ' herd of sheep, horned animal, Billy Goat Dance
[de+P+ -na'g(a)$_N$- horn, antler -ǫdǫ'$_V$- several attached objects]
deyodina'gaǫ:dǫ' a herd of sheep; horned animals; the Billy Goat Dance

•na'gawihdr(a) belt
[at+ -na'g(a)$_N$- horn -(a)wihd$_N$- be inserted]
atna'gawihdra' a belt

•nagęhsrǫni hill s.t.
[-nagęhsr(a)$_N$- hill -ǫni, ǫny$_V$- make]
snagęhsrǫni:' you make hills to plant in I

Legend: H habitual, P punctual, S stative, I imperative, PURP purposive, PURP-H purposive habitual, PURP-PAST purposive past, PURP-P purposive punctual, PURP-I purposive imperative; see §8.6, §8.11 in Appendix J. Alphabetization in stems ignores length (:), and any h's or glottal stops (') that are not between vowels. See §2.2 of the User Guide for explanation.

•na'gow lack a spirit, be ominous, be imbued with potentially dangerous power
[de'+(s+) P+]
o:nęh dejagona'go:wahs she is ominous H

•(h)na'gǫ: under, beneath, below, on the bottom
[o+ -(h)na'gǫh$_V$- bottom]
ohna:gǫ: under
ohna'gǫh tga:yęh it lies underneath, below S

•(')nahgǫd bee swarm, bee sting
[P+ -(')nahg(a)$_N$- sting -ǫd$_V$- attached]
ęsa'na̱hgǫ:dę' (you will get a) bee sting P
o'nahgǫ:t it (skin) is inflamed; a bee sting S

•(h)na'gǫ̱hka:'
[-(h)na'gǫh$_V$- bottom -ka:'- type of]
hna'gǫ̱hka:' underwear

•(')nahgǫta' bee
[ga+ -(')nahg(a)$_N$- bee sting -ǫd$_V$- attached]
g'anahgǫta' a bee

•nagrad be born
[ę+ contains: -nagre', nagrad$_V$- live]
ǫna:gra:s the birthing H
a'ǫnagra:t birth (lit.: s.o. was born) P
agęnagra:dǫh I was born S

•nagre' live
[A+]
gae:nagre' where they (f/m) live; an area S

•nagre' be rare
[(tę') not de+s+ga+ contains: -nagre', nagrad$_V$- live]
dehsganagre' it is rare S

•nahg(wa) drum, barrel
[ga+]
ganahgwa' a bass drum; a barrel

•(')nahg(wa) wife, marriage
see: (')nahk(wa) wife, marriage
ganahkwa' a marriage

•na'gwiy cotton batting
[o+]
ona'gwi:ya' cotton batting

•na'gy(ę, ani) imitate, mock, mimic
[(d+)TR+]
ętsna'gyę:' you will imitate, mock, mimic, s.t. P
ędisana'gyę:' it will imitate, mock, mimic you P

•nahaita'corn napper
see: nęhaita' corn bug, corn napper
ganahaita' a corn napper (an insect similar to a preying mantis)

•nahawenye(:) crazy, insane
[de+ -nǫh(a), nah(a)$_N$- scalp -(a)węnye(:)$_V$- stir, mix]
degena̱ha:we:nye' I am crazy H
dęsęna̱hawęnye:' you will go insane P

•nai be proud
enai: she is proud in a boastful manner S

•nai: pride, boastfulness
[ga+ contains: -nai$_V$- be proud]
ganai: pride; boastfulness

•(h)nai:' oily, greasy
[o+ -(h)n(a)$_N$- oil, gas -i:'$_V$- be stuck onto s.t.]
ohnai:' it is oily, greasy S

•nai'd(a) peacock
[ga+ contains: -nai$_V$- be proud]
ganai'da' a peacock; pride; boastfulness

•na'j(a) pail
[ga+]
gana'ja' a pail

•na(')j(da) grain
[occurs in:]
ganajayę:twęh a wheat field; a grain field
[stem: -na(')ja(da)$_N$- wheat, grain -yętw, yęto$_V$- plant]

•na(ʼ)j(da) grain (continued)
ganaʼjawęhę:s grain auger
[ga+ stem: -naʼjawęhęs- auger; consists of: -na(ʼ)ja(da)$_N$- wheat, grain -węhę(h)d$_V$- climb s.t.]
•najʼaehs thresher
[ga+ -na(ʼ)ja(da)$_N$- wheat, grain -(ʼ)ehsd$_V$- hit with s.t.]
ganajʼaehs a grain threshing machine
•naʼjagęʼd rice
[o+ -na(ʼ)ja(da)$_N$- wheat, grain -(ʼ)gęd$_V$- be light-coloured]
onaʼjagę:t rice
•naʼjagęʼdo:ʼ radiator
[ga+ -naʼj(a)$_N$- pail, drum -gęʼdo:ʼ$_V$- be stuck under s.t.]
ganaʼjagęʼdo:ʼ a radiator
•naʼjaoweh iron kettle
[ga+-naʼj(a)$_N$- pail, drum -o:weh traditional]
ganaʼjʼaǫweh traditional cooking pots with the feet; an iron kettle
•naʼjashǫ:ʼǫh cooking pots
[ga+-naʼj(a)$_N$- pail, drum -shǫ:ʼǫh several objects]
ganaʼjashǫ:ʼǫh cooking pots
•naʼjawęhęs auger
[ga+ -na(ʼ)ja(da)$_N$- wheat, grain -węhę(h)d$_V$- climb s.t.]
ganaʼjawęhę:s a grain auger
•(h)naji: motor oil, black grease
[o+ -(h)n(a)$_N$- oil, gas -ji(:,h)$_V$- dark]
ohna:ji: motor oil; black grease
•naʼjod boil
[-naʼj(a)$_N$- pail, drum -od$_V$- stand]
ęhsnaʼjo:dęʼ you will boil s.t. P
ganaʼjo:t it is boiled (lit.: it is a standing pot) S
•naʼjohaiʼtaʼ cleaner
[e+ -naʼj(a)$_N$- pail, drum -ohaeʼd$_V$- clean with s.t.]
enaʼjǫhaiʼtaʼ a pot cleaner
•naʼj(oh(s)gwa) cup
[ga+]
ganaʼjǫhsgwaʼ a cup
•naʼjǫ: drum, water drum
[ga+ -naʼj(a)$_N$- pail, drum -ǫ:$_V$- resemble]
ganaʼjǫ: a drum; a water drum
•nakd(a) bed, seat
[ga+]
gana:kdaʼ a bed; a seat
•nakdahe: upstairs
[g+yo+ -nakd(a)$_N$- bed, seat -(h)e:ʼ$_V$- sitting up on top of s.t.]
gyonakdahe: upstairs
•nakdahe: loft
[o+ -nakd(a)$_N$- bed, seat -(h)e:ʼ$_V$- sitting up on top of s.t.]
onakdahe: a loft
•nakdiyohsd make oneself comfortable
[(at+) -nakd(a)$_N$- bed, seat -iyohsd$_V$- make nice, good]
agatnakdi:yohs I made myself comfortable P
•nakdowektaʼ bedspread
[e+ -nakd(a)$_N$- bed, seat -(hr)owegd$_V$- cover with s.t.]
enakdowe:ktaʼ a bedspread
•(ʼ)nahk(wa) wife, marriage
[ga+]
ganahkwaʼ a marriage
aknaʼgwaʼ my wife
•naʼkwad be maddening, irritating
[o+ contains: -naʼkwę(h,ʼ), naʼgǫ$_V$- be angry]
onaʼkwat it is irritating, maddening S
•naʼkwę(h,ʼ), naʼgǫ- be angry
[P+]
aknaʼkwęhs s.t. makes me angry H
ahonakwęh he became very angry P
aknaʼkwęʼǫh I am angry S
•naʼnawęʼ
see: nawęʼ [N+/naʼ+] thaw, melt
ganaʼnawęʼs it melts H

Legend: H habitual, P punctual, S stative, I imperative, PURP purposive, PURP-H purposive habitual, PURP-PAST purposive past, PURP-P purposive punctual, PURP-I purposive imperative; see §8.6, §8.11 in Appendix J. Alphabetization in stems ignores length (:), and any h's or glottal stops (ʼ) that are not between vowels. See §2.2 of the User Guide for explanation.

•na'nawę̨hd wet s.t., melt s.t., liquefy s.t.
see: nawę̨hd [ga+N+/na'+] wet s.t., melt s.t., liquefy s.t.
ahan'ana:wę̨ht he wet it P

•na'nawę̨hdah melt s.t., liquefy s.t.
see: nawę̨hdah melt s.t., liquefy s.t.
gana'nawę̨'dahǫh it has been melted S

•(h)naned level
[o+ -(h)n(a)$_N$- oil, gas -ned$_V$- keep -nyǫ' several]
ohna'neda:nyǫ' several levels

•(h)naned lining, insulated wall
see: (i)hnaned lining, insulated wall
degahnane:t lining; an insulated wall

•na'no:' be cold, cool
see: no:' [P+N/na'+] be cold, cool
ona'no:' it is cold, cool S

•na'nohsta' refrigerator
[ga+na'+ -nohsd$_V$- chill s.t.]
gana'no̱hsta' a refrigerator

•nahnǫh be full
[occurs in:]
ga:gwanahnǫh the full moon (which brings rain) S
[ga+ stem: -(r)agwanahnǫh- full moon; consists of: -(r)ag(wa)$_N$- the sun, the moon -nahnǫh$_V$- be full]

•(')na'sę: poison
[o+ -(h)n(a)$_N$- oil, gas -(a's)ę'$_V$- fall, reduce]
o'na'sę: poison
onahsę: water hemlock

•nahsgǫni tame
[at+ -nahsg(wa)$_N$- domestic animal, pet -ǫni, ǫny$_V$- make]
ahatna̱hsgǫni' he raised a pet P
watnahsgǫ:ni: it has been made into a pet S

•na'sgǫni make oneself comfortable
[at+ -na'sg(wa)$_N$- mattress -ǫni, ǫny$_V$- make]
ę̨satn'asgǫ:ni' you will get comfortable in bed P

•na'sgw skip
[de -na'sg(wa)$_N$- lower body -(h)gwę̨hę̨gye'$_V$- go along lifting, picking up]
deyagona'sgwę̨hę̨gye' she is skipping along S

•nahsg(wa) tame animal, pet, domestic animal
[ga+]
ganahsgwa' a tame animal; a pet; a domestic animal

•na'sg(wa), nahsg(wa) mattress, having to do with the lower body
[o+ occurs in:]
ona'sgwa' a mattress
dehanahsgwe:s he jumps far horizontally S
[de+A+ -na'sg(wa)$_N$- lower body -es$_V$- long]
deyagona'sgwę̨hę̨gye' she is skipping along S
[de -na'sg(wa)$_N$- lower body -(h)gwę̨hę̨gye'$_V$- go along lifting, picking up]

•na'sgwes, nahsgwes jump far
[de+A+ -na'sg(wa)$_N$- lower body -es$_V$- long]
dehanahsgwe:s he jumps far horizontally S

•na'sgweso's, nahsgweso's jump high
[de+A+ -na'sg(wa)$_N$- mattress -esǫ's$_V$- several long objects]
dehanahsgwe:so's he jumps high S

•(h)nasǫ(:) oil oneself
[at+ -(h)n(a)$_N$- oil, gas -sǫ$_V$- stir]
hatna:sǫ' he is oiling himself H
ahatna:sǫ' he oiled himself P
satna:sǫ: oil yourself I

•nahsǫd join
[de+ -nahs(a)-$_N$ -ǫd(ę)$_V$- be attached]
dę̨hsnahsǫ:dę' you will join P
dega̱nahsǫ:dǫ' many things are joined together (for example, on a train) S

•nahsǫta', nohsǫta' particle
[de+ga+ -nahsǫd$_V$- join]
deganǫhsǫ:ta' (deganahsǫ:ta') a particle (lit.: joiners)
•(h)natę: have dry skin
see: (i)hnatę: [A+] have dry skin
sehna:tę:, sihna:tę: you have dry skin S
•(h)natęhsdǫh cradle-robber
see: (i)hnatęhsdǫh cradle-robber
ohnatęhsdǫh dried-up skin (a derogatory term referring to s.o. with a younger woman or man)
•na'tr(a) food, lunch
[ade+]
adęn'atra' lunch; groceries
•na'traęni feed
[TR+adę+ -na'tr(a)$_N$- food, lunch -ęni$_V$- lay s.t. down for someone's benefit]
shǫgwadęna'traę:ni: the food he has given us S
•(h)na'ts(a) buttock, behind, ass
ohna'tsa' a buttock; an ass
sn'atsa'geh on your buttocks
•(h)na'tsa'e(g) spank
[TR+ -(h)na'ts(a)$_N$- buttock -(')e(g)$_V$- hit]
ęhyan'atsa'e:k he will spank you P
•(h)na'tsagęnye' fidgety
[P+at+ -(h)na'ts(a)$_N$- buttock -gęni, gęny$_V$- compete]
satna'tsagę:nye' you are fidgety H
•(h)na'tsędǫh shake one's behind
[de+...at+ -(h)na'ts(a)$_N$- buttock -ędǫh$_V$- shake s.t.]
dęhsatn'atsę:dǫ' you will shake your behind P
•naw(a) pond, swamp
[ga+ … -gǫ: in]
ganawagǫ: in the pond; in the swamp
•(h)naw(a), (h)nǫw(a) running water
[occurs in:]
ohnawada:se: whirlpool
[-(h)naw(a)$_N$- running water -dase:$_V$- whirl]
ohnawadeht strong currents
[o+ stem: -(h)nawadehd- strong current; consists of: -(h)naw(a)$_N$- running water -dehd$_V$- bold, bright, strong]
•nawad(a) clay, plaster, white-wash
[o+]
onawada' clay; plaster; white-wash
•(h)nawadase: whirlpool
[o+ -(h)naw(a)$_N$- water, running -dase:$_V$- whirl]
ohnawada:se: a whirlpool
•(h)nawadehd strong currents
[o+ -(h)naw(a)$_N$- flowing water -dehd$_V$- bold, bright, strong]
ohnawadeht strong currents
•(h)nawadeni, (h)nawadeny, (h)nǫwadeni, (h)nawǫdeny strain
[N+ -(h)naw(a)$_N$- running water -deni, deny$_V$- change]
ęhsnǫwade:ni' you will strain P
ganǫwade:nyǫ: it is being strained S
•(h)nawaędahgw filter water
[contains: -(h)naw(a)$_N$- water, running -ędahgw$_V$- raise from the ground]
ęhsnǫwaęhdahk you will filter the water P
•(h)nawaǫd well, spring
[o+ -(h)naw(a)$_N$- water, running -ǫd$_V$- stand -ǫnyǫ' several]
ohnawaǫ:dǫnyǫ' many wells, springs
•nawę wet
[A/P+N+ occurs in:]
ji'dana:wę: butterfly (lit.: s.t. is wet, referring to the transformation)
[-ji'd(a)- cry -nawę:$_V$- be wet]
•nawę' thaw, melt
[N+/na'+ -nawę$_V$- be wet]
gana'nawę's it melts H
ęhsgan'ana:wę' it will thaw again, melt again P
ona'nawę'ǫh it has thawed, melted S

Legend: H habitual, P punctual, S stative, I imperative, PURP purposive, PURP-H purposive habitual, PURP-PAST purposive past, PURP-P purposive punctual, PURP-I purposive imperative; see §8.6, §8.11 in Appendix J. Alphabetization in stems ignores length (:), and any h's or glottal stops (') that are not between vowels. See §2.2 of the User Guide for explanation.

•nawęhd wet s.t., melt s.t., liquefy s.t.
[ga+N+/naˀ+ contains: -nawę$_V$- be wet]
ganaˀnawęht it is melted S
•nawęhd wet s.t., melt s.t., liquefy s.t.
[N+/naˀ+ contains: -nawę$_V$- be wet]
ahanaˀna:węht he wet it P
onaˀnawęhdǫh it has been melted S
•nawęˀd(a) sugar, candy
nawęˀdaˀ sugar; candy
•nawęˀdah melt s.t., liquefy s.t.
[ga+N+/naˀ+ -nawę$_V$- be wet]
ganaˀnawęˀdahǫh it has been melted S
•nawęˀdaweht onęhęˀse: sweet corn
nawęˀdaweht it is sweet; rich
onęhęˀse: new corn
•hne:ˀ in fact
see: Appendix I
•ne:ˀ that
see: Appendix I
•neˀ that
see: Appendix I
•ne:ˀ gwahs hwaˀ it's that one for sure
see: Appendix I
•neˀ ǫ:weh that really
see: Appendix I
•neˀag sin
gri̱hwaneˀa:s I am a sinner H
ęgrihwane:ˀa:k I will sin P
agrihwaneˀagǫh I have sinned S
•neˀd(a:) roe
[o+]
oneˀda: roe (fish eggs)
•neˀd(a), nǫd(a) valley
[ga+ … -gǫ:- in, under]
ganeˀdagǫ: in, under the valley
onǫdagǫ: in the valley
•neˀd(a), nǫd(a) hill
[o+ stem: -nǫd(a), neˀd(a)$_N$- hill
-(h)e:ˀ$_V$- sitting up on top of s.t.]
onǫda̱he:ˀ a hill
•nedadęhdaę(:) lay a floor
[-neda:dęhd(a)$_N$- floor -ę(:)$_V$- lay s.t. down]
ęhsneda:dęhdaęˀ you will lay a floor P
•(h)neˀdr(a) soil, ground
ohneˀdrˀageh on the ground
•neˀdraˀdanih be nauseous, nauseated
[P+]
akneˀdraˀdanih I am nauseated, nauseous H
•(ˀ)neg pray, hope
[-(r)ih(wa)$_N$- word, matter, affair
-(ˀ)neg$_V$- pray]
sri̱hwanˀekaˀ you are always praying H
ęhsrihwˀane:k you will pray P
saihwˀane:gęh you are praying S
•(h)neg(a) water, liquid
[o+ -(h)neg(a)$_N$- water, liquid -ˀgeh- on, at]
ohnegˀageh on the water
•(h)nega:ˀ level
[ga+ -(h)neg(a)$_N$- water, liquid -a:ˀ$_V$- hold, contain, include]
ga̱hne:ga:ˀ a level
•(h)negad be watery
[ga+ -(h)neg(a)$_N$- water, liquid -d$_V$- stand]
ga̱hne:ga:t it is watery S
•(h)negad be drunk, tipsy
[(tęˀ) deˀ+ not P+at+ -(h)neg(a)$_N$- water, liquid -d$_V$- stand]
dihsa:tne:ga:t you are not level; you are tipsy S
•(h)negadase: whirlpool
[o+at+ -(h)neg(a)$_N$- water, liquid -dase$_V$- whirl]
otnegada:se: a whirlpool
•(h)negadeni, (h)negadeny drain s.t.
[N+ -(h)neg(a)$_N$- water, liquid -deni, deny$_V$- change]
snegade:nih drain it (potatoes, etc.) I
•(h)negagaˀǫh pop, soda
[o+ -(h)neg(a)$_N$- water, liquid -gaˀǫh$_V$- be good-tasting]
ohnegagaˀǫh pop; soda

•(h)negagęhyad above the water
[o+ -(h)neg(a)$_N$- water, liquid -gęhyad$_V$- be at the edge of]
ohnegagęhya:t just above the water S

•(h)negagre' rubber coat
[o+ -(h)neg(a)$_N$- water, liquid -gri'$_V$- juice, liquid -e$_V$- go]
ohnegagre' a rubber coat

•(h)negagri' soup, rubber
[o+ -(h)neg(a)$_N$- water, liquid -gri'$_V$- juice, liquid]
ohnegagri' soup; rubber

•(h)negagyęhętw sip
[d+... -(h)neg(a)$_N$- water, liquid -yęhętw, yęhęto$_V$- pull]
ęhtsnegagyęhęto' you will sip through a straw P

•(h)negahe'dahkwa' animal watering place, watering hole, trough
[A+ -(h)neg(a)$_N$- water, liquid -(hr)e'dahkwa'$_V$- place where s.t. is put]
gadihnegahe'dahkwa' an animal watering place; a watering hole; a trough

•(h)negahe be high tide
[de+... -(h)neg(a)$_N$- water, liquid -(h)e:'$_V$- sitting up on top of s.t.]
ętgahnegahe:k it will be high tide

•(h)negahihǫh spring water
[g+yo+ -(h)neg(a)$_N$- water, liquid -(adi)hǫh$_V$- lean against s.t.]
gyohnegahihǫh spring water

•(h)negahkwa' water spout
[de+ga+ -(h)neg(a)$_N$- water, liquid -(h)gw$_V$- lift, pick up]
degahnegahkwa' a water spout

•(h)negahkwa' animal watering place, watering hole, trough
[hadi+ -(h)neg(a)$_N$- water, liquid -(h)gw$_V$- lift, pick up]
hadihnegahkwa' an animal watering place; a watering hole; a trough

•(h)neganawę: lead, lukewarm water, prepubescent boy
[o+ -(h)neg(a)$_N$- water, liquid -nawę:$_V$- be wet]
ohnegana:wę: lead; lukewarm water; a word referring to a prepubescent boy

•(h)neganyo hangover
[P+ -(h)neg(a)$_N$- water, liquid -(r)iyo, nyo$_V$- kill s.t.]
hohneganyohs he has a hangover H

•(h)negatgi' scum
[o+ -(h)neg(a)$_N$- water, liquid -tgi'$_V$- be dirty, ugly]
ohnegatgi' scum; dirty water

•(h)negatsęi, (h)negatsęny divine, witch for water
[-(h)neg(a)$_N$- water, liquid -tsęi, tsęny$_V$- find]
hadihnegatsęnyǫhs they (m) divine, witch for water H

•(h)negayehsd dilute
[de+... -(h)neg(a)$_N$- water, liquid -yehsd$_V$- add]
dehsnegayehs dilute it I

•(h)negeha drink
gahnegęha' it is drinking H
ęyehnegeha' she will drink P
snegehah drink I

•negę: be side by side
[occurs in:]
deyagwęnǫhsane:gę: we all (excl.) are neighbours (lit.: our houses are side by side) S
[de+ -nǫhs(a)$_N$- houses -negę:$_V$- be side by side]

•(h)negę'gwahd tidal wave
[de+...at+ -(h)neg(a)$_N$- water, liquid -ę'gw, (a)hdę'gw$_V$- swell up]
dawatnegę'gwaht a tidal wave

•negę'nage' that is what
see: Appendix I

•ne'gi'ę:' that is the one (emphatic)
see: Appendix I

Legend: H habitual, P punctual, S stative, I imperative, PURP purposive, PURP-H purposive habitual, PURP-PAST purposive past, PURP-P purposive punctual, PURP-I purposive imperative; see §8.6, §8.11 in Appendix J. Alphabetization in stems ignores length (:), and any h's or glottal stops (') that are not between vowels. See §2.2 of the User Guide for explanation.

•ne'gi'gyę:' that's the one
see: Appendix I
•ne'gi'nih and that too; also
see: Appendix I
•ne:'gi'shęh probably
see: Appendix I
•ne:gihshęhwa' maybe that
see: Appendix I
•(h)nego' puddle, water
[o+ -(h)neg(a)$_N$- water, liquid -o'$_V$- submerged -nyǫ' several items]
ohne:go' a puddle; any type of water S
ohnegǫnyǫ' lots of puddles
•(h)negod fire hydrant, fountain
[t+ga -(h)neg(a)$_N$- water, liquid -od$_V$- stand]
tgahnegota' a fire hydrant; a fountain
•(h)negod fountain
[g+yo+ -(h)neg(a)$_N$- water, liquid -od$_V$- stand]
gyo̱hne:go:t fountain
•(h)negoni ferment, brew
[at+ -(h)neg(a)$_N$- water, liquid -ǫni, ǫny$_V$- make]
ęhsatnegǫ:ni' you will ferment s.t. P
•(h)negohs welding machine
[ga+ -(h)neg(a)$_N$- water, liquid -oh$_V$- dip in liquid]
ga̱hne:gohs a welding machine
•(h)negǫgohd filter liquid, strain liquid
[de+...(at+) -(h)neg(a)$_N$- water, liquid -ǫgohd$_V$- surpass]
dęhsne:gǫ:goht you will filter, strain liquid P
deyotnegǫgo̱hdǫh strained water S
•negrę'd(a) morel
[o+]
onegr'ęda' a morel mushroom
•neg(wa) pea
[o+]
one:gwa' peas
•ne'gwatoh and also
see: Appendix I
•ne:'gyę:' it is
see: Appendix I
•ne:'gyę:ne' it is that
see: Appendix I
•nehagwa(h,'), nehago be surprised, amazed
[P+]
akneha:gwahs I'm always amazed H
ǫkneha:go' I was amazed or surprised P
aknehagwa'ǫh I am amazed S
•nehagwahd be amazing
[o+ contains: -nehagwa(h,'), nehago$_V$- be urprised, amazed]
onehagwaht it is amazing, awesome S
•ne:'hęhne:' it also is
see: Appendix I
•ne:'hǫ:ni' that is the reason why; that is why
see: Appendix I
•(h)neka:'dam
[de+ga+ -(h)neg(a)$_N$- water, liquid -(h)awi, (h)a:$_V$- hold, include, bring]
degahne'ka:' a dam
•(h)neka' bartender
[A+ contains: -(h)neg(a)$_N$- water, liquid]
hahne:ka' bartender
•(h)nekę: murky water
[o+ -(h)neg(a)$_N$- water, liquid -(h)ę(:)$_V$- dry]
ohne:kę: it is murky water
•ne:ne' it is
see: Appendix I
•ne:'hne:ne:' and that also is
see: Appendix I
•nenhǫs in-law
[TR+]
hakne:nhǫ:s my father-in-law S
•ne:hni' too, also, and
see: Appendix I
•ne:'hni'ne:' and that also
see: Appendix I

•nenọ(:) warm (weather), mild (weather)
[o+]
one:nọ' it is mild, warm; a warm or hot day S
•ne'onẹh it is now
see: Appendix I
•(')nehs(a) sand
[o+]
o'nehsa' sand
•(')nehsadaihẹ: desert
[o+ -(')nehs(a)$_N$- sand -(')daihẹ:$_V$- hot]
o'nehs'adaihẹ: desert
•(')nehsadase: sand storm
[o+ -(')nehs(a)$_N$- sand -dase$_V$- whirl]
o'nehsada:se: a sand storm
•nehsd(a:) floor, board
[ga+]
ganehsda:' a board
ganehsda:'geh on the floor
•(')nesd(a), (')nosd(a) nudity
[o+]
o'ne:sta', o'no:sta' nudity
•nesda:denyọ' rafter
[ga+ -nehsd(a:)$_N$- floor, board -denyọ'$_V$- several existing objects]
ganehsda:denyọ' rafters (made of board)
•nehsdaod headboards, grave markers, billboards, signs
[ga+ -nehsd(a:)$_N$- floor, board -od$_V$- stand]
ganehsdao:t headboards; grave markers; billboards; signs (lit.: standing board)
•nehshẹhẹ dogfish
[ga+]
ganehshẹhẹ' a dogfish
•(')nehsiyo: sandpiper
[o+ -(')nehs(a)$_N$- sand -iyo:$_V$- be nice, good]
o'nehsi:yo: sandpiper
•neh(wa) skin, leather, rawhide
[ga+]
ganehwa' leather; hide
•nehwiya'g circumcise
[-neh(wa)$_N$- skin -iya'g$_V$- cut]
ẹhadinehwi:ya'k they (m) will circumcise it P
•(')nehsogwahta' sander
[de+at+ -(')nehs(a)$_N$- sand -ogwahd$_V$- dig with s.t.]
dewatnẹhsogwahta' sander H
•netogyẹ:' be it so
see: Appendix I
•netogyẹ(n)họ:weh it is where
see: Appendix I
•ne'tone:' that's the one
see: Appendix I
•ne:'tsọ: that is only; that is all
see: Appendix I
•ne'wa(h)d(ẹ, ani) startle s.o., surprise s.o.
[TR+ contains: -ne'waọ, ne'wa(:)$_V$- be startled]
ẹheyẹne'wa:dẹ' I will startle him P
•ne:'hwa' next
see: Appendix I
•ne'wa(:,ọ) be unexpected, become surprised, be surprising
[ẹ+]
gẹne'waọ:s I get surprised H
agen'ewa:' I was surprised P
one'waọ: s.t. unexpected, surprising S
•neyọ(:) heal
[TR/...at+]
gane:yọhs a medical clinic; a healing place (lit.: it heals) H
ẹjisane:yọ:' it will heal you P
•neyọhs clinic
[ga+ contains: -neyọ(:)$_V$- heal]
gane:yọhs a medical clinic; a healing place (lit.: it heals) H
•nẹ: Exclamation, said when pointing to something
see: Appendix I

Legend: H habitual, P punctual, S stative, I imperative, PURP purposive, PURP-H purposive habitual, PURP-PAST purposive past, PURP-P purposive punctual, PURP-I purposive imperative; see §8.6, §8.11 in Appendix J. Alphabetization in stems ignores length (:), and any h's or glottal stops (') that are not between vowels. See §2.2 of the User Guide for explanation.

•nęh when (for statements only)
see: Appendix I
•nęˀd(a) evergreen, conifer
[o+]
onęˀdaˀ an evergreen; a conifer
•nę:dah this here; said when giving something to someone
see: Appendix I
•nęˀdagayǫh pine
[o+ -nęˀd(a)$_N$- pine -gayǫh$_V$- old (thing)]
onęˀdaga:yǫh white pine
•nęˀdęˀs pine cones
[ga+ -nęˀd(a)$_N$- pine -(aˀs)ęˀ$_V$- fall, drop]
ganęˀdęˀs pine cones
•nęˀdǫd pine cone
[o+ -nęˀd(a)$_N$- pine -ǫd$_V$- attached]
onęˀdǫ:t pine cones
•nęhgwi haul
[(N+)]
knęhgwih(s) I carry it all the time H
ęknęhgwiˀ I will carry, move, tote it P
aknęhgwi: I have moved it S
ga̱heyˀǫdanęhgwih a hearse H
[ga+ -(he)yǫ(ˀda)$_N$- corpse, cadaver -nęhgwi$_V$- haul]
•nęhgwih courier
[A+ -nęhgwi$_V$- haul]
hanęhgwih he is a courier
•nę:gyęh this (one)
see: Appendix I
•nęhaitaˀ corn bug, corn napper
[ga+ -nęh(ę)$_N$- corn -(hr)iˀ$_V$- break up]
ganęhaitaˀ, ganahaitaˀ a corn bug; a corn napper (an insect similar to preying mantis)
•nęh(ę) corn
[o+]
onęhę:ˀ corn
•nęhę(:) guard
[de+…]
dehadinęhę:hęˀ they (m) are guards H
de̱hodinęhę:ˀ they (m) are guarding s.t. (i.e., strikers); security guards S
•nęhęd stand in a line, guard
[de+(d+) P+ contains:-nęhę(:)$_V$- guard]
de̱hadinęhęda:s they (m) are guards; they are participants in a work-bee H
todinęhę:deˀ they are standing there (in a line formation); they are guarding S
•nęhęda:s barn raising, working bee
[de+…A+ contains: -nęhęd$_V$- stand in a line]
de̱hadinęhęˀda:s they (m) will have a working bee, a barn raising
•nęhęsdǫd roasted whole corn
[wa+at+ -nęhęhsd$_N$- whole corn -ǫd$_V$- attached]
watnęhęsdǫ:t whole corn roasted on an open fire
•nęhęsrǫni stand in line
[-nęhęsr(a)$_N$- line -ǫni, ǫny$_V$- make]
ganęhęhsrǫ:ni: a line formed S
swanęhęsrǫ:nih you all stand in line,in a formation I
•nęhohgwaˀ lyed corn soup
[o+ -nęh(ę)$_N$- corn -ohgw$_V$- remove from liquid]
onęhohgwaˀ corn soup (lyed)
•nęhohato lyed corn
[e+ -nęh(ę)$_N$- corn -ohaˀd$_V$- cleaned]
enehohato lyed corn
•nęnog(a:) hickory
[o+]
onęnoga:ˀ hickory wood; a hickory stick
•nęnǫˀ thimbleberry
[contains -nenǫ(:)$_V$- warm (weather), mild (weather)]
nę:nǫˀ thimbleberries
•nęny(a), nǫny(a) husk
[o+]
onǫ:nyaˀ a husk

•nęnyoʼg(wa) pill
[o+]
onęnyʼogwaʼ pills

•(h)nęhs(a) shoulder
ohnęhsaʼ shoulder
snęhsaʼgeh on your shoulders

•(h)nęhsędǫh shrug
[de+...at+ -(h)nęs(a)$_N$- shoulder -ędǫh$_V$- shake s.t.]
atatnęhsę:dǫh he shrugged P

•nęhsgw, nęhsgo steal
[(N+)]
knęhsgwahs I am a thief H
ęhsnęhsgoʼ you will steal P
ganęhsgwęh stolen property, plunder; s.t. robbed S
ahǫgwʼedanęhsgoʼ they stole him (for another group) P
[stem: -ǫgweʼdanęhsgw- kidnap a person; consists of: -ǫgwe(ʼda)$_N$- person -nęhsgw$_V$- steal]

•nęhsgwęh plunder, stolen property
[ga+ contains: -nęhsgw$_V$- steal]
ganęhsgwęh stolen property; plunder; s.t. robbed

•nę:toh right here, over there
see: Appendix I

•nę:toh gwai here (rather than there)
see: Appendix I

•nęts(a) arm
onę:tsaʼ an arm (said, for example, when holding up a doll's arm for show)
snętsaʼgeh on your arm

•nętsadahgw dislocate one's arm
[at+ -nęts(a)$_N$- arm -dahgw$_V$- remove]
asatnętsadahgoʼ your arm came out of its socket P

•nętsaǫnyǫ(:) wave one's arms
[de+... -nęts(a)$_N$- arm -ǫnyǫʼ several objects]
atgęnętsaǫ:nyǫ:ʼ I waved my arms P
desęnętsaǫnyǫ: wave your arms (goodbye) I

•nętses reach, stretch out
[de+A+ -nęts(a)$_N$- arm -es$_V$- long]
desenętse:s stretch out your arms; reach out I

•nętsesǫʼ arm span
[tsaʼde+A+ -nęts(a)$_N$- arm -es$_V$- long -oʼ plural]
tsaʼdehanę:tse:sǫʼ his arm span

•nętsineʼ take, lead s.o. by the arm
[de+TR+ -nęts(a)$_N$- arm -ine$_V$- go]
ętgǫnę:tsi:neʼ I will take you by the arm PURP-P

•nętsiyaʼg break one's limb in two
[de+...ad+N+]
dęgatnętsi:yaʼk I will break my arm P

•nę:tsǫ: just a little bit
see: Appendix I

•nętsǫd sleeve
[ga+ -nęts(a)$_N$- arm -ǫd$_V$- attached]
ganę:tsǫ:t a sleeve

•nętsǫ:gwatoh right now; quickly; immediately;
see: Appendix I

•nętsǫʼn(eg) remove one's support
[de+... -nęts(a)$_N$- arm -ǫʼn(eg)$_V$- remove, take away]
dagenętsǫʼne:k I withdrew my arm (that is, withdrew my support) P
desenętsǫʼne:k remove your arms (that is, retract them); remove your support I

•(h)nęye:s tall
[A+]
ehnę:ye:s she is tall S

•nhaʼ command, hire
kenhaʼs I hire her H
ganhaʼǫh it is hired S

•nha:ʼ stick out
[de+...d+N+ occurs in:]
dęsatnoʼa:nhaʼ you will have a burden strap P
[de+...at+ -nǫʼ(a:), nǫh(a)$_N$- head -nha:ʼ$_V$- stick out]

Legend: H habitual, P punctual, S stative, I imperative, PURP purposive, PURP-H purposive habitual, PURP-PAST purposive past, PURP-P purposive punctual, PURP-I purposive imperative; see §8.6, §8.11 in Appendix J. Alphabetization in stems ignores length (:), and any h's or glottal stops (ʼ) that are not between vowels. See §2.2 of the User Guide for explanation.

•nha:ʼ stick out (continued)
detgano̱hsanha:ʼ it is a house sticking out S
[de+…at+ -nǫhs(a)$_N$- house -nha:ʼ$_V$- stick out]

•nhaʼ order s.t.
[adę+]
ęsadęnhaʼ you will order s.t., hire s.t. P

•(ʼ)nhahgy(a), (ʼ)nhahd(a) large log, timber
[o+]
oʼnhahgyaʼ, onhahdaʼ large lumber logs ; timber

•(ʼ)nhahgyaʼs logger
[A+ -(ʼ)nhahgy(a), (ʼ)nhahd(a)$_N$- log (large) timber -(i)yaʼg$_V$- cut, break, cross]
hadiʼnhahgyaʼs loggers H

•nhahsd encircle
[occurs in:]
ǫnętsanhahstaʼ a bracelet; an armband H
[ǫ+ -nęts(a)$_N$- arm -nhahsd$_V$- encircle]
degęgyohgwanhahsdǫh Circle of Life (a wampum representing the Confederacy) S
[de+ ga+ -(i)gyohg(wa)$_N$- crowd -nhahsd$_V$- encircle]

•nhaʼtr(a) employee, civil servant, minister, Ombudsman, etc.
[A+ contains: -nhaʼ$_V$- hire]
enhaʼtraʼ employee, civil servant, minister, Ombudsman, etc.

•nheʼd(a) porcupine
[ga+]
ganheʼdaʼ a porcupine

•(ʼ)nhehgyęʼ female, genitals
[o+ -(ʼ)nhehgyęʼ$_V$- female]
oʼnhehgyęʼ female genitals (animals only); a female animal

•nhehsr(a) advocacy
[ga+]
ganhehsraʼ to take s.o.'s part; advocacy

•(ʼ)nhęhts(a), (ʼ)nhwęhts(a), tail
[o+]
oʼnhęhtsaʼ, oʼnhwęhtsaʼ the tail of an animal

•(ʼ)nhęhtsędǫh wag
[de+P+ -(ʼ)nhęhts(a)$_N$- tail -ędǫh$_V$- shake s.t.]
deyoʼnhęhtsędǫhǫh it is wagging its tail S

•nhiʼ err, make a mistake
ǫgwa:nhiʼs we all make mistakes H
ęhsa:nhiʼk you will err, make a mistake P
agenhiʼǫh I have made a mistake, an error S

•nhihd calamity
[de+...wa+adę+ contains: -nhiʼ$_V$- err, make a mistake]
adwadęnhiht calamity (lit.: it happened all of a sudden; all at once)

•nhoʼdę: character
[tsęh ni+P+ contains: -oʼdę:$_V$- certain type, kind of thing]
tsęh nihǫnhoʼdę: character

•(h)nodǫ flood
see: (i)hnodǫ flood
ohno:dǫʼ it is flooded S

•nhodǫ(:) lock
genhodǫhaʼ I lock s.t. H
ęge:nho:dǫ:ʼ I will lock it P
age:nho:dǫʼ I have locked it S

•nhodǫgw, nhodǫgo open
[(N+) contains: -nhodǫ(:)$_V$- lock]
genhodǫgwahs I open it, unlock it H
ęhaihwanhodǫ:goʼ he will open the gathering P
[-(r)ih(wa)$_N$- word -nhodǫgw$_V$- open]
agenhodǫ:gwęh I have opened it, unlocked it S
senho:dǫ:goh open the door I

•nhǫdǫhkwaʼ jail, prison
[ǫ+adadę+ contains: -nhodǫ(:)$_V$- lock]
ǫdadęnhodǫhkwaʼgeh a jail; a prison
•nhodǫnyǫ(:) be locked up
[A+ contains: -nhodǫ(:)$_V$- lock -nyǫʼ several]
gadinhodǫ:nyǫʼ they (z) are locked up S
•nhogahęd doorway
[ga+ -nho(ha)$_N$- door -gahęd$_V$- drill, hole]
ganhogahę:t a doorway
•nhoha: close (the door)
[ga+ contains: -nho(ha)$_N$- door]
genhoha:s I close the door H
ęgenhoha: I will close the door P
agenhohahǫh, agenhoha:hǫh I have closed the door S
senhoha: close the door I
•nhohaʼe(g) knock (on a door)
[stem: -nhohaʼeg- knock (on a door); consists of: -nho(ha)$_N$- door -(ʼ)e(g)$_V$- hit]
senhohaʼe:k knock on the door I
•nhohaniyǫd gate, door
[ga+ -nho(ha)$_N$- door -niyǫd$_V$- hang]
ganhohani:yǫ:t a gate; a door
•nhohayęhd banging noise
[-nho(ha)$_N$- door -(y)ęhd$_V$- hit, knock down, strike]
aganhoha:yęh there was a noise made by banging a door
•nhohsgwaǫd cow
[g+yo+ -nhohsg(wa)$_N$- -ǫd$_V$- attached]
gyonhohsgwaǫ:t cow
•nhǫd(a:,ę) put in
[(at+) N+ occurs in:]
ohsgyęʼdanhǫ:t false teeth (lit.: a mouth full of bones) S
[-(h)sgyęʼd(a)$_N$- bone -nhǫd(a:,ę)$_V$- put in]
shenoʼjanhǫ:dęh put her teeth in I
[TR/at+ N+ stem: -noʼj(a)$_N$- tooth -nhǫd(a:,ę)$_V$- put in]
•(ʼ)nhǫhd(a) armpit
[-(a)gǫ: in, under]
onhǫhdaʼ an armpit
senhǫhda:gǫ: your underarm, armpit
•(ʼ)nhǫhs(a) egg
[o+]
oʼnhǫhsaʼ egg(s)
•(ʼ)nhǫhsg(a:) inner thigh
sʼenhǫhsga:ʼgeh on your inner thigh
•(ʼ)nhǫhsdǫd testicles
[de+ha+ -(ʼ)nhǫhsd(a)$_N$- sperm -ǫd$_V$- attached]
dehaʼnhǫhsdǫ:t his testicles
•ni... look for stems beginning with 'i'
•(h)ni bark
gahnih(s) it is barking H
•hniʼ also, and, too
see: Appendix I
•(ʼ)nih father
[TR+]
haʼnih my father S
•nigahę:hęh gʼadroda:ʼ cloth diapers
nigahę:hah, nigahę:hęh it is thin (that is, material)
gʼadroda:ʼ diaper
•nigęʼǫh or, or is it
see: Appendix I
•(ʼ)nigǫh(a) mind
[ga+]
gʼanigǫhaʼ the mind
ǫgwaʼnigǫhaʼ our mind
gʼanihgǫhaʼgeh on the minds
•(ʼ)nigǫhgaę suffer
[(tęʼ) deʼ+ not ...ę+ -(ʼ)nigǫh(a)$_N$- mind -gaę:$_V$- be willing]
desęʼnigǫhgaeʼ you suffer S
•(ʼ)nigǫhgahęhs run out of patience, wait impatiently
[P+]
aknigǫhgahęhs I am running out of patience; I am impatiently waiting H

•(ʼ)nigǫha(:,ʼ) expect, watch
knigǫ:ha:ʼ I am expecting, watching H
ęknigǫhaʼk I will expect it, be watching out for s.t. P
snigǫhaʼk watch out for yourself I

•(ʼ)nigǫha:ʼ be wary, cautious
[A+adat+ -(ʼ)nigǫha(:)$_V$- expect, watch]
wadatnigǫha:ʼ it is wary, cautious H

•(ʼ)nigǫha(:) monitor
[TR+adę+ -(ʼ)nigǫha(:)$_V$- expect, watch]
ǫkiyaʼdęʼnigǫha:ʼ monitors (people) H

•(ʼ)nigǫhad elder
[P+ -(ʼ)nigǫh(a)$_N$- mind -d$_V$- stand]
hodiʼnigǫha:t they (m) have wisdom; male elders

•(ʼ)nigǫhad stupid, foolish, ignorant
[de+P+ not -(ʼ)nigǫh(a)$_N$- mind -d$_V$- stand]
dehoʼnigǫha:t he is ignorant, unthinkingly foolish S

•(ʼ)nigǫhad be a nuisance
[de+ not ...TR+ -yaʼd(a)$_N$- body -(ʼ)nigǫhd$_V$- be wise]
deshayʼadaʼnigǫha:t you are a nuisance S

•(ʼ)nigǫhad be smart
[P+ -(ʼ)nigǫh(a)$_N$- mind -d$_V$- stand]
sʼanigǫha:t you are smart, brilliant S

•(ʼ)nigǫhaʼd(ę, ani) cheat, betray
[TR/adę+ -(ʼ)nigǫh(a)$_N$- mind -dę$_V$- stand for s.o.'s benefit]
gasheʼnigǫhaʼda:nih you betray them continually H
ęhsheʼnigǫhaʼdęʼ you will cheat her, betray her P

•(ʼ)nigǫhaʼd cheat, betray
[TR/adę+ -(ʼ)nigǫh(a)$_N$- mind -d$_V$- stand]
gasheʼnigǫhaʼtaʼ you betray them continually H
ęhsheʼnigǫhaʼt you will cheat s.o. P

•(ʼ)nigǫhadogę undecided, indecisive
[(tęʼ) deʼ+P+ -(ʼ)nigǫh(a)$_N$- mind -dogę(:)$_V$- right, true]
desaʼnigǫhado:gę: you cannot decide which way to go, you are flighty S

•(ʼ)nigǫhahdogęh immature
[(tęʼ) deʼ+P+at+ -(ʼ)nigǫh(a)$_N$- mind -dogę(:)$_V$- right, true]
desathnigǫhahdo:gęh you are immature in mind S

•(ʼ)nigǫhahdǫ(ʼ) faint
[P+ -(ʼ)nigǫh(a)$_N$- mind -(a)hdǫ(:)$_V$- lose, disappear]
ǫknigǫhahdǫʼ I fainted P

•(ʼ)nigǫhaʼe offend
[TR+ -(ʼ)nigǫh(a)$_N$- mind -(ʼ)e$_V$- hit]
ęhsheʼnigǫhaʼe:k you will offend s.o. P

•(ʼ)nigǫhaʼehsd decide
[he+P+ -(ʼ)nigǫh(a)$_N$- mind -(ʼ)ehsd$_V$- hit with s.t.]
haʼhoʼnigohaʼehs his mind settled on s.t., decided on s.t. P

•(ʼ)nigǫha(:,ę) bother s.o., annoy
[de+not TR+ -(ʼ)nigǫh(a)$_N$- mind -(ʼ)nigǫha(:,ę)$_V$- expect, watch]
dehsknigǫha:haʼ you are annoying me H
dęhsnigǫhaę:ʼ you will be annoying P

•(ʼ)nigǫha(ę,nih) unconcerned, indifferent
[taʼde+P+ -(ʼ)nigǫha(ę,nih)$_V$- expect, watch for s.o.'s benefit]
taʼdehoʼnigǫha:nih he is unconcerned, indifferent S

•(ʼ)nigǫhaędaʼ understand
[P+ -(ʼ)nigǫh(a)$_N$- mind -ędaʼ$_V$- finish]
hoʼnigǫhaędaʼs he understands H
ahoʼnigǫhaędaʼ he understood P

•(ʼ)nigǫhaędaʼ misunderstand
[(tęʼ) de+not P+ -(ʼ)nigǫh(a)$_N$- mind -ędaʼ$_V$- finish]
tęʼ dʼehoʼnigǫhaędaʼs he does not understand H

•(ʼ)nigǫhagahe(y) be mentally exhausted
[P+ -(ʼ)nigǫh(a)$_N$- mind -gahe(y)$_V$- be weak, die]
aknigǫhagahe:ʼ my mind got beat; I'm mentally exhausted P
aknigǫhagahe:yǫh I am mentally exhausted S

•(ʼ)nigǫhagęni, (ʼ)nigǫhagęny corrupt, intimidate s.o.
[de+TR+ -(ʼ)nigǫh(a)$_N$- mind -gęni, gęny$_V$- compete]
deshagonigǫhagęnyǫhs he intimidates people all the time H
dęhsheʼnigǫhagę:niʼ you will corrupt s.o.'s mind P

•(ʼ)nigǫhagǫd be uncompromising, steadfast
[(tęʼ) de+ not P+ -(ʼ)nigǫh(a)$_N$- mind -gǫd$_V$- persevere, linger]
deyagʼonigǫha:gǫ:t she cannot be swayed; she is uncompromising, distinguished S

•(ʼ)nigǫhaʼgweni, (ʼ)nigǫhaʼgweny outthink s.o.
[TR+ -(ʼ)nigǫh(a)$_N$- mind -gweni, gweny$_V$- be able to do s.t., succeed]
ęhsheʼnigǫhagwe:niʼ you will outthink her P

•(ʼ)nigǫhahetgęʼ sob, cry uncontrollably
[P+ -(ʼ)nigǫh(a)$_N$- mind -(hr)etgęʼ$_V$- be evil, bad, ugly]
aknigǫhahetgęʼs I am crying, uncontrollably H

•(ʼ)nigǫhaneʼwa(:,ǫ) be mentally surprised, startled
[P+ę+ -(ʼ)nigǫh(a)$_N$- mind -neʼwaǫ, neʼwa(:)$_V$- be startled]
ęsęʼnigǫhaneʼwa: you will be mentally startled P

•(ʼ)nigǫhanidęhd humble, gentle, nice
[P+ -(ʼ)nigǫh(a)$_N$- mind -nidęhd$_V$- cause to be kind]
gʼonigǫha:ni:dęht she is gentle, nice, humble S

•(ʼ)nigǫhahniyaʼd endure
[adę+ -(ʼ)nigǫh(a)$_N$- mind -(h)niyaʼd$_V$- harden, toughen]
ęhsaʼnigǫhahni:yaʼt you will endure P
sadęʼnigǫhahni:yaʼt keep your mind strong I

•(ʼ)nigǫhahniyǫh be stubborn
[P+ -(ʼ)nigǫh(a)$_N$- mind -(h)niyǫh$_V$- be hard, tough]
aknigǫhahni:yǫh I have a strong mind S

•(ʼ)nigǫhahsnoweʼ quick thinker
[A+ -(ʼ)nigǫh(a)$_N$- mind -(h)snoweʼ$_V$- be fast]
haʼnigǫhahsno:weʼ he is a quick thinker S

•(ʼ)nigǫhawęnyaʼd be entertaining
[de+...ę+ -(ʼ)nigǫh(a)$_N$- mind -(a)węnyaʼd$_V$- cause to stir, mix]
deyoʼnigǫhawę:nyaʼt it is entertaining S

•(ʼ)nigǫhawęnye(:) entertain
[de+...TR+ -(ʼ)nigǫh(a)$_N$- mind -(a)węnye(:)$_V$- stir, mix]
desheʼnigǫhawę:nye:ʼ entertain her / them I

•(ʼ)nigǫhayei: crazy, mentally ill
[(tęʼ) deʼ+ not heʼ+A+ -(ʼ)nigǫh(a)$_N$- mind -yei, (y)í$_V$- be right, correct]
tehaʼnigǫhayei: he is not right in the mind S

•(ʼ)nigǫhęh mosquito
[-(ʼ)nigǫh(a)$_V$- mind -(h)ęh$_V$- be in the middle]
nigǫhęh mosquitoes

•(ʼ)nigǫhęʼ be depressed, sad
[d+... -(ʼ)nigǫh(a)$_N$- mind -(h)ę(h,ʼ)$_V$- feel bad]
ętsnigǫhęʼ you will be depressed P
dwaknigǫhęʼǫh I am in sorrow, in mourning; I am sad S

Legend: H habitual, P punctual, S stative, I imperative, PURP purposive, PURP-H purposive habitual, PURP-PAST purposive past, PURP-P purposive punctual, PURP-I purposive imperative; see §8.6, §8.11 in Appendix J. Alphabetization in stems ignores length (:), and any h's or glottal stops (ʼ) that are not between vowels. See §2.2 of the User Guide for explanation.

•(ʼ)nigǫhęhd(ę,ani) make s.o. forget
[TR+ -(ʼ)nigǫh(a)$_{N}$- mind -(a)hdę,ani$_{V}$- lose for s.o.'s benefit]
ęhsheʼnigǫhęhdęʼ you will make s.o. feel better, comfort s.o. (lit.: you will make s.o. forget s.t.) P

•(ʼ)nigǫhęhdǫh be sad
[de+P+ -(ʼ)nigǫh(a)$_{N}$- mind -(a)hdǫ(:)$_{V}$- lose, disappear]
desaʼnigǫhęhdǫh you are sad S

•(ʼ)nigǫhiyo: be satisfied, peaceful
[d+P+ -(ʼ)nigǫh(a)$_{N}$- mind -iyo:$_{V}$- be nice, good]
dwaknigǫhi:yo: I am satisfied, peaceful S

•(ʼ)nigǫhiyo: harmony
[ga+ -(ʼ)nigǫh(a)$_{N}$- mind -iyo:$_{V}$- be nice, good harmony]
gʼaniʼgǫhi:yo: harmony; to be of good mind

•(ʼ)nigǫhiyoh become satisfied
[(d+)P+ -(ʼ)nigǫh(a)$_{N}$- mind -iyoh$_{V}$- become nice, good]
ęhsaʼnigǫhi:yoh you will be satisfied P

•(ʼ)nigǫhiyohsd become comfortable, be at ease
[P+ -(ʼ)nigǫh(a)$_{N}$- mind -iyohsd$_{V}$- become nice, good]
ęhsaʼnigǫhi:yohs your mind will adjust (that is, become comfortable) P

•(ʼ)nigǫhiyohsdę:ʼ be discontent
[(tęʼ) deʼ+ not d/g+P+ -(ʼ)nigǫh(a)$_{N}$- mind -iyohsdę$_{V}$- become nice, good for one's benefit]
degyoʼnigǫhiyohsdę:ʼ it is discontent S

•(ʼ)nigǫhod suggest, advise
[d+...ę+ -(ʼ)nigǫh(a)$_{N}$- mind -odę$_{V}$- stand for s.o.'s benefit]
ętsęʼnigoho:dęʼ you will suggest, present an idea P

•(ʼ)nigǫhodagw persuade, influence
[TR+ -(ʼ)nigǫh(a)$_{N}$- mind -odagw$_{V}$- remove, take away]
ęhseʼnigǫhoda:goʼ you will persuade her, overcome her mind P

•(ʼ)nigǫhoʼdę: think a certain way, have an attitude, a mood
[tsęh that ni+P+ -(ʼ)nigǫh(a)$_{N}$- mind -oʼdę:$_{V}$- type of]
tsęh nisaʼnigǫhoʼdę: your attitude, mood S

•(ʼ)nigǫhoʼdrǫ(:) console s.o.
[TR+ -(ʼ)nigǫh(a)$_{N}$- mind -(a)hdrǫ:(gw)$_{V}$- caress]
ęhsheʼnigǫhoʼdrǫ:ʼ you will console s.o. (lit.: you will caress s.o.'s mind) P

•(ʼ)nigǫhoʼdrǫ(:) worry, despair, desparate
[ę+ -(ʼ)nigǫh(a)$_{N}$- mind -(a)hdrǫ:(gw)$_{V}$- caress]
ęhsęʼnigǫhoʼdrǫ:ʼ you will worry, despair; you will be desparate P
sęʼnigǫhoʼdrǫh you are a worrier S

•(ʼ)nigǫhogw grieve
[de+...ę+ -(ʼ)nigǫh(a)$_{N}$- mind -ogw$_{V}$- scatter]
degęʼnigohogwahs I am broken-hearted (lit.: my mind is scattered) H
agyǫʼnigǫho:goʼ her mind is scattered P

•(ʼ)nigǫhoʼkd(ę) give up
[ę+ -(ʼ)nigǫh(a)$_{N}$- mind -oʼkd$_{V}$- end]
gaǫʼnigǫhǫʼktaʼ they (f/m) are giving up (in spirit) H
ahęʼnigǫhoʼkdęʼ he gave up (his will to live) P

•(ʼ)nigǫhoʼneg revolt, rebel
[d+...ę+ -(ʼ)nigǫh(a)$_{N}$- mind -(ʼ)neg$_{V}$- pray, hope]
ętsęʼnigǫhoʼne:k you will revolt, remove yourself (bodily and in spirit) P

•(ʼ)nigǫhotahsd suggest, advise
[de+TR+ę+ -(ʼ)nigǫh(a)$_{N}$- mind -otahsd$_{V}$- go and cause s.o. to stand]
ętseyęʼnigǫhotahs you will suggest to her, advise her P

•(ʼ)nigǫhowanę wise
[P+ -(ʼ)nigǫh(a)$_N$- mind -owanęh$_V$- be big -ʼs plural]
hodiʼnigǫhowa:nęʼs they (m) are wise; they have the capacity for thinking S

•(ʼ)nigǫhowanęh broad-minded
[A+ -(ʼ)nigǫh(a)$_N$- mind -owanęh$_V$- be big]
snigǫhowa:nęh you have a broad mind S

•(ʼ)nigǫhǫni persuade, influence s.o.
[TR+ -(ʼ)nigǫh(a)$_N$- mind -ǫni, ǫny$_V$- make]
ęhsheʼnigǫhǫ:niʼ you will influence, persuade s.o. P

•(ʼ)nigǫhnyaʼg grieve, be broken-hearted
[de+P+ -(ʼ)nigǫh(a)$_N$- mind -(ni)yaʼg$_V$- cut, break, cross]
dewaknigǫhnyaʼgǫh I am broken-hearted, grieving S

•(ʼ)nigǫhnyaʼg discourage s.o.
[de+TR+ -(ʼ)nigǫh(a)$_N$- mind -(ni)yaʼg$_V$- cut, break, cross]
dęhsheʼnigǫhnyaʼk you will discourage s.o. P

•(ʼ)nigǫhsadǫ be lonesome
[P+ -(ʼ)nigǫh(a)$_N$- mind -(h)sadǫ$_V$- bury s.o., an animal]
akʼnigǫhsa:dǫʼs I am lonesome H
ǫkʼnigǫhsa:dǫʼ I got lonesome P
oʼnigǫhsadǫhk it is lonesome S

•(ʼ)nigǫhsadǫh sadness
[o+ak+ -(ʼ)nigǫh(a)$_N$- mind -(h)sadǫ$_V$- bury s.t.]
oknigǫhsa:dǫh sadness

•(ʼ)nigǫhsadǫhg be mournful
[o+ -(ʼ)nigǫh(a)$_N$- mind -(h)sadǫ$_V$- bury s.t.]
oʼnigǫhsadǫhk it is mournful S

•niha lend s.t.
[at+N+ occurs in:]
satwihsdanihahs you lend money H
[-(h)wisd(a)-$_N$ money -niha-$_V$ lend]

•niha borrow from s.o.
[TR+(N+) occurs in:]
shehwihsdanihahs you borrow from her H
[-(h)wisd(a)-$_N$ money -niha-$_V$ lend]

•niha borrow, rent
[ę+]
sęnihahsgǫ: you are a habitual borrower H
ęhsęnihaʼ you will borrow, rent P

•nihahd(ę, ani) lend
[adę+N+ contains: -niha$_V$- borrow]
sadęhwihsdanihahda:nih you lend money; a lender H
[-(h)wihsd(a)$_N$- money -nihahdani$_V$- lend]

•nihaǫ(:) string
[-nih(a)$_N$- -(r)ǫ$_V$- bead s.t.]
hanihaǫhaʼ he is stringing H
ganihaǫ:ʼ it is strung S

•nihahsd lend
[contains: -niha$_V$- borrow]
ǫnihahstaʼ s.o. lends H

•(ʼ)nikǫ(:) sew
eʼni:kǫhs seamstress H
a:knikǫ:ʼ I should, might sew P
akni:kǫʼ I have sewn S

•(ʼ)nikǫʼ seam
[ga+ contains: -(ʼ)nikǫ(:)$_V$- sew]
gani:kǫʼ a seam

•(ʼ)nikǫgwahs seam ripper, stitch ripper
[ga+ contains: -(ʼ)nikǫgw$_V$- unsew]
gʼanikǫgwahs stitch ripper

•(ʼ)nikǫhaʼ sewing machine
[ga+ contains: -(ʼ)nikǫ(:)$_V$- sew]
ganikǫhaʼ a sewing machine

•(ʼ)nikǫhkwaʼ sewing item
[e+ contains: -(ʼ)nikǫ(:)$_V$- sew -shǫ:ʼǫh several objects]
ęʼnikǫhkwaʼshǫ:ʼǫh sewing room items

Legend: H habitual, P punctual, S stative, I imperative, PURP purposive, PURP-H purposive habitual, PURP-PAST purposive past, PURP-P purposive punctual, PURP-I purposive imperative; see §8.6, §8.11 in Appendix J. Alphabetization in stems ignores length (:), and any h's or glottal stops (ʼ) that are not between vowels. See §2.2 of the User Guide for explanation.

•(ʼ)nikǫhs seamstress
[e+ contains: -(ʼ)nikǫ(:)$_{V}$- sew]
eʼni:kǫhs seamstress
•(h)ninǫ buy
ǫdęhni:nǫh store or storekeeper (f) H
aʼehni:nǫʼ she purchased P
tęʼ dewa:kni:nǫh tęʼ d̲eʼa:kni:nǫh I did not buy it S
tęʼ ta:kni:nǫh I should not or will not buy it I
•(h)ninǫ buy s.t.
aʼehni:nǫʼ she purchased s.t. P
tęʼ dewa:kni:nǫh tęʼ d̲eʼa:kni:nǫh I did not buy it S
•(h)ninǫh store, storekeeper
[A+adę+ -(h)ninǫ$_{V}$- sell]
ǫdęhni:nǫh a store; she is a storekeeper
hadęhni:nǫh he is a storekeeper
•(h)ninǫh grocery store
[g+yǫ+adę+ -(h)ninǫ$_{V}$- store, grocery store]
gyǫdęhni:nǫh a grocery store
•(h)ninǫnyǫʼ consumption
[ga+ -(h)ninǫ$_{V}$- buy -nyǫʼ several objects]
g̲ahninǫnyǫʼ consumption (lit.: things which are bought)
•(h)ninǫnyǫʼ plaza
[g+yǫ+adę+ -(h)ninǫ$_{V}$- sell -nyǫʼ several objects]
gyǫdęhninǫ:nyǫh a plaza
•niʼǫh be stingy, greedy, cheap
[P+]
goniʼǫh she is stingy S
•(ʼ)nihsd(a) stem, hull
[o+]
oʼnihsdaʼ the stem or hull of a berry
•(ʼ)nihsdęhd hull
[-(ʼ)nihsd(a)$_{N}$- stem, hull -(y)ęhd$_{V}$- hit, knock down, strike]
ęhsnihsdęht you will hull strawberries P

•(ʼ)nihsgadeʼ brim
[de+yo+ -(ʼ)nihsg(a)$_{N}$- brim -deʼ$_{V}$- exist]
deyoʼnihsga:deʼ the brim of a hat
•nihsgoʼ late
ęwaknihsgoʼ I will be late P
aknihsgoʼǫhǫ:gyeʼ I am arriving late S
•nihsgyage urinate
gaǫni̲hsgya:gehs they (f/m) urinate H
agaǫnihsgyageʼ they (f/m) urinated P
agęni̲hsgya:ge: I am urinating S
•nihsheʼ be a long time
[tsaʼ+ o+ -nihsheʼ$_{V}$- take time]
tsaʼonihsheʼ a long time; for that length of time
•nihshe:ʼah short duration
[aʼ+ǫ+ -nihsheʼ$_{V}$- take time -ʼah a little bit]
aʼǫnihshe:ʼah a short duration
•(h)niyǫh be hard, tough
[o+(N+)]
ohni:yǫh it is hard S
okyęd̲ahkwahni:yǫh it is a hard chair
[P+(N+) stem: -(a)kyędahkw(a)$_{N}$- chair -(h)niyǫh$_{V}$- hard, tough]
•(h)niyaʼd tighten
[ga+ contains: -(h)niy$_{V}$- hard, tough]
g̲ahniyʼadǫh it is tight, tightened S
•niyo:weʼ, nyo:weʼ to be a certain distance
see: Appendix I
•niyǫd hang
[A+(N+)]
gani:yǫ:t it is hanging S
ganhohani:yǫ:t a gate; a door
[ga+ -nho(ha)$_{N}$- door -niyǫd$_{V}$- hang]
•niyǫdagw unhang
[d+ contains: -niyǫd$_{V}$- hang]
ętsniyǫda:goʼ you will unhang it P
•niyǫdahkwaʼ hook
[e+ contains: -niyǫd$_{V}$- hang -hkwaʼ instrument]
eniyǫdahkwaʼ hook

•niyǫd hang s.t. up
[contains: -niyǫd$_V$- hang]
akni:yǫ:dę' I did hang it up P
akni:yǫ:t I hung it up S

•no:' step-relative
[TR+]
hehsno:' your step-son S

•(h)no(:) pollution
[at+ -(h)n(a)$_N$- oil, gas -o(:)$_V$- be submerged]
ęwa:tno:' there will be pollution P

•no:' cold, cool
[P+N/na'+]
ona'no:' it is cold, cool S

•no'anhahsta' headband
[de+yǫ+at+ -nǫ'(a:), nǫh(a)$_N$- head -nhahsd$_V$- encircle]
deyǫtn'aǫ:nhahsta' a headband

•(h)noda:k'ah shallow
[ni+yo+ -(h)nod(a)$_N$- water -a:k'ah$_V$- short]
niyohnoda:k'ah it is shallow S

•(h)nodes deep
[o+ -(h)nod(a)$_N$- water -es$_V$- long]
ohno:de:s deep water

•(')nodra(h,') be infected
[P+]
g'ono:drahs she has open, weeping sores H
ęhs'ano:dra' sehsohgw'ageh you will have sores on your lips P
o'no:dra' it is infected; an infection S

•(')nodrahs skin rash
[o+ contains: -(')nodra(h,')$_V$- be infected]
o'no:drahs skin rash

•(')nodrahsd become infected, have an allergic reaction
[P+ contains: -(')nodra(h,')$_V$- be infected]
a'agono:drahs s.o. got chicken pox, a skin infection, allergic reactions; s.o. became infected P
s'anodrahsdǫh it has given you an infection, an allergic reaction; you have already had an allergic reaction S

•nogędǫd whiskers
[de+P+ -nogęd(a)$_N$- whisker -ǫd$_V$- attached]
deyodinogędǫ:t whiskers on catfish

•noha' mother
kno:ha' my mother S

•noha:'ah aunt
kno:ha:'ah my maternal aunt S

•nohaehs washing machine, washer
[ga+ -n$_N$- noun -ohae$_V$- clean, wash]
ganohaihs a washing machine

•noha'ta' soap
[e+ / o+ -n$_N$- noun -oha:'d$_V$- clean, wash with s.t.]
enoha:'ta' soap; what one washes with
onoha:'ta' soap

•nohotsgę'ę' beech
[o+]
onohotsgę'ę' a beech tree

•no'j(a) tooth
ono'ja' teeth
sn'oja'geh on your teeth

•no'jatgi:s'ah false teeth
[o+ -no'j(a)$_N$- tooth -tgis$_V$- dirty, ugly objects -'ah small]
ono'jatgi:s'ah false teeth

•no'jes tusk
[ga+ -no'j(a)$_N$- tooth -es$_V$- long]
gano'je:s a tusk

•no'jes fang
[o+ -no'j(a)$_N$- tooth -es$_V$- long]
ono'je:s fang

•no'johai'ta' toothbrush
[ǫ+at+ -no'j(a)$_N$- tooth -ohai'd$_V$- clean, wash with s.t.]
ǫtno'jǫhai'ta' a toothbrush

•no'jonya'ta' teething ring
[ǫ+at+ -no'j(a)$_N$- tooth -ǫnya'd$_V$- cause to grow]
ǫtno'jonya'ta' a teething ring

Legend: H habitual, P punctual, S stative, I imperative, PURP purposive, PURP-H purposive habitual, PURP-PAST purposive past, PURP-P purposive punctual, PURP-I purposive imperative; see §8.6, §8.11 in Appendix J. Alphabetization in stems ignores length (:), and any h's or glottal stops (') that are not between vowels. See §2.2 of the User Guide for explanation.

•noʼjǫni: false teeth
[ti+ga+ -noʼj(a)$_N$- tooth -ǫni, ǫny$_V$- make; be artificial]
tiganʼǫjo:ni: false teeth

•(ʼ)noks(a) bass (fish); oysters; shellfish; sea shells
[o+]
oʼno:ksaʼ bass (fish); oysters; shellfish; sea shells

•(h)noʼs Joe Pye weed
[ga+ -(h)n(a)$_N$- oil, gas -oʼs- be submerged]
ga̱hnoʼs Joe Pye weed

•nohsd become cold, chill down
[N/naʼ+ contains: -no$_V$- be cold, cool; occurs in:]
sagawa:nohs it became cooler P
[-w(a:)$_N$- air -nohsd$_V$- cool down]
owa:nohsdǫh it (weather) got cold S

•(ʼ)nesd(a), (ʼ)nosd(a) nudity
[o+]
oʼne:staʼ, oʼno:staʼ nudity

•noʼsę uncle
[TR+]
haknoʼsęʼ my uncle S

•nohsgaʼd(ę, ani) tickle
[de+TR+]
dęhsnohsgaʼdęʼ you will tickle it P

•nohsgwita:ʼ broom
[ga+ contains: -ęnoʼsgwi, onoʼsgwi$_V$- sweep]
ganohsgwita:ʼ a broom

•(ʼ)noshę: be envious
[P+]
akno:shę: I am envious S

•(ʼ)noshahs be jealous
[o+ contains: -(ʼ)nosh$_V$- be jealous, envious]
seʼno:shahs you are envious H

•(ʼ)noshaʼd jealous, envious
[o+ contains: -(ʼ)nosh$_V$- be jealous, envious]
oʼno:shaʼt it is jealous, envious S

•(ʼ)noshęhsr(a) jealousy
[ga+ contains: -(ʼ)nohs$_V$- be jealous, envious]
ganohshęhsraʼ jealousy

•nohsǫtaʼ particle
[de+ga+ -nahsǫd, nohsǫd$_V$- join]
degano̱hsǫ:taʼ particles (lit.: joiners)

•now(a) guitar, string instrument
[ga+]
gano:waʼ a guitar; any string instrument

•nowagahe:ʼah turtle
[ga+ stem: -nowagahe:ʼah- box turtle; consists of: -nowa(gwa)$_N$- rounded back -(h)e:ʼ$_V$- sitting up on top of s.t. -ʼah diminutive]
ganowagahe:ʼah a box turtle

•nowa(gwa) rounded back
[occurs in:]
honowagwaǫt he has a humped back S
[P+ stem: -nowa(gwa)$_N$- rounded back -ǫd$_V$- attached]

•nowagwaǫd have a rounded or humped back
[P+ stem: -nowa(gwa)$_N$- rounded back -ǫd$_V$- attached]
honowagwaǫt he has a humped back S

•nowę(ʼda) lie
[o+ contains: -nowę(:)$_V$- be a liar]
onowʼędaʼ a lie

•nowę: be a liar
[P+ę+]
sęno:wę: you are a liar S

•nowęhd deny
[adę+ contains: -nowę(:)$_V$- be a liar]
gadęnowęhtaʼ I am in denial; I am denying H
agadęno:węht I denied P

•nowęhd be absurd, unbelievable
[o+ contains: -nowę(:)$_V$- be a liar]
onowęht it is absurd, unbelievable S

•nowęhd lie
[ę+ contains: -nowę(:)$_V$- be a liar]
agę:no:węht I lied P

•nǫ:' costly, dear, expensive
[A+(N+)]
ganǫ:' it is expensive, dear, precious S
•nǫ(:) guard
[at+N+]
hęnatwihsdanǫh they (m) guard the money H
•(')nǫ: remove
see: ǫ'n(eg) remove, take away
gyonǫ: it has been removed S
•nǫ(:,') be unable
[P+]
aknǫha' I am unable H
ęhsa:nǫ:' you will fail P
ęwa:knǫ:' I will fail P
honǫ'ǫh he is unable S
•(h)nǫh handkerchief
see: (i)hnǫh handkerchief
gahnǫh handkerchief
•nǫ'(a:), nǫh(a) head
onǫ'a:' a head (owner unknown)
sanǫ'a:'geh on your head
•nǫ'aędǫ nod one's head, shake one's head
[de+...at+ -nǫ'(a:), nǫh(a)$_N$- head -ędǫh$_V$- shake s.t.]
desatnǫ'aędǫh nod; shake your head I
•nǫ'aohai'ta' shampoo
[ǫ+at+ -nǫ'(a:), nǫh(a)$_N$- head -ohai'd$_V$- cause to clean]
ǫtnǫ'ao:hai'ta' shampoo
•nǫ'aos(a) cabbage
[o+ contains: -nǫ'(a:), nǫh(a)$_N$- head]
onǫ'ao:sa' cabbage
•nǫ'aowekta' kerchief
[ǫ+at+ -nǫ'(a:), nǫh(a)$_N$- head -owekd$_V$- cover with s.t.]
ǫtnǫ'ao:wekta' a kerchief
•nǫd feed
[TR+ (N+)]
knǫ:dęh, knǫ:dęhs I feed it all the time H
ęhsnǫ:t you will feed P
knǫ:dę: I have fed it S
ęgwadęna'tranǫ:t we will give you food P
[TR+adę+ stem: -na'tr(a)$_N$- food, lunch -nǫd$_V$- feed]
•nǫhd be spooky
[P+ag+N+ occurs in:]
ogyanǫhsa:nǫht a weird, odd, spooky house S
•(')nǫhd be in s.t.
[ga+]
g'anǫht it (usually an animal) is in s.t. S
•(')nǫhd(a) bur
[o+]
o'nǫhda' a bur
•(')nǫhda(:,h) get into a vehicle, embark
[at+ contains: -(')nǫh$_V$- put in, get into]
gatn'ǫhda:s H
ęgatnǫhda:' I will embark, get in s.t. P
agatn'ǫhdahǫh, agatn'ǫhda:hǫh S
•(')nǫhda(:,h) give s.o. a ride; put s.o. in s.t.
[TR+ contains: -(')nǫhd$_V$- be in s.t.]
ęhshe'nǫhda:' you will put s.o. in s.t.; you will give him a ride P
•(')nǫhdagowah burdock
[o+ -(')nǫhd(a)$_N$- bur -gowah- large]
o'nǫhdago:wah burdock
•nǫd(a), nęd(a) hill
[o+ -nǫd(a), ned(a)$_N$- hill -ǫnyǫ' several]
onǫdahǫ:nyǫ' hills
•nǫdagǫ: valley
[o+ -nǫd(a), ned(a)$_N$- hill -gǫ: in]
onǫdagǫ: in the valley
•nǫhdahgw, nǫhdahgo disembark
[at+ contains: -(')nǫhd$_V$- be in s.t.]
ęgatnǫhdahgo' I will disembark, get out of a vehicle P

Legend: H habitual, P punctual, S stative, I imperative, PURP purposive, PURP-H purposive habitual, PURP-PAST purposive past, PURP-P purposive punctual, PURP-I purposive imperative; see §8.6, §8.11 in Appendix J. Alphabetization in stems ignores length (:), and any h's or glottal stops (') that are not between vowels. See §2.2 of the User Guide for explanation.

•nǫdahe:ˀ hill
[o+ -nǫd(a), ned(a)$_N$- hill -(h)e:ˀ$_V$- sitting up on top of s.t. -(h)ǫnyǫˀ$_V$- several things sitting up on top of s.t.]
onǫdahe:ˀ a hill
onǫdahǫ:nyǫˀ a hills
•nǫdanh be guilty
[P+ (at+)]
ęhsatnǫda:nhaˀ you will make yourself guilty P
gonǫdanhęh she is guilty S
•nǫdanh innocent
[(tęˀ) deˀ+ not P+ -nǫdanh-$_V$ be guilty]
dehonǫda:nhęh he is innocent S
•(h)nǫda:s gas station attendant
[A+ -(h)n(a)$_N$- oil, gas -ǫda:(h)$_V$- put in, be attached]
hahnǫ:da:s he is a gas station attendant
•(h)nǫde:ˀ sibling
[de+ TR+ adę+]
deyagyadęhnǫ:de:ˀ my brother; my sister (lit.: the one nearest to me in age and gender) S
•(ˀ)nǫdǫd alligator
[de+ga+ -(ˀ)nǫd(a)$_N$- alligator -ǫd$_V$- attached]
degaˀnǫ:dǫ:t an alligator
•(h)nǫdragyehsǫ(:) follow around
[TR+ contains: -(h)nǫdragyeˀ$_V$- follow along -sǫˀ several objects, events]
ęhshehnǫdragehsǫ:ˀ
(**ęhshehnǫdragyęhsǫ:ˀ**) you will follow s.o. around P
•(h)nǫdragyeˀ follow along
[TR+ contains: -(h)nǫdr$_V$- follow]
hǫwahnǫdra:gyeˀ s.o. is following him along H
•(h)nǫdre follow
[TR+ contains: -(h)nǫdr$_V$- follow -e- go]
hǫwahnǫdreˀ s.o. is following him PURP
ęhehsnǫdręˀ you will follow him PURP-P
dǫdahehsnǫ:dręh you follow him back
•nǫhg relative
[adę+]
sadę:nohk any relative (of yours) S
•nǫhg be sudden
[d+a+w+ ę+]
dawę:nǫhk suddenly; all of a sudden P
•(h)nǫg call
see: (i)hnǫg [heˀ/d+TR+] call
tagihnǫ:s he is calling me H
•nǫhga(:,ǫ) cut hair
[at+ contains: -nǫh(a), nah(a)$_N$- scalp]
gatnǫhgaǫ:s I always cut my hair; I am cutting my hair H
ęgatnǫhga:ˀ I am going to cut my hair P
agatnǫhgaǫ:ˀ I did get my hair cut S
•nǫgehaˀd breast-feed
[TR+ -nǫˀg(wa)$_N$- breast, milk -(h)negehaˀd$_V$- cause to drink]
ęhshenǫgehaˀt you will breast-feed P
•nǫhgęd fair haired
[P+ -nǫh(a), nah(a)$_N$- scalp -(ˀ)gęd$_V$- light-coloured white]
gonǫhgę:t she is fair haired; she has light hair S
•nǫgęˀd(a) catfish
[o+]
onǫgˀęda' a catfish
•nǫgęˀdǫ:t carp
[de+yo+ -nǫgęˀd(a)$_N$- catfish -ǫd$_V$- attached]
deyonǫgęˀdǫ:t a carp
•nǫˀg(wa) milk, breast
[o+]
onǫˀgwaˀ milk
enǫˀgwaˀgeh on her breast
•(ˀ)nǫhgwaˀe(g) beat a drum
[-nahg(wa)$_N$- drum, barrel -(ˀ)e(g)$_V$- hit]
ahaˀnǫhgwaˀe:k he beat the drum, the barrel P

•nǫʼgwahihs milkweed
[ga+ -nǫʼg(wa)$_N$- breast, milk -(hr)ihsd$_V$- bump s.t., s.o.]
ganoʼgwa̱hihs milkweed
•nǫgwahkw wean
[TR+ -nǫʼg(wa)$_N$- breast, milk -(h)kw$_V$- take s.t. from s.o. pick up]
ęhshenǫgwahkwaʼ you will take the milk from the child, wean her P
•(ʼ)nǫh arrow
[ga+]
gʼanǫh an arrow
•nǫhg(wę) cob
[o+]
onǫhgweʼ a corn cob
•nǫhgwijaʼ wet
[o+]
onǫhgwijaʼ it is soaking wet, saturated S
•nǫhaged put down one's head
[de+P+ -nǫʼ(a:), nǫh(a)$_N$- head -ged$_V$- grate, scrape, file]
dęhsanǫha:ge:t you will put your head down P
•nǫhahe:ʼ be happy
[P+ adę+ -nǫh(a), nah(a)$_N$- scalp -(h)e:ʼ$_V$- put, place]
hodonǫhahe:ʼ (**hodęnǫhahe:ʼ**) he is happy S
•nǫhahe:ʼ have on a wig
[P+...at+ -nǫh(a), nah(a)$_N$- scalp -(h)e:ʼ$_V$- sitting up on top of s.t.]
otnǫhahe:ʼ it has a wig on S
•nǫhahe:ʼ mane, scalp
[o+ -nǫh(a), nah(a)$_N$- scalp -(h)e:ʼ$_V$- sitting up on top of s.t.]
onǫhahe:ʼ a mane; a scalp
•nǫhaiyoh white sucker
[o+ -nǫʼ(a:), nǫh(a)$_N$- head -iyoh$_V$- become nice, good]
onǫhai:yoh a white sucker (a fish)
•nǫhakdǫ:, nǫhaʼged hang one's head, bow one's head
[de+P+ -nǫʼ(a:), nǫh(a)$_N$- head -(a)ʼkdǫ$_V$- bent, crooked]
deyonǫha:kdǫ: it is hanging its head (that is, in sadness or shame) S
•nǫhǫkdeʼ be painful
[o+ contains: -nǫhǫkd(ę,anih)$_V$- sick]
onohǫkdeʼ it is painful S
•nǫhǫkdenyǫʼ be painful all over
[P+ contains: -nǫhǫkd(ę,anih)$_V$- sick]
onohǫkde:nyǫʼ there is pain all over S
•nǫhǫkd(ę, ani) be sick
[P+]
aknǫhǫkda:nih I am sick H
•nǫhǫnyǫ(:) thank, greet, welcome
[de+...]
dekenǫhǫnyǫhaʼ I greet her H
dęhshenǫhǫ:nyǫ: you will welcome, greet, thank s.o. P
ganǫhǫnyǫhk, ganǫhǫnyǫh thanksgiving; the Thanksgiving Address S
•nǫhǫnyǫ(:) give thanks
[de+adę+]
dędwadęnǫhǫnyǫ:ʼ we all (incl.) will give thanks P
•nǫhkw love
[TR+]
kenǫhkwaʼ I love her H
•nǫhkw revere, show respect
[de+TR+]
dekenǫhǫkwaʼ she whom I revere H
•nǫʼne:ʼ be forbidden, sacred, holy
[o+(N+)]
onǫʼne:ʼ it is forbidden, sacred, holy S
oihwanǫʼne:ʼ a forbidden idea S
[o+ stem: -(r)ih(wa)$_N$- word -noʼne:ʼ$_V$- forbidden, sacred, holy]
•nǫʼned be next in line, be behind
[s+P+ -nǫʼ(a:), nǫh(a)$_N$- head -ned$_V$- keep]
shonǫʼne:t he is behind him, he is next in line S

Legend: H habitual, P punctual, S stative, I imperative, PURP purposive, PURP-H purposive habitual, PURP-PAST purposive past, PURP-P purposive punctual, PURP-I purposive imperative; see §8.6, §8.11 in Appendix J. Alphabetization in stems ignores length (:), and any h's or glottal stops (ʼ) that are not between vowels. See §2.2 of the User Guide for explanation.

•nǫnheʼ fill
ganǫnheʼs it fills up all the time H
ęganǫnheʼ it will fill up P
•nǫnheʼdr(a) nipple, soother, pacifier
onǫnheʼdraʼ a soother; a pacifier; a nipple
sa̱ʼnǫnheʼdraʼgeh on your nipples
•nǫnhehd fill s.t. up
[contains: -nǫnheʼ$_V$- fill]
ęhsnǫ:nheht, ęhsnę:nheht you will fill in P
•nǫny(a) dance
[ga+]
ganǫ:nyaʼ a dance
•nǫny(a) husk
[o+]
onǫ:nyaʼ a husk
•nǫʼnyad mourn
[P+adę+]
ęhsadęnǫʼnya:t you will mourn P
agadenǫʼnya:dǫ:ʼ I am in mourning S
•nǫhnyaʼd hurt
[o+ contains: -nǫhnyaʼg$_V$- hurt]
onǫhyaʼd hurt, hurting
•nǫnyaę(:) freeze
[-nǫny(a)$_N$- -ę-$_V$ lie]
deganǫnyaę:hęʼ it does not freeze H
ęganǫnyaę:ʼ it will freeze P
onǫnyaę:ʼ it is frozen S
•nǫhnyaʼg hurt
[P+]
aknǫhnyaʼs I am always getting hurt H
ęwaknǫhyaʼk I will get hurt P
honǫhnyʼagǫh he is hurt S
•nǫhnyaʼg hurt s.o., s.t.
[TR+]
ęhshenǫhnyaʼk you will hurt s.o. P
•nǫnyagęnyeʼs pow wow
[de+...at+ -nǫny(a)$_N$- dance -gęni, gęny$_V$- compete]
dęhęnatnǫnyagę:nyeʼs a pow wow (lit: they (m) perform competition dancing)
•nǫnyatgiʼ be a bad dancer
[P+ -nǫny(a)$_N$- dance -tgiʼ$_V$- be dirty, ugly]
gonǫnyatgiʼ she does not dance very well S
•nǫnyots(i) husk corn
[N+ -nǫny(a)$_N$- husk -ots(i)$_V$- remove an outer covering]
ęhsnǫnyotsiʼ, ęhsnęnyotsiʼ you will husk the corn P
snonyo:tsiʼ husk the corn I
•nǫhraʼtęʼ have grey hair
[P+ contains: -nǫʼ(a:), nǫh(a)$_N$- head]
gonǫhraʼtęʼ she has grey hair S
•nǫʼs tire of s.t., get sick of s.t.
[P+]
ǫʼknǫʼs I am sick of it, bored, fed up; I got sick of it P
•nǫʼshehsde:ʼ be boring, tiring
[o+ contains: -nǫʼs$_V$- tire, get sick of s.t.]
onǫʼshesde:ʼ it is boring, tiring S
•(ʼ)nǫhs(a) onion
[o+]
oʼnǫhsaʼ onions
•nǫhs(a) house
[ga+]
ganǫhsaʼ a house
•nǫhsagahęd window
[o+ -nǫhs(a)$_N$- house -gahęd$_V$- drill, hole]
onohsagahę:t a window
onǫhsagahę:dǫʼ windows
•nǫhsanǫh cricket
[ji+ -nǫhs(a)$_N$- house -(ʼ)nǫh$_V$- put in]
jinǫhsanǫh a cricket
•nǫhsdeʼ value s.t., cherish s.t.
[P+ contains: -nǫ:ʼ$_V$- be costly, dear, expensive]
aknǫhsdeʼ I value it S
•nǫʼseh be lazy, idle
[P+ contains: -nǫʼs$_V$- tire of s.t., get sick of s.t.]
aknǫʼseh I am lazy S

•nǫ'seh trout
[o+ contains: -nǫ's$_V$- tire of s.t., get sick of s.t.]
onǫ'seh trout
•nǫhsganyęh riot
[ga+ -nǫhs(a)$_N$- house -gany$_V$- be desperate]
ganǫhsganyęh a riot
•nǫhsgwaǫdǫ' toad
[o+ -(nęh)sg(wa), (nǫh)sg(wa)$_N$- frog -ǫdǫ'$_V$- several attached objects]
onǫhsgwaǫ:dǫ' a toad
•nǫhsgwatro' window
[w+adę+ -nǫhsgwatr(a)$_N$- pane -o'$_V$- submerged]
wadęnǫhsgwa'tro' a window
•nǫhsi'dre' snail
[ga+ -nǫhs(a)$_N$- house -(i)'dre(:)$_V$- drag, drive]
ganǫhsi'dre' a snail
•nǫhsod(a) sickness
[o+ -sǫ:'ǫh several]
onǫhsoda'shǫ:'oh human sicknesses
•nǫhsodaę:' sickness
[o+ -nǫhsod(a)$_N$- sickness -ę$_V$- lie]
onǫhsodaę:' sickness
•nǫhsodaiyǫ:' sickness, illness, epidemic, plague
[o+ -nǫhsod(a)$_N$- sickness -iyǫ:'$_V$-]
onǫhsodai:yǫ:' a sickness; an illness; an epidemic; a plague
•nǫhsodaiyǫ: mud puppy, dogfish
[contains: -nǫhsodiyǫ:- sickness, illness]
nǫhsodai:yǫ: mud puppies; dogfish
•nǫhsodanǫ:' AIDs, disease, HIV
[ga+ -nǫhsod(a)$_N$- sickness -nǫ:'$_V$- be costly, expensive]
ganohsohda:nǫ:' AIDs; disease; HIV
•nǫhsǫd room, vault
[o+ -nǫhs(a)$_N$- house -ǫd$_V$- attached]
onǫhsǫ:t a room; a vault
onǫhsǫdǫ:nyǫ' rooms
heyonǫhsǫ:t the next room
hejonǫhsǫ:t the room after the next room
•nǫhsǫnih carpenter
[A+ -nǫhs(a)$_N$- house -ǫni, ǫny$_V$- make]
hanǫhsǫ:nih he is a carpenter
•nǫhsǫnyani: nursing home
[shagodi+ -nǫhs(a)$_N$- house -ǫnyani$_V$- make for s.o.]
sagodinǫhsonya:ni: a nursing home
•nǫhsǫta' stapler
see: nahsǫta' stapler
deganǫhsǫ:ta' a stapler (short form)
•nǫhtwahsd force, rape
[de+TR+ę+]
tgasheyęnǫhtwahs you force people all the time H
dahshagonǫhtwahs he forced her P
•nǫwag crave
knǫ:wa:s I crave s.t. H
ęknǫwa:k I will crave s.t. P
•nǫhwag be sore, ache
[P+N+ -ya'd(a)$_N$- body]
agya'danǫhwa:s I am sore; I ache H
ǫgya'danǫhwa:k I ached P
•nǫwayęhd barter
[de+ contains: -(y)ęhd$_V$- hit]
dehsnǫwayęhta' you are a bargainer H
dęhsnǫwayęht you will barter, bargain, affirm a deal P
•nǫwayęhdǫ: purchase
[ga+ contains: -nǫwayęhd$_V$- barter]
ganǫwayęhdǫ: a purchase
•nǫhwed sleep over
[ę+...]
ęgęnǫhwe:t I will sleep over P
•nǫhwe' like
enǫhwe's she likes it H
ęyenǫhwe' she will like it P
•nǫhwe' dislike
[de'+ not contains: -nǫhwe'$_V$- like]
tę' degęhnǫhwe's I do not like it H

Legend: H habitual, P punctual, S stative, I imperative, PURP purposive, PURP-H purposive habitual, PURP-PAST purposive past, PURP-P purposive punctual, PURP-I purposive imperative; see §8.6, §8.11 in Appendix J. Alphabetization in stems ignores length (:), and any h's or glottal stops (') that are not between vowels. See §2.2 of the User Guide for explanation.

•nǫhwehstaʼ bedroom
[ǫ+ contains: -nǫhwehsd$_V$- cause to sleep over]
onǫhwestaʼ bedroom
•nǫhwetsoʼd(ę, ani) turn s.o. upside down
[de+TR+]
dęgǫnǫhwe:tsoʼdęʼ I am going to turn you upside down, upend you (said in anger) P
•nǫhwetsoʼd(ǫ) do a handstand, turn upside down
[(de+)...at+]
sadǫhweʼtso:taʼ you do hand-stands all the time H
dęsatnǫhwe:tsoʼdǫʼ you (s) will do a hand stand, turn yourself upside down P
•nǫwęhdraʼ be cantankerous
[A+]
enǫwęhdraʼ she is cantankerous S
•nǫhyani be frugal
[de+P+]
deyagonǫhya:ni:s she is frugal H
•nǫhyanihd be terrible, overwhelming
[de+yo+(adę+) contains: -nǫhyani$_V$- be frugal]
deyodęnǫhyanihdǫh it is overwhelming, terrible S
•nr(a) phallus, penis
onraʼ a phallus
hanraʼgeh on his penis, phallus
•nrahd(a) leaf
[o+]
onrahdaʼ a leaf
•nrahdʼaę:ʼ green
[o+ -nrahd(a)$_N$- leaf -ʼę:ʼ$_V$- be coloured]
onrahdʼaę:ʼ green
•nrahda:s lettuce
[e+ -nrahd(a)$_N$- leaf -g$_V$- eat]
enrahda:s lettuce
•nrahdęhd deleaf, pluck leaves
[-nrahd(a)$_N$- leaf -(y)ęhd$_V$- hit, knock down, strike]
ęhsenrahdęht you will pick off leaves P
•nrahsr(a) mushroom
[o+]
onrahsraʼ a mushroom
•nrahsrod rooster comb
[o+ -nrahsr(a)$_N$- mushroom -od$_V$- stand]
onrahsro:t a rooster comb
•nregęʼd(a) tripe, stomach lining, animal stomach
[o+]
onregʼędaʼ tripe (cow stomach lining); an animal stomach
•nreʼogęʼ swallow
[de+ga+ -nreʼ(a)$_N$- -ogę$_V$- be together, between]
deganręʼo:gęʼ a swallow (a bird)
•nręh(ę) tapeworm
[o+]
onręhęʼ a tapeworm
•nrod hermaphrodite
[o+ -nr(a)$_N$- phallus, penis -od$_V$- stand]
onro:t a hermaphrodite
•nrowektaʼcondom
[ǫ+ade+ -nr(a)$_N$- phallus, penis -owekd$_V$- cover with s.t.]
ǫdenrowe:ktaʼ a condom
•(h)ny(a) stick
[ga+]
ganhyaʼ (**gahnyaʼ**) a stick
•(h)ny(a:) nutmeat
[o+]
ohnya:ʼ nutmeat
•(ʼ)ny(a) finger, hand
oʼnyaʼ fingers
•(ʼ)nya(ę,:) look after
[de+...ę+ -(ʼ)ny(a)$_N$- finger, hand -a:ʼ$_V$- hold, contain, include]
dehseʼnya:ʼ you look after it (all the time) H
dęhsęʼnyaę:ʼ, dęhsęʼnya:ʼ you will look after it P

•nyad(a:) lake, body of water, water
ganyada:ʼgeh to, at, on the lake
ganyadakda:gyeʼ along the lake, the shoreline
•(ʼ)nyaʼdad point out s.o.
[TR+ -(ʼ)ny(a)$_N$- finger, hand -d$_V$- stand]
ęhshęʼnyʼada:t you will point s.o. out P
•(h)nyahdod lift one's head
[A+ -(h)nya(ʼsa)$_N$- neck, throat -od$_V$- stand]
ehnyahdo:t she's got her head up (said of a child who is learning to lift its head by itself) S
•nyadahka:ʼ smelts
[ga+ -nyad(a:)$_N$- lake, body of water, water -ka:ʼ- way, kind]
ganyadahka:ʼ smelts
•(h)nyaʼdr(ę:) hang s.o.
[TR+ contains: -(h)nya(ʼsa)$_N$- neck, throat]
hǫwadihnyaʼdręhs they hang him, them (m) all the time H
ahǫwadihnyadrę:ʼ they hanged him, them (m) P
hǫwadihnyaʼdragǫh they have already hanged him (and his neck broke) S
•nyadahneh chokecherries
[o+ -nyad(a:)$_N$- lake, body of water, water -hneh- at]
onyadahneh chokecherries
•nyahdę: turtle
[ga+]
ganyahdę: turtle
•nyahdęgowah snapping turtle
[ga+ -nyahdę$_N$- turtle -gowah big]
ganyahdęgo:wah a snapping turtle
•nyaʼdiga:ʼ heron
[s+ga+ -nyad(a:)$_N$- lake, body of water, -ig(a:ʼ)$_V$- be in water]
sganyaʼdi:ga:ʼ a heron

•nyag marry
[P+]
age:nya:s I am getting married right now H
ęwagenya:k I will be married P
age:nya:gǫh I am married S
•nyaʼg cut, break, cross
see: (i)yaʼg [(N+)] cut, break, cross
enehsdanyaʼs, enehsdaiyaʼs she is sawing a board H
[-nehsd(a:)$_N$- floor, board -(i)yaʼg$_V$- cut, break]
•(ʼ)nyaganye: sweetmilk pop, flour mush cereal
[de+w+ę+ -(ʼ)ny(a)$_N$- finger, hand -ganye(:)$_V$- shuffle]
dewęʼnyaga:nye:ʼ flour mush; sweetmilk pop (a traditional dish)
•(ʼ)nyagę escape, run away
geʼnya:gęʼs I'm an escaper H
shaʼnya:gęʼ he escaped P
godiʼnyaʼgęʼǫh they (f/m) ran away S
•(ʼ)nyagęhd help s.o. escape
[TR+ contains: -(ʼ)nyagęʼ$_V$- escape, run away]
ęhsheʼnya:gęht you will help s.o. escape P
•nyaʼgǫʼ beaver
[na+ga+ contains: -(ʼ)ny(a)$_N$- finger, hand]
naganyaʼgǫʼ beaver
•nyaʼg shoot
see: (i)yaʼg, iʼaʼg shoot
hadiyʼa:s they (m) are shooting H
•(ʼ)nyagw participate
[de+ -(ʼ)ny(a)$_N$- finger, hand -gw$_V$- gather, choose]
dęyagoʼnya:gwęhęgyeʼ she will have a hand in it S
•nyaʼg(wa) vomit
[o+]
onyaʼgwaʼ vomit; vomitus

Legend: H habitual, P punctual, S stative, I imperative, PURP purposive, PURP-H purposive habitual, PURP-PAST purposive past, PURP-P purposive punctual, PURP-I purposive imperative; see §8.6, §8.11 in Appendix J. Alphabetization in stems ignores length (:), and any h's or glottal stops (ʼ) that are not between vowels. See §2.2 of the User Guide for explanation.

•nyaʼgwahd make oneself vomit, be bulemic
[ade+ contains: -nyaʼgwah, nyaʼgoʼ$_V$- vomit]
gadenyagwahtaʼ I make myself vomit H
agadenyaʼgwaht I made myself throw up P
sadenyagwaht make yourself vomit I

•nyaʼgwah, nyaʼgoʼ vomit
[P+]
agenyʼagwahs I am vomiting; I am a vomiter; I vomit all the time H
ǫgenyʼagoʼ I vomited P
agenyaʼgwahǫh I am vomiting (right now) S

•nyah(a) mush
[o+]
onyahaʼ native mush dishes made with corn

•(h)nyaha: win a bet
[adę+ -(h)ny(a)$_N$- stick -(h)awi, (h)a:$_V$- hold, include, carry, bring]
agęnadęhnyęha:ʼ they (z) won a bet P

•nyahaʼd boil s.t.
[ę+ contains: -nyahę(h,ʼ)$_V$- boil]
sęnyahaʼt boil it I

•nyahe:ʼ collar
[de+ga+ -(h)nya(ʼsa)$_N$- neck, throat -(h)e:ʼ$_V$- sitting up on top of s.t.]
deganyahe:ʼ a collar

•nyahę(h,ʼ) boil
[P+(N+)]
onyahęhs it is boiling H
ęgyǫnyahęh it will boil P
onyahęʼǫh it has boiled S
ohsgwanya̱hęhs rocks are boiling H
[-(h)sg(wa:)$_N$- stone, bullet, rock -nyahę(h,ʼ)$_V$- boil]

•nyaohag squeeze s.o.'s neck
[de+TR+ -(h)nya(ʼsa)$_N$- neck, throat -ohag$_V$- squeeze]
atǫwanyaoha:k s.o. squeezed his neck P

•nyakdreʼ bride
[go+ contains: -nyag$_V$- get married]
gonya:kdreʼ a bride to be (lit.: she is getting married)

•nyaʼksǫ(:) several broken pieces
see: (i)yaʼksǫ(:) [de+...] several broken pieces
degayʼaksǫʼ it is broken S

•nyaʼksǫʼ broken up in different ways
see: (i)yaʼksǫʼ [haʼ+de+...] broken up in different ways
haʼdegayaʼksǫʼ it is broken up in different ways S

•nyaʼkwai: seal
[ga+ -nyaʼ(sa)$_N$- neck -g(wa)- lump -i:ʼ$_V$- stuck onto s.t.]
ganyaʼkwai: seal (this word refers to its lack of a neck)

•(h)nya(ʼsa) neck, throat
ohnyaʼsaʼ a neck
ohnyaʼ the neck; the throat
se̱hnyaʼsʼageh on your neck (the front of the neck)
ohnyaʼsaʼgǫ: in the throat

•(h)nyahsg(a:) button
[contains: -ęʼnihsg(a)$_N$- circle]
ęhnyahsga:ʼ a button

•(h)nyaʼsgaʼohsd hiccough, hiccup
[P+ contains: -(h)nya(ʼsa)$_N$- neck, throat]
hohnyaʼsgʼaohs he is hiccupping, hiccoughing H
ęsahnyʼasgaʼohs you will hiccup, hiccough P

•(h)nyahshę: slow beat
[o+ -(h)ny(a)$_N$- stick -(a)hshę:$_V$- be slow-moving]
ohnyahshę: a slow beat

•(h)nyahsnowe' fast beat
[o+ -(h)ny(a)$_N$- stick -(h)snowe'$_V$- be fast]
ohnyahsno:we' a fast beat
•nyatsǫni braid s.t.
ganya:tsǫ:ni: it is braided S
•(')nyawe clap
[de+...ę+ -(')ny(a)$_N$- finger, hand -(')e$_V$- hit]
desę'nya'we:k, desę'nya'o:k (you (s)) clap I
•nya:węh thank you
see: Appendix I
•nyehd send s.t.
shagodęnyehta' H
ahǫwadę:nyeht he was sentenced (lit.: they sent him) P
hewagadęnyehdǫh I sent it S
•nyehd send s.t.
[he'+...ad+N+ stem: -(r)ih(wa)$_N$- word -nyehd$_V$- send s.t.]
hęswadrihwanyeht you all will send a message P
•nyehd refer s.o.
[he'+TR+adę+ contains: -nyehd$_V$- send s.t.]
hęgǫyadę:nyeht I will refer you (to s.o. else) P
•nyehd send s.o., sentence s.o.
[TR+adę+ contains: -nyehd$_V$- send s.t.]
ahǫwadę:nyeht he was sentenced (lit.: they sent him) P
•(h)nye:h(a) flint corn soup
[o+]
ohnye:ha' flint corn soup
•nyęd(a) stem, shin, leg
onyę:da' a stem
genyęd'ageh on my shin, leg
•(h)nyędahs(a) beak
[ga/o+]
gahnyędahsa', ohnyędahsa' a beak
gahnyędahsa'geh on its beak
•(')nyęde' come for a purpose
[A+ contains: -(')nyędę$_V$- try]
senyę'de' you came for a purpose P
•(')nyędę try, sample, attempt
[ade+]
gade'nyę:dęhs I try all the time H
a:gade'nyę:dę' I might try, attempt it P
sade'nyę:dęh sample it; try it I
•(')nyędęhsd measure
[ade+ contains: -(')nyędę$_V$- try]
wade'nyędęhsdǫh the act of measuring S
•(')nyędęhsd copy, compare
[d+...ade+ contains: -(')nyędę$_V$- try]
ętsadenyę:dęhs you will copy, use as a model or pattern P
dahsadenyę:dęhs copy compare I
•(')nyędęhsdǫh measurement
[w+ade+ contains: -(')nyędę$_V$- try]
wade'nyędęhsdǫh the act of measuring
•nyę'gwaohǫh drifted snow
[-nyę'g(wa)$_N$- drifting snow -(h)ǫ(:)$_V$- lie]
onyę'gwaohǫh drifted snow
•nyę'swadih left
[s+ga+ -nyę'sw(a)$_N$- left -(a)dih$_V$- side]
sganyę'sgwa:dih to its left
•(h)nyętse:s garfish
[ga+ -(h)nyęts(a)$_N$- -es$_V$- long]
gahnyętse:s garfish
•nyo kill someting
see: (r)iyo, nyo [TR+] kill someting
aha:nyo' he killed an animal P
•nyo:' animal
[A+ -nyo:'$_N$- wild animal; contains: -(r)iyo, nyo$_V$- kill someting]
ganyo: wild animals
gadi:nyo:' they (z) are wild animals
ganyo'shǫ:'ǫh wild game; wild animals
•nyoh a term of acknowledgement; o.k.; alright; can be said in response to nya:węh; can be said sarcastically to bug someone.
see: Appendix I

Legend: H habitual, P punctual, S stative, I imperative, PURP purposive, PURP-H purposive habitual, PURP-PAST purposive past, PURP-P purposive punctual, PURP-I purposive imperative; see §8.6, §8.11 in Appendix J. Alphabetization in stems ignores length (:), and any h's or glottal stops (') that are not between vowels. See §2.2 of the User Guide for explanation.

•(ʼ)nyod celebrate, party
[adę+ -(ʼ)ny(a)$_N$- finger, hand -od$_V$- stand]
sadęʼnyotaʼ you celebrate all the time; you are celebrating H
ęhsadęʼnyo:dęʼ you will celebrate P
wadęʼnyo:t a celebration, party S
•(ʼ)nyod celebration, party
[w+adę+ -(ʼ)ny(a)$_N$- finger, hand -od$_V$- stand]
wadęʼnyo:t a celebration; a party
•(h)nyod stand
[A+ -(h)ny(a)$_N$- stick -od$_V$- stand]
gahnyo:t it is standing S
•(ʼ)hnyod rainbow
[o+ -(rǫ)ʼnih(a)$_N$- rainbow, sunbeam, ray -od$_V$- stand]
oʼhnyo:t there is a rainbow
•nyod(a) spoon, canoe
[ga+]
ganyo:daʼ a spoon; a canoe; a birch bark canoe
•(h)nyoʼdę: rhythm, beat
[ni+ga+ -(h)ny(a)$_N$- stick -oʼdę:$_V$- be a certain type, kind of thing]
nigahnyoʼdę: the rhythm; the beat of a piece of music
•nyodowanęh tablespoon
[ga+ -nyod(a)$_N$- spoon, canoe -owanęh$_V$- be big]
ganyodowa:nęh a tablespoon
•(h)nyoʼg(wa) nut
[o+]
ohnyoʼgwaʼ nut
•(h)nyʼogęʼ chipmunk
[ji+ -(h)ny(a)$_N$- stick -ogę$_V$- be together, between, double]
jihnyʼogęʼ chipmunk (this word refers to the stripe on the chipmunk's back)
•(h)nyoʼgwaji: walnut
[ga+ -(h)nyoʼg(wa)$_N$- nut -ji(:,h)$_V$- dark]
ga̱hnyoʼgwaji: a walnut

•(h)nyǫ(ʼǫ)hsr(a) iron, steel, bar
[ga+]
ga̱hnyǫʼǫhsraʼ iron; steel
ga̱hnyǫʼsraʼ a bar of iron, steel
•(ʼ)nyotraʼ mittens
[ę+ contains: -(ʼ)ny(a)$_N$- finger, hand -od$_V$- stand]
ęʼnyo:traʼ mittens
•(ʼ)nyǫdǫʼ glove
[(de+y)o+ -(ʼ)ny(a)$_N$- finger, hand -ǫdǫʼ$_V$- several attached objects]
oʼnyǫdo gloves
deyonyǫ:dǫh gloves
•(h)nyǫʼǫh white
[ga+]
ga̱hnyǫʼǫh it is white S
•(h)nyǫhs(a) melon, squash
[o+]
ohnyǫhsaʼ a melon; a squash
•(ʼ)nyǫhs(a) nose
oʼnyǫhsaʼ a nose
sʼenyǫhsʼageh on your nose
•(ʼ)nyǫhsaʼ moose
[s+ga+ -(ʼ)nyǫhs(a)$_N$- nose]
sganyǫhsaʼ a moose
•(h)nyǫhsaǫweh hubbard squash
[o+ -(h)nyǫhs(a)$_N$- squash -ǫweh- traditional]
ohnyǫhsʼaǫ:weh squash (used for soup at the Longhouse; usually Hubbard squash)
•(h)nyǫhsgwaeʼ cucumber
[o+ cǫntains: -(h)nyǫhs(a)$_N$- melon, squash -g(wa)$_N$- lump]
ohnyǫhsgwa:eʼ a cucumber
•(h)nyǫhsr(a) bar
[ga+]
ga̱hnyǫʼsraʼ a bar of iron, steel
•(h)nyǫhsradeʼ prison, iron beams
[de+ga+ -hnyǫ(ʼǫ)hsr(a)$_N$- iron, steel -deʼ$_V$- exist]
degahnyǫhsra:deʼ prison; iron beams

•(ʼ)nyǫhswahaʼd mischievous, nosy
[de+P+ -(ʼ)nyǫhs(a)$_N$- nose -swahaʼd$_V$- go and sniff s.t.]
dewagʼenyǫhswahaʼt I am mischievous, nosy S

O

•o(:) submerge, boil, cook
[A+(N+)]
hęnadahnyoh they (m) are fishing over there H
[ad+ stem: -(a)hnyo- fish; consists of: -(a)hny(a)$_N$- hook -o(:)$_V$- submerge]
gadahnyoʼs I fish continually H
ęhsahyo:ʼ you will cook, boil the fruit P
[-(a)hy(a)$_N$- fruit, berry -o(:)$_V$- submerge]
i:yoʼ it is in the water; it is submerged in liquid S
shǫnaʼdo: boil the potatoes I
[-(h)ǫnaʼd(a)$_N$- potato -o(:)$_V$- submerge]
•oʼ boiled, stewed
[A+(N+) occurs in:]
ganęhoʼ boiled corn S
[A+(N+) -nęh(ę)$_N$- corn -oʼ$_V$- boiled, stewed]
•o: So? Oh really?
see: Appendix I
•o: tęʼǫh no (very emphatic)
see: Appendix I
•od stand
[A/P+N+ occurs in:]
wadręnotaʼ a stereo; a radio H
[-(r)ęn(a)$_V$- music -od$_V$- stand]
ęhsnaʼjo:dęʼ you will boil it P
[-naʼj(a)$_N$- pail, drum -od$_V$- stand]
gaęno:t music playing S
[-(r)ęn(a)$_N$- song, music -od$_V$- stand]
sejihsdo:dęh turn on the light I
[-jihsd(a)$_N$- light -od$_V$- stand]
•od have s.t. attached
[A/P+N+ occurs in:]
dwanoʼjo:t we all (incl.) have teeth S
[-noʼj(a)$_N$- tooth -od$_V$- stand]
sanę:tso:t you have an arm; your attached arm S
•od exist, be standing
[(d+)A/P+N+ occurs in:]
tganǫhso:t a house is over there S
[-nǫhs(a)$_N$- house -od$_V$- stand]
gatseʼdo:t a standing bottle S
[-(i)tseʼd(a)$_N$- bottle -od$_V$- stand]
•ohda(:,h) tidy up, clean
[de+...ad+]
degaǫ:dohda:s (they (f/m) are) janitors H
dęsadǫhda:ʼ you will tidy it up, clean it P
deyodǫhdahǫh it is tidy, neat S
desadǫhda: clean up I
•oda(:,h) drape
[(N+)]
goda:s I drape it all the time H
ęgoda: I will drape it P
oda:hǫh it is draped S
senhehsoda: harness it (an animal) I
[-nhehs(a)$_N$- lace, ribbon, harness -oda(:,h)$_V$- drape]
•odahd(ę, ani) trip
[de+...+ad+]
dedesadoda:hdanih it trips you all the time H
dęhsadodahdęʼ it will trip you P
•odagw remove, take away; also see ǫdagw remove, take away
[(N+) occurs in:]
hadęnʼojodagwahs he is a dentist H
[A+adę+ stem: -nʼojodagwahs- dentist; consists of: -noʼj(a)$_N$- tooth -odagw$_V$- remove, detach]

Legend: H habitual, P punctual, S stative, I imperative, PURP purposive, PURP-H purposive habitual, PURP-PAST purposive past, PURP-P purposive punctual, PURP-I purposive imperative; see §8.6, §8.11 in Appendix J. Alphabetization in stems ignores length (:), and any h's or glottal stops (ʼ) that are not between vowels. See §2.2 of the User Guide for explanation.

•odagw remove, take away (continued)
agatnoʼjodagoʼ I had my tooth pulled P
[at+ -noʼj(a)$_N$- tooth -odagw$_V$- remove, detach]
otnegoda:gwęh splashing water S
[o+ at+ stem: -(h)neg(a)$_N$- water, liquid -odagw$_V$- remove, detach]
•odagyeʼ go along doing s.t., stand along
[A+(N+) contains: -od$_V$- stand -agyeʼ go along doing s.t.]
gajiʼdoda:gyeʼ s.o. is going along crying H
[-jiʼd(a)$_N$- cry -odagyeʼ$_V$- go along doing s.t.]
•odahkwaʼ an attached or standing instrument
[A/P+ N+ contains: -od$_V$- stand -ahkwaʼ instrument; occurs in:]
ǫdręnodahkwaʼ musical instruments S
[ǫ+ad+ -(r)ęn(a)$_N$- song -odahkwaʼ$_V$- an attached or standing instrument]
•ohda:s janitor
[de+...ad+ -ohda(:,h)$_V$- tidy up, clean]
degaǫ:dohda:s they (f/m) are janitors
•odaihs(i) undrape
[de+ contains: -oda(:,h)$_V$- drape]
ętsodaihsiʼ you will undrape s.t. P
•odais(i) comb one's hair
[de+…ad+ / TR+]
degadodaishǫhs I am combing my hair H
dęgadodai:siʼ I am going to comb my hair P
dęgǫyodai:siʼ I am going to comb your hair P
dewagadodaihsǫhǫgyeʼ I am going along combing my hair S
desadodai:siʼ you comb your hair I
•odais(i) rescue s.o., save s.o.
[TR+ ad+]
ęhsheyʼadodaisiʼ you will help her escape; you will save her P

•odais(i) get loose, escape
[ad+]
ahadodaisi:ʼ he got loose, escaped P
•odahs(i) appear unintentionally
[taʼ+...ad+ contains: -od$_V$- stand]
taʼsadodahsiʼ you appeared unintentionally P
•odekǫnyaʼtaʼgeh onǫhsǫ:t dining room
ǫdekǫnyaʼtaʼgeh a dining room
onǫhsǫ:t a room
•odę put somewhere
[N+ contains: -od$_V$- stand]
ahsnętso:dęʼ you put on its (a doll's) arm P
[-nęts(a)$_N$- arm -odę$_V$- put]
sehtseʼdo:dęh you put the bottle there I
[-(i)tse(ʼda)$_N$- bottle -odę$_V$- put]
•oʼdę: be a certain type, kind of thing
[ni+ N+ occurs in:]
nigaęnoʼdę: a type of song S
[ni+ga+ stem: -(r)ęn(a)$_N$- song, music -oʼdę:$_V$- type of]
•odǫ(:,ʼ) be several standing objects
[A/P+ N+ contains: -od$_V$- stand; occurs in:]
ęyohnawao:dǫ:k there will be wells, water, springs P
[-(h)naw(a)$_N$- running water -odǫʼ$_V$- several standing objects]
waʼę:no:dǫʼ saplings; young trees S
[w+ stem: -(a)ʼęn(a)$_N$- stick, pole, rod -odǫʼ$_V$- several standing objects]
•odǫnyǫʼ be many standing objects
[A/P+ N+ contains: -od$_V$- stand -ǫnyǫʼ plural; occurs in:]
ohahodǫ:nyǫʼ many side roads S
[-(h)ah(a)$_N$- road -odǫnyǫʼ$_V$- many standing objects]

•odrah sprinkle
[(N)+ occurs in:]
hǫwadi̱hnegodrahs baptism; to christen s.o. (lit.: they sprinkle him, them) H
[-(h)neg(a)$_N$- water, liquid -odrah$_V$- sprinkle]
ęhęnodrah they (m) will sprinkle on P
hǫwatnegodrahǫh they (m) have been baptized S
[-(h)neg(a)$_N$- water, liquid -odrah$_V$- sprinkle]

•odrahsd sprinkle on
[contains: -odrah$_V$- sprinkle]
hęnodra̱hsta' they (m) sprinkle on H
honodra̱hsdǫh they (m) are going along sprinkling; they (m) have sprinkled S

•odrǫhgwa(ǫhǫ:) shiver, twitch
[(de+) -ya'd(a)$_N$- body -odrǫhgwa(ǫhǫ:)$_V$- shiver, twitch]
desay'adodrǫhgwaǫhǫ' you twitch all the time; you're a twitcher H

•odrǫhgwaǫni shiver
[(de+) -ya'd(a)$_N$- body -odrǫhgwa(ǫhǫ:)$_V$- shiver, twitch -sgǫ: easily]
saya'dodrǫhgwaǫnihsgǫ: you are always shivering H

•(')og axe, chop
gę̱'ohs I am a chopper H
ęhsa'o:k it will chop you P
age'o:gǫh I did chop; I have chopped S

•o:g be blistered
[P+(N+) contains: -o' $_V$- submerged; occurs in:]
ǫgra:do:k I blistered my heel P
[P+(N+) -(r)a(k)d(a)$_N$- heel -og $_V$- be blistered]

•o'gad rough
see: (r)oga'd [P+(N+)] rough
ao:ga't it is rough S

•ohga(:,h) coat, clean s.t.
sǫhga:s you coat s.t. all the time (i.e., for a living) H
ęhsohga:' you will coat s.t. (with a paste, etc.) P
sǫhga:hǫh you have coated it S

•ogę: be between
[de+...adad+ occurs in:]
detniy'ada:do:gę: between you and me (our bodies) S
[de+...adad+ stem: -ya'd(a)$_N$- body -ogę$_V$- together, between]

•ogę' be together, between
[N+]
jihny'ogę' chipmunk (this word refers to the stripe on the chipmunk's back) S
[-jihnew(a)$_N$- stripe -ogę$_V$- between]

•ogę'ǫh be between
[de+...ad+ occurs in:]
deyodogę'ǫh it is in between; a duel between two people S
[de+yo+ad+ stem: -ogę'ǫh- a duel; consists of: -ogę$_V$- be together, between]

•ogę'ǫh duel
[de+yo+ad+ contains: -ogę$_V$- be together, between]
deyodogę'ǫh a duel between two people (lit.: it is in between)

•ogw scatter
[de+ N+ occurs in:]
dewagyęgwaogwahs small puffballs (already gone to seed) H
[de+wa+ag+ stem: -yęgwaogwahs- puffball; consists of: -yę'g(wa)$_N$- tobacco, smoke, cigarettes -ogw$_V$- scatter]
awadę̱hsiyo:go' it frayed P
[(de+)...ade+ -(h)siy(a)$_N$- line, string -ogw$_V$- scatter]
deyoda̱hsiyo:gwęh it is frayed S

•ogwahd distribute
[de+...ad+(N+) contains: -ogw$_V$- scatter]
degadogwahta' I scatter s.t. H

Legend: H habitual, P punctual, S stative, I imperative, PURP purposive, PURP-H purposive habitual, PURP-PAST purposive past, PURP-P purposive punctual, PURP-I purposive imperative; see §8.6, §8.11 in Appendix J. Alphabetization in stems ignores length (:), and any h's or glottal stops (') that are not between vowels. See §2.2 of the User Guide for explanation.

•ogwahd distribute (continued)
dę̨satnesogwaht you will distribute sand P
[-nehs(a)$_N$- sand -ogwahd$_V$- distribute]
desadogwahdǫh you have distributed it S

•oʼgwad dig
[P+ (N+)]
oʼgwa:s it digs H
aʼoʼgwa:t it dug P
ei:hoʼgwa:s she is researching, instigating
[-(r)ih(wa)$_N$- word -oʼgwad$_V$- dig]

•ogwę̨h chaos, disorder
[de+yo+ad+ contains: -ogw$_V$- scatter]
deyodogwę̨h disorder; chaos

•ogwę̨hę̨:gyeʼ now and then, now and again
see: Appendix I

•ogyeʼ float
[P+ contains: -gye$_V$- fly]
ogyeʼ it is floating along (in the water) PURP

•oh dip in liquid
[heʼ+ contains: -o(:)$_V$- submerge]
he:gohs I am dipping it in all the time H
hę̨:goh I will dip it in P
hewagohǫh I have already dipped, submerged it S

•oha(:,ę) attach s.t.
ę̨hsohaę̨ʼ you will attach s.t. P
oha:ʼ it is attached (to s.t.) S

•ohae, ohai clean, wash
[(ad+) n/N+ occurs in:]
ǫhjohai:s she is washing her hands H
[-(a)hj(iʼda)$_N$- hand -ohae$_V$- wash]
ę̨sahyǫ̱hai:ʼ you will wash fruit P
[-(a)hy(a)$_N$- fruit, berry -ohae$_V$- clean, wash]
agatgǫhsǫ̱hai: I did wash my face S
[at+ -gǫhs(a)$_N$- hand -ohae$_V$- wash]
odę̨nǫ̱hai:ʼ it is washed, clean S
satgǫhsǫ̱hae wash your face I

•ohag squeeze
[de+ad/N/(h)sd+ occurs in:]
degahstǫdroha:s a bailer (for hay, straw) H
[-(h)stǫdr(a)$_N$- hay, straw -ohag$_V$- squeeze]
dę̨hstǫ̱ha:k you will squeeze it P
dewakdǫ̱ha:gǫh I am squeezing it S
dehstoha:k squeeze it I

•ohaihǫ(:) go and wash
[(ad+)n/N+ contains: -ohae$_V$- clean, wash; occurs in:]
geksohaihǫh I am washing dishes H
[(ad+)n/N+ -ks(a)$_N$- dish -ohaihǫ$_V$- go and wash]
seksohaihǫ: wash the dishes I

•ohehdaʼ gegwai where it starts; the bottom
ohehdaʼ dirt; earth
gegwai a direction; a side

•oheg gather
see: (r)oheg [(N+)] gather
gae:yohe:s they (f/m) are gathering H

•ohę̨dae:ʼ ohyaʼ peach
ohę̨hdaę̨:ʼ it is furry
ohyaʼ fruit

•ohę̨hda:eʼ ohyaʼ gra̱he:t a peach tree
ohę̨hdae:ʼ ohyaʼ peaches
gra̱he:t a living tree

•ohikdadeht awę̨hę̨ʼ ohǫ:daʼ rose bushes
ohikdadeht rose bushes
awę̨hę̨ʼ flower
ohǫ:daʼ bush

•ohǫnʼadaʼ eyahkwaʼ gaʼahdraʼ a potato basket
ohǫnʼadaʼ potato
eyahkwaʼ container
gaʼahdraʼ basket

•ohǫ:ʼ gathering
see: (r)ohǫ:ʼ gathering
gaohǫ:ʼ the act of gathering

•oi'a: torch s.t., throw flames at s.t.
[N+ occurs in:]
hegę'dǫhgoia:s dragon (lit.: flame thrower) H
[he+ga+ -idǫhg(wa)$_N$- flame -oi'as$_V$- torch s.t.]
dewadejihsdoy'a:s static H
[de+wa+ade+ -jihsd(a)$_N$- light, -oi'as$_V$- torch s.t.]

•o'jin(a) skate
[ad+]
ado'ji:na' skate

•o'jinehd skate
[de+...ad+ -o'jin(a)$_N$- skate -ehd$_V$- do on purpose]
degaǫ:do'jinehta' they (f/m) figure-skate H

•o'jinehdǫ:' skating
[ad+ contains: -o'jinehd$_V$- skate]
ado'jinehdǫ:' skating

•ojitgwa' ohya' lemons
oji:tgwa:' yellow
ohya' fruit

•oji'tgwa:ji: ohya' oranges
ojitgwa:ji: orange
ohya' fruit

•ojitgwaji: ohya' gra̲he:t an orange tree
ojitgwa:ji: ohya' oranges
gra̲he:t a living tree

•o'kd be the end of s.t., edge of s.t.
[ad+(N)+ occurs in:]
heyotaho'k the end of the trail, path, row S
[-(h)ah(a)$_N$- road -o'kd$_V$- end]

•o'kd lack
[d+...ad+]
dawad'okdahs it lacks; it is not enough H
dawadokdę' it lacked; it was not enough P

•o'kda' lack
[d+...ad+ contains: -o'kd$_V$- end]
gyodo'kda̲'ǫh it is lacking S

•o'kdagye's end times
[ni+yo+ad+ contains: -o'kd$_V$- end]
niyod'okda:gye's up to these times H

•o'kda'ǫh be the end of s.t., the edge of s.t.
[tsęh hǫ where he'+yo+ad+ -o'kda'$_V$- come to an end]
tsęh hǫ heyodokda'ǫh the edge

•o'kdahsd come to the end
[d+...ad+N+ occurs in:]
ǫgataho'ktahs I came to the end of the trail, the row P
[-(h)ah(a)$_N$- road -o'kdahsd$_V$- come to the end]

•o'kdahs lack
[d+...ad+]
dawad'okdahs it lacks; it is not enough H

•o'kd(ę,ani) be dissatisfied with s.t., lack
[d+...ad+ contains: -o'kd$_V$- end]
dawad'okdę' it lacked; it was not enough P
dwagad'okda:nih I am dissatisfied S

•o'kd(ę,ani) finish s.t.
[(N+)]
agahahokdę' I finished one row P
[-(h)ah(a)$_N$- road -o'kdę$_V$- finish s.t.]

•ona'ga:' gajihwa' a horn war club; a club; a hammer
ona'ga:' horns; antlers
gajihwa' a hammer

•ona'ga' ohya' a banana
ona'ga:' horns; antlers
ohya' fruit

•ona'ga:' ohya' gra̲he:t a banana tree
ona'ga' ohya' banana
gra̲he:t a living tree

•o:nęh now, when
see: Appendix I

•o:nę to:hah, nęto:hah, to:hah almost
see: Appendix I

•o:nęh g'ihya:' so long for now
see: Appendix I

Legend: H habitual, P punctual, S stative, I imperative, PURP purposive, PURP-H purposive habitual, PURP-PAST purposive past, PURP-P purposive punctual, PURP-I purposive imperative; see §8.6, §8.11 in Appendix J. Alphabetization in stems ignores length (:), and any h's or glottal stops (') that are not between vowels. See §2.2 of the User Guide for explanation.

•onę:diˀ so now
see: Appendix I
•onęˀdo:t ohyaˀ a pineapple
onęˀdǫ:t a pine cone
ohyaˀ fruit
•onęˀe:ˀ now, again
see: Appendix I
•o:nęgwaˀ suddenly; already
see: Appendix I
•onęhęˀ eyahkwaˀ ga̱ˀahdraˀ a corn basket
onęhę:ˀ corn
eyahkwaˀ container
gaˀahdraˀ basket
•onęhęˀ ohnaˀ corn oil
onęhę:ˀ corn
ohnaˀ oil
•onęhęˀ onaˀda:ˀ corn bread
onęhę:ˀ corn
onaˀda:ˀ bread
•onęhę:ˀ otetraˀ corn flour
onęhę:ˀ corn
oteˀtraˀ flour; powder
•onęhęˀǫ:weh onyahaˀ flint corn mush (native dish)
onęhęˀǫ:weh flint corn
onyahaˀ native mush dishes made with corn
•onoˀsgwi, ęnohsgwi sweep
[de+...ę+]
degonˀosgwihs I am sweeping H
dęgęnˀosgwiˀ I will sweep P
dewagęnoˀsgwi: I have swept S
•onoˀsgwita:ˀ broom
[de+yag+ contains: -onoˀsgwi$_V$- sweep]
deyaganoˀsgwita:ˀ broom
•onyeˀs driver
[ad+ -owi, ǫny$_V$- drive]
hadonyeˀs he drives it; he is a driver H
•oˀǫ: Oh really?
see: Appendix I

•ohsgaˀ(w) clear s.t.
[N+ occurs in:]
hadihędohsga:s the clear the land H
[-(h)ęd(a)$_N$- field -ohsgaˀ(w)$_V$- clear]
ahadi̱hędohsga:ˀ they (m) cleared the fields, the land P
hodihędohsgˀawęh they have cleared the land S
•ohsriyaˀgǫh be a certain age
[ni+P+ -(o)hsr(a)$_N$- year, winter -(i)yaˀg$_V$- cut, break, cross]
do: nisohsriyaˀgǫh? how old are you? S
•o:sˀuh several small objects
[ni+A/P+N+ contains: -u:ˀuh$_V$- be small]
niyonaˀdao:s:ˀuh cookies
[-naˀd(a:)$_N$- bread -osˀuh$_V$- several small objects]
•otgahnye̱dahkwaˀ onǫhsǫt a gym
otgahnye̱dahkwaˀ a place where people play; a playground
onǫhsǫt a room
•otgoˀdaˀ ohyaˀ elderberries
otgoˀdaˀ sumac
ohyaˀ fruit
•otgwęhjˀiaˀ otgoˀdaˀ red sumac
otgwęhjˀia:ˀ red
otgoˀdaˀ sumac
•otsa:do:t dega:dęh a jet; an airplane
otsa:do:t there is fog
dega:dęh an airplane
•otseˀdaˀ ohyaˀ pear
otseˀdaˀ a bottle; a jar
ohyaˀ fruit
•otseˀdaˀ ohyaˀ gra̱he:t a pear tree
otseˀdaˀ ohyaˀ pear
gra̱he:t a living tree
•ots(i) remove an outer covering
[N+ occurs in:]
grawihsdotsǫˀs I peel H
[-rawihsd(a)$_N$- peel -ots(i)$_V$- remove an outer covering]

•ots(i) remove an outer covering (continued)
ęhsrawihsdo:tsi' you will peel P
agra'wihsdo:tsǫ I am peeling S
srawihsdotsih peel I
desęhsotsih take your shoes off I
[de+... -(ę)hs(a)$_N$- foot -ots(i)$_V$- remove an outer covering]

•o:'uh be small
[ni+A/P+N+ contains: -u:'uh$_V$- be small]
nigayao:'uh small bag S
[-y(a:)$_N$- bag -o'uh$_V$- be small]

•owanęh be big
[A/P+N+ occurs in:]
gahwajiyowanęh a large family S
[-(h)wajiy(a)$_N$- family -owanęh$_V$- be big]

•owanęhah be fairly big
[A/P+N+ contains: -owanęh$_V$- be big -hah fairly; occurs in:]
gęhwajiowanę:hah my family is fairly big S
[A/P+N+ -(h)wajiy(a)$_N$- family -owanęhah$_V$- be fairly big]

•owanę's be several big objects
[de+A/P+N+ contains: -owanęh$_V$- be big; occurs in:]
ohahowa:nę's big highways S
[de+A/P+N+ -(h)ah(a)$_N$- road -owanę's$_V$- several big objects]

•oweg cover; see also (')howeg cover
[TR+ (N+)]
ge'ho:we:s I am covering s.t. H
ęhse'ho:we:k you will cover s.t. P
age'howe:gǫh I did cover s.t. S
segǫ'dro:we:k you put the pillowcase on I
[-gǫ'dr(a)$_N$- pillow, etc. -oweg$_V$- cover s.t.]

•oweks(i) uncover s.t.
[TR+(N+) contains: -oweg$_V$- cover]
ęhsna'sgowe:ksih you will uncover the bed P
[-na'sg(wa)$_N$- mattress -oweks(i)$_V$- cover]

•owę(:) split in two, halve s.t.
[de+ (N+) occurs in:]
degaiho:węhs computer H
[de+ga+ -(r)ih(wa)$_N$- word -owę(:)$_V$- split in two]
atgo:wę:' I split it open P
deyodahyo:wę' the fruit is split S
[-(a)hy(a)$_N$- berry, fruit -owę(:)$_V$- split in two]
deso:wę: halve it I

•owę(:) split in two from within
[de+ad+(N+)]
adwado:wę:' it split P
deyo:do:wę' it is split S

•ohwę'ga:' oya:na' skis
ohwę'ga:' a splint
oya:na' a tire; a track; anything that leaves long tracks

•owi, ǫny drive
[ad+]
gado:wih, gado:wihs I drive all the time H
hadonye's he drives it; he is a driver H
hęhsa:do:wih you will drive over there P
aga:do:wi: I did the driving S
ha'sa:do:wih drive it over there; herd the animals I

•owihshę(:) rest, relax
[ad+]
gadowihshęhę' I rest all the time H
a'ǫdowihshę:' she rested P
agadowishę' I have rested S

•owi:ya:'ah eksa:'ah a baby girl
owi:ya:'ah a baby
eksa:'ah she is a child (under 12)

Legend: H habitual, P punctual, S stative, I imperative, PURP purposive, PURP-H purposive habitual, PURP-PAST purposive past, PURP-P purposive punctual, PURP-I purposive imperative; see §8.6, §8.11 in Appendix J. Alphabetization in stems ignores length (:), and any h's or glottal stops (') that are not between vowels. See §2.2 of the User Guide for explanation.

•owi:ya:ʼah godaʼstaʼ a baby's sleeper, night gown
owi:ya:ʼah a baby
godaʼstaʼ agyaʼdawiʼtraʼ a nightgown
•owi:ya:ʼah gokwaʼ baby food
owi:ya:ʼah baby
gakwaʼ food
•owi:ya:ʼah gonǫʼgwaʼ baby formula
owi:ya:ʼah baby
onǫʼgwaʼ milk
•owi:ya:ʼah gǫna:kdaʼ a baby crib
owi:ya:ʼah baby
gana:kdaʼ bed
•owi:ya:ʼah haksa:ʼah a baby boy
owi:ya:ʼah baby
haksa:ʼah he is a child (under 12)
•oyaʼ ni:yoht s.t. different
o:yaʼ other
ni:yoht what it is like
•ohyajiwa:gę ohyaʼ gra̱he:t a crabapple tree
ohyaji:wa:gę: crabapples; tart, sour fruit
ohyaʼ fruit
gra̱he:t a living tree

Ǫ

•ǫ: resemble
[P+(N+) occurs in:]
oʼgrǫ: it looks like snow S
[-(a)ʼgr(a)$_N$- snow -ǫ:$_V$- resemble]
•ǫ: be a number (of things)
[ni+A+ y+]
ni:yǫ: amount of things S
do: ni:yǫ: how many S
[do: how ni+y+]
•ǫ: many different things
[haʼde+ y+]
haʼde:yǫ: many different things S
•ǫ: be an equal number of things
[tsaʼde+ y+]
tsaʼde:yǫ: an equal number or amount S
•ǫ: be a certain amount of things
[tsęh, shęh that ni+ y+]
shę ni:yǫ: the amount of S
•ǫ(:) put objects on a string
see: (r)ǫ(:) put objects on a string
hanihaǫhaʼ he is stringing H
degayaǫ:ʼ it is beaded S
•ǫh I guess
see: Appendix I
•ǫd be attached
[(heʼ+) A/P+(N+) occurs in:]
wa̱hyaʼ niyǫ:taʼ a variety of hanging fruits H
ęgahsa̱heʼdǫ:dęʼ beans will sprout P
[-(h)saheʼd(a)$_N$- bean -ǫdę$_V$- be attached]
aǫ:t it is attached; it is sticking out S
heyaǫ:t it protrudes S
heyohsgwaǫ:t a rock formation that protrudes out; a cliff S
[-(h)sg(wa)$_N$- rock -ǫd$_V$- attached]
desejihsdǫgwaǫdęh tie a knot I
[-jihsdǫg(wa)$_N$- knot -ǫdę$_V$- be attached]
•ǫd have s.t.
[P+N occurs in:]
okdehǫ:t it has roots S
[o+ -kdeh(a)$_N$- edible root -ǫd$_V$- attached]
honowagwaǫ:t he has a humped back S
[ho+ -nowag(wa)$_N$- humped back -ǫd$_V$- attached]
•ǫd lack s.t.
[taʼde+ not contains: -ǫd$_V$- be attached]
taʼdegawa:yǫ:t it has no wings S
[-way(a)$_N$- fin, wing -ǫd$_V$- be attached]
•ǫd be baked
[at+ A+N contains: -ǫd$_V$- be attached]
watǫnʼadǫ:t baked potatoes S
[wa+ at+ -(h)ǫnaʼd(a)$_N$- potato -ǫd$_V$- attached]

•ǫd(a) log
see: (r)ǫd(a) log
gaǫ:daʼ a log

•ǫda:(ʼ,h) put in, put on
[ad+(N+)]
sǫ:da:s you put s.t. in H
ęhsǫda:ʼ you will put an object in there P
ahada̲hdiʼtrǫda:ʼ he put his socks on P
[-(a)dahdiʼtr(a)$_{N}$- sock -ǫda:(ʼ,h)$_{V}$- put in, on]
agǫda:hǫh I have put it in S

•ǫdaʼd shake, shiver
[P+ N+ -yaʼd(a)$_{N}$- body -ǫdaʼd$_{V}$- shake, shiver]
sayaʼdǫdaʼtaʼ you are nervous, shaking, shivering H
ęsayʼadǫ:daʼt you will shiver, shake P

•ǫdadeʼ beam
see: (r)ǫdadeʼ beam
gaǫdadeʼ a beam

•ǫdadenyǫʼ log rafter
see: (r)ǫdadenyǫʼ log rafter
gaǫdade:nyǫʼ log rafters

•ǫdaʼehs woodpecker
see: (r)ǫdaʼehs woodpecker
gaǫdaʼehs a woodpecker

•ǫdagw remove, take away; also see (o)da(h)gw remove, take away
ęsǫdagoʼ you will remove, detach s.t.

•ǫdahǫh beam
see: (r)ǫdahǫh beam
degaǫdahǫh a beam

•ǫdahsd put in
[(at+) contains: -ǫda:(h)$_{V}$- put in]
hęnǫda:staʼ they (m) put it in there all the time H

•ǫdahkwaʼ an attached instrument, etc. that sticks out somehow
[A/P+(at+) N+ contains: -ǫd$_{V}$- attached]
ǫtnaʼdaǫdahkwaʼ a bread pan S
[o+at+ -naʼd(a:)$_{N}$- bread -ǫdahkwaʼ$_{V}$- attached instrument]
deyǫtwęʼgaǫdahkwaʼ snowshoes S
[de+yo+at+ -(h)węʼg(a:)$_{N}$- splint -ǫdahkwaʼ$_{V}$- attached instrument]

•ǫdataʼ contain
[wa+ad+ contains: -ǫda:(h)$_{V}$- put in]
wadǫda:taʼ it contains s.t.; a container H

•ǫdatgę: dead tree
see: (r)ǫdatgę: dead tree
aǫdatgę: a dead tree

•ǫdeʼnyędęhsda̲hkwaʼ ganyo:daʼ a measuring spoon
ǫdeʼnyędęhsda̲hkwaʼ s.t. that measures
ganyo:daʼ a spoon; a canoe

•ǫdehsgyǫwataʼtaʼ ohyaʼ grapefruit
ǫdehsgyǫwataʼtaʼ s.o. loses weight, diets
ohyaʼ fruit

•ǫdehsgyǫwataʼtaʼ ohyaʼ gra̲he:t a grapefruit tree
ǫdesgyǫwataʼtaʼ **ohya**ʼ grapefruit
gra̲he:t a living tree

•ǫdǫʼ several attached objects; have several things
[P+N contains: -ǫd$_{V}$- attached -ǫʼ plural]
onrahdǫ:dǫʼ leaves on a tree S
[o+ -nrahd(a)$_{N}$- leaf -ǫdǫʼ$_{V}$- several attached objects]
oʼnihsgaǫdǫʼ it has wheels S
[o+ -ęʼnihsg(a)$_{N}$- wheel -ǫdǫʼ$_{V}$- several attached objects]

•ǫdǫhne:ʼ suppose
[A+ contains: -(a)dǫh$_{V}$- say]
gǫdǫhne:ʼ I suppose S

•ǫdǫʼ many attached objects; have many things
[P+N contains: -ǫd$_{V}$- attached -ǫnyǫʼ plural]
onǫhsǫdǫ:nyǫʼ rooms in a house S
[o+ -nǫhs(a)$_{N}$- house -ǫdǫnyǫʼ$_{V}$- several attached objects]

•ǫdǫʼ many attached objects; have many things (continued)
hodęihǫdǫnyǫʼ his appointed responsibilities S
[ho+ adę+ -(r)ih(wa)$_N$- word, matter, affair --ǫdǫnyǫʼ$_V$- several attached objects]

•ǫgęhdahkwaʼ, ǫgohdahkwaʼ path
[ǫ+ad+ contains: -ǫgohd$_V$- surpass -ahkwaʼ instrument]
ǫdǫhgo̱hdahkwaʼ a path

•ǫgęhdahkwaʼ, ǫgohdahkwaʼ path, shortcut
[he+yǫ+ad+ contains: -ǫgohd$_V$- surpass]
heyǫdogęhda̱hkwaʼ path, short-cut

•ǫgęhdahkwaʼ, ǫgohdahkwaʼ trail
[de+yǫ+ad+ -ǫgohd$_V$- surpass]
deyǫdogęhda̱hkwaʼ trail

•ǫgohd surpass, go past
hadǫgo̱htaʼ he goes past all the time H
aha:dǫ:goht he went past P
hodǫgo̱hdǫh he has gone past S

•ǫgohd surpass, go past , go under s.t.
[de+…ad+N+]
dęhsadʼęhę:gǫht you will go under the fence P
[-(a)dęʼh(ę)$_N$- fence -ǫgohd$_V$- surpass]

•ǫgohd filter, strain, penetrate
[de+…(N+)]
dęsǫ:goht you will penetrate P
dehsǫ:goht filter it; strain it I
dęhsne:gǫ:goht you will filter, strain liquid
[de-(h)neg(a)$_N$- water, liquid -ǫgohd$_V$- surpass]

•ǫgohd exaggerate
[heʼ+…]
hęhso:goht you will exaggerate, go above and beyond P

•ǫgohd be exceptional, above average, too much
[trehs contains: -ǫgohd$_V$- surpass]
(trehs) aǫgo̱hdǫh it is exceptional, above average, too much S

•ǫgohd(ę, ani) deceive s.o.
[TR+ad+ contains: -ǫgohd$_V$- surpass]
ęhseyadogo̱hdęʼ you will outdo s.o.; you will go right over her, go right past her, deceive her P

•ǫgw, ǫgo keep
see: (r)ǫgw, (r)ǫgo [(a)d+ (N+)] keep
ęhsadǫgweʼdaǫgoʼ you will adopt a person

•(ʼ)ǫhg(wa:) sod
[o+]
oʼǫhgwa:ʼ sod; moss

•ǫgweh ojiʼnǫwaʼ a praying mantis
ǫ:gweh person
ojiʼnǫ:waʼ a bug; an insect

•ǫ:gweh okdehaʼ ginger root; ginseng
ǫ:gweh a person
okdehaʼ edible roots

•ǫgwe(ʼda) person
[A+]
ǫ:gweh a person; a human
hǫ:gweh a man (lit.: he is a person)
agǫ:gweh a woman (lit.: she is a person)

•ǫgweʼdadeʼ stranger
[ti+yǫ+ -ǫgwe(ʼda)$_N$- person -deʼ$_V$- exist, be different]
tiyǫgwedadeʼ a stranger

•ǫgweʼdaęʼ middle age
[haʼde+yag+ -ǫgwe(ʼda)$_N$- person -ę$_V$- lie on the ground]
haʼdeyagǫgweʼdaę:ʼ middle age

•ǫgweʼdagǫnyǫ be choosy, discriminate
[P+ad+ -ǫgwe(ʼda)$_N$- person -gǫnyǫ$_V$- be clean, discriminating]
hodǫgweʼdagǫnyǫhs he is choosy about who he associates with; he discriminates H

•ǫgweʼdahetgęʼ be cruel, mean
[P+ -ǫgwe(ʼda)$_N$- person -(hr)etgęʼ$_V$- be evil, bad, ugly]
agǫgwʼedahetgęʼ she is a cruel, mean person S

•ǫgweʼdanęhsgw, ǫgweʼdanęhsgo kidnap a person
[TR+ -ǫgwe(ʼda)$_N$- person -nęhsgw$_V$- steal]
ęhsǫgweʼdanęhsgoʼ you will kidnap s.o. P

•ǫgweʼdiyohsd compose oneself
[ad+ -ǫgwe(ʼda)$_N$- person -iyohsd$_V$- make nice, good]
agadǫgweʼdi:yohs I made myself nice (put on my public face or facade) P

•ǫgwęhęhdǫh new-born baby
[(ya)go+ -ǫgwe(ʼda)$_N$- person -(y)ęhd$_V$- hit, knock down, strike]
gogwęhęhdǫh new born baby

•ǫgyaʼktaʼ saw
see: (r)ǫgyaʼktaʼ saw
deyaǫgyaʼktaʼ, deyǫgyaʼktaʼ a buzz saw (lit.: it cuts logs)

•ǫ:hah be few, little
[ni+yo+ -ǫ$_V$- number (of things) -hah diminutive]
niyǫ:hah a few; a little bit S

•ǫhę be alone, be a loner
see: (r)ǫhę [neʼ a+] be alone, be a loner
neʼ aǫhę:ʼęh all alone; the most S

•ǫhęʼjih private
[P+ contains: -(r)ǫhę$_V$- be alone -jih really]
gonohęʼjih they are private people S

•ǫhkwad itchy
[a+]
aǫhkwat it is itchy S

•ǫhne:ʼ maybe
see: Appendix I

•ǫʼn(eg) remove, take away, subtract
[de+(N+)]
tsǫʼnehs you subtract, take away all the time H
ętsǫʼne:k you will subtract P
disǫʼnǫ: you have taken away S
dahsǫʼne:k subtract it I
de·se·nęt·sǫ́ʼne:k remove your arms (that is, retract them); remove your support I
[stem: -nęts(a)$_N$- arm -ǫʼn(eg)$_V$- remove, take away]

•ǫʼn(eg) move away, shrink
[ad+]
dwadǫʼne:s it moves away all the time; it shrinks H
ęwadoʼne:k it (an animal) will move away P
sadoʼne:k get away, move away I

•ǫʼn(eg) remove oneself
[d+...ad+]
ętsadǫʼne:k you will remove yourself P

•ǫʼneksǫ(:) remove several things
[contains: ǫʼn(eg)$_V$- remove, take away -sǫ(:) several]
sǫne:ksǫ: you remove several things I

•ǫhneʼts(a) stair, ladder
[(o)+ad+]
adǫhnʼetsaʼ, odǫhnʼetsaʼ a ladder; stairs

•ǫhnetsod stairs, ladder
[wa+ad+ -ǫhneʼts(a)$_N$- ladder -od$_V$- stand]
wadǫhnetso:t stairs, ladder

•ǫnęhd swallow
[heʼ+]
hegǫnęhtaʼ I swallow H
hęgǫ:nęht I will swallow P
hewagǫnęhdǫh I have swallowed S
haʼsǫ:nęht swallow I

•ǫnęhtge: gulp
[heʼ+ contains: -ǫnęhd$_V$- swallow -ge: big]
haʼgǫnęhtge: I took a big swallow, a gulp P

Legend: H habitual, P punctual, S stative, I imperative, PURP purposive, PURP-H purposive habitual, PURP-PAST purposive past, PURP-P purposive punctual, PURP-I purposive imperative; see §8.6, §8.11 in Appendix J. Alphabetization in stems ignores length (:), and any h's or glottal stops (ʼ) that are not between vowels. See §2.2 of the User Guide for explanation.

•ǫnheʼ be alive
[P+]
agǫ:heʼ she is alive
ǫnheʼ it is alive
•ǫnhegyeʼs spirit
[tsęh A+ contains: -ǫnheʼ$_V$- be alive]
tsęh sǫnhe:gyeʼs your spirit
•ǫnheʼtr(a) heart, spirit
[P+ad+ contains: -ǫnheʼ$_V$- be alive]
sadǫnheʼtraʼ your soul, heart, spirit
odǫnhehtra:gǫ: in the heart
•ǫnhi:s life expectancy
[tsęh that ni+A+ contains: -ǫnheʼ$_V$- be alive -is$_V$- long]
tsęh nisǫ:nhi:s your life expectancy
•ǫnhed be born, be alive
[ad+ contains: -ǫnheʼ$_V$- be alive]
sagadǫnhe:t I am alive again P
sadǫ:nhe:dǫh you were born S
•ǫnhehg live on, be sustained by s.t.
[P+ contains: -ǫnheʼ$_V$- be alive]
agǫnhehgǫh s.o. lives on it; she is sustained by it S
•ǫnhegyeʼ be stillborn
[(tęʼ) deʼ+ not P+ contains: -ǫnheʼ$_V$- be alive]
deagǫnhe:gyeʼ she was stillborn; she came to be not living S
•ǫnhi:(ʼ) be fully alive
[P+ad+ contains: -ǫnheʼ$_V$- be alive]
agadǫnhi: I am alive; I am born; I am full of life S
•ǫnhoʼg be premature, mentally challenged
[d+P+ad+ contains: -ǫnheʼ$_V$- be alive]
todǫ:nhoʼk he is mentally challenged; he was born premature S
•ǫni, ǫny make
[(N+)]
gǫ:nih I make, earn H
agǫ:niʼ I did make, earn P
ga̱hwęʼgaǫni: it is made into a splint S
[-(h)węʼg(a:)$_N$- splint -ǫni, ǫny$_V$- make]

•ǫni, ǫny use in place of s.t. else, replace
[ti+...]
tigǫ:nihs I use s.t. in place of s.t. else H
•ǫni, ǫny make for s.o.
[TR+(N+)]
ashagonǫhsǫ:niʼ he built a house for her P
[-nǫhs(a)$_N$- house -ǫni, ǫny$_V$- make
•ǫni, ǫny start from, originate, emerge
[t+heʼ...+adad+ contains: -ǫni, ǫny$_V$- make]
tęwadadǫ:niʼ it will emerge or appear unintentionally; it will do it by itself P
•ǫni, ǫny be plentiful
[(N+) contains: -ǫni, ǫny$_V$- make]
odahyǫ:ni: plentiful fruit S
[-(a)hy(a)$_N$- fruit, berry -ǫni, ǫny$_V$- make]
•ǫni, ǫny be little, few
[(tęʼ) deʼ+ not contains: -ǫni, ǫny$_V$- make]
deʼoda̱hyǫ:ni: not much fruit on the trees S
[-(a)hy(a)$_N$- fruit, berry -ǫni, ǫny$_V$- make]
•ǫni, ǫny start from, originate, emerge
[d+A+adad+]
dwada:dǫ:nih where it starts from H
•ǫni, ǫny tease s.o.,s.t.
[d+...+at+ (N+)]
tęnatna̱hsgǫ:nih they (m) are teasing the animal(s) H
[-nahsg(wa)$_N$- domestic animal -ǫni, ǫny$_V$- make]
•ǫnihagyeʼ(s) make continually
[(N+) contains: -ǫni, ǫny$_V$- make]
honǫni̱ha:gyeʼs they (m) are making, earning it (continually) S
•ǫhny(a) river flats
see: (r)ǫhny(a) [(a)+ ... -ʼgeh on, at] river flats
ǫhnyaʼgeh on the river flats

•ǫny, ǫwi breathe
[ad+]
sadǫ:nyeʼs you are breathing H
sadǫ:wih breathe I

•ǫnyahnǫ(:) include, designate
[A+ contains: -ǫni, ǫny$_V$- make -ahnǫ(:) go and do several things]
haǫ:nya̲hnǫʼ he has included, designated it S

•ǫnyahnǫ(:) move
[ad+ -ǫni, ǫny$_V$- make -ahnǫ(:) go and do several things]
sadonyahnǫh you move all the time H
ęsadonyahnǫ:ʼ you will make yourself move P

•ǫnyahnǫ(:) be growing
[at+ N+ contains: -ǫni, ǫny$_V$- make -ahnǫ(:) go and do several things]
otǫdǫnyahnǫʼ growing bushes, saplings S
[-(h)ǫd(a)$_N$- bush -ǫni, ǫny$_V$- make -ahnǫ(:) go and do several things]

•ǫnyeʼd cause s.t. to breathe, gill
[ad+ contains: -ǫwi, ǫny$_V$- breathe]
wadǫnyʼetaʼ how it breathes; it's a breather; the gill H

•ǫny(ę, ani) make for s.o.
[TR+(N+) contains: -ǫni, ǫny$_V$- make]
ahǫwadinǫhsǫnyęʼ they (m) built him a house P
[-nǫhs(a)$_N$- house -ǫni, ǫny$_V$- make]

•ǫnyeʼtaʼ lung
[ǫ+ad+ contains: -ǫwyeʼd$_V$- cause to breathe]
ǫdǫnyeʼtaʼ a lung

•ǫnyǫʼ be in some place; be included
[A+ contains: -ǫni, ǫny$_V$- make]
gaǫ:nyǫʼ it included some; it is in there S

•ǫ:s long
[(i)+y+ contains: -es$_V$- long]
i:yǫ:s it is long S

•ǫ:s be short
[(tęʼ) deʼ+ not A/P+(N+) contains: -es$_V$- long]
tęʼ dʼeyǫ:s it is not long S

•ǫʼs benefit s.o., happen for s.o.'s benefit
[P+ad+]
ęyagodǫʼse̲ha:k it will be happening for them (f/m) H
godǫʼse:ʼ it benefitted her S

•(ʼ)ǫhs(a) vine
[o+]
oʼǫhsaʼ vines

•ǫ:sʼah, e:sʼah be longish
[ni+y+ -es$_V$- long -ʼah diminutive]
niyǫ:sʼah just a little bit long S

•ǫʼsd benefit s.o.
[P+ad+ contains: -ǫʼs$_V$- benefit s.o.]
godǫʼstaʼ it always benefits her H
ęya:go:dǫʼs it will be for her benefit P

•ohsohda̲hkwaʼ eya:taʼ a paintbrush
ǫhsohda̲hkwaʼ s.t. used for colouring
eya:taʼ s.o. spreads it

•ǫsʼǫʼs, e:sʼǫʼs several long objects
[A/P+N+ contains: -es$_V$- long]
onrahde:sǫʼs long leaves S
[-nrahd(a)$_N$- leaf -es$_V$- long]

•ǫhsweʼd(ę) be short of breath
[A+ad+]
hadǫhswʼetaʼ he is short of breath H
ahadǫ̲hsweʼdęʼ he will be short of breath P

•ǫhsweʼdanih be hungry
[P+ad+]
agadǫ̲hsweʼdanih I am hungry H

•ǫhsweʼdęhd famine, hunger
[o+ad+ contains: -ǫhsweʼd$_V$- be short of breath; be hungry]
odǫhsweʼdęht famine; hunger

•ǫtgadeʼ be fun, s.t. that feels good
[ad+ contains: -ǫtgad(ǫ:)$_V$- enjoy]
odǫtgadeʼ it is fun, a good feeling S

•ǫtgadeʼ unhappy
[(tęʼ) deʼ+ not ad+ -ǫtgadeʼ$_V$- be fun]
deʼagadǫtgadeʼ I am not happy S

Legend: H habitual, P punctual, S stative, I imperative, PURP purposive, PURP-H purposive habitual, PURP-PAST purposive past, PURP-P purposive punctual, PURP-I purposive imperative; see §8.6, §8.11 in Appendix J. Alphabetization in stems ignores length (:), and any h's or glottal stops (ʼ) that are not between vowels. See §2.2 of the User Guide for explanation.

•ǫtgadǫ(:) enjoy oneself, have a good time
[ad+]
ędwadǫtga:dǫ: we all (incl.) will have a good time, enjoy ourselves P
ǫgwadǫtga:dǫʼ we all are having fun S

•ǫtgadǫʼ be unhappy
[(tęʼ) deʼ+ not P+ad+ -ǫtgad(ǫ:)$_{V}$- enjoy]
dewagadǫtga:dǫʼ I am not happy S

•ǫtgahiʼdahkwaʼ gani:yǫ:t a mobile (a hanging toy)
ǫtgahiʼdahkwaʼ a toy
gani:yǫ:t it is hanging

•ǫtgeʼ ataʼtkwaʼ hair dryer
ǫtgeʼ s.o.'s hair
ataʼtkwaʼ a dryer

•ǫtgǫhsa̱hsohtaʼshǫ:ʼǫh eyahkwaʼ make-up bag
ǫtgǫhsa̱hsohtaʼshǫ:ʼǫh make-up items
eyahkwaʼ containers

•ǫts(a) knee
ǫtsaʼ a knee
sǫtsaʼgeh on your knee

•ǫtsod pray on one's knees
[de+...ad+ -ǫts(a)$_{N}$- knee -od$_{V}$- stand]
dęhęnadǫtsotaʼ they (m) pray on their knees H
dęyǫdǫtso:dęʼ she will become Christian; she will kneel in prayer P

•ǫtw burn
[ad+]
wadǫ:twahs what it burns (in the way of fuel) H

•ǫhwadęʼ brother's child
[TR+]
heyǫhwa:dęʼ my nephew S

•ǫhwad(ę,ani) show
[TR+]
gǫyǫhwadanih I am showing you s.t. H
agǫhwada:nih it has shown me s.t. P

•ǫhwatahsd show s.o. s.t.
[TR+ contains: -ǫhwad(ę,ani)$_{V}$- show]
ęsayǫhwa:tahs it will show you s.t. P

•ǫʼwesahd, ǫʼwesęh(d) enjoyable
[a+ contains: -ǫʼwes$_{V}$- enjoy s.t.]
aǫʼwe:sęh(t), aǫʼwesah(t) it is enjoyable; a good feeling S

•ǫʼwesahd, ǫʼwesęh(d) be unpleasant
[(tęʼ) deʼ+ not P+ contains: -ǫʼwes$_{V}$- enjoy]
deʼaǫwe:saht it is unpleasant S

•ǫʼwesahs have a good time, enjoy oneself
[P+ contains: -ǫʼwes$_{V}$- enjoy]
agǫʼweshahs I am having a good time, enjoying s.t. H

•ǫʼwes(ę,gwani) enjoy s.t.
[P+ contains: -ǫʼwes$_{V}$- enjoy]
agǫʼwehsgwa:nih I enjoy it H
ęwagǫʼwe:sęʼ I will enjoy myself P

•ǫhwęj(a) earth, land, ground
[o+ … -gǫ: in, under]
ohwęjagǫ: under the earth, ground

•ǫhwęjadeʼ country
[o+ad+ -ǫhwęj(a)$_{N}$- earth -deʼ$_{V}$- exist]
odǫhwęja:deʼ a country

•ǫhwęjadeʼ peninsula
[heʼ+yo+ -ǫhwęj(a)$_{N}$- earth, land -deʼ$_{V}$- exist]
heyohwęja:deʼ a peninsula

•ǫhwęjaihęh earthquake
[d/g+…yo+ -ǫhwęj(a)$_{N}$- earth, land -ęhę(:,w) $_{V}$- direct, convey]
agyǫhwęjaihęh there was an earthquake (lit.: the land shook) P

•ǫhwęję(:) landslide, cave-in
[-ǫhwęj(a)$_{N}$- earth, land -ę$_{V}$- lie on the ground]
aǫhwęjęʼ there was a landslide, a cave-in P

•ǫhwęjędǫh earthquake
[a+g+yo+ -ǫhwęj(a)$_{N}$- earth, land -ędǫh$_{V}$- shake s.t.]
agyǫhwęhję:dǫh there was an earthquake P

•ǫhwęjohǫh necessity
[de+yo+at+ contains: -ǫhwęjoni, ǫhwęjoh$_V$- want, need]
deyotwęjǫ̲hǫh a necessity S

•ǫhwęjoni want, need
[de+P+ad+ (-sgǫ: easily)]
desadǫhwęjoni̲hsgǫ: you always want s.t. H
dęhsadǫhwę:jǫ:niʼ you will want s.t. P

•ǫhwęjohsd want, need
[de+P+ad+ contains: -ǫhwęjoni, ǫhwęjoh$_V$- want, need]
adwagadǫhwęjohs I did want s.t. P

•ǫhwęhsdaga: wheeze
[o+ -(h)węhsd(a)$_N$- -ga:$_V$- make a rattling or grinding noise]
ohwęhsdaga: it is wheezing S

•ǫwi, ǫny breathe
[ad+]
sadǫ:nyeʼs you are breathing H
sadǫ:wih breathe I

•ǫhwidaʼd swing
[ad+]
sadǫhwidaʼtaʼ you swing (all the time); you're a swinger H
a:sadǫhwi:daʼt you will swing P
sadǫhwidaʼdǫh you are swinging S
sadǫhwi:daʼt swing I

•ǫwihshęʼ pant
see: (r)ǫwihshęʼ [P+] pant
gaǫ:wi̲hshęʼǫh she is panting S

•ǫhwihshe(y) be breathless
[A+ -ǫhwihsr(a)$_N$- breath -(ga)hey, (gę)hey, (i)hey, (ga)he:, (gę)he:, (i)he:$_V$- die, be weak, be exhausted]
haǫwihshe:yǫhs he is out of breath; his breath is ebbing away H

•ǫwihsręhd breathe
[ad+ -ǫhwihsr(a)$_N$- breath -(y)ęhd$_V$- hit, knock down, strike]
ęyǫdowihsręht she will breathe P
godoihsręhdǫh she is breathing S

•ǫwihsriyaʼ(g) be breathless
[ad+ -ǫhwihsr(a)$_N$- breath -(i)yaʼg$_V$- cut, break, cross]
hadǫhsriyaʼs (hadǫwi̲hsri:yaʼs) he is out of breath; he is dying H

•ǫhwihsroʼkd be breathless
[ad+ -ǫhwihsr(a)$_N$- breath -oʼkd$_V$- end]
hadǫhwi̲hsroʼktaʼ he is out of breath H

•ǫhy(a) heavens, sky
see: (r)ǫhy(a) [ga+ … ʼgeh on, at] heavens, sky
gaǫhyʼageh in the heavens; in the sky

•ǫhyadagyeʼ skyline, horizon
see: (r)ǫhyadagyeʼ skyline, horizon
gaǫhyada:gyeʼ skyline; horizon

•ǫhyadeʼ heaven
see: (r)ǫhyadeʼ heaven
gaǫ:hyadeʼ in existing heaven

•ǫhyaʼę:ʼ blue
see: (r)ǫhyaʼę:ʼ blue
aǫhyaę:ʼ, ǫhyaʼę:ʼ blue

•ǫhyagahne:ʼ stream crane
[de+ga+ -(r)ǫhy(a)$_N$- sky -gahne(:)$_V$- go and watch]
degaǫhyaga̲hne:ʼ a stream crane

•ǫhyagę be in agony, groan, be in pain
see: (r)ǫhyagę be in agony, groan, be in pain
saǫhyagę: groan I

•ǫhyagęʼd labour, make s.o. work hard
see: (r)ǫhyagęʼd [TR+] labour, make s.o. work hard
ęhsaǫhyagʼędahk it's going to make you groan P

•ǫhyaʼgęd light blue
see: (r)ǫhyaʼgęd light blue
aǫhyagę:t light blue

Legend: H habitual, P punctual, S stative, I imperative, PURP purposive, PURP-H purposive habitual, PURP-PAST purposive past, PURP-P purposive punctual, PURP-I purposive imperative; see §8.6, §8.11 in Appendix J. Alphabetization in stems ignores length (:), and any h's or glottal stops (ʼ) that are not between vowels. See §2.2 of the User Guide for explanation.

R

•(r)a(:,h) spread
ihsra:s you spread it on all the time H
ęhsra:' you will spread P
agrahǫh I did spread it already S
i:drah spread it on I
•(r)ad, yad, wad spread s.t.
[contains: -(r)a(:,h)$_V$- spread]
eya:ta' s.o. spreads it H
•(r)ade' climb
sra:de' you are climbing S
•(r)adrǫ(:) tear s.t., shred s.t.; also see (r)atsǫ(:) tear s.t., shred s.t.
ęhsra:drǫ:' you will tear, shred P
awadratsǫ:' it got torn, ripped P
•(r)age(:,w) wipe
grage:wahs I am erasing or wiping H
ęgra:ge:' I will erase or wipe P
agra:ge:węh I have erased, wiped it S
•(r)agw, (r)ago choose, take out
gragwahs I am taking it out right now; I always take it out H
ęhsra:go' you will choose or take out P
agra:gwęh I have picked it out; I have chosen that one S
•(r)ahg(wa:) sun dog
[o+ad+]
odrahgwa:' a sun dog
•(r)ahg(wa), wahg(wa) spot
[o+ -ǫnyǫ' several objects]
owahgwaǫnyǫ' spots
•(r)a(h)g(wa:) celestial body
[ga+]
ga:gwa:' a celestial body (for example, the sun, the moon)
•(r)agwahd(a) ball of foot, sole
[-agǫ: on, in]
a:gwahda', ogwahda' the sole; the ball of foot
sragwahdagǫ: on the ball, sole of your foot
swa:gwahda:gǫ: on your (p) soles
•(r)agwaę' be limp
[A+ad+ -(r)ag(wa)$_N$- -ę$_V$- lie]
wadragwaę' it is limp S
•(r)agwagye's sun, moon
[ga+ -(r)ag(wa)$_N$- celestial body-gye$_V$- fly]
ga:gwa:gye's the sun; the moon
•(r)agwase: new moon
[ga+ -(r)ag(wa:)$_N$- celestial body -(a)se:$_V$- new]
gahgwase:' new moon
•(r)agwęh fraction
[g+yo+ad+ -(r)agw$_V$- choose, take out]
gyodra:gwęh fractions
•(r)a(k)d(a) heel
srada'geh on your heel
ga:dageh a heel
•(r)a'kwa' container
[wa+ad+ -(r)a(:,h)$_V$- spread]
wadra'kwa' a container
•(r)anawę'doh sweeten
ęhsranawę'doh you will sweeten P
•(ra)nega(:,ǫ) explode, split
[de+...ad+N+]
dewadranegaǫ:s it is exploding H
•(ra')nęd(a:'g), (ya')nęd(a:'g) stick, cling [(N+)]
owa'nę:da:s it sticks to it; it adheres to it H
a'owa'nę:da:'k, a'owa'nę:da:' it is stuck P
owa'nęda:gǫh it is stuck on s.t. S
sa·ya'da·nę́·d'a·gǫh your body is stuck to s.t.
[-ya'd(a)$_N$- body -(ra')nęd(a:'g), (ya')nęd(a:'g)$_V$- stick, cling]
•(r)a'sw, ra'sro luck
[ad+]
adra'swa' luck
adra'swahe:tgę' bad luck
[ad+ -ra'sro, ra'sw$_N$- luck -(hr)etgę'$_V$- be evil, ugly]

•(r)a'swahe:tgę' bad luck
[ad+ -ra'sro, ra'sw$_N$- luck -(hr)etgę'$_V$- be evil, ugly]
adra'swahe:tgę' bad luck
•(r)aswiyohsd(ę, ani) lucky
[P+ad+ -ra'sro, ra'sw$_N$- luck -iyohsdę$_V$- become nice, good]
ǫgadraswiyǫhsdę' I got lucky P
•(r)atę climb
gratęhs I climb H
ęhsra:tę' you will climb P
agra:tę: I did climb S
dahsra:tęh, dadra:tęh climb (over here) I
•(r)a'tę' grey hair
[P+ contains: -nǫ'(a:), nǫh(a)$_N$- head]
gonǫhra'tę' she has grey hair S
•(r)atsǫ(:), (r)adrǫ(:) tear s.t., shred s.t.
[ad+ -(r)adrǫ(:), (r)atsǫ(:)$_V$- tear s.t., shred s.t.]
wadra:tsǫhs it gets torn all the time H
awadratsǫ:' it got torn, ripped P
ęhsra:drǫ:' you will tear it, shred it
odra:jǫ it is torn S
•(ra')wisd(a) slice, peeling
[o+]
owa'wihsda' a slice; a peeling
•(ra')wisd(a) bat (animal)
[contains: -(ra)hwisd(a)$_N$- a thin slice of s.t.]
adra'wihsda' a bat (the animal)
•(ra')wisdots(i) peel
[-rawihsd(a)$_N$- peel -ots(i)$_V$- remove an outer covering]
grawihsdotsǫ's I peel H
ęhsrawihsdo:tsi' you will peel P
agra'wihsdo:tsǫ I am peeling S
srawihsdotsih peel I
•(hr)e, (hr)ę put, place
[(N+)]
kre:ha' I am setting (it on s.t.) H
ęhshrę' you will set it on s.t. P
hewa:kre:' I put, placed it over there S
itręh you place it I
dęsa'ęnahę' you will put on the stick P
[-(a)'ęn(a)$_N$- stick, rod -(hr)e, (hr)ę$_V$- put, place]
•(hr)e(n) cut
[(N+)]
kre:nahs I cut it all the time H
ękre:' I will cut it P
akre:nęh I did cut it S
ahǫwadiy'adáhe:' they gave him an operation P
[-ya'd(a)$_N$- body -(hr)e(n)$_V$- cut]
•(hr)ehn(a) cargo, bundle, load
[ga/o+]
ohehna', gahehna' cargo; a bundle; a load
•(hr)ehnǫni pack
[at+ -(hr)ehn(a)$_N$- cargo, bundle -ǫni, ǫny$_V$- make]
satrehnǫ:nih pack I
•(hr)ena'tr(a) blade
[o+]
ohęn'atra' a blade
•(hr)ena'tra'se:' scissors
[de+ga+ -(hr)ena'tr(a)$_N$- blade -(a)'se:'$_V$- cousin, be double]
degahęna'tra'se:' scissors
•(hr)ena'trǫd blade
[o+ -(hr)ena'tr(a)$_N$- blade -ǫd$_V$- attached]
ohęn'atrǫ:t a blade
•(hr)ena'traho'dę: spatula
[o+ -(hr)ena'tr(a)$_N$- blade -o'dę:$_V$- type of]
ohenatraho'dę: a spatula
•(hr)etgę' be evil, bad, ugly
[A+(N+)]
gahetgę' it is ugly S
e'ni·gǫ·há·het·gę' she is evil-minded
[-(')nigǫh(a)$_N$- mind -(hr)etgę$_V$- be evil, bad, ugly]

Legend: H habitual, P punctual, S stative, I imperative, PURP purposive, PURP-H purposive habitual, PURP-PAST purposive past, PURP-P purposive punctual, PURP-I purposive imperative; see §8.6, §8.11 in Appendix J. Alphabetization in stems ignores length (:), and any h's or glottal stops (') that are not between vowels. See §2.2 of the User Guide for explanation.

•(hr)etgęʼ go bad, get wrecked
[P+(N+) occurs in:]
ǫgeʼdrehdahetgęʼ my car broke down P
[P+(N+) -(ʼ)drehd(a)$_N$- vehicle, car -(hr)etgęʼ$_V$- be evil, bad, ugly]
odrehda̱hetgʼęǫh a car is broken down S
•(hr)etgęhd ruin, wreck, damage
[contains: -(hr)etgę$_V$- be evil, bad, ugly]
ęhshe:tgęht you will damage, ruin, wreck s.t. P
ga̱hetgęhdǫh it is ruined, wrecked S
•(hr)etgęhd become moody
[ad+ contains: -(hr)etgęʼ$_V$- be evil, bad, ugly]
aʼǫtehtgęht s.o. turned funny, moody, etc. P
•(hr)etgęhd go bad
[d+ contains: -(hr)etgęʼ$_V$- be evil, bad, ugly]
dawatehtgęht it went bad P
•(hr)etgędǫni be in a funny mood, an odd mood
[P+at+ contains: -(hr)etgęʼ$_V$- be evil, bad, ugly]
hotehtgędǫ:ni: he is in a funny or odd mood; he is moody S
•(hr)etgęh wreck s.t.
[contains: -(hr)etgęʼ$_V$- be evil, bad, ugly]
ęhsre:tgęh you will wreck it P
•(hr)etgęsʼah unattractive
[A+ contains: -(hr)etgęʼ$_V$- be evil, bad, ugly -ʼah diminutive]
hahe:tgę:sʼah he is unattractive S
•(hr)ewahd apologize, repent
[s+...adat+]
tsadatrewahtaʼ you are repenting right now; you repent all the time H
sa̱hęnada:tre:waht they (m) repented P
•(hr)ewahd punish s.o.
[TR/at+]
satrewa̱htaʼ you are being punished right now H
ęhshehe:waht you will punish her P
satrewa̱hdǫh you have been punished S
•(hr)ęd lead
ęhsrę:t you will be the lead P
ohę:dǫ: ahead; in front; the front S
•(hr)ewahdǫ:ʼ repentance, punishment
[adat+ contains: -(hr)ewahd$_V$- punish]
adatrewahdǫ:ʼ repentance; punishment
•(hr)ęʼda(:,h) burn s.t.
[(N+)]
kręʼda:s I (always) burn s.t. H
ęhsręʼda:ʼ you will burn s.t. P
satwihsdʼęda:s you burn your money H
[at+ -(h)wihsd(a), (hr)ihsd(a)$_N$- metal, money : -(hr)ęʼda:$_V$- burn s.t.]
•(r)ędagyeʼ soar
[(de+) ad+ -(r)ęd$_V$- hover]
odrędagyeʼs it is soaring (for example, a bird) S
•(r)ędeʼ soar
[P+ stem: -(r)ęd$_V$- hover]
odrę:deʼ it is hovering (for example, a hummingbird)
•(r)ęh(a) stack
[occurs in:]
dęsadʼęhodęʼ, dęhsręʼho:dęʼ you will stack things, put one thing on top of the other
[de+...(ad+) stem: -(r)ęʼhodę- stack things; consists of: -(r)ęʼh(a)$_N$- bundle -odę$_V$- stand things up]
•(r)ęhod stack
[de+...(ad+) -(r)ęʼh(a)$_N$- bundle -odę$_V$- stand things up]
dęsadʼęho:dęʼ, dęhsręʼho:dęʼ you will stack things, put one thing on top of the other
•(r)ęhod stack things
[de+...N+]
degaiʼęho:t it is piled up S
dehsręʼho:dęʼ stack things up I

•(r)ęn(a) song, music
[ga+]
gaę:na' a song
gaę:naga:yǫh an old song
[-(r)ęn(a)$_N$- song, music -gayǫh$_V$- old (thing)]
•(r)ęnaehnę' mantis, praying mantis
[wa+ad+ contains: -(r)ęnaę$_V$- pray]
wadręnaehnę' (ojinǫ:wa') a praying mantis
•(r)ęnaę(:) pray
[ad+ -(r)ęn(a)$_N$- song, music -ę$_V$- lie]
tęnadręnaiha' they (m) are praying H
honadręnaę:' they (m) (Christians) are praying S
•(r)ęnanhǫdagw take over a song from s.o.
[TR+]
ahǫwaęnanhǫda:go' he took over the song P
[-(r)ęn(a)$_N$- song -nhodǫgw$_V$- open]
•(r)ęnahsre: hum
ahaęnahsre:' he followed the song; he sang along P
[-(r)ęn(a)$_N$- song, music -(i)hsre(:)$_V$- follow, chase]
•(hr)ęna'tra'a:s stab
[de+TR+ -(hr)ena'tr(a)$_N$- knife -(')a:s, (')i:s$_V$- pierce]
dęhshehęna'tra'a:s you will stab s.o. P
•(hr)ęna'tra'ehsd stab
[de+TR+ -(hr)ena'tr(a)$_N$- knife -(')ehsd$_V$- hit with s.t.]
dehsehena'tra'ehsta' you stab it repeatedly H
dęgǫhęna'tra'ehs I will stab you P
dewagehęna'tra'ehsdǫhǫgye' I am going along stabbing things S
•(rę)nawę'd(a) sugar, candy
nawę'da' sugar
ęhsranawę'doh you will sweeten
[-(rę)nawę'd(a)$_N$- sugar, candy -oh$_V$- dip in liquid]
•(r)ęnod sing
[ad+ -(r)ęn(a)$_N$- song, music -od$_V$- stand]
gęnadręno:ta' they (z) are singers H
godrę:no:t she is singing S
•(r)ęnǫda:(h) record songs
[ad+ -(r)ęn(a)$_N$- song, music -oda:(h)$_V$- put in]
ahaę:nǫ:da: he recorded, taped songs P
•(r)ęnodahkwa' kingfisher
[gęn+ad+ -(r)ęn(a)$_N$- song, music -odahkwa'$_V$- s.t. standing]
gęnadręnodahkwa' kingfisher (bird)
•(r)ęnota' radio, stereo
[wa+ad+ -(r)ęn(a)$_N$- song, music -od$_V$- stand]
wadręnota' a radio; a stereo
•(r)ęnotge: loud music
[ga+ -(r)ęn(a)$_N$- song, music -od$_V$- stand -ge: big]
gaęnotge: loud, amplified music
•(r)ęnǫni compose
[ad+ -(r)ęn(a)$_N$- song, music -ǫni, ǫny$_V$- make]
gaǫdręnǫ:nih (they (f/m) are) composers H
ahadręnǫ:ni' he made a song P
gonadręnǫ:ni: they (f/m) composed a song S
sadrę:nǫ:nih make a song I
•(r)hę tomorrow
ęyo:hę' it will be tomorrow P
•(hr)i' break up
[de+...(N+)]
degahi's it breaks, it is breakable H
dęgahi' it will break P
deyohi'ǫh it is broken S
deyohgwęnyahi'ǫh torn clothes
[de+yo+ stem: -(a)hgwęny(a)$_N$- clothes -(hr)i'$_V$- break up]

Legend: H habitual, P punctual, S stative, I imperative, PURP purposive, PURP-H purposive habitual, PURP-PAST purposive past, PURP-P purposive punctual, PURP-I purposive imperative; see §8.6, §8.11 in Appendix J. Alphabetization in stems ignores length (:), and any h's or glottal stops (') that are not between vowels. See §2.2 of the User Guide for explanation.

•(r)i, (w)i be ripe
[occurs in:]
ęwahyaiˀ it will ripen
[-(a)hy(a)$_N$- fruit, berry -(r)i, (w)i$_V$- be ripe]
•(hr)ihd slice, mash, grind
[de+...(N+) contains: -(hr)iˀ$_V$- break up]
dęhsriht you will break s.t. P
degahehdahihdǫh land that is disced or worked S
[de+ -(h)ehd(a)$_N$- land -hrihd$_V$- break up]
dehsriht grind it I
•(r)ihgwa:dǫˀ sun dog
[de+yo+ad+ -(r)ihg(wa)$_N$- moon -dǫˀ$_V$- several standing objects]
deyodri̱hgwa:dǫˀ a circle around the moon or sun (indicating bad weather); a sun-dog
•(r)ihgwagwenǫni full moon
[de+...ad+ -(r)ihg(wa)$_N$- moon -gwenǫni$_V$- be full]
adwadri̱hgwagwenǫ:ni: there was a full moon P
deyodri̱hwagwenǫ:ni: there is a full moon S
•(r)iho... look for stems beginning with (r)ih(wa)
•(r)ihoˀdad work
[ad+ contains: -(r)ihoˀd$_V$- work]
hęnadri̱hoˀda:s they (m) work; they are workers H
ęgaǫ:drihoˀda:t they (f/m) are going to work P
sadrihoˀda:t work I
•(r)ihoˀdahǫh disagree
[(tęˀ) de+ not P+ contains: -(r)ihoˀd$_V$- work]
dewagrihoˀdahǫh I am not in complete agreement S
•(r)ihodahǫh be confused, mixed up
[de+ not P+ad+ contains: -(r)ihoˀd$_V$- work]
dewagadrihoˀdahǫh I am confused; mixed up; s.t. is blocking my thinking S
•(r)ihodahse:ˀ confused
[de+ not P+ad+ contains: -(r)ihoˀd$_V$- work]
dewagadrihodahse:ˀ I am confused; I cannot make up my mind S
•(r)ihoˀdahstaˀ tool, equipment
[ǫ+ad+ -(r)ihoˀdahsd$_V$- work with an instrument]
ǫdrihoˀda:staˀ tools; equipment
•(r)ihoˀdeˀ be working
[P+ contains: -(r)ihoˀd$_V$- work]
hoihoˀdeˀ he is working S
•(r)ihoˀdę: be soft, loose
[P+(N+) contains: -(r)ihoˀd$_V$- work]
ohehda̱hoˀdę: soft ground S
[P+(N+) -(h)ehd(a)$_N$- land, dirt, earth, ground -(r)ihoˀd$_V$- work]
•(r)ihoˀdę: way, manner, belief
[(tsęh) that ni+P+ -(r)ih(wa)$_N$- word -oˀdę:$_V$- certain type, kind of thing]
tsęh niyǫgwaihodę our ways, beliefs
nisaihoˀdę: your manner
•(r)ihoˀgaˀd speak sharp words
[P+ -(r)ih(wa)$_N$- word -gaˀd$_V$- sharp]
hoiho:gaˀt he speaks sharp words S
•(r)ihowanahd praise, flatter
[TR+ -owanahd$_V$- enlarge]
ęhshehowa:naht you will praise her, uplift her spirits, flatter her P
•(r)ihowanęh special, important
[(g)+(y)o+ -(r)ih(wa)$_N$- word -owanęh$_V$- be big]
gyoihowa:nęh the most important S
oihowa:nęh it is important; a great or worthy commendation; it is special
•(r)ihowęhs computer
[de+ga+ -(r)ih(wa)$_N$- word -owę(:)$_V$- split in two]
degaiho:węhs a computer

•(r)ihowi be slow, feeble, clumsy
[P+ad+ -(r)ih(wa)$_N$- word -owi, ǫny$_V$- drive]
hodriho:wi: he is clumsy S

•(r)ihǫd agent
[A+ ad+ -(r)ih(wa)$_N$- word -ǫd$_V$- attached -ǫʼ plural]
honadriħǫ:dǫʼ they (m) are agents

•(r)ihǫd appoint, delegate
[TR+ -(r)ih(wa)$_N$- word -ǫd$_V$- attached]
ahǫwaihǫdęʼ they delegated him a duty P
shǫgwaihǫ:t he has appointed us S

•(r)ihǫni incite, cause
ętrihǫ:niʼ, ęsrihǫ:niʼ you will incite, be the cause of s.t. P

•(r)ihǫny(ę, ani) read
[adad+ -(r)ih(wa)$_N$- word -ǫnyę, ǫnyani$_V$- make for oneself]
ǫdadriħǫnyanih she is reading H
wadadriħǫnyani: reading material (lit.: it has been read) S
sadadriħo:nyęh read I

•(r)ihǫnyanih teacher
[A+(adę+) -(r)ih(wa)$_N$- word -ǫnyę, ǫnyani$_V$- make for oneself]
hadęihǫnya:nih he is a teacher H
ǫdęihǫnya:nih she is a teacher H
hai:hǫnya:nih he is a teacher H

•(r)ihǫnyani:ʼ education
[ga+ -(r)ih(wa)$_N$- word -ǫnyę, ǫnyani$_V$- make for oneself]
gai:hǫnya:ni:ʼ education

•(r)ihu:ʼuh be sensitive, unimportant
[ni+P+ -(r)ih(wa)$_N$- word -u:ʼuh$_V$- be small]
niwagriħu:ʼuh I am sensitive S
niyoihu:ʼuh it is of little importance S

•(hr)ihsd(a) tin, metal, money
see: (h)wihsd(a), (hr)ihsd(a) tin, metal, money
gai:sdaʼ tin; metal
satwihsdʼęda:s you burn your money H
[at+ -(h)wihsd(a), (hr)ihsd(a)$_N$- metal, money : -(hr)ęʼda:$_V$- burn s.t.]

•(r)ihsdanega(:,ǫ) scream
[de+...ad+ -(h)wihsd(a), (hr)ihsd(a)$_N$- metal, money -(wa)nega(:,ǫ)$_V$- explode, split]
dehsadrihsdanegaǫhs you are bursting out screaming, crying H
dęhsadrihsda:ne:ga:ʼ you will burst out screaming, crying; you will make a loud outburst P
desadrihsdane:ga:ʼ scream (lit.: split your voice) I

•(r)ihsdataʼ iron
[e+ stem: -(r)ihsdataʼ- iron; consists of: -(h)wihsd(a), (hr)ihsd(a)$_N$- metal, money -taʼ- be dry]
ei:sda:taʼ s.t. to iron with; an iron

•(r)ihsdiʼdr survey
[-(h)wihsd(a), (hr)ihsd(a)$_N$- metal, money -(i)ʼdre(:)$_V$- drag, drive]
hadihsdiʼdrehs they (m) are surveying the land; surveyors H
gaihsdiʼdrǫ: it has been surveyed S

•(r)ihsdowanęh loud
[P+ -(h)wihsd(a), (hr)ihsd(a)$_N$- metal, money -owanęh$_V$- be big]
odihsdowanęh they (z) are loud S

•(r)ihsdohas typewriter
[de+ga+ -(h)wihsd(a), (hr)ihsd(a)$_N$- metal, money -ohag$_V$- squeeze]
degaihsdo:ha:s a typewriter

•(r)ihsdowa:ʼ mullet
[s+ga+ -(h)wihsd(a), (hr)ihsd(a)$_N$- metal -owa:ʼ$_V$- bitter]
sgai:sdo:wa:ʼ mullet

•(r)i:sgędri: wren
[s+ga+]
sgai:sgędri: a marsh wren

•(r)ihsgyaʼksǫʼ cut up s.t.
[-(h)wihsd(a), (hr)ihsd(a)$_N$- metal -(i)yaʼksǫʼ$_V$- cut, break several things]
ęhsrihsgyaʼksǫʼ you will slice s.t. up P

Legend: H habitual, P punctual, S stative, I imperative, PURP purposive, PURP-H purposive habitual, PURP-PAST purposive past, PURP-P purposive punctual, PURP-I purposive imperative; see §8.6, §8.11 in Appendix J. Alphabetization in stems ignores length (:), and any h's or glottal stops (ʼ) that are not between vowels. See §2.2 of the User Guide for explanation.

•(r)isr(a) leggings
[ga+]
gai:sraʼ leggings

•(r)ihsres shoe upper
[de+yo+ -(r)ihsr(a)$_N$- leggings -es$_V$- long]
deyoihsre:s an upper (part of a shoe)

•(hr)ihtaʼ grinder, cutter
[de+ga+ contains: -(hr)ihd$_V$- break up with s.t.]
degahihtaʼ a grinder; a cutter

•(r)ih(wa) word, affair, business, message, matter, idea, reason
[o+]
oihwaʼ a message; it matters; it is its fault; a word; an affair; business
oihwageh the reason; the idea for s.t.
oihwaǫ:weh a sacred idea

•(r)ihwad sentence
[j+o+ -(r)ih(wa)$_N$- word -d$_V$- stand, be one object]
joihwa:t one written sentence

•(r)ihwahdę̱di, (r)ihwahdęgy ceremony
[ad+ -(r)ih(wa)$_N$- word -(a)hdę̱di, (a)hdęgy$_V$- leave, go away]
ęwadri̱hwahdę:diʼ the ceremony will start P
odrihwa̱hdę:gyǫ: ceremonies S

•(r)ihwahdęgyaʼd do a ceremony
[ad+ -(r)ih(wa)$_N$- word -(a)hdęgyaʼd$_V$- cause to leave, go away]
edwadri̱hwahdęgyaʼt we all (incl.) did the ceremony P

•(r)ihwadogę traitor
[(tęʼ) deʼ+ not P+ -(r)ih(wa)$_N$- word -dogę(:)$_V$- be right, true]
dehoihwado:gę: he is a traitor S

•(r)ihwadogę be reliable
[P+ -(r)ih(wa)$_N$- word -dogę(:)$_V$- be right, true]
hoihwado:gę: he is a reliable person S

•(r)ihwahdǫʼd suicide
[adad+ -(r)ih(wa)$_N$- word -(a)hdǫʼd$_V$- cause to disappear]
awadadrihwa̱hdǫʼt suicide (lit.: s.o. did away with themselves)

•(r)ihwahdǫ(ʼ) be extinct
[-(r)ih(wa)$_N$- word -(a)hdǫʼ$_V$- disappear]
oihwahdǫʼǫh it is extinct S

•(r)ihwaʼe(g) demand s.t., insist on s.t.
[d+... -(r)ih(wa)$_N$- word -(ʼ)e(g)$_V$- hit]
ętrihwa̱ʼe:k you will demand s.t., insist on s.t., force s.t. P
dahsrihwa̱ʼe:k you insisted P

•(r)ihwaʼehsd demand a report, an account
[de+ TR+ -(r)ih(wa)$_N$- word -(ʼ)ehsd$_V$- hit with s.t.]
atgaǫgrihwaʼehs they wanted a report P

•(r)ihwaʼehsd accuse s.o.
[TR+ad+ -(r)ih(wa)$_N$- word -(ʼ)ehsd$_V$- hit with s.t.]
ahodri̱hwaʼe:s he was accused P

•(r)ihwaʼehsd blame s.o.
[TR+ -(r)ih(wa)$_N$- word -(ʼ)ehsd$_V$- hit with s.t.]
ęhshehwaʼehs you will blame s.o. P

•(r)ihwaʼehsd(ę, ani) demand an audience from s.o.
[TR+ -(r)ih(wa)$_N$- word -(ʼ)ehsd(ę,ani)$_V$- hit with s.t. for s.o.'s benefit]
ęhǫwadihwaʼehsdęʼ they will unravel his message, demand an audience from him P

•(r)ihwaʼehsdǫ:ʼ report
[ga+ -(r)ih(wa)$_N$- word -(ʼ)ehsd$_V$- hit with s.t.]
gaihwaʼehsdǫ:ʼ a report

•(r)ihwaʼestaʼ drumstick, baseball bat
[e+ -(r)ih(wa)$_N$- word -(ʼ)ehsd$_V$- hit with s.t.]
ehwaʼestaʼ a drumstick; a baseball bat

•(r)ihwaę(:) innocent
[sgaho'dę' nothing de'+ not P+ -(r)ih(wa)$_N$- word -ę$_V$- lie]
sgaho'dę' dehoiwaę' he is innocent S

•(r)ihwaędahgw responsibility
[-(r)ih(wa)$_N$- word -ędahgw$_V$- raise from the ground]
ęgaihwaędahk it will become s.o.'s responsibility P
gaihwaędahgǫh their collective responsibility S

•(r)ihwaęda's decide, agree, conclude
[de+P+ -(r)ih(wa)$_N$- word -ęda'$_V$- finish]
atoihwaę:da's he came to a decision, a conclusion P
dehsaihwaęda's decide I

•(r)ihwaędǫhgw gossip
[de+...ad+ -(r)ih(wa)$_N$- word -ędǫhgw$_V$- un-shake s.t.]
deyǫdrihwaędǫhkwa' a female gossiper H
dęsadrihwaędǫhk you will gossip P

•(r)ihwaętwa(hd) spread the news, bring forth a message
[de+s+... -(r)ih(wa)$_N$- word -(y)ętw(ahd)$_V$- broadcast s.t.]
dehaihwaętwahs he brings forth the message all the time H
dęshaihwaętwaht he will bring forth a message P
dehshoihwaętwęh he is bringing forth the message right now S

•(r)ihwaga'de' chatterbox, talkative
[P+ -(r)ih(wa)$_N$- word -ga'de'$_V$- many]
goihwaga'de' she is a chatterbox S

•(r)ihwage: be quick-witted
[ha'+de+A/P+N+ -(r)ih(wa)$_N$- word -(a)ge:$_V$- be two or more]
ha'dehoihwage: he is quick-witted; he has lots of business, different ideas, many ideas; he is into everything S

•(r)ihwagehde' responsibility
[ga+ -(r)ih(wa)$_N$- word -gehd$_V$- have around one's neck]
gaihwagehde' a responsibility

•(r)ihwahsgęnh fight over
see: (hs)gęnh [de+...(r)ihwa/N+] fight over
saǫhwęjahsgęnhęh you are fighting over the land right now S
[-ǫhwęj(a)$_N$- earth, land -(hs)genh$_V$- argue for, advocate]

•(r)ihwagęnya'd complain, instigate
[P+ -(r)ih(wa)$_N$- word -gęnya'd$_V$- cause to compete]
hoihwagęnya't he is an instigator S

•(r)ihwagenh argue for, advocate
[de+ -(r)ih(wa)$_N$- word -genh$_V$- argue for, advocate]
dehaihwagenhahs he is a lawyer H
dęhsrihwage:nha' you will argue, debate, protest P
deyagodihwage:nhęh they (f/m) are arguing S

•(r)ihwagwaihsǫh be righteous, fair
[P+ad+ -(r)ih(wa)$_N$- word -gwaihs(i)$_V$- be straight]
godrihwagwaehsǫh she is fair, righteous S

•(r)ihwagwaihs(i) be a witness
[P+ad+ -(r)ih(wa)$_N$- word -gwaihs(i)$_V$- be straight]
ęhsrihwagwaihsi' you will be a witness P

•(r)ihwagweny accomplish, achieve, lead
[-(r)ih(wa)$_N$- word, affair, matter -gweni, gweny$_V$- be able to do s.t., succeed]
ęhsrihwagwę:ni' you will accomplish P
saihwagwe:nyǫ: you are able to perform (that is, run, dance, orate, etc.) S

Legend: H habitual, P punctual, S stative, I imperative, PURP purposive, PURP-H purposive habitual, PURP-PAST purposive past, PURP-P purposive punctual, PURP-I purposive imperative; see §8.6, §8.11 in Appendix J. Alphabetization in stems ignores length (:), and any h's or glottal stops (') that are not between vowels. See §2.2 of the User Guide for explanation.

•(r)ihwagwenyaʼs be a success
[adad+ -(r)ih(wa)$_{N}$- word, affair, matter -gweni, gweny$_{V}$- be able to do s.t., succeed]
ahsadadrihwagwe:nyaʼs you are a success P

•(r)ihwagwenyęʼs achieve s.t.
[adad+ -(r)ih(wa)$_{N}$- word, affair, matter -gweni, gwenyę$_{V}$- be able to do s.t., succeed for oneself]
ęsadadrihwagwe:nyęʼs you will achieve P

•(r)ihwagwęniyoʼ be a boss, reside, dwell
[A+ -(r)ih(wa)$_{N}$- word -gwęniyoʼ$_{V}$- be the main thing]
grihwagwęni:yoʼ where I reside, dwell (lit.: where I'm the boss) S

•(r)ihwagwęniyohsd sanction, charter, give authority
[A+ -(r)ih(wa)$_{N}$- word -gwęniyohsd$_{V}$- make the main thing]
ęhsrihwagwę:ni:yohs you will sanction, charter, give authority to s.o. P

•(r)ihwagyaǫ accident
[w+ad+ -(r)ih(wa)$_{N}$- word -(a)gyaǫʼ$_{V}$- be tricked, fooled]
wadrihwagyaǫ:s there are continuous accidents H

•(r)ihwagyęhętw participate, partake
[heʼ+... -(r)ih(wa)$_{N}$- word -yęhętw, yęhęto$_{V}$- pull]
hedwaihwagyęhę:tohs, hedwaihwagyęhę:twahs we all partake; we all (incl.) pull forth the words, the ideas all the time H
hęjidwaihwagyęhętoʼ we all (incl.) will bring the idea back again P
heyǫgwaihwadihętwęh, heyǫgwaihwagyęhętwęh we have pulled forth the ideas; we are participating right now S

•(r)ihwahę, (r)ihwahe present an idea, submit an idea
[-(r)ih(wa)$_{N}$- word -(hr)e, (hr)ę$_{V}$- put, place]
ęhsrihwahęʼ you will present an idea P

•(r)ihwahe:ʼ presentation
[ga+ -(r)ih(wa)$_{N}$- word -(hr)e, (hr)ę$_{V}$- put, place]
gaihwa̱he:ʼ a presentation

•(r)ihwahę, (r)ihwahe commit a crime, do wrong
[de+...ad+ -(r)ih(wa)$_{N}$- word -(hr)e, (hr)ę$_{V}$- put, place]
atadri̱hwahęʼ he went afoul of the law; he did s.t. wrong P

•(r)ihwakahǫʼ alliance
[de+ga+ -(r)ih(wa)$_{N}$- word -kahǫ$_{V}$- adjoin, assemble, put together]
degaihwakahǫʼ an alliance

•(r)ihwahkwaʼ choir
[de+A+ -(r)ih(wa)$_{N}$- word -(h)gw$_{V}$- lift, pick up]
de̱hadi:hwa̱hkwaʼ a choir (lit.: they (m) are gospel singers)

•(r)ihwaneʼaksrǫ(:) swear
[-(r)ih(wa)$_{N}$- word; contains: -neʼag$_{V}$- sin]
ęhsrihwaneʼaksrǫ:ʼ you will swear, use profane language P

•(r)ihwaʼneg pray, hope
[-(r)ih(wa)$_{N}$- word, matter, affair -(ʼ)neg$_{V}$- pray]
sri̱hwanʼekaʼ you are always praying H
ęhsrihwʼane:k you will pray P
saihwʼane:gęh you are praying S

•(r)ihwanegę:ʼ prayer
[ga+ -(r)ih(wa)$_{N}$- word; contains: -(ʼ)neg$_{V}$- pray, hope]
gaihwane:gę:ʼ a prayer; to pray

•(r)ihwanhodǫgw, (r)ihwanhodǫgo open a gathering
[-(r)ih(wa)$_N$- word -nhodǫgw$_V$- open]
ęhaihwanhodǫ:go' he will open the gathering P

•(r)ihwahniya'd affirm, agree
[-(r)ih(wa)$_N$- word -(h)niya'd$_V$- harden]
ęhsrihwa̱hni:ya't you will affirm it, agree P

•(r)ihwahniya'd marry s.o. off
[TR+ -(r)ih(wa)$_N$- word -(h)niya'd$_V$- harden]
shagodi:hwahniy'adǫh they got married by the Chiefs; a marriage ceremony usually sanctioned by the Chiefs S

•(r)ihwanǫhwe' disapprove
[(tę') de'+ not A+ -(r)ih(wa)$_N$- word -nǫhwe'$_V$- like]
desrihwanǫhwe's you disapprove H

•(r)ihwanǫhkw care for, respect
[TR+ -(r)ih(wa)$_N$- word -nǫhkw$_V$- love]
a:goi:hwanǫhkwa:k I should care for, respect your ideas P

•(r)ihwaohes be a researcher
[A+ -(r)ih(wa)$_N$- word -(r)oheg$_V$- gather]
eihwaohe:s she is a researcher
haihwaohe:s he is a researcher

•(r)ihwaǫni heal up
[ad+ -(r)ih(wa)$_N$- word -ǫni, ǫny$_V$- make]
ęhswadrihwaǫni' you will heal up P

•(r)ihwahs' plan, promise, make an agreement
[-(r)ih(wa)$_N$- word -(h)s'$_V$- plan, promise]
srihwahs'ahs you promise, make an agreement all the time H
ęhsrihwa̱hs'a:' you will plan an idea; you will promise, make an agreement P
haihwihs'ǫhǫgye' he is going along making promises, making agreements S

•(r)ihwahs'(a) agreement, plan
[ga+ -(r)ih(wa)$_N$- word -(h)s'$_V$- plan, promise]
gaihwi̱hsa' (**gaihwa̱hsa'**) an agreement

•(r)ihwahsde' burden, preoccupation
[o+ -(r)ih(wa)$_N$- word -(a)hsde'$_V$- heavy]
oihwahsde' a mental burden; a preoccupation

•(r)ihwahsehd have a secret
[ad+ -(r)ih(wa)$_N$- word -(a)hsehd$_V$- hide s.t.]
ahęnadrihwa̱hseht they (m) hid their idea (that is, they schemed) P
odrihwasehdǫh it is secret S

•(r)ihwahsehdǫ:' secret
[a+ad+ -(r)ih(wa)$_N$- word -(a)hsehd$_V$- hide s.t.]
adrihwa̱hsehdǫ:' a secret

•(r)ihwahsrǫni be in charge, come to an arrangement
[(ad+) -(r)ih(wa)$_N$- word -(h)srǫni$_V$- fix]
hadi:hwahsrǫ:nih they (m) who are in charge H
ęhsrihwa̱hsrǫ:ni' you will come to an arrangement P

•(r)ihwahsrǫni reconcile, make peace
[s+...(ad+) -(r)ih(wa)$_N$- word -(h)srǫni$_V$- make]
ęjijadri̱hwahsrǫ:ni' you two will reconcile P
wadrihwahsrǫ:ni: peace; to make peace with someone S

•(r)ihwate'd explain s.t.
[de+... -(r)ih(wa)$_N$- word -(a)te'd$_V$- brighten, make clear]
degaihwate'ta' a dictionary H
dęhsrihwate't you will explain P

•(r)ihwate'ta' dictionary
[de+ga+ -(r)ih(wa)$_N$- word -(a)te'd$_V$- brighten, make clear]
degaihwate'ta' a dictionary

Legend: H habitual, P punctual, S stative, I imperative, PURP purposive, PURP-H purposive habitual, PURP-PAST purposive past, PURP-P purposive punctual, PURP-I purposive imperative; see §8.6, §8.11 in Appendix J. Alphabetization in stems ignores length (:), and any h's or glottal stops (') that are not between vowels. See §2.2 of the User Guide for explanation.

•(r)ihwa tgahǫ(:), (a)tgaha(:) oversee, supervise
[P+ -(r)ih(wa)$_N$- word -(a)tgahǫ(:), (a)tgaha(:)$_V$- pay attention, watch]
hodrihwatgaha:ʼ he is a supervisor, overseer H
ęhsadri̱hwatga̱hǫ:ʼ you will oversee, supervise P

•(r)ihwatgihd talk dirty, use bad language
[ad+ -(r)ih(wa)$_N$- word -tgihd$_V$- make dirty, ugly]
hodrihwatgihdǫh he is talking dirty S

•(r)ihwatsʼ earn s.t., fulfill s.t.
[de+...(ad+) -(r)ih(wa)$_N$- word -(a)tsʼ$_V$- use up]
atadri̱hwa:tsʼa:ʼ he earned it; he fulfilled it P
dehodi:hwa̱htsʼa:ʼ they are earning, fulfilling it S

•(r)ihwahtsęnyahsgǫ: find fault
[P+ -(r)ih(wa)$_N$- word -tsęi, tsęny$_V$- find -sgǫ: easily]
saihwahtsęnyahsgǫ: you find faults H

•(r)ihwawaʼs support s.o., back s.o.
[TR+ -(r)ih(wa)$_N$- word -(h)wawaʼs$_V$- support]
hehwawʼaseh I did agree with him, support him H
ęhehsrihwa:waʼs you will back up his ideas P

•(r)ihwahwinyǫʼd report
[TR+ -(r)ih(wa)$_N$- word -iyǫʼd $_V$- put in]
ętrihwa̱hwinyǫʼt you will report P

•(r)ihwayaʼg denounce, disapprove
[de+... -(r)ih(wa)$_N$- word -(i)yaʼg$_V$- cut, break, cross]
dęhsrihwaya:ʼk you will denounce it, disapprove of it P

•(r)ihwayena(w) accept advice
[-(r)ih(wa)$_N$- word -yena(w), yenaǫ, yena(:)$_V$- catch, receive, accept]
ęhsri:hwaye:na:ʼ you will accept advice, a suggestion, etc. P

•(r)ihwaętw(ahd) broadcast s.t.
[-(r)ih(wa)$_N$- word -(y)ętw(ahd)$_V$- plant; cause to plant]
de̱haihwaętwahs he brings forth the message all the time H
dęshaihwaętwaht he will bring forth a message P
dehshoihwaętwęh he is bringing forth the message right now S

•(r)ihwęhd bring down an idea
[-(r)ih(wa)$_N$- word -(y)ęhd$_V$- knock down, hit]
ętrihwęht you will bring the idea down P

•(r)ihwędaʼ wear out
[-(r)ih(wa)$_N$- word -ędaʼ$_V$- finish]
agaihwę:daʼ it wore out (for example, clothing) P

•(r)ihwęhd(ę, ani) give s.o. a message
[TR+ -(r)ih(wa)$_N$- word contains: -ęhd(ę,ani)$_V$- cause to direct, convey for s.o.]
ęgǫihwęhdęʼ I will give you a significant message P

•(r)ihwęhę(:) convey a message
[haʼ+... -(r)ih(wa)$_N$- word -ęhę(:,w)$_V$- direct, convey]
hehaihwęhęhs he always takes the message; he is a messenger H
hęhaihwęhę:ʼ he will take the message P
hehoihwęhę: he has taken a message S

•(r)ihwiyoʼ certain, sure
[o+ -(r)ih(wa)$_N$- word; contains: -iyo:$_V$- be nice, good]
oihwi:yoʼ it is certain, for sure S

•(r)ihwiyohsd become Christian, convert to Christianity
[-(r)ih(wa)$_N$- word -iyohsd$_V$- become nice, good]
ahsrihwi:yohs you became a Christian; you converted to Christianity P

•(r)iyo, nyo kill someting
[TR+ (ad / adę+)]
gęna:dri:yohs they kill H
aha:nyoʼ he killed (an animal) P
hodę:nyo: he has killed s.o. S

•(r)iyo, nyo commit suicide
[adad+-(r)iyo, nyo$_{V}$- kill someting]
awadadri:yoʼ it killed itself; suicide P

•(r)iyo: war, fight
[w+ad+ contains: -(r)iyo, nyo$_{V}$- kill s.t.]
wadri:yo: a war; a fight

•(r)iyohsd(ę, ani) make s.o. fight
[TR+ad+ contains: -(r)iyo, nyo$_{V}$- kill s.t.]
ęgasheyadriyohsdęʼ you will make them fight P

•(r)iʼyǫde:s weasel
[s+ga+ad+ -(r)iʼyǫd(a)$_{N}$- -es$_{V}$- long]
sgadriʼyǫde:s a weasel

•(r)ogaʼd be rough
[P+(N+)]
ao:gaʼt it is rough S
ohaho:gaʼt a rough road
[o+ stem: -(h)ah(a)$_{N}$- road -(r)ogaʼd$_{V}$- rough]

•(r)oheg gather
[(N+)]
gae:yohe:s they (f/m) are gathering H
ęhsrohe:k you will gather P
agrohe:gǫh I have gathered S
saʼnigǫhaohe:k gather your mind I
[-(ʼ)nigǫh(a)$_{V}$- mind -(r)oheg$_{V}$- gather]

•(r)oheg congregate, flock, gather together
[ad+]
gęnadrǫhe:s they (z) are flocking H
ędwadrǫhe:k we all (incl.) will gather together P

•(r)oheg(ę, ani) accumulate for oneself
[adad+ contains: -(r)oheg$_{V}$- gather]
ęhsadadrohe:gęʼ you will accumulate (things, ideas, etc.) for yourself P

•(r)ohektaʼ meeting place, gathering place, venue
[ǫ+ad+ -(r)ohegd$_{V}$- cause to gather]
ǫdrohektaʼ a meeting place; a gathering place; a venue

•(r)ohǫ:ʼ gathering
[ga+ contains: -(r)oheg$_{V}$- gather]
gaohǫ:ʼ the act of gathering

•(hr)owi, (hr)ǫny tell
[TR/...at+]
gatrowih, gatrowihs I tell all the time H
ędwa:tro:wiʼ we all (incl.) will tell P
aga:tro:wi: I have told S
sheho:wih tell her I

•(hr)owi, (hr)ǫny recount, retell
[s+TR/...at+]
ętsa:tro:wiʼ you will recount, retell P

•(r)ǫ(:) put objects on a string
[occurs in:]
hanihaǫhaʼ he is stringing H
[stem: -nihaǫ- string s.t.; consists of: -niha$_{N}$- -(r)ǫ$_{V}$- bead s.t.]
degayaǫ:ʼ it is beaded S
[de+ -ya$_{N}$- -(r)ǫ$_{V}$- bead s.t.]
sagyęhsaǫ: bandage yourself I
[(ag+) -yęhs(a)$_{N}$- bandage -(r)ǫ$_{V}$- bead s.t.]

•(r)ǫd(a) log
[ga+]
gaǫ:daʼ a log

•(r)ǫdadeʼ beam
[ga+ -(r)ǫd(a)$_{N}$- log -deʼ$_{V}$- exist]
gaǫdadeʼ a beam

•(r)ǫdadenyǫʼ log rafter
[ga+ -(r)ǫd(a)$_{N}$- log -denyǫʼ$_{V}$- several existing things]
gaǫdade:nyǫʼ log rafters

•(r)ǫdaʼehs woodpecker
[ga+ -(r)ǫd(a)$_{N}$- log -(ʼ)ehsd$_{V}$- hit with s.t.]
gaǫda̲ʼehs a woodpecker

Legend: H habitual, P punctual, S stative, I imperative, PURP purposive, PURP-H purposive habitual, PURP-PAST purposive past, PURP-P purposive punctual, PURP-I purposive imperative; see §8.6, §8.11 in Appendix J. Alphabetization in stems ignores length (:), and any h's or glottal stops (ʼ) that are not between vowels. See §2.2 of the User Guide for explanation.

•(r)ǫdahǫh beam
[de+ga+ -(r)ǫd(a)$_N$- log -(adi)hǫh$_V$- lean against]
degaǫdahǫh a beam
•(r)ǫdatgę: dead tree
[a+ -(r)ǫd(a)$_N$- log -tgę:$_V$- be spoiled, rotten, rotten]
aǫdatgę: a dead tree
•(r)ǫgw, (r)ǫgo keep, adopt
[ad+ (N+)]
sadwiyaǫ:gwahs you adopt babies H
[-wiy(a)$_N$- child -(r)ǫgw$_V$- keep]
ęsadrǫ:goʼ you will keep P
agadwiyaǫ:gwęh I have adopted a baby S
•(r)ǫhgw(ę, ani) threaten, scare s.o.
[TR+ (ad+)]
sheyadrǫhgwa:nih you are threatening, scaring s.o. H
ęhsheyadrǫhgwęʼ you will threaten, scare s.o. P
•(r)ǫgyaʼktaʼ saw
[de+ya+ -(r)ǫd(a)$_N$- log -(i)yaʼkd$_V$- cut, break with s.t.]
deyaǫgyaʼktaʼ, deyǫgyaʼktaʼ a buzz saw
•(r)ǫhę be alone, be a loner
[neʼ a+]
neʼ aǫhę:ʼęh all alone; the most S
•(r)ǫhny(a) river flats
[-ʼgeh on, at]
ǫhnyaʼgeh on the river flats
•(hr)ǫhwaʼs wait for s.o.
[TR+ -(hr)ǫhw$_V$- cause to wait]
ęgǫhǫhwaʼs you will wait for me P
dahskrǫhwaʼs wait for me I
•(hr)ǫhw(ę, ani) bar a pathway
[de+... contains: -(hr)ǫhw$_V$- cause to wait]
dęhsrǫhwęʼ you will bar s.t., put up a barrier P

•(hr)ǫhwahkwaʼ barrier
[de+wa+at+ -(hr)ǫhw$_V$- cause to wait -hkwaʼ instrument]
dewatrǫhwakwaʼ a barrier
•(r)ǫʼwęsd abuse
[ad+]
dehshagodrǫʼwe̱hstaʼ he abuses s.o. H
•(r)ǫwihshęʼ pant
[P+]
gaǫ:wi̱hshęʼǫh she is panting S
•(r)ǫhy(a) heavens, sky
[ga+ … ʼgeh on, at]
gaǫhyʼageh in the heavens; in the sky
•(r)ǫhyaʼd be unwilling, stubborn
[P+ad+ -(r)ǫhyaʼd$_V$- be unwilling, stubborn]
godrǫhyaʼt she is unwilling, stubborn S
•(r)ǫhyaʼdahgw balk, be reluctant
[ad+ contains: -(r)ǫhyaʼd$_V$- be unwilling, stubborn]
ahadrǫhyaʼdahk he balked at the suggestion P
hodrǫhyadahgǫh, hodrǫhyadahgwęh he is balking S
•(r)ǫhyadagyeʼ skyline, horizon
[ga+ -(r)ǫhy(a)$_N$- sky -dagyeʼ$_V$- be ongoing]
gaǫhyada:gyeʼ the skyline; the horizon
•(r)ǫhyadeʼ heaven
[ga+ -(r)ǫhy(a)$_N$- sky -deʼ$_V$- exist]
gaǫ:hyadeʼ in existing heaven
•(r)ǫhyaʼę:ʼ blue
[(a+) -(r)ǫhy(a)$_N$- sky -ʼę:ʼ$_V$- be coloured]
aǫhyaę:ʼ, ǫhyaʼę:ʼ blue
•(r)ǫhyagę be in agony, groan, be in pain
grǫhya:gęhs I am always in pain H
ęgrǫhyagęʼ I will be in pain; I will labour P
agrǫhyagę: I am in agony, in pain S
saǫhyagę: groan I

•(r)ǫhyagęʼd labour, make s.o. work hard
[TR+ contains: -(r)ǫhyagę$_{V}$- be in agony, labour, groan]
ęhsaǫhyagʼędahk it's going to make you groan P

•(r)ǫhyaʼgęd light blue
[a+ -(r)ǫhy(a)$_{N}$- sky -(ʼ)gęd$_{V}$- light-coloured, white]
aǫhyʼagę꞉t light blue

S

•(h)sadaęʼ foggy
[de+…at+ -(h)sad(a)$_{N}$- fog -ę$_{V}$- lie on the ground]
deyotsadaęʼ it is foggy S

•(h)sadę come by horseback
[d+...P+ contains: -(h)seʼ$_{V}$- ride horseback]
ędyagohsa꞉dęʼ she will come by horse-back P

•(h)sadę mount a horse
[P+ contains: -(h)seʼ$_{V}$- ride horseback]
ęwagęhsa꞉dęʼ I will mount a horse P

•(h)sadę carry s.o. on one's back
[TR+ contains: -(h)seʼ$_{V}$- ride horse-back]
gohsa꞉dęhs a horse (old word)
ęhshehsa꞉dęʼ you will carry s.o. on your back P

•(h)sadęhs horse
[go+ contains: -(h)seʼ$_{V}$- ride horseback]
gohsa꞉dęhs a horse (old word)

•(h)sadǫ(꞉) bury s.o., an animal
ęgehsadǫ꞉ʼ I will bury it (an animal) P

•(h)sadǫ(꞉) bury an object
[at+]
ęgatsadǫ꞉ʼ I will bury s.t. over there P

•(h)sadǫgw, (h)sadǫgo unearth s.t.
[s+...at+ contains: -(h)sadǫ$_{V}$- bury s.t.]
ętsatsadǫ꞉goʼ you will unearth it P

•(h)sag investigate, inquire, look for
see: (i)hsag [(N+)] investigate, inquire, look for
ęgihsa꞉k I will seek it, look for it P

•(h)sag look for a mate
see: (i)hsag [de+] look for a mate
dedwadęhsa꞉s we are looking for mates H

•(h)sa꞉, (h)sag(a) mouth
[o+]
ohsa꞉ʼ a mouth
gahsagahę꞉t a mouth
[ga+ -(h)sag(a)$_{N}$- mouth -gahęd$_{V}$- drill, hole]

•(h)sagahǫ꞉ʼ large-mouthed bass
[s+ga+ -(h)sag(a)$_{N}$- mouth -kahǫ$_{V}$- adjoin, abutt]
sgahsagahǫ꞉ʼ a large-mouthed bass

•(h)sagahęd mouth
[ga+ -(h)sag(a)$_{N}$- mouth -gahęd$_{V}$- drill, hole]
gahsagahę꞉t mouth
gęhsagahę꞉t my mouth
swahsagahę꞉t your (p) mouths

•(h)saheʼd(a) bean
[o+]
ohsaheʼdaʼ beans

•(h)saheʼdagriʼ coffee, bean soup
[o+ -(h)saheʼd(a)$_{N}$- bean -griʼ$_{V}$- juice, liquid]
ohsaheʼda꞉griʼ bean soup; coffee

•(h)saheʼdase꞉ string bean, yellow bean, green bean
[o+ -(h)saheʼd(a)$_{N}$- bean -(a)se꞉$_{V}$- new]
ohsaheʼda꞉se꞉ string beans; yellow beans; green beans

•saide(꞉) beg, freeload
[de+…at+]
desatsai꞉deʼs you are a freeloader H
dęgatsai꞉de꞉ʼ I will freeload P
dewagatsai꞉de꞉ʼ I did freeload S
desatsaide꞉ beg I

Legend: H habitual, P punctual, S stative, I imperative, PURP purposive,PURP-H purposive habitual, PURP-PAST purposive past, PURP-P purposive punctual, PURP-I purposive imperative; see §8.6, §8.11 in Appendix J. Alphabetization in stems ignores length (꞉), and any h's or glottal stops (ʼ) that are not between vowels. See §2.2 of the User Guide for explanation.

•(h)saihsd(a) snake, serpent
[o+]
oshaihsdaʼ a snake; a serpent
•sahnihd be ambitious, tireless, zealous
[P+at+]
gotsahniht she is a good worker, tireless, active, industrious, etc. S
•sanoʼ raccoon
sa:no:ʼ a raccoon
•saʼsaʼ mockingbird, chatterbox
saʼsaʼ a mockingbird; a chatterbox
•(h)s(d) use
ehstaʼ she uses it; people use it H
ę:yehs she will use s.t. P
gǫhsdǫhǫgyeʼ she is arriving wearing that S
ihsehs use it I
•(h)sd(a:) drop of water, raindrop
[o+]
ohsda:ʼ rain
•(h)sd(a:) scale
see: (ih)sd(a:) scale
ohsda:ʼ, ohsdaiʼ the scale (of a fish)
•(h)sdaʼa:ʼ pine tree
[o+ -(h)sd(a:)$_{N}$- drop of water -a:ʼ$_{V}$- hold, include]
osdaʼa:ʼ a pine tree
•(h)sdadenyǫ sprinkle
[o+ -(h)sd(a:)$_{N}$- drop (of water) -denyǫ$_{V}$- several existing objects]
odesda:denyǫ: it is sprinkling S
•(h)sdae:ʼ scale
see: (ih)sdae:ʼ scale
osdae:ʼ scales
•(h)sdaga(:) the sound of rain
[o+ -(h)sd(a:)$_{N}$- drop (of water) -ga:$_{V}$- make a rattling or grinding noise]
osda:ga: the sound of the rain S
•(h)sdagriʼ rain water
[o+ -(h)sd(a:)$_{N}$- drop (of water) -griʼ$_{V}$- juice, liquid]
osda:griʼ rain water

•(h)sdag(wa) dirt, dirty clothes
[ga/o+]
gahsda:gwaʼ, ohsda:gwaʼ dirt; dirty clothes
•(h)sdagwaę(:) be dirty, soiled
[P+ -(h)sdag(wa)$_{N}$- dirt, dirty -ę$_{V}$- lie]
aʼohsdagwaę: it got dirty, soiled P
ohsdagwaę: it is soiled, dirty, stained S
•(h)sdaowanęh rain hard
[ga+ -(h)sd(a:)$_{N}$- drop (of water) -owanęh$_{V}$- be big]
gahsdaowa:nęh it is raining hard S
•(h)sdaowanahd rain hard
[ga+ -(h)sd(a:)$_{N}$- drop (of water) -owanahd$_{V}$- make big]
agasdao:wanaht it rained hard P
•(h)sdaǫdi, (h)sdaǫgy rain
[(y)o+ -(h)sd(a:)$_{N}$- drop (of water) -ǫdi, -ǫgy$_{V}$- throw]
ęyohsdaǫdiʼ it is going to rain P
osdaǫ:gyǫ: it is raining S
•(h)sdahsǫ be worn out
[o+ade+ -(h)sdahsǫ$_{V}$- several used objects]
odehsdahsǫ: it is worn out S
•(h)sdaʼsǫ:ʼǫh vanilla, seasoning, etc.
[de+ye+ -hsd$_{N}$- tool, utensil -shǫ:ʼǫh several things]
deyehstaʼsǫ:ʼǫh vanilla; seasoning; etc.
•(h)sdateʼd shine s.t.
[de+... -(h)sd(a:)$_{N}$- drop (of water) -teʼd$_{V}$- pound]
dęgehsda:teʼt I am going to shine it P
dęgahsdatęʼdǫh it is shined, waxed, polished S
•(h)sdateh shiny, smooth, silver
[de+yo+ -hsd$_{N}$- tool, utensil -(a)te$_{V}$- be bright, clear]
deyohsda:teh it is shiny, smooth (like silver); silver S

•(h)sdenyę'ge: rock slide, avalanche
[contains: -(h)sd(ęha)$_N$- stone -(a's)ę'$_V$- fall, reduce -ge: big]
agahstenyę'ge: rock slide, falling rocks, avalanche

•(h)sdęhd scale fish
see: (ih)sdęhd scale fish
ęsehsdęht you will take the scales off (the fish) P

•(h)sdędo' foundation
[de+ga+ -(h)sd(ęha)$_N$- stone -dǫ'$_V$- several standing objects]
degahstę:do' a foundation

•(h)sdęhes mountain
[de+ga+ -(h)sd(ęha)-$_N$ stone -es$_V$- long]
degahsdęhe:s a high mountain

•(h)sdęhod monument
[t+ga+ -(h)sd(ęha)-$_N$ stone -od$_V$- stand]
tgahsdęho:t a monument

•(h)sdęhod mountain, etc.
[ga+ -(h)sd(ęha)-$_N$ stone -od$_V$- stand]
gahsdęho:t a mountain
gahsdęho:dǫ' mountains; a pile of boulders

•(h)sdęhyai old person
[P+]
gohsdęhyai she is an older woman S

•(h)sdęhowę' volcano
[a+d+wa+ade+ -(h)sd(ęha)$_N$- stone -owę(:)$_V$- split in two]
adwadesdęho:wę' a volcano

•(h)sdi:s trade cloth
[o+ -hsd$_N$- tool, utensil -is$_V$- long]
ohsdi:s trade cloth

•(h)sdihsd care
[ad+(N+/(r)ih(wa)+)]
hadrihwahsdi:hsta' he takes care of the event all the time; he pays attention to what is going on H
ęhadrihwahsdihs he will take care of the event P

•(h)sdihsra:s moth
see: (ih)sdihsra:s moth
gadihsdihsra:s moth

•(h)sdohag squeeze
see: ohag [de+ad/N/(h)sd+] squeeze
dęhsdǫha:k you will squeeze P

•(h)sdow(a) headdress
[ga+]
gahsdo:wa' a headdress

•(h)sdowaheha' pow wow
[A+ -(h)sdow(a)$_N$- feather -(hr)e, (hr)ę$_V$- put, place]
hadihsdowaheha' a pow wow (lit.: they (m) put on their headdresses and perform)

•se' after all, just
see: Appendix I

•(h)se' ride horseback
[P+]
hohse' he is riding a horse S

•sehd(a) nape of the neck, willow
[o+ -agǫ: in]
osehda' a willow; the nape of the neck
sesehdagǫ: on the nape of your neck

•sehdehjih morning
[stem: -sehdehjihah$_N$- morning -geha:' kind]
shedehjihahgeha:' morning kind

•sehdǫg tick
[o+]
osehdǫk a wood tick

•(h)sęh(ę) frost
[o+]
ohsęhę' frost

•(h)sęhęyęhta' goldenrod
[ga+ -(h)sęh(ę)$_N$- frost -(y)ęhd$_V$- hit, knock down, strike]
gahsęhęyęhta' goldenrod

•(h)sęn(a) name
[ga+]
gahsę:na' a name

Legend: H habitual, P punctual, S stative, I imperative, PURP purposive, PURP-H purposive habitual, PURP-PAST purposive past, PURP-P purposive punctual, PURP-I purposive imperative; see §8.6, §8.11 in Appendix J. Alphabetization in stems ignores length (:), and any h's or glottal stops (') that are not between vowels. See §2.2 of the User Guide for explanation.

•(h)sęnaˀse:ˀ surname, family name
[de+A+ -(h)sęn(a)$_N$- name -(a)ˀse:ˀ$_V$- be double]
degahsęnaˀse:ˀ a surname
dehswahsęnaˀse:ˀ your (p) surname, family name (lit.: your (p) double name, joiner name)
dehahsęnaˀse:ˀ his surname

•(h)sęniyohsd compliment, flatter
[TR+ -(h)sęn(a)$_N$- name -iyohsd$_V$- make nice]
gǫwahsęniyǫhstaˀ it is complimentary, flattering H

•(h)sęnowanhęˀ become famous
[A+ -(h)sęn(a)$_N$- name -owanhę$_V$- become big]
ahsehsęnowanheˀ you became famous P

•(h)sęnowanęh be important, famous
[A+ -(h)sęn(a)$_N$- name -owanęh$_V$- be big]
hahsęnowa:nęh he is an important person; he is famous, prominent S

•(h)sęnǫni store, put away
[-(h)sęn(a)$_N$- name -ǫni,ǫny$_V$- make]
se̱hsę:nǫ:nih you are storing it right now H
asehsęnǫ:niˀ you did store it P
ga̱hsę:nǫ:ni: stored items S
se̱hsę:no:nih store it; put it away I

•(h)sęnǫni preserve, can s.t.
[ad+N+]
sadahya̱hsęnǫnih you preserve fruit I
[-(a)hy(a)$_N$- fruit, berry -(h)sęnǫni$_V$- store, put away]

•(h)sętrǫni fatten
[TR+ -(h)sętr(a)$_N$- fat -ǫni, ǫny$_V$- make]
ęhsahsętrǫ:niˀ it will make you fat P

•sgahoˀdęˀ anything, something
see: Appendix I

•sgaoˀdę:ˀęh, something
see: Appendix I

•sga:t e:gęh one acre
sga:t one
e:gęh an acre (lit.: s.o. has seen it)

•(h)sgeh(a) louse
[o+]
ohsgehaˀ a louse

•(h)sgehai:ˀah muslin
[o+ -(h)sgeh(a)$_N$- louse -i:ˀ$_V$- stuck onto s.t. -ˀah diminutive]
osgehai:ˀah muslin

•(h)sgęˀdr(a) rust
[o+]
ohsgęˀdraˀ rust

•(h)sgęˀdraga: rattling noise
[de+yo+ -(h)sgęˀdr(a)$_N$- rust -ga:$_V$- make a rattling or grinding noise]
deyohsgˀędra:ga: a tinny, metallic rattling noise

•(h)sgęˀdrod mouldy, rusty
[-(h)sgęˀdr(a)$_N$- rust -od$_V$- be attached]
awahsgˀędro:dę:ˀ it got mouldy; it got rusty P

•(h)sgęna:ˀ have a stroke
[P+ -(h)sgęn(a)$_N$- stroke -a:ˀ$_V$- hold, contain, include]
ahohsgęna:ˀ he had a stroke P

•(h)sgęnh fight over s.t.
[de+...(r)ihwa/N+]
saǫhwęjahsgęnhęh you are fighting over the land right now S
[-ǫhwęj(a)$_N$- earth, land -genh$_V$- argue for, advocate]

•sgihyoˀts(a) jowl
sgihyoˀtsaˀ jowls

•(ˀ)sgoh immerse, drown s.o.
[ade+]
ęhsadˀesgoh you will go into the water P

•(h)sgogyeˀ float
[A+ -(h)sg$_N$- -ogye$_V$- float]
gahsgo:gyeˀ it (s.t. alive) is floating PURP

•(ʼ)sgoh baptize s.o.
[TR+]
hǫwadʼihsgohs baptism (lit.: s.o. baptizes them) H
ahǫwadiʼsgoʼ they (m) have baptized him, them (m) P

•(ʼ)sgǫd(ę) roast, fry
[ade+ -ʼsg$_N$- roast -ǫd(ę)$_V$- attached]
ęhsadʼesgǫ:dęʼ you will roast P
wadeʼsgǫ:t it is roasting, frying S
sadeʼsgǫ:dęh fry it I

•(h)sgoh(a) branch
[o+]
ohsgohaʼ a branch

•(ʼ)sgohs baptism
[TR+ -(ʼ)sgoh$_V$- immerse, drown]
hǫwadʼihsgohs baptism (lit.: s.o. baptizes them)

•(ʼ)sgǫdahkwaʼ barbecue equipment
[ǫ+ade+ -ʼsg$_N$- roast -ǫdahkwaʼ$_V$- attached object]
ǫdeʼsgǫdahkwaʼ barbecue equipment

•(h)sg(wa:) stone, rock, boulder, bullet
[ga+]
gahsgwa:ʼ a stone; a rock; a boulder; a bullet

•(h)sg(wa:) testicles
[A+ contains: -(h)sg(wa:)$_N$- stone, bullet, rock -ʼgeh on, at]
hahsgwaʼgeh his testicles

•sgwaʼahd(a) frog
see: (nęh)sg(wa), (nǫh)sg(wa) frog, toad
sgwaʼahdaʼ frog

•(h)sgwadahgw neuter, geld
[TR+ -(h)sg(wa:)$_N$- stone, bullet, rock -dahgw$_V$- remove]
ęhǫwaʼsgwa:dahgoʼ they will geld, neuter, fix him (lit.: they will remove his testicles) P
gahsgwa:da̱hgwęh a neutered animal; a gelding S

•(h)sgwadǫʼ rock formation
[de+ga+ -(h)sg(wa:)$_N$- stone, bullet, rock -dǫʼ$_V$- several standing objects]
degahsgwa:dǫʼ rocks piled in an arrangement

•(h)sgwaę(ʼda) coltsfoot
[(o+)]
ohsgwaęʼdaʼ, sgwaęʼdaʼ coltsfoot (a plant)

•(h)sgwaohcs stonegather sucker
[gadi+ -(h)sg(wa:)$_N$- stone, bullet, rock -oheg$_V$- gather]
gadiʼsgwao:he:s a stonegather sucker (a fish)

•(h)sgwaowanęʼs be well-endowed
[de+A+ -(h)sg(wa:)$_N$- stone, bullet, rock -owanęʼs$_V$- several big objects]
dehahsgwaowanęʼs he has big rocks; he is well-endowed S

•(h)sgwaǫd cliff, outcropping
[he+yo+ -(h)sg(wa:)$_N$- stone, bullet, rock -ǫd$_V$- attached]
heyoʼsgwaǫ:t a rock formation that protrudes; a cliff

•(h)sgwaǫd headstone
[ga+ -(h)sg(wa:)$_N$- stone, bullet, rock -od$_V$- stand]
gahsgwao:t a headstone

•(h)sgwaǫdi, (h)sgwaǫgy gravel
[ga+ -(h)sg(wa:)$_N$- stone, bullet, rock -ǫdi, -ǫgy$_V$- throw]
ga̱hswaǫgyǫ: gravel has been put down
nigahsgwaǫgyǫ: gravel somewhere

•sgwa:yęh otter
[-(h)sg(wa:)$_N$- stone, bullet, rock -yę$_V$- lie on the ground]
sgwa:yęh an otter

•(h)sgweg shut s.o. up
[TR+ -(h)s(a)$_N$- mouth -gweg$_V$- close]
ęhshe:sgwe:k you will shut her up P

•(h)sgwiʼdr(a) wrinkle
[o+]
ohsgwiʼdraʼ wrinkles

Legend: H habitual, P punctual, S stative, I imperative, PURP purposive, PURP-H purposive habitual, PURP-PAST purposive past, PURP-P purposive punctual, PURP-I purposive imperative; see §8.6, §8.11 in Appendix J. Alphabetization in stems ignores length (:), and any h's or glottal stops (ʼ) that are not between vowels. See §2.2 of the User Guide for explanation.

•(h)sgwiʼdrahe:ʼ be wrinkly
[s+ga+N+ -(h)sgwiʼdr(a)$_N$- wrinkle -(h)e:ʼ$_V$- sitting up on top of s.t ts:ǫ just]
sgahsgwʼidra̱he:ʼ tsǫ: you are pruny, wrinkly S

•(h)sgyęʼd(a:) bone
[o+]
ohsgyęʼda:ʼ bone; bare bones

•(h)sgyęʼdiyaʼg fracture
[de+...ade+ -(h)sgyęʼd(a:)$_N$- bone -(i)yaʼg$_V$- cut, break, cross]
deyodehsgyęʼdiyaʼgǫh it (bone) is fractured S

•(h)sgyęnaʼgyagǫh pale
[de+P+ -(h)sgyęnaʼd(a)$_N$- -(i)yaʼg$_V$- cut, break, cross]
dehohsgyęnaʼgyʼagǫh he is pale S

•(h)sgyęʼwatę, (h)sgyǫʼwatę thin
[P+ contains: -(h)sgyǫʼw(a), (h)sgyęʼw(a)$_N$- bone -tę(:)$_V$- dry]
hohsgyęʼwatę:, hohsgyǫʼwatę: he is skinny S

•(h)sgyǫʼ(wa) blue beech
[o+ contains: -(h)sgyǫʼw(a), (h)sgyęʼw(a)$_N$- bone]
ohsgyǫʼwaʼ blue beech (a tree)

•(h)sgyǫʼwataʼd diet, lose weight
[ade+ -(h)sgyǫʼw(a), (h)sgyęʼw(a)$_N$- bone -taʼd$_V$- dry out]
ǫdehsgyǫwataʼtaʼ s.o. loses weight, diets H
agaǫ:dehsgyǫwa:taʼt they (f/m) dieted P

•(h)sgyǫʼwatę, (h)sgyęʼwatę be thin, skinny
[P+ -(h)sgyǫʼw(a), (h)sgyęʼw(a)$_N$- bone -tę(:)$_V$- be dry]
hohsgyęʼwatę:, hohsgyǫʼwatę: he is skinny S

•(h)sh(a) string
[occurs in:]
ohshai:s a long string; a rope
[o+ -sh(a)$_N$- string -is$_V$- be long]

•(h)shadenyoh tendons
[o+ -sh(a)$_N$- string -denyǫʼ$_V$- several existing objects]
ohsha:de:nyoh tendons

•shaʼged, shaʼkdǫ fold s.t.
[de+...]
dęsehsage:t (dęsehshaʼge:t) you will fold it once, bend it P

•shaʼged, shaʼkdǫ bend (forwards)
[de+...at+]
dewatsaʼkdǫhs it bends all the time; it is flexible H
dęwatsaʼge:t it will bend P
deyotsaʼkdǫ: it is bent; a curve; a bend S
desatsaʼge:t bend forwards I

•shaʼged, shaʼkdǫ bend (backwards)
[ohnaʼgę:ʼ behind haʼde+...at+]
ohnaʼgę:ʼ haʼdesatsaʼge:t bend backward I

•shaine govern
[TR+]
ǫgwahshaineʼ they govern us H

•shaʼkdǫnyǫgw, shaʼkdǫnyǫgo fold s.t. up
[de+ contains:-shaʼged, shaʼkdǫ$_V$- bend]
dęsehsaʼkda:nyǫ:goʼ you will fold s.t. up P

•(h)shaǫd be tied up
[A+ -sh(a)$_N$- string -ǫd$_V$- attached]
ge̱hshaǫ:t I am tied up S

•(ʼ)shahsdeʼ be strong tough, powerful
[A+(N+) contains: -(ʼ)shahsd$_V$- be strong]
gahsha:sdeʼ it is strong, tough, powerful S

•(ʼ)sha(h)sdeʼ weak
[(tęʼ) deʼ+ not A+(N+) contains: -(ʼ)shahsd$_V$- be strong]
tęʼ degahshahsdeʼ no, it is not strong S

•(ʼ)sha(h)sdeʼ exponents
[tsę̨h that ni+ga+ contains: -(ʼ)shahsd$_V$- be strong]
tsę̨h nigaʼshahsdeʼ exponents

•(ʼ)shahsdǫh use one's strength
[ade+ contains: -(ʼ)shahsd$_V$- be strong]
gadeshahsdǫhaʼ I use my strength H
ęhsadesha:sdǫh you will use your strength P

•(h)sheʼ(a) dough
[o+]
ohsheʼaʼ dough

•shę̨h, tsę̨h of, because, how, that
see: Appendix I

•shęhoʼdęʼ whatever
see: Appendix I

•shęnhǫ:weh where abouts
see: Appendix I

•shęniyo:(weʼ) how much, how many, how far, until
see: Appendix I

•s(h)ęnǫni be happy, glad
[at+]
agatsęnǫ:niʼ I got happy P
agatsęnǫ:ni: I am glad, happy S

•s(h)ęnǫnyaʼd happiness, gratefulness, joy, etc.
[o+at+ contains: -s(h)ęnǫni$_V$- be happy, glad]
otsęnǫnyaʼt a happy feeling; gratefulness, thankfulness, joy

•(ʼ)shęny(ǫgw), (ʼ)shęni overpower
[TR+ contains: -(ʼ)shahsd$_V$- be strong]
sheʼshę:nyǫhs you are always overpowering s.o.; you are overpowering s.o. right not H
ęhsheʼshę:niʼ you will overpower s.o. (physically) P
sheʼshęnyǫgwęh you have overpowered s.o. (before; a long time ago) S

•shohih bite
[at+]
ǫtsohihs she bites it H
ęyǫtsohih she will bite it P
gotsohihǫh I have bit it S
dasatsohih bite I

•(h)shoʼgwaǫd rattle snake
[o+ -(h)shoʼg(wa)$_N$- -ǫd$_V$- attached]
ohshoʼgwaǫ:t a rattle snake

•si there
see: Appendix I

•sigwa:dih over there; common way of telling a dog to move
see: Appendix I

•si:gyęh that, way over there
see: Appendix I

•(h)siha:ʼ stand in a bunch or group, congregate
[A/P+N+]
gadihs̲iha:ʼ they (z) are congregated S
ojihsǫdahsiha:ʼ stars showing S
[-jihsǫd(a)$_N$- star, -(h)siha:ʼ$_V$- stand in a bunch or group, congregate]

•(h)sin(a) leg
ohsi:naʼ leg
s̲ehsinʼageh on your leg

•(h)sinhahstaʼ garters
[ǫ+at+ -(h)sin(a)$_N$- leg -nhahsd$_V$- encircle]
ǫtsinhahstaʼ garters; leg bands

•si(hne:ʼ) over there
see: Appendix I

•si:nhǫ:(weh), si:hǫ:(weh) way over there
see: Appendix I

•hsinodahd(ę,ani) bar s.o.'s way
[de+TR+ -(h)sin(a)$_N$- leg -odahd(ę, ani)$_V$- trip]
ętsheyahsinodahdęʼ you will trip s.o., bar s.o.'s way with your leg P

•(h)sinǫd kettle
[de+ga+ -(h)sin(a)$_N$- leg -ǫd$_V$- attached]
degahsi:nǫ:t kettle (lit.: it has legs attached)

Legend: H habitual, P punctual, S stative, I imperative, PURP purposive, PURP-H purposive habitual, PURP-PAST purposive past, PURP-P purposive punctual, PURP-I purposive imperative; see §8.6, §8.11 in Appendix J. Alphabetization in stems ignores length (:), and any h's or glottal stops (ʼ) that are not between vowels. See §2.2 of the User Guide for explanation.

•(h)sis shoot
hǫwahsi:sahs he is always getting shot by s.o. H
ahohsi:s he was shot P
hohsi:sęh he has been shot S

•(h)siy(a) thread, string, cord, line
[o+]
ohsi:yaʼ a thread; a string; a cord
ohsi:yǫ:t an attached cord; a string; an umbilical cord
[-(h)siy(a)$_N$- line, string -od$_V$- attached]

•(h)siyaniyǫd fringe
[ga+ -(h)siy(a)$_N$- line, string -niyǫd$_V$- hang]
ga̱hsiyani:yǫ:t a fringe

•(h)siyaǫnyahnǫ:ʼ be a fluid dancer
[-(h)siy(a)$_N$- line, string -ǫnyahnǫ$_V$- go along making several things]
ahahsiyaǫ:nyahnǫ:ʼ he is a fluid dancer P

•(h)siyogw, (h)siyogo fray
[(de+)...ade+ -(h)siy(a)$_N$- line, string -ogw$_V$- scatter]
awadę̱hsiyo:goʼ it frayed P
deyoda̱hsiyo:gwęh it is frayed S

•(h)siyǫni: be fringed
[-(h)siy(a)$_N$- line, string -ǫni, ǫny$_V$- make]
ga̱hsi:yǫ:ni: it is fringed S

•(h)siyǫd thread, string, cord, line, umbilical cord
[o+ -(h)siy(a)$_N$- line, string -ǫd$_V$- attached]
ohsi:yǫ:t an attached cord; a string; an umbilical cord

•(h)sna(ʼda) muscle, hamstring, calf, outer thigh
[o+]
ohsnaʼdaʼ hamstrings; calves (of the legs); outer thighs
sę̱hsnaʼdʼageh on your calf

•(h)snaʼda:s Muscular Dystrophy
[ga+ -(h)sna(ʼda)$_N$- muscle, hamstring, calf -g$_V$- eat]
ga̱hsnaʼda:s Muscular Dystrophy

•(h)snagri have muscle cramps
[P+ -(h)sna(ʼda)$_N$- muscle, hamstring, calf -gri$_V$- wrinkle]
ǫgehsnagri:k I had muscle cramps; I got a cramp P

•(h)snagriksǫ(:) cramp
[P+ -(h)sna(ʼda)$_N$- muscle, hamstring, calf -gri$_V$- wrinkle -sǫʼ plural]
ǫgehsnagrihksǫ:ʼ I got cramps P

•(h)snowad hurry up
[de+...ade+ contains: -(h)snow$_V$- fast]
desadę̱hsno:wa:t hurry up I

•(h)snoweʼ be fast
[o+]
ohsno:weʼ it is fast, quick S

•(h)snoweʼ fast
[A/P+N+]
ohnyasnoweʼ a fast beat S
[o+ stem: -(h)ny(a)$_N$- stick -(h)snoweʼ$_V$- fast]

•(h)snye care for, look after
[de+TR+]
dę̱haheyǫʼda̱hsnyehaʼ he is a funeral director H
[de+... -(he)yǫ(ʼda)$_N$- corpse, cadaver -(h)snye$_V$- care for, look after]
dę̱hǫwadihsnyeʼ they care for them S

•(h)snye(h,ʼ) clean s.t. up
[de+...at+N+ occurs in:]
degatnǫhsahsnyeh I am cleaning up the house H
[de+...at+ stem: -nǫhs(a)$_N$- house -(h)snye(h,ʼ)$_V$- clean s.t. up]
dęgatnǫhsahsnyeʼ I will clean up the house P
degahsnyeʼǫ:ʼ it cleans up S

•(h)snye(h,ʼ) groom onself
[de+TR+/adad+ contains: -(h)snye$_V$- care for, look after]
desadadehsnyeh tidy up; groom yourself I

•(h)sod grandparent
hehso:t my grandfather S
gę̱hso:t my grandmother S

•(h)sohd(a) hand, paw
ohsohdaʼ a hand; a paw
sę̱hsohdʼageh on your hand

•(h)soda:ʼ soldier
[A+ -hs(a)$_N$- -oda(:,h)$_V$- drape]
hadihso:da: they (m) are military (the word refers to putting the gun over their shoulders)
hahso:da:ʼ a soldier (lit.: he drapes it)

•(h)sohdǫd hand (of a clock)
[ga+ -(h)sohd(a)$_N$- hand, finger, paw -ǫd$_V$- attached]
ga̱hsohdǫ:t hands on a clock

•(h)soʼg limp
[P+]
go̱hsoʼkaʼ she is limping H

•(h)sohgae: smacking sound
[a+g+yo+ -(h)s(a:)$_N$- mouth -ga:, gae$_V$- make a rattling or grinding noise]
agyohsagae: the sound of smacking lips

•(h)sohgǫd pitcher
[ga+ -(h)sohg(wa)$_N$- lip -ǫd$_V$- attached]
ga̱hsohgǫ:t a pitcher

•(h)sohg(wa) lip
ohsohgwaʼ lips
sę̱hsǫhgwʼageh on your lip
gę̱hsohgwʼageh on my lip

•(h)sogwa:ʼ fork
[ga+ -(h)sohg(wa)$_N$- lip -a:ʼ$_V$- contain]
ga̱hsogwa:ʼ a fork

•(h)sohgwahd(a) big-headed sucker
[at+ -(h)sohg(wa)$_N$- lip -(a)hd$_V$- resemble]
atsokwa̱hdaʼ (**atsogwa̱hdaʼ**) a big-headed sucker

•(h)sohgwahs west
[de+wa+at+ -(ę)hs(a)$_N$- foot -ogw$_V$- scatter]
dewatsohgwahs the west

•sohǫ:t turkey
sohǫ:t a turkey

•(h)sotwahs sunset
[haʼde+w+at+ -(ę)hs(a)$_N$- foot -otw$_V$- burn as fuel]
haʼdewatso:twahs towards the sunset; a direction

•(h)sotwahs fleas
[de+wa+at+ -(ę)hs(a)$_N$- foot -(h)sotw$_V$- jump, hop]
dewatsotwahs fleas (lit.: it jumps, hops)

•sowa:s dog
so:wa:s a dog

•sǫ: go:wę̨h whose (is that)?
see: Appendix I

•sǫ: hne:ʼ naht who is that?
see: Appendix I

•sǫ ʼǫ naht who, which person
see: Appendix I

•(h)sǫhg(a:) upper lip
sę̱hsǫhga:ʼgeh on your upper lip

•sǫga:(ʼah) someone
see: Appendix I

•sǫhehka: ęhniʼda:ʼ the moon
(ah)sǫhehka:ʼ the night kind
ęhniʼda:ʼ a month; a moon

•sǫhehka:ʼ ga:gwa:ʼ the moon
(ah)sǫhehka:ʼ the night kind
ga:gwa:ʼ a celestial body (for example, the sun, the moon)

•sǫnyǫs omen
[w+at+]
watsǫ:nyǫ:s omen

•sǫ(ʼǫh) who (short form)
see: Appendix I

Legend: H habitual, P punctual, S stative, I imperative, PURP purposive, PURP-H purposive habitual, PURP-PAST purposive past, PURP-P purposive punctual, PURP-I purposive imperative; see §8.6, §8.11 in Appendix J. Alphabetization in stems ignores length (:), and any h's or glottal stops (ʼ) that are not between vowels. See §2.2 of the User Guide for explanation.

•(h)sʼǫh be ready
see: (i)hsʼǫh [P+ade+] ready
sadehsʼǫh? Are you ready? (used by Cayuga speakers, but may be an Onondaga phrase) S

•(h)sǫwahd(a) nail, wire, needle
[ga+]
ga̱hsǫwa̱hdaʼ nails; wire; a needle

•(h)sre(:) follow, chase
see: (i)hsre(:) [TR+] follow, chase
ahǫwadihsre:ʼ they chased him, followed him PURP-P

•(h)srę̨ʼdǫni glare, grouchy
[ade+ contains: -(a)hsrǫhę̨(ʼda)$_N$- anger, temper -ǫni, ǫny$_V$- make]
agade̱hsrę̨ʼdǫ:ni: I am grouchy, glaring S
sadehsrę̨ʼdǫ:ni: glare; make yourself look mad I

•(h)srǫhę̨: cross, angry
[A+]
ehsrohę̨: she is habitually cross, cantankerous S

•(h)srǫni fix, repair
[(N+) contains: -hsr$_N$- noun -(h)srǫni$_V$- fix, repair]
sasehsrǫ:nih deyodewane:gaǫ: fix the flat tire I

•(h)srǫnihs repairman
[s+A+ -(h)srǫni$_V$- fix, repair]
shahsrǫ:nihs repairman

•(h)srǫnihsʼǫh ready
[P+ade+ contains: -(h)srǫni$_V$- fix, repair]
agade̱hsrǫni̱hsʼǫh I am ready S

•(h)srǫnyaʼd made from
[contains: -(h)srǫni, (h)srǫny$_V$- fix, repair]
ga̱hsrǫnyadǫh it is made from s.t. S

•(h)srǫnyahnǫ(:) make several things
[contains: -(h)srǫni, (h)srǫny$_V$- fix, repair -ahnǫʼ go and do several things]
aknihsrǫnyahnǫh we two (incl.) are making several things H
ę̨yagwadehsrǫnyahnǫ:ʼ we all (excl.) will prepare things P

•(h)staʼ tool, utensil
[e+ contains -hsd$_N$- tool, utensil]
ehstaʼshǫ:ʼǫh tools; utensils; what one uses)

•(h)sdoda: handcuff s.o.
[de+TR+ -hsd$_N$- tool, utensil -oda(:,h)$_V$- drape]
atǫwadihstoda:ʼ they handcuffed him, them (m) P

•(h)sdoʼdr(a) feather
[o+]
ohsdoʼdrʼageh on its feathers

•(h)stoʼdrę̨hd pluck
[-(h)stoʼdr(a)$_N$- feather -(y)ę̨hd$_V$- hit, knock down, strike]
ę̨sehstoʼdrę̨ht you will pluck feathers P
sehstoʼdrę̨ht pluck it I

•(h)stoʼdrę̨hd moult
[ade+ -(h)stoʼdr(a)$_N$- feather -(y)ę̨hd$_V$- hit, knock down, strike]
awadehstoʼdrę̨ht it moulted P

•(h)stǫdr(a) straw, hay
[o+]
ohstǫ:draʼ straw; hay

•(h)stǫdriyaʼs mower
[ga+ -(h)stǫdr(a)$_N$- straw, hay -(i)yaʼg$_V$- cut, break]
ga̱hstǫ:dri:yaʼs a hay mower

•(h)stǫdroha:s bailer
[de+ga+ -(h)stǫdr(a)$_N$- straw, hay -ohag$_V$- squeeze]
degastǫdroha:s a hay bailer

•stǫ:hah a little bit
see: Appendix I

•(h)stǫwisd hurt
[P+ (ade+)]
sadehstǫwi:staʼ you hurt yourself all the time H
ę̨jisahstǫ:wi:s you will rehurt yourself P

•sw, sho smell
[P+(N+)]
age:swahs I smell it (now) H
ęwageshoʼ I will smell it P
•swahd smell s.t. on purpose, sniff s.t.
[TR+ade+ contains: -sw, sho$_{V}$- smell]
ęwadehswaht it will smell it P
sade:swaht smell I
•swahdahnǫ(:) sniff s.t.
[TR+ade+ contains: -swahd$_{V}$- smell s.t. on purpose -hnǫ(:) go and do things]
sadehswahdahnǫ: sniff I
•(h)swahęh hate, dislike
gǫhswahęhs I hate you H
ęhsehswa̲hęh you will hate, dislike P
•(h)swahęhde:ʼ hatred
[o+ contains: -(h)swahęhd$_{V}$- cause to hate, dislike]
ohswahęhde:ʼ hatred
•(h)swahęʼdǫ: hatred
[o+ contains: -(h)swahęʼd$_{V}$- cause to hate]
ohswahęʼdǫ: hatred
•(h)swaʼn(a), (h)sweʼn(a) upper back
ohsweʼnaʼ the upper back
se̲hsweʼnʼageh on your upper back
degahswʼane:t pie
[de+ga+ -(h)swaʼn(a), (h)sweʼn(a)$_{N}$- reinforced, backed -d$_{V}$- stand]
•(h)swaʼned pie
[de+ga+ -(h)swaʼn(a), (h)sweʼn(a)$_{N}$- reinforced, backed -d$_{V}$- stand]
degahswaʼne:t pie
•(h)swaʼned reinforce, back
[ga+ -(h)swaʼn(a), (h)sweʼn(a)$_{N}$- upper back -d$_{V}$- stand]
ga̲hswaʼne:t reinforcement; backing
•(h)swaʼned support s.o., s.t., agree with s.o., back s.o.
[TR+ -(h)swaʼn(a), (h)sweʼn(a)$_{N}$- upper back -d$_{V}$- stand]
hadihswʼane:taʼ they (m) are advocates, backers, supporters H
ęhsehswʼane:dęʼ you will back up s.t. (that is, reinforce it) P
shehswaʼne:t you are supporting, backing them S
•swahyowa:ʼ ohyaʼ gra̲he:t apple tree
swahyo:wa:ʼ apples; crabapples
ohyaʼ berry; a fruit
gra̲he:t a living tree
•(h)sweʼn(a), (h)swaʼn(a) upper back
ohsweʼnaʼ upper back
se̲hsweʼnʼageh on your upper back
•(h)swęʼd(a) coal, ember
[o+]
ohswędaʼ coal; a ember
•(h)swęʼdaę:ʼ black
[-(h)swęʼd(a)$_{N}$- coal, ember -ʼę:ʼ$_{V}$- be coloured]
swęʼdʼaę:ʼ black
•swęʼgaiyoʼ hawk, small eagle
[o+ -swęʼg(a)$_{N}$- hawk -iyo:$_{V}$- be nice, good]
oswęʼgai:yoʼ a hawk; a small eagle
•(ʼ)syade clan
oʼsya:de:nyǫʼ clans S
•(h)sy(a) herd
[ga+ -(h)sya$_{N}$- herd -dagyeʼ$_{V}$- ongoing]
gahsyada:gyeʼ a passing herd

T

•(h)ta(:,ę) talk, speak
ge̲hta:haʼ I talk H
agehtaę:ʼ, agehta:ʼk I did talk P
gohta:ʼ she is speaking S
•tʼah unusual, queer
[ti+yo+ contains: -d$_{V}$- stand -ʼah diminutive]
tiyo:tʼah it is queer, unusual, odd S

Legend: H habitual, P punctual, S stative, I imperative, PURP purposive, PURP-H purposive habitual, PURP-PAST purposive past, PURP-P purposive punctual, PURP-I purposive imperative; see §8.6, §8.11 in Appendix J. Alphabetization in stems ignores length (:), and any h's or glottal stops (ʼ) that are not between vowels. See §2.2 of the User Guide for explanation.

•taʼd dry s.t. out
[N+ occurs in:]
ęhsnęhęta'ʼt you will dry corn P
[N+ -nęh(ę)$_N$- corn -(h)aʼd, taʼd$_V$- dry]
ganęhętaʼdǫh dried corn S
•taʼdahkwaʼ dryer
[a+ contains: -taʼd$_V$- dry]
ataʼda̱hkwaʼ a dryer
•(h)tagw, (h)tago discuss
[de+ contains: -(h)ta:$_V$- talk, speak]
dęSwahta:goʼ we all (incl.) will discuss P
•(h)tahahsd talk to s.o.
[TR+ contains: -(h)ta:$_V$- talk, speak]
ęhshetahahs you will talk to her P
•tahyǫni: wolf
[(o+)]
otahyǫ:ni:, tahyǫ:ni: a wolf
•tea:ǫt muskrat
[t+he+a+ -ǫd stand]
tea:ǫt a muskrat
•teʼd pound
[(N+)]
geteʼtaʼ I am a pounder H
ęgeteʼt I will pound P
ageteʼdǫh I did pound S
seteht pound (corn, etc.) I
dęgehsdateʼt I am going to shine it
[de-(h)sd(a:)$_N$- drop (of water) -teʼd$_V$- pound]
•tedę(:) past day
te:dę:ʼ yesterday P
gyote:dęhk, gyote:dęht the other day; the day before yesterday S
•teojiʼ ironwood, red oak
teo:jiʼ ironwood (a tree); red oak
•teʼtr(a) flour, powder
[o+ contains: -teʼd$_V$- pound]
oteʼtraʼ flour; powder
•teʼtra: power oneself
[ade+ -teʼtr(a)$_N$- flour, powder -a:ʼ$_V$- hold, contain, include]
gadeteʼtra:s I am powdering myself H
ęgadeteʼtra: I am going to powder myself P
•teʼtrahtaʼ powder
[ǫ+ade+ contains: -teʼtr(a)$_N$- flour, powder]
ǫdeteʼtra̱htaʼ powder
•teʼtrohataʼ bath powder
[ǫ+ade+ -teʼtr(a)$_N$- flour, powder -oha:ʼd$_V$- clean, wash with s.t.]
ǫdeteʼtroha:taʼ bath powder
•tę: be dry, evaporated
[N+ occurs in:]
oʼwahatę: dry meat S
[-(ʼ)wah(a)$_N$- meat -tę(:), hę(:)$_V$- be dry, evaporated]
•tęʼ no
see: Appendix I
•tęʼ gaʼtoh nowhere
see: Appendix I
•tęʼ gwahs ǫ:weh not really
see: Appendix I
•tęʼ hne:ʼ not that
see: Appendix I
•(tęʼ) sga̱hoʼdęʼ nothing
see: Appendix I
•tęʼ tǫ ne:ʼ not really
see: Appendix I
•tęʼ hwę:dǫh never; not ever
see: Appendix I
•tęʼ daǫ it will never happen
see: Appendix I
•tęʼ gęh no?
see: Appendix I
•tęʼ giʼdaǫ No, it will not happen.
see: Appendix I
•tęʼ gihne:ʼ not really
see: Appendix I
•tęʼ gini:ʼ no, not me
see: Appendix I
•tęʼ seʼ not really
see: Appendix I

•tęhsd dry out, evaporate
[N+ contains: -tę:, hę:$_V$- be dry, evaporated]
sagagaho'jatęhs the grass dried up P
[N+ -gaho'j(a)$_N$- grass -tęhsd, hęhsd$_V$- dry out, evaporate]
•tgahnegoy'a:s oji'a:' shower curtain
tgahne'goy'a:s a shower
oji'a:' curtains; lace
•tgę: be spoiled, rotten
[P+(N+)]
otgę: it is rotten; decayed; spoilage S
o'wahatgę: spoiled meat S
[-(')wah(a)$_N$- meat -tgę:$_V$- be spoiled, rotten]
•tgęh become rotten
[P+(N+) contains: -tgę:$_V$- be spoiled, rotten]
a'o:tgęh it became spoiled, rotten P
•tgęhets(a) handle
[ga+]
gatgęhetsa' a handle
•tgęhetses ladle, dipper
[ga+ -tgęhets(a)$_N$- handle -es$_V$- long]
gatgęhetse:s a ladle; a long-handled spoon; a dipper
•tgi' be dirty, ugly
[P+(N+)]
ot.gi' it is ugly, dirty, soiled
niyo:tgi' how dirty or filthy it is S
hoya'datgi' he is dirty, has dirty ways
[-ya'd(a)$_N$- body -tgi'$_V$- be dirty, ugly]
•tgihd turn bad, storm
[ade+ contains: -tgi'$_V$- be dirty, ugly]
awadetgiht it was bad weather, stormy P
odetgihdǫh it is storming right now S
•tgi'tr(a) junk
[ga+ contains: -tgi'$_V$- be dirty, ugly]
gatgi'tra' junk
•tgo'd(a) sumac
[o+]
otgo'da' a sumac
•tgwę(')da) wallet, purse, pocketbook, suitcase
[ga+]
gatgwę'da' a wallet; a purse; a pocketbook; a suitcase
•tgwęhdod cap
[-tgwęhd(a)$_N$- -od$_V$- stand]
gatgwęhdo:t cap
•tgwęhę:' sometimes
see: Appendix I
•tgwęhji'(a) red
[o+]
otgwęhj'ia:' red
•tgwęhj'iaji: maroon, dark red
[o+ -tgwęhji'(a)$_N$- red -ji(:,h)$_V$- be dark]
otgwęhj'ia:ji: maroon; dark red
•tgwęhs(a) blood
[occurs in:]
gatgwęhsanahnǫh pure-bred (lit.: full of the same blood)
[-tgwęhs(a)$_N$- blood -nahnǫh$_V$- be full]
•tgwęhsa:s leukemia
[ga+ -tgwęhs(a)$_N$- blood -g$_V$- eat]
gatgwęhsa:s leukemia
•tigahsro:ni' ono'ja' false teeth
tigahsro:ni' s.t. artificial
ono'ja' teeth
•to: that, there
see: Appendix I
•to nhǫ: (weh), to hǫ: (weh) there, where
see: Appendix I
•to: niyo:(we') that far
see: Appendix I
•to niyǫ: that much
see: Appendix I
•to tsǫ: that is enough! (that is, stop pouring)
see: Appendix I
•to:gyęh that (one)
see: Appendix I
•toh geh and then; that's when
see: Appendix I

Legend: H habitual, P punctual, S stative, I imperative, PURP purposive, PURP-H purposive habitual, PURP-PAST purposive past, PURP-P purposive punctual, PURP-I purposive imperative; see §8.6, §8.11 in Appendix J. Alphabetization in stems ignores length (:), and any h's or glottal stops (') that are not between vowels. See §2.2 of the User Guide for explanation.

•to:hah there
see: Appendix I
•tǫ(:hwaˀ) that one
see: Appendix I
•tragwęˀd(a) flint
[o+]
otragwęˀdaˀ flint (the stone)
•tragwęˀdaˀe slap
[TR+ -tragwęˀd(a)$_N$- flint -(ˀ)e$_V$- hit]
ęhsetragwęˀda̱ˀe:k you will slap it (on the cheek) P
•trehs more than usual (denotes something extreme)
see: Appendix I
•tręˀd(a) housefly, fly
[o+]
otręˀdaˀ a housefly; a fly
•tręˀdagowah horsefly
[o+ -tręˀd(a)$_N$- fly -go:wah big]
otręˀdago:wah a horsefly
•trǫhgeh tsǫ: barely
see: Appendix I
•tsahgo:wah pigeon
[-tsah$_N$- -go:wah big]
tsahgo:wah a pigeon
•tsaˀd struggle, revolt
[ade+]
sadetsaˀtaˀ you struggle all the time H
ęhsadetsaˀt you will struggle, squirm to get loose, revolt P
sadeˀtsaˀdǫh you are going along struggling S
•tsad(a) mist, steam, fog
[o+]
otsa:daˀ mist; steam; fog
•tsadęˀ be damp
[o+ -tsad(a)- mist, steam, fog -ęˀ$_V$- lay down]
otsadęˀǫh it is damp S
•tsaˀgęd(a) corn tassel
tsaˀgę:daˀ a corn tassel
•tsahnihg frighten, scare
ęsetsahnihk you will be scared of it P
otsahnihk it is frightening, scary S
•tse(ˀda) bottle, jar
see: (i)tse(ˀda) bottle, jar
gatseˀdaˀ, gętseˀdaˀ a bottle; a jar
•tseˀdahęh pint
see: (i)tseˀdahęh pint
tsaˀdegatseˀda̱hęh one pint
•tseˀdoˀ cold packing
see: (i)tseˀdoˀ cold packing
gętseˀdoˀ cold packing (part of the process of canning)
•tseˀdod standing bottle
see: (i)tseˀdod standing bottle
gatseˀdo:t a standing bottle; a belly button
•tseˀdod belly button, navel
see: (i)tseˀdod belly button, navel
getseˀdo:t my navel
•tseˀdod hubbard squash
see: (i)tseˀdod hubbard squash
otseˀdo:t hubbard squash
•tsenę tame animal, pet
[ga+]
gatse:nęˀ a tame animal; a pet
gadi:tse:nęˀ farm animals (lit.: they (z) are domesticated, tame)
age:tse:nęˀ my pet
•tsenę be a slave
[A+ contains: -tsenę$_N$- tame animal]
setse:nęˀ you are tied up (meaning: you are a slave to your work; lit.: you are an animal)
•tsehsd(a) syrup, honey, gum
[o+]
otsehsdaˀ syrup; honey; gum
•tsehsd(a) sturgeon
[s+ga+ contains: -tsehsd(a)$_N$- syrup, honey, gum]
sgatsehsdaˀ a sturgeon
•tsehsdaˀd stick to s.t.
[contains: -tsehsd(a)$_N$- syrup, honey, gum]
etsehsda:taˀ glue H

•tsehsdata' glue
[e+ contains: -tsehsdad$_V$- stick to s.t.]
etsehsda·ta' glue

•tsesdaę be sticky
[o+ -tsehsd(a)$_N$- syrup, honey, gum, rubber -ę$_V$- lie]
otsehsdae:' it is sticky S

•tsę be a glutton
[P+ade+]
hode:tsę: he is a glutton S

•tsę:! exclamation
see: Appendix I

•tsęh, shęh of, because, how, that
see: Appendix I

•tsęh ǫ:weh it is really
see: Appendix I

•tsęi, tsęny find
[(N+)]
getshę:nye's, getshę:nyǫhs I am a finder of things H
a:yetsęi:' she might find it P
agetsęnyǫ: I have found it S
ha'ǫdagya'datsęi:' she found her over there
[ag+ -ya'd(a)$_N$- body -tsęi, tsęny$_V$- find]

•tsęhsd gobble, gorge oneself, be a glutton
[ade+ contains: -tsę(:)$_V$- be a glutton]
ęhsadetsęhs you will be a glutton; you will gobble, gorge yourself P

•tsgę('da) rope
[ga+]
ga:tsg'ęda' a rope

•tsgę'ę(da) fruit pit, seed
[o+]
otsgę'ę' a peach pit
ęhsetsgę'ędahgo' you will remove seeds P
[-tsgę'ęd(a)$_N$- pit -(h)gw, (h)go$_V$-.re-move]

•tsgę'ędahgw, tsgę'ędahgo deseed
ęhsetsgę'ędahgo' you will remove seeds P
[-tsgę'ęd(a)$_N$- pit -(h)gw, (h)go$_V$- re-move]

•tsgo'd balsam fir
[o+]
otsgo'da' a balsam fir

•tsgod sit
see: (i)tsgod [A+] sit
etsgo:t she is sitting S

•tsgodę' re-elect
see: (i)tsgodę' [TR+] re-elect
ahǫwaditsgo:dę' they elected him, them (m) P

•tsgodǫ' several living things sitting
see: (i)tsgodǫ' [A+] several living things sitting
gadi:tsgo:dǫ' they (z) are sitting S

•tsgwahe:' sit on s.t., perch on s.t.
see: (i)tsgwahe:' [A+] sit on s.t., perch on s.t.
gitsgwahe:' I am perched up on s.t.; I am sitting on s.t. S

•tsihsdę(h,') be, get numb
[o+]
a'otsihsdęh it got numb P
otsihsdę'ǫh it is numb S

•tsǫ: that is all; just; only
see: Appendix I

•tsǫ' one after another, one at a time
[s+ A/P+ N+ contains: -d$_V$- stand -sǫ' plural]
jǫhsi'datsǫ' one foot apart P
[s/j+o+ -(a)hsi'd(a)$_N$- foot -tsǫ'$_V$- one after another. one at a time]
sg'adrehdatsǫ' each car P
[s +ga+ -(')drehd(a)$_N$- vehicle -tsǫ'$_V$- one after another. one at a time]

•(')tsǫhsd sneeze
[de+P+]
desa'tsǫhstahk you have sneezed, you were sneezing H
dęsa'tsǫhs you will sneeze P

Legend: H habitual, P punctual, S stative, I imperative, PURP purposive, PURP-H purposive habitual, PURP-PAST purposive past, PURP-P purposive punctual, PURP-I purposive imperative; see §8.6, §8.11 in Appendix J. Alphabetization in stems ignores length (:), and any h's or glottal stops (') that are not between vowels. See §2.2 of the User Guide for explanation.

•twęhs(a) liver
[o+]
otwęhsa' a liver
•twętwęt duck
twę:twę:t a duck

U

•u'drugye:'ah be narrow
[ni+w+]
niwu'drugye:'ah it is narrow S
•u:'uh be small
[ni+A+]
niyagu:'uh she is small; a little female; a small girl S
•u:'uh be small
[ni+A/P+N+]
nihahwajiyu:'uh his family is small
[-(h)wajiy(a)$_N$- family -u:'uh$_V$- be small]
•u:s'uh be several small objects
[ni+A/P+N+]
niwę'nhotru:s'uh a number of small balls
[-ę'nhotr(a)$_N$- wheel -u:s'uh$_V$- several small objects]

W

•w(a:) air, wind
[o+]
o:wa:' air; wind
•w(a:) moth
[o+]
o:wa:' a moth
•wa(:,h) spread
see: (r)a(:,h) spread
ęhsra:' you will spread P
•wad spread s.t.
see: (r)ad, yad, wad spread s.t.
eya:ta' s.o. spreads it H
•wad be inflated
[ga+ -w(a:)$_N$- air -d$_V$- stand]
gawa:t it is inflated S
•(h)wahd(a) maple
[o+]
ohwahda' a maple tree
•wadadwę:ni:yo' so:wa:s a wild dog; a stray dog
wadadwę:ni:yo' a stray animal
so:wa:s a dog
•wadahgw deflate
[(ade+) -w(a:)$_N$- air -dahgw$_V$- remove]
awadewa:dahgo' it deflated P
gawa:dahgwęh it is deflated S
•(h)wadased encircle
[de+...at+ -(h)wad(a)$_N$- year -(a)hsehd$_V$- whirl]
dęwatwadahsedahk it (a year) will encircle it P
•wadasehs tornado
[de+ga+ -w(a:)$_N$- air -dase$_V$- whirl]
degawa:da:sehs a tornado
•wade' windy
[o+ -w(a:)$_N$- air -de'$_V$- exist]
owa:de' it is windy; a wind; it is a breeze S
•wade' climb
see: (r)ade' climb
sra:de' you are climbing S
•wa'de'sgǫ:t o'wahǫh fried meat
wade'sgǫ:t it is roasting, frying
o'wahǫh meat
•wadęhi:' oyę:da' a cord of wood
wadęhi:' it is stacked
oyę:da' wood; firewood
•wadęhsǫ' ojihgwa' roasted corn mush
wadęhsǫ' it is roasted
ojihgwa' porridge; mush

•wadęhsǫʼ onęhę:ʼ roasted white corn
wadęhsǫʼ it is roasted
onęhę:ʼ corn
•wadrǫ(:) tear s.t., shred s.t.
see: (r)adrǫ(:) tear s.t., shred s.t.
ęhsra:drǫ:ʼ you will tear, shred it P
•(h)waʼe tap
[-(h)w(a)$_N$- -(ʼ)e$_V$- hit]
hohwaʼe: he is tapping S
•waęhę: wind direction
[ni+g+yo+ -w(a:)$_N$- air -ęhę(:)$_V$- direct, convey]
nigyowaęhę: the direction of the wind
•waęhęwiʼ hurricane
[ga+ -w(a:)$_N$- air; contains: -ęhę(:)$_V$- direct, convey]
gawaęhę:wiʼ a hurricane
•wage(:,w) wipe
see: (r)age(:,w) wipe
ęgra:ge:ʼ I will erase, wipe it P
•wagw, wago choose, take out
see: (r)agw, (r)ago choose, take out
ęhsra:goʼ you will choose, take out P
•wahg(wa), (r)ahg(wa) spot
[o+ -ǫnyǫʼ several objects]
owahgwaǫnyǫʼ spots
odrahgwa:ʼ a sun dog
[o+ad+ -wahg(wa), (r)ahg(wa)$_N$- spot]
•wa(h)g(wa:) orb, circular in shape
see: (r)ag(wa:) celestial body, s.t. circular in shape
ga:gwa:ʼ a celestial body (for example, the sun, the moon)
•wagwahd(a) ball of foot, sole
see: (r)agwahd(a) ball of foot, sole
a:gwa̲hdaʼ, ogwahdaʼ a sole; the ball of foot
•waʼgyęh an exclamation to get someone's attention
cf: Appendix I
•(ʼ)wah(a) meat
[occurs in:]
oʼwahǫh meat
[o+ stem: -(ʼ)wah(a)$_N$- meat -(adi)hǫh$_V$- lean across]
oʼwahatgę: spoiled meat
[stem: -(ʼ)wah(a)$_N$- meat -tgę:$_V$- be spoiled, rotten]
•(ʼ)wahadenyǫʼ muscle
[o+ -(ʼ)wah(a)$_N$- meat -deni, deny$_V$- change]
oʼwahade:nyǫʼ muscles
•(ʼ)wahahihdǫh hamburger
[de+ga+ -(ʼ)wah(a)$_N$- meat -(hr)ihd$_V$- break up]
degaʼwa̲hahihdǫh hamburger meat
•(ʼ)wahaisgyaʼs meat slicer
[ga+ -(ʼ)wah(a)$_N$- meat -(hr)ihsd(a)- metal -(i)yaʼg$_V$- cut, break]
gʼawahai:sgyaʼs a meat slicer
•(ʼ)wahaʼ butcher
[A+ad+ -(ʼ)wah(a)$_N$- meat]
hadwahaʼ he is a butcher
•(ʼ)wahahninǫh butcher
[A+ad+ -(ʼ)wah(a)$_N$- meat -(h)ninǫ$_V$- sell]
hadwahahni:nǫh he is a butcher, a seller of meat
•(ʼ)waha:s cancer
[ga+ -(ʼ)wah(a)$_N$- meat -g$_V$- eat]
gaʼwaha:s cancer
•waʼ(heh) just now
cf: Appendix I
•waʼhehge:haʼ finally, at long last
cf: Appendix I
•waʼhetsǫ: just now
cf: Appendix I
•(ʼ)wahǫdahkwaʼ roasting pan
[ǫ+at+ -(ʼ)wah(a)$_N$- meat -ǫdahkwaʼ$_V$- roaster]
ǫtwahǫdahkwaʼ a roasting pan
•(ʼ)wahǫh meat
[o+ stem: -(ʼ)wah(a)$_N$- meat -(adi)hǫh$_V$- lean across]
oʼwahǫh meat

Legend: H habitual, P punctual, S stative, I imperative, PURP purposive, PURP-H purposive habitual, PURP-PAST purposive past, PURP-P purposive punctual, PURP-I purposive imperative; see §8.6, §8.11 in Appendix J. Alphabetization in stems ignores length (:), and any h's or glottal stops (ʼ) that are not between vowels. See §2.2 of the User Guide for explanation.

•waihǫh good at s.t.
[A+(N+)]
sewaihǫh you are good at s.t. S
hanǫnyawaihǫh he is a good dancer S
[-nǫny(a)$_N$- dance -waihǫh$_V$- be good at s.t.]
•wai'yo:wi's pigeon hawk
[contains: -owi, ǫny$_V$- drive]
gawai'yo:wi's pigeon hawk
•wa'jih after awhile; wait
cf: Appendix I
•wa'ji:hah presently, a little later, after a bit; after a while
cf: Appendix I
•wajihkę:' (gyę:') almost, just about
cf: Appendix I
•wajihsd(a) peelings, rind, bark
[o+]
owaji̱hsda' peelings; the bark of a tree
•wa'jihsda'ǫh birch
[de+yo+ contains: -wajihsd(a)$_N$- peelings, rind -(hwę'ga)'oh$_V$- notch]
deyo'wajihsda̱'ǫh a birch tree
•wa'jihtsǫ: soon, in a while, pretty soon
cf: Appendix I
•wa'jihya:' wait a minute, a while; wait
cf: Appendix I
•(h)wajiy(a) family
[ga+]
gahwa:ji:ya' a family
•(h)wajiyade' family line, lineage
[A+ -(h)wajiy(a)$_N$- family -de'$_V$- exist]
gaehwajiyade' their (f/m) family line
•(h)wajiyǫnih be barren
[(tę') de'+ not A+ -(h)wajiy(a)$_N$- family -ǫni, ǫny$_V$- make]
tę' deyǫtwaji:yǫ:nih she is barren H
•wa(k)d(a) heel
see: (r)a(k)d(a) heel
srada'geh on your heel
ga:dageh a heel

•wanawę'doh sweeten
see: (r)anawę'doh sweeten
ęhsranawę'doh you will sweeten P
•wa'ne:' today, now
cf: Appendix I
•(wa)nega(:,ǫ) get a flat tire
[de+P+ade+ -w(a:)$_N$- air -(wa)negaǫ, (wa)nega(:)$_V$- explode, split]
adyagodewane:ga:'s she got a flat tire P
deyodewane:gaǫ: flat tire S
•wa'nęd(a:'g) stick, cling
see: (ra')nęd(a:'g), (ya')nęd(a:'g) stick, cling
owa'nę:da:s it sticks to it; it adheres to it H
•wa:nohsd become cold, chill down
see: nohsd [N/na'+] become cold, chill down
sagawa:nohs it became cooler P
•wa:nohsd become cold, chill down
[-w(a:)$_N$- air -nohsd$_V$- cool down]
sagawa:nohs it became cooler P
owa:nohsdǫh it (weather) got cold S
•waǫda:(',h) inflate s.t.
[N+ -w(a:)$_N$- air -ǫda:(h)$_V$- put in]
gawaǫda:s an air pump H
gawaǫ:da:hǫh it is inflated S
sewaǫ:da:' inflate it (a tire, a balloon) I
•waǫda:s pump, air pump
[ga+ -w(a:)$_N$- air -ǫda:(h)$_V$- put in, attached]
gawaǫda:s an air pump
•(')wahs(ha:) earring
[ga+]
g'awahsha:' earrings
•(')wahsaǫhkwa' earring
[de+yǫ+at+ contains: -(')wahs(a:)$_N$- earring]
deyǫtwahsaǫ:kwa' earrings
•(')wahsd(a) pin
[ga/o+]
gawahsda', o'wahsda' a clothespin

•(ʼ)waǫni: welt
see: (iʼ)waǫni:welt
giaʼwao:ni: welts
owao:ni: welts
•watę climb
see: (r)atę climb
ęhsra:tęʼ you will climb P
•waʼwisd(a) slice, peeling
see: (raʼ)wisd(a) slice, peeling
owaʼwihsdaʼ a slice; a peeling
•waʼwisdots(i) peel
see: (raʼ)wisdots(i) peel
ęhsrawihsdo:tsiʼ you will peel P
•way(a) fin, wing
[o+]
owa:yaʼ a fish fin; wings
•waye:s wing span
[tsaʼde+A+ -way(a)$_N$- fin, wing -es$_V$- long]
tsaʼdehawa:ye:s his wing span
tsaʼdegawa:ye:s its wing span
•wayęhǫhsdǫh right-handed
[A+ -wayę(n)$_N$- heart, spirit -(h)ǫhsd$_V$- by lying across]
hawayęhǫhsdǫh he is right-handed S
•wayęnęda' complete, finish
[-wayę(n)$_N$- heart, spirit -ędaʼ$_V$- finish]
hawayęnę:daʼs he finishes H
aʼewayę:nę:daʼ she finished P
gawayanędaʼǫh it is ready, prepared S
•wayęnheʼsgǫ: clever, educated
[P+ contains: -wayę(n)$_N$- heart, spirit -sgǫ: easily]
howayęnheʼsgǫ: he is a fast learner, a quick study H
•wayęnheʼsgǫ: slow learner
[(tęʼ) deʼ+not P+ contains: -wayę(n)$_N$- heart, spirit -sgǫ: easily]
dęhowayęnheʼsgǫ: he has difficulty learning H
•wayęnǫni care for, do carefully
[ade+ -wayę(n)$_N$- heart, spirit -ǫni, ǫny$_V$- make]
sadewayę:nǫ:nih you care for it / things all the time H
ęhsheyadewayę:nǫ:niʼ you will take care of them, care for them P
hodewayęnǫni: he has done it carefully S
•wayę(h)sd learn
[ade+ contains: -wayę(n)$_N$- heart, spirit]
ǫdewayę:staʼ she is a novice, learner, beginner H
ęhsadewa:yę:s you will learn P
sadewayę:sdǫh you are learning S
•wayę(h)sd(ę, ani) train, educate, teach
[TR+ contains: -wayę(h)sd$_V$- learn]
ęhshewayę:sdęʼ you will train, educate, teach s.o. P
gawayęhsda:ni: it has been taught S
•wayęhsdǫ:ʼ learning process
[wa+ade+ contains: -wayę(h)sd$_V$- learn]
wadewayęhsdǫ:ʼ the process of learning
•wayęsdǫh tidy, neat
[d+wa+ade+ contains: -wayę(h)sd$_V$- learn]
dwadewayę:sdǫh gagehǫʼ it is tidy, neatly placed S
•wayęstaʼ learner, novice, apprentice
[A+ade+ contains: -wayę(h)sd$_V$- learn]
gaǫdewayę:staʼ they (f/m) are apprentices; they are learning together
•wayǫd angel
[de+gae+ -way(a)$_N$- fin, wing -ǫd$_V$- attached]
degae:wa:yǫ:t angels
•weʼ be a distance, an amount
[ni+yo+]
niyo:weʼ how far (distance) S
•(h)węhd(a:) ear of corn
[o+]
ohwęhda: ears of corn

•wenǫ be a stranger, be a certain age
see: enǫ be a stranger, be a certain age
[ni+d+p]
nita:we:nǫh a male stranger; he's that age (lit.: where he comes from) H
nigyawe:nǫ: where it came from S

•wenǫ go somewhere
see: enǫ go somewhere
[ti+P+]
tiyo:ne:nǫ: where they have gone S

•wenǫh be a stranger
see: enǫh stranger
[ni+d+P -enǫ$_V$- originate from someplace, come from someplace]
nita:we:nǫh a male stranger; he's that age (lit.: where he comes from)
nijagowe:nǫh a female stranger (lit.: where she comes from)

•wenǫgyeʼ move forward
see: enǫgyeʼ move forward
[ohę:dǫ: he+…]
ohę:dǫ: heʼsenǫgyeʼ you're moving forward H

•wenǫgyeʼs roam
see: enǫgyeʼ roam
[ti+…]
tigęnenǫgyeʼs they (z) are roaming about H

•wenǫhah be middle-aged
see: enǫhah be middle-aged
[ni+d+P+ -enǫ$_V$- originate from someplace, come from someplace -hah diminutive]
nitawe:nǫ:hah a middle-aged male
nigyagawe:nǫ:hah a middle-aged female

•(h)weʼnǫni wrap s.t.
[-(h)weʼn(a)$_N$- round, circle -ǫni, ǫny$_V$- make]
sweʼnǫ:nih wrap it I

•(h)weʼnǫni be round
[de+yo+at+ -(h)weʼn(a)$_N$- round, circle -ǫni, ǫny$_V$- make]
deyotweʼnǫ:ni: it is round S

•(h)weʼnǫnihsd make s.t. round
[de+...at+ -(h)weʼn(a)$_N$- round, circle -ǫni, ǫny$_V$- make]
desatwʼenǫ:nihs make it round I

•we:ʼǫ: will s.t.
see e:ʼǫ: will s.t. [P+]
hawe:ʼǫ: he has willed it S

•weodę be mouldy
[-we$_N$- mould -od$_V$- stand]
agaweodęʼ it got mouldy P

•wetʼah pretend
see etʼah pretend [a+w+]
a:we:tʼah implied; pretend P

•wetʼahshǫ:ʼǫh make-believe, pretend
see: etʼahshǫ:ʼǫh make-believe, pretend [a:+w+ -etʼah$_V$- pretend -sǫ:ʼǫh plural]
a:wetʼahshǫ:ʼǫh make-believe; pretend

•(w)ę(:)hdad run
[de+…]
degaǫ:węhda:s they (f/m) run H
da:gaǫ:węhda:t they (f/m) might run P
dewagęhdadǫh I have run S

•(h)wędahd clear out
[de+... -(h)węd(a)$_N$- hole, opening -(a)hd$_V$- be like, resemble]
dęhsehwędaht you will make a clearing P

•(w)ędagę: be a wimp, timid, weak, cowardly
[P+]
gowędagę:, agawęda:gę: she is a wimp, timid S

•(h)wędeʼ gap, opening
[de+ya(ǫ)+ -(h)węd(a)$_N$- hole, opening -deʼ$_V$- exist]
deyaǫhwę:deʼ a gap; an opening

•wędehd forfeit
[ad/adad+]
sadwędehtaʼ you forfeit things all the time H
awadadwę:deht it (for example, a pet) forfeited (its life) P

•wędęnawę: wet (weather)
[-węd(a)$_{N}$- day -(naʼ)nawę:$_{V}$- be wet]
awędęnawę it got wet P

•hwę:dǫh ever, when
cf: Appendix I

•hwędǫgwaʼ sometime
cf: Appendix I

•(h)węʼg(a:) wood chip, splint
[o+]
ohwęʼga:ʼ a splint; a wood chip

•(hwęʼga)ʼoh notch s.t.
[A+hwęʼga/N+]
g̱ahwęʼg̱a̱ʼo:ʼo: it is notched S

•węhęd climb s.t.
[de+…ad/N+ occurs in:]
g̱ahehnawęhę:s bail elevator H
[-(hr)ehn(a)$_{N}$- cargo, bundle -węhę(h)d$_{V}$- climb s.t.]
ęhsenedawęhę:t you will go uphill P
[-nǫd(a), ned(a)$_{N}$- hill -węhę(h)d$_{V}$- climb s.t.]
deyodʼawęhędǫh it went over the fence; it is going over the fence S
[-(a)dęʼh(ę)$_{N}$- fence -węhę(h)d$_{V}$- climb s.t.]

•węhoʼdaʼ sweet flag
[a+ -(a)węh(ę)$_{N}$- flower -odaʼ$_{V}$- stand up]
awęhoʼdaʼ sweet flag (a plant)

•węhodaʼs bloom, flower
[ga+ -(a)węh(ę)$_{N}$- flower -odaʼ$_{V}$- stand up]
gawęho:daʼs a blooming plant; a flower

•węhǫtaʼ flowering plant
[ga+ -(a)węh(ę)$_{N}$- flower -ǫd$_{V}$- attached]
gawęhǫtaʼ a flowering plant

•(h)węj(a) earth, land
ohwęjʼageh on earth
[o+ -(h)węj(a)$_{N}$- land, earth -ʼgeh at, on]
ohwęjageh on the earth, land

•(h)węjaʼgahęd cave
[o+ -ǫhwęj(a)$_{N}$- earth, land -gahęd$_{V}$- drill, hole]
ohwęjaʼg̱ahęt a cave

•(h)węjohǫh necessity
[de+yo+at+ -ǫhwęjoni, ǫhwęjoh$_{V}$- want, need]
deyotwęjohǫh a necessity

•węn(a) word, voice, speech
[o+]
owę:naʼ a word; the voice; speech

•węnaʼd give up
agewęnaʼtaʼ agwęnaʼtaʼ I give up (all the time) H
esa:wę:naʼt you gave up P
agewęnaʼdǫh I have given up S

•węnad voiceless syllable
[tęʼ deʼ+ not ga+ -węn(a)$_{N}$- voice, word -d$_{V}$- stand]
tęʼ dega:wę:na:t voiceless syllable

•węnadehd be harsh-speaking, be a smart-aleck
[P+ -węn(a)$_{N}$- voice, word -dehd$_{V}$- bold, bright, strong]
sawęnadeht you are a harsh-speaking person; you are smart-alecky S

•węnadenyeʼs, węnadenyǫʼs translator
[de+A+ -węn(a)$_{N}$- voice, word -deni, deny$_{V}$- change]
deyewęnadenyeʼs she is a translator; she is translating now H
ḏehawęnadenyeʼs he is a translator H

•węnadęnyǫhs reach puberty
[de+A+ad+ -węn(a)$_{N}$- voice, word -deni, deny$_{V}$- change]
dehadwęnadęnyǫhs he is reaching puberty (lit.: his voice is changing) H

Legend: H habitual, P punctual, S stative, I imperative, PURP purposive, PURP-H purposive habitual, PURP-PAST purposive past, PURP-P purposive punctual, PURP-I purposive imperative; see §8.6, §8.11 in Appendix J. Alphabetization in stems ignores length (:), and any h's or glottal stops (ʼ) that are not between vowels. See §2.2 of the User Guide for explanation.

•węnaʼehsd stutter
[P+ -węn(a)$_N$- voice, word -(ʼ)ehsd$_V$- hit with s.t.]
sawęnaʼehstaʼ you stutter H

•węnagadad interpret, raise a song
[ę+ -węn(a)$_N$- voice, word -gadad$_V$- raise s.t. up]
hadęwęnaga:da:s he is an interpreter H
ędwaęnagada:t we all (incl.) will raise the song P

•węnagadas interpreter
[A+adę+ -węn(a)$_N$- voice, word -gadad$_V$- raise s.t. up]
hadęwęnaga:da:s he is an interpreter H

•węnagayǫh high language, formal language
[o+ -węn(a)$_N$- voice, word -gayǫh$_V$- old (thing)]
owęnaga:yǫh high language; formal language

•węnahǫg receive retribution
[-węn(a)$_N$- voice, word -(h)ǫ:$_V$- lie]
ęhsawęnahǫ:k your words will come back on you; you will be revenged, repaid for your words P

•węnahsais smart weed
[go+ -(a)węʼnahs(a), (a)węʼnohs(a)$_N$- tongue -is$_V$- long]
gowęna̱hsais smart weed (a plant)

•węnaʼsęhd harsh words
[o+ -węn(a)$_N$- voice, word -(aʼ)sęhd$_V$- hand down, bring down]
owęna̱hsęht harsh words

•węnahsnoweʼ auctioneer
[A+ -węn(a)$_N$- voice, word -(h)snoweʼ$_V$- fast]
hawęna̱hsno:weʼ he is an auctioneer H

•węnayenahs tape recorder, transcriber, recorder
[ga+ -węn(a)$_N$- voice, word -yena(w), yenaǫ, yena(:)$_V$- catch, receive, accept]
gawęnaye:nahs a tape recorder; a transcriber

•węnayęhd jeer, jest
[ad+ -węn(a)$_N$- voice, word -(y)ęhd$_V$- hit, knock down, strike]
ęhsadwęna:yęht you will jeer, jest, throw words at s.o. P

•węnihsgaǫ:dǫʼ adoʼji:naʼ roller skates, roller blades
węnihsgaǫ:dǫʼ wheels
adoʼjinaʼ skates

•węnistaʼ slow marker
[ga+ -węn(a)$_N$- voice, word -isd$_V$- make long]
gawęnihstaʼ a slow marker

•węnitgęʼǫ:ʼ speech
[ga+ -węn(a)$_N$- voice, word -itgęʼ$_V$- rise]
gawęnitgęʼǫ:ʼ a speech

•węniyoʼ wild
[A+ ad/adad+]
gęnadagwęni:yo, gęnadadwę:ni:yoʼ they (z) are wild S

•węnod bay, howl
[ad+ -węn(a)$_N$- voice, word -od$_V$- stand]
awadwęno:dęʼ it did bay, howl P
odwę:no:t it is baying S

•węnodahgǫh spoken language
[ga+ -węn(a)$_N$- voice, word -odahgw$_V$- remove, take away]
gawęnǫdahgǫh spoken language

•węnodęʼ language
[ni+A+ -węn(a)$_N$- voice, word -od$_V$- stand]
nigawęno:dęʼ language
nigawęnodęʼs language words
nidwawęno:dę: our language

•węnohgr(a) weed
[a+]
awęno̱hgraʼ weeds

•węnohgra: cause an allergic reaction
[P+]
gowęno̱hgra:ʼs poison ivy; any plant that causes a skin infection H

•węnohgra: cause an allergic reaction (continued)
ęhsawęnogǫ̱hgra:ʼ (**ęhsawęnohgra:ʼ**) it will give you an allergic reaction P

•węnohgra:s poison ivy, allergenic plant
[go+ -węnohgr(a)$_{N}$- weed -węnohgra:$_{V}$- cause an allergic reaction]
gowęnǫ̱hgra:ʼs poison ivy; any plant that causes a skin infection

•węnǫda(:) speak
[ad+ -węn(a)$_{N}$- voice, word -ǫda:(h)$_{V}$- put in]
a:gadwę:nǫ:dahk I should use that language P

•węnǫdas tape recorder
[ga+ -węn(a)$_{N}$- voice, word -ǫda:(h)$_{V}$- put in, attached]
gawę:nǫ:da:s a tape recorder

•węnǫdataʼ tape recorder
[ga+ -węn(a)$_{N}$- voice, word -ǫda:(h)$_{V}$- put in, attached]
gawęnoda:taʼ a tape recorder

•węnǫdi, węnǫgy ventriloquist
[he+P+ad+ -węn(a)$_{N}$- voice, word -ǫdi, -ǫgy$_{V}$- throw]
hę:sadwęnǫ:diʼ you will throw your voice (as a ventriloquist) P

•(h)węʼsd(a) foam
[ga+ -(h)węʼsd(a)$_{N}$- foam -oʼ$_{V}$- be submerged]
ga̱hwęʼsdoʼ foam

•(h)węʼsdod head of foam
[o+ -(h)węʼsd(a)$_{N}$- foam -od$_{V}$- attached object]
ohwęʼsdo:t a head of foam (on a beer)

•(h)węʼsdǫni whip s.t.
[-(h)węʼsd(a)$_{N}$- foam -ǫni, ǫny$_{V}$- make]
ęhswęʼsdo:niʼ you will whip (for example, meringue) P

•(h)węʼsdotaʼ beer
[ga+ -(h)węʼsd(a)$_{N}$- foam -od$_{V}$- stand]
ga̱hwęʼsdotaʼ beer (lit.: it has a head on it)

•węʼyǫhg(a:) thumb
[a+]
awęʼyǫ̱hga:ʼ thumb
gwęʼyǫhga:ʼgeh on my thumb

•węyǫhs(a) heart, spirit
[a+]
awęyǫ̱hsaʼ the heart; the spirit

•(w)ih, (r)ih be undercooked
[(tęʼ) deʼ+ not yo+]
deyo:wi:h it is undercooked S

•(w)i, (r)i be ripe
[occurs in:]
ęwahyaiʼ it will ripen
[-(a)hy(a)$_{N}$- fruit, berry -(r)i, (w)i$_{V}$- be ripe]

•(ʼ)wi: corner
[he+yo+ -(iʼ)w(a)$_{N}$- welt -i:ʼ$_{V}$- stuck onto s.t.]
heyoʼwi: a corner

•widr(a) ice
[o+]
owi:draʼ ice

•widradęhda:ʼ ice patch
[o+ -widr(a)$_{N}$- ice -dęhda:ʼ$_{V}$- lie spread out on the ground]
owidradęhda:ʼ an ice patch

•widrano: ice cream
[o+ -widr(a)$_{N}$- ice -no:$_{V}$- be cold, cool]
owidrano: ice cream

•widrataʼ butter
[o+ -widr(a)$_{N}$- ice -taʼ$_{V}$ dried out]
owidra:taʼ butter

•widrateh glassy, icy, glass tumbler
[de+yo+ -widr(a)$_{N}$- ice -(a)te$_{V}$- bright, clear]
deyowidra:teh it is glassy, icy; a glass tumbler S

•wiʼdreʼ ice patch
[o+ -widr(a)$_{N}$- ice -e$_{V}$- go]
owi:dreʼ ice patch

Legend: H habitual, P punctual, S stative, I imperative, PURP purposive, PURP-H purposive habitual, PURP-PAST purposive past, PURP-P purposive punctual, PURP-I purposive imperative; see §8.6, §8.11 in Appendix J. Alphabetization in stems ignores length (:), and any h's or glottal stops (ʼ) that are not between vowels. See §2.2 of the User Guide for explanation.

•widroʼ floating ice, ice cube
[o+ -widr(a)$_N$- ice -oʼ$_V$- be submerged]
owi:droʼ floating ice in the water; ice cubes

•wihjih overcooked
[o+ contains -(r)i, (w)i$_V$- ripe -jih overly]
owihjih it is overcooked S

•(h)wihsd(a), (hr)ihsd(a) tin, metal, money
[ga+]
gai:sdaʼ tin; metal
hęnatwi̲hsda:nǫh they (m) guard the money
[at+ -(h)wihsd(a), (h)rihsd(a)$_N$- metal, money -nǫ(:)$_V$- guard]

•(h)wihsdʼaehs clock
[ga+ -(h)wihsd(a), (h)rihsd(a)$_N$- metal, money -(ʼ)e$_V$- hit]
ga̲hwihsdʼa̲ehs a clock

•(h)wihsdanǫ:ʼ gold, expensive item
[ga+ -(h)wihsd(a), (hr)ihsd(a)$_N$- metal, money -nǫ:ʼ$_V$- be costly, expensive]
ga̲hwihsdanǫ:ʼ gold; anything expensive

•(h)wihsdaę(:) reserve, economize
[at+ -(h)wihsd(a), (hr)ihsd(a)$_N$- metal, money -ę$_V$- lie]
ęhsatwi̲hsdaęʼ you will economize P
satwihsdaęʼ you will reserve (money) S

•(h)wihsdahihd make change
[de+... -(h)wihsd(a), (hr)ihsd(a)$_N$- metal, money -(hr)ihd$_V$- cause to break up]
dęhswihsda̲hiht you will make change P

•(h)wihsdaniʼǫhsd economize
[at+ -(h)wihsd(a), (hr)ihsd(a)$_N$- metal, money -niʼǫhsd$_V$- be stingy, greedy, cheap with s.t.]
satwihsdaniʼǫhs you economize H
ęhsatwihsdaniʼǫhs you will economize P

•(h)wihsdęda:ʼ waste money
[at+ -(h)wihsd(a), (hr)ihsd(a)$_N$- metal, money -(hr)ęʼda(:,h) $_V$- burn]
satwihsdʼęda:s you burn your money H
agatwi̲hsdęʼda:ʼ I wasted my money P

•(h)wihsdǫni: profit
[w+at+ -(h)wihsd(a), (hr)ihsd(a)$_N$- metal, money -ǫni, ǫny$_V$- make]
watwihsdǫ:ni: profit

•(h)wihsǫd milk snake
[(o+) -(h)wihs(a)- -ǫd$_V$- attached]
(o)hwihsǫ:t a milk snake

•wiy(a) young, offspring, baby
[o+]
owi:yaʼ young; offspring (for example, of an animal); a baby

•wiy:ʼah baby
[o+...-ʼah little]
owi:ya:ʼah a baby

•wiyad be pregnant
[P+ -wiy(a)$_N$- child, offspring -d$_V$- stand]
gowi:ya:t she is pregnant; she has a baby in her S

•wiyahdǫʼd abort
[adad+ -wiy(a)$_N$- child, offspring -(a)hdǫʼd$_V$- cause to lose]
ǫdadwiyahdǫtaʼ abortion H
agadadwiya̲hdǫʼt I had an abortion P
agadadwiya̲hdǫʼdǫh I did have an abortion S

•wiyahdǫʼtaʼ abortion
[ǫ+adad+ -wiy(a)$_N$- child, offspring -(a)hdǫʼd$_V$- cause to lose]
ǫdadwiyahdǫtaʼ abortion

•wiyaędaʼ(dreʼ) pregnant, expecting
[P+ -wiy(a)$_N$- child, offspring contains: -ędaʼ$_V$- finish]
gowiyaędʼadreʼ she is with child S

•wiyahkwaʼ uterus, placenta
[e+ -wiy(a)$_N$- child, offspring -(h)gw$_V$- lift, pick up]
ewiya:hkwaʼ the uterus; the placenta

•wiyanęhsgw, wiyanęhsgo kidnap a child
[TR+ -wiy(a)$_N$- child, offspring -nęhsgw$_V$- steal]
ahawiyanęhsgo' he stole a child, kidnapped a child P
gawiyanęhsgwęh a kidnapped child S

•wiyanǫ(:) babysit
[ad+ -wiy(a)$_N$- child, offspring -nǫ(:)$_V$- guard]
ęgadwiya:nǫ:' I will babysit P
sadwiya:nǫh you babysit all the time; you are babysitting right now S

•wiyatsęny, wiyatsęi foundling, illegitimate child
[ga+ -wiy(a)$_N$- child, offspring -tsęi, tsęny$_V$- find]
gawiyatsę:nyǫ: a child born out of wedlock; a foundling;an illegitimate child

•wiyę's miscarriage
[P+ ago+ -wiy(a)$_N$- child, offspring -(a')sę'- drop]
agowi:yęhs she has a miscarriage

•wiyǫdi, wiyǫgy miscarriage, abandon a child, abort
[P+ -wiy(a)$_N$- child, offspring -ǫdi, -ǫgy$_V$- throw]
sǫgwi:yǫ:di' I had a miscarriage again P

•wiyǫdi, wiyǫgy abandon one's child
[P+ad+ -wiy(a)$_N$- child, offspring -ǫdi, -ǫgy$_V$- throw]
ęhsadwiyǫ:di' you will abandon your baby, child P
wadwiyǫgyǫ: an abandoned child S

Y

•y(a) other, different
[o+]
o:ya' other; another

•ya: bag
[ga+]
ga:ya:' a bag; a pouch; a mattress; a tick (that is, a mattress bag into which straw is stuffed)

•(h)ya:' refers to a period of time
see: Appendix I

•ya(:,h) spread
see: (r)a(:,h) spread
ęhsra:' you will spread it P

•yad spread s.t.
see: (r)ad, yad, wad spread s.t.
eya:ta' s.o. spreads it H

•ya'd(a) body
oya'da' a body
sya'da'geh on your body

•ya'd(a) doll
[ga+]
gaya'da' a doll

•yad(a) basement, track, ditch, hole
[o+]
oya:da' a basement; a track; a ditch; a hole

•ya'da:' picture
[ga+ contains: -ya'd(a)$_N$- body -ǫnyǫ' plural]
gaya'da:' a picture
gaya'daǫ:nyǫ' pictures

•ya'dadaihę: be hot (living thing)
[P+ -ya'd(a)$_N$- body -(')daihę:$_V$- be hot]
agya'dadaihę: I am hot S

•ya'dade' human conditions
[shęh that d+wa+ -ya'd(a)$_N$- body -de'$_V$- exist]
shęh dwaya'dade' human conditions

•ya'dadehd be active, nimble, energetic
[P+ -ya'd(a)$_N$- body -dehd$_V$- be bold, bright, strong]
agya'dadeht I am nimble, active, energetic S

•yaʼdadih lean
[ag+ -yaʼd(a)$_{N}$- body -(a)dih$_{V}$- side]
ęsagyadaʼdih you will lean against s.t. P

•ya:dadǫhs circus
[de+A+ag+ -ya:$_{N}$- bag -(h)adad$_{V}$- rise up]
de̱henagya:dadǫhs a circus (lit.: they put up tents)

•yaʼdahdrǫgw quiver, shudder
[P+ -yaʼd(a)$_{N}$- body -(a)hdrǫgw$_{V}$- caress]
ęsayʼadahdrǫ:gǫʼ you will quiver, shudder P

•yaʼdahdrǫgw caress s.o.
[TR+]
hehsyaʼda̱hdrǫ:gwahs you are caressing him now H
ęhesyaʼdahdrǫ:gǫʼ you will caress him P
hehsyaʼda̱hdrǫ:gwęh you did caress him S

•yaʼdagenh help
[TR+ -yaʼd(a)$_{N}$- body -genh$_{V}$- argue for, advocate]
a:hyayaʼdage:nhaʼ he would help you P

•yaʼdagęhe(y) physically weak, slow
[-yaʼd(a)$_{N}$- body -(ga)hey, (gę)hey, (i)hey, (ga)he:, (gę)he:, (i)he:$_{V}$- die, be weak, exhausted]
agyaʼdagęhe:ʼ I got limp, weak P
agyaʼdagęhe:yǫ: I am physically weak, slow S

•yaʼdagęnye(:) rake s.o. over the coals
[TR+ -yaʼd(a)$_{N}$- body -gęni, gęny$_{V}$- compete]
ahǫwadiyaʼdagę:nye:ʼ they raked him over the coals (lit.: they dragged him around) P

•yaʼdagrahs goat
[ga+ -yaʼd(a)$_{N}$- body -grahs$_{V}$- stink]
gayaʼdagrahs goat

•yaʼdahgw lose weight
[d/g+P+ag+ -yaʼd(a)$_{N}$- body -(h)gw$_{V}$- lift, pick up]
dǫgyaʼda:goʼ I lost weight (lit.: lost part of my body) P
dyagoyada:gwęh she has lost weight S

•yaʼdahgwaʼd push ups
[d/g+...ad+ -yaʼd(a)$_{N}$- body -(h)gwaʼd$_{V}$- cause to lift up]
degaǫ:dagyaʼdahgwataʼ they (f/m) are doing push ups H
dęgaǫ:dagyaʼdahgwaʼt they (f/m) will do push ups P

•yaʼdagweg constipate
[ag+ -yaʼd(a)$_{N}$- body -gweg$_{V}$- close]
ǫgyaʼdagwe:s she gets bound up; constipated H
ęsagyaʼda:gwe:k you will get constipated P
gogyaʼdagwe:gǫh she is constipated S

•yadagyeʼ gulley
[o+ -yad(a)$_{N}$- hole, ditch -(a)gyeʼ$_{V}$- alongside]
oyadagyeʼ a gulley

•yaʼdahe(n) operate
[TR+ -yaʼd(a)$_{N}$- body -(hr)e(n)$_{V}$- cut]
hǫwadiyaʼdahe:neh they operate on him H
ahǫwadiyadahe: they gave him an operation P

•yaʼdahkwaʼ hen hawk
[de+ga+ -yaʼd(a)$_{N}$- body -(h)gw$_{V}$- lift, pick up]
degayʼadahkwaʼ a hen hawk

•yaʼdanega(:,ǫ) hernia
[de+P+ag+ -yaʼd(a)$_{N}$- body -(wa)negaǫ, (wa)nega(:)$_{V}$- explode, split]
dewagagyaʼdanegaǫ: I have a hernia S

•yaʼdahniyaʼd strong
[ag+ -yaʼd(a)$_{N}$- body -(h)niyaʼd$_{V}$- harden]
ędwagyadahni:yaʼt we all will be strong in body P

•yaʼdanǫhwag ache, be sore
[P+ -yaʼd(a)$_N$- body -nǫhwag$_V$- be sore, ache]
agyaʼdanǫhwa:s I am sore; I ache H
ǫgyaʼdanǫhwa:k I ached P

•yaʼda:s self-centred, bold
[A+adag+ -yaʼd(a)$_N$- body -(a)ʼda(ni)$_V$- rely on]
hadagyʼada:s he has a high opinion of himself; he is self-centred; he is bold H

•yaʼdahshęʼ be late
[P+ -yaʼd(a)$_N$- body -(a)hshę:$_V$- be slow-moving]
ǫgyaʼda̲hshęʼ I was late P
ǫgyada̲hshęʼǫhǫgyeʼ I am arriving late S

•yaʼdahshę: be slow-moving
[P+ -yaʼd(a)$_N$- body -(a)hshę:$_V$- slow-moving]
agyaʼda̲hshę: I am slow S

•yaʼdahsrǫnyaʼd dress up
[ag+ -yaʼd(a)$_N$- body -(h)srǫnyaʼd$_V$- cause to fix, repair]
ǫgyaʼda̲hsrǫnyʼataʼ s.o. dresses up H

•yaʼdatsęi, yaʼdatsęny find s.o.
[TR+ -yaʼd(a)$_N$- body -tsęi, tsęny$_V$- find]
haʼǫdagyaʼdatsęi:ʼ she found her over there P

•yaʼdawadǫh be righteous
[o+ -yaʼd(a)$_N$- body -wadǫh$_V$-]
oyaʼdawa:dǫh a righteous person

•yaʼdawę brother's child
[TR+]
keyaʼdawę my brother's children S

•yaʼdawiʼd put on (clothes), clothe one-self
[ag+ -yaʼd(a)$_N$- body -awiʼd$_V$- insert]
sagyaʼdawiʼtaʼ you are always putting it on; you are doing it right now H
ęsagyaʼda:wi:t you will put on (clothes) P
sagyaʼdawiʼdǫh that's what clothing you have on S

•yadeʼ climb
see: (r)adeʼ climb
sra:deʼ you are climbing S

•yadeʼ basement
[o+ -yad(a)$_N$- hole, ditch -e$_V$- go]
oya:deʼ a basement; a track; a ditch

•yaʼde:s water snake
[s+ga+ -yaʼd(a)$_N$- body -es$_V$- long]
sgayaʼde:s a water snake

•yaʼdinyǫd re-elect
[heʼ+s+TR+ -yaʼd(a)$_N$- body -inyǫʼd$_V$- put in]
hǫsaʼhǫwadiyaʼdinyǫ:t they re-elected him, them (m)P

•yaʼditgęʼsǫ(:) have nightmare
[P+ -yaʼd(a)$_N$- body -itgęʼ$_V$- rise -ǫ several]
ǫgyaʼditgęhsǫ:ʼ I had nightmares

•yaʼdohae bathe
[ag+ -yaʼd(a)$_N$- body -ohae$_V$- clean, wash]
hagyaʼdo̲hai: he is bathing H
ęwagyʼado̲hai: it is going to give me a bath P

•yaʼdohaiʼtaʼ, yaʼdohaʼtaʼ bath tub
[ǫ+ag+ -yaʼd(a)$_N$- body -ohae$_V$- clean, wash]
ǫgyaʼdo̲haiʼtaʼ, ǫgyaʼdo̲ha:ʼtaʼ a bath tub

•yaʼdowehd think about, consider
[de+]
deyeyaʼdowe̲htaʼ she is a thinker, a seer H
dęhsyaʼdo:weht you will be a seer, a thinker P
dewagyaʼdowe̲hdǫh I have already thought about it; I am thinking about it S
desyaʼdo:weht be a thinker, a seer I

•yaʼdowehdǫ:ʼ thinking
[ga+ -yaʼdowehd$_V$- think about, consider]
gayaʼdowehdǫ:ʼ the idea of thinking

Legend: H habitual, P punctual, S stative, I imperative, PURP purposive, PURP-H purposive habitual, PURP-PAST purposive past, PURP-P purposive punctual, PURP-I purposive imperative; see §8.6, §8.11 in Appendix J. Alphabetization in stems ignores length (:), and any h's or glottal stops (ʼ) that are not between vowels. See §2.2 of the User Guide for explanation.

•yaʼdowehtaʼ fortune teller, seer, thinker
[de+A+ contains: -yaʼdowehd$_{V}$- think about, consider]
dęhayaʼdowęhtaʼ he is a fortune teller, a seer, a thinker
•(h)yadǫ(:) write
ehyadǫhaʼ she is a secretary, stenographer, court recorder, transcriber H
ehya:dǫh she writes H
ękya:dǫ:ʼ I will write P
•yaʼdǫh direction
(tsęh) niyoyaʼdǫh a direction S
•(h)yadǫ(:) have a reading
[(a)k+ contains: -(h)yadǫ(:)$_{V}$- write]
ęgakyadǫ:ʼ I will have a reading; I will have my fortune told P
•yaʼdǫda: represent, be an ambassador
[TR+ag+ -yaʼd(a)$_{N}$- body -ǫda:(h)$_{V}$- put in]
ęhshagogyaʼdǫ:dahk he will be an ambassador, represent s.o. (lit.: they will put his body in) P
•yaʼdǫdaʼd shake, shiver
[P+ -yaʼd(a)$_{N}$- body -ǫdaʼd$_{V}$- shake, shiver]
sayaʼdǫdaʼtaʼ you are nervous, shaking, shivering H
agyaʼdǫdaʼdǫh I shiver S
•yaʼdǫdaʼtaʼ Parkinson's disease
[go+ -yaʼd(a)$_{N}$- body -ǫdaʼd$_{V}$- shake, shiver]
goyaʼdǫdaʼtaʼ Parkinson's disease
•yaʼdǫdi, yaʼdǫgy pounce on s.t.
[he+P+ag+ -yaʼd(a)$_{N}$- body -ǫdi, -ǫgy$_{V}$- throw]
hęsagyʼadǫ:diʼ you will pounce on it P
•yaʼdǫhaktaʼ girdle
[de+yǫ+ag+ -yaʼd(a)$_{N}$- body -ohakd$_{V}$- squeeze with s.t.]
deyǫgyaʼdoha:ktaʼ a girdle
•(h)yadǫhaʼ secretary, stenographer, transcriber
[e+ contains: -(h)yadǫ(:)$_{V}$- write]
ehyadǫhaʼ she is a secretary, a stenographer, a court recorder, a transcriber
•(h)yadǫhkw(a) pencil, pen
[e+ contains: -(h)yadǫ(:)$_{V}$- write]
ehyadǫhkwaʼ a pencil; a pen
•yaʼdǫni: robot, puppet
[ti+ga+ -yaʼd(a)$_{N}$- body -ǫni, ǫny$_{V}$- make, be artificial]
tigayʼado:ni: a robot; a puppet, etc.
•ya:dǫhs circus
[de+A+ag+ -ya:$_{N}$- bag -d$_{V}$- stand]
dęhęnagya:dǫhs circus (lit.: they (m) put up tents)
•(h)yadǫhsr(a) paper
[ga+ contains: -(h)yadǫ(:)$_{V}$- write]
gahyadǫhsraʼ paper
•(h)yadǫhsraędiʼ smart, educated
[A+ -(h)yadǫhsr(a)$_{N}$- paper -(y)ędei, (y)ędí$_{V}$- know]
syadǫhsraędiʼ you are smart, educated H
•yadreʼ grandchild, descendant
[TR+]
keya:dreʼ my granddaughter S
heya:dreʼ my grandson S
•yadrǫ(:) tear s.t., shred s.t.
see: (r)adrǫ(:) tear s.t., shred s.t.
ęhsra:drǫ:ʼ you will tear, shred P
•yaʼg cut, break, cross
see: (i)yaʼg [(N+)] cut, break, cross
swaǫ:gyaʼgǫh you all have cut the log S
[-(r)ǫd(a)$_{N}$- log -(i)yaʼg$_{V}$- cut, break]
•yaʼg shoot
see: (i)yaʼg shoot
hadiyʼa:s they (m) are shooting H
•yaʼg(a:) waist
oyaʼga:ʼ a waist
syʼaga:ʼgeh on your waist
•ya:gehdeh knapsack
[P+ -ya:$_{N}$- bag -gehd$_{V}$- have around one's neck]
hoya:gehdeh his knapsack

•yage(:,w) wipe
see: (r)age(:,w) wipe
ęgra:ge:ʼ I will erase, wipe it P
•ya:gewahtaʼ eraser
[e+ -(r)age(:,w)$_V$- wipe]
eya:gewahtaʼ an eraser
•yagęʼ go out
gya:gęʼs I am going out H
ęhsya:gęʼ you will go out P
heyoyagęʼǫh that's where it went out S
•yahgęhd(a) morel
yahgęhdaʼ a morel; a black type of mushroom
•yagęhdahgw come out
[d+ contains: -yagęʼ$_V$- go out]
dagayagęhdahk it came out suddenly P
•yagw, yago choose, take out
see: (r)agw, (r)ago choose, take out
ęhsra:goʼ you will choose, take out P
•yag(wa:) orb, circular in shape
see: (r)ag(wa:) body, circular in shape
ga:gwa:ʼ a celestial body (for example, the sun, the moon)
•ya:gwah tick mattress, mattress
[ǫ+ag+ -ya:$_N$- bag -gw$_V$- gather, choose, pick]
ǫgya:gwah a tick mattress
•yagwahd(a) ball of foot, sole
see: (r)agwahd(a) ball of foot, sole
a:gwa̱hdaʼ, ogwahdaʼ the sole; the ball of foot
•(h)yagwaǫd blighted fruit
[o+ -ahya- fruit -g(wa)$_N$- bump -ǫd$_V$- attached]
ohya:gwaǫt fruit with bumps, blight
•ya(k)d(a) heel
see: (r)a(k)d(a) heel
sradaʼgeh on your heel
ga:dageh a heel
•yaʼksǫ(:) several broken pieces
see: (i)yaʼksǫ(:) [de+...] several broken pieces
degayʼaksǫʼ it is broken S
•yaʼksǫʼ broken up in different ways
see: (i)yaʼksǫʼ [haʼ+de+...] broken up in different ways
haʼdegayaʼksǫʼ it is broken up in different ways S
•yahk(wa) pants
[o+]
oyahkwaʼ pants
•yahkwaʼ container
[e+ -(r)a(:,h)$_V$- spread]
eyahkwaʼ containers
•yan(a) tire, track
[o+]
oya:naʼ a tire; its track; anything that leaves tracks
•yanaʼ, yanǫʼ be addicted
[P+ag+ contains: -yanǫʼ$_V$- dream]
hogyanaʼǫh he is possessed, addicted (with gambling, women, etc.) S
agagyanǫʼǫh I am addicted S
•yanaʼdahnǫʼ, yęnaʼdahnǫʼ calico, printed fabrics
[o+ag+ contains: -yęnaʼd, yanaʼd$_V$- mark s.t. -hnǫʼ several]
ogyanadahnǫʼ patterned material; calico; printed fabric
•ya:nawęʼdahkwaʼ sugar bowl
[e+ contains: -(rę)nawęʼd(a)$_N$- sugar, candy]
eya:nawęʼda:kwaʼ a sugar bowl
•yanawęʼdoh sweeten
see: (r)anawęʼdoh sweeten
ęhsranawęʼdoh you will sweeten P
•yaʼnęd(a:ʼg) stick, cling
see: (raʼ)nęd(a:ʼg), (yaʼ)nęd(a:ʼg) stick, cling
owaʼnę:da:s it sticks to it; it adheres to it H
•yanotgę: slow runner
[P+]
hoyano:tgę: he is a slow runner, walker; he has a slow gait S

Legend: H habitual, P punctual, S stative, I imperative, PURP purposive, PURP-H purposive habitual, PURP-PAST purposive past, PURP-P purposive punctual, PURP-I purposive imperative; see §8.6, §8.11 in Appendix J. Alphabetization in stems ignores length (:), and any h's or glottal stops (ʼ) that are not between vowels. See §2.2 of the User Guide for explanation.

•yanowe' be fast
[A/P+N+ occurs in:]
gadrehdaya:no:we' a train; a fast car S
[ga+ stem: -(')drehdayanowe'- train; consists of: -(')drehd(a)$_N$- vehicle, car -yanowe'$_V$- fast]
•yahnǫ(:) grope
hehsyahnǫha', hehsyahnǫh you are picking at s.t. (for example, your food); you are a groper H
hęhsyahnǫ:' you will grope, touch, pick at s.t. P
•yanǫ', yana' be addicted
[P+ag+ contains: -yanǫ'$_V$- dream]
hogyana'ǫh he is possessed, addicted (with gambling, women, etc.) S
agagyanǫ'ǫh I am addicted S
•yanǫ'(dr) dream
[P+ag+]
ogya:nǫ's it dreams H
ęyogyanǫ'k it will dream P
hogyan'ǫdrǫh he is dreaming S
•yanǫdahkwa' ski
[de+yǫ+ag+ -yan(a)$_N$- tire, track -ǫdahkwa'$_V$- attached instrument]
deyǫgyanǫda̱hkwa' skiing
•yanǫhg strange, bizarre
[o+ag+ contains: -yanǫ'$_V$- dream]
ogya:nǫhk it is strange, bizarre S
•yanre' good, nice, beautiful
[o+]
oya:nre' it is nice, good, beautiful S
•yaod put up a tent
[P+ag+ -ya:$_N$- bag -od$_V$- stand]
hogyao:t he has put up a tent S
•yaǫ(:) bead s.t.
[de+ -y(a)$_N$- other, different -(r)ǫ$_V$- bead s.t.]
desyaǫha' you are beading H
degayaǫ:' it is beaded S
•yaǫda: facsimilie; be similar, be an imitation
[de+s+ga+ -y(a)$_N$- other, different -ǫda:(h)$_V$- put in, attached]
dehsgayaǫ'da' a facsimilie; it is an imitation of s.t.; it is similar; it is almost the same H
•yaǫ'd(a) dead body, cadaver
see: (he)yǫ'd(a) [o+] dead body, cadaver
oyǫ'da' a dead body; a cadaver S
•yaǫ'datgę: be decomposed
[o+ -(he)yǫ('da)$_N$- corpse, cadaver -tgę:$_V$- be rotten]
oyaǫ'datgę: a state of decomposition S
•yaǫ'datre(n) make an incision
[d+...(N+) -(he)yǫ('da)$_N$- corpse, cadaver -(hr)enahnǫ$_V$- go and make several cuts]
dehadiyaǫ'datręnahnǫ' they (m) made an incision in a cadaver H
atadiyaǫda'trenahnǫ:' they (m) made an incision in a cadaver P
•ya's parrot
[de+ga+ag+ -(i)ya'g$_V$- cut, break]
dega:gya's a parrot
•yahsd name s.o., s.t.
[contains: -yahsǫ(:)$_V$- be named]
hodiyahsdǫh they (m) have named it S
•yahshe: two or more living things
[de/ni+A+]
de̱hadiyahshe: two males; they (m) are two S
•yahsǫ(:) call s.o.'s name
[d+/ha'+TR+ contains: -yahsǫ$_V$- be named]
tgyahsǫha', haya:sǫh I call them; I am a bingo caller H
hęhsheyahsǫ:' you will call s.o.'s name (over there) P
•yahsǫh be named
[A+ stem: -yahsǫh$_V$- be named]
gadiya̱h·sǫh they (z) are called, named
haya:sǫh his name
•yahsǫd cross
[de+ga+ -yahs(a)$_N$- cross -ǫd$_V$- attached cross]
degaya̱hsǫ:t a cross

•yahsǫha' be a bingo caller
[d+A+ -yahsǫ(:)$_V$- name s.o.]
tgyahsǫha' I call them; I am a bingo caller

•yahsǫnyǫ(:) be named
[A+ contains: -yahsǫ$_V$- be named -ǫnyǫ' plural]
gadiyahshǫ:nyǫ' their (z) names S

•yahsǫnyǫ(:) call s.o.'s name
[d+/ha'+TR+ contains: -yahsǫ$_V$- be named -ǫnyǫ' plural]
tseyahsǫnyǫh you are going along calling s.o.'s name; you call s.o.'s name all the time H
ętseyahsǫ:nyǫ:' you will be calling s.o.'s name P

•yahsǫta' Catholic
[de+A+ -yahs(a)$_N$- cross -ǫd$_V$- attached]
dęhadiyahsǫta' Catholics (lit.: they (m) cross themselves)
dęgaeyahsǫ:ta' Catholics; nuns

•ya'ta' movie, television
[ga+ contains: -ya'd(a)$_N$- body]
gaya'ta' movies; television

•ya'ta' be a photographer
[A+ contains: -ya'd(a)$_N$- body]
haya'ta' he is a photographer

•yatę climb
see: (r)atę climb
ęhsra:tę' you will climb P

•ya'tgahiye' be quick
[A+ -ya'd(a)$_N$- body -gahiye'$_V$- quick]
gya'tgahi:ye' I am quick S

•ya'tgaǫ be active, quick
[A+ -ya'd(a)$_N$- body -gaǫ:'$_V$- be active, quick]
haya'tgaǫ:' he is quick to move; he is active, always moving around S

•ya'tgęni beat in a physical contest
[TR+ -ya'd(a)$_N$- body -gęni, gęny$_V$- compete]
ęhsheya'tgę:ni' you will beat s.o. (in a race) P

•ya'wisd(a) slice, peeling
see: (ra')wisd(a) slice, peeling
owa'wihsda' a slice; a peeling

•ya'wisdots(i) peel s.t.
see: (ra')wisdots(i) peel s.t.
ęhsrawihsdo:tsi' you will peel P

•ye(:) do s.t., conduct oneself
[ni+ d+ ag+ -ye(:)- do]
tsęh nidwagyęha' the way we conduct ourselves H
tsęh nędwa:gye:' the way we will conduct ourselves P
nigyagoyę: the way she does s.t. S
naǫsaǫgwayęhęk what we all should be doing or how we all should conduct ourselves S
sgęnǫ:'ǫh nętsye: take your time (lit.: do it slowly) I

•ye(:) take one's time
[sgęnǫ:'ǫh slowly ni+ d+ ag+ -ye(:)- do]
sgęnǫ:'ǫh nętsye: take your time (lit.: do it slowly) I

•ye: touch
[he'+...]
hehsye:ha' you are a toucher H
hęhsye:' you will touch P
hehsa:yę: you did touch s.t. S

•ye(:) be quiet
[ta'de+ag+ contains: -ye(:)- do]
ta'desagyę: you are quiet S

•ye(h,:) wake up, awaken
igyehs I wake up (all the time) H
ęhsyeh you will wake up P
sa:ye: you are awake S
i:jeh wake up I

•yehd wake s.o. up
[TR+ contains: -ye(h,:)$_V$- wake up, awaken]
ęhsyeht you will wake up s.t. P
hehsyeht wake him up I

•yehwad rise early
[contains: -ye(,:)- wake up, awaken]
syehwa:t you are an early riser S

Legend: H habitual, P punctual, S stative, I imperative, PURP purposive, PURP-H purposive habitual, PURP-PAST purposive past, PURP-P purposive punctual, PURP-I purposive imperative; see §8.6, §8.11 in Appendix J. Alphabetization in stems ignores length (:), and any h's or glottal stops (') that are not between vowels. See §2.2 of the User Guide for explanation.

•yei, (y)í be right, correct
[t+ga+]
tga:yei:, tgayi: it is right, correct S
•yei, (y)í be bad, false, wrong
[(tęʼ) deʼ+ not d+A+ contains: -yei, (y)í$_V$- be right, correct]
tęʼ detga:yeiʼ, tęʼ detga:yi:ʼ it is bad, false, wrong S
•yei, (y)í be enough
[toh that haʼde+ contains: -yei, (y)í$_V$- be right, correct]
toh haʼdegayei:ʼ you get enough S
•yenahs police
[TR+ contains: -yena(w), yenaǫ, yena(:)$_V$- catch, receive, accept]
shago:ye:nahs a policeman
ǫdę:ye:nahs a policewoman
shagodiye:nahs a policemen
gaǫdęye:nahs a policewomen
•yenahsgeh police station
[shagodi+ -yena(w), yenaǫ, yena(:)$_V$- catch, receive, accept -ʼgeh on, at]
shagodiyenahsgeh a police station
•yena(w), yenaǫ, yena(:) catch, receive, accept
[TR+(N+)]
gye:nahs, gye:naǫ:s I catch it H
agye:na:ʼ I caught it; I received it P
agye:naǫ: I have caught it, received it S
ję:na: grip it; hold it I
gahyadǫhsra:ye:nahs a paper clip
[ga+ -(h)yadǫhsr(a)$_N$- paper -yena(w), yenaǫ, yena(:)$_V$- catch, receive, accept]
•yena(w) wrestle
[de+...adag+ -yena(w), yenaǫ, yena(:)$_V$- catch, receive, accept]
dehęnada:gye:nahs wrestlers; they (m) are wrestling H
ęhsadagye:na:ʼ you will wrestle P
desadagye:na: wrestle I
•yena(w), yenaǫ, yena(:) grab s.t.
[d/heʼ+...]
daję:na: grab it I
•yena(w), yenaǫ, yena(:) work together
[de+...]
atadiye:naʼ they (m) did it together (that is, they were accomplices) P
dedwa:ye:na: let's work together, help each other I
•yenawahd cling to s.t.
[TR/ag+(N+) contains: -yena(w), yenaǫ, yena(:)$_V$- catch, receive, accept]
ǫgyenawahtaʼgeh a hand railing H
ęhsagyena:waht you will retain a venue, book a venue, hold onto s.t., cling to s.t. P
ogyenawahdǫh area (lit.: s.t. is clinging to s.t.) S
sagyʼena:waht cling to it; hang on I
•yenawahdǫh venue
[w+ag+ -yenawahd$_V$- cling to s.t.]
wagyenawahdǫh a reserved or booked venue
•yenawaʼkǫ(:) work together, be accomplices
[de+ contains: -yena(w), yenaǫ, yena(:)$_V$- catch, receive, accept]
degadiyenawaʼkǫʼ they (z) are accomplices H
dedwayenawʼakǫ: let's work together I
•yenawaʼs help, assist s.o.
[TR+ contains: -yena(w), yenaǫ, yena(:)$_V$- catch, receive, accept]
gaǫdagyenawaʼseh they help her H
ęgǫyena:waʼs I will help you P
sheyenaʼwaʼs help her I
•yenawaʼseh be a helper, an assistant
[TR+ contains: -yenawaʼs$_V$- help s.o.]
ǫkiyenawʼaseh they are helpers (lit.: they help us) H
•yes be easy
[w+ag+]
wagye:sęh it is easy S
•yesahd waste, be wasteful
[P+ag+ contains: -yes$_V$- easy]
sagyehsahtaʼ you are wasteful H
ęhsa:gye:saht you will waste P

•yesahd abandon s.o.
[TR+ contains: -yesahd$_V$- be wastful]
ahọwagye:saht he abandoned her; he left her P

•yesahd(ahn) condemn, slander, insult
[TR+ contains: -yesahd$_V$- be wastful]
sheyehsa̱hta' you always insult, slander s.o. H
ẹhsye:saht you will condemn, slander, insult s.o. P
sheyehsa̱hdahnọh you are slandering, insulting s.o. S

•yesa'geh be generous
[P+ag+ contains: -yes$_V$- easy -'geh on]
gogyes'ageh she is generous, generous to a fault S

•yesahsdọ: extravagant, wasteful
[P+ag+ contains: -yesahd$_V$- be wasteful]
gogyehsa̱hsdọ: she is extravagant, wasteful S

•yesahsdọh sale, bargain
[w+ag+ -yesahsd$_V$- cause to be wasteful]
wagyesa̱hsdọh sales; bargains

•yehsd mix, add
[(de+)...(N+)]
degayẹ̱hsta' I am adding it H
dẹsyehs you will mix them all together P
degahnegayẹ̱hsdọh water is mixed in it; it is diluted S
[de+ (h)neg(a)$_N$- water, liquid -yehsd$_V$- add]
dehsnegayehs dilute it (lit.: add water) I

•yehsd add
[he'+/d+]
ẹtyehs you will add P
hegayẹ̱hsdọh it has been added S

•yehsdahnọ' herb, spice, mixture
[de+ga+ contains: -yehsd$_V$- add -ahnọ' go and do several things]
degayehsdahnọ' a mixture; it mixed together to make it good (for example, herbs, spices, etc.)

•ye'shọ(:) continue on
[ha'+...adag+ -ye(:)$_V$- do -họ go and do several things]
ha'gadagye'shọ' it continues on endlessly H

•yehta' alarm clock
[go+ contains: -yehd$_V$- wake s.o. up]
goyehta' alarm clock

•yẹ: do
see: ye(:) do
nigyagoyẹ: the way she does s.t. S

•yẹ: touch
see: ye: [he'+...] touch
hehsa:yẹ: you did touch s.t. S

•(y)ẹ' lie on the ground
[ga+]
ga:yẹ' it is lying on the ground S

•(y)ẹ(:) put down, place, set down
[A+(N+) -(y)ẹ$_V$- lie]
hayẹhẹ' he puts, places it there (continuously) H
ẹhsyẹ:' you will put it there P
niga:yẹ' where it is at, where it is placed S
ijẹ: put it down; leave it alone I
agahyaẹ:' I have fruit
[-(a)hy(a)$_N$- fruit, berry -ẹ$_V$- lie]

•(y)ẹ' a group of things lying on the ground
see: ẹ' [A/P+(N+)] a group of things lying on the ground, be lying on the ground covering a large area
ganawaẹ:' a swamp; a pond S
[ga+ -naw(a)$_N$- pond, swamp -ẹ$_V$- lie on the ground]

•yẹ(:) sit down
[ag+ contains: -(y)ẹ$_V$- lie]
ẹhswagyẹ:' you all will sit P
sagyẹ: sit down I

Legend: H habitual, P punctual, S stative, I imperative, PURP purposive, PURP-H purposive habitual, PURP-PAST purposive past, PURP-P purposive punctual, PURP-I purposive imperative; see §8.6, §8.11 in Appendix J. Alphabetization in stems ignores length (:), and any h's or glottal stops (') that are not between vowels. See §2.2 of the User Guide for explanation.

•(y)ęʼ gamble, bet, play a game
[de+A+ contains: -(y)ę$_{V}$- lie]
de̱hodi:yęʼ, detodi:yęʼ they (m) are gambling, betting S

•(y)ęʼ lack s.t.
[deʼ+ not P+ (N+) contains: -(y)ę$_{V}$- lie]
tęʼ dewa:gyęʼ it is not mine; I do not have S
dewagwiyaęʼ I do not have a child
[deʼ+ not -wiy(a)$_{N}$- child, offspring -ę$_{V}$- lie]

•(y)ęʼ have s.t.
[P+(N+) -(y)ę$_{V}$- lie]
hodi:yęʼ they (m) have; they have laid S
agahyaę:ʼ I have fruit
[-(a)hy(a)$_{N}$- fruit, berry -ę$_{V}$- lie]

•(y)ę(:) be quiet, still
[taʼde+P+ag+ contains: -(y)ę$_{V}$- lie]
taʼdesagyę: you are quiet S

•(y)ę(:) put things side by side, lie side by side, be lying side by side
[tsaʼ+de+ contains: -(y)ę(:)$_{V}$- put down, lay down]
tsaʼdęhsyę:ʼ you will put, lay them side by side P
tsaʼde:ga:yęʼ they are (lit.: it is) lying or sitting side by side S

•yę: bead
[o+]
o:yę:ʼ beads

•yęhd begin, be first
[d/g+...ag+ contains: -(y)ęhd$_{V}$- cause to lie]
dawa:gyę:t the first one; the beginner P
gyogyęhdǫh the first one, the beginning S

•yęd(a) wood
[o+]
oyę:daʼ wood; firewood

•(y)ędaʼ become, acquire, finish
[A/P+(N+) contains: -(y)ę$_{V}$- lie]
ęsayę:daʼ you will acquire, obtain P
tsaʼga:yę:daʼ when it became P
awahyę:daʼ the berry season is over P
[stem: -(a)hy(a)$_{N}$- fruit, berry -(y)ędaʼ$_{V}$- finish]

•(y)ędaʼ settle
[ha+t+ga contains: -(y)ę$_{V}$- lie]
hatgayę:daʼ it is settled P

•yędeʼ be good at s.t.
[P+(N+) contains: -(y)ęde(:,ʼ)$_{V}$- recognize -sgǫ: easily]
sayędehsgǫ: you are always really good at it H
ęsayędeʼǫhǫ:k you will be really good at it P
sayędeʼǫh you are really good at s.t. S
sak·wa·yę·déʼǫ: you are a good cook S
[-k(wa)$_{N}$- food -(y)ędeʼ$_{V}$- be good at s.t.]

•yęde(:) recognize s.t.
[TR+]
ęgyę:de:ʼ I will recognize it P
ta:gaesayę:de: they will not recognize you (this word could refer to a disguise) I

•yędehd be recognizable, obvious, conspicuous
[o+ contains: -(y)ęde(:,ʼ)$_{V}$- recognize]
oyę:deht it is recognizable, plain to be seen, conspicuous S

•(y)ędei, (y)ędí know
[(N+)]
dejidwayę:di: we all (incl.) do not know any longer S
degehsęnaę:dí: I do not know its name
[-(h)sęn(a)$_{N}$- name -(y)ędei, (y)ędi$_{V}$- know]

•yędehteʼ emerge unintentionally, come to mind
[P+ contains: -(y)ęde(:,ʼ)$_{V}$- recognize]
aǫyędehteʼ it emerged unintentionally PURP

•(y)ędǫʼ have several things, possessions, bonds
[P+(N+) contains: -(y)ę$_{V}$- lie]
sayę:dǫʼ you own s.t.; your bonds S

•yęʼg(wa) tobacco, cigarettes
[o+]
oyęʼgwaʼ tobacco; cigarettes

•yęʼgwae tan, dry
[de+… -yęʼg(wa)$_{N}$- tobacco, smoke, cigarettes (ʼ)e$_{V}$- hit]
ęhsyęʼgwae:k you will smoke it (meat, etc.); you will tan it P

•yęgwaę(:) be smoky, hazy
[de+… -yęʼg(wa)$_{N}$- tobacco, smoke, cigarettes -ę$_{V}$- lie]
deyoyęgwaę:ʼ it is a smoky, hazy day S

•yęʼgwaǫweh Indian tobacco
[o+ -yęʼg(wa)$_{N}$- tobacco, smoke, cigarettes -ǫweh- traditional, real]
oyęʼgwʼaǫweh Indian tobacco (ceremonial, home-grown and not processed)

•yęhętw, yęhęto pull
[he+/d+]
tgagyęhętwahs I am a puller H
ętgagyęhę:toʼ, ętgatyęhę:toʼ I will pull P
heyagogyęhętwęh she is pulling from there S

•yęhętw, yęhęto retract
[he+…ag+]
hehswagyęhęhtwęh you all retracted S

•yęnaʼd, yanaʼd mark s.t., be an actor, an actress
[ag+]
ǫgyanʼataʼ she is an actress H
ęgya:naʼt I will mark s.t. P
ogyanʼadǫh it is marked S

•yęnaʼtaʼ, yanaʼtaʼ be an actress, an actor, a clown, a performer
[A+ag+ contains: -yęnaʼd, yanaʼd$_{V}$- mark s.t.]
ǫgyanʼataʼ she is an actress H
hagyęnaʼtaʼ he is an actor, a clown, etc. H
gaǫ:gyanaʼtaʼ they (f/m) are performers (for example, figure skaters, actors, etc.) H

•yęhs(a:) bandage
[o+]
oyęhsa:ʼ a bandage

•yęhsa(:,ǫ) bandage (oneself)
[ag+ -yęhs(a)$_{N}$- bandage -(r)ǫ$_{V}$- bead]
sagyęhsaǫ: bandage yourself I

•yęse(:) skin s.t.
syę:sehs you skin animals all the time H
ęhsyę:se:ʼ you will skin (s.t.) P
sayę:se: you are skinning it right now S

•yęhsr(a) blanket
[o+]
oyęhsraʼ blankets

•yęhsrod flag
[ga+ -yęhsr(a)$_{N}$- blanket -od$_{V}$- stand]
gayęhsro:t a flag

•yętw, yęto plant
[(N+)]
gayę:twahs it is planted H
ęknǫhsayę:toʼ I will plant onions P
[(N+) stem: -(ʼ)nǫhs(a)$_{N}$- onion -yętw, yęto$_{V}$- plant]
gayę:twęh a seeded field; it is planted S

•(y)ętw(ahd) broadcast s.t.
[-(r)ih(wa)$_{N}$- word -(y)ętw(ahd)$_{V}$- cause to plant, broadcast]
dęhaihwaętwahs he brings forth the message all the time H
dęshaihwaętwaht he will bring forth a message P
dehshoihwaętwęh he is bringing forth the message right now S

•yętwagw, yętwago harvest
[(N+) contains: -yętw, yęto$_{V}$- plant -gw undo]
hayętwagwahs he is harvesting H
ahayętwa:goʼ he did harvest P
hoyętwagwęh he harvested it S

•yętwahkwaʼ planting tool
[e+ contains: -yętw, yęto$_{V}$- plant -hkwaʼ instrument]
eyętwahkwaʼ a planting tool

•yętwahsǫ(:) garden
[ga+ contains: -yętw, yęto$_V$- plant -sǫ plural]
gayętwahsǫʼ a garden; it is planted
•yid do s.t. right
[de+ contains: -yei, (y)í$_V$- be right, correct]
de̱hsyi:dahs you do things right H
•yoh be an in-law
[TR+]
ǫgya:gyoh my brother-in-law; my sister-in-law S
•yoʼd(a) gums
syʼo̱daʼgeh on your gums
•(ʼ)yohgod tail (of a fish)
[ga+ -(ʼ)yohg(wa)$_N$- tail, skirt -d$_V$- stand]
gayohgo:t a fish tail
•(ʼ)yohg(wa) skirt, tail, feather
oʼyohgwaʼ a skirt; a tail; a feather
gʼayǫhgwʼageh on its (a bird's) tail
•(ʼ)yohg(wa) Avocet blue stocking
[ga+ contains: -(ʼ)yohg(wa)$_N$- skirt, etc.]
gayohgwaʼ an Avocet blue stocking (a bird)
•yoʼg(wa:) cheek
oyoʼgwa:ʼ cheeks
swayoʼgwa:ʼgeh on your (p) cheeks
•yoheg gather
see: (r)oheg [(N+)] gather
gae:yohe:s they (f/m) are gathering H
•(h)yohs(a) elbow
swahyohsʼageh on your (p) elbows
•(h)yohsgwi(n) crawl
[de+…ak+ contains: -(h)yohs(a)$_N$- elbow -in(e)$_V$- go]
desakyo̱hsgwi:neʼ you are crawling H
agyǫkyo̱hsgwi:ʼ she crawled (that is, she learned how to crawl) P
desakyo̱hsgwi: crawl I
•(h)yoʼtiyehd, (h)yuʼtiyehd be sharp
[o+ contains: -(h)y(a)$_N$- blade -oʼtiy$_V$- sharp]
ohyuʼti:yeht, ohyoʼti:yeht it is sharp S
•yoʼts(a) chin
oʼyo:tsaʼ a chin
syʼotsaʼgeh on your chin
•yǫ arrive
e:yǫhs she arrives (at the same time as) H
aʼe:yǫʼ she arrived P
go:yǫ: she has arrived S
•yǫ come in
[d+ contains: -yǫ$_V$- arrive]
itgyǫhs I come in (from the same place) all the time H
daga:di:yoʼ they (z) came in P
dajǫh come in I
•yǫ go in, arrive
[he+ contains: -yǫ$_V$- arrive]
haʼgyǫʼ I went in P
heho:di:yǫ: they (m) arrived, they went in there S
•yǫ go back inside
[he+s+ contains: -yǫ$_V$- arrive]
hǫsaha:yǫʼ he went back inside; he arrived back there P
haʼjǫh, haʼsyǫh go in; enter I
•yǫ return, come back
[s+ contains: -yǫ$_V$- arrive]
sha:yǫʼ he returned P
sho:yǫ: he returned S
•yǫ: discards
[w+ag+ contains: -yǫ$_V$- arrive]
wagyǫ: s.t. thrown away; discards
•yǫʼd bring s.t., score a goal
[contains: -yǫ$_V$- arrive]
aha:yǫʼt he scored; he brought it P
•yǫʼd bring s.t. back
[s+ contains: -yǫ$_V$- arrive]
ęhsgae:yǫʼt they (f/m) will bring it back P
•yǫʼd(a) dead body, cadaver
see: (he)yǫʼd(a) [o+] dead body, cadaver
oyǫʼdaʼ a dead body; a cadaver S

•yǫʼdatgę: be decomposed
[o+ -(he)yǫ(ʼda)$_N$- corpse, cadaver -tgę:$_V$- be rotten]
oyaǫʼdatgę: a state of decomposition S

•yǫdi, yǫgy smile
[P+]
agyǫ:dih I am smiling H
aho:yǫ:diʼ he smiled P
hoyǫgyǫhne:ʼ he has already smiled; he did smile S

•yǫdih opossum, possum
[o+ contains: -yǫdi, yǫgy$_V$- smile]
oyǫdih an opossum

•yǫgyaʼd be amusing, laughable
[o+ contains: -yǫdi, yǫgy$_V$- smile]
oyǫ:gyaʼt it is amusing, laughable S

•yǫgyaʼd laugh, smile
[P+ contains: -yǫdi, yǫgy$_V$- smile]
gyǫgyaʼtaʼ I am really laughing H
ęhsyǫ:gyaʼt you will smile P

•yǫgyatge: guffaw
[P+ contains: -yǫdi, yǫgy$_V$- smile -ge: big]
ęsyǫgyatge: you will laugh loudly, guffaw P

•yǫgyęʼni: have the giggles, smile
[P+ contains: -yǫdi, yǫgy$_V$- smile]
hoyǫgyęni: he is a smiler, a giggler S

•yǫhǫ(:) arrive
[contains: -yǫ $_V$- arrive]
ęgae:yǫhǫ:ʼ they (f/m) will arrive P

•yǫʼse go visit, live with s.o.
[contains: -yǫ $_V$- arrive tsǫ: just]
ęgagyǫsehaʼ I am going to go and visit P
hogyǫʼse: tsǫ: he is a live-in (lit: he's just visiting, living with her) S

•yǫw(a) gut, intestine
[o+]
oyǫ:waʼ guts; intestines

•yǫwadahgw, yǫwadahgo eviscerate
[-yǫw(a)$_N$- guts, intestines -dahgw$_V$- remove]
ęhsyǫwadahgoʼ you will gut s.t. P

•(h)yuʼtiyehd sharp
[o+ -(h)y(a)$_N$- blade -oʼtiy$_V$- be sharp]
ohyuʼti:yeht, ohyoʼti:yeht it is sharp S

•yuʼts(a), yoʼts(a) chin
oʼyo:tsaʼ a chin
swayuʼtsaʼgeh on your (pl.) chins

Legend: H habitual, P punctual, S stative, I imperative, PURP purposive, PURP-H purposive habitual, PURP-PAST purposive past, PURP-P purposive punctual, PURP-I purposive imperative; see §8.6, §8.11 in Appendix J. Alphabetization in stems ignores length (:), and any h's or glottal stops (ʼ) that are not between vowels. See §2.2 of the User Guide for explanation.

Appendix A: Weekdays, Months, Periods of Time

1 MONTHS

January
Ga·ya'da·gó:wah (referring to dolls)

February
Gan·ráh·da̱h·gah (referring to leaves)

March
Ga·nę̨s·gwa·ǫ·tá:'ah (referring to frogs)

April
Ga·nę̨s·gwa·ǫ:ta'go:wah (referring to frogs)

May
Ga·ná'gaht (referring to horns, antlers)

June
Hyá·ikneh (referring to ripe fruit)

July
Hya·ik·neh·gó:wah (referring to ripe fruit)

August
Jíhs·gę̱h·neh (referring to fireflies, grasshoppers, or crickets)

September
Sá'gę̱h·neh (referring to the beginning of the cough season)

October
Sa'gę̱h·neh·gó:wah (referring to coughs)

November
Jo:to:' (referring to cold)

December
Jo:to:'gó:wah (referring to cold)

month
ę̱h·ní'da:' a month, a moon

ę·wa·dę̱h·ní'do'kta:k every month will end

tsa·de·wę̱h·ní·da̱·hę' middle of the month

ę·swę́·ni'·da:' it will be a new month again

ę̱h·ní'da·se:' it is a new month

swę̱h·ní'da:t one month

de·węh·n'idá:ge: two months

wę̱h·ni'da·dé:nyǫ' months

2 WEEKDAYS AND WEEKS

Monday

A·wę·dę·dá'ǫh Monday (lit.: end of the day)

Ę·wę:dę́:da' Monday (future)

Tsa'wę:dę́:da' Monday (past)

Tuesday

Dek·ní: ha·dǫ't Tuesday (lit.: second day)

Dek·ní: ha·dǫ́'tgę̱h·ę:' Tuesday (past)

Wednesday

Ah·sę́h Ha·dǫ't Wednesday (lit.: third day)

Ah·sę́h Ha·dǫ́'tgę̱·hę:' Wednesday (past)

Thursday

Geí: Ha·dǫ't Thursday (lit.: fourth day)

Geí: Ha·dǫ́'tgę̱·hę:' Thursday (past)

Friday

Hwíhs Ha·dǫ't Friday (future) (lit. fifth day)

Hwíhs Ha·dǫ́'tgę̱·hę:' Friday (past)

Saturday

Nak·do·ha·ehs Saturday (lit.: bed washing day)

He·jo·nak·dóh·a·ehs Saturday (future)

Tsi·yo·nak·dóh·a·ehs Saturday (past)

Sunday

A·wę·da·do·gę́:dǫh Sunday (lit.: true or right day)

Ę·ya·ǫ·da·do·gę́h·te' Sunday (future)

Tsi·ya·ǫ·da·do·gę́h·dǫh Sunday (past)

day

ę́:deh daylight; day

wę̱h·níhs·ra·de' this day

wę̱h·nihs·ra·dé:nyo' every day, many days

dwę̱h·nihs·ra·dé:nyǫhk days past

ha'wę̱h·ni̱hs·ra·den·yǫ́:gye' days ahead

da·wę̱h·ni̱hs·ra·ę·dǫ́:gye' the coming days

ęhs·wę̱h·ni̱hs·rá·ę·da' another day (formal language)

tsa'de·wę̱h·níhs·ra̱h·ęh half a day

ah·sę́h nę·yó:da:' three days from now

he·jó·hę'drǫh every other day

today

wa'ne:' today

tomorrow

ę·yó:hę' it will be tomorrow

day after tomorrow

hę·jó:hę' the day after tomorrow

yesterday

té:dę:' yesterday

day before yesterday, other day

gyo·té:dęhk, gyo·té:dęht the other day; the day before yesterday

gyo·te·dę̱hs·hǫ́:'ǫh several days past (an indefinite amount of time)

week

o·yá' deg·ya·dǫ·dá:drehk last week (lit.: between weeks)

shę́h na·deg·ya·dǫ́·da·i: during the week (lit.: between the two Sundays)

Tsa'deg·ya·dǫ·da·í:
tsa'deg·ya·dǫ́·da·de' during the week

sgá:t ę·ya·ǫ:da·do·géh·te' one week

week before last

tsa'deg·ya·dǫ́·dad·rehk week before last

3 PERIODS OF TIME IN THE DAY

half-past

tsa'de·yo̱h·sę:nǫ́' ni·yo·dǫ·góh·dǫh it is half-past the hour

o'clock

oh·wíhs·da'e: o'clock

hwih·shǫ', hwih·shǫ́:'ǫh five-ish (around five o'clock)

sgá:t ę·gah·wi̱hs·dá'e:k it will be one hour, one o'clock

period

shę́h ni·wa·dę̱h·nihs·rí:ne's the time of day

de·wę·dí:ya's it cuts the day (that is, a period of time)

de·węh·ni̱hs·rí:ya's it cuts the day (that is, a period of time)

ha'gáh·e:' the time has arrived

ni·yo·dok·dá:gye's up to these times

ni·ga·há:wi' a period of time

dawn, daybreak

da·wę:dó:dę' dawn, daybreak

morning, brunch

she·de̱h·jí:hah early morning

tsi·shé·de̱h·jih (earlier) this morning

she·deh·ji·hah·né:hah brunch time; mid-morning; early morning

noon

ga·ǫ:hya̱h·ęhs·hǫ́:'ǫh around mid sky

tsi·ga·ǫh·yá·hęh at noon (past)

tsa'de·gá·ǫh·ya̱h·ęh right at noon

evening, tonight

o'gá:s'ah evening

o'ga·se̱h·né:hah eveningish

ęg·yo'gá:hah it will be early night

de·yá'ga:s the night is coming; early night

da·ó'ga̱h·ne' early night is coming

ę·yó'ga: it will be tonight

twilight, dusk

wę·dá:jihs dusk; twilight

night

sǫ́:de' last night

gyo̱h·sǫ́:dehk the other night

ha'dę·wa̱h·sǫ·dá·ę:da' when night has set in, arrived

ah·sǫ́h·eh night

oh·sǫ·dag·wé:gǫh all through the night, all night

ha'de·wa̱h·sǫ́·da·ge: many nights, every night

night (continued)

wah·sǫ·dǫ́:ni: the night is marked (that is, a time has been designated)

ęh·sah·sǫ·dǫ́:ni' you will mark the night (that is, set a time)

midnight

ǫ·dah·sǫ·da:di̲h·áhs·dǫh past midnight

tsa'de·wa̲h·sǫ́:tęh at midnight (lit.: in the middle of the night)

4 SEASONS

summer

gęn·héh·neh summer

dę·yo·gęn·hǫ́:di' it will be summer

fall, autumn

gę·nę·na·géh·neh fall; autumn

winter

go̲hs·réh·neh winter time

tsi·góhs·reh winter past

spring

ga·gwí·de̲h·neh springtime, in the spring

tsi·ga·de̲h·gwí:deh last spring

ga·gwi·de̲h·jí:hah early spring

season

shę́h ni·yot·gę·i:sdǫ̲hǫ:gyé'
de·yo·wá:węn·ye' seasons

dǫ·sa·go·wa:dé:ni' the wind is changing (refers to changing seasons)

de·ga·wa·dé:nyǫhs season

year

ni·yóhs·ra·ge: years

sgá:t dę·wat·wa·dá:se' one year (lit.: it will go around once)

sgá:t e·yóhs·ra:t one year

ohs·ré:dahs year

jo̲h·srá:tshǫ' yearly

Appendix B: Numbers, Money

1	**sgá:t**
2	**dek·ní:**
3	**ah·sę́h**
4	**gé·i:**
5	**hwíhs**
6	**hyé·iʼ**
7	**já:dahk**
8	**deg·rǫʼ**
9	**gyo̲h·dǫ́:**
10	**wa̲h·shę́:**
11	**sgá:t ska·eʼ** (**sgá:t sga̲·heʼ**)
12	**dek·ní: ska·eʼ** (**dek·ní: sga̲·heʼ**)
13	**ah·sę́h ska·eʼ** (**ah·sę́h sga̲·heʼ**)
14	**geí: ska·eʼ** (**geí: sga̲·heʼ**)
15	**hwíhs ska·eʼ** (**hwíhs sga̲·heʼ**)
16	**hye·íʼ ska·eʼ** (**hye·íʼ sga̲·heʼ**)
17	**ja:dáhk ska·eʼ** (**ja:dáhk sga̲·heʼ**)
18	**de·grǫ́ʼ ska·eʼ** (**de·grǫ́ʼ sga̲·heʼ**)
19	**gyo̲h·dǫ́: ska·eʼ** (**gyo̲h·dǫ́: sga̲·heʼ**)
20	**de·wáhs·hę:**
21	**de·wahs·hę́: sga:t**
22	**de·wahs·hę́: dek·ni:**
23	**de·wahs·hę́: ah·sęh**
24	**de·wahs·hę́: gé·i:**
25	**de·wahs·hę́: hwihs**
26	**de·wahs·hę́: hyé·iʼ**
27	**de·wahs·hę́: já:dahk**
28	**de·wahs·hę́: deg·rǫʼ**
29	**de·wahs·hę́: gyo̲h·dǫ:**
30	**ah·sę́h ni·wáhs·hę:**
31	**ah·sę́h ni·wahs·hę́: sga:t**
40	**geí: ni·wáhs·hę:**
50	**hwíhs ni·wáhs·hę:**
60	**hye·íʼ ni·wáhs·hę:**
70	**ja:dáhk ni·wáhs·hę:**
80	**de·grǫ́ʼ ni·wáhs·hę:**
90	**gyo̲h·dǫ́: ni·wáhs·hę:**
100	**sgá:t de·wę́ʼnyʼa·wʼe:**
200	**dek·ní: de·wę́ʼnyʼa·wʼe:**

300 **ah·sę́h na'dew'ęn·yá:w'e:**

400 **ge·í: na'dew'ęn·yá:w'e:**

500 **hwíhs na'dew'ęn·yá:w'e:**

600 **hye·í' na'dew'ęn·yá:w'e:**

700 **ja:dáhk na'dew'ęn·yá:w'e:**

800 **de·grǫ́' na'dew'ęn·yá:w'e:**

900 **gyo̱h·dǫ́: na'dew'ęn·yá:w'e:**

1000 **wa̱h·shę́: na'dew'ęn·yá:w'e:**

once
sgá:t hę·wá:dra:s

twice
dek·ní: hę·wá:dra:s

three times
ah·sę́h hę·wá:dra:s

first
da·wá:gyę:t

first
gyo·gyę́h·dǫh

second
dek·ní: wa·dǫ́'ta'

third
ah·sę́h wa·dǫ́'ta'

last
hes·gá:gǫ:t

1¢, penny
sgag·wén'ida:t one penny, one cent

5¢
hwíhs ni·yo·gwę·ní'da·ge: five pennies

5¢, a nickel
hwíhs·gwę·nihs

10¢, a dime
wa̱h·shę́:gwę·nihs

15¢
hwihs·ga·e·gwę́:nihs

20¢
de·wahs·hę:gwę́:nihs

25¢, a quarter
de·gah·si·ǫ́'trage: twenty-five cents; a quarter (lit.: two bits)

50¢
geí: ni·gah·si·ǫ́'tra·ge: fifty cents (lit.: four bits)

75¢
hyeí' ni·gah·si·ǫ́'tra·ge: 75 cents (lit.: six bits)

$1
sga̱h·wíhs·da:t

$2
de·gah·wi̱hs·dá:ge:

$3
ah·sę́h ni·gah·wi̱hs·dá:ge:

change
gwę·ni̱hs·hǫ́:'ǫh

money
oh·wíhs·da'

Appendix C: Nations, Kin

1 FIRST NATIONS, RACES, NATIONALITIES

Aboriginal

Ǫ·gweh·ǫ́:weh First Nations, Indian people, Aboriginal, Native

O·ya·ji̱·hó:nǫʼ other Indian people; strangers, aliens

African-American

Hah·ǫ́ʼjiʼ Black man

Ahkwesahsne

Og·we·sa̱hs·neh·ó:nǫʼ Akwesasne people

Algonquian

Tsaʼgá:nhaʼ Algonquians (Potawatomi, Odawa, Ojibwe, Chippewa)

see: Delaware

American

Gwahs·dǫ̱h·on·ǫ̱h·geh·ó:nǫʼ

Bear Clan

hah·nya·gwá·i he is Bear Clan

eh·nya·gwá·i she is Bear Clan

ga·eh·nya·gwá·i they (f/m) are Bear Clan

ge̱h·nya·gwá·i I am Bear Clan.

ha·dih·nya·gwá·i ga̱h·sya:deʼ they (m) are Bear Clan

Caughnawaugan

Ga̱h·na·wa·geh·ó:nǫʼ Caughnawaugan (lit.: people living near the rapids)

Cayuga people

Ga·yo·go̱h·ó:nǫʼ Cayuga (lit.: people of the pipe)

Cherokee people

O·yadʼa·geh·ó:nǫʼ

Chippewa see: Algonquian

clan

oʼs·ya:dé:nyǫʼ clans

clan mother

Ho·naʼgá:ʼ eh·a:ʼ clan mother (lit.: she holds his horns)

Delaware

De·wáʼgan·haʼ Delaware; Algonquians living near Six Nations (lit.: s.t. is tied)

Dutch
Oh·wę'gá:' deh·o·nę:so·wé:ksǫ' Dutch (lit.: they (m) wear wooden shoes)

Eskimo see: Inuit

faithkeeper
god·ríh·ǫ:t (she is a) faithkeeper

go·nád·rih·ǫ:t they (f/m) are faithkeepers

ho·nád·rih·ǫ:t they (m) are faithkeepers

hod·ríh·ǫ:t (he is a) faithkeeper; agent

First Nations see: Aboriginal

Five Nations
Hwíhs Ni·yǫh·wę·já:ge: Five Nations (the original Confederacy)

Hawk Clan
ho·dih·sw'ę·gá·i·yo' they are Hawk (Clan)

a·geh·sw'ę·gá·i·yo' I am Hawk (Clan)

go·dih·sw'ę·gá·i·yo' they (f/m) are Hawk (Clan)

Heron clan
De·ga·ǫh·yá·gah·ne:' Great Blue Heron clan

Huron people **Oh·weh·na·geh·ó:nǫ'**

Indian see: Aboriginal

Indian
O·ni·gah·ęhs·rá'
Ho·nǫt·no'á:nhah·węh Indians (from India) (lit.: people who wear turbans)

Inuit
O·to·we·geh·ó:nǫ' Eskimo (lit.: people living in the north)

First Nations see: Aboriginal

Longhouse
ga·e·nǫh·ses·gę·hó:nǫ' they (f/m) are Longhouse people

ha·di·nǫh·ses·gę·hó:nǫ' they (m) are Longhouse people

Ho·di·nǫh·sǫ:ní:dǫh Longhouse People (the hierarchy)

go·di·nǫh·sǫ́:ni: Longhouse people

oh·ę́·dǫh·sǫ' the head ones (Longhouse officials)

Lower End People
Ga·ne·da·geh·ó:nǫ' Lower End People (lit.: people of the valley)

Metis **Deh·o·na·det·gwęh·sá·yęhs·dǫh** Metis (lit.: they have mixed blood)

Mohawk people
Gan·yę'gęh·ó:nǫ' Mohawk (lit.: people of the flint)

moiety
ǫg·wat·nǫh·sóh·dahg·węh our moiety, side; grouped clans, sides

ǫ·gwat·nǫh·só'kda'ǫh our clan, side; our end of the Longhouse

ǫg·yá'sehs·hę' the opposite side (lit.: our cousins)

Native see: Aboriginal

Negro see: Black

Odawa see: Algonquian

Ojibwe see: Algonquian

Oklahoman
Ga̱h·na·wi·yoʼge̱·hó:nǫʼ Oklahoman (lit.: people living near the beautiful rapids)

Oneida people
Oh·nyah·ęh·ó:nǫʼ Oneida (lit.: people of the standing stone)

Onondaga people
O·nǫ·da·geh·ó:nǫʼ Onondaga (lit.: people of the hills)

Oriental
De̱·ho·di·gah·a·dí:yo:t Orientals (lit.: their (m) eyes are stretched)

O.jit·gwáʼ Ni̱·hęh·nó:dę: Orientals (lit.: they have yellow skin)

Osage people
Wa·sah·se̱·hó:nǫʼ

Potawatomi see: Algonquian

Sandpiper clan
Oʼneh·sí:yoʼ

Seneca people
O·nǫ·do·wáʼga:ʼ Seneca (lit.: people of the great mountain)

Sour Spring people
Ga·nǫh·gwat·ro̱h·ó:nǫʼ

Three Fires Confederacy
Ah·sę́h Ho·di·jihs·dá·ę:ʼ Three Fires Confederacy (consisting of the Ojibwe, Potawatomi, and Odawa)

Turtle clan
gen·yáh·dę: I am of the Turtle (clan)

ag·wán·ya̱h·dę: we all are of the Turtle (clan)

Tuscarora people
Dahs·gá·o:węʼ

Tutelo
Ho·nǫh·wę·ja:dó:gę

De·yo·di:hó:nǫʼ

Upper End people
Da·gęh·yat·ge̱·hó:nǫʼ Upper End people (lit.: people living at the top of the mountain)

Wolf clan
ho·tah·yǫ́:ni:
(he is) Wolf clan

a·ga·ta̱h·yǫ́:niʼ
I am Wolf clan

2 KINSHIP TERMS (ENGLISH-CAYUGA)

aunt [-haʼg]
a·gé:haʼk my aunt (old word)

aunt [-noha:ʼah]
ga·ke·no̱h·aʼahs·hǫ́:ǫh my aunts

ho·no:há:ʼah his aunt on maternal side

knoh·á:ʼah my aunt (maternal)

sa·no:há:ʼah your (s) aunt

boyfriend
ǫg·yá:tsih my friend, my boyfriend, my girl friend

see: friend [-(a)tsih]

brother
de·yag·ya·dęh·nǫ́:de:ʼ my brother, my sister

see: sibling [-(a)dęnǫde:ʼ]

brother (older)
heh·jíʼah my older brother

see: sibling (older) [-(h)jiʼah]

brother (younger)
heʼgę́:ʼęh my younger brother

see: sibling (younger) [-(ʼ)gę:ʼęh]

brother-in-law
ǫg·yá:gyoh my brother-in-law, sister-in-law

see: sibling-in-law [-(a)gyoh]

brother's child [-ǫhwadęʼ]
ga·ke·yǫh·wá:dęʼ my brother's children; my nieces and nephews

brother's child [-(a)ʼdawę]
he·yáʼda·węʼ nephew

ke·yáʼda·wę my brother's kids

buddy
ǫg·wa·dá·oʼshǫʼ we all are buddies, friends

see: friend (ceremonial) [-(a)daoʼ]

cousin [-(a)ʼse:ʼ]
ǫg·waʼsé:shǫʼ our cousins (lit.: we all are cousins)

ǫg·yáʼse:ʼ my cousin (lit.: we two are cousins)

ǫg·yaʼsé:ʼshęh our cousins

daughter
keh·á:wahk my daughter

see: offspring [-(h)awahg]

daughter-in-law [-yǫh]
keh·sé:yǫh daughter-in-law

descendant
ga·ke·yad·réʼshǫʼ my grand-children

see: grand-child

father [-(ʼ)nih]
haʼnih my father

hoʼnís·hęʼ he has a father

sa·dę·nih·ó:nǫʼ relatives on your (s) father's side

father-in-law
hak·né:nhǫ:s my father-in-law

see: in-law [-nenhǫs]

friend [-(a)tsih]
go·ná:tsih they (z) are friends

gyá:tsi: Friend (term of address)

ho·ná:tsih his friend; they (m) are friends

ǫg·yá:tsih my friend, my boyfriend, my girl friend

friend (ceremonial friend) [-(a)daoʼ]
o·dá·ot·raʼ friendship

ho·na·dá·oʼshǫʼ they (m) are friends

ǫ·gwa·dá·oʼshǫʼ we all are buddies, friends

ǫg·wá:da·oʼ we all are friends

ǫg·yá:da·o: my ceremonial friend; Friend (term of address)

friend (ceremonial friend) (continued)
a·ga·ǫ·dá·oʼtsę:ʼ they (f/m) became ceremonial friends

girlfriend
ǫg·yá:tsih my friend, my boyfriend, my girl friend

see: friend [-(a)tsih]

godfather
haʼní:hah my godfather

see: father [-(ʼ)nih]

grand-child [-adreʼ]
ga·ké·yad·reʼ my grand-children (said when reckoning a bloodline)

ga·ke·yad·réʼshǫʼ my grand-children

he·yá:dreʼ my grand-son

ke·yá:dreʼ my grand-daughter

grand-daughter
ke·yá:dreʼ my grand-daughter

see: grand-child, descendant [-adreʼ]

grand-father
heh·so:t my grand-father

see: grand-parent [-(h)sod]

grand-mother
ǫ·géh·so:t my grand-mother

see: grand-parent [-(h)sod]

grand-parent [-(h)sod]
e·tíh·so:t our grand-mother

kso:t Grand-mother (term of address; term of respect for an old person)

ha·géh·so:t grand-father

heh·so:t my grand-father

hoh·só:tsęʼ he has a grand-parent

ǫ·géh·so:t my grand-mother

grand-son
he·yá:dreʼ my grand-son

see: grand-child [-adreʼ]

husband
he·gę́h·jih my husband

see: spouse [-gęhjih old (person]

in-law [-nenhǫ:s]
hak·né:nhǫ:s my father-in-law

he·né:nhǫ:s my son-in-law

ǫk·né:nhǫ:s my (a male's) mother-in-law

see:sibling-in-law [-(a)gyoh]

kin
ǫ·dę́·nǫhk·sǫʼ relatives, kin, etc.

see: relative [-nǫhg]

mother [-noha]
knó:haʼ my mother

e·tí·nǫ·haʼ our mother; women

ǫ·dát·nǫh·aʼ her mother

ǫ·kí·nǫ·haʼ our mother

ho·nó:haʼtsęʼ he has a mother

see: aunt

mother-in-law
ǫk·né:nhǫ:s my (a male's) mother-in-law

see: in-law [-nenhǫs]

neighbour
[-nǫhsa- house -kahǫʼ side-by-side]
de·swę·nǫh·sá·kah·ǫʼ your neighbour

swę·nǫh·sa·káh·ǫʼ your neighbours

nephew [-ǫhwadęʼ]
he·yǫ́h·wa:dęʼ my nephew

he·yáʼ·dʼawęʼ nephew

see: brother's child [-(a)ʼdawę]

niece [-(h)awa:kʼah]
keh·a·wá:kʼah my niece (maternal)

ga·geh·e·yǫh·wa:dęʼ my brother's children; my nieces and nephews

see: brother's child [-ǫhwadęʼ]

offspring [-(h)awahg]
heh·á:wahk my son

keh·á:wahk my daughter

relative [-nǫhg]
ag·wa·dę·nǫ́h·ksǫʼ we are relatives

ag·ya:dę́:nǫhk my relative

ke·nǫ́hk·sǫʼ my relatives

ǫ·dę́·nǫhk·sǫʼ relatives, kin, etc.

ǫ·gwa·dę·nǫ́hk·sǫʼ our relatives

sa·dę́:nohk any relative (of yours)

she·nǫ́hk·sǫh (your) relatives

sa·dę·ni̱h·ó:nǫʼ relatives on your (s) father's side

see: father [-(ʼ)nih]

sibling [-(h)nǫde:ʼ]
de·ga·dęh·nǫ́:de: my sibling

de·yag·ya·dęh·nǫ́:de:ʼ my brother, my sister (my nearest sibling)

sibling (older) [-(h)jiʼah]
ho·jíʼaʼ his older sister

keh·jíʼah my older sister

heh·jíʼah my older brother

hǫ·wáh·ji̱ʼah his older brother

ga·keh·jiʼáhs·hǫʼ my older brothers, sisters

keh·jiʼ my older sister (term of address for your relative)

shed·wáh·jiʼah our older brother

sibling (younger) [-(ʼ)gę:ʼęh]
heʼgę́:ʼęh my younger brother

hǫ·wa·gę́:ʼęh his younger brother

keʼgę́:ʼęh my younger sister

sha·goʼgę́:ʼęh his younger sister

sibling-in-law [-(a)gyoh]
go·ná:gyoh their (f/m) or her in-laws

ho·ná:gyoh their (m) in-laws

ǫ·gyá:gyoh my brother-in-law, sister-in-law

sister
de·yag·ya·dęh·nǫ́:de:ʼ my brother, my sister

see: sibling [-(a)dęhnǫde:ʼ]

sister (older)
keh·jíʼah my older sister

see: sibling (older) [-(h)jiʼah]

sister (younger)
keʼgę́:ʼęh my younger sister

see: sibling (younger) [-(ʼ)gę:ʼęh]

sister-in-law
ǫg·yá:gyoh my brother-in-law, sister-in-law

see: sibling-in-law [-(a)gyoh]

son
heh·á:wahk my son

see: offspring [-(h)awahg]

son-in-law
he·né:nhǫ:s my son-in-law

see: in-law [-nenhǫs]

spouse, husband, wife
[-gęhjih old (person)]
he·gę́h·jih my husband

ke·gę́h·jih my wife

step-daughter
ǫk·no:ʼ my step-mother

see: step-relative [-no:ʼ]

step-father
hak·no:ʼ my step-father

see: step-relative [-no:ʼ]

step-mother [-naʼehs]
sa·náʼehs your step-mother

ǫk·no:ʼ my step-mother

see: step-relative [-no:ʼ]

step-relative [-no:ʼ]
hak·no:ʼ my step-father

hehs·no:ʼ your step-son

hǫ·wá:no:ʼ her step-son

ǫ·dá:tno:ʼ her step-daughter

ǫk·no:ʼ my step-mother

she·no:ʼ your step-daughter

step-son
hehs·no:ʼ your step-son

see: step-relative [-no:ʼ]

uncle [-noʼsę]
ga·ké·nʼo·sęh my uncles

ga·ke·nʼo·sęhs·hǫ́:ʼǫh my uncles

hak·nóʼsęh he is my uncle

ho·wánʼo·sęh his uncle

wife
ke·gę́h·jih my wife

see: spouse [-gęhjih old (person)]

3 CAYUGA-ENGLISH KINSHIP TERM PRONOMINAL PREFIXES

[ag- my]
a·gé:haʼk my aunt (old word)

a·gǫ́·gwʼedaʼ my relatives (lit.: my people)

[eti- our relative (female or mixed group)]
e·tíh·so:t our grand-mother

e·tí·nǫh·aʼ our mother; women

[k-, g- my female relative]
knoh·á:ʼah my aunt (maternal)

knó:haʼ my mother

kso:t grand-mother (term of address; term of respect for an old person)

[gadę- my relative (of the same generation)]
de·ga·dęh·nǫ́:de: my sibling

[gadę- my relative (of the same generation)] (continued)
ga·dę́h·nǫhk·sǫʼ my relatives

[gake- my relative(s) (female or mixed group)]
ga·keh·jiʼáhs·hǫʼ my older brothers, sisters

ga·ke·nǫh·aʼahs·hǫ́:ʼǫh my aunts

ga·ke·nǫh·sęhs·hǫ́:ʼǫh my uncles

ga·ke·yǫh·wá:dęʼ my brother's children; my nieces and nephews

ga·keyʼad·réʼshǫʼ my grand-children

[(ya)go- her or their (mixed group) relatives]
go·ná:gyoh their (f/m) or her in-laws

[ha- my father / godfather]
haʼnih my father

haʼníh·aʼ (my) godfather

[hag-, hak- my older male relative]
hak·né:nhǫ:s my father-in-law

hak·nóʼsęh he is my uncle

ha·géh·so:t grand-father

hak·no:ʼ my step-father

[he(y)- my male relative]
heh·so:t my grand-father

he·gę́h·jih my husband

he·yǫ́h·wa·dęʼ my nephew

he·yá:dreʼ my grand-son

heh·jíʼah my older brother

heh·á:wahk my son

he·né:nhǫ:s my son-in-law

heʼgę́:ʼęh my younger brother

he·yáʼdawęʼ nephew

[hehs- your male relative]
hehs·no:ʼ your step-son

[hǫwa- his or her male relative]
hǫ·wa·gę́:ʼęh his younger brother

hǫ·wáh·ji̲ʼah his older brother

hǫ·wá:no:ʼ her step-son

hǫ·wánʼo·sęh his uncle, her uncle

[ho- his relative]
hoʼnís·hęʼ he has a father

hoh·só:tsę: he has a grand-parent

ho·noh·á:ʼah his aunt on maternal side

ho·nóh·aʼtsęʼ he has a mother

ho·jíʼaʼ his older sister

[hon-, hodi- their (males only) relatives]
ho·ná:gyoh their (m) in-laws

[ke- my relative(s) (female or mixed)]
keh·á:wahk my daughter

ke·nǫ́hk·sǫʼ my relatives

ke·yá:dreʼ my grand-daughter

keh·jíʼ·ah my older sister

ke·gę́h·jih my wife

keʼgę́:ʼęh my younger sister

keh·a:wá:kʼah my niece (maternal)

keh·sé:yǫh daughter-in-law

ke·yáʼda·wę my brother's kids

[ǫd- someone's relatives]
ǫ·dę́·nǫhk·sǫ' relatives, kin, etc.

[ǫdat-, ǫdad- her female relative]
ǫ·dát·nǫh·a' her mother

ǫ·dá:tno:' her step-daughter

[ǫg- my female relative]
ǫ·géh·so:t my grand-mother

ǫk·né:nhǫ:s my mother-in-law (only a man can say this)

ǫk·no:' my step-mother

[ǫgwa- our relatives (same generation, belonging to all of us)]

ǫg·wa·dá·o'shǫ' we all are buddies, friends

ǫg·wa:dá·o' we all are friends

ǫg·wa'sé:shǫ' our cousins (lit.: we all are cousins)

[ǫgya- our relatives (same generation, either only two people are involved, or two people are related to the person in question)]
ǫg·yá:tsih my friend, my boyfriend, my girl friend

ǫg·ya:dá·o: my ceremonial friend; Friend (term of address)

ǫg·ya'sé:'shęh our cousins

ǫg·yá'se:' my cousin (lit.: we two are cousins)

ǫg·ya:gyoh my brother-in-law, sister-in-law

[ǫki- our older female relative(s)]
ǫ·kí·nǫ·ha our mother

[sa- your (singular) relative(s)]
sa·noh·á:'ah your (s) aunt

sa·ná'ehs your step-mother

sa·dę·nih·ó:nǫ' relatives on your (s) father's side

sa·dę́:nohk any relative (of yours)

[shago- his female relative(s)]
sha·go'gę́:'ęh his younger sister

[she- your (singular) female relatives]
she·nǫ́hk·shǫh (your) relatives

she·no:' your step-daughter

[shedwa- our (but not your) male relative]
shed·wáh·ji'ah our older brother

[s-hǫwa- the next youngest or oldest sibling]
shǫ·wa·gę́:'ęh the next younger sibling

shǫ·wáh·ji'ah the next older sibling

[swa-, swę- your relatives (belonging to all of you)]
swę·nǫh·sa·káh·ǫ' your neighbours

[(y)agwa- all of our (but not your) relatives]
de·yag·wę·nǫh·sa·né:gę' we all (excl.) are neighbours

ag·wa·dę·nǫ́h·ksǫ' we are relatives (but you aren't)

[(y)agya- our two (but not your) relative; my (but not your) relative]
de·yag·ya·nǫh·sa·né:gę: my neighbour

[(y)agya- our two (but not your) relative; my (but not your) relative] (continued)
de·yag·ya·dẹh·nǫ́:de:ʼ my brother, my sister (lit.: the one nearest to me in age and gender)

ag·ya:dẹ́:nǫhk my relative

4 KINSHIP TERMS ORGANIZED BY GENERATION

grand-parents
gẹhso:t, ǫgéhso:t my grand-mother

hehso:t my grand-father

parent's generation
agé:haʼk my aunt (old word)

knohá:ʼah my aunt

knoʼsẹh, haknóʼsẹh my uncle

knó:haʼ my mother

haʼnih my father

siblings
gakehjiʼashǫ́:ʼ(ǫh) my older siblings

hehjíʼah my older brother

kehjíʼah my older sister

degadẹhnǫ́:drǫʼ my siblings (the ones nearest to me in age and gender)

degadẹhnǫ́:de:ʼ, deyagyadẹhnǫ́:de:ʼ my sibling

heʼgẹ́:ʼẹh my younger brother

keʼgẹ́:ʼẹh my younger sister

cousins
ǫgwaʼsé:ʼshǫʼ my cousins (lit.: we all are cousins)

ǫgyáʼse:ʼ my cousin (lit.: we two are cousins)

children's generation
hehá:wahk my son

kehá:wahk my daughter

kehawá:kʼah my niece (maternal)

gakeyǫhwá:dẹʼ my brother's children; my nieces and nephews

heyǫhwá:dẹʼ my nephew

gakeyaʼdá:wẹh my brother's children

heyáʼdawẹh my nephew

keyáʼdawẹh my brother's kids

grand-children's generation
gakeyadréʼshǫʼ my grand-children

heyá:dreʼ my grand-son

keyá:dreʼ my grand-daughter

5 KINSHIP TERMS OF ADDRESS

Dodama: term of addess for a maternal grand-mother

Doda term of addess for a grand-parent

Doda Grace Great Aunt Grace (term of address for maternal great aunt)

Gyá:tsi: Friend (term of address)

Kẹhso:t, Kso:t grand-mother (term of address; term of respect for an old person)

Kno:há:ʼah my aunt (maternal); term of address

Knó:ha' my mother; term of address

Kno'sęh my uncle (term of address)

Gwadre:' grand-child (term of address said by any old person to a young child)

Sgę:nǫ́: Degyadęhnǫ́:de:' Hello brother / sister! (said by a brother, sister, if they haven't seen each other in a while)

Kehji' my older sister (pet name for your relative)

Ǫgya:dáo:' my ceremonial friend (term of address)

Yahso:t grand-parent, grand-child (term of endearment)

6 IN-LAWS, STEP-RELATIVES, OTHER RELATIVES

in-law

hakné:nhǫ:s my father-in-law

ǫkné:nhǫ:s my mother-in-law (only a man can say this)

ǫgehsé:yǫh my mother-in-law (said by a woman)

ǫgyá:gyoh my brother-in-law, sister-in-law

hené:nhǫ:s my son-in-law

kehsé:yǫh my daughter-in-law

relative

sadęnihó:nǫ' your relatives on your (s) father's side

agǫ́gw'eda' my relatives (lit.: my people)

kenǫ́hksǫ' my relatives

agya:dę́:nǫhk my relative

spouse

hegę́hjih my husband

kegę́hjih my wife

step-relative

ǫkno:' my step-mother

ǫkná'ehs my step-mother

hakno:' my step-father

sheno:' your step-daughter

hehsno:' your step-son

Appendix D: Chiefs' Names

ONONDAGA CHIEFS

Entangled
Ta·do·dá·ho'

The Best Soil Uppermost
Oh·né'dra·ę:'

He Looks Around
Tat·gah·dǫhs

Bitter Throat
Hon·ya'da·jí:wahk

Top of the Water
A·wę́'gęh·ya:t

He Is of Wide Body
Ta·yát·gwa·i:

He Is Out of Sight in Water, He Went Down Current
Ho·no·wi·yéh·dǫh

Her Voice Suspended, Her Voice Scattered
Go·wę·nę'shę́:dǫh

He Is a Spiller, He Is Spilling It
Hah·í:hǫh

He Laid Down a Stick for Him
Ho·wah·nya·yę́·ni:

He Has Bruised Himself
Sho·gwá:sęh

He Is Seeing Them
Sho·gó·gęh·e'
He Has an Axe Placed in Between
Ho'd·ra·há:hǫh

Opposite Side of the Pond, Opposite Side of the Swamp
Sganá·wa·dih

SENECA CHIEFS

Handsome Lake
Sgan·ya·dá·i:yo'

Skies of Equal Length
Tsa'de·gá·ǫh·ye:s

Large Forehead
Sho·gę'jó:wa:'

Threatened
Ga·nó:ga·i:

He Is Falling Over
Nis·ha·yé·nahs

Hold Unto
Sad·yé·na·wahk

Curled Hair
Ga·nǫh·gi:'dá:wi'

Door Partly Open
De·yo·nin·ho·gá:węh

CAYUGA CHIEFS

He Looks Both Ways
Ha·gá'ę:yǫh

Coming on Its Knees
Ga·ji'nǫ·dá·wę·heh

It Is Bruised
Ga·dag·wá:sęh

He Has Long Wampum, He Has a Long Intestine Again
Sho·yǫ́:we:s

He Will Put Bodies One on Top of the Other
Hag·yá'drǫh·ne'

It Touches the Sky
De·yǫh·yǫ́:go:

Double Cold
De·yo·to·wéh·gǫh

Mossy Place
De·yoh·ǫ·wé:tǫ:'

Putting It on Top
Ha·dǫ·dá:heh·a'

Not Sitting on It Any Longer
Dehs·gáh·e:'

MOHAWK CHIEFS

Between the News
De·ga·ih·ó:gę'

He Who Seeks a Wampum Belt, He Who Makes a Wampum Belt
Ha·yę́h·wa·ta'

News Is Different from Another, Two of Same News
Tsa'de·gá·ih·wa·de'

He Is Biggest Tree Top
Sa·ę'hó:wa:'

Double Life, Our Sustenance
Dyǫn·héh·gwęh

Doubtful, High Hill, Wide Branch, Large Flower
A·węh·e'gó:wah

Dragging Horns
Tę·na·gá·i:ne'

Attaching Rattles
Hahs·da·węd·rǫ́:ta'

He Is a Good Woodrift, He Is a Big Branch
Shohs·goh·á·o·wa:'

ONEIDA CHIEFS

Carrying a Quiver Around His Neck or Shoulder
Ho'dáts·heh·de'

Standing Corn Cobs
Ga·nǫh·gwe·i·yó:dǫ'

Open Voice
De·yoh·a'gwę́:de'

He Is of a Longhouse
Sho·nǫ́h·se:s

Shouting Loudly
Had·wę·ná·i:kǫh

He Lowers His Body
Hag·ya'do·nę́h·ta'

It Is Shaking Its Ears
De·wa·dah·ǫh·dę́:dǫhs

Slow-Moving Body
Hon·ya'das·há:yę:

He Is Buried, He Is Dampened
Ho·wat·sa·dę́h·ǫh

MISCELLANEOUS

chief
ha·di·go·wá:nę'̜s they (m) are big; chiefs

ho·di·ya·néh·sǫ' (they (m) are) chiefs

ho·yá:neh (he is) a chief; Confederacy Chief

ho·ya:néh hahs·hę·no·wá:neh chiefs

chief title
ga·ya:né:da chief title

clan mother
Ho·yáne·ta' the chief's clan mother

Go·yá:neh clan mother

Divided Body
De·o'ja'já'gǫh (a chief's name)

funeral (for a chief)
a·ga'hnyé:nę' something fell over; the passing of a chief (high language)

a'ǫg·wa'hnyé:nę's we all are experiencing the passing of a chief

Pine Tree Chief
Hǫ·wah·nyoh·so·dá:hǫh Pine Tree Chief

subchief
Hǫ·wa·ǫ·dá:nǫh, Há·ǫ·da·nǫh He Is the Watcher of the Log; a subchief

Appendix E: Place Names

Ahkwesahsne Territory (includes Cornwall, Ont., St. Regis, N.Y.)
Gwé·sa̲hs·neh, O·gwé·sa̲hs·neh (lit.: where partridges live)

Albany, N.Y.
Sga·nę·dá:dih (lit.: beyond the pine; on the other side of the pine)

Allegheny, N.Y.
O·hí:yoʼ (lit.: nice flowing stream)

Ancaster, Ontario
see: Mohawk Valley, N.Y.

Brantford, Ont.
Tga·na·da̲·há·e:ʼ (lit.: where the town sits up on top of the hill)

Buffalo, N.Y.
Kyod·ró:wę:, Gyod·ró:wę: (lit.: where there is a split fork)

Burlington, Ont.
Deg·yoʼne̲h·sáh·ǫh (lit.: where the sand banks are)

Caledonia, Ont.
Tga·ná·da·ę:ʼ (lit.: there the town lies)

Canada
Ca·na·dag·wá:dih, Ka·na·dag·wá:dih the Canadian side

Os·wé:gęʼ This word refers to the town of Ohsweken on Six Nations Reserve; it also refers to Six Nations and to Canada

see: Six Nations Reserve, Ont.

Cattaraugus, N.Y.
Ga·da:gráhs·gę·hę:ʼ Cattaraugus (lit.: where it smelled like mud)

De·yo·ya·dá·ęʼ No Ditch, Cattaragus

Sgi·hę́:dih Pinewoods, Cattaraugus (lit.: alongside the river)

O·nę́ʼda·gǫ: Pinewoods, Cattaraugus (lit.: under the pine woods)

Ga·ná·da·se:ʼ Newtown, Cattaraugus (lit.: new town)

Caughnawaga, Que., Kahnawake, Que.
Ga̲h·ná·wa·geh (lit.: on the rapids)

Cayuga, Ont.
Ni·ga·naʼjú:ʼuh (lit.: small pail)

Cold Spring, N.Y.
Gyoh·né·ga·no: (lit.: cold water there)

Cornplanter Reserve, Pennsylvania
Ga·yę́t·wa̱h·geh Cornplanter Reserve, near Warren, Pennsylvania (lit.: where it is planted)

Cornplanter Reserve (continued)
Gyo·nǫh·sa·dé:geh a place on Cornplanter Reserve (lit.: the house burnt there)

Cornwall, Ont
see: Ahkwesahsne

Deseronto, N.Y.
Ta·yę·da·né:gę' (lit.: firewood side-by-side there)

Dunnville, Ont.
Det·gah·ne·gah·a'gó:wah (lit.: where the big dam is)

England
Gwa·gó·wa̱h·neh (lit.: where the queen is)

Europe
Sgan·ya·da:di·gó:wah (lit.: across the ocean)

Ǫh·wę·ja·gá·yǫ̱h·neh (lit.: the old country)

Gibson Reserve, Ont.
Wáh·ta' (lit.: maple tree)

Grand River
Gi·hę'go·wáh·neh (lit.: to the big river)

Hagersville, Ont.
Tga·nę·no·gá·he:' (lit.: a hickory log is across)

Hamilton, Ont.
Ga̱·hę́·na·gǫ: (lit.: in the bay)

Jarvis, Ont.
see: York, Ont.

Jordan, Ont.
Dwa̱h·yá·yęt·węh (lit.: fruit is planted there)

Kahnawake, Que.
see: Caughnawaga

Kanesatake, Que., Oka, Que.
Ga·neh·sa·dá:geh (lit.: on the sand)

Kingston, Ont.
Det·gah·nyǫ̱h·sráh·dǫ' (lit.: where there is a jail, or standing bars)

Lake Ontario
see: Ontario

Long Lake, N.Y., Skaneateles, N.Y.
Sga·nyá·da·es (lit.: long lake)

Longhouses
Ga·ne·da·gǫ́: ga·nǫ́h·se:s Lower Cayuga Longhouse

Ga·nǫh·gwa'tró' ga·nǫ́h·se's Upper Cayuga Longhouse

De·wa'ga·géh ga·nǫ́h·se:s Seneca Longhouse

Da·ge·ga·géh ga·nǫ́h·se:s Onondaga Longhouse

Mohawk Territory
Gan·yę'geh·ó·nǫ̱h·geh any Mohawk territory

Mohawk Valley, N.Y., Ancaster, N.Y.
Tga·ná'jǫ̱h·a:' (lit.: pot attached to something)

New York, N.Y.
Ga·nǫ́:nyo' (lit.: expensive)

Niagara Falls
Tga̲h·ná·wę̱h·ta', Ga̲h·ná·wę̱h·ta' (lit.: a waterfall flows there)

Niagara-on-the-Lake, Ont.
Tga·na̲h·wá·i:'

Ohsweken, Ont.
Gye̲h·ahs·hę·dáh·kwa' This word is used locally to refer to Ohsweken, Ont. (lit.: counselling place)

see also: Six Nations Reserve, Ont.

Oka, Que.
see: Kanesatake, Que.

Oklahoma
Ga̲h·na·wi·yó'geh (lit.: place of the beautiful rapid)

Oneida, N.Y.
O·nę́·yot·ga:' Oneida people; Oneida, New York (lit:. standing stone)

Oneida, Ont.
Oh·nyá·hęh Oneida, Ontario (lit.: dry stick)

Onondaga, Ont.
O·nǫ́n·da·geh, O·nǫ́·da·geh (lit.: on the hill)

Ontario, Lake Ontario
Ga·nya·dá·i·yo' (lit.: beautiful lake)

Ottawa, Ont.
Tga·ya'da·gwę·ni·yó'geh (lit.: leading place)

Philadelphia, PA
Tga·na·da·ę'gó:wah (lit.: big town lying there)

Pittsburgh, PA
De·yo·ha·téh·sǫ' (lit.: bright things here and there)

Sandy's Road
De·yo·yę·gwá:kęh (lit.: smokes are joined)

Six Nations Reserve, Ont., Ohsweken, Ont.; Canada
Os·wé:gę' This word refers to the town of Ohsweken on Six Nations Reserve; it also refers to Six Nations and to Canada

Hye·í Ni·yǫh·wę·já:ge: Six Nations

Da·gęh·ya·tó:no' Upper End People

Ga·ne·da·ge·hó:nǫ' Lower End People

Da·gę́h·ya:t Upper End (lit.: top of the mountain)

Ga·né·da·geh Lower End (lit.: in the valley)

Ga·nǫ́hgw'at·ro' Sour Springs (lit.: medicine in the water there)

Skaneateles, N.Y.
see: Long Lake, N.Y.

St. Catharines, Ont.
Deg·yot·nǫh·sá:kdǫ: (lit.: a crooked house there)

St. Regis, N.Y.
see: Ahkwesahsne

Tonawanda, N.Y.
Tah·na·wá:de' (lit.: rapids exist there)

O'néh·sa·gǫ: In the Sand (a place near Tonawanda, N.Y.)

Toronto, Ont.
Tgá·ǫ:do' (lit.: log in the water)

Tuscarora, N.Y. (near Lewiston, N.Y.)
Dahs·ga·o·wę́ʼ(geh) (lit.: place of split stone)

Tyendinaga, Ont.
Det·ga·yędáne·gęʼ, Ta·yę·dané:gęʼ (lit.: land of two logs)

United States
Gwahs·dǫ·hó·nǫh·geh

De·yoh·wę·jah·kah·sǫ́·gwah·nǫʼ states (in the United States)

Warren, PA
Ga̱h·ná·wa·gǫ: (lit.: in the rapids)

Washington, D.C.
Ha·na·da·gán·ya̱hs·geh (lit.: place of the President or Destroyer of Towns)

York, Ont., Jarvis, Ont.
Tga·gwę́:troʼ (lit.: silt in the water)

Appendix F: Traditional and Ceremonial Language

1 HIGH LANGUAGE

accomplish a task
ah·a·ih·wá:is he accomplished or completed a task (for example, a speech); he carried out a responsibility

amulet
go·yá'da·nǫh amulet (lit.: her amulet)

charm society, charm
O·tsi·nǫh·gę́'da'

consensus
sga·íh·wa:t one mind (said when consensus is reached in the High Council); one idea

consider
ę·gát·gǫ·drahk I will sleep on it, consider it

cookhouse
Ǫt·gah·dęhs·dáh·kwa'geh Cookhouse

gahs·dǫ́h·gwa·ge: Cookhouse

ga·nǫh·sá·ǫ:weh the cookhouse (at the Longhouse)

sa·dáh·gahs·dǫ: go and cook in the cookhouse (lit.: endure)

ę·ga·ǫ·dáh·gahs·dǫ: go and cook in the cookhouse (lit.: they (f/m) will endure)

death
ę·sa·tah·í:t'a:' you will earn the heavenly road

a'ǫ·tah·í:t'a' she went on the heavenly road (refers to a woman who is done with this world)

de·ja·gǫh·wíhs·ra:t she no longer has breath; she's dead

die out
a·wa·dri̱h·wáh·dǫ' it died out, faded away (an idea)

a·ga·ih·wáh·dǫ' it became extinct, died out (this is an old word)

dę·ga·ih·wa·gǫ́:dǫ:' it will smother itself, die out slowly on its own, peter out (for example, a language at a critical state)

ta:ga·ih·wa·gǫ́:dǫ:' (it) smothered, died out slowly on its own, petered out

a·ga·ih·wa·gǫ́:dǫ:' it died out (high language)

forsake

ǫg·wát·sǫʼnyo:t we all turned our backs to the bush; we all forsook religion, family, etc. (high language)

funeral

ah·a·yag·yé:nęʼ he fell over (refers to passing on)

aʼǫg·waʼhnyé:nęʼs we all are experiencing the passing of a chief

ę·hǫ·wa·dí·nǫh·da: there will be a funeral for him (lit.: they will put him in)

de·yǫt·nǫh·sǫ́:goht she will go by the Longhouse (funeral)

ę·sat·gah·óh·a:t you will cleanse your eyes with something (that is, wash death off of you before or after a funeral so nothing will happen to your baby)

oʼwahs·dǫ·dáh·kwaʼ the little sticks they make for a funeral ceremony

deh·a·dihs·da:téʼdah·kwaʼ wax for the sticks

honour

ah·a·yęg·wah·sǫ́:nyeht he honoured them with tobacco

hoop

węʼnihs·ga·ní:yǫ:t a hanging hoop

węʼníhs·ga·ę:ʼ a hoop (lying down)

węʼníhs·ga:ʼ, ęʼníhs·ga:ʼ a circle hoop; a wheel

invitation

aʼǫ·ki·nę́:tsa:ʼ a nation-to-nation invitation (preceded by a speech; high language)

Longhouse

Ga·nǫ́h·se:s Longhouse

Ga·nǫh·sé:sǫʼs Longhouses

man

ho·dihs·gęʼá·gęh·dah men (high language)

marry

sha·go·di:h·wah·ní·ya·dǫh they got married by the Chiefs; marriage ceremony sanctioned by the Chiefs

message

Ga·ih·wa·weh·tá:hǫh (any) inserted message

ę·ha·teh·náht·gęh·da:t he will carry a large load or bundle; he will carry a message

ę·héh·nǫn·yęʼ I will put a load on him, put a bundle on him (that is, give him a message to convey)

ę·hǫ·wa·dih·eh·nǫ́:nyęʼ they will make him a load or bundle to carry; they will send him with a message

rattle

gahs·dáwʼęd·raʼ rattle; horn rattle

o·wa·jihs·dáʼ gahs·dáwʼęd·raʼ bark rattle

ǫ·tǫ·wi·sa·dah·kwáʼ gahs·dáwʼęd·raʼ box turtle rattle

o·naʼgá:ʼ gahs·dáwʼęd·raʼ horn rattle

ok·dáʼ gahs·dáwʼęd·raʼ nut rattle; shell rattle

ga·nyah·dę·go:wáh gahs·dáwʼęd·raʼ snapping turtle rattle

rattle (continued)
oh·nyoh·sa·ǫ:wéh ga̱hs·dáw'ęd·ra' squash rattle

ga·ihs·dá' ga̱hs·dáw'ęd·ra' tin rattle

ga·nyah·dę́: ga̱hs·dáw'ęd·ra' turtle rattle

recognize
de·ye·ti·nǫ́h·ǫh·kwa' we refer to them as (something)

des·hed·wa·nǫ́h·ǫh·kwa' we refer to him as

dę·ga·ke·nǫ́h·ǫh·kwa:k I will recognize them as my kin

ded·wa·nǫh·ǫ́h·kwa' we all (incl.) refer to it as

righteous
o·ya'da·wá:dǫh a righteous person

speech
de·yo·ih·wa·do·gę́h·dǫh a shortened speech

tidy up
de·sa·da·déhs·nyeh groom yourself; prepare yourself mentally

2 BETTING

betting
hah·sah·e'dá:gwahs he picks out the beans (for a game)

shę·dá·ę you lay the field (take bets)

ę·yǫ·de·sah·e'da·nǫ́:na:' she will be the bean watcher

collect bets
há·oh·e:s he collects the bets; he gathers

Dish Game
Oh·ę́:da' the field (of Iroquois origin only; refers to the Dish Game)

Indian bone dice
de·yǫ·dets·gę'ih·dréh·da̱h·kwa'

Thrower of Sticks
heh·o'ę·nǫ́:gye's

win a throw
a'eh·ę·dá·ę:' she won the throw (when all the stones come up the same)

a'eh·ę·da·ę·dǫ́:nyǫ:' (she won the throw) repeatedly, one right after the other (refers to a betting game and a perfect score)

ah·ah·ę·dá·ę:' they (m) won the throw in a betting game

3 CEREMONIES

All Eaten Up
Gah·sǫ:' (restricted ceremony for charms)

Clean Up
De·yak·wet·nǫ́h·sǫ·ta' (ceremony)

Devil Dance
Ga'no·gę·yǫ:' Grinding the Arrow (forbidden ceremony)

Eagle Feather
Ga·nré'a' Eagle Feathers (for making friends; the one who asks for the friendship holds the feathers)

False Face
Ga·jíh·sa' Husk Face; False Face

Finish Planting

Go·tę·dihs'án·hǫ' (ceremony)

Four Main Ceremonies

Ga·yę·do·wá:nęh Peach Pit Game

Ge·í: Ni·wah·sǫ·dá:ge: Four Nights Ceremony (part of Sustenance dances or **ga·ę·nah·sǫ́:'ǫh**)

Ge·í: Ni·yo·ih·wá:ge: Four Ceremonies

ah·a·dǫ́:dę' men's chant; he is singing adǫ́:wa'

hę·na·dǫ·wíh·sręh·ta' they are accompanying adǫ́:wa' (singing he' he' he')

Ga·yę·do·wa:nę́h Ga.ję' Peach Pit Dish game

Ohs·do·wa·gó:wah Great Feather Dance

Sdá·ohs Great Feather Dance

Ga·néh·ǫ:' Drum Dance

Gathering of Fruit, Strawberry Ceremony

A·dah·yá·oh·ǫ:' Gathering of Fruit Ceremony (done during the Strawberry Ceremony)

Gathering of the Sugar

Ęd·wa·na·wę'dá·oh·e:k Gathering of the Sugar Ceremony (done during Drying Up the Trees)

Green Bean Ceremony

Ę·hę·na·deh·sah·e'dá·oh·e:k (lit.: they (m) gather the green beans)

Husk Face

Ga·jíh·sa' Husk Face, False Face

Maple Sap Ceremony

Ha·dit·sehs·dǫ́:da:s (lit.: they (m) are putting the sap in the tree)

O·deh·a·dǫ́:ni: Maple Sap Ceremony; woods (trees)

Ę·ha·di·ya·ǫ·dá:ta't Drying Up the Trees Ceremony (ceremony done at the ending of the maple sap run)

Sha·di·yá·ǫ·da·ta' Dry Up the Trees (ceremony done at the end of the maple sap run)

Ots·hes·da·dǫ́:da:s Tree or Sap Dance

Medicine Mask

O.jihs·gwa·gwáh·a' (Seneca ceremony; lit.: they come after their mush)

Midwinter

Ga·nah·á·o·wi:' Midwinter Ceremony

Ga·ih·wa·nǫhs·gwa'gó:wah, Ga·ih·wa·nahs·gwa'gó:wah Midwinter Ceremony

Ho·di·nah·á·o·wih they (m) are having the Midwinter Ceremony

Ę·yǫg·wa·nah·á·o·wi' we all will have the Midwinter Ceremony

Ǫ·gwa·nah·á·o·wih we all are having the Midwinter Ceremony

Tsa'de·gohs·ráh·ęh Ga·ih·wa·yá·ǫ·ni: Midwinter Ceremony

ę·ta·di·na'dá:gwah·e' The Corn Husk Mask society will come after their (m) bread

dę·ta·di·jih·gwa·gwáh·e' they (m) will come back for their mush (said of False Faces)

Moon Ceremony
Ah·sǫh·eh·ká: E·tíh·so:t Moon Ceremony

Ęs·ha·go·di·wę·nǫ:góht Ah·sǫh·eh·ká:ʼ Ęh·níʼdag·yeʼs
Moon Ceremony (lit.: uplifting the stature of the moon)

dę·ya·goʼnya:gwę́·hę·gyeʼ she will have a hand in it

Our Uncles Ceremony
E·ti·noʼsę́h Ę·hę·nat·noʼá·o:wa·naht Our Uncles Ceremony (lit.: they (m) become bigheads)

Shake Pumpkin Ceremony
Ga̲h·í·dǫh·ǫ: Shake Pumpkin Ceremony

Hę·nah·iʼdóhs Ho·dihs·da·węʼdráʼ ah·sę́h sga·éʼ ni·yo·dihs·yá:ge Shake Pumpkin Rattle Ceremony; there are thirteen types

Hę·náh·iʼdohs Gourd Society Dance (part of Shake Pumpkin)

Ga̲h·a·di·yáʼgǫʼ Crossing the Forest Song (goes with Shake Pumpkin; restricted)

Sun Ceremony
Ę·hǫ·wa·di·wa·nǫ:góht Ę·deh·ge̲h·á:ʼ Gá:gwa:ʼ Sun Ceremony

Thanksgiving Ceremony
Ga·nǫ́h·ǫn·yǫhk

Thanksgiving Opening
Oh·ę·dǫ́: Ga·ih·wa̲h·deh·gǫ́h Ga·nǫ́h·ǫn·yǫhk

Thunder Ceremony
Hǫ·wa·di·wę·nǫ·goh·táʼ Ha·di·wę·nó·dag·yeʼs

White Dog Feast
Ga·ní·yǫ·dǫʼ White Dog Feast (lit.: a lot of them are hanging there)

4 GAIHWI:YO:

Gaihwi:yo:
Ho·na·de·jíhs·da·ne:t Fire Keepers

Ho·de·ji̲hs·dá:ne:t Fire Keeper

Ęh·se·ji̲hs·táʼdraʼ you will go with the fire (refers to going to the **Gaihwi:yo:** convention)

ah·ǫ·wa·dih·sa̲h·ǫ́:dęʼ they committed him to the main fire (refers to sending a delegate to the **Gaihwi:yo:** convention)

Ga·jihs·da·gwę·ní:yoʼ the Main Fire

Handsome Lake
Sgan·ya·dá·i·yo: Handsome Lake

Dǫ·sah·a·ih·wá·ęt·waht He Who Seeded the News; He Who Spread the News (refers to Handsome Lake)

He Breaks the Wires
Deh·ah·sǫ·wáhg·yaʼs He Breaks the Wires (Handsome Lake's nephew)

5 GAMES

Bowl Game, Dish Game
Ga·ję́ʼge̲h·a:ʼ

Dingball, Double Ball Game
De·węʼnhot·rá·na̲h·sǫ:t (a medicine game)

Door Keepers' Dance

De·yǫhs'idá·dih·ahs (a medicine dance; lit.: every other step dance; the Hado'i:s also dance this with their grandchildren)

Ho·na·den·hoh·at·gáh·a:' they (m) are the Keepers of the Door (referring to the Mohawks)

Football

Wę́·sęh·twahs football (a medicine game)

Hoop and Javelin Game

Ja·ga:wé:nih

Horseshoes, Moccasin Game

A·tę·nah·dáh·gwa·ę:' they (m) played horseshoes (a game); the moccasin game

Snowsnake

Gah·ne·gá:hǫh head lead on a stick (a snowsnake term)

Ha·di·yęh·dáh·kwa' Pitch Hole

6 MEDICINE

Football

Wę́·sęht·wahs (a medicine game)

Great Black Leaves

On·rah·da·ji'gó:wah (medicine)

Great Distorted Root

Ok·deh·at·gi'gó:wah (medicine)

Grinding Dishes

Gak·sa·gá:nye:' (medicine ceremony)

Love Medicine

O·nǫ́h·weht (restricted)

Tug O' War

Dę·ha·dih·nyó:da:s they (m) are having a tug o' war (a ceremony or healing ritual)

A·ta·dih·nyó:da: they (m) had the tug o' war

7 SONGS

o·nę́h di' o·wa·ę·na·gá·e: let the song begin

hehs·ga·ę·ná:gǫ:t the last song

ęd·wa·ę·na·gé:tsgo' we all (incl.) will raise the song

Ga·ę·na·weh·tá:hoh an inserted song

ęhs·wa·ę·ná·gan·ye: you all will sing

ah·a·ę·ná·gan·ye: he chanted, he trilled the music

ę·ha·ę·ná·gan·ye' he will trill the song

ha·ę·na·gá:nyeh he is trilling the song

earth songs

Oh·wę·ja·geh·geh·á:' Ga·ę:na·shǫ́:'ǫh

Roll Call Chant

A·ta·da·dí:trahk Roll Call Chant (lit.: He Picked Up The Cane)

see: §8, §13.1

8 SOCIAL DANCES AND SONGS

Standing Quiver Dance

Ga·dá:tro:t

Moccasin Dance

Ga·yó:wah

Old Moccasin Dance
Ga·yo·wa·gá:yǫh

Robin Dance
Jihs·go·goʼg̱eh·a:ʼ

Duck Dance
Twę·twę́t·g̱eh·a:ʼ

Alligator Dance
De·gaʼnǫ·dǫ́t·g̱eh·a:ʼ

Pigeon Dance
Tsah·go·waʼg̱eh·a:ʼ

Raccoon Dance
Sa·no·g̱eh·a:ʼ

Chicken Dance
Daks·ha·eʼdohs·g̱eh·a:ʼ

One Side Male Dance, Male Dance
Ęhsga:nyé:ʼ Sga·di·ga·jí:nah
De·yéh·nyo·taʼ (a dance or ceremony done with a paternal cousin, uncle, etc.)

Sga·di·ga·jí:nah (a social dance done with a paternal cousin, uncle, etc.)

Sharpened Stick Dance
Waʼę·no·tí:yǫʼ

Ferrying Dance
Ǫ·da·d̲eh·nyóh·aʼ

Naked Dance
Daʼnus·daʼg̱eh·a:ʼ

Shake The Bush Dance
Gahs·goh·á·ǫ:ʼda·dǫʼ

Gartered Dance
Ot·sín·hah·ǫʼ

Women's Old Shuffle Dance
Ęs·ga:nyé:ʼ Ga·ę·na·gá·yǫ̱h·ka:ʼ

Women's New Shuffle Dance Song
Ęhs·ga:nyé:ʼ Gá·ę·na·se:ʼ

Northern Dance
O·to·we·géh·a:ʼ

Cherokee Stomp Dance
O·ya·da·géh·a:ʼ

Rabbit Dance
Gwaʼyǫ́·g̱eh·a:ʼ

Delaware Skin Dance
Ga·néhwʼa·e:ʼ

Round Dance
Ǫt·wa·da·séʼtaʼ

Friendship Dance
De·yǫ·dat·nǫh·ǫn·yǫ́ʼd̲ah·kwaʼ (a social dance; a welcoming dance)

Standing Quiver Dance
Ga·dá:tro:t

Changing Rib Tumbling Dance
O·dehs·wa·dé:nyo:ʼ

see: §9, §10, §13.2

9 RESTRICTED DANCES

Dark Dance
De·yo·d̲ah·sǫ·dá·e·gǫh (for the Little People; restricted)

Devil Dance
De·yǫ·da·nę́t·sǫ·taʼ Linking Arm Dance (forbidden dance)

Devil Dance (continued)
Ga·na'jit·gę́·hǫh Taking Out Kettle (forbidden dance)

Ga·jí·ha·ya' Taking out the Cork (forbidden dance)

10 MISCELLANEOUS DANCES

Big Dance; Creator's Dance
Ga·nǫn·yo·wá:nęh

Big Green Corn Dance
Gah·ko·wa:nah

Fishing Dance
Ǫ·da·dęh·nyóh·a'

Great Leather Dance
Ohst·nǫ́h·sǫ·ta'

Harvest Dance
Deh·ę́:gwis

Medicine Dance
A·wa·da·núk·da·nǫ: (a Seneca dance)

Shaking the Bottle
Ga·di·tse'dǫ́d'adǫ'

Small Green Corn Dance
O·dag·woh·óh Ni·ga·kwá:'ah

Strike the Stick, Little Horses Dance
O·wę́'na·ę:'

Thunder Ceremony, Rain Dance, War Dance
Wa·sá:seh War Dance (of the Osage); Rain Dance; Thunder Ceremony

Ho·nę́·ni'je: they (m) are doing the War Dance

Women's Dance
Ęs·gá:nye:' (lit.: shuffling feet)

11 CURING DANCES

Bear Dance
Hnya·gwá·i:'gęha:'

Buffalo Dance
De·yo·di·na'gá·ǫ·dǫ'

Eagle Dance, Strike the Stick
Ga·ne'gwá:'e:', Gan·re'gwá:'e:'

Rain Dance, War Dance
Wa·sá:seh War Dance (of the Osage); Rain Dance

Little Horses Dance
Wa'ę́n'a·e:'

Women's Old Shuffle Dance
Ęs·ga:nyé:' Ga·ę:na·gá·yǫh·ka:'

12 SACRED SOCIETY DANCES

Dress-up Society Dance
Ǫ·dę·ya'dahs·rǫ́:nih (a Tutelo Ceremony)

Ghost Society Dance
Oh·gí:we: (takes place in spring and fall; but only in fall at Sour Springs)

Gourd Society Dance
Hę·náh·i'dohs Gourd Society Dance (part of Shake Pumpkin)

13 SUSTENANCE DANCES AND SONGS

Four Nights Ceremony
Ge.í: Ni.wah.sǫ.dá:ge: Four Nights Ceremony (part of Sustenance dances or gaęnahsǫ́:ˀǫh)

Seed Blessing Ceremony
Dęd.wa.nah.a.ǫg.wę́t.ra.ęˀ Seed Ceremony
De.ye.ti.yaˀtah.ah.gwá:dęˀ Seed Ceremony (lit.: we will walk the seeds)

13.1 SUSTENANCE SONGS

Ga.ę:naˀsǫ́:ˀah, Ga.ę:naˀsǫ́:ˀǫ́h songs, songs for Our Sustenance

Gyon.heh.gǫ́h o.di.á.ę:naˀ Sustenance songs

A.tǫ:wí:sę:ˀ Seed Blessing Songs

ę.ga.ǫ.tǫ́:wi:s they (f/m) will sing the seed songs (also used as lullabies)

ǫ.tǫ:wí:sas Seed Songs (for women)

Gyǫn.heh.gǫ́h o.di.yá.ę.naˀ what we all (incl.) live on; Our Sustenance; Women's Old Shuffle Dance Song

13.2 SUSTENANCE DANCES

Corn Dance, Song
O.nę.hę́:ˀ **o.di.á.ę:na**ˀ Corn Dance or Song

Bean Dance
O.sah.eˀdáˀ **o.di.á.ę:na**ˀ

Four Nights Ceremony
Ge.í: Ni.wah.sǫ.dá:ge: (part of Sustenance dances or gaęnahsǫ:ˀǫh)

Squash Dance
Ohn.yǫh.sáˀ **o.di.á.ę:na**ˀ

Women's Old Shuffle Dance
Ęs.ga:nyé:ˀ **Ga.ę:na.gá.yǫh.ka:**ˀ

14 IMPORTANT AND MYTHICAL FIGURES

Corn Bug
O.nę́.hęt.gǫˀ (a bug with evil power)

Creator
Shǫg.wayˀa.díhsˀǫh he is the Creator (of our bodies)

Death
Oh.sǫ.do.wah.gó:wah Angel of Death, Spirit of Death (lit.: the big blackness)

Devil
Ha.wę:ní:yo: the Devil's own name for himself (lit.: he has good words; you can hear this in Gaihwi:yo:)

Ga.jí.ha.yaˀ the devil

Sha.goh.e.wáh.taˀ The Punisher (the Devil)

Dry Fingers (legendary figure)
Oˀnyá:tę:

Exploding Wren (legendary figure)
De.wat.nǫh.só:węhs

Great Bear (legendary figure)
Hnya.gwa.iˀgó:wah

He Hits With A Head (legendary figure)
Sha·go·nǫ:ʼa·ę̨ʼyę́h·taʼ

He Paddles or Ferries People (legendary figure)
Sha·go·ga·wé:haʼ

He Takes Out People's Feces (legendary figure)
Sha·go·dá:da̲hg·wahs

Little Dry Hand (legendary figure)
Oh·soh·da·tę́:ʼah

Little People
Ji·gáh·ęh the Little People

Peacemaker
Ho·nǫh·so·ní:dǫh the Peacemaker (lit.: He Strengthens the Longhouse; refers to the Creator's Messenger for the Great Law)

Punisher, Devil
Sha·goh·e·wáh·taʼ The Punisher (the Devil)

Red Jacket
Sha·go·yeh·wáh·taʼ Red Jacket

Sharp Legs (legendary figure)
Oh·si·na·tí:yeht

Stone Giant (legendary figure)
Ga·néh·wa:s

Thunderers
Ha·di·wę·nó·da·gyeʼs

White Beaver (legendary figure)
Na·gá·nya·gę:t

Appendix G: Government and Business

Aboriginal Affairs
Ǫg·we·hǫ·wéh O·ih·wa·géh·sǫ'
[Ǫgwehǫ:weh First Nations people Oihwagehsǫ' affairs, statistics]

Aboriginal Trappers' Federation
Ǫg·we·hǫ·wéh Ho·nę·nig·yohg·wa·ę́' Hę·nad·ri̱hs·dá·ę·hę'
[Ǫgwehǫ:weh First Nations people honęnigyohgwaę' their (m) crowd, group, association hęnadri̱hsdaęhę' they (m) are trappers]

Aboriginal Education Council
Ǫg·we·hǫ·wéh Ga·i·hǫn·yá:ni:' Hę·nág·ye̱·hę'
[Ǫgwehǫ:weh First Nations people gaihǫnyę:ni:', gaihǫnya:ni:' it teaches hęnagye̱hę' they (m) do it]

administer
ha·di:h·wa·hę́:de' an administration (lit.: they (m) administer)
[-(r)ihwahęde' administrate]

ha·ih·wa·hę́:de' he is an administrator

e·ih·wa·hę́:de' she is an administrator

administration building
ga·nǫh·sag·wę:ní:yo'
[ga+...-nǫhsagwęniyo' administration building; consists of: -nǫhs(a)- house -gwęniyo- main]

advisory council
Tę·nę'ni·gǫ·hó:ta' the Advisory Council (lit.: they give ideas, suggestions)
[d+...-(')nigǫhod- suggest, advise]

Ha·di:h·wa·do·gę́hs·ta' Advisory Council (lit.: they (m) set it straight)
[A+...-(r)ihwadogęhsta' Advisory Council; consists of: -(r)ih(wa)- word -dogęhsd- make right, true]

affairs
hę·nahs·he:dáhs o·ih·wa·géh·sǫ' affairs, statistics
[hęnahshedahs they (m) count oihwagehsǫ' things]

agency
gęg·yohg·wa·gé·hǫ' associations; councils; agencies; groups; lit.: crowds lying about
[ga+...-(i)gyohg(wa)- crowd -gehǫ' lie about]

ambassador
gon·ha'trá' sha·gogy'ada·nǫhg·wá:nih ambassadors, commissioners, etc.
[gonha'tra' s.o.'s assistant
shagogya'danǫhgwa:nih he represents s.o.]

arbitrate
dę·ha·di:h·wa·gé:nha' arbitration; they (m) will be arbitrators
[de+...-(r)ih(wa)- word -genh- argue for, advocate]

archive
o·ih·wa·gá:yǫh archives
[o+...-(r)ihwagayǫh archive; consists of -(r)ih(wa)- word -gayǫh old (thing)]

o·ih·wa·gá·yǫh·sǫ' archives

arm (of an organization)
he·ga·nęt·sa:dé'
de·yǫ·ki·yǫh·wę·já'nya:' an arm, branch, division of an organization
[heganętsa:de' an arm, branch, division (of an organization); a municipality
deyǫkiyǫhwęja'nya:' they look after our land for us]

he·ga·nęt·sa:dé'
de·yo·de·kah·sǫg·wá·hǫ' divisions (of an organization)
[heganętsa:de' an arm, branch, division (of an organization); a municipality
deyodekahsǫgwahǫ' they are divided]

he·ga·nęt·sá:de' an arm, branch, division (of an organization); a municipality
[he+...-nęts(a)- arm -de' exist]

arts
hę·nag·ye·náh·ta' the arts (lit.:they (m) perform)
[A+...-agyena'd-, agyana'd- act]

arts council
Hę·nag·ye·nah·tá' Gęg·yóhg·wa·ę'
[hęnagyenahta' they (m) perform the arts
gęgyohgwaę' association; council; agency; group]

arts foundation
O·ih·wag·we:gǫ́h
Ha·diy'a·dahs·dah·nǫ́h
Ho·nahs·dí:hsdǫh
[oihwagwe:gǫh everything; the whole idea
hadiy'adahsdahnǫh they (m) put in s.t.
honahsdi:hsdǫh foundation, board, etc. (lit.: they (m) care for it)]

assembly
Ho·nǫh·wę·jag·wę:ní:yo' assembly
[honǫhwęjagwę:ni:yo' they (m) are the main body]

Assembly of First Nations
Ho·nǫh·wę·jag·wę·ni:yó'
Ho·nę·nig·yohg·wahs·rǫ́:ni:
[honǫhwęjagwę:ni:yo' assembly (lit.: they (m) are the main body)
honęnigyohgwahsrǫ:ni: they (m) fix the crowds]

assistant
ę·ya·go·yę·na·wá'syag·ye' s.o. will be helping
[TR+...-yenawa's- help]

association
gęg·yohg·wa·gé·hǫ' associations; councils; agencies; groups (lit.: crowds lying about)
[ga+...-(i)gyohg(wa)- crowd -gehǫ' lie about]

Association of (Canadian) Courts
Ha·di·hah·sę'dah·kwa'go·wáh·geh Courts; Association of (Canadian) Courts
[A+...-(h)ahsę'dahkwa'gowahneh court association; consists of: -(h)ahsę'dahkwa' court -gowah big, great -geh at, on]

Association of Colleges and Universities Student Services
He:tgę́h Tga:déh
Hę·na·de·wa·yęhs·tá'
Hǫ·wa·di·ye·na·wá'seh
[he:tgę' tga:de' it is superior
hęnadewayęhsta' they (m) are learners
hǫwadiyenawa'seh services (lit.: they help them)]

assurance
ad·rih·wag·ya·ǫhs·rá' ha·dí·gan·ya's insurance; assurance
[adrihwagyaǫhsra' disaster
hadiganya's they (m) pay]

Attourney General
Dę·ha·ih·wa·gen·has·gó:wah he is the Attorney General (lit.: big lawmaker)
[de+A+...-(r)ihwagenhahs lawyer -gowah big, great]

auditor
hę·nat·wihs·da:nǫ́h ha·dík·dǫh·a'
[hęnatwihsdanǫh they (m) guard the money
hadikdǫha' they (m) examine it]

hę·nat·wihs·da:nǫ́h ho·nát·gah·a:'
[hęnatwihsdanǫh they (m) guard the money
honatgaha:' they (m) are watching]

Auditor General
Hat·wihs·da·nǫh·gó:wah (o·hę:dǫ:)
[A+...-(a)twihsdanǫhgowah Auditor General; consists of: -(h)wihsd(a)- metal, money -nǫ- guard -gowah big, great]

Better Business Bureau
Ho·nah·dęg·ya'dǫ́h
Ta·di·dag·wá·ihs·hǫhs
[honahdęgya'dǫh business, industry
tadidagwaihshǫhs where they (m) keep straight the ways]

bailiff
hǫ·wa·ih·wáw'ase' a bailiff (lit.: he is a judge's aide)
[TR+...-(r)ihwawa's- help]

bank
eh·wihs·dá·ę·dah·kwa' bank
[-(h)wihsd(a)-, (hr)ihsd(a)- metal, money -(y)ędahkwa' place where s.t. is put]

Bank of Canada
Eh·wihs·da·ę·dah·kwa'go·wáh·neh
[-(h)wihsd(a), (hr)ihsd(a) metal, money -(y)ędahkwa' place where s.t. is put -gowah big, great -(h)neh place]

bilingualism
de·ga·wę·ná:ge:
[de...-węn(a) voice, language -age: two]

Bill of Rights, Charter of Rights and Freedoms
Tǫ·wa:na:wí: Ga·ya'da·gęn·hahs·rá'
Ga·yá·nęhs·ra'
[tǫwa:na:wi: he has given us rights
gaya'dagęnhahsra' helpfulness
gayanęhsra' rights; laws; code]

board

ho·nad·rih·wahs·dí:hsdǫh board, bureau, office, department, foundation, institute, etc.
[P+...-(a)drihwahsdihsdǫh chairman, board; consists of: -(r)ih(wa)- word, affair -(h)sdihsd- care for]

bonds

sa·yę́·dǫ' you own s.t., your bonds
[P+...-(y)ędǫ' several owned objects]

branch

he·ga·nęt·sa:dé'
de·yǫ·ki·yǫh·wę·já'nya:' an arm, branch, division (of an organization); a municipality
[heganętsa:de' an arm, branch, division (of an organization); municipality
deyǫkiyǫhwęja'nya:' they look after our land for us]

he·ga·nęt·sá:de' an arm, branch, division (of an organization); a municipality
[he+...-nęts(a)- arm -de' exist]

bureau

ho·nad·rih·wahs·dí:hsdǫh board, bureau, office, department, foundation, institute, etc.

business

ho·nah·dęg·yá'dǫh business, industry
[honahdęgya'dǫh their (m) business]

business association

ho·nah·dęg·ya'dǫ́h gęg·yóhg·wa·ę'
[honahdęgya'dǫh business; industry
gęgyohgwaę' association; council; agency; group]

Cabinet

Gwa·go:wáh Ga·ǫg·we'dá'
Gęg·yohg·wa·gé·hǫ'
[Gwa:go:wah royalty, king, the King
gaǫgwe'da' person, human
gęgyohgwagehǫ' associations; councils; agencies; groups (lit.: crowds lying about)]

Canada Act

Ga·ya·nęhs·rá' Ǫg·wahs·há·i·ne'
[gayanęhsra' rights, laws, code
ǫgwahshaine' they govern us]

Canada Council

Oh·wihs·dá' Tę·náht·ga's
[ohwihsda' money
tęnahtga's they (m) forfeit, let go of it]

Canada Post Corporation

Gah·ya·dǫhs·ra·nęhg·wíh
Gęg·yóhg·wa·ę'
[gahyadǫhsranęhgwih post office (lit.: it hauls paper)
gęgyohgwaę' association; council; agency; group]

candidate

dę·hę́h·da:t a candidate (lit.: he will run)
[-(w)ęhdad- run]

capital city

Ga·na·dag·wę:ní:yo'
[ga+...-nadagwęniyo' capital; consists of -nad(a)- town, community -gwęniyo' main]

census

hę·na·dǫg·we'dahs·hé:dahs a census (lit.: they (m) count people)
[A+...-(a)dǫgwe'dahshedahs census; consists of: -ǫgwe('da)- person -(a)hshed- count]

chairman

hod·rih·wahs·díhs·dǫh a chairman (lit.: he looks after the message); he is taking care of this event
[P+...-(a)drihwahsdihsdǫh chairman; consists of: -(r)ih(wa)- word, affair -(h)sdihsd- care for]

ho·yę·da̱h·kwáhs·dihs·dǫh a chairman (lit.: he looks after the chair)
[P+...-(a)kyędahkwahsdihsdǫh chairman; consists of: -(a)kyędahkw(a)- chair -(h)sdihsd- care]

Charter of Rights and Freedoms, Bill of Rights

Tǫ·wa:na:wí: Ga·yaʼda·gęn·hahs·ráʼ Ga·yá·ne̱hs·raʼ
[tǫwa:na:wi: he has given us rights
gayaʼdagęnhahsraʼ helpfulness
gayane̱hsraʼ rights; laws; code]

chief

ha·di·go·wá:nęʼs they (m) are big; chiefs
[A+...-gowanęʼs big ones]

Chief Justice

Sha·go·dęn·yéh·taʼgo:wah
[TR+...-(a)dęnyehtaʼ judge -gowah big, great]

child welfare

ek·saʼshǫ:ʼǫ́h hǫ·wa·dihs·wáʼne·táʼ
[eksaʼshǫ:ʼǫh they (f/m) are children
hǫwadihswaʼnetaʼ they support them]

children's aid office

ha·dik·sa·shǫʼǫ́h de̱h·ǫ·wa·díhs·nyeʼ
[hadiksaʼshǫ:ʼǫh they (m) are children
de̱hǫwadihsnyeʼ they care for them]

citizenship

dę·hǫ·wa·di·den·yéʼs tsę́h ni·ho·nǫh·wę́jʼodę:h
[de̱hǫwadidenyeʼs citizenship (lit.: they (m) change them (m))
tsęh that
nihonǫhwęjʼodę: what kind of land]

de̱·hǫ·wa·dí·den·yeʼs citizenship (lit.: they (m) change them (m))
[de+...-deni-, deny- change]

coalition

sgęg·yohg·wá:t o·dǫ́ʼǫh
[sgęgyohgwa:t one crowd, body
odǫʼǫh it has become]

sgʼa·ni·gǫ·há:t o·dǫ́ʼǫh
[sgʼanigǫha:t one mind
odǫʼǫh it has become]

de̱·ho·di:h·wá·ę·dʼa·seh
coalition (lit.: they come to one mind)
[de+P+...-(r)ihwaędaʼs- decide, agree]

code

ga·yá·ne̱hs·raʼ rights; laws; code
[ga+...-yanehsr(a) rights; laws; code]

ga·ya·ne̱hs·ráʼgeh on the rights, laws, code

commissioner

gon·haʼtráʼ sha·gog·yaʼda·nǫhg·wá·nih
ambassadors, commissioners, etc.
[gonhaʼtraʼ s.o.'s assistant
shagogyaʼdanǫ̱hgwa:nih he represents s.o.]

consensus

de·ga·ih·wá·ę·daʼs
[de+ga+...-(r)ihwaędaʼs- decide, conclude]

conservation
de·hę·nọh·wę́·ja̱hs·nye' land preservation; land conservation (lit.: they (m) look after the land)
[de+A+...-ọhwęjahsnye' conservation, preservation; consists of: -ọhwęj(a)- earth, land -(h)snye- care for, look after]

ho·nọh·wę·ját·ga̱·ha:' conservation (lit.: they pay attention to the earth)
[P+...-ọhwęjatgaha:' conserve, conservation; consists of: -ọhwęj(a)- earth, land -(a)tgah- pay attention, watch]

Constitution
Ga·ya·ne̱hs·ra'gó:wah
[ga+...-yanehsra'gowah Constitution; consists of: -yanehsr(a)- law, rights -gowah big, great]

Constitution Act
Ga̱h·ya·dọhs·rag·wę:ní:yo'
[ga+...-(h)yadọhsragwęniyo' Constitution Act; consists of: -(h)yadọhsr(a)- paper -gweniyo' main]

Consumer's Affairs
Ga̱h·ni·nọh·nyọ́'
O·de·dag·wa·ih·sọ́·hag·ye'
[ga̱hninọhnyọ' consumption (lit.: things which are bought)
odedagwaihsọhagye' it is being straightened out]

corporation
dę̱h·o·nag·yéhs·dọh they (m) form a corporation
[de+P+...-(a)gyehsdọh be mixed together]

correctional services
ọ·da·dę̱n·ho·dọh·kwá' o·íh·wa·geh
[ọdadęnhodọ̱hkwa' jail, prison (lit.: place where s.o. is locked up)
oihwageh the reason, idea for s.t.]

counselor
ha·háhs·hę·hę' he is a counselor
[A+...-(h)ahshęhę' counsel, give advice]

council
gęg·yóhg·wa·ę' association; council; agency; group
[ga+...-(i)gyohgwaę' crowd; group]

gęg·yohg·wa·gé·họ' associations; councils; agencies; groups (lit.: crowds lying about)
[ga+...-(i)gyohg(wa)- crowd -gehọ' lie about]

country
o·dọh·wę·já:de' country
[o+...-(a)dọhwęjade' country; consists of: -ọhwęj(a)- earth -de' exist]

court
ha·di·hah·sę'da̱h·kwa'go·wáh·geh Courts; Association of (Canadian) Courts
[A+...-(h)ahsę'dahkwa'gowahneh court association; consists of: -(h)ahsę'dahkwa' court -gowah big, great -geh at, on]

ha·di·hahs·hę́'da̱h·kwa' a court (lit.: place where they (m) counsel)
[A+...-(h)ahshę'dahkwa' court]

courthouse
dę̱·ha·di·hah·sę·dáh·kwa' courthouse
[de+A+...-(h)ahshę'dahkwa' court]

crown
gwa:gó:wah royalty; king; the King; the crown

Crown corporation
Gwa:go:wáh De̱·ho·nag·yéhs·dǫh Crown corporation
[gwa:go:wah royalty, king, the King de̱honagyehsdǫh they (m) form a corporation]

Crown Council
Gwa:go:wáh
Des·ha·go·dih·wa·gé:nhahs
[gwa:go:wah royalty, king, the King deshagodihwage:nhahs they argue for us]

CSIS
de·ha·di·nę·hę·dá:s
ho·nad·ri̱h·wah·se̱h·dǫ́h
oh·wę·já·ę:dǫnyǫ' intelligence agency, spy agency
[dehadinęhęda:s they (m) are guards honadri̱hwahse̱hdǫh they are secretive ohwęjaę:dǫnyǫ' lands; countries]

Cultural Affairs
Ti·yǫg·we'da·de·jíh Go·íh·wa·geh
[Tiyǫgwe'dadejih culture (lit.: all sorts of people)
goihwageh s.o.'s affairs]

culture
Ti·yǫg·we'da·de·jíh culture
[tiyǫgwedadejih all sorts of people; consists of: -ǫgwe('da)- people -ade' exist -jih really]

curator
ek·dǫ·da̱h·kwa'géh hohs·díhs·dǫh he is a museum director; a curator
[ekdǫda̱hkwa'geh museum
hohsdihsdǫh he is a director]

department
ho·nad·ri̱h·wahs·dí:hs·dǫh board; bureau; office; department; foundation; institute; etc.
[P+...-(a)drihwahsdihsdǫh be a chairman, board, etc.; consists of: -(r)ih(wa)- word, affair -(h)sdihsd- care for]

Department of Energy and Mines
Oh·wę·ja·géh Wah·dęgy'atá'
Oh·wę·ja·gǫh·sǫ́'
Ho·nad·rih·wahs·dí:hs·dǫh
[ohwęjageh on earth
wahdęgya'ta' a starter
oh·wę·ja·gǫh·sǫ' under the earth
honadrihwahsdi:hsdǫh department]

development
ho·dis·rǫ·ní·hag·ye' development (lit.: they (m) are developing)
[P+...-(h)srǫnihagye' be going along making s.t.]

director
gohs·díhs·dǫh she is a director; principal; head; etc.
[P+...-(h)sdihsdǫh director, principal, head; consists of: -(h)sdihsd- care for]

ga·i·hǫn·ya·ní:' gohs·díhs·dǫh she is an education director
[gaihǫnyę:ni:' it teaches
gohsdihsdǫh she is a director, etc. etc.]

director (continued)
o·wę:ná' hohs·díhs·dǫh he is a language director
[owę:na' word
hohsdihsdǫh he is a director]

de·gahs·nye'ǫ́:' hos·díhs·dǫh he is a maintenance director
[degahsnye'ǫ:' it cleans up
hohsdihsdǫh he is a director]

de·ga·ǫ·doh·dá:s o·hę́:dǫ: maintenance director
[degaǫdohda:s they (f/m) tidy up
ohę:dǫ: ahead; in front; the front]

ga·ih·wa·o·hǫ́:' hohs·díhs·dǫh he is a research director
[gaihwaohǫ:' gathered news or ideas
hohsdihsdǫh he is a director]

division (of an organization)
he·ga·nęt·sa:dé'
de·yǫ·ki·yǫh·wę·já'nya:' an arm, branch, division (of an organization)
[heganętsa:de' an arm, branch, division (of an organization); a municipality
deyodekahsǫgwahǫ' divisions (of an organization)]

economic development (office)
o·hę:dǫ́: ha'wa·ta·hi:né'
got·ga·nǫ·ní·hag·ye'
[ohę:dǫ: ahead; in front; the front
ha'watahi:ne' it is walking over there
gotganǫnihagye' prosperity (lit.: s.o. is prospering]

education (postsecondary)
he:t·gę́h tga:déh hę·na·de·wá·yęh·sta' higher learning, postsecondary education
[he:tgę' tga:de' it is superior
hęnadewayęhsta' they (m) are learners]

elect
dę·hę·nę·nig·yǫhg·wah·gę́:ni' they (m) will have an election
[de+...-ęnigyohgwagęni vote, elect; consists of: -(i)gyohg(wa)- crowd -gęni- compete]

dęh·sę·nig·yohg·wa·gę́:ni' you will vote, cast lots

hǫ·sá'hǫ·wa·di·yá'din·yǫ:t they re-elected him, them (m)
[hǫsa'-TR+...-ya'dinyǫd elect, re-elect; consists of: -ya'd(a)- body -inyǫ'd- put in]

sa·hǫ·wa·dits·gó:dę' they re-elected him, them (m)
[s+...-itsgodę' re-elect; consists of: -(n)itsg(wa)- having to do with the lower body or torso -odę' put in]

a·hǫ·wa·dits·ó:dę' they elected him, them (m)

ha'ha:yǫ́' né:' tó a·hǫ·wa·di:ts·gó:dę' they elected him, them (m)

election
dę·hę·nę·nig·yóhg·wa:gę́:ni' they (m) will have an election
[de+...-ęnigyohgwagęni vote, elect; consists of: -(i)gyohg(wa)- crowd -gęni- compete]

employee
sen·há'tra' you are an employee
[A+...-nha'tr(a)- employee, minister; consists of: -nha' command, hire]

Employment and Immigration, Human Resources Development
Hę·na·dęn·há'ˀs
Dẹ·hę·na·dǫgwˀedá·den·yeˀs
[hęnadęnhaˀs they (m) order it
dẹhęnadǫgwˀedadenyeˀs human development (lit.: they change people)]

employment office
Dẹ·ha·di·hoˀdęhs·rag·wę·ní:yoˀ
[de+A+...-(r)ihoˀdęhsragwęniyoˀ employment office; consists of: -(ri)hoˀdęhsr(a)- work -gweniyoˀ main]

environment
tsęh ni·yoh·dǫ·hǫg·yéˀ tsęh hǫh·wę·ja·dá:dǫh environment
[tsęh that
niyohdǫhǫgyeˀ what it is being like
hǫhwęjadadǫh he has created the earth]

FBI
de·ha·di·nę·hę·dá:s
ho·nad·rịh·wah·sẹh·dǫ́h
oh·wę·já·ę:dǫn·yǫˀ intelligence agency; spy agency
[dehadinęhęda:s they (m) are guards
honadrịhwahsẹhdǫh they are secretive
ohwęjaę:dǫnyǫˀ lands; countries]

federal
ha·di·go·wáh·shǫˀ they (m) are federal
[A+...-gowahshǫˀ big ones]

federation
de·ga·na·da·węn·yeˀtaˀgéh federation
[de+... -(a)dawęnyeˀd- stir up (a)ˀgeh-on]

fish and wildlife
ga·na·dad·wę:ni:yóˀ ga·dí:nyo:ˀ
[gęnadadwę:ni:yoˀ they (z) are wild
gadi:nyo:ˀ wild animals]

forest industry
ha·diˀnhahg·yáˀs ho·nah·dęg·yáˀdǫh
[hadiˀnhahgyaˀs they (m) cut down the forest
honahdęgyaˀdǫh business; industry]

foundation
ho·nad·rịh·wáhs·dihs·dǫh board; bureau; office; department; foundation; institute; etc.
[P+...-(a)drihwahsdihsdǫh chairman, board; consists of: -(r)ih(wa)- word, affair -(h)sdihsd- care for]

govern
ǫg·wahs·há·i·neˀ they govern us
[TR+...-shaineˀ govern s.o.]

government
de·yǫ·ki·yǫh·wę·jáˀnya:ˀ they look after our land, take care of business (refers to a title, an office)
[de+TR+...-ǫhwęjaˀnya:ˀ title, office; consists of: -ǫhwęj(a)- earth, land -(ę)ˀnya:ˀ govern, watch]

Governor General, Prime Minister
gwa:go:wáh gon·háˀtraˀ
[gwa:go:wah royalty; king; the King
gonhaˀtraˀ s.o.'s assistant]

grant
hǫ·wa·dịh·wíhs·da·wihs a subsidy; a grant (lit.: they give him, them (m) money)
[TR+...-(h)wihsdawihs subsidy, grant; consists of: -(h)wihsd(a) metal, money -awi-, -ǫ- give]

group
ho·nę·nig·yóhg·wa·ęˀ their (m) crowd, group, association
[A+...-(i)gyohg(wa) crowd -(y)ęˀ exist]

group (continued)
gęg·yohg·wa·gé·hǫʼ (associations; councils; agencies; groups (lit.: crowds lying about)
[ga+...-(i)gyohg(wa) crowd -gehǫʼ lie about]

health
A·daʼga·i·dęhs·ráʼ O·íh·wa·geh health
[adagaidęhsraʼ health
oihwageh the reason, the idea for s.t.]

Health Canada
a·daʼga·e·dęhs·ráʼ de·ho·dí:h·wah·ja:ʼ
[adagaidęhsraʼ health
dehodi:hwahtsʼa:ʼ they are earning, fulfilling it]

higher education
he:t·gę́h tga:déʼ hę·na·de·wá·yęh·staʼ
higher learning, postsecondary education
[he:tgęʼ tga:deʼ it is superior
hęnadewayęhstaʼ they (m) are learners]

House of Commons, Legislature
hę·nag·yę·dah·kwáʼ
ha·di·ya·nęhs·rǫ́:nih
[hęnagyędahkwaʼ their (m) chair
hadiyanęhsrǫ:nih they (m) make the laws]

Human Resources Development, Employment and Immigration
Hę·na·dęn·háʼs
Dę·hę·na·dǫgwʼedá·den·yeʼs
[hęnadęnhaʼs they (m) order it
dęhęnadǫgweʼdadenyeʼs human development (lit.: they change people)]

Human Rights Commission
He·yǫg·weʼda:gwe:gǫ́h
Go·ya·nęhs·ra·ę́ʼ Gęg·yóhg·wa·ęʼ
[heyǫgweʼda:gwe:gǫh all humans everywhere
goyanęhsraęʼ s.o.'s laws, rights
gęgyohgwaęʼ association; council; agency; group]

industry
ho·nah·dęg·yáʼdǫh business; industry
[honahdęgyaʼdǫh their (m) business]

Inspector General
Hak·do·haʼgó:wah
[A+...-kdohaʼgowah Inspector General; consists of: -kdo- examine, inspect -gowah big, great]

institute
ho·nad·rih·wáhs·dihs·dǫh board; bureau; office; department; foundation; institute; etc.
[P+...-(a)drihwahsdihsdǫh chairman, board; consists of: -(r)ih(wa)- word, affair -(h)sdihsd- care for]

insurance
ad·rih·wag·ya·ǫhs·ráʼ ha·dí·gan·yaʼs
insurance; assurance
[adrihwagyaǫhsraʼ disaster
hadiganyaʼs they (m) pay]

intelligence agency
oh·sǫ·da·gǫ́h·sǫʼ an intelligence agency (lit.: it is dark, murky)
[o+...-(a)hsǫdagǫhsǫʼ dark, murky; consists of: -(a)hsǫd(a) night, blackness -(a)gǫ: in -sǫʼ plural]

de·ha·di·nę·hę·dá:s
ho·nad·rih·wah·sęh·dǫ́h
oh·wę·já·ę:dǫn·yǫʼ intelligence agency; spy agency
[dehadinęhęda:s they (m) are guards
honadrihwahsęhdǫh they are secretive
ohwęjaę:dǫnyǫʼ lands; countries]

jail
ǫ·da·dęn·hó·dǫh·kwa' jail; prison (lit.: place where s.o. is locked up)
[ǫ+...-(adę)nhodǫ(:)- be locked up]

judge
sha·go·dęn·yéh·ta' judge
[TR+...-(a)dęnyehd- send s.o., judge s.o.]

jury
des·ha·go·diy'adó·węh·ta' a jury (lit.: they decide for them)
[de+...-ya'dowehd think about, consider]

justice
ga·ih·wahs·rǫ́:nih justice; rules
[ga+...-(r)ihwahsrǫni be just ; consists of: -(r)ih(wa)- word -(h)srǫni- fix, repair]

king
gwa:gó:wah royalty; king; the King; the Crown
[gwagowah royalty]

hǫ·wa·dig·wa:gó:wah their king

labour board
ga·i·ho'dęhs·rá' ga·ya·nęhs·rá' ha·díhs·re'
[gaiho'dęhsra' work
gayanęhsra' rights; laws; code
hadihsre' they (m) follow]

labour relations board
ga·i·ho'dęhs·rá' ga·ya·nęhs·rá' ho·ná·dihs·dǫh
[gaiho'dęhsra' work
gayanęhsra' rights; laws; code
honahsdi:hsdǫh foundation; board; etc.]

land
sah·wę́:ja', sǫh·wę́:ja', sa·ǫh·wę́:ja'
your land; property; real estate
[P+...-ǫhwęj(a) earth, land]

land claim
hę·nǫh·wę·jáhs·gen·hahs land claims (lit.: they (m) fight for the land)
[A+...-ǫhwęjahsgenhahs land claim; consists of: -ǫhwęj(a)- earth, land -gęni- compete]

land owner, land title
ho·nǫh·wę·já·ę:dǫ' land owners; land titles
[P+...-ǫhwęjaędǫ' land owner, land title; consists of: -ǫhwęj(a)- earth, land -(y)ędǫ' own several things]

ho·nǫh·wę·jáhs·no' land titles
[P+...-ǫhwęjahsno' land title; consists of: -ǫhwęj(a) earth, land -(h)sno' care for, look after several things]

law
ga·yá·nęhs·ra' rights; laws; code
[ga+...-yanehsr(a) law, rights]

ga·ya·nęhs·rá'geh on the rights, laws, code

lawmaker
ga·e·ya·nehs·rǫ́·ni they (f/m) are lawmakers
[A+...-yanehsrǫnih Parliament; governing body, lawmaker; consists of: -yanehsr(a)- law, rights -ǫni-, -ǫny- make]

swa·ya·nęhs·rǫ́:nih you all are lawmakers

lawyer
dę·ha·ih·wá·gen·hahs he is a lawyer [de+A+...(r)ihwagenhahs lawyer; consists of: -(r)ih(wa)- word, affair -genh- argue for, advocate]

dę·ha·dih·wá·gen·has they (m) are lawyers

dę·ha·ih·wa·gen·has·gó:wah he is the Attorney General [de+A+...(r)ihwagenhahsgowah Attourney General; consists of: -(r)ihwagenhahs- lawyer -gowah big, great]

leader
gǫ·wa·di·gó·wa·nęh their leader [TR+...-gowanęh big]

shed·wa·go·wá:nęh he is our leader

sha·go·hę:dǫ́: (gyoh·wę́·jade') leader (of a land, country, or territory) [shagohę:dǫ: a leader gyǫhwęjade' existing land]

Legislature, House of Commons
Hę·nag·yę·dah·kwá'
Ha·di·ya·nęhs·rǫ́:nih
[hęnagyędahkwa' their (m) chair hadiyanęhsrǫ:nih they (m) make the laws]

licensing and control board
hǫ·wa·di̲h·ya·dǫhs·ra:wíhs
ga·ya·ne̲hs·rá'geh
[hǫwadi̲hyadǫhsra:wihs licensing body (lit.: they give them paper) gayane̲hsra'geh the rights; laws; code]

licensing body
hǫ·wa·di̲h·ya·dǫhs·ra:wíhs licensing body [TR+...-(h)yadǫhsr(a)- paper -(a)wi-, -ǫ- give]

Member of Parliament, MLA, etc.
Han·há'tra' he is a Member of Parliament [A+...-nha'tra' employee, minister]

Ha·din·ha'tra'shǫ:'ǫh they (m) are employees, etc.

minister
gon·há'tra'shǫ' they (f/m) are ministers [P+...-nha'tra' employee, minister; consists of: -nha'- command, hire]

ha·din·ha'trá'shǫ' they (m) are ministers or aides [A+...-nha'tra' employee, minister]

gwa:go:wáh gon·há'tra' Governor General, Prime Minister [gwa:go:wah royalty; king; the King gonha'tra' s.o.'s assistant]

ministry
hǫ·wa·dis·hahs·dęhs·rá:wi: ministry [TR+...-shahsdęhsrawi: ministry; consists of: -shasdęhsr(a)- power, strength -awi-, -ǫ- give]

multilingualism
ta'de·ga·wę́·na·ge: all kinds of languages; multilingualism [ta'de... -węn(a) voice, word -(a)ge: all kinds of]

municipal
ha·di·hah·shę́·hę' they (m) are municipal (lit:. they (m) counsel) [A+...-(h)ahshęhę' counsel]

municipality
he·ga·nęt·sá:de' an arm, branch, division (of an organization); a municipality
[he+…-nęts(a)- arm -de' exist]

national
he·yǫh·wę·ja:gwé:gǫh national (lit.: it is all over the earth)
[he'+ yo+…-ǫhwęj(a) land, earth -gwegǫh be all over the place]

Native Council on Justice
Ǫg·we·hǫ:wéh Ho·dih·wa'géh Ha·di·ya·nehs·rag·wáhs·hǫhs
[Ǫgwehǫ:weh First Nations people hodihwa'geh on their (m) word hadiyanehsragwaishǫhs they (m) straighten out the laws]

natural resources
ga·wa·yę·nah·tá:' oh·wę·ja·géh·gę·ha:'
[gawayęnahta:' resources (lit.: it causes it to be cared for)
ohwęjagehgęha:' earthly things; resources]

nature
na·ha·wa·yę́·nan·he' nature (lit.: his finished creation)
[na+ha+…-wayęnanhe' nature; consists of: -wayęnǫni care for, do carefully]

office
ho·nad·rih·wáhs·dihs·dǫh board; bureau; office; department; foundation; institute; etc.
[P+…-(a)drihwahsdihsdǫh chairman, board; consists of: -(r)ih(wa)- word, affair -(h)sdihsd- care for]

office (continued)
de·yǫ·ki·yah·węh·jáhs·nye' they look after our land (refers to a title, an office)
[de+TR+…-ǫhwęhjahsnye' title, office; consists of: -ǫhwęj(a)- earth, land -(h)snye- care for, look after]

de·yǫ·ki·yǫh·wę·já'nya:' they look after our land, take care of business (refers to a title, an office)
[de+TR+…-ǫhwęja'nya:' title, office; consists of: -ǫhwęj(a)- earth, land -(ę)'nya:' govern, watch]

Ombudsman
en·há'tra' ombudsman, etc.
[e+…-nha'tra' ombudsman; consists of: -nha'tra' employee, minister]

parks and wildlife federation
de·ga·na·da·węn·ye'ta'géh ga·dí:nyo:'
[degęnadawęnye'ta'geh federation (lit.: where they (z) stir it up)
gadi:nyo:' wild animals]

Parliament
Ga·nǫh·so·wa·nęh·gó:wah
[ga+…-nǫhsowanęhgowah Parliament; consists of: -nǫhs(a)- house -owanęh be big, great -gowah big, great]

ha·di·ya·nehs·rǫ́·nih a governing body; Parliament (lit.: they (m) are lawmakers)
[A+…-yanehsrǫnih Parliament, governing body, lawmaker; consists of: -yanehsr(a)- law, rights -ǫni-, -ǫny- make]

people's council
ǫg·wéh he·ye·ih·wah·win·yǫ́'t'ageh
[ǫ:gweh person
heyeihwahwinyǫ'ta'geh place into which people take their ideas]

postsecondary education, higher learning
he:tgę́h tga:déh hę.na.de.wá.yęh.sta'
[he:tgę' tga:de' it is superior
hęnadewayęhsta' they (m) are learners]

Premier
O.hę.dǫh.gó:wah (ne') Premier (of)
[o+...-(h)ędǫh leader -gowah big, great]

preservation, conservation
de.hę.nǫh.wę́.jahs.nye' land preservation; land conservation (lit.: they (m) look after the land)
[de+A+...-ǫhwęjahsnye' conservation, preservation; consists of: -ǫhwęj(a)- earth, land -(h)snye- care for, look after]

president
sha.go.hę:dǫ́: gyoh.wę́.ja.de' leader (of a land, country, or territory)
[shagohę:dǫ: a leader
gyǫhwęjade' existing land]

Ha.na.da.gá:nyahs he is the President of the United States (lit.: he destroys towns)
[A+...-nadaganyahs President; consists of: -nad(a) town, community -riyo-, -nyo- fight, kill]

Prime Minister, Governor General
gwa:go:wáh gon.há'tra'
[gwa:go:wah royalty; king; the King
gonha'tra' s.o.'s assistant]

sha.go.hę:dǫ́: gyoh.wę́.ja.de' leader (of a land, country, or territory)
[shagohę:dǫ: a leader
gyǫhwęja:de' existing land]

principal
gohs.díhs.dǫh she is a director, principal, head, etc.
[P+...-(h)sdihsdǫh director, principal, head; consists of: -(h)sdihsd- care for]

prison
ǫ.da.dęn.hó.dǫh.kwa' jail; prison (lit. place where s.o. is locked up)
[ǫ+...-(a)dęnhodǫ(:) be locked up]

Privy Council
Gwa:go:wáh Hǫ.wa.dih.nya'so.dá.hǫh
[Gwa:go:wah royalty; king; the King
hǫwadihnya'sodahǫh Senate (lit.: where they hang their necks or nod their heads)]

property
sah.wę́:ja', sǫh.wę́:ja', sa.ǫh.wę́:ja' your land, property, real estate
[P+...-ǫhwęj(a) earth, land]

province
de.yǫh.wę.jah.kah.sǫ́:gwęh a province (lit.: divided lands)
[de+yo+...-ǫhwęjahkahsǫgwęh province; consists of: -ǫhwęj(a)- earth, land -kahs(i)- share, divide]

provincial
ha.di:gó:wahs they (m) are provincial
[A+...-gowahs provincial; consists of: -gowah big, great -'s plural]

re-elect
hǫ.sa'hǫ.wa.di.yá'din.yǫ:t they re-elected him, them (m)
[hǫsa'+TR+...-ya'dinyǫd elect, re-elect; consists of: -ya'd(a)- body -inyǫ'd- put in]

real estate
sah.wę́:ja', sǫh.wę́:ja', sa.ǫh.wę́:ja' your land, property, real estate
[P+...-ǫhwęj(a)- earth, land]

Receiver General
Hat·wihs·da·nǫh·go:wáh o·hę́:dǫ:
[hatwihsdanǫhgo:wah Auditor General ohę:dǫ: ahead; in front; the front]

resources
ǫh·wę·ja·géh·gęh·a:ʼ earthly things; resources
[-ǫhwęj(a) earth, land -(a)ʼgeh on -geha:ʼ type of]

right
dwa·gá:wi: a given right (lit.: it is given)
[d+wa+...-(a)wi: right; consists of: -awi-, -ǫ- give]
tsǫg·wá:wi: what he has given us; rights

Royal Canadian Mounted Police
Sha·go·di·ye·nahs·gó:wah
[TR+...-yenahsgowah RCMP; consists of: TR+...-yenahs police -gowah big, great]

royalty
gwa:gó:wah royalty; king; the King; the Crown
[gwa:gowah royalty]

hǫ·wa·dig·wa:gó:wah their king

ga·ih·go·wáh·sǫʼ they (f/m) are royalty
[A+...-(r)ihgowahsǫʼ royalty; consists of: -(r)ih(wa) word -(g)owah great, big -sǫʼ plural]

rules
ga·ih·wahs·rǫ́:nih justice; rules
[ga+...-(r)ihwahsrǫni justice, rules; consists of: -(r)ih(wa)- word -(h)srǫni- fix, repair]

sales tax
ha·di·gá:he·haʼ a sales tax (lit.: they (m) put a price on top of s.t.)
[A+...-ga:hehaʼ sales tax; consists of: -ga(:) price -(hr)e, (hr)ę put, place]

ǫ·ki·gá:gwahs sales tax
[TR+...-ga:gw tax s.o.; consists of: -ga(:) price -gw gather, choose, pick]

Secretary of State
Sha·goh·ya·dǫh·seh·gó:wah Secretary of State
[TR+...-(h)yadǫhsehgowah Secretary of State; consists of: -(h)yadǫ(:) write -gowah great]

Senate
(Gwa:go:wáh)
Hǫ·wa·dihn·yaʼso·dá·hǫh
[-(h)nyaʼsodahǫh Senate; consists of: -(h)nyaʼs(a) neck -odahǫh be draped over]

service
hǫ·wa·di·ye·na·wáʼseh services
[TR+...-yenawaʼseh services; consists of: -yenawaʼs help s.o.]

social work(ers)
ga·ih·wa·jiyʼat·gáh·a:ʼ they (f/m) are social workers
[A+...-(h)wajiyatgaha:ʼ social workers; consists of: -(h)wajiy(a) family -(a)tgahǫ(:), (a)tgaha(:) pay attention, watch]

go·nat·wa·jiyʼat·gáh·a:ʼ they (f/m) are social workers

ga·ih·wa·jiyʼat·gá·ǫ·haʼ they (f/m) are social workers

ga·ǫh·wa·ji·yaʼt·gá·ǫ·haʼ they (f/m) are social workers

spy
ho·nat·gwęh·ę́:gye's spies (lit.: they (m) are shadowing around)
[P+ -(a)tgwęhęgye's spy; consists of: -gw gather, pick, get]

statistics
o·ih·wa·géh·sǫ' affairs; statistics
[o+...-(r)ihwagehsǫ' affairs, statistics; consists of: -(r)ihw(a)- word, matter, affair -(a')geh on -sǫ' several]

Statistics Canada
Hęnahs·he:dáhs O·ih·wa·géh·sǫ'
[hęnahshe:dahs they (m) count things oihwagehsǫ' affairs, statistics]

stock exchange, stock market
dę·hę·nat·wihs·da·dé:nyǫhs a stock exchange; stock market; the Dow Jones; the TSE; etc. (lit.: where they (m) exchange money)
[de+A+...-(a)twihsdadenyǫhs stock exchange, etc.; consists of: -(h)wihsd(a)- metal, money -deni-, -deny- change]

subsidy
hǫ·wa·dih·wíhs·da·wihs a subsidy; a grant (lit.: they give him, them (m) money)
[TR+...-(h)wihsdawihs subsidy, grant; consists of: -(h)wihsd(a)- metal, money -awi-, -ǫ- give]

tax
ǫ·ki·gá:gwahs sales tax
[TR+...-ga:gw tax s.o.; consists of: -ga(:)- price -gw- gather, choose, pick]

taxation department
ha·di·ga:he·há'geh
[A+ -ga:heha'geh taxation department; consists of: -ga(:)- price -(hr)e-, -(hr)ę- put -(')geh on]

title
de·yǫ·ki·yah·węh·jáh·snye' they look after our land (referring to a title, an office)
[de+TR+...-ǫhwęhjahsnye' title, office; consists of: -ǫhwęj(a)- earth, land -(h)snye- care for, look after]

de·yǫ·ki·yǫh·wę·já'nya:' they look after our land, take care of business (referring to a title, an office)
[de+TR+...-ǫhwęja'nya:' title, office; consists of: -ǫhwęj(a)- earth, land -(ę)'nya:' govern, watch]

Trans-Canada Highway
De·yoh·wę·jíy'agǫh
[de+y+...-ǫhwęjiya'gǫh Trans-Canada Highway; consists of: -ǫhwęj(a)- earth, land -(i)ya'g- cross]

urban design and development
e·nag·rehs·ra·ę́' ho·dis·rǫ·ní·hag·ye'
[enagrehsraę' s.t. is urban hodisrǫnihagye' they (m) are developing s.t.]

vote
dęh·sę·nig·yohg·wa·gę́:ni' you will vote, cast lots
[de+...-ęnigyohgwagęni- vote, elect; consists of: -(i)gyohg(wa)- crowd -gęni- compete]

dę·hę·nę·nig·yǫhg·wah·gę́:ni' they (m) will have an election

welfare office
to·na·dę·ní·dę'ǫh welfare office
[d+P+...-(a)dęnidę- be kind]

Appendix H: **Ganǫhǫnyǫhk** (The Thanksgiving Address)

ah·a·ih·wá:is
he accomplished or completed a task (for example, a speech); he carried out a responsibility
[-(r)ih(wa)- word -i:s be long]

ah·ǫh·ya·gę́·dahk, ah·a·ǫh·yág'ę·dahk
it made him work hard; he laboured
[-(r)ǫhyagę'd- labour, work hard]

a·i:dwę·nǫ́h·dǫn·yǫ:'
we all (incl.) should or would think about
[-ęnǫhdǫnyǫ:- think, wonder about]

a·ǫ:hę́:'ęh
the most
[-(r)ǫhę- be alone]

a·ǫ'wé:saht
a happy, glad feeling; s.t. pleasant
[-ǫ'wesahd- be enjoyable]

a·tad·ri̲h·wá:ts'a:'
he earned it; he fulfilled it
[-(a)drihwats'a:' earn s.t., fulfill s.t.]

a·to·wa·yę:ní:ya'k
it broke his spirit
[de+...-wayę(n)- heart, spirit -(i)ya'g- cut, break]

a·wá:dǫ'
it has become; it became
[-(a)dǫ- become]

da·ga·ya·gę́h·dahk
it came out suddenly
[d+...-yagęhdahgw- come out suddenly]

da·ne:'
that it

da·ne:'hni'
that also

da·ne:o:nęh
and now

da:ne·toh
that is all

da:nę:dah
now this also

ded·wa·nǫh·ǫ́h·kwa'
we all (incl.) refer to it as
[de+...-nǫhǫhkw- recognize, refer to s.o. as]

de·jid·wa·yę́:di:
we all (incl.) do not know any longer
[-(y)ędei-, (y)ędí- know]

des·hed·wa·nǫ́h·ǫh·kwa'
we refer to him as
[de+...-nǫhǫhkw- recognize, refer to s.o. as]

de·wáh·ǫh·de:s
deer
[de+w+ -(a)hǫhde:s deer]

de·ye·ti·nǫ́h·ǫh·kwa'
we refer to them as
[de+...-nǫhǫhkw- recognize, refer to s.o. as]

de·yo·wá:węn·ye'
stirring winds
[de+...-w(a:)- air -(a)węnye(:)- stir, mix]

de·yǫg·wahg·wę́h·ęg·ye's
we all are continually picking it up
[de+...-(h)gw- lift, pick up]

de·yǫg·węh·si'da·gę́d·rahg·węh
earth (lit.: where we put our feet)
[de+...-(a)hsi('da)-, -(ę)hs(a)- foot -gędrahgw- foundation]

de·yǫ·ki·yę́'nya·dǫ'
they protect us with their hands; angels
[de+...-(')ny(a)- finger, hand -(')nyadǫ- protect]

dęd·wa·dat·nǫ́h·ǫn·yǫ:'
we all (incl.) will greet each other
[de+...-nǫhǫnyǫ(:)- thank, greet]

dęd·wa·nǫh·ǫ́:nyǫ:'
we all (incl.) will thank s.t.
[de+...-nǫhǫnyǫ(:)- thank, greet]

dęs·ha·ih·wá·ęt·waht
he will bring forth a message
[de+s+...-(r)ihwaętwahd- spread the news, bring forth a message]

dęs·hed·wa·nǫ́h·ǫn·yǫ:'
we will thank him
[de+...-nǫhǫnyǫ(:)- thank, greet]

dęt·gá·na·nuhs, dęt·gá·na·nohs
it becomes cold
[de+...-(na')nohsd- become cold]

dę·toh·a·té'tǫk, dę·toh·a·té'dǫh·ǫ:k
he will brighten
[de+d+...-(a)te'd- brighten up]

dę·wa·nǫh·ǫ́:nyǫ:'
it will give thanks
[de+...-nǫhǫnyǫ(:)- thank, greet]

dę·ya·go·da'ǫh·ǫ́:gye'
they (f/m) will be standing along (to be born)
[de+...-da'ǫhǫgye' stand along; consists of: -da' stand up, stop]

dę·ya·go·da·węn·yéh·a:k
they (f/m) will be walking about
[de+...-(a)węnye(:)- stir, mix]

dę·ya·go'nya:gwę́h·ęg·ye'
she will have a hand in s.t.
[de+...-(')nyagw- participate in s.t.]

dę·ye·ti·nǫ́h·ǫn·yǫ:ʼ
we will thank her / them
[de+...-nǫhǫnyǫ(:)- thank, greet]

dó:gwaʼ
how; a certain amount; a measure

Dǫ·sah·a·ih·wá·ęt·waht
He Who Seeded the News; He Who Spread the News (referring to Handsome Lake)
[dǫsa+ha+ -(r)ihwaętwahd- spread the news, bring forth a message]

dwa·da:dǫ́:nih
where it starts from
[d+...(a)dad+ -ǫni, ǫny- start from, originate]

dwa·nó:haʼ
our mother
[-no:haʼ mother]

dwę·nǫ́h·dǫn·yǫh
we all (incl.) are experiencing in thought; we are in mind of s.t.
[-ęnǫhdǫnyǫ- think, wonder about]

e:ʼ
again

ek·saʼshǫ́:ʼǫh
they are children
[-ksa(ʼda)- child]

e·tíh·so:t
our grandmother
[-(h)sod- grandparent]

ę·déh·ka:ʼ
the day kind (things used only during the day)
[-ęd(a)- day -ka:ʼ kind of]

ęd·wa·de·wa·yę·nǫ́:niʼ
we all (incl.) will do it carefully; we all will do right
[(a)de+ -wayęnǫni- care for]

ęd·wa:tró:wiʼ
we all (incl.) will tell
[-(a)t+ -(hr)owi, (hr)ǫny- tell]

ęd·wá:yę:ʼ
we all (incl.) will set forth; we all will set down
[-(y)ę:- set down]

ęd·wé:he:k
we all (incl.) will in thought
[-e- think, hope, want]

ę·ga:gwé:niʼ
it can be; that is enough
[-gweni, gweny- be able to do s.t., succeed]

ę·gah·ne·go·wa·nę́ʼse:k
there will be big bodies of water
[-(h)neg(a)- water, liquid -(g)owanęʼs several big objects]

ę·gan·ya·dá·i:nyǫ:k
there will be lakes
[-nyad(a:)- lake, body of water, water -i:ʼ exist]

ę·gih·ę·dé:nyǫk
there will be streams, rivers
[-ihę- river, stream, creek -denyǫʼ several existing things]

ęh·níʼdagyeʼs
phases of the moon
[-ęhniʼd(a)- month, moon -dagyeʼ continue on, be ongoing]

ęh·oʼda·ih·aʼdǫ́h·ǫk
he will be warming s.t.
[-(ʼ)daihaʼd- warm up]

ęh·oh·do·gaʼdǫh·ǫ́꞉gyeʼ
he will be growing along
[-(a)hdogaʼd- grow s.t.]

ęhs·yaʼgyé꞉nęht
you can knock it down
[-yaʼd(a)- body -yaʼgyenęhd- knock s.t. down]

ęs·wa·da̱h·ǫh·si·yóhs·dęʼ
you will listen
[-(a)hǫhsiyohsd- listen to s.o., obey]

ę·wa·dę̱h·níʼdoʼkta꞉k
every month will end
[-ęhniʼd(a)- month -oʼkd- end]

ę·ya·go·deʼnyę·dę́hs·dǫ̱h·ǫ꞉k
she will be measuring things
[-(ʼ)nyędęhsd- measure]

ę·ya·go·dǫ́ʼse̱h·a꞉k
it will be happening for them (f/m)
[(a)d+…-ǫʼs happen for s.o.'s benefit]

ę·ya·go̱h·do·ga·dǫ́h·ǫg·yeʼ
she will be continually growing it, them
[-(a)hdogaʼd- grow s.t.]

ę·ya·go·yaʼda·da·ih·áʼdǫ̱h·ǫ꞉k
it will warm their (f/m) bodies
[-yaʼd(a)- body -(ʼ)daihaʼd- warm up]

ę·ya·gǫn·héh·gǫ̱h·ǫ꞉k
they (f/m) will live on it; what will sustain them
[P+…-ǫnhehg- live on, be sustained by s.t.]

ę·yeh·aʼdá·na·wę꞉ʼ
they (lit.: she) will wet their cores, throat
[-(h)aʼdanawę꞉ʼ quench one's thirst]

ę·yoh·na·wá·o꞉dǫ꞉k
there will be wells, water, springs
[-(h)naw(a)- running water -odǫʼ- several standing objects]

ę꞉yo·no̱h·dǫ́n·yǫh·ǫk
they (z) will be experiencing in thought; they will feel well
[-ęnǫhdǫnyǫ(꞉)- think, wonder, feel well]

ę·yǫn·heh·gǫ́h·ǫk
it will live on
[P+…-ǫnhehg- live on, be sustained by s.t.]

ę·yǫ·no̱h·dǫ́꞉nyǫ꞉ʼ
they (z) will experience in thought
[-ęnǫhdǫnyǫ(꞉)- think, wonder, feel well]

ga·di·dak·sé·nǫg·yeʼs
they (z) are running about, roaming
[-daksenǫgyeʼ roam, run about]

ga·dig·ye·nǫ꞉gyeʼ(s)
they (z) are flying, floating about in the air (for example, seeds, etc.)
[-gyenǫgyeʼs fly, float along]

ga·díh·si̱h·a꞉ʼ
they (z) are congregated
[A+…-(h)siha꞉ʼ stand in a bunch or group, congregate]

ga·dí꞉nyo꞉ʼ
wild animals
[-nyo꞉ʼ wild animal]

ga.dó:gę:
a certain way; together; a certain thing
[-dogę- right, true]

ga:gwa:gyeˀs
the sun; the moon
[-(r)agw(a)- heavenly body -gyeˀs fly]

gah.ne.go.wá:nęˀs
big waters
[-(h)neg(a)- water, liquid +owanęˀs several big objects]

gah.wa.ji.yáˀgęha:ˀ
the family kind
[-(h)wajiy(a)- family -geha:ˀ kind]

ga.ih.wa.ęt.gwáh.nǫˀ, ga.ih.wa.ę.dah.gwáh.nǫˀ
their (f/m) collective responsibility; delegations
[-(r)ihwaędahgw- responsibility]

ga.ih.wa.néˀak.sraˀ
sin
[ga+…-(r)ihwaneˀaksr(a)- sin]

gˀa.ni.gǫh.á:geh
on the minds
[-(ˀ)nigǫh(a)- mind -(aˀ)geh on]

ga.nǫ́h.ǫn.yǫhk, ga.nǫ́h.ǫn.yǫh
the Thanksgiving Address
[ga+…-nǫhǫnyǫh(g)- Thanksgiving Address]

gan.ya.dá.i:nyǫˀ
lakes
[-nyad(a:)- lake, body of water, water -inyǫˀ several existing things]

ga.ǫ:hya.dá:gyeˀ
on-going skies; the heavens
[-(r)ǫhy(a)- sky -dagyeˀ be ongoing]

gá.ǫ:hya.deˀ
in existing heaven
[-(r)ǫhy(a)- sky -deˀ exist]

gá.ǫ:nyǫˀ
it included some; it is in there
[ga+…-ǫnyǫˀ be in some place, be included]

ga.yaˀda.gén.hah.sraˀ
helpfulness
[ga+…-yaˀdagenhahsr(a)- helpfulness]

gé.i:
four

gę.dę́.ǫh.sraˀ
pity; mercy; compassion
[ga+…-(i)dęǫhsr(a)- pity]

gih.ę́.den.yǫˀ
streams; rivers; creeks
[-(r)ihę- river, stream, creek -denyǫˀ several existing things]

gǫh.do.ga.dǫ́h.ǫg.yeˀ
she is growing s.t.
[-(a)hdogaˀd- grow s.t.]

go.yaˀda.gǫ́h.sǫh.taˀ
human survivors
[P+…-yaˀdagǫhsohtaˀ survivor]

gǫ.wa.di.gó.wa.nęh
their leader
[TR+…-(g)owanęh lead s.o.]

gwaˀ tí:gę:
plainly; clearly; as it is
[-gę- see]

gwa·toh
it will be also

gwé:gǫh, ag·wé:gǫh, og·wé:gǫh
everything; all
[-gwegǫh all]

gyog·yę́h·dǫh
the first one; the beginning
[-yęhd- begin, be first]

gyo·ih·o·wá:neh
the most important
[d/g+...-(r)ih(wa)- word, affair -owanęh big]

gyǫn·héh·gǫh
what we all (incl.) live on; Our Sustenance
[-ǫnhehg- live on s.t., be sustained by s.t.]

ha'de·węh·níhs·ra·ge:
many days
[ha'de+...-ęhnihsr(a)- day -(a)ge: be a variety of things]

ha'de·ya·wę·noh·grá·ge:
a variety of weeds
[ha'de+...-węnohgr(a)- weed -(a)ge: be a variety of things]

ha·dih·á:wi's
they (m) carry along
[-(h)awi, (h)a:- hold, include, carry, bring]

ha·di·ǫh·ya'gęh·ó:nǫ'
they (m) are the heavenly kind
[-(r)ǫhy(a)- sky -(a')geh on -ho:nǫ' dwellers of]

Ha·di·wę·nó·dag·ye's
Thunderers; the Thunder Dance
[-węn(a)- voice, word -odagye's go along doing s.t.]

ha'ho'ni·góh·a'ehs
his mind settled on s.t.; he decided
[he+P+...-(')nigǫha'ehsd- decide]

ha·ná:gre'
he lives
[-nagre' live]

há·ǫh·a'geh
about him
[-haǫha' he alone -(a')geh on]

há·ǫ:nyah·nǫ'
he has included, designated
[-ǫnyahnǫ' include, designate]

ha·wé:'ǫ:
he has willed
[P+...-e:'ǫ: will s.t.]

ha'węh·nihs·ra·den·yǫ́:gye'
the days ahead
[ha'de-...-ęhnihsr(a)- day -denyǫ' all kinds of existing things]

he·gáhg·wę's
to the sun-down; the direction of the sunset; west
[-(h)gwę- set]

hes·ho'ni·goh·í:yo:
his mind is good over there
[-(')nigǫh(a)- mind -iyo nice, good]

hę̨d·wa·ih·wak·yę́·to',
hę̨d·wa·ih·wag·yę̨h·ę́·to'
we all (incl.) will participate in s.t.
[he+...-(r)ihwagyęhętw- participate, partake]

hę'hne:'
too; also; and

hę·ja:gǫ́:nęht
they (f/m) will swallow again
[he+...-ǫnęhd- swallow]

hę·nód·rah·sta'
they (m) sprinkle on
[-odrahsd- sprinkle]

ho·de·wa·yę·nǫ́:ni:
he has done it carefully
[(a)de+...-wayęnǫni- care for]

ho·dę·ih·ǫ́·dǫn·yǫ'
his appointed responsibilities; his assigned duties
[P+(a)d+...-(r)ihǫd- have appointed responsibilities]

ho·di·dag·wá·ihs·hǫ:
they (m) keep straight the ways
[-d(a)- way -gwaihs(i)- straight]

ho·dí·yahs·dǫh
they (m) have named it
[-yahsd- name s.o.]

ho·ih·wa·káhs·hǫg·weh
he has divided into parts or duties
[-(r)ih(wa)- word -kahsǫgw- divide into parts]

ho·nǫ·nih·á:gye's
they (m) are making, earning it
[-ǫni, ǫny- make]

Hos·gę'ę·geh·da·gó:wah
the Great Warrior
[-(h)sgyę'd(a:)- bones -gowah great]

ho·yę́t·wa'ǫh
he has planted already
[-yętw, yęto- plant]

i'geh
on my side

i:'hya:'
me first

jih·sǫ́:dahk
strawberry
[jihsǫdahk strawberry]

Ǫg·yǫhs·rah·ni·yǫ́hs·dǫh,
Ǫg·yǫ·wihs·rah·ni·yǫ́hs·dǫh
Our Sustenance; it strengthens our breathing
[-ǫhwihsr(a)- breath -(h)niyǫhsd- strengthen]

na'ga:tgwé:ni'
the best I could do
[-gweni, gweny- be able to do s.t.]

nah·a·wa·yę́·nan·he'
his finished creation; s.t. natural (lit.: what he has laid out)
[-wayęn- complete, finish]

na·ǫ·sa·ǫg·wa·yę́h·ę:k
what we all should be doing; how we all should conduct ourselves
[-ye(:)- do]

ne'
the

ne:ʼ
that, it (is)

ne:ʼah·sǫh
still, yet

ne:ʼdiʼneʼ
so it is

ne:ʼgiʼhne:ʼ
and just

ne:ʼgwa·tǫh
and also

ne:ʼgyę:ʼ
it is

ne:ʼgyęʼhne:
it is that

ne:hęʼhne:ʼ
too; also; and

ne:hne:ʼ
in fact

ne:ʼhne:neʼ
and that also is

ne:ʼhniʼ
also; and; too

ne:ʼhniʼneʼ
and

ne:ʼneʼ
it is

neʼo:nęh
it is now

ne·tog·yę:ʼ
be it so

ne·tog·yęnʼhǫ́:weh
it is where

ne:ʼtoh·ne:ʼ
and then

ne:ʼtsǫ:
it is only thing; that is all

nę:dah
this here

nę:toh
right here; over there

ni·gah·a:ʼ
how much it holds
[-(h)awi, (h)a:- hold, include, carry, bring]

ni·gęg·yo̱h·góʼdę:
an assembled crowd; a kind of crowd
[-(i)gyohg(wa)- crowd -oʼdę:- type of]

nig·ya:gó:yę:
the way she does s.t.
[-ye(:)- do]

nig·yó:yę:
what it is doing
[-ye(:)- do]

nih·ǫ·wá·i:hǫ:t
what he has appointed him
[TR+…-(r)ihǫd- appoint s.o.]

nis·ha·gó·i:hǫt
their duty; what he appointed them; their appointed duties.
[TR+…-(r)ihǫd- appoint s.o.]

ni·to:dí:yę:
as they (m) are continually doing s.t.
[-ye(:)- do]

ni·tó:yę:
what he is doing
[-ye(:)- do]

ni·ya·got·gę·ihs·dǫ́h·ǫg·ye'
she is travelling; as she is moving
[-gęihsdǫhǫgye' travel along]

ni·yé:ha:'
she holds
[-(h)awi, (h)a:- hold, include, carry s.t.]

ni·yo·dok·dá:gye's
up to these times
[(a)d+...o'kdagye's be at the end, edge]

ni·yóhs·ra·ge:
years
[ni+...-(o)hsr(a)- year, winter -(a)ge: be several]

ní:yoht
what it is like
[ni+...-(a)hd- be like, resemble]

ni·yǫg·we·dá:ge:
that many people
[ni+...-ǫgwe('da)- person -(a)ge: be several]

nyea:
the men's response at certain points in the Thanksgiving Address

odá'a·ǫt
web
[o+ -da'(a)- web -ǫd- attached]

O·deh·a·dǫ́:ni:
Maple Sap Ceremony; woods (trees)
[-(a)dehadǫ:ni: Maple Sap Ceremony; consists of: -(h)ad(a)- forest -ǫni, ǫny- make; grow]

od·wę·nǫhg·rǫ́n·yah·nǫ'
the growing weeds
[(a)d+...-węnohgr(a)- weed -ǫnyahnǫ' grow]

oh·ę́:dǫ:
ahead; in front; the front
[-(h)ęd- lead]

oh·na'ne·dá:nyǫ'
several levels
[-(h)naned- level -nyǫ' plural]

oh·na·wá·ǫ:dǫn·yǫ'
many wells; springs
[-(h)naw(a)- running water -ǫdǫnyǫ' several existing objects]

oh·né·ga·nohs
water
[-(h)neg(a)- water, liquid -(na')no- cold, cool]

oh·wáh·da'
maple
[o+...-(h)wahd(a)- maple]

oh·wę́·ja·de'
existing earth; land
[-ǫhwęj(a) earth, land -de' exist]

oh·wę́·ja·geh
on earth
[-ǫhwęj(a) earth, land -(a')geh on]

o·ih·o·wá:nęh
it is important; glory; a great or worthy commendation; it is special
[-(r)ih(wa)- word, affair -owanęh special, important]

o·ih·wag·wé:gǫh
everything; the whole idea
[-(r)ih(wa)- word -gwegǫh all]

o·jih·sǫ·dáh·sih·a:ʼ
stars showing
[-jihsǫd(a)- star -(h)siha:ʼ stand in a bunch or group, congregate]

o·nah·do·gę́h·ęg·yeʼ
they (z) are growing (plants and vegetation)
[-(a)hdogaʼd- grow s.t.]

ó:nęh
now; when

o·nǫ́hg·wa·traʼ
medicines
[o+...-nǫhgwatr(a)- medicine]

o·tǫ·dǫn·yáh·nǫʼ
growing bushes; saplings
[(a)d+ -(h)ǫd(a)- bush-ǫnyahnǫʼ grow]

o·tsę́·nǫn·yaʼt
a happy feeling; gratefulness; thankfulness; joy
[o+ (a)t+...-s(h)ęnǫnyaʼd happiness]

ǫg·wá·dǫ·se:
it is for us all; it is beneficial; we deserve it
[(a)d+...-ǫʼs be for s.o.'s benefit]

ǫg·waʼni·gǫ́h·aʼ
our mind
[-(ʼ)nigǫh(a)- mind]

Sgan·ya·dá·i:yoʼ
Beautiful Lake (Seneca Chief Title); Handsome Lake (the Messenger)
[s+ga+ -nyad(a:)- lake -iyoʼ good]

sgá:t
one

sgę́:nǫʼ
it is well
[-ęnǫ- well]

sgę·nǫ́:ʼǫh
it is slow; slowly
[-ęnǫ:ʼǫh slow]

sha·gó·ih·ǫ:t
he has appointed s.o.
[TR+...-(r)ihǫd- appoint]

shed·wa·go·wá:nęh
he is our leader
[TR+...-gowanęh lead]

shed·wah·jí:ʼah
our older brother
[-(h)jiʼah older sibling]

shęh, tsęh
of; because; how

shęh·oʼdęʼ
whatever

shę·nhǫ́:weh
whereabouts

shę·ní:yǫ:
the amount of
[-ǫ:- a number (of things)]

shǫg·wa·dę·naʼtrá·ę:ni:
the food he has given us
[-naʼtraęni- feed s.o.]

shǫg·wá:wi:
he has given us
[-awi, ǫ- give]

Shǫg·wa·yaʼdíhsʼǫh
the Creator; he is the Creator of our bodies
[-yaʼd(a)- body -ihsʼǫh- create]

sǫh·eh·ká:ʼ gá:gwa:ʼ
moon

ta·dihs·nyé:gyeʼs
they (m) look after all
[-(h)snye- care for, look after]

ta·ǫ:h·wę·já:deʼ
where his land exists
[-ǫhwęj(a)- earth, land -deʼ exist]

tęʼ
no

tę·né·da̱h·kwaʼ
where they (m) come from
[d+…-edahkw- come from]

toʼsę́h·dǫh
he has handed down
[d+…-(aʼ)sęhd- hand down, bring down]

tsaʼga:yę́:daʼ
when it became
[-yędaʼ become, acquire]

tsaʼha·ǫh·wę·já:da:t, tsaʼhǫh·wę·já:da:t
when he made the earth
[-ǫhwęj(a)- earth, land -dad- create]

tsaʼha·wa·yę:nę́:daʼ
what he finished or completed
[-wayęnędaʼ complete, finish]

wá:dǫh
it is said
[-(a)dǫh say]

wa̱h·ya·ni·yǫ́:taʼ
hanging fruit
[-(a)hy(a)- fruit, berry -niyǫd- hang]

waʼne:ʼ
today

Appendix I: Particles

1. ENGLISH-CAYUGA PARTICLE INDEX

above
  see: he:tgęh

after all
  see: seʼ

afterwards
  see: waʼji:hah
  see: waʼjih

again
  see: e:ʼ
  see: onęʼe:ʼ

aha!
  see: hoho:

all
  see: da:netoh
  see: gwe:gǫh, agwe:gǫh, ogwe:gǫh
  see: ne:ʼtsǫ:

almost
  see: o:nę to:hah, nęto:hah, to:hah
  see: wajihkę:ʼ (gyę:ʼ)

already
  see: o:nęgwa'

also
  see: neʼgiʼnih
  see: neʼgwatoh
  see: ne:ʼhęhne:ʼ
  see: hęʼhne:ʼ
  see: hę'ni:'
  see: ne:hniʼ
  see: ne:ʼhniʼne:ʼ
  see: hniʼ

amount
  see: do:gwaʼ

and
  see: neʼgiʼni
  see: hęʼhne:ʼ
  see: ne:hniʼ
  see: neʼgiʼnih

anything
  see: sgahoʼdęʼ

anywhere
  see: ga'toh
  see: tę' ga'toh

around
see: gaęgwaˀ nhǫ:(weh)

as for
see: iˀgeh

as is
see: gwa’ ti:gę:

barely
see: trǫhgeh tsǫ:

be
see: gę:
see: gwatoh
see: ne:ˀ
see: ne:ˀgyę:ˀ
see: ne:ˀgyę:neˀ
see: ne:ˀhne:ne:ˀ
see: ne:neˀ

because
see: giˀ gyę:ˀ
see: shęh, tsęh

before
see: gao:ˀ
see: gaoˀ nawahtgeh
see: gaoˀ shęh nyo:(weˀ)

both
see: dejaǫ:

clearly
see: gwaˀ ti:gę:

come on!
see: haoˀ

difference
see: hę:gyeh

distance
see: niyo:weˀ, nyo:weˀ

don’t
see: ahgwih

enough
see: To tsǫ:

ever
see: hwę:dǫh

everything
see: gwe:gǫh, agwe:gǫh, ogwe:gǫh

exclamations
see: aju!
see: hoho:
see: hotgǫ’ǫh
see: nę:
see: tsę:!
see: wa’gyęh

excuse me!
see: waˀgyęh

fact
see: hne:ˀ

far
see: gaę nyo:weˀ, gaę niyo:weˀ
see: i:nǫh
see: shęniyo:(weˀ)
see: to: niyo:(weˀ)

finally
see: waˀhehge:haˀ

first
see: hya:ˀ

generally
see: gę:s

good-bye
see: o:nẹh g'ihya:'

greatest
see: gyaọhẹ:'ẹh

guess
see: ọh

happen
see: tẹ'daọ
see: tẹ'gi'daọ

he
see: haọhẹ' haọha'

hello
see: hai'
see: gwe:

here
see: da...gwa:dih
see: nẹ:toh
see: nẹ:toh gwai

here!
see: nẹ:dah

hers
see: go:wẹh

hey!
see: hotgọ'ọh

his
see: ho:wẹh

how
see: do:
see: shẹh, tsẹh

how much
see: do:gwa'

how far
see: dodinyo:we'
see: gaẹ nyo:we', gaẹ niyo:we'

I
see: i:'

if
see: gẹh
see: gyẹ:gwa'

immediately
see: gọdagye'

instead
see: gihne:

is
see: gẹ:
see: gwatoh
see: ne:'
see: ne:'gyẹ:'
see: ne:'gyẹ:ne'
see: ne:'hne:ne:'
see: ne:ne'

isn't
see: degẹ:

isn't it so?
see: ẹ:'

it
see: aọhẹ'

its
see: o:wẹh

just
see: gi'
see: gi' gyẹ:'
see: gitsọ:
see: gwahs wahetsọ:

just (continued)
see: gyę:'gwahne:hwa'
see: he:gę:
see: nę:tsǫ:
see: se˺
see: tsǫ:
see: wa˺hetsǫ:
see: wajihkę:˺ (gyę:˺)

know
see: do:ga˺

later
see: wa˺ji:hah

less
see: gao:˺

let
see: do:˺ i:˺

little
see: nę:tsǫ:
see: stǫ:hah

long
see: wa˺hehge:ha˺

look!
see: nę:

lots
see: i:so˺

many
see: i:so˺
see: shęniyo:(we˺)

matter
see: hę:gyeh

maybe
see: (gat)gi˺shęhwa˺
see: gihshęh
see: gihshęhwa˺
see: gyę:gwa˺
see: gyę:˺gwahne:hwa˺
see: ne:gihshęh
see: ne:gihshęhwa˺
see: ǫhne:˺

me
see: i:˺
see: tę˺gini:˺

me first
see: i:˺hya:˺

me too
see: hę˺ni:˺

measure
see: do:gwa˺

mine
see: aga:węh

more
see: ahsǫh
see: trehs

most
see: aǫ:hę:˺ęh
see: gyaǫhę:˺ęh

move!
see: sigwa:dih

much
see: i:so˺
see: shęniyo:(we˺)

nearby
see: i:wa:k˺ah

never
  see: tę̓ hwę:dǫh

next
  see: hwa̓
  see: hya:̓
  see: ne:̓hwa̓

no
  see: hę̓ęh
  see: tę̓

No!
  see: o: tę̓ǫh

no?
  see: tę̓gęh

not
  see: o: tę'ǫh
  see: tę̓
  see: tę̓ gini:'
  see: tę̓ hne:̓

nothing
  see: (tę̓) sga̱ho̓dę̓

now
  see: da:nę:dah
  see: dane:onęh
  see: da:onęh
  see: ne̓onęh
  see: nętsǫ:gwatoh
  see: onę:di̓
  see: onę̓e:̓
  see: o:nęh
  see: wa̓(heh)
  see: wa̓hetsǫ:
  see: wa̓ne:̓

now and again
  see: ogwęhę:gye'

now and then
  see: ogwęhę:gye̓

nowhere
  see: ga̓toh
  see: tę̓ ga̓toh

o.k.
  see: hao̓

o.k., then
  see: Hao̓ d̓ęnyoh.

of
  see: shęh, tsęh

Oh really?
  see: o:
  see: o̓ ǫ:

one
  see: ne̓gi̓gyę:̓

only
  see: he:gę:
  see: tsǫ:
  see: i:s tsǫ:
  see: ne:'tsǫ:

or
  see: nigę̓ǫh

ouch
  see: agi:
  see: aju!

ours
  see: aga:węh

outdoor
  see: ahsdeh

outside
see: ahsdeh

over here
see: da...gwa:dih

over there
see: sigwa:dih
see: si:gyęh
see: si(hne:')
see: si:nhǫ:(weh), si:hǫ:(weh)

perhaps
see: (gat)gi' shęhwa'
see: gyę:gwa'

plainly
see: gwa' ti:gę:

please!
see: wa' gyęh

presently
see: wa' ji:hah

probably
see: ne:' gi' shęh

question
see: ęhę'
see: ę:'
see: gęh

quickly
see: nętsǫ:gwatoh

really
see: gwahs ǫ:weh
see: ne' ǫ:weh
see: tę' gihne:'
see: tę' gwahs ǫ:weh
see: tę' se'
see: tę' tǫ ne:'
see: tsęh ǫ:weh

really?
see: o:

reason
see: ne:' hǫ:ni'

right away
see: gǫdagye'

say
see: awę'

say!
see: hotgǫ' ǫh

she
see: gaǫhę'

side
see: gao:'
see: gwa:dih, gwai
see: i' geh gwadih

so be it
see: netogyę:'

so
see: di'
see: onę:di'

so?
see: o:

someone
see: sǫga:(' ah)

someplace
see: gaęgwa' nhǫ:(weh)

something
  see: sgaho'dę'
  see: skao'dę:'ęh, sga̱ho'dę:'ęh

sometime
  see: hwędǫgwa'
  see: tgwęhę:'

somewhere
  see: g'atoh
  see: g'ato:hah
  see: hǫ(weh), nhǫ:(weh)

soon
  see: wa'jihtsǫ:

still
  see: ahsǫh

suddenly
  see: o:nęgwa'

thank you
  see: nya:węh

that
  see: dane:'
  see: dane:'hni'
  see: gyę'hne:'
  see: ne'
  see: ne:'
  see: negę'nage'
  see: ne'gi'gyę:'
  see: ne'gi'ę:'
  see: ne'tone:'
  see: shęh, tsęh
  see: si:gyęh
  see: to:
  see: to:gyęh
  see: tǫ(:hwa')

the
  see: ne'

theirs (f/m)
  see: gona:węh

theirs (m)
  see: hona:węh

theirs (z)
  see: ona:węh

then
  see: di'
  see: toh geh

there
  see: nę:toh
  see: si
  see: sigwa:dih
  see: si:gyęh
  see: si(hne:')
  see: si:nhǫ:(weh), si:hǫ:(weh)
  see: to:
  see: to:hah
  see: to nhǫ: (weh), to hǫ: (weh)

thereabouts
  see: gaęgwa' nhǫ:(weh)

they (f/m)
  see: gonǫ:hę'

they (m)
  see: honǫ:hę'

they (z)
  see: onǫ:hę'

this
  see: nę:dah
  see: nę:gyęh

time
  see: ne:' gwahs hwa'

today
 see: waˀneːˀ

too
 see: hęˀhneːˀ
 see: hniˀ
 see: neˀgiˀnih
 see: neːhniˀ

too much
 see: jitrehs

uh-oh
 see: hohoː

until
 see: shęniyoː(weˀ)

up
 see: heːtgęh

wait
 see: waˀjih

wait!
 see: waˀjihyaːˀ

way
 see: gaoːˀ
 see: neˀgiˀęːˀ

we
 see: iːˀ

welcome
 see: nyoh

well
 see: gweː

what
 see: dęˀ
 see: dęˀhoˀdęˀ
 see: hoˀdęˀ
 see: ne'gi'gyęː'

what the...?!
 see: hoh

whatever
 see: shęhoˀdęˀ

when
 see: hwęːdǫh
 see: nęh
 see: oːnęh

where
 see: danhǫweh
 see: gaęːdiˀ
 see: (gaę) hǫː(weh)
 see: netogyę(n)hǫːweh
 see: shęnhǫːweh
 see: toː
 see: to nhǫː(weh), to hǫː(weh)

whether
 see: gęh

which
 see: gaę
 see: sǫ ˀǫ naht

while
 see: waˀjihtsǫː
 see: waˀjihyaː'

who
 see: sǫ(ˀǫh)
 see: sǫː hneːˀ naht
 see: sǫ ˀǫ naht

whose
 see: sǫː goːwęh

why
see: dę̓ hne:̓
see: ne:̓ hǫ:ni̓

wow!
see: hotgǫ̓ ǫh

yes
see: ęhę̓
see: ę:̓

yet
see: ahsǫh

you
see: i:s

yours
see: sa:węh

2. CAYUGA-ENGLISH PARTICLES

aga:wẹh
it is mine, ours
[(a)wẹh have, own]

agi:
ouch!

ahgwih
Don't...

(Ahgwih) ẹdihsa'dre:. Don't drive over here.

Ahgwih hẹhsa'dre:. Don't drive over there.

Ahgwih dẹhsnigọhaẹ'. Don't bother it.

Ahgwih ẹhsa:sdi:s. Don't disturb it; don't handle it.

aju!
ouch! (exclamation, said when you touch something cold or hot)

aọhẹ'
it (lit.: it is alone)
[(a)ọhẹ' alone]

aọ:hẹ:'ẹh
the most

ahsdeh
outside, outdoor

ahsọh, ahsọ(h)
still, yet, some more; More! (Said when you want someone to pour a drink.)

Ahsọ gẹh? Do you want some more?

Ahsọh ne:' ahahsowẹh. He's still angry.

Ahsọ hodre:nọ:t. He's still singing.

Ahsọh ni:' agọtsanọhwa:s ne' dagaihọ:ni' gyotedẹhshọ:'ọh agahyagwẹhne:'. My knees are still sore because of the other day (when) I picked fruit.

Ahsọh awagahyagwẹhẹgye'se:k gyẹ:gwa' ta:waknọhy'agọ:k. I would still be picking fruit if I didn't get hurt. (I would still have been picking fruit if I hadn't been hurt).

Ahsọh e'nihs desatwẹ:jo:nih! You still want more!

awẹ'
it is said

da
here (does not occur alone)

see: **dagwa:dih, da...gwa:dih**

see: **dane:'**

see: **dane:'hni'**

see: **dane:onẹh**

see: **da:netoh**

see: **da:nẹ:dah**

see: **danhọweh**

see: **da:onẹh**

see: **nẹ:dah**

dagwa:dih
over here, this side here
[da, gwa:dih]

dane:', dane(:')
that it
[da, ne:']

dane:ʼhniʼ, dane(:ʼ)hni(ʼ)
that also
[da, ne:ʼ, hniʼ]

Dane:ʼhniʼ dwę:dǫh. That is also what we mean.

dane:ʼonęh, dane(:ʼ)onę(h)
and now that
[da, ne:ʼ, o:nęh]

Dane:onęh to niya:węhdreʼ. And now this is what is going to happen.

da:netoh
that is all
[da, neʼ, to]

da:nę:dah
now this also
[da, nę:, nę:dah]

Da:nę:dah haʼgaheʼ gaoʼ ędihswatrihs ęhswadahǫhsi:yohs. Now is the time to come closer and listen.

danhǫweh, da(n)hǫweh
this is where
[hǫ(weh), nhǫ:(weh), da]

Da:nhǫ:weh hǫ: hęʼdrǫʼ ne:ʼ haksaʼgo:wah. This is where he lives, the good-looking man.

da:onęh
and now
[da, o:nęh]

degę:hęh, (tęʼ) degę:hęh
not too many
[gę:]

dejaǫ:
both (of you two)

dęʼ, dę(ʼ)
what (short form); why
[dęʼ, hoʼdęʼ]

Dęʼ hne:ʼ i:se:ʼ? What do you want?

Dęʼ hne:ʼ ni:yoht shęh ahadone:k? Why did he leave?

Agyaʼdahsdeʼ dęhni:ʼ. I'm heavy.

Dęʼ ni:s ętsahtgaʼ? What will you give, donate?

Dęʼ ni:s saʼnigǫhoʼdę:? What are your thoughts?

Dęhne:ʼ ni:yoht tsęh toh nahsye:ʼ. Why did you do that?

dęʼ hne:ʼ, dę(ʼ) hne(:ʼ)
what? why?; what is that? why me? (or any similar expression of exasperation)
[dęʼ, hne:ʼ]

Dęʼ hne:ʼ i:se:ʼ? What do you want?

Dęʼ hne:ʼ ni:yoht i:se:ʼ? Why do you want it that way?

Dęʼ hne:ʼ ni:yoht shęh ahadone:k? Why did he leave?

Dęhne:ʼ ni:yoht tsęh toh nahsye:ʼ. Why did you do that?

dęʼhoʼdęʼ dę(ʼ)ho(ʼ)dę(ʼ)
what
[dęʼ, hoʼdęʼ]

Dęʼ hne: hoʼdęʼ? What kind?

Haoʼ dahskro:wih dęʼ ni:ʼ (hoʼ dęʼ) nęga:gye:ʼ. O.k., you tell me what to do!

Haoʼ dęhskro:wiʼ dęʼ niʼ (hoʼ dęʼ) nęga:gye:ʼ. Tell me what to do.

di', di(')
so, then

Do:gęhs di' gęh? Is that true (then)?

Gaę di' nhǫ:weh nihswe's o:nęh? Where then are you now?

Hwę:dǫh di' ęje:yǫ'? When then is she going to return?

I:s di' gęh hne:'? How about you then?

Nę' di' ni:s? How about you then?

Ne:' di' gęh? Is that it then? (that is, is that what you were referring to?)

Sanǫhǫkda:ni' gę di'? Are you sick (then)?

Ęhsne' gęh di'? Are you coming along (then)?

Ęhę: sgęnǫh. Nę' di' ni:s? I'm fine thanks. And you (then)?

Do: di' nęyonishe'? How long will it take (then)?

do:, do(:)
how (or other terms involving measurement)

Daskro:wi' do: niyowihsdae' ęsahdę:di'. You tell me at what time you're going to leave.

Do: nitga:de'? How high?

Do: gwa' nęyonishe'. A certain length of time.

Do: i:'! Let me!; How about me?

Do: ni:wa's? How big?

Do: niga:gǫ? How many people?

Do: niya:ga'? How big is it/she?

Do: niyo:? How many, how much?

Do: nidihse:no:'? How old are you? (singular)

Do:gwa' ni:yǫ: ęsaga:dę'. It is going to cost you a certain amount.

Do: gwa' na'ǫnihshe'? How long did it take?

Do: di' nęyonishe'? How long will it take?

do: i:'
let me!
[do, i:']

dod'inyo:we', dod(')inyo:(we')
how far is it then?
[do, di', niyo:(we'), nyo:(we')]

do:ga'
I do not know

do:gwa'
how; certain amount, a measure
[do, gwa']

Do: gwa' nęyonishe'. A certain length of time.

Do:gwa' ni:yǫ: ęsaga:dę'. It is going to cost you a certain amount.

e:', e(:')
again

Agahdrǫ's onęh e: jitrehs satshę:nǫ:nih. I'm frightened now (again) because you're too happy.

I:' gęh e: sgwatro:wi:? Are you talking about me again? (joking)

Onęh e: agri'sdowa:neh.... (now again) I'm loud, noisy

e:ʼ (continued)

i:hs gyęʼhne:ʼ tsǫ: e:ʼ toh nahsye:ʼ You're the only one that did that again

jidwahshe:t e:ʼ. Let's count again!

jidwahshe:t giʼ gyeʼ e:ʼ. Let's count it again then!

Hehshę:da:ge:ʼ e:ʼ. He's lying over there again!

O:nęh e:ʼ i:s toh haʼsegǫhe:k. You're getting into someone else's fight again, butting in.

Ahsǫh e:ʼnihs desaʼtwę:jo:nih! You still want more (again)!

Neʼgiʼę:ʼ e:ʼ toh iheʼs. He's here again!

Tsę: eʼneʼ satro:wi:. You're talking about that again! (Expression of disgust.)

ę:ʼ, ę(:ʼ)

Isn't it so? Yes? (question marker; asking for confirmation)

Ę: nʼaganǫhsa:dih ita:t. He's standing on the other side of the house.

Enǫhweʼs ę:ʼ? She likes it...(doesn't she?) (This is a statement with some doubt; it asks for some confirmation.)

ęhęʼ

yes; expressions using this word include:

Ęhęʼ gęh? Is that right?

Ęhęʼ seʼ. It is so.

gaʼ, g(ʼ)a

(does not occur alone)

see: **gʼatoh**

see: **gʼato:hah**

see: **tęʼ gaʼtoh**

gaę, gaę(:)

which, where, somewhere

Gaę diʼ nhǫ:weh nihsweʼs o:nęh? Where then are you now?

Gaę niyeyaʼda:ʼ? Which person? Which woman?

Gaę ni:ga: i:seʼ a:se:k? Which one do you want to eat?

Gaęgwaʼ nhǫ:(weh) tǫwaʼnigǫha:ʼ. She waits for him somewhere, someplace.

Gaę nǫdahse:? Where do you come from?

Gaę nhǫ nǫdi:se:nǫ:? Where are you from?

Gaę nhǫ tsiʼdrǫʼ? Where do you live?

Gaę hwaʼ nhǫ hejisaihoʼdeʼ? Where do you work?

Gaę niyo:weh heha:we:nǫ:. How far has he gone?

gaęnhǫ:weh, (gaę) hǫ(:weh), (gaę) nhǫ(:weh)

what place, where

[gaę, hǫ(weh), nhǫ:(weh)]

Gaę diʼ nhǫ:weh nihsweʼs o:nęh? Where then are you now?

Gaę diʼ nhǫ:weh heha:we:nǫ:? Where then has he gone?

Gaęgwaʼ nhǫ:(weh) tǫwaʼnigǫha:ʼ. She waits for him somewhere, someplace.

gaęnhǫ:weh (continued)
Gaę nhǫ nǫdi:se:nǫ:? Where are you from?

Gaę nhǫ tsi'drǫ'? Where do you live?

Gaę hwa' nhǫ hejisaiho'de'? Where do you work?

gaę nyo:we', gaę n(i)yo:(we')
How far?
[gaę, niyo:(we'), nyo:(we')]

Gaę niyo:weh heha:we:nǫ:. How far has he gone?

gaę:di', gaę(:)di(')
where is it then (emphasizing where)
[gaę, di']

Gaę di' nhǫ:weh nihswe's o:nęh? Where then are you now?

Gaę di' nhǫ:weh heha:we:nǫ:? Where then has he gone?

gaęgwa' nhǫ:weh, gaęgwa(') (n)hǫ:(weh)
somewhere around; someplace, thereabouts
[gaę, gwa', hǫ(weh), nhǫ:(weh)]

Gaęgwa' nhǫ:(weh) tǫwa'nigǫha:'. She waits for him somewhere, someplace.

gao:', gao(:')
this side, this way; at this time; before; less

gao' shę nyo:' to: nęya:węh before that happens

gao' nawahtgeh tsa'gaǫdri:yo'. The time before, they fought.

Gao' nǫdahse:'. Come this way.

Da:nę:dah ha'gahe' gao' ędihswatrihs ęhswadahǫhsi:yohs. Now is the time to come closer and listen.

gao' nawahtgeh, gao(') nawahtgeh
before that time
[gao:', nawahtgeh]

Gao' nawahtgeh tsa'gaǫdri:yo'. The time before, they fought.

gao' shęh nyo:(we'), gao(') tsęh nyo:(we')
before that time
[gao:', shęh/tsęh, niyo:(we'), nyo:(we')]

gao' shę nyo:' to: nęya:węh before that happens

gaǫhę'
she, her (lit.: she is alone)
[(a)ǫhę' alone]

(gat)g'ishęhwa', (gat)gi(')shęhwa(')
maybe, perhaps
[gi', shęh, tsęh, hwa']

Ne' gihshęhwa' e:dǫh. Maybe that's the one she means.

g'atoh, g(')ato(h)
nowhere, somewhere, anywhere
[ga', to, to:hah]

G'atoh tsǫ: ta:se:tsęi:. Nowhere only will you find it

g'ato:hah, g(')ato(:)hah
somewhere
[ga', to, to:hah]

G'ato:hah todahsdǫh. He's hiding somewhere.

G'atohah tsǫ: ęse:tsaę'. You will find it someplace.

gę:, gę(:)
be the one
[gę:]

Tę' ne:' degę:. It's not the one.

Trehs gi' gę'. My goodness!

gęh, gę(h)
particle indicating a question; whether, if, etc.
[gęh]

Ahsǫ gęh? Do you want some more?

Dahe' gęh tę' nigę'ǫh? Is he coming or not?

Daskro:wih sanǫhǫkda:ni' gęh? Tell me whether you're sick.

Daskro:wih ędwe: gęh. Tell me if you're coming along.

Do:gęhs di' gęh? Is that true?

Dǫdahe' gęh? Is he coming back?

Do:gęhs gęh? Is that the case? Is that true?

Enǫhwe's gęh? Does she like it?

Hǫgweh gęh agǫgweh nigę'ǫh Kim eya:sǫh? Was it a man or a woman whose name is Kim?

Hǫgweh gęh agǫgweh nigę'ǫh? Is it a man or a woman?

Hǫgwe'di:yo: gęh? Is he a kind person?

I:s di' gęh hne:'? How about you then?

Ihse: gęh to: ne: dwa:ye:? Do you think we should do it that way?

Ne:' di' gęh? Is that it then? (that is, is that what you were referring to?)

O: gęh? Said when really questioning someone.

Sanǫhǫkda:ni' gi' gęh? Are you really sick? Are you sick for sure?

Sanǫhǫkda:ni' gę di'? Are you sick?

To gę'ǫh ni:yoht? I wonder if it's like that?

To: gęh ha'se' shęh nho: dedwatgęnyo:? Are you going to the fair?

Tę' gęh dehse: to: ne:' dwa:ye'? Don't you think we should do that?

Tę' gęh dehsho:yǫ:? Did he not come home?

Tę' gęh? Isn't it?

Ędwe:' gęh? Are you coming along with us?

Ęhę' gęh? Is that right?

Ęhsne' gęh di'? Are you coming along?

Ęsgoho:wi' to gęh ne: hęyę:'. I will tell you if she's going.

Ęshe' gęh? Are you going to come?

Gayogǫho:nǫh gę' ni:s nahsya'dodę'? Are you Cayuga?

Sǫgwehǫ:weh gęh? Are you Indian?

I:' gęh sgi:dǫh? Do you mean me?

I:' gęh sgwatro:wi:? Are you talking about me? (a little bit paranoid)

I:' gęh e: sgwatro:wi:? Are you talking about me again? (joking)

Sgęnǫjih gęh? Are you well?

Snigǫha:' gęh? Are you expecting, watching for something?

gęh (continued)
I:s gęhne:ʼ? Was that you?

Ętne:ʼ gęh? Do you want to come along with me?

gę:s
generally, used to, usually, basically

I:soʼ agidahsgęhę:ʼ gę:s. I used to sleep a lot.

Jiʼ gę:s trehs sheno:wę:. You lie too much; you're too much of a liar (generally).

Ne:ʼ gę:s ga:dǫh. That's what I usually say.

Ji gę:s trehs jahsę: tsęh nisnihnę:ye:s. You're (generally) too fat for your height.

Ahsǫheh ge:s agahdrǫni:h. I'm (usually) afraid of the dark.

Tsigǫgweʼda:seʼ gę:s gahyagwahsgęhę:ʼ. When I was a young person I usually picked berries.

Knǫhweʼs gę:s tsigǫgweʼda:seʼ tiga:gwe:gǫh gę:s agahyagwęhęgyeʼsgęhę:ʼ. When I was young, I used to love going all over and picking fruit.

Ogwęhę:gyeʼ gę:s ahsyǫʼ. Now and again (that is, in general) you'll be here.

giʼ, gi(ʼ)
just, really

Giʼ trehs aǫgohdǫh. It's (just) beyond.

Ne:ʼ giʼ e:dǫh. That's (just) what she means.

Ne:ʼ giʼ gi:dǫh. That's (just) what I mean.

Ne:ʼ giʼ hę:dǫh. That's (just) what he means.

O: tęʼǫ: giʼ, gatgʼishęh ne:ʼ hwaʼ (Just) maybe I will, maybe I won't (come along)

O:nęh giʼ hodehsronihsʼǫh. He is (just) ready now.

O:nęh giʼ ęgoyęʼęsętwahsǫʼǫh. I'm (just) now going to kick you around.

Sanǫhǫkda:niʼ giʼ gęh? Are you really sick? Are you sick for sure?

To giʼ shęh ha:ge:. just maybe I should go there.

Trehs giʼ gęʼ. My goodness!

Tęʼ gʼatoh. Tęʼ giʼ dehe:gę: Nowhere. I just didn't see him.

Tęʼ giʼ gwah dewagadaʼgaideʼ. I'm just not feeling well.

Waheʼ giʼ gatahi:neʼ. I'm just getting on my way.

Agaʼtsęnǫ:ni: giʼ tsęh sadaʼgaideʼ. I'm just happy that you are well.

Hoihoʼdeʼsri:yo: giʼ ne:ʼ. He just has a good job.

Ahi:ʼ giʼ to na:ya:węh. I just thought that's what should happen.

Ahi:ʼ ˋgiʼ to nęya:węh. I just thought that's what would happen.

Neʼgiʼgyęʼ asiʼ. That's just what you said.

Neʼgiʼgyęʼ gaǫ:dǫh. That's just what the women say.

Neʼgiʼgyęʼ hana:dǫh. That's just what the men say.

gi' (continued)
Hęgyehgi'! just leave well enough alone!

Tę'gi'daǫ: to na:ya:węh. No, it (just) will not happen.

Tę'gihne:' dedo:gęhs de'sa:dǫh. No, it's not really true what you're saying.

Tę'gidaǫ tayagogaę:. No, she (just) will never agree to...

Tę'gini:' to ta:gye:. No, I (just) will not do that.

gi' gyę:', gi(') gyę(:')
just (because)
[gi', gyę:']

Jidwahshe:t gi' gye' e:'. Let's (just) count it again then!

Ne:' gi' gyę:'. Just because.

g'ihne:', g(')ihne(:')
instead
[gi', hne:']

g'ihshęh, g(')ihshęh, g(')itsęh
maybe
[gi', shęh, tsęh]

O: tę'ǫh, gatg'ishęh gye:gwa'. Maybe, maybe not.

O: tę'ǫh, gatg'ishęh ne:' hwa'. Maybe, maybe not.

Tę' g'i shęh. Maybe not

g'ihshęhwa', g(')ihshęhwa('), g(')ihtsęhwa(')
maybe that
[gi', shęh, tsęh, hwa']

Tę' gi' shęh hwa'. Maybe not.

g'itsǫ:, g(')itsǫ(:)
just that, just there
[gi', tsǫ:]

To: gitsǫ: ni:yǫ:. That's just all there is.

gona:węh
it is theirs (f/m)
[(a)węh have, own]

gonǫ:hę'
they (f/m) (lit.: they (f/m) are alone)
[(a)ǫhę' alone]

go:węh
it is hers
[(a)węh have, own]

gǫdagye'
immediately, right away
[gǫdagye']

Gǫdagye' ętsahdę:di'. You will leave right away!

gwa', gwa(')
referring to a measure of time (does not occur alone)

see: **do:gwa'**

see: **gaęgwa' nhǫ:(weh)**

see: **gwa' ti:gę:**

see: **gwatoh**

see: **gyę:gwa'**

see: **gyę:'gwahne:hwa'**

see: **hwędǫgwa'**

see: **ne'gwatoh**

see: **nętsǫ:gwatoh**

see: **o:nęgwa'**

gwa' ti:gę:, gwa(') ti:gę:
plainly, clearly, as it is
[gwa', ti:gę:]

gwa:dih, gwai
to one side

Si:hne:' gwai hęhsadi'. Throw that over there!

see: **sigwa:dih**

gwahs
(does not occur alone)

see: **gwahs ǫ:weh**

see: **gwahs wahetsǫ:**

see: **ne:' gwahs hwa'**

see: **tę' gwahs ǫ:weh**

gwahs ǫ:weh
really
[gwahs, ǫ:weh]

Gwahs ǫ:weh a:yę' tę' desho:tǫ:de'. It really seems like he doesn't (want to) hear; he has selective hearing.

Gwahs ǫ:weh tsa'ho:ya:t honi'ǫh. He can't help himself, he's really really stingy.

gwahs wahetsǫ:
just now; just a few seconds ago
[gwahs, wa'(heh), tsǫ:]

Gwahs wa'hetsǫ: to: na'a:węh. That just happened.

gw'atoh, gw(')ato(h)
it will be also; also
[gwa', to]

Ne' gwatoh gi:dǫh. I also mean that.

gwe:
well! (surprise or sarcasm); can also mean 'hello'

Gwe: a:ye' sanǫhyagǫh! Well, it looks like you're hurt!

gwe:gǫh, agwe:gǫh, ogwe:gǫh
everything, all

gyaǫhę:'ęh
the most, the greatest
[aǫhę:'ęh]

ne' gyaǫhę:'ęh gyonǫ'shehsde:' the most sickening, tiring, aggravating

gyę:', gyę(:')
(does not occur alone)

see: **gi' gyę:'**

see: **gyę:gwa'**

see: **gyę:'gwahne:hwa'**

see: **gyę'hne:'**

see: **ne:'gyę:'**

see: **ne:'gyę:ne'**

see: **netogyę:'**

see: **netogyę(n)hǫ:weh**

see: **wajihkę:' (gyę:')**

gyę:'gwa', gyę(:')gwa(')
maybe, if, perhaps, what if, if only
[gyę:', gwa']

Gyę:gwa' ahagwe:ni'? Maybe if he could do it, if he is able?

Gyę:gwa' ahogaę', ahagaę'? Maybe if he would agree, if he's willing?

Gyę:gwa' o:nęh ahahdę:di'? What if he should leave now?

gyę:ˀgwaˀ (continued)
O: tęˀǫh, gatgˀishęh gye:gwaˀ. Maybe, maybe not.

A:ga̱hyagwa̱hse:k se hę ni:ˀ gyę:gwaˀ a:wagadagaide:k. I would be a fruit picker too if I were well.

A:ga̱hya:goˀ gyę:gwaˀ a:sgyena:wahs. I would pick fruit if only you would help me.

Ahsǫh awaga̱hyagwęhęgyeˀse:k gyę:gwaˀ ta:waknǫhyˀagǫ:k. I would still be picking fruit if I didn't get hurt. (I would still have been picking fruit if I hadn't been hurt).

gyę:ˀgwaˀhne:ˀhwaˀ, gyę(:ˀ)gwa(ˀ)hne:(ˀ)hwa(ˀ)
just maybe
[gyę:ˀ, gwaˀ, hne:ˀ, hwaˀ]

gyęh, gyę(h)
(does not occur alone)

see: **nę:gyęh**

see: **si:gyęh**

see: **to:gyęh**

see: **waˀgyęh**

gyęˀhne:ˀ, gyę(ˀ)hne(:ˀ)
that is
[gyę:ˀ, hne:ˀ]

I:hs gyęˀhne:ˀ That's you!

I:hs gyęˀhne:ˀ toh nahsye:ˀ. Are you the one that did it.

I:hs gyęˀhne:ˀ tsǫ: e:ˀ toh nahsye:ˀ You're the only one that did that again

haiˀ
hello (a word attributed to Oneida or Tutelo)

haoˀ
o.k.; come on!

Haoˀ dahskro:wih dęˀ ni:ˀ (hoˀ dęˀ) nęga:gye:ˀ. O.k., you tell me what to do!

haoˀ dˀęnyoh, hao(ˀ) d(ˀ)ęnyoh
O.k. then.
[haoˀ, dęˀ, nyoh]

haǫhęˀ, haǫhaˀ
he (lit.: he is alone)
[(a)ǫhęˀ alone]

he:gę:
just, only, all

Ne:ˀ he:gę: agyǫhsętoh. All she did was cry.

he:tgęh
up, above

hęˀ, hę(ˀ)
refers to also, too (does not occur alone)

see: **hęˀhne:ˀ**

see: **hęˀni:ˀ**

see: **ne:ˀhęhne:ˀ**

hęˀęh
no (a slang-like expression)

hę:gyeh, hę:gye(h)
it doesn't matter; it doesn't make any difference

Hęgyehgiˀ! Leave well enough alone!

Aweˀ hęgyeh tsǫ:. Let it go! (It's not worth bothering.)

hę'hne:', hę(')hne(:')
too, also, and
[hę', hne:']

Honahsę: hę' ne' dẹhęnadęhnọ:drọ'. Your brothers are fat.

hę'ni:', hę(')ni(:')
me too
[hę', ne', i:']

Ęgahyagwahse:k hę ni:' nęh ęgahdo:k. I'll be a fruit picker when I grow up.

A:gahyagwahse:k se hę ni:' gyę:gwa' a:wagadagaide:k. I would be a fruit picker too if I were well.

hne:', hne(:')
in fact

Dę' hne:' i:se:'? What in fact do you want?

Dę' hne: ho'dę'? What kind in fact?

I:s di' gęh hne:'? How about you then in fact?

Ne:' hne:' go:węh. That's hers in fact.

Tę' hne:' dehoyętwęh. No, in fact he did not plant. (emphatic)

Dęhne:' ni:yoht tsęh toh nahsye:'. Why in fact did you do that?

I:s gęhne:'? Was that in fact you?

Ne:'hęhne:' gaọgwe'da'. Also in fact that is her family, one of her people.

Ne:'hne:ne' gaihwagwę:ni:yo. That in fact is the main thing, the main item.

Tę'gihne:' dedo:gęhs de'sa:dọh. No, it's not in fact really true what you're saying.

hni', hni(')
also, and, too

Dę' hni' ho'dę' hoiho'dęhsro'de'? And what does he do?

Dane:'hni' dwę:dọh. That is also what we mean.

ho'dę', ho(')dę(')
what
[dę', ho'dę']

Gado:gę: shęh ho'dę' a'ọgwayọdahk. A certain something brought us together (that is, a meeting).

hoh!
what the...?! (expression of surprise)

hoho:!
Aha! Uh-oh! Yes! (exclamation, said in anticipation of something bad or good; for example, someone's about to win at bingo, or have a fight)
[hoho:]

hona:węh
it is theirs (males only)
[(a)węh have, own]

honọ:hę'
they (males) (lit.: they (males) are alone)
[(a)ọhę' alone]

hotgọ'ọh
Say! Hey! Wow! What the...?! For Heaven's sake! (exclamation; said when something is out of the ordinary).

Hotgọ'ọh asyọ'! For heaven's sake, you got here! What the... you made it!

ho:wę̱h
it is his
[(a)wę̱h have, own]

hǫ:, hǫ(:)
there (does not occur alone)

see: **danhǫweh**

see: **gaęgwa' nhǫ:(weh)**

see: **(gaę) hǫ:(wch)**

see: **hǫ(weh), nhǫ:(weh)**

see: **netogyę(n)hǫ:weh**

see: **shę̱nhǫ:weh**

see: **si:nhǫ:(weh), si:hǫ:(weh)**

see: **to nhǫ: (weh), to hǫ: (weh)**

see: **danhǫweh**

hǫ:ni'
referring to a reason why (does not occur alone)
see: **ne:'hǫ:ni'**

hǫ(:weh), (n)hǫ(:weh)
to be somewhere

Da:nhǫ:weh hǫ: hę'drǫ' ne:' haksa'go:wah. This is where he lives, the good-looking man.

Shę̱nhǫweh hehehta' onę'dagǫhsǫ', agę'. Where he goes, under the pines it's been said.

Si:nhǫ:weh tgani:yǫ:t sagya'dawi'tra'. Your coat is hanging way over there.

To hǫ: hę:ge' dwagye:sę̱h. There I will go where it's cheap (shopping).

hwa', hwa(')
next (the 'a' is sometimes nasalized) (does not occur alone)

see: **(gat)gi'shę̱hwa'**

see: **gihshę̱hwa'**

see: **ne:gihshę̱hwa'**

see: **ne:' gwahs hwa'**

see: **ne:'hwa'**

see: **tǫ(:hwa')**

hwę̱dǫgwa', hwę̱dǫgwa(')
sometime
[hwę:dǫh, gwa']
Hwę̱dǫgwa' toniyawę̱hdre'. Sometime it's going to happen. (i.e. a prediction)

Hwę̱dǫgwa' toniyawę'ǫh It happened sometime in the past.

hwę:dǫh, hwę(:)dǫ(h)
ever, when

Daskro:wi' hwę:do' ęsahdę:di'. Tell me when you're going to leave.

Hwę:dǫh di' ęje:yǫ'? When then is she going to return?

Hwę:dǫh ne:' to nęya:wę̱h? When is that going to happen?

Hwę:dǫh ęyǫhdę:di'? When is she going away?

hya:', hya(:')
refers to a period of time (does not occur alone)

see: **i:'hya:'**

see: **o:nę̱h g'ihya:'**

see: **wa'jihya:'**

i:ʼ, ni:ʼ, (n)i(:ʼ)
me, I, we, us
[(neʼ), i:ʼ]

Do: i:ʼ! Let me!; How about me?

... ni:ʼ gaǫgyahstaʼ. They call me … (not common)

Gayogo̲ho:nǫh ni:ʼ. I'm Cayuga.

Gǫgwehǫ:weh ni:ʼ. I'm Indian.

I:ʼ gęh sgi:dǫh? Do you mean me?

I:ʼ tgegowa:nęh. I'm the oldest.

I:ʼ gęh sgwatro:wi:? Are you talking about me? (a little bit paranoid)

I:ʼ gęh e: sgwatro:wi:? Are you talking about me again? (joking)

Agyaʼdahsteʼ dęhni:ʼ. I'm heavy.

Tęʼ ni: toh ta:ge:ʼ. No, I'm not going there.

E̲gatrǫnyahnese:k ni:ʼ I'll be the teller (that is, I'll go around and announce something)

Tęʼ niʼ ta:gye:na: I refuse to accept it.

Ahsǫh ni:ʼ agǫtsanǫhwa:s neʼ dagaihǫ:niʼ gyotede̲hshǫ:ʼǫh agahyagwęhne:ʼ. My knees are still sore because of the other day (when) I picked fruit.

Tęʼgini:ʼ to ta:gye:. No, I will not do that.

i:ʼgeh, i(:ʼ)geh
as for me
[i:ʼ, geh]

i:ʼgeh gwa:dih
on my side; referring to a matrilineage
[gwadih, gwai]

i:ʼhya:ʼ, i(:ʼ)hya(:ʼ)
me first
[i:ʼ, hya:ʼ]

i:nǫh
far

I:nǫh tgidrǫʼ. I live far away.

I:nǫh tgasgwiʼdraę:ʼ. Far away this Old Prune lives/sits.

i:s, i(:h)s
you

i:s tsǫ:
only you; you'll do.
[i:s, tsǫ:]

i:soʼ
much, many, lots

I:soʼ gʼadrehdʼashǫ:ʼǫh ho:yęʼ ǫtgahiʼdahkwaʼ He has many toy cars.

I:soʼ agidahsge̲hę:ʼ gę:s. I used to sleep a lot.

Aǫgo̲hdǫh ǫgeʼdra̲hehs i:soʼ. I ate too much

I:soʼ go̲hwihsdaęʼ Onehagwat giʼ. She has a lot of money; it's amazing how much!

i:soʼ degade̲nǫhǫnyǫh. I am very thankful.

i:wa:kʼah
nearby

I:wa:kʼah dǫdahotrihsdo̲hǫgyeʼ. He's getting nearer and nearer again.

jih, ji(h)
refers to a measure of amount or time (does not occur alone)

see: **jitrehs**

see: **waʼjih**

see: **wajihkę:ʼ (gyę:ʼ)**

see: **waʼjihtsǫ:**

see: **waʼjihya:ʼ**

jitrehs
too much

[jih, trehs]

Agahdrǫʼs onę e: ji trehs satshę:nǫ:nih. I'm frightened now because you're too happy again.

A:yeʼ ji trę̱hs tsishedę̱hjih agahyagoʼ. It seems to me I picked too much fruit this morning.

naht
(does not occur alone)

see: **sǫ: hne:ʼ naht**

see: **sǫ ʼǫ naht**

nawahtgeh
(does not occur alone)

see: **gaoʼ nawahtgeh**

neʼ, ne(ʼ)
that, the

Dęʼ hoʼdęʼ eya:sǫh neʼ sanǫ:haʼ? What is the name of your mother?

Dęʼ hoʼdęʼ gaeyasǫhǫnyǫʼ neʼ... What are the names of your ...(female relatives)?

Honahsę: hęʼ neʼ dehenadę̱hnǫdrǫʼ. Your brothers are also fat.

tsę̱h nigaha:ʼ neʼ ekǫnyaʼtaʼsǫ:ǫh the kinds of things you cook with

Neʼ aǫhę:ʼę̱h tahnaʼtsowa:nę̱h. He has the biggest ass.

Ahsǫh ni:ʼ agǫtsanǫ̱hwa:s neʼ dagaihǫ:niʼ gyotedę̱hshǫ:ʼǫh agahyagwę̱hne:ʼ. My knees are still sore because of the other day (when) I picked fruit.

Neʼgiʼgyęʼ asiʼ. That's what you said.

Neʼgiʼgyęʼ gaǫ:dǫh. That's what the women say.

Neʼgiʼgyęʼ hana:dǫh. That's what the men say.

Neʼ gihshę̱hwaʼ e:dǫh. Maybe that's the one she means.

Neʼ gwatoh gi:dǫh. I also mean that.

neʼ gyaǫhę:ʼę̱h gyonǫʼshehsde:ʼ the most sickening, tiring, aggravating

Neʼtone:ʼ, tęʼtone:ʼ tega:yei:ʼ. That's the one that's 'not all there.'

Neʼ ǫ:weh gaǫde:nǫhk. They're really related.

Neʼseʼ hǫwę:dǫh. He's the one she means.

Tsę: eʼneʼ satro:wi:. You're talking about that again! (Expression of disgust.)

Tęʼ gę̱h neʼ desa:wę̱h? Isn't that yours?

ne:ʼ, ne(:ʼ)
that is, it is

Tigaʼdrẹhda:deʼ ne:ʼ ahahni:nọʼ. He bought a different car.

Hwę:dọh ne:ʼ to nęya:węh? When is that going to happen?

Ihse: gęh to: ne: dwa:ye:? Do you think we should do it that way?

Nęne:ʼ i:s. Dęʼ nis hoʼdęʼ nisaʼnigọhoʼdęʼ? How about you? What are your thoughts?

Ne:ʼhwaʼ ęyotshęnọ:niʼ This time she will be happy.

Ne:ʼ gaihọ:nih. That's what makes it that way.

Ne:ʼ giʼ e:dọh. That's what she means.

Ne:ʼ giʼ gi:dọh. That's what I mean.

Ne:ʼ giʼ hę:dọh. That's what he means.

Ne:ʼ hne:ʼ go:węh. That's hers.

Ne:ʼ go:węh. That's hers. (a little more definite than Ne:ʼ hne:ʼ go:węh.)

Ne:ʼ gę:s ga:dọh. That's what I usually say.

Ne:ʼ gwahs gahwajiyagwani:yoʼ It's the main (that is, matrilineal) family.

Ne:ʼ he:gę: agyọhsętoh. All she did was cry.

Ne:ʼ hęʼ hne:ʼ ho:węh nę:gyeh. This is also his.

Ne:ʼ nęh gwaʼ hę:gyọh. When I get there.

Ne:ʼ tsọ: dehoyaʼdohdọh. That's just what he's thinking about. (that is, he's preoccupied.)

Ne:ʼ diʼ gęh? Is that it then? (that is, is that what you were referring to?)

Netoh ni:yọ: ho:yęʼ. That's how many he has.

O: tęʼọh, gatgʼishęh ne:ʼ hwaʼ. Maybe, maybe not.

O: tęʼọ: giʼ, gatgʼishęh ne:ʼ hwaʼ Maybe I will, maybe I won't (come along)

To gęʼọ: ne:ʼ ni:yoht? I wonder if it's like that?

To: ni:yoʼ ne:ʼ hesheʼs. That's your birthday. (lit.: that's when you come around again.)

Tęʼ gęh dehse: to: ne:ʼ dwa:yeʼ? Don't you think we should do that?

Ęsgoho:wiʼ to gęh ne: hęyę:ʼ. I will tell you if she's going.

Gowędagę: ne:ʼ tsọ niyesgyęda'. She's a wimp because she's just a small person.

Agyęʼ ne:ʼ desatgọhe:jo:nih. I have what you want.

Hoihoʼdeʼsri:yo: giʼ ne:ʼ. He has a good job.

Nę:ʼ tsọ: niwatonaʼdaʼ. It's a small, puny potato

Da:nhọ:weh họ: hęʼdrọʼ ne:ʼ haksaʼgo:wah. This is where he lives, the good-looking man.

Dane:ʼhniʼ dwę:dọh. That is also what we mean.

Dane:onęh toniya:węhdreʼ. And now this is what is going to happen.

Neʼtone:ʼ, tęʼtone:ʼ tega:yei:ʼ. That's the one that's 'not all there.'

ne:ʼ (continued)
Ne:ʼgyę:ʼ gi:dǫh. That is what I mean.

Ne:ʼhęhne:ʼ gaǫgweʼdaʼ. Also that is her family, one of her people.

Ne:ʼhne:neʼ gaihwagwę:ni:yo. That is the main thing, the main item.

Ne:ʼhwaʼ gi:dǫh. I mean that this time.

Ne:ʼǫh. That, I guess.

Ne:ʼ ǫh neʼo:nęh haʼgahe:ʼ edwadrihoʼda:t. And it is now time for us to work.

Tęʼ tǫ ne:ʼ dedo:gehs. No, it's not really true.

ne:ʼ gwahs hwaʼ, ne(:ʼ) gwahs hwa(ʼ)
it's that one for sure
[ne:ʼ, gwahs, hwaʼ]

Gwahs hwaʼ esagaę: You're willing / giving permission this time.

neʼ ǫ:weh
that really
[neʼ, ǫ:weh]

Neʼ ǫ:weh gaǫde:nǫhk. They're really related.

negęʼnageʼ, negę(ʼ)nage(ʼ)
that is what

Negęʼnageʼ gi:dǫh. That's what I meant to say.

neʼgiʼę:ʼ, ne(ʼ)gi(ʼ)ę(:ʼ)
that is the one (emphatic)
[neʼ, giʼ, ę:ʼ]

Neʼgiʼę:ʼ e:ʼ toh iheʼs. He's here again!

neʼgiʼgyę:ʼ, ne(ʼ)gi(ʼ)gyę(:ʼ)
that's the one, that's it, that's what

Neʼgiʼgyęʼ asiʼ. That's what you said.

Neʼgiʼgyęʼ gaǫ:dǫh. That's what the women say.

Neʼgiʼgyęʼ hana:dǫh. That's what the men say.

neʼgiʼnih, ne(ʼ)gi(ʼ)ni(h)
and that too; also
[neʼ, giʼ, hniʼ]

ne:ʼgiʼshęh, ne(:ʼ)gi(ʼ)shę(h), ne(:ʼ)gi(ʼ)tsę(h)
probably
[ne:ʼ, giʼ, shęh, tsęh]

ne:ʼgiʼshęhwaʼ, ne(:ʼ)gi(ʼ)shęhwa(ʼ), ne(:ʼ)gi(ʼ)tsęhwa(ʼ)
maybe that
[ne:ʼ, giʼ, shęh, tsęh, hwaʼ]

neʼgwʼatoh, ne(ʼ)gwato(h)
and also
[neʼ, gwaʼ, to]

Neʼgwatoh haʼhǫwadiha:ʼ. They also took him.

ne:ʼgyę:ʼ, ne(:ʼ)gyę(:ʼ)
it is
[ne:ʼ, gyę:ʼ]

Ne:ʼgyę:ʼ gi:dǫh. That is what I mean.

ne:ʼgyę:neʼ, ne(:ʼ)gyę(:)ne(ʼ)
it is that
[ne:ʼ, gyę:ʼ, neʼ]

Ne:ʼgyę:neʼ to:gyęh. That is the one.

ne:ˀhęˀhne:ˀ, ne(:ˀ)hę(ˀ)hne(:ˀ)
it also is
[ne:ˀ, hęˀ, hne:ˀ]

Ne:ˀhęhne:ˀ gaǫgweˀdaˀ. Also that is her family, one of her people.

ne:ˀhne:ne:ˀ, ne(:ˀ)hne(:)ne(:ˀ)
and that also is
[ne:ˀ, hne:ˀ, neˀ]

ne:hniˀ, ne(:)hni(ˀ)
too, also, and
[ne:ˀ, hniˀ]

ne:ˀhniˀne:ˀ, ne(:ˀ)hni(ˀ)ne(:ˀ)
and that also
[ne:ˀ, hniˀ]

ne:ˀhǫ:niˀ, ne(:ˀ)hǫ:niˀ
that is the reason why; that is why
[ne:ˀ, hǫ:niˀ]

Ne:ˀ hǫ:niˀ to: ni:yoht. That's (the reason) why it's that way.

ne:ˀhwaˀ, ne(:ˀ)hwa(ˀ)
next, this (coming) time
[ne:ˀ, hwaˀ]

Ne:ˀhwaˀ ęyotshęnǫ:niˀ This time she will be happy.

Ne:ˀhwaˀ gi:dǫh. I mean that this time.

ne:neˀ, ne(:)ne(ˀ)
it is
[ne:ˀ, neˀ]

neˀo:nęh, neˀo:nę(h)
it is now
[neˀ, o:nęh]

ne:toh, ne(:)to(h)
it is that
[neˀ, to]

Netoh ni:yǫ: ho:yęˀ. That's how many he has.

neˀtogyę:ˀ, ne(ˀ)togyę(:ˀ)
be it so
[neˀ, to, gyę:ˀ]

Netogyę:ˀ haˀhoyˀada:węh. That's what happened to him over there

neˀtogyę:ˀhǫ:weh, ne(ˀ)togyę(:ˀ)(n)hǫ:weh
it is where
[neˀ, to, gyę:ˀ, hǫ(weh), nhǫ:(weh)]

neˀtone:ˀ, ne(ˀ)tone(:ˀ)
that's the one
[neˀ, to, ne:ˀ]

Neˀtone:ˀ shagohsgane:s. She is the one he desires.

ne:ˀtsǫ:, ne(:ˀ)tsǫ(:)
that is only; that is all
[ne:ˀ, tsǫ:]

Ne:ˀtsǫ: hǫwayˀada:ˀs. He's the only one she depends on.

Ne:ˀ tsǫ: dehoyadowęhdǫh. That's all he's thinking about (that is, he's preoccupied.)

nę:
Look! Here, take this! (exclamation, said when pointing to something)

nę:dah
this way; Here, take this! (said when giving something to someone)
[nę:, da]

Nęh toh hędwa:yǫ' nę:dah nędwa:ye:'. When we arrive there, we will do it this way.

nę:gyęh, nę:gyę(h)
this (one)
[nę:, gyęh]

Ne:' hę' hne:' ho:węh nę:gyeh. This is also his.

nęh, nę(h)
when (only at the beginning of embedded clauses; for statements, not questions)
[nęh, o:nęh]

Nęh toh hędwa:yǫ' nę:dah nędwa:ye:'. When we arrive there, we will do it this way.

Ne:' nęh dwahęgyǫh. When I get there.

nę:toh, nę(:)to(h)
right here, over there
[nę:, to]

Nętoh ni:yǫ: ho:yę'. That's how many he has.

nę:toh gwai, nę(:)to(h) gwai
here (rather than there)
[nę:, to, gwa:dih]

Nę:toh gwai hę'drǫ' Allan. Allan lives on this side.

nę:'tsǫ:, nę(:')tsǫ(:)
just a little bit
[nę:', tsǫ:]

Nę:tsǫ:gwatoh niyǫ: hohwihsdaę:'. Also right now he has very little money.

Nę:tsǫ: niyǫ: hohwihsdaę:'. Right now he has very little money.

nę'tsǫ:gw'atoh, nę(')tsǫ(:)gw(')ato(h)
right now; quickly; immediately;
[nę', tsǫ:, gwa', to]

Hohsę: nętsǫ:gwatoh nihahnę:ye:s. He's stout and he's also short.

nigę'ǫh, nigę'ǫ(h)
or, or is it, if it is
[nigę'ǫh, ǫh]

Hǫgweh gęh agǫgweh nigę'ǫh Kim eya:sǫh? Was it a man or a woman whose name is Kim?

Hǫgweh gęh agǫgweh nigę'ǫh? Is it a man or a woman?

To' ge'ǫ ni:yoht. I wonder if it's like that.

niyo:we', nyo:we', niyo(')(:we'), nyo(')(:we')
to be a certain distance
[niyo:(we'), nyo:(we')]

To: ni:yo' ne:' heshe's. That's your birthday. (lit.: that's when you come around again.)

To: ni:yo' nę' heha:we:noh. That's as far as he has gone.

Toniyo:we' hę'se' wa'he' hęhsyǫ'. You'll get that far before you arrive.

Agwa'nigǫha' shęniyo:we' hędwawayę:nęda'. We're waiting until the time we're finished.

nya:węh, nya:wę(h)
thank you

nyoh
you're welcome; all right; o.k. (a term of acknowledgement); can also be said in response to nya:węh; one can also say it sarcastically to bug someone.

o:, o(:)
So? Oh really?

O: gęh? Said when really questioning someone.

ogwęhę:gye', ogwęhę(:)gye(')
now and then, now and again
[ogwęhę:gye']

Ogwęhę:gye' gę:s ahsyǫ'. Now and again you'll be here.

ona:węh
it is theirs (animals)
[(a)węh have, own]

onę:di', onę(:)di(')
so now
[o:nęh, di']

Onędi' to:hah hęgahe:' ędwęnihę:'. Now it is almost time for us to quit.

onę'e:', onę'e(:')
now, again
[o:nęh, nęh, e:']

Onę'e:' toh hodaditsgo:t. Now again he has himself sitting there.

o:nęhgwa', o:nę(h)gwa(')
suddenly; already
[o:nęh, gwa']

O:nęgwa' edwawayęnęda'. We're finished already.

o:nęh, o:nę(h), (o:)nę(h)
now, when, at this time

Gaę di' nhǫ:weh nihswe's o:nęh? Where then are you now?

Gyę:gwa' o:nęh ahahdę:di'? What if he should leave now?

O:nęh gi' ha'gahe:' ęshetrohna'. It is time for me to take him back.

O:nęh gi' hodehsronihs'ǫh. He is ready now.

O:nęh gi' ęgoyę'ęsętwahsǫ'ǫh. I'm now going to kick you around.

O:nęh to:hah to: heshe:'. He's almost ready to return (come back).

O:nęh to:hah ęsha:yǫ'. He's almost ready to go back.

Agahdrǫ's onę e: ji trehs satshę:nǫ:nih. I'm frightened now because you're too happy.

Onę e: agri'sdowa:neh. I'm loud, noisy again.

O:nęh e:' i:s toh ha'segǫhe:k. You're getting into someone else's fight again, butting in.

Dane:onęh toniya:węhdre'. And now this is what is going to happen.

o:nęh g'ihya:', o:nę(h) g(')ihya(:')
so long for now; good-bye
[onęh, gi', hya:']

o:nęh to:hah, (o:)nę(h) to:hah, to:hah
almost
[o:nęh, to:hah]

O:nęh to:hah John ęhshodǫhswe'dę'. Now almost John is going to get hungry again.

onǫ:hę'
they (animals) (lit.: they (animals) are alone)
[(a)ǫhę' alone]

o'ǫ:, o'ǫ(:)
Oh really?
[o:, ǫh]

o: tę'ǫ:, o: tę'ǫ(:), o: tę'ǫ(h)
no! (very emphatic); maybe not
[o:, tę', ǫh]

O: tę'ǫh, gatg'ishęh gye:gwa'. Maybe, maybe not.

O: tę'ǫh, gatg'ishęh ne:' hwa'. Maybe, maybe not.

O: tę'ǫ: gi', gatg'ishęh ne:' hwa' Maybe I will, maybe I won't (come along)

o:węh
it is its; it belongs to it
[(a)węh have, own]

ǫh, ǫ(h), ǫ(:)
I guess, I wonder (if)

To gę'ǫ ni:yoht? I wonder if it's like that?

To 'ǫ ni:yoht. I wonder if it's like that.

To 'ǫ: ni:yohdǫhne:. I wonder if it used to be like that; I wonder if that's how it was.

Agi'd'aǫh ǫ tsę n'aonishe' hohta:'. I slept while he spoke.

Ne:'ǫh. That, I guess.

Ne:' ǫh ne'o:nęh ha'gahe:' edwadriho'da:t. And it is now time for us to work.

ǫhne:', ǫhne(:')
maybe
[ǫh, ne:']

Mary ǫhne:' gohwihsdaga'de'. Maybe Mary has a lot of money.

ǫ:weh
(does not occur alone)

see: **gwahs ǫ:weh**

see: **ne' ǫ:weh**

see: **tę' gwahs ǫ:weh**

see: **tsęh ǫ:weh**

sa:węh
it is yours
[(a)węh have, own]

se', se(')
after all, just, so, also, too

Ęhę' se'. It is so.

Agahyagwęhne:' sehę'ni:'. I've also picked fruit (I've experienced this)

A:ga̱hyagwa̱hse:k se hę ni:' gyę:gwa' a:wagadagaide:k. I would be a fruit picker too if I were well.

Ne'se' hǫwę:dǫh. He's (just) the one she means.

sga̱ho'dę', sga̱ho(')dę(')
anything, something, nothing

Sga̱hǫ'dę' dawatehtgęht. Something's not right.

Tę' sga̱ho'dę' desęnǫhdǫ'. No, you don't know anything (lit.: nothing).

shęh, tsęh, shę(h), tsę(h)
of, because, how, that (etc.) (many examples of tsęh do not translate well into English)

Dega'dręhdagęha'gye' shę ahęnǫ:da:'. They put the cars in two at a time.

Shęh tganǫhso:t ita:t. He's standing at the house.

Dę' hne:' ni:yoht shęh ahadone:k? Why did he leave?

Gado:gę: shęh ho'dę' a'ǫgwayǫdahk. A certain something brought us together (for example, a meeting).

Tę' gi' shęh hwa'. Maybe not.

To hęgye' tsęh age:ji:yo'. I'm really crippled.

Ji gę:s trehs jahsę: tsęh nisnihnę:ye:s. Yout two are too fat for your height.

Agatshęnǫ:ni: tsęh ahsyǫh. I'm happy you've arrived.

Aga'tsęnǫ:ni: gi' tsęh sada'gaide'. I'm happy that you are well.

Agahsę: tsę age:ji:yoh. I'm slow because I'm lame.

Shęh knętsa'geh ǫknǫhnyak. My arm hurts.

tsęh nigaha:' ne' ekǫnya'ta'sǫ:ǫh the kinds of things you cook with

Aǫgǫhdǫh ǫge'drahehs tsęh nagadekǫ:ni'. I ate too much.

tsęh hǫ ha'ge:' where I went

tsęh nǫda:ge:', tsęh na'dǫ:da:ge:' where I'm coming from

Ohsga:naht tsęh niyehnatsi:yo:. She has an attractive bum.

Ohsga:naht tsęh nihahnatsi:yo:. He has an attractive bum.

Sekdǫ: tsęh niyoga'ǫhsro'dę:. Taste it!

Agahyago' tsęh n'aonishe' odahyǫ:ni:. I did pick fruit while it was plentiful.

ǫ:gweh tsęh niyagoiho'dę' how people are (that is, human activities)

tsęh nęya:węh what will happen

Dękde:ni' tsęh niwagriho'dę:. I'm going to change my outlook.

ahęnadrihwahseht tsęh nihęnagye:ha'. They hid their ideas of what they are up to, what they are doing (that is, they are scheming).

Hętsyę:' tsęh hǫ hesa:gwęh. You will put it back where you got it.

Knigǫha:' tsęh niyoht dęgatahahk. I watch how I walk.

Knigǫha:' tsęh hǫ:weh dęgatahahk. I watch where I walk

Dęhne:' ni:yoht tsęh toh nahsye:'. Why did you do that?

Agwa'nigǫha' shęniyo:we' hędwawayę:nęda'. We're waiting until the time we're finished.

Tsęh ǫ:weh nito:ne:nǫ:. Where they really come from.

shęho'dę', tsęho'dę', shęho(')dę('), tsęho(')dę(')
whatever, a certain something
[shęh, tsęh, ho'dę']

Gado:gę: shęh ho'dę' a'ǫgwayǫdahk. A certain something brought us together (for example, a meeting).

shęnhǫ:weh, shę(n)hǫ:we(h), tsę(n)hǫ:we(h)
where abouts
[shęh, tsęh, hǫ(weh), nhǫ:(weh)]

tsęh hǫ ha'ge:' where I went

Hętsyę:' tsęh hǫ hesa:gwęh. You will put it back where you got it.

Knigǫha:' tsęh hǫ:weh dęgatahahk. I watch where I walk

Hęhsahshę:da' tsęh hǫweh dedihsawihs. You will trod, step where you're not wanted (that is, trespass).

Shęnhǫweh hehehta' onę'dagǫhsǫ', agę'. Where he goes, under the pines it's been said.

shęniyo:we', shęn(i)yo:(we'), tsęn(i)yo:(we')
(how) much, (how) many, (how) far, until
[shęh, tsęh, niyo:(we'), nyo:(we')]

Agwa'nigǫha' shęniyo:we' hędwawayę:nęda'. We're waiting until the time we're finished.

si, si(:), si(h)
there

Si:gyęh tga:yę', de:sehk. That lying over there, pick it up!

Si:hne:' gwai hęhsadi'. Throw that over there!

Si:nhǫ:weh tgani:yǫ:t sagya'dawi'tra'. Your coat is hanging way over there. (lit.: Way over there, hanging, your coat.)

Sihne:' sigwadih ha'se:. Get over there! (speaking generally to an animal)

sigwa:dih
over there; move it! (a common way of telling a dog to move)
[si, gwa:dih]

Sihne:' sigwadih ha'se:. Get over there! (speaking generally to an animal)

si:gyęh, si:gyę(h)
that, way over there
[si, gyęh]

Si:gyęh tga:yę', de:sehk. That lying over there, pick it up!

sihne:', si(hne:')
over there
[si, hne:']

Si:hne:' gwai hęhsadi'. Throw that over there!

Sihne:' sigwadih ha'se:. Get over there! (speaking generally to an animal)

si:nhǫ:weh, si(:n)hǫ:(weh)
way over there
[si, hǫ(weh), nhǫ:(weh)]

Si:nhǫ:weh tgani:yǫ:t sagya'dawi'tra'. Your coat is hanging way over there. (lit.: Way over there, hanging, your coat.)

sga̱ho'dę:'ęh, sga̱ho(')dę:'ęh
something
[sga̱ho'dę:'ęh, ho'dę']

sǫ'ǫh, sǫ('ǫh), sǫ(:)
who (short form)

Daskro:wi' sǫ: nhaht daǫdekǫnyahne'. Tell me who's coming to eat.

Sǫ'ǫh hne:' naht gaǫdę:nǫhk. I'm wondering who her people are.

sǫˀǫh (continued)

Sǫ:go:węh tǫ gadrehdase:ˀ. Who owns that new car?

Sǫga:ˀah gęh hǫwayędi:? Does someone know him? Who knows him?

sǫ: go:węh
whose (is that)?
[sǫ(ˀǫh)]

Sǫ:go:węh tǫ gadrehdase:ˀ. Who owns that new car?

sǫ: hne:ˀ naht
who (is that?)
[sǫ(ˀǫh), hne:ˀ, nˀaht]

Sǫˀǫh hne:ˀ naht gaǫdę:nǫhk. I'm wondering who her people are.

sǫˀǫh naht, sǫ(ˀǫh) naht, sǫ(:) naht
who, which (person, one)
[sǫ(ˀǫh), nˀaht]

Daskro:wiˀ sǫ: nhaht daǫdekǫnyahneˀ. Tell me who's coming to eat.

Daskro:wiˀ sǫ: nhaht daǫdekǫnyahneˀ. Tell me who's coming to eat.

Daskro:wiˀ sǫ: nhaht gado:gę: dęwa:dǫ:t. Tell me who is going to dine with us.

Sǫˀǫh hne:ˀ naht gaǫdę:nǫhk. I'm wondering who her people are.

sǫga:(ˀah)
someone
[sǫ(ˀǫh)]

Sǫga:ˀah gęh hǫwayędi:? Does someone know him? Who knows him?

sdǫ:hah
a little bit

Sdǫ:hah segęi:s. Move a little bit.

tęˀ, tę(ˀ)
no, not

Dąheˀ gęh tęˀ nigęˀǫh? Is he coming or not?

Gwahs ǫ:weh a:yęˀ tęˀ desho:tǫ:deˀ. It really seems like he doesn't (want to) hear. (selective hearing)

Sanǫhǫkda:niˀ tęˀ nigeˀǫ? Are you sick or not?

Tęˀ gęh dehse: to: ne:ˀ dwa:yeˀ? Don't you think we should do that?

Tęˀ gęh dehsho:yǫ:? Did he not come home?

Tęˀ gˀatoh. Tęˀ giˀ dehe:gę: Nowhere. I didn't see him.

Tęˀ giˀ shęh hwaˀ. Maybe not.

Tęˀ gˀi shęh. Maybe not

Tęˀ gęh? Isn't it?

Tęˀ giˀ gwah dewagadaˀgaideˀ. I'm not feeling well.

Tęˀ dewagadaˀgaideˀ. I'm not well.

I:wiˀ ge:s agatganǫ:niˀ, deˀęgwahe tęˀ seˀ. I'm wealthy, but then not really.

Tęˀ toh degahe:ˀ. It's not setting there.

Tęˀ tǫdesaˀdre: to:gyęh! Don't (or you won't) drive that over here!

Tęˀ toh teˀgahe:ˀ. It's not setting way over there.

Tęˀ taˀdeyagodawęnyeˀ. No, she's not walking about

tę' (continued)
(Tę') ta:hayę:toh. No he won't plant.

Tę' hne:' dehoyętwęh. No, he did not plant. (emphatic)

Tę' ni: toh ta:ge:'. No, I'm not going there.

Tę' toh ta:ge:. No, I will not go.

Tę' daǫ toh ta:ge:. No, I will definitely not go.

Tę' ni' ta:gye:na: I refuse to accept something.

Ne'tone:', tę'tone:' tega:yei:'. That's the one that's 'not all there.'

Tę' sga̱ho'dę' desęnǫhdǫ'. No, you don't know nothing.

Tę' tǫ ne:' dedo:gehs. No, it's not really true.

Tę'gihne:' dedo:gęhs de'sa:dǫh. No, it's not really true what you're saying.

Tę'gidaǫ tayagogaę:. No, she will never agree to...

Tę'gini:' to ta:gye:. No, I will not do that.

Tę' gęh ne' desa:węh? Isn't that yours?

tę'daǫ, t(')ędaǫ(:)
it will never happen, definitely not
[tę', da, ǫh]

Tę' daǫ toh ta:ge:. No, I will definitely not go.

Tę' daǫ a:hǫwayenawa's. (Definitely not); no one will help him.

Tę'daǫ: to na:ya:węh. It will never happen.

Tę'gi'daǫ: to na:ya:węh. No, it will not happen.

tę' g'atoh, tę(') g(')ato(h)
nowhere, anywhere
[tę', ga', to]

Tę' g'atoh d'ega:yę' It's not laying anywhere.

Tę' g'atoh. Tę' gi' dehe:gę: Nowhere. I didn't see him.

tę' gwahs ǫ:weh, tę(') gwahs ǫ:weh
not really
[tę', gwahs, ǫ:weh]

Tę' gwahs ǫ:weh ǫgweh degę:. No, you're not really human.

tę' hne:', tę(') hne(:')
not (that)
[tę', hne:']

Tę' hne:' hwa to ta:ya:węh. No, that'll never really happen this time.

tę' hwę:dǫh, tę(') hwę:dǫ(h)
never; not ever
[tę', hwę:dǫh]

Tę' hwę:dǫh tǫ: sǫsadonhe:k. You'll never come alive again.

Tę' hwę:dǫh to tǫ: ęsha:gye'. No, he'll never do that.

Tę' hwę:dǫh to ta:gye'. I would never do that.

tę' sga̱ho'dę', (tę') sga̱ho(')dę(')
nothing
[tę', sgaho'dę', ho'dę']

Tę' sga̱ho'dę' desęnǫhdǫ'. No, you don't know nothing.

tę' tǫ ne:', tę(') to ne(:')
not really
[tę', to, ne:']

Tę' tǫ ne:' dedo:gehs. No, it's not really true.

t'ęgęh, t(')ęgę(')
no?
[tę', gęh]

Tę' gęh ne' desa:węh? Isn't that yours? (lit.: that's yours, no?)

tę'gi'daǫ, tę(')gi(')daǫ(:)
No, it will not happen; definitely not
[tę', gi', da, ǫ:]

Tę'gi'daǫ: to na:ya:węh. No, it will not happen.

Tę'gidaǫ tayagogaę:. No, she will (definitely not) ever agree to...

tę'g'ihne:', tę(')g(')ihne(:')
not really
[tę', gi', hne:']

Tę'gihne:' dedo:gęhs de'sa:dǫh. No, it's not really true what you're saying.

tę'g'ini:', tę(')g(')ini(:')
no, not me
[tę', gi', i:']

Tę'gini:' to ta:gye:. No, I will not do that.

tę' nigę'ǫh, tę(') nigę'ǫh
isn't it
[nigę'ǫh, ǫh]

Dahe' gęh tę' nigę'ǫh? Is he coming or not?

Sanǫhǫkda:ni' tę' nige'ǫ? Are you sick or not?

tę'se', tę(')se(')
not really
[tę', se']

I:wi' ge:s agatganǫ:ni', de'ęgwahe tę' se'. I'm wealthy, but then not really.

tgwęhę:', tgwęhę(:')
sometimes

Tgwęhę:' hahkdǫhs. Sometimes he comes (around).

to:, to(:), to(h)
that, there, where

gao' shę nyo:' to: nęya:węh before that happens

Gwahs wa'hetshǫ: to: na'a:węh. That just happened.

Hwę:dǫh ne:' to nęya:węh? When is that going to happen?

Ihse: gęh to: ne: dwa:ye:? Do you think we should do it that way?

Ne:' hǫ:ni' to: ni:yoht. That's (the reason) why it's that way.

O:nęh to:hah to: heshe:'. He's almost ready to return (there).

To gę'ǫ ni:yoht? I wonder if it's like that?

To gi' shęh ha:ge:. Maybe I should go there.

To 'ǫ ni:yoht. I wonder if it's like that.

To 'ǫ: ni:yohdǫhne:. I wonder if it used to be like that; I wonder if that's how it was. (lit.: That, I wonder, if it used to be)

to: (continued)

To: gẹh ha'se' shẹh nho: dedwatgẹnyo:? Are you going (there) to the fair?

To: ni:yo' ne:' heshe's. That's your birthday. (lit.: that's when you come around again.)

To: ni:yo' nẹ' heha:we:noh. That's as far as he has gone.

Toh geh gẹnhowe' toh na'a:weh? Where did it happen?

To' ge'ǫ ni:yoht. I wonder if it's like that.

Tẹ' gẹh dehse: to: ne:' dwa:ye'? Don't you think we should do that?

Tẹ' hwẹ:dǫh tǫ: sǫsadonhe:k. You'll never come alive again (from there).

Tẹ' hwẹ:dǫh to tǫ: ẹsha:gye'. No, he'll never do that.

Tẹ' hwẹ:dǫh to ta:gye'. I would never do that.

Ẹsgoho:wi' to gẹh ne: hẹyẹ:'. I will tell you if she's going (there).

To hẹgye' tsẹh age:ji:yo'. I'm really crippled (there).

I:hs gyẹ'hne:' toh nahsye:'. Are you the one that did it.

i:hs gyẹ'hne:' tsǫ: e:' toh nahsye:' You're the only one that did that again

Tẹ' toh degahe:'. It's not setting there.

Tẹ' tǫdesa'dre: to:gyẹh! Don't (or you won't) drive that over here!

Tẹ' toh te'gahe:'. It's not setting way over there.

to hǫ: ha:gi'drǫ:da'k where I would dwell (over there)

Tẹ' ni: toh ta:ge:'. No, I'm not going there.

Tẹ' toh ta:ge:. No, I will not go (there).

Tẹ' daǫ toh ta:ge:. No, I will definitely not go (there).

To hǫ: hẹ:ge'. There I will go.

To hǫ: ha'ge'. I went there.

I:wi to na:ya:wẹh. I want, intend that to happen.

Ahi:' gi' to na:ya:wẹh. I thought that's what should happen.

Ahi:' gi' to nẹya:wẹh. I thought that's what would happen.

dewagegaẹhs to ha:ge:'. I'm unwilling to go there.

O:nẹh e' i:s toh ha'segǫhe:k. You're getting into someone else's fight again, butting in (there).

Dane:onẹh toniya:wẹhdre'. And now this is what is going to happen (there).

Dẹhne:' ni:yoht tsẹh toh nahsye:'. Why did you do that?

To: gitsǫ: ni:yǫ:. That's all there is.

Ne' gwatoh gi:dǫh. I also mean that.

Ne'tone:', tẹ'tone:' tega:yei:'. That's the one that's 'not all there.'

To hǫ: hẹ:ge' dwagye:sẹh. There I will go where it's cheap (shopping).

Toh tsǫ: niyowe' hẹsẹ'drǫ:'. That's only as far as it will take you.

to: (continued)

To:gyęh hǫgweʼdase:ʼah shǫgwahyadǫ:nih. That young man does our writing.

Tęʼ hne:ʼ hwa to ta:ya:węh. No, that'll never really happen this time.

Tęʼgiʼdaǫ: to na:ya:węh. No, it will not happen (there).

Waʼji:hah to hęgyǫʼ. I will arrive (there) after a while.

to:gyęh, to:gyę(h)

that (one)

[to, gyęh]

Tęʼ tǫdesaʼdre: to:gyęh! Don't (or you won't) drive that over here!

Ne:ʼgyę:neʼ to:gyęh. That is the one.

To:gyęh hǫgweʼdase:ʼah shǫgwahyadǫ:nih. That young man does our writing.

to:hah

there

O:nęh to:hah to: heshe:ʼ. He's almost ready to return (there).

O:nęh to:hah ęsha:yǫʼ. He's almost ready to go back (there).

Onędiʼ to:hah hęgahe:ʼ ędwęnihę:ʼ. Now it is almost time for us to quit (there).

toh geh, to(h) geh

and then; that's when; then; where

[to, geh]

Toh geh gęnhoweʼ toh naʼa:weh? Where did it happen?

to: hǫ:weh, to(:) (n)hǫ(:weh)

there, where

[to nhǫ: (weh), to hǫ: (weh), hǫ]

to hǫ: ha:giʼdrǫ:daʼk where I would dwell (over there)

To hǫ: hę:geʼ. There I will go.

To hǫ: haʼgeʼ. I went there.

to hǫ:weh ha:yęh where he puts or places it

To hǫ hayęhęʼ. He's always putting it there.

To hǫ: sre:hah. That's where you put it.

To hǫ: hę:geʼ dwagye:sęh. There I will go where it's cheap (shopping).

to: niyo:weʼ, to(:) n(i)yo(:we)ʼ

that far, when

[to, niyo:(weʼ), nyo:(weʼ)]

To: ni:yoʼ ne:ʼ hesheʼs. That's your birthday. (lit.: that's when you come around again.)

To: ni:yoʼ nęʼ heha:we:noh. That's as far as he has gone.

Toniyo:weʼ hęʼseʼ waʼheʼ hęhsyǫʼ. You'll get that far before you arrive.

To tsǫ:, To tsǫ(:)

That is enough! (that is, stop pouring)

[to, tsǫ:]

Toh tsǫ: niyoweʼ hęsęʼdrǫ:ʼ. That's only as far as it will take you.

tǫ(:hwaʼ)
that one
[to, hwaʼ]

Tęʼ hwę:dǫh tǫ: sǫsadonhe:k. You'll never come alive again.

Tęʼ hwę:dǫh to tǫ: ęsha:gyeʼ. No, he'll never do that.

Sǫ:go:węh tǫ gadrehdase:ʼ. Who owns that new car?

Tǫ:hwaʼ gi:dǫh. I mean that one.

Tęʼ tǫ ne:ʼ dedo:gehs. No, it's not really true.

trehs
more (than usual) (denotes something extreme)

Jiʼ gę:s trehs sheno:wę:. You lie too much; you're too much of a liar.

Giʼ trehs aǫgohdǫh. It's beyond.

Ji gę:s trehs ja̱hsę: tsęh nisnihnę:ye:s. You're too fat for your height.

Agahdrǫʼs onę e: ji trehs satshę:nǫ:nih. I'm frightened now because you're too happy.

Trehs also occurs in expressions such as:

Trehs giʼ gęʼ. My goodness!

trǫhgeh tsǫ:, trǫhge(h) tsǫ(:)
barely
[trǫh, geh, tsǫ:]

Trǫhgeh tsǫ: ǫgwahdęgyaʼdǫh. We're just barely able to make it go (for example, a ceremony).

Trǫhgeh tsǫ: jǫgwaihoʼdeʼ. We're barely working.

tsę:!
exclamation (of disgust) (pronunciation: [tsæ:])

Tsę: eʼneʼ satro:wi:. You're talking about that again! (expression of disgust.)

tsęh ǫ:weh, shęh ǫ:weh
it is really
[shęh, tsęh, ǫ:weh]

Tsęh ǫ:weh nito:ne:nǫ:. Where they really come from.

tsǫ:, tsǫ(:)
that is all; just; only

Gʼatohah tsǫ: ęse:tsaęʼ. You will (just) find it someplace.

Ne:ʼ tshǫ: dehoyaʼdohdǫh. That's just what he's thinking about. (that is, he's preoccupied.)

Gowędagę: ne:ʼ tsǫ niyesgędaʼ. She's a wimp because she's just a small person.

i:hs gyęʼhne:ʼ tsǫ: e:ʼ toh nahsye:ʼ You're the only one that did that again

Nę:ʼ tsǫ: niwatonaʼdaʼ. It's (just) a small, puny potato.

Tiga:gwe:gǫh tsǫ: agahyagwęhęgyeʼs aknǫhaʼ a:knǫnheht agaʼahdraʼ. I'm just going along picking fruit here and there (because) I'm unable to fill my basket.

Trǫhgeh tsǫ: ǫgwahdęgyaʼdǫh. We're just barely able to make it go (for example, a ceremony).

To: gitsǫ: ni:yǫ:. That's all there is.

Aweʼ hęgyeh tsǫ:, Awęʼ hęgyeh tsǫ:. Let it go! (it's just not worth bothering.)

tsǫ:, tsǫ(:) (continued)
Toh tsǫ: niyowe' hęsę'drǫ:'. That's only as far as it will take you.

Trǫhgeh tsǫ: jǫgwaiho'de'. We're (just) barely working.

G'atoh tsǫ: ta:se:tsęi:. (Just) nowhere will you find it

Wa'hetsǫ: aha:tgęh. He just now got up.

wa'gyęh, wa(')gyę(h)
Listen! Excuse me! (exclamation to get someone's attention)
[wa'gyęh, wa'(heh), gyęh]

Wa'gyęh desa'draihęh! Would you hurry up!

wa'heh, wa('heh)
just (now)

Gwahs wa'hetshǫ: to: na'a:węh. That just happened.

Wahe' gi' gatahi:ne'. I'm (just now) getting on my way.

Toniyo:we' hę'se' wa'he' hęhsyǫ'. You'll (just) get that far before you arrive.

Wa'hetsǫ: aha:tgęh. He just now got up.

Wa'gyęh desa'draihęh! Would you hurry up (just now)!

Wa'heh ahsyǫ'. You finally arrived (just now).

Wa'hehge:ha' ahakǫ:ni'. At long last he (just now) decided to cook.

wa'hehge:ha', wa(')hehge:ha(')
finally, at long last
[wa'(heh)]

Wa'hehge:ha' ahakǫ:ni'. At long last he decided to cook.

wa'hetsǫ:, wa(:)hetsǫ(:)
just now
[wa'(heh), tsǫ:]

Gwahs wa'hetsǫ: to: na'a:węh. That just happened.

Wa'hetsǫ: aha:tgęh. He just now got up.

wa'jih, wa(')ji(h)
after awhile; wait
[wa'(heh), jih]

Wa'jih, ęhtsya'dę'. Wait, you might fall.

wa'ji:hah, wa(')ji:hah
presently, a little later, after a bit; after a while; afterwards; later
[wa'(heh)]

Wa'ji:hah to hęgyǫ'. I will arrive after a while.

wa'jihkę:' gyę:', wajihkę:' (gyę:')
almost, just about
[wa'(heh), jih, gyę:']

wa'jihtsǫ:, wa(')jihtsǫ(:)
soon, in a while, pretty soon
[wa'(heh), jih, tsǫ:]

wa'jihya:', wa(')jihya(:')
wait a minute, a while; wait!
[wa'(heh), jih, hya:']

wa'ne:', wa(')ne(:')
today, now
[wa'(heh), ne:']

Appendix J: Cayuga Grammatical Sketch

1 OVERVIEW OF CAYUGA GRAMMAR

Cayuga has three parts of speech: nouns, verbs, and particles.

Nouns name a person, place, thing, quality, event, etc.

Verbs express activities such as walking, eating, etc. In Cayuga, verbs also describe characteristics and function like the English predicate adjectives *be short, be green*, etc. As well, in Cayuga there is a type of verb which describes an object's position.

Particles are neither nouns nor verbs. (Their characteristics are discussed in §5; see Appendix I for a list with examples). Some particles in Cayuga function like English pronouns such as *he, she,* etc., while some act like adverbs such as *today, soon, quickly,* etc.

Other unique features of Cayuga include noun incorporation, and sentence structure or word order. Noun incorporation occurs when a noun is added into a verb, resulting in a single word. A comparable type of word in English is the verb *to babysit*, which contains the noun *baby* and the verb *sit*.

Cayuga sentence structure, or word order, is more fluid than that of English. For example, a noun denoting the receiver of the action can occur either before or after the verb in Cayuga. (In contrast, such a noun typically occurs after the verb in English). For example, the sentence *I'm picking strawberries* can be expressed with either of the following word orders:

Ga̱hya:gwáhs *I'm picking*	jihsǫ́:dahk. *strawberries*
Jihsǫ:dáhk *strawberries*	ga̱hyá:gwahs. *I'm picking*

Details on nouns, verbs, particles, noun incorporation, and sentence structure follow below.

2 NOUNS

The types of nouns in Cayuga include:

- Basic nouns
- Onomatopoeic animal names (these words imitate the sound that the animal makes)
- Other animal names (non-onomatopoeic)
- Body parts
- Verbal nouns
- Deverbal nouns (nouns formed from verbs)
- Compound nouns

These types of noun all have the same function—they name people, places, things, qualities, events, etc. However, they are classified below on the basis of how they are formed.

2.1 BASIC NOUNS

Unpossessed basic nouns end with -aʼ and begin with either ga-, ǫ-, or a-, and you have to memorize which prefix the noun takes. (Ga-, o-, and a- are the 3rd zoic pronominal prefixes. To find out more about the pronominal prefixes, see §8.3).

ga-nǫ́hs-aʼ *house(s)*
o-nǫhs-owaːnęh *a big house*

o-ʼnhǫ́hs-aʼ *egg(s)*
s-ga-ʼnhǫ́hsaː-t, j-o-ʼnhǫ́hsaː-t *one egg*

a-węʼyǫhgaː-ʼ *thumb(s)*
g-wʼęyǫhgáː-ʼgeh *on my thumb(s)*

Basic nouns are singular or plural in meaning, depending on the context. (For more discussion of this point, see §2.1 in the User Guide).

2.2 ONOMATOPOEIC WORDS

Onomatopoeic words name an animal and imitate the sound made by the animal. Some examples include:

gaʼgaːʼ *crow*
twę́ːtwęːt *duck*
duwísduwiːʼ *killdeer*
hihiː *great horned owl*

Unlike the basic nouns, these nouns have no prefixes or endings.

2.3 ANIMAL NAMES

Another type of animal name is shown below. These are not onomatopoeic, and they do not have prefixes or endings.

hnyagwáiʼ *bear*
daguːs, dagoːs *cat*
sóːwaːs *dog*
drę́ːnaː *skunk*

Many such nouns begin with <ji> or <jʼi>:

jʼidę́ːʼęh *bird*
jikjíːyeːʼ *chickadee*
jíhsguguʼ *robin*

2.4 BODY PART NOUNS (INALIENABLE)

Body part nouns (also called inalienable nouns) are unlike basic nouns in several respects: while basic nouns take the ending —a', body part nouns take the ending —a'geh, meaning *on*. (This is the external locative suffix, which is described in §7.5).

snętsá'geh *on your arm*
knętsá'geh *on my arm*

The first letter of the above nouns designate the owner of the body part: <s> at the beginning of snętsá'geh means *your (one person)*, and the <k> at the beginning of knętsá'geh means *my*. Units such as s- and k- are examples of pronominal prefixes, which are described in §8.3.

2.5 VERBAL NOUNS

Verbal nouns are technically verbs because they have the same types of prefixes and suffixes as verbs. However, verbal nouns *function* like *nouns*—they designate people, places, things, qualities, events, etc. For example, the verbal noun hagę́hjih literally has the verbal or sentence meaning *he is an old man*, but hagę́hjih is often used in the noun sense of *an old man*. Various types of verbal nouns are described below.

2.5.1 *Human beings (verbal nouns)*

Nouns denoting human beings have prefixes which designate the number (singular, plural, etc.) and gender (male, female) of the person described. Examples of such verbal nouns include:

nihú:'uh
  little boy (lit.: he is small)
eksá:'ah
  girl child (lit.: she or someone is a child)
hadiks'ashǫ́:'ǫh
  male children (lit.: they (males) are children)
agǫ́:gweh
  girl, woman (lit.: she or someone is a person)
hǫgwé'dase:'
  young man (lit.: he is a new person)
nitawenǫ́:hah
  middle-aged male (lit.: he has come from somewhere, with diminutive suffix; see §7.5)

2.5.2 *Kinship terms (verbal nouns)*

Kinship terms often describe a *relationship* between one person and another. For example, the following kinship term has a prefix, he-, which designates two groups of people, *I / my* and *he / him*.

he-'gę́:'ęh *my younger brother*

Used with other types of verbs, the prefix he- has a similar meaning, as shown in the next example:

he-nǫ́hwe's *I like him*

A small group of kinship terms takes the same prefixes as body part nouns (that is, the agentive series of pronominal prefixes, described in §2.4, §8.3). For example, the <k> at the beginning of the following words means *I* or *my*:

k-nohá:'ah *my maternal aunt*
k-nó:ha' *my mother*
k-no'sęh *my uncle*

Kinship terms, and the pronominal prefix system they use, are listed in Appendix C.

2.5.3 Habitual aspect verbs (used as verbal nouns)

Habitual aspect verbs (see §8.7) can describe a habitual or ongoing activity, and they often denote professions, machinery or instruments. Examples include the following. ('Something' is abbreviated as 's.t.' here and in the remainder of this appendix).

haheyǫdanę̲hsrǫ́:ni:
undertaker (lit.: he fixes the bodies)
sha'drehdǫ́:nihs
mechanic (lit.: the one who fixes cars)
ganǫ'gwadáhgwahs
milking machine (lit.: it gathers milk)
degáhihta'
grinder (lit.: it grinds s.t.)
degáyę̲hsta'
blender, food processor (lit.: it mixes s.t.)
dewáwęnyehs
mixer (lit.: it stirs s.t.)
ganóhaehs
washing machine (lit.: it washes s.t.)
wadrę́nota'
radio (lit.: words are put in s.t.)

2.5.4 Descriptive verbal nouns

These verbal nouns describe the typical characteristics or functions of a person, place, or thing. They are not habitual aspect verbs, but instead occur in some other aspect (see §8.7). Some examples are:

dewáhǫhde:s
deer (lit.: it has two long ears)
Hǫwadi̲hnya'sodáhǫh
the Senate (lit.: they are hanging their necks, or nodding off)

2.5.5 Instrumental verbal nouns

This type of verbal noun takes the instrumental ending -hkwa', meaning *instrument used for...* (see §7.5). Examples include the following.

ganǫhsanóhsda̲hkwa'
air conditioner (lit.: it is used for cooling the house)
akyę́da̲hkwa'
chair (lit.: it is used for sitting)
gye̲hey'ǫdaędáhkwa'
funeral home (lit.: place used for holding bodies)

The instrumental suffix often combines with three special incorporating verbs to produce new nouns. Examples from the Cayuga-English dictionary section are repeated below to illustrate.

•ędahkwa' a place where s.t. is put
[contains: -(y)ę$_{V}$- lie on the ground]
ehwihsdaędahkwa' a bank
[e+ -(h)wihsd(a)$_{N}$- money -ędahkwa'- place where s.t. is put]

•odahkwa' an attached or standing instrument
[A / P+ N+ contains: -od$_{V}$- stand -ahkwa' instrument; occurs in:]
ǫdręnodahkwa' musical instruments S
[ǫ+ad+ -(r)ęn(a)$_{N}$- song -odahkwa'$_{V}$- an attached or standing instrument]

•ǫdahkwa' an attached instrument, etc. that sticks out somehow
[A / P+(at+) N+ contains: -ǫd$_{V}$- attached]
ǫtna'daǫdahkwa' a bread pan S
[o+at+ -na'd(a:)$_{N}$- bread -ǫdahkwa'$_{V}$- attached instrument]

2.6 DEVERBAL NOUNS

Deverbal nouns are formed from verbs via the addition of a suffix. (In the word *deverbal* the prefix de- means *from*, while 'deverbal' means *formed from verbs*).

English also has deverbal nouns; for example, 'location' is formed by taking the verb 'locate' and adding the suffix '-tion' (with a few spelling and sound changes).

In Cayuga, a deverbal noun is formed by adding the *nominalizer* and *noun stem former* endings -tr-aʼ or -sr-aʼ to a verb (see §7.5). Some examples include the following words.

o-yę́-hsr-aʼ *blanket, quilts*
adeʼnyędę́h-sr-aʼ *measurements*
ga̱-hyádǫ-hsr-aʼ *paper*

The above are based on the following verbs.

gá:-yę-ʼ *it is lying on the ground*
ęhs-adʼenyę́:dę-ʼ *you will try, measure*
e-hyá:dǫ-h *she writes*

2.7 COMPOUND NOUNS

Compound nouns consist of two (or more) words which together denote one object. Typically, the first word of the compound is more specific in meaning while the second word is more general.

Examples of compound nouns include:

hnyagwaíʼ	oʼwáhǫh	*bear meat*
bear	*meat*	

naganyaʼgǫ́ʼ	oʼwáhǫh	*beaver meat*
beaver	*meat*	

In some compound nouns, the second noun indicates a possessor (as shown by the literal translation beneath each of the two following examples).

owi:ya:ʼáh	gokwaʼ	*baby's food*
baby	*her food*	

owi:ya:ʼáh	gonohá:ʼtraʼ	*baby's soap*
baby	*her soap*	

3 VERBS:

Types of Cayuga verbs include:

- active, intransitive verbs
- interactive, transitive verbs
- adjectival verbs (also called stative verbs; these are both intransitive and transitive)
- positional verbs (intransitive)

The verb types are overviewed below.

3.1 ACTIVE INTRANSITIVE VERBS

Active, intransitive verbs describe an activity in which *someone does something*, either intentionally or unwittingly. Examples include the following.

deyagodáwęnyeʼ *<u>she</u> is walking about*
agadekǫ́:ni: *<u>I</u>'m eating*
desęnaʼsgwáhgwęh *(<u>you</u>) jump!*
desahsagá:węh *(<u>you</u>) yawn!*
sadǫ́:nyeʼs *<u>you</u>'re breathing*

In general—there are exceptions—if the action described by the verb is intentional, then the verb takes *agent* pronominal prefixes in the habitual and punctual aspects, and *patient* pronominal prefixes in the stative aspect. In contrast, if the action described by the verb is unintentional, then *patient* pronominal prefixes are used in the habitual, punctual, and stative aspects. (See §8.3.1, 8.3.2, and 8.7).

3.2 INTERACTIVE OR TRANSITIVE VERBS

Interactive, transitive verbs describe an activity or interaction in which *someone does s.t. to someone else*. Examples include:

tęʼ ta:kní:nǫh *I shouldn't or won't buy it*
hehó:gyǫ: *he has thrown it*
ahékǫnyeʼ *I cooked a meal for him*
atagʼedréhdaʼehs *he hit me with his vehicle*

3.3 ADJECTIVAL VERBS

Adjectival verbs (also called stative verbs) describe characteristics of people or things. They can be transitive (allowing incorporated nouns) or intransitive (not allowing incorporated nouns). Examples include:

niwú:ʼuh *how small it is*
nigá:dę:s *how thin it is*
í:yǫs *it is long*
egówaneh *she is big, pregnant*
agriʼsdowá:neh *I'm loud, noisy*

Adjectival verbs are used in Cayuga where predicate adjectives and adjectives would be used in English. To illustrate, the following sentence fragment can be translated as *fat chickens*:

onahsę́: daksaheʼdóhs
they are fat *chicken*

In this sentence, the verb onáhsę:, which literally means *they (animals) are fat*, modifies the meaning of the noun daksáheʼdohs. In this sense, the verb onáhsę: functions like an adjective.

Some adjectival verbs can also include (or incorporate) the noun which is being described. In this case, the verb expresses as much as a whole English sentence:

hǫgweʼdí:yo: *he's a charming or nice person*
shayáhkwase: *you have new pants*

(Verbs which have incorporated nouns are discussed further in §4 and §8.5).

One type of adjectival verb functions either like a pronoun, or like a sentence designating ownership. This verb fully conjugated is:[1]

agá:węh *(it is) mine, ours*
sá:węh *(it is) yours*
hó:węh *(it is) his*
gó:węh *(it is) hers*
ó:węh *(it is) its*
honá:węh *(it is) theirs (males only)*
goná:węh *(it is) theirs (females or mixed)*
oná:węh *(it is) theirs (animals)*

3.4 POSITIONAL VERBS

Positional verbs describe an object's position. Examples of positional verbs include:

detgáʼnha:ʼ *it is sticking out*
gadę́hda:ʼ *it is lying spread out on the floor or the ground*
gagéhǫʼ *things are lying around*
g̱ahe:ʼ *it is sitting on top of s.t.*
ganí:yǫ:t *it is hanging*

Positional verbs often incorporate the noun whose position is being described.

---

[1] These examples are from Michelson (1994).

An example is the following, which contains the basic noun oyę́hsra' *blanket* and the verb ganí:yǫ:t *it is hanging.*

gayęhsraní:yǫ:t *hanging blanket*

4 NOUN INCORPORATION

Verbs which have incorporated nouns are formed by taking a noun such as oyę́hsra' *blanket*, and then removing its prefixes and suffixes to leave the stem -yęhsra-. The stem is then incorporated into a verb such as gadę́hda:' *it is lying spread out on the ground.* The result is a verb which describes both the object and its position:

ga-yęhsra-dę́hda:' *it is a blanket lying spread out on the ground.*

Other examples of noun incorporation include the following.

ga-hǫ́:w-a' *boat* (noun)
w-adíhǫh *it is leaning* (verb)
ga-hǫw-adíhǫh *it is a leaning boat* (verb with incorporated noun)

o-háh-a' *road* (noun)
ni-w-ú:'uh *it is small* (verb)
ni-yo-hah-ú:'uh *it is a small road* (verb with incorporated noun)

All of the following words contain the incorporated noun -yęhsr-, and, in some cases, the *joiner vowel* -a-. Except for the first example, the letters to the right of the noun are the verb stem, and the letters to the left of the noun are prefixes; in the first example, the ending -a' is the Noun Stem Former, described in §7.5.

o-yę́hsr-a' *blanket*
ga-yę́hsr-a-ę' *it is a blanket lying on the ground*
ga-yęhsr-a-ní:yǫ:t *it is a hanging blanket*
o-yęhsr-owá:nęh *it is a big blanket*
o-yę́hsr-ase: *it is a new blanket*
o-yęhsr-a-gá:yǫh *it is an old blanket*
o-yę́hsr-a-tgi' *it is an ugly blanket*

Note in the above examples that the prefix meaning *it* is either ga- or o-. In general—there are exceptions—for unpossessed adjectival verbs, prefix selection is the same as if the verb did not have an incorporated noun. For positional verbs, the pronominal prefix is the same as the incorporating noun.

5 PARTICLES

Particles are short words containing one vowel only; they are neither nouns nor verbs. Appendix I lists many Cayuga particles.

Particles have many functions. For example, there are:

- interrogative particles such as hwę́:dǫh *when?* (for forming questions).
- subordinating particles such as tsę́h / shę́h *that, etc.* (for forming embedded sentences).
- exclamations, interjections such as agí: *ouch!* (the equivalents of *oh, uh-oh,* etc.)
- demonstrative particles such as sí:gyęh *that (one) way over there* (for pointing out objects) equivalent to words such as *this, that*, etc.
- pronominal particles such as í:hs *you* (for emphatic pronouns) equivalent to words such as *I, you,* etc.

- adverbial particles, including:
- particles of time such as é:ʼ *again* (equivalent to words such as *yesterday, tonight,* etc.)
- particles of place such as sihǫ:weh, sinhǫ́:weh *over there* (equivalent to words such as *there, here*, etc.)
- particles of degree or measurement such as dó: *how (much)* (equivalent to words such as *so much, very,* etc.)

Individual particles are short and contain only one vowel (whereas most nouns and verbs have at least two vowels). Because they are short, particles often join together to form larger units. For example, individual particles such as the following often form combinations.

nę́h *look; say; here, take this*
síh *over there*
tóh *there, that much*
gyę́h *the one*

nę́:gyęh *this* (nę́h and gyę́h)
sí:gyęh *that (one) way over there* (síh and gyę́h)
tó:gyęh *that* (tóh and gyę́h)

In contrast, particles that typically join together, such as dęʼhoʼdęʼ *what (kind)* can be broken up by the insertion of other particles such as hne: *in fact*:

dęʼ hne: hoʼdęʼ... *what, in fact...*

Another example is the following sentence, meaning *O.k., tell me what to do*, in which the particle combination dęʼhoʼdęʼ is interrupted by the particle ní:ʼ (a variant of the particle meaning *I*).[2]

Haóʼ dahskro:wíh dęʼ ní:ʼ
o.k., tell me what I

hoʼdę́ʼ nęgá:gye:ʼ.
what I will do

By convention, Cayuga speakers spell particle groups as a single word. (See §5.6 of the User Guide for further discussion).

A final characteristic which sets particles apart is their meaning. Unlike (most) nouns and verbs, the meaning of a particle is often hard to define, and highly dependent on the context of the sentence; some particles simply have no good English translation. Appendix I gives example sentences for many particles to help illustrate their meaning.

5.1 PRONOMINAL PARTICLES

As mentioned earler, some particles function as the equivalent of English pronouns, demonstratives, etc. Particles that are used as pronouns include:

í:ʼ, ní:ʼ I, we[3]
í:hs, ní:hs you

The remaining pronouns are technically verbs:[4]

háǫhęʼ, háǫhaʼ *he (lit.: he is alone)*
gáǫhęʼ *she (lit.: she is alone)*
áǫhęʼ *it (lit.: it is alone)*
honǫ́:hęʼ *they (males) (lit.: they (males) are alone)*
gonǫ́:hęʼ *they (females or mixed) (lit.: they (females or mixed) are alone)*

[2] The <n> at the beginning of the particle <i:ʼ> is a contracted form of the particle <neʼ>.

[3] The forms <ni:ʼ> and <ni:hs> are contractions of <neʼ i:ʼ> and <neʼ i:hs>; the words <ni:hs> and <i:hs> are also spelled as <ni:s> and <i:s>.

[4] These examples are from Michelson (1994).

onǫ́:hęʼ *they (animals) (lit.: they (animals) are alone)*

Cayuga pronouns are used for contrast, or to emphasize or point out something contrary to expectation; otherwise they are not required in a sentence. For example, in the following sentence, the particle haǫhęʼ emphasizes *who* spoke, but is optional.

Haǫhę́ʼ ahęʼ *He spoke.*
he alone he spoke

Such a sentence would be used to point out that *he* said something (as opposed to *she* or *they*).

A Cayuga sentence does not require a pronoun. For example, the verb ahęʼ *he spoke* is also an acceptable sentence in Cayuga. The pronominal word can be omitted here (and usually is) because the verb ahęʼ already expresses the meaning of *he*.

6 SENTENCES

A sentence is a group of words expressing a complete thought. Some of Cayuga's many sentence types are overviewed below.

At their simplest, sentences can consist of particles or combinations of particles:

Dęʼ hne:ʼ. *That's why.*
Dó: í:ʼ! *Let me!*
Nę́:dah. *Here, take this.*
Trehs giʼ gęʼ. *My goodness!*
Ęhę́: sgę́:nǫh. *I'm fine thanks.*
Nęʼ diʼ ní:hs ? *And you?*

However, sentences can be much more complicated, as in the following sentence which means *I'm just going along picking fruit here and there (because) I'm unable to fill my basket.*

Tiga:gwe:gǫ́h tsǫ:
here and there just

agahyagwęhęgyéʼs aknǫ:háʼ
I'm going along picking I'm unable

a:knǫnhéht agáʼahdraʼ.
I would fill it my basket

One of the most striking features of Cayuga is that the verb can express the meaning of an entire sentence.

Degaǫdatgǫhsóhae:
They are washing each other's faces.

Cayuga verbs not only include the meanings conveyed by pronouns in English, they can also include (or incorporate) an object noun as well. To illustrate, the verb degaǫdatgǫhsóhae: *they are washing each other's face* consists of smaller units that have identifiable meanings. The approximate meanings of each part of the verb are shown next.

type of unit	*unit*	*meaning*
prepronominal	de	*back-and-forth motion*
pronominal	gaǫ	*they*
semireflexive	dat	*each other*
noun	gǫhs	*face*
verb	ohae:	*are.washing*

Other examples of verbs that are complete sentences include:

ahadadrihwagwé:nyęʼ *he had earned it for himself*
hahnaʼtsí:yo: *he has a nice bum*

Sentences can be formed from a verb plus a particle modifying the meaning of the verb or of the sentence. The particle can precede the verb:

Ahsǫ́h hodrę́:nǫ:t.
still he is singing
He's still singing.

G'ato:háh todáhsdǫh.
somewhere he is hiding
He's hiding somewhere.

Sgęnǫshǫ:'ǫ́h satahí:ne'
slowly go along
Amble along slowly!

The particle can also follow the verb:

Jidwahshé:t e:'
let's count again
Let's count again!

Agahyaksé' ęyo:hę́' shedehjí:hah
I'm going to pick fruit tomorrow morning
I'm going to pick berries tomorrow morning

A particle can also appear on either side of the verb:

I:só' agidahsgęhę́:' gę:s
much I used to sleep generally
I used to sleep a lot.

Sentences can also consist of a verb plus a noun. In many cases, the order of the noun and the verb is not crucial to the basic meaning of the sentence (as it is in English). Instead, in Cayuga, the order of words indicates which ideas are emphasized or focussed on in the sentence. For example the following sentences are equally good ways of saying *I'm picking strawberries.*

gahya:gwáhs jihsǫ́:dahk
I'm picking strawberries

jihsǫ:dáhk gahyá:gwahs
strawberries I'm picking

As an example of fluid word-order, one can combine the following words in many different ways to make sentences which have largely the same meaning (*you're the only one that did it again*).

í:hs *you*
é:' *again*
gyę́' *the one*
hné: *in fact*
tsǫ́: *only*
tóh *that*
nahsye:' *you did it*

i:hs e:' gyę'hne: tsǫ: toh nahsye:'
i:hs gyę' e:' hne: tsǫ: toh nahsye:'
i:hs gyę'hne: e:' tsǫ: toh nahsye:'
i:hs gyę'hne: tsǫ: e:' toh nahsye:'
i:hs gyę'hne: tsǫ: toh e:' nahsye:'

While the Cayuga word order is more fluid, there are subtle rules governing the order of words in a sentence. In general, the beginning of the sentence is for words which are emphasized, or for words which convey the focus or topic of conversation.

7 NOUN MORPHOLOGY (PREFIXES AND SUFFIXES)

7.1 OVERVIEW

Noun prefixes and noun suffixes (endings) are listed below. (Not all variants are listed; see §8.3.4). The terms *agent* (pronominal prefix) and *patient (*pronominal prefix) are discussed in §8.3. Terms such as 'inclusive' or 'exclusive' are described in §8.3.1 and §8.3.2.

Noun prefixes

agent	*patient*	*translation*
k-	ak-	*I*
kni-	ǫkni-	*we two (inclusive)*
akni-	—	*we two (exclusive)*
dwa-	ǫgwa-	*we all (inclusive)*
agwa-	—	*we all (exclusive)*
ha-	ho-	*he*
e-	go-	*she, someone, one*
ga-	o-	*it (animal or thing)*
s-	sa-	*you (singular)*
sni-	sni-	*you two*
swa-	swa-	*you all*
hadi-	hodi-	*they (males)*
gae-	godi-	*they (females or mixed)*
gadi-	odi-	*they (animals, objects)*

Either the Noun Stem Former -aʼ, or the joiner vowel -a precedes the remaining noun suffixes.

Noun suffixes

-aʼ	*Noun Stem Former*
-go:wah	*augmentative suffix*
-nehaːʼ, -gehaːʼ, -kaːʼ	*customary suffixes*
-gęhęːʼ	*decessive suffix*
-ʼah, -hah	*diminutive suffixes*
-agǫː	*internal locative suffix*
-hneh -ʼgeh	*external locative suffixes*
-kʼah, -akdagyeʼ	*other locative suffixes*
-sraʼ, -traʼ	*nominalizer suffixes*
-shǫʼ, -shǫːʼǫh (-sǫʼ, -sǫːʼǫh)	*pluralizer suffixes*
-hoːnǫʼ	*populative suffix*
-ǫːweh	*typicalizer suffix*

7.2 UNPOSSESSED, BASIC NOUNS

Unpossessed, basic nouns begin with ga-, o-, or a-, followed by the noun stem, and ending with the Noun Stem Former (NSF) suffix -aʼ.

ganǫ́hsaʼ *house*; consists of:

agent	*noun stem*	*NSF*
ga+	-nǫhs-	-aʼ

oʼnhǫ́hsaʼ *egg*; consists of:

patient	*noun stem*	*NSF*
o+	-ʼnhǫhs-	-aʼ

awęʼyǫhgaːʼ *thumb*; consists of:

agent	*noun stem*	*NSF*
a+	-węʼyǫhgaː-	-aʼ

7.3 BODY PART (INALIENABLE) NOUNS

Nouns denoting attached body parts (see §2.4) begin with an agentive pronominal prefix, followed by the noun stem, and ending with the *joiner vowel plus locative* suffix combination -aʼgeh.

knętsáʼgeh *on my arm*; consists of:

agent	*noun stem*	*locative*
k+	-nęts-	-aʼgeh

Inalienable nouns and certain adjectival verbs use the same (agentive) prefixes to convey similar meanings, as illustrated by the following examples.

k- *I, my*
 khnę́ːyeːs *I am tall*
 knętsáʼgeh *on my arm*

kni- *we two / our two (includes listener)*
 kni̲hnę́ːyeːs *we two are tall*
 kninę́tsaʼgeh *on the arms of the two of us*

akni- *we two / our two (excludes listener)*
akniihnę́:ye:s *we two are tall*
akninętsá'geh *on the arms of the two of us*

dwa- *we all / all of our (includes listener)*
dwahnę́:ye:s *we all are tall*
dwanę́tsa'geh *on the arms of all of us*

agwa- *we all / all of our (excludes listener)*
agwahnę́:ye:s *we all are tall (but not you)*
agwanętsá'geh *on the arms of all of us (but not you)*

ha- *he, his*
hahnę́:ye:s *he is tall*
hanę́tsa'geh *on his arms*

e- *she, her, someone*
ehnę́:ye:s *she / someone is tall*
enę́tsa'geh *on her arms*

ga- *it, its (object or animal)*
ga̱hnę́:ye:s *it (animal) is tall (nonsensical)*
ganę́tsa'geh *on its (an animal's) arms (nonsensical)*

s- *you (one person), your*
shnę́:ye:s *you are tall (one person)*
snętsá'geh *on your arm (one person)*

sni- *you two, the two of you(r)*
sni̱hnę́:ye:s *you two are tall*
sninę́tsa'geh *on the arms of two of you*

swa- yo*u all, all of you(r)*
swa̱hnę́:ye:s *you all are tall*
swanę́tsa'geh *on the arms of all of you*

hadi- *they (males only), their*
hadihnę́:ye:s *they are tall (males only)*
hadinętsá'geh *on their arms (males only)*

gae- *they (females or mixed group), their*
gaehnę́:ye:s *they are tall (females or mixed group)*
gaenętsá'geh *on their arms (females or mixed group)*

gadi- *they (animals, things), their*
gadihnę́:ye:s *they are tall (animals; nonsensical)*
gadinętsá'geh *on their arms (animals; nonsensical)*

7.4 OTHER POSSESSED NOUNS (ALIENABLE NOUNS)

Possession in basic or 'alienable' nouns (see §7.2) is conveyed with a patient pronominal prefix. Alienable nouns and certain adjectival verbs use the same (patient) pronominal prefixes to convey similar meanings, as illustrated by the following examples.

ak- *I, my*
aknǫhǫkdá:nih *I am sick*
aknǫ́hsa' *my house*

ǫkni- *we two, our two (there is no distinction between inclusive and exclusive for patient prefixes)*
ǫkninǫhǫ́kdanih *we two are sick*
ǫknínǫ̱hsa' *the house belonging to the two of us*

ǫkni- *we all / all of ours (there is no distinction between inclusive and exclusive for patient prefixes)*
ǫgwanǫhǫ́kdanih *we all are sick*
ǫgwánǫ̱hsa' *the house belonging to all of us*

sa- you (singular), *your*
sanǫhǫkdá:nih *you are sick*
sanǫ́hsa' *your house*

sni- *you two, the two of you(r)*
sninǫhǫkdá:nih *you two are sick*
sninǫ́hsa' *the house belonging to the two of you*

swa- *you all, all of you(r)*
swanǫhǫkdá:nih *you all are sick*
swanǫ́hsa' *the house belonging to all of you*

ho- *he, his*
honǫhǫkdá:nih *he is sick*
honǫ́hsa' *his house*

go- *she, someone, her*
gonǫhǫkdá:nih *she or someone is sick*
gonǫ́hsa' *her or someone's house*

o- *it (object or animal)*
onǫhǫkdá:nih *it (animal) is sick*
onǫ́hsa' *its house (note:* ganǫ́hsa' *means 'a house')*

hodi- *they (males only), their*
hodinǫhǫ́kdanih *they are sick (males only)*
hodínǫhsa' *their house (males only)*

godi- *they (females or mixed group), their*
godinǫhǫ́kdanih *they are sick (females or mixed group)*
godínǫhsa' *their house (females or mixed group)*

odi- *they (animals or objects), their*
odinǫhǫ́kdanih *they are sick (animals)*
odínǫhsa' *their house (animals)*

7.5 NOUN SUFFIXES

Suffixes that can be added to nouns are shown below. Nouns with and without suffixes are given in order to illustrate the basic meanings of the suffixes.

augmentative suffix: *big*
dagu:s *cat*
dagu:sgó:wah *big cat*

customary suffixes: *a way, type, kind*
ǫgwehǫ́:weh *Indian*
ǫgwehǫwéhnęha:' *Indian way, language*
ǫgwehǫwéhgęha:' *Indian kind, type*

ahsǫ́heh *night*
ahsǫ́hehka:' *the night kind*

decessive suffix: *former*
akyę́dahkwa' *chair*
akyędahkwá'gęhę:' *former chair*

diminutive suffixes: *smallness; otherwise non-obvious meanings*
ęyó'ga:' *it will be night*
o'gá:s'ah *evening*

ne' owí:ya' *its baby*
owi:yá:'ah *baby*

gwa'yǫ:' *rabbit*
gw'ayę́:'ah *Cottontail rabbit*

tsishéhdęhjih *this morning*
shedęhjí:hah *early morning*

internal locative suffix: *in, under, etc.*
gahǫ́:wa' *boat*
gahǫ́wagǫ: *in a boat*

external locative suffixes: *on, at, etc.*
otó:we' *it's cold*
otów'egeh *north*

Arnie
Arnígeh, Arníhneh *at Arnie's place*

other locative suffixes: *beside, alongside*
akyę́dahkwa' *chair*
akyędahkwá:'k'ah *beside the chair*

ganǫ́hsa' *house*
ganǫhsakdá:gye' *along the house*

nominalizer suffixes: (see §2.6)
dó: gade:nyę́:dęh *Oh, let me try!*
ade'nyędę́hsra' *measurements*

g̲ahna'tso:t *its (attached) behind*
atna'tsotra' *pants (lit.: s.t. attached to the behind)*

pluralizer suffixes: *several, a number of*
agétgw'ęda' *my suitcase*
agetgw'ędá'sǫ' *my suitcases (that is, a bunch of suitcases, bundled together or thought of as a unit)*
agetgw'ęda'sǫ́:'ǫh *my suitcases (that is, ones that are scattered around*

populative suffix: *people living at*
G̲ahnawiyó'geh *Oklahoma*
G̲ahnawiyo'g̲ehǫ́:nǫ' *Oklahomans*

typicalizer suffix: *Indian, real, traditional*
ǫ́:gweh *person*
ǫgwehǫ́:weh *Indian*

8 VERB MORPHOLOGY

8.1 OVERVIEW

Prefixes and suffixes (endings) within the Cayuga verb follow a specific order or template, which is outlined below.

1. prepronominal prefixes
2. pronominal prefixes
3. semireflexive and reflexive prefixes
4. incorporated nouns
5. verb stems (with any derivational suffixes already attached; see §8.6)
6. primary aspect suffixes
7. secondary aspect suffixes
8. postaspectual suffixes

The individual prefixes and suffixes are listed below with the exception of the pronominal prefixes, which are listed in following sections. For prepronominal prefixes, see §8.2; for pronominal prefixes, see §8.3; for semireflexive and reflexive prefixes, see §8.4; for incorporated nouns, see §4, §8.5, and the Cayuga-English dictionary; for verb stems, see the Cayuga-English dictionary; for derivational suffixes, see §8.6; for primary aspect suffixes, see §8.7; for secondary and post-aspect suffixes, see §8.8-§8.11.

1. prepronominal prefixes (not all pronunciation variants are shown here; see §8.2.3).

a. modal
a'- *factual*
ę- *future*
a:- *optative* or *indefinite*

b. non-modal
d- *cislocative*
ti- *contrastive*
ts- *coincident*

de- *dualic*
de'- *negative*
ni- *partitive*
s- *repetitive*
ha'- *translocative*

3. derivational prefixes
ad- *semireflexive*
adad- *reflexive*

5. derivational suffixes for verb stems
-hd / -ht *causative*
-hs, -nih *datives* or *benefactives*
-hn -'n, -dr *dislocatives*
-hsǫ:', -nyǫ:', hnǫ:',
-ǫnyǫ:' *distributives*
-s' *eventuative*
-sgǫ: *facilitative*
-'d / -'t, -nhe' *inchoatives*
-hkwa' *instrumental*

-jih *intensifier*
-agyeʼ, -ǫgyeʼ, -ęgyeʼ *progressives*
-e *purposive*
-goʼ, -gwęh, -ahsih *reversives*
-ge: *augmentative*

6. primary aspect suffixes

-hs, -haʼ, ʼs *habituals*
-ǫh, -ęh, -: *statives*
-eʼ *purposive* [5]
-ʼ *punctual*
-:, -h, or
ø (nothing) *imperative*

7, 8. secondary and post-aspectual suffixes
-gęhę:ʼ *past*
-hk *former*
-(e):k *continuative* or *modalizer*
-ʼs, -shǫʼ, -sǫʼ *pluralizers*
-hne:ʼ *remote*

8.2 PREPRONOMINAL PREFIXES

There are two types of prepronominal prefixes, the modal prefixes, which indicate the verb's mood or mode, and the non-modal prefixes, which have a variety of functions.

8.2.1.1 MODAL PREPRONOMINAL PREFIXES

Modal prepronominal prefixes convey attitudes such as uncertainty, definiteness, and possibility. The most common variants of the modal prepronominal prefixes are illustrated below with example words. The approximate meanings are underlined in the English glosses.

future
ę- ękní:nǫʼ *I will buy it*

factual
a- akní:nǫʼ *I bought it (a fact)*
aʼ- aʼé:yǫʼ *she arrived (a fact)*
ǫ- ǫgí:daʼ *I slept, or I'm sleeping (a fact; said when you want to be left alone)*

optative or *indefinite*
a:- a:kní:nǫʼ *I might / should / could / would buy it*
ae- aeswá:gęʼ *you all might / should / could / would see it*
aǫ- aǫgé:gęʼ *she might / should / could / would see me*

8.2.2 *Non-modal prepronominal prefixes*

The non-modal prepronominal prefixes have various meanings and functions. Examples with and without the prefixes are shown in order to illustrate the basic meaning of each prefix. The most common pronunciations are also shown:

partitive—an amount
ni- nigá:nǫ:ʼ *how much it costs*
cf. ganǫ:ʼ *it's expensive*

coincident—while
tsi- tsịhǫgweʼdá:se: *when he was young*
cf. hǫgwéʼda:se: *he is a young man*

contrastive—different
ti- tigaʼdręhdá:deʼ *it's a different car from the others*

cislocative—here, there (closer to speaker)
t- tga̱he:ʼ *it is sitting there*
cf. ga̱he:ʼ *it's sitting here*

[5] Michelson (1994) recognized the importance of the purposive as a distinct aspectual category in Iroquoian.

da- dasrá:tę̱h, dadrá:tę̱h *climb (over here)!*
cf. haʼsrá:tę̱h, haʼdrá:tę̱h *climb (over there)!*

g- gyʼedrǫʼ *she's at home (here)*
cf. eʼdrǫʼ *she is home*

de- desáʼdre: *drive over here*
cf. heʼsáʼdre: *drive over there*

translocative—way over there (farther from speaker)
heʼ- heʼgáhe:ʼ *it's sitting way over there*
cf. gahe:ʼ *it's sitting here*

he- heyéʼdrǫʼ *she's at home, way over there*
cf. eʼdrǫʼ *she is home*

dualic—two; back-and-forth motion
de- deganǫhsá:ge: *two houses*
cf. niganǫhsá:ge: *a number of houses*

repetitive—one, the one, again
s- shoyę́:twę̱h *he planted it again*
cf. hoyę́:twę̱h *he planted it*
j- jotó:weʼ *it is cold again*
cf. otó:weʼ *it is cold*
ji- jidwáhshe:t *let's count again*
cf. dwahshe:t *let's count*

8.2.3 Combinations of prepronominal prefixes

Many of the possible combinations of prepronominal prefixes are listed below.[6]

a- *factual*
agaedá:graʼ *they fell down*

a:- *optative*
a:gahyá:goʼ *I would pick fruit*

ad- *dualic and factual*
adwagahsíha:s *I choked*

adi- *dualic and factual*
adigyatnę:tsí:yaʼk *we two (exclusive) broke our arm*

ae- *optative*
aeswá:gęʼ *you all might / should / could / would see it*

ag- *dualic and factual*
agyagwatnę:tsí:yaʼk *we all (exclusive) broke our arm*

aǫ- *optative*
aǫgé:gęʼ *she might / should / could / would see me*

aǫda- *cislocative and optative*
aǫdasagyʼǫséhaʼ *you would come and visit*

aǫsa-, ǫ:sa- *repetitive and optative*
aǫsagahdę́:diʼ, ǫ:sagahdę́:diʼ *I might, should go home*

at- *dualic and factual*
atgaeyé:naʼ *they (females or mixed) did it together*

da- *cislocative and factual*
daga:dí:yǫʼ *they (animals) came in*

da- *dualic*
dahsge:gáih *you bite me*

da:- *dualic and optative*
da:gatnę:tsí:yaʼk *I might break my arm*

daǫda, dǫ:da- *dualic, cislocative, and optative*
dǫ:dá:ge:ʼ *I would come back*

daǫsa, dǫ:sa- *dualic, repetitive, and optative*
dǫ:sáedaʼ *she stood up again*

---

[6] This list is adapted from Foster (1993); example words were provided by Cayuga dictionary project members.

de- *dualic*
dedwadagyénawahs *let us all help one another*

d'e, de'-, de- *negative*
de'agadǫ́tgade' *I'm not happy*
de'agǫnhé:gye' *she was stillborn; she came to be not living*

dedi- *negative and cislocative*
hęhsahshę́:da' tsęh hǫ:wéh dedíhsawihs *you will trod, step where you're not wanted (that is, trespass)*

deg- *dualic and cislocative*
Degyotnǫhsá:kdǫ: *St. Catharine's, Ont.*

de'ji- *negative and repetitive*
dejidwayę́:di: *we do not know any longer*

des- *dualic and repetitive*
Tę' gęh deshó:yǫ: ? *Did he not come home?*

d'es, des- *negative and repetitive*
desga:ní:yǫ:t *it is not hanging any longer*

det-, ded- *dualic and cislocative*
detge' *I am coming back*

d'et, det-, d'ed-, ded- *negative and cislocative*
detgá:yę' *it is no longer laying there*

d'ej-, dej- *negative and repetitive*
deja:gó:yǫ: *she didn't return*

dę- *dualic and future*
dęhsná'net'a:' *you will double it, reinforce s.t.*

dędi- *dualic, cislocative, and future*
dędíhs'adre:' *you will drive over there*

dęg- *dualic, cislocative, and future*
dęgyá:kne:' *we two will come back*

dęj- *dualic, repetitive, and future*
dęjǫtnǫhsǫ́:goht *she will go in one door and out the other door (at a funeral)*

dęji- *dualic, repetitive, and future*
dęjidwanǫ́hǫnyǫ:' *we will thank again*

dęs- *dualic, repetitive, and future*
dęshaihwáętwaht *he will bring forth a message*

dęt-, dęd- *dualic, cislocative, and future*
dętga:dǫ́:goht *I will pass that way*

di- *cislocative*
disáhdęgyǫ: *you come from there*

dǫ- *cislocative and factual*
dǫgáhdǫ:' *(where) I lost it*

dǫda- *dualic, cislocative, and factual*
dǫdá:ge' *I'm coming back*

dǫsa- *dualic, repetitive, and factual*
dǫsagakenǫhǫ́:nyǫ:' *I thanked them again; I greeted them again*

e- *factual*
esáhdǫ:' *you lost it*

edi- *dualic and factual*
edidwatnę:tsí:ya'k *we all broke our arm*

ę- *future*
ęgátnǫhga:' *I'm going to cut my hair*

ędi- *cislocative and future*
ędis'anigǫhí:yoh *your mind will become adjusted*

ęg- *cislocative and future*
ęgyo'gá:hah *early evening*

ęj- *repetitive and future*
ęjé:kse:k *she can eat it again*

ęji- *repetitive and future*
ęjidwana'dáiksǫ:' *we will snack (lit.: bite the bread)*

ęs- *repetitive and future*
ęshahé:waht *he will punish again*

ęt- *cislocative and future*
ętsę'nigǫ́ho'ne:k *you will revolt, remove yourself (bodily and in spirit)*

ha:- *translocative and optative*
to hǫ́: ha:g'idrǫ́:da'k *where I would dwell*

ha', ha- *translocative and factual*
ha'ge' *I am going there*

ha'de- *translocative and dualic*
ha'deg'adréhdage: *all kinds of cars*

ha'dę- *translocative, dualic, and future*
ha'dę́:syehs *you will put them all together*

haǫsa-, hǫ:sa-, hǫ:sa- *translocative, repetitive, and optative*
to é: hǫsá:ge:' *I would go again*

ha't- *translocative, dualic, and factual*
ha'tgęnętsáǫnyǫ:' *I waved my arms*

ha't- *translocative and dualic*
ha'tsę́nętse:s *you reach out!*

he, he'- *translocative*
he'sá:dih *throw it away from me!*

hej- *translocative and repetitive*
hejónǫhsǫ:t *the next room*

heji- *translocative and repetitive*
Gaę hwa' nhǫ hejisáiho'de' ? *Where do you work again?*

hes- *translocative and repetitive*
I:wa:k'áh heshohdrihsdǫ́hǫgye'. *He's getting nearer and nearer*

hę- *translocative and future*
hęsyę:' *you will put it there*

hęs- *translocative, repetitive, and future*
hęsge' *I am going back there*

hęt- *translocative, repetitive, and future*
hętsyę:' *you will put it back in its place*

hęj- *translocative, repetitive, and future*
hęja:gǫ́:nęht *they (f / m) shall swallow again*

hęji- *translocative, repetitive, and future*
hęjísasha:' *you will remember back in time*

hǫ:sa-, hǫsa- *translocative, repetitive, and factual*
hǫ:sahá:yǫ' *he went back inside; he arrived*

j- *repetitive*
jodrę́:no:t *it is singing again*

ji- *repetitive*
jidwahshé:t e:' *let's count again (emphatic)*

na:- *partitive and optative*
I:wí: to na:yá:węh *I want, intend that to happen*

na', na, n'a- *partitive and factual*
tsę na'á:węh *how it happened*

na'daǫda, na'dǫ:da- *partitive, dualic, cislocative, and optative*
na'dǫ:dá:ge' *I should come this way*

na'de, n'ade- *partitive and dualic*
na'degáǫdre' *how far apart they are (f / m)*

na'deg- *partitive, dualic, and cislocative*
tsęh nadegyadǫ́dai: *during the week*

na'det- *partitive, dualic, and cislocative*
na'dé:tge' *I am coming back over here, returning*

na'dęt- *partitive, dualic, and cislocative and future*
na'dę́:tge:' *I'll come back over here, return*

na'dǫda- *partitive, dualic, cislocative, and factual*
tsęh na'dǫ:dá:ge:' *where I'm coming from*

naǫsa- *partitive, repetitive, and optative*
naǫsaǫgwayę́hę:k *what we should be doing*

nę- *partitive and future*
nęwú:k'uh *it will be small*

nhe- *partitive and translocative*
nhé:yoht *suddenly it occurred*

ni- *partitive*
nigahnę́:ya' *it is short*

nidi- *partitive and cislocative*
nidihsé:no: *you (singular) come from (that is, you are X years old)*

nig- *partitive and cislocative*
nigyagawé:no' *she comes from (that is, she is X years old)*

nij- *partitive and repetitive*
nijagowé:nǫh *female stranger (lit.: where she comes from)*

nis- *partitive and repetitive*
Nishayé:no:s *Hold unto (Seneca Chief Title)*

nit- *partitive and cislocative*
nita:wé:nǫh *male stranger (lit.: where he comes from)*

nǫ:-, ni- *partitive*
nǫ:gé'syáo'dę:h, niwagehsyáo'dęh *I'm... clan*

nǫda- *partitive, cislocative, and factual*
nǫdá:ge:' *I come from*

nǫdi- *partitive, cislocative, and factual*
Gaę nhǫ nǫdi:sé:nǫ: ? *Where are you from?*

nǫ:sa- *partitive, repetitive, and factual*
see naǫsa-

ǫ- *factual*
ǫgáhdrǫ'k *It frightened me; I got frightened*

s- *repetitive*
sgayá'da:t *one (living thing)*

sa- *repetitive and factual*
sagę'nho'trá:twaht *I missed the ball*

sa- *repetitive*
sasnęht *get down from there*

t- *cislocative*
tadínagre' *that's where they live over there*

tae, te:- *contrastive and optative*
tę' taeswa:gęh, te:swa:gęh *you all shouldn't see it*

ta', ta- *contrastive and factual, or contrastive, translocative, and factual*
tę' taha:yę́:toh *no, he won't plant*

ta'de- *contrastive and dualic, or contrastive, translocative, and dualic*
ta'degawá:yǫ:t *it has no wings*

ta'dę- *contrastive, dualic, and future, or contrastive, translocative, dualic, and future*
ta'dęjatáhahk *you two will walk side by side*

te', te- *contrastive and translocative*
tę' toh te'gáhe:' *it's not sitting way over there*

te: see tae-
tę' te:sagáę: *you are not willing*

ti- *contrastive*
tiga'drehdá:de' *a different car*

tǫde, tǫdi- *contrastive, cislocative, and factual*
tę' tǫdes'adré: tó:gyęh *you won't drive that over here*

tsa'- *coincident and factual, or coincident, translocative, and factual*
tsa'ga:yę́:da' *when it became (lit: when it landed; when it set down)*

tsa'de- *coincident and dualic, or coincident, translocative, and dualic*
tsa'dé:wa's *they are the same size*

tsa'deg- *coincident, dualic, and cislocative*
tsadegy'adǫ́dadrehk *the week before last*

tsa'dę- *coincident, dualic, and future,* or *coincident, translocative, dualic, and future*
tsa'dę́hsyę:' *you will lay them side by side*

tsi- *coincident*
tsiyeksa'da:sé:'ah *when she was a teenager*

tę- *contrastive and future,* or *contrastive, translocative, and future*
tęhayętó:'ah *he'll just plant it any old way or helter-skelter*

8.3 PRONOMINAL PREFIXES

There are three types of pronominal prefixes, the agent series, the patient series, and the interactive or transitive series. Each type is discussed below.

8.3.1 Agent pronominal prefixes

The following table shows a verb (-hnęye:s *to be tall*) that takes agent pronominal prefixes; in the dictionary, this verb's grammatical information would state [A+].[7]

k-hnę́:ye:s *I am tall*
first person singular 1A

kni̲-hnę́:ye:s *we two are tall*
first and second dual inclusive 1indA

akni-hnę́:ye:s *we two are tall (doesn't include listener)*
first and third dual exclusive 1exclA

agwa-hnę́:ye:s *we all are tall (doesn't include listener)*
first and third plural exclusive 1expA

dwa̲-hnę́:ye:s *we all are tall*
first and second plural inclusive 1inpA

ha-hnę́:ye:s *he is tall*
third person singular masculine MA

e-hnę́:ye:s *she / someone is tall*
third person singular feminine-indefinite FA

ga̲-hnę́:ye:s *it is tall*
third person singular zoic-neuter NA

s-hnę́:ye:s *you (singular) are tall*
second person singular 2A

sni̲-hnę́:ye:s *you two are tall*
second person dual 2dA

swa̲-hnę́:ye:s *you all are tall*
second person plural 2pA

[7] Linguistic terms included in this section and the next are from Michelson (1988:45-46).

hadi-hnę́:ye:s *they (males) are tall*
third person non-singular masculine MdpA

gae-hnę́:ye:s *they (females or mixed) are tall*
third person non-singular feminine FdpA

gadi-hnę́:ye:s *they (animals) are tall*
third person non-singular zoic-neuter ZdpA

hodi-nǫhǫ́kdanih *they (males only) are sick*
third person non-singular masculine MdpP

godi-nǫhǫ́kdanih *they (females or mixed) are sick*
third person non-singular feminine FdpP

odi-nǫhǫ́kdanih *they (animals) are sick*
third person non-singular zoic ZdpP

8.3.2 Patient pronominal prefixes

The following table shows a verb (-nǫhǫkdanih *to be sick*) that takes patient pronominal prefixes; in the dictionary, such a verb's grammatical information would specify [P+].

ak-nǫhǫkdá:nih *I am sick*
first person singular 1P

ǫkni-nǫhǫ́kdanih *we two are sick*
first person dual 1dP

ǫgwa-nǫhǫ́kdanih *we all are sick*
first person plural 1pP

sa-nǫhǫkdá:nih *you (singular) are sick*
second person singular 2P

sni-nǫhǫkdá:nih *you two are sick*
second person dual 2dP

swa-nǫhǫkdá:nih *you all are sick*
second person plural 2pP

ho-nǫhǫkdá:nih *he is sick*
third person singular masculine MP

go-nǫhǫkdá:nih *she / someone is sick*
third person singular feminine-indefinite FP

o-nǫhǫkdá:nih *it is sick*
third person singular zoic-neuter 3znP

8.3.3 Transitive or interactive pronominal prefixes

The following table illustrates a verb (-gę' *to see, punctual aspect*) that takes transitive or interactive pronominal prefixes; in the dictionary, such a verb's grammatical information would specify [TR+]. Each word in the following table ends with the verb and begins with the factual prefix a-, a'-, or e-. Sometimes the epenthetic vowel -e- occurs between the pronominal prefix and the verb. Other words are sometimes provided in order to show further variants.

a-hé:-gę' *I...him*

a-sha:kní:-gę' *she / he / someone and I...him*

a-sha:gwá:-gę' *they and I...him / them (males)*

a-she:tní:-gę' *you (singular) and I...him*

a-she:dwá:-gę' *you all and I...him*

a-hehsé:-gę' *you (singular)...him*

a-she:sní:-gę' *you two...him; he...you two*

a-she:swá:-gę' *you all...him; he...you all*

a-ho:wá:-gę' *she / he / someone...him*

a-hǫwadí:-gę' *they...him; she / he / someone ... them (males)*

a-ha:g-é:-gę' *he...me*

a-shǫ:kní:-gę' *he...us two*

a-shǫ:gwá:-gę' *he...us all*

e-hyá:-gę' *he...you (singular)*

a-sha:gó:-gę' *he...her / someone / it / them (females or mixed)*

a-ké:-gę' *I...her / someone*

a-ga:ké:-gę' *I...them*

a'-a:kí:-gę' *she / he / someone / they and I...her / someone / them*

a'-e:tí:-gę' *you (singular) / you all and I...her / someone / them*

a-shé:-gę' *you (singular)...her / someone*

a-ga:shé:-gę' *you (singular)...them*

a'-e:tsí:-gę' *you two / you all...her / someone / them she / someone / them...you two / you all*

a-gaǫdad-é:-gę' *they ... her; she / someone / they(females or mixed)...them (females or mixed*

gaǫdagyenawa'seh *they help her, etc.*

a-shagodí:-gę' *they (males or animals)...her / someone / them (females or mixed)*

a-gowadí:-gę' *she / he / someone / they...it*

a'-ǫ:g-é:-gę' *she / someone...me*

a-gaǫg-é:-gę' *they...me*

a'-ǫ:kí:-gę' *she / someone / they...us*

a'-e:sá:-gę' *she / someone...you (singular)*

a-gaesá:-gę' *they...you (singular)*

a-gǫ́:-gę' *I...you (singular)*

a-kní:-gę' *she / he / someone and I...it*

a-gwá:-gę' *they and I...it*

a-sg-é:-gę' *you (singular)...me*

e-skní:-gę' *you (singular) / you two...us two*

e-sgwá:-gę' *you...us*

In addition to taking these prefixes, active transitive verbs can also take the agent and patient series prefixes. For example, the verb *to buy* can take the agentive prefix meaning *I*, as in a:-k-hní:nǫ' *I should buy something*. As shown in this example, when agent prefixes are used in active transitive verbs, an object noun (translated as *something* or *it* above) is implied. Conversely, when an active, transitive verb such as *to see* takes a patient prefix such as (w)ag(e)- *me*, the subject *it or something* is implied, as in tę' de-wa:g-é:-gęh *(it) did not see me.*

8.3.4 Pronominal prefix allomorphy

The agent, patient, and interactive prefixes all have pronunciation variants, which are determined by the first consonant or vowel of the following verb stem, as well as by the last segment of the preceding prepronominal prefix. Changes triggered by the first consonant or vowel of the following verb stem are listed in §8.3.4.1 and following. Changes triggered by the last segment of the preceding prepronominal prefix are listed below. Abbreviations include:

c-stem: verb stem beginning with a consonant

a-stem: verb stem beginning with the vowel [a]

i-stem: verb stem beginning with the vowel [i]

e-stem: verb stem beginning with the vowel [e] or [ę]

o-stem: verb stem beginning with the vowel [o] or [ǫ]

u-stem: verb stem beginning with the vowel [u]

* the vowel of the stem deletes when the prefix is added

The initial segments of some pronominal prefixes are sometimes deleted. The segments which can delete are in brackets in the following table. These segments are generally present after any prepronominal prefix that ends with a vowel; they are absent otherwise.

(w)ag-	*I*
(y)ǫkni-	*we two*
(y)ǫgwa-	*we all*
(h)sa-	*you (singular)*
(h)sni-	*you two*
(h)swa-	*you all*
(ya)go-	*she / someone*
(y)o-	*it*
(y)odi-	*they (animals)*
(y)akni-	*we two (not including listener)*
(y)agwa-	*we all (not including listener)*
(h)s-	*you (singular)*
(y)e-	*she / someone*
(y)aki-	*she / he / someone / they and I...her / someone / them*
(y)eti-	*you (singular) / you all and I...her / someone / them*
(y)etsi-	*you two / you all...her / someone / them; she / someone / them...you two / you all*
(y)ǫdad-	*she / someone...her / someone*
(y)ǫg-	*she / someone...me*
(y)ǫki-	*she / someone / they...us*
(y)esa-	*she / someone...you (singular)*
(h)sg-	*you (singular)...me*

8.3.4.1 Patient, c-stem

c-stem *(-nǫhǫkdanih to be sick)*

ak-nǫhǫkda:nih I

ǫkni-nǫhǫ́kdanih *we two*

ǫgwa-nǫhǫ́kdanih *we all*

sa-nǫhǫkdá:nih *you (singular)*

sni-nǫhǫkdá:nih *you two*

swa-nǫhǫkdá:nih *you all*

ho-nǫhǫkdá:nih *he*

go-nǫhǫkdá:nih *she / someone*

o-nǫhǫkdá:nih *it*

hodi-nǫhǫ́kdanih *they (males only)*

godi-nǫhǫ́kdanih *they (females or mixed)*

odi-nǫhǫ́kdanih *they (animals)*

Before stems beginning with a consonant other than [n] or [h], the prefix meaning *I* is -ag-, followed by an epenthetic -e-:

ag-ę́:-gaʼs *I like the taste of it*

ag-ę́:-swahs *I'm smelling it I*

8.3.4.2 Patient, a-stem

a-stem *(-atowinyǫʼse: to have a cold).* An asterisk indicates that the vowel of the stem deletes.

ag-atowíny'ǫse: *I*

ǫgy-atowíny'ǫse: *we two*

ǫgw-atowíny'ǫse: *we all*

*sa-towinyǫ́'se: *you (singular)*

*ja-towinyǫ́'se: *you two*

*swa-towinyǫ́'se: *you all*

*ho-towinyǫ́'se: *he*

*go-towinyǫ́'se: *she / someone*

*o-towinyǫ́'se: *it*

hon-atowíny'ǫse: *they (males only)*

gon-atowíny'ǫse: *they (females or mixed)*

on-atowíny'ǫse: *they (animals)*

8.3.4.3 Patient, i-stem

i-stem (-ida'ǫh *to be sleeping, stative aspect).* An asterisk indicates that the vowel of the stem deletes or merges with the prefix vowel.

ag-íd'aǫh *I*

*ǫkní-d'aǫh *we two*

*ǫgwę-d'aǫh *we all*

*sę-dá'ǫh *you (singular)*

*sni-dá'ǫh *you two*

*swę-dá'ǫh *you all*

*ho-dá'ǫh *he*

*go-dá'ǫh *she / someone*

*o-dá'ǫh *it*

*hodí-d'aǫh *they (males only)*

*godí-d'aǫh *they (females or mixed)*

*odí-d'aǫh *they (animals)*

8.3.4.4 Patient, e-stem

e-stems (-ęne'waǫ: *to be surprised, stative aspect;* -ęne'wahdę' *to startle someone, punctual aspect*). Less common variants are shown in brackets. An asterisk indicates that the vowel of the stem deletes or merges with the prefix vowel.

ag-ęn'ewáǫ:, ę-wag-ęné'wa̲hdę' *I*

ǫkn-ęn'ewáǫ: (ǫgy-ęn'ewáǫ:), ę-yǫkn-ęné'wa̲hdę' *we two*

ǫgw-ęn'ewáǫ:, ę-yǫgw-ęné'wa̲hdę' *we all*

s-ęné'waǫ:, ę-hs-ęn'ewáhdę' *you (singular)*

sn-ęné'waǫ:, ę-hsn-ęn'ewáhdę', (ę-j-ęn'ewahdę') *you two*

sw-ęné'waǫ:, ę-hsw-ęn'ewáhdę' *you all*

haw-é:'ǫ: *he has willed*

*(ho-né'waǫ:), (*ę-ho-n'ewáhdę') *he*

gaw-ęn'ewáǫ:., (*go-né'waǫ:), *ę-yǫ-ne'wáhdę', (*ę-yago-né'wa̲hdę') *she / someone*

aw-ęn'ewáǫ:, (*o-né'waǫ:), (*ę-yo-n'ewáhdę') *it*

hon-ęn'ewáǫ:, ę-hon-ęné'wa̲hdę' *they (males only)*

gon-ęn'ewáǫ:, ę-yagon-ęn'ewáhdę' *they (females or mixed)*

on-ęn'ewáǫ:, ę-yon-ęné'wa̲hdę' *they (animals)*

8.3.4.5 Patient, o-stem

o-stems (-ǫtsanǫhwa:s *to have a sore knee;* -odaihsi' *to comb someone's hair, punctual aspect).* Less common variants are shown in brackets.

ag-ǫtsanǫ́hwa:s, dę-wag-odáihsi' *I*

ǫkn-ǫ̲tsanǫ́hwa:s, dę-yǫkn-odáihsi' *we two*

ǫgy-ǫtsanǫ́hwa:s, (dę-yǫgway-odáihsi') *we all*

s-ǫtsánǫ̲hwa:s, (dę-hsay-odáihsi') *you (singular)*

sn-ǫtsánǫ̲hwa:s, dę-hsn-odáihsi' *you two*

j-ǫtsánǫ̲hwa:s, (dę-hsway-odáihsi') *you all*

ha-ǫtsanǫ́hwa:s, (h-ǫtsánǫ̲hwa:s), (dę-hoy-odáihsi') *he*

ga-ǫtsanǫ́hwa:s, (gwa-ǫtsanǫ́hwa:s), (g-ǫtsánǫ̲hwa:s), (dę-yagoy-odáihsi') *she / someone*

a-ǫtsanǫ́hwa:s, (ǫtsanǫhwa:s), (dę-yoy-odaihsi') *it*

hon-ǫtsanǫhwa:s, (hodin-ǫtsánǫ̲hwa:s), (dę-hon-odáihsi') *they (males only)*

gon-ǫtsanǫ́hwa:s, (godin-ǫtsánǫ̲hwa:s), dę-yagon-odáihsi' *they (females or mixed)*

on-ǫtsanǫ́hwa:s, (odin-ǫtsánǫhwa:s), dę-yon-odáihsi' *they (animals)*

8.3.4.6 Agent, C-stem

c-stem (-hnę:ye:s *to be tall)* Other words are also provided in order to show variants in the c-stem pronominal prefixes.

k-nę́:ye:s, k-hnę́:ye:s *I*

kni̲-hnę́:ye:s *we two (including listener)*

dę-tní̲-hsdate't *we two will shine it*

akni-hnę́:ye:s *we two (not including listener)*

agwa-hnę́:ye:s *we all (not including listener)*

dwa̲-hnę́:ye:s *we all (including listener)*

s-hnę́:ye:s *you (singular)*

s-é:-ge:t *scrape it*

da-hs-ra:tęh, da-d-ra:tęh *climb (over here)!*

sni̲-hnę́:ye:s *you two*

swa̲-hnę́:ye:s *you all*

ha-hnę́:ye:s *he*

e-hnę́:ye:s *she / someone*

ga̲-hnę́:ye:s *it*

hadi-hnę́:ye:s *they (males only)*

gae-hnę́:ye:s *they (females or mixed)*

gadi-hnę́:ye:s *they (animals)*

8.3.4.7 Agent, a-stem

a-stem (-ahsi'dagrahs *to have smelly feet).* An asterisk indicates that the vowel of the stem deletes or merges with the prefix vowel.

g-a̲hsí'dagrahs *I*

gy-a̲hsí'dagrahs *we two (including listener)*

agy-ahs'idá:grahs *we two (not including listener)*

*agw-ahs'idá:grahs *we all (not including listener)*

*dw-ahsí'dagrahs *we all (including listener)*

s-ahsí'dagrahs *you (singular)*

j-a̱hsí'dagrahs *you two*

*sw-a̱hsí'dagrahs̱ *you all*

*h-ahsí'dagrahs *he*

*ǫ-hsí'dagrahs *she / someone*

*w-a̱hsí'dagrahs *it*

hęn-ahs'idá:grahs *they (males only)*

*gaǫ-hs'idá:grahs *they (females or mixed)*

gęn-ahs'idá:grahs *they (animals)*

8.3.4.8 Agent, i-stem

i-stem *(-idagra' to fall, trip, punctual aspect)*; the *future* prefix ę- precedes the pronominal prefixes in these examples. An asterisk indicates that the vowel of the stem deletes or merges with the prefix vowel.

ę-g-ídagra' *I*

*ę-kn-ídagra', *ę-tn-ídagra' *we two (including listener)*

*ę-yakn-idá:gra' *we two (not including listener)*

*ę-yagwę-dá:gra' *we all (not including listener)*

*ę-dwę́-dagra' *we all (including listener)*

*ę-hs-ídagra' *you (singular)*

*ę-hsn-ídagra' *you two*

*ę-swę́-dagra' *you all*

*ę-hę́-dagra' *he*

*ę-yę́-dagra' *she / someone*

*ę-gę́-dagra' *it*

*ę-had-idá:gra' *they (males only)*

*ę-gae-dá:gra' *they (females or mixed)*

ę-gad-idá:gra' *they (animals)*

8.3.4.9 Agent, e-stem

e-stem (-ęne'wahdę' *to startle someone, punctual aspect).* The *future* prefix ę- precedes the pronominal prefixes in these examples. An asterisk indicates that the vowel of the stem deletes or merges with the prefix vowel. Less common variants are shown in brackets.

ę-g-ęn'ewáhdę' *I*

ę-kn-ęn'ewáhdę', ę-tn-ęn'ewáhdę' *we two (including listener)*

ę-yakn-ęné'wa̱hdę', (ę-yagy-ęné'wa̱hdę') *we two (not including listener)*

ę-yagw-ęné'wa̱hdę' *we all (not including listener)*

ę-dw-ęn'ewáhdę' *we all (including listener)*

ę-hs-ęn'ewáhdę' *you (singular)*

ę-hsn-ęn'ewáhdę' *you two*

ę-hsw-ęn'ewáhdę' *you all*

ę-h-ęn'ewáhdę' *he*

ę-yag-ęné'wa̱hdę', (*ę-yǫ-n'ewáhdę') *she / someone*

ę-w-ęn'ewáhdę' *it*

ę-hęn-ęné'wa̱hdę' *they (males only)*

*ę-gaǫ-né'wa̱hdę', (ę-ga:g-ęn'ewáhdę'), *they (females or mixed)*

ę-gęn-ęné'wa̱hdę' *they (animals)*

8.3.4.10 Agent, o-stem

o-stem (-ǫgweʼdi:yo: *to be a nice person*; -odaihsiʼ *to comb someone's hair, punctual aspect*). An asterisk indicates that the vowel of the stem deletes or merges with the prefix vowel. Less common variants are shown in brackets.

g-ǫgweʼdí:yo:, dę-g-odáihsiʼ *I*

kn-ǫgweʼdí:yo:, tn-ǫgweʼdí:yo:, (gy-ǫgweʼdí:yo:), dę-kn-odáihsiʼ *we two (including listener)*

akn-ǫgweʼdí:yo:, dę-yakn-odáihsiʼ *we two (not including listener)*

agy-ǫgweʼdí:yo:, dę-yagy-odáihsiʼ *we all (not including listener)*

dę-gy-odáihsiʼ *we all (including listener)*

s-ǫgweʼdí:yo:, dę-hs-odáihsiʼ *you (singular)*

sn-ǫgweʼdí:yo:, dę-hsn-odáihsiʼ, (dę-hsniy-odáihsiʼ) *you two*

j-ǫgweʼdí:yo:, (dę-hsway-odáihsiʼ) dę-j-odáihsiʼ *you all*

h-ǫgweʼdí:yo:, dę-h-odáihsiʼ *he*

ag-ǫgwʼedí:yo:, dę-yag-odáihsiʼ *she / someone*

*ǫgweʼdí:yo:, dę-y-odáihsiʼ *it*

hęn-ǫgwʼedí:yo:, dę-hęn-odáihsiʼ *they (males only)*

ga:g-ǫgweʼdí:yo:, dę-ga:g-odáihsiʼ *they (females or mixed)*

gęn-ǫgwʼedí:yo:, dę-gęn-odáihsiʼ *they (animals)*

8.3.4.11 Agent, u-stem

u-stem (-u:ʼuh *to be small*; -u:sʼuh *to be several small objects)*; the *partitive* prefix ni- occurs before the pronominal prefixes in these examples. An asterisk indicates that the vowel of the stem deletes or merges with the prefix vowel.

ni-g-ú:ʼuh *I*

*ni-kn-ú:ʼuh, nitnú:ʼuh *we two (including listener)*

*ni-ya:kn-ú:ʼuh *we two (not including listener)*

*ni-ya:gy-ú:ʼuh *we all (not including listener)*

*ni-gy-ú:ʼuh *we all (including listener)*

ni-s-ú:ʼuh *you (singular)*

*ni-sn-ú:ʼuh *you two*

*ni-j-ú:ʼuh *you all*

*ni-h-ú:ʼuh *he*

*ni-ya:g-ú:ʼuh *she / someone*

*ni-w-ú:ʼuh *it*

*ni-hę:n-ú:sʼuh *they (males only)*

ni-ga:g-ú:sʼuh *they (females or mixed)*

*ni-gę:n-ú:sʼuh *they (animals)*

8.3.4.12 Interactive, C-stem

C-stem *(-gęʼ to see, punctual aspect)*; the *factual* prefix a-, aʼ-, or e- occurs before the pronominal prefixes in these examples. Other words are sometimes included in order to illustrate prefix variants. Sometimes an epenthetic -e- occurs between the prefix and the verb.

a-hé:-gę', a-hí:-gę' *I...him*

a-sha:kní:-gę' *she / he / someone and I...him*

a-sha:gwá:-gę' *they and I...him / them (males)*

a-she:tní:-gę' *you (singular) and I...him*

a-she:dwá:-gę' *you all and I...him*

a-hehs-é:-gę' *you (singular)...him*

a-she:sní:-gę' *you two...him; he...you two*

a-she:swá:-gę' *you all...him; he...you all*

a-hǫ:wá:-gę' *she / he / someone...him*

a-hǫwadí:-gę' *they...him; she / he / someone ... them (males)*

a-ha:g-é:-gę' *he...me*

a-shǫ:kní:-gę' *he...us two*

a-shǫ:gwá:-gę' *he...us all*

e-hyá:-gę' *he...you (singular)*

a-sha:gó:-gę' *he...her / someone / it / them (females or mixed)*

a-ké:-gę', a-kí:-gę' *I...her / someone*

a-ga:ké:-gę', a-ka:ké:-gę' *I...them*

a'-a:kí:-gę' *she / he / someone / they and I...her / someone / them*

a'-e:tí:-gę' *you (singular) / you all and I...her / someone / them*

a-shé:-gę' *you (singular)...her / someone*

a-ga:shé:-gę', a-ka:shé:-gę' *you (singular)...them*

a'-e:tsí:-gę' *you two / you all...her / someone / them; she / someone / them...you two / you all*

a'-ǫdad-é:-gę' *she / someone...her / someone*

a-ǫdat-gwé:ni' *she won a competition (for herself)*

ha'-ǫdag-ya'datsę́i:' *she found her over there*

a-gaǫdad-é:-gę' *she / someone / they (females or mixed)...them (females or mixed)*

gaǫdag-yenawa'seh *they help her*

a-shagodí:-gę' *they (males or animals)...her / someone / them (females or mixed)*

a-gowadí:-gę' *she / he / someone / they...it*

a'-ǫg-é:-gę' *she / someone...me*

a-gaǫg-é:-gę' *they...me*

a'-ǫ:kí:-gę' *she / someone / they...us*

a'-e:sá:-gę' *she / someone...you (singular)*

a-gaesá:-gę' *they...you (singular)*

a-gǫ́:-gę' *I...you (singular)*

a-sg-é:-gę' *you (singular)...me*

ę-hsg-ǫ' *you will give me*

de-hsk-nigǫ̱há:ha' *you are annoying me*

e-skni:-gę' *you (singular) / you two...us two*

e-sgwá:-gę' *you...us*

For remaining prefix variants, look in §8.3.4.1 (patient, C-stem) and §8.3.4.6 (agent, C-stem).

8.3.4.13 Interactive, a-stem

a-stem (-ahǫdǫha' *to be asking someone, habitual aspect).* [8] An asterisk indicates that the vowel of the stem deletes or merges with the prefix vowel. Less common variants are shown in brackets.

hey-ahǫdǫ́ha', hiy-ahǫdǫ́ha' *I...him*

*shagy-ahǫdǫ́ha', (shakniy-ahǫ́dǫha') *she / he / someone and I...him*

*shagw-ahǫdǫ́ha' *they and I...him / them (males)*

*shegy-ahǫdǫ́ha' *you (singular) and I...him*

*shedw-ahǫdǫ́ha', shetwahǫdǫ́ha' *you all and I...him*

hehs-ahǫdǫ́ha' *you (singular)...him*

*shej-ahǫdǫ́ha' *you two...him; he...you two*

*shesw-ahǫdǫ́ha' *you all...him; he...you all*

*hǫw-ahǫdǫ́ha' *she / he / someone...him*

*hǫwęn-a̲hǫ́dǫha', (*hǫwan-a̲hǫ́dǫha') *they...him; she / he / someone ... them (males)*

hag-ahǫdǫ́ha' *he...me*

*shǫgy-ahǫdǫ́ha' *he...us two*

*shǫgw-ahǫdǫ́ha' *he...us all*

*ę-hy-a:tró:wi' *he will tell you (singular)*

*shago-hǫdǫ́ha' * *he...her / someone / it / them (females or mixed)*

key-ahǫdǫ́ha' *I...her / someone*

gakey-a̲hǫ́dǫha', (kakey-a̲hǫ́dǫha') *I...them*

akiy-a̲hǫ́dǫha' *she / he / someone / they and I...her / someone / them*

etiy-a̲hǫ́dǫha' *you (singular) / you all and I...her / someone / them*

shey-ahǫdǫ́ha' *you (singular)...her / someone*

gashey-a̲hǫ́dǫha', ka:sheyahǫdǫ́ha' *you (singular)...them*

etsiy-a̲hǫ́dǫha' *you two / you all...her / someone / them; she / someone / them...you two / you all*

ǫdad-a̲hǫ́dǫha' *she / someone...her / someone*

gaǫdad-ahǫdǫ́ha' *she / someone / they(females or mixed)...them(females or mixed)*

*shagon-a̲hǫ́dǫha' *they (males or animals)...her / someone / them (females or mixed)*

*gǫwęn-a̲hǫ́dǫha', gǫwana̲hǫ́dǫha' *she / he / someone / they...it*

ǫg-ahǫdǫ́ha' *she / someone...me*

gaǫg-a̲hǫ́dǫha' *they...me*

ǫkiy-a̲hǫ́dǫha' *she / someone / they...us*

*es-ahǫdǫ́ha' *she / someone...you (singular)*

*gaes-a̲hǫ́dǫha' *they...you (singular)*

gǫy-ahǫdǫ́ha' *I...you (singular)*

sg-ahǫ́dǫha' *you (singular)...me*

sgy-a̲hǫ́dǫha' *you (singular) / you two...us two*

sgw-a̲hǫ́dǫha' *you...us*

---

[8] The a-stem and i-stem interactive verb forms are courtesy of Sasse & Keye (1999); some modifications and additions have been made.

For remaining prefixes, look in §8.3.4.2 (patient, a-stem) and §8.3.4.7 (agent, a-stem).

8.3.4.14 Interactive, i-stem

i-stem (-ihnǫ:s *to be calling someone, habitual aspect*).[9] An asterisk indicates that the vowel of the stem deletes or merges with the prefix vowel.

*he-hnǫ:s *I...him*

*shakn-íhnǫ:s *she / he / someone and I...him*

*shagwę́-hnǫ:s *they and I...him / them (males)*

*shetn-íhnǫ:s *you (singular) and I...him*

*shedwę́-hnǫ:s, shetwę́hnǫ:s *you all and I...him*

*hehs-íhnǫ:s *you (singular)...him*

*shesn-íhnǫ:s *you two...him, he...you two*

*sheswę́-hnǫ:s *you all...him, he...you all*

*hǫwę́-hnǫ:s *she / he / someone...him*

*hǫwád-i̱hnǫ:s *they...him, she / he / someone ... them (males)*

hag-íhnǫ:s *he...me*

*shǫkn-íhnǫ:s *he...us two*

*shǫgwę́-hnǫ:s *he...us all*

*ę-hyę́-hnǫksa' *he...you (singular)*

*shagó-hnǫ:s *he...her / someone / it / them (females or mixed)*

*ke-hnǫ:s *I...her / someone*

*gaké-hnǫ:s, kakéhnǫ:s *I...them*

*akí-hnǫ:s *she / he / someone / they and I...her / someone / them*

*etí-hnǫ:s *you (singular) / you all and I...her / someone / them*

*shé-hnǫ:s *you (singular)...her / someone*

*gashé-hnǫ:s, kashehnǫ:s *you (singular)...them*

*etsí-hnǫ:s *you two / you all...her / someone / them, she / someone / them...you two / you all*

ǫdád-i̱hnǫ:s *she / someone...her / someone*

gaǫdad-íhnǫ:s *she / someone / they(females or mixed)...them(females or mixed)*

*shagódi̱-hnǫ:s *they (males or animals)...her / someone / them (females or mixed)*

*gǫwádi̱-hnǫ:s *she / he / someone / they...it*

ǫg-íhnǫ:s *she / someone...me*

gáǫg-i̱hnǫ:s *they...me*

*ǫkí-hnǫ:s *she / someone / they...us*

*esę́-hnǫ:s *she / someone...you (singular)*

*gáesę-hnǫ:s *they...you (singular)*

*gǫ̱-hnǫ:s *I...you (singular)*

sg-i̱hnǫ:s *you (singular)...me*

*skni̱-hnǫ:s *you (singular) / you two...us two*

*sgwę̱-hnǫ:s *you...us*

For remaining prefixes, look in §8.3.4.3 (patient, i-stem) and §8.3.4.8 (agent, i-stem).

[9] The a-stem and i-stem interactive verb forms are courtesy of Sasse & Keye (1999); some modifications and additions have been made.

8.3.4.15 Interactive, e-stem

e-stem (-ęneʼwahdęʼ *to startle someone*). The *future* prefix ę- precedes the pronominal prefixes in these examples. An asterisk indicates that the vowel of the stem deletes or merges with the prefix vowel.

ę-hey-ęnéʼwa̲hdęʼ *I...him*

*ę-shagy-ęnéʼwa̲hdęʼ[10] *she / he / someone and I...him*

*ę-shagw-ęnéʼwa̲hdęʼ *they and I...him / them (males)*

*ę-shetn-ęnéʼwa̲hdęʼ *you (singular) and I...him*

*ę-hshedw-ęnéʼwa̲hdęʼ *you all and I...him*

*ę-hehs-ęnéʼwa̲hdęʼ *you (singular)...him*

*ę-shesn-ęnéʼwa̲hdęʼ *you two...him, he...you two*

*ę-shesw-ęnéʼwa̲hdęʼ *you all...him, he...you all*

*ę-hǫw-ęnéʼwa̲hdęʼ *she / he / someone...him*

*ę-hǫwan-ęnʼewáhdęʼ *they...him, she / he / someone ... them (males)*

ę-hag-ęnéʼwa̲hdęʼ *he...me*

*ę-shǫgy-ęnéʼwa̲hdęʼ[11] *he...us two*

*ę-shǫgw-ęnéʼwa̲hdęʼ *he...us all*

*ę-hy-ęnʼewáhdęʼ *he...you (singular)*

[10] This ę-initial stem takes a different variant than the e-stems; e-stems normally take the variant shakn- (Foster 1993).

[11] This ę-initial stem normally takes a different variant than the e-stems; e-stems take the variant shǫkn- (Foster 1993).

*ęshagonéʼwa̲hdęʼ[12] *he...her / someone / it / them (females or mixed)*

ę-key-ęnéʼwa̲hdęʼ *I...her / someone*

ę-gakey-ęnʼewáhdęʼ, ę-kake-yęnʼewa̲hdęʼ *I...them*

ę-yakiy-ęnʼewáhdęʼ *she / he / someone / they and I...her / someone / them*

ę-yetiy-ęnʼewáhdęʼ *you (singular) / you all and I...her / someone / them*

ę-shey-ęnéʼwa̲hdęʼ *you (singular)...her / someone*

ę-gashey-ęnʼewáhdęʼ, ę-kashey-ęnʼewáhdęʼ *you (singular)...them*

ę-yetsiy-ęnʼewáhdęʼ *you two / you all...her / someone / them, she / someone / them...you two / you all*

ę-yǫd-ęnéʼwa̲hdęʼ *she / someone...her / someone*

ę-gaǫdad-ęnéʼwa̲hdęʼ *she / someone / they(females or mixed)...them(females or mixed)*

*ę-shagon-ęnʼewáhdęʼ *they (males or animals)...her / someone / them (females or mixed)*

*ę-gowan-ęnʼewáhdęʼ *she / he / someone / they...it*

ę-yǫg-ęnéʼwa̲hdęʼ *she / someone...me*

ę-gaǫg-ęnʼewáhdęʼ *they...me*

ę-yǫkiy-ęnʼewáhdęʼ *she / someone / they...us*

[12] This ę-initial stem takes a different variant than the e-stems; e-stems normally take the variant shakaw- (Foster 1993).

ę-yes-ęné'wąhdę' *she / someone...you (singular)*

ę-gaes-ęn'ewáhdę' *they...you (singular)*

*ę-gǫ-n'ewáhdę' *I...you (singular)*

ę-hsg-ęn'ewáhdę' *you (singular)...me*

*ę-skn-ęn'ewáhę' *you (singular) / you two...us two*
*ę-sgw-ęn'ewáhdę' *you...us*

For remaining prefixes, look in §8.3.4.4 (patient, e-stem) and §8.3.4.9 (agent, e-stem).

8.3.4.16 Interactive, o-stem

o-stem (-ǫ' *to give someone something, punctual aspect;* -odaihsi' *to comb someone's hair, punctual aspect*); the *future* prefix ę- or the dualic and future prefixes dę - precede the pronominal prefixes in these examples. An asterisk indicates that the vowel of the stem deletes or merges with the prefix vowel. Less common variants are shown in brackets.

ę-hé:y-ǫ', dę-hey-odáihsi' *I...him*

ę-hshá:khn-ǫ', (dę-hshakhniy-odáihsi') *she / he / someone and I...him*

*ę-shá:gy-ǫ', (dę-hshagway-odáihsi') *they and I...him / them (males)*

*ę-hshé:tn-ǫ', (ę-hshe:thní:y-ǫ') *you (singular) and I...him*

(dę-hshetniy-odáihsi') *you (singular) and I...him*

(ę-hshe:dwá:y-ǫ')[13], (dę-hshedway-odáihsi)' *you all and I...him*

*ę-héhs-ǫ', *dę-hehs-odáihsi' *you (singular)...him*

*ę-hshé:sn-ǫ', (ę-she:sní:y-ǫ'), (dęhshehsniyodáihsi') *you two...him, he...you two*

*ę-hshé:j-ǫ', (ę-hshe:swá:y-ǫ'), (dęhsheswayodáihsi') *you all...him, he...you all*

ę-hǫ:wá:y-ǫ', dę-hǫway-odáihsi' *she / he / someone...him*

*ę-hǫ:wę́:n-ǫ', *ę-hǫ:wá:n-ǫ', (ę-hǫwadí:y-ǫ'), (dę-hǫwadiy-odáihsi'), *dę-hǫwęn-odáihsi' *they...him, she / he / someone ... them (males)*

ę-há:g-ǫ', dę-hag-odáihsi' *he...me*

*ę-shǫ́:kn-ǫ', *dę-hshǫkn-odáihsi', (dę-hshǫkniy-odáihsi') *he...us two*

(ę-hshǫ:gwá:y-ǫ')[14], (dę-hshǫgway-odáihsi') *he...us all*

ę-hyá:y-ǫ', dę-hyay-odáihsi' *he...you (singular)*

*ę-shága-ǫ', (ę-hsha:gó:y-ǫ'), *dę-hshaga-odáihsi', (dę-hshagoy-odáihsi') *he...her / someone / it / them (females or mixed)*

ę-ké:y-ǫ', dę-key-odáihsi' *I...her / someone*

ę-ga:ké:y-ǫ' ę-ka:ké:y-ǫ', dę-gakey-odáihsi' *I...them*

---

[13] These forms normally take the prefix variant shegy- before o-stems (Foster 1993).

[14] These forms normally take the prefix variant shǫgy- before o-stems (Foster 1993).

ę-ya:kí:y-ǫʼ, dę-yakiy-odáihsiʼ *she / he / someone / they and I...her / someone / them*

ę-ye:tí:y-ǫʼ, dę-yetiy-odáihsiʼ *you (singular) / you all and I...her / someone / them*

ę-shé:y-ǫʼ, dę-hshey-odáihsiʼ *you (singular)...her / someone*

ę-ga:shé:y-ǫʼ, ę-ka:shé:y-ǫʼ, dę-gahshey-odáihsiʼ *you (singular)...them*

ę-ye:tsí:y-ǫʼ, dę-yetsiy-odáihsiʼ *you two / you all...her / someone / them,, she / someone / them...you two / you all*

ę-yǫ́dad-ǫʼ *she / someone...her / someone*

ę-gaǫdá:d-ǫʼ *she / someone / they(females or mixed)...them(females or mixed)*

*ę-sha:gó:n-ǫʼ, *dę-hshagon-odaihsiʼ, (dę-hshagodiy-odáihsiʼ) *they (males or animals)...her / someone / them (females or mixed)*

*ę-gǫ́wan-ǫʼ, *dę-gǫwan-odáihsiʼ, (dę-gǫwadiy-odáihsiʼ) *she / he / someone / they...it*

ę-yǫ́:g-ǫʼ, dę-yǫg-odáihsiʼ *she / someone...me*

ę-gáǫg-ǫʼ, dę-gaǫg-odáihsiʼ *they...me*

ę-yo:kí:y-ǫʼ, dę-yǫkiy-odáihsiʼ *she / someone / they...us*

*ę-yé:s-ǫʼ, (ę-yésay-ǫʼ), *dę-yes-odáihsiʼ, (dę-yesay-odáihsiʼ) *she / someone...you (singular)*

*ę-gáes-ǫʼ, (ę-gaesá:y-ǫʼ), *dę-gaes-odáihsiʼ, (dę-gaesay-odáihsiʼ) *they...you (singular)*

ę-gǫ́:y-ǫʼ, dę-gǫy-odáihsiʼ *I...you (singular)*

ę-hsg-ǫʼ, dę-hsg-odáihsiʼ *you (singular)...me*

(ę-hskní:y-ǫʼ)[15], (dę-hskniy-odáihsiʼ) *you (singular) / you two...us two*

(ę-sgwá:y-ǫʼ)[16], (dę-sgway-odáihsiʼ) *you...us*

For remaining prefix variants, look in §8.3.4.5 (patient, o-stem) and §8.3.4.10 (agent, o-stem).

8.4 SEMIREFLEXIVE AND REFLEXIVE PREFIXES

The semireflexive and reflexive prefixes occur after the pronominal prefixes. Examples of verbs with and without each type of prefix are contrasted below.

8.4.1 The reflexive prefix

Examples without and with the reflexive prefix include the following.

a-g-é:-gęʼ *I saw (no reflexive)*
a-g-adad-é:-gęʼ *I saw myself (with reflexive)*
a-gádat-gęʼ *I saw myself (with reflexive)*

Other variants of the reflexive prefix include:

a-ha-dad-í:yaʼk *he shot himself*
dedwa-dag-yénawahs *let all of us help one another*

[15] These forms also take the prefix variant skn- before o-stems.

[16] These forms also take the prefix variant sgy- before o-stems.

8.4.2 The semireflexive prefix

Examples without and with the semireflexive prefix include the following.

shago-gǫhs-oháe: *he is washing her face (no prefix)*
h-at-gǫhs-ǫháe: *he is washing his (own) face (with prefix)*

Other variants of the semireflexive prefix include:

adǫhwihsę́hde:ʼ *it is restful*
awagyʼadohái:ʼ *it washed its body*
dędwadęnǫ́hǫnyǫ:ʼ *we will give thanks*
agęsʼidóhai: *I did wash my feet*

8.5 NOUN INCORPORATION

Incorporated nouns occur after pronominal prefixes or (semi-)reflexive prefixes and before the verb stem. Noun incorporation was discussed previously in §4. The following examples contrast verbs with and without the incorporated noun ohyaʼ *fruit, berry* in its incorporated form -(h)y(a)-.

ohyajiwá:gę: *(it is) tart, sour fruit*
cf. ojíwagę: *it is tart, sour, salty*

ohyágaʼǫh *good-tasting fruit*
cf. ogáʼǫh *it is good-tasting*

ohyówaneh *big fruit*
cf. gagówanęh *it is big*

niyohyú:ʼuh *small fruit*
cf. niwú:ʼuh *it is small*

wahyaniyǫ́:taʼ *hanging fruit*
cf. ganí:yǫ:t *it is hanging*

ohyá:jih *dark fruit*
cf. gahǫ́:jih *it is dark*

ohyá:tgę: *spoiled, rotten fruit*
cf. otgę: *it is rotten*

8.6 DERIVATIONAL SUFFIXES

Suffixes can occur after the verb stem. Suffixes that derive new verb forms are listed below. The table compares verbs with the suffix and verbs without in order to illustrate the basic meanings added by the suffixes. A joiner vowel, -a-, can occur between the verb stem and the suffix; aspect suffixes also occur after the suffixes shown below.

oppositive or reversive -hsi *to do the opposite*
ęsatrǫnyáhsiʼ *you will take your clothes off*
cf. satrǫ́:nih *get dressed*

inchoative -heʼ *become, get*
agówanheʼ *it became big*
cf. gowá:nęh *it is big*

inchoative -ʼt, -ʼd *become, get*
ęwaʼdáihaʼt *it will get hot*
cf. oʼdáihę: *it is hot*

inchoative -ʼ, -(ę)ʼ *become, get*
agagwiyǫ́:dęʼ *it got buds*
cf. ogwí:yǫ:t *it has buds*

causative -hd, -ht *cause to do s.t.*
ęhsé:tgiht *you will dirty it up*
cf. otgiʼ *it is dirty*

causative -ʼt, -ʼd *cause to do s.t.*
wahdę́hgyaʼtaʼ *a starter (for a vehicle; lit.: it starts it)*
cf. ęwadrihwahdę́:di-ʼ *the ceremony will start*

causative-instrumental -(h)st, -(h)sd
degadidáhsta' *stable, barn, bus stop (lit.: it makes them stand up)*
cf. gá:di:t *they (animals) are standing*

instrumental -hkwa'
ehyádǫhkwa' *pencil*
cf. ehyá:dǫh *she writes*

benefactive or dative -ę, -ni *do for someone*
ahadadrihwagwę́:nyę' *he had earned it for himself*
cf. ęhsrihwagwę́:ni' *you will accomplish*
ǫdadrihǫ́nyanih *she is reading (lit.: making words for herself)*

benefactive or dative -hs *do for someone*
ha'hohahó'ktahs *the road ran out for him (figuratively: he died)*
cf. awatahó'kdę' *the road ended*

distributive -ǫnyǫ' *several here and there*
ohnawáodǫnyǫ' *springs*
cf. ohnáwao:t *well, spring*

distributive -hnǫ' *several here and there*
gahá'dǫhnǫ' *a clothesline (lit.: things are hanging up to dry*
cf. ohá'dǫh *it is dry*

distributive -hsǫ' *several here and there*
hoyę́twahsǫ' *he planted several things*
cf. hoyę́:tweh *he has planted*

distributive -ǫ' *several here and there*
aknǫhsó:dǫ' *I have several houses*
cf. aknǫ́hso:t *I have a house*

facilitative -(h)sgǫ: *do easily*
sęníhahsgǫ: *you are a habitual borrower*
cf. ęhsę́niha' *you will borrow, rent*

eventuative -(h)s' *do eventually*
sadehsrǫníhs'ǫh *you are ready*
cf. ęhsehsrǫ́:ni' *you will create, fix s.t.*

intensifier -jih *really*
sgę:nǫjih gęh ? *are you really well?*
cf. sgę:nǫh *you are well*

dislocative -'dr *go and do something*
sędá'drah *you go to sleep*
cf. sę́:da' *you sleep*

dislocative -'n *go and do something*
ęyǫdawę́'na' *she will go swimming*
cf. ęyǫ́dawę:' *she will swim*

dislocative -hn *go and do something*
ahęnadáhnyǫhna' *they went fishing*
cf. ahęnadáhnyo:' *they (m) fished*

dislocative -h *go and do something*
sihsá:kah *go and look for it*
cf. sihsa:k *look for it*

dislocative -(h)s *go and do something*
hayę́twahse' *he is going to plant*
cf. ęháyęto' *he will plant*

purposive and dislocative[17] -'dre' *go and do something*
ehsę́d'adre' *You are / are you going to bed?*
cf. ęsę́d'adra' *you will go to sleep*

purposive and dislocative -hne' *go and do something*
ahęnadáhnyǫhne' *they are / are they going fishing?*
cf. ahęnadáhnyǫhna' *they went fishing*

purposive and dislocative -ke' *go and do something*
agaesá:ke' *they are / are they going to look for it?*
cf. agaehsá:ka' *they (f) went looking for it*

---

[17] The purposive -e- always occurs after the dislocative.

purposive and dislocative -hse’ *go and do something*

ahayętwáhse’ *he is / is he going to plant?*

cf. ęhayętwáhsa’ *he will go planting*[18]

progressive -ęgye’, -ǫgye’ *be going along doing something*

agahyagwę́hęgye’ *(as) I’m going along in a row picking fruit*

cf. agáhyagwęh *I have picked fruit*

augmentative -ge: *big*

ganǫ́hsotge: *it’s a standing big house*

cf. ganǫ́hso:t *it’s a standing house*

8.7 PRIMARY ASPECT SUFFIXES

Traditional descriptions recognize three primary aspects, the habitual, punctual, and stative. Michelson (1994) argues for the existence of a fourth primary aspect, the purposive. Only the habitual, punctual, and stative forms are discussed in this section; for the purposive, see §8.11.

The habitual, punctual and stative aspects are expressed through suffixes on the verb. However, for each aspect, there are several possible suffixes. The suffix is partly determined by the last sound of the verb stem, but is otherwise not predictable, and must be memorized for each verb.

The following table lists rules of thumb about which of the primary aspect suffixes are required by a given verb. However, to be certain about the aspect suffixes for individual verbs, look in the Cayuga-English dictionary, or ask a Cayuga speaker.

[18] This example is from Foster (1993).

The table in this section should be interpreted as in the following example:

end of verb stem	*with habitual*	*with punctual*	*with stative*
-hsd	-hsta’	-hs (d deletes)	-hsdǫh

If the verb stem ends with -hsd (in the grammtical information sections of the dictionary entries) then:

- the habitual verb ends with -hsta’
- the punctual verb ends with -hs (the final ‘d’ deletes)
- the stative verb ends with -hsdǫh

So, for example, the verb -(a)drihwahsdihsd- *to look after an event* would be conjugated as follows:

hadrihwahsdíhsta’ *he takes care of the event all the time; he pays attention to what is going on* (HABITUAL form)

ęhadri̱hwáhsdihs *he will take care of the event* (PUNCTUAL form)

hodrihwahsdíhsdǫh *(a) chairman (lit.: he looks after the message) (he is) taking care of this event* (STATIVE form)

Abbreviations include:

(i) the letter <i> is not found in all forms

-V any vowel

Note: Where two patterns are shown, you must ask a speaker or consult the dictionary about which of the two patterns will be used for a particular verb. In addition, some verbs are irregular and do not follow the patterns shown below.

end of verb stem	*with habitual*	*with punctual*	*with stative*
-a:	-a:’(s)	-a:’	-a: -a:hǫh
-d	-s (d deletes)	-t	-dǫh
-hd	-hta’	-ht	-hdǫh
-’d	-’ta’	-’t	-’dǫh
-di ? -gy	-gye’s	-di’	-gyǫh -gyǫ:
-e’	e’(s) e:’	e:’	ǫ:
-g	-ka’	-k	-gęh -gǫh
-g	-s (g deletes)	-k	-gǫh
-gw	-gwahs	-go’	-gwęh
-h	-hs	-h	-hǫh
-’	-’s	-’	-’ǫh
-hsd	-hsta’	-hs (d deletes)	-hsdǫh
-’s	-’seh	-’s	
-ǫd	-ǫta’	-ǫdę’	-ǫt
-ǫny, -ǫni	-ǫnih(s)	-ǫni’	-ǫni:
-Vę	-Vęhę’	-Vę:’	-Vę:’
-Vn	-Vnahs	-V:’ (n deletes)	-Vnęh
-ni, -ny	-nyǫhs -nye’s	-ni’	-nyǫ: -nyǫh
-od	-ota’	-odę’	-ot
-Vs	-Vsahs	-Vs	-Vsęh
-s(i)	-sǫhs	-si’	-sǫ: -sǫh
-s’	-s’ahs	-s’a:’	-s’ǫh
-tw	-twahs	-to’	-twęh

end of verb stem	*with habitual*	*with punctual*	*with stative*
-V	-Vhs	-V’	-V:
-V	-Vha’	-V’	-V(:)’
-ę, nih	-nih	-ę’	-ni:
-nye	-nyeh	-nye:’	-nye’
-Vw,:	-Vwa’s	-V:’ (w deletes)	-Vwęh
wi, ny	-wihs -nye’s	-wi’	-wi:

8.8 SECONDARY ASPECT SUFFIXES

The following tables illustrate prefixes and suffixes which can be added to the habitual, punctual, or stative verb forms in order to create additional tense or modal distinctions. Two verbs, -(a)trowi, (a)trǫny- *tell s.o.*, and -(a)hyagw, (a)hyago- *pick fruit, berries* are illustrated.[19] Approximate translations are provided, but since meanings are so context-dependent, see individual dictionary entries for example translations.

The meaning of habitual aspect verbs can be modified by secondary aspect suffixes, as shown below. Abbreviations include [A+] (agent pronominal prefix required) and [P+] (patient pronominal prefix required.

habitual aspect verbs [A+] *to be doing on a continual basis or regularly*

g-atró:wih(s), g-ahyá:gwahs

[19] The tables in this and the following sections were completed by consulting Michelson (1994). Forms listed there were re-elicited and double-checked with three Cayuga speakers to produce these tables.

habitual past [A+ habitual verb +gęhę:ˀ *past*] *to be doing in the past on a continual basis or regularly; something one used to be doing*
g-atrowi̲hs-gę́hę:ˀ, g-a̲hyagwa̲hs-gę́hę:ˀ

future habitual [ę+ A+ habitual verb +a:k, +e:k *continuative, modalizer*] *to be doing in the future on a continual basis or regularly*
ę-g-atrowíh-a:k, ę-g-ahyagwáhs-e:k

indefinite habitual [a:- A+ habitual verb +a:k, +e:k *continuative, modalizer*] *to possibly be doing in the future on a continual basis or regularly*
a:-g-atrówi̲h-a:k, a:-g-a̲hyágwa̲hs-e:k

Punctual aspect verbs can be modified by modal prefixes, as shown below.

factual punctual [a A+ verb stem +ˀ *punctual*] *an event that has occurred or is occurring at one point in time*
a-g-a:tró:wi-ˀ, a-gáhyago-ˀ

future punctual [ę A+ verb stem +ˀ *punctual*] *an event that will occur at one point in time*
ę-g-a:tró:wi-ˀ, ę-g-áhyago-ˀ

indefinite punctual [a: A+ verb stem +ˀ *punctual*] *an event that might, should, or could occur at one point in time*
a:-g-atró:wi-ˀ, a:-g-a̲hyá:go-ˀ

Stative aspect verbs can be modified by secondary aspect suffixes, or by using agentive [A+] pronominal prefixes, as shown below.

stative [P+ verb stem +:, +ęh, +ǫh *stative*] *a state of affairs that has taken place or that is taking place*
ag-a:tró:wi-:, ag-áhyagw-ęh

agentive stative [A+ verb stem +:, +ęh, +ǫh *stative*] *a state of affairs that is done; the result of an event*
w-atró:wi-:, w-a̲hyá:gw-ęh

stative past [P+ stative verb form +(h)ne:ˀ *remote or* +hk *former (not shown)*] *a state of affairs that has taken place; a state of affairs that existed in the past*
ag-atrowí-hne:ˀ, ag-ahyagw-ę́h-ne:ˀ

future stative [ę- P+ stative verb form +a:k +(e):k *continuative, modalizer*] *a state of affairs that will take place; a state of affairs that will be in the future*
ę-wag-atrówi̲h-a:k, ę-wag-a̲hyá:gw-ę:-k

[a:- P+ stative verb form +a:k +(e):k *continuative, modalizer*] *a state of affairs that might take place; a state of affairs that might be in the future*
a:-wag-a:tró:wi:-k, a:-wag-áhyagw-ę-:k

8.9 ASPECT SUFFIXES WITH PROGRESSIVE VERB FORMS

Stative verbs can take the progressive suffix -agyeˀ-, -ęgyeˀ-, after which additional aspect suffixes can be added.

stative [P+ verb stem +:, +ęh, +ǫh *stative*] *a state of affairs that has taken place or that is taking place*
ag-a:tró:wi-:, ag-áhyagw-ęh

progressive habitual [P+ stative verb form +agyeˀs, +ęgyeˀs] *an activity that one is going along and doing on a continual basis*
ag-atrowíh-agyeˀs,
ag-ahyagwę́h-ęgyeˀs

progressive habitual past [P+ stative verb form +agye'ʼs +gęhę:ʼ *past*, -ęgyeʼs +gęhę:ʼ *past*] *an activity that one used to go along and do on a regular basis*
ag-atrowih-agyéʼs-gęhę:ʼ,
ag-ahyagwęh-ęgyéʼs-gęhę:ʼ

progressive future habitual [ę- P+ stative verb form +agyeʼs +a:k, +e:k *continuative, modalizer*, +ęgyeʼs +a:k, +e:k *continuative, modalizer*] *an activity that one will go along and do on a regular basis*
ę-wag-atrowih-ágyʼes-e:k,
ę-wag-ahyagwęh-ę́gyʼes-e:k

progressive indefinite habitual [a:- P+ stative verb form +agyeʼs +a:k, +e:k *continuative, modalizer*, +ęgyeʼs +a:k, +e:k *continuative, modalizer*] *an activity that one might go along and do on a regular basis*
a:-wag-atrowih-agyéʼs-e:k,
a:-wag-ahyagwęh-ęgyéʼs-e:k

progressive stative [P+ stative verb form +agyeʼ, +ęgyeʼ] *while one is going along and doing something (another activity takes place)*
ag-atrowíh-agyeʼ, ag-ahyagwę́h-ęgyeʼ

progressive indefinite stative [a:+ P+ stative verb form +agyeʼ, +ęgyeʼ] *an activity that one might, should, etc. go along and do*
a:-wag-atrowíh-agyeʼ,
a:-wag-ahyagw-ę́h-ęgyeʼ

progressive indefinite stative [a:+ P+ stative verb form +agyeʼ +a:k, +e:k *continuative, modalizer*, +ęgyeʼ +a:k, +e:k *continuative, modalizer*] *an activity that one should have been going along and doing*
a:-wag-atrowíh-agye:-k,
a:-wag-ahyagwę́h-ęgye:-k

8.10 ASPECT SUFFIXES WITH DISLOCATIVE VERB FORMS

Verbs with a dislocative suffix can take the following additional aspect forms:

dislocative stem
-atrǫnyahn-, -ahyagwah-

dislocative habitual [A+ dislocative stem +eʼs] *something one is being sent to do all the time*
g-atrǫ́nyahn-eʼs, g-ahyá:gwah-s

dislocative habitual past [A+ dislocative habitual stem +gęhę:ʼ *past*] *something one used to be sent to do all the time*
g-atrǫnyahnéʼs-gęhę:ʼ,
g-ahyagwahs-gę́hę:ʼ

dislocative future habitual [ę+A+ dislocative habitual stem +a:k, +e:k *continuative, modalizer*] *something one will be sent to do all the time*
ę-g-atrǫnyáhnʼes-e:k,
ę-g-ahyagwáhs-e:k

dislocative indefinite habitual [a:+A+ dislocative habitual stem +a:k, +e:k *continuative, modalizer*] *something one might be sent to do all the time*
a:-g-atrǫnyahnéʼs-e:k,
a:-g-ahyágwahs-e:k

factual punctual [a- A+...-ʼ] with dislocative stems [-agatrǫnyahn-, -agahyaks-]

dislocative factual punctual [a- A+ dislocative stem +aʼ *joiner vowel and punctual*] *something one went and did*
a-g-atrǫnyáhn-aʼ, a-g-áhyaks-aʼ

dislocative future punctual [ę- A+ dislocative stem +aʼ *joiner vowel and punctual*] *something one will go and do*
ę-g-atrǫnyáhn-aʼ, ę-g-áhyaksaʼ

dislocative indefinite punctual
[a:- A+ dislocative stem +a' *joiner vowel and punctual*] *something one might go and do*
a:-g-atrǫ́nya̲hn-a', a:-g-a̲hyá:ks-a'

stative [P+...:, ęh] with dislocative stems [agatrǫnyahn-, agahyaks-]

dislocative stative [P+ dislocative stem +ǫh, +ǫ:, +ęh] *something one has gone and done, or something one is going and doing now*
ag-atrǫnyáhn-ǫh, ag-áhyaks-ǫ:

dislocative stative past [P+ dislocative stative +hne:' *remote*] *one went there and did something (and one is back now)*
ag-atrǫnyáhn-ǫh-k, ag-áhyaks-ǫh-k

dislocative future stative [ę+P+ dislocative stative -k *modalizer*] *something one will have gone and done (by the time someone else does something else)*
ę-wag-atrǫ́nya̲hnǫ:-k,
ę-wag-a̲hyáksǫh-k

dislocative indefinite stative [a:+P+ dislocative stative -k *modalizer*] *something one would have gone and done (by the time someone else would have done something else)*
a:-wag-atrǫnyáhnǫ:-k,
a:-wag-áhyaksǫh-k

8.11 ASPECT SUFFIXES WITH PURPOSIVE VERB FORMS

Purposive aspect verbs with a dislocative and purposive suffix can take the following additional aspect forms:

Purposive verb [-e to go]; purposive stems [-agatrǫnyahne-, -ahyakse-]

purposive habitual [A+(dislocative stem) +e +'s] *something one goes and does all the time*
ę tsǫ́: i-t-s-e-'s *you wander all the time; you are over there*

purposive [A+(dislocative stem) +e +' *punctual*] *something one has come to do*
g-atrǫ́nya̲hn-e-', g-a̲hyá:ks-e-'

purposive past [A+(dislocative stem) +e: +'*punctual*] *something one came and did*
g-atrǫ́nya̲hn-e:-', g-a̲hyá:ks-e:-'

purposive factual punctual [a+ A+ (dislocative stem) +e +'] *something one* will *go and do; something one is going to do now*
a-g-atrǫnyáhn-e-', a-g-áhyaks-e-'

purposive future punctual [ę+ A+ (dislocative stem) +e +'] *something one will go and do*
ę-t-h-e-' he will come this way

purposive indefinite punctual [a:+ / ǫ:+ (dislocative stem) +e +'] *something one might go and do*
na'dǫ:dá-h-e-' *he would come this way*

9 BIBLIOGRAPHY

Chafe, W. 1967. *Seneca morphology and dictionary.* (Smithsonian Contributions to Anthropology 4). Washington, D.C.: Smithsonian Institution.

Foster, M. 1974. *From the earth to beyond the sky: An ethnographic approach to four Longhouse Iroquois speech events.* (The Mercury Series, Ethnology Division, Paper 20). Ottawa: National Museum of Man.

Foster, M. 1993. *Course notes for Ling. 29-381.* Carleton University.

Michelson, K. 1988. *A comparative study of Lake-Iroquoian accent.* Studies in Natural Language and Linguistic Theory. Dordrecht: Kluwer Academic Publishers.

Michelson, K. 1994. *Language Patterns in Ontario Oneida, Cayuga, and Mohawk.* Ontario Training and Adjustment Board.

Mithun, M. 1979. Iroquoian. In L. Campbell & M. Mithun (eds). 133-212. *The languages of Native America.* Austin: University of Texas Press.

Mithun, M. & R. Henry. 1984. Watęwayę́stanih. *A Cayuga teaching grammar.* Brantford, Ontario: Woodland Indian Cultural Educational Centre.

Sasse, H-J., and A. Keye. 1998. *Far more than one thousand verbs of* Gayogo̱ho:nǫʼ *(Cayuga). A handbook of Cayuga morphology.* ms. Universität zu Köln, Köln, Germany and Woodland Cultural Centre, Brantford, Ontario.